PINSON
ON
REVENUE LAW

AUSTRALIA AND NEW ZEALAND
The Law Book Company Ltd.
Sydney : Melbourne : Perth

CANADA AND U.S.A.
The Carswell Company Ltd.
Agincourt, Ontario

INDIA
N. M. Tripathi Private Ltd.
Bombay
and
Eastern Law House Private Ltd.
Calcutta and Delhi
M.P.P. House
Bangalore

ISRAEL
Steimatzky's Agency Ltd.
Jerusalem : Tel Aviv : Haifa

MALAYSIA : SINGAPORE : BRUNEI
Malayan Law Journal (Pte.) Ltd.
Singapore and Kuala Lumpur

PAKISTAN
Pakistan Law House
Karachi

PINSON

ON

REVENUE LAW

comprising
Income Tax; Capital Gains Tax; Corporation Tax;
Inheritance Tax; Value Added Tax; Stamp Duties;
Tax Planning

SEVENTEENTH EDITION

BY

BARRY PINSON, Q.C., LL.B., F.T.I.I.
A Bencher of Gray's Inn

with

ROGER THOMAS, M.A., B.C.L.
of Lincoln's Inn, Barrister

LONDON
SWEET & MAXWELL
1986

First edition	1962	Eleventh edition	1977
Second edition	1965	Twelfth edition	1978
Third edition	1968	(First Supplement)	1979
Fourth edition	1970	Thirteenth edition	1980
Fifth edition	1971	Fourteenth edition	1981
Sixth edition	1972	Fifteenth edition	1982
Seventh edition	1973	(First Supplement)	1983
Eighth edition	1974	Sixteenth edition	1985
Ninth edition	1975	Seventeenth edition	1986
Tenth edition	1976		

Published by
Sweet & Maxwell Limited of
11 New Fetter Lane London
Computerset by Promenade Graphics Limited, Cheltenham
Printed in Great Britain by
Richard Clay Limited, Bungay, Suffolk

British Library Cataloguing in Publication Data

Pinson, Barry,
  Pinson on revenue law—17th ed.
  1. Taxation—Law and legislation—Great
  Britain
  I. Title   II. Thomas, Roger, *1955–*
  344.1034   KD5359

ISBN 0–421–37000–9

PREFACE

Since the first edition of this book appeared over 20 years ago the dimensions and complexity of revenue law have grown to such an extent that any book which now aims to be comprehensive will be bulky and may be unreadable.

This book does not aim to be comprehensive. It is offered as a statement of the fundamental principles of revenue law and it aims to state those principles in as readable and intelligible a form as the subject-matter and the need for conciseness allow. The principles it states are those which practitioners in the field, whether lawyers or accountants, will need to have at (or near) their fingertips. The text will not reveal the solution to every problem but it is hoped that it will provide a useful starting point which will lead on to consideration of the statutes and cases and, where necessary, more detailed reference books. No attempt has been made to theorise about taxation or to consider the law as it might have been or is in remote jurisdictions. The selection of topics aims to meet the needs of those who practise, or hope to practise, and who have to consider the impact of taxation on ordinary transactions.

The book is in five parts. Part 1 deals with taxes on income and on capital gains. This Part is in four divisions dealing with (A) the taxation of the income of non-corporate bodies; (B) the taxation of companies; (C) the taxation of capital gains; and (D) administration, assessments and back duty. Part 2 is on inheritance tax. Part 3 states the principles of the law relating to stamp duties as briefly as the subject allows. Part 4 deals with value added tax and Part 5, entitled "Tax Planning," deals with a number of topics which straddle different areas of revenue law.

This edition incorporates the changes in revenue law since the publication of the last edition, including those made by the Finance Acts of 1985 and 1986. These changes include the abolition of development land tax and the introduction of inheritance tax.

In the realm of case law, the *Ramsay* decision continues to create ripples of uncertainty for tax advisers while its implications and limitations are slowly worked out by the courts. The most recent cases are noted in Chapter 36.

I wish to express my thanks to my colleagues—to Roger Thomas who has updated or rewritten, as necessary, the chapters on value added tax, inheritance tax and stamp duties; and to Richard Fitzgerald, who made a number of valuable suggestions for the improvement of Chapters 14 and 15 (on companies).

Thanks are once again due to the many readers who have contributed by their criticism to the improvement of the book and to the editorial staff of Sweet & Maxwell who assisted in its production.

BARRY PINSON

The law is stated as at August 30, 1986

CONTENTS

PART 1: TAXES ON INCOME AND CAPITAL GAINS

DIVISION A: THE TAXATION OF THE INCOME OF NON-CORPORATE BODIES

DIVISION B: THE TAXATION OF COMPANIES

DIVISION C: THE TAXATION OF CAPITAL GAINS

PART 3: STAMP DUTIES

PART 4: VALUE ADDED TAX

WORKS CITED

The following works and periodicals are cited by the means of abbreviations which appear in the left-hand column:

B.T.E. *British Tax Encyclopedia*, General Editor: Philip Lawton. (Sweet & Maxwell.)

Simon Simon's *Taxes*, 3rd edition. (Butterworths.)

Sergeant and Sims *Sergeant and Sims on Stamp Duties*, 8th edition, by B. J. Sims, LL.B., F.T.I.I., Solicitor. Assistant editors: E. N. E. Sims, Solicitor; R. D. Fulton, LL.B., Solicitor. Consultant editor A. K. Tavaré LL.B., Solicitor. (Butterworths.)

Dymond Dymond's *Capital Transfer Tax*, by Reginald K. Johns, I.S.O., LL.B. and Roy R. Greenfield, LL.B.

B.T.R. The *British Tax Review*, edited by John Avery Jones. This is published six times a year and deals with all aspects of taxation. It contains a section entitled Current Tax Intelligence which is invaluable for keeping up to date. (Sweet & Maxwell.)

S.T.C. Simon's *Tax Cases*.

S.T.I. Simon's *Tax Intelligence*.

Other books are cited but without abbreviations.

TABLE OF CASES

TABLE OF STATUTES

PART 1

TAXES INCOME AND CAPITAL GAINS

DIVISION A

THE TAX OF THE INCOME OF NON-CORPORATE BODIES

CHAPTER 1

INTRODUCTION

1. PREFATORY

Sources: income taxation

1–01   The principal Act charging income tax and corporation tax is the Income and Corporation Taxes Act 1970. Matters of administration and procedure are dealt with in the Taxes Management Act 1970. Capital allowances are dealt with in the Capital Allowances Act 1968 and in the Finance Act 1971.

The Acts of 1970 are consolidating and not codifying statutes. It is therefore necessary to refer to decided cases for many of the fundamental principles of income taxation. Tax cases are reported in the official *Law Reports* published by the Council of Law Reporting and also in the *Reports of Tax Cases* (cited as T.C.) published by the Stationery Office under the directions of the Board of Inland Revenue. Where there is a discrepancy between the official reports and the *Tax Cases,* the former are to be preferred.[1]

There are a number of extra-statutory concessions which are applied in practice.[2] The Revenue produce a number of explanatory booklets[3] and now publish Statements of Practice.[4]

Annual nature of tax

1–02   All taxes on income are annual taxes which are renewed each year by Act of Parliament. Proposals made by the Chancellor of the Exchequer in his Budget speech are at once agreed to by resolution of the House of Commons: and because such a resolution would otherwise lack the force of law, the Provisional Collection of Taxes Act 1968 provides that resolutions which vary an existing tax or renew a tax shall have limited statutory force

---

1. *Fairman* v. *Perpetual Investment Building Society* [1923] A.C. 74 at pp. 78–79; [1931] W.N. 121. The official *Law Reports* include summaries of the arguments of counsel which are often of some value and which are not always in the *Tax Cases.* On the other hand, the *Tax Cases* usually include the case stated by the Commissioners. It is the practice not to report a case in the *Tax Cases* until it is disposed of by the final court to which appeal is made: this causes considerable delay in publication. In proceedings in the House of Lords the *Law Reports* should be cited in preference to the *Tax Cases: Practice Note* [1970] 1 W.L.R. 1400. In *Murphy* v. *Ingram* [1973] Ch. 434 at p. 438; 49 T.C. 410 at p. 420 B, Megarry J. expressed the view (giving reasons) that the *Law Reports* should generally be cited, not only in the House of Lords. The actual decision in that case was reversed on appeal: [1974] Ch. 363; 49 T.C. 410.
2. See Revenue Booklet I.R.1. (1985) and containing Extra Statutory Concessions in operation in June 1985. For a recent judicial onslaught on extra-statutory concessions, see Walton J. in *Vestey* v. *I.R.C.* (1978) 54 T.C. 503 at p. 544 G.
3. See list in [1978] S.T.I. 154–155 and [1979] S.T.I. 74.
4. [1978] S.T.I. 349. These will be designated SP1/78 *et seq.* The Revenue have published an index of administrative practices which came into existence before July 18, 1978: see Press Release in [1979] S.T.I. 274–289 and 382 and a cumulative index: see [1983] S.T.I. 214. For a looseleaf collection, see Dearden Farrow, *Inland Revenue Practices and Concessions,* published by Oyez Publishing Ltd.

until the Finance Act embodying the resolution is passed.[5] This Act must be passed within about four months from the date of the resolution and, in practice, the Finance Act usually receives the Royal Assent on about July 31. Changes made by the Act may be retrospective to Budget Day or to some other date specified in the Act.

The annual nature of tax is reflected in the method by which individuals and companies are assessed to tax. For individuals the tax year commences on April 6 in one year and ends on April 5 in the following year and such a year is termed a "year of assessment"[6]; for companies liable to corporation tax, the year commences on April 1 in one year and ends on March 31 in the following year and such a year is termed a "financial year."[7] The term "assessment" describes the administrative act by which income is made liable to tax and every such assessment is made for a year of assessment (or a financial year, as the case may be) irrespective of the period for which the taxpayer renders accounts.

2. The Six Schedules

1–03 The general scheme of the Income Tax Acts[8] is to charge tax according to the source from which income arises. Thus section 1 of the Income and Corporation Taxes Act 1970 charges tax for each year of assessment in respect of "all property, profits or gains" described or comprised in Schedules A, B, C, D, E and F to the Act and in accordance with the provisions applicable to those Schedules. Schedules D and E are further subdivided into Cases.

1–04 The following table shows how "income" is classified by reference to the source from which it arises, and how the basis on which the amount of taxable income is measured or computed differs as between the Schedules. References to sections are (unless otherwise stated) to those of the Income and Corporation Taxes Act 1970.

	Tax is charged on:	Basis on which income is computed:
1–05 SCHEDULE A (s. 67)	Annual profits or gains arising in respect of certain rents or receipts from land in the United Kingdom.	The rents or receipts to which the taxpayer becomes entitled in the year of assessment *less* the deductions authorised by the Act.

Note: Schedule A was originally Case VIII of Schedule D and was introduced as such by the Finance Act 1963. Before 1963, Schedule A existed in a different form.

---

5. There are similar provisions relating to stamp duty, which have permanent statutory effect until repealed or varied: F.A. 1973, s.50.

6. See the definition of "year of assessment" and "the year 1970–71" in I.C.T.A. 1970, s.526(5). The possibility of changing the end of the tax year to March 31 has been considered but the Chancellor saw no case for recommending any change: [1980] S.T.I. 799.

7. I.C.T.A. 1970, ss.238(1), 527(1).

8. "The Income Tax Acts" means, except in so far as the context otherwise requires, all enactments relating to income tax, including the provisions of the Corporation Tax Acts which relate to income tax: I.C.T.A. 1970, s.526(1)(*b*).

1–06 SCHEDULE B
(s. 91)

Income from the occupation of woodlands in the United Kingdom managed on a commercial basis and with a view to the realisation of profits.

One-third of the G.A.V. for the current year of assessment.

1–07 SCHEDULE C
(s. 93)

Profits arising from public revenue dividends payable in the United Kingdom; or payable in the Republic of Ireland, being dividends on Government stock registered or inscribed in the books of the Bank of Ireland in Dublin; and overseas public revenue dividends payable through a banker or other person in the United Kingdom, if paid by means of coupons.

The income of the current year of assessment.

Schedule C thus applies to interest payable on certain securities of the United Kingdom and of foreign governments, where the interest is paid in the United Kingdom. The tax is assessed on the paying authority and is deducted from the interest which is paid.

1–08 SCHEDULE D
(ss. 108–109)

CASE I

Profits of a trade.

CASE II

Profits of a profession or vocation.

Normal Basis: the profits of the taxpayer's accounting year ending in the preceding year of assessment. Special rules for opening and closing years (ss. 115–118).

Example: Brown, a solicitor, prepares annual accounts made up to December 31 each year. The profits of the accounting year ended December 31, 1985, constitute the statutory income (Case II) of the year of assessment 1986–87.

CASE III

Interest, annuities or other annual payments; discounts; small maintenance payments, etc.

Normal Basis: the income arising in the preceding year of assessment. Special rules for opening and closing years (ss. 119–121).

CASE IV

Income arising from securities out of the United Kingdom not charged under Schedule C.

CASE V

Income arising from possessions out of the United Kingdom.

Normal Basis: the income arising in the preceding year of assessment. Special rules for opening and closing years (ss. 122–124).

Income arising under Cases IV and V is assessable only if the taxpayer is resident in the United Kingdom. In some cases, tax is payable only on the income which is received in the United Kingdom.

CASE VI

Any annual profits or gains not falling under any other Schedule or Case; and certain income specifically directed to be charged under Case VI.	The profits of the current year of assessment (s. 125).

1–09 SCHEDULE E
(s. 181)

Income arising from offices, employments and pensions; and certain income specifically directed to be charged under Schedule E, *e.g.* some social security benefits (s. 219)	The emoluments or other income of the current year of assessment.

Schedule E is divided into three Cases, of which Cases II and III apply where there is a foreign element.

1–10 SCHEDULE F
(s. 232)[9]

Dividends and other distributions made by companies resident in the United Kingdom.	The dividends etc. of the year of assessment.

1–11 Capital gains tax is, as its name implies, a tax on gains of a capital (not income) nature. Such gains are not taxed as income except where statute deems them to be so.

1–12 It will be observed from the table that there are, broadly speaking, six sources of income:

(1) income from the ownership or occupation of land (Schedules A and B);

(2) profits of a trade, profession or vocation (Schedule D, Cases I and II) and other profits brought into charge (Schedule D, Case VI);

(3) emoluments of an office or employment (Schedule E, Case I);

(4) "pure income" comprising interest, annuities and other annual payments (Schedule D, Case III);

(5) foreign income (Schedule C; Schedule D, Cases IV and V; Schedule E, Cases II and III);

(6) dividends and other distributions made by United Kingdom companies (Schedule F).

Corporation tax is merely a tax levied on the profits of certain companies

---

9. For the year 1973–74 and subsequent years of assessment, this means I.C.T.A. 1970, s.232, as substituted by F.A. 1972, s.87.

from the sources above referred to. Before 1965 both companies and individuals were charged to income tax. Since the Finance Act 1965 companies have been separately charged to corporation tax in order that changes in the rates of company taxation can be made without affecting individuals, and vice versa.

Where a taxpayer has numerous sources of income falling under different Schedules, it is necessary to aggregate the statutory income computed under each Schedule for the purpose of determining his income in the year of assessment. Under some Schedules (*e.g.* Schedule E) the statutory income of a year of assessment is the income of that year; whereas under all the Cases of Schedule D (other than Case VI) statutory income is measured by reference to the profits or income of a preceding period. It follows that income as computed for the purpose of the Income Tax Acts for a year of assessment may bear no relation to the taxpayer's incomings in that year.

Relationship between the Schedules

1–13   The six Schedules are mutually exclusive so the Revenue cannot charge under one Schedule income which properly falls under another.

> Thus in *Fry* v. *Salisbury House Estate Ltd.*[10] a company formed to acquire, manage and deal with a building let out the rooms as unfurnished offices. The company provided a staff of lift-operators and porters and also certain services at an additional charge. It was held that the income from rents was assessable only under Schedule A and not (as the Revenue contended) under Schedule D. Profits made on services supplied to tenants were assessable under Schedule D.

In *Mitchell and Edon* v. *Ross*[11] specialists holding part-time appointments under the National Health Service (Schedule E) also engaged in private practice (Schedule D, Case II). A claim was made to set against the Schedule D receipts certain expenses incurred in connection with the Schedule E appointments which were not allowable under the rules applicable to Schedule E. The House of Lords rejected the claim and Lord Radcliffe said this:

> "Generally speaking, the . . . schedules of taxable categories are distinguished from each other by distinctions as to the nature of the source from which the chargeable profit arises. The source may be property in the ordinary sense such as land, securities, copyright, office, or it may be an activity sufficiently coherent, trade or profession, for example, to be regarded as itself the stock upon which profits grow. That is not an exhaustive account, but it is, I think, a sufficient general introduction. Before you can assess a profit to tax you must be sure that you have properly identified its source or other description according to the correct schedule, but, once you have done that, it is obligatory that it should be charged, if at all, under that schedule and strictly in accordance with the rules that are there laid down for assessments under it. It

---

10. [1930] A.C. 432; 15 T.C. 266 (H.L.). At this time Schedule A was a tax on the net annual value of the building. In consequence of this decision, statute provided for the assessment of "excess rents" under Case VI of Schedule D. Now rents are assessed under Schedule A.
   11. [1962] A.C. 814; 40 T.C. 11 (H.L.).

is a necessary consequence of this conception that the sources of profit in the different schedules are mutually exclusive."

Where income falls under more than one Case of the same Schedule the Revenue may elect the Case under which to make the assessment.[12]

Profits not chargeable to tax

1–14   A profit or gain which does not fall within the charging provisions escapes tax. Suppose, for example, that Adam sells his house at a profit. If Adam is a property dealer and the house is part of his trading stock, the profit is assessable under Case I of Schedule D; otherwise the profit is a "capital profit" which escapes tax, unless the capital gains tax applies. It will be apparent from this example that the taxable quality of a payment must be determined by reference to the circumstances surrounding the payment. Where Adam is not trading with the house, there is no "source" which the Acts recognise as income-producing; but the possibility of a taxable capital gain must be considered.

A profit or gain which clearly falls within one of the Schedules may nevertheless escape tax if the source from which it comes does not exist in the year when the profit arises.[13] Thus when a trader or professional man dies or retires and sums are later received for goods supplied or services rendered during the course of the trade or profession, such receipts are not chargeable to tax in the year of receipt,[14] except where statute otherwise provides.[15] Similarly, payments made to an employee after his employment has terminated escape tax, unless they are deferred remuneration or statute imposes a charge to tax.[16]

3. THE SCOPE OF THE INCOME TAX ACTS

1–15   The Income Tax Acts apply to the United Kingdom, that is, to England, Wales, Scotland and Northern Ireland, but not to the Channel Islands or the Isle of Man. The territorial sea of the United Kingdom is deemed to be part of the United Kingdom and there are provisions to ensure that profits arising from the exploitation of the natural resources of the United Kingdom part of the Continental Shelf shall be charged to United Kingdom tax.[17]

Broadly speaking, all income which arises in the United Kingdom is liable to United Kingdom income tax, irrespective of the nationality, domicile or residence of the recipient; and foreign income is assessable to tax only if the recipient is resident in the United Kingdom. Where income is

12. *Liverpool & London & Globe Insurance Co.* v. *Bennett* [1913] A.C. 610; 6 T.C. 327 (H.L.). Where the Revenue make an assessment under the wrong Case of Schedule D, *e.g.* Case VII and not Case I, the court has a discretion to deal with the assessment under the right Case: see T.M.A. 1970, s.56(6) applied in *Bath and West Counties Property Trust Ltd.* v. *Thomas* (1978) 52 T.C. 20; [1978] S.T.C. 30.
13. On the doctrine of "the source," see *Brown* v. *National Provident Institution* [1921] 2 A.C. 222; 8 T.C. 57 (H.L.).
14. *Bennett* v. *Ogston* (1930) 15 T.C. 374; *Carson* v. *Cheyney's Executors* [1959] A.C. 412; 38 T.C. 240.
15. See *post,* §§ 2–88 *et seq.*
16. See *post,* §§ 3–24 *et seq.*
17. F.A. 1973, s.38.

liable to double taxation (*e.g.* in the country where it arises and in the country where the recipient resides), relief may be available.[18]

Exemptions from tax

1–16   The following income is exempt from income tax:

(1) Scholarship and similar income.[19]

(2) Certain social security benefits and payments of child benefit.[20]

(3) Accumulated interest and any terminal bonus or other sum payable in respect of United Kingdom savings certificates.[21]

(4) Interest on post-war credits.[22]

(5) Interest on tax reserve certificates.[23]

(6) The first £70 interest on ordinary (but not investment) deposits with the National Savings Bank. The £70 exemption applies to both husband and wife, *i.e.* the exemption is £140 on a joint account or £70 each on separate accounts.[24] (The exemption for Trustee Savings Bank interest has been abolished.[25])

(7) Dividends and interest paid by a Building Society, if the society has an arrangement with the revenue.[26] (This exemption applies only to income tax at the basic rate.)

(8) Terminal bonuses under certified contractual saving schemes (*e.g.* SAYE).[27]

(9) Interest on damages for personal injuries awarded by a court in the United Kingdom[28] and, by concession, a foreign court.[29]

(10) Certain pensions in respect of death due to war service, etc.,[30] and certain gallantry awards.[30a]

(11) Payments under job release schemes under the the Job Release Act 1977.[31]

(12) Income from investments or deposits of a superannuation fund (called a "gross fund").[32]

Interest from certain United Kingdom Government securities belonging to persons not ordinarily resident in the United Kingdom is exempt from tax.[33]

---

18. See *post*, § 7–25.
19. I.C.T.A. 1970, s.375, and see § 3–44.
20. *Ibid.* s.219 as amended by F.A. 1977, s.23 and F.A. 1978, s.20(4). But see F.A. 1981, ss.27–30.
21. F.A. 1981, s.34.
22. Income Tax (Repayment of Post-War Credits) Act 1959, s.2(4).
23. I.C.T.A. 1970, s.98. These were at one time issued by the Treasury as a means by which money could be invested to meet liability for tax. Tax reserve certificates have now been replaced by Certificates of Tax Deposit, the interest on which is taxable.
24. I.C.T.A. 1970, s.414 amended by F.A. 1977, s.26.
25. F.A. 1980, s.59.
26. I.C.T.A. 1970, s.343.
27. *Ibid.* s.415.
28. *Ibid.* s.375A.
29. [1979] S.T.I. 263.
30. F.(No. 2)A. 1979, s.9.
30a. I.C.T.A. 1970, s.368 and F.A. 1980, s.26.
31. F.A. 1977, s.30.
32. I.C.T.A. 1970, s.208.
33. *Ibid.* s.99(1).

The Crown

1–17   Generally, all persons having a source of income which is chargeable to tax are liable to tax, irrespective of personal incapacity. The Crown is not liable to tax unless statute otherwise provides. By section 524 of the Income and Corporation Taxes Act 1970, the provisions of the Income Tax Acts relating to the assessment, charge, deduction and payment of income tax are made to apply to public offices and departments of the Crown, except in so far that these provisions would require the payment of any tax which would be ultimately payable by the Crown. The section enables public offices and departments of the Crown to deduct tax from annual payments, etc. made by them and enables the Revenue to recover the tax so deducted.[34]

Charities

1–18   A charity (defined as any body of persons or trust established for charitable purposes only) enjoys the following main exemptions from tax[35]:

(a) exemption from tax under Schedules A and D in respect of the rents and profits of any lands, etc., if applied[36] to charitable purposes only;

(b) exemption from tax under Schedule B in respect of any lands occupied by a charity;

(c) exemption from tax on interest annuities, dividends, etc., if applied[36] to charitable purposes only[37];

(d) profits of a trade carried on by a charity are exempt from tax under Schedule D if the profits are applied solely to the purposes of the charity *and* either (i) the trade is exercised in the course of the actual carrying out of a primary purpose of the charity; or (ii) the work in connection with the trade is mainly carried out by beneficiaries of the charity.

For other exemptions from tax, reference should be made to sections 360 to 377 of the Income and Corporation Taxes Act 1970 and to standard works on income tax.

4. THE UNIFIED SYSTEM OF PERSONAL TAXATION

1–19   Sections 32 to 39 of the Finance Act 1971 introduced a new method of charging tax on the income of individuals which applies in the year 1973–74 and in subsequent years of assessment. This has been called the "unified system" of direct personal taxation. The significance of the term "unified"

---

34. See *post*, §§ 5–30 *et seq.*
35. I.C.T.A. 1970, s.360. There are anti-avoidance provisions in F.A. 1986, ss.30–31 and Sched. 7. See [1986] S.T.I 431.
36. As to what constitutes an "application" to charitable purposes, see *I.R.C.* v. *Helen Slater Charitable Trust Ltd.* [1982] Ch. 49; (1981) 55 T.C. 230 (C.A.).
37. Thus a charity is able to recover basic rate income tax on payments made under covenants. If tax rates go down, a charity recovers less.

will appear from the following comparison between the unified system and the system in operation in years up to and including the year 1972–73.

The pre-1973 system

Before the year 1973–74, individuals were subject to income tax and in some cases surtax. Each Finance Act contained a section charging income tax for the appropriate year of assessment at a rate which was called "the standard rate." Thus section 62 of the Finance Act 1972 charged income tax for the year 1972–73 at the standard rate of 38.75 per cent. An individual's entire income was not taxed at the standard rate for he was entitled to personal reliefs and allowances which increased in amount with the number of his dependants and which had the effect of relieving altogether a portion of his income from tax. Only a proportion of an individual's earned income was subject to income tax, by reason of the earned income relief available to earned but not unearned (such as investment) income. Hence the pre-1973 system discriminated against unearned income by taxing it (in effect) at higher rates, thereby discouraging saving.

Where the total income of an individual exceeded a certain amount, he was liable to surtax in addition to income tax. Surtax was a progressive tax the rate of which increased with each successive slice of the taxpayer's income above the figure at which liability began. The rates of surtax were fixed each year by the Finance Act. Section 10 of the Finance Act 1973, for example, fixed the surtax rates for 1972–73. Each Finance Act fixed the rates of surtax for the preceding fiscal year; surtax was technically a deferred instalment of income tax.

Assume, for example, that a trader's accounting period ends on March 31 in each year. His profits for the year ended March 31, 1970, formed his statutory income for the year of assessment 1970–71: see the example in § 1–08. Income tax was payable at the standard rate, with the benefit of the personal reliefs and allowances fixed by the Finance Act 1970, the income tax being payable in two instalments during the year 1971. Surtax on the profits for the year ended March 31, 1970, was payable in 1972 at rates fixed by the Finance Act 1971. This dual system of income tax and surtax therefore involved some complication.

The post-1973 unified system

1–19A   The unified system of personal taxation involves the abolition of earned income relief as such and the abolition of surtax as such. For the year 1973–74 and subsequent years of assessment there is a single tax on all income, namely, income tax. The concept of a "standard rate" of tax disappears in favour of a new concept of "basic rate" to be fixed annually by Parliament. Section 66 of the Finance Act 1972 fixed the basic rate of income tax for 1973–74 at 30 per cent. This rate of 30 per cent. corresponded roughly to tax at the standard rate of 38.75 per cent. less earned income relief; earned income relief disappears and instead all income (including unearned or investment income) is taxed at the lower rate formerly applicable only to earned income. Personal taxation is simplified by removing the separate charge of surtax.

Not all income is taxed only at the basic rate, for when the total income of an individual exceeds a certain figure, income tax at higher rates is payable. A table showing the higher rates of income tax is in § 8–05.

For the year 1973–74 and subsequent years, investment income was subject to income tax at an additional rate or rates, commonly called "the investment income surcharge." This was abolished for the year 1984–85 and subsequent years by section 17(2) of the Finance Act 1984.

Trustees are not liable to higher rate income tax because trustees are not "individuals" for tax purposes. For the same reason trustees were not liable to the investment income surcharge, except in the case of accumulated income.[38] For 1984–85 and subsequent years, trustees remain liable to the additional rate tax on accumulated income: see § 9–02.

Husband and wife

1–20   A husband and wife living together are treated as one unit for tax purposes. Their separate incomes are therefore added together and income tax is charged on the total joint income as if it were the income of one person.[39] This principle of aggregation may cause hardship where each spouse has a substantial income, and the principle is subject to some modification in the case of a wife's earned (but not investment) income.[40]

Parent and child

1–21   The income of a minor is treated as his income and not that of his parent (subject to an exception in the case of income paid to or for the benefit of a minor under a settlement made on him by his parent; see §§ 10–23 and 10–35). In March 1974 the Labour Government announced its intention to aggregate a minor's income with that of his parents but this proposal was never implemented.

Companies

1–22   Companies are subject to corporation tax, not income tax; hence the new unified system of taxation does not affect companies as such. The manner in which companies are taxed is discussed in Chapter 14.

5. COLLECTION OF TAX

1–23   The Income Tax Acts provide two principal methods of collecting tax on income:

   (1) *By direct assessment.* Tax which is due under, for example, Schedule D, Cases I and II, is collected by direct assessment. After the

---

38. F.A. 1973, s.16, *post,* § 9–02.
39. For details, see *post,* §§ 8–23 *et seq.*
40. See *post,* § 8–29. In 1986 the Conservative Government published a Green Paper on "The Reform of Personal Taxation" (Cmnd. 9756) on which the Financial Secretary has commented: see [1986] S.T.I. 297.

amount of tax which is due has been determined by the Inspector, a formal assessment is made which (unless appealed against) becomes final; and the tax is collected by the Collector of Taxes.

(2) *By deduction at source.* A high proportion of income tax is collected by the Revenue at the source where the income arises. In the case of the employee, for example, tax is deducted from his salary under the Pay As You Earn system (PAYE) and the employer is made accountable to the Revenue for the tax so deducted. The necessity for assessing the employee is thereby removed and the administrative work of the Revenue is reduced. Income tax at the basic rate is collected at the source in the case of annuities and other annual payments.[41] Bank interest and interest on government stock is in some cases paid without deduction and assessed under Schedule D, Case III.[42]

The following illustration shows how the system of collection operates:

A (who has £5,000 a year) covenants to pay B £800 a year for the joint lives of A and B. This covenant gives B a new source of income falling under Case III of Schedule D and reduces A's total income by £800. A is nevertheless assessed to tax on £5,000, for no deduction is allowed in respect of the payment to B. Under the collection machinery of section 52 of the Income and Corporation Taxes Act 1970 A is entitled to deduct tax at the basic rate when making the payment to B, who is then said to have "suffered tax by deduction at the source." A thus recoups the tax to which he has already been assessed, and has acted as a collector for the Revenue of the basic rate tax on B's income.

This system is explored in Chapters 5 and 8. The mechanics of assessments and appeals against assessments are considered in Chapter 17.[43]

Date of payment[44]

1–24   Income tax is generally payable on January 1 in the year of assessment to which the tax relates. But income tax on the professional and trading income of an individual is payable in two equal instalments on January 1 and the following July 1. Generally, income tax charged at a rate other than the basic rate on income from which tax has been deducted before its receipt (*e.g.* higher rate tax on building society interest, dividends, interest from most bank deposits and most government stocks and trust income) is payable on or by December 1[45] following the end of the year for which it is assessed. Interest is payable on overdue tax.[46]

---

41. See *post*, §§ 5–30 *et seq.*
42. See *post*, § 8–19(4).
43. Some readers may find it useful to read Chapter 17 before continuing further.
44. I.C.T.A. 1970, s.4.
45. Changed from July 6 in relation to tax for 1980–81 and subsequent years: F.A. 1980, s.61(1), (5).
46. T.M.A. 1970, s.86, as substituted by F.(No.2)A. 1975. The rate of interest is now 8.5 per cent. per annum: the Income Tax (Interest on Unpaid Tax and Repayment Supplement) Order 1986 (S.I. 1986 No.1181), in [1986] S.T.I. 509.

CHAPTER 2

SCHEDULE D CASES I AND II: PROFITS OF A TRADE, PROFESSION OR VOCATION

1. THE SCOPE OF THE CHARGE

2–01 TAX under Schedule D is charged on the profits of a trade (Case I), profession or vocation (Case II) carried on wholly or partly in the United Kingdom.[1] Trades, professions and vocations carried on outside the United Kingdom are considered later.[2]

Trade is defined in section 526(5) of the Income and Corporation Taxes Act 1970 to include "every trade, manufacture, adventure or concern in the nature of trade." Farming and market gardening in the United Kingdom are included: see § 2–18A.

Profession is not defined in the Act but has been said to "involve the idea of an occupation requiring either purely intellectual skill, or manual skill controlled by the intellectual skill of the operator"[3] (*e.g.* barrister, solicitor, surgeon).

Vocation means "the way a person passes his life"[4] (*e.g.* author).

The method of computing profits and losses under Cases I and II of Schedule D is similar and generally no practical importance attaches to the distinction between a trade, on the one hand, and a profession or vocation on the other. The important distinction is that between the activity which constitutes the carrying on of a trade, profession or vocation (the profits or losses from which are dealt with under income tax rules) and the activity which does not (the gains or losses from which are dealt with under capital gains tax rules). Trading profits of an individual are subject to income tax (at the basic and higher rates) whereas capital gains are subject to capital gains tax. Non-trading activities are less generously treated as regards relief from capital gains tax and capital taxes; and there are many areas of revenue law in which trading companies are treated differently from (and more favourably than) other companies. In this chapter, the terms "trade" and "trading" should be read as including professions and vocations, unless otherwise stated.

2. WHAT CONSTITUTES TRADING

2–02 The term "trade" is not precisely defined in the Tax Acts. Section 526(5) merely extends its ordinary meaning to include "every trade, manufacture, adventure or concern in the nature of trade." It was said in one case that

---

1. I.C.T.A. 1970, ss.108, 109.
2. See *post*, §§ 7–02 *et seq*.
3. *Per* Scrutton L.J. in *I.R.C.* v. *Maxse* [1919] 1 K.B. 647; 12 T.C. 41 (C.A.).
4. *Partridge* v. *Mallandaine* (1886) 18 Q.B.D. 276 at p. 278; 2 T.C. 179 at p. 180 (bookmaker). *Cf. Graham* v. *Green* [1925] 2 K.B. 37; 9 T.C. 309 (where a person whose sole means of livelihood was betting on horses at starting prices was held not to be carrying on a vocation).

the words "in the nature of trade" govern only the word "concern" but this is of doubtful authority.[5]

Whether or not an activity is a trade in this extended sense is a mixed question of law and fact. A person does not trade if he simply procures others to trade: he must be involved in the buying and selling or rendering of services.[6] If there is regular buying and selling, or rendering of services, this is clearly trading and the annual profits or gains thereof are assessable to tax; but an isolated or casual transaction may be "an adventure or concern in the nature of trade": see §§ 2–05 *et seq.* In *Erichsen* v. *Last*[7] the Master of the Rolls said:

> "There is not, I think, any principal of law which lays down what carrying on trade is. There are a multitude of things which together make up the carrying on of trade, but I know no one distinguishing incident, for it is a compound fact made up of a variety of things."

Appeals to the High Court

2–03　　The question whether a profit is the result of trading is decided initially by the Inspector of Taxes. If he decides that it is, an assessment is made against which the taxpayer may appeal to the Commissioners. From the Commissioners an appeal lies to the High Court, but only by the way of case stated on a point of law.[8] The High Court has no jurisdiction to rehear the case and shows a marked reluctance to interfere with the findings of the Commissioners if there was evidence before the Commissioners to justify those findings. Lord Denning remarked in one case[9] that:

> "the powers of the High Court on an appeal are very limited. The judge cannot reverse the Commissioners on their findings of fact. He can only reverse their decision if it is 'erroneous in point of law.' Now here the primary facts were all found by the Commissioners. They were stated in the case. They cannot be disputed. What is disputed is their conclusion from them. And it is now well settled, as well as anything can be, that their conclusion cannot be challenged unless it was unreasonable, so unreasonable that it can be dismissed as one which could not reasonably be entertained by them. It is not sufficient that the judge would himself have come to a different conclusion."

In the case from which this extract is taken, the Commissioners had found that a dividend-stripping transaction carried out by the taxpayer was not an adventure or concern in the nature of trade and Lord Denning's remarks were directed to the decision of the Commissioners on that issue. Appellate courts show a marked reluctance to interfere with decisions of the Commissioners where the issue is essentially one of fact, and this reluctance must always be kept in mind when considering decisions of the courts in such cases. But while paying proper regard to the facts found by the

---

5. See, generally, *Johnston* v. *Heath* (1970) 46 T.C. 463 at pp. 469–470.
6. *Ransom* v. *Higgs* (1974) 50 T.C. 1; [1974] S.T.C. 539 (H.L.).
7. (1881) 8 Q.B.D. 414 at p. 416; *cf.* 4 T.C. 422 at p. 423 (C.A.), where the text differs.
8. T.M.A. 1970, s.56. See § 17–18.
9. *J. P. Harrison (Watford) Ltd.* v. *Griffiths* (1962) 40 T.C. 281 at pp. 298–299 (a dissenting judgment).

Commissioners and to the inferences drawn by them from those facts, the court will itself decide questions of law, such as whether receipts are capital or income receipts or whether expenditure is incurred on capital or revenue account, and questions of construction of statutes, including the question as to the meaning of "trade" in the Tax Acts.[10] The duty of the court when hearing appeals from Commissioners in tax cases was stated by Lord Radcliffe in *Edwards* v. *Bairstow and Harrison*[11] as follows:

> "I think that the true position of the Court in all these cases can be shortly stated. If a party to a hearing before Commissioners expresses dissatisfaction with their determination as being erroneous in point of law, it is for them to state a Case and in the body of it to set out the facts that they have found as well as their determination. I do not think that inferences drawn from other facts are incapable of being themselves findings of fact, although there is value in the distinction between primary facts and inferences drawn from them. When the Case comes before the Court, it is its duty to examine the determination having regard to its knowledge of the relevant law. If the Case contains anything *ex facie* which is bad law and which bears upon the determination it is, obviously, erroneous in point of law. But, without any such misconception appearing *ex facie*, it may be that the facts found are such that no person acting judicially and properly instructed as to the relevant law could have come to the determination under appeal. In those circumstances, too, the Court must intervene. It has no option but to assume that there has been some misconception of the law and that this has been responsible for the determination. So there, too, there has been error in point of law. I do not think that it much matters whether this state of affairs is described as one in which there is no evidence to support the determination or as one in which the evidence is inconsistent with and contradictory of the determination or as one in which the true and only reasonable conclusion contradicts the determination. Rightly understood, each phrase propounds the same test. For my part, I prefer the last of the three, since I think that it is rather misleading to speak of there being no evidence to support a conclusion when in cases such as these many of the facts are likely to be neutral in themselves and only to take their colour from the combination of circumstances in which they are found to occur."

Thus if the court is satisfied that the only reasonable conclusion to which the Commissioners could come on the facts found by them is that a trade was (or was not) carried on, it will set aside any determination of the Commissioners to the contrary.

Judicial Decisions

2–04   The *Law Reports* abound in decisions on the question whether an activity constitutes trading. Only by study of these cases can one come to recognise the incidents which distinguish the trading from the non-trading activity. Some of these incidents are now considered.

---

10. See generally *Edwards* v. *Bairstow and Harrison* [1956] A.C. 14 (H.L.); 36 T.C. 207; *Jeffrey* v. *Rolls-Royce Ltd.* (1962) 40 T.C. 443, *per* Viscount Simonds at p. 490. See *Tyrer* v. *Smart* (1978) 52 T.C.533 (H.L.) in § 3–05, note 26. See *ACT Construction Ltd.* v. *Customs and Excise Commissioners* [1980] S.T.C. 716 (C.A.), *per* Lord Denning at p. 720.

11. [1956] A.C. 14 at p. 35; 36 T.C. 207 at p. 229. See also *Ransom* v. *Higgs* (1974) 50 T.C. 1 (H.L.), *per* Lord Simon at pp. 95–96.

The single speculation

2–05   It is wrong to suppose that the profit on a transaction escapes tax because the transaction is "isolated." Numerous decisions show that a single speculation or deal may constitute "an adventure or concern in the nature of trade."

> Thus in *Martin* v. *Lowry*[12] an agricultural machinery merchant who had had no previous connection with the linen trade purchased from the Government its entire surplus stock of aeroplane linen amounting to some 44 million yards. Failing to sell the linen outright to manufacturers, he set up an organisation to facilitate its disposal to the public; he advertised extensively, rented offices and engaged a manager and staff. By this means he disposed of the linen over a period of about 12 months and realised a profit of about £1,900,000. It was held that, although there was a single purchase and the taxpayer envisaged a "single gigantic speculation," the operations constituted trading.

Martin v. *Lowry* was a case of a single purchase and of a disposal through a selling organisation over a considerable period. But a single purchase followed by a single immediate sale may likewise constitute trading.

> Thus in *Rutledge* v. *I.R.C.*[13] the taxpayer, while on business in Berlin for a cinema company in which he was interested, purchased one million rolls of toilet paper for £1,000. Within a short time after his return to England he sold the entire consignment to one person at a profit of over £10,000. It was held that this was an adventue in the nature of trade.

2–06 This case, and the preceding case, illustrate that the commercial nature of a transaction may be deduced from the nature and quantity of the subject-matter. A person who purchases a vast consignment of linen or toilet paper must be taken to have intended to resell it and thus to be engaged in a commercial speculation. Where the property purchased is income-producing or has some value as an investment or some other intrinsic value (*e.g.* a work of art), its subsequent realisation at a profit may not constitute trading.

> Thus in *I.R.C.* v. *Reinhold*,[14] the taxpayer (a director of a company carrying on the business of warehousemen) bought four houses. He admitted that he bought them for resale and that he had once before engaged in a property deal. The Court of Session held that the fact that property was purchased with a view to resale did not of itself establish that the transaction was an adventure in the nature of trade, and that the Commissioners were justified in treating the profit as not assessable.

Lord Keith stated the position as follows:

> "It is not enough for the Revenue to show that the subjects were purchased with the intention of realising them some day at a profit. This is the expectation of most, if not all, people who make investments. Heritable property is a not uncommon subject of investment and generally has the feature, expected of

---

12. [1927] A.C. 312; 11 T.C. 320 (H.L.).
13. (1929) 14 T.C. 490. See also *I.R.C.* v. *Fraser* (1942) 24 T.C. 498: woodcutter buys whisky in bond, does not take delivery, resells at a profit: held to be trading; and *J. P. Harrison (Watford) Ltd.* v. *Griffiths* (1962) 40 T.C. 281 at p. 303.
14. (1953) 34 T.C. 389. *Cf. Cooke* v. *Haddock* (1960) 39 T.C. 64 where the interest on moneys borrowed to purchase land exceeded the net income from the land; this is not consistent with normal investment policy. See also *Turner* v. *Last* (1965) 42 T.C. 517; *Johnston* v. *Heath* (1970) 46 T.C. 463.

investments, of yielding an income while it is being held. In the present case the property yielded an income from rents. . . . The intention to resell some day at a profit is not *per se* sufficient in this case to attract tax."

Stock exchange transactions

2–06A   Modern case law recognises that a transaction involving the purchase and sale of shares on a stock exchange may fall into one of three categories: (i) trading; (ii) investment; and (iii) "gambling."

Thus in *Lewis Emanuel & Son Ltd.* v. *White*[15] Pennycuick, J. said (at p. 377):

" . . . it is certainly true, at any rate in the case of an individual, that he may carry out a whole range of financial activities which do not amount to a trade but which could equally not be described as an investment, even upon a short term basis. These activities include betting and gambling in the narrow sense. They also include, it seems to me, all sorts of stock exchange transactions. For want of a better phrase, I will describe this class of activities as gambling transactions. . . . "

In that case the company claimed to have made losses from *trading* in shares and claimed loss relief. The Crown rejected the claim loss relief but could not, on the facts, contend that the company was an investor. The Crown, having no other alternative contended that the company had entered into *gambling transactions* and not trading transactions. The judge rejected this contention on the ground that the company was a trading company without power to engage in gambling transactions. He said this (at p. 378):

"An individual may do as he pleases: a corporation must act within the limitation of its memorandum of association. All companies have power to invest; many companies have power to deal in securities; few companies can have power to enter into gambling transactions—i.e. by definition, transaction otherwise than by way of investment or trade. When a transaction can be brought within the scope of an authorised object—e.g. investment or dealing—one would not readily treat the transaction as having been carried out *ultra vires* in pursuit of an authorised object—e.g. gambling."

It is thought that many adventures carried out by individuals on the Stock Exchange are properly categorised as "gambling transactions" in the sense in which the phrase was used by Pennycuick J, rather than as "investment", and that this is the legal basis for the Revenue's practice of not treating ordinary stock exchange transactions as trading transactions. The older cases which tended to regard such transactions as "investment" are probably now suspect.[16]

2–06B   The difference between dealing in shares and investment may be expressed as follows: *share dealing* is the employment of cash resources in the purchase of a stock of shares, primarily with the object of turning over the stock in order to make a profit on resale. Shares acquired by a share

---

15. (1965) 42 T.C. 369. See also *Salt* v. *Chamberlain* (1979) 53 T.C. 143; [1979] S.T.C. 750.
16. See, *e.g. I.R.C.* v. *Fraser* (1942) 24 T.C. 498 at p. 502.

dealer, like other trading stock, are not bought to hold nor primarily for the yield in dividend. Characteristics of share dealing include:

(1) the purchase of shares expected to yield profit on resale in the short term;

(2) seizing every opportunity of profit as soon as the opportunity arises;

(3) a high level of activity in seeking out profitable deals, often involving the establishment of a commercial organisation for the purpose; and

(4) a rapid and continuous turnover.

2–06C   By contrast, *share investment* is the employment of cash resources in the purchase of growth stock, *i.e.* shares which are expected to appreciate in value and which, because of inflation and other factors, are a preferred alternative to holding cash. Shares bought as investments are bought to be held until growth has been achieved or seems unlikely to be further achieved, when the shares will be sold and the sale proceeds re-invested in other growth stocks. Characteristics of investment in shares include:

(1) the purchase of share expected to grow in value over the long term;

(2) selling shares when the potential for growth seems exhausted or has been achieved and re-investing the sale proceeds in shares having greater potential;

(3) the enjoyment of dividend income while the shares are held; and

(4) possibly not much activity, except when the portfolio undergoes a periodic review.

It is in the context of the above distinctions that the well-known passage in *Californian Copper Syndicate* v. *Harris*[17] should be read:

> "It is quite a well settled principle . . . that where the owner of an ordinary investment chooses to realise it, and obtains a greater price for it than he originally acquired it at, the enhanced price is not [a trading profit]. But it is equally well established that enhanced values obtained from realisation or conversion of securities may be so assessable, where what is done is not merely a realisation or change of investment, but an act done in what is truly the carrying on, or carrying out, of a business. The simplest case is that of a person or association of persons buying and selling lands or securities speculatively, in order to make gain, dealing in such investments as a business, and thereby seeking to make profits."

Some transactions are plainly trading or investment. In others the question is one of degree.[18]

Commodities

2–06D   Difficult questions sometimes arise in relation to purchases and sales of commodities or other non-income producing assets, such as bullion or Krugerrand, which are often offered as a form of "investment." In one case a profit on the sale of silver bullion purchased with *borrowed* money as

---

17. (1905) 5 T.C. 159 at p. 165.
18. See *Cooper* v. *C. & J. Clarke Ltd.* (1982) 54 T.C. 670; [1982] S.T.C. 335: shoe manufacturing company incurring losses on a short-term speculation in gilts as an "investment" of surplus funds. General Commissioners held to be a trading loss. *Held*, that the Commissioners' decision could not be set aside as wrong in law, since the case fell into the "no-man's land" of fact and degree.

a hedge against devaluation was held to be a trading profit (confirming the decision of the General Commissioners).[19] In another case, however, where a high taxpayer left the management of his investments to a merchant bank who purchased and sold silver bullion in the ordinary course of the management of the investments, the Special Commissioners decided that the profit realised for the sale of bullion was not a trading profit, distinguishing *Wisdom's* case on the ground that the bullion was there purchased with borrowed money.[20]

Adaptations

2–07   The trading (as distinct from the investment) nature of a transaction may in some cases be deduced from the method of handling or treating its subject-matter.

> Thus in *Cape Brandy Syndicate* v. *I.R.C.*,[21] three individuals in the wine trade formed a syndicate (independently of their firms) and acquired a quantity of Cape brandy. This was shipped to the United Kingdom, blended with French brandy, recasked and sold in lots to different purchasers over a period of about 18 months. It was held that the resultant profit was assessable as profit of a trade.

"This case," said Rowlatt J., "presents some curious features. It is quite clear that these gentlemen did far more than simply buy an article which they thought was going cheap, and resell it. They bought it with a view to transport it, with a view to modify its character by skilful manipulation, by blending, with a view to alter, not only the amounts by which it could be sold as a man might split up an estate, but by altering the character in the way it was done up so that it could be sold in smaller quantities. They employed experts—and were experts themselves—to dispose of it over a long period of time. . . . They did not buy it and put it away, they never intended to buy it and put it away and keep it. They bought it to turn over at once obviously and to turn over advantageously by means of the operations which I have indicated."[22]

> Similarly in *I.R.C.* v. *Livingston*,[23] three men (only one of whom was in the ship business) purchased as a joint venture a cargo vessel with a view to converting it into a steam drifter and selling it. They had never previously done this. They sold the converted ship at a profit, which was held assessable as the profit of an adventure in the nature of trade.

The test (said Lord President Clyde at p. 542) is "whether the operations involved in it are of the same kind, and carried on in the same way, as those which are characteristic of ordinary trading in the line of business in which the venture was made." All the operations carried on by the three men were characteristic of those carried on by professional ship-repairers.

---

19. *Wisdom* v. *Chamberlain* (1969) 45 T.C. 92 (C.A.).
20. The Revenue did not appeal from the decision of the Special Commissioners which is therefore unreported.
21. [1921] 2 K.B. 403; 12 T.C. 358 (C.A.).
22. In (1921) 12 T.C. 358 at p. 364. Not reported on this point in the *Law Reports*.
23. (1927) 11 T.C. 538.

Repetition

2–08   An important fact in deciding whether or not a trade (as distinct from an adventure or concern in the nature of trade) is carried on is whether the taxpayer has engaged in repeated transactions of the same kind.

> Thus in *Pickford* v. *Quirke*[24] the taxpayer was one of a syndicate who purchased the shares of a mill-owning company, liquidated the company, and sold its assets (at a profit) to another company formed for the purpose. The taxpayer had engaged in four transactions of this nature, each resulting in a profit to him. It was held that although the transactions, considered separately, were capital transactions, they together constituted the carrying on of a trade.

It follows that if there are successive purchases and resales of property over a period of time, the repetitious nature of the transactions is evidence of trading.

Profit motive

2–09   The fact that the taxpayer does not intend to make a profit or carries on activities which are not directed primarily to profit-making does not preclude the assessment of a profit which in fact emerges. The question whether there is trading must be determined objectively. If commercial methods are used, this points to trading.[25] Moreover, the fact that the taxpayer is bound by statute or otherwise to apply a profit for a particular purpose is irrelevant to the question whether the profit is the consequence of trading.[26]

Transactions designed to secure fiscal advantages

2–10   In a number of cases the question has arisen whether a loss on the purchase and resale of shares arose in the ordinary course of a trade of dealing in shares, where the transaction was a device to secure some fiscal advantage, as by dividend stripping. The principles may be summarised as follows. A share dealing which is clearly part of a trade of dealing in shares will not cease to be so merely by virtue of the dealer's intention to obtain a fiscal advantage[27]; but what is in reality merely a device to secure a fiscal advantage will not become part of a trade of dealing in shares because it is given the trappings normally associated with a share dealing within the trade of dealing in shares.[28]

---

24. (1927) 13 T.C. 251 (C.A.) (an Excess Profits Duty case). See also *I.R.C.* v. *Rolls-Royce Ltd.* (1962) 40 T.C. 443 (H.L.).
25. *Grove* v. *Y.M.C.A.* (1903) 4 T.C. 613: restaurant carried on by Y.M.C.A. held to be a trading activity. *Cf. Religious Tract and Book Society* v. *Forbes* (1896) 3 T.C. 415: colportage business held not to be a trade.
26. *Mersey Docks and Harbour Board* v. *Lucas* (1883) 8 App.Cas. 891; 2 T.C. 25.
27. *Griffiths* v. *J. P. Harrison (Watford) Ltd.* [1963] A.C. 1; 40 T.C. 281 (H.L.).
28. *Lupton* v. *F.A. & A.B. Ltd.* [1972] A.C. 634; 47 T.C. 580 (H.L.); *Thomson* v. *Gurneville Securities Ltd.* [1972] A.C. 661; 47 T.C. 633 (H.L.); *Finsbury Securities Ltd.* v. *Bishop* (1966) 43 T.C. 591 (H.L.). For an article on the cases in this and the preceding note, see [1972] B.T.R. 6, and see *Newstead* v. *Frost* (1980) 53 T.C. 525; [1980] S.T.C. 123 (H.L.).

Business knowledge

2–11   The business knowledge of the taxpayer or of his associates[29] may indicate the commercial nature of a transaction. In the *Cape Brandy*[30] case, Rowlatt J. referred to the expert knowledge of the members of the syndicate; and in *I.R.C.* v. *Fraser*,[31] Lord Normand said that "It is in general more easy to hold that a single transaction entered into by an individual in the line of his own trade (although not part and parcel of his ordinary business) is an adventure in the nature of trade than to hold that a transaction entered into by an individual outside the line of his own trade or occupation is an adventure in the nature of trade."

Mere realisation

2–11A   The mere act of selling property does not constitute trading. The concept of trading generally implies purchasing property with the object at the time of purchase of resale at a profit although the cases establish that the taxpayer's object at the time of purchase is a matter to be determined objectively in the light of all surrounding circumstances including, for example, inferences to be drawn from the nature of the commodity purchased: see §§ 2–05 *et seq.* Where property is purchased as an investment (*e.g.* income-producing land or shares) or to be used or enjoyed (*e.g.* a private residence or an old master), a surplus which emerges on a subsequent sale is not a trading profit even if steps have been taken (*e.g.* the obtaining of planning permission in respect of land or the restoration of an old master) to obtain the best possible price on resale. Where a landowner lays out part of his estate with roads and sewers and sells it in lots for building, he does this as a landowner and not as a speculator or trader.[32] Similarly, if land is purchased as an investment and the landowner, realising that his investment is no longer a sound one, decides to sell off the land this is not trading.[33]

Property not originally purchased for resale in the course of trade may be "appropriated" to trading stock. An established trader in old masters might, for example, elect to deal with a painting acquired by inheritance by exhibiting it for sale in his gallery in the ordinary course of his trade; or a non-trader, wishing to embark on a trade of *buying and selling* paintings, might initiate the trade by using assets acquired by inheritance as opening stock-in-trade. In such cases the paintings are said to be appropriated to trading stock with the consequences (i) that there is a notional disposal of the assets for capital gains tax purposes at their market value at the time of appropriation[34] and (ii) that the assets are brought into trading stock at their market value at that time.[35]

---

29. *Burrell, Webber, Magness, Austin and Austin* v. *Davis* (1958) 38 T.C. 307.
30. [1921] 2 K.B. 403; 12 T.C. 358 (C.A.); *ante*, § 2–07.
31. (1942) 24 T.C. 498: see note 13, *supra.*
32. *Hudson's Bay Co. Ltd.* v. *Stevens* (1909) 5 T.C. 424, *per* Farwell L.J. at p. 437; *Rand* v. *Alberni Land Co. Ltd.* (1920) 7 T.C. 629. *Cf. Alabama Coal, etc., Co. Ltd.* v. *Mylam* (1926) 11 T.C. 232.
33. *West* v. *Phillips* (1958) 38 T.C. 203; *Eames* v. *Stepnell Properties Ltd.* (1967) 43 T.C. 678; *Simmons* v. *I.R.C.* (1980) 53 T.C. 461; [1980] S.T.C. 350 (H.L.).
34. C.G.T.A. 1979, s.122, discussed *post*, § 16–11.
35. See *post*, § 2–48. Thus any profit which arises before appropriation bears capital gains tax and only the subsequent profit (if any) is taxed as a trading profit.

Thus in *Pilkington* v. *Randall*[36] the taxpayer purchased his sister's share of inherited land with a view to making a profit by resale after development, and it was found as a fact that he appropriated his own inherited share to trading stock at the same time.

Although an established trader may appropriate non-trading assets to trading stock, assets purchased by a non-trader for an admitted non-trading purpose do not subsequently become trading stock where the purchaser does nothing more than take steps to realise the assets to the greatest advantage, having no intention of making any further purchases.[37]

Where land which is acquired with a non-trading purpose is subsequently developed with the sole or main object of realising a gain from disposing of the land when developed, any gain of a capital nature which is obtained from the disposal of the land, so far as attributable to the period after the intention to develop was formed, is chargeable to income tax under Case VI of Schedule D under provisions contained in section 488 of the Income and Corporation Taxes Act 1970.[38]

Company transactions

2–12   The tests for determining whether an activity is trading are the same for companies as for individuals. But as Pennycuick J. pointed out in the passage quoted in § 2–06A, an indivdual may do as he pleases whereas a company must act within the limitations of its memorandum of association: if it acts *ultra vires*, its acts may be unlawful. This leads on logically to the conclusion that if, for example, a company is formed specifically for the purpose of dealing in shares or in land (*i.e.* if dealing is its substantive main object[39]), there is an initial presumption (no more) that its transactions in shares or in land are dealing transactions. The objects clause can never, however, be conclusive as to the nature for tax purposes of a company's activities. In *I.R.C.* v. *Hyndland Investment Co. Ltd.*[40] the Lord President (at p. 699) said:

> "The first point that strikes one is that the company in its Memorandum of Association describes its objects as being the acquisition of land and other heritable property, and the holding of the same as an investment, and the division of the income thereof. That is not, however, conclusive, because the question is not what business does the taxpayer profess to carry on, but what business does he actually carry on."

The professed objects are no more than one of the factors to be taken

---

36. (1966) 42 T.C. 662 (C.A.). But see *McClelland* v. *Australia Taxation Commissioner* [1971] 1 W.L.R. 191 (P.C.) (where M. sold part of inherited land in order to buy out her brother's interest in the remaining land: *held* to be a capital accretion and not an "undertaking or scheme" producing assessable income).

37. *Taylor* v. *Good* (1974) 49 T.C. 277 (C.A.). And see *Simmons* v. *I.R.C.* (1980) 53 T.C. 461; [1980] S.T.C. 350 (H.L.).

38. See *post*, §§ 40–16 *et seq.*

39. See generally *Re Horsley & Weight Ltd.* [1982] Ch. 442 (C.A.) and *Rolled Steel Products (Holdings) Ltd.* v. *British Steel Corp.* [1984] B.C.L.C. 466 (C.A.).

40. (1929) 14 T.C. 694. And see *W. M. Robb Ltd.* v. *Page* (1971) 47 T.C. 465: factory built by trading company in course of its trade but shown as fixed capital in accounts, profit on sale held a trading receipt.

into account in determining a transaction is a trading transaction or not.[41] Where the memorandum of association is so constructed as to give the company all the powers of an individual, in so far as they are capable of being exercised by a legal entity, the objects clause will throw no light on the nature of the company's activities.

It follows that individuals who wish to incorporate a company for the purpose of dealing in shares should ensure that this is the *substantive main object* of the company and that there is no more than a *power* to invest. But this will not establish dealing unless the company's activities, viewed objectively, constitute share dealing.

Share transactions

2–13   If the shares of a company are sold at a profit, the share-vendor's profit is not assessable under Case I of Schedule D unless he can be shown to be a dealer in shares. This was the basis of a common device for avoiding tax on land deals: the dealer caused the land to be conveyed to a company under his control and, later, when a profit was to be made, sold the shares in the company. By the Finance Act 1960 profits on the sale of shares in land-owning companies were made assessable under Case VI of Schedule D as if the shareholders had themselves bought and sold the land.[42]

In one case a company (A Limited) owned certain land. To procure the development of the land and turn it to account, another company (B Limited) was formed with capital subscribed equally by A Limited and C, an individual. A Limited and C provided capital to finance the purchase of the land by B Limited from A Limited and its development. On completion of the development A Limited sold its shares in B Limited to C. It was held that the profit made by A Limited was taxable as a trading profit. A Limited had employed this device as a special method of dealing with land in which, in reality, it continued to retain an interest.[43]

Share exchanges, etc.

2–13A   Where shares which are held as circulating capital (*e.g.* trading stock) are exchanged for other shares or securities, *e.g.* on a takeover, the shares acquired on the exchange have to be valued and any profit on the transaction is taxable under Case I of Schedule D. Section 46 of the Finance Act 1977 now affords a measure of relief where, if the shares had been held as fixed capital, roll over relief would have been available under the capital gains tax rules: see §§ 40–28 *et seq.* Thus if a bank holds as circulating capital 30 per cent. of the shares of Company A (called "the original hold-

---

41. *Balgownie Land Trust Ltd.* v. *I.R.C.* (1929) 14 T.C. 684 at p. 692. See, *e.g.* cases in note 17 to § 2–06.
42. See now I.C.T.A. 1970, ss.488–489 discussed *post*, §§ 40–16 *et seq.*
43. *Associated London Properties Ltd.* v. *Henriksen* (1944) 26 T.C. 46. *Cf. Fundfarms Developments Ltd.* v. *Parsons* (1969) 45 T.C. 707 in which a property development company purchased shares in a land-owning company as an indirect means of acquiring the land and subsequently realised a loss on the liquidation of the company so acquired. *Held*, not a trading loss; the transaction, though of a trading or commercial character, did not form part of the normal business of the company.

ing") which it transfers in exchange for an issue of shares or debentures (called "the new holding") in Company B, the bank incurs no tax liability under Case I of Schedule D until it sells the new holding in Company B. Section 46(3) of the Finance Act 1977 provides that in making any computation in accordance with the provisions of the Taxes Act applicable to Case I of Schedule D of the profits or losses of the business, the transaction shall be treated as not involving any disposal of the original holding, and the new holding shall be treated as the same asset as the original holding. The section applies where the securities comprised in the new holding are issued after April 19, 1977. The clearance procedure under section 88 of the Capital Gains Tax Act 1979 is available where relief under section 46(3) is claimed: see § 40–31.

Illegal trading

2–14   Once it is established that an activity constitutes trading, any profits thereof which are illegally obtained are nevertheless assessable to tax.[44] The trader cannot rely on the incidental illegality to avoid tax.[45] For this reason, profits derived from *ultra vires* trading are taxable.[46] It is doubtful if systematic crime can itself constitute a trade.[47]

Trading after discontinuance

2–15   The mere realisation of assets *after* the permanent discontinuance of a trade, *e.g.* by a liquidator in the course of winding up a company or by personal representatives in the course of administration, is not trading if it is incidental to the liquidation or administration.[48]

> Thus in *I.R.C.* v. *Nelson*[49] a whisky broker was compelled through ill-health to close his business. He closed his bank account, instructed his accountant to wind up the business, and notified creditors and customers. Within a few days, one of his customers purchased the business including a stock of whisky which was its principal asset; but the Special Commissioners found the purchaser wanted only the whisky and not the business. *Held,* there was evidence on which the Commissioners could properly find that the transaction took place *after* trading had ceased and was not a realisation in the course of trade.

If a trader decides to have a "closing down" sale of stock, he will be treated as realising assets in the course of trade until the stock is finally sold off.[50]

If the liquidator or personal representative does something more than merely realise assets, *e.g.* if he also makes purchases, he may be held to be

---

44. *Mann* v. *Nash* [1932] 1 K.B. 752; 16 T.C. 523 (diddler machines); *Southern* v. *A.B.* [1933] 1 K.B. 713; 18 T.C. 59.
45. *Minister of Finance* v. *Smith* [1927] A.C. 193 (J.C.).
46. See *Lewis Emanuel* v. *White* (1965) 42 T.C. 369 at p. 377; *ante* § 2–06.
47. In *Partridge* v. *Mallandaine* (1886) 2 T.C. 179 at p. 181. Denman J. expressed the view that the profits of systematic crime were assessable; but the report in (1886) 18 Q.B.D. 276 has been considerably revised. In *Lindsay* v. *I.R.C.* (1933) 18 T.C. 43 at p. 55. Lord Clyde expressed a contrary view; so also Lord Denning in *J. P. Harrison (Watford) Ltd.* v. *Griffiths* (1962) 40 T.C. 281 at p. 299. See also *I.R.C.* v. *Alexander von Glehn & Co. Ltd.* [1920] 2 K.B. 553; 12 T.C. 232, especially Scrutton L.J.
48. *Cohan's Executors* v. *I.R.C.* (1924) 12 T.C. 602 (C.A.).
49. (1939) 22 T.C. 716.
50. *O'Kane & Co.* v. *I.R.C.* (1922) 12 T.C. 303 (H.L.).

trading,[51] unless such purchases were necessary to facilitate the disposal of the existing assets.[52]

If the deceased trader was one of a number of partners, the participation of his personal representatives in the trading activities of the continuing partners will not necessarily constitute trading.[53]

Certain tax advantages which may be obtained by postponing the realisation of stock until after discontinuance have been nullified by statute: see § 2–38.

Mutual trading

2–16 Where a number of persons contribute to a common fund for their mutual benefit, as in the case of a mutual insurance body,[54] a municipal undertaking or a members club,[55] any surplus received by the members on the division of the fund is tax free. "As the common fund is composed of sums provided by the contributors out of their own moneys, any surplus arising after satisfying claims obviously remains their own money. Such a surplus resulting from miscalculation or unexpected immunity cannot in any sense be regarded as taxable profit. This was clearly laid down in the case of *New York Life Insurance Co.* v. *Styles:*"[56]

> "The cardinal requirement is that all the contributors to the common fund must be entitled to participate in the surplus and that all the participators in the surplus must be contributors to the common fund; in other words, there must be complete identity between the contributors and the participators. If this requirement is satisfied, the particular form which the association takes is immaterial."[57]

Thus the principle applies if the association is carried on through the medium or machinery of an incorporated company. The cardinal requirement referred to is satisfied if, at any given time, the contributors comprise the same group of persons as those who are entitled to participate in a surplus: it matters not that the group is a fluctuating body with a changing membership.[58] The mutual principle can be usefully employed by farmers, fruit growers and others who wish to form a "Co-operative" Society for the purpose of acquiring and holding equipment to be used in common by the members.

---

51. *Weisberg's Executrices* v. *I.R.C.* (1933) 17 T.C. 696.
52. *I.R.C.* v. *Old Bushmills Distillery Co. Ltd.* (1928) 12 T.C. 1148: liquidator purchased spirit to blend with the company's stock of whisky, also bottles and casks to facilitate sale. *Held*, not trading. *Cf. Alabama Coal* v. *Mylam* (1926) 11 T.C. 232.
53. *Marshall and Hood's Executors and Rogers* v. *Joly* (1936) 20 T.C. 256; *cf. Newbarns Syndicate* v. *Hay* (1939) 22 T.C. 461 (C.A.).
54. *New York Life Insurance Co.* v. *Styles* (1889) 14 App.Cas. 381; 2 T.C. 460 (H.L.).
55. *I.R.C.* v. *The Eccentric Club Ltd.* [1924] 1 K.B. 390; 12 T.C. 657 (H.L.).
56. (1889) 14 App.Cas. 381; 2 T.C. 460 (H.L.). The decision of the Judicial Committee in *Fletcher* v. *Income Tax Commissioner* [1972] A.C. 414 (J.C.) merits study. For a useful article, see Robert Burgess "The Mutuality Principle" [1976] B.T.R. 361.
57. *Municipal Mutual Insurance Ltd.* v. *Hills* (1932) 16 T.C. 430 (H.L.), *per* Lord Macmillan at p. 448; see also *Jones* v. *South-West Lancashire Coal Owners' Association Ltd.* [1927] A.C. 827; 11 T.C. 790 (H.L.).
58. *Faulconbridge* v. *National Employers' Mutual General Insurance Association Ltd.* (1952) 33 T.C. 103.

2–17   If a mutual association trades with outsiders, the profits of that trade are taxable. Thus in *Carlisle and Silloth Golf Club* v. *Smith*,[59] profits on green fees charged by a golf club to outsiders were held to be taxable; and in *N.A.L.G.O.* v. *Watkins*,[60] profits derived from the admission of non-members of a trade union to a holiday camp established for union members were held to be taxable. Where such profits are derived from a trade or adventure or concern in the nature of trade, tax will be charged under Case I of Schedule D. In other cases, liability will fall under Case VI of Schedule D.

2–18   The mutual trading doctrine has presented opportunities for the avoidance of tax.

> Thus in *Brogan* v. *Stafford Coal & Iron Co. Ltd.*[61] the appellant company and a number of other colliery companies were members of a mutual indemnity company formed to insure their members against accident claims. The mutual company insured only its own members and its only source of income was premiums paid by the members, such premiums being deductible as trading expenses of the member-companies.[62] On the nationalisation of the collieries, the mutual company ceased to carry on business and a substantial surplus was received on the liquidation of the mutual insurance company by the appellant company. The House of Lords held that this surplus was not taxable, notwithstanding that the premiums were deductible.

The decision in *Brogan's* case was nullified by section 21 of the Finance Act 1964 (now s.347 of the Income and Corporation Taxes Act 1970), under which the surpluses received in similar cases are now taxable. The provisions of the Corporation Tax Acts relating to distributions apply in some cases to distributions by a mutual concern.[63]

Farming, etc.

2–18A   All farming and market gardening in the United Kingdom is treated as the carrying on of a trade within Case I of Schedule D; so also is any occupation of land in the United Kingdom where the land is managed on a commercial basis with a view to the realisation of profits.[64] Commercial woodlands are discussed in § 6–04.

3. The Computation of Profits

A. General Matters

2–19   Tax under Schedule D Cases I and II is charged on the "annual profits or gains" of the trade, profession or vocation.[65] The word "annual" in this context means that only profits of an income nature (as distinct from capi-

---

59. [1913] 3 K.B. 75; 6 T.C. 198. See also *Fletcher* v. *Income Tax Commissioner* [1972] A.C. 414 (J.C.), where the "outsiders" (hotel guests) came to enjoy club facilities through "hotel membership" and the mutual principle was held not to apply.
60. (1934) 18 T.C. 499.
61. (1963) 41 T.C. 305 (H.L.).
62. *Thomas* v. *Richard Evans & Co. Ltd.* [1927] 1 K.B. 33; 11 T.C. 790 (C.A.).
63. I.C.T.A. 1970, s.346.
64. *Ibid.* s.110.
65. *Ibid.* ss.108–109.

tal profits) are chargeable to tax; the word does not mean that profits are chargeable only if they are recurrent.[66] Thus the profits of an isolated transaction in the nature of trade are "annual profits."[67] The Tax Acts do not prescribe general rules as to the manner in which annual profits or gains should be determined for tax purposes. The Acts assume that the trader will prepare an account showing his profit or loss for the accounting period and that this account will be prepared in accordance with correct principles of commercial accounting.[68] The profit or loss disclosed by this account will be the profit or loss for the purposes of Case I or II of Schedule D, as appropriate, subject to any adjustments which may be required by the Tax Acts or may be needed to comply with established principles of revenue law:

> " . . . first, . . . the ordinary principles of commercial accounting must, as far as practicable, be observed, and, secondly, . . . the law relating to income tax must not be violated . . . that is to say, by one means or another the full amount of the profits or gains must be determined."[69]

2–19A   The role of the evidence of accountants in the determination of profit has been considered by the courts in a number of cases. In *Odeon Associated Theatres Ltd.* v. *Jones*[70] the Special Commissioners found as a fact on the basis of expert evidence from accountants that, in accordance with the principles of sound commercial accounting at the relevant time, the disputed expenditure [on deferred repairs] would be dealt with as a charge to revenue in the purchasers' accounts. The court could find no reason in law for dissenting from this finding of fact and the expenditure was accordingly allowed as a deduction for tax purposes. The *Odeon* case led some commentators to suppose that the question whether expenditure was of a capital or revenue nature was a matter for accountancy evidence alone, but in *Heather* v. *P.-E. Consulting Group Ltd.*[71] it was held that the question of capital or revenue was a question of law for the court to decide. In the *Odeon* case Buckley L.J. said:

> "As Lord Reid observed in *Regent Oil Co.* v. *Strick*,[72] 'The question [whether a particular outlay can be set against income or must be regarded as a capital outlay] is ultimately a question of law for the court, but it is a question which must be answered in light of all the circumstances which it is reasonable to take into account, and the weight which must be given to a particular circumstance

---

66. *Scottish Provident Institution* v. *Farmer* (1912) 6 T.C. 34; *Ryall* v. *Hoare* [1923] 2 K.B. 447 at p. 454; 8 T.C. 521 at p. 526.
67. *Martin* v. *Lowry* [1926] 1 K.B. 550 at pp. 556, 558; 11 T.C. 297 at pp. 310, 311, 312; affirmed [1927] A.C. 312; 11 T.C. 320.
68. *Whimster & Co.* v. *I.R.C.* (1926) 12 T.C. 813, *per* Lord President Clyde.
69. *Duple Motors Ltd.* v. *I.R.C.* (1961) 39 T.C. 537, *per* Lord Simonds at p. 566.
70. (1971) 48 T.C. 257 (C.A.). For the facts, see § 2–62. See also *Pitt* v. *Castle Hill Warehousing Co. Ltd.* (1974) 49 T.C. 638; *E.C.C. Quarries Ltd.* v. *Watkis* (1975) 51 T.C. 153; [1975] S.T.C. 578.
71. [1973] Ch. 189; 48 T.C. 293 (C.A.). For the facts see § 2–53, note 69.
72. [1966] A.C. 295 at p. 313; 43 T.C. 1 at p. 29 (H.L.). For the facts see § 2–56. "If a trader acquires a rapidly wasting asset . . . he would not generally strike his balance of profits and gains without taking account of the annual wasting or diminution of the asset. But if his expenditure in acquiring it has to be regarded as capital expenditure he cannot do that for income tax purposes." (Lord Reid in [1966] A.C. 295 at p. 314D.)

in a particular case must depend rather on common sense than on a strict application of any single legal principle.' In answering that question of law it is right
that the court should pay regard to the ordinary principles of commercial
accounting so far as applicable. Accountants are, after all, the persons best
qualified by training and practical experience to suggest answers to the many
difficult problems that can arise in this field. Nevertheless, the question
remains ultimately a question of law."

The principle has recently been re-affirmed by the House of Lords in
Willingale v. *International Commercial Bank Ltd.*, which is discussed in
§ 2–21A.

Cash or earnings basis

2–20   As a general rule, the profits of the trade must be computed for tax purposes by crediting sums *earned* in the accounting period and not merely
sums actually received. If a trader contracts to sell goods in year 1 for
delivery in year 2, payment to be due on delivery, the amount due should
be credited as a trading receipt of year 2 because, by delivery, the trader
will have fulfilled the condition entitling him to payment.[73] The goods in
such a case are replaced in the trader's books by a debt and so the profit (if
any) has been "earned" or "realised." If the contract in such a case provided for delivery to be made in year 2 but for payment to be made in (say)
year 3, the trader should nevertheless bring in the price as a trading receipt
of year 2. If the position were otherwise, a trader who purchased goods for
£500 and sold them for £600 in the same accounting period on the terms
that the price should be paid in a later period or periods, would show (in
respect of that transaction) a trading loss whereas, on normal accounting
principles, he would have earned a profit of £100. Lord Simon stated the
principle as follows in *I.R.C.* v. *Gardner, Mountain and D'Ambrumenil
Ltd.*[74]:

> "In calculating the taxable profit of a business on income tax principles . . .
> goods supplied, which are not to be paid for until a subsequent year, cannot,
> generally speaking, be dealt with by treating the taxpayer's outlay as pure loss
> in the year in which it was incurred and bringing in the remuneration as pure
> profit in the subsequent year in which it is paid, or is due to be paid. In making
> an assessment to income tax under Schedule D the net result of the trans-
> action, setting expenses on the one side and a figure for remuneration on the
> other side, ought to appear (as it would appear in a proper system of account-
> ancy) in the same year's profit and loss account, and that year will be the year
> when the . . . goods were delivered . . . this may involve in some instances, an
> estimate of what the future remuneration will amount to. . . . "[75]

The principle applies only where the trader has fulfilled *all* the conditions

---

73. *J. P. Hall & Co.* v. *I.R.C.* [1921] 3 K.B. 152; 12 T.C. 382 (C.A.); *I.R.C.* v. *Newcastle
Breweries Ltd.* (1927) 12 T.C. 927 (H.L.); *New Conveyor Co. Ltd.* v. *Dodd* (1945) 27 T.C. 11.
74. (1947) 29 T.C. 69 at p. 93 (H.L.). See also Whiteman and Wheatcroft, §§ 9–03 *et seq.*
For a case in which trade expenses were "bunched" into a single year and partially disallowed,
see § 2–70, note 34.
75. A trader who failed to recover the sum earned would be entitled to bad debt relief: see
post, § 2–68.

entitling him to payment; and it applies not only to a contract of sale but also to a contract for the supply of services. In one case a company was refused planning consent in year 1. On selling the land in year 5 the company became entitled to compensation in respect of the earlier refusal. It was held that since the compensation was payable only when the company sold the land, it should be credited as a trade receipt of year 5.[76]

If the trader receives payment in money's worth, this must be brought in at market value, subject to the statutory exception in § 2–13A.[77]

> In *Emery & Sons* v. *I.R.C.*[78] a firm of builders sold freehold houses for a cash payment and a rentcharge reserved out of the land. It was held that the realisable value of the rentcharge should be added to the cash payment in computing the receipts of the firm.

2–21   In the case of professions and vocations, the Revenue may allow profits to be calculated by reference to actual cash received in the accounting period, no account being taken during any accounting period of uncollected fees. The accounts of barristers and authors are often rendered on this "cash" (or "receipts") basis but there is no rule of law to prevent them rendering accounts on an earnings basis, if they choose to do so. In the case of other professions (*e.g.* solicitors) the Revenue may allow accounts to be submitted on a cash basis, except in the early years when the earnings basis is usually obligatory. Thereafter, the Revenue may allow a change to a cash basis (usually only on the taxpayer giving an undertaking to render bills promptly), but no deduction is allowed from the profits computed on a cash basis in respect of fees already brought into charge on an earnings basis.[79] Such fees may thus be taxed twice.[80] Once an assessment has been made on a cash basis for any year, it is not open to the Revenue to make additional assessments on an earnings basis for that year; but the Revenue can make original assessments for other years on an earnings basis.[81]

Profits not yet earned

2–21A   The converse of the principle stated in § 2–20 is that a trader who is assessed on the "earnings basis" cannot be taxed on profits which have not yet been earned. The question whether a profit had been earned arose in

---

76. *Johnson* v. *W. S. Try Ltd.* (1946) 27 T.C. 167 (C.A.).

77. *Gold Coast Selection Trust Ltd.* v. *Humphrey* [1948] A.C. 459; 30 T.C. 209. In *Varty* v. *British South Africa Co.* (1965) 42 T.C. 406 (H.L.) a company had an option to acquire shares at 20s. each which it exercised when the shares were worth 43s. 6d. It was held that the exercise of the option was not a realisation: no trading profit or loss would arise until the shares were sold.

78. [1937] A.C. 91; 20 T.C. 213. When a builder sells leasehold houses for a premium and a ground rent, only the premium is brought in as a Case I trading receipt: *Hughes* v. *Utting* [1940] A.C. 436. The ground rent remains part of the builder's stock-in-trade and must be brought in at cost price, see *post* §§ 2–34 *et seq.*). If the ground rents are sold, the proceeds of the sale must be brought in, as Case I trading receipts of the accounting period when the sale occurs.

79. *I.R.C.* v. *Morrison* (1932) 17 T.C. 325.

80. This apparent inequity was at one time compensated by the immunity from tax (now abolished) of post-cessation receipts: *post*, §§ 2–88 *et seq.*

81. *Rankine* v. *I.R.C.* (1952) 32 T.C. 520; *Wetton Page & Co.* v. *Attwooll* (1962) 40 T.C. 619.

Willingale v. *International Commercial Bank Ltd.*[82] in relation to bills purchased by a bank at a discount. A typical transaction was as follows. In 1970 the bank purchased, for £1,000, a bill having a face value of £1,500 which was due to mature in 1975. From the date of purchase onwards the bill's market value increased as the maturity date drew nearer and, in its accounts for each year, the bank credited a fractional part of the profit which the bank expected to make assuming the bills were held to maturity. Accountancy evidence showed that this was an appropriate method of applying the principles of commercial accountancy, consistent with that adopted by the clearing banks, since it gave a fair and realistic picture of the position from year to year. There was also evidence that it would have been equally appropriate as a matter of accountancy treatment to bring in any profit only when a bill either matured or was sold.

The Revenue contended that the bank should be treated as having earned the profit attributable to the bill in each of the five years, *i.e.* that the accountancy treatment actually adopted by the bank should be applied for tax purposes. The bank contended that the profit on the bill was not "earned" or "realised" until the year in which the bill matured or was sold prior to maturity. (The Revenue did not contend that the profit realised in year 5 should be related back to the earlier years.)

The House of Lords (by a majority), affirming the decision (by a majority) of the Court of Appeal, decided as follows. First, it affirmed the principle stated in § 2–19A that the principles of commercial accountancy must yield to the overriding principles of tax law where there is any conflict between the two. Secondly, the court held that it was an established principle of tax law that a profit cannot be taxed until it is "earned" or "realised." A trader cannot be taxed on "contingent profits." Put in another way, neither profit or loss may be "anticipated" save in the exceptional case of stock-in-trade: see § 2–35. (There was an alternative contention by the bank that the bills were stock-in-trade but, in the absence of any finding by the Commissioners to this effect, this contention was not dealt with by the court.) Thirdly, the court held that no profit was earned by the bank until the bank was entitled to receive payment on the bill, whether by reason of its maturity or on sale prior to maturity. As Ormrod L.J. said:

> "I am unable to see how it can be argued that the bank becomes legally entitled as a matter of contract to those separate increments in each of the five accounting years. The obligation of the person signing the bill is simply to pay £1,500 in five years time to the then holder of the bill. This seems to be an obligation which is different in kind from a contract to borrow money at an annual interest even if the interest is not payable until the end of the five-year period. The argument for the Crown is ultimately reduced to the proposition that just as the money earns interest in the latter case, so in the former it earns discount. This is like saying that because two roads run from A to B, they are the same road. Money "earns" interest because the lender becomes legally entitled to it during the year of account; in the instant case the bill appreciates in value in

---

82. (1978) 52 T.C. 242; [1978] S.T.C. 75 (H.L.). The example of a "typical transaction" in the text is oversimplified. Whether or not the value of a bill would "increase" with time would depend on interest trends and, in the case of non-sterling bills, changes in the value of the foreign currency relative to sterling.

the bank's safe, very much as stock-in-trade may increase in value in the trader's stores. The bank holds a single large debt, not a succession of five small ones."

Liabilities not yet matured

2–21B　　*Owen v. Southern Railway of Peru Ltd.*[83] was concerned with present liabilities to make payments in the future. Under Peruvian law S. was bound to pay its employees compensation on the termination of their employment. The amount of the compensation depended, in the case of each employee, on *inter alia* the length of his service with S. and his pay at the end of the period of service. In the year in question S. claimed to deduct £x, being the amount of the provision made in the accounts in respect of the sum total of compensation payments that might become payable in future years. Correct accountancy practice required that provision should be made in the accounts for the payments in question. The House of Lords held that there was no rule of law preventing a deduction for payments to be made at a future date; but the sum claimed as a deduction must be shown to be an accurate estimate of the claimant's liability. The £x claimed by S. did not satisfy this condition. As Lord Radcliffe said:

> "When account is taken of all the circumstances I should have thought that the sums charged were a very long way from affording a scientific appraisement of the additional burden arising in respect of the year's services, and were, therefore, *in the nature of a rough reserve against the future rather than a measured provision.*"

Post-cessation receipts

2–22　　The term "post-cessation receipts" describes sums which are received after the permanent discontinuance of a trade, profession or vocation for work done, or services rendered, before discontinuance. The liability of such receipts to tax under special provisions contained in the Tax Acts depends upon whether a cash or earnings basis was adopted.[84]

B. Trading Receipts

2–23　　Once it is established that an activity constitutes trading, the annual profits or gains thereof are assessable under Case I of Schedule D. But not *all* profits are so assessable, for some may be of a capital nature. Capital profits are not taxed as income but may fall within the scope of the tax on capital gains, discussed later in this book.

> If a manufacturer acquires a new factory and disposes of his old factory at a profit, such profit is not assessable under Schedule D, for it is an accretion to capital.

This conclusion can be reached by saying that the factory forms part of the *fixed* capital of the manufacturer and that a sum realised on the disposal of fixed capital does not have to be brought into the computation of the

---

83. (1956) 36 T.C. 634 (H.L.). *Cf. I.R.C.* v. *Titaghur Jute Factory Co. Ltd.* (1977) 53 T.C. 675; [1978] S.T.C. 166.
84. This subject is considered, *post,* §§ 2–88 *et seq.*

profits for income tax purposes: it is a capital receipt, not a revenue receipt. Alternatively, it can be said that it is excluded because it is not a receipt *of the trade* because the trade of manufacturer does not include dealing in factories. In *Mallet* v. *Staveley Coal & Iron Co. Ltd.*[85] Lord Hanworth M.R. distinguished fixed and circulating capital:

> "I think one has to keep clear in one's mind that in dealing with any business there are two kinds of capital, one the fixed capital, which is laid out in the fixed plant, whereby the opportunity of making profits or gains is secured, and the other the circulating capital, which is turned over and over in the course of the business which is carried on."

It is not always easy, however, to determine whether an asset belongs to one category or the other, and little or no assistance can be obtained by examining the nature of the asset itself. This difficulty is referred to by Romer L.J. in *Golden Horse Shoe (New) Ltd.* v. *Thurgood*[86]:

> "Land may in certain circumstances be circulating capital. A chattel or chose in action may be fixed capital. The *determining factor must be the nature of the trade in which the asset is employed.* The land upon which a manufacturer carries on his business is part of his fixed capital. The land with which a dealer in real estate carries on his business is part of his circulating capital. The machinery with which a manufacturer makes the articles that he sells is part of his fixed capital. The machinery that a dealer in machinery buys and sells is part of his circulating capital, as is the coal that a coal merchant buys and sells in the course of his trade."

Again, the character of an asset may change in the course of business: thus land originally acquired as an investment may later become part of the owner's circulating capital or stock-in-trade. Indeed, the value of the distinction between fixed and circulating capital as a criterion for determining the nature of a receipt may be questioned; but it is thought that the distinction has some value if it is recognised that the character of the asset is but one of a number of factors which are material. Where a receipt comes from the sale of ordinary trading stock or from the rendering of services, it will be brought into the computation of the annual profits or gains for tax purposes. A sum realised on the sale of a fixed asset may be a trading receipt. If, for example, the asset is sold on terms which secure to the vendor a right to future commission on sales by the purchaser the commission thus received is a trading receipt of the vendor.[87] The question in such cases is whether there is a sale of an asset providing for the payment of capital sums by instalments on a sale coupled with a collateral bargain for the sharing of commission.[88]

2–24   A sum received by a trader for undertaking *not* to carry on some trading activity may not be a receipt of the trade.

Thus in *Higgs* v. *Olivier*,[89] following the production of the film *Henry V* and to

---

85. [1928] 2 K.B. 405 at p. 413; 13 T.C. 772 at p. 780 (C.A.).
86. [1934] 1 K.B. 548 at p. 563; 18 T.C. 280 at p. 300 (C.A.).
87. *Orchard Wine and Spirit Co.* v. *Loynes* (1952) 33 T.C. 97.
88. *Lamport & Holt Line Ltd.* v. *Langwell* (1958) 38 T.C. 193 (C.A.).
89. [1952] Ch. 311; 33 T.C. 136. *Cf.* payments made to employees for restrictive covenants: *Beak* v. *Robson* [1943] A.C. 352; 25 T.C. 33; *post*, § 3–05.

assist in its promotion, Sir Laurence Olivier entered into a covenant under which he received £15,000 in consideration of an undertaking by him to appear in no other film for any company other than the covenantee company for a period of 18 months.

It was held that the sum was not taxable. It did not come to the recipient as income of his vocation; it came to him for refraining from carrying on one facet of his vocation, namely "that part of it which showed him as an actor on the celluloid stage." It should be observed that there was a finding of the Special Commissioners in that case that the covenant formed no part of the agreement under which the appellant made the film. Where, however, a trader agrees to some restriction on his trading activities as part of an arrangement to obtain supplies of raw material, the sums receivable by him are trading receipts.

Thus in *Thompson* v. *Magnesium Electron Ltd.*,[90] the respondent company entered into two agreements with I.C.I.:
  (i) an agreement for the purchase of chlorine at a stated price per ton; and
  (ii) an agreement not to manufacture chlorine or caustic soda (its by-product), in consideration of a payment of £x for each ton of caustic soda which the respondent company would have produced if it had manufactured its own chlorine, for which latter purpose it was to be treated as having produced an agreed number of tons for each ton of chlorine purchased from I.C.I.

It was held that the two agreements should be read together as an arrangement for the supply of chlorine and that the sums received under agreement (i) were taxable.

In *I.R.C.* v. *Biggar*[90a] a grant paid under the EEC Dairy Herd Conversion Scheme to a farmer who agreed to switch from dairy farming to raising cattle for beef was held to be a receipt of the trade of farming.

In this case the General Commissioners held that the grant was a capital receipt, in reliance on the decision in *Higgs* v. *Olivier* (above); but Lord Emslie (allowing the Revenue's appeal) explained the difference between the cases as follows (at p. 687):

"In *Higgs* Sir Laurence Olivier would, but for the restrictive covenant, have carried on acting in and producing and directing films as well as carrying on his vocation on the legitimate stage on radio and elsewhere. The restriction which he accepted severely limited his ability to exploit his art and exposed him to inevitable loss. In [the *Biggar*] case there is no question of there being a restriction of this kind which is capable of being equiparated with sterilisation of part of a taxpayer's capital assets. The scheme was a conversion scheme in terms of which on the one hand the taxpayer agreed to stop producing milk and milk products and, on the other hand, to begin producing meat instead. They agreed, in short, to continue to farm to their full capacity. Only the product changed."

There are many cases where the problem of distinguishing an income from a capital receipt presents great difficulty and, as Lord Macmillan said

90. (1944) 26 T.C. 1 (C.A.).
90a. (1982) 56 T.C. 254; (1982) S.T.C. 677 (C.S.).

in one such case, "the task of assigning it to income or capital is one of much refinement." Some of these cases must now be considered.

(1) *The compensation cases*

2–25   The problems now to be considered arise where a trader is deprived of some profitable asset and receives compensation by way of damages or otherwise for loss suffered or anticipated. It should be kept in mind that the cases discussed below preceded the introduction of the tax on capital gains and that compensation payments are often taxable as capital gains: see § 16–08.

2–26   *Compensation for sterilisation of assets.* The leading case is *Glenboig Union Fireclay Co. Ltd.* v. *I.R.C.*,[91] where the facts were as follows:

> The appellants manufactured fireclay goods and sold raw fireclay. They were lessees of fireclay fields in the neighbourhood of the Caledonian Railway and a dispute arose with the railway company as to their right to work the fireclay under the railway. An action by the railway company to restrain the appellants was eventually unsuccessful, but during its pendency the appellants were restrained from working the fields (but incurred expense in keeping them open). When the House of Lords decided against the railway company, that company exercised its statutory powers to require part of the fireclay to be left unworked on payment of compensation. *Held,* that the amount received for compensation was a capital receipt, not subject to tax.

Lord Wrenbury stated the principle (at p. 465) as follows:

> "Was that compensation profit? The answer may be supplied, I think, by the answer to the following question: Is a sum profit which is paid to an owner of property on the terms that he shall not use his property so as to make a profit? The answer must be in the negative. The whole point is that he is not to make a profit and is paid for abstaining from seeking to make a profit. . . . It was the price paid for sterilising the asset from which otherwise profit might have been obtained."

It must not be supposed, however, that *all* payments for sterilisation of assets are capital receipts. In the *Glenboig* case, the asset of which the appellants were deprived was a capital asset (*i.e.* fixed capital); moreover, sterilisation was complete. If the appellants had been dealers in fireclay beds (which would then be circulating capital or stock-in-trade), or if the asset had been only partially sterilised or sterilised in the last year of its effective life, the payment might be regarded as of an income nature. The real test, it seems, is whether the thing in respect of which the taxpayer has recovered compensation is the depreciation of one of the capital assets of his trading enterprise or a mere restriction of his trading opportunities.

2–27   The *Glenboig* case should be contrasted with *Burmah Steam Ship Co. Ltd.* v. *I.R.C.*[92] where the facts were as follows:

> Repairers of a vessel exceeded the time stipulated by contract for the completion of an overhaul and damages were paid in compromise of a claim for loss of profit. The payment was held to be a trading receipt.

---

91. (1921) 12 T.C. 427 (H.L.).
92. (1931) 16 T.C. 67 (Ct. of Sess.).

The character of a payment for sterilisation of assets is not determined by the manner in which the compensation payment is calculated. In the *Glenboig* case, for example, the compensation was estimated on the basis of the profits lost to the appellants; yet the payment was held to be a capital receipt.

> "There is no relation," said Lord Buckmaster, "between the measure that is used for the purpose of calculating a particular result and the quality of the figure that is arrived at by means of the application of that test."

2–28   *Compensation for cancellation of business contracts.* In *Van den Berghs Ltd.* v. *Clark*[93] an English company manufacturing margarine and other butter substitutes had a Dutch company as its principal trade rival. In 1908 and 1913 certain "pooling agreements" were entered into between the companies under which each company retained its separate identity but agreed to conduct business on certain agreed lines to the mutual advantage of both companies. After some years these agreements became unworkable and it was agreed that they should be rescinded and that the Dutch company should pay the English company £450,000 "as damages." It was held that this was a capital receipt. The following passage in Lord Macmillan's judgment[94] is frequently cited:

> "The three agreements which the appellants consented to cancel were not ordinary commercial contracts made in the course of carrying on their trade; they were not contracts for the disposal of their products, or for the engagement of agents or other employees necessary for the conduct of their business; nor were they merely agreements as to how their trading profits when earned should be distributed as between the contracting parties. On the contrary *the cancelled agreements related to the whole structure of the appellant's profit-making apparatus.* They regulated the appellants' activities, defined what they might and what they might not do, and affected the whole conduct of their business. I have difficulty in seeing how money laid out to secure, or money received for the cancellation of so fundamental an organisation of a trader's activities can be regarded as an income disbursement or an income receipt. . . . It is not the largeness of the sum that is important but the nature of the asset that was surrendered."

This passage is the foundation of the distinction, often made, between payments for the cancellation of ordinary trading contracts (which are taxable as income under Case I of Schedule D) and payments for the cancellation of contracts affecting the structure of the taxpayer's profit-making apparatus (which are not).

2–29   In contrast to the decision in the *Van den Berghs* case is *Kelsall Parsons & Co.* v. *I.R.C.*[95] The appellants were manufacturers' agents; that is, they had contracts with a number of manufacturers whose products they sold on

---

93. [1935] 431; 19 T.C. 390. See also *Barr, Crombie & Co. Ltd.* v. *I.R.C.* (1945) 26 T.C. 406; *I.R.C.* v. *Fleming & Co. (Machinery)* (1951) 33 T.C. 57; *Wiseburgh* v. *Domville* (1956) 36 T.C. 527 (C.A.); *Keir & Cawder Ltd.* v. *I.R.C.* (1958) 38 T.C. 23; *Sabine* v. *Lookers Ltd.* (1958) 38 T.C. 120 (C.A.); *Creed* v. *H. & M. Levinson Ltd.* (1981) 54 T.C. 477; (1981) S.T.C. 486.

94. [1935] A.C. 431 at pp. 442–443; 19 T.C. 390 at pp. 431–432.

95. (1938) 21 T.C. 608 (Ct. of Sess.). See also *Elson* v. *James G. Johnston Ltd.* (1965) 42 T.C. 545; *Fleming* v. *Bellow Machine Co. Ltd.* (1965) 42 T.C. 308.

a commission basis. They had sold Ellison products for some time under agency contracts which had occasionally been varied, and the agreement in force in 1934 was due to expire on September 30, 1935. In May 1934, however, Ellisons requested that the agency agreement should be terminated and, in due course, £1,500 was paid as compensation for the premature determination. This amount was held to be a taxable receipt.

The *Kelsall Parsons* case can be distinguished from the *Van den Berghs* case in the following respects:

(a) In the *Kelsall Parsons* case, the taxpayer was a manufacturers' agent, so the acquisition and loss of an agency was a normal incident of the business.

> "The agency agreements," said Lord Normand at p. 621, "so far from being a fixed framework, are rather to be regarded as temporary and variable elements of the . . . profit-making enterprise."

(b) In the *Kelsall Parsons* case, the abandoned agreement had only one year to run (a factor to which importance was attached) and the compensation was "really a surrogatum for one year's profits." In the *Van den Berghs* case, however, the cancelled agreements had 13 years to run.

There are numerous reported cases in which the courts have been called on to decide whether a payment is taxable as income, within the *Kelsall Parsons* principle, or escapes tax as income under the *Van den Berghs* principle.[96]

(2) *Unclaimed balances and released debts*

2–30   In *Morley* v. *Tattersall*,[97] a firm of bloodstock auctioneers received sums from sales for which they were liable to account to the vendors, their clients. These sums were not trade receipts; they were the clients' money. Substantial sums were never collected by the clients and remained in the firm's hands as "unclaimed balances"; and, in due course, when such balances seemed unlikely ever to be claimed, they were transferred to the credit of the individual partners. It was held that these sums were not trading receipts of the firm. The following passage from the judgment of Sir Wilfrid Greene M.R. (at p. 65) shows clearly the basis of the decision:

> "I invited Mr. Hills to point to any authority which in any way supported the proposition that a receipt which at the time of its receipt was not a trading receipt could by some subsequent operation *ex post facto* be turned into a trading receipt, not, be it observed, as at the date of receipt, but as at the date of the subsequent operation. It seems to me, with all respect to that argument, that it is based on a complete misapprehension of what is meant by a trading receipt in income tax law. . . . It seems to me that the quality and nature of a receipt for income tax purposes is fixed once and for all when it is received."

---

96. Some of these cases are cited *ante*, § 2–28 in note 93. See *London & Thames Haven Oil Wharves Ltd.* v. *Attwooll* (1966) 42 T.C. 491 (C.A.); *Rajas Commercial College* v. *Gian Singh* [1977] A.C. 312; [1976] S.T.C. 282 (J.C.); *I.R.C.* v. *Biggar* (1982) 56 T.C. 254; [1982] S.T.C. 677 (C.S.) *ante*, § 2–24; *Lang* v. *Rice* (1984) 57 T.C. 80; [1984] S.T.C. 172 (C.A., N.I.).
    97. (1938) 22 T.C. 51 (C.A.).

2–31   This case was distinguished in *Jay's the Jewellers Ltd.* v. *I.R.C.*,[98] where a company of pawnbrokers had unclaimed balances representing the proceeds of sale of unredeemed pledges. Some of these balances became the property of the pawnbroker after a period of time by virtue of the Pawnbrokers Act 1872, and these were held to have become trade receipts when they became the pawnbroker's property. The statute had changed the character of the balances. Other unclaimed balances were outside the Pawnbrokers Act but they became statute-barred after six years under the Statutes of Limitation. Atkinson J. decided that these also became trade receipts of the pawnbroker. It is not clear from the report whether this part of the case was fully argued but, in the author's view, this part of the decision cannot be reconciled with the decision of the Court of Appeal in *Tattersall*'s case.[99]

2–32   In *Elson* v. *Prices Tailors Ltd.*,[1] the defendant tailors took "deposits" from customers who ordered garments. Where garments were not collected, the deposits were eventually transferred to an "Unclaimed Deposits Account" and would ordinarily be returned to dissatisfied customers. It was held:

(i) that the payments were true deposits and were therefore strictly irrecoverable by the customers;
(ii) that they were trading receipts because they were paid to the defendant company subject to the consequence that they would be used in the company's business, and they were receipts of the year when the payments were made (following *Smart* v. *Lincolnshire Sugar Co.*[2]).

Morley v. *Tattersall* and *Jay's the Jewellers Ltd.* v. *I.R.C.* were distinguished because in those cases the balances in the traders' hands were originally their clients' property and they were not receipts of the trade.

2–33   *Released, remitted or forgiven debts.* In *British Mexican Petroleum Co. Ltd.* v. *I.R.C.*,[3] it was held that where a trade debt is incurred in an accounting period and the creditor later releases or forgives the debt (or part of it) (a) the accounts for the earlier period cannot be reopened and (b) no assessment can be made in the year of release, for there is then no trade receipt. This decision was nullified by section 36 of the Finance Act 1960 (now s.136 of the Income and Corporation Taxes Act 1970), as respects releases effected after April 5, 1960. Now, where a deduction has been allowed for any debt incurred for the purposes of a trade and the

---

98. (1947) 29 T.C. 274.
99. Although the debts in *Tattersall's* case might not have been technically statute-barred, it is not thought that this is sufficient grounds of distinction.
1. (1962) 40 T.C. 671.
2. (1937) 20 T.C. 643 (H.L.), where Government advances to sugar manufacturing companies were repayable in certain contingencies and it was held that they became trade receipts in the year of payment and not in the year when the contingency of repayment ceased. What was decisive was that these payments were made in order that the money might be used in the business: Lord Macmillan at p. 670.
3. (1932) 16 T.C. 570 (H.L.).

whole or part of that debt is thereafter released, the amount released is treated as a trading receipt of the period in which the release is effected.[4] The section does not apply to debts incurred on capital account which are later released.

(3) *Trading stock*

2–34   In computing the profits of a trade, profession or vocation, it is necessary to bring into account the value of the stock-in-trade at the beginning and end of the accounting period. The following account shows the relevance of stock valuation in the ascertainment of profits:

	£		£
Opening stock	1,000	Sales during the year	15,000
Purchases during the		Closing stock	1,300
year	12,000		
Gross profit	3,300		
	£16,300		£16,300

The trader in this example begins the year with £1,000's worth of stock. During the year he purchases a further £12,000 of stock. He takes £15,000 in sales. Note that the stock must be again valued at the close of the year before the gross profit can be ascertained. The closing stock becomes the figure for opening stock in the next accounting period.

2–35   The trader values his stock, item by item, at the close of each accounting period. The higher the figure for closing stock, the higher the gross profit; the lower the figure, the lower the profit. In *I.R.C.* v. *Cock, Russell & Co. Ltd.,*[5] judicial approval was given to the rule of accounting that, when valuing stock, the trader may value each item at its cost price or its market price whichever is the lower. He may value one item at cost and another at market price: thus he may "pick and choose." Market price means the best price obtainable in the market in which the trader sells.[6] The practical effect of the rule is that where an item of stock increases in value during the accounting period, such increase does not enter into the computation of profits; yet if an item of stock decreases in value, so that a loss may be anticipated,[7] the decrease will be taken into account.[8-12] This is an exception

---

4. This can have important repercussions when shares of a tax-loss company are purchased. It is not uncommon in such a case for trade creditors who are associated with the company to release their debts in order to facilitate the sale of the shares to outsiders. S.136 might have the effect of extinguishing the losses.
    5. (1949) 29 T.C. 387.
    6. *B.S.C. Footwear Ltd.* v. *Ridgway* [1972] A.C. 544; 47 T.C. 495 (H.L.): thus in the case of the retail trade, it means the retail market.
    7. In the case cited in note 5 Lord Pearson said *obiter* that goods should not be written down below cost price unless there really is a loss, actual or prospective. They should not be written down where a reduced profit only is anticipated.
    8–12. Generally tax law permits no relief for unrealised losses on (for example) future contracts, the rule applicable to stock is a departure from the general rule: *Naval Colliery Co. Ltd.* v. *I.R.C.* (1928) 12 T.C. 1017, *per* Lord Warrington; *Whimster & Co.* v. *I.R.C.* (1925) 12 T.C. 813.

to the general principle of tax law, under which neither profits nor losses may be "anticipated": see § 2–21A.

2–36   *The Emery formula.* Where a builder or developer erects houses on plots of land owned by him and grants leases for lump sum payments (premiums) and rents reserved out of the land (ground rents), the freehold reversions which the builder retains form part of his stock-in-trade and must be brought into account at the lower of cost or market price.[13] The formula for ascertaining cost in such cases was determined by the Special Commissioners in *John Emery & Sons* v. *I.R.C.*[14] The effect of the formula is that part of the building costs which goes to improve the ground rent which the builder retains must be eliminated in computing his building profits.[15]

2–37   *Work in progress.* There are in many trades, at the end of each accounting period, unfinished products in hand, such as goods in process of manufacture, films in the course of production, or houses in course of erection. Each unit of "work in progress" may be valued in the same way as stock-in-trade[16] that is, at the lower of cost or market price. In arriving at a figure for the cost of a product, however, some account must be taken of the cost of production and for this purpose a distinction is made between *direct costs* (which are readily attributable to a given item, such as the wages of a person engaged in making the product) and *indirect costs* (which, though part of the total cost of production, cannot be attributed to any one item, *e.g.* general overheads). Where the value of work in progress is computed by the "direct cost" method, only direct costs are taken into account; whereas, where the "on-cost" method is used, a proportion of indirect costs is added to the direct costs. There is no rule of law requiring one method to be used rather than another.[17] The relief for the rise in the cost of replacement of stock[18] also applies to work in progress.

2–38   *Valuation of stock on discontinuance of a trade.* It has been observed that the mere realisation of assets after the permanent discontinuance of a trade does not constitute trading.[19] Any tax advantages which could hitherto be gained by this rule (*e.g.* by a company purchasing an appreciating asset, such as whisky, going into liquidation when the whisky reached maturity and selling it in the liquidation) were nullified by provisions now in section 137 of the Income and Corporation Taxes Act 1970. This section requires

---

13. *Utting* v. *Hughes* (1940) 23 T.C. 174 (H.L.).
14. (1937) 20 T.C. 213. This aspect of the case is not reported in [1937] A.C. 91. The formula is sometimes referred to as the "Macnaghten formula" because of Macnaghten J.'s reference to it in *Heather* v. *Redfern* (1944) 26 T.C. 119 at p. 124. The formula, he said, is a simple rule of three sum: As A, the premiums, plus B, the selling value of the ground rents, is to B, so is C, the total expenses of the builder, to D, the cost of the ground rents or reversions.
15. *McMillan* v. *I.R.C.* (1924) 24 T.C. 417 (Ct. of Sess.).
16. Trading stock is defined in I.C.T.A. 1970, s.137(4), to mean property such as is sold in the ordinary course of the trade or would be so sold if it were mature or if its manufacture, preparation or construction were complete. It thus includes work in progress.
17. *Duple Motor Bodies Ltd.* v. *Ostime* (1961) 39 T.C. 537 (H.L.).
18. See *ante*, § 2–35A.
19. See *ante*, § 2–15.

that, where a trade is discontinued, any trading stock (including work in progress) belonging to the trader "at" the discontinuance must be valued at the amount realisable on a sale in the open market at the discontinuance. Any latent profit is thereby brought into account in the final chargeable period.

2–39 Section 137 provides two exceptions which apply:

(1) If the stock is sold or transferred for valuable consideration to a person who carries on or intends to carry on[20] a trade in the United Kingdom so that the cost thereof is a deductible expense in computing his (the purchaser's) profits. In this case, the vendor brings into account the actual consideration for the transfer.

(2) If the discontinuance is caused by the death of a sole proprietor.[21] In this case the figure for closing stock remains undisturbed.

Where (1) applies the Revenue lose nothing, for the profit will eventually come into charge when the purchaser sells the stock in the course of his trade. The explanation of (2) is that section 137 is an anti-avoidance section and is designed to prevent tax avoidance by "artificial cessations" when stock figures are low and market values high. Section 137 applies where the discontinuance of trading and the sale are simultaneous as well as where the sale or transfer take place *after* the discontinuance.[22]

2–40 *Valuation of work in progress on discontinuance of a profession or vocation.* Section 137 of the Income and Corporation Taxes Act 1970 applies only to discontinued trades. Section 138 of the Income and Corporation Taxes Act 1970 contains similar provisions which apply to work in progress on the discontinuance of a profession or vocation. Subsection (1) provides that where, on such a discontinuance, a valuation is taken of the work of the profession or vocation in progress at the discontinuance, that work shall be valued as follows:

(a) if the work is transferred for money or other valuable consideration to a person who carries on or intends to carry on a profession or vocation in the United Kingdom, and the cost of the work may be deducted by that person as an expense in computing for any such purpose the profits or gains of that profession or vocation, the value of the work shall be taken to be the amount paid or other consideration given for the transfer;

(b) if the work does not fall to be valued under (a), its value shall be taken to be the amount which would have been paid for a transfer thereof on the date of the discontinuance as between parties at arm's length.

---

20. I.C.T.A. 1970, s.137(1)(*a*). Thus where a partnership is "converted" into a company and stock is sold to the company, the exception applies.

21. *Ibid.* s.137(3). But where a business passes on death to the trader's husband or wife who has been living with him or her, the discontinuance provisions are not enforced unless claimed. See Concession No. A7.

22. *Moore* v. *R. J. Mackenzie & Sons Ltd.* (1971) 48 T.C. 196.

2-41   It should be observed that the subsection imposes no obligation to value work in progress: it provides that *if* a valuation of work in progress is taken, it shall be made in accordance with the section. The subsection applies only if accounts have been rendered in such a form that normal accountancy practice demands a valuation of work in progress; thus if accounts have been rendered on a cash basis (*i.e.* crediting only sums actually received) no adjustment to those accounts is required by section 138 of the Income and Corporation Taxes Act 1970 on the discontinuance of the profession or vocation. Where accounts have been rendered on a cash basis and there is a discontinuance, the Revenue might require accounts to be rendered on an earnings basis in respect of the final accounting period[23] (assuming that accounts have not already been accepted on a cash basis prior to the date of discontinuance). Work in progress would then have to be brought in at the time of discontinuance, valued in accordance with section 138 of the Income and Corporation Taxes Act 1970, but the taxpayer would be entitled to bring in the value of work in progress as at the beginning of that accounting period.[24] Thus only the increase in value of the work in progress in the final accounting period would be brought into charge under section 138.

2-42   Work in progress is defined for the purposes of section 138(5) as including:

(a) any services performed in the ordinary course of the profession or vocation, the performance of which was wholly or partly completed at the time of the discontinuance and for which it would be reasonable to expect that a charge would have been made on their completion if the profession or vocation had not been discontinued, and

(b) any article produced, and any such material as is used, in the performance of any such services.

The definition thus includes completed but unbilled work as well as uncompleted or partly completed work.

(4) *Section 485 and the rule in Sharkey* v. *Wernher*[25]

2-43   Generally, a trader is free to dispose of his stock on any terms he pleases and is entitled, for example, to sell at an under-value for the purpose of avoiding liability to income tax. There is no rule of law which demands that a trader shall realise the maximum profit; nor can tax be levied on a profit which is forgone. This general rule is subject to some important exceptions which must now be considered.

---

23. As in *Rankine* v. *I.R.C.* (1952) 32 T.C. 520, *ante*, § 2–21.
24. *Bombay Commissioner of Income Tax* v. *Ahmedabad New Cotton Mills Co. Ltd.* (1929) 8 A.T.C. 575. But see *Pearce* v. *Woodall Duckham Ltd.* (1978) 51 T.C. 271; [1978] S.T.C. 372 (C.A.) where the Court of Appeal held that a sum thrown up in consequence of a change in the method of valuing work in progress was a profit of the year of change.
25. [1956] A.C. 58; 36 T.C. 275 (H.L.).

2–44　　(a) *Section 485 of the Income and Corporation Taxes Act 1970.* Where on a sale between "associated persons" property is sold at a price less than the price which it might have been *expected to fetch* if the parties to the transaction had been independent persons dealing at arm's length, then, in computing the income, profits or losses of the seller for tax purposes, the like consequences are to ensue as would have ensued if the property had been sold for the price it *would have fetched* if the transaction had been between independent persons dealing at arm's length.[26] There is an important exception where the buyer is resident in the United Kingdom and is carrying on a trade therein, where the price of the property has to be taken into account as a deduction in computing the profits or gains or losses of that trade for income tax purposes.[27]

> Thus if a trading company sells property at an under-value to an associated investment company, the receipts of the trading company will be adjusted in accordance with section 485 on a direction being made by the Board.

The section contains similar provisions for adjustment of the profits or losses of the buyer where property is sold in excess of its arm's length value.[28]

Persons are "associated" for the purpose of section 485 if the buyer is a body of persons (including a partnership)[29] over whom the seller has control, or vice versa, or both seller and buyer are bodies of persons over whom some other person has control.

2–45　　"Control" has the meaning ascribed to it in section 534 of the Income and Corporation Taxes Act 1970, which, in relation to a body corporate, means the power of a person to secure

> "(a) by means of the holding of shares or the possession of voting power in or in relation to that or any other body corporate, or
>
> (b) by virtue of any powers conferred by the articles of association or other document regulating that or any other body corporate,
>
> that the affairs of the first-mentioned body corporate are conducted in accordance with the wishes of that person, and, in relation to a partnership, means the right to a share of more than one-half of the assets, or of more than one half of the income, of the partnership."

In applying this test a person is deemed to possess all the rights and powers of any nominee for him or of any person who is connected[30] with him.[31] There are similar provisions for the adjustment of the consideration in the case of "lettings and hirings of property, grants and transfers of rights, interests or licences and the giving of business facilities of whatever kind," where the parties to the transaction are associated.[32]

---

26. I.C.T.A. 1970, s.485(1). Note the contrast in the italicised words. The Inland Revenue has published notes, primarily designed for the guidance of overseas companies, entitled "The transfer pricing of multinational enterprises": see [1981] S.T.I. 212.
27. *Ibid.* s.485(1), proviso.
28. *Ibid.* s.485(2).
29. *Ibid.* s.485(5).
30. The definition of "connected persons" is found in I.C.T.A. 1970, s.533: see § 16–18A.
31. F.A. 1975, s.17(1) enacting a new I.C.T.A. 1970, s.485(5A).
32. I.C.T.A. 1970, s.485(6).

The Commissioners are given extensive powers to obtain information for the purpose of this provision, in particular, as regards any related transaction which may have a bearing on market value. The powers include the right of a properly authorised person to enter premises and inspect documents.[33]

Section 485 has fulfilled an important role in enabling the Inland Revenue to examine prices at which goods are sold to overseas subsidiaries of United Kingdom companies. The importance of section 485 in this respect will diminish in view of the new provisions relating to controlled foreign companies which are discussed in §§ 14–85 *et seq*.

2–46   (b) *The rule in Sharkey* v. *Wernher*.[34] The rule is that where a trader disposes of part of his stock-in-trade not by way of sale in the course of trade but for his own use, enjoyment or recreation, he must bring into his trading account for tax purposes as a receipt the market value of that stock at the time of such disposition. The facts of the case were as follows:

> Lady Wernher owned a stud farm, which was a trade assessed under Case I of Schedule D. She also owned racing stables where horses were trained and this activity was admitted to be merely recreational. Lady Wernher transferred five horses from the farm to the stables, having debited in the stud farm accounts the cost of breeding the horses. Some figure (it was admitted) had to be brought into the stud farm accounts as a receipt. *Held*, that the figure to be brought in was the market value of the horses.

This case shows that a person can make a taxable profit by trading with himself; and that unrealised profits may be assessable to tax. The practical consequence of the decision is that a farmer or grocer who (for example) takes his own produce or stock for domestic consumption must credit his account as if he had sold it in the normal course of trade, at the retail market value. The same problem arises (said Viscount Simonds)

> "whether the owner of a stud farm diverts the produce of his farm to his own enjoyment or a diamond merchant, neglecting profitable sales, uses his choicest jewels for the adornment of his wife, or a caterer provides lavish entertainment for a daughter's wedding breakfast. Are the horses, the jewels, the cakes and ale to be treated for the purpose of income tax as disposed of for nothing or for their market value or for the cost of their production?"[35]

The answer given by the House of Lords (Lord Oaksey dissenting) was their market value.

2–47   It should be observed that the rule applies only to dispositions of trading assets such as stock-in-trade[36]: property which never becomes part of such assets is outside the rule. The rule applies in all cases where a trader disposes of his stock otherwise than in the normal course of trade. Thus a sale

---

33. See generally F.A. 1975, s.17.
34. [1956] A.C. 58; 36 T.C. 275 (H.L.).
35. [1956] A.C. 58 at pp. 69–70; 36 T.C. 275 at p. 297.
36. Thus a solicitor who gives advice without reward cannot be required to bring in as a receipt of his profession the fee he foregoes. In *Mason* v. *Innes* [1967] Ch. 1079; 44 T.C. 326 (C.A.) the Revenue contended unsuccessfully that the rule applied to a gift by an author of his rights in an unpublished novel. Such a gift would now attract capital gains tax.

at an under-value to secure some tax advantage is subject to review by the Revenue, even in cases to which section 485 of the Income and Corporation Taxes Act 1970 does not apply.

In *Petrotim Securities Ltd.* v. *Ayres*,[37] Petrotim (a company dealing in securities) purchased War Loan which it sold four days later at less than one-tenth of its costs and of its realisable market value at the date of sale. It was held that neither the purchase nor the sale was a trading transaction and that both should therefore be expunged from the company's accounts. Petrotim also sold for £205,000 securities forming part of its trading stock which it acquired some time previously for £478,573, and which had a market value of £835,505. It was held that the sale was not a trading transaction. It was further held in the *Petrotim* case[38] that the principle in *Sharkey* v. *Wernher*[39] applied and that a figure equal to the market value of the securities at the date of disposal should be brought in as a receipt. These decisions were affirmed by the Court of Appeal.[40] In one case it was held that a sale of land at an under-value by a land-dealing company to its parent company was a sale otherwise than in the ordinary course of trade.[41]

2–48   If a trader starts a business with stock provided gratuitously, he may bring in the stock at its market value at that time: he will not be taxed on the basis that the value of the opening stock is nil.[42] But this principle was held not to apply in a case in which the Commissioners had held that the acquisition of the stock was "a commercial acquisition."[43]

(5) *Interest, etc.*

2–49   Interest earned by a trader whose stock-in-trade is money and who earns the interest by the use of that money, as by borrowing at one rate and lending at a higher rate, is a trading receipt and will be brought into the profit and loss account. But, for tax purposes, a distinction is drawn between interest from which income tax is deducted before its receipt by the trader (which has to be excluded from the receipt in the tax computation[44]) and interest paid in full without deduction (which is not so excluded). This distinction is said to be based on the proposition that, if interest taxed by deduction were treated as a trade receipt for tax purposes, it would be

37. (1963) 41 T.C. 389.
38. *Ibid.* at p. 402.
39. [1956] A.C. 58; 36 T.C. 275 (H.L.).
40. (1963) 41 T.C. 405 (C.A.).
41. *Skinner* v. *Berry Head Lands Ltd.* (1970) 46 T.C. 377.
42. *Ridge Securities* v. *I.R.C.* (1963) 44 T.C. 373 at p. 392.
43. *Jacgilden (Weston Hall) Ltd.* v. *Castle* [1971] Ch. 408; 45 T.C. 685, where R, having agreed to buy land for £72,000 and paid a deposit, directed the vendor to convey the land to the appellant company by which time the land was worth £150,000. *Held,* the company could deduct only the price actually paid. "The *Sharkey* v. *Wernher* line of authority has never . . . been applied to a case where the price at which property passed had been negotiated at a fair and proper price . . . " (*ibid.* at p. 700).
44. See *F. S. Securities Ltd.* v. *I.R.C.* (1964) 41 T.C. 666 (H.L.) which related to the taxation of dividends payable under deduction of tax; but the same principle has been held to apply to interest and other sums paid under deduction: *Bucks* v. *Bowers* (1969) 46 T.C. 267.

taxed twice because there is no provision for giving relief for tax already suffered by deduction in the Case I assessment: see the discussion in § 5–23.

(6) *Know-how*

2–50   In *Evans Medical Supplies Ltd.* v. *Moriarty*[45] the House of Lords held that a sum received by a trading company on the sale of know-how was not taxable as a trading receipt. In *Jeffrey* v. *Rolls-Royce Ltd.*,[46] the House of Lords held that a sum received for imparting know-how was taxable. Section 21 of the Finance Act 1968 clarified the position in provisions now contained in section 386 of the Income and Corporation Taxes Act 1970.

The provisions of section 386 may be summarised as follows:

(a) Where a person buys know-how for use in a trade carried on or to be carried on by him, he is entitled to writing-down allowances in respect of his expenditure, if the expenditure is not otherwise deductible for corporation tax or income tax purposes. The allowances are spread over a six-year period.[47] The expression "know-how" is defined in section 386 as meaning

> "Any industrial information and techniques likely to assist in the manufacture or processing of goods or materials, or in the working of mine, oil-well or other source of mineral deposits (including the searching for, discovery, or testing of deposits or the winning of access hereto), or in the carrying out of any agricultural, forestry or fishing operations."[48]

(b) Where a person disposes of know-how which has been used in a trade carried on by him and he continues to carry on the trade after the disposal, the amount or value of any consideration he receives is treated for all purposes as a trading receipt, if it is not otherwise chargeable to tax as a revenue or income receipt.[49] The purchaser may be entitled to writing-down allowances under (a), above.

(c) Where a person disposes of a trade or part of a trade *together with* the know-how used therein, any consideration received is dealt with both in relation to the vendor and the purchaser, if he provided the consideration, and for all tax purposes, as a payment for goodwill.[50] The effect of this treatment is, first, that the purchaser is not entitled to writing-down allowances under (a) above; secondly, the "capital gains tax regime" applies to both parties. This rule is not excluded in relation to transactions between persons under common control[51] so that if, for example, the vendor and

---

45. (1957) 37 T.C. 540.
46. (1962) 40 T.C. 443. See also *Musker* v. *English Electric Co. Ltd.* (1964) 41 T.C. 556 (H.L.); *Coalite & Chemical Products Ltd.* v. *Treeby* (1971) 48 T.C. 171; *John & E. Sturge Ltd.* v. *Hessel* (1975) 51 T.C. 183; [1975] S.T.C. 573 (C.A.); *Thomsons (Carron) Ltd.* v. *I.R.C.* (1976) 51 T.C. 490; [1976] S.T.C. 317.
47. I.C.T.A. 1970, s.386(1). The section applies as from March 19, 1968.
48. *Ibid.* s.386(7). An undertaking which has the effect of restricting the activities of a person may be treated as a disposition of know-how: see *ibid.* s.386(8).
49. *Ibid.* s.386(2).
50. *Ibid.* s.386(3).
51. *Ibid.* s.386(6).

purchaser are in the same group of companies, the normal "no gain no loss" rule will apply.[52]

(d) The provision summarised in (c) does not apply to either of the persons concerned if they so elect by written notice given jointly to the Inspector within two years of the disposal. The effect of an election is that the transaction is not treated as relating to goodwill: accordingly, the purchaser may be entitled to writing-down allowances under (a), above, but the vendor is taxed under Case VI of Schedule D.[53] This right of election is excluded in "common control" situations[53a]—presumably to prevent the persons concerned electing themselves into a position where writing-down allowances become available.

(7) *Voluntary payments*

2–50A   A voluntary payment of an income character may be a trading receipt, as is illustrated by the case of *British Commonwealth International Newsfilm Agency* v. *Mahany*,[54] discussed in § 5–18. But not all voluntary payments are of an income nature.

In *Walker* v. *Carnaby Harrower, Barnham & Pykett*[55] the taxpayers, a firm of accountants, had for many years acted as auditors to a group of companies. As a result of a group re-organisation the taxpayers were asked if, after completing the 1962 audit, they would not seek re-appointment. Their charges of £2,567 for the 1962 audit were duly paid and later the taxpayers, as a firm, received an unsolicited *ex gratia* payment, also of £2,567, as compensation for the loss of their office as auditors. It was held that the payment was not taxable. Pennycuick J. said:

> " . . . [the taxpayers] were carrying on the business of chartered accountants, which consists in rendering services of a certain professional character in return for reward. They rendered those services to these six companies over a number of years and duly received their reward for so doing. At the end of their final term of office they had no legal claim of any description to receive any further payment from the companies. The companies then proceeded to make the wholly voluntary payment to the respondent firm. It is, I think, irrelevant that the companies elected to make that payment in an amount identical to a penny with the fees paid to the firm during their last year of office. It seems to me that a gift of that kind made by a former client cannot reasonably be treated as a receipt of a business which consists in rendering professional services. The subject-matter of the assessment under Cases I and II is the full amount of the profits or gains of the trade or profession. Those profits have to be computed, it is well established, upon ordinary commercial principles. It does not seem to me that ordinary commercial principles require that bringing into account of this sort of voluntary payment, not made as the consideration for any services rendered by the firm, but by way of recognition of past services or by way of consolation for the termination of a contract. . . . "

A similar point arose in *Simpson* v. *John Reynolds & Co. (Insurances)*

---

52. *Ibid.* ss.272 *et seq.*
53. *Ibid.* s.386(3), proviso (a) and s.386(4).
53a. *Ibid.* s.386(6).
54. (1962) 40 T.C. 550.
55. (1969) 46 T.C. 561.

Ltd.[56] where a voluntary payment was made to a firm of insurance brokers by a client company which, following its takeover by a public company, was no longer able to place its business with the brokers. The payment was held not to be taxable as a trading receipt. Russell L.J. said the following:

> "First, this was a wholly unexpected and unsolicited gift. Secondly, it was made after the business connection had ceased. Thirdly, the gift was in recognition of past services rendered to the client company over a long period, though not because those past services were considered to have been inadequately remunerated. Fourthly, the gift was made as a consolation for the fact that those remunerative services were no longer to be performed by the taxpayer for the donor; and, fifthly, there is no suggestion that at a future date the business connection might be renewed."

The Crown had contended that the fact that a payment was made without legal obligation did not *per se* elude the fiscal grasp. Russell L.J. said (at p. 712F):

> "This is true. Gifts made or promised during the relevant connection may well be caught. It was also pointed out that the fact that payments are made after the connection has ceased does not *per se* elude the fiscal grasp. This also is true: for it may be part of the connection that such payments after its determination are to be expected. But that does not in my view lead to the suggested conclusion that when both of those circumstances are present—that is to say, where the gift is wholly voluntary and made unexpectedly after the business connection has come to an end—the payment is within the statutory language. The Crown contended, as I understand it, as a general proposition, that in the case of a business connection that was a trade connection, and the trade of the donee as a whole continued with persons other than the donee, a gift made for the reasons given in the present case *must* be caught: for it was not made merely out of personal affection or regard. Or, the Crown submitted, that viewed as a whole the circumstances of this case showed that this sum did accrue or arise from the trade. For my part, I am unable to accept this. The impact of the argument would, it seems to me, be very wide indeed. A legacy to a doctor or a solicitor expressed to be in gratitude for his professional services to the testator or the testator's late spouse (*ex hypothesi* operative after the connection had ceased) would apparently, according to the Crown's argument . . . be liable to income tax, granted that the solicitor or the doctor had not at the time of the death retired from practice. That is a suggestion I have certainly never met."

By contrast, in *I.R.C.* v. *Falkirk Ice Rink Ltd.*[57] a donation to a trading company which operated an ice rink on a commercial basis, made in order to supplement its trading revenue from curling and to ensure the continuation of its ability to continue to provide curling facilities in the future, was held to be a trading receipt. It was a supplement to its trading revenue.

Literary awards to authors may escape income tax as voluntary payments.[58]

---

56. (1975) 49 T.C. 693 (C.A.). See also *Murray* v. *Goodhews* (1977) 52 T.C. 86; [1978] S.T.C. 207 (C.A.) and *Rolfe* v. *Nagel* (1981) 55 T.C. 585; [1982] S.T.C. 53 (C.A.). In *Poulter* v. *Gayjon Processes Ltd.* [1985] S.T.C. 174 a subsidy paid to a manufacturer by the Department of Employment for the purposes of relieving unemployment in the trade was held to be a trading receipt.
57. (1975) 51 T.C. 42; [1975] S.T.C. 434. *Cf.* the *British Commonwealth* case in § 5–18.
58. See [1979] S.T.I. 76.

C. Trading Expenses

2–51   Not all expenses incurred in the course of trading are deductible in computing annual profits or gains for tax purposes. Section 130 of the Income and Corporation Taxes Act 1970 contains a list of prohibited deductions which are followed, in some cases, by words of exception. There is no enumeration of permitted deductions. Thus section 130(*a*) does not provide that money wholly and exclusively laid out or expended for the purposes of a trade may be deducted, but that no sum shall be deducted in respect of any disbursements or expenses, not being money wholly and exclusively laid out or expended for the purposes of the trade. It is, however, obvious that if no deduction of expenses from gross receipts was allowed, it would be impossible to arrive at the balance of the profits and gains of a trade on which tax under Case I of Schedule D is to be assessed. Accordingly, it has long been settled that the effect of the provisions now contained in section 130 is that the balance of the profits and gains of a trade must be ascertained in accordance with the ordinary principles of commercial accounting, by deducting from the gross receipts all expenditure properly deductible from them on those principles, save in so far as any amount so deducted falls within any of the statutory prohibitions contained in section 130, in which case the amount disallowed must be added back.[59] Generally, any expenditure which is justified by commercial expediency and is incurred for the purpose of enabling a person to carry on and earn profits in the trade is deductible, even if those profits may arise *in futuro*.[60] The principles of commercial accounting will be determined by the court on the evidence before it: see § 2–19.

2–52   Expenditure in earning profits must be distinguished from the application of profits after they have been earned.[61] The payment of income tax is an application of profits after they have been earned: it is not an expense of earning profits.[62]

Two conditions must be satisfied before an item of expenditure is deductible:

(1) it must be revenue and not capital expenditure;
(2) the expenditure must be incurred wholly and exclusively for the purposes of the trade.[63]

Hence the cost of fixed assets (*e.g.* business premises) is not deductible,[64] even if paid by instalments[65]; nor is a sum set aside to cover depreciation of capital assets.[66] Expenditure incurred in anticipation of the commence-

---

59. See the remarks of Lord Sumner in *Usher's Wiltshire Brewery Ltd.* v. *Bruce* [1915] A.C. 433 at p. 467; 6 T.C. 399 at p. 436.
60. *Vallambrosa Rubber Co. Ltd.* v. *Farmer* (1910) 5 T.C. 529.
61. *Mersey Docks and Harbour Board* v. *Lucas* (1883) 2 T.C. 25 (H.L.); *Racecourse Betting Control Board* v. *Young* (1959) 38 T.C. 426 (H.L.).
62. *Ashton Gas Co.* v. *Att.-Gen.* [1906] A.C. 10 (H.L.).
63. I.C.T.A. 1970, s.130(*a*).
64. *Watney* v. *Musgrave* (1880) 5 Ex.D. 241; 1 T.C. 272 (premium for lease); *European Investment Trust Co. Ltd.* v. *Jackson* (1932) 18 T.C. 1 (C.A.).
65. *Green* v. *Favourite Cinemas Ltd.* (1930) 15 T.C. 390.
66. But capital allowances may be claimed: see Chap. 13.

ment of trading (*e.g.* the cost of forming a company) is not deductible,[67] subject to the statutory exception in § 2–75B. Capital expenditure is dealt with in the provisions relating to capital allowances (Chap. 13) and capital gains tax (Chap. 16).

(1) *Capital and revenue expenditure distinguished*

2–53   In *Vallambrosa Rubber Co. Ltd.* v. *Farmer,*[68] Lord Dunedin suggested that expenditure which is made once and for all is normally capital expenditure, whereas recurrent expenditure (or expenditure which is likely to recur) is revenue expenditure. In *British Insulated and Helsby Cables Ltd.* v. *Atherton,*[69] Viscount Cave L.C. carried the matter a stage further:

> "But when an expenditure is made, not only once and for all, but with a view to bringing into existence an asset or an advantage for the enduring benefit of a trade, I think that there is very good reason . . . for treating such an expenditure as properly attributable not to revenue but to capital."

The expenditure in that case was of £30,000, to form the nucleus of a pension fund which would endure throughout the life of the company. Whether an item of expenditure is capital or revenue expenditure is ultimately a question of law for the court; and in one case[70] Lord Greene M.R. remarked that "in many cases it is almost true to say that the spin of a coin would decide the matter almost as satisfactorily as an attempt to find reasons." The procedure by coin-spinning has not as yet commended itself to the Commissioners, however, so the quest for legal principles must continue. The passage from the speech of Viscount Cave L.C. (above) indicates that there are two elements which determine whether expenditure is capital expenditure. First, it must be made "once and for all." Secondly, it must be made "with a view to bringing into existence an asset or an advantage for the enduring benefit of a trade." This second "limb" has been said to be inappropriate as concentrating too much attention on the *reason* why the expenditure was incurred rather than on the *subject-matter* that was acquired by means of the expenditure.[71] The courts seem now to have accepted an "identifiable asset test," making the obtaining of or the enrichment of some capital asset as the key factor in capital expenditure. The test is: can a capital asset be identified for which the payment was made?[72]

---

67. *Royal Insurance Co.* v. *Watson* [1897] A.C. 1; 3 T.C. 500.
68. (1910) 5 T.C. 529 (Ct. of Sess.).
69. [1926] A.C. 205 at p. 214; 10 T.C. 155 at p. 192. *Cf. Heather* v. *P-E Consulting Group Ltd.* [1973] Ch. 189;. 48 T.C. 293 (C.A), in which annual payments made by a company to establish a fund to acquire shares for the benefit of the employees were held to be of a revenue nature and deductible in computing profits (C.A.). See also *Strick* v. *Regent Oil Co. Ltd.* (1965) 43 T.C. 1 (H.L.) and *Jeffs* v. *Ringtons Ltd.* (1985) S.T.C. 809.
70. *British Salmson Aero Engines Ltd.* v. *I.R.C.* [1938] 2 K.B. 482; 22 T.C. 29 (C.A.). " . . . reported cases are the best tools that we have, even if they may sometimes be blunt instruments": Lord Wilberforce in *Tucker* v. *Granada Motorway Services Ltd.* (1979) 53 T.C. 92 at p. 107A (H.L.). See also Lord Radcliffe in *Comr. of Taxes* v. *Nchanga Consolidated Copper Mines Ltd.* [1964] A.C. 948 at 959.
71. *Tucker* v. *Granada Motorway Services Ltd.* (1979) 53 T.C. 92 at p. 115D (Lord Fraser).
72. *Tucker* v. *Granada Motorway Services Ltd.* (1979) 53 T.C. 92 at p. 108A (Lord Wilberforce) and see the dicta of Walton J. in *Watney Combe Reid* v. *Pike* [1982] S.T.C. 733 at pp.752C *et seq.*. Also *Whitehead* v. *Tubbs* (*Plastics*) *Ltd.* (1984) S.T.C. 1 (C.A.).

In *Tucker* v. *Granada Motorway Services Ltd.*[73] the taxpayer company had a lease of a motorway service area for 50 years from 1964. The rent payable consisted of two elements: a fixed rent of £15,000 per annum and an additional rent equal to a percentage of the previous year's gross takings. The gross takings included tobacco duty in the selling price of tobacco. As tobacco duty increased, the rent increased and it became difficult to operate the service area profitably. A variation of the terms of the lease was accordingly negotiated. In consideration of a lump sum payment of £122,220 made by the taxpayer company in 1974 (being six times the additional rent due on tobacco duty in the year ended July 31, 1973) the lessor agreed to exclude this duty from the additional rent.

The House of Lords held that the lump sum payment was capital expenditure: it was expenditure on a capital asset (namely the lease) and it made the lease a more valuable asset. Lord Wilberforce said (at p. 107 B):

> "I think that the key to the present case is to be found in those cases which have sought to identify an asset. In them it seems reasonably logical to start with the assumption that money spent on the acquisition of the asset should be regarded as capital expenditure. Extensions from this are, first, to regard money spent on getting rid of a disadvantageous asset as capital expenditure and, secondly, to regard money spent on improving the asset, or making it more advantageous, as capital expenditure. In the latter type of case it will have to be considered whether the expenditure has the result stated or whether it should be regarded as expenditure on maintenance or upkeep, and some cases may pose difficult problems."

It is true that the object of the payment was to increase the taxpayer's share of profits: but this commercial objective could not obscure the fact that, both in substance and in form, the payment was to secure a variation in the lease.

2–54   The cost of an item from the resale of which a trader makes his profit is generally deductible: the item is part of the trader's "circulating capital." There is, however, an important distinction between the purchase of the raw material of a trade (revenue expenditure) and the purchase of an asset from which the trader obtains his raw material (capital expenditure).

> Thus in *Stow Bardolph Gravel Co. Ltd.* v. *Poole,*[74] the company who were dealers in sand and gravel claimed as a deduction the cost of a contract giving them the exclusive right to excavate gravel. The contract was unlimited in time and imposed no obligation on the company to excavate the gravel; the price was not related to the quantity of gravel excavated; and there were options to acquire other reserves of gravel. *Held* to be capital expenditure.

This distinction was maintained in *H. J. Rorke Ltd.* v. *I.R.C.,*[75] notwithstanding evidence that the payments in that case were a normal and recurrent incident of the trade and that, since the purchaser had a lease for one

---

73. (1979) 53 T.C. 92; [1979] S.T.C. 393 (H.L.).

74. (1954) 35 T.C. 459 (C.A.); see also *Golden Horse Shoe (New) Ltd.* v. *Thurgood* [1934] 1 K.B. 548; 18 T.C. 280 (C.A.); *Saunders* v. *Pilcher* (1949) 31 T.C. 314 (C.A.); *Hopwood* v. *C. N. Spencer Ltd.* (1964) 42 T.C. 169.

75. (1960) 39 T.C. 194.

year only, no "enduring benefit" was obtained. "They were not payments made for the purchase of coal but payments to put the company into the position to get coal" (p. 205).

Examples of revenue expenditure

2–55   In *Mitchell* v. *B. W. Noble Ltd.*[76] a lump sum was paid to a director who, though liable to dismissal, agreed to retire to avoid undesirable publicity. *Held* to be deductible. " . . . a payment to get rid of a servant in the interests of the trade is a proper deduction." (*Per* Rowlatt J.). The payment was made "not in order to secure an actual asset to the company but to enable the company to continue to carry on, as it had done in the past . . . unimperilled by the presence of one who . . . might have caused difficulty." (*Per* Hanworth M.R.).

Similarly in *Anglo-Persian Oil Co. Ltd.* v. *Dale*[77] a lump sum paid by a principal to his agent for the cancellation of an onerous long-term agency agreement, the payment being in the course of a change in the principal's business methods and to effect an economy in the business, was allowed as a deduction. "The agency contract was not a capital asset and the result of terminating it was simply to relieve the company of an obligation to make recurring payments under the contract."[78]

In *Southern* v. *Borax Consolidated Ltd.*[79] costs incurred by a company in defending its title to certain land were allowed as a deduction.

In *Morgan* v. *Tate & Lyle Ltd.*[80] T. carried on the business of sugar refiners. Threatened with the nationalisation of the sugar refining industry, T. incurred expenses on a propaganda campaign designed to show that nationalisation would harm "workers, consumers and stockholders alike." *Held*, that the expenses were deductible. The money was spent "to preserve the very existence of the company's trade." (*Per* Lord Morton at p. 410.)

In *I.R.C.* v. *Carron Company*[81] the cost of obtaining a new charter which provided a better administrative structure for the company was held to be deductible " . . . what matters is the nature of the advantage for which the money was spent. This money was spent to remove restrictions which were preventing profits from being earned. It created no new asset. It did not even open new fields of trading which had previously been closed to the Company." (*Per* Lord Reid at p. 68.) The "identifiable asset test" was not satisfied: see § 2–53.

Examples of capital expenditure

2–56   *Mallet* v. *Staveley Coal and Iron Co. Ltd.,*[82] where a colliery company with long-term mining leases found that some of the seams of coal it had contracted to work were unprofitable. The lessor agreed to release the company from its

---

76. [1927] 1 K.B. 719; 11 T.C. 372 (C.A.) and see *Nevill & Co. Ltd.* v. *Federal Commissioner of Taxation* (1936) 56 C.L.R. 290: "The purpose was transient and, although not in itself recurrent, it was connected with the ever-recurring question of personnel" (*per* Dixon J.).

77. [1932] 1 K.B. 124; 16 T.C. 253 (C.A.).

78. *Tucker* v. *Granada Motorway Services Ltd.* (1979) 53 T.C. 92 at p. 115H (Lord Fraser).

79. [1941] 1 K.B. 111; 23 T.C. 597.

80. [1955] A.C. 21; 35 T.C. 367 (H.L.).

81. (1968) 45 T.C. 18 (H.L.). And see *Cooper* v. *Rhymney Breweries Ltd.* (1965) 42 T.C. 509 (cost of publicity campaign to achieve Sunday opening in the Principality of Wales *held* to be revenue expenditure).

82. [1928] 2 K.B. 405; 13 T.C. 772 (C.A.).

obligations under the leases on payment of a lump sum. *Held*, this was not deductible. The company was "getting rid of a permanent disadvantage or onerous burden, arising with regard to the lease which was a permanent asset of the business." (*Per* Sargant L.J.)

Associated Portland Cement Manufacturers Ltd. v. *Kerr*,[83] where lump sum payments to retiring directors in consideration of covenants that they would not thereafter carry on a similar business were held to be capital expenditure.

Strick v. *Regent Oil Co. Ltd.*,[84] where R.—in order to secure exclusive sales of its products at service stations—paid substantial sums to dealers for the benefit of "ties" ranging from 5 to 21 years. The form of the transaction was a lease from the dealer to Regent Oil for a lump sum calculated by reference to estimated petrol sales over the "tie" period, with a lease back from Regent Oil to the dealer for the same time less three days. The rent payable under both leases was nominal. *Held*, that the lump sums paid by Regent Oil were capital expenses, having regard to the nature of the asset which the expenditure secured.

(2) *Wholly and exclusively for the purposes of the trade*

2–57   Section 130(*a*) of the Income and Corporation Taxes Act 1970 disallows any disbursements or expenses, not being money wholly and exclusively laid out or expended for the purposes of the trade, profession or vocation. Section 130(*b*) disallows any disbursements or expenses of maintenance of the parties, their families or establishments, or any sums expended for any other domestic or private purposes distinct from the purposes of a trade, profession or vocation.

In *Bentleys, Stokes & Lowless* v. *Beeson*[85] the appellants, a firm of solicitors, had incurred expenses in entertaining clients. The question arose whether such expenses were wholly and exclusively incurred for professional purposes. The Crown contended that the expenses could not be wholly divorced from the relationship of host and guest and that the "wholly and exclusively" test was not satisfied. The Court of Appeal allowed the expenses.

The sole question for the consideration of the court was whether the expenditure in question was "exclusively" laid out for business purposes having regard to the fact that entertaining inevitably involves the characteristic of hospitality. Romer L.J. said (at p. 504):

" . . . it is quite clear that the [business] purpose must be the sole purpose. The paragraph says so in clear terms. If the activity be undertaken with the object both of promoting business and also with some other purpose, for example, with the object of indulging an independent wish of entertaining a friend or stranger or of supporting a charitable or benevolent object, then the paragraph is not satisfied although in the mind of the actor the business motive may predominate. For the statute so prescribes. *Per contra*, if in truth the sole subject is business promotion, the expenditure is not disqualified because the nature of the activity necessarily involves some other result, or the attainment or furtherance of some other objective, since the latter result or objective is necessarily inherent in the act."

---

83. (1945) 27 T.C. 103 (C.A.).

84. [1966] A.C. 295; 43 T.C. 1 (H.L.). The speeches in this case merit careful study. See also *B.P. Australia Ltd.* v. *Comr. of Taxation of the Commonwealth of Australia* [1966] A.C. 224 (J.C.).

85. (1952) 33 T.C. 491 (C.A.). Business entertaining expenses are now disallowed by statute; see *post*, §§ 2–71 *et seq*.

2–58   The court held that the primary purpose of the expenditure was a business purpose and so allowed the deduction.[86] The test is a subjective, not an objective one. The relevant question is: what was the object of the person making the disbursement in making it? not what was the effect of the disbursement when made?[87] It follows from the principle enunciated by Romer L.J. that where expenditure is incurred for a dual purpose, one a business purpose and one not, no part of the expenditure is deductible.[88] Logically, where the taxpayer admits some degree of non-business purpose by claiming a percentage deduction for private use from total expenditure, disallowance of the whole should follow; but the Revenue do not in all cases so apply the law. The *Bentleys* case may be contrasted with *Norman* v. *Golder*[89] where a sick shorthand-writer unsuccessfully claimed as a deduction expenses involved in getting well. Lord Greene M.R. said:

> "It is quite impossible to argue that doctors' bills represent money wholly and exclusively laid out for the purposes of a trade, profession, employment or vocation of the patient. True it is that if you do not get yourself well and so incur expenses to doctors you cannot carry on your trade or profession and if you do not carry on your trade or profession you will not earn an income, and if you do not earn an income the Revenue will not get any tax. The same thing applies to the food you eat and the clothes that you wear. But expenses of that kind are not wholly and exclusively laid out for the purposes of trade, profession or vocation. They are laid out in part for the advantage and benefit of the taxpayer as a living human being."

If Company A incurs expenditure to sustain the trade of Company B, the expenditure is not deductible unless the trades are interlinked and it can be shown that the expenditure was incurred to ensure the prosperity of Company A's trade.[90] A starting point in determining the purpose of a company in making expenditure is the minutes of directors' meetings.[90a]

---

86. See *Usher's Wiltshire Brewery* v. *Bruce* (1914) 6 T.C. 399 at p. 437 (Lord Sumner); *Morgan* v. *Tate & Lyle Ltd.* (1954) 35 T.C. 367 at p. 417 (Lord Reid).

87. *Robinson* v. *Scott Bader Co. Ltd.* (1981) 54 T.C. 757; [1980] S.T.C. 241 at p. 249C affirmed [1981] S.T.C. 436 (C.A.) (when the taxpayer seconded one of its employees to a French subsidiary company and paid for his services and it was held that the purpose was to protect the taxpayer's trade and not to protect its investment in the French company: *held*, the sums paid were deductible). *Cf. Garforth* v. *Tankard Carpets Ltd.* (1980) 53 T.C. 342; [1980] S.T.C. 251.

88. *Bowden* v. *Russell and Russell* (1965) 42 T.C. 301 (a solicitor combining attendance at foreign law conference with holiday; no deduction allowed). And see *Mallalieu* v. *Drummond* [1983] S.T.C. 665 (H.L.) (cost of woman barrister's black clothes required for wearing in court *held* not to satisfy the "wholly and exclusively" test).

89. (1944) 26 T.C. 293 (C.A.). See also *Murgatroyd* v. *Evans-Jackson* (1966) 43 T.C. 581 (professional man entered nursing home to enjoy facility of private room, telephone, etc., which he could use as office; cost not deductible); *Prince* v. *Mapp* (1969) 46 T.C. 169 (guitar player played professionally and as hobby—cost of operation on finger not allowable expense); *Knight* v. *Parry* (1972) 48 T.C. 580; [1973] S.T.C. 56 (expenses of solicitor in refuting allegations of professional misconduct disallowed); *Kilmorie (Aldridge) Ltd.* v. *Dickinson* (1974) 50 T.C. 1; *Caillebotte* v. *Quinn* (1975) 50 T.C. 222 (self-employed carpenter incurring extra costs on meals when away from home: *held*, not allowable). *Mason* v. *Tyson* (1980) 53 T.C. 333; [1980] S.T.C. 284 (expenditure incurred by chartered surveyor in redecorating flat above his office in which he occasionally slept and worked: *held*, not allowable).

90. *Milnes* v. *J. Beam Group Ltd.* (1975) 50 T.C. 675; [1975] S.T.C. 487 (where Company A guaranteed loans to an associated company and it was not established that a sum paid by Company A in discharging its liability was made wholly and exclusively for the purpose of the trade of Company A); *cf. Morley* v. *Lawford* (1928) 14 T.C. 229. See the cases in note 87.

90a. *Watney Combe Reid* v. *Pike* [1982] S.T.C. 733 at p. 751G.

2–59   It appears that the word "wholly" in the phrase "wholly and exclusively" relates to *quantum*. Thus if an employee is paid a salary which is excessive having regard to the services he renders, the excess may be disallowed as a deduction[91]; and the same rule applies to excessive pensions.[92]

Expenditure is incurred "for the purpose of the trade" if it is incurred "for the purpose of enabling a person to carry on and earn profits in the trade . . . ."[93]

Specific Items of Expenditure

2–60   *Rent and premiums for business premises.* Rent paid for business premises is deductible in computing trading profits, even if the premises are temporarily out of use.[94] If premises are used partly for business and partly for domestic purposes, the Revenue allow a deduction in respect of such part of the rent as is attributable to the business but disallows the remainder.[95] A premium for a lease is treated as non-deductible capital expenditure (except possibly in the case of very short leases[96]); but deduction is allowed to a trader who pays a premium for (or a sum on the assignment of) business premises when the payment is chargeable on the recipient.[97] When a capital asset is acquired by means of payment of "rent," the payment will be disallowed.[98]

2–61   *Sale and lease-back transactions.* A trader who sells his business premises, whether freehold or leasehold, for a capital sum and takes from the purchaser a lease or sub-lease at a rent is generally entitled to deduct the whole of the rent as an expense of his trade. Any chargeable gain accruing on the transaction is subject to capital gains tax. This general principle is subject to two statutory exceptions.

First, if the rent under the lease is in excess of a commercial rent, the excess will be disallowed as a deduction, under section 491 of the Income and Corporation Taxes Act 1970.

Secondly, where a lease with not more than 50 years to run (called "the original lease") is assigned or surrendered in consideration of a capital sum and the lessee[99] takes a lease back at a rent, the lease back (called "the new

91. *Copeman* v. *Flood* [1941] 1 K.B. 202; 24 T.C. 53: but *quaere* if this decision can be reconciled with the principle enunciated by Romer L.J. in the *Bentleys* case, *supra*.
92. An agreement to provide a pension may be *ultra vires* and void: see *Re W. & M. Roith Ltd.* [1967] 1 W.L.R 432. But see *Re Horsley & Weight Ltd.* [1982] Ch. 442 (C.A.); *Rolled Steel Products Ltd.* v. *B.S.C.* (1984) B.C.L.C. 466 (C.A.).
93. *Strong* v. *Woodfield* (1906) 5 T.C. 215 at p. 220, *per* Lord Davey, as explained in *Morgan* v. *Tate & Lyle Ltd.* (1954) 35 T.C. 367 at pp. 410 (Lord Gordon) and 421 (Lord Reid).
94. *I.R.C.* v. *The Falkirk Iron Company Ltd.* (1933) 17 T.C. 625. The position is the same where the premises have been sub-let: *Hyett* v. *Lennard* (1940) 23 T.C. 346.
95. I.C.T.A. 1970, s.130(*c*).
96. See dicta of Lord Reid in *Strick* v. *Regent Oil Co. Ltd.* [1966] A.C. 295 at pp. 315F and 325G.
97. *Ibid.* s.134, as amended by F.A. 1978, s.32. For the taxation of premiums, see *post*, §§ 6–16 *et seq.*
98. *Littlewoods Mail Order Stores Ltd.* v. *McGregor* (1969) 45 T.C. 519 (C.A.); *I.R.C.* v. *Land Securities Investment Trust Ltd.* (1969) 45 T.C. 495 (H.L.).
99. Defined to include a partner or associate of the original lessee: see F.A. 1972, s.80(7).

lease") being for a term not exceeding 15 years,[1] a proportion of the capital sum is taxable as income under section 80 of the Finance Act 1972. The rent will be allowed as a deduction, subject to the provisions of section 491 (above). The proportion of the capital sum which is taxable as income is found by applying the formula $\dfrac{16-n}{15}$ where "n" is the term of the new lease expressed in years.[2]

> Thus if the new lease is for a term of 15 years, one-fifteenth of the capital sum is taxable; if for a term of one year, the whole of the capital sum is taxable.

"Top slicing" relief is available to prevent the capital sum being treated as income of a single year of assessment.[3] That part of the capital sum which is chargeable as income is outside the charge to capital gains tax.[4]

Section 80 of the Finance Act 1972 applies only where the new lease is "a lease . . . of or including the whole or any part of the land which was the subject of the original lease."[5] Difficulties in applying this provision may arise in practice in cases where, for example, the original lease is surrendered to a landlord who demolishes the existing premises, rebuilds a tower block on the site of the old premises, and grants to the original lessee a lease of a floor which was airspace before the demolition. Section 80(4) of the Finance Act 1972 provides that where the property which is the subject of the new lease does not include the *whole* of the property which was the subject of the original lease, the consideration received by the lessee should be treated as reduced to that portion thereof which is reasonably attributable to such part of the property which was the subject of the original lease as consists of, or is included in, the property which is the subject of the new lease.

> Thus if one-third of the property included in the original lease is included in the new lease, only one-third of the capital sum is taken into account in applying the section.

2–62   *Repairs and improvements.* A deduction is allowed for the sum actually expended on repairs to business assets,[6] provided the expenditure is revenue and not capital expenditure.

> In *Law Shipping Co. Ltd.* v. *I.R.C.*[7] a trader purchased a ship in a state of disrepair. After the completion of the voyage on which it was then embarked, repairs were necessary to obtain the Lloyd's certificate which was essential if the ship was to remain a profit-earning asset. The Revenue claimed that the cost of the repairs was capital expenditure to the extent that it was attributable to the state of disrepair of the ship at the time of purchase. The Court of Session upheld the Revenue's claim and disallowed the expenditure. (Part of the cost of the repairs was attributable to deterioration during the last voyage

---

1. There are anti-avoidance provisions which cause the section to apply when the term of the new lease is "artificially" extended beyond 15 years: see F.A. 1972, s.80(2).
2. F.A. 1972, s.80(3).
3. *Ibid.* s.80(5).
4. See *post,* § 16–19.
5. F.A. 1972, s.80(1)(*a*).
6. I.C.T.A. 1970, s.130(*d*).
7. (1924) 12 T.C. 621. See also *I.R.C.* v. *Granite City Steamship Co. Ltd.* (1927) 13 T.C. 1.

when the ship was in the appellant's ownership. This was conceded to be revenue expenditure.)

In another case where a trader acquired business premises in a state of dilapidation, the cost of reinstating the premises was disallowed.[8]

> In *Odeon Associated Theatres Ltd.* v. *Jones*[9] the taxpayer purchased a cinema in 1945 which, owing to war time restrictions on building, had not been kept in repair. Some years later the taxpayer carried out repairs which were outstanding at the time when the cinema was purchased. There was no element of improvement in the repairs and the price paid for the cinema was not diminished on their account. The Special Commissioners found as a fact that, on the principles of sound commercial accounting, the deferred repairs would be dealt with as a charge to revenue in the taxpayer's accounts. The Court of Appeal held that the cost of the repairs was deductible as revenue expenditure.

The *Law Shipping*[10] case was distinguished on the grounds (i) that in that case there was no evidence of accountancy practice[11]; (ii) that the cinema was a profit-earning asset even though in a state of disrepair; and (iii) that the purchase price for the cinema was unaffected by the state of disrepair.[12]

2–63   The cost of improvements (as distinct from repairs) is not deductible for income tax or corporation tax purposes,[13] although the cost may be deductible for the purposes of capital gains tax (as explained in § 16–30). The terms "repair" and "improvement" are not defined in the Tax Acts but the following passage from the judgment of Buckley L.J., in *Lurcott* v. *Wakely & Wheeler*,[14] in which he contrasts the terms "repair" and "renew," is frequently cited in tax cases as indicating the difference between repair and improvement.

> " 'Repair' and 'renew' are not words expressive of a clear contrast. Repair always involves renewal; renewal of a part; of a subordinate part. A skylight leaks; repair is effected by hacking out the putties, putting in new ones, and renewing the paint. A roof falls out of repair; the necessary work is to replace the decayed timbers by sound wood; to substitute sound tiles or slates for those which are cracked, broken, or missing; to make good the flashings, and the like. Part of a garden wall tumbles down; repair is effected by building it up again with new mortar, and, so far as necessary, new bricks or stone. Repair is restoration by renewal or replacement of subsidiary parts of a whole. Renewal, as distinguished from repair, is reconstruction of the entirety, meaning by the entirety not necessarily the whole but substantially the whole subject-matter under discussion."

The judge refers in this extract to *the entirety* and in many cases it becomes material to determine what constitutes the entirety. If, for example, a factory chimney falls into disrepair and is rebuilt, the question

---

8. *Jackson* v. *Laskers Home Furnishers Ltd.* (1957) 37 T.C. 69. See also *Bidwell* v. *Gardiner* (1960) 39 T.C. 31.

9. (1971) 48 T.C. 257 (C.A.).

10. (1924) 12 T.C. 621.

11. As to the weight to be given to evidence of accountancy practice, see *Heather* v. *P-E Consulting Group Ltd.* [1973] Ch. 189; 48 T.C. 293 (C.A.) and the discussion in § 2–19A.

12. Other points of contrast are discussed in a Note in [1972] B.T.R. 51.

13. I.C.T.A. 1970, s.130(g).

14. [1911] 1 K.B. 905 (C.A.). See *Morcom* v. *Campbell-Johnson* [1956] 1 Q.B. 106.

may arise whether the entirety was the factory (a subsidiary part of which was rebuilt—this would be "repair") or the chimney (the whole of which was renewed—this would be "improvement").[15] In some cases the Crown has contended that the question whether expenditure on (say) rebuilding is to be regarded as capital or revenue expenditure is a different question from the question whether the expenditure is on improvements or repairs. The author doubts whether these can properly be regarded as separate questions.[16]

2–64   *Damages and losses*. No sum can be deducted in respect of "any loss not connected with or arising out of" a trade.[17] In *Strong & Co. Ltd.* v. *Woodifield*,[18] damages paid to an hotel guest for injury sustained in the hotel when part of the building collapsed were disallowed. The basis of this decision appears to be that the loss was not sufficiently incidental to the trade of *hotel keeper* to be outside the specific prohibition quoted above. Damages paid to a guest who was injured, *e.g.* by bad food served in the hotel, would apparently be deductible.

2–65   Penalties incurred by a trader for breaches of the law committed in the course of trading are not allowable.[19] This apparently is because the penalties are not incurred by the trader in his capacity as a trader.[20]

If money is lent by a trader and the loan is not repaid, a deduction is allowed only if the trade is, or includes, moneylending.[21]

2–66   *Compensation payments*. A payment made by a company to get rid of a director or employee is an allowable expense if the payment is made in the interests of the company's trade[22]; but a payment which is made on the occasion of the acquisition of the company's shares by outsiders will often

---

15. *O'Grady* v. *Bullcroft Main Collieries Ltd.* (1932) 17 T.C. 93: "If you replace in entirety, it is having a new one and it is not repairing the old one"; *Margrett* v. *Lowestoft Water and Gas Co.* (1935) 19 T.C. 481; *Samuel Jones and Company (Devonvale) Ltd.* v. *I.R.C.* (1951) 32 T.C. 513; *William P. Lawrie* v. *I.R.C.* (1952) 34 T.C. 20; *Thomas Wilson (Keighley) Ltd.* v. *Emmerson* (1960) 39 T.C. 360; *Wynne-Jones* v. *Bedale Auction Ltd.* (1977) 51 T.C. 426; [1977] S.T.C. 50; *Brown* v. *Burnley Football and Athletic Co.* (1980) 53 T.C. 357; [1980] S.T.C. 424; *ACT Construction* v. *Customs and Excise* [1980] S.T.C. 716 (C.A.).
16. Cf. *Phillips* v. *Whieldon Sanitary Potteries Ltd.* (1952) 33 T.C. 213; *Conn* v. *Robins Brothers Ltd.* (1966) 43 T.C. 266; *Hodgins* v. *Plunder & Pollack* [1957] I.R. 58.
17. I.C.T.A. 1970, s.130(*e*). And see *Allen* v. *Farquharson Bros. & Co.* (1932) 17 T.C. 59 at p. 64 where Finlay J. distinguishes "disbursements" in s.130(*a*) from "loss" in s.130(*e*).
18. [1906] A.C. 448; 5 T.C. 215. See also *Fairrie* v. *Hall* (1948) 28 T.C. 200: damages for libel held not deductible as a trading expense of a sugar broker.
19. *I.R.C.* v. *Alexander von Glehn & Co. Ltd.* [1920] 2 K.B. 553; 12 T.C. 232 (C.A.) (fines are not paid for the purpose of earning profits; they are unfortunate incidents which follow after the profits have been earned (Scrutton L.J.)). The treatment of legal costs in this case was not argued separately, it being assumed that, if the fines were non-deductible, so also would be the costs.
20. *Morgan* v. *Tate & Lyle Ltd.* (1954) 35 T.C. 367 at pp. 419 (Lord Reid) and 430 (Lord Keith). See also *Spofforth & Prince* v. *Golder* (1945) 26 T.C. 310.
21. *Hagart and Burn-Murdoch* v. *I.R.C.* [1929] A.C. 386; 14 T.C. 433; *Rutherford* v. *I.R.C.* (1939) 23 T.C. 8; and *Bury and Walkers* v. *Phillips* (1951) 32 T.C. 198. And see *Reid's Brewery Co.* v. *Male* [1891] 2 Q.B. 1; 3 T.C. 279, where a loss on loans to clients was allowed. See also *Jennings* v. *Barfield & Barfield* (1962) 40 T.C. 365.
22. *Mitchell* v. *B. W. Noble Ltd.* [1972] 1 K.B. 719; 11 T.C. 372 (C.A.), *ante*, § 2–55.

be disallowed. In *James Snook & Co. Ltd.* v. *Blasdale,*[23] Donovan J. said that in such a case:

> "The mere circumstance that compensation to retiring directors is paid on a change of shareholding control does not of itself involve the consequence that such compensation can never be a deductible trading expense. But it is essential that the company should prove to the Commissioners' satisfaction that it considered the question of payment wholly untrammelled by the terms of the bargain its shareholders had struck with those who were to buy their shares and came to a decision to pay solely in the interests of its trade."

"Golden handshakes" which are tax-free in the hands of the recipient are in some cases disallowed as sums not incurred wholly and exclusively for the purposes of the payer's trade.

2–66A   *Payments to redundant employees.* Payments which are made after, or in anticipation of, the permanent discontinuance of a trade are not normally allowable as a deduction in computing trading profits (or as management expenses of an investment company).[24] There is a limited statutory exception which applies to payments to redundant employees in addition to those made under statutory schemes (which are deductible under section 412 of the Income and Corporation Taxes Act 1970). Additional payments to redundant employees may also be deductible.[25]

2–67   *Tax.* In one case it was held that the Argentine "substitute tax" for which the appellant was liable was deductible as expenditure incurred wholly and exclusively for the purposes of the appellant's trade.[26]

2–67A   *Relief for Class 4 National Insurance Contributions.* These are contributions at a graduated rate payable under Section 9(2) of the Social Security Act 1975, by individuals who carry on a trade, profession or vocation. In and from 1985–86, an individual may claim to deduct in computing his total income for a year of assessment one-half of the amount as finally settled of his Class 4 contributions for the year. The claim must be made within six years from the end of the year of assessment.[26a]

2–68   *Bad debts.* An amount to which a trader is entitled, *e.g.* for goods supplied by him, enters into the computation of his profits in the period when the sum falls due.[27] If, later, the trader is able to prove that the debt is a bad or doubtful debt, the Revenue allow a deduction—in the latter case, to

23. (1952) 33 T.C. 244 at p. 251; *Godden* v. *Wilson's Stores (Holdings) Ltd.* (1962) 40 T.C. 161 (C.A.); *George Peters & Co. Ltd.* v. *Smith* (1963) 41 T.C. 264. *Cf. I.R.C.* v. *Patrick Thompson Ltd.* (1956) 37 T.C. 145.

24. *I.R.C.* v. *The Anglo Brewing Co. Ltd.* (1925) 12 T.C. 803; *Godden* v. *A. Wilson's Stores (Holdings) Ltd.* (1962) 40 T.C. 161 (C.A.). But see *O'Keefe* v. *Southport Printers Ltd.* [1984] S.T.C. 443.

25. F.A. 1980, s.41 (applying to payments made on or after April 1, 1980). In practice, s.41 is applied to cases of partial discontinuance: see I.R. Press Release in [1981] S.T.I. 584.

26. *Harrods (Buenos Aires) Ltd.* v. *Taylor-Gooby* (1964) 41 T.C. 450 (C.A.). As regards the deduction of VAT, see Chap. 35.

26a. F.A. 1985, s.42.

27. See *ante*, § 2–20.

the extent that the debt is estimated to be a bad debt.[28] A debt may be a bad debt even though the debtor continues to trade.[29] If an allowance is given and the debt is later paid, the amount must be brought in as a trading receipt of the year when it is paid.[30]

2–69   *Defalcations.* In *Curtis* v. *Oldfield*[31] the managing director of a company had used the company's bank account to pay his own private bills. It was held that the loss so incurred by the company was not deductible. In this connection, the remarks of Rowlatt J. are important:

> "If you have a business . . . in the course of which you have to employ sub-ordinates, and owing to the negligence or the dishonesty *of the subordinates,* some of the receipts of the business do not find their way into the till, or some of the bills are not collected at all, or something of that sort, that may be an expense connected with and arising out of the trade in the most complete sense of the word."

In a later case it was contended that there is no logical distinction to be drawn between petty theft by a subordinate employee and massive defal-cation by a director. But Brightman J. said this[32]:

> "In my view there is a distinction. I can quite see that the Commissioners might find as a fact that a £5 note taken from the till by a shop assistant is a loss to the trader which is connected with and arises out of the trade. A large shop has to use tills and to employ assistants with access to those tills. It could not trade in any other way. That it seems to me, is quite a different case from a director with authority to sign cheques who helps himself to £15,000, which is then lost to the company. I find it difficult to see how such a loss could be regarded fairly as "connected with or arising out of the trade." In the default-ing director type of case, there seems to me to be no relevant nexus between the loss of the money and the conduct of the company's trade. The loss is not, as in the case of the dishonest shop assistant, an incident of the company's trading activities. It arises altogether outside such activities. That, I think, is the true distinction."

The distinction drawn in this passage between defalcations by subordin-ates and defalcations by directors does not provide the only criterion to the solution of the problem. If, for example, the rules of a trading establish-ment require that cash dealings with customers in excess of (say) £5,000 shall be handled only by a director, a loss arising through misappropriation of cash receipts by such a director would, it is thought, be allowable.

2–70   *Legal and other professional charges.* The costs of a tax appeal arising out of a disputed assessment of trading profits are not allowable.[33] In prac-tice, the fees paid to an accountant in agreeing tax computations with the Inspector are allowed; so also are fees paid in seeking advice on liability to

---

28. I.C.T.A. 1970, s.130(*i*).
29. *Dinshaw* v. *Income Tax Commissioners* (*Bombay*) (1934) 50 T.L.R. 527 (J.C.).
30. *Bristow* v. *Dickinson* [1946] K.B. 321; 27 T.C. 157 (C.A.). If the trade has been discon-tinued at the date of payment, the sum will be assessed as a post-cessation receipt under the I.C.T.A. 1970, s.143; *post,* §§ 2–88 *et seq.*
31. (1925) 9 T.C. 319.
32. *Bamford.* v. *A. T. A. Advertising Ltd.* (1972) 48 T.C. 359 at p. 368.
33. *Smith's Potato Estates Ltd.* v. *Bolland* [1948] A.C. 508; 30 T.C. 267 (H.L.). See also *Meredith* v. *Roberts* (1968) 44 T.C. 559.

tax. Legal expenses incurred in the course of a trade, *e.g.* in recovering debts, in settling disputes and in the preparation of service agreements are allowed; but the costs of acquiring premises or a lease thereof will normally be disallowed as capital expenses. The cost of renewing a short lease is usually allowed.[34]

2–71 *Business entertaining expenses.* The rules which apply to Cases I and II of Schedule D allow the deduction of entertaining expenses incurred for the purposes of a trade[35]; but section 411 of the Income and Corporation Taxes Act 1970 disallows as a deduction all expenses incurred in providing business entertainment, including expenses allowances made for that purpose. "Business entertainment" is defined in section 411(5) as meaning

> "entertainment (including hospitality of any kind[36]) provided by a person, or by a member of his staff,[37] in connection with a trade carried on by that person, but does not include anything provided by him for bona fide members of his staff unless its provision for them is incidental to its provision also for others."

2–72 There is an exception in the case of expenses incurred by a United Kingdom trader in the entertainment of an "overseas customer," meaning:

(1) any person who is not ordinarily resident nor carrying on a trade in the United Kingdom and who avails himself, or may be expected to avail himself, in the course of a trade carried on by him outside the United Kingdom, of any goods, services or facilities which it is the trade of the United Kingdom trader to provide, and

(2) any person who is not ordinarily resident in the United Kingdom and is acting, in relation to such goods, services or facilities, on behalf of an overseas customer within (1) or on behalf of any government or public authority of a country outside the United Kingdom.[38]

The word "trade" in section 411 includes a business, profession or vocation. Subject to (2), the expense of entertaining a "non-trader" is not allowable.

Expenditure incurred by a publisher of newspapers in giving hospitality to informants, contributors and other contacts, in order to gather material, has been disallowed.[39]

---

34. In *Stephenson* v. *Payne, Stone, Fraser & Co.* (1968) 44 T.C. 507, a firm of accountants formed a service company to provide them with all their administrative requirements, and in the first year the charge made to the firm exceeded the cost by £15,000. *Held*, that the £15,000 was not an allowable expense of the year. And see *ante*, § 2–20.

35. *Bentleys, Stokes and Lowless* v. *Beeson* (1952) 33 T.C. 491 (C.A.): *ante*, § 2–57.

36. Gifts are included, with an exception for certain small gifts bearing advertisements for the donor.

37. This means employees and directors: I.C.T.A. 1970, s.411(7).

38. See I.C.T.A. 1970, s.411(6). S.411(8) does not preclude the deduction of gifts to bodies established for charitable purposes only: F.A. 1980, s.54.

39. *Fleming* v. *Associated Newspapers Ltd.* [1973] A.C. 628; 48 T.C. 382 (H.L.). This case contains some illuminating observations on the construction of obscure and almost unintelligible statute law. See also the VAT case of *Customs and Excise Commissioners* v. *Shaklee International* [1981] S.T.C. 776 (C.A.) and *Celtic Football and Athletic Co. Ltd.* v. *Customs and Excise Commissioners* [1983] S.T.C. 470.

2–72A   *Business travelling expenses.* The cost of travelling on business is a deductible expense. In *Horton* v. *Young*[40] it was held on the facts that a self-employed bricklayer's home was his "base of operations" and that the expense he incurred in travelling between his home and building sites was an allowable deduction in computing his profits under Case I of Schedule D. This may be contrasted with *Newsom* v. *Robertson*[41] where it was held that a Chancery barrister's chambers in Lincoln's Inn were his base, and that the home in which he did a large part of his work was not. It is thought that the principle in *Horton* v. *Young* would apply to the case of a barrister who practised on circuit, who seldom visited his chambers, and who used his home as the centre of his professional activities; the costs of travelling between home and the courts in which he practised (as well as the costs of travelling between courts) would be allowed as a deduction.

In *Sargent* v. *Barnes*[42] a dentist travelled 11 miles from his home to his surgery. En route, about one mile from his home, was a dental laboratory at which the dentist called each morning to collect completed work and each evening to deliver work. The dentist claimed that his day's work commenced and ended at the laboratory and that the expenses of travelling from the laboratory to the surgery and back were deductible. It was held that they were not. Oliver J. said this:

> "I do not think, however, that the findings in the present case can justify the assertion that, looked at realistically, there was here really a profession being carried on in two places. . . . The taxpayer had made arrangements at somebody else's premises for a dental mechanic to carry out what was, no doubt, an essential function for his practice. If he had made those arrangements in an outbuilding in the curtilage of his own house, it would not, in my judgment, mean that he was carrying on a dental practice from his home, so as to justify an assertion that the expenses of travel from his home to his surgery were exclusively for the purposes of his practice."

The judge added that this was an area in which it was difficult and, he thought, positively dangerous to seek to lay down any general proposition designed to serve as a touchstone for all cases.

2–73   *Annual payments.* No deduction can be made *in computing* profits in respect of any annuity or other annual payment (other than interest) payable out of the profits or gains.[43] The types of payment which fall within this prohibition are discussed *post*, §§ 5–04 *et seq.* The prohibition applies only to payments which are charged on the profits: it does not apply to payments which are made in earning profits.[44] Many annuities and annual payments are a charge on income and are deductible as such: see § 8–31 (individuals) and § 14–08 (companies).

---

40. [1972] 1 Ch. 157; 47 T.C. 60 (C.A.).
41. [1953] Ch. 7; 33 T.C. 452 (C.A.).
42. (1978) 52 T.C. 335; [1978] S.T.C. 322.
43. I.C.T.A. 1970, s.130(*l*).
44. *Gresham Life Assurance Society* v. *Styles* [1892] A.C. 309; 3 T.C. 185: annuities paid by a society whose business it was to grant annuities; *held* to be deductible.

2–74 *Patent royalties.* No deduction is allowed for any royalty or other sum paid in respect of the user of a patent.[45] Expenses of obtaining a patent may be allowed.[46]

2–75 *Interest.* Interest paid as a business expense, whether short interest or yearly interest, is deductible[47] except in the case of companies where yearly interest (other than bank interest) is not deductible as a business expense but is a charge on income.[48] Other provisions relating to interest are discussed *post,* §§ 8–57 *et seq.*

–75A *Incidental costs of obtaining loan finance.*[49] The incidental costs of obtaining loan finance are deductible in computing profits for the purposes of Case I or II of Schedule D or as expenses of management of an investment company. The loan must be "a qualifying loan" or "qualifying loan stock," which means a loan the interest on which is deductible in computing profits (see § 2–75) or as a charge on income (see §§ 14–08 *et seq.*); but a loan or loan stock which carries a right of conversion into, or to the acquisition of, shares or other securities not being a qualifying loan or qualifying loan stock is non-qualifying if the right is actually exercised[49a] within three years from the date when the loan was obtained or the stock was issued. "Incidental costs of obtaining finance" means expenditure on fees, commissions, advertising, printing and other incidental matters (excluding stamp duty), being expenditure wholly and exclusively incurred for the purpose of obtaining the finance (whether or not it is in fact obtained), of providing security for it or of repaying it. The section does not give relief for losses resulting from changes in the rate of exchange between different currencies or sums paid to secure protection against such losses, nor does it give relief for a premium payable on repayment or other sum payable in consequence of the loan being provided at a discount.

–75B *Relief for pre-trading expenditure.*[50] Expenditure incurred before a trade is commenced is not deductible: see § 2–52. There is a limited statutory exception which applies to expenditure incurred on or after April 1, 1980 and within three years before the commencement, provided the expenditure would have been deductible had it been incurred after the commencement. Thus capital expenditure is excluded. The expenditure is treated for income tax purposes as if it were the amount of a loss sustained in the trade in the year in which it is set up and commenced: see Chapter 12.

–75C *Voluntary contributions to local enterprise agencies.*[51] Where a person carrying on a trade, profession or vocation makes a contribution whether in cash or in kind to an "approved local enterprise agency," a sum equal to

45. I.C.T.A. 1970, s.130(*n*).
46. See *ibid.* s.132 for details.
47. *Ibid.* s.130(*l*).
48. *Ibid.* s.251(2), (3) and s.248; see *post,* §§ 14–08 *et seq.*
49. F.A. 1980, s.38 applying to expenditure incurred on or after April 1, 1980.
49a. See F.A. 1984, s.43 (applying to expenditure incurred on or after April 1, 1983).
50. F.A. 1980, s.39, the period of three years was extended from one year by the F.A. 1982, s.44.
51. F.A. 1982, s.42.

the amount or value of the contribution is deductible as a trade expense; and a similar contribution by an investment company may be treated as an expense of management: see § 6–31. This applies to contributions made on or after April 1, 1982 and before April 1, 1992. A local enterprise agency is a body which has as its sole objective the promotion or encouragement of industrial and commercial activity or enterprise in a particular area in the United Kingdom with particular reference to encouraging the formation and development of small businesses. The agency must be approved by the Secretary of State. There is no right of deduction if the contributor or anyone connected with him receives or is entitled to receive any benefit from the agency; and there are elaborate provisions to ensure that members of the agency and persons directing its affairs do not derive benefit from the contribution.

2–76   *Employees seconded to charities.* Section 28 of the Finance Act 1983 (as extended) allows an employer which makes available to a legal charity, on a temporary basis, the services of an employee, to have the same tax deductions the employer would have had if the seconded employee had remained in the employer's service. The section as originally enacted applied only to company employers. It now applies to others, such as partnerships or sole traders.[52] The section applies to expenditure on or after April 1, 1983.

2–77   *Pensions.* Pensions paid by employers are deductible in computing profits if the expenditure is incurred wholly and exclusively for the purposes of the trade. A pension which is paid voluntarily may fulfil this condition.[53] A pension which is excessive may be disallowed as expenditure incurred not wholly and exclusively for the purposes of the payer's trade.[54]

2–78   *Payments to provide pensions.*[55] An employer who wishes to provide his employee or employees with a pension may do so in one of the following ways:

(1) By contributing to a pension fund established for the purpose. An initial contribution made by an employer to establish a pension fund is not deductible,[56] unless the pension scheme is an "exempt approved" scheme. Ordinary annual contributions are usually deductible.[57]

(2) By purchase of an annuity from an insurance company. The cost of

---

52. F.A. 1984, s.33.
53. *Smith* v. *Incorporated Council of Law Reporting* [1914] 3 K.B. 674; 6 T.C. 477.
54. See *ante*, § 2–59.
55. See also *post*, §§ 39–08 *et seq.*
56. *British Insulated and Helsby Cables Ltd.* v. *Atherton* [1926] A.C. 205; 10 T.C. 155.
57. *Morgan Crucible Co. Ltd.* v. *I.R.C.* [1932] 2 K.B. 185; 17 T.C. 311. And see *Southern Railway of Peru Ltd.* v. *Owen* [1957] A.C. 334; 36 T.C. 634: *ante*, § 2–21B. See also F.A. 1970, s.21.

purchasing an annuity for an employee in substitution for a pension already awarded is deductible.[58]

(3) By paying premiums on a policy assuring retirement benefits. The premiums are deductible if the policy moneys are held upon trust for the employees[59] and the arrangement is approved by the Revenue or if the premiums are a proper business expense.[60]

If the employer makes contributions to a pension fund which is not an "exempt approved scheme" within section 21 of the Finance Act 1970, any relief in respect of those contributions will be governed by section 130 of the Taxes Act 1970. To qualify for relief the payment must not be of a capital nature[61] and must be wholly and exclusively for the purposes of the employer's trade.

4. THE BASIS OF ASSESSING PROFITS[62]

A. The Normal Basis

2–79 The normal basis on which profits arising under Cases I and II of Schedule D are assessed is the "preceding year basis"; that is, in each year of assessment, ending on April 5, the assessment is based on the profits of the accounting period ending in the preceding year of assessment.

Example
A trader prepares yearly accounts to December 31 each year. In 1982–83, he is assessed on the profits of the year ended December 31, 1981. (The accounting year to December 31, 1981, is described as the "basis period" for the year 1982–83.)

B. Rules for Opening Years

2–80 The normal preceding year basis cannot, of course, be applied in the opening year of a business. Accordingly, sections 115–117 of the Income and Corporation Taxes Act 1970 contain special provisions which apply from the date when a trade, profession or vocation has been set up and commenced. These "commencement provisions" are as follows:

Basis of Assessment

First tax year s. 116(1)	The profits from the date of commencement to the following April 5. If the first accounting period covers one year not ending on or about April 5, such profits must be computed by apportioning the profits of the accounting period on a time basis.

---

58. *Hancock* v. *General Reversionary and Investment Co. Ltd.* [1919] 1 K.B. 25; 7 T.C. 358. *Cf. Morgan Crucible Co. Ltd.* v. *I.R.C.* [1932] 2 K.B. 185; 17 T.C. 311: sum paid by company in purchasing annuity out of which the company could itself pay voluntary pensions; *held*, not deductible.

59. See note 56, *supra*.

60. *Dracup & Sons Ltd.* v. *Dakin* (1957) 37 T.C. 377.

61. *British Insulated and Helsby Cables Ltd.* v. *Atherton* [1926] A.C. 205; 10 T.C. 155.

62. The basis of assessing profits in the case of companies chargeable to corporation tax is discussed in Chap. 14. The Inland Revenue are reviewing the feasibility of moving from the previous year basis of assessment to a current year basis for unincorporated businesses: [1978] S.T.I. 480.

Thus if a trader commences business on January 1, 1982, and his first accounts, prepared to December 31, 1982, show a profit of £1,200, the first tax year is 1981/82 (because the business started in that year) and the assessment is $\frac{3}{12}$ths of £1,200 = 300.

Second tax year   The profits for one year from the date of commencement of
s. 116(2)   the business.

Thus is the first accounts cover a period of one year, the profits of that period form the basis of assessment. If the first accounts cover a period of less than a year, the assessment for the second tax year must be computed by apportioning the profits shown by the accounts of the first two years. (See *Example* in § 2–81.)

Third tax year   Generally, the normal preceding year basis.
s. 115.

Election for actual basis: s.117

2–81   The taxpayer has an option with regard to the second and third tax year (but not for one without the other) to have the assessments based on the actual profits of the tax years themselves, *i.e.* from April 6 to the following April 5 in each of those years. Such profits are computed by apportioning on a time basis the profits disclosed by the accounts which overlap the two tax years. The option is exercisable by notice to the Inspector within seven years from the end of the second tax year and can be revoked during that time.

Example
A trader starts business on December 6, 1977. His trading profits for the first three years are as follows:

		£
Accounting year ended December 5, 1978	....	1,200
,, ,, ,, ,, ,, 1979	....	1,800
,, ,, ,, ,, ,, 1980	....	2,400

Assessments are as follows:

1977–78 4/12ths of the actual profits in year ended December 5, 1978	....	400
1978–79 Actual profits to December 5, 1978	....	1,200
1979–80 ,, ,, ,, ,, ,, 1978	....	1,200
1980–81 ,, ,, ,, ,, ,, 1979	....	1,800
1981–82 ,, ,, ,, ,, ,, 1980	....	2,400

Alternative assessments for the second and third years if the taxpayer elects for the "actual basis" are as follows (other years being unaffected by the exercise of the option):

Basis of Assessment

1978–79	April 6, 1978—December 5, 1978: 8/12ths × 1,200 = 800 December 6, 1978—April 5, 1979: 4/12ths × 1,800 = 600	1,400
1979–80	April 6, 1979—December 5, 1979: 8/12ths × 1,800 = 1,200 December 6, 1979—April 5, 1980: 4/12ths × 2,400 = 800	2,000

Note. Where the profits of the trade are rising, as in this example, the option would not normally be exercised. If, however, the profits of the first three accounting years had been £1,200, £900 and £600 the assessments for the second and third years would have been respectively £1,200 and £1,200 (on the normal basis) or £1,100 and £800 (on the alternative basis) and the option would be exercised.

2–82 The method of computing profits in the opening years of a business is highly artificial and may often result in assessable profits being substantially more or less than actual profits during the same period. Generally, the profits for the first accounting period should be kept as low as possible.[63] and in the case of trades with fluctuating profits the greatest care should be taken in selecting the closing date of the first accounting period.[64]

C. Rules for Closing Years

2–83 When a trade, profession or vocation is *permanently* (not merely temporarily) discontinued, section 118 of the Income and Corporation Taxes Act 1970 applies. This section contains special provisions (called the "cessation provisions") which govern the assessment of profits in the tax year in which the trade, etc., is discontinued and in the two previous tax years. These provisions are as follows:

Basis of Assessment

Final tax year s. 118(1)(*a*)	Actual profits from April 6 to the date of discontinuance.
Penultimate tax year s. 118(1)(*b*) and Pre-penultimate tax year s. 118(1)(*b*)	Assessments for these years will have already been made on the normal preceding year basis. If the aggregate of the *actual* profits of these two years exceeds the aggregate of the profits computed on the normal preceding year basis, the profits of these two years must be computed on the actual basis and any further assessment or adjustment made. No reduction in the assessments will be allowed if the aggregate of the actual profits is less than the aggregate of the profits as assessed on the normal preceding year basis. "Actual profit" is found by apportioning the profits of the accounting periods which overlap the penultimate tax year.[65]

Example of the cessation provisions

The trading profits in the final years of a business (up to March 5, 1975, when the business was permanently discontinued) are as follows:

	£
Accounting year ended December 5, 1981	2,400
,, ,, ,, ,, ,, 1982	2,100
,, ,, ,, ,, ,, 1983	3,000
,, ,, ,, ,, ,, 1984	3,600
Period from December 6, 1984 to March 5, 1985	900

---

63. See *Stephenson* v. *Payne, Stone, Fraser & Co.* (1968) 44 T.C. 507: *ante,* § 2–70.
64. For the practice of the Board of Inland Revenue when there is a change of accounting date, see the Notes published by the Board and printed in B.T.E., § 6–148. For tax planning and other considerations affecting the choice of accounting dates, see Tolley, *Tax Planning.*
65. *Wesley* v. *Manson* [1932] A.C. 635; 16 T.C. 654 (H.L.).

Assessments are as follows

Basis of Assessment

Final year 1984–85   Actual Profits April 6, 1984 to March 5, 1985

April 6, 1984—December 5, 1984:

$8/12\text{ths} \times 3,600 = 2,400$

December 6, 1984—March 5, 1985:

$= 900$ } 3,300

Penultimate
year 1983–84   Normal basis: £

Actual profits to December 5, 1982   2,100

Actual year basis:

April 6, 1983—December 5, 1983:

$8/12\text{ths} \times 3,000 = 2,000$

December 6, 1983—March 5, 1984:

$4/12\text{ths} \times 3,600 = 1,200$ } 3,200

Pre-penultimate
year 1982–83   Normal basis:

Actual profits to December 5, 1981   2,400

Actual year basis:

April 6, 1982—December 5, 1982:

$8/12\text{ths} \times 2,100 = 1,400$

December 6, 1982—April 5, 1983:

$4/12\text{ths} \times 3,000 = 1,000$ } 2,400

For the penultimate and pre-penultimate years, assessments on the normal basis (£2,100 + £2,400) will have already been made when the business ceases. The Revenue have the power to make a further assessment for 1983–84 on £1,100, *i.e.* the amount by which assessment on the actual basis exceeds assessment on the normal basis. If, in the example, the assessed profits had been £2,100 + £2,400 and the actual profits £3,200 + £2,300, there would be a further assessment of £1,100 for the first year and a £100 reduction of the assessment for the second year.

A cessation may result in a saving of income tax. In this example the trading profits from December 6, 1980 to the date of cessation are £12,000, whereas the assessable profits are £8,900. There are provisions designed to prevent avoidance of tax by artificial cessation.[66]

Farming and market gardening

2–84A   There are special provisions which apply in and from 1977–78 for averaging over a two-year period the fluctuating profits of a person (or partnership) carrying on the trade of farming or market gardening.[67]

---

66. See I.C.T.A. 1970, ss.483–484.
67. See F.A. 1978, s.28.

D. The Application of the Rules on Changes of Ownership

2–85 The new business provisions apply when in any year of assessment a trade, profession or vocation has been "set up and commenced"[68]; the cessation provisions apply when it is "permanently discontinued."[69] It is often a difficult question of fact whether a new business has been set up.[70] Where, for example, a new branch is opened, it may be contended that this is an extension of an existing trade rather than a setting up of a new trade. Where a trader discontinues one of several *distinct* trades carried on by him, the cessation provisions apply to the discontinued trade. If, on the other hand, part of a *single* trade is discontinued (as where a department in a store is closed), the cessation provisions do not apply. It is often a difficult question of fact, especially where the trading activities are diverse but are controlled under a single organisation, to decide whether the discontinuance of one activity constitutes the discontinuance of a separate trade or the discontinuance of a mere department of a trade.

Changes in ownership of trade, etc.

2–86 By section 154(1) of the Income and Corporation Taxes Act 1970, where there is a change in the *persons* engaged in carrying on a trade, profession or vocation,

> the amount of the profits or gains of the trade, profession or vocation, on which tax is chargeable and the persons on whom it is chargeable, must be determined as if the trade, profession or vocation, had been permanently discontinued at the date of the change and a new trade, profession or vocation, had been then set up and commenced.

If, therefore, on October 5, 1983, A sells his business as a going concern to B, A is assessed as if his trade were discontinued on that date (so the cessation provisions apply); and B is assessed as if he had set up a new business (so the commencement provisions apply).

2–87 The commencement provisions apply to the new owner by virtue of section 154 only if, notwithstanding the change of ownership, the trade itself continues.[71] The new owner must *succeed* to the former trade. Whether a "succession" has taken place is a question of fact,[72] but the following propositions may be advanced:

(1) If a person takes over the whole of a trade as a going concern, he

---

68. I.C.T.A. 1970, s.116(1).
69. *Ibid.* s.118(1) and see § 2–15.
70. See *Merchiston Steamship Co. Ltd.* v. *Turner* (1910) 5 T.C. 520; *Kirk and Randall Ltd.* v. *Dunn* (1924) 8 T.C. 663; *H. and G. Kinemas Ltd.* v. *Cook* (1933) 18 T.C. 116.
71. *I.R.C.* v. *Barr* (1954) 35 T.C. 293 (H.L.).
72. *Alexander Ferguson & Co. Ltd.* v. *Aikin* (1898) 4 T.C. 36. For succession generally, see B.T.E. (I.T.), § 6–10. The terms "succeed" and "succession" are not used in s.154, but the terms were used in the earlier legislation and it is assumed that this requirement exists under the present law. *Cf.* § 13–19A (capital allowances).

succeeds to that trade, even if he already has a trade of the same nature and the newly acquired trade is merged with it.[73]

The new owner must produce accounts (i) for the existing trade, on the normal preceding year basis; and (ii) for the new trade, on the "new business" basis, *i.e.* he must treat them as separate trades for tax purposes even though they may be managed as a single trade. This may cause inconvenience and difficulty. Further, if the profits of the acquired trade are high in the first accounting period, these will form the basis of its tax liability for three years.

(2) If a person merely takes over the assets of a trade, with no intention of taking over the business as a going concern, there is no succession.[74]

The new owner's existing trade absorbs the acquired assets and the basis of which profits were assessed remains the same.

If the new owner has acquired only part of a trade carried on by the vendor, it may be a difficult question of fact for the Commissioners to decide if a succession has occurred.

5. POST-CESSATION RECEIPTS

2–88   The term "post-cessation receipts" describes sums which are received after the permanent discontinuance of a trade, profession or vocation for work done, or services rendered, before discontinuance. The position before the Finance Act 1960 was as follows:

(1) If the pre-cessation profits were assessed on an *earnings* basis, post-cessation receipts were not assessable as such because the sums received would normally have already been brought into account while the trading was continuing. In the case of a receipt which had not previously been brought in, the Revenue could reopen the account for the period to which the sum related and raise an additional assessment.[75]

(2) If the pre-cessation profits were assessed otherwise than by reference to earnings, as in the case of a professional man assessed on a *cash* basis, post-cessation receipts escaped tax. They were not taxable under Case II, because the profession had ceased; and attempts by the Revenue to tax them under other Cases of Schedule D failed.[76]

2–89   The Finance Act 1960 brought into charge to tax some post-cessation receipts of a trade, profession or vocation which previously escaped tax, and the Finance Act 1968 closed a number of gaps left by the 1960 Act.

---

73. *Bell* v. *National Provincial Bank* [1904] 1 K.B. 149; 5 T.C. 1 (C.A.); *Briton Ferry Steel Co. Ltd.* v. *Barry* [1940] 1 K.B. 463; 23 T.C. 414; *I.R.C.* v. *Watson & Philip Ltd.* [1984] S.T.C. 184 (C.S.). *Cf. Laycock* v. *Freeman, Hardy & Willis* [1939] 2 K.B. 1; 22 T.C. 288 (C.A.).

74. *Watson* v. *Lothian* (1902) 4 T.C. 441; *Reynolds, Sons & Co. Ltd.* v. *Ogston* (1930) 15 T.C. 501.

75. As in *Severne* v. *Dadswell* (1954) 35 T.C. 649.

76. *Stainer's Executors* v. *Purchase* [1952] A.C. 280; 32 T.C. 367 (H.L.); *Carson* v. *Cheyney's Executors* [1959] A.C. 412; 38 T.C. 240 (H.L.). See also *Hume* v. *Asquith* (1968) 45 T.C. 251: royalties paid to legatee of deceased author; held, not chargeable to tax.

These enactments have now been consolidated in sections 143 to 151 of the Income and Corporation Taxes Act 1970.

Earnings and conventional basis distinguished

2–90   The enactments charging tax on post-cessation receipts distinguish the case where the pre-cessation profits were computed "by reference to earnings" from the case where they were computed "on a conventional basis (that is to say, were computed otherwise than by reference to earnings)."

The profits or gains of a trade, profession or vocation in any period are to be treated as computed by reference to earnings where all credits and liabilities accruing during that period as a consequence of the carrying on of the trade, profession or vocation, are brought into account in computing those profits or gains for tax purposes.[77] This is termed the "earnings basis."

The expression "conventional basis" is used to describe any method of computing profits otherwise than by reference to earnings,[78] such as the "cash basis." If profits are computed on a "bills delivered" basis, work in progress being disregarded, or if a figure is brought in for completed but unbilled work, partly completed work being disregarded, profits are computed on a conventional basis.

Receipts after discontinuance

2–91   The following sums arising from the carrying on of a trade, profession or vocation during any period before the discontinuance are chargeable to tax under Case VI of Schedule D, if not otherwise chargeable to tax:

(1) where the profits or gains for that period were computed by reference to earnings, all such sums in so far as their value was not brought into account in computing the profits or gains for any period before the discontinuance[79];

(2) where those profits or gains were computed on a conventional basis, any sums which, if those profits or gains had been computed by reference to earnings, would *not* have been brought into the computation for any period before the discontinuance because either (i) the date on which they became due, or (ii) the date on which the amount due in respect thereof was ascertained, fell after the discontinuance.[80]

2–92   *Exceptions.*[81] Some post-cessation receipts are expressly excepted from these provisions, namely:

(a) sums received by or on behalf of a person not resident in the United

---

77. I.C.T.A. 1970, s.151(2).
78. *Ibid.* s.151(3).
79. *Ibid.* s.143(1), (2)(*a*).
80. *Ibid.* s.143(1), (2)(*b*).
81. *Ibid.* s.143(3).

Kingdom representing income arising outside the United Kingdom; and

(b) a lump sum paid to the personal representatives of an author as consideration for the assignment by them of the copyright in the author's work[82]; and

(c) sums realised by the transfer of trading stock belonging to a trade on its discontinuance, or by the transfer of the work of a profession or vocation in progress on discontinuance.[83]

Further, the provisions do not apply to the post-cessation receipts of a partnership resident outside and not trading within the United Kingdom, because the profits of such a partnership would not be chargeable to tax under Case I or Case II of Schedule D.

2–93   *Released debts.* We have seen that where a deduction has been allowed for any debt incurred for the purposes of a trade, profession or vocation and the whole or any part of the debt is subsequently released, a sum equal to the amount released is treated as a receipt of the chargeable period in which the release is effected.[84] Where the trade, profession or vocation has been permanently discontinued before the release was effected, the sum referred to is treated as a post-cessation receipt.[85]

2–94   *Bad debts.* Where relief is given under section 130(*i*) of the Income and Corporation Taxes Act 1970 in respect of a bad debt and the debt is subsequently paid, a sum equal to the amount paid is treated as a trading receipt of the chargeable period in which payment is made.[86] Where the trade, profession or vocation has been permanently discontinued before payment is made, the sum paid is treated as a post-cessation receipt.[87]

Other receipts after discontinuance or change of basis

2–95   The provisions in paragraphs (1) and (2) in § 2–91 were introduced by the Finance Act 1960 in order to nullify the decision of the House of Lords in the *Cheyney*[88] case. As regards paragraph (2), it will be observed that sums which would have been brought into the computation on a hypothetical earnings basis escaped tax, such as the post-cessation receipts of a professional man assessed on a cash basis; so also sums which would not have been brought in for some reason other than (i) or (ii). The Finance Act 1968 contained provisions designed to tax post-cessation receipts which escaped tax under the Act of 1960 and generally to prevent avoidance of tax on a change in the basis of computing profits. To illustrate this last-mentioned point: suppose that a professional man was assessed on a cash basis in years 1, 2 and 3. In year 4 his profits were computed by reference to

---

82. See *post*, §§ 5–62 *et seq.*
83. See *ante*, §§ 2–38—2–42.
84. See *ante*, § 2–33.
85. I.C.T.A. 1970, s.143(4).
86. See *ante*, § 2–68.
87. I.C.T.A. 1970, s.143(5).
88. [1959] A.C. 412; 38 T.C. 240 (H.L.).

earnings. Profits earned in years 1, 2 and 3 which were received in year 4 would escape tax in year 4 because they were not earned in that year and the Revenue could not (having accepted accounts on a cash basis for years 1, 2 and 3) reopen the assessments for those years.[89]

2–96   The Act 1968—in provisions now contained in Chapter V of Part VI of the Income and Corporation Taxes Act 1970—provided:

> (1) that all sums received after discontinuance arising from the carrying on of a trade, profession or vocation during any period before the discontinuance, including sums received as consideration for the transfer of work in progress on the discontinuance of a profession or vocation,[90] should if not otherwise chargeable to tax (*e.g.* under the provisions in § 2–91), be chargeable under Case VI of Schedule D on being received.[91]
>
> Thus the post-cessation receipts of a professional man previously assessed on a cash basis (including the proceeds of sale of work in progress) are now taxable under section 144(1), subject to the relief mentioned in § 2–100, *post*;
>
> (2) that sums which dropped out of the computation or otherwise escaped assessment on a change of basis should be charged under Case VI of Schedule D when received after the change and before discontinuance[92]:
>
> See the illustration in § 2–95. The profits received in year 4 which would previously have escaped tax are taxed under section 144(2).
>
> (3) that work in progress which escaped assessment on a change of basis should likewise be charged under Case VI.[93]

Where relevant, the exceptions mentioned in § 2–92 also apply to these charging provisions.

Permanent discontinuance

2–97   For the purposes of the above provisions, any reference to the permanent discontinuance of a trade, profession or vocation includes a reference to the occurring of any event which, under section 154 or 251(1) of the Income and Corporation Taxes Act 1970, is to be treated as equivalent to the permanent discontinuance of a trade, profession or vocation.[94]

Method of charge

2–98   A sum which is chargeable under section 143 or 144 of the Income and Corporation Taxes Act 1970 is assessable under Case VI of Schedule D in the year of assessment in which the sum is received, except that if the sum

---

89. See *ante*, § 2–21.
90. I.C.T.A. 1970, s.144(3).
91. *Ibid*. s.144(1).
92. *Ibid*. s.144(2).
93. *Ibid*. s.144(4).
94. *Ibid*. s.146. See *ante*, § 2–86.

is received not later than six years after the discontinuance or, as the case may be, a change of basis, by the person by whom the trade, profession or vocation was carried on before the discontinuance or change (or by his personal representatives), the recipient may, by notice in writing sent to the Inspector within two years after that year of assessment, elect that the tax chargeable shall be charged as if the sum in question were received on the date on which the discontinuance took place or, as the case may be, on the last day of the period at the end of which the change of basis took place.[95]

2–99   Sums assessable under sections 143 to 144, above, are treated as earned income if the profits of the trade, profession or vocation were so treated[96] and there are provisions for deducting from the assessable sum certain expenses, unrelieved losses and unabsorbed capital allowances which would have been deductible before the discontinuance or change of basis.[97]

Reliefs for individuals[98]

2–100   Some relief is given to individuals from the charge imposed by section 144 of the Income and Corporation Taxes Act 1970. The relief is available only to individuals born before April 6, 1917. Briefly, an individual aged 65 or more on April 6, 1968, is taxed on $\frac{5}{20}$ths of his post-cessation receipts; if he was aged 64, he is taxed on $\frac{6}{20}$ths of his post-cessation receipts—and so on; so that an individual aged 51 on April 6, 1968, would be taxed on $\frac{19}{20}$ths of his post-cessation receipts, while an individual who was aged 50 or less would be taxed on the whole of the receipts without any relief.

---

95. *Ibid.* s.149.
96. *Ibid.* s.148.
97. *Ibid.* s.145.
98. *Ibid.* s.150.

CHAPTER 3

THE TAXATION OF EMOLUMENTS:
SCHEDULE E

1. THE SCOPE OF THE CHARGE

3–01 UNDER the Income Tax Act 1918, tax under Schedule E was charged only "in respect of every public office or employment of profit." Income from other employments was charged under Schedule D. The Finance Act 1922 transferred to Schedule E the emoluments which were previously charged under Schedule D, other than foreign emoluments. These continued to be charged under Case V of Schedule D as income from a foreign possession. The Finance Act 1956 which applied for years from and including 1956–57, brought all emoluments of all employments into charge under Schedule E and removed the distinction which hitherto existed between public offices and employments of profit and other offices and employments. This distinction must nevertheless be kept in mind when reading cases relating to years before 1956–57. The rules of Schedule E are now contained in Part VIII of the Income and Corporation Taxes Act 1970 as amended and extended by later legislation.

3–02 Tax is charged under Schedule E on the emoluments of the offices and employments which fall under one of the three Cases into which the Schedule is divided.[1] Case I applies to the emoluments of a chargeable period[2] in which the person holding the office or employment is resident and ordinarily resident in the United Kingdom, subject to a deduction or exception if he performs the duties of the office or employment wholly outside the United Kingdom or the emoluments are foreign emoluments. Cases II and III apply where some foreign element is involved. Cases in which a foreign element is present are discussed in Chapter 7. It should be assumed that the discussion in the present chapter is directed to Case I of Schedule E. Social security benefits (if not exempt) are specifically brought into charge under Schedule E.[3]

Tax is chargeable under Schedule E only if the following three conditions are satisfied:

(1) *There must be an "office" or "employment"*

3–03 The term "office" is not defined in the Income and Corporation Taxes Act 1970, but has been judicially described as a subsisting, permanent, substantive position which has an existence independent of the person who

---

1. I.C.T.A. 1970, s.181(1), para. 1.
2. "Chargeable period" means an accounting period of a company or a year of assessment: *ibid.* s.526(5).
3. I.C.T.A. 1970, ss.219 and 219A.

fills it, which goes on and is filled in succession by successive holders.[4] A director of a company holds an office[5]; so also do consultants with part-time appointments under the National Health Service[6]; so also do trustees and executors.[7] An auditorship is an office.[8] An engineer appointed under statutory powers to act as inspector at a public local inquiry, who performs functions of a temporary nature (being *functus officio* once his report has been delivered) and is remunerated by fee according to the time spent on performing his functions has been held *not* to hold an office: "there is no office of inquirer or inspector created by the act, but merely a provision authorising the Minister to 'cause to be held' the appropriate enquiry."[9]

The term "employment" signifies something in the nature of a "post." Where a person works for more than one employer it is often a difficult question whether there are a number of separate employments (each chargeable under Schedule E) or whether the employments are mere engagements undertaken in the course of exercising a single profession or vocation (Schedule D). Where the activities of the taxpayer do not consist of obtaining a post and staying in it but consist of a series of engagements and moving from one to the other, as in the case of an actor, he may be treated as carrying on a profession.[10] In *Fall* v. *Hitchin*[11] it was held that the word "employment" in Schedule E is coterminous with the words "contract of service" and that income derived by a ballet dancer from a contract with Sadler's Wells having the attributes of a contract of service was taxable under Schedule E, notwithstanding the fact that the dancer carried on a profession as such and entered into the contract in the normal course of carrying on that profession. This decision narrows the scope of *Davies* v. *Braithwaite*[12] to contracts entered upon in the course of carrying on a profession which are contracts for services. The two cases are, however, difficult to reconcile since the modern cases[13] show that the test for distinguishing a contract of service from a contract for services is whether the propositus carries on business on his own account, and *ex hypothesi* a person who carries on a profession does so. It is interesting to note that the Solicitor-General, arguing the case for the Crown in *Davies* v. *Braithwaite*, contended that the Schedule E rules were not applicable to a person who carries on a profession whether or not the profit arises under a contract for services or a contract of service.[14]

4. Rowlatt J. in *Great Western Railway Co.* v. *Bater* [1920] 3 K.B. 266 at p. 274; approved in *McMillan* v. *Guest* [1942] A.C. 561 at p. 564; 24 T.C. 190 at p. 201.
5. *McMillan* v. *Guest, supra.*
6. *Mitchell and Edon* v. *Ross* [1960] Ch. 498; 40 T.C. 11 (C.A.) (on this point).
7. *Att.-Gen.* v. *Eyres* [1909] 1 K.B. 723.
8. *Ellis* v. *Lucas* (1966) 43 T.C. 276; followed in *I.R.C.* v. *Brander & Cruickshank* (1971) 46 T.C. 574 (H.L.).
9. *Edwards* v. *Clinch* [1981] Ch. 1; 56 T.C. 367; [1981] S.T.C. 617 (H.L.).
10. *Davies* v. *Braithwaite* [1931] 2 K.B. 628; 18 T.C. 198 (an actress). The tax status of "freelance" workers in the film and allied industries has recently been reviewed by the Inland Revenue: see I.R. Press Release in [1983] S.T.I. 150 and [1984] S.T.I. 55.
11. (1972) 49 T.C. 433; [1973] S.T.C. 66.
12. See note 10, *supra.*
13. *Ready Mixed Concrete (South-East) Ltd.* v. *Minister of Pensions and National Insurance* [1968] 2 Q.B. 497; *Market Investigations Ltd.* v. *Minister of Social Security* [1969] 2 Q.B. 173; *Global Plant Ltd.* v. *Secretary of State for Social Services* [1972] 1 Q.B. 139.
14. See [1931] 2 K.B. 628 at pp. 631–632.

An individual may hold an office or employment and carry on a profession at the same time,[15] in which case the rules of Schedule E apply to the office or employment.

> Thus in *I.R.C.* v. *Brander & Cruickshank*[16] a firm of advocates in Scotland, although not holding themselves out as professional registrars, acted as secretaries and registrars for companies and performed the duties imposed on the holders of such offices by the Companies Acts. The registrarships were acquired in the ordinary course of the firm's practice as advocates. It was held that the registrarships were offices and that a payment of £2,500 on the termination of a registrarship was a payment to which the Schedule E rules applied, and being less than £5,000 was accordingly exempt from tax: see § 3–25.

In practice, and as a matter of convenience, receipts from offices held by persons carrying on a profession are often treated as receipts of the profession.[17] Hence accountants bring in their fees from auditorships in computing profits chargeable under Case II of Schedule D. A strict application of the law would require that each auditorship should be treated as a separate office in respect of which a separate claim for expenses should be made in accordance with the Schedule E expenses rules discussed in § 3–35; moreover, in the case of partners, since a partnership is not treated as a separate legal entity in England and there is no provision for joint Schedule E assessments in the partnership name,[18] the Schedule E rules ought strictly to be applied to each partner's share of the Schedule E income. The cases cited in note 16 show that the Schedule E rules are applied to terminal payments[19] notwithstanding the practice of convenience above referred to. In one case[20] a company trading as merchant bankers (Schedule D) entered into agreements with other companies to provide managerial and secretarial services for fees which the Crown conceded were properly chargeable under Schedule E; nevertheless, it was held that compensation received by the banking company on the termination of one of its Schedule E agreements was chargeable under Case I of Schedule D on the ground that the banking company acquired the Schedule E source of income in the course of its trade. The terminal payment was so linked to the trade as to be identified as one of its products; but this conclusion could be reached only in a case in which there was a clear finding that the trader sought the office as part of his profession.[21] In *Brander & Cruickshank*[22] the office was acquired incidentally in the course of carrying on the profession of advocates.

A "salaried partner" does not *qua* partner hold an office or employment and his "salary" is accordingly not assessable under Schedule E: see § 11–05.

---

15. See, *e.g.* the case in note 6, *supra*, summarised *ante*, § 1–13.
16. (1971) 46 T.C. 574 (H.L.) (H.L.Sc.). See also *Ellis* v. *Lucas, supra. Cf. Walker* v. *Carnaby Harrower, Barnham & Pykett* (1969) 46 T.C. 561 in § 2–50A.
17. See I.R. Press Release of March 20, 1980, in [1980] S.T.I. 128.
18. See *post*, §§ 11–03 *et seq.* A partnership is treated as a separate legal entity in Scotland.
19. Discussed *post*, §§ 3–24 *et seq.*
20. *Blackburn* v. *Close Brothers Ltd.* (1960) 39 T.C. 164.
21. See Lord Donovan in *I.R.C.* v. *Brander & Cruickshank* (1971) 46 T.C. 574 at p. 595.
22. See note 16, *supra*.

3-03A   *Workers supplied by agencies.* There are statutory provisions which
apply Schedule E to payments made to workers supplied to clients by
agencies. Thus if a secretary (S) is supplied to a client by an agency and S is
subject to, or to the right of, supervision, direction or control as to the
manner in which she renders her services, remuneration received by S
under her contract with the agency is chargeable to income tax under
Schedule E (if not so chargeable apart from the statute) provided the services are rendered under the terms of a contract between S and the
agency.[23] The services rendered by S are treated as if they were the duties
of an office or employment held by S and the payments she receives are
treated as emoluments therefrom. The section does not apply where S renders services under the terms of a contract between S and the client, and in
this respect the distinction between an "employment agency" and an
"employment business" may be important.[24]

Section 38 deals with the case when the worker (S) goes on the books of
an employment agency. It does not cover the case when S forms her own
company (S Limited) which employs her, and when S Limited supplies S's
services to a client, in consideration of payments to S Limited.[25]

(2) *There must be "emoluments"*

3-04   Emoluments are defined as including salaries, fees, wages, perquisites
and profits whatsoever.[26] The inclusion of "perquisites and profits" shows
that the word "emoluments" is not limited to remuneration in the sense of
a reward for specific services. Examples of emoluments are given in
§§ 3-09 *et seq.*

> Thus in *Laidler* v. *Perry*[27] it was the practice in a group of companies to give
> every christmas to staff employees and staff pensioners a gift voucher with
> which goods up to £10 in value could be bought. The vouchers were given to all
> employees without regard to their rate of pay or the way in which they per-

---

23. F.(No. 2)A. 1975, s.38. Certain entertainers and models are excepted: see *ibid.* s.38(5).
See *Brady* v. *Hart* [1985] S.T.C. 498.
24. See Employment Agencies Act 1973, s.13(2)(3).
25. Clause 34 of the Finance Bill 1981 introduced provisions to deal with this situation, but
the clause was withdrawn for further consideration: see [1981] S.T.I. 185, explaining the background to this legislation, and the consultative paper in [1981] S.T.I. 578. The Chancellor
announced on April 7, 1982, that no legislation is proposed for the time being: see [1982]
S.T.I. 164 and 166.
26. I.C.T.A. 1970, s.183(1). Statute may provide that something shall be chargeable as an
emolument, *e.g.* sick pay (F.A. 1981, s.30).
27. (1965) 42 T.C. 351 (H.L.). In *Holland* v. *Geoghegan* (1972) 48 T.C. 482, refuse collectors' compensation for loss of salvage was held to be an emolument of the employment:
" . . . the main purpose of the Borough was to get the respondent back to work, and the
money when received by him was a form of substituted remuneration for his former rights to
share in the proceeds of sale of the salvage" (p. 492H). And see *Tyrer* v. *Smart* (1978) 52 T.C.
533; [1967] S.T.C. 141 (C.A.), where employees of a group of companies with at least five
years' service were given a right to subscribe for shares on preferential terms on the occasion
of the group going public. *Held,* in the High Court and Court of Appeal, not an assessable
emolument: the employees who subscribed for shares did so as private investors. This
decision was reversed in the House of Lords: [1979] S.T.C. 34 (H.L.). See also *Beecham
Group Ltd.* v. *Fair* [1984] S.T.C. 15 where garage allowance to salesman who stored the
employer's stock and the company car was *held* to be an emolument.

formed their duties. The purpose of the gift vouchers was to promote goodwill. *Held* that the gift vouchers were assessable as emoluments.

(3) *The emoluments must derive* from *the office or employment*

3–05 The office or employment must be the *source* of the payment.[28]

In *Hochstrasser* v. *Mayes*[29] I.C.I. established a housing scheme to assist those of their married male employees whose jobs demanded mobility. If the employee sold his house at a loss, I.C.I. (subject to certain options reserved to I.C.I.) guaranteed him against the loss. *Held*, that a sum paid to an employee in respect of such a loss was not an emolument from the employment.

This case shows that, to render a benefit chargeable to tax, the office or employment must be the *causa causans* of the benefit; it is not sufficient that it is the *causa sine qua non*.[29a] In another case an employee was required, as a condition of entering upon his employment to enter into a restrictive covenant with his employer which was to take effect on leaving his employer's service; and it was held that a lump sum paid in consideration for such a restrictive covenant was not an emolument from the employment.[30] "It is quite true that, if he had not entered into the agreement to serve as a director and manager, he would not have received £7,000. But that is not the same thing as saying that the £7,000 is profit from his office of director so as to attract tax under Schedule E."[31] Another illustration of the principle under discussion is given by Lord Denning M.R. in his judgment in *Jarrold* v. *Boustead*[32]:

"Suppose there was a man who was an expert organist but was very fond of playing golf on Sundays. He is asked to become the organist of the parish church for the ensuing seven months at a salary of £10 a month for the seven months, but it is expressly stipulated by this strange parish council that, if he takes up the post, he is to give up Sunday golf for the rest of his life. Thereupon he says that, if he is to give up golf, he wants an extra £500 and they agree to pay it. In such a case the £500 is not a payment for his services as an organist for seven months. It is a payment for relinquishing what he considered to be an advantage to him."

---

28. In *Pritchard* v. *Arundale* (1972) 47 T.C. 680, a transfer of shares to a former partner in a firm of accountants, in consideration of his undertaking to serve a company, was held not to be an assessable emolument. It was an inducement to him to give up an established position and status and not a reward for future services. *Cf. Glantre Engineering Ltd.* v. *Goodhand* (1982) 56 T.C. 165.
29. [1960] A.C. 376; 38 T.C. 673 (H.L.). *Cf. Hamblett* v. *Godfrey* [1986] S.T.C. 213 where £1,000 paid to a civil servant emloyed at GCHQ for accepting the withdrawal of her right to belong to a trade union and certain other rights under employment protection legislation was held to be an emolument.
29a. But see the remarks of Lord Simon of Glaisdale on outmoded and ambiguous concepts of causation expressed in latin, in *Brumby* v. *Milner* (1976) 51 T.C. 583 at p. 613 D (H.L.)
30. *Beak* v. *Robson* [1943] A.C. 352; 25 T.C. 33 (H.L.). The position is the same where the covenant is to take effect during the currency of the agreement: *Hose* v. *Warwick* (1946) 27 T.C. 459. Payments for restrictive covenants are chargeable to higher rate income tax under I.C.T.A. 1970, s.34: *post*, § 3–24, para. (4).
31. *Beak* v. *Robson, supra, per* Viscount Simon L.C. at pp. 355 and 41, respectively.
32. (1964) 41 T.C. 701 at p. 729. In this case, signing-on fees paid to Rugby League players on relinquishing amateur status were held not to be taxable. As to liability to higher-rate tax, see *post*, § 3–24(4).

An employee may receive a present in such circumstances that the employment is not its source.[33]

When a director wrongly directs moneys from a company into his own pocket and, by virtue of his fiduciary obligation to the company to preserve its assets, holds those moneys as trustee for the company, such moneys are not received as an emolument of the office.[34]

Basis of charge

3–06   Tax under Schedule E is charged on the full amount of the emoluments falling under the appropriate Case, subject to such deductions only as are authorised by the Tax Acts.[35] The permissible deductions are considered later.[36]

It seems that emoluments are not chargeable to tax unless they are received by or credited to or otherwise placed at the disposal of the employee. If an employee assigns his right to emoluments to a third person, they will be treated as having been received by the employee.[37] If the emoluments, when received, relate to services rendered in the past, they must be treated as income of the years in which the services were rendered.[38]

> Thus in *Heasman* v. *Jordan*,[38a] a special bonus paid to an employee in 1945 for overtime during the war years (it being understood that the overtime would not be "overlooked") was held to be taxable as an emolument of the years when the services were rendered.

Where emoluments otherwise chargeable under Schedule E are formally waived or repaid before any assessment has become final and conclusive, it seems to be the Revenue's practice not to claim Schedule E tax, provided the employer's profits or losses are adjusted so as to make no deduction in respect of such emoluments.[39]

3–07   Payments made to an employee after his employment has ceased are not chargeable under Schedule E[40] unless they are remuneration for past services or are expressly charged to tax, *e.g.* pensions[41] and "golden handshakes."[42] Tax under Schedule E is charged on the emoluments of the

---

33. See *post*, §§ 3–09 *et seq.*
34. *Rose* v. *Humbles* (1971) 48 T.C. 103, *per* Buckley J. at p. 117H.
35. I.C.T.A. 1970, s.183(1).
36. See *post*. §§ 3–35 *et seq.*
37. *Smyth* v. *Stretton* (1904) 5 T.C. 36; *cf. Edwards* v. *Roberts* (1935) 19 T.C. 618 (C.A.); *Hibbert* v. *Fysh* (1962) 40 T.C. 305 (earnings of undischarged bankrupt).
38. *Heasman* v. *Jordan* [1954] Ch. 744; 35 T.C. 518. As to the time limit for assessments in such cases, see T.M.A. 1970, s.35. See also *Bray* v. *Best* [1986] S.T.C. 96, in § 3–13A. *Quaere* if remuneration paid some years in advance can be "spread forward."
38a. [1954] Ch. 744; 35 T.C. 518. And see *Board of Inland Revenue* v. *Suite* [1986] S.T.C. 292 (J.C.)
39. See *post* § 15–24. As to inheritance tax, see *post*, § 18–04A.
40. See, *e.g. Cowan* v. *Seymour* [1920] 1 K.B. 500; 7 T.C. 372; *post*, § 3–09.
41. I.C.T.A. 1970, ss.181–182.
42. *Ibid.* s.187: *post* §§ 3–24 *et seq.*

current year of assessment, *e.g.* the statutory income for the year 1986–87 includes the total of the emoluments of that year. Income tax is collected under the Pay As You Earn (PAYE) system (see § 3–53). Where the tax collected under PAYE is the same in amount as would be payable under a Schedule E assessment, the need for such an assessment is dispensed with unless required by the taxpayer.[43]

Annual payments

3–08   The remuneration of executors and trustees by annual payments is discussed later.[44]

2. TAXABLE EMOLUMENTS

Gifts and other voluntary payments

3–09   Gifts are not, as such, chargeable to income tax for they are not "income."[45] If however, a gift is made to an employee by virtue of his employment, its taxable quality differs and it is chargeable under Schedule E.[46] A gift which is attributable to the personal qualities of the employee or to his relationship to the donor is not made by virtue of the employment[47]; it is a "mere present."[48]

> In *Cowan* v. *Seymour,*[49] the appellant acted without remuneration as the secretary of a company from the date of its incorporation until he was appointed its liquidator. On completion of the liquidation there remained a sum in hand which under the Memorandum of Association was divisible among the ordinary shareholders; but they, by unanimous resolution, voted this sum to the chairman and the appellant in equal shares. *Held*, that the sum was not assessable under Schedule E.

Sterndale M.R. was influenced by two considerations: (i) that the payment was made by the shareholders and not by the employer; and (ii) that the employment had already terminated before the payment was voted.[50] It is more difficult in practice to prove that payments made by the employer are not assessable emoluments than those made by a third person. Other con-

---

43. *Ibid*. 1970, s.205.
44. See *post*, § 5–22.
45. *R.* v. *Supplementary Benefits Commission, ex p. Singer* [1973] 1 W.L.R. 713 (D.C.). Gifts are not assessable under Case VI of Schedule D: *post*, § 4–01. Gifts are disposals for purposes of the taxation of capital gains (*post*, § 15–18) and may attract capital transfer tax or inheritance tax.
46. Collins M.R. in *Herbert* v. *McQuade* [1902] 2 K.B. 631 at p. 649; 4 T.C. 489 at p. 500 (C.A.).
47. See, *e.g. Bridges* v. *Hewitt* (1957) 37 T.C. 289 (C.A.).
48. *Blakiston* v. *Cooper* [1909] A.C. 104 at p. 107; 5 T.C. 347 at p. 355. For a case in which all the authorities are reviewed, see *I.R.C.* v. *Morris* (1967) 44 T.C. 685 (Ct. of Sess.): employee of Atomic Energy Authority seconded to Scottish Electricity Board received £1,000 from Board as a mark of appreciation after his employment with the Board had terminated; *held*, not an assessable emolument. And see *Ball* v. *Johnson* (1971) 47 T.C. 155: award to bank clerk for passing examinations; *held*, not to be remuneration for services, upholding the decision of General Commissioners; *Moore* v. *Griffiths* (1972) 48 T.C. 338: bonus prizes paid to World Cup footballer; *held* to be a testimonial and not a reward for services.
49. [1920] 1 K.B. 500; 7 T.C. 372 (C.A.).
50. But Sterndale M.R. was not prepared to hold that all voluntary payments made after an employment has terminated are not assessable. It is thought that the payment in *Cowan* v. *Seymour* would now be assessable under I.C.T.A. 1970, s.187: *post*, § 3–25.

siderations which affect the taxable quality of a gift or similar payment are illustrated by the following cases:

3–10   (a) *Tips.* In *Calvert* v. *Wainwright*,[51] the tips of a taxi-driver were held to be taxable emoluments; but Atkinson J. remarked that an especially large tip given on a special occasion (such as Christmas) by a regular customer might escape tax as a mere present.

3–11   (b) *Easter offerings.* In *Blakiston* v. *Cooper*[52] the Easter "freewill offerings" of an incumbent, most of which were raised by collections on Easter Sunday, were held to be taxable.

> "It was suggested," said Lord Ashbourne, "that the offerings were made as personal gifts to the vicar as marks of esteem and respect. Such reasons no doubt played their part in obtaining and increasing the amount of the offerings, but I cannot doubt that *they were given to the vicar as vicar*, and that they formed part of the profits accruing by reason of his office."

3–12   (c) *Benefit matches.* In *Moorhouse* v. *Dooland*[53] moneys collected for a professional cricketer for meritorious performances at matches were held to be assessable, where the cricketer had a contractual right to talent money. In *Seymour* v. *Reed*,[54] on the other hand, where a benefit match was held for a professional cricketer on the occasion of his retirement following a lifetime's service to cricket, the gate money was held not to be taxable.

> "Its purpose," said Lord Cave, "is not to encourage the cricketer to further exertions, but to express the gratitude of his employers and of the cricket-loving public for what he has already done, and their appreciation of his personal qualities."

3–13   (d) *Bonuses.* The ordinary bonus paid by an employer at his discretion in addition to salary is taxable[55]; so also are long service payments.[56] Moreover, the employee's tax liability is not avoided by the employer's declaration that he did not intend the payment to be remuneration or that he intended it to be a gift.[57]

---

51. [1947] K.B. 526; 27 T.C. 475. See also *Wright* v. *Boyce* (1958) 38 T.C. 160 (C.A.), where Christmas presents of cash received by a huntsman from followers of the hunt were held to be assessable even though (i) the gifts were spontaneous and there was no organised collection and (ii) his contract of service conferred no right to the gifts (*cf.* the "benefit" matches). The payments were made pursuant to a custom and the expectation of receiving Christmas presents went with the office.
52. See note 48, *supra.*
53. [1955] Ch. 284; 36 T.C. 1 (C.A.). See especially the judgment of Jenkins L.J.
54. [1927] A.C. 554; 11 T.C. 625.
55. *Denny* v. *Reed* (1933) 18 T.C. 254.
56. But see Concession A22 ("long service awards"). Tax is not charged on awards to directors and employees to mark long service if the period of service is not less than 20 years and no similar award has been made to the recipient within the previous 10 years. The concession now applies to tangible articles and shares in the employing company (or another group company) provided the cost or value does not exceed £20 per year of service.
57. *Weston* v. *Hearn* (1943) 25 T.C. 425; *Radcliffe* v. *Holt* (1927) 11 T.C. 621. See also *Davis* v. *Harrison* (1927) 11 T.C. 707; *Corbett* v. *Duff* (1941) 23 T.C. 763.

3–13A   (d) *Distributions on winding up of trust.* In *Bray* v. *Best*[57a] a trust had been established for the benefit of employees of Company X. Company X was taken over by Fisons and, after the employers of Company X had become employees of Fisons, the trustees distributed the trust funds on a fair and equitable basis. The distributions were held to be emoluments. Distributions to *all* employees are inherently unlikely to be anything but emoluments.

Money's worth: benefits in kind and fringe benefits

3–14   The term emoluments includes not only money payments but also "substantial things of money value . . . capable of being turned into money."[58] This brings within the charge under Schedule E a variety of "fringe benefits" or "benefits in kind." It should be observed that the words of Lord Halsbury distinguish two types of benefit;

(1) benefits not convertible into money, such as free travel, free board and lodging,[59] free meals, free uniform or free education, and

(2) benefits convertible into money.

Benefits of the first type are not assessable (subject to the exception hereinafter mentioned and the special legislation affecting directors and certain employees[60]) even if their value was taken into account in determining the employee's remuneration; whereas convertible benefits are assessable, although it is not the practice of the Revenue to tax all such benefits.[61] A cash payment in lieu of any of the benefits referred to in (1) would be assessable.[62] Meal or luncheon vouchers are by concession exempt from tax if they are (a) non-transferable and used for meals only; (b) available to lower paid staff if their issue is restricted; (c) limited to a value of 15p for each working day.[63] The tax treatment of other vouchers is considered later.[64]

3–15   *Examples*
    (i) In *Machon* v. *McLoughlin*[65] a male attendant at an asylum was paid a salary out of which he was bound to pay 10s. a week for board, lodging, etc. *Held,* that he was taxable on his gross salary. "If a person is paid a wage with some

---

57a. [1986] S.T.C. 96.

58. *Per* Lord Halsbury in *Tennant* v. *Smith* [1892] A.C. 150 at p. 156; 3 T.C. 158 at p. 164. Lord Watson used the words "that which can be turned to pecuniary account."

59. *Daly* v. *I.R.C.* (1934) 18 T.C. 641 (free maintenance of a priest in a communal presbytery house).

60. See *post,* §§ 3–40 *et seq.*

61. Thus in *Wright* v. *Boyce* (1958) 38 T.C. 160 (C.A.), only gifts in cash appear to have been assessed.

62. *Corry* v. *Robinson* (1933) 18 T.C. 411 (C.A.): colonial allowance of civil servant; *Sanderson* v. *Durbridge* (1955) 36 T.C. 239: allowance for meals on overtime; *Evans* v. *Richardson* (1957) 37 T.C. 178: army lodging allowance.

63. Concession A3. "The luncheon voucher concession is not and never has been linked to the cost of a ham sandwich": *per* Lord Cockfield in [1982] S.T.I. 46.

64. See *post,* § 3–17A.

65. (1926) 11 T.C. 83 (C.A.).

advantage thrown in, you cannot add the advantage to the wage for the purpose of taxation unless that advantage can be turned into money. That is one proposition. But when you have a person paid a wage with the necessity—the contractual necessity if you like—to expend that wage in a particular way, then he must pay tax upon the gross wage and no question of alienability or inalienability arises."

(ii) In *Weight* v. *Salmon*[66] the directors by resolution each year gave S. the privilege of subscribing for unissued shares of the company at par value, which was below the market value at which they were readily realisable. *Held*, that the difference between the two values was assessable to tax.

(iii) In *Heaton* v. *Bell* [67] B. was employed by a company which introduced a voluntary car loan scheme for employees who earned less that £2,000 per annum and were not directors. The company purchased the car and paid tax and insurance. B. applied to join the scheme and an agreed amount was deducted from his weekly wage. An employee joining the scheme could withdraw on 14 days' notice, when the weekly deduction would cease. B was assessed under Schedule E on the weekly wage without any deduction in respect of the amount paid under the scheme. *Held*, (i) (Lord Reid dissenting) that the true effect of the contractual arrangements was that the emoluments of an employee who joined the scheme remained unaltered, so the assessment was correctly made. *Cf.* Lord Reid, who held that the employee had agreed to accept a reduced wage plus the free use of a car; (ii) (Lord Hodson and Lord Upjohn dissenting) that even if Lord Reid's view of the effect of the agreement was right, the assessment was correctly made because B. could convert his free use of the car into money by withdrawing from the scheme and no longer suffering any reduction of salary.

(iv) In *Clayton* v. *Gothorp*[68] the discharge of an obligation to repay a loan was held to give rise to an assessable emolument.

(v) In *Jenkins* v. *Horn*[69] the employee was paid in gold sovereigns. If the salary due to him was £60 the employer purchased from X £60's worth of sovereigns (which had a nominal value of between £1 and £4). The employee resold the sovereigns to X receiving a little less than £60. *Held*, that he was assessable under Schedule E on the market value, not the nominal value, of the sovereigns.

For a written answer to a parliamentary question itemising tax-free benefits in kind, see [1979] S.T.I. 220 and 489.

Medical insurance

3–15A   Section 68 of the Finance Act 1976 treated as emoluments of an employment, and accordingly as chargeable to tax under Schedule E, an amount equal to the expense incurred by the employer or others, and not made good by the employee, in connection with the provision for the employee, and for others being members of his family or household[70] of insurance against the cost of medical treatment (defined so as to include, *inter alia*,

---

66. (1935) 19 T.C. 174 (H.L.). And see F.A. 1976, s.67 in § 3–51.
67. [1970] A.C. 728; 46 T.C. 211 (H.L.).
68. (1971) 47 T.C. 168; and see F.A. 1976, s.66(3) in § 3–50.
69. (1979) 52 T.C. 591; [1979] S.T.C. 446.
70. References to members of a person's family or household are to his spouse, his sons and daughters and their spouses, his parents and his servants, dependants and guests: F.A. 1976, s.72(4).

procedures for diagnosing any physical or mental ailment, infirmity or defect). The section applied only where the provision was made by reason of the employment,[71] and only where the provision was not otherwise chargeable as income.

Section 68 ceased to apply in and from the year 1982–83.[72] The effect is that only persons who are employed in director's or higher-paid employment (see § 3–41) are taxed on the benefit of medical insurance, only under section 61 of the Finance Act 1976 (see §§ 3–43 *et seq.*). There is an exception for the cost of treatment outside the United Kingdom (and for insurance against such cost) where the need for treatment arises from duties performed abroad.

Discharging obligations of employee

3–16   If an employer discharges out of his own resources some obligation which his employee has incurred to a third person, otherwise than in performing the duties of the employment, the sum paid by the employer is a taxable emolument: it is "money's worth."[73] Thus if an employer pays his employee's income tax or pays a salary expressed to be free of tax, the tax must be added to the salary for the purpose of determining the gross emoluments of the employee.[74]

> In *Barclays Bank Ltd.* v. *Naylor*,[75] a liability incurred by the employee in respect of his child's school fees was settled not by the employer, but (at the request of the employee) by trustees out of a fund established by the employer for the purpose, the income whereof was payable to the employee's child. *Held*, that this was not income of the employee: "the way in which the employer contributed to the education expenses . . . was not by paying the school bills . . . out of own money, but by providing the child with an income out of which the bills . . . could be met" (p. 268).

3–17   Where an employer discharges an obligation incurred by his employee to a third person, the measure of the taxable emolument is the cost to the employer of discharging the obligation. Where, however, the employer purchases something which he then gives to his employee, the measure of the taxable emolument is the value of the benefit to the employee.

> Thus in *Wilkins* v. *Rogerson*,[76] a company decided to give certain employees a suit, overcoat or raincoat as a Christmas present. The tailor was instructed to give each employee a fitting and send the account to the company. There was

---

71. See definitions in F.A. 1976, s.72. See also § 3–43.
72. F.A. 1981, s.72.
73. *Nicoll* v. *Austin* (1935) 19 T.C. 531 (company paid sums for rates, light, heat, telephone and upkeep of gardens of directors' residence; *held*, that the amount so paid was an assessable emolument).
74. *Hartland* v. *Diggines* [1926] A.C. 289; 10 T.C. 247 (H.L.). and see *Richardson* v. *Worrall* [1985] S.T.C. 693.
75. [1961] Ch. 7; 39 T.C. 256.
76. *Wilkins* v. *Rogerson* [1961] Ch. 133; 39 T.C. 344 (C.A.). Contrast § 3–46. *Cf. Richardson* v. *Worrall* [1985] S.T.C. 693 where the *Wilkins* case was held not to apply where an employee was supplied with free petrol under a credit card arrangement.

no contractual relationship between the tailor and the employee. *Held*, that this was a "perquisite or profit" of the employment and that the measure of the emolument was the value of the suit to the employee, *i.e.* its second-hand value. [If the employer had paid for a suit previously ordered by the employee, the measure of the emolument would have been the cost of the suit.]

Vouchers and credit-tokens

3–17A   If an employer provides a voucher,[77] stamp or similar document, capable of being exchanged for money, goods or services, the employee is treated as receiving emoluments equal to the expense incurred by the employer in providing the voucher.[78] The charge is levied in the year of assessment in which the employer incurs the expense or, if different and later, the year in which the employee receives the voucher. A voucher is for this purpose treated as received by an employee if it is appropriated to him, whether by attaching it to a card held for him or in any other way. Where, if the employee had actually purchased the goods, etc. his expenditure would have qualified for relief under section 189 of the Taxes Act 1970 (see § 3–35), there is no charge under section 36.

There is a different rule for a voucher which is a *cash voucher* meaning (briefly) a voucher which can be exchanged for a sum of money not substantially less than the cost of providing it.[79] In this case the charge to tax arises at the moment when the employee receives the voucher or it is appropriated to him, *i.e.* it is treated as "pay" of an amount equal to the amount for which it can be exchanged and tax must be deducted under the PAYE system.[79] Where no vouchers are involved but there is a supply of goods or services, as in *Wilkins* v. *Rogerson*, the principle in that case applies. Likewise it seems that if property is directly given to an employee for his actual use (without the interposition of a voucher) and that property is subject to some restriction affecting its transferability, the restriction may be taken into account in determining the value of the benefit.[80] Thus if an employer provides his employee with a non-transferable season ticket, the employee would not be taxed (without an express statutory provision) on the cost of the ticket.[81] There is, however, such an express statutory provision which applies in and from 1982–83 since section 70 of the Finance Act 1981 amends section 36 (above) to include a "transport voucher," defined as any ticket, pass or other document or token intended to enable a person to obtain passenger transport services.[82]

3–17B   Section 36A of the Finance (No. 2) Act 1975 (which was introduced in the Finance Act 1981) contains similar provisions which apply to the provision of credit-tokens in connection with an employment and treat the

---

77. Voucher includes a cheque voucher, *i.e.* a cheque provided for an employee to enable him to pay for goods or services. For transport vouchers, see below.
78. See F.(No. 2)A. 1975, s.36. For guidance as to what expenses should be included and what excluded, see SP 6/85 in [1986] S.T.1. 484.
79. *Ibid.* s.37.
80. See *Ede* v. *Wilson* (1945) 26 T.C. 381.
81. For earlier parliamentary questions on season tickets, see [1978] S.T.I. 255 at pp. 508 and 556.
82. Transport vouchers issued to lower-paid employees of British Rail and other passenger transport undertakings are excluded: F.(No. 2)A. 1975, s.36(3A) inserted by F.A. 1982, s.44.

employee as receiving an emolument equal to the expense incurred by the employer. Credit-token is elaborately defined to include any document, etc., given to a person which, when produced, will enable that person to get money, goods or services on credit, whether from the provider of the token or from some third party at the provider's expense.[82a]

Share options: non-approved schemes

3–18   In *Abbott* v. *Philbin*[83] the facts were that an employee accepted an offer from his employing company in year one to acquire for £20 a 10-year non-assignable option to purchase up to 2,000 shares at 68s. 6d., their then market price. In year two he exercised the option as regards 250 shares, then worth 82s. each. It was held that the benefit, namely the value of the option less the cost of acquiring it, arose in year one. The effect of this decision was that liability under Schedule E arose on the *grant* of an option on the then value of the right conferred on the director or employee; no Schedule E liability arose on the *exercise* of the option. In practice, the tax liability on the grant of the option was often small because of the difficulty of putting more than a nominal value on the option rights at that time. The director or employee might, of course, be liable to capital gains tax on the transfer of the shares or the assignment of the option rights.

3–19   The tax position was altered by section 25 of the Finance Act 1966 which, on the 1970 consolidation, was re-enacted in section 186 of the Taxes Act 1970. Section 186 provides that where, on or after May 3, 1966, a person realises a gain by the exercise, or by the assignment or release, of a right to acquire shares in a body corporate obtained by that person as a director or employee of that or any other body corporate, he is chargeable to income tax under Schedule E on an amount equal to the amount of his gain as computed in accordance with the section.[84] In such a case no tax is charged on the *grant* of the option.[85] Where an option is exercised in respect of shares, the gain is the difference between (i) the amount a person might reasonably expect to obtain from a sale in the open market of such shares at the time the option is exercised and (ii) the amount or value of the consideration given whether for the shares or for the grant of the option right, the value of any services to be performed by the director or employee being disregarded in computing the consideration. The gain is deductible for the purposes of capital gains tax if the shares are later sold.[86]

> *Example*
> X is granted an option to purchase 100 shares at £1 each, the cost of the option being £10. X later exercises the option when the shares are worth £250. X is assessed under section 186 on £250 less £110 = £140. X later sells the shares for £300. The chargeable gain is £300 less (£110 + £140) = £50.

82a. F.(No. 2)A. 1975, s.36A(4) inserted by F.A. 1982, s.45.
83. [1961] A.C. 352; 39 T.C. 82 (H.L.).
84. I.C.T.A. 1970, s.186(1).
85. *Ibid.* s.186(2). But see the exception in § 3–19A.
86. *Ibid.* s.186(12).

Similarly, where the option rights are assigned or released, the gain is the difference between (i) the amount or value of the consideration for the assignment or release and (ii) the amount or value of the consideration given for the grant of the option right. By way of exception to these general rules, where the option right is granted before May 3, 1966, the gain is not to exceed the difference between the market value of the shares at the time of the realisation of the gain and their market value on May 3, 1966.[87]

Tax chargeable under section 186 can in some cases be paid by instalments over three years, if the person chargeable so elects and the tax payable exceeds £250.[88] Where the option is granted before April 6, 1984 and exercised after April 5, 1983, the period is extended from three to five years. The instalment facility is withdrawn for options granted after April 6, 1984.[89]

3–19A   If an option obtained on or after April 11, 1972, is capable of being exercised later than seven years thereafter and the amount payable to exercise it is less than the market value of the equivalent shares when the option is obtained, a Schedule E assessment can be raised on the *grant* of the option on the difference between these two amounts.[90] When a Schedule E charge is so raised, the tax payable will be deducted from tax charged under section 186 on the exercise or assignment of the right.[90]

3–20   Section 186 of the Taxes Act 1970 applies only if the right is obtained by a person as a director or employee of a body corporate; and a right to acquire shares is treated as obtained by a person as a director or employee of a body corporate—

(a) if it is granted to him by reason of his office or employment as a director or employee of the body corporate who is chargeable to tax in respect of that office or employment under Case I of Schedule E, or

(b) if the right is assigned to him and was granted by reason of any such office or employment of his to some other person,

and paragraph (a) applies to a right granted by reason of a person's office or employment after he has ceased to hold it if it would apply to a right so granted in the last year of assessment in which he did hold it.[91–92]

Approved share option schemes

3–20A   Section 38 of the Finance Act 1984 applies where a director or employee of a body corporate obtains a right to acquire shares in accordance with the provisions of a scheme which is approved by the Board under Schedule 10

---

87. *Ibid.* s.186(8). Subject to this subsection, s.186 applies to an option right whenever granted.
88. F.A. 1982, s.40, applying from 1982–83.
89. F.A. 1984, s.39.
90. F.A. 1972, s.77. See *Abbott* v. *Philbin* in § 3–18.
91–92. I.C.T.A. 1970, s.186(9).

to that Act. It applies to options granted after April 5, 1984. Where an option is granted under such an approved scheme:

(a) no tax charge arises on the grant of the option;
(b) no tax charge arises on its exercise under section 186 of the Income and Corporation Taxes Act 1970 as is the case with non-approved schemes (see § 3–19); and
(c) no tax charge arises under section 79(4) of the Finance Act 1972 on any appreciation in the value of the shares between the grant of the option and its subsequent exercise (see § 3–20C).

No tax charge arises, therefore, until the option having been exercised the shares are subsequently disposed of; in which case the normal capital gains tax rules apply. Hence the employee can take advantage of the annual exemption and the 30 per cent. tax rate—a great benefit to higher rate taxpayers. The market value rule in section 29(A) of the Capital Gains Tax Act 1979 does not apply: see § 16–18.

To qualify for approval, a number of conditions must be satisfied. Briefly, the participants must be full-time directors or full-time employees of the company granting the option or of, for example, a subsidiary company if the scheme is a group scheme. Where the company is a close company, no one is eligible to participate who has a more than 5 per cent. interest in that company or in a company which controls it. There is a limit on the number of option shares which may be held at any one time by any one person which is, roughly, the greater of £100,000 or four times the emoluments of the participant in the year of assessment or (if greater) the preceding year. There is a time limit of three years before an employee may exercise his option. Once an option is exercised the employee must wait a further three years before he can exercise a further part of his option.

Share incentive schemes

3–20B   The legislation summarised in §§ 3–19 *et seq.* applied to share option schemes, *i.e.* when the director or employee was granted and subsequently exercised an *option* to acquire shares. It did not apply if a director or employee subscribed for shares to which certain restrictions were attached for a prescribed period (*e.g.* restrictions as to voting and the right to receive dividends so long as a loan to the subscriber remained outstanding) and those shares became more valuable on the lifting of the restrictions; except that a Schedule E liability would arise if the amount subscribed was less than the value of the shares at the time of subscription.[93] Section 79 of the Finance Act 1972 accordingly extended the charge under Schedule E to such share incentive schemes. The section applies where a person, on or after April 6, 1972, acquires shares or an interest in shares in a body corporate in pursuance of a right conferred on him or opportunity offered to him as a director or employee of that or any other body corporate and not

---

93. See *Weight* v. *Salmon* (1935) 19 T.C. 174 (H.L.) in § 3–15.

in pursuance of an offer to the public.[94] Section 186(9) of the Taxes Act 1970, summarised in § 3–20, applies for the purpose of determining whether a person acquires a right or opportunity "as a director or employee."[95] Section 79 may apply to shares acquired by a person who is to become a director or employee.[96] There are two separate charges to tax under section 79:

(1) *The tax on appreciation in value*

3–20C   Where the market value of the shares at the end of a prescribed period exceeds their market value at the time of the acquisition, the acquirer is chargeable to tax under Schedule E for the year of assessment in which the prescribed period ends on an amount equal to the excess, the amount chargeable being treated as earned income.[97] Hence the director or employee is taxed on any unrealised appreciation in the value of his shares or interest in shares. If the acquirer has an interest less than full beneficial ownership, *e.g.* if he is entitled only to a share in a trust fund made up of the company's shares, he is taxed only on such part of the appreciation in value as corresponds to his interest.[97] There are provisions for a reduction in the amount chargeable where, in accordance with the terms on which the acquisition of the shares was made, the consideration for the acquisition is subsequently increased (*e.g.* on the acquirer leaving the company's service prematurely) or the shares are disposed of for a consideration which is less than their market value at the time of the disposal.[98] In such cases the increase in market value over the prescribed period would not provide a proper measure of the benefit received.

3–20D   The prescribed period referred to above is a period ending at the earliest of the following times:

(a) the expiration of seven years from the acquisition of the shares or interest in the shares;

(b) the time when the acquirer ceases to have any beneficial interest in the shares; and

(c) in relation only to a person who acquires shares (*i.e.* not merely an *interest* in shares), the time when the shares cease to be subject to restrictions specified in section 79(2A).[99]

The assessment is made for the year in which the period ends.[1] A person whose beneficial interest in shares is reduced is treated as ceasing to have

---

94. F.A. 1972, s.79(1), (1A) and (1B). For a case which turned on the words "opportunity offered" see *Cheatle* v. *I.R.C.* (1982) 56 T.C. 111; [1982] S.T.C. 376. And see s.79(10) as to offers to connected persons. As to the furnishing of information, see *ibid.* Sched. 12, Pt. VII, paras. 3–5.
95. *Ibid.* Sched. 12, Pt. VII, para. 7.
96. *Ibid.* Sched. 12, Part VII, para. 6.
97. *Ibid.* s.79(4). The charge to tax on the appreciation in the value of shares is excluded in the case of approved profit-sharing schemes: see § 3–20A.
98. *Ibid.* s.79(5).
99. *Ibid.* s.79(6).
1. *Ibid.* s.79(4). See § 3–20 EE.

an interest in such a part of the shares as is proportionate to the reduction.[2] A person who disposes of shares or an interest in shares otherwise than by a bargain at arm's length with a person who is not connected with him is deemed not to cease to have a beneficial interest in the shares.[3] But a Schedule E charge will arise on a gift of shares to a connected person, including a transfer by way of gift to trustees of a settlement made by the transferor. Increases in market value chargeable under section 79 of the Finance Act 1972 are deductible for capital gains tax purposes on the occasion of the first disposal of the shares after their acquisition.[4]

3–20E The charge discussed in § 3–20C does not apply[5–6] if:

(a) the acquisition was made in pursuance of arrangements under which employees of a body corporate receive as part of their emoluments shares or interests in shares of that body or of a body controlling it to an extent determined in advance by reference to the profits of either body[7]; or

> Thus ordinary profit-sharing schemes are excluded. The shares or interest in shares in such cases will be assessable emoluments under the general rules of Schedule E.[8]

(b) the acquisition was of shares which immediately after the acquisition were subject to none of the specified restrictions (see § 3–20EE), and were not exchangeable for shares subject to such restrictions, where the majority of the available shares of the same class was acquired otherwise than in pursuance of a right conferred or opportunity offered to a director or employee of the company. Shares are "available shares" if they are not held by or for the benefit of an associated company of the body; and shares are exchangeable for other shares if (whether by one transaction or a series of transactions) they can be exchanged for or converted into other shares[9]:

> (i) Thus if X, a director of P Limited, is offered shares in P Limited and the majority of the shares in P Limited are owned by (say) the public, section 79 will not apply provided the conditions as to the absence of restrictions, etc., are satisfied.
> (ii) Assume, however, that P Limited in example (i) forms a subsidiary company, S Limited, and subscribes for 90 per cent. of its shares. X then obtains the remaining 10 per cent. by virtue of his office or

---

2. *Ibid.* s.79(6)
3. F.A. 1972, s.79(11). For the meaning of "connected person," see I.C.T.A. 1970, s.533, *post,* § 16–18A.
4. *Ibid.* s.79(9).
5–6. *Ibid.* s.79(1)(2)(8).
7. *Ibid.* s.79(8), to be read subject to F.A. 1973, s.19 and Sched. 8 (Pt. I), in the case of arrangements made or modified after March 22, 1973. Control is defined in I.C.T.A. 1970, s.534.
8. See *Brumby* v. *Milner* (1975) 51 T.C. 583; [1975] S.T.C. 534 (H.L.) where it was held that the distribution of capital on the termination of a profit-sharing scheme was taxable in the year of distribution. *Cf. Bray* v. *Best* [1986] S.T.C. 96 (trust for benefit of employees; assets distributed on a take-over and after employments had been transferred; *held* to be emoluments from former employment: see § 3–13A).
9. F.A. 1972, s.79(2)(*c*)(i).

employment with P Limited, or S Limited. Section 79 applies because the shares held by P Limited in S Limited are not "available shares." Of the available shares, all will be held by X, *i.e.* the majority of available shares will not be acquired otherwise than in pursuance of rights conferred on directors, etc.

(c) the acquisition was of shares which immediately after the acquisition were not subject to specified restrictions (see § 3–20EE) and not exchangeable for shares subject to such restrictions, where the majority of the available shares of the same class were acquired by persons who were or had been employees or directors of or of a body controlled by, the body in which they were shares and who were together able as holders of the shares to control that body.[10]

Thus, if P Limited forms a subsidiary company, S Limited, and, later, directors or employees of P Limited acquire the majority of the shares in S Limited (excluding those owned by P Limited), so that S Limited is a director/employee-controlled company, section 79 does not apply provided the shares are unrestricted, as required by the section.

3–20EE   *Specified restrictions*. The restrictions which are referred to in paragraphs (b) and (c) in § 3–20E are:

(i) restrictions not attaching to all shares of the same class; or
(ii) restrictions ceasing or liable to cease some time after the acquisition; or
(iii) restrictions depending on the shares being or ceasing to be held by directors or employees of any body corporate (other than such restrictions imposed by a company's articles of association as require shares to be disposed of on ceasing to be so held).[11]

The exemption in paragraph (b) requires that the shares are not subject to *any* such restrictions. The exemption in paragraph (c) above is not, however, lost if the shares are subject to the restriction in (iii). This is an exemption which applies to a director- or employee-controlled company and it is not fatal that the holding of shares is made conditional on continuation in office or employment.

There is treated as a restriction attaching to shares any contract, agreement, arrangement or condition by which the owner's freedom to dispose of the shares or any interest in them or to exercise any right conferred by them is restricted, or by which such a disposal or exercise may result in any disadvantage to him or a person connected with him, except where the restriction is imposed as a condition of a loan which is not a related loan.[12]

(2) *The tax on special benefits*

3–20F   Some share incentive schemes provide for participants to receive, in their capacity as holders of incentive shares, benefits not received by shareholders generally. Accordingly it is provided that where the person making

---

10. *Ibid*. s.79(2)(*c*)(ii). Control has the meaning given in T.A. 1970, s.534.
11. *Ibid*. s.79(2A).
12. See F.A. 1973, s.19 and Sched. 8, paras. 5–7, where "related loan" is defined.

the acquisition referred to in § 3–20B receives, by virtue of his ownership of or interest in the shares, any benefit not received by the majority of ordinary shareholders who acquired their shares otherwise than pursuant to a share incentive scheme, he is chargeable to tax under Schedule E for the year of assessment in which he receives the benefit on an amount equal to the value of the benefit, the amount so chargeable being treated as earned income.[13]

–20G   This charge does not apply[14] if:

(a) the acquisition was made before March 27, 1974, and the benefit mentioned was received in pursuance of a scheme approved (whether before or after the acquisition or receipt) under Schedule 12 to the Act,[15] or

(b) the acquisition was made under such arrangements as are mentioned in paragraph (a) in § 3–20E above.

–20H   Where any amount is chargeable to tax under section 79 on a person acquiring any shares or interest in shares, the amount so chargeable is deductible in computing any chargeable gain on the first disposal of the shares, whether by that or another person.[16]

The Finance Act 1984

3–20I   This Act amends the above provisions in two respects. First, it removes the charge under section 79 of the Finance Act 1972 where, by an arrangement with his employer, an employee acquires by deductions from his salary units in an authorised unit trust, under a scheme approved by the Revenue. Secondly, it removes the charge that would otherwise arise under section 79 where there is an offer to the public and directors and employees are given the opportunity to take up shares at a discount.

The Finance Act 1986

3–20J   Section 26 of this Act counters a number of devices which have been used to avoid the Schedule E charge under section 79 of the Finance Act 1972.

Provision of living accommodation

3–21   *History.* Before the year 1977–78, an employee was not assessable to tax under Schedule E on the value of accommodation which he was *required* to occupy for the more efficient performance of his duties.[17] This was because the employee was regarded as a "representative occupier," occupying the

---

13. F.A. 1972, s.79(7).
14. *Ibid.* s.79(1)(3).
15. See note 2, *supra.*
16. F.A. 1972, s.79(9).
17. *Langley* v. *Appleby* (1976) 53 T.C. 1; [1976] S.T.C. 368 (police officer required by the express terms of his contract to occupy particular premises, such occupation enabling him to perform his duties more effectively).

accommodation on behalf of his employer.[18] An employee who was *entitled* (but not *required*) to occupy accommodation provided by his employer was formerly assessed on its annual value under Schedule A but not under Schedule E. When the Schedule A charge was abolished in 1963–64, a Schedule E charge was introduced by what became section 185 of the Income and Corporation Taxes Act 1970. Section 185 proved unsatisfactory in many respects[19] and was repealed in and from the year 1977–78, when it was replaced by new provisions, now section 33 of the Finance Act 1977.

3–21A *Position from 1977–78 onwards.* Section 33 of the Finance Act 1977 states that where living accommodation is provided for a person in any period *by reason of his employment* (see § 3–22), and is not otherwise made the subject of any charge to him by way of income tax, he is to be treated for Schedule E purposes as being in receipt of emoluments of an amount equal to the value to him of the accommodation for the period, less so much as is properly attributable to that provision of any sum made good by him to those at whose cost the accommodation is provided. The value of the accommodation to the employee in any period is the rent which would have been payable for the period if the premises had been let to him at an annual rent equal to their annual value as ascertained under section 531 of the Taxes Act. "Annual value" is there defined as the rent which might reasonably be expected to be obtained on a letting from year to year if the tenant undertakes to pay all usual tenant's rates and taxes, and if the landlord undertakes to bear the costs of the repairs and insurance and the other expenses, if any, necessary for maintaining the subject of the valuation in a state to command that rent.[20] For any period, however, in which those at whose cost the accommodation is provided pay rent at an annual value greater than the annual value so ascertained under section 531, the value of the accommodation to the employee is an amount equal to the rent payable by them for the period. From any amount which is treated as emoluments under section 33, the employee can deduct as a Schedule E expense such amounts (if any) as would have been so deductible if the accommodation had been paid for by the employee out of his emoluments. As to the expenses which are so allowable, see §§ 3–35 *et seq.* Section 33 applies to all employees, including persons in director's or higher-paid employment (see §§ 3–41 *et seq.*).

Note that section 33 does not treat as an emolument the cost of purchasing accommodation which is owned by the employer; the employer is taxed only on the value of its use to him.

---

18. In *Tennant* v. *Smith* [1892] A.C. 150; 3 T.C. 158, it was thought that this rule applied only if the benefit was non-convertible, *e.g.* if the employee had no power to sell or lease the accommodation; but this view was rejected in *I.R.C.* v. *Miller* [1930] A.C. 222; 15 T.C. 25 (H.L.).

19. A working party was set up in July 1976 to undertake a review of the tax treatment of representative occupation and to make recommendations.

20. I.C.T.A. 1970, s.531. This definition of annual value corresponds with the definition of "gross value" for rating purposes in England: see General Rate Act 1967, s.19(6). Rates are differently assessed in Northern Ireland but the Taxing Acts apply there also. A concession has been introduced as a result of the 1985 rating valuation in Scotland: see (1985) S.T.I. 466.

Section 21 of the Finance Act 1983 levies, as from April 6, 1984, an additional tax charge made under a new section 33A of the Finance Act 1977, when section 33 (in the text) applies (or would apply but for the sum made good by the employee), if the cost of the accommodation including improvements exceeds £75,000. The charge is a percentage of the excess over £75,000, the percentage being the official rate of interest prescribed by the Treasury for the purposes of Finance Act 1976, s.66(9) (beneficial loan arrangements): see § 3–49. This has been 12 per cent. since October 6, 1982. If the rent paid by the employee exceeds the value of the accommodation, as determined under section 33 (so that some part of the rent can be said to be attributable to the cost of the accommodation), this excess can be deducted from the amount which is chargeable under section 33. When the new section 33A applies the employee is treated as being in receipt of emoluments as so calculated (this being in addition to the amount chargeable under section 33).

3–21B   *Exceptions.* There are a number of cases where accommodation provided for the employee gives rise to no assessable emolument. These cases are as follows[21]:

(a) where it is necessary for the proper performance of the employee's duties that he should reside in the accommodation;

(b) where the accommodation is provided for the better performance of the duties of his employment, and his is one of the kinds of employment in the case of which it is customary for employers to provide living accommodation for employees;

> This may apply, for example, to accommodation provided for police officers or fire officers.

(c) where there being a special threat to the security of the employee, special security arrangements are in force and he resides in the accommodation as part of those arrangements.

In these cases there is no charge to tax under Schedule E either by virtue of section 33 or 33A of the Finance Act 1977 or section 183 of the Taxes Act 1970 (see § 3–06 and §§ 3–16 *et seq.*) or otherwise in respect of a liability for rates on the premises being discharged for or on behalf of the employee or the employee being reimbursed for the discharge of that liability. These exceptions are wider and more precise in their scope than the old exception for the "representative occupier."[22]

3–21C   Exceptions (a) and (b) do not apply (and there may be a tax liability under section 33) if the accommodation is provided by a company and the employee is a director of the company or of an associated company unless,

21. F.A. 1977, s.33(4).
22. See the case cited in n. 17, *supra*.

for each employment of his which is employment as director of the company or an associated company, the following conditions are fulfilled, that is:

(a) he has no material interest in the company; and

(b) either his employment is as a full-time working director or the company is non-profit making (meaning that neither does it carry on a trade, nor do its functions consist wholly or mainly in the holding of investments or other property) or is established for charitable purposes only.[23]

Accommodation provided for the employee's family or household

3–22   If by reason of a person's employment accommodation is provided for others being members of his family or household, he is to be treated as if it were accommodation provided for him.[24] Living accommodation provided for an employee, or for members of his family or household, by his employer, is deemed to be provided by reason of his employment unless:

(a) the employer is an individual, and can be shown that he makes the provision in the normal course of his domestic, family or personal relationships; or

(b) the accommodation is provided by a local authority for an employee of theirs, and it can be shown that the terms on which it is provided are no more favourable than those on which similar accommodation is provided by the authority for persons who are not their employees but are otherwise similarly circumstanced.[25]

Special rules apply where the provision of living accommodation gives rise to a charge to tax under section 33 of the Finance Act 1977 (see § 3–21B) where the person is employed in director's or higher-paid employment. This is discussed in § 3–47.

Expenses allowances

3–23   If an employer reimburses his employee for expenses which he has incurred wholly, exclusively and necessarily in the performance of his duties, the amount paid does not form part of the employee's emoluments.[26] If a lump sum is paid to an employee as an expenses allowance, it is not in practice treated as an emolument if it is of a reasonable amount.[27]

---

23. F.A. 1977, s.33(5). For definitions, see F.A. 1976, s.72.
24. *Ibid.* s.33(6).
25. *Ibid.* s.33(7).
26. *Pook* v. *Owen* [1970] A.C. 244; 45 T.C. 571 (H.L.).
27. But see *McLeish* v. *I.R.C.* (1958) 38 T.C. 1, where the allowance was found excessive. *Cf. Napier* v. *National Business Agency* [1951] 2 All E.R. 264; 30 A.T.C. 180 (C.A.) where N. was employed at a salary of £13 a week plus £6 a week for expenses. Both the employer and N. knew N.'s expenses could not exceed £1 a week. N. was dismissed and sued on the basis that his weekly salary was £13. *Held,* the service agreement was unenforceable as being contrary to public policy, it being intended to mislead the Revenue. The provisions relating to salaries were not severable from the rest of the agreement and could not be enforced.

There are special provisions affecting expenses allowances paid to directors and employees remunerated at the rate of £8,500 a year or more.[28]

In *Donnelly* v. *Williamson*[29] a teacher received a car-mileage allowance for attending functions such as parent-teachers' meeting. Attendance formed no part of the duties of her employment. It was held that the allowance was not an emolument of her employment: "repayment of expenses is not emolument."

3. TERMINAL PAYMENTS[30]

3–24   Before 1960, a sum paid to an employee or office-holder on the termination of his office or employment or in consideration of a variation of its terms was dealt with as follows:

(1) If there was a previous arrangement that the sum would be paid (such as a provision in articles of association), the sum was treated as deferred remuneration and taxed under Schedule E.[31]

(2) If the payment was in anticipation of future services, it was treated as advance remuneration and taxed under Schedule E.[32]

(3) If the payment was not related to services rendered or to be rendered but was paid as consideration for the release of the employers' obligations under the service agreement or was a genuine redundancy payment (see § 3–25A), it escaped tax.

> Thus in *Chibbett* v. *Robinson*,[33] payments by way of compensation for loss of office voted by shareholders on the liquidation of a company were held not to be taxable.
>
> In *Hunter* v. *Dewhurst*[34] a company director was paid £10,000 as compensation for loss of office on ceasing to be chairman of the company. "It seems to me," said Lord Atkin, "that a sum of money paid to obtain a release from a contingent liability under a contract of employment, cannot be said to be received 'under' the contract of employment, is not remuneration for services rendered or to be rendered under the contract of employment, and is not received 'from' the contract of employment."
>
> In *Tilley* v. *Wales*[35] a lump sum paid to commute a pension was held not to be taxable because it was "in the nature of a capital payment which is substituted for a series of recurrent and periodic sums which partake of the nature of income" (*per* Viscount Simon L.C.).

(4) A payment made in consideration of the employee entering into a

---

28. See *post*, §§ 3–40 *et seq*.

29. (1981) 54 T.C. 636; [1982] S.T.C. 88.

30. For an Inland Revenue consultative paper on this subject, see [1979] S.T.I. 353.

31. *Henry* v. *Foster* (1932) 16 T.C. 605 (H.L.); *Dale* v. *De Soissons* (1950) 32 T.C. 118 (C.A.); *cf. Henley* v. *Murray* (1950) 31 T.C. 351 (C.A.); *Williams* v. *Simmonds* (1981) 55 T.C. 17; [1981] S.T.C. 715; *McGregor* v. *Randall* [1984] S.T.C. 223 (C.A.).

32. *Cameron* v. *Prendergast* [1940] A.C. 549; 23 T.C. 122; *Tilley* v. *Wales* [1943] A.C. 386; 25 T.C. 136.

33. (1924) 9 T.C. 48. See also *Clayton* v. *Lavender* (1965) 42 T.C. 607 and *Comptroller-General of Inland Revenue* v. *Knight* [1973] A.C. 428, (J.C.).

34. (1932) 16 T.C. 605 (H.L.).

35. [1943] A.C. 386; 25 T.C. 136.

restrictive covenant was not chargeable to income tax.[36] Such payments were, however, chargeable to surtax, for which purpose the amount paid was grossed up at the standard rate.[37] For 1973–74 and subsequent years, the payment is treated as a net amount of income received after deduction of income tax at the basic rate; the tax notionally deducted is not repayable; where the recipient is assessed at higher rates, the notional tax is allowed as a credit; and the income is treated in the recipient's hands as income not brought into charge to income tax for the purposes of sections 52 and 53 of the Taxes Act 1970.[38]

The Finance Act 1960 charged under Schedule E payments which hitherto escaped tax under paragraph (3), above. Payments already taxable under paragraphs (1) and (2) were unaffected by the Act; and the payments referred to in paragraph (4) were expressly excluded. These statutory provisions are now in sections 187 to 188 of the Income and Corporation Taxes Act 1970.

Income and Corporation Taxes Act 1970, ss.187 to 188

3–25   Section 187 charges tax under Schedule E on any payment to which the section applies which is made to the holder or past holder of any office or employment, or to his personal representatives, whether the payment is made by the employer or by any other person. Payments made to the spouse or any relative or dependant of the employee, or on his behalf or by his direction, are treated as made to him; and any valuable consideration other than money must be treated as a payment of money equal to the value of the consideration at the date of the gift. There is a statutory obligation on the employer to deliver particulars of the payment to the Inspector within 14 days after the end of the year of assessment in which the payment is made. Personal representatives can be assessed in respect of payments made to the deceased. There is an exemption from tax on a payment not exceeding £25,000; and where a payment exceeds this amount only the excess over £25,000 is taxable.[39] Section 187 applies

"to any payment (not otherwise chargeable to tax[40]) which is made, whether in pursuance of any legal obligation or not, either directly or indirectly in con-

---

36. *Beak* v. *Robson* [1943] A.C. 352; 25 T.C. 33: *ante*, § 3–05. Such a payment is not deductible in computing the employer's profits under Schedule D: *Associated Portland Cement Manufacturers Ltd.* v. *Kerr* (1945) 27 T.C. 103 (C.A.): *ante*, § 2–56.

37. I.C.T.A. 1970, s.34. This section applies to any undertaking "the tenor or effect of which is to restrict [the individual] as to his conduct or activities": this would seem sufficiently wide to cover an undertaking of the kind imposed on the organist in Lord Denning's illustration in *Jarrold* v. *Boustead*: *ante*, § 3–05.

38. I.C.T.A. 1970, s.34(1) as amended by F.A. 1971, Sched. 6, para. 15. And see *post*, §§ 5–30 *et seq.*

39. I.C.T.A. 1970, s.188(3), as amended, which also contains provisions to prevent avoidance by payments made by associated employers. The question whether payments of compensation are deductible as a trading expense is referred to *ante*, § 2–66. The tax free sum of up to £25,000 is not chargeable to capital gains tax: *post*, § 16–29. Figure increased from £5,000 by F.A. 1978, s.24 and from £10,000 by F.A. 1981, s.31(1).

40. Thus a payment which was a distribution within Schedule F would fall outside s.187 and the exemption and rulings in § 3–26 would not apply.

sideration or in consequence of, or otherwise in connection with, the termination of the holding of the office or employment or any change in its functions or
emoluments, including any payment in commutation of annual or periodical
payments (whether chargeable to tax or not) which would otherwise have been
made as aforesaid."[41]

The types of payment referred to in (3) in § 3–24 are within this section.
Payments which are chargeable under Schedule E apart from the section
continue to be so chargeable and do not attract the £25,000 exemption and
the other reliefs which apply to payments which are chargeable under the
Act. It should be observed that section 187 is not confined to payments by
way of compensation for loss of office; it applies also to those retirement
gratuities which would otherwise escape tax. The PAYE system applies to
any lump sum payments on the cessation of an employment to the extent
that the payment exceeds £25,000.[42]

Non-statutory redundancy payments

3–25A   The Board of Inland Revenue has issued a Statement of Practice (SP1/
81) indicating what they regard as a genuine redundancy payment, qualifying for the £25,000 tax exemption. The Statement, reproduced in full, is as
follows[43]:

> "1. Section 412, Income and Corporation Taxes Act 1970, provides that any
> statutory redundancy payment shall be exempt from liability under Schedule
> E, with the exception of any liability under Section 187 of the Taxes Act.
>
> 2. A payment made under a non-statutory redundancy scheme may in law be
> taxable in full under Schedule E if the scheme is part of the conditions under
> which the employees agree to give their services, or if there is an expectation of
> payment on their part. However, in practice the Inland Revenue accept that in
> the case of a genuine redundancy the only tax liability on lump sum payments
> made under redundancy schemes is under Section 187, even though the pay-
> ment may be calculated by reference to the length of service or the amount of
> remuneration, or is conditional on continued service for a short period consist-
> ent with the reasonable needs of the employer's business.
>
> 3. As a general guide, redundancy is regarded as genuine for this purpose
> if—
>
> > (a) payments are made only on account of redundancy as defined in Section
> > 81 of the Employment Protection (Consolidation) Act 1978;
> > (b) the employee has been continuously in the service of the employer for at
> > least two years;
> > (c) the payments are not made to selected employees only; and
> > (d) they are not excessively large in relation to earnings and length of ser-
> > vice.
>
> The Revenue also accept that a scheme may be devised to meet a specific case

---

41. I.C.T.A. 1970, s.187(2). Payments made before April 6, 1960, are outside the charge;
so also are payments made after that date in respect of obligations incurred or employments
terminating before that date: *ibid.* s.187(6).

42. See *Employers Guide to PAYE*, para. 51.

43. [1981] S.T.I. 128. But see *Malaysian Comptroller-General of Inland Revenue* v. *Knight*
(1973) 51 A.T.C. 203; *Haywood* v. *Malaysian Comptroller-General of Inland Revenue* (1974)
53 A.T.C. 280.

of redundancy, for example the imminent closure of a particular factory, or couched in general terms to embrace redundancies as and when they arise.

4. This practice is designed to distinguish between payments which are made in cases of genuine redundancy and those which are no more than terminal bonuses given as a reward for services and which are taxable in full. It follows that each case must be considered in the light of its particular facts. Where an employer wishes to be satisfied in advance that a proposed scheme will fall within the Revenue guidelines Inspectors will be prepared to give an advance clearance on being informed of the full facts."

Exemptions and reliefs

3–26　Section 188 of the Income and Corporation Taxes Act 1970 contains a list of payments to which section 187 (above) does not apply including:

(a) any payment made in connection with the termination of the holding of an office or employment by the death of the holder, or made on account of injury to or disability of the holder of an office or employment[44];

(b) any sum paid in consideration of the employee entering into a restrictive covenant and chargeable to tax under section 34 of the Income and Corporation Taxes Act 1970[45];

(c) payments under approved retirement benefit schemes.[46]

The taxation of terminal payments in cases where a foreign element is involved is considered in § 7–16.

Where, as part of an arrangement relating to the termination of an employment, an agreement is reached between the parties for the employer to make a special contribution into an approved retirement benefit scheme in order to provide benefits for the employee, the Inland Revenue will not seek to charge such a payment under section 187 provided that the retirement benefits are within the limits and in the form prescribed by the rules of the scheme. Similarly, they will not seek to charge the payment under section 187 where the employer purchases an annuity for his former employee from a Life Office, so long as the transaction is approved under Chapter II, Part II of the Finance Act 1970.[47]

Methods of assessing terminal payments

3–27　A payment which is chargeable to tax under section 187 of the Income and Corporation Taxes Act 1970 is treated as earned income and as received (a) in the case of a payment in commutation of annual or other periodical payments, on the date when the commutation is effected; and (b) in the case of any other payment, on the date of the termination or

---

44. I.C.T.A. 1970, s.188(1)(a). The word "disability" covers not only a condition resulting from a sudden affliction but also continuing incapacity to perform the duties of an office or employment arising out of the culmination of a process of deterioration of physical or mental health caused by chronic illness: See SP 10/81 in [1981] S.T.I. 571.

45. *Ibid.* s.188(1)(b); see *ante*, § 3–24, para. (4).

46. *Ibid.* s.188(1)(c); see *post*, § 3–34.

47. SP 2/81 in [1981] S.T.I. 129.

change in respect of which the payment is made.[48] Relief may be available by virtue of section 188(3) of the Act (which exempts from tax under section 187 the first £25,000 of the terminal payments) and under Schedule 8. Prior to the enactment of the Finance Act 1981 the relieving provisions were of extreme complexity.[49] These have been simplified as respects income treated as received after April 6, 1981.[50] The terminal payment is treated as falling into slices of £25,000 which are dealt with as follows[51–52]:

The first £25,000	exempt from tax
The second £25,000	tax relief at 50 per cent.
The third £25,000	tax relief at 25 per cent.
The fourth £25,000	no tax relief

The stages in computing the tax payable on a terminal payment may be summarised as follows:

(1) Calculate the individual's tax liability ignoring the terminal payment.

(2) Calculate the individual's tax liability treating as income so much of the terminal payment as falls into the second slice. Thus if the terminal payment is £100,000, add in £25,000. If the terminal payment is £30,000, add in £5,000.

(3) Take the difference between (1) and (2). This difference is the "extra tax" attributable to the second slice. Deduct 50 per cent. This gives the tax liability attributable to the second slice.

(4) Calculate the individual's tax liability treating as income so much of the terminal payment as falls into the third slice.

(5) Take the difference between (1) and (4). This difference is the extra tax attributable to the third slice. Deduct 25 per cent. This gives the tax liability attributable to the third slice.

(6) Calculate the individual's tax liability treating as income so much of the terminal payment as falls into the fourth slice.

(7) Take the difference between (1) and (6). This difference is the extra tax attributable to the fourth slice.

(8) The total tax liability on the terminal payment is the sum of the amounts in (3), (5) and (7).

The PAYE Regulations apply to payments chargeable to tax under section 187 and the appropriate amount of tax must be deducted by the payer. If the payer fails to deduct tax he cannot recover the amount overpaid from the recipient (for this is a case of money paid under a mistake of law[53]). There are only two cases in which the payer is exonerated from liability to account for tax.[54]

---

48. *Ibid.* s.187(4).
49. See the 15th edition at § 3–27.
50. I.C.T.A. 1970, Sched. 8, as amended by F.A. 1986, s.45 for reasons explained in I.R. Press Release in [1986] S.T.I. 401.
51–52. For a worked example, see [1981] S.T.I. 184.
53. *Bernard & Shaw Ltd.* v. *Shaw* (1951) 30 A.T.C. 187.
54. See Income Tax (Employments) Regs. 1973 (S.I. 1973 No. 334), para. 26(3) and (4) and see *R.* v. *I.R.C., ex p. Chisholm* (1981) 54 T.C. 722; [1981] S.T.C. 253.

4. Pensions

3–28   It is usual for employers to offer pension schemes for the benefit of their employees. There are many different types of scheme but the tax problems, so far as employees are concerned, are as follows:

(1) *Whether contributions made by the employee are deductible in computing his emoluments*

3–29   The employee's contributions may take the form of payments (usually by deduction from salary) into a pension fund established by the employer, or of payments to an insurance company which has made arrangements with the employer to provide pensions. In either case, the contributions are not deductible in computing the employee's emoluments, unless the pension scheme is an "exempt approved" scheme within the meaning of section 21 of the Finance Act 1970: the contributions are treated as an application of income, not as expenditure incurred in earning the income.[55] The types and conditions of approval are considered later.[56–57]

(2) *Whether contributions made by the employer are to be treated as additional emoluments of the employee*

3–30   Under most types of pension scheme, contributions are made by the employer in respect of each employee in his service. By virtue of section 23 of the Finance Act 1970, where any sum is paid pursuant to a scheme (called a "retirement benefits scheme"[58]) for the provision of relevant benefits for any employee, the sum so paid, if not otherwise chargeable to income tax as income of the employer, is deemed to be income of the employee assessable under Schedule E for the year of assessment in which the sum is paid. The section applies whether the sum paid is a contribution to a pension fund established by the employer or a premium on a life policy. "Relevant benefits" means[58]

3–31   "any pension, lump sum, gratuity or other like benefit given or to be given on retirement, or on death or in anticipation of retirement, or in connection with past service, after retirement, or death or to be given on or in anticipation of or in connection with any change in the nature of the service of the employee in question. . . . "

It includes benefits payable to the employee's wife or widow, children, dependants or personal representatives.[59] It does not include any benefit which is to be offered solely by reason of the disablement by accident of a person occurring during his service or of his death by accident so occurring and for no other reason.[60] The section applies not only to the case where the employer pays a contribution towards the provision of the employee's retirement or other benefits; it applies where there is an agreement

---

55. *Smyth* v. *Stretton* (1904) 5 T.C. 36.
56–57. See *post*, §§ 39–08 *et seq.*
58. F.A. 1970, s.25(1) defines "retirement benefits scheme" and s.26(1) defines "relevant benefits."
59. F.A. 1970, s.23(5).
60. See F.A. 1970, s.26(1), defining "relevant benefits."

between employer and employee for the provision of future retirement or other benefits, such as a service contract with a director under which he is entitled to a pension on retirement. In such a case, an estimate has to be made of the annual cost to the employer of securing the benefits under a contract with a third person, such as an insurance company, and the annual cost so estimated is treated as an emolument of the employee and taxed accordingly.[61] It should be noted that a service agreement between a company and a single employee may be a "retirement benefits scheme": the word "scheme" is deceptive. The provisions of section 23 should be kept in mind when negotiating service agreements for directors and employees. A director or employee who feels disheartened by the amount of tax payable on a proposed increase in salary may wish to forgo the increase in return for increased benefits after retirement. Section 23 may treat as "emoluments" the actual or estimated cost of providing those benefits.

Exemption from the consequences of section 23

3–32 Section 24 of the Finance Act 1970 provides that certain schemes are to be exempt from the provisions of section 23 of that Act. The main exemption is for approved schemes, but statutory schemes and those set up by a foreign government for its own employees are also exempt. It is further provided that employees who are resident and working overseas will not be liable to a Schedule E charge under section 23 if they are not liable to United Kingdom tax on their earnings.[62]

[The next paragraph is 3–34]

(3) *Whether pensions are taxable*

3–34 All pensions paid under any scheme which is approved or being considered for approval are chargeable to tax under Schedule E and PAYE should be operated on the payment.[63] Pensions paid by a person outside the United Kingdom to a resident of the United Kingdom are chargeable under Case V of Schedule D (see § 7–07). Pensions are ordinarily treated as earned income and not as investment income.[64] There are provisions for excluding from the charge under Schedule E lump sum benefits paid on retirement pursuant to approved schemes.[65]

5. EXPENSES ALLOWABLE UNDER SCHEDULE E

3–35 Section 189(1) of the Income and Corporation Taxes Act 1970 provides that:

"If the holder of an office or employment is necessarily obliged to incur and defray out of the emoluments thereof the expenses of travelling in the performance of the duties of the office or employment, or of keeping and maintain-

---

61. See *ibid*. s.23(2) and (3).
62. *Ibid*. s.24(2) as substituted by F.A. 1974, s.21(7).
63. *Ibid*. Sched. 5, Pt. II, para. 1. It seems that no specific case of Schedule E applies.
64. See *post*, § 8–07.
65. See F.A. 1973, s.14; but see F.A. 1972, s.73 and F.A. 1971, Sched. 3, para. 9.

ing a horse to enable him to perform the same, or otherwise to expend money wholly, exclusively and necessarily in the performance of the said duties, there may be deducted from the emoluments to be assessed the expenses so necessarily incurred and defrayed."

Two conditions must exist before an expense is allowable:

3–36   (1) The expense must be incurred in the performance of the duties of the office or employment. Expenditure which is incurred merely to enable a person to perform the duties, or to perform them more efficiently, does not satisfy this test.

> In *Simpson* v. *Tate*,[66] a county medical officer of health joined certain medical and scientific societies so that he might keep up to date on matters affecting public health. A claim to deduct the subscriptions paid to the societies was refused on the ground that the expense was incurred not in the performance of the duties but so that the officer might keep himself fit to perform them.

A deduction was similarly refused in *Blackwell* v. *Mills*[67] where the taxpayer was bound as a condition of his employment to incur the expense. "The test," said Donovan L.J. in another case, "is not whether the employer imposes the expense but whether the duties do, in the sense that, irrespective of what the employer may prescribe, the duties cannot be performed without incurring the particular outlay."[68]

3–37   (2) The expense must be necessary to the office or employment, in the sense that the job must generate the need for the expenditure.

> In *Roskams* v. *Bennett*, B.[69] (who was district manager of an insurance company) was unable, through defective eyesight, to drive a car and found it necessary to maintain an office at home. A claim in respect of the additional household expenses was refused.

3–38   It follows that the cost of travelling from the place where the employee lives to the place where he is employed is not deductible; and that the expense incurred by a person who practises a profession in one place of travelling to another place where he is employed is not deductible.[70]

---

66. [1952] 2 K.B. 214; 9 T.C. 314. Certain fees and subscriptions to approved bodies are deductible under I.C.T.A. 1970 s.192. A list of approved bodies is published: [1986] S.T.I. 251.
67. (1945) 26 T.C. 468. See also *Lupton* v. *Potts* (1969) 45 T.C. 643: examination fees paid to the Law Society by solicitor's articled clerk; *held*, not deductible. The clerk paid the fees "not to benefit or fulfil an obligation to an employer but to benefit himself because he wanted to become a solicitor."
68. *Brown* v. *Bullock* (1961) 40 T.C. 1 at p. 10 (C.A.). Cf. *Elwood* v. *Utitz* (1965) 42 T.C. 482 (C.A., N.I.): the sum must be defrayed "in doing the work of the office"; *Nolder* v. *Walters* (1930) 15 T.C. 380 at p. 387. See also *McKie* v. *Warner* (1961) 40 T.C. 65; *Owen* v. *Burden* (1971) 47 T.C. 476 (C.A.); *Ward* v. *Dunn* (1978) 52 T.C. 517; [1979] S.T.C. 178.
69. (1950) 32 T.C. 129. See also *Marsden* v. *I.R.C.* (1965) 42 T.C. 326 (car expenses of Inland Revenue investigator).
70. In *Mitchell and Edon* v. *Ross* [1962] A.C. 814; 40 T.C. 11 (H.L.), an unsuccessful attempt was made by consultants holding appointments under the National Health Service (Schedule E) and also carrying on private practice (Schedule D) to offset certain Schedule E expenses against the Schedule D receipts on the basis that they in fact practised a single profession. See *ante*, § 1–13.

(i) In *Ricketts* v. *Colquhoun*,[71] the Recorder of a provincial borough who was a barrister residing and practising in London claimed to deduct from his emoluments as Recorder the travelling expenses between London and the borough and hotel expenses in the borough. *Held,* that the travelling expenses were attributable to the Recorder's own choice of residence and were not necessary to the office as such; nor were any of the expenses incurred "in the performance of" his duties as Recorder.

(ii) In *Pook* v. *Owen*[72] O., a general medical practitioner in Fishguard, also held two part-time hospital appointments as obstetrician and anaesthetist 15 miles away in Haverfordwest. Under the appointments O. was on stand-by duty to deal with emergency cases and was required to be available by telephone. His responsibility for the patient began from the moment he received a call, but not every call resulted in a visit to the hospital. Under his appointment O. was paid travelling expenses at a fixed rate per mile up to a single journey of 10 miles. O. bore the cost of travelling the additional five miles of the journey from Fishguard. *Held,* (i) distinguishing *Ricketts* v. *Colquhoun* (Lord Donovan and Lord Pearson dissenting), that the duties of O.'s office were performed in two places, namely, in the hospital and in the place where he received the telephone call and that the travelling expenses from one place to the other were incurred in the performance of the duties; and (ii) (Lord Pearson dissenting and Lord Wilberforce doubting) that the travelling allowance paid by the hospital was a reimbursement for actual expenditure incurred by O., and was not an assessable emolument.[73]

In the past it has often been supposed that the Schedule E expenses rule should be applied "objectively" without taking account of the duties imposed on the taxpayer by the express terms of his office or employment. This approach may be wrong.

In *Taylor* v. *Provan*[74] T., who lived and worked in Canada and the Bahamas and who was not resident in the United Kingdom, accepted a special assignment to advise certain United Kingdom companies on terms that he should be free to perform the bulk of his duties outside the United Kingdom and should be reimbursed expenses of travelling to and from the United Kingdom. A majority of the House of Lords held on the special facts of the case that, although T. chose to live and work outside the United Kingdom, the expenses of travelling were nevertheless incurred in the performance of the duties.

This case shows that travelling expenses from home to work, where the terms of employment contemplate that home shall be a place of work, may in some cases be deductible.

3–39   The prohibition against the deduction of business entertainment expenses and the exception in the case of the "overseas customer," which has already been mentioned with regard to Schedule D,[75] also applies to Schedule E. The Rules of Schedule E relating to allowable expenses have been the subject of much comment and criticism.[76]

---

71. [1926] A.C. 1; 10 T.C. 118.
72. [1970] A.C. 244; 45 T.C. 571 (H.L.). See also *Taylor* v. *Provan* [1975] A.C. 194; 49 T.C. 579 (H.L.).
73. *Semble* the principle in (ii) applies not only to expenditure incurred in performing the duties of the office or employment but also to expenditure to put the person in a position to perform such duties. *Cf.* § 3–42.
74. [1975] A.C. 194; 49 T.C. 579 (H.L.).
75. See *ante,* § 2–71.
76. See Cmd. 9474, paras. 118–143.

6. Legislation Affecting Directors and Certain Employees[77]

3–40   It has been observed that many expenses allowances and benefits in kind escape tax under the ordinary rules applicable to Schedule E. There are, however, special provisions (now contained in sections 60 to 72 of the Finance Act 1976, as amended), which apply to persons in "director's or higher-paid employment" (as defined) under which, with some exceptions, all expense allowances and the cash equivalent of all benefits in kind provided for them are treated as taxable emoluments, subject to the right to claim a deduction under section 189 (see § 3–35) for money expended wholly, exclusively and necessarily in performing the duties of the office or employment or under section 192 in respect of fees, contributions or subscriptions falling within that section. These provisions in the Finance Act 1976 apply in and from 1977–78 and supersede provisions (now repealed) in sections 195 to 203 of the Income and Corporation Taxes Act 1970.

3–41   These special provisions in sections 60 to 72 of the Finance Act 1976 ("the special provisions") apply only to persons in "director's or higher-paid employment."[78]

Directors. The special provisions apply to a person employed as a director of a company and the word "director" is widely defined in section 72(8) of the Finance Act 1976 to include *inter alia* any person in accordance with whose directions or instructions the directors of a company are accustomed to act, excluding a person giving advice in a professional capacity. The special provisions do not apply to a director with no material interest in the company if either (a) his employment is as a full-time working director or (b) the company is non-profit making (meaning that neither does it carry on trade, nor do its functions consist wholly or mainly in the holding of investments or other property) or is established for charitable purposes only.[79] "Full-time working director" means a director who is required to devote substantially the whole of his time to the service of the company in a managerial or technical capacity.[80] A person has a material interest if (broadly) he controls, directly or indirectly, more than 5 per cent. of the company's ordinary share capital.[81] Directors who are so excluded from the special provisions will be caught by them if their emoluments are such that the next paragraph applies.

Other employees. The special provisions apply to all persons in employment with emoluments at the rate of £8,500 a year or more.[82] The figure of £8,500 has to be calculated on the assumption that the special provisions

---

77. See I.R. Booklet No. 480: *Notes on Expenses Payments and Benefits for Directors and Certain Employees*.
78. F.A. 1976, s.69(1) and (3) (substituted by F.A. 1978, s.23).
79. *Ibid.* s.69(5).
80. *Ibid.* s.72(9).
81. *Ibid.* s.72(10).
82. *Ibid.* s.69(1) and (3), substituted by F.A. 1978, s.23. The rate of £8,500 has applied in and from 1979–80.

apply and on the further assumption that all benefits in respect of medical insurance (see § 3–15A) and cash vouchers (see § 3–17) are included.[83] The special provisions apply whether the employer is a company, firm or an individual. Separate employments with the same employer are treated as one employment; so also are separate employments with employers under common control.[84]

The effect of the special provisions is as follows:

(1) *Expenses allowances*[85]

3–42   Any sum paid in respect of expenses (whether by way of reimbursement of expenses actually incurred or "round sum allowances" or otherwise) to a person in director's or higher-paid employment is, if not otherwise chargeable to tax as his income, treated as emoluments of the employment and accordingly is chargeable to income tax under Schedule E. If the director or employee is able to show that the allowance was expended wholly, exclusively and necessarily in the performance of the duties of the office or employment, a claim for a deduction under section 189 (see § 3–35) may be made. The onus of showing that the conditions of section 189 of the Income and Corporation Taxes Act 1970 have been satisfied is thus thrown on the director or employee.

(2) *Benefits in kind*

3–43   There is legislation in section 33 of the Finance Act 1977 which deals with the provision of living accommodation, whether for a director or other employee. This has been discussed in §§ 3–21A *et seq.* Subject to this legislation, section 61 of the Finance Act 1976 (which applies in and from 1977–78) treats as the emolument of an employment and accordingly as chargeable to income tax under Schedule E an amount equal to the "cash equivalent" of certain benefits provided for a person who is in director's or higher-paid employment (see § 3–41) where the benefit is provided by reason of his employment. The persons providing a benefit are those at whose cost the provision is made. The section applies whether the benefit is provided for the director or employee or for others who are members of his family or household,[86] except that where the employer is an individual the section does not apply to payments or provisions which can be shown to have been made in the normal course of the individual's domestic, family or personal relationships.[87] Section 61(2) provides as follows:

> "The benefits to which [section 61] applies are accommodation (other than living accommodation[88]), entertainment, domestic or other services, and other benefits and facilities of whatsoever nature (whether or not similar to any of

---

83. *Ibid.* s.69(2).
84. *Ibid.* s.69(3), (4).
85. *Ibid.* s.60.
86. References to members of a person's family or household are to his spouse, his sons and daughters and their spouses, his parents and his servants, dependants and guests: F.A. 1976, s.72(4).
87. *Ibid.* s.72(3).
88. For the separate treatment of living accommodation, see §§ 3–21A and 3–47.

those mentioned above in this subsection), excluding however those taxable under sections 64 to 68 below in this chapter, and subject to the exceptions provided for by the next following section."[89]

The section does not apply where the cost of providing the benefit is chargeable under the ordinary rules of Schedule E apart from the special provisions applicable to persons in director's or higher-paid employment. Thus if an employer discharges an obligation which his employee has incurred to pay £x to a third person and the £x is chargeable under Schedule E under the principle in *Nicoll* v. *Austin* (see § 3–16), section 61 of the Finance Act 1976 is not needed and does not apply.

> In *Rendell* v. *Went*[90] a company which employed the appellant met the legal costs involved in defending the appellant on a charge of causing the death of a pedestrian by reckless or dangerous driving. If the charge had been proved the appellant would have been liable to be imprisoned and the company did not wish to be deprived of his services. *Held,* that the expense incurred by the company was a benefit or facility giving rise to a charge to tax.

3–44   Section 61 of the Finance Act 1976 applies only to benefits provided for a director or employee *by reason of his employment.*[91] Section 72(3) provides that all sums paid to an employee by his employer in respect of expenses, and all such provision as is mentioned in the chapter of which section 72 forms part which is made for an employee, or for members of his family or household, by his employer, shall be deemed to be paid to or made for him or them by reason of his employment; but this does not apply to any such payment or provision made by the employer, being an individual, as can be shown to have been made in the normal course of his domestic, family or personal relationships. The exception meets the case where an individual employs a friend or member of his family. The benefit of medical insurance is taxed under section 61 in and from 1982–83 (see § 3–15A).

The application of section 61 to a scholarship scheme for employees' children has recently been considered by the courts; and in the context it will be recalled that section 375 of the Income and Corporation Taxes Act 1970 provides that scholarship income "shall be exempt from income tax, and no account shall be taken of any such income in computing the amount of income for income tax purposes" (see § 1–16).

> In *Wicks* v. *Firth*[92] I.C.I. established an educational trust for children of all employees or officers of I.C.I. and of certain nominated subsidiaries. The trustees of a fund, which I.C.I. provided, interviewed children who had been accepted for university or similar courses and, in appropriate cases, made awards. It was common ground that the awards were scholarships. In the test case the parents were in director's or higher-paid employment and they were assessed under section 61 of the Finance Act 1976 on the cash equivalent of the benefit, namely, the amount awarded. The taxpayers claimed the benefit of

---

89. F.A. 1976, ss.64 and 65 (cars): § 3–48; s.66 (beneficial loan arrangements): § 3–45; s.67 (employee shareholdings): § 3–47; s.68 (medical insurance): § 3–15A.
    90. (1964) 41 T.C. 641 (H.L.) (a case under the law before 1977–78).
    91. F.A. 1976, s.61(1).
    92. (1982) 56 T.C. 318; [1982] S.T.C. 76 (C.A.).

exemption in section 375 of the 1970 Act (above). The House of Lords held by a majority that this exemption applied.

Legislation has nullified the effect of this decision.[92a] It is now clear that the exemption in section 375 applies only to the person who holds the scholarship.

3–45   Section 61 does not apply to a benefit consisting in the provision by the employee's employer for the employee himself, or for the spouse, children or dependants of the employee, of any pension, annuity, lump sum, gratuity or other like benefit to be given on the employee's death or retirement[93]; nor does section 61 apply to a benefit consisting in the provision by the employee's employer of meals in any canteen in which meals are provided for the staff generally.[94] Section 61 does not apply to accommodation in the employer's premises, or to supplies or services, used by the employee solely in performing the duties of his employment.[95]

The measure of the charge under section 61

3–46   Where tax is charged under section 61 on a benefit, the measure of the charge under Schedule E is "an amount equal to whatever is the *cash equivalent* of the benefit."[96] This means an amount equal to the *cost* of the benefit, less so much (if any) of it as is made good by the employee to the provider of the benefit.[97] Generally, the cost of a benefit is the amount of any expense incurred in or in connection with its provision, including a proper proportion of any expense relating partly to the benefit and partly to other matters.[98]

This represents a radical departure from the normal Schedule E rule under which tax on many benefits in kind is charged on the value of the benefit to the employee. In *Wilkins* v. *Rogerson*, for example (see § 3–17), the taxable emolument was an amount equal to the secondhand value of the suit provided for the employee. If in such a case the employee were in director's or higher-paid employment, the tax charge in and from 1977–78 would be on an amount equal to the cost of the suit.

Where an employer purchases an asset, such as a house or television set, and places it at an employee's disposal, or at the disposal of others being members of his family or household, tax is levied on the *annual value* of the use of the asset plus the total of any expense incurred in or in connection with the provision of the benefit (excluding however the expense of acquiring or producing it incurred by the person to whom the asset belongs and excluding also any rent or hire charge payable for the asset by the provider of the benefit).[99] The annual value of the use of the asset[1]:

92a. See F.A. 1976, s.62A as amended by F.A. 1984, s.31. And see [1984] S.T.I. 62.
93. F.A. 1976, s.62(6).
94. *Ibid*. s.62(7).
95. *Ibid*. s.62(3).
96. *Ibid*. s.61(1).
97. *Ibid*. s.63(1).
98. *Ibid*. s.63(2).
99. *Ibid*. s.63(4), as amended by F.A. 1980, s.51(1)(*a*).
1. *Ibid*. s.63(5).

(a) in the case of land, is its annual value being the rent which might reasonably be expected to be obtained on a letting from year to year if the tenant undertakes to pay all usual tenant's rates and taxes, and if the landlord undertakes to bear the costs of the repairs and insurance, and the other expenses, if any, necessary for maintaining the subject of the valuation in a state to command that rent;

> Thus if a company buys a freehold house for one of its directors, who has the use of it, the director is taxed under Schedule E on the annual value. If the company pays the outgoings (rates, electricity, etc.), the director is taxed on their cost: see § 3–43 and § 3–47.

(b) in any other case, is 20 per cent.[2] of the market value of the asset at the time when it was first applied (by those providing the benefit in question) in the provision of any benefit for a person, or for members of his family or household, by reason of his employment.

Where the person providing the benefit rents or hires the asset which he then puts at the employee's disposal, and the amount of the rent or hire-charge equals or exceeds the annual value, the tax charge is levied by reference to the former.[3]

Where the benefit consists in the transfer of an asset by any person, and since that person acquired or produced the asset it has been used or has depreciated, the cost of the benefit is deemed to be the market value of the asset at the time of transfer or, if higher, its market value when it was first applied for the person's benefit *less* the total amounts taken into account under (b) above.[4]

> Thus if a company buys hi-fi equipment for £1,000 and places it at the disposal of a director, who uses it in his home, the director is taxed under Schedule E on the annual value, which under (b) above is £200 annually. If after two years the director buys the equipment from the company, he is taxed under Schedule E on £1,000 less £400 less the price he pays the company. (If at the time of the purchase by the director its then market value exceeded £1,000, the higher market value would be substituted in the equation.)

There are special provisions which apply to cars: see § 3–48.

Expense connected with living accommodation: representative occupiers

3–47   We have seen in § 3–21A that all employees, whether or not in director's or higher-paid employment, are taxable under section 33 of the Finance Act 1977 on the annual value of living accommodation provided for them, subject only to three exceptions in § 3–21C where there is no tax either on the annual value or on any liability for rates which the employer discharges. Two of these exceptions remove any tax charge in respect of the emoluments of representative occupiers. Where there would be a tax charge under section 33 but for these exceptions, section 63A of the

---

2. Increased from 10 per cent. as respects assets first applied after April 5, 1980: F.A. 1980, s.49(3), (4).
3. F.A. 1976, s.63(6), as substituted by F.A. 1980, s.51(1)(*b*).
4. *Ibid.* s.63(3) and 63(3A), inserted by F.A. 1980, s.49(2), (4).

Finance Act 1976[5] prevents persons in director's or higher-paid employment being taxed (as a benefit in kind) on the full amount of expenditure incurred in providing one or more of the following:

(a) heating, lighting, or cleaning the premises concerned;
(b) repairs (other than structural repairs) to the premises, their maintenance or decoration;
(c) the provision in the premises of furniture, or other appurtenances or effects which are normal for domestic occupation.

The tax charge under section 61 of the Finance Act 1976 is limited in the case of such expenditure to 10 per cent. of the net amount of the emoluments of the employment for the year (for which purpose the expenditure falling into categories (a)–(c) is left out of account) plus capital allowances and certain pension contributions.

> Thus if X is employed as a teacher at a boarding school at a salary of £9,000 a year and is required to live in a house provided by the school, the cash equivalent of any benefits in categories (a)–(c) is taxable under section 61 of the Finance Act 1976, subject to the 10 per cent. limit.

There are provisions which prevent tax being avoided by dividing an employment between different associated employers.

Cars and benefits associated with cars

3–48   Where a person in director's or higher-paid employment or a member of his family or household has the use (but not the ownership) of a car which is available for his or their private use[6] and the car is made available by reason of the employment, an amount equal to the cash equivalent of the benefit is treated under section 64 of the Finance Act 1976 as emoluments of the employment chargeable to income tax under Schedule E, except where it is chargeable under Schedule E apart from the section.

The cash equivalent is set out in Tables in Schedule 7 to the Finance Act 1976, as amended from time to time by Treasury Order. The cash equivalent depends on the original market value of the car, its cylinder capacity and its age at the end of the year of assessment.[7]

The charge under section 64 covers the use of the car. If a driver is provided, the benefit is separately charged under section 61 of the Finance Act 1976 (see § 3–43) under the provision relating to benefits in kind.

No business or insubstantial business travel. If the car is not used for the employee's business travel or its use for such travel does not amount to more than 2,500 miles in the relevant year, the cash equivalent to be taxed under section 64 is the amount shown in the Tables referred to above plus 50 per cent.[8]

---

5. Inserted by F.A. 1977, s.34.
6. See *Gilbert* v. *Hemsley* (1981) 55 T.C. 419; [1981] S.T.C. 703.
7. The tables which apply from April 6, 1986 and April 6, 1987, are set out in [1985] S.T.I. 652 and [1986] S.T.I. 314.
8. F.A. 1976, s.64 as amended by F.A. 1981, s.68(6), (7).

Two or more cars. If a person is taxable under section 64 of the Finance Act 1976 in respect of two or more cars which are made available concurrently, the cash equivalent in the case of each of those cars (other than the one which in the period for which they are concurrently available is used to the greatest extent for the employee's business travel) is the amount shown in the Table plus 50 per cent.

Pooled cars.[9] Broadly, cars which are included in a car pool for a number of employees, which are kept overnight on the employer's premises, and where any private use is merely incidental to the employee's other use of the car during the year, attract no tax charge under either section 61 or 64 of the Finance Act 1976.

3–48A   *Car fuel.*[10] When a person employed in director's or higher-paid employment or a member of his family or household has fuel for a car provided by reason of the employment, an amount equal to the cash equivalent of the benefit of the fuel is treated under section 64A of the Finance Act 1976 as an emolument of the employment.[11] No other charge to tax is levied in connection with the provision of the fuel. The cash equivalent is set out in Tables in Section 64A.[12]

Beneficial loan arrangements

3–49   (1) *Loans.* Beneficial loans are not caught by the tax charge on "benefits in kind" (see § 3–43) because, generally, no expense is incurred by the employer in providing the loan; and loans are generally not taxable as emoluments under Schedule E because the benefit of the loan is not convertible into money (see § 3–14).

Section 66(1) of the Finance Act 1976, which takes effect in and from the year 1977–78, provides that where a person employed in director's or higher-paid employment (§ 3–41) has the benefit of a loan which is obtained by reason of his employment, being a loan which is interest-free or at a rate less than the official rate (as defined),[13] the cash equivalent of the benefit (as defined)[14] shall be treated as emoluments of the employment. The section applies whether the loan is to the employee or to a relative of his, except that no tax charge arises in the case of a loan to a relative where the employee is able to show that he derived no benefit from the loan. The cash equivalent (roughly) is the difference between the interest actually charged, if any, and the official rate. There is no charge to tax if the cash equivalent does not exceed £200[15–16]; and there are provisions for

---

9. *Ibid.* s.65.

10. For a consultative document, see [1981] S.T.I. 161.

11. s.64A was inserted by F.A. 1981, s.69(1) to take effect in and from 1982–83.

12. The tables which apply from April 6, 1986 and April 6, 1987, are set out in [1985] S.T.I. 653 and [1986] S.T.I. 330.

13. F.A. 1976, s.66(9). The official rate as from October 6, 1982, is 12 per cent. per annum: see The Income Tax (Official Rate of Interest on Beneficial Loans) Order 1982 in [1982] S.T.I. 431.

14. *Ibid.* s.66(8) and Sched. 8, Pt. II.

15–16. Increased from £50 for 1980–81 and subsequent years: F.A. 1980, s.50(1).

excluding the section where the interest on the loan would be eligible for relief under section 75 of the Finance Act 1972 (see §§ 8–57 *et seq.*). The section took effect in and from 1977–78 with a reduced tax charge for the two years 1977–78 and 1978–79.

Where the amount of interest paid on a loan for the year of assessment in which it is made is not less than interest at the official rate applying for that year and the loan is for a fixed and unvariable period and at a fixed and unvariable rate of interest, section 66(1) will not apply by reason only of a later increase in the official rate.[17]

There is a concession under which cheap bridging loans to enable an employee to change his residence as a result of a transfer within his employer's organisation are treated as non-taxable benefits.[18]

The Inland Revenue do not propose to charge as taxable benefits under section 66 of the Finance Act 1976 amounts advanced by an employer in respect of expenses necessarily incurred by an employee in performing the duties of his employment, if: (a) the maximum amount advanced at any one time does not exceed £1,000; (b) the advances are spent within six months; and (c) the employee accounts to his employer at regular intervals for the expenditure of the sum advanced.[19]

3–50   (2) *Loans released or written off.* In many cases the act of releasing or writing off a loan made to an employee will give rise to an assessable emolument under the ordinary rules of Schedule E.[20] However, section 66(3) of the Finance Act 1976 (which generally applies for the year 1976–77 and subsequent years) provides that where in the case of a person employed in director's or higher-paid employment (as defined)[21] there is in any year released or written off the whole or part of a loan (whether to the employee himself or to a relative of his and whether or not such a loan as is mentioned in § 3–49), the benefit of which was obtained by reason of his employment, an amount equal to that which is released or written off shall be treated as emoluments of the employment chargeable to income tax under Schedule E. Section 66(3) does not apply in the case of a loan to a relative if the employee shows he derived no benefit from it. Further, section 66(3) does not apply to amounts otherwise chargeable to income tax as income of the employee, except that it applies to amounts chargeable only under section 187 of the Taxes Act: thus sums released or written off on the occasion of the termination of a director's or higher-paid employment are taxed without the benefit of the £25,000 exemption (see § 3–25). Section 66(3) cannot be avoided by the employer deferring the release or writing off of the loan until after the director's or higher-paid employment has terminated, except that no charge arises where the release or writing off takes effect on or after the employee's death.

---

17. F.A. 1980, s.50(2); and see s.50(3) as to loans made before April 6, 1978, when there was no official rate.
18. See [1985] S.T.I. 216.
19. SP 7/79 in [1979] S.T.I. 178.
20. See *Clayton* v. *Gothorp, ante,* § 3–15.
21. F.A. 1976, s.69.

Employee's shareholdings acquired at an undervalue: treatment as notional loan

3–51   Section 67 of the Finance Act 1976 applies where, after April 6, 1976, a person employed or about to be employed in director's or higher-paid employment ("the employee"), or a person connected with him, acquires shares in a company (whether the employing company or not) and the shares are acquired at an undervalue (as defined) in pursuance of a right or opportunity available by reason of the employment. The section applies for 1976–77 and subsequent years and has the effect of treating the undervalue as if the employee had the benefit of an interest-free loan of an equivalent amount (called "the notional loan") within section 66(1) of the Act (see § 3–49). The tax charge imposed by section 67 does not apply to the extent that the acquisition at an undervalue gives rise to a Schedule E emolument apart from that section, *e.g.* under the principle in *Weight* v. *Salmon* referred to in § 3–15. Payments or further payments for the shares go to reduce the amount outstanding of the notional loan but, subject thereto, the loan is treated as outstanding until: (a) the whole amount outstanding is made good; or (b) the debt is released; or (c) the beneficial interest in the shares is disposed of; or (d) the employee dies. In case (a) the tax charge under section 66(1) comes to an end. In cases (b) and (c) the employee is taxed under section 66(3) (see § 3–46) as if an amount equal to the outstanding loan had been released or written off. In case (d) there is no Schedule E charge but the shares will form part of the employee's estate for the purposes of capital transfer tax. In cases (a)–(c) the tax charge arises notwithstanding the cessation of the employment.

3–52   *Sale of shares acquired by employees.* Where after April 6, 1976, shares are acquired as mentioned in § 3–51 (but whether or not at an undervalue) and those shares are subsequently disposed of by surrender or otherwise so that neither the employee nor any person connected with him any longer has a beneficial interest in them and the disposal is for a consideration which exceeds the then market value of the shares, the amount of the excess is treated as an emolument of the employee's employment and is accordingly chargeable to income tax under Schedule E for the year in which the disposal is effected. The charge to tax arises even if the employment has ceased but it does not apply to a disposal effected after the employee's death.

7. THE PAY AS YOU EARN SYSTEM[22]

3–53   It would be out of place in a book dealing with the principles of Revenue Law to consider in any detail the administrative machinery by which the tax due from directors and employees in respect of their emoluments is col-

---

22. See I.C.T.A. 1970, s.204, and the Income Tax (Employment) Regs. 1973 (S.I. 1973 No. 334). These are printed in Simon, Vol. G, immediately after I.C.T.A. 1970, s.207. The system is explained in detail in the *Employer's Guide to Pay As You Earn* (April 1979) issued by the Board of Inland Revenue under reference P7. See *Clark* v. *Oceanic Contractors* (1982) 56 T.C. 183; [1983] S.T.C. 35 (H.L.). (PAYE in relation to foreign company making payments from abroad to employees in the designated area of the North Sea).

lected. Briefly, every person liable to assessment under Schedule E has a code number allocated to him by the Revenue. The code number is determined by the total of reliefs and allowances due to the taxpayer. The employer is supplied with tax tables by reference to which he is able to calculate the amount of tax to be deducted from the salary, the object of these tables being to secure that the tax payable for the year of assessment is spread over the year. Where reliefs or allowances change during the year (*e.g.* through marriage), the code number is revised and an adjustment follows in the amount of tax deducted. The employer is bound to account to the Collector of Taxes within 14 days from the end of each month for the tax which he ought to have deducted from the employee's emoluments. The obligation to deduct tax arises "on the making of any payment of, or on account of, any income. . . . " A company which places moneys *unreservedly* at the disposal of a director or employee, *e.g.* by crediting a bonus to a current account with the director, makes a *payment* at the time of such crediting.[23–24]

8. Approved Profit Sharing Schemes

3–54 The Finance Act 1978[25] has introduced elaborate provisions which enable employers to establish trusts and provide funds to enable the trustees to buy ordinary shares in the employing company and appropriate and hold them on trust for individual employees of the company. Such profit sharing schemes, if approved by the Revenue, enjoy certain tax advantages. The provisions take effect as respects schemes approved after April 5, 1979. The Board of Inland Revenue has announced its willingness, where possible, to give an informal opinion in advance of a formal application for approval, provided that full particulars of the proposed scheme and the relevant documentation are provided. There is a right of appeal to the Special Commissioners against refusal or withdrawal of approval. Only a brief outline of the relevant provisions is given below. Amendments made by later legislation have been incorporated in the text.

Conditions for approval

3–55 The scheme must provide for the establishment of a body of trustees resident in the United Kingdom who, out of moneys paid to them by the company, will acquire shares (*e.g.* by purchase or subscription) and appropriate the shares so acquired to eligible individuals. The initial market value of the shares appropriated to any one participant in a year of assessment is the greater of £1,250 and 10 per cent. of the individual's salary for

---

23–24. I.C.T.A. 1970, s.204 and *Garforth* v. *Newsmith Stainless Ltd.* (1978) 52 T.C. 522; [1979] S.T.C. 129.
25. F.A. 1978, ss.53–61 and Sched. 9. The Revenue have published two pamphlets on the tax treatment of profit sharing schemes. These are IR 35 entitled "Income Tax—Profit Sharing" (for employees) and IR 36 entitled "Approved Profit Sharing Schemes" (for companies and professional advisers). The Revenue have issued a consultative paper on the tax treatment of rights issues under approved profit-sharing schemes: see [1981] S.T.I. 480.

either that year or the preceding year, with a maximum of £5,000.[26] Such appropriations may be made year by year. Generally, every full-time employee or director of the company concerned who has been such during a qualifying period not exceeding five years must be eligible to participate in the scheme on similar terms. The shares purchased must be shares in the employing company or in a company which has control of it or of a member of a consortium which has control of it; and the shares must be either shares of a class quoted on a recognised Stock Exchange or shares in a company which is not under the control of another company. Thus employees of a subsidiary company cannot be given an interest in the shares of that company (unless its shares are quoted) but must take an interest in shares in the parent company. The shares in question must be fully paid up and not redeemable, and they must be subject to no restrictions, other than restrictions which attach to all shares of the same class.[27] There are a number of conditions as to the individuals eligible to participate. For example, an individual is not eligible unless, at the time of appropriation or within 18 months previously, he was a director or employee of the company concerned or, where the scheme is a group scheme, of a participating company. Individuals with a material interest (as defined) in a close company whose shares are appropriated are ineligible.

It is a condition of approval that every participant in the scheme will be bound to permit his shares to remain in the hands of the trustees during the "period of retention" and that he will be bound not to assign, charge or otherwise dispose of his beneficial interest in the shares during that period. The *period of retention* in relation to any participant's shares means the period from the date on which they are appropriated to him and ending on the second anniversary of that date or, if sooner, the date on which the participant ceases to be an employee or director of the company by reason of injury, disability or dismissal through redundancy (as defined) or the date on which the participant reaches pensionable age (as defined) or the date of the participant's death. A participant can direct the trustees to transfer the shares appropriated to him at any time after the period of retention but if the direction is given before the release date (see § 3–56), the transfer must be by way of sale at the best price obtainable. After the release date the participant can deal with the shares as he pleases. He can, if he wishes, sell his interest to the trustees.

Tax treatment

3–56   On the appropriation of shares to a participant under an approved profit sharing scheme no charge arises under Schedule E (see § 3–02) or under section 67 of the Finance Act 1976 (see § 3–51); nor does any charge arise on the appreciation in value of the shares under section 79 of the Finance Act 1972 (see § 3–20C). The full benefit of the exemption from income tax is obtained only if the participant holds his shares until the *release date* or

---

26. F.A. 1983, s.25. See also [1983] S.T.I. 150.
27. See F.A. 1986, s.22, with regard to restrictions requiring an employer to sell his shares if he leaves the employment.

until his death, if sooner. The release date in relation to a participant's shares means the fifth anniversary from the date on which the shares were appropriated to him. If trustees dispose of any of a participant's shares before the release date or (if sooner) the date of his death, the participant is chargeable to income tax under Schedule E for the year of assessment in which the disposal takes place on the *appropriate percentage* of the "locked-in value" of the shares at the time of the disposal. Generally, the locked-in value means the initial market value of the shares, which is generally their market value at the date on which the shares were appropriated to the participant. (Locked-in value has a different meaning where, since the initial appropriation to the participant, there has been a capital receipt in respect of such shares.)

If the event giving rise to the tax charge occurs during the period of retention, the appropriate percentage of the locked-in value which is chargeable to income tax is 100 per cent.; if it occurs after the expiry of the period of retention and before the fifth anniversary, the appropriate percentage is as follows:

Before 4th anniversary	100%
After 4th but before 5th anniversary	75%
On or after date on which the participant ceases to be an employee or director as a result of injury, disability or redundancy, or attains pensionable age	50%

Any tax charge under Schedule E is collected (so far as possible) under the PAYE system.

For the purposes of the capital gains tax, a participant is treated as absolutely entitled to the shares as against the trustees, notwithstanding the conditions which restrict his disposal of them; hence the treatment accorded to settled property (see §§ 16–21 *et seq*) is excluded. The normal capital gains tax rules apply on a disposal of the appropriated shares.

Dividends on scheme shares belong to the participants, with normal tax consequences (see § 8–20). A rights issue in excess of a statutory limit may give rise to a charge to tax under Schedule E.[28]

Sums expended by the employing company in contributing to an approved profit sharing scheme are deductible in computing trading profits or as management expenses in the case of an investment company.

---

28. F.A. 1982, s.42.

CHAPTER 4

SCHEDULE D, CASE VI

1. THE SCOPE OF THE CHARGE

4–01 TAX under Schedule D Case VI is charged in respect of:

(1) certain classes of income specifically directed to be charged under Case VI, such as post-cessation receipts,[1] gains of a capital nature arising from "artificial transactions" in land (see §§ 40–16 *et seq.*) and from sales of income derived from personal activities (§§ 40–21 *et seq.*); and

(2) any "annual profits or gains" not falling under any other Case of Schedule D and not charged by virtue of any other Schedule.[2]

Case VI is a residual Case and many different types of income have been brought within (1). These are discussed elsewhere in this book.[3] It might be supposed from (2) that Case VI charges tax on all profits not otherwise chargeable. This, however, is not the case, for the following principles limiting the scope of the charge are firmly established:

First, capital profits are not assessable under Case VI. This is because "annual profits" describes profits of an income nature as distinct from capital profits.[4]

Secondly, under the rule in *Jones* v. *Leeming,*[5] a profit derived from a transaction of purchase and resale is not assessable under Case VI.

In *Jones* v. *Leeming,*[5] L. and three others obtained options to purchase two rubber estates in the Malay Peninsula, which they later sold at a profit. The Commissioners found that the transaction was not a concern in the nature of trade. *Held,* that the profits were not assessable under Case VI.

"It seems to me," said Lawrence L.J., "that in the case of an isolated transaction of purchase and resale of property there is really no middle course open. It is either an adventure in the nature of trade, or else it is simply a case of sale and resale of property."[6] A sum paid as consideration for the surrender or withdrawal of a legal claim is not assessable under Case VI, for such a transaction would involve the realisation of an asset; nor does Case VI apply where the claimant has only a moral claim or nuisance value.[7]

---

1. See *ante*, §§ 2–88 *et seq.*
2. I.C.T.A. 1970, s.109.
3. Examples are balancing charges (§§ 13–12 *et seq.*); see also Sections 2 and 3 of Chap. 40.
4. *Scottish Provident Institution* v. *Farmer* (1912) 6 T.C. 34, *per* Lord Dunedin at p. 38.
5. [1930] A.C. 415; 15 T.C. 333 (H.L.).
6. *Leeming* v. *Jones* [1930] 1 K.B. 279 at p. 301; 15 T.C. 333 at p. 354.
7. *Scott* v. *Ricketts* (1967) 44 T.C. 303 (C.A.). A sum paid for the surrender of a legal claim might now be chargeable to capital gains tax: see C.G.T.A. 1979, s.20(1)(*c*): § 16–08.

Thirdly, only profits or gains which are *ejusdem generis* with the profits or gains specified in the preceding five Cases of Schedule D are chargeable under Case VI.[8] For this reason, voluntary gifts,[9] betting winnings,[10] receipts by finding[10] and "reverse premiums" are not chargeable under Case VI.

2. ANNUAL PROFITS ASSESSABLE UNDER CASE VI

4–02 A profit may be assessable under Case VI as an "annual" profit even though it arises from a service rendered on an isolated occasion and outside the normal business of the taxpayer. Thus in *Ryall* v. *Hoare,*[10] a commission paid to directors for guaranteeing an overdraft without security was held to be assessable; and the same principle was applied in *Lyons* v. *Cowcher*[11] where a commission was paid for underwriting shares. In *Brocklesby* v. *Merricks,*[12] a contention that a sum paid to an architect for services rendered by him was in the nature of a voluntary gift was rejected in view of evidence of an enforceable contract for remuneration for those services. In *Hale* v. *Shea*[13] the whole of an annual sum paid to a retiring partner by the continuing partner, as consideration both for the retiring partner's share of profits and his agreement to act as consultant if so requested, and which on the construction of the relevant document it was found impossible to apportion as between the two items of consideration, was held to be assessable under Case VI, and not to be earned income.

The question whether a payment is made for services, or is a gift, or is the price of an asset, is a question of fact.

> In *Hobbs* v. *Hussey*[14] the appellant (who was not an author by profession) contracted with a newspaper to write his reminiscences in a series of articles for £1,500. The contract involved the sale of the appellant's copyright in the series, which had not been written at the time the contract was made. An assessment was raised on the £1,500.

It was argued that the payment was for the sale of copyright and, therefore, escaped assessment under the rule in *Jones* v. *Leeming*[15]; but the court held that the true nature of the transaction was the performance of services and that any sale of copyright was merely incidental thereto.[16]

> In *Alloway* v. *Phillips*[17] the taxpayer was the wife of a man who took part in the great train robbery and who escaped from prison to Canada. In 1967–68

---

8. *Att. Gen* v. *Black* (1871) L.R. 6 Ex. 308; 1 T.C. 54.
9. *Turner* v. *Cuxon* (1888) 22 Q.B.D. 150; 2 T.C. 422.
10. *Ryall* v. *Hoare* [1923] 2 K.B. 447; 8 T.C. 521. See also *Norman* v. *Evans* (1964) 42 T.C. 188 (sums received under leasing arrangement for racehorses, which included half the prize money, held to be assessable under Case VI).
11. (1926) 10 T.C. 438.
12. 1934) 18 T.C. 576 (C.A.). *Cf. Bloom* v. *Kinder* (1958) 38 T.C. 77.
13. (1964) 42 T.C. 260. See § 8–12 note 25.
14. [1942] 2 K.B. 491; 24 T.C. 153. See also *Housden* v. *Marshall* (1959) 38 T.C. 233.
15. See *ante*, § 4–01.
16. *Cf. Trustees of Earl Haig* v. *I.R.C.* (1939) 22 T.C. 725; *Beare* v. *Carter* [1940] 2 K.B. 187; 23 T.C. 353, where the sums were held to be capital receipts. It would seem that the taxpayers in *Hobbs* v. *Hussey* and *Housden* v. *Marshall* would have escaped tax if there had been an outright sale of copyright in articles written by them; but liability for capital gains tax would not have to be considered in such a case.
17. (1980) 53 T.C. 372; [1980] S.T.C. 490 (C.A.).

when she was resident in Canada and not in the United Kingdom she entered into a contract with the *News of the World* to co-operate in writing a number of articles relating to the robbery, life "on the run," etc. The agreed fee was £39,000 but was not paid until 1973–74 when a Case VI assessment was made. *Held*, that the income arose under a contract which was "property" situated in the United Kingdom, being a chose in action which was enforceable here; and that the Case VI assessment was properly made for the year in which payment was received (see also § 7–07). The income did not arise from services provided outside the United Kingdom.

The income from leasing chattels otherwise than in the course of a trade may be assessed under Case VI.[18] The profits of theatrical backers are now treated as assessable under Case VI, if Cases I and II of Schedule D do not apply.[19]

4–02A   The income from the letting of furnished accommodation is assessed under Case VI[20] save in the exceptional case when the activities of the lessor extend beyond the mere provision of accommodation and constitute the carrying on of a trade.[20a] The Finance Act 1984 treats income from holiday lettings of furnished accommodation as income derived from the carrying on of a trade.[20b]

4–03   It will be observed that all the cases which have been referred to of income assessable under Case VI are cases of casual profits for services rendered, where there is no office or employment to bring the profits under Schedule E and no trade, profession or vocation to bring them under Schedule D, Cases I or II. A case in which income of a different character was held to be assessable under Case VI was *Cooper* v. *Stubbs*,[21] where the facts were as follows:

> S. was a member of a firm of cotton brokers and cotton merchants and it was the practice of such firms to deal in "futures," *i.e.* to make contracts to purchase cotton in the future, not with a view to taking delivery but as a hedge against fluctuations in the market. S. had a number of private dealings in futures. The Commissioners found that these were *gambling* transactions and that the profits were not assessable under Case I of Schedule D. *Held*, that Case VI applied.

They were, said Warrington L.J. "dealings and transactions entered into with a view to producing, in the result, income or revenue for the person

---

18. See *Norman* v. *Evans, supra*, note 10.
19. Hence losses can be set off against other Case VI income: see § 4–05. At one time backers' profits were treated as Case III income and losses as capital losses.
20. *Wylie* v. *Eccott* (1913) 6 T.C. 128; and see *Ryall* v. *Hoare* (1923) 8 T.C. 521 *per* Rowlatt J. at p. 526. See also I.C.T.A. 1970, s.67; Rule 4 of Schedule A, giving the landlord an option to be assessed under Schedule A: *post*, § 6–11. As to the deductions which are allowed in computing profits of furnished lettings, see Simon's *Taxes*, B7.206.
20a See *Gittos* v. *Barclay* (1982) 55 T.C. 633; [1982] S.T.C. 390 when General Commissioners held there was no trade and Goulding J. felt unable to say this was a view no reasonable commissioners could properly have formed; also *Griffiths* v. *Jackson* (1983) 56 T.C. 583; [1983] S.T.C. 184. As to the treatment of caravan-letting, see [1984] S.T.I. 386.
20b. See F.A. 1984, s.50 (where holiday letting is narrowly defined) and Sched. 11.
21. [1925] 2 K.B. 753; 10 T.C. 29 (C.A.).

who entered into them." It would seem from this decision that profits from activities which are *ejusdem generis* with trade but which lack some fundamental characteristic of trade may nevertheless be assessable under Case VI. *Cooper* v. *Stubbs* was followed in *Leader* v. *Counsell*,[22] where subscribers purchased a stallion and sold rights to nominations to the stallion. It was held that the profits were assessable under Case VI, this not being a case (as the taxpayer contended) which was excluded from Case VI as being a transaction of purchase and resale of property (see § 4–01). It is thought that the transactions in *Cooper* v. *Stubbs* (above) would now be held to constitute the carrying on of a trade notwithstanding the element of speculation involved.[23]

3. COMPUTATION OF PROFITS UNDER CASE VI

4–04 Tax under Case VI is charged on the full amount of the profits or gains arising (*i.e.* received[24]) in the year of assessment.[25] Although there is no express provision in the Act for deduction of expenses, it seems clear from the use of the phrase "profits or gains" that the charge is limited to the excess of the receipts over such expenses as are necessary to earn them. In this respect Case VI differs from Case III, considered in the next chapter, under which no relief for expenses is available. Case VI income is investment income, unless statute otherwise provides. See § 8–07(4) and § 8–07(9).

Losses

4–05 Where a loss is sustained in a transaction falling under Case VI, relief is available under section 176 of the Income and Corporation Taxes Act 1970 by setting off the loss against other Case VI income of the same or a subsequent year. No relief is available against income from any other source or against income of an earlier year, so the taxpayer with a source of Case VI income is less favourably treated in respect of losses than a taxpayer with a source of income falling under Case I or II of Schedule D.

An individual with casual profits from writing, for example, is more favourably treated as regards losses if he can satisfy the Revenue that he is carrying on the vocation of an author (to which Case II of Schedule D applies), for losses may be relieved against other income of the same or any following year.[26]

---

22. [1942] 1 K.B. 364; 24. T.C. 178.
23. Since the decision in *Edwards* v. *Bairstow and Harrison* (*ante*, § 2–03) the courts have been less reluctant to interfere with the decision of Commissioners on the question whether a transaction can in law constitute "trading."
24. *Grey* v. *Tiley* (1932) 16 T.C. 414.
25. I.C.T.A. 1979, s.125.
26. *Ibid.* s.171 discussed *post*, §§ 12–02 *et seq.* and see § 12–12.

CHAPTER 5

THE TAXATION OF PURE PROFIT INCOME: SCHEDULE D

CASE III: SECTIONS 52 AND 53

1. THE CHARGING PROVISION

5–01 TAX under Schedule D Case III is charged[1] on the following:

(1) Any interest of money, whether yearly or otherwise, or any annuity or other annual payment, whether such payment is payable within or out of the United Kingdom, either as a charge on any property of the person paying the same by virtue of any deed or will or otherwise, or as a reservation out of it, or as a personal debt or obligation by virtue of any contract, or whether received and payable half-yearly or at any shorter or more distant periods, but excluding any payment chargeable under Schedule A;

(2) all discounts[2];

(3) income from securities bearing interest payable out of the public revenue, except income charged under Schedule C[3];

(4) certain income specifically directed to be charged under Case III, such as:

    (i) small maintenance payments[4];

    (ii) savings bank interest (if not exempted)[5];

    (iii) loan and share interest paid by industrial and provident societies without deduction of tax.[6]

In this book, only income falling under (1) and (4)(i) is discussed in any detail. Note that dividends and other distributions from the resources of a company are not taxed under Schedule D: see §§ 14–40 *et seq.*

---

1. I.C.T.A. 1970, s.109. The charge is on the persons receiving or entitled to the income: *ibid.* s.114.

2. In practice, most discounts are trading receipts and Case III of Schedule D does not apply: see § 5–18. There are now statutory provisions for the taxation of "deep discount securities" *i.e.* securities issued at a discount of more than 15 per cent. of the amount payable on redemption or, if less, of more than $\frac{1}{2}$ per cent. for each complete year between issued date and redemption date. See F.A. 1984, s.36 and Sched. 9; also *Ditchfield* v. *Sharp* [1983] S.T.C. 590 (C.A.).

3. In practice, Schedule C usually applies: see § 5–17.

4. I.C.T.A. 1970, s.65: see § 5–05.

5. See *ante*, § 1–16.

6. I.C.T.A. 1970, s.340.

2. INTEREST, ANNUITIES AND OTHER ANNUAL PAYMENTS

Interest, annuities and annual payments

5–02   *Interest* has been judicially defined as "payment by time for the use of money."[7] In one case Lord Wright said[8]:

> "The essence of interest is that it is a payment which becomes due because the creditor has not had his money at the due date. It may be regarded either as representing the profit he might have made if he had had the use of the money, or, conversely the loss he suffered because he had not that use. The general idea is that he is entitled to compensation for the deprivation."

Where a loan transaction provides for the payment of a premium on redemption, it depends on the nature of the transaction and the surrounding circumstances whether the premium is "interest" or merely a sum paid to recompense the lender for the risk taken in advancing the loan. Generally, where a loan is made at or above a commercial rate of interest, any sum payable on redemption by way of premium will not be treated as interest.[9] Capital gains tax is payable on such a sum if the debt is "a debt on a security."[10] Interest awarded by the court under the Law Reform (Miscellaneous Provisions) Act 1934, s.3, is income chargeable under Case III.[11] In one case where a debenture provided for the payment of "interest" which exceeded the amount of the principal advanced and was payable within a few days after the advance, it was held that this was not interest in law.[12]

5–02A   If a principal debtor defaults in payment of interest and the debt is discharged by a third person pursuant to a contract of indemnity, the payment by the third person has been held itself to be a payment of "interest."[13] Under a contract of *indemnity*, the indemnifier may fall under a primary obligation to perform the debtor's obligations. The position is different in the case of a contract of *guarantee* and the proposition that "if a guarantor of rent pays under the guarantee, he pays rent"[14] must be open to question

---

7. *Bennett* v. *Ogston* (1930) 15 T.C. 374, *per* Rowlatt J. at p. 379.
8. *Riches* v. *Westminster Bank Ltd.* [1947] A.C. 390; (1947) 28 T.C. 159 at p. 189. See *Re Euro Hotel (Belgravia) Ltd.* (1975) 51 T.C. 293 at pp. 300–303; [1975] S.T.C. 682. ("The payments are not compensation for delay in payments but for delay in performance of other obligations"); also *Chevron Petroleum (U.K.) Ltd.* v. *B.P. Development Ltd.* (1981) 57 T.C. 137, [1981] S.T.C. 689.
9. *Lomax* v. *Dixon* [1943] K.B. 671; 25 T.C. 353 (C.A.). See especially Lord Greene at pp. 682 and 367 respectively. *Cf. Davies* v. *Premier Investment Co. Ltd.* (1945) 27 T.C. 27.
10. C.G.T.A. 1979, s.134: *post,* § 16–14.
11. *Riches* v. *Westminster Bank Ltd.* [1947] A.C. 390; 28 T.C. 159 (H.L.). Interest on damages in respect of personal injuries or death may be exempt from tax under I.C.T.A. 1970, s.375A: see *Paterson* v. *Chadwick* [1974] 1 W.L.R. 890 and *Mason* v. *Harman* [1972] R.T.C.I.
12. *Ridge Securities Ltd.* v. *I.R.C.* (1964) 44 T.C. 373 at pp. 393F–394. See also *Cairns* v. *MacDiarmid* (1983) 56 T.C. 556; [1983] S.T.C. 178 (C.A.) (interest payable in advance under tax avoidance scheme. Such schemes were legislated against: see § 8–58A).
13. See *Re Hawkins decd.* [1972] Ch. 714; *cf. Westminster Bank Executor and Trustee Co. (Channel Islands) Ltd.* v. *National Bank of Greece S.A.* (1970) 46 T.C. 472 at pp. 485 and 494.
14. *Holder* v. *I.R.C.* (1932) 16 T.C. 540 (H.L.) at p. 565, *per* Lord Atkin.

in view of more recent authority.[15] The difference between "yearly" and "non-yearly" or "short" interest is discussed in § 5–57.

5–03   *Annuity* describes an income which is purchased (usually from an insurance company) with a principal sum which then ceases to exist. It also describes an annual payment which is granted by an instrument. All annuities are "annual payments,"[16] but not all annual payments are properly described as annuities.

5–04   *Other annual payments*. The meaning of this phrase was considered by the Court of Appeal in *I.R.C.* v. *Whitworth Park Coal Co. Ltd.*[17] and the following propositions held to be established:

(1) Other annual payments must be construed *ejusdem generis* with interest and annuity. (Thus if X joins a firm of solicitors on terms that he contributes £10,000 on joining plus £2,000 a year for five years, the latter payments are not annual payments.)

(2) The payment must be made under some binding legal obligation, *e.g.* a court order or contract[18] or deed poll, *e.g.* a voluntary deed of covenant. Gifts, however recurrent, are not annual payments.[19] Payments made by trustees in the exercise of a discretion vested in them may be annual payments within Case III, even though the trustees might (consistently with their trust) have made no payment[20]; once the trustees exercise their discretion in favour of a beneficiary, the payment is one to which the beneficiary was entitled by virtue of the gift made by the settlor and has the character of income in his hands.[21] Dividends which are not due unless and until they are declared are not annual payments[22]; nor is a payment which is *ultra vires* the company making it.[23]

(3) The payment must possess the quality of recurrence, which it may do even though the amount may be variable and/or the payments contingent.

---

15. *Lep Air Services* v. *Rolloswin* [1973] A.C. 331 at p. 348, *per* Lord Diplock. And see *Holder* v. *I.R.C.* (1932) 16 T.C. 540 (H.L.) at p. 567, *per* Lord Thankerton.

16. Note that T.M.A. 1970, s.106(2), discussed in § 5–48, makes void agreements for the payment of "interest, rent or other annual payment" without allowing for deduction of tax. The section clearly applies to annuities, although they are not expressly mentioned.

17. [1958] Ch. 792 at pp. 815 *et seq., per* Jenkins L.J.; 38 T.C. 531 at pp. 548 *et seq.*

18. *Peters' Executors* v. *I.R.C.* (1941) 24 T.C. 45 (C.A.) (oral agreement made on separation of spouses).

19. *Gibbs* v. *Randall* (1980) 53 T.C. 513; [1981] S.T.C. 106: "Mere voluntary, unenforceable payments, however regular in amount, are not income for tax purposes; nor are they money to which the recipient is entitled" (*per* Goulding J. at p. 523G).

20. *Lindus and Hortin* v. *I.R.C.* (1933) 17 T.C. 442; *Cunard's Trustees* v. *I.R.C.* (1946) 27 T.C. 122 (C.A.). These were cases in which trustees were empowered to augment income of a life-tenant out of the *capital* of the trust fund: see *post* § 9–17.

21. *Drummond* v. *Collins* [1915] A.C. 1011 at pp. 1019–1021; 6 T.C. 525 (H.L.) at pp. 540–541, *per* Lord Wrenbury.

22. *Canadian Eagle Oil Co.* v. *R.* [1946] A.C. 119 at p. 135; 27 T.C. 205 at p. 245, *per* Viscount Simon.

23. *Ridge Securities Ltd.* v. *I.R.C.* (1964) 44 T.C. 373 at pp. 395–396 (where the alleged annual payments were unlawful gifts by the company). As to what is *ultra vires*, see the cases in § 2–59, note 92.

Thus in *Moss' Empires Ltd.* v. *I.R.C.*[24] the appellants guaranteed to make up the profits of a company if they fell below a certain amount. It was held that the payments under the guarantees were "annual" even though they were both variable and subject to a contingency.

The fact that payments are to be made weekly or monthly does not prevent the payments being "annual" provided they may continue beyond a year.[25] Periodic payments under separation agreements and under orders made by the court, *e.g.* on divorce, are examples of annual payments.

Not all "annual payments" fall within the scope of Case III of Schedule D: see §§ 5–12 *et seq*.

Small maintenance payments[26]

5–05   Small maintenance payments are payments made under an order made by a court in the United Kingdom (a) by one of the parties to a marriage (including a marriage which has been dissolved or annulled) to or for the benefit of the other party to that marriage for that other party's maintenance, or (b) to any person under 21 for his own benefit, maintenance or education (see § 38–18), or (c) to any person for the benefit, maintenance or education of a person under 21. Payments within (a) and (b) must not exceed £48 weekly or £208 monthly. Payments within (c) must not exceed £25 weekly or £108 monthly. Such payments are made without deduction of tax and the recipient is assessable under Case III of Schedule D on payments falling due in the year of assessment. A payment which cannot be taxable in the hands of the recipient under Case III cannot be a small maintenance payment.[26a]

Building society interest

5–05A   There are special provisions which apply to interest paid by building societies, under which interest is deducted by the society which accounts to the Revenue: See § 8–19.

The Finance Act 1984 applies a similar regime ("the composite rate scheme") to interest paid by banks to individuals who are resident in the United Kingdom. These provisions apply from April 6, 1985.[26b] The composite rate scheme applies only to "relevant deposits," as defined, and there are many deposits which are excluded, *e.g.* deposits of £50,000 or more for at least 28 days. The composite rate for 1986–87 is 25.25 per cent.

---

24. [1937] A.C. 785; 21 T.C. 264 (H.L.).

25. *Taylor* v. *Taylor* [1938] 1 K.B. 320.

26. I.C.T.A. 1970, s.65 as amended by F.A. 1982, s.33. The weekly and monthly limits stated in the text apply to all payments falling due after April 5, 1986, whether under orders in force at that date or under orders made, varied or revived after that date: The Income Tax (Small Maintenance Payments) Order 1986 (S.I. 1986 No. 328) in [1986] S.T.1. 89.

26a. *McBurnie* v. *Tacey* [1984] S.T.C. 347 (payment ordered under the Supplementary Benefits Act 1976, s.18 and exempt from tax as a social security contribution under I.C.T.A. 1970, s.219).

26b. F.A. 1984, ss. 26–27 and Sched. 8.

3. THE BASIS OF ASSESSMENT UNDER CASE III

5–06   Generally tax is charged on the full amount (without any deduction) of the income arising in the year preceding the year of assessment.[27]

> Thus if A has a bank deposit account, he is assessed in 1980–81 on the income which arises in 1979–80, *i.e.* on the interest credited to his account in the year 1979–80.

Income does not "arise" until it is received by or credited to the tax-payer[28]: thus if interest is credited half-yearly in June and December, A (in the example) is not taxed in 1980–81 on the interest his deposit earns between the interest date in December 1979 and April 5, 1980; for this interest is credited in June 1980 and is taxed (on the preceding year basis) as income of 1981–82.

If A sells an interest-bearing security to B for a price which includes accrued interest, the interest is not income of A for tax purposes.[29] If B buys an interest-bearing security in (say) May 1980 and he receives interest in respect of the period from (say) February to August 1980, he is liable to income tax on the whole of that interest and not merely on the part accruing after May.[30]

5–07   There are special rules which apply where the taxpayer acquires a fresh source of Case III income or where a source ceases. Normally, in the year when the income first arises and in the next year, the assessment is on the income actually arising in those years.[31]

> Thus if A opens a bank deposit account on May 15, 1980, he is assessed in 1980–81 on the interest credited up to April 5, 1981; and he is assessed in 1981–82 on the interest credited up to April 5, 1982.

In the next year, 1982–83, the normal preceding tax year basis applies[31a] and A is assessed on the interest credited in 1981–82, *i.e.* in the same amounts as for 1981–82; but this is subject to the taxpayer's right to elect that the first assessment on the preceding tax year basis should be adjusted to the actual income arising in that year. The taxpayer has six years in which so to elect.[32]

Where a source of Case III income ceases, tax for the year of cessation is assessed on the income arising in that year, and the assessment for the penultimate year (which will have already been made on the preceding tax year basis) will be adjusted to the actual basis, if this gives a greater tax

---

27. I.C.T.A. 1970, s.119. The examples that follow relate to deposits outside the composite rate scheme in § 5–05A.
28. *Whitworth Park Coal Co. Ltd.* v. *I.R.C.* [1961] A.C. 31; 38 T.C. 531 (H.L.).
29. *Wigmore* v. *Summerson & Sons Ltd.* (1926) 9 T.C. 577. There are provisions to counter avoidance of higher rate tax and investment income surcharge by such sales, if they are systematic: see I.C.T.A. 1970, s.30 and *McCarney* v. *Freilich* (1981) 53 T.C. 575; [1981] S.T.C. 79 (*held*, s.30 does not authorise assessment to basic rate tax) and see I.C.T.A. 1970, ss.469–479.
30. *Schaffer* v. *Cattermole* (1980) 53 T.C. 499; [1980] S.T.C. 650 (C.A.).
31. I.C.T.A. 1970, s.120.
31a. *Moore* v. *Austin* [1985] S.T.C. 673.
32. *Ibid.* s.120(1)(*c*). See *Beese* v. *Mackinlay* [1980] S.T.C. 228.

liability.[33] If the taxpayer acquires a new source, or an addition to an existing source, of Case III income the commencement provisions apply thereto.

> Thus in *Hart* v. *Sangster*[34] it was held that a deposit of £2 million in an existing deposit account constituted a new source of income to which the commencement provisions of Case III applied.

It is understood not to be the practice of the Revenue to apply this principle strictly.

Small maintenance payments are assessed under Case III on a current year basis: see § 5–05.

Deduction of tax at the source

5–08   Interest, annuities and other annual payments taxable under Case III of Schedule D are generally subject to the system by which income tax at the basic rate is deducted by the payer and collected from him by the Revenue. This system is discussed in detail in Section 5 of this chapter.

If interest on a debt is payable subject to deductions of income tax but then ceases to be payable subject to deduction, the debt is treated as a new source of income for the purposes of applying the Case III commencement provisions referred to above. Likewise if the debt begins to be payable subject to deduction of income tax, the cessation provisions apply as if the debt were a source of income which the creditor ceased to possess at that time.[35]

"Receivability without receipt"

5–09   Case III income is taxed on an arising basis and it has been held that income "arises" for this purpose when it is received,[36] or enures for the taxpayer's benefit.[37] Thus if interest, an annuity or other annual payment which is due in a year is not paid in that year, whether through default on the part of the debtor or a waiver of rights before the income arises on the part of the creditor, no Case III income arises in that year: "Receivability without receipt is nothing."[38] Where payment is made by cheque, there is no receipt by the drawee until he receives the proceeds, either in cash or by crediting the sum to his account.[38a]

---

33. *Ibid*. s.120(1)(*c*).
34. (1956) 37 T.C. 231 (C.A.). A transfer of money on deposit with a bank to current account may cause a cessation of the Case III source, namely, the deposit: *Cull* v. *Cowcher* (1934) 18 T.C. 449.
35. I.C.T.A. 1970, ss.120(4), 121(2).
36. See note 28 above.
37. See *Dunmore* v. *McGowan* (1978) 52 T.C. 307; (1978) S.T.C. 217 (C.A.); *Macpherson* v. *Bond* [1985] S.T.C. 678.
38. *Leigh* v. *I.R.C.* [1928] 1 K.B. 73; (1928) 11 T.C. 590, 595, *per* Rowlatt J. And see *Lambe* v. *I.R.C.* [1934] 1 K.B. 178; (1934) 18 T.C. 212; *Dewar* v. *I.R.C.* [1935] 2 K.B. 351; (1935) 19 T.C. 561 (C.A.).
38a. *Parkside Leasing Ltd.* v. *Smith* [1985] S.T.C. 63. and see "More on Receivability and Receipt": [1986] B.T.R. 152 (John Tiley).

5–10   If payment is made in arrears the question arises whether this is Case III income of the year in which payment is made or of the earlier year in which payment was due; and this may be an especially important consideration if the payee's income, or rates of tax, differ in the two years. If the payment is one from which tax is not deducted before receipt, such as interest paid by a bank, the income is income of the year in which payment is made and is taxed on the basis set out in §§ 5–06 *et seq.* If, however, the payment is one from which tax is deducted before receipt, the position differs according to whether deduction is made under section 52, 53 or 54 of the Income and Corporation Taxes Act 1970. In cases where section 52 applies, the income is income of the year in which payment is due; but where section 53 or section 54 applies, it is income of the year when payment was made: see § 8–18.

5–11   Tax reliefs available to the person who makes payments which are Case III income of the payee are governed by similar principles: that is, no relief is given until payment is actually made; and relief is given (broadly speaking) in the same year as that in which the payee is taxed.

4. THE SCOPE OF CASE III

The concept of pure profit income

5–12   The Case III charging provisions give no relief for expenses; indeed, it is assumed that no expense will be incurred in earning Case III income. Where expense has to be incurred in earning income, such income disqualifies itself from treatment as Case III income. The phrase "pure income profit" or "pure profit income" or "pure income" has been used to describe this category of income:

> "The words of Case III . . . make this much plain: that the legislature is there taxing sums which are a profit in the true sense of the word in the hands of the recipient. The full amount is to suffer the tax and there is to be no deduction from the full amount. When I receive interest from my debtor or an annuity from whomsoever is obliged to pay me one, I receive a sum which comes to me in its entirety as a profit. I do not have to set some expenses against the interest or the annuity to find out what the profit content is. It is all profit—at least in contemplation of Case III. To distinguish such a receipt from a receipt against which expenses must be set in order to discover the profit, various expressions are used. Interest and annual payments caught by Case III are said to be income *eo nomine* or 'pure income' or 'profit income.' It does not matter much what label one uses so long as one makes it plain what is being labelled. I will use the term 'profit income' to denote that kind of annual payment which the legislature has in mind under Case III, namely an annual payment which for tax purposes is all profit in the recipient's hands."[39]

5–13   The following examples show what is, and is not, Case III income. By a separation agreement a husband agrees or is ordered to pay his wife £x a year. This is an "annual payment" within Case III of Schedule D. It is pure

---

39. *I.R.C.* v. *Corporation of London* (*as Conservators of Epping Forest*) (1953) 34 T.C. 293, *per* Donovan J. at p. 303 (whose actual decision was reversed by the House of Lords).

profit income of the wife. By contrast, A agrees to pay his garage (B) £x a year in consideration of B agreeing to maintain A's car at no further cost to A. B is a trader taxed under Case I of Schedule D on the excess of his trading receipts (including the £x received from A) over his trading expenses (including the actual cost of maintaining A's car). The £x in this case is not pure profit income of B. Similarly, if C pays his club £x a year and is entitled to certain benefits or facilities in consideration for his subscription, the £x is not pure profit income of the club. In neither of these cases is the £x an annual payment within Case III of Schedule D. The £x is no more than an element to be taken into account in determining the taxable income of the recipient. To such a payment it would be inappropriate to apply the system by which income tax at the basic rate is deducted by the payer (see §§ 5–30 *et seq.*) which applies only to annual payments, etc., within Case III of Schedule D.

5–14 In *Earl Howe* v. *I.R.C.*[40] the question arose whether premiums paid on a policy of assurance were annual payments within the scope of Case III of Schedule D. If they were, Earl Howe (the payer) would have been entitled to deduct them in computing his total income. In a frequently quoted passage Scrutton L.J. said this:

" . . . if a man agrees to pay a motor garage £500 a year for five years for the hire and upkeep of a car, no one suggests the person paying can deduct income tax from each yearly payment. So, if he contracted with a butcher for an annual sum to supply all his meat for a year, the annual instalment would not be subject to tax as a whole in the hands of the payee, but only that part of it which was profits. . . . "

The premiums were thus held not to be Case III income of the payee (in whose hands they were a trading receipt) and the Earl's claim to a deduction failed. The principle so stated by Scrutton L.J., which takes trading and professional receipts outside the ambit of Case III, is sometimes called "the *Earl Howe* principle."

5–15 In the more recent case of *Campbell* v. *I.R.C.*[41] Lord Donovan said that the problem whether an annual payment was Case III income of the recipient

" . . . must continue to be resolved, in my opinion, on the lines laid down by Scrutton L.J. in *Earl Howe's* case. One must determine, in the light of all the relevant facts, whether the payment is a taxable receipt in the hands of the recipient without any deduction for expenses or the like—whether it is, in other words 'pure income' or 'pure profit income' in his hands, as those expressions have been used in the decided cases. If so, it will be an annual pay-

---

40. [1919] 2 K.B. 336; 7 T.C. 289. See also *Asher* v. *London Film Productions Ltd.* [1944] 1 K.B. 33 (where, following the cancellation of his service agreement. A entered into an agreement under which he was to receive 60 per cent. of the takings (if any) in excess of £110,000 from two motion pictures: *held*, to be annual payments from which the payer could properly deduct tax.)
41. [1970] A.C. 77; 45 T.C. 427 (H.L.).

ment under Case III. If, on the other hand, it is simply gross revenue in the recipient's hands, out of which a taxable income will emerge only after his outgoings have been deducted, then the payment is not such an annual payment. . . . "

Payments outside the scope of Case III

The following classes of payment fall outside the scope of Case III of Schedule D:

5–16   (1) *Payments chargeable under Schedule A.* Such payments are expressly excluded by section 109(2) of the Income and Corporation Taxes Act 1970. Thus rentcharges and any other annual payments reserved in respect of, or charged on or issuing out of land in the United Kingdom, are chargeable only under Schedule A: see §§ 6–10 *et seq.*

5–17   (2) *Payments chargeable under Schedule C.* Income from interest-bearing securities payable out of the public revenue which is chargeable under Schedule C is not chargeable under Case III of Schedule D. In practice Schedule C usually applies. Securities chargeable under Case III include $3\frac{1}{2}$ per cent. War Loan and stock held on the National Savings Stock Register or Trustee Savings Bank Register.

5–18   (3) *Payments which are not pure profit income of the recipient.* This concept has been discussed in general terms in §§ 5–12 *et seq.* Payments which are receipts of a trade, profession or vocation carried on by the recipient are not pure profit income of the recipient and so fall outside the scope of Case III. The principle was illustrated in the extract from the speech of Scrutton L.J. in *Earl Howe's* case: (see § 5–14); and it explains why, for example, copyright royalties earned by an author carrying on a vocation as such are not chargeable under Case III.[42]

> In *British Commonwealth International Newsfilm Agency Ltd.* v. *Mahany*[43] the appellant company was set up by the Rank Organisation ("Rank") and the BBC to provide a newsfilm service. Under a deed of covenant Rank and the BBC each agreed to make annual payments to the appellant company equal to half its annual deficit. Pursuant to this covenant Rank paid the appellant company its "share" of the deficit, deducting tax at the standard rate. The appellant company claimed repayment of the tax so deducted, which it could do if the annual payments were Case III income of the appellant company. *Held,* refusing the claim (i) that the payments were trade receipts of the appellant company because they were supplements to its trading revenue and were made to preserve its trading stability: they were trade subsidies; and (ii) that the payments were not therefore Case III income of the appellant company.

5–19   Payments which are made to a non-trader but are made in consideration of the provision of benefits or facilities to the payer are also disqualified from treatment as Case III income. Thus club subscriptions are not Case

---

42. *Stainer's Executors* v. *Purchase* [1952] A.C. 280; 32 T.C. 367 (H.L.); *Carson* v. *Cheyney's Executors* [1959] A.C. 412; 38 T.C. 240 (H.L.).
43. (1962) 40 T.C. 550 (H.L.).

III income and, if they are paid under deduction of tax, the club cannot recover the tax from the Revenue.

> In *I.R.C.* v. *National Book League*,[44] the League (a charity) raised its membership subscription except for members who entered into seven-year covenants to pay their subscriptions at the then existing rates. Club facilities were available to members. A number of members executed covenants expressed as net sums after deduction of tax and the League claimed to recover tax in respect of the sums so paid on the ground that they were annual payments within Case III of Schedule D. *Held*, refusing the claim, that the payments were not annual payments.

The evidence in the *Book League* case

> "clearly established that the so-called annual payment was simply a club subscription in return . . . for the 'annual provision by the League of goods and services,' and so was clearly within the scope of the decision in *Earl Howe's* case."[45]

It should be noted that the principle in the *Earl Howe* case takes trading and professional receipts which are Case I or II income outside the charge under Case III: hence this is not a case in which the Revenue has an option to assess under one case or the other as it chooses.[46]

5–20   It does not follow from the principles stated in §§ 5–18 and 5–19 that *only* income which is pure bounty in the hands of the recipient falls within Case III of Schedule D. If an individual purchases an annuity from an insurance company, this is Case III income of the individual notwithstanding the absence of any bounty towards him; and property can be sold in exchange for an annuity.[47] It is only where the *Earl Howe* principle takes a payment out of the category of pure profit income that Case III does not apply. It is thought that the *Earl Howe* principle does not apply to annuities: see § 5–23.

5–21   The fact that the payee has expense to incur and the payer makes covenanted payments equal to the expense so incurred does not prevent the payments being pure profit income of the payee.[48] Maintenance payments may be related to expenses the payee has to incur.

5–22   *Annual payments to executors and trustees.* Executors or trustees may be rewarded for their services by an annuity or other annual payment. Consistently with the principle in the *Earl Howe* case it appears to be the practice of the Revenue to treat such remuneration as Case III income, except in the case of a professional executor or trustee who brings the payments

---

44. [1957] Ch. 488; 37 T.C. 455 (C.A.).
45. *Campbell* v. *I.R.C.* (1970) 45 T.C. 427, *per* Lord Donovan at p. 474C.
46. *Stainer's Executors* v. *Purchase* (1952) 32 T.C. 367, *per* Jenkins L.J. at pp. 402–403.
47. For other examples, see *Campbell* v. *I.R.C.* (1970) 45 T.C. 427, *per* Lord Donovan at pp. 473–474. See also paras. 5–27 *et seq.*
48. See the *Epping Forest* case *ante*, § 5–12.

into the computation of the profits of his profession under Case II of Schedule D.[49]

5–23   *Interest and annuities.* It is not clear from the Case III charging provision (see § 5–01) if the principle in the *Earl Howe* case applies to interest and annuities or only to annual payments. If the principle were so applied, interest or annuities which formed a constituent part of the trading receipts of a trader would fall outside the scope of Case III and outside the system by which basic rate income tax is deducted by the payer on making the payment: see §§ 5–55 *et seq.* Also the tax relief for interest payments applies only to Case III and bank interest: see §§ 8–57 *et seq.* Interest earned by a trader whose stock-in-trade is money and who earns interest by the use of that money, as by borrowing at one rate and lending at a higher rate, is clearly capable of being a Case I trading receipt. Annuities also are capable of being Case I trading receipts in certain circumstances.[50] If the *Earl Howe* principle applied to interest and annuities, they would be excluded from the Case III charge on the authority of the *British Commonwealth* case discussed in § 5–18. The author is inclined to the view that the *Earl Howe* principle does not apply to interest and annuities. Interest and annuities are in all cases "chargeable" under Case III although, in some cases, they may be charged at the Revenue's option (see § 1–13) under Case I of Schedule D: see also § 8–57. This view appears to accord with Revenue practice. Assume, for example, that interest is paid to a finance company in circumstances where the interest could constitute a trade receipt. Assume that the payer deducts income tax on making the payment, so treating the payment as if Case III applied. Revenue practice is to exclude sums so paid under deduction of tax in computing Case I trading profits but to allow the payer such tax relief as is appropriate to the payment of interest chargeable under Case III: see § 2–49.

5–24   (4) *Payments which are not income of the recipient.* Annual payments which lack the quality of "income" in the hands of the recipient fall outside the scope of Case III of Schedule D, which applies only to income.

> In *Campbell* v. *I.R.C.*[51] a company carrying on business as tutors covenanted for seven years to pay 80 per cent. of its trading profits (less capital allowances) to trustees of a charitable trust, there being an understanding (held on the facts to constitute a legally binding obligation) that the trustees would apply the sums received together with any income tax recoverable in purchasing the company's business. The trustees claimed to recover the tax under what is now section 360(1)(c) of the Income and Corporation Taxes Act 1970 on the ground that the payments were annual payments within Case III of Schedule D which formed part of the income of the trustees. *Held,* that the payments were not income of the trustees.

This was a case, said Lord Donovan (at p. 473C), "where a person wishing

---

49. *Jones* v. *Wright* (1927) 13 T.C. 221.
50. Interest treated as a trading receipt under Case I is taxed in the year of trading: *Bennett* v. *Ogston* (1930) 15 T.C. 374 at p. 379.
51. (1970) 45 T.C. 427 (H.L.).

to sell an asset provides the prospective purchaser with the purchase price. That seems to me as clear a case of a gift of capital as one could want." Viscount Dilhorne reached the same conclusion by a different route (at p. 463C):

> " . . . in my opinion the condition as to the return of the money to (the company) deprived the payments of the character of income just as much as if, instead of the return of the money, the condition or counter-stipulation had been the provision of goods or services by the (trustees to the company)."

The correctness of this approach to the problem may be questioned since the existence of a condition to provide goods or services (as in the *National Book League* case: see § 5–19) does not deprive the payments of the character of income; it merely disqualifies the income from being treated as Case III income: see §§ 5–18 *et seq.*

5–25   *Campbell*[52] was a case in which the company financed the purchase by trustees of an asset which the company owned, the finance being provided by a seven-year covenant. There were three classes of transaction involved: (i) the provision of finance by the company under the covenant; (ii) the application of the covenanted sums in the purchase of the asset from the company; and (iii) the transfer of the asset to the trustees. *Campbell* was concerned only with the character for tax purposes of the payments made to the trustees under (i). The principles which govern the character for tax purposes of the payments made to the company under (ii), *i.e.* the character of annual payments made as the price of an asset, are considered in a later section of this chapter: see § 5–27.

5–26   (5) *Payments which have a source outside the United Kingdom.* Income which arises from securities or possessions out of the United Kingdom is chargeable under Case IV or V of Schedule D and not under Case III.

> Thus in the *Greek Bank* case,[53] the A Bank issued bonds on which interest was payable in London or Athens, at the holder's option. The B Bank guaranteed A's liability under the bonds. The C Bank was universal successor of B. The A and B Banks were incorporated in Greece and neither Bank was resident in or carried on business in the United Kingdom. The C Bank was also incorporated in Greece and not resident in the United Kingdom but carried on business through a branch office in London. The proper law of the bonds and of the guarantee was English law. The C Bank paid interest to the plaintiff and deducted standard rate income tax. The plaintiff sued, claiming that the C Bank had no right to deduct such tax. *Held,* on the facts, that the interest arose from a foreign source and that Case III did not apply. Hence income tax was wrongly deducted.

Annual payments distinguished from instalments of capital

5–27   There is authority for the propositions (1) that if A sells property to B for £10,000 to be paid by instalments of £1,000 without interest, the whole of each instalment is capital; whereas (2) if A sells property to B for 10 instal-

---

52. *Ibid.*
53. *Westminster Bank Executor and Trustee Co.* (*Channel Islands*) v. *National Bank of Greece S.A.* [1971] A.C. 945; 46 T.C. 472 (H.L.).

ments of £1,000 (*i.e.* with no reference to a lump sum), the whole of each instalment is income.[54] Proposition (1) rests on the principle that paying for property by instalments is like paying off a debt by instalments: the instalments take their character as capital from the antecedent debt or the lump sum expressed in the contract.[55] Proposition (2) rests on the principle that if A purchases an annuity with money or money's worth, the annuity is wholly income.

> In *I.R.C.* v. *Ramsay*[56] R. agreed to purchase a dental practice for £15,000. R. was to pay £5,000 at once and the balance by 10 yearly instalments equal to one-fourth of the net profits of the practice in each of those years. If the annual payments came to more or less than the balance of the purchase price (£10,000), that price was to be treated as correspondingly increased or diminished. *Held,* that the yearly payments were capital and were not deductible in computing R.'s total income for surtax purposes.

These propositions have the attraction of simplicity but they fail to take account of the fact that a commercial bargain which provides for payment by instalments over a period of years will invariably require the purchaser to pay interest. Not surprisingly, therefore, there have been a number of cases in which the courts have had to consider whether, if property is sold for a lump sum payable by instalments, the instalments can be dissected into capital and income (being the interest element). If an asset has a market value of £10,000 and payment is to be made by instalments, there are two principal ways in which interest can be included in the instalments:

(a) By the purchaser agreeing to purchase the asset for £10,000 and to pay instalments of £1,000 plus interest at an agreed rate. Assume an instalment comes to £1,200. It is clear that the instalment will be treated for tax purposes as made up of capital (£1,000) and income (£200).[57]

(b) By increasing the lump sum to allow for interest so that, *e.g.* the purchaser agrees to pay (say) £30,000 by 10 instalments of £3,000. In the early case of *Foley* v. *Fletcher*[58] (in which the purchaser treated the whole of each instalment as income, apparently on the ground that some part of it must have represented interest but, since the contract did not enable him to quantify that part, he was entitled to treat the whole as income), the court refused to dissect the instalments into capital and income on the ground that there was no war-

54. *I.R.C.* v. *Ramsay* (1935) 20 T.C. 79, *per* Romer L.J. at p. 98; *I.R.C.* v. *Wesleyan and General Assurance Society* (1948) 30 T.C. 11, *per* Lord Greene M.R. at p. 16.

55. *Dott* v. *Brown* [1936] 1 All E.R. 543 (C.A.); *Jones* v. *I.R.C.* [1920] 1 K.B. 711; 7 T.C. 310. In *I.R.C.* v. *Mallaby-Deeley* (1938) 23 T.C. 153 at p. 169 Sir Wilfrid Greene M.R. said: " . . . If there is a real liability to pay a capital sum, either pre-existing or then assumed, that capital sum has a real existence, and, if the method adopted of paying it is a payment by instalments, the character of those instalments is settled by the nature of the capital sum to which they are related. If there is no pre-existing capital sum, but the covenant is to pay a capital sum by instalments, the same result will follow."

56. (1935) 20 T.C. 79 (C.A.).

57. *Secretary of State for India* v. *Scoble* [1903] A.C. 299; 4 T.C. 618 (H.L.). In this case the instalments were described as an *annuity* but it was held that this did not determine the character of the payments for tax purposes.

58. (1853) 3 H. & N. 769; 157 E.R. 678.

rant for this in the Taxing Acts and held that the whole of each instalment was capital. The significant feature of this case was that there was no *evidence* that the property was worth less than the lump sum provided for in the contract.

In *Vestey* v. *I.R.C.*[59] V. sold shares valued at £2 million for the sum of £5.5 million payable without interest by 125 yearly instalments of £44,000. Although the agreement contained no provision for interest there was evidence before the Commissioners that the shares were worth £2 million; that if one pays £2 million by annual instalments over 125 years with interest on the unpaid balance at 2 per cent. per annum, the instalments amount to £44,000 per annum; and that the purchasers were so advised by an actuary and acted on this advice. *Held*, that the instalments should be dissected into capital and income.

It follows that proposition (1), above, is true only if the lump sum for which the property is agreed to be sold is the value of the property at the time of the contract of sale.

5–28   In *I.R.C.* v. *Church Commissioners*,[60] the Church Commissioners owned properties which were let to Investment Trust Ltd. ("Land Securities") for rents totalling £40,000 per annum. By an agreement of January 5, 1960, the Church Commissioners agreed to sell the properties to Land Securities for yearly rentcharges issuing out of the properties which were payable for 10 years and totalled £96,000 per annum. On paying the rentcharges, Land Securities deducted income tax at the standard rate. The Church Commissioners, being a charity, claimed repayment of the income tax so deducted.

The Revenue rejected the claim on two grounds. First, the claim was rejected on the broad ground (so expressed in argument) that there is a general principle of tax law that where a capital asset is transferred, or a capital obligation is discharged, or a capital payment is made, in consideration of a series of cash receipts of a *fixed amount over a fixed* period, so that the total debt may be immediately calculated, then those cash receipts are, in the hands of the recipient, partly income and partly capital, whether the parties call the series of cash receipts "rent" or "annuity" or "annual sums" or "rent charges" or "instalments," and whether the payments are secured or unsecured. Secondly, the claim was rejected on the narrower ground, and in reliance on the decision in *Vestey* (see § 5–27, above) that the real bargain between the parties as revealed by certain documents which had been admitted in evidence as showing the negotiations leading up to the agreement of January 5, 1960, was such as to require dissection of the rentcharges into an income and capital element.

5–29   The House of Lords unanimously allowed the Church Commissioners' claim, holding, as regards the first ground, that the propositions stated in the first sentence of § 5–27, above, are now too firmly entrenched in tax law to be displaced otherwise than by legislation. As regards the second ground, it was held that on the true construction of the agreement of Janu-

---

59. *Vestey* v. *I.R.C.* (1961) 40 T.C. 112.
60. [1977] A.C. 329; 50 T.C. 516; [1976] S.T.C. 339 (H.L.).

ary 5, 1960, the payments were of an income character and that the admitted evidence merely confirmed that the bargain had always been conceived in income terms. In this respect the present case was distinguishable on its facts from the *Vestey* case which Lord Wilberforce described as "the high water mark of dissection cases." The large difference between the purchase price of £5½ million and the £2 million which represented the value of the shares at the date of the contract, the fact that the payment was spread over 125 years and the absence in the contract in the *Vestey* case of any provision for interest made that case distinguishable from the *Church Commissioners* case. Significantly, too, the Church Commissioners merely replaced one form of income (rents) with another (rentcharge income).

It seems unlikely that the principles outlined above are affected by the decisions in *Ramsay* and *Dawson* in §§ 36–10 *et seq*. A sale for a series of capital instalments cannot be treated as a sale for an annuity, or vice versa.

5. COLLECTION OF TAX AT THE SOURCE: SECTIONS 52 AND 53

5–30   Interest, annuities and other annual payments are the most important forms of income falling under Case III of Schedule D. Annuities and annual payments (and interest in some cases) are subject to the system by which basic rate income tax is deducted by the payer at the time when he makes the payment and collected from him by the Revenue. This system of collection must now be examined in some detail. The system applies to payments made by the Crown: see § 1–17. Interest is separately considered in §§ 5–55 *et seq*. of this chapter.

The Income and Corporation Taxes Act 1970 distinguishes between annuities and other annual payments charged with tax under Case III of Schedule D which are payable out of "profits or gains brought into charge to tax" (s.52) and those not so payable (s.53).

> *Example*
> X, who carries on a trade, covenants to pay £160 to Y on June 30 each year. In the year ended December 31, 1982, X's trading profits are £1,400; in the year ended December 31, 1983, X's profits are nil. These profits are the income of X for the years 1983–84 and 1984–85 respectively. Section 52 applies to the payment of £160 due in 1983–84; section 53 applies to the payment of £160 due in 1984–85.

Payments out of chargeable profits: section 52

5–31   Under section 52 of the Income and Corporation Taxes Act 1970, where any annuity or other annual payment charged with tax under Case III of Schedule D (not being interest) is payable wholly out of profits or gains brought into charge to income[61] tax, the payer is taxed on the whole of his profits without distinguishing the payment. The payer is entitled, on making the payment, to deduct and retain out of it a sum representing the amount of income tax thereon, *i.e.* income tax at the basic rate in force for the year of assessment in which the amount becomes due.[62]

---

61. Thus s.52 does not apply to payments made by companies chargeable to corporation tax: s.53 applies (I.C.T.A. 1970, s.240(4), *post*, § 14–09).
62. I.C.T.A. 1970, s.52(1)(*c*), read with F.A. 1971, s.36(*a*).

Thus, in the example in § 5–30, in the year in which the payment due on June 30, 1983, falls (1983–84), X has sufficient statutory income to support the annual payment. X deducts tax at the basic rate at the time the payment is due (£160 @ (say) 30 per cent. = £48) and pays Y the balance of £112, retaining the amount deducted.

The effect of section 52 can be seen if the position of each of the parties in the example is considered.[63]

5–32   *The payee.* The recipient of an annuity or other annual payment is entitled only to the net amount after deduction of tax at the basic rate for the year in which the payment is due, and is bound (under penalty) to allow the deduction.[64] Payment of the net amount is a full discharge by the payer of his obligation to the payee.[65] The amount deducted is treated as income tax paid by the payee. The gross amount of the payment will enter into the computation of the payee's total income so that (a) if he is not liable to bear tax at the basic rate, he can make a repayment claim; and (b) if he is liable to higher rate income tax, the gross amount forms part of his total income for the year by reference to which basic rate tax was deducted[66]: see §§ 8–16 *et seq.*

5–33   *The payer.* A person who is liable to pay an amount by way of annuity or other annual payment is treated as having alienated part of his income to the payee. In strictness, therefore, if X (having trading income of £5,000) covenants to pay £2,000 annually to Y, Y ought to be assessed on £2,000 (under Case III of Schedule D) and X on £3,000 (under Case I). Section 52 however, directs that X should be assessed on the *whole* of his profits without distinguishing the payment; moreover, the annual payment is not deductible in the computation of X's trading profits, even if it was incurred for the purposes of X's trade.[67] X is relieved from tax on the income he alienates to Y in two ways: (a) when he makes the payment, X is entitled to deduct tax at the basic rate and to retain the amount deducted; (b) X is entitled to deduct the gross amount of the payment (£2,000) in the computation of his total income.

For an example see § 8–33.

Payments not made out of chargeable profits: section 53

5–34   Under section 53 of the Income and Corporation Taxes Act 1970, where any annuity or other annual payment charged with tax under Case III of Schedule D (not being interest) is not payable or not wholly payable out of profits or gains brought into charge to income tax, *i.e.* if it is payable wholly

---

63. For a judicial analysis of ss.52 and 53 (then Rules 19 and 21 respectively) see *Allchin* v. *Corporation of South Shields* [1943] A.C. 607; 25 T.C. 445 (H.L.), *per* Viscount Simon L.C. at pp. 618, 460, respectively; *I.R.C.* v. *Frere* [1965] A.C. 402; 42 T.C. 125 (H.L.), *per* Viscount Radcliffe.
64. I.C.T.A. 1970, s.52(1)(*d*); T.M.A. 1970, s.106; F.A. 1971, s.36(*a*).
65. *Ibid.* s.52(1)(*e*).
66. *Ibid.* s.528(3)(*a*).
67. *Ibid.* s.130(*l*).

or in part out of a source other than profits or gains brought into charge,[68] the person by or through whom the payment is made must, on making the payment, deduct a sum representing the amount of income tax thereon, *i.e.* income tax at the basic rate in force for the year in which the payment is made.[69] Such person must then deliver to the Inspector an account of the payment and an assessment will be duly made to enable the Revenue to collect the tax so deducted.[70] Failure to deliver an account renders the person in default liable to a penalty.

> Thus in the example in § 5–30, in the year in which the payment due on June 30, 1984, fell (1984–85), X had insufficient income to support the annual payment. X deducts tax at the basic rate (under s.53), but must account to the Revenue for the tax deducted.

All the provisions of the Income Tax Acts relating to persons who are to be chargeable with income tax, to income tax assessments, and to the collection and recovery of income tax apply (so far as they are applicable) to the charge, assessment, collection and recovery of income tax under section 53.[71]

5–35   It should be observed that section 53 provides for the assessment of the person "by or through whom" the payment is made. Thus it applies to those who pay as agents as well as to those who pay as principals.

> In *Rye and Eyre* v. *I.R.C.*,[72] the appellants were solicitors of an individual who was about to form a company to produce a play written by M. Sacha Guitry whose usual place of abode was outside the United Kingdom. Under an agreement made by the individual with the author's agent, advance copyright royalties became payable to M. Guitry, which the solicitors remitted in full without deducting tax. Section 53 applied to the payment of royalties by virtue of section 25 of the Finance Act 1927, now section 391 of the Income and Corporation Taxes Act 1970. *Held,* that the solicitors were assessable in respect of the tax they ought to have deducted, for they were persons "through whom" the royalties were paid.

Where a person, acting in one capacity, pays interest to himself in another capacity, this is a payment "through" him.

> Thus in *Howells* v. *I.R.C.*,[73] a solicitor lent money to a builder on the security of properties in the course of development and was entitled to interest. The solicitor later acted for the builder in connection with the sale of the properties and he retained, out of the proceeds of sale, the principal due to him and the *net amount* of interest. *Held,* that the solicitor was liable to account to the Revenue under section 53 for income tax on the interest. [Section 53 then applied to interest as well as to annuities and other annual payments.]

The solicitor in *Howells's* case ought to have retained the gross amount of

---

68. *Ibid.* s.56.
69. F.A. 1971, s.36(*b*). An annuity payable out of a superannuation fund to a U.K. resident may be taxed under Schedule E and not by deduction under s.53: see I.C.T.A. 1970, s.208(3).
70. I.C.T.A. 1970, s.53(2). Such an assessment is not made under any of the Schedules and so falls outside T.M.A. 1970, s.86(2) relating to interest on overdue tax. But see F.A. 1972, s.104 and Sched. 20 and T.M.A. 1970, s.87.
71. I.C.T.A. 1970, s.53(3). See T.M.A. 1970, ss.71 *et seq.*
72. [1935] A.C. 274; 19 T.C. 164 (H.L.).
73. [1939] 2 K.B. 597; 22 T.C. 501.

interest due to him out of which to meet his liability to account for basic rate income tax. Since, in practice, the solicitor in such a case will often have no means of knowing whether section 52 or section 53 applies, it is probably safer to effect the transaction by exchange of cheques, the solicitor accounting to his client for the proceeds of sale and the client accounting to his solicitor for the net amount of interest. In this way the solicitor is exonerated from any possible liability to account for tax.

5–36   The duty to account under section 53 arises only if and when "payment" is actually made.

> In *I.R.C.* v. *Oswald*,[74] it was held that the capitalisation of interest on non-payment thereof by a mortgagor was not a "payment" of interest.

The word "payment" in this context has been said to include everything which is in a commercial sense a "payment," including the making of credit entries in books of account.[75]

Which section applies?

5–37   The question whether section 52 or section 53 of the Income and Corporation Taxes Act 1970 applies to a payment is important to the payer because this determines his title to the sum which he deducts when making the payment. If section 52 applies, he may retain it; but if section 53 applies, he must generally account for it to the Revenue.[76] As regards the payee, if section 52 applies the payment is included in his total income for the year when the payment is *due*; if section 53 applies the payment is included in his total income for the year when the payment is *made*: see § 8–18.

Section 52 applies to a payment which is "payable wholly out of profits or gains brought into charge to tax." Section 53 applies in any other case, *e.g.* if or to the extent that the profits are insufficient to cover the payment or if the payment can lawfully be made only out of capital.[77] Tax in section 52 means income tax, so section 53 applies to payments made by companies chargeable to corporation tax.[78] A payment which is deductible in computing profits chargeable to income tax is not payable *out of* such profits and section 53 applies.

5–38   "Profits or gains brought into charge to income tax" means income determined in accordance with the rules which apply for computing total income: see § 8–16. These rules require that income should be computed in accordance with the charging provisions applicable to the appropriate Schedule.[79] In the case, for example, of a trader whose accounting year ends on December 31 and whose only income is derived from the trade, his

---

74. [1945] A.C. 360; 26 T.C. 435 (H.L.).
75. *Rhokana Corporation Ltd.* v. *I.R.C.* [1937] 1 K.B. 788 at p. 808; 21 T.C. 552 at p. 573, *per* Lord Wright M.R.
76. See *ante*, §§ 5–30 *et seq.* See concession A16 in § 5–42.
77. *Sugden* v. *Leeds Corporation* [1914] A.C. 483; 6 T.C. 211 (H.L.).
78. I.C.T.A. 1970, s.240(4).
79. *Att.-Gen.* v. *L.C.C.* [1901] A.C. 26; 4 T.C. 265 (H.L.).

income for the year 1982–83 will be the profits for the year ended December 31, 1982[80]; and any capital allowances or losses which are brought forward must be deducted from the profits for the purpose of determining whether the payer has sufficient profits or gains brought into charge to support the payment.[81]

5–39   In *Chancery Lane Safe Deposit and Offices Co. Ltd.*v. *I.R.C.*[82] Lord Morris said this:

> " . . . the perplexing words 'payable . . . out of profits or gains brought into charge to tax' were fully analysed in the *Central London* case. The words 'payable out of' are words which might often be used to denote an actual payment out of some actual fund. In [sections 52 and 53] the words involve a different conception. There is a statutory figure of 'profits or gains brought into charge to tax.' It is an assessment based at any rate so far as trading profits are concerned upon the actual results of the previous year. It is not, therefore, an actual fund. If the word 'fund' is used in reference to it it must be classed as a notional fund. An annual payment, on the other hand, is not something notional; it is actual and real. But since, as Lord Macmillan has pointed out, you cannot make an actual payment out of a notional fund the word 'payable' comes to mean notionally payable. It denotes, therefore, a right which the taxpayer may decide to exercise: he may attribute his payment as being within and under the statutory figure of his profits or gains brought into charge to tax. He can say that in paying tax on his profits or gains brought into charge to tax he has paid tax on the amount of a smaller annual payment which he has to make: he may, therefore, deduct tax in making such annual payment: the recipient must allow that deduction if it is made. It may be, however, that the taxpayer cannot link his annual payment with 'profits or gains brought into charge to tax': there may not be any: in that event the annual payment cannot be 'payable out' of them: there cannot be any attribution to them. In that situation the taxpayer must deduct tax when making his annual payment. He is, so to speak, collecting the tax for the Revenue, to whom he must pay it. The same result will follow if the taxpayer firmly decides not to link and in fact does not link his annual payment with profits or gains. This may be so if he decides to make his annual payment out of capital."

5–40   Where the payer of an annuity or other annual payment has a mixed fund of (i) profits or gains brought into charge to income tax and (ii) profits or gains not so charged (*e.g.* capital) and the payment can lawfully be made in full out of either fund, the payment will normally be treated as made out of (i), with the result that section 52 applies, irrespective of the actual resources out of which the payment is made or is shown by the accounts to have been made.[83] Thus in *Postlethwaite* v. *I.R.C.*[84] in which trustees paid an annuity out of a mixed fund consisting of capital and accumulated income, Wilberforce J. said:

---

80. *Att.-Gen.* v. *The Metropolitan Water Board* [1928] 1 K.B. 833; 13 T.C. 294 (C.A.).
81. *Trinidad Petroleum Development Co. Ltd.* v. *I.R.C.* [1937] 1 K.B. 408; 21 T.C. 1 (C.A.); thus when losses are brought forward under I.C.T.A. 1970, s.171 (*post* § 12–02), and profits are rendered insufficient to cover annual payments, s.53 applies.
82. [1966] A.C. 85; 43 T.C. 83 (H.L.). See also Lord Wilberforce in *I.R.C.* v. *Plummer* [1980] A.C. 896 at p. 909; 54 T.C. 1 at p. 41A, (comment on "the second argument").
83. *Edinburgh Life Assurance Co.* v. *Lord Advocate* [1910] A.C. 143; 5 T.C. 472; *Sugden* v. *Leeds Corporation* [1914] A.C. 483; 6 T.C. 211 (H.L.); *Allchin* v. *Coulthard* [1942] 2 K.B. 228 at pp. 233 *et seq.*; [1943] A.C. 607 at p. 626; 25 T.C. 445 at p. 465.
84. (1963) 41 T.C. 224.

" . . . I think it is not disputed that, there being in the trustees' accounts a mixed fund consisting partly of capital and partly of taxed income, and the trustees not having made any express declaration as to how the annuity was to be paid, it is open to the taxpayer [in that case the annuitant] to claim that payment has been made out of that portion of the trust fund which yields him the most favourable result for the purposes of taxation. That follows from the analogy of *Sugden* v. *Leeds Corporation*; and following that, it would be open to the taxpayer to say that the payment must be considered as having been made out of the former income element of the fund. I think it is accepted by both sides that the manner in which the trust accounts have been presented is not material in this respect."

5-41   Where, however, the payer of an annuity or other annual payment has secured some fiscal or other advantage by debiting the payment to capital[85] or has made a deliberate decision to charge the payment to capital,[86] section 53 applies even though the payer has sufficient taxed income to support the payment.

Thus in *Chancery Lane Safe Deposit and Offices Co. Ltd.* v. *I.R.C.*,[87] the appellant company borrowed to finance building works. Interest on the borrowings was charged to capital so as not to reduce the fund distributable as dividend. *Held*, that the company could not make an inconsistent attribution for tax purposes.

5-42   If in the year when a payment is due and made the payer has insufficient chargeable income to cover the payment, the payer cannot avoid the consequences of section 53 by relating the payment back to accumulated profits of earlier years.

Thus in *Luipaard's Vlei Estate and Gold Mining Co. Ltd.* v. *I.R.C.*[88] a company made no profits for four years. During those years the company paid debenture interest and deducted tax. [Section 53 then applied to interest.] The Revenue sought to recover from the company the tax so deducted (on the basis that section 53 applied to the payments), but the company contended that the debenture interest should be treated as having been paid out of the accumulated profits of past years. It was held that only profits of the year when the interest was paid could be regarded as profits out of which the debenture interest was paid. "You cannot look for the fund brought into charge to tax outside the year in which the interest is paid and the amount deducted. . . . "

There is a concession (A16) under which, where annuities, annual payments, etc. (other than interest) are paid in a later year than the due year but in the due year could have been paid wholly or partly out of taxed income, an allowance is made, in fixing the amount to be paid over under

---

85. *Corporation of Birmingham* v. *I.R.C.* [1930] A.C. 307; 15 T.C. 172 (H.L.) (corporation paid interest out of an account drawn to show a deficit recoverable from Exchequer subsidy. Cost of interest shown as gross amount, *i.e.* consistent only with [section 53]. *Held*, that corporation could be assessed).
86. *Central London Ry.* v. *I.R.C.* [1937] A.C. 77; 20 T.C. 102 (H.L.); applied in *B. W. Nobes & Co. Ltd.* v. *I.R.C.* (1965) 43 T.C. 133 (H.L.); *Chancery Lane Safe Deposit and Offices Co. Ltd.* v. *I.R.C.* [1966] A.C. 85; 43 T.C. 83 (H.L.); *Fitzleet Estates Ltd.* v. *Cherry* (1977) 51 T.C. 708; [1977] S.T.C. 95. For payments made by companies liable to corporation tax, see *post*, § 14–10(1).
87. [1966] A.C. 85; 43 T.C. 83 (H.L.).
88. [1930] 1 K.B. 593; 15 T.C. 573 (C.A.).

section 53, for the tax which the payer would have been entitled (under section 52) to deduct and retain if the payments had been made at the due dates.

5–43   *Foreign cases.* Where the proper law of a deed is English law, the position *as between the parties* is that the payer (whether resident within or outside the United Kingdom) is entitled to deduct tax from an annual payment, whether it is payable within or out of the United Kingdom. There is no such right of deduction in the case of a deed the proper law of which is foreign law.[89–90] Note the words in italics. The position may arise when the payer is bound as a matter of contract law to make his payments without deducting tax; but he may nevertheless be bound to account to the Revenue for income tax. *Proper* law is not the key factor in determining the Revenue's right to assess: see § 5–26.

Foreign currency loans to United Kingdom residents commonly include a grossing-up provision under which (in effect) the lender, if assessed to United Kingdom tax, can recover the amount assessed from the borrower.

6. FAILURE TO DEDUCT TAX

5–44   What is the position if a person paying an annuity or other annual payment fails to deduct tax, as he is entitled to do under section 52 of the Income and Corporation Taxes Act 1970 or bound to do under section 53?

(1) *As between payer and payee*

Generally the payer cannot recover the tax by action from the payee, for this is a case of money paid voluntarily under a mistake of law.[91] The payer has a remedy in only three cases:

(a) Where payments are made by instalments, any under-deduction during a tax year can be made good out of any subsequent payments in the same tax year.[92]

(b) Where the basic rate of tax is increased by the Finance Act, so that tax is under-deducted from earlier payments, an adjustment can be made in the next payment after the passing of the Act. If there is no "next payment," the amount under-deducted may be recovered as if it were a debt.[93]

(c) Where the failure to deduct (or under-deduction) is through a mistake of fact.[94]

89–90. *Keiner* v. *Keiner* (1952) 34 T.C. 346. (H. by a deed executed in America, agreed to make payments to his divorced wife. H, when resident in the U.K., deducted tax in reliance on what are now ss.52 and 53. *Held*, that H had no right to deduct tax).
91. *Re Hatch* [1919] 1 Ch. 351.
92. *Taylor* v. *Taylor* [1938] 1 K.B. 320 (C.A.), explained in *Hemsworth* v. *Hemsworth* [1946] K.B. 431. *Cf. Johnson* v. *Johnson* [1946] P. 205 (C.A.).
93. I.C.T.A. 1970, s.521. As to overdeductions in the year 1986–87, when the basic rate was reduced from 30 to 29 per cent., see I.C.T.A. 1970, s.522 and (1986) S.T.I. 171.
94. *Turvey* v. *Dentons (1923) Ltd.* [1953] 1 Q.B. 218.

(2) *As between the parties and the Revenue*

5–45   Failure to deduct income tax at the basic rate in a case to which section 52 applies does not normally concern the Revenue, for the Revenue recover the tax in the assessment on the profits or gains of the payer, the whole of which are taxed without distinguishing the annuity or other annual payment.[95] Failure to deduct in a case to which section 53 applies does, however, concern the Revenue who may either (i) assess the payee under section 53 in the year in which the payment is made, or (ii) assess the payee[96] under the Schedule and Case appropriate to the nature of the income and in accordance with the rules applicable thereto[97]: thus an annuity or other annual payment may be assessed under Case III of Schedule D on the basis discussed in §§ 5–06 *et seq.* Failure to deduct will not expose the payer to any penalty, notwithstanding that under section 53 the obligation to deduct is mandatory. In no case can relief be claimed under section 33 of the Taxes Management Act 1970,[98] for a failure to deduct is not an error or mistake in a return or statement made by the payer for purposes of assessment.

5–46   In practice, a person who pays an annuity or annual payment gives the payee a certificate stating the gross amount of the payment, the amount of income tax deducted, and the actual amount paid. He is bound to give such a certificate on the request in writing of the recipient, who may enforce the due performance of this duty.[99] Where no such certificate is given, it may be uncertain whether the recipient is to be treated as having received untaxed income (in which case he could be assessed to basic rate tax) or income taxed by deduction at source.

5–47   Where the recipient of an annual payment is assessed the onus lies on him to show either that the payment was made out of profits or gains brought into charge to tax, or alternatively, that the payment was a net amount from which tax had been deducted.[1]

In *Stokes* v. *Bennett*[2] a husband resident abroad had been ordered by an Eng-

---

95. For an example of a case in which the Revenue was unable to recover tax from the payer, see *Hume* v. *Asquith* (1968) 45 T.C. 251 (as regards the B royalties). At that time the payee could not be assessed where [section 53] applied. There is no longer any prohibition against assessment of the payee: I.C.T.A., 1970, s.52(1), (*a*), was repealed as from 1973–74 by F.A. 1971, ss.37(2), 38 and Sched. 14, Pt. II.

96. *Lord Advocate* v. *Edinburgh Corporation* (1905) 7 F. (Ct. of Sess.) 972.

97. *Grosvenor Place Estates Ltd.* v. *Roberts* [1961] Ch. 148; 39 T.C. 433 (C.A.); where a tenant under a long lease failed to deduct tax as required by the now repealed s.177 of the Income Tax Act 1952: *held*, that the landlord could be assessed under Case VI of Schedule D.

98. See *post*, § 17–09.

99. I.C.T.A. 1970, ss.55 and 232(4), relating to payments by companies.

1. See *Hume* v. *Asquith* (1968) 45 T.C. 251 at pp. 271–272 (as regards the C royalties) where the appellant taxpayer failed to discharge this onus.

2. *Stokes* v. *Bennett* [1953] Ch. 566; 34 T.C. 337. *Cf. Hemsworth* v. *Hemsworth* [1946] K.B. 431, where apparently the covenantee was expressed to be entitled to a gross amount and Denning J. held that, in the absence of notification that tax had been deducted, the payment must be taken to have been made without deduction. And see *Butler* v. *Butler* [1961] P. 33 (C.A.).

lish divorce court to pay his wife £22 per month free of tax. (It was agreed that an order in that form was to be construed as an order to pay a gross sum of such an amount as after deducting tax would leave £22.) There was no evidence that the husband had any English income which had suffered United Kingdom income tax; nor was there evidence that he had ever purported to deduct tax. However, the order of the court referred to a net sum and the husband had in fact paid that sum over some years. *Held*, that the husband must be presumed to have paid a net sum after deduction of standard rate tax, so that no assessment to standard rate tax could be raised on the wife under Case III. [The "standard" rate was the equivalent of "basic" rate under the preunified system: see § 1–19.]

7. TAX FREE PAYMENTS

5–48   A person who agrees to make annual payments may wish to ensure that the payee receives a fixed amount of, say, £x per annum, neither more nor less. Such a wish is commonly expressed in connection with separation agreements. This objective is not easy to achieve; for if A agrees to pay B £x per annum, B is entitled only to £x less tax at the basic rate, which may vary from year to year; and if A agrees to pay B in full without deduction of tax this provision is ineffective. This is because under section 106(2) of the Taxes Management Act 1970 every agreement for payment of interest, rent or other annual payment in full without allowing any deduction authorised by the Taxes Acts is void. The subsection does not make the agreement void *in toto*, but only the provision for non-deduction of tax[3]; so that, in the result, B is entitled to £x less tax, as before. The prohibition in section 106(2) applies only to *agreements*, such as a separation agreement, a deed of covenant (even if unilateral) and any settlement which contains an element of bargain.[4] It does not apply, for example, to wills. The effect of section 106(2) is that only an agreement to pay a taxable sum is permissible,[5] but formulae can be devised which will satisfy this requirement and yet, at the same time, provide the recipient with a sum which will remain constant despite changes in the basic rate of income tax. The conventional formula provides for the payment of

> such a sum as after the deduction of income tax at the basic rate for the time being in force will leave the sum of £x per annum in the payee's hands.

5–49   This takes effect as a covenant to pay an amount equal to £x grossed up at the current basic rate[6]: the payee receives a constant annual sum of £x irrespective of changes in the basic rate of tax (hence payment by bankers' order can be easily arranged) and the only variable factor is the gross cost of the agreement to the grantor and the amount which is deductible in computing his total income.[7] Thus if the agreement provides for a net annual sum of £500, the gross cost will be £704.23 if the basic rate is 29 per cent.

---

3. In *Whiteside* v. *Whiteside* [1950] Ch. 65 (C.A.), the court refused rectification of an instrument which infringed s.106(2).
4. *Brooke* v. *Price* [1917] A.C. 115 (settlement following a divorce). *Cf. Re Goodson's Settlement* [1943] Ch. 101.
5. *Re Maclennan* [1939] 1 Ch. 750, 755.
6. *I.R.C.* v. *Cook* [1946] A.C. 1; 26 T.C. 489.
7. As to total income, see Chap. 8.

and £714.29 if the basic rate is 30 per cent.[8] Two points should be noted in connection with the conventional formula:

(1) If the payee is liable to higher rate income tax on the covenanted sum (which must be grossed up at the basic rate for the purpose of computing the payee's total income: see § 8–18), the payer is not bound to indemnify the annuitant in respect of such tax[9];

(2) if the payee is entitled to claim repayment in respect of the tax notionally deducted by the payer, he is not accountable to the payer for the tax so reclaimed.[10]

It follows that where the conventional formula is used, the recipient who is liable to tax in excess of the basic rate will be left with £x less the amount of tax in excess of the basic rate which is attributable to £x; whereas the recipient who is not a basic rate taxpayer will be left with £x plus any repayment due in respect of tax deducted at the basic rate. Practically speaking this is unavoidable. Forms of words other than those referred to as "the conventional formula" may be used but care should be taken to ensure that the consequences referred to in (1) and (2) ensue. An agreement to pay a specified sum "free of tax" has been held to oblige the payer to pay such a sum as after deduction of income tax at the basic rate equals the specified sum.[11]

Wills

5–50   The provisions of section 106(2) of the Taxes Management Act 1970 do not apply to wills and there is accordingly no objection to a testator directing the payment of an annuity of £x per annum tax free. This takes effect as a direction to pay such a sum as after deduction of tax at the basic rate will leave £x. In practice, however, tax free annuities in wills should be avoided for two reasons:

(1) The words "tax free" mean free of all income tax, so that if in any year the annuitant is liable to tax at any rate in excess of the basic rate, the trustees must indemnify him in respect of the amount of such tax which is attributable to the gross amount of the annuity.[12]

(2) The annuitant may be accountable to the deceased's personal representatives or will trustees for a proportion of any repayment which he receives.

> In *Re Pettit*,[13] an annuity was given by will free of duty and income tax. The annuitant was not liable to tax at the standard rate and recovered part of the tax which he had suffered by deduction in respect of the annuity. *Held*, that he was not entitled to retain the whole of the tax so

---

8. To "gross up" £500 when the basic rate is (say) 30 per cent., multiply by 100 and divide the result by 70 (100 minus 30).
9. *Re Bates* [1925] Ch. 157 where the earlier cases were reviewed.
10. *Re Jones* [1933] Ch. 842.
11. *Ferguson* v. *I.R.C.* [1970] A.C. 442; 46 T.C. 1 (H.L.).
12. *Re Reckitt* [1932] 2 Ch. 144 (C.A.); *Re Bates* in note 9, *supra*. For a glimpse of the difficulties which can arise, see *I.R.C.* v. *Duncanson* (1949) 31 T.C. 257.
13. [1922] 2 Ch. 765. See also *Re Lyons* [1952] Ch. 129.

reclaimed, but was accountable to the trustees for a proportion thereof. This is the proportion which the gross amount of the annuity bears to the annuitant's total gross income.[14]

The annuitant in such a case is under a duty to the trustees to make the necessary claim for repayment[14]; and an annuitant who is a married woman can be compelled to apply for separate assessment.[15]

Court orders

5–51   A court order, not being an agreement, may provide for the making of tax free payments.[16] An order to pay £x "tax free" obliges the payer to pay such a sum as after deduction of income tax at the basic rate equals £x.[17] It is common practice in divorce proceedings, however, to order the payment of a sum "less tax."[18] An order to pay £x less tax takes effect as an order to pay £x from which sum the payer will deduct tax at the basic rate under section 52 or section 53 of the Income and Corporation Taxes Act 1970, as appropriate. The rule in *Re Pettit* does not apply to court orders.[19]

Small maintenance payments are subject to special provisions.[20]

Pre-war tax free annuities

5–52   By section 422 of the Income and Corporation Taxes Act 1970, any provision made[21] before September 3, 1939, and not varied on or after that date, for the payment of a stated amount free of income tax, is to take effect in each year of assessment as if the stated amount were reduced in accordance with the following fraction:

The stated amount $\times \dfrac{100 - A}{72.5}$ where A is the basic rate of income tax for the year expressed as a percentage.

8. PURCHASED LIFE ANNUITIES

5–53   Until 1956, when a life annuity was purchased, the entire annuity was taxed as income of the annuitant, no account being taken of the capital content in the payments. Through recommendations in the Report of the Committee on the Taxation Treatment of Provisions for Retirement,[22] section 27 of the Finance Act 1956 was passed (now section 230 of the Income and Corporation Taxes Act 1970) providing that the capital element in each periodic payment of a purchased life annuity should be exempt from tax. The

---

14. *Re Kingcome* [1936] Ch. 566, where the court made a declaration that the annuitant was a trustee of her statutory right to recover the overpaid tax.

15. *Re Batley* [1952] 1 All E.R. 1036.

16. *Spilsbury* v. *Spofforth* (1937) 21 T.C. 247; *cf. Blount* v. *Blount* [1916] 1 K.B. 230; *Burroughes* v. *Abbott* [1922] 1 Ch. 86 (agreements made to give effect to court orders).

17. *Ferguson* v. *I.R.C.* [1970] A.C. 442.

18. *Wallis* v. *Wallis* [1941] P. 69.

19. *Jefferson* v. *Jefferson* [1956] P. 136.

20. *Ante*, § 5–05.

21. Where an annuity is granted by will, provision is "made" when the testator dies, not when the will is executed: *Berkeley* v. *Berkeley* [1946] A.C. 555. See also *Re Westminster's Deed of Appointment* [1959] Ch. 265 (C.A.).

22. Cmd. 9063, paras. 496–505.

capital content is found by dividing the purchase price of the annuity by the normal expectation of life of the annuitant at the date when the annuity commences, and this remains constant throughout the life of the annuitant. Tax is then charged each year on the amount by which the annuity payment exceeds this annual capital content, whether or not the annuitant survives the period of normal expectation. The question whether an annuity is subject to these provisions, and the amount of the capital content, is determined by the Inspector, subject to a right of appeal.[23]

Exceptions[24]

5-54   The following annuities are excepted from these provisions:

(1) An annuity which would in any event be treated wholly or partly as capital. An annuity for a *fixed term* is so treated.

(2) Annuities granted in consideration of sums which qualify for relief under the provisions relating to retirement annuities[25] or for life assurance relief.[26] A life annuity which also combines a life policy is within this exception.

(3) Annuities purchased in pursuance of any direction in a will, or to provide for an annuity payable by virtue of a will or settlement out of income of property disposed of by the will or settlement (whether with or without resort to capital).

(4) Annuities purchased under a sponsored superannuation scheme[27] or approved trust scheme,[28] or an annuity purchased in recognition of another's services (or past services) in any office or employment. The full amount of the annuity is taxable but, in the latter case, may be treated as earned income.[29]

9. INTEREST

5-55   Until the Finance Act 1969 the system of deduction of tax at source which now applies to annuities and annual payments applied also to interest, except that for some purposes a distinction was made between "yearly" or "annual" and "non-yearly" or "short" interest. The pre-1969 system is not further discussed in this book.[30] Suffice it to say that sections 52 and 53 of the Income and Corporation Taxes Act 1970 now expressly exclude interest. All interest of money, whether yearly or otherwise, and whether payable within or out of the United Kingdom, is chargeable under Case III of Schedule D,[31] provided the instrument under which the obligation to pay interest arises does not create a foreign source of income outside the scope

---

23. See I.C.T.A. 1970, ss.230–231; Income Tax (Purchased Life Annuities) Regulations 1956 (S.I. 1956 No. 1230).
24. I.C.T.A. 1970, s.230(7).
25. *Ibid.* s.227.
26. *Ibid.* s.19; *post*, § 8–54.
27. *Ibid.* s.226.
28. *Ibid.* s.226(5), (6).
29. See *post*, § 8–07.
30. For the pre-1969 law, see the 3rd edition of this book.
31. I.C.T.A. 1970, s.109; see § 5–01.

of the Schedule D charge.[32] Interest is payable in full without deduction of tax, except where statute otherwise provides.

These statutory provisions are to be found:

(1) in section 54 of the Income and Corporation Taxes Act 1970: see §§ 5–56 to 5–58; and

(2) in section 26 of and Schedule 7 to the Finance Act 1982 under which, on and after April 1 1983, mortgage interest will in most cases be payable under deduction of tax: see §§ 8–60C and 8–65.

5–56   Section 54 applies where any yearly interest of money chargeable to tax under Case III is paid

(a) otherwise than in a fiduciary or representative capacity, by a company or local authority, or

(b) by or on behalf of a partnership of which a company is a member, or

(c) by any person to another person whose usual place of abode is outside the United Kingdom.[33]

In these three cases, the person by or through whom the payment is made is bound, on making the payment, to deduct out of it a sum representing the amount of income tax thereon at the basic rate for the year in which the payment is made,[34] except that this requirement does not apply:

(i) to interest payable in the United Kingdom on an advance from a bank carrying on a bona fide banking business in the United Kingdom, or

(ii) to interest paid by such a bank in the ordinary course of that business, or[35]

(iii) to interest paid on a quoted Eurobond (defined as a bearer security carrying a right to interest which is quoted on a recognised stock exchange and issued by a company.[35a]

In these cases the interest is paid without deduction of tax. Exception (i) applies only where the interest is paid by the person to whom the advance is made; it does not apply to payments made by a guarantor under a guarantee.[36] Exception (iii) applies only where the person by or through whom the payment is made is not in the United Kingdom. Payment can be made without deduction by a person in the United Kingdom, but only if the beneficial owner of the interest is not resident in the United Kingdom or the bond is held in a recognised clearing system.[36a]

---

32. See *ante*, § 5–26.
33. If a solicitor pays interest gross on the faith of an assurance by the recipient's solicitor that to the best of his knowledge the recipient's usual place of abode is in the United Kingdom, the Revenue will not hold the paying solicitor accountable for the tax that ought to have been deducted: see I.R. statement in (1981) 78 L.S.Gaz. 1022.
34. I.C.T.A. 1970, s.54(1), as amended by F.A. 1971, s.37 and Sched. 6, para. 22. As to payments "through" others, see *ante*, § 5–35.
35. I.C.T.A. 1970, s.54(2).
35a. See F.A. 1984, s.35 and S.T.I. (1983) 552. And see SP 8/84 in [1984] S.T.I. 707.
36. *Holder* v. *I.R.C.* [1932] A.C. 624; 16 T.C. 540 (H.L.). As to whether a payment by a guarantor is itself a payment of "interest" see § 5–02A.
36a. See F.A. 1984, s.35 and [1983] S.T.I. 552.

Where a bank carrying on a *bona fide* banking business in the United Kingdom makes a loan in foreign currency carrying yearly interest on such terms that the interest falls to be brought into account as a trading receipt of the business carried on in the United Kingdom (and it is brought into account accordingly), the interest is in practice treated for the purposes of Section 54 (and Section 251) as payable in the United Kingdom and consequently not liable to deduction of income tax at source, notwithstanding any provision on the loan agreement for payment to be made by the debtor abroad.[37]

Where there is an obligation to deduct tax under section 54, the provisions in section 53 relating to the obligation to render an account to the Inspector apply.[38] The Inland Revenue have published a statement summarising the duties and liabilities of solicitors who pay interest to clients under the Solicitors' Account (Deposit Interest) Rules 1975.[39]

5–57   *Yearly and short interest.* Section 54 of the Income and Corporation Taxes Act 1970 applies only to "yearly interest." Non-yearly or "short" interest is always payable in full without deduction of tax. The main factor which determines whether interest is "yearly" or "short" is the degree of permanence of the loan[40]: if the obligation to pay interest is to continue for less than a year, the interest is "short" interest. Interest paid on unpaid purchase money when completion is delayed has been held to be yearly interest.[41] Interest on damages is yearly interest.[42]

5–58   *Bank interest.* Interest paid on an advance from a bank carrying on a bona fide banking business in the United Kingdom is payable without deduction, whether the interest is yearly or short.

Tax relief for interest paid is discussed in §§ 8–57 *et seq.*

10. PATENTS AND COPYRIGHTS

Patents

5–59   Sections 52 and 53 of the Income and Corporation Taxes Act 1970, relating to deduction of basic rate income tax, which are discussed *ante*, §§ 5–30 *et seq.*, apply to "any royalty or other sum paid in respect of the user of a patent."[43] A *royalty* commonly assumes the form of a periodic payment made to an inventor by a manufacturer under an agreement by which the inventor grants to the manufacturer a licence (exclusive or non-exclusive)

---

37. SP 6/1973.
38. *Ibid*. s.54(3); see *ante*, § 5–34.
39. See (1981) 78 L.S.Gaz. 1022.
40. *Hay* v. *I.R.C.* (1924) 8 T.C. 636; *I.R.C.* v. *Frere* [1965] A.C. 402; 42 T.C. 125 (H.L.); *Corinthian Securities Ltd.* v. *Cato* [1970] 1 Q.B. 377; 46 T.C. 93 (C.A.). In *Cairns* v. *Macdiamid* (1983) 56 T.C. 556; [1983] S.T.C. 178 a tax avoidance transaction included the payment of interest on a loan in circumstances where the loan was not intended to last for more than a few days. *Held*, that the interest was not annual interest.
41. *Bebb* v. *Bunny* (1854) 1 K. & J. 216; 69 E.R. 436.
42. *Jefford* v. *Gee* [1970] 2 Q.B. 130, at p. 149C.
43. I.C.T.A. 1970, ss.52(2)(*a*) and 53(1)(*b*).

to exploit the inventor's patent; and the royalty may be an agreed sum for each article manufactured or produced. The words *other sum* include a lump sum awarded to an inventor in respect of the past user of a patent.[44] In one case a non-exclusive licence to use a patent was granted in consideration of the payment of a lump sum plus a royalty and it was held (contrary to the taxpayer's contention) that the lump sum was an income receipt notwithstanding that there was no evidence that the lump sum was arrived at by reference to some anticipated quantum of user.[45] The phrase "royalty or other sum" does not include capital payments, such as a lump sum payment for the grant of an *exclusive* licence[46]; but such a payment may be assessable under section 380 of the Income and Corporation Taxes Act 1970 (see § 5–61) or may be liable to capital gains tax.

5–60   Patent royalties, like annual payments, are payable less income tax at the basic rate. Patent royalties may be "annual payments" within Case III of Schedule D; but in most cases they are trade or professional receipts and therefore lack the quality of being pure profit income of the recipient.[47] Where a lump sum royalty or other payment is made in respect of the past user of a patent, there are provisions which allow the payee to spread the payment backwards over a period of years corresponding to the period of past user.[48]

5–61   Where a person resident in the United Kingdom sells any patent rights for a capital sum, he is chargeable under Case VI of Schedule D; but the sum may be "spread forward" over a period of six years.[49] If in a similar case the vendor is not resident in the United Kingdom and the patent is a United Kingdom patent, the vendor is chargeable under Case VI but the purchaser is entitled to deduct tax under section 53 of the Income and Corporation Taxes Act 1970 as if the capital sum were an annual sum payable otherwise than out of profits or gains charged to tax.[50] If the purchaser is also non-resident, his liability to account for the amount he deducts may be difficult to enforce.

Copyrights

5–62   Sections 52 and 53 of the Income and Corporation Taxes Act 1970 do not apply to copyright royalties, which are payable in full without deduction of tax. If the recipient is an author by profession and the royalties are receipts of that profession, they are taxed under Case II of Schedule D or, if the

---

44. *Constantinesco* v. *R.* (1927) 11 T.C. 730 (H.L.); *Mills* v. *Jones* (1929) 14 T.C. 769 (H.L.).
45. *Rustproof Metal Window Co.* v. *I.R.C.* (1947) 29 T.C. 243 (C.A.). See also *Murray* v. *I.C.I. Ltd.* [1967] Ch. 1038; 44 T.C. 175 (C.A.).
46. *British Salmson Aero Engines Ltd.* v. *I.R.C.* (1938) 22 T.C. 29 (C.A.).
47. *Rank Xerox Ltd.* v. *Lane* [1979] Ch. 113; (1978) 53 T.C. 185; [1978] S.T.C. 449 (C.A.). This point was not in issue in the House of Lords.
48. I.C.T.A. 1970, s.384.
49. *Ibid.* s.380(1).
50. *Ibid.* s.380(2).

profession has ceased, as post-cessation receipts.[51] If the recipient is not an author by profession, the royalties may be taxable under Case VI of Schedule D.[52]

Where an author assigns the copyright in a work, wholly or partially, or grants an interest in the copyright by licence, and he receives a lump sum payment (including a non-returnable advance on account of royalties), the sum is taxable as a receipt of his profession by reference to the year in which it is received, or under Case VI of Schedule D.[53] In the absence of specific relief, the lump sum might therefore be swallowed in tax as income of a single year of assessment. Two alternative forms of relief are available:

5–63   (1) *Relief by spreading the payment backwards*[54]: If the author was engaged on the making of a literary, dramatic, musical or artistic work for a period of more than 12 months, he can claim to spread the lump sum payment backwards over a period of two or three years depending on the period of engagement on the making of the work. If this exceeded 24 months, the lump sum can be treated as if it had been received in three equal annual instalments, the last being received on the date of actual receipt; if it was less than 24 months, the lump sum can be treated as received in two such instalments. A claim for the relief should be made to the Inspector.[55]

5–64   (2) *Relief by spreading the payment forwards*[56]: This relief applies only to the case where the author etc. of the established work sells the residual rights in that work. If not less than 10 years after the first publication of a work the author assigns the copyright therein, wholly or partially, or grants an interest in the copyright by licence in consideration of a lump sum payment (including a non-returnable advance on account of royalties), and the duration of the assignment or grant is not less than two years, he can claim to spread the payment forwards over a period of years depending on the duration of the grant or licence. Except where the duration is less than six years, the payment can be treated as becoming receivable in six equal annual instalments, the first being received on the date of actual receipt; if the duration is less than six years, the payment can be treated as becoming receivable in equal annual instalments corresponding to the number of whole years throughout the duration of the assignment or grant. The relief is available in the case of payments falling to be included in computing profits or gains for the year 1967–68 or any subsequent year of assessment. There are special provisions to meet the cases where, during the period of

---

51. Discussed, *ante*, §§ 2–88 *et seq.*
52. See *ante*, §§ 4–02 *et seq.*
53. *Mackenzie* v. *Arnold* (1952) 33 T.C. 363 (C.A.). The rule in *Sharkey* v. *Wernher* (*ante*, § 2–46) does not apply to an assignment by way of gift or at an undervalue: *Mason* v. *Innes* [1967] Ch. 1079; 44 T.C. 326 (C.A.). The transaction would be a capital gains tax disposal, credit being given in computing the capital gains tax payable for income tax on any sum received by the assignor.
54. I.C.T.A. 1970, s.389.
55. T.M.A. 1970, s.42 and Sched. 2.
56. I.C.T.A. 1970, s.390.

"spread," the author dies or his profession is otherwise permanently discontinued.

Relief is not available under one of the above heads if relief has already been claimed under the other head.

CHAPTER 6

THE TAXATION OF INCOME FROM LAND:
SCHEDULES A AND B

1. INTRODUCTION

6–01 THE feudal structure of English society in the early years of development of the common law made land the subject of special treatment under English law, and it is not surprising that income from land should be differentiated from other sources of income under the Income Tax Acts. The taxation of income from land was put on an entirely new basis by the Finance Act 1963 which became fully effective in and from the year 1964–65, and this chapter is concerned principally with the provisions of that Act, which have now been incorporated in the Income and Corporation Taxes Act 1970. In order that the effect of these provisions may be fully understood, the reader must know something of the law which previously applied and it is the purpose of this Introduction to summarise, in broad outline, the pre–1963 law.

Income from land was taxed under Schedules A and B. Schedule A in its pre–1963 form was a tax on income from the ownership of land capable of actual occupation, except that certain quarries, mines and other concerns were excluded from the charge. For the purpose of taxing income from land, all property in the United Kingdom had a gross annual value representing the value at which it was worth to be let by the year in the open market on the footing that the landlord was responsible for all repairs and that the tenant was liable for rates. From the gross annual value so found by valuation, a statutory repairs allowance was deducted and tax was levied on the resultant net annual value. Schedule A tax was not restricted to the income which landlords derived from letting property: it was also levied on owner-occupiers and, in their case, the net annual value represented a "notional income" from the land. As between landlord and tenant, Schedule A tax was (subject to exceptions) levied on the occupier of the property and the Income Tax Act 1952 contained elaborate provisions to enable the tenant who paid the tax to pass it on to the landlord by deduction from rent. There was an exception in the case of property let on a "long lease" when the rent was treated as an annual payment chargeable under Case VI of Schedule D and paid under deduction of tax. The long lease became an attractive proposition for tenants of luxury flats in the higher income groups because the rent (being an annual payment) was deductible in computing total income for purposes of surtax. The distinction between the short and the long leases has no place in the system introduced by the Act of 1963.

6–02 It was originally intended that a revaluation of property for purposes of Schedule A tax should be made every five years, but the last general valuation was made in 1935–36 ("the preparatory year") for 1936–37 ("the year of revaluation"). As time passed and rents increased the annual values determined for Schedule A purposes became more and more unrealistic, for the Revenue had no power to revalue property between years of revaluation unless there had been such a change in the character of the property (*e.g.* by structural conversion or development) as to create a new unit of assessment. For this reason the Finance Act 1940 introduced provisions for taxing under Case VI of Schedule D rents received by landlords to the extent that the rents exceeded the annual value for Schedule A. These "excess rent assessments" were made on the landlord; they were not levied on the tenant and the tax passed on to the landlord by deduction.

Maintenance claims

6–03   A statutory repairs allowance was deducted in ascertaining the net annual value of property. This allowance was a fixed fraction of the gross annual value. Where the taxpayer's expenditure on maintenance, repairs, insurance and management of the property, averaged over five years, exceeded the statutory repairs allowance, there were provisions to enable the taxpayer to obtain relief by way of maintenance claim.[1]

Schedule B

6–04   Tax under Schedule B was charged in respect of the occupation of land in the United Kingdom which was chargeable under Schedule A, except that dwelling-houses and land occupied for the purposes of carrying on a trade, profession or vocation were excluded. Farming and market gardening used at one time to fall within Schedule B until these activities were made statutory trades subject to tax under Case I of Schedule D.[2] Schedule B thus applied to amenity lands, lands occupied for non-profit-making purposes (*e.g.* sports grounds), sporting rights and woodlands. The basis of assessment was one-third of the gross annual value and the tax was additional to Schedule A tax. The tax was assessed on the occupier, who had no right of recoupment.

The Finance Acts 1963 and 1969

6–05   The Finance Act 1963 introduced a new code for the taxation of income from land. Schedule A in its original form ceased to have effect in and from the year 1963–64 except that, for the year 1963–64 only, Schedule A tax and the excess rent provisions were preserved for the purpose of taxing landlords on rental income. There was no Schedule A tax (and accordingly no maintenance relief) for owner-occupiers and tenants with a beneficial occupation in 1963–64.[3]

---

1. For details, see the first edition of this book, pp. 19–23.
2. I.C.T.A. 1970, s.110. For the history of the relevant provisions, see *Sargent* v. *Eayrs* (1973) 48 T.C. 573; [1973] S.T.C. 50 and see § 2–18A.
3. F.A. 1963, s.20.

The Finance Act 1963 introduced a new Case VIII of Schedule D to tax income from land. The Finance Act 1969 renamed Case VIII of Schedule D "Schedule A."[4]

Furnished lettings

–05A   The assessment of income derived from the letting of furnished accommodation is dealt with under Case VI of Schedule D and statutory provisions in the Finance Act 1984: see § 4–02A.

Woodlands

6–06   In and from the year 1963–64, Schedule B tax is restricted to the occupation of woodlands in the United Kingdom managed on a commercial basis and with a view to the realisation of profit.[5] Tax under Schedule B is charged on the occupier (which includes every person having the use of lands[6]) on the assessable value of his occupation in the chargeable period, that is on an amount equal to one-third of the woodlands' annual value, or a proportionate part of that amount if the period in respect of which he is chargeable is less than one year.[7] A person who has the use of woodlands wholly or mainly for the purpose of felling, processing or removing timber or clearing or preparing timber for replanting is not an "occupier" for the purposes of Schedule B.[7a] The annual value of land is taken to be the rent which might reasonably be expected to be obtained on a letting from year to year if the tenant undertook to pay all usual tenant's rates and taxes, and if the landlord undertook to bear the costs of the repairs and insurance and the other expenses, if any, necessary for maintaining the subject of the valuation in a state to command that rent; but the annual value of any woodlands is determined in accordance with this formula as if the land, instead of being woodlands, were let in its natural and unimproved state.[8] Disputes as to annual value are determined by the General Commissioners.[9]

6–07   Under section 111 of the Income and Corporation Taxes Act 1970, any person occupying woodlands managed by him on a commercial basis and with a view to the realisation of profits may elect to be assessed under Schedule D instead of under Schedule B. He is then assessed on the basis

---

4. F.A. 1969, s.60 and Sched. 20, para. 1 (an amendment which was made for the purposes of the 1970 Consolidation).
5. I.C.T.A. 1970, s.91. In December 1980 the Chancellor confirmed in answer to a parliamentary question that no change in the arrangements for taxing woodlands was then proposed: [1980] S.T.I. 873.
6. *Ibid.* s.92(3).
7. *Ibid.* s.92(1), (2).
7a. *Ibid.* s.92(4), which applies to any use commencing after March 13, 1984, and nullifies the decision in *Russell* v. *Hird* (1983) T.C. 127; [1983] S.T.C. 541.
8. I.C.T.A. 1970, s.92(2) applying the definition of "annual value" in s.531.
9. *Ibid.* s.531(3).

of profits (if any) instead of on the basis of annual value. Grants from the Forestry Commission are taken into account in the computation of profits. The election must extend to all such woodlands on the same estate; except that woodlands planted or replanted within the previous 10 years can be treated (at the occupier's option) as forming a separate estate. The election has effect for the year of assessment to which it relates and for all future years so long as the woodlands are occupied by the person making the election.

Where profits derived from "commercial woodlands" exceed their assessable value for Schedule B purposes, as would normally be the case where the woodlands have reached maturity, taxation under Schedule B is preferable. Where, however, the woodlands are immature or otherwise unproductive of profits, taxation under Schedule D is preferable because (a) relief for losses may be claimed[10]; and (b) relief for capital expenditure on machinery and plant, forestry buildings, fences, etc., may be available.[11] Once an election has been made under section 111 it applies until there is a change of occupation. A new occupier is at once assessed under Schedule B, unless he elects for assessment under Schedule D.

6–08   Where the occupier elects to be assessed under Schedule D, the profits or gains arising to him from the occupation of the woodlands are to be deemed to be profits or gains of a trade. But this does not mean that the occupier is to be treated as carrying on a trade or that the woodlands are trading stock:

> "Merely by deeming the offspring to be something which it is not, the section does not change the nature of the parent. Merely to deem the profits or gains arising from the occupation of the woodlands to be the profits or gains of a trade is not, in my judgment, to say that the occupation of the woodlands is to be deemed to be a trade. . . . "[12]

Thus there is no tax liability under Case I of Schedule D on a sale of the woodlands.[13]

6–09   There is a distinction between occupying woodlands on a commercial basis (when Schedule B applies, subject to the right of election under section 111) and carrying on a trade in relation to the products of the woodlands (when Schedule D, Case I applies as regards the trade itself).

> In *Collins* v. *Fraser*[13] the taxpayer manufactured boxes and crates from timber provided from his own woodlands. The mill was some distance from the woodlands. The General Commissioners found that the activities fell within Schedule B to the point when the timber was transported from the woodlands. Megarry J. held that the activities ceased to be referable to the Schedule B occupation when something more was done than market the timber.

---

10. See *post*, Chap. 12.
11. See *post*, Chap. 13.
12. *Coats* v. *Holker Estates Co.* (1961) 40 T.C. 75, *per* Plowman J. at p. 80.
13. *Collins* v. *Fraser* (1969) 46 T.C. 143.

2. THE TAXATION OF ANNUAL PROFITS OR GAINS FROM RENTS AND OTHER RECEIPTS FROM LAND (OTHER THAN PREMIUMS)

The charging provisions

6–10   By section 67 of the Income and Corporation Taxes Act 1970, tax under Schedule A is charged on "the annual profits or gains arising in respect of any such rents or receipts" as follow, that is to say:

   (a) rents under leases[14] of land in the United Kingdom;

   (b) rentcharges, ground annuals and feu duties, and other annual payments reserved in respect of, or charged on or issuing out of, such land; and

   (c) other receipts arising to a person from, or by virtue of, his ownership of an estate or interest in or right over such land or any incorporeal hereditament or incorporeal heritable subject in the United Kingdom. Thus payments for easements or other rights to use land are taxed under Schedule A.[15]

It will be convenient to refer to the above-mentioned sources of income as "rents, etc." It should be observed that rents, etc., are not made taxable as such. Schedule A charges tax on the profits or gains arising in respect of rents, etc., and it is therefore necessary to visualise an income and expenditure account in which rents, etc., are credited and certain outgoings are debited. The Act contains a general provision authorising the deductions provided for by sections 72 to 77.[16] Receipts of a capital nature are not taxed under Schedule A: thus, if A realises a profit on the sale of his dwelling-house, this may be said to be a receipt which arises by virtue of his ownership thereof, but it escapes tax under Schedule A because it is not an annual profit or gain. He might, however, be liable to capital gains tax.[17] There are special provisions relating to the taxation of premiums which are discussed later.[18]

6–11   *Exceptions.* The following income from land is not assessed under Schedule A:

   (1) Yearly interest and payments charged under section 112 (mines, quarries and other concerns) and section 156 or 157 (mining etc. rents and royalties) of the 1970 Act. These are expressly excluded

---

14. Lease includes an agreement for a lease and any tenancy; it does not include a mortgage or heritable security: I.C.T.A. 1970, s.90(1). As to nature of rent under a lease, see *T. & E. Homes Ltd.* v. *Robinson* (1979) 52 T.C. 567; [1979] S.T.C. 351 (C.A.).

15. And see I.C.T.A. 1970, s.67(3), for the position where the occupier is taxed under Schedule B. In *Lowe* v. *J. W. Ashmore Ltd.* (1970) 46 T.C. 597 receipts from sales of turf were held to be taxable under (c). See also *Jeffries* v. *Stevens* (1982) 56 T.C. 134; [1982] S.T.C. 639 at p. 651 (payments made by a company, described as "rents" in its accounts, where the company had neither a lease nor a license: *held*, chargeable under (c)).

16. I.C.T.A. 1970, s.71(1). For the allowed deductions, see §§ 6–27 *et seq.*

17. See *post*, Chap. 16.

18. See *post*, §§ 6–16 *et seq.* See also § 2–61.

from Schedule A.[19] Mineral royalties are taxed on a special basis: briefly, half the royalty is taxed as income and half as capital gain.[20]

(2) Furnished lettings. Where rent is paid under a lease entitling the tenant to the use of furniture, and tax in respect of the payment for its use is chargeable under Case VI of Schedule D,[21] tax will be charged on the rent under Case VI unless the landlord, by notice in writing to the Inspector given within two years after the end of the year of assessment, requires that this provision shall not apply.[22] Schedule A would then apply and consequential adjustments would follow. A landlord of a furnished letting would elect for a Schedule A assessment if he was advised that the deductions allowed under the provisions applicable to Schedule A were more favourable to him than those normally permitted in the case of furnished lettings.[23] Where payment for a furnished letting in the United Kingdom is made (whether in the United Kingdom or elsewhere) to a person, whether the landlord or not, whose usual place of abode is outside the United Kingdom, the tenant must deduct tax from the payment and account therefore to the Revenue under section 53 of the Income and Corporation Taxes Act 1970 as if it were an annual payment not payable out of profits or gains brought into charge.[24] It therefore behoves a tenant of a furnished letting to insert in his lease a covenant by the landlord to notify the tenant if the person to whom the rent is payable changes his usual place of abode to a place outside the United Kingdom.

(3) Income from land outside the United Kingdom. This is outside the charging provisions of Schedule A.

Rents receivable but not received

6-12   Tax under Schedule A is charged by reference to the rents, etc., to which a person *becomes entitled* in the year of assessment.[25] The principle that receivability without receipt gives rise to no tax liability has no place in this sphere of income taxation: a person is charged on rents, etc., which he is entitled to receive, whether or not he receives them and whether or not he demands payment. Section 87, however, allows a person to claim relief in respect of rents, etc., which are not received and which would be chargeable under Schedule A in two cases:

(1) if the non-receipt was attributable to the default of the person by whom the rent was payable and the claimant proves that he has taken reasonable steps available to him to enforce payment;

---

19. I.C.T.A. 1970, s.67(1), para. 3.
20. F.A. 1970, s.29 and Sched. 6.
21. See *ante*, § 4–02A.
22. I.C.T.A. 1970, s.67(1), para. 4 and s.67(2). And see § 4–05 as to losses.
23. The wear and tear allowance is usually 10 per cent. of rents less rates or other sums for services normally borne by the tenant: I.R. letter of October 13, 1977.
24. I.C.T.A. 1970, s.89. See *ante*, § 5–34.
25. *Ibid*. s.67(1), para. 2.

(2) if the claimant waived payment and the waiver was made without consideration and was reasonably made in order to avoid hardship.

Consequential adjustments will then be made. If relief is given and the rent, etc., is subsequently received, the claimant (or his personal representatives) must notify the Inspector in writing within six months of the receipt. There are penalties for non-compliance.[26] The rent, etc., will then be treated as income of the year to which it relates and will be assessed accordingly; and for this purpose the Inspector has power to make assessments for more than six years back but the assessment must be made within six years from the end of the year when payment was received.[27]

Basis of assessment

6–13   Tax under Schedule A is assessed on a current year basis. Thus tax in 1985–86 is levied on the annual profits or gains from rents, etc., in the year ended April 5, 1986. Since, however, tax for 1985–86 is due on or before January 1, 1986,[28] and assessments have to be made in advance of this date, the assessment has to be provisional followed by an adjustment (either by way of additional assessment or repayment claim) when the profits of the year are finally agreed.[29] The provisional assessment (for 1985–86 in the above example) is to be made on the basis that all sources of income and all amounts relevant in computing profits or gains are the same as for the last preceding year of assessment (*i.e.* the year ended April 5, 1985).[30] A person who ceases to own property after the beginning of a year of assessment may have this excluded from the provisional assessment for the following year by notifying the Inspector in writing before January 1 in that year. Thus (in the above example) property sold in the year ended April 5, 1985, will be excluded from the computation of the provisional assessment for 1985–86 if notice is given before January 1, 1986. It will not be excluded, however, unless the taxpayer can show that his provisional assessment for 1985–86 will be less than it would have been if he had not ceased to possess the property.

Collection

6–14   (1) *From derivative lessees.*[31] Where any tax under Schedule A is charged to a person who is not the occupier of the land (such as a lessor or licensor) but the tax is not paid by that person (referred to as "the person in default") the tax may be recovered from any lessee of the land or any part thereof (referred to as "a derivative lessee") whose interest is derived directly or indirectly from the person in default. The amount demanded from a derivative lessee in any period must not exceed the amount of the rent, etc., arising from the land which is due from him at the end of the

---

26. T.M.A. 1970, s.98.
27. I.C.T.A. 1970, s.87(1).
28. *Ibid.* 1970, s.4(1).
29. *Ibid.* s.69.
30. *Ibid.* s.69.
31. *Ibid.* s.70(1).

period and payable to the person in default or another derivative lessee; and there are provisions which allow the derivative lessee from whom tax has been collected to deduct the tax from any subsequent payment arising from the land and due to the person in default or another derivative lessee. If the subsequent payments are insufficient to cover the tax paid, the difference can be recovered from the Revenue.

(2) *From agents.*[32] Where any person (referred to as "the agent") is in receipt of rents, etc., on behalf of another person (referred to as "the principal") and any tax under Schedule A charged on the principal has not been paid, the collector may require the agent to pay in or towards satisfaction of the tax sums received by the agent on behalf of the principal on account of rents, etc. An agent who fails to comply with the requirements of a notice served on him by the Inspector is liable to penalties.

Returns[33]

6–15   For the purpose of obtaining particulars of profits or gains chargeable to tax under Schedule A, the Inspector has power to require information from a number of sources. Thus lessees and licensees (including former lessees and licensees) may be required to give information as to the terms of the lease or licence; a lessee (or former lessee) may be required to state the consideration given for the grant or assignment to him of the tenancy; and any person who as agent manages land or is in receipt of rents, etc. (which might include a solicitor or accountant), may be required to furnish the particulars relating to payments arising from land. There are penalties for non-compliance.

3. The Taxation of Premiums

6–16   A code of taxation of income from land would not be complete unless premiums on leases were brought into charge. If premiums were not made chargeable to tax as income, landlords seeking to avoid income tax would grant leases at a premium and not at a rent, for a lump sum premium would escape tax under section 67 of the Income and Corporation Taxes Act 1970 (see § 6–10), because it is not an annual profit or gain. Only capital gains tax would be chargeable. Section 80(1) accordingly provides as follows:

> "Where the payment of any premium is required under a lease, or otherwise under the terms subject to which a lease is granted, and the duration of the lease does not exceed fifty years, the landlord shall be treated for the purposes of the Tax Acts as becoming entitled when the lease is granted to an amount by way of rent (in addition to any actual rent) equal to the amount of the premium reduced by 1/50th of that amount for each complete period of twelve months (other than the first) comprised in the duration of the lease."

The term "premium" is defined to include any like sum, whether payable to the immediate or a superior landlord or to a person connected with

---

32. *Ibid.* s.70(2).
33. T.M.A. 1970, s.19.

either of them within section 533 of the 1970 Act[34–35]; and any sum (other than rent) paid on or in connection with the granting of a tenancy is presumed to have been paid by way of premium except in so far as other sufficient consideration for the payment is shown to have been given.[36]

6–17 The reader will recall that rents are not taxed as such. The charge under Schedule A is on the annual profits or gains arising in respect of rents, etc., and a premium (or the appropriate part of it) is treated as rent and so falls into charge under section 67. It will be convenient, however, to refer in this chapter to premiums as being "chargeable." The following is an example of the operation of the section:

> A grants a lease for a term of 21 years at a premium of £5,000. The chargeable portion of the premium is £5,000 less 40 per cent. thereof = £3,000. If the term had been 50 years, the chargeable portion would be £5,000 less 98 per cent. thereof = £100. Where the term exceeds 50 years, the premium escapes tax under Schedule A (subject to the qualifications in § 6–18).

Premiums and sums which are taxed as premiums received by a dealer in land are treated as trading receipts only to the extent that section 80, 81 or 82 of the 1970 Act does not apply.[37]

The duration of the lease

6–18 It will be appreciated from the example just given that the longer the term of the lease, the lower is the charge to tax. A lease for a term exceeding 50 years escapes the charge under Schedule A; and in the case of leases for 50 years or less, the discount increases as the term increases. In ascertaining the duration of a lease, the following provisions have effect[38]:

(a) where any of the terms of the lease (whether relating to forfeiture or to any other matter) or any other circumstances render it unlikely that the lease will continue beyond a date falling before the expiry of the term of the lease and the premium was not substantially greater than it would have been (on certain assumptions specified in the Act) had the term been one expiring on the date,[39] the lease shall not be treated as having been granted for a term longer than one ending on that date; and

(b) where the terms of the lease include provision for the extension of the lease beyond a given date by notice given by the tenant, account may be taken of any circumstances making it likely that the lease will be so extended; and

(c) where the tenant, or a person connected with him, is or may become entitled to a further lease or the grant of a further lease (whenever

---

34–35. See the definitions in I.C.T.A. 1970, s.90.

36. I.C.T.A. 1970, s.90(2). *Quaere* why the word "tenancy" is used in the definition and not "lease."

37. *Ibid*. s.142.

38. *Ibid*. s.84.

39. F.A. 1972, s.81(2) amending I.C.T.A. 1970, s.84 as from August 25, 1971, in order to counteract a number of tax avoidance schemes.

commencing) of the same premises or of premises including the whole or part of the same premises, the term of the lease may be treated as not expiring before the term of the further lease.

Paragraph (a) catches the lease which contains an "escalator clause," *i.e.* a clause reserving a rent which increases to such an extent as to induce the premature determination of the lease by the lessee.

Work carried out by the tenant

6–19   The tax on premiums is not avoided by the landlord requiring the tenant to carry out work on the demised premises, for section 80(2) of the Income and Corporation Taxes Act 1970 provides as follows:

> "Where the terms subject to which a lease is granted impose on the tenant an obligation to carry out any work on the premises, the lease shall be deemed for the purposes of this section to have required the payment of a premium to the landlord (in addition to any other premium) of an amount equal to the amount by which the value of the landlord's estate or interest, immediately after the commencement of the lease, exceeds what its then value would have been if the said terms did not impose that obligation on the tenant."

There is a proviso that this subsection shall not apply in so far as the obligation requires the carrying out of work payment for which would, if the landlord and not the tenant were obliged to carry it out, be deductible from the rent under sections 72 to 76 of the Act.[40]

Thus, if L grants a lease for a term of 21 years to T at a rent and in consideration of a covenant by T to carry out structural alterations, it is necessary to find out to what extent the value of L's reversionary interest immediately following the grant of the lease is increased by virtue of T's covenant. The amount so found is treated as a premium and discounted according to the length of the term. There is an element of double discounting in this case, for the greater length of the term not only increases the amount of the discount but also reduces the value of the works to the hypothetical purchaser. It is thought that no tax would be chargeable in respect of the value of work of a temporary nature.

Delayed premiums

6–20   The charge on premiums is not avoided by arranging for a lump sum to be paid by the tenant on some occasion subsequent to the grant of the lease. The following provisions are relevant in this connection:

(1) By section 80(3) of the Income and Corporation Taxes Act 1970 where, under the terms subject to which a lease is granted, a sum becomes payable by the tenant in lieu of the whole part of the rent for any period, that sum is treated as a premium payable in the year when it first becomes payable by the tenant. The premium is dis-

---

40. See *post*, §§ 6–27 *et seq.*

counted on the basis that the duration of the lease excludes any
period other than that in relation to which the sum is payable.

(2) By section 80(3) where, under the terms subject to which a lease is
granted, a sum becomes payable by the tenant as consideration for
the surrender of the lease, that sum is treated as a premium payable
in the year when it becomes payable by the tenant. The premium is
discounted on the basis that the duration of the lease extends from
its commencement to the date of surrender. It should be noted that
this provision does not apply to a surrender which is negotiated after
the term has commenced.

(3) By section 80(4) where, as consideration for the variation or waiver
of any of the terms of a lease, a sum becomes payable by the tenant
otherwise than by way of rent, this sum is treated as a premium in
the year when the contract providing for the variation or waiver is
entered into. The premium is discounted on the basis that the
duration of the lease is the period during which the variation or
waiver is to have effect.

Premiums payable by instalments[41]

6–21 Where a premium (or a sum which is treated as a premium under one of
the provisions discussed under the above head "Delayed premiums") is
payable by instalments, the tax chargeable by reference to the premium
may, if the recipient satisfies the Board that he would otherwise suffer
hardship, be paid at his option by such instalments as the Board may allow
over a period not exceeding eight years and ending not later than the time
at which the last of the first-mentioned instalments is payable.[42]

Charge on assignment of lease granted at undervalue[43]

6–22 The tax on premiums which has been discussed could be avoided in the
following way. Suppose A wished to grant a lease to B at a premium and to
avoid tax on the premium. A could grant a lease to a company which he
controlled or to a collaborator, which lessee would then assign the lease to
B for a consideration equal to the desired premium. Whereas a premium
taken on the *grant* of a lease is chargeable under section 80(1), a lump sum
taken on the *assignment* of a lease escapes tax (unless it falls into charge as
a trading receipt of a dealer in land or as a taxable capital gain). To prevent
this form of avoidance, section 81(1) provides as follows:

"Where the terms subject to which a lease of a duration not exceeding fifty
years was granted are such that the grantor, having regard to values prevailing
at the time it was granted, and on the assumption that the negotiations for the
lease were at arm's length, could have required the payment of an additional

---

41. I.C.T.A. 1970, s.80(6) as substituted by F.A. 1972, s.81(1) with effect from April 11,
1972: *ibid.* s.81(6).
42. Where the premium is not payable by instalments, see *post*, § 6–26.
43. I.C.T.A. 1970, s.81.

sum (hereinafter referred to as "the amount foregone") by way of premium, or additional premium, for the grant of the lease, then, on any assignment of the lease for a consideration—

(*a*) where the lease has not previously been assigned, exceeding the premium (if any) for which it was granted, or

(*b*) where the lease has been previously assigned, exceeding the consideration for which it was last assigned,

the amount of the excess, in so far as it is not greater than the amount foregone reduced by the amount of any such excess arising on a previous assignment of the lease, shall in the same proportion as the amount foregone would under section 80(1) . . . have fallen to be treated as rent if it had been a premium under the lease, be treated as profits or gains of the assignor chargeable to tax under Case VI of Schedule D."

6–23   Suppose that A grants a lease to B for a term of 21 years and that A demands a premium of £200, but could have demanded £380. On an assignment of the lease by B, B is chargeable on his profit on the assignment up to the amount foregone by A. Thus, if B assigns to C for £350, B is chargeable on his profit (£150) up to the amount foregone (£180), *i.e.* B is treated as receiving a premium of £150, which will be discounted according to the duration of the lease. If C later assigns the lease to D, any profit made by C on the assignment is taxable up to the amount foregone by A (£180) less £150 (the amount charged against B).

The Revenue can therefore recover tax from successive assignors until the lost tax is recovered. Assignors could unwittingly incur tax liability as a result of tax avoidance by the original lessor, whether deliberate or not, and a measure of protection is afforded by section 81(2) under which if there is submitted to the Inspector, by the grantor or any assignor or assignee of the lease, a statement showing whether or not a charge to tax arises or may arise, and if so the amount on which the charge arises or may arise, then if the Inspector is satisfied as to the accuracy of the statement he shall so certify. The assignee of a lease should, of course, seek indemnities against liability which might arise under the section.

Charge on sale of land with right to reconveyance[44]

6–24   Another method by which the tax on premiums could be avoided is as follows. Suppose A wished to take a premium of (say) £8,000 on the grant of a lease to B for seven years and that A wished to avoid tax on the premium. The transaction could be carried out by A selling the land to B for (say) £15,000 on terms that B would reconvey the land to A at the end of seven years for £7,000. To prevent this form of avoidance, section 82(1) of the Income and Corporation Taxes Act 1970 provides as follows:

"Where the terms subject to which an estate or interest in land is sold provide that it shall be, or may be required to be, reconveyed at a future date to the vendor or a person connected with him, the vendor shall be chargeable to tax under Case VI of Schedule D on any amount by which the price at which the

---

44. *Ibid.* s.82.

estate or interest is sold exceeds the price at which it is to be reconveyed or, if the earliest date at which, in accordance with those terms, it would fall to be reconveyed is a date two years or more after the sale, on that excess reduced by 1/50th thereof for each complete year (other than the first) in the period between the sale and that date."

Thus, in the example, A will be taxed under Case VI on £8,000 discounted on the footing that there was a lease of duration of seven years.

Section 82(1) presupposes that the date of the reconveyance and the reconveyance price are fixed by the terms of the sale. Section 82(2) deals with the case where the date of the reconveyance is not so fixed, *e.g.* where gravel-bearing land is sold with a provision for reconveyance when extraction is complete.

Section 82(3) deals with the case where land is sold with an arrangement for a lease back to the vendor or a person connected with him. Transactions of this nature are common as methods of financing the development of land and there is an express proviso excluding the operation of the subsection where the lease is granted and begins to run within one month after the sale.

Premiums: capital gains tax

6–25 Schedule A does not charge tax on a premium where the duration of the lease exceeds 50 years; but there may be liability to capital gains tax. Likewise a liability to capital gains tax might arise in respect of the portion of a premium which escapes Schedule A.

4. PREMIUM TOP-SLICING

6–26 Where a premium (or a sum which is treated as such) is chargeable as income of a single year of assessment, the Act allows an *individual* who is chargeable to avoid having the payment swallowed up in tax by claiming "top-slicing relief." The relief is not available where the person chargeable is not an individual, *e.g.* a company; nor where the premium is payable by instalments. No attempt is made here to summarise the detailed provisions of Schedule 3 to the Income and Corporation Taxes Act 1970 by reference to which relief is given. Broadly speaking the chargeable portion of the premium (called the "chargeable sum") is spread over the duration of the lease (called "the relevant period") to give what is termed the "yearly equivalent." If, for example, the chargeable sum is £2,100 and the relevant period is seven years, the yearly equivalent is £300. Outgoings are to be set against rents, etc., as far as possible and only the balance that remains is set against the yearly equivalent. There is then calculated the top rate of tax in the claimant's total income, including what (if anything) remains of the yearly equivalent after deducting outgoings. Tax is then charged at this top rate on the whole of the chargeable sum. If nothing remains of the yearly equivalent after deducting outgoings, tax is charged at the rate applicable to the highest part of the remainder of the claimant's total income for the year of assessment.

5. Deductions

What is deductible

6–27   In computing the profits or gains arising to a person in a year of assessment, certain deductions are allowed from the rent or receipts to which he
becomes entitled—including premiums which are treated as rent.[45] These
are contained in sections 72 to 77 of the Income and Corporation Taxes
Act 1970. The person chargeable may, under section 72, deduct payments
made by him (but not mere liabilities incurred by him):

   (a) in respect of maintenance, repairs, insurance or management;
   (b) in respect of services provided under the terms of the lease other
        than services for which he received separate consideration;
   (c) in respect of rates or other charges on the occupier which the person
        chargeable was obliged to defray;
   (d) in respect of any rent, rentcharge, ground annual or other periodical
        payment reserved in respect of, or charged on or issuing out of,
        land.

6–28   Maintenance refers to expenditure necessary to maintain the value of
property. Repairs has a similar meaning. It is difficult to differentiate these
terms and no useful purpose is served by attempting to do so; for the
important distinction is that between expenditure on maintenance and
repairs (which is deductible) and expenditure on replacements, additions
and improvements (which is not deductible).[46] Insurance refers to premiums paid on a policy insuring the building but not its contents. Premiums
on a leasehold redemption policy are not allowable.[47] Management
includes all the ordinary expenses of managing property, such as the cost of
obtaining estimates for repairs, architects' and surveyors' fees,[48] accountants' fees, legal expenses of recovering arrears of rent, the cost of advertising property for letting,[49] etc. Capital allowances may be claimed for
expenditure on machinery or plant provided for use or used by a lessor for
the maintenance, repair or management of the demised premises.[50]

It is the view of the Inland Revenue that there is no material difference
in the law relating to expenditure on dilapidations under Schedule A and
under Case I of Schedule D as interpreted in *Law Shipping Co. Ltd.* v.
I.R.C. and *Odeon Associated Theatres Ltd.* v. *Jones*.[51] Thus expenditure
on maintenance and repairs will be disallowed as a deduction under Schedule A if it relates to dilapidations attributable to a period before the currency of the relevant lease and the expenditure would have been
disallowed under Case I if the property had been acquired as a fixed asset

---

45. *Ibid.* s.71(1).
46. For the distinction between "repairs" and "improvements," see the discussion, *ante*, § 2–63.
47. *Pearce* v. *Doulton* (1947) 27 T.C. 405.
48. *London and Northern Estates Co. Ltd.* v. *Harris* [1939] 1 K.B. 335; 21 T.C. 187.
49. *Southern* v. *Aldwych Property Trust Ltd.* [1940] 2 K.B. 266; 23 T.C. 707.
50. I.C.T.A. 1970, s.78; *post*, § 13–19.
51. See *ante*, § 2–62.

of a trade at the commencement of the lease; and it will be allowed under Schedule A if it would have been allowed under Case I. It is arguable that the decision in the *Law Shipping*[51] case had no relevance to maintenance claims under Schedule A in the pre–1963 form and now has no relevance to the computation of profits or gains under Schedule A in its present form. Where maintenance and repairs of property are obviated by improvements, additions and alterations, so much of the outlay as is equal to the estimated cost of the maintenance and repairs is (with some qualifications) allowed as a deduction in computing liability in respect of rents under Schedule A.[52]

Principles of deduction

6–29 As a general principle, payments made by the landlord in respect of premises may only be deducted from rent payable in respect of those premises and must relate to expenditure incurred (or, in the case of maintenance and repairs, to dilapidations occurring) during the currency of the lease. No deduction is allowable with respect to dilapidations outstanding at the commencement of the lease or in respect of expenditure incurred by a predecessor in title.[53]

There is an exception to this general principle in the case of a lease at a full rent, when a deduction is allowed for payments made in respect of expenditure incurred prior to the commencement of the lease in a "previous qualifying period" (as defined), *e.g.* when a previous lease at a full rent with the same lessor was subsisting or when no lease was subsisting and the lessor was entitled to possession (called a "void period").[54] Thus where a lessor grants successive leases at a full rent, the allowable expenditure may be carried forward and deducted from the future rent: the right to carry forward expenditure is lost only by a period of owner-occupation or by a letting which is not at a full rent. A lease is a lease at a full rent if the rent reserved under the lease (including an appropriate sum in respect of any premium under the lease) is sufficient, taking one year with another, to defray the cost to the lessor of fulfilling his obligation under the lease and of meeting any expenses of maintenance, repairs, insurance and management of the premises subject to the lease which fall to be borne by him.[55]

6–30 There are cases in which payments made in respect of demised premises may be deducted from rents from other premises demised by the same lessor. Broadly speaking, where rent is payable under a lease at a full rent (including a tenant's repairing lease) and the rent is insufficient to absorb the expenditure, the excess may be set off against rent from another lease at a full rent which is not a tenant's repairing lease.[56] "Tenant's repairing

---

52. Concession No. B4.
53. I.C.T.A. 1970, s.72(2).
54. *Ibid*. s.72(3)–(7).
55. *Ibid*. s.71(2).
56. *Ibid*. s.72(4).

lease" means a lease where the lessee is under an obligation to maintain and repair the whole, or substantially the whole, of the premises comprised in the lease.

6. Management Expenses

6–31 A company which owns tenanted property as an investment bears corporation tax on its annual profits or gains arising in respect of rents or receipts from land, computed under the rules applicable to Schedule A; and, in particular, may deduct the cost of managing *the properties*.[57] In addition, tax relief is allowed in respect of the cost of managing *the company*. Before the introduction of corporation tax, the relief was given by way of repayment of income tax[58]; now it is given by way of deduction in computing the profits liable to corporation tax.[59] The same relief for management expenses is available to any company whose business consists mainly in the making of investments and the principal part of whose income is derived therefrom.

6–32 A proportion of director's fees may be claimed as management expenses but these will be closely scrutinised.[60] Brokerage and stamp duty paid on a change of investments are not allowable management expenses.[61] A loss arising when rents were misappropriated by a fraudulent agent was held not to be a cost of management for the purposes of a Schedule A maintenance claim[62]; but different principles apply to a management expenses claim.

---

57. See *ante*, § 6–27.
58. I.T.A. 1952, s.425.
59. I.C.T.A. 1970, s.304; see *post*, §§ 14–20 *et seq*.
60. See *Berry Investments Ltd.* v. *Attwooll* (1964) 41 T.C. 547.
61. *Capital and National Trust* v. *Golder* (1949) 31 T.C. 265; *Sun Life Assurance Society* v. *Davidson* (1957) 37 T.C. 330. See § 14–21.
62. *Pyne* v. *Stallard-Penoyre* (1964) 42 T.C. 183.

CHAPTER 7

THE TAXATION OF FOREIGN INCOME

1. SCHEDULE D

7–01 INCOME which arises from a source within the United Kingdom is generally liable to United Kingdom tax, irrespective of the nationality, domicile, residence or presence of the recipient. There is an exception in the case of interest on certain United Kingdom government securities in the beneficial ownership of a person not ordinarily resident in the United Kingdom.[1] There are also exceptions under double taxation agreements: see § 7–25. Foreign income is chargeable to United Kingdom tax only if the recipient is resident in the United Kingdom.[2] All income which originates from a source outside the United Kingdom is "foreign income" including, for example:

(1) income from a property situated outside the United Kingdom[3];
(2) dividends from a company resident outside the United Kingdom[4];
(3) income from a trust where the fund is situated outside the United Kingdom[5];
(4) income from a trade, profession or vocation carried on *wholly* outside the United Kingdom.[6]

The taxation of foreign income under Schedule C has already been mentioned.[7] Income from employments which have a foreign element is discussed later in this chapter.[8] The taxation of companies and capital gains are discussed in later chapters.[9] Other foreign income is taxed (if at all) under Case IV or Case V of Schedule D.[10]

Case I

7–02 Tax is charged under Case I of Schedule D in respect of any trade carried on in the United Kingdom *or elsewhere* on the annual profits or gains thereof[11]; but it has been held that, notwithstanding the italicised words, Case I does not apply to a trade carried on wholly outside the United King-

---

1. I.C.T.A. 1970, s.99. Ordinary residence is discussed *post*, § 7–24. The exemption applies only when the securities are owned by the claimant at the time when the interest arises; thus it will not apply when the securities are sold before the coupon date. The exception does not apply to securities in the beneficial ownership of U.K. controlled foreign companies (§ 14–85) and offshore funds (§ 7–34).
2. *Ibid.* s.108. Residence is discussed *post*, §§ 7–17 *et seq.*
3. The general principles as to the situation of property are discussed *post*, § 23–09.
4. *Bradbury* v. *English Sewing Cotton Co.* [1923] A.C. 744; 8 T.C. 481 (H.L.).
5. *Baker* v. *Archer-Shee* [1927] A.C. 844; 11 T.C. 749 (H.L.).
6. *Colquhoun* v. *Brooks* (1889) 14 A.C. 493; 2 T.C. 490 (H.L.).
7. See *ante*, § 1–07.
8. See *post*, §§ 7–12 *et seq.*
9. Chaps. 14 to 16.
10. See *post*, §§ 7–06 *et seq.*
11. I.C.T.A. 1970, s.109(2), Case I.

dom.[12] The income of such a trade is foreign income; the trade is a "foreign possession"; and United Kingdom tax can be levied only under Case V of Schedule D.[13]

The question therefore arises: when is a trade carried on wholly or partly within the United Kingdom so as to bring Case I of Schedule D into operation? If a company whose trading operations are carried on wholly abroad is controlled from the United Kingdom, so that the company is resident in the United Kingdom,[14] the company is treated as trading partly within the United Kingdom.[15] In one case it was held that a foreign business owned by an individual in the United Kingdom who had the sole right of control of the business was carried on partly within the United Kingdom, even though in fact the individual had at no time exercised control within the United Kingdom. "It is a matter . . . of power and right, and not of the actual exercise of right or power."[16]

7–03   In the case of a trade which is controlled from outside the United Kingdom there is an important distinction between trading *with* and trading *partly within* the United Kingdom. If the activities of the trade consist of selling goods, the place where contracts are concluded may be decisive.

> Thus in *Grainger & Son* v. *Gough*[17] the question arose whether a French wine merchant was trading within the United Kingdom. He had appointed a firm in the City of London to be agents in Great Britain for the sale of his wines. The agents canvassed for orders and were remunerated on a commission basis; but no orders were accepted in Great Britain. Orders were transmitted to France where the French wine merchant exercised his discretion whether or not to accept them. No offers were accepted on behalf of the French wine merchant in Great Britain. It was held (Lord Morris dissenting) that no part of the trade was carried on in the United Kingdom.

But the place where contracts are made is not the only test and may be inappropriate in the case of a non-mercantile business. In one case, for example, Atkin L.J. propounded the test: where do the operations take place from which the profits in substance arise?[18] Thus if goods are manufactured by X in the United Kingdom and their sale by X is negotiated in the United Kingdom and delivery takes place in the United Kingdom, the clear fact that X is trading within the United Kingdom cannot be altered by executing the contract of sale abroad.

The mere act of purchasing goods from the United Kingdom (*e.g.* for resale abroad) is not trading within the United Kingdom.[19]

---

12. *Colquhoun* v. *Brooks* (1889) 14 A.C. 493; 2 T.C. 490 (H.L.).

13. For the method of assessment, see §§ 7–09, *et seq.*

14. *Unit Construction Co.* v. *Bullock* [1960] A.C. 351; 38 T.C. 712 (H.L.), *post*, § 7–24.

15. *San Paulo (Brazilian) Ry. Co.* v. *Carter* [1896] A.C. 31; 3 T.C. 407 (H.L.).

16. *Ogilvie* v. *Kitton* (1908) 5 T.C. 338, *per* Lord Stormonth-Darling at p. 345. It is difficult to reconcile this decision with the later decision of the House of Lords in *Egyptian Hotels Ltd.* v. *Mitchell* [1915] A.C. 1022; 6 T.C. 542 (H.L.).

17. [1896] A.C. 325; 3 T.C. 462 (H.L.) and see *Maclaine* v. *Eccott* [1926] A.C. 424; 10 T.C. 481 (H.L.).

18. *Smidth & Co.* v. *Greenwood* [1922] A.C. 417; 8 T.C. 193 at p. 204 (H.L.). See also *Firestone Tyre & Rubber Co. Ltd.* v. *Lewellin* (1957) 37 T.C. 111 especially the speech of Lord Radcliffe (H.L.).

19. *Att.-Gen.* v. *Sully* (1860) 2 T.C. 149n. (Exch.Ch.).

Case II

7–04   Tax is charged under Case II of Schedule D in respect of any profession or vocation which is carried on wholly or partly within the United Kingdom; but not in respect of a profession or vocation carried on wholly abroad.[20] Where the activities of a profession or vocation are normally carried on in the United Kingdom by a resident of the United Kingdom, it is difficult in practice to show that activities carried on abroad constitute a separate profession.

> Thus in *Davies* v. *Braithwaite*,[21] an actress resident in the United Kingdom was held assessable to tax in respect of earnings from an American contract which she fulfilled during a year in which she also acted in the United Kingdom. It could not be said that the acting in the United States was a "separate profession" from the acting in the United Kingdom.

The actress in this case entered into a variety of contracts of employment in the course of carrying on a profession within Case II of Schedule D.[22] The fees from the American contract were thus subject to United Kingdom tax, whether or not remitted to the United Kingdom.[23] If the American contract had been a "Schedule E contract" and the duties had been performed wholly outside the United Kingdom, fees paid under that contract but not remitted to the United Kingdom would at that time have escaped United Kingdom tax.

There are to be special rules, applicable from April 6, 1987, which provide for tax to be deducted at source on payments made to non-resident entertainers and sportsmen who perform in the United Kingdom.[23a]

Method of assessment

7–05   The Income Tax Acts contain special provisions to enable the Revenue to assess the profits of non-residents trading in the United Kingdom. They may be assessed and charged in the name (*inter alia*) of any factor, agent, receiver, branch or manager in the United Kingdom, whether or not the factor, etc., has the receipt of the profits or gains.[24] There are provisions for the charge to be based on a percentage of turnover if the profits cannot be otherwise ascertained[25] and for taxation on the basis of merchanting profit.[26]

Cases IV and V

7–06   Case IV of Schedule D charges tax in respect of income arising from *securities* out of the United Kingdom, except income charged under Schedule C.[27] "Securities" in Case IV was held in *Singer* v. *Williams*[28] to denote

---

20. I.C.T.A. 1970, s.109(2), Case II.
21. (1931) 18 T.C. 198 at pp. 205 *et seq.* Not reported on this point in [1931] 2 K.B. 628.
22. *Cf. Fall* v. *Hitchen* (1973) 49 T.C. 433; [1973] S.T.C. 66. See *ante*, § 3–03.
23. See *post*, § 7–08.
23a. F.A. 1986, s.44 and Sched. 11; and see [1986] S.T.I. 398.
24. T.M.A. 1970, ss.78–85.
25. *Ibid.* 1970, s.80.
26. *Ibid.* s.81.
27. I.C.T.A. 1970, s.109(2).
28. [1921] 1 A.C. 41; 7 T.C. 419.

"a debt or claim the payment of which is in some way secured. The security would generally consist of a right to resort to some fund or property for payment; some form of secured liability is postulated." A debenture or mortgage is a security; stocks and shares are not.[28]

Case V of Schedule D charges tax in respect of income arising from *possessions* out of the United Kingdom.[29] "Possessions" in Case V is a very wide term which embraces all sources of income other than securities, including income from trades, professions and vocations; income from stocks and shares; income from a foreign trust fund[30]; income from unsecured overseas pensions[31]; and alimony.[32] Note that dividends from companies resident outside the United Kingdom are taxed under Case V of Schedule D and not under Schedule F[33]: see § 14–58. Income derived from a partnership controlled outside the United Kingdom may constitute Case V income of partners resident in the United Kingdom.[34] Until 1956, emoluments of foreign employments fell within Case V but these are now assessable (if at all) under Schedule E: see *post*, §§ 7–12 *et seq.*

Foreign income which arises under a trust is not liable to United Kingdom tax if the beneficiary is resident abroad and the income is mandated direct to the beneficiary, even if the trustees are resident in the United Kingdom.[35]

Case VI

7–07   This is a residual head of charge taxing annual profits or gains from "property"—property situated in the United Kingdom in the case of a non-resident and the property situated anywhere in the case of a resident person.[36] The "property" often takes the form of a contract to render services: see § 4–02.

2. THE BASIS OF COMPUTATION UNDER SCHEDULE D

Cases I and II of Schedule D

7–08   The basic rule is that tax is charged under Cases I and II of Schedule D on the whole of the profits from trading, etc., within the United Kingdom, whether or not the profits are remitted to the United Kingdom and whether or not the trader is resident in the United Kingdom. Thus the solicitor who carries on his practice from an office in London is chargeable

29. I.C.T.A. 1970, s.109(2).
30. *Drummond* v. *Collins* [1915] A.C. 1011; 6 T.C. 525 (where the income was paid at the discretion of the trustees).
31. *Aspin* v. *Estill* [1986] S.T.C. 323. Some pensions are exempt from tax: see I.C.T.A. 1970, ss.213–218.
32. *I.R.C.* v. *Anderström* (1927) 13 T.C. 482.
33. *Rae* v. *Lazard Investment Co. Ltd.* (1963) 41 T.C. 1 (H.L.); but *cf. Courtauld's Investments* v. *Fleming* (1969) 46 T.C. 111. See generally Whiteman and Wheatcroft, *Income Tax,* (2nd ed.), para. 12–04.
34. See I.C.T.A. 1970, s.153; *post,* § 7–24. For an example, see *Newstead* v. *Frost* (1980) 53 T.C. 525; [1980] S.T.C. 123 (H.L.).
35. *Williams* v. *Singer* [1921] 1 A.C. 65; 7 T.C. 387.
36. I.C.T.A. 1970, s.108, para. 1.

to tax under Case II on profits arising from work done outside, as well as within, the United Kingdom. This is because the *source* of his income is a United Kingdom source, being the profession he practises in the United Kingdom; he does not have a separate source of income in each country in which he does business.

Cases IV and V

7–09   Tax is charged under Cases IV of Schedule D (on income from securities) and under Case V (on income from possessions) on the full amount of the income *arising* in the year preceding the year of assessment, whether the income has been or will be received in the United Kingdom or not.[37] This basis (called "the arising basis") did not apply as respects income arising up to and including the year 1973–74 in three cases:

(1) To the income of any person who satisfies the Commissioners that he is not domiciled in the United Kingdom or that (being a British subject or a citizen of the Republic of Ireland) he is not ordinarily resident in the United Kingdom.

(2) To any income which is immediately derived by a person from the carrying on by him of any trade, profession or vocation, either solely or in partnership.

(3) To any income which arises from a pension.

In these three cases, tax was charged on the full amount of the sum *received* in the United Kingdom in the year preceding the year of assessment.[38] This was commonly described as the "remittance basis," as contrasted with the normal "arising basis."

For the year 1974–75 and subsequent years of assessment the remittance basis applies only to (1) in § 7–09, the arising basis applying to cases (2) and (3).[39–40] A deduction of one-tenth is allowed in charging income arising from foreign pensions and annuities.[40–41] Since the remittance basis no longer applies in case (2), no saving of United Kingdom income tax can be achieved by individuals establishing foreign trading partnerships and accumulating profits outside the United Kingdom, unless case (1) applies.[42]

Where the arising basis applies, income tax paid in the place where the income arises may be deducted, unless this is forbidden by the Income Tax Acts or some other relief is given, *e.g.* under a double taxation agreement. Any annuity or other annual payment payable out of the income to a non-resident may likewise be deducted.[43] Foreign income tax on profits which are not chargeable to tax in the United Kingdom cannot be deducted from

37. I.C.T.A. 1970, s.122(1). There are special rules which apply where a source of income is first acquired or ceases. As to Case V losses, see [1980] S.T.I. 107.
38. I.C.T.A. 1970, s.122(3).
39–40. F.A. 1974, ss.22(1) and 23(1).
40–41. F.A. 1974, s.22(1), (3).
42. See, *e.g. Newstead* v. *Frost* (1980) 53 T.C. 525; [1980] S.T.C. 123 (H.C.).
43. I.C.T.A. 1970, s.122(1)(*b*).

income which is so chargeable.[44] The remittance basis does not apply to companies within the charge to corporation tax.[45]

What constitutes a remittance?[46]

7–10   Income is remitted to the United Kingdom if the money or the equivalent of money in normal commercial usage (*e.g.* a cheque or bill of exchange) is received in the United Kingdom, either by the resident taxpayer himself or by another person to whom the taxpayer has directed payment to be made[47] (*e.g.* a creditor), unless the amount remitted has ceased to be the property of the taxpayer before it reaches the United Kingdom.[48] Capital which is remitted to the United Kingdom is not assessable to tax.[49] If income is invested abroad and the investments are later sold and the proceeds of sale remitted to the United Kingdom, this is a remittance of income.[50] Foreign income of a person ordinarily resident in the United Kingdom which is applied abroad in repaying debts in the United Kingdom is deemed to be remitted to the United Kingdom.[51] There are other cases of constructive, or deemed, remittance.[52–53]

Basic periods

7–11   Cases IV and V of Schedule D charge tax on the income which arises (or is received) in the year preceding the year of assessment. There is, however, a different basis period where a fresh source of foreign income arises.[54] Where the remittance basis applies, tax is charged as if a new source arose when the income was first remitted to the United Kingdom, so if the recipient was not resident in the United Kingdom in that year, the normal preceding year basis will apply if he later becomes resident.[55] Where a non-resident with an existing source of foreign income later acquires a United Kingdom residence, this is not a new "source."[56]

Losses

7–11A   The methods by which tax relief for losses is given are discussed in Chapter 12. The Finance Act 1974 contains provisions enabling losses to be relieved against foreign income which, in consequence of the changes made by that Act, is now liable to United Kingdom tax.

---

44. *Scottish American Investment Co.* v. *I.R.C.*, 1938 S.C. 234.
45. I.C.T.A. 1970, s.243(1).
46. See especially *Thomson* v. *Moyse* [1961] A.C. 967; 39 T.C. 291 where the law is reviewed by the House of Lords. It was held that the sale of a cheque in London drawn on a bank abroad was a remittance of the sum realised. See also *Harmel* v. *Wright* (1974) 49 T.C. 149; [1974] S.T.C. 88.
47. *Timpson's Executors* v. *Yerbury* [1936] 1 K.B. 645; 20 T.C. 155 (C.A.).
48. *Carter* v. *Sharon* (1936) 20 T.C. 229. But see *Harmel* v. *Wright,* above.
49. *Kneen* v. *Martin* [1935] 1 K.B. 499 (C.A.); 19 T.C. 33 (remittance of proceeds of sale of investments); *cf. Scottish Provident Institution* v. *Allan* [1903] A.C. 129; 4 T.C. 591 (where interest was intermixed with capital to an extent that made segregation impossible: the onus lies on the taxpayer to show that what is remitted is capital).
50. *Patuck* v. *Lloyd* (1944) 26 T.C. 284 (C.A.).
51. See I.C.T.A. 1970, s.122(4).
52–53. See I.C.T.A. 1970, s.122(5)–(7).
54. See I.C.T.A. 1970, s.123.
55. *Carter* v. *Sharon* (1936) 20 T.C. 229. See Concession A11 as to the year of commencement or cessation of permanent residence.
56. *Back* v. *Whitlock* [1932] 1 K.B. 747; 16 T.C. 723.

Relief for expenses connected with foreign trades etc.

7–11B   Section 35 of the Finance Act 1986 allows a deduction for certain expenses incurred after April 5, 1984 by an individual domiciled in the United Kingdom who carries on a trade, profession or vocation wholly outside the United Kingdom, whether solely or in partnership. Travelling expenses to and from the United Kingdom and board and lodging expenses in the overseas location are allowable deductions under section 130(a) Income and Corporation Taxes Act 1970, if the individual's absence from the United Kingdom is wholly and exclusively for the purposes of performing the functions of the overseas trade. If the taxpayer is absent for a continuous period of 60 days or more for that purpose, the cost of journeys by his spouse and child are allowed, but limited to two return journeys by the same person in any year of assessment.

Section 36 of the Finance Act 1986 allows a deduction for the cost of travelling between overseas locations where an individual carries on separate trades.

3. EMPLOYMENTS WITH A FOREIGN ELEMENT

7–12   The Schedule E charging provisions were restructured by the Finance Act 1974, primarily in order to bring into charge to tax emoluments, wherever earned, of persons resident and ordinarily resident in the United Kingdom and to get rid of the provisions under which emoluments earned by such persons outside the United Kingdom previously escaped United Kingdom tax provided they were not remitted to the United Kingdom during any year of assessment in which the office or employment existed.[57] The changes made by the 1974 Act operated for 1974–75 and subsequent years and take effect subject to double taxation agreements.

The charging provisions

7–12(1)   Schedule E is now divided into three Cases. The expression "foreign emoluments" which is used in connection with the Cases is defined in § 7–14. The meaning of residence, ordinary residence and domicile is discussed in §§ 7–17 *et seq.*

Case I[58] applies where the person holding the office or employment is resident and ordinarily resident in the United Kingdom. The charge is on any emoluments for the chargeable period,[59] *i.e.* the whole of the emoluments are chargeable to tax, subject to the following exceptions:

(1) *Foreign duties performed in periods of long absence from the United Kingdom (365 days or more): 100 per cent. deduction.*[60] This exception meets the case where the job keeps the employee outside the United Kingdom for a consecutive period of at least 365 days, ignor-

---

57. For the law before 1974–75, see 7th ed. at §§ 7–12 *et seq.*
58. I.C.T.A. 1970, s.181(1) substituted by F.A. 1974, s.21(1).
59. Chargeable period means an accounting period of a company or a year of assessment: I.C.T.A. 1970, s.526(5).
60. F.A. 1977, s.31 and Sched. 7.

ing short intervening periods spent in the United Kingdom. More precisely: where in any year of assessment the duties of an employment (including an office[61]) are performed wholly or partly outside the United Kingdom[62] and any of those duties are performed during a *qualifying period* which falls wholly or partly in that year of assessment, no tax is chargeable on the emoluments attributable to that qualifying period or such of it as falls in the year of assessment. In charging tax under Case I of Schedule E on the amount of the emoluments in question, a deduction equal to the whole of them is allowed. A *qualifying period* means[63] a period of at least 365 consecutive days entirely consisting of days of absence[64–65] from the United Kingdom; except that where a period of absence from the United Kingdom is preceded by an earlier such period or periods, all the periods of absence, and the intervening days (but not more than 62) can be added together to see if there are 365 days in all. If there are, the 100 per cent. deduction is allowed provided that out of the total number of days constituting the resulting period the number of days spent in the United Kingdom does not exceed one-sixth of the total number of days in that period. In reckoning the emoluments attributable to a qualifying period there can be included any emoluments covering a period of leave immediately following the period.

(2) *Foreign emoluments.* When the emoluments are foreign emoluments (see § 7–14), a deduction of 50 per cent. of their amount is allowed, for certain persons who were in the relevant employment before March 13, 1984. The deduction is 25 per cent. for 1987–88 and 1988–89.[66–73] The relief disappears after April 6, 1989.[74] Subject to this limited exception, there is no relief from income tax for foreign emoluments chargeable under Case 1.

If the duties are performed wholly outside the United Kingdom in the chargeable period, Case I will not apply[75]; but Case III will apply to emoluments received in the United Kingdom: see § 7–12(3).

> Thus a person domiciled in the United States of America, employed by an American corporation and posted to the United Kingdom for a tour of duty with its United Kingdom branch will pay United Kingdom tax under Case I on half the emoluments from his United Kingdom job. If he also has a directorship with a foreign company and performs the

---

61. *Ibid.* para. 11.
62. Where an employment is in substance one the duties of which fall in the year of assessment to be performed in the United Kingdom, there shall be treated as so performed any duties performed outside the United Kingdom the performance of which is merely incidental to the performance of the other duties in the United Kingdom: *ibid.* para. 8. For the location of duties performed on ships or aircraft: *ibid.* para. 7.
63. *Ibid.* para. 1(2), (3).
64–65. A person is not regarded as absent from the United Kingdom on any day unless he is so absent at the end of it: *ibid.* para. 6.
66–73. F.A. 1984, s.30(9)–(12).
74. The reasons are explained in [1984] S.T.I. 198.
75. F.A. 1974, Sched. 2, para. 4.

duties of that office wholly outside the United Kingdom, he will be charged on a remittance basis under Case III in respect of the emoluments of the foreign directorship.

7–12(2)   *Case II*[76] applies where the person holding the office or employment is not resident or, if resident, is not ordinarily resident in the United Kingdom. Thus it applies to a person who normally lives and works abroad (and so is ordinarily resident outside the United Kingdom) but who works in the United Kingdom for periods sufficiently short to become resident but not ordinarily resident there or so short as to become neither resident nor ordinarily resident. The charge is on the whole of the emoluments for the chargeable period[77] in respect of duties performed in the United Kingdom unless the emoluments are foreign emoluments (see *post*, § 7–14) when a deduction of one-half of their amount may be allowed.[78] Emoluments for duties performed outside the United Kingdom are not taxable under Case II but are taxable under Case III[79] if the person is resident in the United Kingdom and remits the emoluments to the United Kingdom.

7–12(3)   *Case III*[79] applies to persons resident in the United Kingdom (whether ordinarily resident there or not) and applies to emoluments *received* in the United Kingdom in circumstances (mentioned above) in which Cases I and II do not apply.

Emoluments are treated as received in the United Kingdom if they are paid, used or enjoyed or in any manner or form transmitted or brought to the United Kingdom.[80–82]

Non-residents

7–13   Persons who are neither resident nor ordinarily resident in the United Kingdom can be charged to tax in respect of an office or employment only under Case II of Schedule E on the emoluments attributable to the duties performed in the United Kingdom. If the emoluments are foreign emoluments, a deduction of one-half of their amount may be allowed.

Foreign emoluments

7–14   The expression "foreign emoluments" means emoluments of a person not domiciled in the United Kingdom from an office or employment under or with any person, body of persons or partnership resident outside, and not resident in, the United Kingdom.[83]

The expression foreign emoluments describes the emoluments of an individual whose home is outside the United Kingdom but who works in the United Kingdom for a non-resident company. Note that the word "foreign" does not refer to the place where the duties are performed. Foreign emolu-

---

76. I.C.T.A. 1970, s.181(1) substituted by F.A. 1974, s.21(1).
77. Chargeable period means an accounting period of a company or a year of assessment: I.C.T.A. 1970, s.526(5).
78. I.C.T.A. 1970, s.181(1), para. 1 and F.A. 1974, Sched. 2, para. 3.
79. See *post*, § 7–12(3).
80–82. I.C.T.A. 1970, s.184(4). See also § 7–10.
83. I.C.T.A. 1970, s.181(1), para. 1.

ments may be taxable under any one of the three Cases of Schedule E, depending on the residence and ordinary residence of the taxpayer.

Place of performance of duties

7–15   There are a number of rules which apply for determining the place where duties of an office or employment are to be treated as performed. These are as follows:

(1) Under section 184(2) of the Income and Corporation Taxes Act 1970 where an office or employment is in substance one the duties of which fall in the year of assessment to be performed outside the United Kingdom, duties of an incidental character performed in the United Kingdom are to be treated as performed outside the United Kingdom. *Semble,* a close examination of all duties performed in and out of the United Kingdom should be made to see to what extent the duties performed in the United Kingdom are incidental to those performed outside the United Kingdom.[84] (Section 184(2) is ignored in determining when duties are performed or whether a person is absent from the United Kingdom in applying exception (1) in § 7–12(1).)[85]

(2) Under section 184(3) the following duties are to be treated as performed in the United Kingdom:

(a) the duties of any office or employment under the Crown of a public nature[86] of which the emoluments are payable out of public revenue; and

(b) any duties which a person performs on a vessel engaged on a voyage not extending to a port outside the United Kingdom, or which a person resident in the United Kingdom performs on a vessel or aircraft engaged on a voyage or journey beginning or ending in the United Kingdom, or on a part beginning or ending in the United Kingdom of any other voyage or journey.[87]

Expenses in connection with work done abroad

7–15A   Section 32 of the Finance Act 1977, which has effect for 1977–78 and subsequent years of assessment, gives a special relief to employees who are resident and ordinarily resident in the United Kingdom and who hold an office or employment ("the overseas employment") the duties of which are performed wholly outside the United Kingdom. When the emoluments are

---

84. See *Robson* v. *Dixon* (1972) 48 T.C. 527; *post,* § 7–20. The Revenue generously state that they "would normally concede on *de minimis* grounds a single take-off and landing in the United Kingdom in a year in considering whether any duties were performed in this country by an airline pilot of British nationality owning a house in the United Kingdom who was otherwise resident abroad": *Hansard,* Vol. 898, col. 431. (October 28, 1975).

85. F.A. 1977, Sched. 7, para. 9.

86. Duties performed by civil servants are of a public nature, whatever the rank or grade of the servant: *Graham* v. *White* (1971) 48 T.C. 163. And see *Wienand* v. *Anderton* (1976) 51 T.C. 570; [1977] S.T.C. 12.

87. As to modifications to this provision in applying F.A. 1977, Sched. 7, see *ibid.* para. 7.

not foreign emoluments: see § 7–14. The following expenses are treated for the purposes of section 189(1) as necessarily incurred for the purposes of the overseas employment:

(a) expenses incurred by the employee in travelling from the United Kingdom to take up the overseas employment and in returning to the United Kingdom on its termination;

(b) where the employee holds two or more offices or employments, one outside the United Kingdom, and he travels from one place of duty to the other (either or both of such places being out of the United Kingdom), the expenses of travelling are treated as incurred in performing the duties to be performed at his destination[88];

(c) where a person is absent from the United Kingdom for a continuous period of 60 days or more for the purpose of performing duties outside the United Kingdom, travelling expenses incurred by the employee in visiting (or being visited by) his spouse or child are (within stringent limits) allowed;

(d) where in order to enable him to perform the duties of an overseas employment, board and lodging outside the United Kingdom is provided (or the cost is reimbursed), the cost (or the amount reimbursed, as the case may be) is deductible.

The reliefs for travelling expenses in (a) and (c) have been found to be unduly restrictive and are relaxed by provisions contained in section 34 of the Finance Act 1986 which generally take effect from April 6, 1984. Originally only expenses incurred in travelling from or to the point of departure or arrival (*e.g.* an airport) in the United Kingdom were allowed; but the relief now applies to travelling to and from any place in the United Kingdom.

Travelling expenses of non-domiciled employees

7–15B   Section 37 of the Finance Act 1986 allows a Schedule E deduction for travelling expenses paid or reimbursed by his employer to an employee working in, but not domiciled in, the United Kingdom. The deduction is for the cost of travelling from his usual place of abode to any location in the United Kingdom to perform duties there, and the return journey. There is no limit on the number of journeys in respect of which the travelling expenses are deductible. If the employee is present in the United Kingdom for a continuous period of sixty days or more to perform duties there, a deduction is allowed for the cost of journeys undertaken by his spouse or child in order to accompany or visit him; but the deduction is limited to two return journeys for any one individual in a particular tax year. There is a five year limit for which the relief is available.

Section 37 generally applies from April 6 1984, except that the five year limitation generally applies only from April 6 1986.[88a]

---

88. This involves a departure from normal Schedule E principles, which draw a distinction between travelling *on* the job (deductible) and travelling *to* the job (non-deductible).
88a. F.A. 1986, s.38.

Terminal payments

7–16   The provisions discussed in §§ 3–24 *et seq.* apply to offices and employments in which a foreign element is involved, but subject to an exception
where the holder's service included "foreign service" (as defined).[89]

4. THE NATURE OF RESIDENCE AND ORDINARY RESIDENCE

7–17   The Tax Acts contain no definition of the terms "residence" and "ordinary
residence," which accordingly have their ordinary dictionary meaning. In
the case of an individual, "residence" describes the country where he lives.
"Ordinary residence" is broadly equivalent to habitual residence and contrasts with casual or occasional residence.[90] The question whether an individual is ordinarily resident in the United Kingdom in any year of
assessment has to be answered by examining his pattern of life over a
period of years: in this respect, the concept of ordinary residence
resembles domicile more than residence. A person may be resident but not
ordinarily resident in the United Kingdom in a year of assessment; conversely, he may be ordinarily resident but not resident.[91] It will be seen
from the cases referred to below that an individual who is physically absent
from the United Kingdom for an entire year of assessment is normally not
resident there; but it is clear that such a person may be treated as ordinarily
resident if, for example, he was ordinarily resident in the previous year and
returned to the United Kingdom as a resident in the following year. Thus
an individual cannot escape capital gains tax by physically absenting himself from the United Kingdom for one year of assessment during which he
disposes of his assets, for he will be treated as ordinarily resident (though
not resident) in the United Kingdom in that year. The purchase of accommodation in the United Kingdom is some indication of "ordinary"
residence.

The concept of "ordinary residence" is important as regards (a)
immunity from income tax[92] and inheritance tax[93] in respect of certain
British Government securities; (b) immunity from capital gains tax[94]; (c)
the taxation of emoluments[95]; (d) the application of section 478 of the
Income and Corporation Taxes Act 1970[96]; and (d) the application of section 45 of the Finance Act 1981.[97]

Confusion as to the ordinary residence status of someone who comes to
the United Kingdom for some temporary purpose, especially employment,
and who has accommodation for his use in this country, has prompted the

---

89. I.C.T.A. 1970, s.188(2) as amended.
90. *I.R.C.* v. *Lysaght* [1925] A.C. 234; 13 T.C. 511 (H.L.) and see *R.* v. *Barnet London
Borough Council, ex p. Nilish Shah* [1982] Q.B. 688 (C.A.) (a case on eligibility for an award
under the Education Act 1962 and the Local Education Authority Awards Regulations 1979).
See also *R.* v. *Secretary of State for the Home Department, ex p. Margueritte* [1983] Q.B.180
(C.A.).
91. *Cf.* F.A. 1965, s.20; *post,* § 16–04.
92. See *ante,* § 7–01.
93. See *post,* § 19–26.
94. See *post,* § 16–04.
95. See *ante,* §§ 7–12 *et seq.*
96. See *post,* § 7–26.
97. See *post,* § 7–29.

Board of Inland Revenue to issue a Statement of Practice on the subject.[98] A person who comes to the United Kingdom is not usually regarded as having become ordinarily resident here until he has been in this country for at least three years, unless it is clear from before then that he intends to be here for three years or more. In general it is the Board's practice to regard someone who comes to the United Kingdom, whether to work here or not, as ordinarily resident for tax purposes:

(a) from the date of his arrival if he has, or acquires during the year of arrival, accommodation for his use in the United Kingdom which he occupies on a basis that implies a stay in this country of three years or more,

(b) from the beginning of the tax year in which such accommodation becomes available.

If in the event an individual, who has been regarded as ordinarily resident solely because he has accommodation here, disposes of the accommodation and leaves the United Kingdom within three years of his arrival he would normally be regarded as not ordinarily resident for the duration of his stay if this were to his advantage.[98]

The six months rule

7–18   Section 51 of the Income and Corporation Taxes Act 1970 provides that a person who is in the United Kingdom for some temporary purpose only and not with a view or intent of establishing his residence there, and who has not actually resided in the United Kingdom at one time or several times for a period equal in the whole to six months in any year of assessment, shall not be chargeable as a United Kingdom resident; but that a person who has so actually resided shall be so chargeable. Thus physical presence in the United Kingdom in a year of assessment for some temporary purpose will not make a person resident in the year unless the physical presence is for a period or periods totalling six months in the year of assessment. Six months is regarded as equivalent to 183 days, whether or not the year is a leap year. Fractions of a day will be taken into account to measure the period spent in the United Kingdom[99] except that, under the present practice of the Revenue, days of arrival and days of departure are normally ignored.[1] An individual physically present in the United Kingdom for more than six months, but not in the same year of assessment, is not thereby made resident.

Presence for less than six months

7–19   It follows from section 51 of the Income and Corporation Taxes Act 1970 (*ante*, § 7–18), that a person who is physically present in the United Kingdom for less than six months in a year of assessment may nevertheless be

98. This is SP 3/81. [1981] S.T.I. 200 and 202.
99. *Wilkie* v. *I.R.C.* [1952] Ch. 153; 32 T.C. 395.
1. See Inland Revenue booklet, "Residents and Non-residents: Liability to Tax in the United Kingdom," I.R. 20, para. 8.

treated as resident there if his presence has a "residential quality." The following numbered paragraphs exemplify this proposition.

(1) *Place of abode in the United Kingdom.* A person who has his home abroad but also has a place of abode available for his occupation in the United Kingdom will be treated as resident in the United Kingdom in any year of assessment in which he visits the United Kingdom, however short his visit. If he visits in four or more consecutive years, or intends to do so from the start, he will be treated as ordinarily resident also.[2]

> Thus in *Lloyd* v. *Sulley*,[3] a merchant who carried on business in Italy (where he ordinarily resided) owned a house in the United Kingdom where he lived with his family for several months in a year. It was held that he was resident in the United Kingdom, for his occupation of the house had the characteristics of a settled residence. The same conclusion was reached in a case where the establishment was leased to,[4] and in another where it was owned by,[5] a company controlled by the taxpayer. By contrast a different conclusion was reached in a case where a merchant living in Madras had a family home in Scotland (where his children lived during the year of assessment) but which the merchant did not visit during the year.[6]

Hence *ownership* of the place of abode is immaterial. Note that physical presence within the United Kingdom is necessary for residence as distinct from ordinary residence. A house owned by a visitor but let on terms which give him no right of occupation is not in practice regarded as available for his use.[7]

7–20   There is an important statutory qualification[8] to the proposition in (1) in § 7–19 which applies where a person works full-time abroad in a trade, profession, vocation, office or employment where all the duties thereof are performed outside the United Kingdom. In this case the question whether he is resident in the United Kingdom must be decided without regard to any place of abode maintained there for his use; and if (in the case of an office or employment) the office or employment is one of which the duties fall in the year of assessment to be performed outside the United Kingdom, merely incidental duties performed within the United Kingdom are treated as performed abroad. Thus a man who works full-time abroad but who keeps his house in the United Kingdom (*e.g.* for use when on leave) is not treated as resident in the United Kingdom merely by virtue of his ownership of the house and of his visits when on leave. Further, if his job brings him to the United Kingdom, the duties performed here are disregarded.

> But in *Robson* v. *Dixon*[9] a pilot employed by K.L.M. Airlines and based in Amsterdam occasionally landed in the United Kingdom *en route* to his destination. It was held that the landings in the United Kingdom were not "merely

---

2. *Ibid.* para. 21.
3. (1884) 2 T.C. 37, *per* Lord Shand at p. 44.
4. *Cooper* v. *Cadwalader* (1904) 5 T.C. 101.
5. *Loewenstein* v. *De Salis* (1926) 10 T.C. 424.
6. *Turnbull* v. *Foster* (1904) 6 T.C. 206.
7. See Inland Revenue booklet in note 1 at para. 28.
8. I.C.T.A. 1970, s.50.
9. (1972) 48 T.C. 527.

incidental to the performance of the other duties outside the United Kingdom." The duties performed here had the same quality as those performed elsewhere.

7–21   (2) *Regular visits.* A person who maintains no place of abode in the United Kingdom may nevertheless be held to be resident there if he pays regular visits to the United Kingdom (although for less than 183 days in each year of assessment) if these visits form part of his habit of life. The Revenue's practice in applying this rule is as follows:

> "A visitor who has no accommodation available will be regarded as becoming resident and ordinarily resident after his visits for four consecutive years have averaged three months or more a year. If it is clear when he first comes that he proposes to make such visits, he may be treated as resident and ordinarily resident in the United Kingdom from the start."[10]

Thus a person who comes to the United Kingdom for a period of study or education expected to last more than four years will be regarded by the Revenue as resident and ordinarily resident from the date of his arrival in the United Kingdom.[11] A person who comes to the United Kingdom to work for a period of at least two years is treated as resident for the whole period but not as ordinarily resident until he has been in the United Kingdom for at least three years.[12]

By contrast, a person who visits the United Kingdom over a number of years merely in the course of travel will not be treated as resident there.

Although the purpose of the visitor is relevant in determining whether or not his visits have a residential quality, it is immaterial that the visitor has no freedom of choice, *e.g.* because his presence in the United Kingdom is an exigency of his business.[13]

> In *Levene* v. *I.R.C.*[14] a retired businessman who had been resident and ordinarily resident in the United Kingdom went to live abroad where he lived in hotels, having no fixed abode. For five years thereafter he spent four or five months each year in the United Kingdom obtaining medical advice, visiting relatives, etc.—this being part of his regular system of life. *Held,* he remained resident in the United Kingdom having left the United Kingdom for "occasional" residence abroad (see § 7–22).

> In *I.R.C.* v. *Lysaght*[15] a director sold his house in England and went to live with his family in Ireland. He returned to England each month for directors' meetings, remaining for about a week on the company's business and staying in hotels. *Held,* he was resident in the United Kingdom.

7–22   (3) *Former residence.* Section 49 of the Income and Corporation Taxes Act 1970 provides that where a British subject or citizen of the Republic of Ireland, whose ordinary residence has been in the United Kingdom, leaves the United Kingdom for the purpose only of occasional residence abroad,

---

10. See Inland Revenue booklet in note 1 at para. 21.
11. *Ibid.* paras. 23–24; *Miesegaes* v. *I.R.C.* (1957) 37 T.C. 493 (C.A.).
12. *Ibid.* para. 25.
13. *I.R.C.* v. *Lysaght* [1928] A.C. 234 at p. 248; 13 T.C. 511 at pp. 534–535; *Inchiquin* v. *I.R.C.* (1948) 31 T.C. 125.
14. [1928] A.C. 217; 13 T.C. 486, *per* Viscount Cave.
15. *I.R.C.* v. *Lysaght* [1928] A.C. 234 at p. 248; 13 T.C. 511 at pp. 534–535; *Inchiquin* v. *I.R.C.* (1948) 31 T.C. 125.

he will be treated during his absence as actually residing in the United Kingdom. In *Levene* v. *I.R.C.*[16] the observation that the appellant "changed his sky but not his home" graphically describes the state of mind of an individual with an "occasional" residence abroad. Section 49 creates a presumption that a person ordinarily resident in the United Kingdom retains that ordinary residence; but this presumption may be displaced by proof of abandonment of his United Kingdom residence.

> In *Reed* v. *Clark*[16a] the taxpayer was a British subject domiciled in England who, before and after the year 1978–79, was resident in the United Kingdom. He planned to spend 1978–79 working outside the United Kingdom but was also advised that he could avoid United Kingdom income tax on the sale of certain copyrights if he was physically absent from the United Kingdom throughout 1978–79 and sold the rights during that year. He was further advised that he could avoid United States tax if he received payment before January 1, 1978. The taxpayer accordingly left England shortly before April 5, 1978 and returned to England shortly after April 6, 1979. *Held* (i) the Commissioners' determination that the taxpayer was not resident in the United Kingdom for the year 1978–79 was the only true and reasonable conclusion that could be drawn from their findings of primary fact and (ii) section 49 Taxes Act 1970 did not bring the taxpayer into charge to tax. Although the taxpayer intended to avoid liability to income tax, he did not leave the United Kingdom for the purposes of "occasional residence abroad."

Residence in the year of assessment

7–23   The question whether a person is resident or ordinarily resident in the United Kingdom has to be determined for the year of assessment. Strictly, each tax year has to be looked at as a whole and a person is either resident or not resident for the whole year. He cannot be regarded as resident for part only. There is, however, a published concession[17] which applies when a person leaves the United Kingdom for permanent residence abroad so as to become not ordinarily resident in the United Kingdom or becomes a new permanent resident not previously ordinarily resident in the United Kingdom. In such cases, he is treated as ceasing to be resident (or becoming resident, as the case may be) on the date of departure (or arrival).

Residence of corporations and partnerships

7–24   A corporation is resident in the country (or countries) where its real business is carried on; which is where the central management and control resides.[18] Central management and control (in the sense of the highest level of control) is usually invested by the constitution of the company in its board of directors and therefore normally lies in the country where the board meets; but if in fact control is exercised elsewhere, the company will be treated as resident elsewhere. The Revenue have published a Statement of Practice which seeks to draw out the implications of the decisions of the

---

16. [1928] A.C. 217; 13 T.C. 486, *per* Viscount Cave.
16a. [1985] S.T.C. 323.
17. Concession A11. See Inland Revenue booklet in note 1 at para. 11.
18. *De Beers Consolidated Mines* v. *Howe* [1906] S.T.C. 198; and see *Unit Construction* v. *Bullock* [1960] A.C. 351; 38 T.C. 712 (H.L.).

Courts, and which indicates how the Revenue will apply the "central control and management test."[18a] A company resident in the United Kingdom may not lawfully cease to be so resident without Treasury consent.[19]

The residence of a partnership is determined on principles similar to those governing corporations. If the control and management of the firm is situate abroad, the trade or business of the firm is deemed to be carried on by persons resident outside the United Kingdom and the firm is deemed to reside outside the United Kingdom, notwithstanding the fact that some of the members are resident in the United Kingdom and some of the trading operations are conducted within the United Kingdom[20]; but the profits of trading operations within the United Kingdom are chargeable to United Kingdom taxation.[21]

5. DOUBLE TAXATION RELIEF

7-25 Income arising in one country to which a person resident in another country is entitled may be subject to tax in both countries. Under English law relief in respect of the foreign tax may take one of the following forms:

(1) *Double taxation conventions*[22]

Many conventions have been entered into between the United Kingdom and foreign governments providing relief from double taxation. Each convention is different but, broadly speaking, the relief may take one of two forms:

(a) Certain classes of income are made taxable only in one of the countries concerned, *e.g.* in the country where the taxpayer resides.

(b) Other income is taxable in both countries but (in the case of United Kingdom residents) the foreign tax is allowed as a credit against United Kingdom taxes.

Where the taxpayer is resident in both countries, the relief in (a) is usually not available.

(2) *Unilateral relief*

Where there is no double taxation convention in force, relief is given in accordance with section 498 of the Income and Corporation Taxes Act 1970 by allowing the foreign tax to be credited against United Kingdom tax in respect of the income.

18a. See SP 6/83 in [1983] S.T.I. 360. See also [1981] S.T.I. 39 (consultative document).
19. I.C.T.A. 1970, s.482. In March 1986 the Chancellor announced that section 482 had been reviewed and that it would be inappropriate to make any changes to the legislation; but the list of general consents was being reviewed: [1986] S.T.I. 187.
20. *Ibid.* s.153(1).
21. *Ibid.* s.153(2).
22. *Ibid.* s.497.

(3) *Relief by deduction*

Where neither (1) nor (2) applies the foreign tax may be deducted in computing the amount of foreign income which is assessable to United Kingdom income tax.

6. ANTI-AVOIDANCE LEGISLATION

7-26   Income of a person neither resident nor domiciled within the United Kingdom, which arises outside the United Kingdom, escapes United Kingdom income tax. If it were not for the provisions of sections 478–481 of the Income and Corporation Taxes Act 1970, an individual who was resident in the United Kingdom could thus avoid United Kingdom income tax by transferring income-producing property to trustees of a foreign settlement made by the individual, of which the individual was a beneficiary. Section 478(1) counters this form of avoidance by providing that where an individual who is *ordinarily* resident (see § 7–17) in the United Kingdom makes a transfer of assets in consequence of which (whether directly or through associated operations) income becomes payable to persons resident or domiciled outside the United Kingdom, and the individual has power to enjoy that income—the words "power to enjoy" being widely defined[23]— the income shall be treated as the individual's income for all the purposes of the Tax Acts.

> *Example*
> X, a United Kingdom ordinarily resident individual, owns a block of shares, dividends on which attract higher rate income tax. Hoping to avoid tax, X forms a Bahamian settlement including (say) X and his wife as beneficiaries and transfers the shares to the trustees. The settlement provides for accumulation of income, which may eventually be appointed to X in a capital form by the trustees.
> The effect of section 478 is to deem the income which accrues to the Bahamian trustees to be income of X for tax purposes, because X has power to enjoy that income.

7-27   Section 478(1) applies where an individual has power to enjoy the income of a non-resident person. Section 478(2) applies in another case, namely, where the individual receives or is entitled to receive a capital sum the payment whereof is in any way connected with the transfer or any associated operation; and the expression "capital sum" is defined as meaning any sum paid or payable by way of loan or repayment of a loan and any other sum paid or payable otherwise than as income, being a sum which is not paid or payable for full consideration in money or money's worth.[24] Again, the charge is on the income accruing to the non-resident person.[25]

---

23. *Ibid.* s.478(5) as amended by F.A. 1981, s.46(5).
24. *Ibid.* s.478(2) and s.478(2A) and (2B) added by F.A. 1981, s.46(3), (4).
25. As to the extent of the charge, see R.S. Boyd, "Requiem for a man of straw" [1980] B.T.R. 442.

7-28   The House of Lords decided in the *Vestey* case.[26] that section 478 does not apply where the individual having power to enjoy the income of the non-resident person did not make the relevant transfer of assets. Thus if X transfers income-producing property to the trustees of a foreign discretionary settlement of which X's children and remoter issue (but neither X nor his wife) are beneficiaries, section 478 cannot be invoked against any one or more of the beneficiaries save in very exceptional circumstances. *e.g.* if the beneficiary and X have conspired together to cause the settlement to be made.

7-29   Section 45 of the Finance Act 1981 introduces new provisions which are designed to apply where section 478 does not apply and thus to "fill the gap" left by the decision in the *Vestey* case.[26] Section 45 applies where (a) by virtue or in consequence of a transfer of assets, either alone or in conjunction with associated operations, income becomes payable to a person resident or domiciled outside the United Kingdom, and (b) an individual *ordinarily* resident (see § 7-17) in the United Kingdom who is not liable to tax under section 478 by reference to the transfer *receives a benefit* provided out of assets which are available for the purpose by virtue or in consequence of the transfer or of any associated operations. Note that no charge to tax arises under the section unless there is a receipt of benefit; but difficult questions arise in practice in seeking to apply these words to actual situations, *e.g.* providing cheap loans or cheap accommodation: *cf.* the more detailed provisions in section 80 of the Finance Act 1981 in § 16-26. These are provisions to prevent a double charge to tax under section 45 and section 80 of the Finance Act 1981.[27] Section 45 applies irrespective of when the transfer or associated operation took place but only to benefits received and relevant income arising on or after March 10, 1981.[28] Tax is charged under Case VI of Schedule D.[29]

Where an amount of income of a non-resident person is attributed to a beneficiary under section 478 or section 45 (above), it cannot be attributed a second time to the same or another beneficiary. Where there is a choice as to the person in relation to whom any amount of income can be taken into account, it is taken into account in relation to such of them, and if more than one in such proportions respectively, as appears to the Board to be just and reasonable. Any decision of the Board is subject to review on appeal to the Special Commissioners.[30]

7-30   A benefit is chargeable under section 45 only to the extent that it represents income arising to the person resident or domiciled outside the United Kingdom either during the year of assessment in which the benefit is received or in some previous year or years.[31]

---

26. *Vestey* v. *I.R.C.* [1980] A.C. 1148; 54 T.C. 503 (H.L.).
27. F.A. 1981, s.45(6).
28. *Ibid.* s.45(9).
29. *Ibid.* s.45(4).
30. *Ibid.* s.46(1)–(2).
31. *Ibid.* s.45(2), (3).

Thus if X transfers £50,000 into a foreign trust to hold on discretionary trusts for the benefit of X's children and grandchildren (but excluding X and any wife of X) and the trustees invest and accumulate the income outside the United Kingdom for eventual distribution to one or more of the beneficiaries, no charge to tax under section 45 arises until actual distributions representing accumulated income are made.

7–31   Section 45 applies where the individual is ordinarily resident in the United Kingdom; but the "remittance basis" applies if the individual is domiciled outside the United Kingdom as respect any benefit not received in the United Kingdom.[32]

7–32   There are provisions which exempt transactions in respect of which the Board is satisfied either (a) that tax avoidance was not the purpose or one of the purposes for which the transfer or associated operations or any of them were effected; or (b) that the transfer and any associated operations were bona fide commercial transactions and were not designed for the purpose of avoiding liability to taxation.[33]

The Revenue have wide powers to obtain information for the purposes of both section 478 and section 45 (above).

7–33   There are provisions for preventing a double charge to tax, both under section 478 and or section 45 (above) and under the new provisions which apply to controlled foreign companies: see §§ 14–85 *et seq*.

Roll-up funds

7–34   In 1982–83 the roll-up fund emerged. Such funds were operated by off-shore companies incorporated mainly by United Kingdom merchant banks. The investing public subscribed for redeemable preference shares in an offshore fund, which invested the subscription moneys in the money markets at wholesale interest rates. The preference shares carried no right to any dividend but the moneys invested (with the profits they earned) could be realised at any time by redeeming the shares. This was a "disposal" for capital gains tax purposes but many investors were able to take advantage of the annual exemption which, in 1983–84, was £5,300 for individuals. At one time it was supposed that income accruing to investors would be taxed under section 478 of the Income and Corporation Taxes Act 1970 (see § 7–26) but it later became apparent that this was not to be the case. Further legislation was required.

The Finance Act 1984[34] deals comprehensively with offshore funds by charging income tax on any increase in the value of the shares between

---

32. *Ibid.* s.45(5). *Cf.* §§ 7–09 and 7–10.
33. I.C.T.A. 1970, s.478(3), which applies also to F.A. 1981, s.45 by virtue of s.45(8). "Taxation" in this subsection includes capital gains tax or capital transfer tax or inheritance tax: see *Sassoon* v. *I.R.C.* (1943) 25 T.C. 154.
34. F.A. 1984, ss.92–100.

January 1, 1984 and the time of disposal. No charge to income tax arises unless and until the shares are actually disposed of. Any gain which had accrued before January 1, 1984, was liable only to capital gains tax—again, deferred until the time of actual disposal. The capital gains tax rules about disposals apply, subject to some modifications: First, there is a deemed disposal on the death of the shareholder giving rise to a tax charge (*cf.* § 16–19); Secondly, the rules about paper-for-paper and similar transactions (see § 16–13) are modified so as to "trigger" a tax charge where, *e.g.* a shareholder in an offshore funds exchanges his shares for shares in another offshore fund.

CHAPTER 8

TOTAL INCOME: THE COMPUTATION OF THE TAX LIABILITY OF AN INDIVIDUAL UNDER THE UNIFIED SYSTEM

INTRODUCTION

8–01 IN the earlier chapters of this book we have seen what income is chargeable to tax and the detailed provisions of the Schedules and Cases under which income is so chargeable. In this chapter we see how, for each year of assessment ending on April 5, the taxable income of an *individual* is determined and charged to tax. The word "individual" does not include personal representatives or trustees, nor does it include companies.

1. THE METHOD OF CHARGING TAX

8–02 The rates of tax and the "bands" of income taxed at those rates are determined annually by Parliament.[1] The Finance Act 1986, the Budget Resolutions for which were passed on March 18, 1986, fixes the rates and bands for 1986–87.

Basic and higher rate income tax

8–03 Section 32 of the Finance Act 1971 (as amended) prescribes the method of charging income tax. The first band of an individual's *taxable income* is charged at the basic rate. Taxable income means the amount of an individual's income after making deductions for personal reliefs, etc., as explained in §§ 8–15 *et seq.* For the year 1986–87 the basic rate is 29 per cent. and the basic rate band ends at £17,200.[2] The amount up to which income is chargeable at the basic rate is known as *the basic rate limit.*[3]

8–04 Income of an individual in excess of the basic rate limit is not charged at the basic rate but is charged at a higher rate or rates in accordance with a statutory table.[2] Tax at these higher rates may be conveniently referred to as "higher rate tax." The table applicable for 1986–87 is as follows:

---

1. F.A. 1971, s.32.
2. F.A. 1986, s.16.
3. F.A. 1980, s.24(3).

Tax Rates 1986–87

	Bands		Tax	Taxable income	Total tax
		%			
Basic rate band	17,200 @		29 = 4,988	17,200	4,988
Higher rate bands	1st	3,000 @	40 = 1,200	20,200	6,188
	2nd	5,200 @	45 = 2,340	25,400	8,528
	3rd	7,900 @	50 = 3,950	33,300	12,478
	4th	7,900 @	55 = 4,345	41,200	16,823
Remainder			60 over	41,200	—

There is an expanded table in § 8–70.

Section 24(4) of the Finance Act 1980 provides for the indexation of income tax thresholds and allowances by reference to the retail prices index. Indexation applies unless Parliament otherwise determines. In 1986–87, the main thresholds and allowances were increased by the statutory indexation figure of 5.7 per cent., rounded up[3a]; but indexation was not applied to the higher rate bands.

Additional rates on investment income

8–05   For years up to and including the year 1983–84, where an individual's taxable income included investment income in excess of a certain amount, income tax was charged at an additional rate or rates, *i.e.* additional to basic rate income tax and to higher rate tax.[4] This additional rate tax was referred to as the "investment income surcharge." For the year 1983–84, for example, investment income in excess of £7,100 was charged at an additional rate of 15 per cent. The investment income surcharge was abolished for the year 1984–85 and subsequent years of assessment.[5]

What is earned income?

8–06   When the investment income surcharge was in force, it was necessary to define "investment income." Section 32(3) of the Finance Act 1971 defined investment income as "any income other than earned income." This definition is no longer required and section 32(3) has been repealed, but the meaning of "earned income" continues to have importance, *e.g.* in the tax treatment of husband and wife: see § 8–10.

8–07   Earned income is defined in section 530 of the Income and Corporation Taxes Act 1970 to include (in relation to an individual) the following:

(1) Remuneration from an office or employment, including the annual value of property which the employee is entitled to occupy rent free.[6]

3a. The Income Tax (Indexation) Order 1986 S.I. No. 529 in (1986) S.T.I. 235.
4. For details, see the 15th edition.
5. F.A. 1984, s.17, and Sched. 7.
6. I.C.T.A. 1970, s.185. See *ante*, §§ 3–21 *et seq.*

In *Dale* v. *I.R.C.*[7] it was held that an annuity payable under a will to a trustee for acting as such was income of an office of profit and therefore earned income.

In *White* v. *Franklin*,[8] F. was the managing director of a family company and held no shares. To induce F. to stay with the company, his mother and brother settled shares in the company on him for so long as he should be engaged in the management of the company. *Held,* that the settlement income paid to F. was earned income.

(2) Pensions given in respect of past service in an office or employment, whether the pension is paid to the servant or his wife or parent and whether contributory or not.

(3) Payments in connection with the termination of an office or employment which are assessable under section 187 of the Income and Corporation Taxes Act 1970.[9]

(4) Any income charged under Schedule A, Schedule B or Schedule D which is *immediately derived* (see § 8–08) by the individual from the carrying on or exercise by him of his trade, profession or vocation, either as an individual or, in the case of a partnership, as a partner *personally acting* therein. It follows from the words "personally acting" that the income of a "sleeping" partner (including, as a general rule, that of a limited partner), and the income of beneficiaries under a trust derived from a business carried on by the trustees, is not earned income.[10] Interest paid to a partner (other than a sleeping or limited partner) in respect of capital contributed by him to the partnership is earned income.

(5) Post-cessation receipts.[11]

(6) Income from patent rights actually devised by the recipient.[12]

(7) Annuities payable under approved retirement annuity contracts.[13]

(8) Annuities payable to retired partners, within limits: see § 8–09.

(9) Profits or gains of an individual from any commercial letting of furnished holiday accommodation to which the Finance Act 1984 applies.[14]

8–08   *Trades and professions.* The words "immediately derived" in § 8–07(4) are narrowly construed so as to exclude income which is not exclusively attributable to the carrying on of a trade, etc.

Thus in *Bucks* v. *Bowers*[15] merchant bankers held securities and foreign investments in the course of their business. The share of income of a partner derived from these sources was held not to be earned income on the ground that the

---

7. [1954] A.C. 11; 34 T.C. 468 (H.L.).
8. (1965) 42 T.C. 283.
9. I.C.T.A. 1970, s.187(4). See *ante*, §§ 3–27 *et seq*.
10. *Fry* v. *Sheil's Trustees* (1915) 6 T.C. 583; *M'Dougall* v. *Smith* (1919) 7 T.C. 134; *Hale* v. *Shea* (1964) 42 T.C. 260 in § 4–02, shows that an indivisible payment which is partly in consideration of an agreement to render services if required and partly in consideration of the transfer of goodwill is not earned income of the recipient.
11. I.C.T.A. 1970, s.148. See *ante*, §§ 2–88 *et seq*.
12. *Ibid.* s.383.
13. *Ibid.* s.226(1).
14. F.A. 1984, s.50 and Sched. 11, para. 1. See *ante*, § 4–04A.
15. (1970) 46 T.C. 267. In this case Pennycuick J. appears to have attached some importance to the fact that the interest was paid under deduction of tax; but this, it is thought, is not relevant in applying the words "immediately derived."

source of the income was not the trade but the loan obligations and foreign investments.

In *Pegler* v. *Abell*[16] it was held that an annuity received by a retired partner was not earned income because it was derived not from the past carrying on by the partner of his profession but from the contractual liability of the continuing partners to the retired partner.

In *Northend* v. *White & Leonard & Corbin Greener and others*[17] the taxpayer claimed to treat as earned income his share of interest, being interest earned by a firm of solicitors when depositing clients' funds with a bank which the firm was entitled to retain under section 8(3) of the Solicitors Act 1965. *Held,* not to be earned income.

Templeman J. said this (at pp. 324–325):

" . . . if the Solicitors Act 1965 had not been passed, or if the firm had not carried on the exercise of the profession of solicitors, there would have been no deposit account and no interest. But, it does not follow that the interest was 'immediately derived' from the carrying on of the profession. To produce the interest there must be an intervening event which could not be described as the 'carrying on of the profession of solicitor'; namely, the loan of money by a customer [the firm] to a bank on terms that interest should be paid. The fact that the money lent did not belong to the customer did not prevent the interest deriving from the intervening event; namely, the loan and the contract between the customer and the bank."

He accordingly held that the interest was not "exclusively attributable" to the carrying on of the practice.

Contrast *Peay* v. *Newton*[18] where the proceeds of the sale of the goodwill of a hairdressers' business (taxable under Case VII of Schedule D as a short-term capital gain: see § 16–03A) was held to be exclusively attributable to and immediately derived from the carrying on of the business which was sold.

8–09 *Partnership retirement annuities.* In *Pegler* v. *Abell*[19] a retirement annuity paid to a partner was held not to be earned income, on the ground that it was not immediately derived from the carrying on by him of his profession but from the contractual liability imposed under the partnership deed on the continuing partners: see § 8–08. Section 16 of the Finance Act 1974 gives some relief from the effect of this decision. It provides that where a person ceases to be a member of a partnership on retirement, because of age or ill health or on death, and annual payments are made to him or his widow or a dependant of his, such payments are within specified limits to be treated as earned income. The section applies to annual payments which are made under the partnership agreement, or under an agreement replacing it or supplementing it or supplementing an agreement replacing it, or to payments made under an agreement made with an individual who acquires the whole or part of the business. Note that the section does not apply where retirement is due otherwise than to age or ill health.

16. (1973) 48 T.C. 564; followed in *Lawrence* v. *Hayman* (1976) 51 T.C. 376; [1976] S.T.C. 227; and see § 8–09.
17. (1975) 50 T.C. 121; [1975] S.T.C. 317.
18. (1970) 46 T.C. 653.
19. (1972) 48 T.C. 564.

The limit referred to may be roughly expressed as 50 per cent. of the average of the retired or deceased partner's share of profits in the best three of the last seven years of assessment in which he was required to devote substantially the whole of his time to acting as a partner, subject to upwards adjustment where the index of retail prices increases: see § 11–13.

8–10   *Husband and wife.* In cases where the income of a wife is deemed to be the income of her husband (see § 8–23) the income, if earned income, is treated as earned income of the husband.[20]

Persons other than individuals

8–11[21]   This chapter is concerned only with the taxation of *individuals*. It should be noted, however, that the levy of income tax at the *basic* rate is not confined to individuals; but only individuals are liable to higher rate tax: see § 8–04. Trustees may be liable to additional rate tax: see § 9–02.

A company resident outside but not within the United Kingdom may be liable to income tax at the basic rate: see § 14–02. Dividends received by such a company from a United Kingdom resident company are not assessed to income tax at the basic rate but will notionally have suffered such tax under the imputation system: see §§ 14–01B *et seq.*

2. The Computation of Taxable Income

8–15   In order to compute the amount of an individual's taxable income in a year of assessment, it is first necessary to determine the amount of his total income. Certain deductions are allowed *in computing* total income, *e.g.* for sums paid under deduction of tax such as annuities and other annual payments. These are called "charges on income": see § 8–31. Other deductions are allowed *from* total income, *e.g.* for personal reliefs.

In the following sections of this chapter are considered:

(1) The meaning of total income (§§ 8–16 *et seq.*).
(2) Charges on income and other deductions (§§ 8–31 *et seq.*), personal reliefs (§§ 8–36 *et seq.*) and deductions in respect of interest (§§ 8–57 *et seq.*).
(3) The allocation of deductions in quantifying and taxing income (§§ 8–68 *et seq.*).

There then follows in § 8–69 a number of specimen computations showing how the provisions are applied in practice.

3. Total Income

8–16   Section 8(1) of the Taxes Management Act 1970 authorises the Revenue to require a person to deliver a return of his income, computed in accordance with the Income Tax Acts and specifying each separate source of income

20. I.C.T.A. 1970, s.530(1).
21. The next paragraph is § 8–15.

and the amount of income from each source. Section 528(1) of the Income and Corporation Taxes Act 1970 provides that:

> " 'total income,' in relation to any person, means the total income of that person from all sources estimated in accordance with the provisions of the Income Tax Acts. . . . "

Thus total income means income under Schedules A to F, as set out in section 1 of the Income and Corporation Taxes Act 1970. The return will show income of the following categories on which tax will be charged in accordance with the following rules:

8–17 (1) *Income not taxed by deduction before receipt.* The income from each source must be stated, computed by reference to the rules of the appropriate Schedule and Case and making whatever deductions are appropriate to each source. Thus a statement of Schedule A income will show rents received and the amounts deductible from those rents. Income falling under all Schedules, other than Schedule D, is taxed on a current year basis, *e.g.* income of the year ended April 5, 1985, forms part of the total income of the year 1984–85. Income falling under all the cases of Schedule D, other than Case VI, is taxed on a preceding year basis.

> Thus if X carries on a profession and makes up annual accounts to April 30, X's profits for the year ended April 30, 1984, form part of his total income for the year 1985–86: see § 2–79. The total income for the year 1985–86 will include interest (other than bank interest) credited to X in 1984–85: see § 5–06.

A partner's share of partnership income forms part of his total income, as illustrated in § 11–06.

8–18 (2) *Income taxed by deduction before receipt.* A return of income computed in accordance with the Income Tax Acts will include particulars of income from which tax has been deducted before receipt,[22] *e.g.* annuities and other annual payments. Such income must be grossed up at the basic rate for the purpose of computing total income.

> Thus an annuity of £70 net is returned as a receipt of £100, if the basic rate of income tax is 30 per cent. (It is a receipt of £98.59 if the basic rate is 29 per cent.

Difficulties sometimes arise when a sum which is due in one year is paid in a later year. Is the sum income of the year in which it was due or of the year in which it was paid? It seems from section 528(3)(*a*) of the Income and Corporation Taxes Act 1970 that it forms part of the total income of the year by reference to which basic rate tax was deducted. If section 52 of the Act applies to the payment (see §§ 5–31 *et seq.*) this is the year when payment was due; whereas, if section 53 (see §§ 5–34 *et seq.*) or section 54 (see § 5–56) of the Act applies, this is the year when payment was made.[23] Where the sum has to be related back to an earlier year, additional assess-

---

22. T.M.A. 1970, s.8(8).
23. F.A. 1971, s.36.

ments to higher rate income tax and investment income surcharge may have to be made for that earlier year.

Tax credit. The effect of including in total income the grossed up amount of annuities and annual payments is that income tax at the basic rate and at higher rates is charged on the grossed up amount. To avoid a double charge to tax, the taxpayer is entitled to credit against income tax so charged an amount equal to the basic rate tax which was deducted before receipt. For an example, see Computation B in § 8–69.

8–19 (3) *Building society interest.* Building society interest is subject to special provisions.[24] The societies pay income tax at a special rate but the investor (who receives his interest "free of tax") is treated as having had tax at the basic rate deducted before receipt. The interest must be grossed up at the basic rate for the purposes of estimating total income, but a credit is given against total tax payable equal to tax at the basic rate on the grossed up amount; but no refund in tax can be obtained by an investor not liable to basic rate income tax. Building society interest is assessed on a current year basis.[25]

> Thus if X receives £70 of building society interest, £100 is included in X's total income (assuming basic rate tax of 30 per cent.). But X gets credit against the total tax payable by him of basic rate tax on £100, *i.e.* £30. In the result X is assessed only to higher rate tax on this income. If X is not liable to basic rate income tax, he cannot recover any part of the £30 treated as deducted.

This example shows that investment in a building society should be avoided by an individual who is not liable to income tax at the basic rate.

(4) *Bank interest.* Most bank interest is treated in a similar way to building society interest. The bank is taxed under the composite rate scheme[26] and pays the depositor net interest which is grossed up at the basic rate for the purpose of computing total income.

8–20 (5) *Dividends and other distributions chargeable under Schedule F.* A return of income must separately state the amount or value of the distribution and the amount of the tax credit[27] (see § 14–01B); and the amount to be included in total income in respect of a dividend chargeable under Schedule F is the actual amount or value of the dividend or other distribution plus the tax credit. A dividend is treated as income of the year by reference to which advance corporation tax is calculated.[28] The shareholder deducts the tax credit from the total tax payable by him.

> Thus if in 1985–86 (when the basic rate is 30 per cent.) X receives a dividend of £70 from a United Kingdom company, this carries a tax credit of 3/7ths of £70. £100 is included in X's total income, *i.e.* the dividend plus the tax credit, but X

---

24. I.C.T.A. 1970, s.343 and see F.A. 1980, s.58.
25. But see *ante*, § 5–05A.
26. F.A. 1984, ss.26–27 and Sched. 8.
27. T.M.A. 1970, s.8(9).
28. I.C.T.A. 1970, s.528(3)(*b*) and see *post*, § 14–59.

gets credit against the total tax payable by him equal to £30. If X is not liable to basic rate income tax, he can make a repayment claim in respect of the whole, or some part of, the £30. See also Computation B in § 8–69.

8–21   (6) *Trust income.* A beneficiary must include in his total income an amount equal to his share of the trust income, grossed up at the basic rate of income tax. The beneficiary is entitled to a tax credit against the total tax payable by him equal to the tax attributable to his share of that income. See Computation B in § 8–69.

8–22   (7) *Salary.*[29] Income tax on salary is deducted before receipt under the PAYE system: see § 3–53. The gross amount is included in total income and the recipient is entitled to a credit for the tax suffered by deduction. Salary is earned income.

Aggregation of income: husband and wife[30]

8–23   Subject to the options discussed in §§ 8–26 and 8–29, and except in the first year of marriage (unless the marriage takes place on April 6),[31] the separate incomes of husband and wife must be aggregated for the purpose of determining total income. This is because a woman's income chargeable to income tax, so far as it is income for a year of assessment or any part of a year of assessment (being a part beginning with April 6) during which she is a married woman "living with her husband," is deemed for income tax purposes to be his income and not to be her income.[32] Hence the husband is assessed on the joint income,[33] there being included as income of the woman any sum which (aggregation apart) would have been included in computing her total income.[34] A married woman is treated for tax purposes as "living with her husband" unless either:

(a) they are separated under an order of a court of competent jurisdiction or by deed of separation; or

(b) they are in fact separated in such circumstances that the separation is likely to be permanent.[35]

8–24   Where one spouse is resident in the United Kingdom for a year of assessment but the other is not, or both are resident in the United Kingdom but one is absent throughout the year of assessment, they are treated for that

---

29. *Ibid.* ss.204–207.

30. See Inland Revenue publication: "Taxation of Wife's Earnings" (1977) I.R. 13. A government Green Paper on the taxation of the family, including the personal tax allowances and the principle of aggregation, has been published and is summarised in [1980] S.T.I. 853.

31. F.A. 1976, s.36(1) and (2). Although the income of husband and wife are not aggregated in the first year of marriage, there are provisions to enable one spouse to transfer specified unutilised reliefs to the other where the transferring spouse has insufficient income: see F.A. 1976, s.36(7) and (8).

32. I.C.T.A. 1970, s.37(1), as amended by F.A. 1976, s.36(2). In the year of marriage, any income of the wife is apportioned on a time basis and the post-marital income treated as income of the husband. If the wife's income is assessed in a preceding year basis, income apportioned to the husband will include earnings of an earlier year: *Leitch* v. *Emworth* (1929) 14 T.C. 633.

33. I.C.T.A. 1970, s.37(2).

34. *Ibid.* s.37(1), proviso, and (4).

35. *Ibid.* s.42(1).

year as if they were permanently separated.[36] Hence their separate incomes are not aggregated for that year.

8–25   A husband whose wife's income is substantial would be in difficulties if his wife declined to fund tax on her income for which he is chargeable under the aggregation rule. Section 40 of the Income and Corporation Taxes Act 1970 enables the Revenue to collect tax from the wife in certain circumstances; and section 41 of that Act entitles a husband to disclaim liability for the tax on his deceased wife's income.

Options for separate assessment

8–26   Either husband or wife may apply to be separately assessed. The application must be made within six months before July 6 in any year of assessment except that, in the case of persons married during the year of assessment, an application has effect for the year for which it is made and for subsequent years, until the application is withdrawn.[37]

8–27[37a]   The effect of an application is that the provisions of the Income Tax Acts governing the assessment, charge, and recovery of income tax apply as if the husband and wife were not married.[38] An application does not have the effect of reducing the total amount of tax payable by husband and wife. Their incomes are aggregated for the purpose of determining the measure of the joint tax liability and reliefs and allowances are apportioned between them.[39] Separate assessment has the effect that each spouse pays his or her respective share of the tax bill. Since the aggregation rule in § 8–23 does not normally apply in the first year of marriage, the option is not needed in that year and is excluded.[40] If the application for separate assessment is not made, the husband can be assessed to tax on his wife's investment income even if they have later come to live apart and she is not prepared to tell him what her income is.[41]

Although a repayment of tax in respect of the wife's income has to be made to her husband if there has been no application for separate assessment, the wife is beneficially entitled to the amount repaid.[42]

Election for non-aggregation of wife's earned income

8–29   The provisions discussed in §§ 8–23 *et seq.* requiring that the income of husband and wife should be aggregated for tax purposes are a disincentive to wives who might otherwise go out to work. Accordingly the provisions

---

36. *Ibid.* s.42(2). See *Gubay* v. *Kington* [1984] S.T.C. 99 (H.L.) (a capital gains tax case in which one spouse was resident and the other not). See also *I.R.C.* v. *Addison* [1984] S.T.C. 540.

37. I.C.T.A. 1970, s.38(1), (3), (4).

37a. The next paragraph is § 8–29.

38. *Ibid.* s.38(1).

39. *Ibid.* ss.38(2) and 39.

40. F.A. 1976, s.36(1) and (2).

41. *Hotter* v. *Spackman* [1982] S.T.C. 483 (C.A.).

42. *Re Cameron, decd.* (1982) 54 T.C. 774; (1965) 42 T.C. 539. But see F.A. 1978, s.22, which allows tax repayment to wives in some cases.

were modified as from the year 1972–73. Section 23 of the Finance Act 1971 provides that where a man and his wife living with him jointly so elect, the wife's earnings and their other income shall be chargeable to tax separately, as provided in Schedule 4 to that Act. "Wife's earnings" is defined[43] as earned income of hers, excluding income arising in respect of any pension, superannuation or other allowance, deferred pay or compensation for loss of office given in respect of the husband's past services in any office or employment. These words of exclusion prevent a husband negotiating a "split" pension—part payable to the husband and part payable to his wife—in order to have the two parts taxed separately.

Where notice of election is given, the wife's earnings (but not her other income) are charged to income tax as if she were a single woman with no other income and the husband's other income (including the wife's investment income) is charged as if the wife's income were nil. Any payments made by her which give rise to relief, such as interest in certain circumstances, must be set solely against the wife's earnings: any excess will be unrelieved.[44] Income tax charged on the wife's earnings is taxed on and recovered from her. Section 23 states the procedure for electing. Notice of election must be given by husband and wife jointly not earlier than six months before the beginning of the year of assessment concerned and not later than 12 months after the end of the year. The Board of Inland Revenue may extend the time limit. The election, once given, remains effective until husband and wife give joint notice of withdrawal, which may be given up to 12 months after the end of the year of assessment concerned. Election for non-aggregation does not mean that husband and wife make separate tax returns. This consequence ensues only if they elect for separate assessment: see §§ 8–26 *et seq*. For 1986–87, the election will normally be worthwhile only if the combined income of the married couple, before deduction of allowances and reliefs, exceeds £26,520 and the earnings of the wife are not less than £6,986.[44a]

Aggregation of income: parent and child

8–30   For the three years 1969–70 to 1971–72 (both inclusive), an infant's income so far as it was income for a year (or part of a year) of assessment during which he or she was unmarried and not regularly working was treated as income of the infant's parent or parents.[45]

Section 16(1) of the Finance Act 1971 provided that for the year 1972–73 and subsequent years of assessment the provisions for aggregation should cease to have effect. The income of an infant child is therefore not now taxed as if it were the income of his parent, except in the case of income of the infant under a settlement made by his parent as explained in §§ 10–23 *et seq*.

43. F.A. 1971, Sched. 4, para. 1.
44. *Ibid*. Sched. 4, para. 4.
44a. See I.R. leaflet I.R. 13 (Wife's Earnings Election) in [1986] S.T.I. 592.
45. I.C.T.A. 1970, ss.43–48.

4. Charges on Income and Other Deductions

Charges on income

8–31   A return of income computed in accordance with the Income Tax Acts will include particulars relating to "charges on income," which are defined as "amounts which fall to be deducted in computing total income."[46] These include annuities or other annual payments.[47] The gross amount of any sum payable under deduction of tax by reason of section 52 of the Income and Corporation Taxes Act 1970 (see § 5–31), *e.g.* annuities or annual payments, is allowable as a deduction in computing total income; whereas interest paid under deduction of tax by reason of section 54 of that Act (see § 5–56) is deductible only where statute so allows (see §§ 8–57 *et seq.*).

Difficulties may arise when a sum which is due in one year is paid in a later year. Is the sum deductible in the year in which it falls due for payment, or in the year in which it is actually paid? It seems from section 528(3)(*b*) of the Income and Corporation Taxes Act 1970, that it is deductible in the year by reference to which basic rate tax is deductible. See and compare § 8–18.

8–32   *Add back of retained tax.* We have seen in § 8–18 that, to avoid a double charge to tax, an individual is entitled to a tax credit where tax at the basic rate has been deducted from income he receives. Where an individual pays an annuity or other annual payment, the gross amount is deductible in computing his total income (see § 8–31) and therefore reduces tax liability at the basic and higher rates (see § 8–05). But where section 52 of the Income and Corporation Taxes Act 1970 applies to the payment, the payer is entitled to retain the tax he deducts on making the payment (see § 5–31). To prevent the individual (in effect) obtaining double relief for tax, he is charged to tax on an amount equal to the tax he so deducts.[48]

Example (1985–86)

8–33   X has earned income of £10,000. He pays Y, his ex-wife, maintenance of £2,000 (gross), *i.e.* £1,400 net after deduction of tax at 30 per cent. (£600), which was the then basic rate. X's tax liability is as follows:

	£
Earned income	10,000
less personal relief (1985–86)	2,205
	7,795
less maintenance	2,000
	5,795

---

46. T.M.A. 1970, s.8(8).

47. I.C.T.A. 1970, s.528(1), (2), (3), (*b*) and Sched. 13. The absence of any general principle allowing the deduction of interest seems to follow from the speech of Viscount Radcliffe in *Frere* v. *I.R.C.* [1965] A.C. 402; 42 T.C. 125 (H.L.).

48. I.C.T.A. 1970, s.3(*a*) read with s.52(1)(*b*).

Tax
	£
£5,795 at 30%	1,738.50
Add back retained tax	
£2,000 at 30%	600
	2,338.50

This example shows that X acts as a tax collector for the Revenue when, on paying Y, he deducts £600 and accounts for this amount in his own tax computation.

8–34 *Add back of income under the settlement provisions.* There are a number of provisions in the Income Tax Acts relating to settlements which, for tax purposes, deem income to be the income of the settlor and not income of any other person. These provisions are discussed in Chapter 10. Where they apply, sums are added back in computing the total income of the settlor. Sums so added back are investment income, even if the settlor's only income is income other than investment income.[49–52] See §§ 10–04 *et seq.*

8–34A Where husband and wife elect for non-aggregation of the wife's earnings (see § 8–29), charges on the wife's income are deductible only from her earnings. Charges on the husband's income are deductible from their joint income excluding the wife's earnings.

Other deductions

8–35 Interest is in some cases deductible in computing total income: see §§ 8–57 *et seq.*
Deductions are in some cases given in respect of losses and capital allowances: see Chapters 12 and 13.
Deductions in respect of personal reliefs are discussed in §§ 8–36 *et seq.*
Deductions are allowed in respect of small maintenance payments: see § 5–05.

5. PERSONAL RELIEFS

8–36 An individual who makes a claim in that behalf is entitled to personal reliefs.[53] Claims for reliefs are made to the Inspector, subject to a right of appeal to the Commissioners where relief is refused.[54] Claims are normally made by the individual making an entry in his tax return in the section headed "Allowances." These reliefs reduce the amount of the income on which he is liable to tax. Where the taxpayer's income in any year is insufficient to absorb in full the reliefs to which he is entitled, they are to that

---

49–52. *Ang* v. *Parrish* (1980) 53 T.C. 304; [1980] S.T.C. 341.
53. I.C.T.A. 1970, s.5.
54. T.M.A. 1970, s.42.

extent lost: there is no provision for carrying forward unabsorbed personal reliefs.

8–37　　Where an individual is entitled to deduct tax at the basic rate on making a payment, *i.e.* where there is a charge on his income equal to the gross amount of the payment (see § 8–31), personal reliefs are restricted to the extent that they reduce the income below an amount equal to the amount of the charge.[55]

> Thus if X, having income of £3,000, makes a deed of covenant for £100 in favour of Y, X's personal reliefs are limited to reliefs on £2,900. This ensures that the Revenue collect basic rate income tax on £100.

8–38　　Personal reliefs may be claimed only by persons resident in the United Kingdom, except in the case of certain classes of non-resident listed in section 27 of the Income and Corporation Taxes Act 1970, who may claim in respect of their United Kingdom income a proportion of the personal reliefs.[56]

8–39　　Before the introduction of the unified system, reliefs were given by deducting from the amount of tax a sum equal to tax at the standard rate on an amount specified as the amount of the relief. Under the unified system, the amount specified as the amount of the relief (shown in the second column of the following Table) is deducted from the individual's total income.[57] Hence income tax at the basic and higher rates is charged on the balance of an individual's income, after deducting personal reliefs and any other allowable deductions. For unified tax the amounts of the personal reliefs have been adjusted to allow for the abolition of earned income relief.

8–40　　The following Table shows the reliefs which are available in 1986–87:

	Allowance £	Paragraph where discussed
Personal relief: married	3,655 ⎱	8–42
: single	2,335 ⎰	
Wife's earned income relief	2,335 (max)	8–44
Age allowance: married	4,505 ⎱	8–43
: single	2,850 ⎰	
Housekeeper	100	8–46
Additional allowance	1,320	8–47
Widow's bereavement allowance	1,320	8–49
Dependent relative	100 or 145	8–51
Son's or daughter's services	55	8–52
Blind person	360	8–53

55. I.C.T.A. 1970, s.25, substituted by F.A. 1971, s.33(5).
56. See generally the Revenue booklet (I.R. 20) on "Residents and Non-residents. Liability to Tax in the United Kingdom"— paras. 60 *et seq.*
57. F.A. 1971, s.33(2); and see § 1–19.

8–41 The following personal allowances may be claimed in the year 1986–87:

1. *Personal relief*[58]

8–42 A married man is entitled to deduct £3,655 from his total income if he proves:

(1) that for the year of assessment he has his wife living with him (in the sense in which those words are defined in § 8–23); or

(2) that he wholly maintains his wife during the year of assessment and is not entitled in computing his total income for the year to make any deduction in respect of the sums paid for his wife's maintenance: see § 8–31.

Accordingly, if a husband and wife are permanently separated and the wife is wholly maintained under payments made by the husband on a voluntary basis, he is entitled to the married man's deduction of £3,655, but if he maintains her under a court order or deed so that the payments are annual payments which are a charge on his income, he is entitled only to the single person's deduction of £2,335.

A married man not within (1) or (2) and a single individual, including a widow or widower and including a child, is entitled to the single person's allowance of £2,335. A man is not entitled to the married man's allowance for a woman to whom he is not married, even though they are living together as man and wife.

The difference between the married man's allowance and the single person's allowance in 1986–87 is £1,320. In the year when a man marries, the allowance of £3,665 is reduced by one-twelfth of £1,320, *i.e.* by £110, for each complete month in that year prior to the date of marriage. The "month" referred to begins with the sixth day of one month and ends with the fifth day of the next.[59] A man who is entitled to a married man's allowance by virtue of a previous marriage existing in the year will continue to receive the amount of the allowance due by virtue of that previous marriage.

Where husband and wife jointly elect that the wife shall be taxed on her earnings as if she were a single person with no other income (see § 8–29), each of them is entitled only to the single person's deduction of £2,335. See Computation D in § 8–69.

8–43 *Persons aged 65 or more with small incomes: age allowance.*[60] In 1986–87 a person whose total income does not exceed £9,400 and who proves that, at some time in the year of assessment, he or his wife living with him (see § 8–23) is aged 65 or more, is entitled to a personal relief of £4,505 if married and £2,850 if single. If the total income exceeds £9,400, the allowance

---

58. I.C.T.A. 1970, s.8(1). In *Nabi* v. *Heaton* [1983] S.T.C. 344 (C.A.) it was held that "wife" in I.C.T.A. 1970, s.8(1) could not be read in the plural.
59. I.C.T.A. 1970, s.8(3).
60. *Ibid.* s.8(1A) and (1B).

is reduced by £2 for every £3 of income over £9,400 until it is the same as the personal allowance in § 8–42.

2. *Relief on wife's earned income*[61]

8-44   Where a husband and wife are living together (see § 8–23) and they have not elected for non-aggregation of the wife's earnings (see § 8–29), their separate incomes are aggregated for tax purposes. Personal reliefs are given to the husband against the total income; no reliefs are given to the wife as such.

If, however, a husband's total income includes any earned income of his wife, the husband is entitled to an additional deduction from total income of £2,335 or, if less, the amount of his wife's earned income. This allowance is given in addition to the personal relief in § 8–42.

The following income of the wife (though earned) is excluded for this purpose:

(a) Pensions and similar payments made to the wife in respect of her husband's past services; and

(b) benefits under the Social Security Act 1975 (other than the wife's Category A retirement pension); and

(c) unemployment benefit.

This additional deduction is not given where husband and wife elect for non-aggregation of the wife's earnings: see § 8–29. Each spouse then gets the single person's allowance only.[62–65] See Computation C in § 8–69. The additional deduction is not available where, in the first year of marriage, the aggregation rule in § 8–23 does not apply.

3. *Child relief*

8-45   For many years a relief from tax was available in respect of a child or children. The effect of the relief was to reduce the amount of tax which would otherwise be payable by the husband, or by husband and wife if each were separately assessed. Alongside, there existed a system of family allowances taxable under Schedule E. The Child Benefit Act 1975 and Regulations made thereunder abolished family allowances as from April 4, 1977, and substituted a system of non-taxable child benefits payable usually to the mother and in respect of all children including the first child. In consequence of the introduction of child benefits, the system of tax allowances for children was phased out and sections 23 to 26 of the Finance Act 1977 implemented Government policy in this respect.

4. *Housekeeper relief*[66]

8-46   The sum of £100 is deductible from the total income of a widower who has a person resident with him in the capacity of a housekeeper being either a relative of his or of his deceased wife or (there being no such rela-

---

61. *Ibid*. s.8(2).
62–65. F.A. 1971, s.23(1) and Sched. 4, para. 3.
66. I.C.T.A. 1970, s.12, as amended. See *Barentz* v. *Whiting* (1965) 42 T.C. 267 (C.A.).

tive able or willing to act in that capacity) some other person who is employed as a housekeeper. The same relief may be claimed by a widow, the relation in this case being a relative of her or her deceased husband. The relief is not allowed where the relative is a man who has claimed and been allowed the higher personal relief applicable to married persons or a married woman living with her husband where the husband has claimed and been allowed the higher personal relief applicable to married persons (see § 8–42); nor where the claimant is entitled to the additional reonal relief in § 8–50.[67] Also the relief is not allowed unless the claimant proves that no other individual is entitled to relief in respect of the relative or, if so entitled, has relinquished his claim thereto.

5. *Additional relief for widows and others in respect of children (or additional personal allowance for one-parent families)*[68]

8–47 A sum equal to the difference between the higher (married persons) relief and the lower (single persons) relief—£1,320 in 1986–87—is deductible from the total income of a person who proves that he has a "qualifying child" (as defined) resident with him. This additional relief may be claimed by widows, widowers and other persons not entitled for the year to the higher personal relief given to married persons (see § 8–43) and by any married man who is so entitled to the higher personal relief but whose wife was throughout the year totally incapacitated by physical or mental infirmity. There are provisions for apportioning the relief where more than one person is eligible.

The claimant must show that neither he nor any other person is entitled to the relief in § 8–49 or that such entitlement has been relinquished.

The relief is not available in the case of a person who is entitled to the single person's allowance in consequence only of electing for the non-aggregation of wife's earnings: see § 8–29.

8–48 A qualifying child is one who is receiving full-time instruction at any university, college, school or other educational establishment *or* is undergoing training for any trade, profession or vocation, in such circumstances that the child is required to devote the whole of his time to the training for a period of not less than two years.[69]

If the necessary conditions are satisfied, the claim may be made notwithstanding that the child is over 18 or marries during the year of assessment.

> In *Heaslip* v. *Hasemer*,[70] a child attended the house of a music teacher for regular lessons and the teacher gave her work to do at home. A claim for child relief was rejected (1) because there was no educational establishment; and (2) because the instruction was not full-time. The court would not accept that there was "constructive instruction" while the pupil practised at home under her tutor's directions.

---

67. F.A. 1971, s.15(5).
68. I.C.T.A. 1970, s.14.
69. *Ibid.* s.10(5) and (6).
70. (1927) 13 T.C. 212.

An educational establishment is one whose primary function is education in the sense of training the mind, as distinct from training in manual skills.[71]

6. *Widow's bereavement allowance*[72]

8–49 This allowance is available to any widow whose husband was entitled to the married man's allowance at the time of his death or would have been so entitled but for an election for non-aggregation of his wife's earnings: see § 8–29. The allowance is the amount of the difference between the married and single allowance—£1,330 in 1986–87.

8–50 The allowance was formally available only in the year of assessment in which the death occurred. Where the husband dies after April 6, 1982, the allowance is available also for the following year, unless the widow re-marries before April 6, which follows the death.

7. *Dependent relative relief*[73]

8–51 The maximum amount of the dependent relative deduction is £100, or £145 when the claimant is a single woman. For the purposes of this allowance, husband and wife are treated as separate persons where they elect for non-aggregation of wife's earnings, so each can claim for his or her own dependent relative. The allowance is deductible from the total income of a person who proves that he maintains at his own expense any person, being a relative of his or of his wife, who is incapacitated by old age or infirmity from maintaining himself, or who maintains his own or his wife's mother (whether incapacitated or not) if she is a widow or divorced or separated from her husband. The amount of the relief is reduced, if the total income of the person maintained exceeds the basic retirement pension (as defined[74]), by the amount of the excess. No relief is given where the dependant's income exceeds the basic retirement pension by more than £100 (or £145 where the claimant is a single woman). If two or more persons jointly maintain a relative, the relief is apportioned in the ratio of their respective contributions.

8. *Claimant depending on services of a son or daughter*[75]

8–52 The sum of £55 is deductible from the total income of a person who, by reason of old age or infirmity, is compelled to depend upon the services of a son or daughter resident with and maintained by him. A married man is not entitled to the allowance unless his wife is old or infirm. This allowance

---

71. *Barry* v. *Hughes* (1972) 48 T.C. 586; [1972] S.T.C. 103.
72. I.C.T.A. 1970, s.15A as amended.
73. *Ibid.* s.16.
74. *Ibid.* s.16(2A).
75. *Ibid.* s.17.

should not be claimed where the larger housekeeper allowance (see § 8–48) can be claimed. A person cannot claim both.

9. *Reliefs for blind persons*[76]

8–53 The sum of £360 is deductible from the total income of a person who (or whose wife) is a registered blind person. Where both husband and wife are registered blind persons, the allowance is £720. A person entitled to relief under § 8–52 must relinquish that relief as a condition of claiming blind person's relief.

10. *Life insurance relief*

8–54 Before 1979–80 tax relief was given on premiums on certain policies of life insurance, the relief being a percentage of the premiums paid (subject to upper limits). The relief was complicated and is summarised in § 8–54 in the fifteenth edition of this book.

8–55 The method of giving relief on premiums was altered in and from 1979–80. The payer became entitled to deduct and retain a percentage of the amount of each premium, such percentage being $17\frac{1}{2}$ per cent. in 1979–80 and 1980–81 and 15 per cent. thereafter.[77] No claim had to be made and the relief was given whether or not the payer (if a United Kingdom resident) had income chargeable to tax. The life offices were compensated for their loss of premium income by means of deficiency payments made by the Revenue. The effect of giving relief by deduction was to remove policies from the tax system, in the sense that premiums no longer entered into the computation of an individual's tax liability.

6. RELIEF FOR INTEREST PAID[78–81]

8–57 By changes made by section 19 of the Finance Act 1974, which apply to interest paid after March 26, 1974, interest is not deductible in computing total income for tax purposes. There are exceptions to this rule which apply where the loan is applied for a qualifying purpose and transitional provisions which give tax relief on interest payable under obligations incurred on or before March 26, 1974. The exceptions are summarised below. Where the exceptions apply and a claim for relief is made, tax relief is available to a person who pays in any year of assessment:

(a) annual interest chargeable to tax under Case III of Schedule D (see §§ 5–01 *et seq.*); or

(b) interest payable in the United Kingdom on an advance from a bank carrying on a bona fide banking business in the United Kingdom or from a person bona fide carrying on a business as a member of the

---

76. *Ibid.* s.18.
77. F.A. 1976, s.34, Sched. 4, para. 5 (as amended) and para. 5A.
78–81. For a more detailed treatment of this topic, see the Revenue publication "Tax Treatment of Interest Paid" I.R. 11.

Stock Exchange in the United Kingdom or bona fide carrying on the business of a discount house in the United Kingdom.

Relief is given by allowing the interest to be deducted from or set off against the income for the year of assessment, income tax being discharged or repaid accordingly.[82] As regards (a), it is thought that the word "chargeable" does not require that the interest should be actually charged under Case III. All annual interest is chargeable under Case III although in some cases it may be charged under Case I: see § 5–23.

8–58　　Interest paid on a bank overdraft or under credit card arrangements is not eligible for relief,[83] except under the transitional provisions summarised in § 8–67.

8–58A　　*Anti-avoidance legislation.* Section 38 of the Finance Act 1976 denies tax relief in respect of any payment of interest if a scheme has been effected or arrangements have been made such that the sole or main benefit that might be expected to accrue to the claimant from the transaction under which the interest is paid was the obtaining of a reduction in tax liability by means of such relief.[84] The purpose is to counteract tax avoidance schemes which involve payments of interest in advance on artificial borrowings.[85]

Relief in respect of interest paid may be available in the following circumstances:

1. *Interest paid as a business expense*

8–59　　Interest paid as a business expense, whether short interest or yearly interest, is deductible, except in the case of interest paid by companies where yearly interest (other than some bank interest) is not deductible as a business expense but may be allowed as a charge on income: see § 2–75.[85a]

2. *Loans for purchase or improvement of land*[86]

8–60　　Interest is eligible for relief under section 75 of the Finance Act 1972, if paid by a person owning an estate or interest in land in the United Kingdom on a loan to defray money applied:

(a) in purchasing the estate or interest, or one absorbed into or given up to obtain, the estate or interest; or

(b) in improving or developing the land, or buildings on the land including (i) payments in respect of maintenance or repairs incurred by reason of dilapidation attributable to a period before the estate or interest was acquired (but not otherwise including payments in

---

82. F.A. 1972, s.75 as amended.
83. *Ibid.* s.75(1A) as inserted by F.A. 1974, s.19(1).
84. See Inland Revenue Press Release in [1976] S.T.I. 208.
85. As to the test to be applied *cf. Crown Bedding Co. Ltd.* v. *I.R.C.* (1946) 34 T.C. 107 at p. 118. For such a scheme, see *Cairns* v. *MacDiarmid* (1982) 56 T.C. 556; [1983] S.T.C. 178 (C.A.).
85a. But see FRP2/IRII/I, para. 30.
86. F.A. 1972, s.75 and Sched 9, paras. 1–9 as applied by F.A. 1974, s.19.

respect of maintenance or repairs, or any other payments deductible from rent: see §§ 6–27 *et seq*.), and (ii) certain payments in respect of street works, as defined; or

(c) in paying off another loan where the claimant could have obtained relief under section for interest on that other loan if it had not been paid off (and, if free of interest, assuming it carried interest).

The section does not apply to a loan unless made "in connection with the application of the money" *and* either on the occasion of its application or within a reasonable time from the application of the money; and the section does not apply to a loan where the proceeds are applied for some other purpose before being applied as so described. Interest on loans to purchase existing rentcharges, mortgages or charges do not qualify. There are provisions to prevent relief being given more than once and anti-avoidance provisions to prevent claims resulting from transactions between spouses, between a settlor and the trustees of his settlement, and between connected persons.

Interest on a loan to purchase or improve land, buildings or a caravan or house-boat is eligible for relief only if one of two conditions is satisfied[87]:

(1) *Main residence*

8–60A   Loan interest (including mortgage interest) is eligible for relief if, at the time when the interest is paid, the land, etc., is used as the only or main residence of the borrower or of a dependent relative or former or separated spouse of his. The relief is available only for loans up to the "qualifying maximum," which is £30,000 for 1986–87.[88] Where the loan exceeds the qualifying maximum, only a proportion of the interest is eligible for relief. If, for example, the loan is £40,000 only 30,000/40,000ths of the interest is eligible. Previous loans have in some cases to be taken into account in determining whether the qualifying maximum has been exceeded. This applies to an earlier loan made after March 26, 1974, in respect of a main residence so that if, for example, A borrows £30,000 to purchase a main residence, interest on a subsequent loan to finance improvements will be ineligible for relief. There are special provisions which apply to bridging loans and to cases where interest is payable before the land, etc., is used as a residence; also to cases where the borrower lives in job-related accommodation.

The legislation does not say how the "main" residence is to be determined.[89] This is a question of fact.

In *Frost* v. *Feltham*[90] the taxpayer was the tenant and licensee of a public house in Essex, in which he was required to reside. The taxpayer purchased a house in Wales in the joint names of himself and his wife and claimed tax relief on mortgage interest. This was the only house the taxpayer had ever purchased

---

87. F.A. 1974, s.19(2) and Sched. 1, paras. 4–8.
88. *Ibid*. Sched. 1, para. 5 (1), as amended. Parliament may determine the qualifying maximum each year. See F.A. 1986, s.20, which specifies a maximum of £30,000 for 1986–87.
89. *Cf.* C.G.T.A. 1979, s.101 in § 16–41.
90. (1980) 55 T.C. 10; [1981] S.T.C. 115.

and he and his wife equipped it as a home and spent some time there each month. The General Commissioners held that the property was the taxpayer's only or main residence. The Crown's appeal from their decision was dismissed.

The judge said that the question:

" . . . is not whether it was his only or main residence during that period, but whether it was used as such. . . . If someone lives in two houses the question which does he use as the principal or more important one cannot be determined solely by reference to the way in which he divides his time between the two."

(2) *Let property*

8–60B   Where (1) does not apply, loan interest is eligible for relief if, in any period of 52 weeks comprising the time at which the interest is payable, the land, etc., is let at a commercial rent for more than 26 weeks and, when not so let, is either available for letting at a commercial rent or used as the main residence of the owner or is prevented from being available for letting by reasons of works of construction or repair. Where the borrower owns the land for less than 26 weeks in the year of assessment, it must be let at a commercial rent throughout that period. Interest relief in respect of let property is available only against rental income derived from that or any other let property.[91] There is no restriction by reference to a qualifying maximum, as in (1).

Relief will be available under these provisions where *e.g.* an individual borrows to buy property which he lets to a partnership of which he is a member. If the partners pay rent, this will be a deductible business expense; and interest paid by the individual will be set against his share of rental income.[91a]

8–60C   *Deduction of tax from mortgage interest.* Interest on loans for house purchase from building societies, banks, etc., was at one time payable without deduction of tax. Tax relief was given in PAYE codings or in assessments. Frequent changes in interest rates made the system costly to administer and the Finance Act 1982 accordingly introduced a system for deduction of tax at source which applies where a *qualifying borrower* makes a payment of *relevant loan interest* to a *qualifying lender*. The words in italics are defined in Section 26 and Schedule 7 to the Finance Act 1982. The new system (called MIRAS) applies to interest paid in and after 1983–84.

3. *Loan applied in acquiring interest in close company*[92]

8–61   Interest is eligible for relief under section 75 of the Finance Act 1972 on a loan to an individual to defray money applied:

(a) in acquiring any part of the ordinary share capital of a close com-

---

91. F.A. 1974, Sched. 1, para. 7. It seems unnecessary that the other let property should itself be let at a commercial rent for the period stated in para. 4(1)(*b*).
91a. And see SP 4/85 in (1985) S.T.I. 60, which states the practice where the individual lets the property rent-free but the partnership pays the interest.
92. F.A. 1974, s.19(2) and Sched. 1, paras. 9–10 and paras. 13–16. And see *post*, §§ 15–07 *et seq*.

pany satisfying any of the conditions of paragraph 3A(2) of Schedule 16 to the Finance Act 1972; or

(b) in lending money to such a close company which is used wholly and exclusively for the purposes of the business of the company or of any associated company (being a close company satisfying any of these conditions); or

(c) in paying off another loan where relief could have been obtained under the section for interest on that other loan if it had not been paid off (and, if free of interest, assuming it carried interest).

The conditions in (a) restrict the relief to loans to purchase capital of close companies which are (i) trading companies, (ii) companies which are members of a trading group and (iii) companies of which the whole, or substantially the whole, of the income is estate or trading income, or interest and dividends or other distributions received from a 51 per cent. subsidiary, itself within (i), (ii) or (iii). It is not necessary that the company should be close at the time the interest is paid, provided it is close when the money is applied.[93] Relief is given only:

(a) if when the interest is paid the company continues to satisfy any of the conditions (above) and either (i) the individual has a material interest (as defined)[94] in the company or (ii) the individual holds any part of the ordinary share capital and from the time of the loan to the payment of the interest has worked for the greater part of his time in the actual management or conduct of the company or of an associated company[95]; and

(b) if he shows that in the period from the application of the proceeds of the loan to the payment of the interest he has not recovered any capital from the close company: if capital is so recovered and is not used to repay the loan, the individual is treated as having repaid the loan to the extent of the capital recovered and the amount of interest eligible for relief is reduced accordingly. An individual is treated as having recovered an amount of capital if he receives consideration for the sale of ordinary share capital of the company, or by way of repayment of any part of the ordinary share capital; if the company repays a loan or advance; or if he receives consideration for the assignment of a debt due from the company. In each case the capital recovered is the amount or value so received or repaid, save that a sale or assignment otherwise than by way of a bargain at arm's length is deemed to be made at market value; and

(c) if the company exists wholly or mainly from the purpose of holding investments or other property, no property held by the company is used as a residence by the individual.

---

93. Statement of Practice SP 3/78: [1978] S.T.I. 497. And see the Concession in (1985) S.T.I. 58 which applies where the close company is reorganized.
94. See I.C.T.A. 1970, s.285(6) as applied by F.A. 1974, Sched. 1, para. 16. A person has a material interest who alone, or with associates (see *post*, § 15–04), controls more than 5 per cent. of the ordinary share capital or would, on a statutory apportionment, have more than 5 per cent. of the distributable income apportioned to him: see *post*, §§ 15–28 *et seq.*
95. F.A. 1974, Sched. 1, paras. 9–10 as amended by F.A. 1982, s.49.

The condition in (c) does not apply where the individual has worked for the greater part of his time in the actual management or conduct of the business of the company, or of an associated company of the company.

The section does not apply to a loan unless made "in connection with the application of the money" and either on the occasion of its application or within a reasonable time from the application of the money; and the section does not apply to a loan where the proceeds are applied for some purpose before being applied as specified in the section.

The Finance Act 1980[96] removed the former requirement that the individual should have worked for the greater part of his time in the management or conduct of the business of the company. The stated purpose was to encourage individuals to invest in small companies where their main occupation was elsewhere. Condition (c) prevents an individual obtaining interest relief on, for example, second residences, by the device of funding a company with borrowed money.

The Finance Act 1981 introduced new provisions for the relief of interest on loans applied in acquiring an interest in a co-operative, *i.e.* a common ownership enterprise or a co-operative enterprise as defined in section 2 of the Industrial Common Ownership Act 1976.[97]

4. *Loan to acquire ordinary share capital in employee-controlled company*[97a]

8–61A   Interest paid after April 5, 1983, is eligible for relief under section 75 of the Finance Act 1972 if it is interest on a loan to an individual to defray money applied in acquiring any part of the ordinary share capital of an employee-controlled company. A company is employee-controlled if at least 50 per cent. of the issued ordinary share capital of the company and the voting power in the company is beneficially owned by persons who (or whose spouses) are full-time employees (as defined) of the company; but an individual who beneficially owns more than 10 per cent. of such ordinary share capital or voting power is treated as earning the excess otherwise than as a full-time employee. For this purpose shares beneficially owned by an individual and his or her spouse are aggregated, unless both of them are full-time employees of the company. Thus if an individual owns 15 per cent. of the voting power in the company, the excess over 10 per cent. is disregarded in applying the "at least 50 per cent. rule." If an individual owns 9 per cent. and his wife owns 8 per cent., the excess over 10 per cent. is disregarded unless both of them are full-time employees.

A number of conditions have to be satisfied for the interest to be eligible for relief. The company must be an unquoted company resident only in the United Kingdom which is either a trading company or the holding company of a trading group; and this condition must be satisfied from when the individual acquires the shares up to the time when the interest is paid.

---

96. F.A. 1980, s.28 applying to interest paid after March 26, 1980.
97. F.A. 1974, Sched. 1, para. 10A inserted by F.A. 1981, s.25(3).
97a. *Ibid.* Sched. 1, paras. 10C and 10D (inserted by F.A. 1983, s.24 and amended by F.A. 1984, s.24. And see [1983] S.T.I. 523.

5. *Loan applied in acquiring an interest in a partnership*[98]

8–62 This relief is similar to the relief in § 8–61. Under section 75 of the Finance Act 1972 interest is eligible for relief on a loan to an individual to defray money applied—

(a) in purchasing a share in a partnership; or

(b) in contributing money to a partnership by way of capital or premium, or in advancing money to the partnership, where the money contributed or advanced is used wholly for the purposes of the trade, profession or vocation carried on by the partnership; or

(c) in paying off another loan where relief could have been obtained under section 75 for interest on that other loan if it had not been paid off (and, if free of interest, assuming it carried interest).

Relief is given only—

(a) if throughout the period from the application of the proceeds of the loan until the interest was paid, the individual has been a member of the partnership otherwise than as a limited partner; and

(b) if he shows that in that period he has not recovered any amount of capital from the partnership (the provisions in this respect being similar to those summarised in § 8–61).

The section does not apply to a loan unless made "in connection with the application of the money," etc. (see § 8–60). As regards (a) the Finance Act 1981 removed the former requirement that the individual personally acted in the conduct of the trade, etc., carried on by the partnership. The purpose is to provide some encouragement to individuals to invest in partnerships where their main occupation is elsewhere. The relief is not lost if the partnership is incorporated into a close company.[98a]

6. *Loan to purchase machinery or plant used by a partnership or in an office or employment*[99]

8–63 Section 44 of the Capital Allowances Act 1968 provides that in taxing a trade carried on in partnership, the same capital allowances or balancing charges shall be made in respect of machinery or plant used in the trade and belonging to one or more of the partners, but not being partnership property, as would be made in the case of machinery or plant belonging to the partners and being partnership property. For any year of assessment in which a partnership is entitled to an allowance or liable to a charge under section 44, the individual to whom the machinery or plant belongs is entitled to relief on interest paid by him in that year in a loan to defray money applied as capital expenditure on the provision of that machinery or plant. Relief will not be given in respect of interest falling due and payable more than three years after the end of the year of assessment in which the debt was incurred.

Thus a partner in a firm of solicitors can claim interest relief (for the

---

98. F.A. 1974, s.19(2) and Sched. 1, paras. 11–12 and paras. 13–16 (as amended).
98a. See the I.R. Concession in (1985) S.T.I. 58.
99. F.A. 1972, Sched. 9, paras. 10–15 as applied by F.A. 1974, s.19.

three year period mentioned) on a loan to purchase a car which is used in the practice.

Where the holder of an office or employment is entitled in any year to a capital allowance, or liable to a balancing charge, on machinery or plant purchased for use therein (see § 13–23), and he pays interest in that year on a loan to defray money applied as capital expenditure on the provision thereof, the interest so paid may be deducted from the emoluments of the year in which the interest is paid. The three-year limitation period mentioned in the preceding paragraphs applies.

7. Loan to pay capital transfer tax[1] or inheritance tax

8–64　　Interest on a loan to the personal representatives of a deceased person is eligible for relief if the proceeds are applied:

  (a) in paying, before the grant of representation, capital transfer tax (or inheritance tax) in respect of personal property to which the deceased was beneficially entitled immediately before his death; or
  (b) in paying off another loan where relief could have been obtained under the section for interest on that other loan if it had not been paid off.

Relief will not be given in respect of interest on so much of any loan as is applied in paying tax in respect of property situate in Great Britain which did not vest in the personal representatives or in respect of property which, if it had been situate in Great Britain, would not have vested in them. A certificate of the Board as to the amount of tax paid will be sufficient evidence for the purposes of claiming tax relief. Interest paid on a loan within (a), above, in respect of any period ending within one year from the making of the loan will be deducted from or set off against the income of the personal representatives for the year in which the interest is paid.

8. Loans to purchase life annuity[2]

8–65　　Interest on loans to purchase life annuities for persons aged 65 or more, secured on land in the United Kingdom or in the Republic of Ireland in which the borrower has an interest, are eligible for relief in some cases.

9. Further provisions relating to interest

8–66　　Where credit is given for any money due from the purchaser under any sale, this is to be treated as the making of a loan to defray money applied by the purchaser in making the purchase. Thus if V sells land to P for £10,000 and the purchase money is left unpaid, V is to be treated as having made a loan of £10,000 to P, who may be entitled to relief in respect of interest paid to V.[3] Interest in excess of a reasonable commercial rate is ineligible for relief to the extent of the excess.[4] There are provisions for apportionment in the case of a debt which does not wholly fulfil the con-

---

1. F.A. 1974, Sched. 1, paras. 17–22, as amended by F.A. 1975, Sched. 12, para. 19.
2. *Ibid*. Sched. 1, para. 24.
3. F.A. 1972, Sched. 9, para. 14.
4. *Ibid*. s.75(2).

ditions required by the relevant sections.[5] Relief will be given under the sections only on the making of a claim[6–7]; and an appeal on the claim lies to the General Commissioners, or to the Special Commissioners if the appellant so elects.

7. RELIEF FOR INVESTMENT IN CORPORATE TRADES: BUSINESS EXPANSION SCHEME

8–67 Sections 52 to 67 of the Finance Act 1981 introduced provisions designed to encourage individuals to invest in new corporate trading ventures by providing income tax relief on the sum invested. This "business start up scheme" was not a great success. Section 26 of and Schedule 5 to the Finance Act 1983 introduced a new business expansion scheme to replace it.[8]

Tax relief under the business expansion scheme is available to a qualifying individual who subscribes for new ordinary shares ("eligible shares") in a qualifying unquoted company. The investor may deduct the amount he subscribes from his total income for the year of assessment in which the shares are issued; but relief cannot exceed £40,000 in any year and, generally, the total amount subscribed in the year must not be less than £500. Relief for a smaller amount may be obtained by investing through an approved investment fund.

An individual qualifies for the relief if he subscribes for shares on his own behalf, is resident and ordinarily resident in the United Kingdom throughout the year of assessment in which the shares are issued and is not "connected with" the company at any time during the period from the incorporation of the company (or two years before the issue of the shares if later) until five years after the issue of the shares.

A company is a qualifying company if it is incorporated in the United Kingdom and satisfies certain tests throughout the three years from the date of the issue of the shares (or, if later, three years from the time when the company commenced trading). The company must be an unquoted company and must not be quoted on the unlisted securities market. It must be resident in (and only in) the United Kingdom; and it must exist wholly or substantially for the purpose of carrying on one or more qualifying trades wholly or mainly in the United Kingdom. Trades which consist of activities such as commodity dealing, leasing, banking and farming do not qualify; neither do companies having a substantial interest in land.[9] The company must carry on the trade on a commercial basis with a view to the realisation of profits.

A claim must be made for the relief to be given. If the investor disposes of the eligible shares within five years of their issue otherwise than by way of a bargain made at arm's length, the relief is withdrawn. If he disposes of them during that period by way of bargain made at arm's length, the relief is reduced by the consideration he receives. Relief may also be withdrawn

---

5. *Ibid.* Sched. 9, para. 15.
6–7. *Ibid.* s.75(1) as amended by F.A. 1974, s.19(1).
8. See [1983] S.T.I. 152.
9. See F.A. 1986, s.40 and Sched. 9.

or restricted if the investor receives value from the company or if he receives back the capital he has invested.

Capital gains tax is payable when the scheme shares are disposed of, except in the case of shares issued to the disposer after March 18, 1986.[9]

8. The Allocation of Deductions in Quantifying and Taxing Income

8–68 The rules are as follows:

(1) Deductions from total income under Chapter II of Part I of the Taxes Act (personal reliefs) must be made *after* any other deductions. Thus deductions in respect of charges on income are made before deductions in respect of personal reliefs.[10]

(2) Deductions in respect of charges on income can be made from income of different descriptions in the order which will result in the greatest reduction in liability to income tax.[11]

The computations that follow are for the year 1984–85 when the basic rate of income tax was 30 per cent. and the single person's allowance was £2,005.

Computation A

8–69 X, who is unmarried and carries on a profession, has a Case II profit of £25,000 in his accounting period of 12 months to December 31, 1983. He made a loan to Y who paid interest of £4,000 (gross) in December 1983. Trust income to April 5, 1985, is £2,000. X receives dividends of £700 (tax credit £300). X pays interest (deductible) of £3,000 in 1984–85. X's tax liability in 1984–85 is as follows:

	£
Professional earnings	25,000
Loan interest (gross)	4,000
Trust income (gross)	2,000
Dividends (£700) plus tax credits (£300): see § 14–59.	1,000
	32,000
less interest	3,000
	29,000
less personal relief	2,005
Taxable income	26,995

Tax 1984–85

£			£
15,400	@	30%	4,620
2,800	@	40%	1,120
4,900	@	45%	2,205
3,895	@	50%	1,947.50
26,995			9,892.50

---

10. F.A.1971, s.34(3).
11. *Ibid.* s.34(1) and (2).

less tax credit on trust income	600	
less £2,000 @ 30% (§ 8–21)		
tax credit on dividends (§ 14–56)	300	
		900.00
Total tax		8,992.50

Computation B

H's salary to April 5, 1985, is £16,000. H receives interest of £600 (gross) in December 1983. H, who is divorced and unmarried, pays his ex-wife (W) maintenance of £3,000 gross in the year 1984–85. H deducts income tax at the basic rate of 30 per cent. (£900) and pays W £2,100: see § 5–31. H's income tax liability for 1984–85 is as follows:

	£
Salary	16,000
Untaxed interest	600
	16,000
less maintenance payment	3,000
	13,600
less personal relief (single)	2,005
	11,595

Tax

Tax	11,595	@	30%	= 3,478.50
Add back retained tax (§ 8–32)				
	£3,000	@	30%	= 900
				£4,378.50

Computation C

Facts as in Computation B. W's tax position in 1984–85 is as follows. (It is assumed that W has no income other than the maintenance payments).

	£
Maintenance payments	3,000
less personal relief (single)	2,005
	995

Tax	995	@	30%	= £298.50

W's repayment claim.

		£
Tax deducted by H (3,000 @ 30%)	=	900
Tax payable by W (above)		298.50
Tax repayable		601.50

		£
Thus W receives: from H		1,400
from the Revenue		535.50
		2,701.50

Comments on Computations B and C

These computations show:

(1) That H gets relief from higher rate tax because the gross amount of £3,000 is deductible in computing his total income.

(2) That H discharges his obligation to pay £3,000 to W by paying only £3,000, less income tax at the basic rate (£900). The Revenue recovers this from H under section 3 of the Taxes Act 1970: see § 8–32. H thus acts as a tax collector for the Revenue.

(3) That W receives £2,701.50 from an outlay by H of £2,100, the difference of £601.50 being an amount equal to tax at the basic rate of 30 per cent. on the personal relief of £2,005 to which W is entitled.

(4) If the £3,000 were not a charge on H's income, H's tax liability would be on £16,600 less H's personal relief. This demonstrates in practical terms the proposition that an income settlement has the effect of removing the top slice of the settlor's income and making it the income of the beneficiary for tax purposes.

8–70   *1986–87*

Tax rates on earned income

Total taxable income	Total tax	Tax as percentage of total income
£	£	%
17,200	4,988	29
20,200	6,188	30.64
25,400	8,528	33.58
33,300	12,478	37.48
41,200	16,823	40.84
50,000	22,103	44.20
55,000	25,103	45.64
60,000	28,103	46.83
80,000	40,103	50.12

Taxable income is defined in § 8–03.

CHAPTER 9

TRUST INCOME

1. THE CHARGE ON THE TRUSTEES

A. *Income arising to trustees: basic rate income tax*

9–01   Income received by trustees in the course of administering a trust is assessed to tax at the basic rate, unless the income has already suffered basic rate tax by deduction or is a distribution from a United Kingdom company. There is no provision in the Income Tax Acts specifically charging trustees to basic rate tax on trust income,[1] but they are nevertheless assessable under the Schedule appropriate to the source from which the income arises.[2] Thus trustees who carry on a trade are assessed under Case 1 of Schedule D; trustees in receipt of an income from rents are taxed under Schedule A, and so on. Trustees are chargeable persons in respect of capital gains.[3] Trustees are not entitled to personal reliefs because they are not "individuals" for tax purposes[4]; but they may claim other reliefs appropriate to the source of the trust income, *e.g.* loss relief in respect of Schedule D income. No deduction is allowable in computing liability to basic rate income tax for expenses incurred by the trustees in managing the trust[5]; nor can trustees make a management expenses claim.[6] Foreign income which arises under a trust is not liable to United Kingdom tax if the beneficiary who is entitled to the income is resident outside the United Kingdom, if the income is paid direct from the foreign source to the non-resident beneficiary.[7] It appears that a trustee would have a good defence to an assessment to the extent that the income assessed was held in trust for a beneficiary not liable to income tax.

In one case Lord Clyde stated the position as follows[8]:

> "The conclusion on the whole matter seems to be that trustees, albeit only the representatives of ulterior beneficial interests, are assessable generally in respect of the trust income under [sections 68 and 114 of the Income and Corporation Taxes Act 1970][9]; but that—just because they represent those beneficial interests—they may have a good answer to a particular assessment, as regards some share or part of the income assessed, on the ground that such share or part arises or accrues *beneficially* to a *cestui que trust* in whose hands it is not liable to income tax [*e.g.* a person not domiciled in the United Kingdom

---

1. I.C.T.A. 1970, ss.68(1) and 114(1) charge tax under Schedules A and D respectively on "the persons receiving or entitled to the profits or gains or income" in respect of which tax is directed to be charged. T.M.A. 1970, s.72, provides for the assessment of trustees of incapacitated persons, including infants (*ibid*, s.118(1) defining "incapacitated person").
2. I.C.T.A. 1970, s.1. *Williams* v. *Singer* [1921] A.C. 65; 7 T.C. 387; *Reid's Trustees* v. *I.R.C.* (1929) 14 T.C. 512; *Kelly* v. *Rogers* [1935] 2 K.B. 446; 19 T.C. 692 (C.A.).
3. See *post*, Chap. 16.
4. This is clear from many statutory provisions. See *e.g.* the discussion in § 9–02.
5. *Aiken* v. *MacDonald's Trustees* (1894) 3 T.C. 306.
6. See *ante*, § 6–31.
7. *Williams* v. *Singer* [1921] A.C. 65; 7 T.C. 387 (H.L.).
8. See *Reid's Trustees* v. *I.R.C.* (1929) 14 T.C. 512 at p. 525.
9. See note 1, above.

who does not receive the income in the United Kingdom: see § 7–09]. The fact that most trust income is subject to deduction of income tax at the source has probably obscured the speciality which attaches to the representative character of trustees as payers of income tax . . . "

B. *Income arising to trustees: additional rate tax*

9–02   Under the pre-unified system of personal taxation, trustees were not assessable to surtax because they are not "individuals" for tax purposes; and when the unified system was introduced by section 32(1) of the Finance Act 1971, charging higher rate income tax and additional rates of income tax (the "investment income surcharge") on the total income of *individuals*, trustees were liable only to basic rate income tax. Had the law remained unchanged, a settlement authorising or directing the accumulation of income with a view to its eventual distribution in capital form would have been an attractive vehicle for the accumulation of wealth at a relatively low cost in taxation. Not surprisingly, therefore, section 16 of the Finance Act 1973 altered the law in and from 1973–74 by making certain income which arises to trustees liable to income tax at "the additional rate" (but not higher rate income tax) as well as to basic rate income tax. "The additional rate" in this context means the difference between the basic rate and the second higher rate band[10–11]: see § 8–05. The additional rate in 1986–87 is $45 - 29 = 46$ per cent.[12] Thus where the section applies, trust income bears tax at 16 per cent. Hence income being accumulated may, during the period of accumulation, bear a higher rate of income tax than that applicable to the beneficiaries. A single person needs a taxable income of about £55,000 in 1986–87 before he becomes liable to tax at the 45 per cent. rate: see § 8–69.

9–03   Section 16 of the Finance Act 1973 applies to income arising to trustees which is subject to a trust for accumulation and also to income which is payable at their discretion, whether or not the trustees have power to accumulate.[13] Thus income tax at the additional rate is charged on the income of a trust for maintenance and accumulation (see § 37–14). Not all the income is chargeable but only the net amount after defraying expenses of the trustees properly chargeable to income (or which would be so chargeable but for any express provisions of the trust). This includes all expenses the trustees are authorised to incur under the general law. Premiums under policies of assurance effected by the trustees and fees paid to investment advisors have been held not to be deductible in computing the amount of income liable to additional rate tax.[14]

9–04   The charge does not apply to income which, when it arises, is treated as the income of a beneficiary (see § 9–15); nor to income which is treated as income of the settlor under one of the provisions considered in Chapter 10.

10–11. F.A. 1971, s.32(1).
12. F.A. 1973. s.16(1)(*d*).
13. See *I.R.C.* v. *Berrill* (1981) 55 T.C. 429; [1978] S.T.C. 784 (protected life interest—power to accumulate—section 16 held to apply).
14. *Carver* v. *Duncan* [1985] S.T.C. 356 H.L.).

Thus if trustees of a discretionary trust are required to pay an annuity to X, so much of the trust income as is equal to the gross amount of the annuity does not bear the additional rate income tax.

The charge does not apply to income arising under a trust established for charitable purposes only or to income from investments, deposits or other property held for the purposes of a fund or scheme established for the sole purpose of providing relevant benefits within the meaning of section 26 of the Finance Act 1970 (relating to retirement benefits schemes).

Dividends and building society interest received by trustees are treated as income from which income tax from a corresponding gross amount has been deducted.[15]

9–05   Where trustees are participators in a close company and sums are apportioned to them under the provisions discussed in §§ 15–28 *et seq.*, such sums together with the amount of advance corporation tax attributable to them are income chargeable at the additional rate.[16]

Thus if £700 is apportioned to trustees in a year, when the rate of ACT is $\frac{3}{7}$ths, the trustees are assessed under section 16 of the Finance Act 1973 to tax at the additional rate on £1,000.

Dividends on shares in United Kingdom companies received by trustees of a discretionary trust outside the United Kingdom are liable to income tax at the additional rate. Tax is charged on the actual amount of the dividend.[17]

9–06   The term "trustees" in the above paragraphs does not include personal representatives, but where personal representatives, on or before the completion of the administration of an estate, pay to trustees any sum representing income which, if personal representatives were trustees within the meaning of section 16 of the Finance Act 1973, would be income to which the section applies, that sum is to be deemed to be paid to the trustees as income and to have borne income tax at the basic rate.[18]

9–07   The Revenue may, by notice given to trustees under section 8 of the Taxes Management Act 1970, require a return of the income arising to them to include particulars of the manner in which the income has been applied, including particulars as to the exercise of any discretion and of the persons in whose favour it has been exercised.[19]

9–08   Tax at the additional rate normally becomes due and payable by trustees on December 1[20] following the end of the year of assessment in which the relevant income arises to the trustees.

---

15. F.A. 1973, s.16(5).
16. *Ibid.* s.16(3) and (4).
17. *I.R.C.* v. *Regent Trust Co. Ltd.* (1979) 53 T.C. 54; [1980] S.T.C. 140. See also *I.R.C.* v. *Berrill* (1981) 55 T.C. 429; [1978] S.T.C. 784.
18. F.A. 1973, s.16(6).
19. *Ibid.* s.16(8). Forms 31 and 32 are currently in use.
20. I.C.T.A. 1970, s.4(3).

C. *Income distributed by trustees: discretionary settlements*

9–09   We have seen that income which arises to trustees of a discretionary settlement in and from 1973–74 (including a maintenance and accumulation settlement) is liable to basic rate income tax and tax at the additional rate in the year when the income arises, whether or not the income is distributed in that year or is accumulated.[21] A further charge to tax may arise on the trustees in the year when the income is distributed if the tax rate on trust income has increased since the year in which the income arose. Section 17 of the Finance Act 1973 provides that where, in any year of assessment, trustees make a payment to a person in the exercise of a discretion and the sum paid is for all the purposes of the Income Tax Acts *income* of the payee (but would not be his income apart from the payment), the payment shall be treated as a net amount corresponding to a gross amount from which tax has been deducted at a rate equal to the sum of the basic rate and the additional rate in force for the year in which the payment is made.[22]

> Thus if trustees make an income-payment of £550 to a beneficiary in a year of assessment when the basic rate is 30 per cent. and the additional rate 15 per cent., the payment is treated for tax purposes as a payment of £1,000 from which tax of £450 has been deducted, *i.e.* the payment is "grossed up" at 45 per cent.

The sum treated as deducted (£450) is treated as income tax paid by the payee and, subject to the set-off provisions in § 9–10, as income tax assessable on the trustees.[23] Payments out of capital will constitute *income* of the payee if the payments are annual payments within Case III of Schedule 9: see the discussion in § 9–17.

9–10   Section 17(3) of the Finance Act 1973 allows the trustees to set-off against the amount assessable on them income tax already borne by them on the income as it arose, under the provisions summarised in §§ 9–02 *et seq*.

> Thus if trustees of a discretionary settlement receive income in 1974–75 on which they suffer tax at 48 per cent. and the income is distributed as income in 1975–76 when the tax rate on trust income is 50 per cent., the trustees suffer tax at 2 per cent. on the amount distributed in 1975–76.

There are provisions having the same effect to meet the case where income of a close company which is apportioned to trustees in one year and taxed under section 16 of the Finance Act 1973, is actually distributed to the trustees by way of dividend in a later year, and subsequently distributed by the trustees as income.[24–25]

Tax payable by trustees under section 17 of the Finance Act 1973 nor-

---

21. See *ante*, §§ 9–02 *et seq*.
22. F.A. 1973, s.17(1), (2). Trustees in this section do not include personal representatives: *ibid*. s.17(5). SP 3/86 in [1986] S.T.I. 252 deals with double taxation aspects of payments to a non-resident beneficiary from a United Kingdom discretionary trust and estates during the administration period.
23. *Ibid*. s.17(2)(*b*).
24–25. *Ibid*. s.17(3)(*b*) and (*c*).

mally becomes due and payable on December 1 following the end of the year of assessment in which the relevant payment is made.[26] The beneficiaries are entitled to a certificate of tax deducted by the trustees.[27]

[The next paragraph is 9–13.]

2. TOTAL INCOME OF THE BENEFICIARIES

9–13 It will be apparent from Section 1 of this chapter that trust income will have already suffered tax at the basic rate before it reaches the beneficiaries and that, where trust income is to be accumulated or is payable at the discretion of the trustees, it will also have borne additional rate tax. Trustees are under no circumstances liable to higher rate income tax because trustees are not "individuals."[28] The beneficiary must include in his return of total income the amount of trust income to which he is entitled, grossed up at the rate of tax treated as deducted by the trustees.

> This is tax at the basic rate in the case of a beneficiary with a life interest and tax at the sum of the basic and additional rates in the case of a beneficiary under, *e.g.* a discretionary settlement: see § 9–09.

A beneficiary who is liable to a lower rate of tax than that suffered by deduction will be entitled to claim repayment of the excess, relying on the certificate available from the trustees: see § 9–12.

Where trust income is received direct by the beneficiary under the authority of the trustees, the beneficiary may be assessed instead of the trustees.[29]

9–14 The significance of total income was explained in Chapter 8. In the computation of total income, the following rules apply with respect to trust income:

9–15 (1) Income to which a beneficiary is entitled (whether by virtue of the trust instrument or otherwise, *e.g.* under the Trustee Act 1925) forms part of his total income, whether or not he receives it. This is because

> "Where trustees are in receipt of income which it is their duty to pay over to beneficiaries . . . that income is at its very inception the beneficiary's income."[30]

Consequently, the beneficiary avoids no higher rate income tax by

---

26. I.C.T.A. 1970, s.4(3).
27. I.C.T.A. 1970, s.55.
28. See *ante*, § 8–03.
29. See T.M.A. 1970, s.76(1), which protects trustees who authorise the receipt of "profits arising from trust property" by the persons entitled thereto and who make a return in accordance with s.13 of that Act.
30. Sir Wilfrid Greene M.R. in *Corbett* v. *I.R.C.* [1938] 1 K.B. 567, 577 (C.A.); 21 T.C. 449, 460; *Dreyfus* v. *I.R.C.* (1963) 41 T.C. 441; *cf. Cornwell* v. *Barry* (1955) 36 T.C. 268 where the beneficiary had a vested interest in income which was liable to be divested and the court held that income not specifically appropriated to the beneficiary was not his income for tax purposes.

refusing to accept payment of the trust income.[31] Note that trustees are not chargeable at the additional rate on income which, before being distributed, is income of a beneficiary.[32]

> Where trustees hold, *e.g.* securities upon trust for A for life, the source of A's income for tax purposes is the securities, not the trust instrument.[33] *Ergo* it is the location of the securities which determines if the income is from a foreign possession within Case V.

9–16   (2) Sums which a beneficiary is entitled to have applied for his benefit form part of his total income.

> Thus if a testator directs his trustees to pay the rates and other outgoings on a house occupied by his widow (the tenant for life), the amount so paid by the trustees forms part of his widow's total income.[34]

9–17   (3) A payment to a beneficiary out of trust *capital* is *income* of the beneficiary, if the payment is Schedule D Case III income (*i.e.* an annual payment) in the hands of the beneficiary.[35]

> In *Brodie's Will Trustees* v. *I.R.C.*,[36] trustees were directed to pay part of the trust income to the testator's widow; and if in any year the widow's share of income did not amount to £4,000, the trustees were directed to raise and pay the deficiency out of capital. *Held*, that the sums so paid out of capital in seven successive years were "annual payments" within Case III of Schedule D and formed part of the beneficiary's total income.[37]

The position is the same where the beneficiary has no right to demand that his income be augmented but has to rely on the trustees' discretion.[38] Care must therefore be taken in drafting any provision in a will or settlement giving trustees power to advance sums out of capital: payments which have the quality of recurrence will be treated as income of the beneficiary, notwithstanding their origin in capital and notwithstanding the parties' own description of the payment.[39] Hence the power should not be expressed as a power to make up deficiencies in income or to maintain the beneficiary in a particular standard of living but should be expressed in general terms and exercised in such a manner as not to give the quality of income (*i.e.* annual payment) to the payments. In the case of a dis-

---

31. *Cf.* income under Case III of Schedule D: *ante*, § 5–09.
32. See *ante*, § 9–04.
33. *Archer-Shee* v. *Baker* [1927] A.C. 844; 11 T.C. 749 (H.L.).
34. *I.R.C.* v. *Miller* [1930] A.C. 222; 15 T.C. 25. The annual value of the house would no longer form part of the widow's total income. As to the effect of the provisions for compensating the beneficiary against higher rate income tax (then surtax): see *Michelham's Trustees* v. *I.R.C.* (1930) 15 T.C. 737 (C.A.).
35. See *ante*, § 5–04.
36. (1933) 17 T.C. 432. See also *Cunard's Trustees* v. *I.R.C.* (1946) 27 T.C. 122; *Williamson* v. *Ough* [1936] A.C. 384; 20 T.C. 194; *Milne's Executors* v. *I.R.C.* (1956) 37 T.C. 10; *Lawson* v. *Rolfe* (1969) 46 T.C. 199.
37. There would be an assessment on the trustees under I.C.T.A. 1970, s.53 (*ante*, §§ 5–34 *et seq.*) or under F.A. 1973, s.17(1) as appropriate: *ante*, §§ 9–09 *et seq.*
38. *Lindus and Hortin* v. *I.R.C.* (1933) 17 T.C. 442. See also *Peirse-Duncombe Trust (Trustees)* v. *I.R.C.* (1940) 23 T.C. 199, where the deficiency in an annuity was made up out of borrowed moneys and the principle was applied.
39. *Jackson's Trustees* v. *I.R.C.* (1942) 25 T.C. 13.

cretionary settlement, the Revenue has contended that the manner in which trustees resolve to exercise their discretion may give payments made by them out of capital the quality of income.

> In *Stevenson* v. *Wishart*[40] Mrs. H. was a beneficiary under the trust under which the trustees could apply the trust fund and the income for the beneficiaries, as the trustees might in their discretion appoint. From 1978 (when Mrs. H. was aged over 90) until she died in 1981, the trustees appointed sums out of capital to defray medical and nursing home expenses. The entire income was paid to charity. The Revenue claimed that the appointed sums were income of Mrs. H. and assessed the trustees under section 17(2)(*b*) of the Finance Act 1973 (see § 9–09). *Held* that the appointments created no entitlement to income.

Bona fide loans by the trustees are not income of the beneficiary.[41] In one case, the nature of a payment to a beneficiary is determined by the source from which it arises. This is where the beneficiary is absolutely entitled to both income and capital of the fund: the entire income of the fund is income of the beneficiary, and the capital of the fund is capital of the beneficiary.[41a] This rule applies whether the beneficiary is paid in a lump sum or by periodic payments.

9–18 (4) Discretionary payments. Sums actually paid to a beneficiary in the exercise of a discretion, whether statutory or otherwise, are part of the beneficiary's total income.[42] So, for example, sums paid to an infant beneficiary in exercise of the statutory power of maintenance are income of the infant.

9–19 (5) Accumulated income. The question whether income which is accumulated by trustees forms part of the beneficiary's total income depends on whether the beneficiary has a vested or a contingent interest in the income. Whether an interest is vested or contingent must be ascertained by applying general principles of law and especially section 31 of the Trustee Act 1925, as amended by the Family Law Reform Act 1969.[43]

　　(a) *Vested interest.* If the beneficiary has a vested interest, the income forms part of the beneficiary's total income year by year as it arises, even if it is not received by him.[44] Any claim for personal reliefs by the beneficiary and any assessment on him to higher rate income tax must ordinarily be made within six years after the end of the year.

　　(b) *Contingent interest.* Income in which a beneficiary has a contingent interest and which is accumulated does not form part

---

40. [1986] S.T.C. 74. The Revenue have also contended that capital advances to pay school fees should be treated as Case III income of the beneficiary: see [1985] S.T.I. 238.
41. *I.R.C.* v. *Sansom* [1921] 2 K.B. 492; 8 T.C. 20 (C.A.).
41a. *Brodie's Will Trustees* v. *I.R.C.* (1933) 17 T.C. 432, *per* Finlay J. at p. 438.
42. *Drummond* v. *Collins* [1915] A.C. 1011; 6 T.C. 525. See also § 5–04 (2). Higher rate income tax due from a beneficiary under a discretionary trust may be recovered from the trustees: I.C.T.A. 1970, s.36.
43. See *Stanley* v. *I.R.C.* [1944] K.B. 255; 26 T.C. 12 (C.A.).
44. *Hamilton-Russell's Executors* v. *I.R.C.* (1943) 25 T.C. 200 (C.A.).

of his total income, even retrospectively when the contingency occurs and the accumulations are paid to the beneficiary. The income reaches the beneficiary as capital.[45] Higher rate income tax is thus avoided.[46]

Example:
Assume A settles income-producing property on trust for such of his children as shall attain the age of 25 years and that A has two children. The trustees accumulate the whole of the income of each child's share until he attains the age of 18 years when, under section 31 of the Trustee Act 1925, each child's interest in income vests in possession. Each child attains the age of 25 years. The income of each child's share forms part of his total income from the date when he attains 18 years but, before that date, is taxed as income of the trustees at the basic and additional rate.[47] No further income tax is payable on the vesting of each child's share of capital.

Where a foreign element is present, sections 478–481 of the Income and Corporation Taxes Act 1970 (as extended) may be relevant: see § 7–26.

3. INCOME ARISING DURING THE ADMINISTRATION OF AN ESTATE

9–20   Income which arises from an estate during the course of its administration is treated as income of the personal representatives in their representative capacity and is charged to basic rate income tax (but not to higher rate income tax).

The income of an estate has to be taken into account in computing the total income of the beneficiary entitled thereto, and the method by which this is done is provided in Part XV of the Income and Corporation Taxes Act 1970. These provisions apply only during the "administration period"; that is, from the date of death until the date of completion of the administration of the estate.[48] Although the phrase "the completion of the administration" is used frequently in the Acts, the only definition is that contained in section 433(*a*) of the Income and Corporation Taxes Act 1970, which is concerned with the application of Part XV to Scotland. From this definition it would appear that the administration is complete when the residue is ascertained. After the completion of the administration, the total income of the beneficiaries is computed in accordance with the rules already discussed (in Section 2) applicable to trust income.

The method of computing total income under Part XV varies with the nature of the interest of the beneficiary in residue:

(1) *Where the beneficiary has a limited interest in residue*[49]

9–21   A beneficiary with a right to income only (such as a life tenant) has a "limited interest."[50] Such a beneficiary has a right to income from the date of death but the final determination of the exact amount of the income to

---

45. *I.R.C.* v. *Blackwell Minor's Trustees* [1924] 2 K.B. 351; 10 T.C. 235.
46. *Stanley* v. *I.R.C.* [1944] K.B. 255; 26 T.C. 12 (C.A.).
47. See generally Chaps. 10 and 37.
48. I.C.T.A. 1970, s.426(1).
49. *Ibid*. s.426.
50. *Ibid*. s.432(3).

which he is entitled must await the completion of the administration, for the residue cannot be ascertained until all claims against the estate have been determined. The general scheme of the Act is as follows:

(1) Any sums which are paid to the beneficiary during the administration period are treated as part of his total income for the year when they are paid. Where such sums have already suffered tax at the basic rate (which is ordinarily the case where the estate is a United Kingdom estate),[51] they must be grossed up at the basic rate for the year of payment. Clearly this method of computing the beneficiary's income can produce only a provisional figure and adjustments are necessary when the amount of the residue is finally known.

(2) On completion of the administration, the sums already paid to the beneficiary are aggregated with any sums then found due to him, and the aggregate income is deemed to have accrued due and been paid to the beneficiary from day to day during the administration period. This reallocation of the income throughout the period of administration will necessitate fresh computations of total income, and any additional assessments which are required may be made at any time within three years from the completion of the administration.[52]

(2) Where the beneficiary has an absolute interest in residue[53]

9–22   A beneficiary has an absolute interest in residue if he has a right to capital on the residue being ascertained.[54] In this case, the problem is to find what part of any sum which is paid to the beneficiary during the administration period represents capital and what part represents income of the capital still awaiting distribution. The problem is to segregate the income element from the capital element, for only the former enters into the computation of the beneficiary's total income. The method by which this process of segregation is achieved is briefly as follows:

(1) Calculate the "residuary income" of the estate for each year (or part of a year) of assessment during the administration period.[55] This, broadly speaking, is the aggregate income of the personal representatives from all sources, less certain charges on the estate of an income nature (*e.g.* annuities, interest on legacies) and certain management expenses.[56]

(2) Sums which are paid to the beneficiary during the administration period are treated as income up to the amount of the "residuary

---

51. Defined *ibid*. s.432(8). In the case of a "foreign estate" the income is charged to tax at the basic rate under Case IV of Schedule D: *ibid*. s.426(4).
52. *Ibid*. s.431(3).
53. *Ibid*. s.427.
54. *Ibid*. s.432(2).
55. *Ibid*. s.427(2), s.428(1). Income received under deduction of tax by personal representatives which covers a period including the date of death is not income of the deceased: *I.R.C. v. Henderson's Executors* (1931) 16 T.C. 282.
56. *Ibid*. s.432(7), s.428(1).

income." Any excess over this is treated as payment on account of capital.

(3) On completion of the administration, adjustments may be necessary.

4. Legacies and Annuities

General legacies

9–23　　Where a general legatee is entitled to interest,[57] the amount of interest actually paid to the legatee forms part of his total income. Such interest is income falling under Case III of Schedule D. Interest which is not paid (*e.g.* because the legatee declines to accept payment[58]) is not "income" of the legatee.

Specific legacies

9–24　　Income arising from property which is the subject of a specific disposition by will belongs to the legatee from the date of death, unless the will otherwise provides. It therefore forms part of the legatee's total income year by year as it arises.[59]

Annuities

9–25　　An annuity provided by will is payable (unless the will otherwise provides) from the date of death, and therefore forms part of the annuitant's total income from that date. An annuitant is entitled to have a fund set aside which will produce income sufficient to secure the annuity; and where the estate is insufficient to pay the pecuniary legacies in full and also to provide the annuity fund, the annuitant is generally entitled to demand payment of the actuarial value of the annuity (abated with the legacies).[60] In such an event, the annuitant's right is to *capital* only, and all payments to him must be treated as such.[61] A direction in a will to purchase an annuity generally entitles the annuitant to demand the capital value of the annuity, when similar tax consequences ensue.

Purchased life annuities

9–26　　These are considered in §§ 5–53 *et seq*.

---

57. See Snell's *Principles of Equity*, 28th ed., p. 367.
58. *Dewar* v. *I.R.C.* [1935] 2 K.B. 351; 19 T.C. 561 (C.A.): and see § 5–09. For the position where the legacy is abated or payment is delayed and sums are paid on account, see *Re Prince* (1935) 51 T.L.R. 526; *Re Morley's Estate* [1937] Ch. 491.
59. *I.R.C.* v. *Hawley* [1928] 1 K.B. 578; 13 T.C. 327.
60. See Snell's *Principles of Equity*, (28th ed.), p. 364.
61. *I.R.C.* v. *Lady Castlemaine* (1943) 25 T.C. 408.

Chapter 10

INCOME AND CAPITAL SETTLEMENTS

1. Introduction

10–01 THERE are many circumstances in which one person may wish, or be obliged, to provide another person with a source of income. A parent or grandparent may wish to provide a source of income for a child's education or maintenance, or to assist a dependent relative. A person may wish to provide an income for charitable purposes. Divorce and separation are occasions when one spouse may be obliged by law to provide an income for the other or for the children of the marriage.

10–02 A legally enforceable right to a source of income may be provided in one of two ways:

(1) The provider may enter into a deed or other instrument transferring part of his income.

Example
X covenants to pay Y during the joint lives of X and Y or for seven years whichever is the shorter period the sum of £2,000 per annum less income tax at the basic rate.

This type of arrangement may be described as an "income settlement" because X merely transfers part of his income to Y. X's capital (if any) is unaffected.

(2) Where the provider has capital, he may enter into a deed or other instrument transferring part of his capital to trustees, directing them to invest the capital and pay or apply the income so produced to or for the benefit of one or more persons.

Example
X transfers £20,000 to trustees upon trust to invest the same, to divide the capital between X's children if and when they attain the age of 25 years and meanwhile to apply the income for the maintenance, education or benefit of such children.

This type of arrangement may be described as a "capital settlement" because X transfers part of his capital to trustees.

10–03 The terms "income settlement" and "capital settlement" are not used in the Tax Acts but the expressions conveniently describe the differences between the two types of arrangement. Because of these differences, income and capital settlements are dealt with separately in the pages that follow. Although many of the statutory provisions which apply to the one type of settlement apply also to the other, their effect is not the same.

The effect of the statutory provisions

10–04   The object of both types of settlement is to transfer a slice of the settlor's
income from the settlor to another person or persons. In some cases the
settlor is a high rate taxpayer, whereas the beneficiary is taxable at a lower
rate or not at all (*e.g.* a charity). The object of the exercise in such a case is
to transfer income in such a way that it ceases to be part of the settlor's
income taxable at the high rates applicable to him and becomes the beneficiary's income. Whether the settlement is an income settlement or a
capital settlement, the income will have borne basic rate income tax before
it reaches the beneficiary; hence if the beneficiary is exempt from income
tax or not liable to tax at the basic rate on the whole of the income he
derives from the settlor, the beneficiary will be able to make a claim for
repayment of income tax from the Revenue.

10–05   The statutory provisions which are considered in this chapter operate in
one of two ways:

(1) In some cases they deem the income to be that of the settlor for *all*
    income tax purposes. This renders the settlement wholly ineffective
    for tax purposes because (a) the settlor saves no tax because the
    transferred income is added back in computing his tax liability (see
    § 8–34) and (b) it denies the beneficiary any right to claim repay-
    ment of basic rate income tax.
(2) In other cases, they deem the income to be that of the settlor only
    for the purposes of "excess liability." Excess liability means the
    excess of liability to income tax over what it would be if all income
    tax were charged at the basic rate to the exclusion of any other
    rate.[1] This means that the transferred income is deemed to be the
    income of the settlor for the purposes of higher rate income tax,
    with the result that the settlor saves no tax chargeable at these rates;
    but the beneficiary is not deprived of his right to claim repayment of
    basic rate income tax in an appropriate case.

10–06   Although settlements are often used in tax planning where the settlor is a
high rate taxpayer and the beneficiary is a low rate taxpayer, it should be
kept in mind that the tax position of the parties may become reversed
through changed circumstances, in which case deeming the income arising
under the settlement to be the income of the settlor may cause it to be
taxed at a lower rate than the rate at which it would be taxed if the deeming
provision had not applied.

A settlement which is ineffective under the general law, *e.g.* for lack of
certainty[2] or for perpetuity[3] is equally ineffective for any tax purpose.

---

1. I.C.T.A. 1970, s.457(1).
2. See *Re Baden's Deed Trusts* [1971] A.C. 424 (H.L.).
3. *Aked* v. *Shaw* (1947) 28 T.C. 286.

What is a settlement?

10–07 For the purposes of most of the provisions considered in this chapter the word "settlement" is defined as including "any trust, covenant, agreement or arrangement"[4] although, for the purposes of other provisions, it also includes "a transfer of assets."[5]

10–08 Although this definition is sufficiently wide to include commercial transactions, the House of Lords has recently confirmed that the settlement provisions in Part XVI of the Income and Corporation Taxes Act 1970 apply only to transactions in which there is an element of bounty.[6] Lord Wilberforce stated the position as follows:

> "My Lords, it seems to me to be clear that it is not possible to read into the definition an exception in favour of commercial transactions whether with or without the epithet 'ordinary' or 'bona fide.' To do so would be legislation not interpretation: if Parliament had intended such an exception it could and must have expressed it . . . My Lords, it can, I think, fairly be seen that all these provisions, in Part XVI have a common character. They are designed to bring within the net of taxation dispositions of various kinds, in favour of a settlor's spouse, or children, or of charities, cases, in popular terminology, in which a taxpayer gives away a portion of his income, or of his assets, to such persons, or for such periods, or subject to such conditions, that Parliament considers it right to continue to treat such income, or income of the assets, as still the settlor's income. These sections, in other words, though drafted in wide, and increasingly wider language, are nevertheless dealing with a limited field, one far narrower than the field of the totality of dispositions, or arrangements, or agreements, which a man may make in the course of his life. Is there any common description which can be applied to this? The Courts which, inevitably, have had to face this problem, have selected the element of 'bounty' as a necessary common characteristic of all the 'settlements' which Parliament has in mind. The decisions are tentative, but all point in this direction."

The House of Lords thus rejected the Crown's contention that the definition applied to all transactions that did not have a bona fide commercial reason, including a transaction the sole reason for which was to avoid tax.

The expression "arrangement" is extremely wide. A scheme to secure a particular objective may constitute an "arrangement" from its inception even though, at its inception, the final steps have not been worked out.[7] Further, an arrangement may include a combination or series of transactions, some of which may be for consideration or of a commercial character.[8]

---

4. I.C.T.A. 1970, s.454(3) applying for the purposes of Chapter III (ss.445–456) and Chapter IV (ss.457–459). The word "disposition" is so defined in s.434(2) for the purposes of Chap. I (ss.434–436).

5. I.C.T.A. 1970, s.444(2) applying for the purposes of Chapter III (ss.437–444). *Cf.* the definition for the purposes of capital transfer tax in §§ 22–05 *et seq.*

6. *I.R.C.* v. *Plummer* [1980] A.C. 896 54 T.C.1; [1979] S.T.C. 793 (H.L.). See also *Bulmer* v. *I.R.C.* [1967] Ch. 145; 44 T.C. 1; following *Copeman* v. *Coleman* (1939) 22 T.C. 594 and *I.R.C.* v. *Leiner* (1964) 41 T.C. 589. And see *I.R.C.* v. *Levy* (1982) 56 T.C. 68; [1982] S.T.C. 442. The exercise by trustees of a power of appointment is an exercise of bounty by the *settlor*: *Chinn* v. *Collins*, 54 T.C. 311; [1981] S.T.C. 1 (H.L.).

7. *Crossland* v. *Hawkins* (1961) 39 T.C. 493 (C.A.).

8. *Chinn* v. *Collins* (1980) 54 T.C. 311; *per* Lord Wilberforce at p. 351F.

10–09   A court order can constitute a "settlement" and in *Yates* v. *Starkey*[9] (a divorce case) it was held that an order directing the husband to make payments *in trust* for each of his children was a settlement of which the husband was settlor. It was (the court held) immaterial that the order was not a consent order and that the husband was acting under compulsion in making the payments due under the order. Where the court orders that payments be made *directly* to the child, it is Revenue practice not to treat the order as constituting a settlement. Where, however, there is a consent order and the amount ordered is excessive in relation to the legal obligations of the father to maintain his child, the Revenue may contend that there is a settlement.

2. INCOME SETTLEMENTS

10–10   The following is an example of the operative clause in a typical income settlement:

> X covenants to pay Y during the joint lives of X and Y or for seven years, whichever is the shorter period, the sum of £2,400 per annum less income tax at the basic rate, such payments to be made in equal monthly instalments on the first day of each month.

It has been explained in § 5–04 that, provided the agreement between X and Y creates an obligation binding on X (as it will if the agreement is under seal or is otherwise enforceable as a simple contract), the payments made under the agreement are annual payments within Case III of Schedule D. On making the payments X deducts income tax at the basic rate: see § 5–30.

10–11   Let it be assumed that X has an income (all earned) of £9,000 in the year of assessment and that he has covenanted to make Y an annual payment of £2,400, payable by equal quarterly instalments. Ignoring the settlement provisions in the Tax Acts, the tax consequences of this arrangement may be summarised as follows:

1. X discharges his obligation to Y by paying to Y each quarter £600 less income tax at the basic rate. Thus if the basic rate is 30 per cent., X will pay £600 less £180 = £420.
2. Y can reclaim from the Inland Revenue the amount by which the amount deducted by X exceeds Y's tax liability, if any. If Y is a charity or is otherwise exempt from income tax on Case III income, Y can reclaim from the Revenue the whole of the amount deducted by X. If Y is an individual with no other income, and therefore taxable only on his income after deducting the personal reliefs, Y can

---

9. [1951] Ch. 465; (1981) 54 T.C. 32 T.C. 38 (C.A.).

reclaim tax at the basic rate on an amount equal to his personal reliefs.

3. The gross amount of the annual payment (£2,400) is a charge on the income of X: see § 8–31. Hence X is entitled to deduct the £2,400 in computing his total income. The effect is that X avoids higher rate income tax on the annual payment but has to account for the basic rate tax which he deducts: see § 8–32.

10–12 The practical effect of these consequences is clearly demonstrated by the example in § 8–69 (Computations D and E) and the comments there, to which the reader is referred. Briefly, an income settlement enables an individual to transfer a slice of his income so that it ceases to bear income tax at the rate or rates that would otherwise apply to such income, which becomes taxable at the rate or rates applicable to the transferee. Tax law permits these consequences to ensue only where there is a genuine alienation of income which creates a source of Case III income for the transferee. Not all expenditure has this effect. Thus the example in § 10–10 may be contrasted with the case where X gives £2,400 out of one year's income to Y. Such a gift is not Case III income of Y: it is a mere gift of money. The statutory provisions which are discussed in the following paragraphs show the conditions that have to be satisfied for a transfer of income to be effective for tax purposes.

Statutory provisions affecting income settlements

(1) Higher rate and additional rate relief for settlors

10–13 We have seen, in § 10–11, that the gross amount of an annual payment made under an income settlement is a charge on the settlor's income and so escapes income tax at the higher rates. As a result of legislation first enacted in 1965 and now in section 457 of the Income and Corporation Taxes Act 1970, the opportunity for an individual to avoid higher rate income tax by means of an *income* settlement has been severely restricted. Section 457, which applies to all income settlements made on or after April 7, 1965, other than those which are expressly excepted (see §§ 10–14 *et seq.*), deems the income so settled to be the income of the settlor for the purposes of higher rate tax. Taking the example in § 10–11, the tax consequences of such a settlement, if made after April 7, 1965, are exactly as there stated, except that X will not avoid higher rate income tax on the gross amount of the annual payment. But the income arising under the settlement is not deemed to be the income of X for *all* income tax purposes; hence Y's right to recover basic rate income tax is unaffected by section 457. Section 457 restricts reliefs which would otherwise be available to the settlor: it has no impact on the tax position of the beneficiary.

Settlements excepted from section 457. Annual payments which are made in the following circumstances are excepted from the operation of section 457:

10–14   (a) *Annuities to retired partners and their families.*[10] Annual payments made under a partnership agreement to or for the benefit of a former member (as defined[11]) or to the widow or dependants[12] of a deceased former member of the partnership fall outside section 457, if the payments are made under a liability incurred for full consideration. Continuing partners thus normally get full income tax relief on annuities which they pay to retired partners, their widows or dependants: see also § 8–11. Section 457 applies if partners provide an increased annuity for a former member, for there will be no consideration moving from the former member. Section 16 of the Finance Act 1974, as amended (see § 11–13), now allows annuities payable to former partners to be increased by reference to increases in the retail prices index, and section 457(4A) of the Income and Corporation Taxes Act 1970 has been inserted in order to except such increases from section 457. Hence the continuing partners will obtain tax relief where they make good the shortfall in a retired partner's annuity by payments which are annual payments for tax purposes.

10–15   (b) *Purchase of a business on an annuity basis.*[13] Annual payments made by an individual in connection with the acquisition by him of the whole or part of a business fall outside section 457 if they are made under a liability incurred for full consideration:

   (i) to or for the benefit of the individual from whom it is acquired or (if he is dead) his widow or dependants[13a]; or
   (ii) if the vendor was a partnership, to or for the benefit of a former member (as defined[13b]) or the widow or dependants of a deceased former member of that or any preceding partnership[14] or to or for the benefit of an individual from whom the business or part was acquired by that or any preceding partnership or, if he is dead, to or for the benefit of the widow or dependants of such an individual.

In this context the distinction between annual payments and instalments of capital must be kept in mind (see § 5–27). No income tax relief is given to the purchaser of a business for a capital sum paid by instalments.

10–16   (c) *Payments on divorce, nullity and separation.*[15] Annual payments under a settlement made by one party to a marriage by way of provision for the other after the dissolution or annulment of the marriage, or while they are separated under an order of a court or under a separation agreement or

---

10. I.C.T.A. 1970, s.457(1)(*a*).
11. "Former member" in relation to a partnership means an individual who has ceased to be a member of that partnership on retirement or death: *ibid.* s.457(5)(*a*).
12. As to the meaning of "dependants," see *Re Baden's Deed Trusts (No. 2)* [1972] Ch. 607; [1973] Ch. 9 (C.A.).
13. I.C.T.A. 1970, s.457(2), (4).
13a. See note 12, above.
13b. See note 11, above.
14. A partnership becomes a "preceding partnership" of another if it transfers its business or part of its business to another and one or more individuals are members of both, and any preceding partnership of the transferor by reference to any part of the business transferred also becomes a preceding partnership of the transferee: I.C.T.A. 1970, s.457(5)(*b*).
15. I.C.T.A. 1970, s.457(1)(*c*).

in such circumstances that the separation is likely to be permanent, fall out-side section 457 if they are payable to or applicable for the benefit of that other party.

> Thus, if a husband (H) and wife (W) are separated and the separation is likely to be permanent and H agrees to pay £x per annum to W, H is entitled to full tax relief on the gross amount which he pays. If H agrees to pay £y to H's son (S), section 457 applies and H gets no tax relief on the payments to S unless there is a court order directing H to pay S. In that case, section 457 does not apply because there is no "settlement": see § 10–09.

0–16A (d) *Charity covenants*. Annual payments which are covenanted pay-ments to charity (as defined: see § 10–20A) are (without financial limit) outside section 457 if the charity is not a "private indirect charity" (as defined). If it is such a charity, section 457 may apply to part of the cove-nanted payment.[16]

10–17 *Transactions for full consideration*. It was explained in § 10–08 that an element of bounty is an essential characteristic of a "settlement" as that term is defined in Part XVI of the Taxes Act 1970. The test is not whether the transaction was a bona fide commercial transaction. In the *Plummer*[17] case Lord Fraser said this view was supported by the exceptions in § 10–14, § 10–15 and § 10–16 above. Thus in § 10–14 only annuities paid for full consideration are excluded: gratuitous annuities are not excluded. Like-wise the exception in § 10–15 applies only to annual payments made under a liability incurred for full consideration. As to the exception in § 10–16 Lord Fraser said:

> "There is no express requirement in [this paragraph] for full consideration as that would clearly be inappropriate, but it is reasonable to assume that pay-ments in the circumstances mentioned in this paragraph would usually be moti-vated by obligation, legal or moral, rather than by bounty."

Thus if a husband uses the opportunity of separation or divorce to make annual payments far in excess of those which the court would order, the element of bounty present in such a transaction may bring it within the definition of settlement and not within the exception in § 10–16.

10–18 *Reverse annuity transactions*. The principle that the settlement pro-visions in the Tax Acts do not apply to agreements which are bona fide commercial transactions for full consideration in money or money's worth, with no element of bounty, formed the basis of a tax avoidance scheme[18] whereby, for example, a high rate taxpayer covenants to pay £x per annum out of his income to (say) a charity in consideration of a capital sum. The payer claims the annual payment as a deduction in computing his total income for income tax purposes. The capital sum is non-taxable. This device was legislated against by section 48 of the Finance Act 1977.

The section requires that the annual payment in such a case shall be

---

16. *Ibid*, s.457(1A) as amended by F.A. 1986, s.32 and Sched. 7. See [1986] S.T.I. 431 and the I.R. leaflets entitled "Tax Aid" (I.R. 64 and I.R. 65).
17. *I.R.C.* v. *Plummer* [1980] A.C. 896; 54 T.C.1 (H.L.).
18. See *I.R.C.* v. *Plummer*, above.

made without deduction of income tax and shall not be allowed as a deduction in computing income or total income of the payer and shall not be a charge on income for the purposes of the corporation tax. The section does not apply if the capital sum is taxable as income of the payer or if it is received as consideration for any annuity granted in the ordinary course of a business of granting annuities. Nor does the section apply so as to deny full tax relief to the person paying an annuity or other annual payment in any of the cases mentioned in §§ 10–14 to 10–16 above.

Section 48 applies to payments made after March 29, 1977, irrespective of when the liability to make the payments was incurred.

(2) *The period of the settlement*

10–19   To be effective for tax purposes, an alienation of income must be capable of remaining operative for a substantial period of time. Section 434 of the Income and Corporation Taxes Act 1970 provides that where under a disposition[19] income[20] is payable to or applicable for the benefit of a person for a period which cannot exceed six years, such income shall be deemed for all tax purposes to be that of the disponer, if living. "Disposition" (with one qualification mentioned below) includes any trust, covenant, agreement or arrangement.[21]

This section applies only if the period of payment *cannot* exceed six years. (Where the exception for covenanted donations to charity in § 10–20A applies, the following should be read with the substitution of *three* years to *six* years). To avoid the section, therefore, the covenantor must choose either:

(a) A definite period which must exceed six years: hence the "seven-year covenant"; or

(b) an indefinite period which might exceed six years, such as a covenant for the joint lives of the covenantor and covenantee or for seven years, whichever shall be the shorter period.

If an indefinite period is chosen, it is immaterial that, in the events which happen, the payments cease within six years, whether by mutual agreement between the parties[22] or otherwise.

In *I.R.C.* v. *Black*[23] the respondents covenanted to pay a property-owning company which they controlled an annuity equal to a proportion of the difference between the annual letting value of certain property and the income actually produced. There was to be an overall limit of £100,000. The covenant

---

19. As to what constitutes an effective disposition of income, see *I.R.C.* v. *Lee* (1943) 25 T.C. 485; *I.R.C.* v. *Compton* (1946) 27 T.C. 350. *Cf. Russell* v. *I.R.C.* (1944) 26 T.C. 242.

20. As to payments of capital, see *I.R.C.* v. *Mallaby-Deeley* (1938) 23 T.C. 153 (C.A.). "Income" means income under the Tax Acts which is chargeable under those Acts. It does not include a non-resident person's income from foreign property: *Becker* v. *Wright* (1965) 42 T.C. 591 (where the taxpayer had foreign income under a deed of covenant made by a covenantor resident outside the U.K. and unsuccessfully relied on s.434 to escape assessment under Case V of Schedule D.).

21. I.C.T.A. 1970, s.434(2). As to dispositions by more than one settlor, see *ibid.* s.436.

22. If a provision for revocation is contained in the settlement itself, I.C.T.A. 1970, s.445(1) will apply: *post*, § 10–26.

23. (1940) 23 T.C. 715 (C.A.).

was made in 1936 and was to expire in 1944. Within two years, however, the limit had been reached. Since the period *might* have exceeded six years, the covenant was not caught by the section.

It should be kept in mind that a covenant which is not limited to the life of the settlor will bind his personal representatives and, if there is a life interest in the covenantor's residuary estate, some part of the covenanted sums will be payable out of capital under the rule of apportionment in *Re Perkins*.[24] The personal representatives will to this extent be liable to account for tax under section 53 of the Income and Corporation Taxes Act, 1970.[25] It is advisable in such a case to exclude the apportionment rule.

10–20   The period of six years referred to in section 434 is the period during which income is payable, and is therefore reckoned from the date when the first payment is due (which cannot be before the date of execution of the settlement) to the date when the last payment is due.[26] Considerable care is required in drafting a deed to ensure that section 434 does not apply.[27]

Section 434 does not apply to a disposition made for "valuable and sufficient consideration"[28]; so, for example, provision can be made for a retiring partner or his dependants in an appropriate case by covenants made by the continuing partners and expressed to run for a definite period of less than six years: and see § 11–13. Dispositions made on the occasion of separation or divorce may fall within the words of exception.

10–20A   *Covenanted payments to charity.* The period of six years in § 10–19 is reduced to three years in the case of a "covenanted payment to charity": hence the "four year covenant." The amendment has effect in and from 1980–81 in relation to payments made after April 5, 1980. A covenanted payment to charity means "a payment made under a covenant made otherwise than for consideration in money or money's worth in favour of a body of persons or trust established for charitable purposes only whereby the like annual payments (of which the payment in question is one) become payable for a period which may exceed three years and is not capable of earlier transaction under any power exercisable without the consent of the persons for the time being entitled to the payments."[29]

10–21   *Covenants for varying amounts.*[30] Where a settlement provides for the payment of fixed sums which vary in amount throughout its duration, only the amount common to the whole period is outside the mischief of section

---

24. [1907] 2 Ch. 596. See Snell's *Principles of Equity* (28th ed.), p. 343.
25. See *ante*, §§ 5–34 *et seq.*
26. *I.R.C.* v. *St. Luke's Hostel Trustees* (1930) 15 T.C. 682. Separate from the question of reckoning the six-year period is the question whether sums expressed to be payable in respect of a period prior to the date of execution but paid on or after that date are deductible in computing the covenantor's income. *Semble*, they are not deductible unless they are expressed to be payable on or after the execution of the deed: see *I.R.C.* v. *Nettlefold* (1933) 18 T.C. 235.
27. See, *e.g. I.R.C.* v. *St. Luke's Hostel Trustees* (1930) 15 T.C. 682; *I.R.C.* v. *Verdon Roe* (1962) 40 T.C. 541 (C.A.); *I.R.C.* v. *Hobhouse* (1956) 36 T.C. 648.
28. For a discussion on this phrase see *I.R.C.* v. *Plummer* (1978) 54 T.C.1 especially at pp. 29 *et seq.*
29. I.C.T.A. 1970, s.434(1A) inserted by F.A. 1980, s.55(1).
30. For stamp duty see F.A. 1980, s.99; *post* § 28–44.

434. Any excess over this amount in any year is to be treated as income of the settlor for that year. This is because the words of the section require the recurrence in each year of some definable unit of income which is payable for a period which can exceed six years.[31] It seems this requirement is satisfied by a covenant whereby the settlor is to pay a stated fraction of his income (even if it amounts to the whole thereof) or an amount equal to a yearly dividend from a block of ordinary shares.[32]

10–22   *Effect where section 434 applies.* Where a settlement is caught by section 434, the income payable thereunder is deemed for all tax purposes to be the income of the settlor. Such income is deemed to be the highest part of his income and is accordingly liable to tax at the highest rate applicable to him.[33] Under section 435(1) of the Income and Corporation Taxes Act 1970, there are provisions whereby the amount of the income tax chargeable on and paid by the settlor in consequence of the disposition may be recovered from the trustee or other person to whom the income was payable. The result is that the payee cannot recover any part of the basic rate income tax deducted by the settlor; and the settlor bears the same higher rate income tax that would have been payable by him if the settlement had not been made. Having paid such higher rate income tax, the settlor is entitled to recover this from the payee.

(3) *Covenants for the covenantor's own children*

10–23   By section 437 of the Income and Corporation Taxes Act 1970, where under a settlement and during the life of the settlor any income is in any year *paid*[34] to or for the benefit of a child[35] of the settlor who at the time of payment is unmarried and below the age of 18, such income is to be treated for all tax purposes as the settlor's income for that year and not that of any other person. There is an exception in the case of sums not exceeding £5.[36] "Settlement" includes any disposition, trust, covenant, agreement, arrangement or transfer of assets.[37] An income settlement by a parent on his infant, unmarried child is thereby rendered ineffective as a means of creating a source of income in respect of which the child can recover basic rate income tax.[37a] Settlements for the children of others and on grandchil-

---

31. *I.R.C.* v. *Mallaby-Deeley* (1938) 23 T.C. 153 (C.A.).
32. *I.R.C.* v. *Black* (1940) 23 T.C. 715 (C.A.); *D'Ambrumenil* v. *I.R.C.* [1940] 1 K.B. 850; 23 T.C. 440; *cf. I.R.C.* v. *Prince-Smith* (1943) 25 T.C. 84.
33. I.C.T.A. 1970, s.435(3).
34. Income apportioned to a child by virtue of a surtax direction has been held not to have been "paid": see *Houry* v. *I.R.C.* [1960] A.C. 36 (J.C.). This now applies to statutory apportionments: see §§ 15–28 *et seq.*
35. Child includes a step-child, an adopted child and an illegitimate child: I.C.T.A. 1970, s.444(1). A step-child includes a child of a former marriage whose parents are alive: *I.R.C.* v. *Russell* (1955) 36 T.C. 83.
36. I.C.T.A. 1970, s.437(3).
37. *Ibid.* s.444(2). As to arrangements, see *Crossland* v. *Hawkins* [1961] Ch. 537; 39 T.C. 493 (C.A.) and *Mills* v. *I.R.C.* [1975] A.C. 38; 49 T.C. 367 (H.L.). See also § 10–08.
37a. *Harvey* v. *Sivyer* (1985) S.T.C. 434 (deed of separation under which father convenanted to pay a monthly sum to each of his children *held* to be a settlement; childrens claim for repayment of tax refused).

dren of the settlor are outside the scope of section 437, except that reciprocal arrangements between parents to make settlements on each other's children are caught.[38]

The provisions of section 437 cannot be avoided by directing the income to be paid to trustees for the child and directing the trustees to accumulate the income for the child, even if the child's interest in the income so accumulated is contingent. This is because income which *might* become payable to or for the benefit of a child in the future is to be treated as if it were actually paid to him.[39]

10–24 *Effect where section 437 applies.* Where a settlement is caught by section 437, the income payable thereunder is deemed for all tax purposes to be the income of the settlor. Such income is deemed to be the highest part of his income and is accordingly liable to tax at the highest rate applicable to him.[40] Under section 441(1) of the Income and Corporation Taxes Act 1970, there are provisions whereby the amount of the income tax chargeable on and paid by the settlor in consequence of the disposition may be recovered from the trustee or other person to whom the income was payable. The result is that the payee cannot recover any part of the basic rate income tax deducted by the settlor; and the settlor bears the same higher rate income tax that would have been payable by him if the settlement had not been made. Having paid such higher rate income tax, the settlor is entitled to recover this from the payee.

10–25 *Covenants for adult or married children.* Section 437 does not apply where the settlor's child is married or has attained the age of 18 at the time of the payment. In such a case, therefore, the income is not deemed to be that of the settlor for all tax purposes so the covenantee may be able to make a claim for repayment of the basic rate income tax suffered by deduction; but the income is deemed to be that of the settlor for the purposes of higher rate income tax, as explained in § 10–13 above, so the settlor is denied tax relief on the gross amount of the payments.

(4) *Revocable settlements*

10–26 Section 445(1) of the Income and Corporation Taxes Act 1970 provides that if the terms of any settlement[41] are such that any person has or may have power either to revoke or otherwise determine the settlement (so that the liability to make the payments thereunder ceases) or to diminish the amount of any payments thereunder, the sum payable under the settlement or a sum equal to the amount of the possible diminution (as the case may be) is to be treated for all tax purposes as the settlor's income. There is a proviso which excepts a power of revocation or of determination or of

---

38. See the definition of "settlor" in I.C.T.A. 1970, s.444(2).
39. I.C.T.A. 1970, s.438(1).
40. *Ibid.* s.441(3).
41. Defined in I.C.T.A. 1970, s.454(3), to include any disposition, trust, covenant, agreement or arrangement.

diminution which is not exercisable for six years from the time when the first annual payment is payable[42]; but this merely suspends the operation of the section, which applies as soon as the power is exercisable after six years. This period during which the section is held in suspense cannot be extended retrospectively.[43]

Section 445 must be kept in mind where the amount payable under a covenant is to be related to the income of the covenantor or to some other variable sum. In a separation deed, for example, the amount payable in each year may be related to the husband's income in that year; or a covenant to guarantee periodical payments may be related to the profits of the covenantee. Two points should be noted in this connection:

10–27

(1) The section applies only to a *power* to revoke, etc. It is thought that the section does not apply if the amount to be paid is defined by reference to a formula, *e.g.* as a defined fraction of the covenantor's income. Thus if, in a separation deed, a husband reserves power to reduce the amount of the payments if his income falls, the section applies; but it will not apply if he covenants to pay one third of his annual income.

(2) The section applies only to a power contained in the settlement itself.

In *I.R.C.* v. *Wolfson*[44] the settlor controlled a private company. He covenanted to pay periodical sums which were related to the dividends declared by the company, and the Revenue contended that because the settlor could ensure that no dividends were paid, there was therefore a power of revocation. The House of Lords held that the section did not apply because the power was not to be found in the terms of the settlement.

Lest it be thought that the section can always be avoided by the interposition of a company, it should be noted that "settlement" includes an arrangement and that the formation of a company followed by the execution of an income settlement may together constitute a single settlement.[45]

10–28 *Effect where section 445 applies.* Where a settlement is caught by section 445 the income payable thereunder, or the appropriate part thereof, is deemed for all tax purposes to be income of the settlor. Such income is deemed to be the highest part of his income and is accordingly liable to tax at the highest rate applicable to him.[46] Under section 449(3) there are provisions whereby the tax consequently paid by the settlor may be recovered from the trustee or other person to whom the income was actually paid.

---

42. I.C.T.A. 1970, s.445(1), proviso. The period is three years in the case of a covenanted payment to charity: *ibid*. s.445(1A): see § 10–20A.
43. *Taylor* v. *I.R.C.* (1945) 27 T.C. 93 (C.A.); *I.R.C.* v. *Nicolson* (1953) 34 T.C. 354.
44. (1949) 31 T.C. 141 (H.L.).
45. I.C.T.A. 1970, s.454(3); and see *I.R.C.* v. *Payne* (1940) 23 T.C. 610 (C.A.); *Crossland* v. *Hawkins* [1961] Ch. 537; 39 T.C. 493 (C.A.).
46. I.C.T.A. 1970, s.449(5).

(5) *Undistributed income*

10–29 Income is "undistributed" if it is so dealt with that it does not fall to be treated as the income of the person entitled to it.[47] It is thought that income will be treated as distributed if it is applied for the benefit of the beneficiary, *e.g.* by purchase of investments in the beneficiary's name. Income is undistributed if, for example, there is a covenant to pay periodic sums to trustees for an infant beneficiary who is contingently entitled thereto, and the trustees do not distribute the entire income for purposes of maintenance[48]; or if, in a discretionary settlement, the trustees fail to exercise their discretion in respect of the whole of the income.[49]

10–30 (a) *Position where settlor retains interest.* By section 447(1) of the Income and Corporation Taxes Act 1970, if the settlor has an interest in any income arising under or property comprised in a settlement, undistributed income which arises in any year of assessment during the settlor's life is to be treated for all tax purposes as the settlor's income. A settlor is deemed to have such an interest if any income or property which may at any time arise under or be comprised in the settlement is, or will or may become, payable to or applicable for the benefit of the settlor or the wife[50] or husband of the settlor in any circumstances whatsoever.[51] If, therefore, there is any likelihood that there might be undistributed income it is important to see that there is no possibility, however remote, of a resulting trust to the settlor.

10–31 *Exceptions.* By the proviso to section 447(2), the settlor is not to be deemed to have an interest within the section if the income or property can only become payable or applicable to him in the events therein stated.[52] In particular, the settlor has no such interest if there is a resulting trust to him (or his spouse) in the event of the death under 25 or some lower age of some person beneficially entitled to the income of property on attaining that age. If the vesting of capital is postponed until the beneficiary attains an age greater than 25, the deeming provision is excluded until the beneficiary attains 25 but not thereafter.

Effect where section 447 applies. The effect is the same as when section 445 applies: see § 10–28.

---

47. See *ibid*. s.455 for details.
48. It seems that if a beneficiary has a vested interest and the trustees accumulate income because the infant cannot give a valid receipt, such income is "distributed:" see § 9–05.
49. See *Cornwell* v. *Barry* (1955) 36 T.C. 268: child had vested interest in income liable to be divested—no appropriation of income to child—*held*, not income of child for purpose of enabling child to claim personal reliefs and allowances.
50. "Wife" does not include "widow": *Vestey's Executors* v. *I.R.C.* (1949) 31 T.C. 1.
51. I.C.T.A. 1970, s.447(2). In *Glyn* v. *I.R.C.* (1948) 30 T.C. 321, the possibility that the settlor might benefit under a power exercisable jointly with his son was held to be such an interest; but it was said *obiter* that the possibility of a mere voluntary application of income by a beneficiary to a settlor was outside the section notwithstanding the words "in any circumstances whatever."
52. These events are set out in full in § 10–42.

10–32   (b) *Position where income is left undistributed.* Section 450 of the Income
and Corporation Taxes Act 1970 applies if the covenantor pays to the trustees of a settlement any sums which would otherwise be deductible in computing his total income if income remains undistributed in the trustees'
hands at the end of the year of assessment. Such income is disallowed as a
deduction in computing the settlor's total income, unless it is otherwise disallowed under sections 445, 446, 447 or 448 of the Act.[53] This prevents
income settlements being used to build up funds in the hands of trustees for
eventual distribution as capital, the settlor getting relief from higher rate
tax in the process.

Conclusion on income settlements

10–33   Since 1965 the settlor who makes an income settlement gets relief from
higher rate tax only in four exceptional cases. These are cases of payments
of annuities under partnership agreements (see § 10–14), payments
towards the purchase of a business on an annuity basis (see § 10–15), certain payments made in connection with divorce, nullity or separation (see
§ 10–16) and covenanted payments to charity (see § 10–16A).

Even in these exceptional cases no such relief is given unless further conditions are satisfied. First, the period of the settlement must be capable of
exceeding six years (see § 10–19), except where the disposition is for valuable and sufficient consideration (see § 10–20) or is a covenanted payment
to charity (see § 10–16A). Secondly, the payments must not be to infant
unmarried children of the settlor (see §§ 10–23 *et seq.*). Thirdly, the settlement must not be "revocable" in the extended sense in which that word is
used (see §§ 10–26 *et seq.*). Fourthly, the settlor must retain no interest,
subject to certain excepted interests (see §§ 10–31 *et seq.*). Fifthly, the
income must be distributed and not accumulated at the end of each year of
assessment (see § 10–32).

As regards the covenantee, it is not necessary that the settlement should
fall within one of the three exceptional cases referred to above in order that
the amount covenanted to be paid should be treated as the covenantee's
income for tax purposes. But each of the other five conditions referred to
above has to be satisfied.

3. CAPITAL SETTLEMENTS

10–34   A capital settlement is one under which a settlor transfers property, usually
of an income-producing nature, to trustees and directs the trustees to deal
with the capital and the income so produced for the benefit of one or more
persons. The implications of capital settlements as regards capital transfer
tax are considered in Chapter 22 of this book. As regards income tax, the
objective (in most cases) is that the income shall no longer be treated as
part of the income of the settlor for the purposes of income tax but that it
shall be treated in accordance with the principles applicable to trust
income, which are considered in Chapter 9. It will be recalled that trustees

---

53. For s.445, see § 10–26; for s.448, see § 10–44.

bear tax at the basic rate on trust income and, in some cases, at an additional rate. Where, however, the income is distributed to a beneficiary or he is otherwise entitled to it, the income is treated as the beneficiary's income for tax purposes and bears tax at the rate or rates applicable to him. We now consider the statutory provisions which apply to capital settlements, the effect of which has already been briefly mentioned in §§ 10–04 *et seq.*

(1) *Settlements on children*

10–35 It has been seen in § 10–23 that an income settlement for the settlor's unmarried child below the age of 18 has no tax saving effect. This is because, by section 437 of the Income and Corporation Taxes Act 1970, where under a settlement and during the settlor's life, income is in any year paid to or for the benefit of a child of the settlor who at the time of payment is unmarried and below the age of 18, such income is treated for all tax purposes as the settlor's income for that year and not as the income of any other person. "Settlement" includes any disposition, trust, covenant, agreement, arrangement or transfer of assets.[54] The section thus applies to capital as well as to income settlements.

> In *Thomas* v. *Marshall*[55] a father made payments into a Post Office Savings Bank into accounts opened in the names of his infant unmarried children and purchased Defence Bonds in their names. *Held*, that this was a "settlement" within the section and that the interest on the Savings and Bonds must be treated as the father's income.

Accumulation settlements

10–36 There is an important exception to the statutory provision in section 437, which applies to an irrevocable capital settlement where income is lawfully accumulated under a trust or power to accumulate. The exception is in section 438 of the Income and Corporation Taxes Act 1970. "Irrevocable" is defined in section 439 and has an unusually extended meaning. A settlement is not irrevocable (subject to limited exception[56]) if either:

(1) It can be determined by the act or default of any person; or
(2) if in any circumstances any income or property can be applied for the benefit of the settlor, or the husband or wife[57] of the settlor, during the life of a child-beneficiary; or
(3) if it provides for the payment of any penalty by the settlor in the event of his failing to comply with its provisions.

If and so long as income arising under an irrevocable settlement is *accumulated*, such income is not to be deemed under section 437 to be income of the settlor; but *distributed* income (*e.g.* income applied for the mainten-

---

54. I.C.T.A. 1970, s.444(2).
55. [1953] A.C. 543; 34 T.C. 178 (H.L.). For an example of an arrangement, see *Crossland* v. *Hawkins* [1961] Ch. 537; 39 T.C. 493 (C.A.) and the cases cited therein and *Mills* v. *I.R.C.* [1975] A.C. 38; 49 T.C. 367 (H.L.).
56. I.C.T.A. 1970, s.439(1), proviso.
57. "Wife" does not include "widow": *Vestey's Executors* v. *I.R.C.* (1949) 31 T.C. 1.

ance of an infant and unmarried child under section 31 of the Trustee Act 1925) falls within the deeming provision. The section cannot be avoided by the trustees accumulating income (which thus becomes capital) and making advancements out of capital; for it is expressly provided that distributions of capital shall be treated as distributions of income up to the amount of undistributed income.[58] A settlement of capital (*i.e.* income-producing property) under which the income is accumulated is the only method provided for in the Taxing Acts by which a high-rate taxpayer can provide for his own infant unmarried children and avoid higher rate income tax on the income so accumulated. Accumulated income will be liable to the additional rate tax.[59] The requirement that the settlement should be "irrevocable" makes it essential that the settlor and his spouse should be excluded from any possible interest under the settlement, other than such interest as is specifically allowed by the proviso to section 439.

Income derived from appropriations of income

10–37   Section 437 of the Income and Corporation Taxes Act 1970 applies where, by virtue or in consequence of the settlement, income is paid to or for the benefit of a child of the settlor. Where income is *appropriated* to a child to be held for the child contingently on his attaining a specified age (pursuant to a power conferred on the trustees) and is invested for the child's benefit, the investment income derived from the appropriations is income which (so it would seem) does not fall to be treated as income of the settlor under section 437. That income is income of which it can be said—using the language of section 438(1) of the Income and Corporation Taxes Act 1970—that it, or assets representing it, will or may become payable or applicable to or for the benefit of the child in the future; and that subsection is intelligible only on the assumption that such income is *not* income which is "paid to or for the benefit of" a child of the settlor. It would seem, therefore, that income derived from appropriations of income is income of the child, not income of the settlor.

Adjustments between disponer and trustees

10–38   Where income tax is chargeable on and is paid by the settlor in consequence of these statutory provisions, he is entitled to recover the tax so paid from the trustee or other persons to whom the income is payable by virtue or in consequence of the settlement.[60]

(2) Revocable settlements

10–39   Section 446 of the Income and Corporation Taxes Act 1970 applies to a settlement if its terms are such that:

(1) Any person has or may have power to revoke or otherwise deter-

---

58. I.C.T.A 1970, s.438(2)(*b*).
59. See *ante*, § 9–02.
60. I.C.T.A. 1970, s.441.

mine the settlement or any provision thereof or to diminish the property comprised in it or to diminish the amount of any payments which are or may be payable under the settlement to any person other than the settlor or the wife[60a] or husband of the settlor; and

(2) on the exercise of that power the settlor (or the wife[60a] or husband of the settlor) will or may become entitled to the whole or any part of the property then comprised in the settlement or of the income arising from the whole or any part of that property.

Where a settlement is "revocable" as thus defined, the income arising under the settlement from the property comprised in the settlement[61] is to be treated as that of the settlor (and not as the income of any other person) for all tax purposes, except that if the power of revocation extends only to a part of the property comprised in the settlement, only the income arising from that part is deemed to be income of the settlor.

It will be observed that the mere existence of a power coupled with the possibility of benefit, however remote, to the settlor or the wife of the settlor, will bring the section into operation.[62] The effect of the section is to deny the settlor the tax advantages of a capital settlement where its terms are such that he retains power to regain the capital or income for his or his wife's benefit.

The section contains a proviso excepting a power to revoke which cannot be exercised within a period of six years from the time when property is put into the settlement and suspending the operation of the section during that period.

It should be noted that, where section 446 applies, the settlor retains no *interest* in capital or income: there is a mere opportunity to regain such an interest through the exercise of a power by someone, not necessarily the settlor.

Where section 446 applies, there are provisions for adjustment similar to those mentioned in § 10–38.[63]

(3) *Undistributed income*

10–40   Income is "undistributed" if it is so dealt with that it does not fall to be treated as the income of the person entitled to it.[64] Income which is accumulated for the benefit of a beneficiary contingently entitled thereto is undistributed.[65]

10–41   (i) *Position where settlor retains interest.* By section 447(1) of the Income and Corporation Taxes Act 1970 (which has already been referred to in connection with income settlements),[66] if and so long as the settlor has an

---

60a. See note 57, above.

61. For the definition of this phrase, see I.C.T.A. 1970, s.454(1) and (1A), inserted by F.A. 1981, s.44(1)

62. See *Barr's Trustees* v. *I.R.C.* (1943) 25 T.C. 72; *I.R.C.* v. *Kenmare* [1958] A.C. 267; 37 T.C. 383.

63. I.C.T.A. 1970, s.449(3).

64. *Ibid.* s.455 and § 10–29.

65. *Ibid.*

66. See *ante*, § 10–30.

interest in any income arising under or property comprised in a settlement, any income so arising during the settlor's life in any year of assessment is, to the extent to which it is not distributed, treated for all tax purposes as the income of the settlor for that year and not as the income of any other person. A settlor is deemed to have an interest for this purpose if any income or property which may at any time arise under or be comprised in the settlement *could* at any time be payable to or applicable for the benefit of the settlor (or the wife[67] or husband of the settlor) *in any circumstances whatever.*[68] Defective drafting which produces a resulting trust of income or capital to the settlor will cause section 447 to apply. A mere power reserved to the settlor to direct investment policy is not an "interest" for the purposes of this provision[69]; nor is an investment clause under which the trustees can invest in companies in which the settlor has a financial interest.

10–42   Section 447 will apply if the settlement deed provides for the property comprised in the settlement to revert back to the settlor (or the wife or husband of the settlor) because this will constitute a retained "interest"; but, by a proviso to section 447(2), the settlor is not deemed to have an interest:

(a) If and so long as the income or property cannot become payable or applicable as aforesaid except in the event of:
    (i) the bankruptcy of some person who is or may become beneficially entitled to that income or property; or
    (ii) any assignment of or charge on that income or property being made or given by some such person; or
    (iii) in the case of a marriage settlement, the death of both the parties to the marriage and of all or any of the children of the marriage; or
    (iv) the death under the age of 25 or some lower age of some person who would be beneficially entitled to that income or property on attaining that age; or

(b) if and so long as some person is alive and under the age of 25 during whose life that income or property cannot become payable or applicable as aforesaid except in the event of that person becoming bankrupt or assigning or charging his interest in that income or property.

In most family settlements, the settlor will wish the settled property to revert to himself (or his wife) on failure of the primary trusts for the children. The proviso to section 447(2) of the Income and Corporation Taxes Act 1970 enables this wish to be fulfilled. There is generally no objection to the settlor or his spouse being named as the person entitled on the failure of the trusts, where the settlement provides for the vesting of capital in children at an age not exceeding 25 years.

67. "Wife" does not include "widow": *Vestey's Executors* v. *I.R.C.* (1949) 31 T.C. 1.
68. I.C.T.A. 1970, s.447(2); *Hannay* v. *I.R.C.* (1956) 37 T.C. 217. For a recent example, see *I.R.C.* v. *Wachtel* [1971] Ch. 573; 46 T.C. 543.
69. *Vestey's Executors* v. *I.R.C.* (1949) 31 T.C. 1.

Where section 447 applies and the income is deemed to be the settlor's income, there are provisions for adjustment similar to those mentioned in § 10–38.[70]

10–43   (ii) *Position where settlor receives a capital sum.* Section 451 of the Income and Corporation Taxes Act 1970 (as amended[71]) is concerned with capital settlements (including those in which the settlor retains no interest) where the trustees pay a *capital sum* to the settlor. To the extent that the capital sum falls within the amount of *income available* up to the end of the year of assessment in which the sum is paid, it is treated as the income of the settlor for that year. To the extent that the capital sum exceeds the amount of the income available up to the end of that year but falls within the amount of the income available up to the end of the next following year, it is treated as income of the settlor in that next year—and so on for each subsequent year up to a maximum of ten subsequent years.

The amount of *income available* up to the end of any year means the aggregate amount of income arising under the settlement in that year and any previous relevant year which has not been distributed; and a "relevant year" means any year of assessment after the year 1937–38. From the income so available is deducted sums chargeable to tax under other provisions; and there is also deducted tax at the basic and additional rate on the income in question.[72] Hence if by the end of year 5 of a settlement the accumulated income less tax thereon is £50,000, and no part of that £50,000 has been treated as income of the settlor, a *capital* sum up to £50,000 which is paid to the settlor will be treated as the settlor's *income* in year 5. If the capital sum exceeds £50,000, the excess will be carried forward to match undistributed income of year 6, and so on.

The expression "capital sum" means[73]:

(i) Any sum paid by way of loan or repayment of a loan; and
(ii) any sum paid otherwise than as income, being a sum which is not paid for full consideration in money or money's worth;

but it does not include any sum which could not have become payable to the settlor except in one of the events specified in the proviso to section 447(2) of the 1970 Act: see § 10–42.

It may seem strange to the reader that a settlor should be taxed where the trustees merely repay a loan. The Revenue have offered the following explanation[74] for treating repayments of loans on the same basis as loans:

"Suppose taxpayer A creates a settlement by transferring investments to trustees and thereafter withdraws the income on the investments at convenient intervals as loans. Taxpayer B creates a settlement by lending money to his trustees with which they buy the same investments as in case A; the settlor thereafter withdraws the income on the investments in the same amounts and

---

70. I.C.T.A. 1970, s.441.
71. See F.A. 1981, s.42 and F.A. 1982, s.63.
72. I.C.T.A. 1970, s.451(1)(2)(8).
73. *Ibid.* s.451(8).
74. [1980] S.T.I. 614, para. 14.

on the same dates as in case A but in the form of repayments of a loan. Clearly the second case has the same practical results as the first and although some criticism has been directed at the legislation it seems right that the two situations should be treated for tax purposes in the same way."

Section 451(1) charges tax where any capital sum is paid directly or indirectly in any relevant year of assessment by the trustees of a settlement *to the settlor*. This includes a sum paid to the wife or husband of the settlor or to one of them jointly with another person[74a]; and there is treated as paid to the settlor by the trustees any sum which (i) is paid by them to a third party at the direction or by virtue of the assignment by him of his right to receive it; or (ii) is otherwise paid or applied by them for the benefit of the settlor.[75] Thus a settlor who is owed money by the trustees cannot avoid section 451 by directing the trustees to pay his creditors or by assigning his rights to a third person.[76]

Where a sum is treated as income of the settlor for any year, it is treated as income of such an amount as after deduction of tax at the basic and additional rate for that year is equal to the sum; but the settlor is entitled to set off against the tax charged under section 451 an amount equal to (i) the sum of tax at the basic and additional rate for that year on the amount treated as his income or (ii) so much of the sum as is equal to the tax charged. The assessment is under Case VI of Schedule D.

If a loan is made by the settlor in a year of assessment when there is undistributed income, section 451 applies even if the loan is repaid in the same or a subsequent year of assessment; but if a loan is made in a year when there is no undistributed income and is repaid before any undistributed income arises, section 451 does not apply. If one or more loans are made and an equivalent amount of undistributed income is taxed as income of the settlor, such income is not again taxed if the loans are repaid and further loans are made to the settlor. If a repayment of a loan is taxed, there is no further charge under section 451 if the same or a lesser amount is reloaned by and later repaid to the settlor.[77]

Capital sums paid by connected companies

10–43A The previous paragraph deals with the case where the trustees of a settlement pay a capital sum to the settlor. We now consider the position where trustees own shares in a company and a capital sum is paid to the settlor by the company. Section 451 "bites" only where the company is "connected with" the settlement and, for this purpose, section 454(4) of the Income and Corporation Taxes Act 1970[78] provides that a body corporate shall be deemed to be connected with a settlement in any year of assessment if at any time in that year:

(a) it is a close company (or only not a close company because it is resi-

---

74a. I.C.T.A. 1970, s.451(8).
75. I.C.T.A. 1970, s.451(9).
76. *Cf. Potts' Executors* v. *I.R.C.* [1951] A.C. 443; 32 T.C. 211 (H.L.).
77. I.C.T.A. 1970, s.451(3A), (3B).
78. Substituted by F.A. 1981, s.44(2).

dent in the United Kingdom) and the participators then include the trustees of the settlement, or

(b) it is controlled within the meaning of section 534 of the 1970 Act (see § 2–45) by a company falling within paragraph (a) above.

Paragraph (a) brings certain foreign companies within section 451. Paragraph (b) treats as connected with the trustees a subsidiary of a company in which the trustees own shares. It will be convenient to refer to bodies corporate as so defined as "connected companies."

A capital sum (defined as in § 10–43) paid to a settlor by a connected company is taxed only if it can be matched with an *associated payment* made directly or indirectly by the trustees of the settlement to the connected company. Thus if trustees buy shares in an established company which then (being a connected company) makes a loan to the settlor in a year of assessment in which no payment has been made by the trustees to the company, section 451 will not apply to the loan.

Where however a capital sum is paid to the settlor in a year of assessment by a connected company and an associated payment has been or is made directly or indirectly to the connected company by the trustees, the capital sum is treated for the purposes of section 451 (above) as having been paid to the settlor by the trustees of the settlement. To the extent to which the sum falls within the total of the associated payment or payments made up to the end of the year of assessment in which it is paid, the sum is treated as having been paid to the settlor in that year. To the extent to which the sum is not so treated as paid to the settlor in that year and falls within the total of the associated payment or payments made up to the end of the next following year (less what was taken into account in relation to that sum in the previous year), it is treated as having been made to the settlor in the next following year, and so on. If the payment of the capital sum can be matched with an associated payment, it matters not how few shares in the connected company the trustees own.

Associated payment is defined[79] in relation to any capital sum as meaning any capital sum paid to the connected company by the trustees and any other sum paid or asset transferred to the connected company by those trustees which is not paid or transferred for full consideration in money or money's worth being a sum paid or asset transferred in the five years ending or beginning with the date on which the capital sum is paid to the settlor. Note that a capital sum can be matched with an associated payment made later.

(4) *The settlor (or his spouse) as the object of a discretion*

10–44   Sections previously considered have dealt with the cases where the settlor retains an interest in the settlement and there is undistributed income (see § 10–41) and where, having no interest, the settlor might

---

79. I.C.T.A. 1970, s.451A(3).

regain an interest (see § 10–39). Section 448 of the Income and Corporation Taxes Act 1970 deals with the case of a discretionary settlement where the settlor (or the husband or wife of the settlor) is among the class of beneficiaries for whose benefit the trustees might exercise their discretion to pay income or capital. Section 448 applies whether or not the income is undistributed. The section provides that if the terms of a settlement are such that any person has or may have power to pay to or apply for the benefit of the settlor, or the wife[80] or husband of the settlor, the whole or any part of the income or property which may at any time arise under or be comprised in the settlement, being a power exercisable at his discretion, any income arising under the settlement in any year of assessment shall be treated as income of the settlor for that year for all tax purposes and not as the income of any other person.[81] The section does not apply if the discretionary power is exercisable only in the events specified in the proviso to section 447(2), which are set out in § 10–42; and there is a provision which suspends the operation of the section where the power cannot be exercised within a period of six years.[82]

The mere existence of the discretionary power brings the section into operation: it is immaterial that in fact the income is paid or applied to or for the benefit of some other person. A provision in the settlement by which the settlor and his spouse for the time being are expressly excluded from any benefit by the exercise of any power or discretion given by the settlement is sufficient to prevent the section applying.

Where section 448 applies, there are provisions for adjustment similar to those mentioned in § 10–38.

80. "Wife" does not include "widow": *Vestey's Executors* v. *I.R.C.* (1949) 31 T.C. 1.
81. I.C.T.A. 1970, s.448. See *Blausten* v. *I.R.C.* (1971) 47 T.C. 542; *I.R.C.* v. *Cookson* (1977) 50 T.C. 705 (C.A.).
82. *Ibid.* s.448(2).

CHAPTER 11

PARTNERSHIP TAXATION

1. The Existence of a Partnership

1–01 PARTNERSHIP is defined in section 1 of the Partnership Act 1890 as the relationship which subsists between persons carrying on business in common with a view to profit; and section 2 of that Act contains a number of rules for determining whether a partnership exists. This is a question of law which must be determined by reference to the facts of the particular case. The execution of a partnership agreement will not of itself constitute a partnership, unless that agreement is put into effect[1]; on the other hand, individuals may be held to be trading in partnership although no formal partnership agreement exists and although they never intended such a relationship to exist.[2] A partnership agreement is not effectual for tax purposes prior to the date on which it was executed, unless a partnership in fact existed before execution, in which case the deed may operate to confirm such a relationship.

> In *Waddington* v. *O'Callaghan*[3] W., who carried on practice as a solicitor, told his son on December 31, 1928, that he intended to take him into partnership as from that date. Instructions for the drafting of a partnership deed were at once given, and on May 11, 1929, a deed was executed expressed to have effect from the previous January 1. Rowlatt J. held that the facts showed clearly that there was to be no partnership unless and until a deed was agreed upon between father and son. Hence the partnership created by the deed commenced on the date of the deed. "It was a contemplated future partnership the accounts of which were to relate back."

1–02 The position was clearly stated by Slade J. in *Saywell* v. *Pope*[4] as follows:

> "I take it to be clear law that, when persons enter into a written partnership agreement and state therein that they are to be partners as from some date prior to the date of execution of the agreement, or, as in the present case, that the partnership commenced on a date prior to the date of such execution, such a statement cannot in law operate retrospectively. If it takes the latter form and if it is an accurate statement of fact, it may safely reflect the past position. If, however, it is an inaccurate statement of fact, it cannot alter such position with retrospective effect. It may well bind all the parties, as between themselves, to take their accounts and to assume all other obligations on the footing that they have been partners from the stated date. It cannot, however, operate actually to make them partners from the stated date, if they were not in truth partners. If authority for these propositions is needed, it is to be found in the judgment of Rowlatt J. in *Waddington* v. *O'Callaghan*.[5] I might add that, as

---

1. *Dickenson* v. *Gross* (1927) 11 T.C. 614 and see *Alexander Bulloch & Co.* v. *I.R.C.* (1976) 51 T.C. 563; [1976] S.T.C. 514.
2. *Fenston* v. *Johnstone* (1940) 23 T.C. 29 at p. 36. In this case A and B declared that the arrangement between them should not constitute a partnership. A and B were nevertheless held to be partners.
3. (1931) 16 T.C. 187.
4. (1979) 53 T.C. 40 at p. 501; [1979] S.T.C. 824 at pp. 833–834.
5. (1931) 16 T.C. 187.

illustrated by the decision of Rowlatt J. in *Dickenson* v. *Gross*,[6] the execution of a partnership deed will not even operate to create a partnership from the date of the deed in a case where the extrinsic evidence clearly shows that there is no partnership in fact. As the Lord President (Clyde) said in *I.R.C.* v. *Williamson*[7] '. . . you do not constitute or create or prove a partnership by saying that there is one.' "

On the same principles the question whether a partnership has ceased to exist is a question of mixed law and fact.[8] A declaration by the partners that the partnership has terminated or will terminate on a specified date is not necessarily conclusive.

2. THE TAXATION OF PARTNERSHIP INCOME

11–03 Although a partnership, unlike a company, is not a legal entity, separate from its members,[9] it is to an extent treated as such for tax purposes. Thus under section 152 of the Income and Corporation Taxes Act 1970, where a trade or profession[9a] is carried on by two or more persons jointly, the tax in respect of it has to be computed jointly and a joint assessment made in the partnership name. The liability of partners to tax is the *joint* liability of *all* the partners, not the *several* liability of each.[10] An assessment on partnership profits which is made *after* the death of a partner imposes liability only on the surviving partners, unless the deceased was the last surviving partner.[11] A joint return of the partnership income must be made by the "precedent partner" who is usually the partner resident in the United Kingdom who is first named in the partnership agreement.[12] The income of a partnership is computed by applying the ordinary rules applicable to individuals: so, for example, a trading partnership is assessed under Case I of Schedule D on the normal preceding year basis: see §§ 2–79 *et seq*. There are special provisions which apply where one of the partners is a company chargeable to corporation tax.[13]

Where husband and wife are in partnership, the rules requiring the aggregation of a wife's income with that of her husband (see *ante*, § 8–23) are disregarded in applying section 152 (above).[14]

11–04 When the partnership income is determined, it must be allocated to each partner for tax purposes by reference to the share of profits to which he is entitled in the year of assessment of which those profits constitute the statutory income.[15]

---

6. (1927) 11 T.C. 614.
7. (1928) 14 T.C. 335 at p. 340.
8. *Keith Spicer Ltd.* v. *Mansell* [1970] 1 W.L.R. 333 (C.A.).
9. In Scotland a partnership is treated as a separate entity: see the case first cited in note 10.
9a. Note the reference to trade and profession. Not all partnerships within the meaning of the Partnership Act 1890 carry on a trade or profession.
10. *Income Tax Commissioners for the City of London* v. *Gibbs* [1942] A.C. 402; 24 T.C. 221 (H.L.).
11. *Harrison* v. *Willis Bros.* [1966] Ch. 619; 43 T.C. 61 (C.A.); and see *post*, § 17–25.
12. T.M.A. 1970, s.9(1).
13. I.C.T.A. 1970, s.155.
14. *Ibid.* s.37(2), proviso.
15. *Ibid.* s.26 (dealing with the allocation of income for the purposes of personal reliefs). And see *Lewis* v. *I.R.C.* (1933) 18 T.C. 174; *I.R.C.* v. *Blott* (1920) 8 T.C. 101 at p. 111. See *Bucks* v. *Bowers* (1969) 46 T.C. 267 at p. 275 as to the effect of attempting to re-allocate partnership income some years after it arises in order to secure the maximum tax relief.

Example

The adjusted profits of a firm of solicitors for the year ended December 31, 1979, are £6,000. This is the statutory income of the firm for 1980–81. This amount must be divided between the partners in the shares to which they are entitled under the partnership agreement in the year ending April 5, 1981. It is immaterial that they in fact divided profits in different shares in the basis year 1979.

–05   Salary paid to a partner is not assessed under Schedule E, for a partner is not an employee.[16] Interest on capital contributed by a partner is not an annual payment and the partner is therefore credited with the full amount of that interest.[17] The following example shows how these items enter into the computation of the assessable income of a partnership:

–06   *Example*

The adjusted profits of a firm of solicitors for the year ended December 31, 1984, are £10,000. In 1985–86 there are three partners, X, Y and Z who are entitled to profits in the following shares: X: 1/5; Y: 2/5; Z: 2/5. Y and Z have contributed capital on which they receive interest. Y and Z are also entitled to salary. The assessment for 1985–86 is computed as follows:

Line	*Firm* £	X £	Y £	Z £
1 Profits to December 31, 1984 adjusted	10,000			
2 *less* interest on capital and salary	1,150			
3	8,850	1,770	3,540	3,540
4 *add* interest on capital	450	nil	200	250
5 *add* salary	700	nil	400	300
6	£10,000	£1,770	£4,140	£4,090

Explanatory notes:
Line

1 The £10,000 are the profits of the basis period adjusted for tax purposes, less capital allowances. All debits in the partnership accounts for partners' shares of profits, partners' salaries and interest on capital will have been added back and are thus included in the £10,000. This is because these items are not expenses which are deductible in computing profits under Schedule D, Case II. The salary paid to a "salaried partner" (as distinct from the salary paid to a salaried employee) is not deductible because (as with interest on capital contributed) it is an allocation of profit, not an expense in earning profit: see § 2–52.

2 This is the total of the figures in lines 4 and 5 (see below).

---

16. See *Stekel* v. *Ellice* [1973] 1 W.L.R. 191 as to when a "salaried partner" is truly a partner and not an employee. And see *Lindley on Partnership* (15th ed.), pp. 90–91.

17. Annual payments are discussed in Chap. 5. A partner has no statutory right to interest on the capital which he contributes: Partnership Act 1890, s.24(4). But it is common practice to stipulate that each partner shall be entitled to interest at (say) 5 per cent. per annum on the capital for the time being standing to his credit, such interest to be paid in priority to any division of profits.

    3 Each partner has allocated to him a share of £8,850 corresponding to the share of profits to which he is entitled in the year 1985–86.[18]

    4 It is usual for a partner to receive interest on any capital contributed by him. Each partner is credited with the full amount due to him in the current year, for this is not an annual payment.[19]

    5 The salary credited to each partner is the salary to which he is entitled in the current year, 1985–86.

    6 The partnership income allocated to each partner is included in his total income. The profits of each partner (including interest on partnership capital) are treated as earned (not investment) income, unless the partner is a sleeping partner or is not an individual. Interest on capital loaned to the partnership is investment income. Note that the partners' share includes any salary or commission payable to him and any interest on capital contributed by him.[20]

The tax liability of each partner is computed and the total is assessed in the partnership name. The tax is payable by the firm and the amount due from each partner (according to the above computation) is debited to his current account.

11–06A   A partner who is an individual can deduct from his share of profits interest paid by him on a loan to defray money applied in (a) purchasing a share in the partnership, or (b) contributing or advancing capital to the partnership: see § 8–62.

    Charges on income paid by the firm under deduction of tax will be apportioned to the partners in their profit-sharing ratios, unless otherwise agreed between them.

Partnership losses

11–07   Where a firm suffers a loss, the loss is apportioned between the partners in the same way that profits are apportioned. Each partner may claim relief in respect of the share of the loss apportioned to him under section 168, 171 or 172 of the Income and Corporation Taxes Act 1970 as he thinks fit.[21] Terminal losses may be the subject of relief under section 174 of that Act.[22] Where there is a change of partners and the partnership business is treated as discontinued (see § 11–08), losses can nevertheless be carried forward.[23]

Limited partnerships

11–07A   The Limited Partnership Act 1907 introduced the limited partnership. The essential features of this entity are twofold. First, there must be one or more general partners who are liable for all the debts and obligations of the firm. Secondly, there must be one or more limited partners who contribute capital but who are not liable for the debts and obligations of the firm

---

18. See *Gaunt* v. *I.R.C.* (1913) 7 T.C. 219 and Simon's *Taxes* (3rd ed.), E 5. 307. Profits to which no partner is entitled cannot be allocated, *e.g.* profits carried to reserve.

19. If there is other income of the partnership (*e.g.* fees for appointments held by the partners for which the partners are accountable to the partnership), this also must be brought into account and apportioned between the partners in their profit-ratio.

20. *Lewis* v. *I.R.C.* (1933) 18 T.C. 174.

21. These reliefs are considered in Chap. 12.

22. See *post*, § 12–12.

23. I.C.T.A. 1970, s.171(4).

beyond the amount they contribute. Limited partnerships have been relatively uncommon in the United Kingdom (though not in Europe), and the tax problems associated with them escaped the attention of the courts until 1983.

> In *Reed* v. *Young*[24] a limited partnership was formed to produce and exploit motion pictures. Y. was a limited partner who contributed £10,000 out of total limited partner contributions of £150,000. The partnership agreement provided that the limited partners should receive 95 per cent. of the profits or losses pro rata to the capital contributed by them and in 1977–78 Y.'s share of the losses amounted to over £41,000. The Revenue asserted that Y.'s right to set off her losses was limited to £10,000. *Held*, Y. was entitled to relief in respect of the whole £41,000.

The Finance Act 1985 now contains provisions to restrict the share of partnership losses, interest and charges for which a limited partner is entitled to relief.[24a]

3. CHANGE OF PARTNERS

1–08 Where there is a change in the persons engaged in carrying on a trade, profession or vocation, the amount of the profits or gains of the trade, etc., on which tax is chargeable and the persons on whom it is chargeable have to be determined as if the trade, etc., had been permanently discontinued at the date of the change and a new trade, etc., had been then set up and commenced.[25] This provision in section 154 of the Income and Corporation Taxes Act 1970,[26] comes into operation whenever a partner dies or retires or where a new partner is admitted or where a sole trader takes another person into partnership with him.

> Thus, if A, B and C are trading in partnership and A dies (or retires) on March 14, 1981, the firm of A, B and C will be treated as having discontinued business on that date and a new firm of B and C as having commenced business.

The consequences of this provision have already been explained.[26] Because of it, a change of partners, whether deliberate or otherwise, can have serious tax repercussions; and through recommendations made by the Committee on the Taxation of Trading Profits,[27] a right of election was given on a change in the constitution of a partnership.

The death of a trader and the consequent passing of his business to his successor is an occasion for the application of the discontinuance provisions of the Tax Acts. Where, however, a business passes on death to the trader's husband or wife who has been living with her or him, the discontinuance provisions are not enforced unless claimed. But, in any case, losses and capital allowances for which the deceased had not obtained relief are not permitted to be carried forward.[28]

---

24. [1986] S.T.C. 285 (H.L.).
24a. See F.A. 1985, s.48 and Sched. 12.
25. See generally *Commrs. of Income Tax* v. *Gibbs and others* [1942] A.C. at pp. 413 *et seq.*; 24 T.C. at pp. 239 *et seq.*
26. See *ante*, §§ 2–86 *et seq.*
27. Cmnd. 8189, para. 72.
28. Concession No. A7.

Election to exclude section 154(1)

11–09   Under section 154(2) of the Income and Corporation Taxes Act 1970, where there is a change in the persons engaged in carrying on any trade, profession or vocation, and a person so engaged immediately before the change continues to be so engaged immediately after it, all the persons so engaged immediately before and after the change may by notice elect that section 154(1) shall not apply. The notice must be signed by all the persons mentioned (including personal representatives of a deceased partner)[29] and must be sent to the Inspector of Taxes within two years[30] after the date of the change. Where the partners elect for a continuation, the assessment on the firm is made as if no change had occurred, *i.e.* on the usual preceding year basis; but there will be an apportionment for the year of change (usually on a time basis) as between the partners. An election under section 154(2) is not irrevocable: it is the practice of Inspectors to accept a notice of revocation if given (signed by all interested parties) before the expiry of the two-year limit for making an election.[31]

11–10   If there is an election for continuance under section 154(2) and, after the change of partners but before the end of the second year of assessment following that in which the change occurred, there is a permanent discontinuance (including a change of partners which is treated as such), the cessation provisions apply giving the Revenue the right to assess the penultimate and pre-penultimate years on an actual basis. Revised assessments on this basis will extend back into the first partnership, but this is permitted[32] notwithstanding that it may mean additional assessments being raised on the original partners. The election is therefore nullified.

A situation may arise in which it is financially advantageous to the continuing partners but not to the outgoing partner for an election to be made under section 154. For this reason it is common practice to include in partnership agreements a provision that the outgoing partner (or the personal representatives of a deceased partner) will join in the making of an election, if required to do so by the continuing partners. To the extent that this may increase the tax liability of the outgoing partner (or the personal representatives of a deceased partner) it is usual for the continuing partners to indemnify the outgoing partner (or the personal representatives) in respect of any additional tax liability resulting from the election.

Anti-avoidance provisions

11–11   The tax rules in the 1970 Act which apply on a change of partners were capable of being used to avoid tax, usually by "engineering" a change of partners at a favourable time and not electing for continuance under Sec-

---

29. I.C.T.A. 1970, s.154(6).
30. *Ibid.* s.154(2).
31. Inland Revenue Press Notice dated January 17, 1973, in [1973] 1 B.T.R. 811. For a brief discussion of the application of s.154 to the merger of firms, see *Lindley on Partnership* (15th ed.), pp. 985–986.
32. I.C.T.A. 1970, s.154(3)(*b*).

tion 154. Section 47 of the Finance Act 1985 counters this form of avoidance by providing special rules for determining the profits of the "new" partnership where there is change in the partnership after March 20, 1985 and the partners *could* make a continuance election under Section 154(2) but do not do so. The new rules for determining the profits of the new partnership in the years of assessment immediately after the change apply in place of the rules in Section 116: see § 2–80. (The rules for the closing years of the old partnership remain unchanged: see § 2–83). The new rules are as follows:

Basis of assessment

First tax year : Annual profits from date of change to following April 5.
Second, third and
fourth tax years : Actual profits of tax year.
Fifth and sixth tax years: Normal preceding year basis, unless the partners elect for actual

4. PARTNERSHIP ANNUITIES

11–12 An annuity payable to a retired partner or to the widow or dependants of a deceased partner is paid less income tax at the basic rate, as explained in §§ 5–30 *et seq.* The amount of the annuity is deductible in computing the total income of the payer (see § 8–31), provided the annuity is not "caught" by any of the provisions under which income payable under a settlement is treated as income of the settlor (see §§ 10–10 *et seq.* and, in particular, § 10–14). Partnership annuities are frequently paid under commercial arrangements which are not settlements, as explained in §§ 10–08 and 10–17; but see § 11–13.

11–13 A partnership annuity is investment income of the recipient.[33] Section 16 of the Finance Act 1974 provides an exception to this general rule by treating certain partnership annuities as earned income up to a certain limit, the excess over this limit being treated as investment income. Section 16 applies where a person ("the former partner") has ceased to be a partner on retirement, because of age or ill-health or on death, and annual payments are made to the former partner or his widow[34] or a dependant, either under the partnership agreement or under an agreement replacing or supplementing it. The limit up to which the annuity is treated as earned income is related to the former partner's share of profits chargeable to income tax and is 50 per cent. of the average of the former partner's share of profits in the best three of the last seven years of assessment in which he was required to devote substantially the whole of his time to acting as a partner. Where the former partner was a member of more than one part-

---

33. *Pegler* v. *Abell* (1972) 48 T.C. 564; [1973] S.T.C. 23. *Ante,* § 8–09.
34. The Revenue has confirmed that "widow" in this context includes a "widower": see [1981] S.T.I. 193.

nership, his share of profits of all the partnerships of which he was a member have to be aggregated. There are provisions for the automatic increase of the limit where the retail prices index for any December is greater than it was in the December of the year when the partner retired: the limit increases by the same percentage as the index. Partners who ceased to be members before 1974–75 are treated as having ceased to be members in that year.[35] See also § 10–14 (which deals with the tax position of the payers of the annuity).

For 1982–83 and subsequent years the relief is increased still further by allowing indexation of the share of profits by reference to which the annuity is calculated. The profits during each of the first six of the seven years can now be indexed to reflect the increase in the retail prices index from the December of that year up to the month of December in the seventh year. When the retired partner's average has then been determined, the limit up to which the annuity is treated as earned income is then determined by applying the indexation provisions referred to above.[36]

35. F.A. 1974, s.16(3)(4).
36. *Ibid.* s.16(2A).

CHAPTER 12

LOSSES

12–01 A LOSS arises in a trade where, in a year of assessment, trading expenses exceed trading receipts. There are two principal methods of dealing with a trading loss while a business is a going concern, and these are considered in Sections 1 and 2 of this chapter. Other methods of dealing with losses are considered in other sections of this chapter. The methods of dealing with losses of companies liable to corporation tax are considered in Chapter 14. Pre-trading expenditure may qualify for loss relief in certain circumstances: see § 2–75B.

1. CARRYING LOSSES FORWARD: SECTION 171

12–02 Under section 171(1) of the Income and Corporation Taxes Act 1970, where a person has sustained a loss in any trade,[1] profession or vocation carried on by him either solely or in partnership, he may claim to carry forward the loss and set it off against profits of the same trade, etc. assessed to income tax in subsequent years of assessment. The loss can be carried forward indefinitely, but must be set off against the first subsequent assessment and, so far as it remains unrelieved, from the next assessment, and so on.[2] If a loss is partially relieved under some other provision, the unrelieved part may be carried forward. Note that losses may be carried forward against profits of the *same trade*. It is often a difficult question whether one trade is the same as another.[3]

12–03 *Example*
The accounts of a trade are as follows:

	£	Tax year
Accounting year ended December 31, 1979 Profit	2,000	1980–81
Accounting year ended December 31, 1980 Loss	3,500	1981–82
Accounting year ended December 31, 1981 Profit	3,000	1982–83
Accounting year ended December 31, 1982 Profit	5,000	1983–84

The loss of £3,500 in 1980 will produce a nil assessment for 1981–82. If relief under section 171 is claimed, it must be given in the assessment for 1982–83

---

1. Including woodlands where an election under I.C.T.A. 1970, s.111 has been made: s.171(5); see *ante*, § 6–07.
2. *Ibid*. s.171(2). As to the period for making the claim, see *ibid*. s.171(7). Trades, etc., carried on outside the U.K., the profits of which would be chargeable to U.K. tax, are included, with the qualification (since only 75 per cent. of the profits of such a trade are charged to United Kingdom tax) that only 75 per cent. of the losses are relievable: F.A. 1974, s.23(2), (4); see *ante*, § 7–09.
3. See *ante*, §§ 2–85 *et seq*. and *Robroyston Brickworks Ltd.* v. *I.R.C.* (1976) 51 T.C. 230; [1976] S.T.C. 329; *Rolls-Royce Motors Ltd.* v. *Bamford* (1976) 51 T.C. 319; [1976] S.T.C. 162.

(reducing the profit of that year to nil) and 1983–84 (reducing the profit of that year to £4,500).

In a year in which assessable profits are reduced to nil, a trader who is an individual will lose his personal reliefs, unless he has sufficient income apart from the trade to support them. Section 171 cannot be used to "skim off" the top slice of profits so as to leave sufficient to cover personal reliefs but otherwise avoid tax liability.

12–04　Where the Case I profits of a trade are insufficient to enable relief to be given in respect of a loss brought forward under section 171(1), interest or dividends taxed at source which would have been taken into account as trading receipts had they not already been taxed will be treated as if they were trading profits.[4] Thus the carried forward losses of a dealer in securities with insufficient profits to absorb the losses may be set off against interest or dividends derived from the securities.

12–05　Where a person has been assessed under section 53 of the Income and Corporation Taxes Act 1970 in respect of a payment made wholly and exclusively for the purpose of a trade profession or vocation, the amount on which tax has been paid under that assessment must be treated as a loss sustained in the trade, etc., and carried forward under section 171 (above) or under section 172, discussed in § 12–06.[5] Unrelieved interest may in some cases be treated as a loss available for carry-forward.[6]

"Conversion" of business into company

12–06　If a business carried on by an individual, or by individuals in partnership, is transferred to a company in consideration solely or mainly of the allotment of shares of the company, and the individual(s) continue to hold those shares throughout the tax year in question, any unrelieved loss of the former business can be carried forward under section 172 and set off against any income derived by the individual(s) from the company, whether by way of dividends on the shares or otherwise, as if such income were income of the business.[7] The set-off has to be made primarily against income which is directly assessable to tax, such as directors' remuneration or other earned income.[8]

> If an individual or partnership with tax losses is "converted" into a company, care should be taken to arrange the transaction to take advantage of section 172. It is not essential that the vendor(s) should take up all the shares of the company.

This is a method by which carried-forward losses of a business can be set off against income which may derive from a business of an entirely different character.

---

4. I.C.T.A. 1970, s.171(3).
5. *Ibid.* s.173.
6. *Ibid.* s.175.
7. *Ibid.* s.172(1) losses incurred in a foreign business may be relieved under this section where profits of that business would have been subject to U.K. tax: see F.A. 1974, s.23(2).
8. *Ibid.* s.172(2).

2. IMMEDIATE RELIEF FOR CURRENT LOSSES: SECTION 168(1)

12–07   There are many reasons why a taxpayer may not wish to carry forward a loss under section 171 of the Income and Corporation Taxes Act 1970. In the example in § 12–03, no relief for the loss sustained in 1980 was available until 1982–83, and a trader may not wish to wait so long: he may be uncertain whether the future profits of the trade will be sufficient to support the loss. Again, in periods of falling rates of tax, immediate relief may be preferred.

12–08   Section 168 of the Income and Corporation Taxes Act 1970 enables a trader to obtain relief for a loss in the year in which the loss is sustained. Section 168(1) provides that where any person sustains a loss in any trade, profession, employment or vocation carried on by him either solely or in partnership, he may, by notice in writing given within two years after the year of assessment, make a claim for relief from income tax on an amount of his income equal to the amount of the loss. Any unrelieved loss may be carried forward under section 171 or 172.[9]

> *Example*
> In the example in § 12–03 the trader sustained a loss of £3,500 in 1980. In practice the Revenue allow a loss sustained in an accounting period to be treated as a loss of the tax year in which the accounting period ends[10]; so the loss in 1980 would be treated as a loss in 1980–81. If relief under section 168(1) were claimed, the tax for 1980–81 (tax on £2,000) would be repaid and the balance of the loss (£1,500) may be carried forward under section 171.

Generally, relief for a loss under section 168(1) will be given against income of the corresponding class: thus a loss in a trade will be relieved against earned before unearned income.[11]

A trader who suffers a loss in a year cannot set off part of the loss against that year's income (under s.168) and the remainder of the loss against his income in an earlier year (under s.30 of the Finance Act 1978: see § 12–10A). A claim under section 168 cannot be limited to *part* of the loss.[11a]

12–09   It should be noted that relief under section 168, unlike relief under section 171, is not restricted to profits of the *same trade*. Relief is available against *any* income of the trader in the relevant period. Under section 170, however, a loss is not available for relief under section 168 unless it is shown that, in the year of assessment in which the loss is claimed to have

---

9. See *ante*, § 12–02 (s.171); § 12–06 (s.172).
10. Strictly, the loss sustained in a tax year should be computed by apportioning the figures in the trading accounts which overlap the tax year. The Revenue require this method to be adopted in the opening years and in the final year of a trade.
11. I.C.T.A. 1970, s.168(4). Generally, in the case of husband and wife, relief is given against the joint income, after first exhausting the earned (then unearned) income of the spouse sustaining the loss. Alternatively, the loss can be confined to the spouse who sustains it: *ibid.* s.168(3). For the position where, in or after 1972–73, husband and wife jointly elect to have the wife's earnings taxed separately, see F.A. 1971, Sched. 4, para. 4.
11a. *Butt* v. *Haxby* [1983] S.T.C. 239 and see Concession No. A8.

been sustained, the trade was being carried on on a commercial basis and with a view to the realisation of profits in the trade or, where the carrying on of the trade formed part of a larger undertaking, in the undertaking as a whole[12]; and the fact that a trade was being carried on at any time so as to afford a reasonable expectation of profit is conclusive evidence that it was then being carried on with a view to the realisation of profits.[13]

Thus a "hobby-trader" may be unable to set off a loss in that trade against profits of a trade carried on on a commercial basis.

Generally, a loss incurred in a trade of farming or market gardening cannot be relieved under section 168 if in each of the prior five years (as defined) a loss was incurred in carrying on that trade; and when a loss is so excluded from relief, any related capital allowance (as defined) is also excluded from relief.[14]

Subject to some qualifications, the capital allowances to which a trader is entitled (see Chap. 13) may be used to augment a claim for loss relief under section 168.[15]

3. RELIEF IN THE NEXT YEAR: SECTION 168(2)

12–10   Where a trade shows a loss in one year, there will be a nil assessment in the following year. The trader may, however, have another source of income in that following year and, under section 168(2) of the Income and Corporation Taxes Act 1970 he may set off the loss against the income of that year only, provided the trade, profession or vocation is still then being carried on.

Thus in the example in § 12–03, the trader sustained a loss in 1980, producing a nil assessment in respect of the trade for 1981–82. Under section 168(2) the trader can set off the loss against income from another source (*e.g.* investment income) in 1981–82 if the trade was still then being carried on.

Relief under section 168(2) is given before relief under section 168(1).

4. CARRY-BACK OF NEW BUSINESS LOSSES

12–10A   Section 30 of the Finance Act 1978 introduced a new form of relief aimed to encourage individuals to start new businesses. If an *individual* carrying on a trade (including a profession or vocation) sustains a loss in the trade either in the year of assessment in which it is first carried on by him or in any of the next three years of assessment, he may, by notice in writing given within two years after the year of assessment in which the loss is sustained, make a claim for relief. Briefly, the loss may be carried back against income for the three years of assessment last preceding the year in which the loss is sustained, taking income for an earlier year before income for a later year. Relief is not, however, given in respect of a loss sustained in any period unless it is shown that the trade was carried on throughout that

---

12. I.C.T.A. 1970, s.170(1).
13. *Ibid.* s.170(5).
14. *Ibid.* s.180.
15. *Ibid.* s.169.

period on a commercial basis and in such a way that profits in the trade (or, where the carrying on of the trade forms part of a larger undertaking, in the undertaking as a whole) could reasonably be expected to be realised in that period or within a reasonable time thereafter. The relief is available whether the individual carries on the trade solely or in partnership.[16]

Relief is not given in respect of a loss sustained by an individual in a trade if, at the time when it is first carried on by him, he is married to and living with another individual who has previously carried on the trade *and* the loss is sustained in a year of assessment later than the third year of assessment after that in which the trade was first carried on by the other individual.

There are provisions to prevent relief being given for the same loss twice over.

5. Relief for Losses on Unquoted Shares in Trading Companies

Losses of individuals

2–10B   Section 37 of the Finance Act 1980 introduces a new relief whereby losses sustained by *individuals* on equity investment in unquoted trading companies may, at the taxpayer's option, be set off against income, instead of being treated as allowable losses within the capital gains tax rules. Hence income tax relief is available in respect of a capital loss. A number of conditions have to be satisfied. The individual must have *subscribed* for the shares: the relief does not apply if he purchased or inherited them or acquired them by way of gift (except that an individual is treated as having subscribed for shares if his spouse did so and transferred them to him by a transaction *inter vivos*). "Spouse" in this context refers to one of two spouses who are living together: see § 8–23.

The company must be a trading company or the holding company of a trading group, but certain types of trades, etc., are excluded, such as share dealing, land dealing, etc. Further, the company must be a "qualifying trading company" for which purpose the Act stipulates the period of time during which it must have been trading. Only companies which have always been resident in the United Kingdom qualify.

The relief is available where the loss arises on a sale at arm's length for full consideration; on a distribution in the winding up or dissolution of a company (see § 16–12); or on a deemed disposal arising out of a claim that the shares had become of negligible value (see § 16–09).

If the conditions are satisfied, a claim for relief from income tax may be made for the year in which the loss is sustained or for the year immediately following. The time limit for making the claim is two years after the end of the year for which the relief is claimed. Any unused balance of the loss is available to be set off against capital gains. Relief under section 37 is given in priority to relief under section 168 (in § 12–10) or section 30 (in § 12–10A). Section 37 applies to disposals on or after April 6, 1980.

---

16. The set-off rules as between husband and wife are as stated in note 11: see F.A. 1978, s.30(7).

Losses of companies

12–10C   Section 36 of the Finance Act 1981 introduces a new relief, similar to that in § 12–10B, which applies to losses sustained by *investment companies* on equity investment in unquoted trading companies. Hence corporation tax relief against investment income is available in respect of a capital loss. The holding company of a trading company is not treated as an investment company for this purpose. Further, the claimant company must not be associated with, or a member of the same group as, the trading company between the date of the subscription and the date of the disposal.

The claimant company must have *subscribed* for the shares; and it must be an investment company on the date of the disposal and for a continuous period of six years ending on that date. Investment company status for a shorter continuous period ending on the date of the disposal will be sufficient provided the company was not previously a trading company or an excluded company (as defined).[17]

If the conditions for relief are satisfied, a claim may be made to have the loss set off against the income (including surplus franked investment income: see § 14–68) of the accounting period in which the loss was incurred and of the previous 12 months (apportioned between accounting periods as necessary). The relief is given before any deduction for charges on income, expenses of management or other amounts which can be deducted from or set off against or treated as reducing profits of any description. The relief must be claimed within two years after the end of the accounting period in which the loss was incurred. Section 36 applies to disposals on or after April 1, 1981.

6. OTHER METHODS OF DEALING WITH LOSSES

Carry-back of terminal losses[18]

12–11   If a trade, profession or vocation has been permanently discontinued, a loss sustained in the last 12 months of the trade, etc. (called a "terminal loss"), can be set against the profits in the three years preceding the year in which the discontinuance occurred, unless the loss has been relieved under some other provision. The latest profits are relieved first.

In the case of a partnership, this relief is available (i) on a permanent discontinuance of the partnership; and (ii) on a statutory discontinuance caused by a change of partners,[19] as regards the non-continuing partners.

Case VI losses

12–12   Where a person sustains a loss in a transaction the profits from which (if any) would be assessed under Case VI of Schedule D, the loss may be set off against any other Case VI profits of the same year or carried forward

---

17. For definitions, see F.A. 1980, s.37.
18. I.C.T.A. 1970, s.174. Losses in a foreign trade, etc., may be relieved under this section where profits of the trade would have been subject to U.K. tax: F.A. 1974, s.23(2).
19. See *ante*, § 11–08.

and set off against Case VI profits of future years, without time limit.[20] Case VI losses cannot be set off against income assessable under Cases I or II of Schedule D. And see § 4–05.

Other losses

12–13   Losses under Schedule A and under the legislation taxing capital gains are discussed elsewhere.

---

20. I.C.T.A. 1970, s.176.

CHAPTER 13

CAPITAL ALLOWANCES

13–01 THE cost and depreciation of capital assets are not allowable deductions in computing profits under Schedule D,[1] but capital allowances are available in respect of certain types of expenditure including expenditure on:

(1) Machinery and plant;
(2) Industrial buildings and structures;
(3) Agricultural or forestry buildings and works;
(4) Mines, oil wells, etc.; dredging; and scientific research.

The provisions of the Income Tax Act 1952 and of later statutes granting capital allowances were consolidated in the Capital Allowances Act 1968, which applies as respects allowances and certain charges (called balancing charges) falling to be made for chargeable periods ending after April 5, 1968.[2] The Finance Act 1971 introduced a new system of capital allowances in respect of expenditure on plant and machinery incurred on or after October 27, 1970, which does not, however, supersede the Act of 1968.

1. ALLOWANCES ON MACHINERY AND PLANT

13–02 The term "plant" was said by Lindley L.J. in *Yarmouth* v. *France*[3–4] to include·

> "whatever apparatus is used by a business man for carrying on his business—not his stock-in-trade . . . but all goods and chattels, fixed or movable, live or dead, which he keeps for permanent employment in his business. . . . "

Note that the proposition imports three essential qualifications for a subject-matter to be considered plant: (i) it must be "apparatus"; (ii) it must be used by the claimant in carrying on his business; and (iii) it must be kept for permanent employment in the business.

These propositions enunciated by Lindley L.J. have been relied on throughout the cases as indicating the nature of "plant" for the purpose of capital allowances although conditions (ii) and (iii) are in fact statutory requirements embodied in sections 41 and 44 of the Finance Act 1971, condition (iii) being implicit in the requirement that the expenditure should be "capital expenditure." Examples of things held to be plant include a horse, knives and lasts used in shoe manufacture,[5] the books of a practising barrister[6] and a range of light fittings and mural decorations in a hotel.[7]

Although Lindley L.J. used the term "apparatus," it is clear that a building or structure will be plant if it fulfils the function of apparatus in the

---

1. See *ante*, § 2–52.
2. Capital Allowances Act 1968 (C.A.A.), s.96(1). "Chargeable period" means a year of assessment or, in relation to a company, an accounting period: *ibid.* s.94(2).
3.–4. (1887) 19 Q.B.D. 647 at p. 658.
5. *Hinton* v. *Maden & Ireland Ltd.* (1959) 38 T.C. 391 (H.L.).
6. *Munby* v. *Furlong* (1977) 50 T.C. 491; S.T.C. 232 (C.A.), overruling *Daphne* v. *Shaw* (1926) 11 T.C. 256. See *Rose & Co. (Wallpaper & Paints) Ltd.* v. *Campbell* (1967) 44 T.C. 500 (expenditure on pattern books with minimum useful life of two years not capital expenditure).
7. *I.R.C.* v. *Scottish & Newcastle Breweries* (1982) 55 T.C. 252; [1982] S.T.C. 296 (H.L.).

claimant's business.[8] Thus it has been held that the cost of excavating and constructing a dry dock used by a ship repairer[9] and a swimming pool used in a leisure centre[10] was expenditure on plant; also that a grain silo was plant.[11] By contrast, if the only function of a building or structure is to provide shelter from the elements to whomsoever might occupy the building from time to time, it is not plant; nor in such a case does it become plant because the building was specially constructed in a particular way or in a particular location.[12]

13–03   The most difficult area relates to apparatus which, though not a building or structure, is closely integrated with a building or structure, such as central heating equipment, air conditioning equipment, sprinkler systems, electrical installations, etc. At an early stage in the development of the case law a distinction was suggested between (i) the apparatus with which a business is carried on (plant) and (ii) something which was more part of the setting,[13] but the Court of Appeal held that the two were not mutually exclusive.[14] Thus movable office partitioning used in a trade which demanded flexible office accommodation was held to be plant although it was obviously part of the setting and part of the structure of the building.[14] The most recent case concerned the electrical installation at a John Lewis department store which the Special Commissioners had held could not be regarded as a single entity because of the many elements in the installation and the differing purposes they served.[15] This (so held the House of Lords) was a decision on a question of fact and degree, so also was the question whether components in the installation (*e.g.* the lighting installation) were plant. It was clear, however, that their Lordships might have reached a different conclusion had they been judges of fact. The decision cannot be regarded as authority for the proposition that a lighting installation is not plant: indeed, the *Scottish & Newcastle Breweries*[15] case (in which the light fittings in hotels *were* held to be plant) was decided by the House of Lords in the same week as was the *John Lewis* case. The decision leaves open the question whether central heating installations, air conditioning installations and the like are plant; although the Revenue appears to concede that they are.[16]

---

8. C.A.A. 1968, s.14.

9. *I.R.C.* v. *Barclay, Curle & Co.* (1969) 45 T.C. 221 (H.L.). Excavation was expenditure on the "provision" of plant. *Cf. Ben-Odeco Ltd.* v. *Powlson* (1978) 52 T.C. 459; [1978] S.T.C. 460 (H.L.): cost of financing the acquisition of plant *held* to be too remote from its provision to qualify.

10. *Cooke* v. *Beach Station Caravans Ltd.* (1974) 49 T.C. 514.

11. *Schofield* v. *Hall* (1975) T.C. 538; [1975] S.T.C. 351 (C.A.N.I.).

12. *St. John's School* v. *Ward* (1974) 49 T.C. 524; *Benson* v. *Yard Arm Club Ltd.* (1979) 53 T.C. 67; [1979] S.T.C. 266 (C.A.); *Brown* v. *Burnley Football and Athletic Co. Ltd.* (1980) 53 T.C. 357; [1980] S.T.C. 424.

13. *J. Lyons & Co. Ltd.* v. *Att.-Gen.* (1944) 170 L.T. 349.

14. *Jarrold* v. *John Good & Sons Ltd.* (1963) 40 T.C. 81. (C.A.).

15. *Cole Brothers Ltd.* v. *Phillips* (1982) 55 T.C. 188; [1982] S.T.C. 307 (H.L.). See also *Hampton* v. *Fortes Autogrill Ltd.* (1980) 53 T.C. 691; [1980] S.T.C. 80 (false ceilings).

16. "The heating installation of a building may be passive in the sense that it involves no moving machinery, but few would deny it the name of 'plant.' The same could no doubt be said of many air conditioning and water softening installations": Donovan L.J. in *Jarrold* v. *Good* (1963) 40 T.C. 681 at p. 694 (C.A.). See also the News Release issued on August 9, 1977, by the Consultative Committee of Accountancy Bodies including the text of a letter from the Chairman of the Board of Inland Revenue.

Businessmen wishing to invest in expensive equipment need to know for certain if capital allowances will or will not be available before any decision is taken, and it is regrettable that there is so much uncertainty in an area of law which has such a great impact on commercial life.

Expenditure incurred in insulating industrial buildings against loss of heat is deemed to be incurred on machinery or plant.[17] Film production expenditure resulting in the master print of a film may be expenditure on "plant"; likewise expenditure on producing the master copy of records and tapes.[18]

13–04   Certain allowances are available under Part III of the Finance Act 1971 in respect of capital expenditure on machinery or plant.[19] The following is a summary of the allowances available where the expenditure is incurred[20] on or after April 1, 1986. First-year allowances, which were at one time 100 per cent. of the expenditure, are no longer available.[21]

Writing-down allowances

13–05   Where (a) a person carrying on a trade has incurred capital expenditure on the provision of machinery or plant wholly and exclusively for the purposes of the trade and (b) in consequence of his incurring the expenditure, the machinery or plant belongs or has belonged to him, he is entitled to a writing down allowance.[22] The condition that the machinery or plant should "belong" to the trader may be satisfied where it is purchased on hire purchase or similar terms.[23] There is no requirement that the machinery or plant should be "new": expenditure on secondhand equipment qualifies.

The system of writing down allowances may be explained by taking a simple case of a trader who buys one machine in year 1 for £10,000. In year 1 he is entitled to a writing down allowance equal to 25 per cent. of cost, *i.e.* £2,500. In year 2 the writing down allowance is 25 per cent. of the cost of the machine less the allowance previously given, *i.e.* 25 per cent. of £7,500—and so on. The formula "cost less allowances already given" produces what the Act describes as the "qualifying expenditure" (commonly described as the written down value of the machine). Normal writing-down allowances have the effect that 90 per cent. of the cost of an asset is written off for tax purposes after eight years.

13–06   *Pooling.* Where the trader purchases a number of items of machinery or plant, these are treated for the purposes of the writing down allowance as falling into a "pool" made up of all the machinery or plant already belonging to him. The qualifying expenditure is therefore determined by aggre-

---

17. F.A. 1975, s.14.
18. SP 9/79 in [1979] S.T.I. 382.
19. F.A. 1971, s.40.
20. See F.A. 1985, s.56 (time when capital expenditure is incurred).
21. These were phased out by F.A. 1984, s.58 and Sched. 12. Expenditure on ships is the subject of separate provisions.
22. F.A. 1971, s.44. And see *ibid*. s.47(1) for the meaning of "trade."
23. *Ibid*. s.45.

gating the written-down values of all the machinery etc. in the pool. If an item in the pool is disposed of, the qualifying expenditure applicable to the machinery or plant in the pool is diminished by its disposal value (as defined). This reduction of the qualifying expenditure by an amount equal to the disposal value of plant leaving the pool is called a "balancing adjustment."

No writing-down allowances are given in the chargeable period related to the permanent discontinuance of a trade; but any unrelieved capital expenditure is relieved by way of "balancing allowance."

13–07 *Cars.* A car which costs more than £8,000 and is used in a trade qualifies for writing-down allowances but is treated as used in a separate trade.[24] The effect of this treatment is that the car falls into a separate "pool" from other machinery or plant. Generally the writing-down allowance cannot exceed £2,000.

Short-life assets

13–08 It has been seen that writing-down allowances have the effect that 90 per cent. of the cost of an asset is written off for tax purposes over eight years. Some assets, however, may be expected to have a much shorter working life and normal writing-down allowances may give inadequate relief. The Finance Act 1985 accordingly introduced[25] provisions applicable to machinery or plant acquired on or after April 1 1985 under which a taxpayer can give notice to the Inspector electing to have items of machinery or plant specified in the notice treated as short-life assets. Schedule 15 to the Act contains a list of assets which are not eligible for this treatment; but any assets outside the Schedule can be designated. The effect of a notice is that the assets are treated as falling into a pool separate from the main pool of machinery or plant and separate from any "car pool": see §§ 13–06 and 13–07. If the short-life asset is disposed of or ceases to be used in the trade within four years from the end of the chargeable period related to the incurring of the expenditure, a balancing allowance will be given if it fetches (or has a value less than) its written-down value. (Correspondingly, there will be a balancing charge if the asset is sold for more than its written-down value). If the asset has not been sold by the end of the four year period, it is then treated as transferred at its then written-down value to the main pool of machinery or plant.[26]

Leasing

13–09 Where capital expenditure is incurred on machinery or plant which is to be let, or to be comprised in an existing letting, the first question to consider is whether the machinery or plant will become a fixture. In a recent

24. F.A. 1971, Sched. 8, paras. 9–12.
25. F.A. 1985, s.57 and Sched. 15.
26. For an illustration of the effect of a "de-pooling" election, see (1985) S.T.I. 143.

case[27] a developer installed lifts and central heating equipment in buildings in the course of development. On completion of the development, the taxpayer was entitled to a lease. A claim for capital allowances for the expenditure on the lifts and central heating was rejected on the ground that this had become a fixture and therefore "belonged" to the freeholder. The injustice of this position was recognised and resulted in a major change in the law by the Finance Act 1985, which introduced[28] a new code providing for the allocation of capital allowances where machinery or plant becomes a fixture on land. No attempt is made to summarise this code: suffice it to say that, where (as in the case[27] referred to) more than one person has an interest in the land, the person with the most subordinate interest is entitled to the allowances.

Where machinery or plant does not become a fixture, and is purchased to be let, the position may be summarised as follows.

13–10　　Where the lessor carries on a trade of plant leasing, the lessor is entitled to the writing-down allowances available to an ordinary trader.

13–11　　Where the lessor purchases machinery or plant wholly or exclusively for the purpose of being let otherwise than in the course of a trade, he is treated for the purposes of the 1971 Act as having incurred the expenditure for the purposes of a trade begun to be carried on by him, separately from any other trade which he may carry on.[29] Treating the letting as incurred in a separate and notional trade has the effect that "let" machinery or plant falls into a different pool of expenditure from other machinery or plant. No allowance is given in the case of machinery or plant let for use in a dwelling house.[30]

13–12　　Where a lessee incurs capital expenditure on the provision for the purposes of a trade carried on by him of machinery or plant which he is required to provide under the terms of the lease and the machinery or plant does not become a fixture, the machinery or plant is treated as belonging to him for so long as it continues to be used for the purposes of the trade.[31] Thus if a lease of an office-block imposes on the lessee an obligation to replace worn out equipment of a type which does become a fixture, the lessee will qualify for writing-down allowances in respect of his expenditure. The lessee is not required on the determination of the lease to bring any disposal value into account: the lessor "takes over" the machinery or plant at its then written-down value and is entited to the allowances as if he had incurred the expenditure the lessee incurred.[32]

27. *Stokes* v. *Costain Property Investments Ltd.* (1984) S.T.C. 204 (C.A.).
28. F.A. 1985, s.59 and Sched. 17.
29. F.A. 1971, s.46(1). As to the method of giving the allowance, see *ibid*. s.48.
30. *Ibid*. s.46(1), proviso.
31. *Ibid*. s.46(2).
32. *Ibid*. s.46(2)(*b*).

Investment companies, etc.

13–13   Capital allowances may be claimed in respect of machinery or plant used in the maintenance of property or in the management of the business of an investment company.[33]

2. ALLOWANCES IN OTHER CASES

Industrial buildings

13–14   Where a person incurs capital expenditure on the construction of a building or structure which is to be an "industrial building or structure" to be occupied for the purposes of a trade carried on by him or certain lessees, he is entitled to writing-down allowances based on the initial cost of construction.

The rate of writing-down allowance is 4 per cent.[34]

There are provisions for balancing allowances and charges.[35] An industrial building or structure is defined in section 7 of the Capital Allowances Act 1968 to mean a building or structure in use for one or more of the purposes listed in the section, *e.g.* manufacture, certain processes,[36] storage, catching shellfish, etc. Buildings in use as a dwelling-house, retail shop, showroom or office are excluded.

Qualifying hotels are treated as industrial buildings or structures in relation to expenditure incurred after April 11, 1978.[37]

Agricultural land and buildings

13–15   Where a person with a major interest (as defined in any agricultural or forestry land incurs any capital expenditure on the construction of farmhouses,[38] farm or forestry buildings, cottages, fences or other works, he is entitled to writing-down allowances of 4 per cent. of the expenditure for a period of 25 years beginning with the chargeable period related to the incurring of the expenditure.[39] To qualify for the allowances, the expenditure must be incurred for the purposes of husbandry or forestry on the land in question and, in the case of expenditure on the farmhouse, one-third of the expenditure is the maximum which will qualify.[40] There are provisions for balancing adjustments when the ownership of the asset changes or it is demolished or destroyed.[41]

---

33. F.A. 1971, s.47(2).
34. C.A.A. 1968, s.2. Initial allowances are not available for expenditure incurred on or after April 1, 1986.
35. *Ibid.* s.3.
36. See *Buckingham* v. *Securitas Properties Ltd.* (1979) 53 T.C. 292.
37. F.A. 1978, s.38 and Sched. 6.
38. As to what constitutes a farmhouse, see *Lindsay* v. *I.R.C.* (1953) 34 T.C. 289.
39. F.A. 1986, s.56 and Sched. 15.
40. *Ibid.* Sched. 15, para. 2.
41. *Ibid.* Sched. 15, paras. 6 and 7.

13–16   *Miscellaneous allowances.* Allowances are available in respect of specified capital expenditure in connection with the working of a mine, oil well or other source of mineral deposits of a wasting nature[42]; in respect of expenditure on dredging[43]; in respect of expenditure on scientific research[44]; in respect of expenditure on sports grounds[45]; and on the acquisition of know-how for the purposes of a trade.[46]

13–17   *Employees.* An employee who uses machinery or plant in the performance of his duties is entitled to capital allowances on his expenditure.[47]

---

42. F.A. 1986, s.55 and Schedules 13 and 14 (applying from after March 31, 1986). See I.R. Press Release in [1986] S.T.I. 182.
43. C.A.A. 1968, s.67.
44. *Ibid.* ss.90–95.
45. F.A. 1978, s.40.
46. I.C.T.A. 1970, s.386(1). See *ante*, § 2–50.
47. C.A.A. 1968, s.47.

DIVISION B

THE TAXATION OF COMPANIES

CHAPTER 14

CORPORATION TAX AND THE TAX TREATMENT OF DISTRIBUTIONS

14–01A THE profits of companies are chargeable neither to income tax[1] nor capital gains tax[2] but only to corporation tax. The Finance Act 1972 introduced the "imputation system" of company taxation and made substantial changes in the system which had been introduced by the Finance Act 1965. Under the earlier system, the profits of companies were charged to corporation tax at the rate then in force (which was 40 per cent. for the year ended March 31, 1972). When a company paid a dividend it deducted income tax at the current standard rate (which was 38·75 per cent. for the year 1972–73) and accounted to the Revenue for the income tax so deducted. Hence the total tax charge on a company which distributed none of its profits was 40 per cent. If it distributed all its profits the total tax charge was 63·25 per cent. If it distributed (say) 60 per cent. of its profits, the total tax charge was 53·95 per cent. Dividends were treated in substantially the same way as annuities or annual payments paid out of profits or gains not brought into charge to income tax and each member included the grossed-up amount of the dividend in his return of total income. Companies could not deduct the income tax paid on dividends or other distributions in computing profits chargeable to corporation tax; hence the profits of companies were, in a sense, taxed twice—once at the corporation tax rate in the hands of the company and again at the income tax rate when they were distributed to members. One criticism often levelled at this system was that it encouraged companies to retain profits in order to avoid income tax on distributions although, in the case of close companies, there were provisions designed to counteract such avoidance of tax when the retention of profits was not justified by the commercial needs of the company. Another criticism was that the system treated a company and its shareholders as separate entities which (it was said) was juristically correct but commercially unrealistic.

The imputation system

14–01B The essential features of the imputation system (ignoring cases in which there is a foreign element) are as follows:

(1) A company pays corporation tax on its profits, whether distributed or not, at the prescribed rate, which will be assumed in the examples that follow to be 35 per cent. (which is the unreduced rate for the year beginning with April 1986, called "the financial year 1986": see

---

1. I.C.T.A. 1970, s.238(2). Income which arises to a company in a fiduciary or representative capacity is chargeable to income tax: see § 14–03. There is an Inland Revenue booklet on Corporation Tax I.R. 18.
2. *Ibid*. s.238(3).

§ 14–04). There is a lower rate for small companies and for charge-able gains: see § 14–04B.

(2) When making a qualifying distribution (see § 14–41), *e.g.* paying a dividend, the company does not deduct Schedule F income tax as under the pre-imputation system. The company is required to make an advance payment of corporation tax ("ACT") to the Revenue at a rate which, for the financial year 1986 is 29/71ths of the amount or value of the distribution: see § 14–50. This rate applies irrespective of the effective rate of tax suffered by the company on its income.

(3) Advance payments of corporation tax made in respect of dividends or other qualifying distributions paid in an accounting period are available for set-off against corporation tax liability on the profits (excluding chargeable gains) of the period: see §§ 14–51 to 14–53.

Thus a company with an income (excluding chargeable gains) in an account-ing period of £60,000 is assessed after the end of the period to corporation tax at (say) 35 per cent. = £21,000. If the company pays a dividend of £7,100 it must pay an amount equal to 29/71ths of this amount (£2,900) of ACT to the Revenue. The actual corporation tax payable is therefore £21,000 less £2,900 = £18,100. (*Note* that the company needs a fund of £10,000 in order to pay £7,100 to its members when the ACT rate is 29/71ths.)

(4) An individual resident in the United Kingdom who receives a quali-fying distribution (see § 14–41) is liable to Schedule F income tax on the aggregate of the distribution and the tax credit: see § 14–59. The tax credit is set against the tax due: see § 14–56. Note that a rate of ACT of 29/71ths of the amount distributed is equivalent to income tax at the basic rate of 29 per cent. on the aggregate of the distribu-tion and the tax credit.

Thus an individual who receives a dividend of £71 is treated as having Sched-ule F income of £100. If he is liable only to the basic rate of income tax, he has no further tax to pay. An individual with a higher income is liable to higher rate income tax, if appropriate. An individual not liable to the basic rate of income tax can claim repayment from the Revenue: see § 14–56.

(5) An individual resident in the United Kingdom who receives a non-qualifying distribution (see § 14–41) incurs no charge to income tax at the basic rate and has no entitlement to a tax credit. Any liability to higher rate income tax is on the amount of the distribution (with-out the addition of any credit), but any higher rate tax payable is reduced by an amount equal to tax at the basic rate on the amount assessed at higher rates: see § 14–60.

(6) A company resident in the United Kingdom which receives a quali-fying distribution is chargeable neither to income tax nor corpor-ation tax in respect of it. The company is entitled to a tax credit which can be set off against its liability to ACT on its own qualifying distributions: see §§ 14–54 *et seq.* and § 14–63.

14–01C   The new system is described as an "imputation system" because part of the company's liability to corporation tax is imputed to the members and is treated as satisfying their basic rate income tax liability. Effect is given to this imputation by conferring a tax credit on the member in respect of each distribution made to him: see § 8–20. The imputation system removes the bias against distributed profits, for its effect is that a company pays corporation tax at a flat rate on all its profits whether distributed or not.

Non-resident members

14–01D   A member of a company who is not resident in the United Kingdom has no entitlement to a tax credit. He therefore suffers United Kingdom income tax at the basic rate and may (if an individual) be assessed under Schedule F to higher rate income tax, subject to any relevant double taxation arrangement.

Chapter summary

14–01E   In the remainder of this chapter, the taxation of companies is considered in detail under the following main headings:

A. The Corporation Tax.
B. The Tax Treatment of Distributions.
C. Companies Purchasing Their Own Shares.
D. Controlled Foreign Companies.

The special legislation applicable to close companies is considered in Chapter 15. The pre-imputation system is referred to in this edition only so far as necessary to explain the imputation system.

A. THE CORPORATION TAX

1. Introduction

14–02   All companies resident in the United Kingdom became liable to corporation tax on trading profits arising after the end of the period which formed the basis period for the year of assessment 1965–66. In respect of most other sources of income, liability to corporation tax commenced on April 6, 1966.[3–4] A company which is not resident in the United Kingdom but which trades in the United Kingdom through a branch or agency is liable to corporation tax on chargeable profits from the branch or agency.[5]

14–03   A company resident in the United Kingdom is liable to corporation tax on all its profits wherever arising.[6] "Company" means any body corporate or unincorporated association, but does not include a partnership or a local authority.[7] "Profits" means income and chargeable gains.[8] This includes

---

3.–4. F.A. 1965, s.80. Companies resident in the United Kingdom and non-resident companies within the charge to corporation tax are not liable to income tax after the year 1965–66: *ibid.* s.46(2).

5. I.C.T.A. 1970, ss.246 and 527(1). As to the mode of assessing such companies, see T.M.A. 1970, s.85.

6. *Ibid.* ss.238(2) and 243(1).

7. *Ibid.* s.526(5). As to what constitutes an unincorporated association, see generally *Conservative and Unionist Central Office* v. *Burrell* (1981) 55 T.C. 671; [1982] S.T.C. 317 (C.A.). Most clubs are unincorporated associations.

8. *Ibid.* s.238(4)(*a*).

profits accruing for its benefit under any trust or arising under any partnership in any case in which the company would be so chargeable if the profits accrued to it directly; and a company is chargeable to corporation tax on profits arising in the winding-up of the company, but is not otherwise chargeable to corporation tax on profits accruing to it in a fiduciary or representative capacity except as respects its own beneficial interest (if any) in those profits.[9] Thus profits which arise to a company on a sale of assets by its liquidator are chargeable to corporation tax; profits which arise to a company as agent or trustee are chargeable only to income tax.

14–04   Corporation tax (unlike income tax) is levied by reference to financial years.[10] "The financial year 1986" means the year beginning with April 1986, and so on.[11] When an assessment to corporation tax falls to be made before the rates for the financial year are fixed, the Revenue has power to charge tax at rates fixed for the previous year, subject to adjustment later.[12] There are special provisions relating to the profits of a company in liquidation,[13] where the tax liability has to be finally determined before the rate has been fixed for the year.

The rate of corporation tax for the financial year 1986 is 35 per cent.[14] The reducing fraction (explained in § 14–04B) is one-seventh.

Rates for earlier years are in the Table in § 14–100.

Franked and unfranked income

14–04A   Corporation tax is not chargeable on dividends and other distributions received from a company resident in the United Kingdom, nor are such dividends or distributions taken into account in computing income for corporation tax.[15] United Kingdom companies account for advance corporation tax when making a distribution; a United Kingdom resident company receiving a distribution is entitled to a tax credit. The consequences of this are discussed in §§ 14–54 *et seq.*

The general scheme of the Act is that a company should suffer corporation tax (and not basic rate income tax) on its unfranked investment income, such as interest on debentures and investments. Such income is assessed to corporation tax under Case III of Schedule D, credit being given for any income tax the income has already borne.

Special rates for small companies and chargeable gains

14–04B   Under the imputation system "small companies" pay corporation tax at a lower rate called the "small companies rate."[16] The small companies rate for the financial year 1986 is 29 per cent.[17] This rate applies to a company

---

9. *Ibid.* s.243(2).
10. *Ibid.* s.238(1).
11. *Ibid.* s.527(1).
12. *Ibid.* s.243(5).
13. *Ibid.* s.245. See also F.A. 1974, s.37.
14. F.A. 1984, s.18(1)–(3). This Act departed from tradition in fixing the rates of corporation tax in advance for the financial years 1983–1986.
15. I.C.T.A. 1970, s.239.
16. F.A. 1972, s.95.
17. F.A. 1986, s.18.

with taxable profits (including chargeable gains) in the accounting period not exceeding £100,000 but there are tapering provisions for companies with profits between £100,000 and £500,000.[18] There are provisions for apportionment when an accounting period straddles more than one financial year. There are anti-avoidance provisions designed to prevent the fragmentation of businesses into a number of companies in order to get the benefit of the lower rate. The small companies rates for financial years in and from the financial year 1973 are set out in the Table in § 14–100.

Under the new system a company's chargeable gains are taxed at a lower rate than the normal "mainstream" corporation tax rate. This is achieved by excluding a fraction of such gains, called "the reducing fraction," from the charge to corporation tax and charging corporation tax only on the balance.[19] The reducing fraction for the financial year 1986 is one-seventh. The effect of applying the fraction is that chargeable gains are taxed at 30 per cent.

Accounting periods

14–05 Although the rate of tax is levied by reference to financial years, assessments to corporation tax are made on a company by reference to the company's own accounting period[20] and where the accounting period does not coincide with the financial year, the chargeable amount must be calculated by apportioning the profits of the accounting period (after making all proper deductions) between the financial years in which the period falls.[21] The apportionment is made on a time basis.[22]

> Thus if a company's accounts are made up to December 31, 1986, and the period of account is 12 months, one-quarter of the profits fall in the financial year 1985 and three-quarters in the financial year 1986.

The Act contains elaborate provisions for defining accounting periods. An accounting period cannot, for the purpose of corporation tax, be longer than 12 months; and if accounts are prepared for a longer period, the first 12 months will be treated as the accounting period.[23]

14–06 Generally, corporation tax assessed for an accounting period is payable within nine months from the end of that period or, if the assessment is later, within one month from the making of the assessment.[24]

Administration

14–07 Corporation tax is under the care and management of the Board of Inland Revenue, who may do all such acts as are necessary and expedient for raising, collecting, receiving and accounting for the tax.[25] Detailed pro-

18. F.A. 1972, s.95 and F. (No. 2) A. 1983, s.2(2).
19. F.A. 1972, s.93, *post*, § 16–53.
20. I.C.T.A. 1970, s.243(3); and see s.527(1) for definitions of "accounting date" and "period of account."
21. *Ibid*. s.243(3).
22. *Ibid*. s.527(4).
23. *Ibid*. s.247(2)–(7).
24. *Ibid*. s.243(4).
25. T.M.A. 1970, s.1.

visions relating to the administration of the Corporation Tax Acts are contained in the Taxes Management Act 1970.

2. *Charges on Income*

14–08   The general rules governing the computation of the income of a company are discussed in the next section of this chapter; but first it will be convenient to examine the statutory definition of "charges on income" and to see how charges are dealt with under the corporation tax system.

Charges on income *paid* by a company in an accounting period (but not before the year 1966–67), so far as paid out of the company's profits brought in to charge to corporation tax, are allowed as deductions against the total profits for the period as reduced by any other relief from tax, other than group relief.[26] Charges are not a deduction in computing profits; they are deductible after "total profits" have been ascertained and reduced by other reliefs, such as loss relief. It is expressly provided that no payment which is deductible in computing profits shall be treated as a charge on income for the purposes of corporation tax.[27] Dividends or other distributions of a company are not charges on income of the company and, by virtue of the wide definition of "distribution," which is extended in the case of close companies, many payments which fall within the definition of "charges on income" are excluded.[28]

Charges on income defined

14–09   Charges on income are defined[29] as:

   (a) any yearly interest, annuity or other annual payment[30] and any such other payments as are mentioned in section 52(2) of the 1970 Act, but not including sums which are or, but for any exemption would be, chargeable under Schedule A[31]; and

   (b) any other interest payable in the United Kingdom on an advance from a bank carrying on a bona fide banking business[32] in the United Kingdom, or from a person who in the opinion of the Board is bona fide carrying on business as a member of a stock exchange in the United Kingdom or bona fide carrying on the business of a discount house in the United Kingdom[33]; and

---

26. I.C.T.A. 1970, s.248(1). Surplus franked investment income may be treated as an equivalent amount of profits for this purpose: *ibid.* s.254(2)(*b*).

27. *Ibid.* s.248(2). See also *ante*, § 14–17. There is no requirement that a *claim* should be made before a payment is "deductible" in computing profits: see *Wilcock* v. *Frigate Investments Ltd.* (1981) 55 T.C. 530; [1982] S.T.C. 198.

28. *Ibid.* s.248(2). As to the meaning of dividends and other distributions, see *post*, §§ 14–40 *et seq.* and §§ 15–21 *et seq.*

29. *Ibid.* s.248(3).

30. Discussed *ante*, § 5–04.

31. I.C.T.A. 1970, s.52(2), includes patent royalties, mining rents and royalties and payments for easements.

32. See *United Dominions Trust Ltd.* v. *Kirkwood* [1966] 1 Q.B. 783 as to the meaning of "bona fide banking business."

33. Non-yearly interest paid to a bank would fall under (b).

(c) certain donations by companies to charities.

The interest in (b) is to be treated as paid on its being debited to the company's account in the books of the person to whom it is payable.[34] Subject to this last-mentioned exception, charges on income are not deductible unless and until they are actually paid; but charges which are paid in an accounting period are deductible even though they were due in an earlier period. The difficulties created by the use of the words "paid" and "payable" in sections 52 and 53 of the Income and Corporation Taxes Act 1970,[35] do not therefore exist in the case of companies liable to corporation tax. Payments of interest within (b) above, may be deductible as a trading expense of a trading company; but generally the payments within (a) above, may not be deducted in computing income and are therefore deductible as charges on income.[36] A company making payments within (a) above must deduct basic rate income tax from the payments and account to the Revenue for the tax so deducted.[37] Note that the obligation to deduct and account for income tax continues under the imputation system.

The Finance Act 1986 allows non-close companies resident in the United Kingdom to treat as a charge on income one-off donations to charity made in an accounting period up to 3 per cent. of the dividends paid by the company in that period.[37a] Income tax at the basic rate must be deducted from the payment and accounted for. The relief applies to payments made after April 1, 1986. (Regular donations made under covenant may fall under (a) above as "annual payments").

Charges in excess of profits

14-09A Where in an accounting period the charges on income paid by a company exceed the amount of profits against which they are deductible, and include payments made wholly and exclusively for the purposes of a trade carried on by the company, then up to the amount of that excess or of those payments (if less) the charges are deductible as if they were a trading expense for the purposes of computing trading losses.[38] The manner in which losses of trading companies are relieved is considered in §§ 14–24 *et seq.*

There are similar provisions for treating charges on income of an investment company which exceed profits as if they were expenses of management.[39] Charges on income may be surrendered for group relief.[40]

---

34. I.C.T.A. 1970, s.248(3).
35. See *ante*, §§ 5–37 *et seq.*
36. I.C.T.A. 1970, s.251(2)(3).
37. *Ibid.* ss.53–54 and s.240(4); see *ante*, §§ 5–09 *et seq.*; and §§ 5–33 *et seq.*
37a. F.A. 1986, s.29.
38. I.C.T.A. 1970, s.177(8).
39. *Ibid.* s.304(2); see *post*, § 14–22.
40. *Ibid.* s.259(6); see *post*, § 14–41. It is thought that debited bank interest is treated as *paid* for the purposes of *ibid.* s.259(6).

Payments not charges on income

14–10   A payment is not to be treated as a charge on income in the following circumstances:

(1) If the payment (not being interest) is charged to capital[41–42];

(2) if the payment is not ultimately borne by the company, *e.g.* where there is a right of reimbursement against a third party which is effectively exercised[43];

(3) if the payment is not made under a liability incurred for a valuable and sufficient consideration[44]: thus a voluntary annuity is not a charge on income. There is an exception in the case of a covenanted donation to charity (defined in § 14–11, below)[44];

> In *Ball* v. *National and Grindlays Bank*,[45] officers employed by the bank were normally required to spend their whole working lives abroad and had, therefore, to educate their children at boarding schools. The financial burden falling on parents caused much discontent and some resignations or threatened resignations. The bank entered into a deed of covenant with trustees to pay monthly sums to be applied in the education of the children and this scheme in fact abated some of the discontent. *Held*, that payments under the deed were not a charge on income, because there was no valuable consideration representing an adequate or fair equivalent for the bank's expenditure. A business advantage fell short of this requirement.

(4) if, in the case of a non-resident company (which is liable to corporation tax on the profits from trading in the United Kingdom),[46] the payment is not incurred wholly and exclusively for the purposes of a trade carried on by it in the United Kingdom through a branch or agency[47]: thus interest on moneys borrowed for the purposes of its overseas operations is not deductible. The exception in (3) for covenanted donations to charity applies.

14–11   "Covenanted donation to charity" in paragraph (3) of § 14–10 means a payment under a disposition or covenant made by the company in favour of a body of persons or trust established for charitable purposes only, whereby the like annual payments (of which the donation is one) become payable for a period which may exceed three years[48] and is not capable of earlier termination under any power exercisable without the consent of the persons for the time being entitled to the payments.[49] Such a payment is not treated as a distribution.[50] The effect of the words "whereby the like annual payments" etc. is that, for example, a covenant to pay such an

---

41–42. *Ibid.* s.248(5)(*a*). The exception for interest enables, for example, property developers who borrow to finance a development and treat the interest as part of the capital cost to obtain tax relief on that interest: see I.C.T.A. 1970, s.269 and *cf. Chancery Lane Safe Deposit Limited* v. *I.R.C.* [1966] A.C. 85; 43 T.C. 83 (H.L.).
43. I.C.T.A. 1970, s.248(5)(*a*).
44. *Ibid.* s.248(5)(*b*). But see § 10–18 (reverse annuity transactions).
45. [1973] Ch. 127; 47 T.C. 287 (C.A.).
46. I.C.T.A. 1970, s.246.
47. *Ibid.* s.248(5)(*b*).
48. "Three" years was substituted for "six" years by F.A. 1980, s.55(3), (4). *Cf. ante.* § 10–20A.
49. I.C.T.A. 1970, s.248(9).
50. *Ibid.* s.248(8).

amount as the directors in their discretion should determine is not a "covenanted donation to charity," because it cannot be said of any one payment made under such a covenant that it has the quality of recurrence that characterises an annual payment: see § 10–19 *et seq.*

Payments of interest

14–12 A payment of interest is not to be treated as a charge on income unless—

(a) the company exists wholly or mainly for the purpose of carrying on a trade; or

(b) the payment of interest is wholly and exclusively laid out or expended for the purposes of a trade carried on by the company; or

(c) the company is an investment company; or

(d) the payment of interest would on certain assumptions, be eligible for relief under section 75 of the Finance Act 1972.[51]

Payments by companies to non-residents

14–13 A payment of yearly interest, an annuity or other annual payment and a payment of the kind referred to in section 248(3)(*a*) of the Income and Corporation Taxes Act 1970 which is made by a company to a non-resident person is not treated as a charge on income[52] unless the paying company is resident in the United Kingdom and either:

(a) the company deducts income tax from the payment in accordance with section 53 or 54 and accounts for the tax so deducted[53]; or

(b) the company is carrying on a trade and the payment is a payment of interest falling within section 249. Generally, the interest must be payable and paid outside the United Kingdom and the liability must be on a loan incurred for the purposes of trading activities of the company outside the United Kingdom, save where the interest is payable in a currency other than sterling[54]; or

(c) the payment is one payable out of income brought into charge to tax under Case IV or V of Schedule D; or

(d) the payment is of interest payable without deduction under the provisions relating to quoted Eurobonds.[55]

Collection of tax

14–14 Although the income of companies is charged to corporation tax, a company must account for income tax under sections 53 and 54 of the Income and Corporation Taxes Act 1970 on payments it makes by way of interest,

---

51. *Ibid.* s.248(6); and see *ante*, §§ 8–57 *et seq.*

52. *Ibid.* s.248(4).

53. See *ante*, §§ 5–30 *et seq.* Where the company would have deducted tax but for the existence of double taxation relief, the company is treated as if tax had been deducted and accounted for: Double Taxation Relief (Taxes on Income) (General) Regs. (S.I. 1970 No. 488). See Simon's *Taxes*, F4.302.

54. The words "currency other than sterling" were substituted for "the currency of a territory outside the United Kingdom" in relation to payments of interest made on or after April 6, 1982, by F.A. 1982, s.64.

55. F.A. 1984, s.35 and § 5–56.

annuities and annual payments and will suffer income tax by deduction on "unfranked" income. Section 104 of and Schedule 20 to the Finance Act 1972 contain provisions for regulating the time and manner in which companies resident in the United Kingdom should account for income tax, and allow income tax suffered by deduction to be offset against income tax for which they are accountable on their own payments.

3. *General Rules for Computation of Income*

14–15   Corporation tax is assessed and charged on the profits which arise in the accounting period, subject only to such deductions as the Act allows.[56] Profits means income and chargeable gains.[57] The Act states[58] that, except as otherwise provided,

> "the amount of any income shall for purposes of corporation tax be computed in accordance with income tax principles, all questions as to the amounts which are or are not to be taken into account as income, or in computing income, or charged to tax as a person's income, or as to the time when any such amount is to be treated as arising, being determined in accordance with income tax law and practice as if accounting periods were years of assessment."

The way in which income is determined by reference to accounting periods but tax is levied by reference to financial years has already been mentioned.[59] The expression "income tax law" is defined to mean the law which applies to the charge on individuals of income tax; except that it excludes certain enactments which make special provision for individuals in regard to certain matters.[60] The incorporation of "income tax law" into corporation tax implies that both statutory exemptions and provisions imposing a charge to income tax also apply.

14–16   It follows that, for the purposes of corporation tax, income is computed and assessments are made under the like Schedules and Cases as apply for purposes of income tax and in accordance with the rules applicable to those Schedules and Cases.[61]

> Thus if a company carries on a trade, receives rent from land and receives interest, its income in any accounting period must be determined by reference to the rules of Schedule D Case I, Schedule A and Schedule D Case III respectively and assessments to corporation tax will be made under the rules which apply to those Cases of Schedule D, except that income of an accounting period is not to be determined by reference to any preceding year or other period.

The amounts which are so computed for the several sources of income, if more than one, together with any amount to be included in respect of

---

56. I.C.T.A. 1970, ss.129(1), 247(1). For company partnerships, see s.155.
57. *Ibid.* s.238(4)(*a*).
58. *Ibid.* s.250(1).
59. See *ante*, § 14–05.
60. See I.C.T.A. 1970, s.250(2) for details.
61. *Ibid.* s.250(3).

chargeable gains must be aggregated to arrive at the *total profits* of the company.[62]

14–17   Dividends or other distributions are not deductible in computing income from any source[63] nor are they charges on income.[64] Yearly interest, annuities, other annual payments and certain payments which are similarly treated are not deductible in computing income[65] but may be a charge on the income of the company, when they are deductible from total profits.[66]

14–18   Where a company begins or ceases to carry on a trade, or to be within the charge to corporation tax in respect of a trade, *e.g.* where a non-resident company carrying on a trade becomes resident and chargeable to corporation tax, the company's income must be computed as if that were the commencement or, as the case may be, discontinuance of the trade, whether or not the trade is in fact commenced or discontinued.[67] Thus stock-in-trade held at the time of the deemed discontinuance must be valued in accordance with section 137 of the Income and Corporation Taxes Act 1970.[68]

Computation of chargeable gains

14–19   Corporation tax (not capital gains tax) is assessed and charged on the chargeable gains which arise in any accounting period of a company, after setting off allowable losses of that and earlier periods, including periods before the company became liable to corporation tax.[69] The chargeable gains of a company are computed in accordance with the principles applying for capital gains tax,[70] subject to some modifications which are discussed elsewhere in this book.[71] Generally, where the provisions of the capital gains tax refer to income tax or the Income Tax Acts, the reference in relation to a company is to be construed as a reference to corporation tax or the Corporation Tax Acts.[72]

Investment companies: management expenses

14–20   A trading company is normally able to deduct expenses of management in computing its income chargeable to corporation tax under Case I of Schedule D. An investment company with income from land, *e.g.* rents, may deduct expenses of managing its *properties* under the Schedule A rules

---

62. *Ibid.* s.250(3). And see s.527(1), which states when a source of income is within the charge to corporation tax.
63. *Ibid.* s.251(2).
64. *Ibid.* s.248(2).
65. *Ibid.* s.251(2); but yearly interest paid to a U.K. bank may be deductible: *ibid.* s.251(3). And see SP 6/1973 in § 5–56.
66. See *ante*, §§ 14–08 *et seq.*
67. I.C.T.A. 1970, s.251(1).
68. See *ante*, §§ 2–34 *et seq.*
69. I.C.T.A. 1970, s.265(1).
70. *Ibid.* s.265(2).
71. See *post*, §§ 16–53 *et seq.*
72. I.C.T.A. 1970, s.265(3). And see the definitions in s.526(1).

discussed in §§ 6–27 *et seq.*; but expenses of managing the *company* itself, *e.g.* head office administration expenses, may not be allowed under these rules. An investment company with income from stocks and shares would secure no relief for management expenses without the special provisions discussed below.

Section 304(1) of the Income and Corporation Taxes Act 1970 provides that in computing for the purposes of corporation tax the total profits for any accounting period of an investment company resident in the United Kingdom, there shall be deducted any sums disbursed as *expenses of management (including commissions)* for that period, except any such expenses as are deductible in computing income for the purposes of Schedule A. It is further provided that there shall be deducted from the amount treated as expenses of management the amount of any income derived from sources not charged to tax, other than franked investment income and group income.[73] The purpose of this not obviously meaningful provision is apparently to enable the Revenue to deduct (for example) bank deposit interest from expenses of management, thus obviating the need for separate Case III or other assessments on the income so deducted.

14–21   "Investment company" is defined[74] for this purpose as meaning—

> "any company whose business consists wholly or mainly in the making of investments and the principal part of whose income is derived therefrom, but with the exception of a trustee savings bank (as defined) includes any savings bank or other bank for savings."

It follows that no relief under section 304 is available in the case of a mixed trading and investment company where the principal part of the income is derived from trading and the expenses relate to the management of the investments, for such a company is not an "investment company" as defined. The relief will, however, be available if the two enterprises are segregated into separate companies. An authorised unit trust is treated as if it were an investment company[75]: trustees are not otherwise entitled to relief for management expenses.

The Act contains no definition of the phrase "expenses of management," or of the term "disbursed," and reference must accordingly be made to cases decided under section 425 of the Income Tax Act 1952 for illumination.[76] Brokerage and stamp duty paid on a change of investments have been held not to be expenses of management as being so closely linked with the purchases and sales (being necessarily incurred in the course thereof) as to be considered part of the expenses of the purchases and sales and not expenses of the management of the company's business.[77] In a recent case a company's function was to raise money on the

---

73. *Ibid.* s.304(1), proviso.
74. *Ibid.* s.304(5).
75. *Ibid.* s.354(1)(*a*).
76. See Simon's *Taxes* (3rd ed.), D4.408.
77. *Sun Life Assurance Society* v. *Davidson* [1958] A.C. 184; 37 T.C. 330 (H.L); and see *Capital & National Trust Ltd.* v. *Golder* (1949) 31 T.C. 265 (C.A.).

Stock Exchange to finance trading companies in the group operating in the United Kingdom. The company placed an issue of loan stock. The company's parent company in West Germany guaranteed the issue in return for an annual commission on the amount of loan stock outstanding. It was held that the commission was not allowable as an expense of management, since it was part of the cost of raising the money and not severable from it.[78]

4-22 Where the deductible management expenses in any accounting period, together with any charges on income paid in the accounting period wholly and exclusively for the purposes of the company's business, exceed the amount of the profits from which they are deductible, the excess can be carried forward to the succeeding accounting period.[79] The amount carried forward is to be treated for this purpose, including any further application of this carry-forward provision, as if it had been disbursed as expenses of management for that accounting period.[80] A claim may be made by a company to set off management expenses against a surplus of franked investment income.[81]

Capital allowances

4-23 Effect is given to allowances and charges for corporation tax purposes by deductions from or additions to profits.[82] In taxing the trade, capital allowances due for an accounting period are treated as a trading expense of the trade (so reducing profits); balancing charges so due are treated as trading receipts (so increasing profits).[83] Allowances and charges of an investment company are similarly treated.[84] Capital allowances can be added to the expenses of management of an investment company for the purposes of relief by carry-forward.[85]

4. Losses

4-24 Sections 177 to 179 (inclusive) of the Income and Corporation Taxes Act 1970 contain provisions for the relief of losses of companies liable to corporation tax which are similar to those already discussed in connection with income tax.[86] Losses incurred in a trade are computed in the same way that trading income is computed.[87] In the case of a company carrying on a trade so as to be within the charge to corporation tax in respect of it, losses may be relieved in the following ways:

---

78. *Hoechst Finance Ltd.* v. *Gumbrell* (1983) 56 T.C. 594; [1983] S.T.C. 150 (C.A.).
79. I.C.T.A. 1970, s.304(2). Not all charges on income will satisfy the wholly and exclusively test: covenanted donations to charity may not do so (*ante*, § 14–11).
80. I.C.T.A. 1970, s.304(2).
81. *Ibid.* s.254(2)(*c*).
82. C.A.A. 1968, s.73(1).
83. *Ibid.* s.73(2).
84. I.C.T.A. 1970, s.306.
85. *Ibid.* s.304(3).
86. See *ante*, Chap. 12.
87. I.C.T.A. 1970, s.177(6).

14–25   (i) *Carry-forward*. The company may claim to set off a trading loss incurred in an accounting period against trading income from the trade in succeeding accounting periods.[88] The trading income must be derived from the *same trade* as that in respect of which the loss is incurred.[89] "Trading income" means, in relation to any trade, the income which falls or would fall to be included in respect of the trade in the total profits of the company (and thus does not include chargeable gains); but where the trading income is insufficient to support losses carried forward, any interest or dividends on investments which would fall to be treated as trading receipts but for the fact that they have been otherwise taxed are to be treated as if they were trading income.[90] Thus dividends on shares which are trading stock of a share-dealing company may be treated as trading receipts.

If charges on income paid by a company in an accounting period exceed the profits from which they are deductible, the charges may be treated as a trading expense to the extent that they are payments made wholly and exclusively for the purposes of a trade carried on by the company, thereby creating a loss which is available to be carried forward.[91]

14–26   (ii) *Set-off against the profits (including chargeable gains) of current or past accounting periods*. Where a company incurs a trading loss in an accounting period, it may claim to set the loss off against profits[92] (of whatever description) of that accounting period and, if necessary, against the profits of preceding accounting periods in which the trade was carried on; but this is subject to the limitation that a loss cannot be carried back for a period longer than the duration of the accounting period in which the loss is incurred.[93] Thus if a company suffers a trading loss in an accounting period of 12 months, the company may claim to carry the loss backwards and set it off against the profits of the preceding 12 months, even if this includes more than one accounting period. If the company incurs a trading loss in an accounting period of nine months and the preceding accounting period was of 12 months, the loss may be set off against nine-twelfths of those profits and any excess carried forward under the provisions discussed above. No loss relief is available under this provision unless, in the accounting period in which the loss was incurred, either (i) the trade was being carried on on a commercial basis and with a view to the realisation of gain in the trade or in any larger undertaking of which the trade formed part; or (ii) the trade is one carried on in the exercise of functions conferred by or under any enactment (including an enactment contained in a local or private Act).[94] As regards (i), the fact that a trade was being carried on at any time so as to afford a reasonable expectation of gain is conclusive evidence that it was then being carried on with a view to the

---

88. *Ibid*. s.177(1).
89. *Cf.* § 12–02.
90. I.C.T.A. 1970, s.177(7).
91. *Ibid*. s.177(8).
92. Profits includes chargeable gains: *ibid*. s.238(4)(*a*) applied to s.177 by s.527(2).
93. *Ibid*. s.177(2), (3).
94. *Ibid*. s.177(4).

realisation of gain; and where in an accounting period there is a change in the manner in which the trade is being carried on, it will for those purposes be treated as having throughout the accounting period been carried on in the way in which it was being carried on by the end of that period.[95] Losses attributable to capital allowances can be carried back three years.[96]

14–27 (iii) *Relief for terminal losses.* The relief which is given to a trading company liable to corporation tax in respect of terminal trade losses is substantially the same as that given by section 174 of the Income and Corporation Taxes Act 1970.[97] Thus a company can claim to set off a loss incurred in the last 12 months of its life against trading income from the trade (not chargeable gains) of the preceding three years.

14–28 *Case VI losses.* If a company suffers a Case VI loss in respect of which it is chargeable to corporation tax, the company may claim to set the loss off against any other Case VI income liable to corporation tax in the same or any subsequent accounting period.[98] This relief does not apply to a loss incurred in a transaction falling within section 80, 81 or 82 of the Act (premiums, leases at undervalue, etc.).[99]

Company reconstructions

14–29 Where a company (called "the predecessor") ceases to carry on a trade and another company (called "the successor") begins to carry it on, the trade is treated as continuing in the same ownership if on or at any time within two years after the change the trade or an interest amounting to not less than a three-fourths share in it belongs to the same persons as the trade or such an interest belonged to at some time within a year before the change.[1] A trade carried on by a company may be treated as belonging to the persons owning the ordinary share capital (as defined) in proportion to their shareholdings.[2] Where this provision applies, the position with respect to capital allowances, balancing charges and losses is broadly the same as if no change had occurred: thus the losses of the predecessor may be carried forward and offset against the trading income of the successor as if the predecessor had continued trading.[3] The predecessor is not entitled to terminal loss relief except in certain circumstances where the successor ceases to trade within four years of the succession.[4]

Thus if A Limited has accumulated tax losses available to be carried forward

---

95. *Ibid.* s.177(5).
96. *Ibid.* s.177(3A).
97. *Ibid.* s.178. For s.174 see *ante*, § 12–12.
98. *Ibid.* s.179(1).
99. *Ibid.* s.179(2).
1. *Ibid.* s.252(1); and see s.252(6) where there is a series of transfers.
2. *Ibid.* s.253.
3. *Ibid.* s.252(3). But see F.A. 1986, s.42 which restricts the relief when the predecessor is insolvent at the time of the transfer and see explanatory I.R. Press Release in (1986) S.T.I. 186.
4. *Ibid.* s.252(3), (5).

under section 177 of the Act (see § 14–25), and the trade of A Limited is transferred to B Limited, B Limited will be entitled to carry forward the losses (if the 75 per cent. "common ownership test" is satisfied) and set them off against profits *of the transferred trade* but not against profits of the original trade of B Limited.

There are provisions to meet the case where only the *activities* of the predecessor's trade (or part of it) are transferred and not the trade itself.[5]

14-30   The provisions just mentioned were widely used for purposes of avoiding tax and elaborate anti-avoidance provisions will be found in section 483 of the Income and Corporation Taxes Act 1970. Briefly, if in any period of three years there is both a change in the ownership of a company and a "major change[5a] in the nature or conduct of a trade," past losses will not be available for carry forward. A number of schemes to pass on losses to a purchaser have failed.[6]

Group relief

14-31   The Finance Act 1967 introduced a new form of relief called "group relief" by which a member of a group of companies (called "the surrendering company") can surrender its claim to relief for capital allowances, charges on income and management expenses of an investment company to another company which is a member of the same group (called "the claimant company").[7] Two companies are deemed to be members of a group if one is a 75 per cent. subsidiary[8] of the other or both are 75 per cent. subsidiaries of a third company. Group relief is also available in certain other cases, *e.g.* where the surrendering company is a trading company which is owned by a consortium and which is not a 75 per cent. subsidiary of any company where the claimant company is a member of the consortium.[9] There is no requirement that companies should be members of the same group at the time when relief is claimed.[10] There are statutory provisions designed to prevent the formation of "artificial" groups in order to secure group relief.[11]

---

5. *Ibid.* s.252(7).
5a. As to "major change," see *Purchase* v. *Tesco Stores Ltd.* [1984] S.T.C. 304.
6. See, *e.g.* *Pritchard* v. *H. M. Builders (Wilmslow) Ltd.* (1969) 45 T.C. 360 and *Ayerst* v. *C. & K. (Construction) Ltd.* [1976] A.C. 167; 50 T.C. 651, (H.L.) where it was held that a company was divested of the beneficial ownership of its assets upon a resolution or order for winding up.
7. See now I.C.T.A. 1970, ss.258–264.
8. A body corporate is a 75 per cent. subsidiary of another body corporate if and so long as not less than 75 per cent. of its ordinary share capital is owned directly or indirectly by that other body corporate. Ownership means beneficial ownership and ordinary share capital means all the issued share capital (by whatever name called) other than capital carrying a right to a dividend at a fixed rate and with no other right to share by profits: *ibid.* ss.258(5), 526(5) defining "ordinary share capital" and 532.
9. See *ibid.* s.258(2) and the definitions in s.258(8). Consortium relief has been extended by F.A. 1981, s.40 and F.A. 1984, s.46.
10. *A. W. Chapman Ltd.* v. *Hennessey* (1981) 55 T.C. 516; [1982] S.T.C. 214.
11. See F.A. 1973, ss.28–29 and [1973] S.T.I. 451 for the Revenue's view of the effect of these provisions. For a recent case on the meaning of "arrangement," see *Pilkington Bros.* v. *I.R.C.* (1982) 55 T.C. 705; [1982] S.T.C. 103 (H.L.).

14–32 *Trading losses.* If in an accounting period, a company incurs a loss in carrying on a trade, the amount of the loss may be surrendered by that company and claimed by another company in the same group, whether a trading company or not. The loss may then be set off against the total profits of the claimant company in the corresponding accounting period (as defined).[12] Profits means income and chargeable gains.[13] Where a claim for group relief is made by a company which is a member of a consortium, only a fraction of the amount of the loss may be set off corresponding to a member's share in the consortium (as defined). There are special provisions where a company joins or leaves a group or consortium.

The right to group relief is not dependent on the claimant company having made any payment to the surrendering company: it is sufficient that the right to loss relief is surrendered by the one company and claimed by the other. In practice, however, a company in a group which makes a loss in an accounting period may have that loss subsidised by a payment (which in earlier legislation was called a "subvention payment") from a profit-making company in the same group. The legislation relating to subvention payments no longer applies and the phrase "payment for group relief" is now used. This means[14]

> "a payment made by the claimant company to the surrendering company in pursuance of an agreement between them as respects an amount surrendered by way of group relief, being a payment not exceeding that amount."

The agreements referred to must be legally enforceable and must be either under seal or supported by consideration.[15] A payment for group relief is not taken into account in computing profits or losses of either company for corporation tax purposes and is not for any of the purposes of the Corporation Tax Acts regarded as a distribution or a charge on income.

–33/39 *Other cases.* Group relief is available also in respect of capital allowances, management expenses of an investment company and charges on income.[16]

B. The Tax Treatment of Distributions

The meaning of distribution

14–40 The term "distribution" is defined in sections 233 to 237 of the Income and Corporation Taxes Act 1970, as amended. The definition embraces not only dividends but also distributions out of assets of a company representing funds which could have been applied in the payment of dividends. Distributions in respect of share capital in a winding up are excluded.[17]

---

12. I.C.T.A. 1970, ss.259(1), 261.
13. *Ibid.* s.238(4)(*a*).
14. *Ibid.* s.258(4).
15. *Montague L. Meyer Ltd. and Canusa Ltd.* v. *Naylor* (1961) 39 T.C. 577; *Haddock* v. *Wilmot Breeden Ltd.* (1975) 50 T.C. 132; [1975] S.T.C. 255 (H.L.).
16. The next paragraph is § 14–40.
17. I.C.T.A. 1970, s.233(1). It is not clear what the position is where distributions are made in the course of the dissolution of a company *without* winding up, pursuant to the Companies Act 1985, s.427(3)(*d*).

14–41   *Qualifying and non-qualifying distributions.*[18] The imputation system, unlike the earlier system, makes a distinction between qualifying and non-qualifying distributions. Qualifying distributions are dividends and other distributions which are similar to dividends. Non-qualifying distributions, such as issues of bonus debentures or bonus redeemable shares, are distributions which give the recipient a potential claim on the profits of the company at a future date. Qualifying distributions require an advance payment of corporation tax by the company and confer a tax credit on the recipient.[19] Non-qualifying distributions require no advance payment of corporation tax and confer no tax credit on the recipient.

Companies are required to make returns of, and provide information about, non-qualifying distributions.[20] The statutory provisions defining the term distribution cannot easily be summarised. The following are mere guide-lines:

14–42   1. Any dividend paid by a company, including a capital dividend, is a distribution.

14–43   2. The term also includes any other distribution out of assets of a company (whether in cash or otherwise) in respect of shares in the company, except so much of the distribution (if any) as represents a repayment of capital on the shares or is, when it is made, equal in amount or value to any new consideration received by the company for the distribution.[21] Thus if sums are returned to shareholders by way of reduction of capital which are shown to represent no more than the amount subscribed, there is no distribution. Where shares are issued at a premium the premium is treated as share capital for this purpose.[22] There is a distribution if sums in excess of the amount subscribed are returned.[23] Where companies form a 90 per cent. group (as defined), a distribution by one company in respect of shares in another company in the group may be caught.[24]

14–44   3. *Repayment of share capital with or followed by bonus issue.* If share capital is repaid (after April 6, 1965) and at or after the time of repayment the company issues bonus shares (whether redeemable or not), the amount capitalised in the bonus issue is treated as a distribution in respect of the bonus shares, except in so far as that amount exceeds the share capital repaid.[25]

> Assume a company has a share capital of £50,000 in £1 ordinary shares (all subscribed in cash) and a revenue reserve of £80,000. Assume the company reduces its share capital to £25,000 by repaying 50p on each £1 share. This

---

18. F.A. 1972, s.84(4).
19. *Ibid.* s.86; *post*, § 14–54.
20. *Ibid.* ss.105, 108(1).
21. I.C.T.A. 1970, s.233(2)(*b*). "New consideration" is defined in s.237(1).
22. *Ibid.* s.235(4).
23. Note that in the cases of *Hague* and *Horrocks* (*post*, § 40–02), the sums returned did not exceed the amount of the subscribed capital.
24. F.A. 1972, s.106 and Sched. 22, para. 10.
25. I.C.T.A. 1970, s.234(1).

would not of itself constitute a distribution. But if the company issues 50,000 new bonus shares of 50p each and applies £25,000 out of its revenue reserve to pay for them, the overall effect of the transaction is the same as if the original share capital had remained intact and £25,000 had been distributed by way of dividend. Hence the amount paid up on the bonus shares (£25,000) is treated as distributed. If the amount paid up on the bonus shares exceeded £25,000, only £25,000 would be treated as distributed.

A bonus issue does not give rise to a distribution under this provision if:

(a) the share capital repaid consists of fully paid preference shares (defined so as to include only normal fixed interest stock)[26]; or

(b) the bonus issue (on or after April 6, 1973) is of share capital other than redeemable share capital and takes place more than 10 years after the repayment; but this exception does not apply in relation to a company within paragraph D of section 461 of the Income and Corporation Taxes Act 1970.[27] This paragraph embraces closely controlled companies and, in their case, any repayment of non-preference share capital after April 6, 1965, will cause a subsequent bonus issue to be treated as a distribution.[28]

14–45   4. *Bonus issue followed by repayment of share capital.* Where a company (after April 6, 1965) makes a bonus issue which does not rank as a qualifying distribution and subsequently repays the bonus shares, the amount so repaid is treated as a distribution.[29] There is an exception similar to the exception in paragraph 3(b), above, where the repayment is made more than 10 years after the bonus issue, which, again, does not apply to companies within paragraph D of section 461 of the 1970 Act.[30]

14–46   5. *Bonus shares.* An issue of bonus ordinary shares involves no distribution. But if any bonus redeemable share capital or any security is issued by a company in respect of shares in the company or (after April 5, 1972) in respect of securities of the company, this is treated as a distribution[31] and as a non-qualifying distribution.[32] If a shareholder is given the option of taking either cash or bonus shares and elects to take the shares he is liable to higher rate tax, on the basis of the equivalent cash dividend grossed up at the basic rate.[33]

14–47   6. *Interest and other distribution in respect of securities.* Interest and other distributions out of assets of a company in respect of the company's securities are treated as distributions where the securities fall into one of a

---

26. *Ibid.* s.234(2)(*a*) and (3).
27. F.A. 1972, Sched. 22, para. 5. For s.461, see *post,* §§ 40–02 *et seq.*
28. *Cf. I.R.C.* v. *Horrocks* (1968) 44 T.C. 645.
29. I.C.T.A. 1970, s.235.
30. F.A. 1972, Sched. 22, para. 6. For s.461, see *post,* §§ 40–02 *et seq. Cf. Hague* v. *I.R.C.* (1968) 44 T.C. 619 (C.A.).
31. I.C.T.A. 1970, s.233(2)(*c*) substituted by F.A. 1972, Sched. 22, para. 2.
32. See *ante,* § 14–41.
33. F. (No. 2) A. 1975, s.34 and Sched. 8; this provision also applies where a class of shares gives a *right* to receive bonus shares; and where the shares are not issued by reference to an alternative cash dividend the charge is on the (grossed up) market value of the bonus shares issued.

number of specified categories.[34] Interest on bonus redeemable shares or securities within paragraph 5, above, is treated as a distribution. Interest on securities which are convertible directly or indirectly into shares in the company, or securities issued after April 5, 1972, which carry a right to receive shares in or securities of the company, is treated as a distribution, subject to an exception for certain quoted securities. Where the amount of interest is to any extent dependent on the results of the company's business or any part of it, or represents more than a reasonable commercial return for the use of the principal, the interest is treated as a distribution,[35] except that in the latter case only the excess over a reasonable commercial return is so treated. Where companies form a 90 per cent. group (as defined), a distribution by one company in respect of securities in another company in the group may be caught.[36]

14–48   7. *Transfers of assets, etc., to or by members.* Where on a transfer of assets or liabilities by a company to its members or to a company by its members the amount or value of the benefit received by the member (taken at its market value) exceeds the amount or value of any new consideration given by him, the company is treated as making the distribution to him of an amount equal to the difference.[37] Thus if a company sells an asset to a member at an undervalue or a member sells an asset to the company at an overvalue, the company is treated as making a distribution. There is an exception to this rule in the case of inter-group company transactions.

14–49   8. *Reciprocal arrangements.* Where two or more companies enter into arrangements to make distributions to each other's members, all parties concerned can be treated as if anything done by either of those companies had been done by the other; and this applies however many companies participate in the arrangements.[38]

Demergers

14–49A   Section 117 of and Schedule 18 to the Finance Act 1980 introduced provisions for facilitating certain transactions whereby trading activities carried on by a single company or group may be divided so as to be carried on by two or more companies not belonging to the same group or by two or more independent groups. Certain transfers in connection with such "demergers" which would otherwise constitute "distributions" (see §§ 14–40 *et seq.*) are treated as "exempt distributions": see §§ 40–43 *et seq.*

---

34. See I.C.T.A. 1970, s.233(2)(*d*).
35. *Ibid.* s.233(2)(*d*)(iii) and F.A. 1972, Sched. 22, paras. 3(2) and (3). A lender on such terms will be treated as an "equity holder" in the borrowing company for group relief purposes: see F.A. 1973, s.28 and Sched. 12, para. 1(1) and (5). The expression "equity loans" is used to describe loan agreements where the interest is contrived so as to be "dependent on" the results of the borrowing company's business. For anti-avoidance provisions see F.A. 1982, s.60 and for an "explanation" the IR Press Release in [1982] S.T.I. 106.
36. F.A. 1972, s.106 and Sched. 22, para. 10.
37. I.C.T.A. 1970, s.233(3).
38. F.A. 1972, Sched. 22, para. 9.

Advance corporation tax

14–50　　Where a company resident in the United Kingdom makes a qualifying distribution (see § 14–41), it is liable to pay an amount of corporation tax to the Revenue, called "advance corporation tax."[39] Virtually all distributions are qualifying distributions other than issues of bonus redeemable shares and bonus debentures.[40] Advance corporation tax is payable on an amount equal to the amount or value of the distribution and is payable at a rate, called "the rate of advance corporation tax." Up to 1985 the rate of advance corporation tax was such fraction as Parliament should from time to time determine.[41] The rate for the financial year 1985 was 3/7ths.[42] (The rates as from April 6, 1973, are in the Table in § 14–100). For the financial year 1986 onwards, the rate of advance corporation tax will be determined automatically by a fraction which is $\dfrac{I}{100-I}$ when I is the basic rate of income tax for the year of assessment beginning in the financial year for which the rate of ACT is fixed. Thus the rate of advance corporation tax for the financial year 1986 is 29/71ths.[42a] A distribution attracts the rate of advance corporation tax in force for the financial year in which the distribution is made.[43] The expression "franked payment" is used to describe the sum of the amount or value of a qualifying distribution and the amount of the advance corporation tax attracted to it.[43]

> Thus if a company makes a distribution of £7,100 during the financial year 1984, it is required to make a payment of advance corporation tax to the Revenue of £2,900. The company is said to have made a franked payment of £10,000.

The main due dates for the payment of advance corporation tax are 14 days after the end of the quarterly "return periods" (*i.e.* the quarters ended March 31, June 30, September 30 and December 31).

Set-off of advance corporation tax against corporation tax

14–51　　We have seen how the liability of a company to corporation tax is computed by reference to accounting periods.[44] Advance corporation tax paid by a company (and not repaid[45]) in respect of any distribution made by it in an accounting period can be set against its liability to corporation tax "on any income charged to corporation tax for that accounting period."[46] Liability to corporation tax is to that extent discharged.[47] The phrase in quotation marks is defined as meaning the amount of the company's profits for

---

39. F.A. 1972, s.84(1).
40. *Ibid.* s.84(4); see *ante,* § 14–41.
41. *Ibid.* s.84(2). See also s.103.
42. F.A. 1985, s.35.
42a. F.A. 1986, s.17.
43. F.A. 1972, s.84(3).
44. See *ante,* § 14–05.
45. See *post,* § 14–55.
46. F.A. 1972, s.85(1) and (7).
47. *Ibid.* s.85(1).

the period on which corporation tax falls finally to be borne exclusive of the part of the profits attributable to chargeable gains.[48] Hence advance corporation tax cannot be credited against that part of the company's profits which is attributable to chargeable gains, the reason being that chargeable gains attract a lower rate of corporation tax than other profits.[49] The amount of the chargeable gains to be excluded is the amount before any deduction for charges on income, expenses of management or other amounts which can be deducted from or set against or treated as reducing profits of more than one description.[50] There is therefore an order of set-off for those reliefs which take effect against total profits, the rule being that such reliefs must be set off first against income other than chargeable gains.

14–52   *"Excessive distribution."* There is an important restriction on the extent to which a payment of advance corporation tax can be set against corporation tax liability. If in an accounting period a company makes distributions which are in excess of or disproportionate to the profits of that period, *e.g.* out of profits of an earlier period, or because its commercial profits have been reduced for tax purposes by capital allowances, it would be wrong to allow the whole of the payment of advance corporation tax to be used to eliminate the company's corporation tax liability for that period. Hence it is provided that the amount of advance corporation tax to be set against a company's liability for any accounting period shall not exceed the amount of advance corporation tax that would have been payable in respect of a distribution made at the end of that period of an amount which, together with the advance corporation tax so payable in respect of it, is equal to the company's income charged to corporation tax for that period.[51]

The surplus advance corporation tax paid for the accounting period can be carried back to the six preceding accounting periods (against the company's liability for the more recent accounting period before the remote one) and any surplus still remaining may be carried forward to the next accounting period and so on.[52] Other methods of dealing with surplus advance corporation tax are considered later.[53] These are statutory provisions to frustrate the purchase of companies merely for the purpose of obtaining the benefit of surplus advance corporation tax: see § 14–66A.

14–53   A company must make a claim to set advance corporation tax against its liability to corporation tax for any accounting period but a claim is treated as made when the company makes a return under section 11 of the Taxes Management Act 1970.[54]

---

48. *Ibid.* s.85(6). And see s.110(4).
49. See *post*, § 16–53.
50. F.A. 1972, s.85(6).
51. *Ibid.* s.85(2).
52. *Ibid.* s.85(3) and (4), as amended.
53. See *post*, § 14–75.
54. F.A. 1972, s.85(5).

As to the set-off of advance corporation tax by subsidiary companies, see § 14–75.

Tax credits and their utilisation

14–54   The distinction between qualifying and non-qualifying distributions was noted in § 14–41. Where a company resident in the United Kingdom makes a qualifying distribution, and the person receiving the distribution is another company resident in the United Kingdom or a person resident in the United Kingdom, not being a company, the recipient of the distribution is entitled to a "tax credit" equal to the advance corporation tax attributable to the distribution.[55] Distributions by non-United Kingdom resident companies attract no tax credit. Distributions to non-United Kingdom resident members attract no tax credit but there is an exception in the case of a qualifying distribution to a non-United Kingdom resident member who claims personal allowances under section 27 of the Income and Corporation Taxes Act 1970.[56] Such a member is brought within the charge to basic rate income tax, and is entitled to a tax credit and is chargeable on the aggregate of the distribution and the tax credit in the same way as a United Kingdom resident member.[56]

14–55   Where a United Kingdom resident company is entitled to a tax credit it may claim to have the amount of the credit paid to it[57] if:

(a) the company is wholly exempt from corporation tax or is only not exempt in respect of trading income (in which case distributions would be exempt); or

(b) the distribution is one in relation to which express exemption is given (other than the exemption from corporation tax for dividends and other distributions).

Hence an incorporated charity can "cash" its tax credit. Where there is no such right to "cash" the tax credit, it can be set against the recipient company's liability to advance corporation tax on its distributions: see § 14–63.

14–56   A person (other than a United Kingdom resident company) who is entitled to a tax credit can claim to set the credit against his tax liability for the year of assessment in which the distribution is received: see Computation B in § 8–69. He can set it either against income tax chargeable at the basic rate on annuities and other annual payments, etc., or against tax on his total income for the year of assessment; and where the credit exceeds the tax due, he is entitled to claim payment of the excess.[58] This applies not only to United Kingdom resident individuals but also to non-residents entitled to tax credits. The recipient of a distribution who is not liable to income tax at the basic rate can claim payment of any tax credit, subject to

55. *Ibid.* s.85(1)(2). See *ante*, § 14–01B.
56. *Ibid.* s.98. And see § 8–52.
57. *Ibid.* s.86(3). But see s.89(5).
58. *Ibid.* s.86(4).

an exception to prevent exempt persons holding 10 per cent. or more of any one class of shares or securities recovering tax on distributions earned before he acquired his holding.[59]

14–57   It was said in § 14–54 that the *recipient* of a distribution may be entitled to a tax credit. But where the distribution falls to be treated as the income of some person other than the recipient, that person is treated as the recipient; and, accordingly, the question whether there is any entitlement to a tax credit is determined by reference to his residence and not the residence of the actual recipient.[60] Thus if non-United Kingdom resident trustees hold a trust fund upon trust for a United Kingdom resident individual, a distribution which forms part of the income of that resident individual will qualify for a tax credit.[60] Where any qualifying distribution is income of a United Kingdom trust (as defined[61]) the trustees are entitled to a tax credit in respect of it if no other person is entitled.[62]

Income tax on distributions: Schedule F

14–58   The meaning of "distribution" and the distinction between qualifying and non-qualifying distributions has already been discussed in §§ 14–40 *et seq.* For the year 1973–74 and subsequent years of assessment, the recipient of a distribution is chargeable to income tax under the substituted Schedule F.[63] Schedule F charges income tax for a year of assessment in respect of all dividends and other distributions in that year of a company resident in the United Kingdom which are not specially excluded from income tax[64]; and for the purposes of income tax all such distributions are regarded as income however they fall to be dealt with in the hands of the recipient.[65] Hence capital dividends which, as between tenant for life and remainderman, fall to be treated as capital are nevertheless treated as income for Schedule F purposes. Schedule F does not apply to dividends or other distributions of companies not resident in the United Kingdom: these are taxed under Case V of Schedule D. No distribution which is chargeable under Schedule F is chargeable under any other provisions of the Income Tax Acts.[66]

14–59   *Position where distribution carried tax credit.* The charge under Schedule F is on the aggregate of the amount or value of the distribution and any tax credit to which the recipient is entitled, and this aggregate is treated as income of the recipient.[67] Hence an individual who receives a dividend of £7,100 must include in his return of total income for income tax purposes, as his income from the company, the sum of £10,000 being the dividend

---

59. F.A. 1973, s.21. See also *ibid*. s.22.
60. F.A. 1972, s.86(5).
61. *Ibid*. s.110(1).
62. See *ante*, § 14–55.
63. *i.e.* the charging provision in I.C.T.A. 1970, s.232(1) substituted by F.A. 1972, s.87(2).
64. F.A. 1972, s.87(1)(2).
65. *Ibid*. s.87(2).
66. *Ibid*. s.87(3).
67. *Ibid*. s.87(2).

plus the tax credit of £2,900 attributable to it. (This example assumes a rate of advance corporation tax of 29/71ths.) The recipient of a qualifying distribution is entitled, if he so requests, to a statement in writing showing the amount or value of the distribution and (whether or not he is a person entitled to a tax credit in respect of the distribution) the amount of the tax credit to which a recipient who is such a person is entitled.[68]

14–60 *Position where distribution carries no tax credit.* Where the recipient of a distribution (not being a company resident in the United Kingdom) is not entitled to a tax credit in respect of that distribution, *e.g.* because the distribution is a non-qualifying distribution or because the recipient is not resident in the United Kingdom, no assessment to basic rate income tax can be made on that person in respect of the distribution. Higher rate income tax is levied on the amount or value of the distribution, but any higher rate tax payable is reduced by an amount equal to tax at the basic rate on the amount assessed.[69]

> Thus if a company issues bonus redeemable shares this is a non-qualifying distribution. Suppose a shareholder receives such shares having a value[70] of £700. No basic rate income tax is leviable on the £700. Any higher rate income tax is levied on £700 and the amount of tax reduced by an amount equal to tax at the basic rate on £700.

14–61 If in this example the company later repays the bonus shares, this repayment (£700) will be a qualifying distribution (see § 14–41) in respect of which a payment of advance corporation tax (say, £300) will be made by the company. A tax credit (£300) will then be conferred on the recipient. The recipient is entitled if assessed to higher rate income tax in respect of the repayment of the bonus shares, to take credit for tax levied on the previous non-qualifying distribution.[71]

14–62 The amount or value of a distribution which carries no tax credit is treated for the purposes of sections 52 and 53 of the Income and Corporation Taxes Act 1970 as not brought into charge to income tax.[72] The consequences of this are discussed in §§ 5–34 *et seq.*

Franked investment income

14–63 We have seen that a company resident in the United Kingdom which makes a qualifying distribution is liable to pay advance corporation tax to the Revenue: see § 14–50. But companies with investments in other companies receive as well as make distributions and this is taken into account in quantifying the company's liability for advance corporation tax. Briefly, a company can take credit for tax imputed to it: hence advance corporation

---

68. I.C.T.A. 1970, s.232(4) substituted by F.A. 1972, Sched. 24, para. 18.
69. F.A. 1972, s.87(5).
70. *Ibid.* Sched. 22, para. 2(2).
71. *Ibid.* s.87(6).
72. *Ibid.* s.87(5).

tax is payable only to the extent that the company's qualifying distributions exceed distributions received.

14–64   Income of a company resident in the United Kingdom which consists of a distribution in respect of which the company is entitled to a tax credit is called "franked investment income" of the company.[73] Its franked investment income is the amount it receives plus the relevant tax credit. Franked investment income is not chargeable to corporation tax (see § 14–0A).

> Hence if in an accounting period company A receives a dividend from company B of £7,000 (both companies being resident in the United Kingdom), this represents franked investment income of £10,000 (assuming the rate of advance corporation tax to be 3/7ths).
>
> If during the same period company A made a qualifying distribution to its members of £1,400, it would prima facie have to make a payment of advance corporation tax of £600 (3/7ths of £1,400).

14–65   The Act, however, provides that where in any accounting period a company receives franked investment income, it shall not be liable to pay advance corporation tax in respect of qualifying distributions made by it in that period unless the amount of the franked payments made by it in that period exceeds the amount of its franked investment income.[74] In the example in § 14–64 the franked payment made by company A is £1,400 plus £600 = £2,000. Since this is less than the franked investment income received by the company (£10,000), no advance corporation tax is payable in respect of the distribution of £1,400. If (as in the example) the amount of franked investment income received in an accounting period exceeds the amount of the franked payments made in that period, the excess (£8,000 in the example) must be carried forward to the next accounting period and treated as franked investment income received by the company in the next period, and so on.[75] Such an excess is called a "surplus of franked investment income."[76]

14–66   Where franked payments made by a company exceed franked investment income received in the same accounting period, advance corporation tax is payable on an amount which, when the advance corporation tax payable thereon is added to it, is equal to the excess.[77]

Certain companies exempt from tax, such as incorporated charities, can claim to be paid the amount of a tax credit.[78] There are provisions to prevent such a company using its franked investment income to frank distributions made by it and thus obtain relief (in effect) twice over.[79]

---

73. *Ibid.* s.88(1). And see s.88(2). Group income is not franked investment income: see *ante*, § 14–72.
74. *Ibid.* s.89(1).
75. *Ibid.* s.89(3).
76. *Ibid.* s.89(6).
77. *Ibid.* s.89(2).
78. *Ibid.* s.86(3); see *ante*, § 14–55.
79. *Ibid.* s.89(5).

Anti-avoidance provisions

14–66A It has been explained that a surplus of advance corporation tax may be carried forward and credited against corporation tax liability in a subsequent accounting period.[80] Section 101 of the Finance Act 1972 contains provisions designed to frustrate the purchase of companies merely for the purpose of obtaining the benefit of surplus advance corporation tax. The provision is similar to section 483 of the Taxes Act 1970, dealing with tax losses.[81]

Accounting for advance corporation tax

14–67 Schedule 14 to the Finance Act 1972 regulates the time and manner in which advance corporation tax is to be accounted for and paid and the manner in which effect is to be given to the provisions allowing franked investment income of a company to be used to frank its distributions.[82] Companies are required to make returns on a quarterly basis. The return must show the franked payments made in the "return period" and the franked investment income received or brought forward from a previous period. Advance corporation tax is payable on the excess of franked payments in the period over the amount of franked investment income.

Set-off of losses, etc., against a surplus of franked investment income

14–68 There is a surplus of franked investment income where the amount of the franked income received by a company in an accounting period exceeds the amount of the franked payments made by it in that period.[83] Such an excess, as explained in § 14–65, may be carried forward to and treated as franked investment income of the next and subsequent accounting periods. Section 254 of the Income and Corporation Taxes Act 1970[84] provides an alternative method of obtaining relief from tax on that surplus by allowing a company in certain circumstances to claim to treat a surplus of franked investment income in an accounting period as if it were a like amount of profits chargeable to corporation tax in that period and to set against the surplus so treated unrelieved trading losses, charges on income, expenses of management, capital allowances and capital loss relievable against investment income on a claim made under the provisions in § 12–10C. Such deductions must be made first against profits chargeable to corporation tax before resorting to a surplus of franked investment income treated as if it were profits. Thus if, due to an insufficiency of *actual* profits, the company is unable to set off losses, charges, etc., and so obtain relief from corporation tax, it can claim to treat surplus franked investment income as a fund of *notional* profits and so reclaim tax at (effectively) income tax rates (because tax credits are calculated by reference to income tax rates). For

---

80. See *ante*, § 14–52.
81. See *ante*, § 14–30.
82. F.A. 1972, ss.84(5), 89(4).
83. *Ibid*. s.89(6); see *ante*, § 14–65.
84. Substituted by F.A. 1972, s.90(1) and Sched. 15.

the purposes of a claim under section 254, the surplus of franked investment income for an accounting period must be calculated without regard to the part, if any, carried forward from an earlier period. There are various provisions to prevent more than one relief being obtained in respect of the same franked investment income.[85]

14–69   Where a claim is made under section 254 of the 1970 Act, the claimant company receives payment of the amount of the tax credit comprised in the surplus of franked investment income. Section 255 of the Income and Corporation Taxes Act 1970[86] contains similar provisions under which losses brought forward and terminal losses can be set against a surplus of franked investment income.

14–70   *Compensating adjustments.* Where surplus franked investment income is treated as a fund of notional profits chargeable to corporation tax, two compensating adjustments have to be made. The first arises from the fact that losses, charges, etc., are worth less if set against surplus franked investment income rather than actual profits chargeable at corporation tax rates.[87] The second allows the tax credit repaid to be carried forward and deducted from the amounts of advance corporation tax available to be set off against mainstream corporation tax.[88]

Groups of companies

14–71   We have seen that a United Kingdom resident company which makes a qualifying distribution to another such company is required to make a payment of advance corporation tax and that the recipient is entitled to a tax credit.[89] There is an important exception to this principle which applies to dividends (but no other distributions) paid from one member of a group of companies to another member of the same group, where an election is in force under section 256 of the Income and Corporation Taxes Act 1970.[90] In that case no liability to advance corporation tax is incurred and the recipient is entitled to no tax credit. Section 256 applies only where both companies are bodies corporate resident in the United Kingdom and where the company paying the dividends is:

(a) a 51 per cent. subsidiary of the other or of a company so resident of which the other is a 51 per cent. subsidiary; or

(b) a trading or holding company owned by a consortium the members of which include the company receiving the dividends.

14–72   Dividends so treated are referred to as "group income" and are not franked investment income of the recipient company.[91]

---

85. *Ibid.* s.90(2) and (3).
86. Substituted by F.A. 1972, s.90(1) and Sched. 15.
87. See I.C.T.A. 1970, s.254(5)(6).
88. F.A. 1972, s.90(3). See IR 18 (1979), para. 4.31.
89. See *ante*, § 14–54.
90. Substituted by F.A. 1972, s.91(1) and Sched. 15.
91. F.A. 1972, s.88(1) and I.C.T.A. 1970, s.256(1).

14–73   The provisions by which dividends may be treated as group income apply also to payments which are corporation tax charges on income of the company making them: thus interest, annuities and other annual payments can be paid by a subsidiary company to its parent company in full, without deduction of basic rate income tax, where the appropriate election is in force.[92]

14–74   Dividends and other payments received by a company on investments cannot be treated as group income if a profit on a sale of those investments would be treated as a trading receipt of the company.[93] Hence dividends on shares forming part of the trading stock of a company dealing in shares cannot be treated as group income. There are provisions for the recovery of tax in respect of dividends and other payments which were wrongly treated as group income.[94] The Board of Inland Revenue has power to make regulations governing the manner in which claims for group treatment are to be made.[95]

Setting off companies' advance corporation tax against subsidiaries' liability

14–75   It has been explained that advance corporation tax paid by a company is deducted from the corporation tax payable on its income.[96] In a group of companies, it might happen that one member of the group has a liability for advance corporation tax but no corporation tax profits, whereas another member of the same group has profits but no liability to advance corporation tax. Section 92 of the Finance Act 1972 (as amended[97–98]) enables a United Kingdom resident company to surrender advance corporation tax for the benefit of its resident subsidiaries. The subsidiaries must be 51 per cent. subsidiaries (as defined); and the relief only applies to advance corporation tax paid in respect of dividends (not other distributions). Thus if a company makes a bonus issue of ordinary shares which it then repays by way of reduction of capital, this is a qualifying distribution of the amount repaid (see § 14–41 and § 14–43) but the advance corporation tax cannot be surrendered to group subsidiaries under section 92.

C. COMPANIES PURCHASING THEIR OWN SHARES

14–76   The Companies Act 1985 contains provisions which enable companies, if authorised by their Articles, to issue redeemable shares and to purchase their own shares.[99] These provisions came into force on June 15, 1982.[1] Generally, shares can be redeemed or purchased only out of distributable

---

92. I.C.T.A. 1970, s.256(2). For the method of electing, see *ibid.* s.257.
93. *Ibid.* s.256(2).
94. F.A. 1972, s.91(2).
95. *Ibid.* s.91(3).
96. *Ibid.* s.85(1); see *ante*, § 14–51.
97–98. F.A. 1973, s.32 and Sched. 13.
99. C.A. 1985, ss. 159–181.
1. The Companies Act 1981 (Commencement No. 4) Order 1982 (S.I. 1982 No. 672).

profits or out of the proceeds of a fresh issue made for the purpose; but there are special provisions by which private companies can redeem or purchase their own shares out of capital. Readers are referred to the books on company law for a full discussion of these provisions.

14–77   A consultative document published by the Board of Inland Revenue in September 1981[2] suggested five situations where the facility to purchase its own shares could enable certain types of trading company to manage their affairs more flexibly and efficiently:

(1) It could encourage investment in the company's shares. Investors are reluctant to put money into a company if there is no ready market for the shares and they are in a "locked in" position.

(2) It could make it easier for the proprietor of a business to seek equity investment from others without himself surrendering a permanent equity stake.

(3) It may contribute to the efficient management of a business if dissident or apathetic shareholders can be brought out.

(4) When a family shareholder with a significant number of shares retires or dies and there are no children to succeed him, the other members of the family may not be able to afford to buy out his shares. There may be cases where the only option is to sell shares to a third party (resulting in loss of family control), which might have harmful effects on the company's trade.

(5) A similar situation may arise when a shareholder dies and shares have to be sold to meet liabilities to capital transfer tax (or inheritance tax). A purchase by the company may be preferable to a purchase by an outsider.

14–78   The Finance Act 1982 contains provisions to deal with the tax problems created by these new provisions. Generally, where a company makes a payment to its shareholders otherwise than by way of repayment of share capital, the "distribution provisions" in the Corporation Tax Acts apply: the company has to pay advance corporation tax and the amount distributed (plus the associated tax credit) is income of the shareholder. By section 53 of the Finance Act 1982, however, a payment made by a company on or after April 6, 1982, on the redemption, repayment or purchase of its own shares is not a distribution if the company is an unquoted company *and* either a trading company or the holding company of a trading group and one of the following conditions is satisfied:

Condition (1): purchases to benefit the trade[3]

14–79   This condition requires that the redemption, repayment or purchase (a) is made wholly or mainly for the purpose of benefiting a trade carried on by the company or by any of its 75 per cent. subsidiaries, and (b) does not

---

2. [1981] S.T.I. 512.
3. F.A. 1982, s.53(1).

form part of a scheme or arrangement the main purpose or one of the main purposes of which is to enable the owner of the shares to participate in the profits of the company without receiving a divided or the avoidance of tax, and (c) the conditions in paragraphs 1 to 9 of Schedule 9, so far as applicable, are satisfied in relation to the owner of the shares.

These further conditions in Schedule 9 are numerous. In brief, the vendor must be resident and ordinarily resident in the United Kingdom in the year of assessment in which the purchase is made; the shares must have been owned by the vendor throughout the period of five years ending with the date of the purchase; and, if the vendor sells only part of his holding of shares, his interest must be "substantially reduced"—and this is elaborately defined in the Schedule.

Condition (2): sales to pay inheritance tax[4]

14-80   This condition requires that the whole or substantially the whole of the payment (apart from any sum applied in paying capital gains tax charged on the redemption, repayment or purchase) is applied by the person to whom it is made in discharging a liability of his for inheritance tax charged on a death, and is so applied within the period of two years after the death; but this condition is not satisfied to the extent that the liability could without undue hardship have been discharged otherwise than through the redemption, repayment, etc.

Where the conditions in (1) or (2) are satisfied, the capital gains tax rules apply to the disposal of the shares, except where the vendor is a dealer in shares.[5]

14-81   In respect of condition (1) in § 14–79, it may prove difficult in practice to show that a redemption, etc. by a trading company was made wholly or mainly for the purpose of benefiting the trade carried on by that company. To take two extremes, the condition would be satisfied if there was clear evidence that the efficient management of the company was being impaired by the presence of the shareholder being bought out and that he was bought out for that reason; but it would not be satisfied if the main object of the transaction was to get surplus cash out of the company into the pockets of the shareholder and the dispute with him was contrived in order to take advantage of the section. The conditions in section 53 are more likely to be satisfied in situations (3) and (4) in § 14–77 than in situations (1) and (2).

14-82   During the Committee stage debates on the Finance Act 1982, the Financial Secretary said that a statement of practice would be issued on the way that Condition (1) would be interpreted by the Revenue; and SP2/1982 was duly issued on August 3, 1982.[6] The following is an extract from this statement:

---

4. *Ibid.* s.53(2).
5. *Ibid.* s.54.
6. The full text is in [1982] S.T.I. 367.

"1. Section 53 provides that references in the Corporation Tax Acts to distributions of a company shall not include references to a payment made by a company on the redemption, repayment or purchase of its own shares if, among other conditions, the redemption, repayment or purchase is made wholly or mainly for the purpose of benefiting a trade carried on by the company or by any of its 75 per cent. subsidiaries.

2. This test indicates that the sole or main purpose of the transaction is to be to benefit a trade of a relevant company and not, for example, to benefit the vending shareholder (although he usually will also benefit) nor some wider commercial purpose to which he may put the payment he receives nor any business purpose of a relevant company itself if it is not a trade, such as an investment activity which it may also carry on.

3. If the problem being resolved by the transaction is a disagreement over the management of the company, the main purpose may nonetheless be to benefit a trade if, as will usually be the case with a trading company, the disagreement has or can reasonably be expected to have an adverse effect on the running of the trade. It would not be so however if, exceptionally, the disagreement were, for example, over the question whether the company should discontinue trading and become an investment company and the shareholder being bought out advocated the continuance of trading.

4. More generally, with rare exceptions of the kind just mentioned, since it will normally be unsatisfactory to retain an unwilling shareholder it is expected that the condition will be shown to be satisfied where, after taking into account the interests of any associates, the vending shareholder is genuinely giving up his entire interest of all kinds in the company. The case of a boardroom disagreement has already been mentioned; other examples where this might happen are:

a. an outside shareholder has provided equity finance (whether or not with the expectation of redemption or sale to the company); he is now withdrawing his investment:

b. the proprietor of a company is retiring to make way for new management:

c. a shareholder has died leaving shares in his estate and his personal representatives or the beneficiaries do not wish to keep them.

5. Where a shareholder is only reducing (by 25 per cent. or more) his proportionate interest in shares and profits, or retaining some other interest, it is less likely that the condition will be satisfied. It cannot, for example, then usually be argued that the purpose is to remove his continued unwilling presence which could otherwise damage the trade. But the condition might still be satisfied where the intention was that his entire interest should cease but this was to be achieved by more than one transaction (for example, because the company could not afford to buy all his shares at one time): or where the interest he retained was minimal and kept only for sentimental reasons."

14–83/84   There is a procedure for obtaining a clearance.[7] The application, where condition (1) is relied on, is required to state the reasons for the purchase, the trading benefits expected and any other benefits expected to accrue whether or not to the purchasing company. The application where condition (2) is relied on must provide a full explanation of the circumstances in which there would be undue hardship, if the tax liability were to be discharged otherwise than through the purchase by the company of its own

---

7. F.A. 1982, Sched. 9, para. 10 and [1982] S.T.I. 230. And see SP 2/1982 for guidance, in [1982] S.T.I. 369.

shares. An application for clearance under section 464 (see § 40–15) will usually also be necessary.

D. CONTROLLED FOREIGN COMPANIES[8]

Income and Corporation Taxes Act 1970, s.478

14–85   Section 478 of the Income and Corporation Taxes Act 1970 and section 45 of the Finance Act 1981 contain provisions which have the effect of preventing *individuals* who are ordinarily resident in the United Kingdom from avoiding United Kingdom income tax by accumulating income abroad and enjoying that income (whilst still so resident) in a capital form. These provisions are summarised in §§ 7–26 *et seq.* They apply only to individuals: no assessment under these provisions can be made on a company. If, however, an individual owns shares in a United Kingdom resident company which itself has a foreign subsidiary, the individual may be assessed under section 478 on the undistributed income of the foreign subsidiary which he directly enjoys through the United Kingdom resident company.

The provisions about to be considered have the effect of preventing United Kingdom resident *companies* from avoiding corporation tax by the use of subsidiaries in "tax havens."

Power to give a direction

14–86   Sections 82–91 of and Schedule 16 to the Finance Act 1984 enable a charge to corporation tax to be imposed on companies resident in the United Kingdom which have interests in "controlled foreign companies." The sections apply as from April 6, 1984.[9] The charge[10] applies only in an accounting period in which the Board of Inland Revenue so direct and only if the foreign company:

(a) is resident outside the United Kingdom; and

(b) is controlled by persons resident in the United Kingdom; and

(c) is subject to a lower level of taxation in the territory in which it is resident, *i.e.* where the tax payable under the law of the territory ("the local tax") is less than half the amount that would have been payable had the company been resident in the United Kingdom.[11] (The Board have published a list of companies which are not regarded as low tax countries.)[12]

A foreign company which satisfies these conditions is called a "controlled foreign company."[13] Generally, a company which is resident outside the United Kingdom is treated as resident in the territory in which it is

---

8. The Revenue has published explanatory notes dealing with these provisions: see (1985) S.T.I. 78.
9. F.A. 1984, s.91(4).
10. *Ibid.* s.82(1).
11. *Ibid.* s.85.
12. This is the "Excluded Countries List": see (1984) S.T.I. 549, (1985) S.T.I. 469 and (1986) S.T.I. 54.
13. F.A. 1984, s.82(2).

liable to be taxed; but if there is no such territory, it is treated as resident in a territory which is subject to a lower level of taxation.

The charge does not apply unless the United Kingdom company (together with associated or connected persons) would have at least 10 per cent. of the chargeable profits of the controlled foreign company apportioned to it.[14]

14–87   Where a direction is given for an accounting period, the chargeable profits of the controlled foreign company and its creditable tax (if any) for that period are apportioned among the persons (whether resident in the United Kingdom or not) who had an interest in the company at any time during the accounting period. The apportionment is made according to the respective interests of those persons in the controlled foreign company during that period.[15]

There are detailed provisions in Schedule 16 for determining the chargeable profits of a controlled foreign company. Chargeable gains are not included: these can only be apportioned in accordance with the provisions summarised in § 16–55.

14–88   Where chargeable profits are apportioned to a United Kingdom resident company those profits (less any creditable tax) are chargeable to corporation tax.[16] Note that the direction does not have the effect of treating the profits as income of the United Kingdom resident company: hence carried-forward losses cannot relieve that company from liability to corporation tax on the profits apportioned to it. The only reliefs available to the United Kingdom company are those specified in Schedule 18.[17]

Cases in which no direction will be given

14–89   No direction will be given if, for a particular accounting period, the controlled foreign company falls into one of the following five categories[18]:

14–90   (1) *Acceptable distribution policy*.[19] No direction will be given for an accounting period in which a company pursues an acceptable distribution policy as defined in Schedule 17. This requires that at least 50 per cent. of the controlled foreign company's available profits (as defined) are distributed by way of dividend to persons resident in the United Kingdom (or 90 per cent. where the controlled foreign company is not a trading company[20]). The definition of available profits does not include capital profits (defined). Where a dividend is declared to be paid out of the profits of a

---

14. *Ibid.* s.82(5).
15. *Ibid.* ss.82(3), 84(5)–(7) and 87.
16. *Ibid.* s.82(4).
17. *Ibid.* s.87(7).
18. *Ibid.* s.83.
19. *Ibid.* Sched. 17, Pt. I. In practice the Board may wish to give a direction after the end of the accounting period before it is known if an acceptable distribution policy has been pursued: *ibid.* s.83(2).
20. Trading company means a company whose business consists wholly or mainly of the carrying out of a trade or trades: *ibid.* s.91(1).

specified period, little difficulty may arise in applying the test; but the legislation provides detailed rules to meet the case where, *e.g.* a dividend is not paid for a specified period and therefore has to be related to profits of a particular period.

A United Kingdom resident company with a tax haven subsidiary will avoid a direction if the subsidiary distributes (say) 51 per cent. of its profits by way of dividend, and the balance is accumulated in the tax haven. But the provisions discussed in § 7–26 might apply as respects United Kingdom resident individuals holding shares in the United Kingdom company.

14–91 (2) *Exempt activities.*[21] The controlled foreign company is engaged in exempt activities in an accounting period if, throughout that period, it has a business establishment in the territory in which it is resident and its business affairs in that territory are effectively managed there. These conditions are not satisfied by having a mere postal address: the company must have permanent business premises and an adequate staff. Additionally the main business of the controlled foreign company must not consist of investment business (as defined) or dealing in goods (without taking delivery of them) as an intermediary between the United Kingdom and connected or associated persons. The definition of investment business embraces the holding of securities, patents or copyrights, dealing in securities except as a broker, leasing and investing in any manner funds which would otherwise be available for investment in the case of a subsidiary by its parent company in the United Kingdom or someone connected or associated with it. Where in the accounting period the controlled foreign company is engaged in wholesale, distributive or financial business (defined to include, *e.g.* banking and insurance) less than 50 per cent. of its gross trading receipts from that business must be derived directly or indirectly from connected or associated persons. Thus an overseas insurance company which derives 50 per cent. or more of its premium income from the United Kingdom parent would not carry on exempt activities.

The effect of this exemption is to exclude genuine trading companies with a real presence in the foreign territory but to exclude "money box companies" and companies which are merely a vehicle through which goods are invoiced in order to syphon-off profits in the tax haven.

14–92 (3) *The public quotation condition.*[22] No direction may be given if shares carrying not less than 35 per cent. of the voting power in the company are quoted on a recognised stock exchange, if numerous other conditions are satisfied.

14–93 (4) *Profits not exceeding £20,000.*[23] No direction may be given with respect to an accounting period where the chargeable profits of the period do not exceed £20,000, or, if the accounting period is less than 12 months, a proportionately reduced amount.

21. *Ibid.* Sched. 17, Pt. II.
22. *Ibid.* Sched. 17, Pt. III.
23. *Ibid.* s.83(1)(*d*). As to "chargeable profits" see *ibid.* s.82(6).

14–94/99　　(5) *No main tax reduction purpose.*[24] If a transaction or transactions, the results of which are reflected in the profits of an accounting period, achieved a reduction in United Kingdom tax, no direction may be given if either the reduction so achieved was minimal or it was not the main purpose or one of the main purposes of the transaction to achieve it, and it was not the main reason or the main reason for the company's existence in that accounting period to achieve a reduction in United Kingdom tax by a diversion of profits from the United Kingdom.

TABLE OF COMPANY TAX RATES

14–100

Financial Year beginning April 1	Rate of corporation tax %	Small companies rate % (F.A. 1972 s. 95)	Upper and lower limits		A.C.T. Rate
1964	40				
1965	40				
1966	40				
1967	$42\frac{1}{2}$				
1968	45				
1969	45				
1970	40				
1971	40				
1972	40				
1973[25]	52	42	15,000	25,000	3/7
1974	52	42	15,000	25,000	33/67
1975	52	42	30,000	50,000	35/65
1976	52	42	40,000	65,000	35/65
1977	52	42	50,000	85,000	34/66
1978	52	42	60,000	100,000	33/67
1979	52	40	70,000	130,000	3/7
1980	52	40	80,000	200,000	3/7
1981	52	40	90,000	225,000	3/7
1982	52	38	100,000	500,000	3/7
1983	50	30	100,000	500,000	3/7
1984	45	30	100,000	500,000	3/7
1985	40	30	100,000	500,000	3/7
1986	35	29	100,000	500,000	29/71

---

24. *Ibid.* s.83(3) and Sched. 17, Pt. IV.
25. The period from April 6, 1973, to March 31, 1974, is treated as a "financial year": F.A. 1972, s.84(2).

CHAPTER 15

CLOSE COMPANIES

15–01 THE expression "close company" is used to describe a company which is sufficiently closely controlled by its shareholders to enable them to manipulate the company's affairs and so procure certain advantages. Sections 1 and 2 of this Chapter explain what companies are "close companies" and what are not. Inevitably, the legislation is complex and detailed. Sections 3, 4 and 5 of the Chapter show how this legislation is relevant to the tax regime that exists at the present time.

Section 3 is concerned with accommodation and other benefits or facilities for participators and their associates. We have seen in Chapter 3 that a director or employee of a company (whether a close company or not) may be taxed under Schedule E if the company provides him with accommodation or other benefits in kind. There are statutory provisions in § 15–21 which have a similar effect where a close company provides benefits or facilities for individuals who are not employees but are participators or associates of participators. The legislation operates by treating the company as having made a distribution equal to the value of the benefit, giving rise to a liability in the company for advance corporation tax and in the participator for higher rate tax.

Section 4 deals with loans to participators and their associates. There would be a substantial loophole in the tax system if those in control of a close company were able to "borrow" the company's funds without tax liability. There are, accordingly, statutory provisions (see §§ 15–25 *et seq.*) which treats loans to participators and their associates as if the company had distributed an amount equal to the money borrowed.

Section 5 summarises the statutory provisions which prevent the use of close companies as a vehicle for accumulating investment income at the relatively low rates of corporation tax.

1. DEFINITIONS

There are a number of general definitions which apply for the purposes of the statutory provisions relating to close companies.

Participator[1]

15–02 A participator is, in relation to any company, a person having a share or interest in the capital or income of the company. Thus in the case of a company with a share capital, it includes every shareholder; and in a company

---

1. I.C.T.A. 1970, s.303(1). For the position of debenture holders, see § 15–03A.

with no share capital, it includes every member. Without prejudice to the generality of these words, "participator" includes:

(a) any person who possesses, or is entitled to acquire, share capital or voting rights in the company;

(b) any loan creditor of the company (see § 15–03);

(c) any person who possesses, or is entitled to acquire, a right to receive or participate in distributions[2] of the company or any amounts payable by the company (in cash or in kind) to loan creditors by way of premium on redemption; and

(d) any person who is entitled to secure that income or assets (whether present or future) of the company will be applied directly or indirectly for his benefit.

References in (a), (c) and (d) to being entitled to do anything apply where a person is presently entitled to do it at a future date, or will at a future date be entitled to do it.[3] Thus a person who has an option (or right to acquire an option) entitling him to acquire shares at a future date is a "participator" within (a).

There are a number of provisions in the Act which enable a "participator" in one company to be treated as being also a "participator" in another.[3]

Loan creditor

15–03   This definition has to be read in conjunction with paragraph (b) in § 15–02.

Loan creditor, in relation to a company, means a creditor in respect of any debt incurred by the company:

(a) for any money borrowed or capital assets acquired by the company; or

(b) for any right to receive income created in favour of the company; or

(c) for consideration the value of which to the company was (at the time when the debt was incurred) substantially less than the amount of the debt (including any premium thereon),

or in respect of any redeemable loan capital issued by the company.[4]

A person carrying on a business of banking is not deemed to be a loan creditor in respect of any loan capital or debt issued or incurred by the company for money lent by him to the company in the ordinary course of that business.[4]

Note that the term "loan creditor" does not apply only to a person who

---

2. "Distributions" is here to be construed without regard to the extended meaning in I.C.T.A. 1970, ss.284 and 285 (§§ 15–21 *et seq.*); *ibid.* s.303(1)(c). For the meaning of "distribution," see *ante*, §§ 14–40 *et seq.*

3. *Ibid.* s.303(2). See for examples *ibid.* s.284(7) in § 15–21; s.286(9) and s.282(2) in § 15–25.

4. *Ibid.* s.303(7).

lends money to a company. It also applies to a person who sells assets or an annuity to a company, leaving the purchase price owing.

A person who is not the creditor in respect of any debt or loan capital to which the provisions summarised in § 15–03 applies, but nevertheless has a beneficial interest therein (*e.g.* under a trust) is, to the extent of that interest, to be treated as a loan creditor in respect of that debt or loan capital.[5]

–03A   A debenture holder is a participator as being a "loan creditor" unless the holder is excepted as being a bank lending in the ordinary course of banking business. Such a bank is not a participator within the definition of paragraph (a) of § 15–02 (unless he is entitled to voting rights, *e.g.* because his security is in jeopardy), because a debenture gives an interest in the *assets* of a company, not an interest in its *share capital*.[6] A debenture holder who is entitled to interest which is to any extent dependent on the results of the company's business or represents more than a reasonable commercial return for the use of the principal (*i.e.* who is entitled to participate in "distributions": see § 14–47) is a participator within the definition in paragraph (c) in § 15–02.

Associate

5–04   This definition is important because, generally, the rights of "associates" of participators can be attributed to the participators[7] (see § 15–09). An "associate" means,[8] in relation to a participator:

    (a) any relative (see § 15–05) or partner of the participator;
    (b) the trustee or trustees of any settlement in relation to which the participator is, or any relative of his (living or dead) is or was, a settlor ("settlement" and "settlor" having here the same meaning as in section 454(3) of the Income and Corporation Taxes Act 1970) (see §§ 10–07 *et seq.*); and
    (c) where the participator is interested (whether beneficially or as trustee[9]) in any shares or obligations of the company which are subject to any trust, or are part of the estate of a deceased person, any other person interested therein.[10]

The term "associate" has a corresponding meaning in relation to a person other than a participator.[11] In *Willingale* v. *Islington Green Investment*

---

5. *Ibid.* s.303(8).
6. *I.R.C.* v. *R. Woolf & Co. Ltd.* (1961) 39 T.C. 611.
7. I.C.T.A. 1970, s.302(6).
8. *Ibid.* s.303(3).
9. *Willingale* v. *Islington Green Investment Co.* (1972) 48 T.C. 547 (C.A.).
10. Beneficiaries under some types of trust are not "associates" under (c). See I.C.T.A. 1970, s.303(3) proviso. A legatee in an unadministered estate may not be a person interested within (c): see the case in note 12, *post*. It appears from the proviso to s.303(3) that objects of a discretionary trust are persons "interested" within para. (c).
11. *Ibid.* s.303(3). Thus "associate" has the same meaning in relation for example to a director: see s.303(5)(*c*) in § 15–06; also for the purposes of *ibid.* s.461 D(3) in § 40–11.

Co.[12] executors holding shares in a company *qua* executors were held to be associates of a director who held shares in the same company.

Relative and partner

15–05   "Relative" in paragraph (a) of § 15–04 means husband or wife, parent or remoter forebear, child or remoter issue, or brother or sister.[13] Note that this definition does not include "in-laws."

There is no definition of the word "partner" for the purposes of paragraph (a) of § 15–04. General principles of law have to be applied: see § 11–01. Note that although a shareholder's partner can be treated as his associate, and so also a shareholder's relative, a relative of the shareholder's partner cannot be treated as the shareholder's associate: see § 15–09.

Director

15–06   The word "director" is widely defined[14] so as to include any person occupying the position of director by whatever name called, any person in accordance with whose directions or instructions the directors are accustomed to act, and any person who:

(a) is a manager of the company or otherwise concerned in the management of the company's trade or business; and

(b) is, either on his own or with one or more associates (see § 15–04), the beneficial owner of, or able, directly or through the medium of other companies or by any other indirect means, to control 20 per cent. or over of the ordinary share capital of the company.

A person is for this purpose to be treated as owning or, as the case may be, controlling what any associate owns or controls, even if he does not own or control share capital of his own.[15]

> Thus if X has no shares in Y Ltd., but X's relatives or other associates together directly or indirectly control 20 per cent. or more of the ordinary share capital of Y Ltd., X is for the purposes of the close company provisions treated as a director of Y Ltd. if he is concerned in its management although not a member of the Board of Directors.

2. WHAT IS A CLOSE COMPANY?

15–07   There are two main tests for determining what is a close company. These may be called the "control" test (see §§ 15–08 *et seq.*) and the "apportionment" test (see §§ 15–12 *et seq.*). There are also a number of cases in which companies which would otherwise be treated as close companies as satisfying one or other of these tests are excepted and so made "non-close" or "open" companies (see §§ 15–14 *et seq.*).

---

12. (1972) 48 T.C. 547 (C.A.).
13. I.C.T.A. 1970, s.303(4).
14. *Ibid.* s.303(5).
15. *Ibid.* s.303(7).

1. *The control test*

15–08   Section 282(1) of the Income and Corporation Taxes Act 1970 provides that a close company is one which is under the control of (i) five or fewer participators or (ii) of participators (however many) who are directors. The terms "participator" is defined in § 15–02 and "director" in § 15–06.

If there is any group of five or fewer participators who together have "control" in any sense in which that term is defined (see § 15–10), the company is a close company. The following examples illustrate the principle:

> *Example 1*
> A Ltd. has an issued capital of £90 in £1 shares, all carrying equal voting rights. There are nine members with 10 shares each; no member is an "associate" of any other: see § 15–04. Any group of five members would have 50 shares between them, *i.e.* voting control. A Ltd. is therefore a "close" company.

> *Example 2*
> B Ltd. has an issued capital of £90 in £1 shares, all carrying equal voting rights. There are 18 members with five shares each, all disassociated as in Example 1. No group of five members would have more than 25 shares. B Ltd. is therefore an "open" company.

If in Example 2 the shares had unequal voting rights and it was possible to find any group of five or fewer participators who between them had voting control, the company would be a close company.

Attributions

15–09   It is assumed in Example 2 that the 18 members (*i.e.* participators: § 15–02) are "disassociated," *i.e.* that no one is the "associate" of any other in the sense in which the term "associate" is defined in § 15–04. In applying the control test in § 15–10 there can be attributed[16] to any person any rights or powers of—

> (a) a nominee to him, *i.e.* which another person possesses on his behalf or may be required to exercise on his direction or behalf;
> (b) any company (or companies) of which he has control or of which he and associates of his have control; and
> (c) any associate or associates of his.

Such attributions are to be made as will result in the company being treated as under the control of five or fewer participators if it can be so treated.

The meaning of "associate" is in § 15–04 and includes, *e.g.* a relative of a participator; and relative includes child or remoter issue, or brother or sister; but not *e.g.* a brother's child. Section 302(6) provides that there cannot be attributed to a person the rights and powers attributed to an associate: thus if A has a brother (B) who has a child (C), the rights of B can be attributed to A and the rights of C to B; but the rights of C cannot for that reason be attributed to A.

---

16. *Ibid*. s.303(5)(6).

The following example shows how the rules regarding attributions are applied:

> Assume that, in Example 2, the 18 members include X_1 (with five shares) and four children of X_1 (X_2, X_3, X_4 and X_5) with five shares each. X_1 can be treated as owning $5+20 = 25$ shares, 20 being attributed to X_1. Similarly, X_2 can be treated as owning 25 shares, X_1's shares being attributed to X_2, and so on. Thus A Ltd. can be treated as controlled by any two members of the group comprising X_1 and his children.

These provisions prevent a person with control of a close company making the company "open" by off-loading shares to relatives or (generally) by settling them otherwise than in connection with certain approved superannuation funds and retirement schemes and on certain employee-trusts set out in a proviso to section 303(3) of the Taxes Act 1970.

The meaning of control

15–10   In the Examples in §§ 15–08 and 15–09, it has been assumed that "control" means voting control; but the statute treats as having control not only a person (or group of persons) who have the lion's share of the votes; it also brings in a person (or group of persons) who together have the lion's share of the income or would, in the event of a liquidation, have the lion's share of the assets available for distribution. More precisely, section 302(2) provides that a person shall be taken to have control of a company if he (including any rights, etc. attributed to him under the provisions in § 15–09) exercises, or is able to exercise or is entitled to acquire (see § 15–11), control, whether direct or indirect, over the company's affairs, and in particular, but without prejudice to the generality of the preceding words, if he possesses or is entitled to acquire:

    (a) the greater part of the share capital or issued share capital of the company or of the voting power in the company; or

    (b) such part of the issued share capital of the company as would, if the whole of the income of the company were in fact distributed among the participators (without regard to any rights which he or any other person has as a loan creditor), entitle him to receive the greater part of the amount so distributed; or

    (c) such rights as would, in the event of the winding up of the company or in any other circumstances, entitle him to receive the greater part of the assets of the company which would then be available for distribution among the participators.

15–11   Section 302(3) provides that where two or more persons together satisfy any of the conditions of section 302(2), they shall be taken to have control of the company. Section 302(4) provides that a person shall be treated as entitled to acquire something which he is entitled to acquire at a future date, or *will* at a future date be entitled to acquire (but not if he only *may* be so entitled).

> Thus, if C Ltd. has 11 shareholders, all disassociated and with shares carrying equal voting rights, C Ltd. is an open company if no group of five has voting

control or any other rights which confer control. But if D (an individual) has an option to acquire sufficient shares to confer "control," the company can be treated as controlled by D.

The definition of "control" is such that more than one person or group of persons can control the same company at the same time; and one person or group may have one type of control whereas another person or group may have a different type of control. Thus if a company has in issue (i) 100 £1 ordinary shares carrying one vote each and (ii) 200 £1 non-voting 10 per cent. preference shares and (iii) 10 £1 participating preference shares carrying one vote each and the right to 60 per cent. of the profits available for distribution by way of dividend in priority to the ordinary shares, the non-voting preference shares in (ii) have control because they possess the greater part of the share capital; the ordinary shares in (i) have control because they have the greater part of the voting power; and the participating preference shares in (iii) have control within paragraph (b) of § 15–10. A company is a close company if there can be found *any* five or fewer participators who, with their associates, have control in *any* sense: see the example in § 15–09.

2. *The apportionment test*

5–12   Section 282(2) of the Income and Corporation Taxes Act 1970 provides an additional test which, if satisfied in relation to a company, makes the company a close company. We shall see in §§ 15–28 *et seq.* that, in certain circumstances where a close company fails to distribute a sufficient part of its income, a statutory apportionment of that income can be made under Schedule 16 to the Finance Act 1972, as amended by the Finance Act 1980. The persons to whom the income is so apportioned are then taxed (in effect) as if a dividend of an amount computed as provided in the Act had been paid. Section 282(2) of the Income and Corporation Taxes Act 1970 provides that if, on the assumption that it is a close company or on the assumption that it and any other such company or companies are so, more than half of any amount falling to be apportioned under Schedule 16 (including any sum which has been apportioned to it, or could on either of those assumptions be apportioned to it, under that Schedule) could be apportioned among five or fewer participators, or among participators who are directors, the company shall be treated as a close company. This test is especially important in relation to the exemption discussed in § 15–16 and § 15–17, where an example of its operation is given.

15–13   Section 282(2) provides that in ascertaining under that subsection whether any amount could be apportioned among five or fewer participators or among participators who are directors, account shall, in cases where an original apportionment and any sub-apportionment are involved, be taken only of persons among whom that amount could be finally apportioned as the result of the whole process of original apportionment and sub-apportionment; and those persons shall be treated as participators or directors if they are participators or directors of any company in the case of which either an original apportionment or any sub-apportionment could be made. This is an example of a provision such as is referred to in the last sentence in § 15–02 where a participator in one company can be treated as being also a participator in another company.

Companies which are not Close Companies

(1) Non-resident companies

15–14   The expression "close company" does not include a company which is not resident in the United Kingdom.[17] A company is treated as resident in the country or countries from which it is centrally managed and controlled.[18] Lest it be supposed that a company can easily escape the restrictions imposed on close companies by changing its residence from the United Kingdom to some other country, reference should be made to section 482 of the Income and Corporation Taxes Act 1970, which makes it unlawful for a company resident in the United Kingdom to cease to be so resident or to transfer the whole or part of its trade or business to a non-resident person, without obtaining Treasury consent.[19]

(2) Quoted companies

15–15   A company is not to be treated as being at any time a close company if shares in the company carrying not less than 35 per cent. of the voting power in the company (and not being shares entitled to a fixed rate of dividend, whether with or without a further right to participate in profits) have been allotted unconditionally to, or acquired unconditionally by, *and* are at that time beneficially held by, the public, *and* any such shares have within the preceding 12 months been the subject of dealings on a recognised stock exchange, *and* the shares have within those 12 months been quoted in the official list of a recognised stock exchange.[20] The Finance Act 1965 contained no definition of the expression "public"; except that it stated the circumstances in which shares would *not* be treated as held by the public. The absence of any definition of "public" in the Act of 1965 gave rise to many difficulties and the Finance Act 1967 defined the circumstances in which shares should be deemed to be held by the public. The relevant provisions (now in s.283 of the Income and Corporation Taxes Act 1970) are of some complexity and cannot be summarised in an intelligible form. Briefly, shares held by a director or his associate, or by a company controlled by a director or his associate, or by an associated company[21] of the company, or by trustees of a fund held for the benefit of such persons are treated as *not* held by the public; and not more than 85 per cent. of the voting power must

---

17. I.C.T.A. 1970, s.282(1)(*a*).
18. See *ante*, § 7–22.
19. See *ante*, § 7–22.
20. I.C.T.A. 1970, s.283. "Share" includes "stock." "Recognised stock exchange" has the same meaning, as in the Prevention of Fraud (Investments) Act 1958, except that it includes the Belfast Stock Exchange and other exchanges outside the U.K. designated by order of the Board: I.C.T.A. 1970, s.535.
21. *Ibid*. s.302(1).

be held by "principal members," *i.e.* persons with more than 5 per cent. of the voting power in the company.

(3) *Subsidiaries of non-close companies*

15–16   Section 282(4) of the Income and Corporation Taxes Act 1970 provides as follows:

> (4) A company is not to be treated as a close company—
>> (*a*) if—
>>> (i) it is controlled by a company which is not a close company, or by two or more companies none of which is a close company; and
>>> (ii) it cannot be treated as a close company except by taking as one of the five of fewer participators requisite for its being so treated a company which is not a close company;
>> (*b*) if it cannot be treated as a close company except by virtue of paragraph (*c*) of section 302(2) of this Act and it would not be a close company if the reference in that paragraph to participators did not include loan creditors who are companies other than close companies.

If sub-paragraph (i) stood alone, it could be said that a company which is controlled by an open company, or by two or more companies none of which is close, is an open company. Thus if two individuals owned 50 per cent. each of the issued share capital of X Ltd. (which would clearly then be a close company), X Ltd. would cease to be a close company if the individuals granted an option to an open company enabling that company to acquire their shares at a future date. X Ltd. would cease to be close on the granting of the option because the open company would be a participator with control within paragraph (a) in § 15–02. However, sub-paragraph (ii) provides (in effect) that where the participators in a company include an open company or companies and others, the rule is that if you can find five or fewer participators who between them have control *without* including the open company among them, the company is a close company; conversely, if it is necessary to include an open company among the five or fewer participators requisite for close status, the company is not a close company. In the Example, X Ltd. could be treated as controlled by the two individuals *or* as controlled by the open company: therefore, X Ltd. is treated as a close company.

15–17   In applying sub-paragraph (ii), the expanded definition of participator in section 282(2)—see § 15–12 (the apportionment test)—must not be overlooked. Under this test, the participators in one company can be treated as participators in another.

> *Example*
> A Limited has 11 shareholders (including X, Y and Z) with nine shares each, all with equal voting and other rights, and none of whom is the associate of any other. Thus A Ltd. is an open company because no group of five members has control. B Ltd. has an issued capital of 100 shares of £1 each. A Ltd. subscribes for 55 shares in B Ltd. The remaining 45 shares in B Ltd. are held as to 15 shares each by X, Y and Z.

At first sight, B Ltd. would appear to be an open company because it is controlled by an open company, A Ltd., which cannot be excluded in applying the control test to B Ltd. But the apportionment test in § 15–12 demands an enquiry as to whom income of B Ltd. would be apportioned if both A Ltd. and B Ltd. were close companies, and on this hypothesis 45 per cent. of the income would be apportioned to X, Y and Z as members of B Ltd. and 3/11ths of 55 per cent. (15 per cent.) would be apportioned to X, Y and Z as members of A Ltd. Hence X, Y and Z can be treated as participators in both A Ltd. and B Ltd., who together are entitled to more than half the distributable income of B Ltd.: see § 15–13. B Ltd. is therefore a close company.

Section 282(4)(*b*) prevents an otherwise open company becoming a close company merely through taking a substantial loan from a close company giving the lender "loan creditor control": see § 15–03A.

15–18   The subsidiary, resident in the United Kingdom, of a foreign company will be an open company if either the subsidiary company or its foreign parent company satisfy the conditions of exemption referred to in § 15–15 (quoted companies). In this connection it should be noted that foreign stock exchanges are not recognised stock exchanges for the purposes of the relevant provisions, unless a double taxation agreement so provides[22]; so the wholly-owned United Kingdom resident subsidiaries of foreign quoted companies are not necessarily non-close companies. References in section 282(4) to a close company (see § 15–16) are to a company which, if resident in the United Kingdom, would be a close company.[23] Hence the United Kingdom subsidiary of a non-resident parent company under the control of five or fewer participators and not quoted is a close company.

(4) *Crown-controlled companies*

15–19   A company controlled by or on behalf of the Crown, and not otherwise a close company, is not a close company.[24] A company is to be treated as controlled by or on behalf of the Crown if, but only if, it is under the control of the Crown or of persons acting on behalf of the Crown, independently of any other person; and where a company is so controlled, it shall not be treated as being otherwise a close company, unless it can be treated as a close company as being under the control of persons acting independently of the Crown.[25]

(5) *Certain societies*

15–20   The expression "close company" does not apply to a registered industrial and provident society (as defined) or to certain building societies.[26]

---

22. See Double Taxation Relief (Taxes on Income) (France) Order 1968 (S.I. 1968 No. 1869), art. 25(5).
23. I.C.T.A. 1970, s.282(5).
24. *Ibid.* s.282(1)(*c*).
25. *Ibid.* s.282(3).
26. See *Ibid.* s.282(1)(*b*).

(6) *Non-resident participators*

–20A   When a close company, 90 per cent. or more of the ordinary share capital of which is beneficially owned by non-residents, wishes to retain its surplus funds in the United Kingdom, a request that the company should not be liable to apportionment of its income will be favourably considered.[27]

3. EXTENDED MEANING OF DISTRIBUTION[28]

The term "distribution" has an extended meaning in the case of close companies. The tax consequences of a distribution have already been considered: see § 14–50 (advance corporation tax) and § 14–59 (Schedule F income tax).

Accommodation and other benefits or facilities for participators and associates

-21[28a]   If a close company incurs expense in or in connection with the provision for any participator (see § 15–02) of living or other accommodation, of entertainment, of domestic or other services, or of other benefits or facilities of whatever nature, the company is treated as making a distribution to him of an amount equal to so much of that expense as is not made good to the company by the participator.[29] The amount of the expense to be taken into account as a distribution is the same as would, under the Finance Act 1976, be the cash equivalent of the resultant benefit to the participator.[30] The tax charge on distributions will be avoided if the expense is "made good" at any time before the relevant assessment becomes final. There are exceptions from the tax charge in the case of such benefits (taxable under Schedule E) as are mentioned in any of sections 61–68 of the Finance Act 1976 (*i.e.* where the participator is in director's or higher-paid employment: see § 3–40, including the provision of living accommodation), and in the case of expenses incurred in providing death or retirement benefits for the spouse, children or dependants of a person employed by the company.[31–32] References to a participator in this paragraph include an associate (see § 15–04) of a participator; and any participator in a company which controls another company is treated as a participator in that other company.[33]

There are anti-avoidance provisions to counter reciprocal arrangements by which two close companies provide benefits or facilities for participators in the other.[34] There is no "distribution" if the company and the participator are both resident in the United Kingdom and one is the subsidiary of the other or both are subsidiaries of a third company, also so resident, and

---

27. See Concession B22 in (1978) S.T.I. 456.
28. The meaning of the term "distribution" is discussed *ante*, §§ 14–40 *et seq.* The provisions there discussed apply to close as well as to non-close companies.
28a. The next paragraph is § 15–24.
29. I.C.T.A. 1970, s.284(1)(*c*), (2).
30. *Ibid.* s.284(3), as substituted by F.A. 1976, Sched. 9, para. 16, in and from 1977–78.
31.–32. *Ibid.* s.284(2), proviso.
33. *Ibid.* s.284(7). "Control" is defined in § 15–10.
34. *Ibid.* s.284(6).

the benefit to the participator arises on or in connection with a transfer of assets or liabilities of the company to him, or to the company by him.[35]

Disallowed directors' remuneration

15–24   When directors' remuneration is disallowed for corporation tax purposes the disallowance will not rank as a distribution. When such a disallowance has been negotiated with the Inspector of Taxes, the Schedule E liability of the director will be reduced by the amount of that disallowance, provided that the amount disallowed is formally waived and refunded to the company by the director, and a satisfactory settlement of the amount to be apportioned (if any), under Schedule 16 to the Finance Act 1972, for that accounting period is reached.[37–42]

4. LOANS TO PARTICIPATORS AND THEIR ASSOCIATES

15–25   Section 286 of the Income and Corporation Taxes Act 1970 provides that where any loan or advance of money is made by a close company to an individual[43] who is a participator[44] in the company or an associate[45] of a participator, there shall be assessed on and recoverable from the company, as if it were an amount of corporation tax for the accounting period in which the loan or advance is made, an amount equal to such proportion of the amount of the loan or advance as corresponds to the rate of advance corporation tax in force for the financial year in which the loan or advance is made.[46]

> Thus if a close company makes a loan of £7,100 to a participator in the financial year 1986, it must pay to the Revenue an amount equal to $\frac{29}{71}$ths of £7,100 = £2,900.

The section does not apply to a loan or advance made by a close company in the ordinary course of a business which includes the lending of money; nor does it apply to a loan to a director or employee of a close company (or its associated company[47]) if the amount of the loan including outstanding loans made by such close company (or associated companies[47]) to the borrower (or his husband or wife) does not exceed £15,000, provided the borrower works full-time for the close company or any of its associated companies[47] and does not have a material interest[48] in the close company or in any associated company.[49] Section 286 does not apply where the loan

---

35. *Ibid.* s.284(4) and (5), defining "subsidiary."

36–42. Inland Revenue Press Statement [1973] S.T.I. 56; and see §§ 15–28 *et seq.*

43. References to an individual include a company receiving the loan or advance in a fiduciary or representative capacity, and to a company non-resident in the U.K.: I.C.T.A. 1970, s.286(8). Loans to individuals who are trustees are also included: *ibid.* s.287(2), (4).

44. "Participator" is defined in § 15–02. For the purposes of s.286, a parent company is treated as a participator in its sub-subsidiary company: see *ibid.* s.286(9).

45. Defined *ante*, § 15–04.

46. I.C.T.A. 1970 s.286(1).

47. "Associated company" is defined in I.C.T.A. 1970, s.302(1).

48. "Material interest" is defined in I.C.T.A. 1970, s.285(6) as applied by s.286(9): see *ante*, § 15–22.

49. *Ibid.* s.286(3).

or advance is made by a company which is not a close company, but section 287A (inserted by s.44 of the Finance Act 1976) extends it to certain loans made by companies which are or come under the control of close companies. Thus if company S (resident outside the United Kingdom and not close) is controlled by company P (a close company), a loan made by S to a participator in P is treated as made by P.

5–26   It should be noted that the Act does not expressly provide that the loan or advance shall be treated as a dividend or other distribution made by the company: the tax assessed on the company is to be treated "as if it were an amount of corporation tax." Hence the tax paid by the company may not be credited against the company's liability for corporation tax. There are provisions to prevent avoidance of the section by the company channelling a loan to a participator through a non-participator.[50] Where the whole or part of the purchase price is left unpaid on a sale to a company, this is not a "loan" or "advance" by the vendor,[51] but when a person incurs a debt to a company, *e.g.* on a sale of property *by* the company, this is treated as a loan by the company to the extent of the debt, except where the debt is incurred for the supply of goods or services in the ordinary course of the company's business and the credit does not exceed six months or that normally given to the company's customers.[52] A company is treated as making a loan to a person if, for example, the person borrows from a bank which assigns the debt to the company.[53]

Tax is assessable under Section 286 whether or not the whole or any part of the loan or advance has been repaid at the time of the assessment and, subject to any appeal, is due within 14 days after the issue of the notice of assessment.[54] If a close company makes a loan or advance which gives rise to a charge to tax and the loan or advance (or any part of it) is repaid to the company, relief is given by discharge or repayment. A claim for relief must be made within six years from the end of the financial year in which the repayment is made.[54]

15–27   The loan or advance is not treated as income of the borrower at the time it is made; but if the company releases or writes off the whole or part of the debt, the borrower is treated for purposes of computing his total income as having then received income equal to the grossed up equivalent of the amount so released or written off. No repayment of income tax will be made in respect of that income and no assessment will be made on him to basic rate income tax on that income.[55] If the loan or advance was made to a person who has since died or to trustees of a trust which has come to an end, the Act applies to the person from whom the debt is due at the time of

50. *Ibid.* s.286(7).
51. *Cf. Ramsden* v. *I.R.C.* (1957) 37 T.C. 619.
52. I.C.T.A. 1970, s.286(2).
53. *Ibid.* s.286(2).
54. *Ibid.* s.286(4) and (5), as amended by F.A. 1986, s.43 in relation to loans made (or repaid) after March 18, 1986. And see T.M.A. 1970, s.109. For I.R. explanatory Press Release, see (1986) S.T.I. 186.
55. *Ibid.* s.287(1).

release or writing off.[56] Loans taxable under section 451 (see § 10–43) are excepted from the operation of section 286.[57]

5. THE STATUTORY APPORTIONMENT OF INCOME

15–28   A company that exists mainly to hold investments pays corporation tax on its income at the corporation tax rate (35% for the financial year 1986) or the small companies rate (29% for that year, with tapering provisions if the profits exceed £100,000). If tax law did not include special provisions to deal with the situation, there would be an inducement for wealthy individuals to put their investments into close companies under their control, to avoid declaring dividends (which, if declared, would be subject to higher rates of tax) and to allow the investment income to accumulate in the company subject only to the comparatively low rates of tax applicable to companies.

Hence there are statutory provisions in Schedule 16 to the Finance Act 1972 which counteract the avoidance of higher rate tax by the accumulation of investment income, where this cannot be justified by reference to the needs of the company's business activities. Where these provisions apply, the company's income is "apportioned" among the participators so that the company is, in effect, treated as if the profits had been distributed way of dividend.

The power to apportion no longer exists in relation to the trading income of a trading company or of a company which is a member of a trading group. It applies to income (of whatever kind) of companies which are neither trading companies nor members of trading groups and to the investment income of trading companies. The only trading companies to which the rules apply are those with so much estate or investment income (or both) that they fall outside the statutory definition of "trading company" in § 15–38.

A number of terms used in the Schedule and printed in italics in the following paragraphs are defined in § 15–37 *et seq*. The definitions in § 15–02 *et seq*. also apply by virtue of s.94(3) of the Finance Act 1972.

The power to apportion

15–29   Paragraph 1(1) of Schedule 16 provides that the income of a close company for any accounting period may be apportioned by the inspector among the *participators*.[58–61] It is generally thought that the power exists only in the case of a company which is a close company at the end of the accounting period to which the apportionment relates[62] and that no apportionment can be made if a company ceases to be a close company before the end of the accounting period, *e.g.* by a non-close company acquiring control.[62a] As a general rule no such apportionment may be

---

56. I.C.T.A. 1970, s.287(2).
57. *Ibid*. s.287(3).
58–61. Defined *ante*, § 15–02.
62. *Cf. C. H. W. (Huddersfield) Ltd.* v. *I.R.C.* (1961) 41 T.C. 92.
62a. But the possible impact of I.C.T.A. 1970, s.460 should be considered: see §§ 40–02 *et seq*.

made unless the *relevant income* of the company for the accounting period exceeds its *distributions* for the period; and the amount to be apportioned is the amount of the excess.[63] Where the excess is not more than £1,000 no apportionment is made if the company is a *trading company* or *a member of a trading group*.[64] This enables such companies to have some investment income without taking a statutory apportionment. An amount which is apportioned to a close company may be sub-apportioned through that company to its participators.[65]

The general rule stated in the preceding paragraph is subject to two exceptions:

15–30   First, in the case of a company which is not a trading company (*e.g.* an investment company), the inspector can if he sees reason for it apportion the whole of the relevant income for an accounting period, whether or not there is an excess of relevant income over distributions for the period (*i.e.* even if the company has distributed the whole of its relevant income) and whether or not the excess is more than £1,000.[66]

15–31   Secondly, if a company has made annual payments which were deducted in arriving at its distributable income (*e.g.* as charges on income) and which, in the case of an individual, would not have been deductible or would (apart from section 457(1A) of the Income and Corporation Taxes Act 1970[67]) have been treated as his income in computing his total income, the amount so deducted by the company may be apportioned.[68] It has been explained in § 10–13 that an individual is generally unable to avoid higher rate income tax by making an income settlement in favour of a charity. This second exception (for example) prevents such an individual who is a participator in a close company from securing tax relief (beyond the permitted £5,000: see § 10–16A) indirectly by getting the company to make the settlement for him. The provision does not apply to annual payments which consist of interest or are made wholly and exclusively for the purposes of the company's trade.[68]

15–32   Paragraph 3A of Schedule 16 allows interest paid by an investment company to be apportioned in certain circumstances. The object of this paragraph is to prevent an individual or individuals avoiding the provisions which restrict interest relief (see §§ 8–57 *et seq.*) by channelling their borrowing through a company.

---

63. F.A. 1972, Sched. 16, para. 1(2). Certain payments which would not otherwise be treated as distributions, or are exempt distributions, are nevertheless treated as distributions for shortfall purposes, *e.g.* payments made by a company in redeeming or purchasing its own shares (*ante*, § 14–76) or under the demerger provisions (*post*, § 40–33): F.A. 1982, s.56.

64. *Ibid*. Sched. 16, para. 1(3).

65. *Ibid*. Sched. 16, para. 1(4).

66. *Ibid*. Sched. 16, para. 2.

67. The words in parenthesis were added by the F.A. 1980, s.56(4).

68. F.A. 1972, Sched. 16, para. 3. For charges on income, see §§ 14–08 *et seq*. The word "may" indicates that the power to apportion is discretionary. See *R*. v. *Inspector of Taxes and Others, ex p. Lansing Bagnall Ltd.* (1986) S.T.C. 117, where the Inspector supposed the power to be mandatory and notices issued by the inspector were quashed on an application for judicial review. This decision was upheld on appeal: [1986] S.T.I. 562.

Manner of apportionment

15–33   An apportionment (or sub-apportionment) is made according to the respective interests in the company in question of the participators.[69] An inspector who proposes to make an apportionment must serve a notice on the company showing the amount to be apportioned and a further notice showing how the amount is apportioned to each participator or, if the inspector thinks fit, to each class of share; and the manner of apportionment may be reviewed on appeal.[70] The inspector may, if it seems proper to him to do so, attribute to each participator an interest corresponding to his interest in the assets of the company available for distribution among the participators in the event of a winding up or in any other circumstances[71]; and in the case of a non-trading company, the inspector may if it seems proper to him to do so treat a *loan creditor* as having an interest to the extent to which the income to be apportioned, or assets representing it, has or have been expended or applied, or is or are available to be expended or applied, in redemption, repayment or discharge of the loan capital or debt (including any premium thereon) in respect of which he is a loan creditor.[72]

Consequences of apportionment: income tax

15–34   The sum apportioned to an individual (whether by original apportionment or by sub-apportionment) is treated as income of the individual received by him at the end of the accounting period to which the apportionment relates and must therefore be included in the computation of his total income. The apportioned amount is deemed to be the highest part of his total income and is therefore liable to bear tax at the highest rate applicable to the individual. The recipient cannot be assessed to basic rate income tax on the amount apportioned (because liability to this extent is treated as satisfied); but a recipient who is not liable to tax at the basic rate can make no claim for repayment of tax. The sum apportioned is treated for the purposes of sections 52 and 53 of the Taxes Act as income not brought into charge to income tax.[73] A sum apportioned to trustees may attract the additional rate of tax on trust income.[74]

No individual is to be assessed by virtue of an apportionment[74] unless the sum on which he is assessable amounts at least to £1,000 or 5 per cent. of the amount apportioned, whichever is the less.[75]

Where income which has been apportioned to an individual and income is actually distributed to him, there are provisions for excluding from charge the amount already taxed.[76]

---

69. *Ibid.* Sched. 16, para. 4(1). "Participator" is defined in § 15–02.
70. *Ibid.* Sched. 16, paras. 15 and 16.
71. *Ibid.* Sched. 16, para. 4(2).
72. *Ibid.* Sched. 16, para. 4(3).
73. *Ibid.* Sched. 16, para. 5(1)(2).
74. See *ante*, § 9–05.
75. F.A. 1972, Sched. 16, para. 5(4), amended by F.A. 1984, s.32 for accounting period ending on or after April 5, 1984. The amount was previously £200.
76. *Ibid.* Sched. 16, para. 5(5)(8).

The Board are normally prepared to regard a non-resident whose dividend income from United Kingdom companies is effectively relieved from higher-rate tax under a Double Taxation Agreement as exempted from the United Kingdom income tax charge on any close company income apportioned to him.[77]

Payment and collection of income tax

5–35   Income tax chargeable in respect of a sum apportioned to a participator is assessed in the first place on the participator. If the tax so assessed is not paid within 30 days from the date on which the assessment became final and conclusive, or by July 6, in the year next following the year of assessment, whichever is the later, a notice of liability to tax may be served on the company and the tax thereupon is payable by the company on the service of the notice. Where such a notice of liability is served on the company, any interest due on the tax assessed on the participator and not paid by him, and any interest accruing due on that tax after the date of service, is payable by the company. If the company then fails to pay the tax and any interest payable before the expiry of three months from the date of service of the notice, the tax and any interest may, without prejudice to the right to recovery from the company, be recovered from the participator.[78]

Consequences of apportionment: advance corporation tax

15–36   Where a statutory apportionment is made for an accounting period, there are provisions which are designed to put the company into substantially the same position as respects advance corporation tax *as if* a dividend equal to the amount apportioned had been paid at the end of the accounting period. These provisions have to allow for the fact that an apportionment is usually made long after the company's corporation tax liability for the period has been settled, and they are designed, *inter alia*, to avoid unnecessary repayment claims.

It will be recalled that when an *actual* dividend is paid, the company is liable to pay advance corporation tax to the Revenue save to the extent that the company's franked investment income equals or exceeds the sum of the dividend and the advance corporation tax attributable thereto (see §§ 14–63 and 14–64). Any advance corporation tax which is payable can be set off against the company's liability to corporation tax (see § 14–51).

One consequence of an apportionment is that the advance corporation tax attributable to the "notional" dividend is set off against what remains of any surplus franked investment income at the time when the apportionment becomes final and conclusive. This cancels the tax advantage which otherwise would arise to the company through withholding income from distribution and thereby "increasing" surplus franked investment income.[79]

---

77. See Concession B22 in (1978) S.T.I. 456.
78. F.A. 1972, Sched. 16, para. 6.
79. *Ibid.* Sched. 16, para. 7. For details of this complex provision, see Bramwell's *Taxation of Companies*, §§ 12–22 *et seq.*

Definitions

15–37   It was explained in § 15–29 that no apportionment can be made unless the relevant income of the company for the accounting period exceeds its distributions for the period; and that subject to the provisions summarised in §§ 15–31 to 15–33, the amount apportioned is the amount of that excess. For these purposes and for the purposes of provisions discussed later, the following expressions are used.

15–38   "*Trading company*"[80] means any company which exists wholly or mainly for the purpose of carrying on a trade, and any other company whose income does not consist wholly or mainly of investment income, that is to say, income which, if the company were an individual, would not be earned income (see § 8–07). An amount which is apportioned to a company is deemed to be income of the company and to be investment income.

15–39   A company is treated as *a member of a trading group*[81]

(a) if it exists wholly or mainly for the purpose of co-ordinating the administration of a group of two or more companies each of which is under its control and exists wholly or mainly for the purpose of carrying on a trade. The parent company of a group of trading companies may fulfil such a co-ordinating function in which case, although its income may consist substantially if not wholly of dividend income, it will be treated (in effect) as a trading company and not as an investment company; or

(b) if it exists wholly or mainly for the purpose of a trade or trades carried on by a company resident in the United Kingdom which controls it (and is not itself controlled by a third company). A company which carries on research work which is ancillary to the activities of a group of trading companies may fulfil this function.

15–40   The *distributable income*[82] of a company for an accounting period is the amount of its distributable profits (see § 15–41) for the period exclusive of the part attributable to chargeable gains.

15–41   The *distributable profits*[82] of a company for an accounting period is the aggregate of the following amounts:

(a) the amount of any profits on which corporation tax falls finally to be borne (as defined), less the amount of that tax;

(b) an amount equal to the qualifying distributions comprised in any franked investment income, other than franked investment income against which relief is given under section 254 or 255 of the Taxes Act (see §§ 14–68 and 14–70); and

(c) an amount equal to any group income (see § 14–72).

---

80. *Ibid*. Sched. 16, para. 11(1).
81. *Ibid*. Sched. 16, para. 11(2).
82. *Ibid*. Sched. 16, para. 10(2); and see para. 10(7).

15–42   The *distributable investment income*[83] of a company for an accounting period is the amount of the distributable income, exclusive of the part attributable to estate or trading income (see below), less whichever is the smaller of:

> (a) 10 per cent. of the estate or trading income; and
> (b) £1,000 (or £3,000 in the case of a trading company) or, if the accounting period is of less than 12 months, a proportionately reduced amount.

15–43   The *estate or trading income*[84] of a company means income which falls within the following:

> (a) *estate income* is income which is chargeable to tax under Schedule A or Schedule B and income (other than yearly or other interest) which is chargeable to tax under Schedule D and which arises from the ownership or occupation of land (including any interest in or right over land) or from the letting furnished of any building or part of a building; and
> (b) *trading income* is income which is not investment income (see 15–43A); and it includes the income incidental to the trade of a company the activities of which consist wholly or mainly of the carrying on of a trade or life assurance business, insurance business of any other class, banking, moneylending, financing or hire-purchase or similar transactions, or dealing in securities. Thus income derived from investments of such companies may be trading income.[85]

5–43A   *Investment income* means income which, if the company were an individual, would not be earned income: see § 8–07.

15–44   There is an order of set-off of charges on income, expenses of management and other amounts which can be deducted from or set against or treated as reducing profits of more than one description for the purpose of quantifying the amount of each class of a company's income.[86]

The computation of "relevant income"

15–45   (1) *Trading companies and members of trading groups.* Relevant income in the case of a trading company (see § 15–38) or a member of a trading group (see § 15–39) means so much of the company's distributable income (§ 15–40) *other than trading income* for the accounting period as can be distributed without prejudice to the requirements of the company's busi-

---

83. *Ibid.* Sched. 16, para. 10(3). The figure of £3,000 in (b) was increased from £1,000 for accounting periods after March 26, 1980: F.A. 1980, s.44(2).
84. F.A. 1972, Sched. 16, para. 10(4) and 10(4A).
85. *Ibid.* Sched. 16, para. 10(5) and (6).
86. *Ibid.* Sched. 16, para. 10(8), (9).

ness; and for the purpose of arriving at the relevant income, regard is to be had not only to the current requirements of the business but also to such other requirements as may be necessary or advisable for the maintenance and development of *that* business.[87]

15–46   The proposition in § 15–45 is subject to the qualification[88] that, in certain circumstances, income has to be treated as available for distribution and not as having been applied, or as being applicable, to the requirements of the company's business, etc. These provisions are especially important as regards debts incurred by a company for the purpose of acquiring the business, undertaking or property which the company was formed to acquire or which was the first business, undertaking or property of a substantial character in fact acquired by the company. Sums applied out of income[89] in discharging such debts (called "first business loans") will be subject to the apportionment provisions, irrespective of the company's trading requirements.

> Thus if A Limited is formed to acquire A's business in consideration for an issue of redeemable preference shares or loan stock, sums applied out of income in redeeming the shares or repaying the stock will be apportioned irrespective of the trading requirements of A Limited.

15–46A   By amendments made in the Finance Act 1978,[90] regard may be had, for the purpose of arriving at the relevant income of an accounting period, not only to the requirements referred to in § 15–45 but also to any other requirements necessary or advisable for the acquisition of a trade or of a controlling interest (as defined) in a trading company or in a company which is a member of a trading group, including a requirement to repay any debts or meet any other obligations in connection with the acquisition. Hence, if A and B, who carry on a trade in partnership, transfer their trade to a newly formed company in exchange for loan stock, sums applied out of income in discharging the debt to A and B are not now treated as relevant income available for distribution, even if they are "first business loans."[91] This is subject to the qualification that, under the new provisions, regard may not be had to sums expended or applied where the expenditure or application would constitute a distribution by the company, *e.g.* if the acquisition is at an over-value from a participator. Nor may advantage be taken of these relaxed provisions where the purchaser is from, *e.g.* an associated company of the purchaser.

---

87. *Ibid.* Sched. 16, para. 8(1)(*a*) and para. 8(2) as amended to exclude trading income by F.A. 1980, Sched. 9, para. 1: see *ante*, § 15–28. For the Revenue's practice in applying these provisions to groups of companies, see Press Statement in [1973] S.T.I. 55. For a recent case on required standard, see *MacTaggart Scott & Co. Ltd.* v. *I.R.C.* (1973) 48 T.C. 708; [1973] S.T.C. 180 (Ct. of Sess.). For a recent case on the meaning of the words "that business," see *Wilson and Garden Ltd.* v. *I.R.C.* (1982) 56 T.C. 279; [1982] S.T.C. 597 (H.L.).
88. *Ibid.* Sched. 16, para. 12.
89. A sum is not applied out of income if it is an expense to be taken into account in determining income: *Hanstead Investments Ltd.* v. *I.R.C.* (1975) 50 T.C. 419; [1975] S.T.C. 419 (C.A.).
90. F.A. 1972, Sched. 16, para. 8(3)–(5), added by F.A. 1978, s.36 and Sched. 5.
91. *Ibid.* Sched. 16, para. 12, qualifies *ibid.* para. 8(2)(*a*) but *not* the new para. 8(3)–(5).

15–47   (2) *Non-trading companies having estate or trading income.* Where a company is not a trading company or a member of a trading group but its distributable income for an accounting period consists of or includes *estate or trading income* (see § 15–37) (*e.g.* in the case of a land-owning company, its income from rents), the *relevant income* means (i) so much of the estate or trading income as can be distributed without prejudice to the requirements of the company's business so far as concerned with the activities or assets giving rise to estate or trading income, and (ii) its distributable income, if any, other than estate or trading income.[92] There must be treated as available for distribution any sum expended or applied, or available to be expended or applied, out of the income, in or towards the acquisition of an estate or interest in land, or the construction or extension of a building (other than a construction or extension which constitutes an improvement or development of farm land or market garden land).[93]

15–48   (3) *Other companies.* In the case of any other company, *e.g.* a pure investment company, the relevant income for an accounting period is its distributable income for that period.[94] Interest paid by such a company which would not qualify for tax relief if paid by an individual may be apportioned as if it were income.[95]

> Thus no avoidance of income tax is achieved by forming a company to own stocks or shares, for the whole of the distributable income of such a company is apportioned, if it is not distributed.

Maximum amount to be taken as relevant income

15–49   Subject to special provisions applicable to cessations and liquidations (see § 15–53), the relevant income of a company must in no case be taken to exceed the company's distributable investment income (see § 15–42) for the accounting period plus 50 per cent. of the estate or trading income (see § 15–43) for the period.[96]

Special reduction for estate income of trading companies[97]

–50/51   The "relevant income" of a company will normally not exceed its distributable investment income for the accounting period plus 50 per cent. of the estate or trading income for the period. In the case of a trading company or a member of a trading group, the trading income is disregarded. In the case of a trading company, estate income is dealt with as follows. The *appropriate fraction* is $\times \dfrac{x}{x + y}$ where x is the amount of the estate income and y is the amount of the trading income. The *relevant maximum and minimum amounts* are £75,000 and £25,000 respectively where the com-

---

92. *Ibid.* Sched. 16, para. 8(1)(*b*) and para. 8(2).
93. *Ibid.* Sched. 16, para. 12(1)(*d*).
94. *Ibid.* Sched. 16, para. 8(1)(*c*).
95. *Ibid.* Sched. 16, para. 3A, added by Sched. 1, Pt. V to the F.A. 1974.
96. *Ibid.* Sched. 16, para. 9(1).
97. *Ibid.* Sched. 16, para 9(2)(6) as amended by F.A. 1980, Sched. 9, para. 9(2).

pany has no associated company in the accounting period (these figures being adjusted when there are one or more such companies). If the estate income is less than the appropriate fraction of the relevant minimum amount, it is disregarded. If it is less than the appropriate fraction of the relevant maximum amount, it is treated as reduced by half the amount required to make it up to that fraction of the relevant maximum amount.

Distributions for an accounting period[98]

15–52   Generally, no apportionment will be made unless the relevant income of the company for the accounting period exceeds its distributions for that period (see § 15–29). The distributions for an accounting period consist of:

(a) any dividends which are declared in respect of the period and are paid during the period or within a reasonable time thereafter; and
(b) all distribution made in the period except dividends declared in respect of an earlier period.

Where dividends are declared in respect of a period which straddles more than one accounting period, they must be apportioned between the accounting periods in proportion to the distributable income of each such period.

Cessations and liquidations[99]

15–53   Where a close company ceases to carry on the trade, or the business of holding investments, in which its activities wholly or mainly consisted, the relevant income of the company for any accounting period in which that event occurs, or which ends in or within the 12 months ending with that event, is calculated on the whole instead of on 50 per cent. of the estate income (if any) taken into account, and without any deduction in respect of the requirements of the business. The conception underlying this provision is that a company which has ceased to trade has no business requirements to justify the retention of income either in the accounting period with which the cessation occurs[1] or in the previous period. There is an exception where the company shows that distributions of the whole income could not be made without prejudice to the claims of creditors (certain creditors being excluded); in this case, a shortfall in distributions is disregarded to the extent necessary to satisfy the non-excluded creditors. Debts due to participators and their associates will be taken into account only if they are ordinary trading debts or debts for remuneration or rent at a commercial rate.

These provisions also apply where a resolution is passed or an order is made for the winding up of a close company.[2]

---

98. *Ibid.* Sched. 16, para. 10(1).
99. *Ibid.* Sched. 16, para. 13. The operation of this provision may be relaxed in cases of reorganisation carried out for commercial reasons: see [1973] S.T.I. 57.
1. An accounting period ends with the cessation of trade: I.C.T.A. 1970, s.247(3)(c).
2. See F.A. 1972, Sched. 16, para. 13. For capital gains tax, see *post*, § 16–31(v).

Legal restrictions on distributions[3]

15–54 Where a company is subject to any restriction imposed by law as regards the making of distributions, the excess of relevant income over distributions in the period is disregarded to the extent to which the company could not make distributions up to the amount of its relevant income without contravening that restriction. Restrictions contained in a company's articles are not "imposed by law."[4]

Clearances

15–55 There are provisions[5] under which a close company may, at any time after the general meeting at which the accounts for any period are adopted, forward a copy of the accounts to the inspector requesting him to intimate whether or not he proposes to make an apportionment. The inspector has three months from the date of the request in which to make his decision (unless he requires further particulars, when the three months' period runs from the receipt of the particulars). If the inspector does *not* intimate his intention to make an apportionment, he cannot do so unless material information has been withheld or there is a cessation or liquidation within 12 months from the end of the period, when he may reconsider the matter.

---

3. *Ibid*, Sched. 16, para. 14.
4. *Noble* v. *Laygate Investments Ltd.* (1978) 52 T.C. 345; [1978] S.T.C. 430; *Shearer* v. *Bercain Ltd.* (1980) 53 T.C. 698; [1980] S.T.C. 359.
5. F.A. 1972, Sched. 16, para. 18.

DIVISION C

THE TAXATION OF CAPITAL GAINS

CHAPTER 16

THE TAXATION OF CAPITAL GAINS

1. THE SCOPE OF THE CHARGE

16–01 Capital gains tax was introduced by the Finance Act 1965. It applies in and from the year 1965–66. The tax is levied on the total amount of *chargeable gains* which accrue to a person on the *disposal of assets* in a year of assessment (or accounting period, in the case of a company) after deducting *allowable losses*.[1] The expression "chargeable gain" means a gain which accrues after April 6, 1965, such gain being computed in accordance with provisions contained in the Capital Gains Tax Act 1979.[2] "Allowable losses" are computed in the same way.[3] The chargeable gain (or allowable loss) on the disposal of an asset is, roughly, the difference between the cost of the asset (plus any expenditure on improvements) and the consideration in money or money's worth for its disposal. Where an asset was acquired before April 1965 it has, in some cases, to be assumed that the asset was sold and re-acquired for its market value on April 6, 1965. The asset is then treated as if it cost this amount. On certain disposals on or after April 6, 1982 (or April 1, 1982, for disposals by companies) an indexation allowance is given in computing the chargeable gain: see § 16–30B. The purpose of the indexation allowance is to take out of charge to tax such part of the gain on the disposal of an asset as is attributable to inflation, as measured by rises in the index of retail prices.

The main provisions relating to capital gains tax are in the Capital Gains Tax Act 1979, but the provisions dealing with companies' capital gains are in sections 265–281 of the Income and Corporation Taxes Act 1970: see §§ 14–04B, *ante* and 16–53, *post.* The Taxes Management Act 1970 deals with the administration of the capital gains tax (including corporation tax on chargeable gains).

Rates: individuals

16–02   In the case of an individual, the rate of capital gains tax is 30 per cent.[4] Section 5 of the Capital Gains Tax Act 1979 provides that an individual is not chargeable to capital gains tax for a year of assessment if his *taxable amount* for that year does not exceed the exempt amount for the year. The excess over this amount is taxed at 30 per cent. The exempt amount for 1986–87 is £6,300.[5] The Treasury fixes the exempt amount for each year by statutory instrument.[6]

---

1. C.G.T.A 1979, ss.1 and 4(1).
2. *Ibid.* ss.155(1) and 28. The 1979 Act is a consolidation Act, deriving its material from the F.A. 1965 and amending Acts.
3. *Ibid.* ss.155(1) and 29. As to "manufactured" or "artificial" losses, see § 16–38A.
4. *Ibid.* s.3
5. The increase in the general index of retail prices from December 1984 to December 1985 was 5·7 per cent. The increase in the exempt amount for 1986–87 reflects this fact.
6. C.G.T.A. 1979, s.5(1c). The Capital Gains Tax (Annual Exempt Amount) Order 1986 S.I. 1986 No. 527 in (1986) S.T.I. 234.

The expression *taxable amount* means the total amount of chargeable gains accruing to the individual in the year of assessment after deducting (i) any allowable losses accruing in that year and (ii) any unrelieved losses carried forward from a previous year, except that no deduction is made in such a way as to reduce gains below the exempt amount for the year.[7] Thus the benefit of the tax-free amount is preserved and any unrelieved losses are carried forward. Note that the indexation allowance mentioned in § 16–01 is applied to each disposal during the course of a year and determines the amount of the chargeable gain on that disposal; whereas the exempt amount is applied to the taxable amount for a year and thus by reference to all disposals during the year.

Rates: personal representatives and trustees

16–02A   For the year of assessment in which an individual dies and for the two following years of assessment, the exemption which applies to an individual whose gains do not exceed the exempt amount for the year applies to disposals by his personal representatives.[8]

For any year of assessment during the whole or part of which any property is settled property (see § 16–21), the trustees are not chargeable to capital gains tax for a year in which their taxable amount for the year does not exceed half the exempt amount for the year, *i.e.* £3,150 in 1986–87.[9] The excess over this amount is taxed at 30 per cent. The larger relief applicable to individuals applies to certain trusts for mentally disabled persons and persons in receipt of an attendance allowance.[10–12]

Due date

16–03   Capital gains tax is assessed on a current year basis. The tax is payable on or before December 1 following the year of assessment or at the expiration of 30 days beginning with the date of issue of the notice of assessment, whichever is the later.[13] Corporation tax on the chargeable gains of companies is payable within nine months from the end of the accounting period or, if it is later, within 30 days from the date of issue of the notice of assessment.[14]

Short-term gains

16–03A   The Finance Act 1962 introduced a tax on short-term gains, under Case VII of Schedule D. In its final form it was levied on gains which accrued where there was an acquisition of an asset and a disposal within 12 months; and whereas capital gains tax is a flat rate tax, gains charged under Case VII of Schedule D were subject to income tax and surtax. After the

---

7. *Ibid.*, s.5(4).
8. *Ibid.*, Sched. 1, para. 4.
9. *Ibid.*, Sched. 1, para. 6(2). There are provisions to prevent an individual making a number of settlements, each of which qualifies for the relief: see C.G.T.A. 1979, Sched. 1, para. 6(4)–(9).
10.–12. *Ibid.*, Sched. 1, para. 5.
13. *Ibid.* s.7.
14. *Ibid.* s.243(4).

Finance Act 1965, the gains of companies fell outside the ambit of Case VII and within the ambit of the capital gains tax. Gains which were chargeable as short-term gains were not chargeable to capital gains tax.[15]

Case VII of Schedule D was abolished for the year 1971–72 and subsequent years[16] and is not further considered in this edition.

Chargeable persons

16–04 The capital gains tax applies to all gains accruing to a person in a year of assessment during any part of which he is *resident* in the United Kingdom, or during which he is *ordinarily resident* in the United Kingdom.[17] The alternative of "ordinary" residence is introduced to prevent a person normally resident in the United Kingdom avoiding capital gains tax by disposing of assets during a period of "temporary" non-residence. The terms "resident" and "ordinarily resident" have the same meanings as in the Income Tax Acts.[18] An individual who is resident or ordinarily resident but not domiciled in the United Kingdom is taxed on a remittance basis on gains from the disposal of assets situated outside the United Kingdom; losses on the disposal of such assets are not allowable losses.[19] The Act contains provisions for determining the location of assets.[20] Trustees and personal representatives are not "individuals" so the remittance basis does not apply to disposals by them.[21]

Where any trade or business is carried on by two or more persons in partnership and the control and management of the trade or business is situated abroad, partners resident in the United Kingdom are treated for the purposes of the capital gains tax as resident outside the United Kingdom.[22] This artificial treatment does not extend to *ordinary* residence. Its effect, therefore, is that partners who are ordinarily resident in the United Kingdom are chargeable to capital gains tax on the disposal of partnership assets, whereas partners who are not so ordinarily resident are exempt from the charge.

A person who is neither resident nor ordinarily resident in the United Kingdom in a year of assessment is not chargeable to capital gains tax on gains accruing to him in that year, unless he is carrying on a trade in the United Kingdom through a branch or agency (as defined[23]), in which case he is taxable on chargeable gains (and is entitled to relief for allowable losses[24]) which accrue on the disposal:

---

15. C.G.T.A. 1979, s.157(1) and Sched. 6, para. 12.
16. F.A. 1971, s.56(1). For details of the taxation of short-term gains, see the 4th ed. of this book at Chapter 15.
17. C.G.T.A. 1979, s.2(1). See Concession D2 as to the year of commencement or cessation of permanent residence. An unincorporated association is a "person" for capital gains tax purposes: *Frampton* v. *I.R.C.* [1985] S.T.C. 186.
18. *Ibid.* s.18(1); and see §§ 7–17 *et seq.*
19. *Ibid.* ss.14, 29(4). As to the amount to be treated as remitted, see *ibid.* s.14(2). As to delayed remittances, see § 16–06.
20. *Ibid.* s.18(4).
21. *Ibid.* s.48(2).
22. *Ibid.* s.60 applying I.C.T.A. 1970, s.153, *ante*, § 7–24.
23. C.G.T.A. 1979, s.12(3).
24. *Ibid.* s.29(3).

(a) of assets situated in the United Kingdom[25] and used in or for the purposes of the trade at or before the time when the capital gain accrued; or

(b) of assets situated in the United Kingdom[25] and used or held for the purposes of the branch or agency at or before that time, or assets acquired for use by or for the purposes of the branch or agency.[26]

Paragraph (b) applies (for example) to investments which serve a purpose in supporting the trading activities of a branch or agency in the United Kingdom but which are not actually used in the trade itself. This provision does not apply to a person who is exempt from income tax in respect of the profits or gains of the branch or agency under a double taxation agreement.[27] The position with respect to chargeable gains of non-resident companies is discussed below.[28]

Husband and wife

16–04A   Gains and losses of husband and wife are calculated separately for each spouse, losses incurred by one of them being set primarily against that spouse's gains. Chargeable gains accruing to a married woman in any year or part of a year during which she is living with her husband (see § 8–23) are, however, assessed on the husband unless either the husband or wife elect to be separately assessed.[29] Where husband and wife are living together (whether or not an election for separate assessment has been made), unrelievable losses of one spouse in any year are deductible from gains accruing to the other spouse for that year; but this is subject to either spouse's right to elect not to have the losses so dealt with. Such losses must then be carried forward to the next year or years.[30]

As between married persons living together, the exempt amount referred to in § 16–02 is divided between them in proportion to their respective taxable amount, except that they can agree the apportionment if either has allowable losses to carry forward from previous years.[31] If they live together for part only of the year, the part in which they are separated is treated as a separate year of assessment.

As to disposals between husband and wife, see § 16–17.

Chargeable assets

16–05   The capital gains tax is charged on the disposal of assets[32] and all forms of property are assets for this purpose,[33] whether situated in the United Kingdom or not, including:

---

25. The rules for the situation of assets are in C.G.T.A. 1979, s.18(4). A non-sterling bank account of an individual who is domiciled outside the United Kingdom is now treated as a 'foreign asset' unless the individual is resident in the United Kingdom and holds the account at a United Kingdom branch: *ibid.*, s.18(4)(j).
26. *Ibid.* s.12(1).
27. *Ibid.* s.12(2).
28. See *post*, § 16–55.
29. C.G.T.A. 1979, s.45 (tax on married woman's gains).
30. *Ibid.* s.4(2), proviso.
31. *Ibid.* s.5(6) and Sched. 1, paras. 1–3, as amended.
32. *Ibid.* s.1(1).
33. *Ibid.* s.19(1).

(a) options, debts and incorporeal property generally;

(b) any currency other than sterling; and

(c) any form of property created by the person disposing of it, or otherwise coming to be owned without being acquired,[33] *e.g.* a building which the person erects, goods which he manufactures, a pedigree herd bred by him, or the copyright of a book written by him.

The benefit of a contract of personal service is an "asset": it is irrelevant that the rights of the employer cannot be turned to account by transfer or assignment and thus have no market value. There is no requirement that assets must, for capital gains tax purposes, have a market value. Thus, in one case[34] a sum of £50,000 received by a company for releasing a director from his obligations under a service agreement was held to be a capital sum derived from assets within what is now section 20(1) of the Capital Gains Tax Act 1979: see § 16–08 paragraph (c). A right to bring an action to enforce a claim has been held to be an "asset."[35]

> In *Kirby* v. *Thorn EMI plc*[35a] Thorn and its wholly-owned subsidiary (M1) agreed with GE that Thorn would procure the sale of three subsidiaries of M1 by M1 to GE. Thorn covenanted with GE that no company in the Thorn group would compete with the three subsidiaries for five years; and GE paid $575,000 for the covenant. The Revenue assessed M1 to capital gains tax, contending that it was a sum received by M1 for giving up rights: see § 16–08(c). *Held* that the covenant, which had no existence prior to the making of the contract, was not an asset for the purposes of capital gains tax.

Relief for delayed remittances

16–06 Capital gains from the disposal of assets outside the United Kingdom are chargeable gains if the disponer is resident or ordinarily resident in the United Kingdom; and tax is levied on an arising basis or, if the disponer is domiciled outside the United Kingdom, on a remittance basis: see § 16–04. If the disponer is unable to transfer the gains to the United Kingdom due to the provisions of the foreign law or to some executive action of the foreign government or to the impossibility of obtaining foreign currency, the liability to tax is delayed until remittance becomes possible.[36]

2. DISPOSALS

Disposal

16–07 The charge to capital gains tax arises on the *disposal* of an asset.[37] On each such disposal a computation must be made to determine whether a chargeable gain (or allowable loss) has accrued. The term "disposal" is not

---

34. *O'Brien* v. *Benson's Hosiery (Holdings) Ltd.* [1980] A.C. 562; (1980) 53 T.C. 241 (H.L.).
35. *Zim Properties Ltd* v. *Proctor* (1985) S.T.C. 90.
35a. (1986) S.T.C. 200.
36. C.G.T.A. 1979, s.13.
37. *Ibid.* s.1(1). For a case in which a "Tomlin order" recording the terms of a compromise of an action was held to impose an immediate trust for sale and so effect a "disposal" for the purposes of capital gains tax, see *Anders Utkilens Rederi A/S* v. *O/Y Lovisa Stevedoring Co. A/B and Keller Bryant Transport Co. Ltd.* [1985] S.T.C. 301.

defined in the Act so general principles of law have to be applied. Plainly there is a disposal if the beneficial ownership of an asset is transferred from one person to another, whether by sale, exchange, gift or otherwise. The expression "disposal" includes a part disposal of an asset[38]; and there is a part disposal where an interest or right in or over the asset is created by the disposal, as well as where it subsists before the disposal (*e.g.* where a lease is granted by the freeholder as well as where it is assigned by the lease-holder), and generally there is a part disposal where, on a person making a disposal, any description of property derived from the asset remains undisposed of.[38] Hence a computation has to be made if a person disposes of less than his entire interest in an asset in order to apportion the cost of the asset between the part retained and the part disposed of, according to their respective market values: see § 16–31A. A person's holding of shares of the same class in a company is treated as a single asset, so a disposal of part of a shareholding requires a computation on a part disposal basis.

Disposals under contracts

16–07A   a   Where an asset is disposed of and acquired under a contract, the time at which the disposal and acquisition is made is the time the contract is made (and not, if different, the time at which the asset is conveyed or transferred). There is an exception in the case of a conditional contract: if a contract is conditional (and in particular if it is conditional on the exercise of an option) the time at which the disposal and acquisition is made is the time when the condition is satisfied.[39]

Thus if V agrees to sell land to P, contracts are exchanged on January 1 and completion takes place on March 1, V's disposal (and P's acquisition) of the land are treated as made on January 1. A problem arises where a contract for the sale of land is not carried through to completion. It is sometimes said that if V agrees to sell land to P, V becomes a trustee for P who thereby becomes "beneficial owner," provided the contract is specifically enforceable. "Equity looks upon that as done which ought to be done." This reasoning is said to lead to the conclusion that there is a disposal when the agreement for sale is made, whether or not the agreement proceeds to completion. It would follow from this that, if the contract is rescinded or "goes off" through inability of the vendor to make title or of the purchaser to provide the purchase price, there is a further disposal from purchaser to vendor. An alternative view is that it is only where the contracting parties get what they bargain for under the contract that it can be said, with benefit of hindsight, that there was a disposal and that the time of the disposal was the time when the contract was made. In the common case the bargain is that the vendor will make title to the land and the purchaser will pay the balance of the purchase price, whereupon a deed of transfer will be executed. In such a case there will be a disposal on completion, related back to the time of exchange of contracts. This view

---

38. *Ibid.* s.19(2).
39. *Ibid.* s.27 and see *Johnson* v. *Edwards* (1981) 54 T.C. 488; [1981] S.T.C. 660.

appears to derive some support from *Rayner* v. *Preston*.[40] If, in order to avoid stamp duty, the bargain provides that the purchaser will be allowed into possession on payment of the price and that no deed of transfer will be executed unless and until called for by the purchaser, the bargain may be said to be complete before the execution of the deed. In such a case there may be a disposal on exchange of contracts.

The dissenting judgment in Floor v. *Davis*

6–07B   In *Floor* v. *Davis*[41] the shareholders of A Limited wished to sell their shares to C Limited. Substantial gains would accrue on a sale for cash. They accordingly devised a scheme which involved the formation of an intermediate company, B Limited, and its liquidation; and the share structure of B Limited was so arranged that, on the liquidation, the larger part of the assets would pass to a Cayman Islands company. The first part of the scheme involved the transfer of the shares in A Limited to B Limited, in consideration of an issue of shares in B Limited. This was a reorganisation of the share capital of B Limited. (There is no disposal for capital gains tax purposes where a person exchanges shares in one company for shares in another under a reorganisation of share capital: see § 16–13.) B Limited then sold the shares in A Limited to C Limited for cash. (No chargeable gain accrued to B Limited on this disposal). The second part of the scheme involved the liquidation of B Limited in order that a large part of the cash proceeds derived from the sale to C Limited might find their way to the Cayman Islands company.

The majority of the Court of Appeal held that the passing of the winding-up resolution involved an exercise of control by the shareholders of A Limited under which value passed out of their shares in B Limited into the shares in B Limited held by the Cayman Islands company. Such a transaction is treated as a deemed disposal for a notional consideration: see § 16–16. In a dissenting judgment Eveleigh L.J. saw the case:

> "as one in which the court is not required to consider each step in isolation. It is a question of whether or not the shares were disposed of to [C Limited] by the taxpayer. I believe that they were. Furthermore they were in reality at the disposal of the original shareholders until the moment they reached the hands of [C Limited], although the legal ownership was in [B Limited] . . . I do not seek to say that the transfer to [B Limited] was not a transfer. The important feature of the present case is that the destiny of the shares was at all times under the control of the taxpayer who was arranging for them to be transferred to [C Limited]. The transfer to [B Limited] was but a step in the process."[42]

We shall see later that in *Ramsay* v. *I.R.C.*[43–46] Lord Wilberforce and Lord Fraser expressed their approval of the reasoning of Eveleigh L.J. in *Floor* v. *Davis*. Other aspects of this case are considered in § 36–08 *et seq.*

---

40. [1881] 18 Ch.D. 1 (C.A.).
41. [1980] A.C. 695; (1979) 52 T.C. 609P; (H.L.).
42. (1979) 52 T.C. 609 at pp. 633 I–634 B.
43–46. (1981) 54 T.C. 101; [1981] S.T.C. 174 (H.L.) (and see *Furniss* v. *Dawson* [1984] A.C. 474; 55 T.C. 324 (H.L.) where this approval was "explained." *Post*, §§ 36–17 *et seq.*

Extended meaning of disposal

16–08   The term "disposal" has an extended meaning for the purposes of capital gains tax. There is a disposal of assets by their owner where a capital sum is *derived from* assets notwithstanding that no asset is acquired by the person paying the capital sum[47]; and the relevant provision[48] applies in particular to:

(a) capital sums received by way of compensation for any kind of damage or injury to assets or for the loss, destruction or dissipation of assets or for any depreciation or risk of depreciation of an asset[49];

(b) capital sums received under a policy of insurance against the risk of any kind of damage or injury to, or the loss or depreciation of, assets;

(c) capital sums received in return for forfeiture or surrender of rights, or for refraining from exercising rights[50]; and

(d) capital sums received as consideration for use or exploitation of assets.

The disposal is treated as occurring at the time when the capital sum is received.[51] The expression "capital sum" means any money or money's worth which is not excluded from the consideration taken into account in the computation of the chargeable gain, *e.g.* sums chargeable to tax as income.[52]

In *Drummond* v. *Austin Brown*[53] it was held that statutory compensation paid on the termination of a business tenancy, under section 37 of the Landlord and Tenant Act 1954, was not subject to capital gains tax, since it was neither derived from an asset (*i.e.* the lease) or compensation for the loss of an asset. The right to the payment was derived exclusively from the statute.

"Rights" in paragraph (c) of § 16–08 means legal rights as this expression is understood by students of jurisprudence. If A, in the front of a bus queue, gives up his place in the queue to B in return for a sum of money, there is no deemed disposal by A within paragraph (c) because A's "right"

---

47. The words "notwithstanding that no asset is acquired" mean "whether or not an asset is acquired": see *Marren* v. *Ingles*, (1980) 54 T.C. 76; [1980] S.T.C. 500 (H.L.) at § 16–35. *Cf. I.R.C.* v. *Montgomery* (1975) 49 T.C. 679 (in which the meaning of "derived" was discussed at p. 686F). The actual decision in the *Montgomery* case has been reversed: see C.G.T.A. 1979, s.140.

48. C.G.T.A. 1979, s.20(1).

49. That part of a "golden handshake" which escapes income tax under Schedule E will be exempt from capital gains tax under C.G.T.A. 1979, s.31; *post,* § 16–29.

50. See *O'Brien* v. *Benson's Hosiery (Holdings) Ltd.* in § 16–05.

51. C.G.T.A. 1979, s.20(2).

52. *Ibid.* s.20(3). See *post* § 16–29.

53. [1984] S.T.C. 321 (C.A.). See also *Davis* v. *Powell* (1976) 51 T.C. 492; [1977] S.T.C. 32 (where compensation for disturbance paid to a tenant farmer on surrendering his lease, following a notice to quit from his landlord, was not taxable: it was a sum which had to be paid under s.34 of the Agricultural Holdings Act 1948. This, however, was not a case of a *negotiated* surrender: the tenant could not serve a counter-notice to gain the protection of the Act). In *Golding* v. *Kaufman* [1985] S.T.C. 152 a sum paid to relinquish rights under an option agreement was held to be taxable under s.22. Followed in *Powlson* v. *Welbeck Securities Ltd.* [1986] S.T.C. 423.

to his place in the queue is not a right which is capable of enforcement by legal process.[53a]

Roll-over relief is available in certain cases where the capital sum is applied in restoring or replacing an asset which is damaged or injured or is lost or destroyed.[54]

6–09 The occasion of the entire loss, destruction, dissipation or extinction of an asset is treated as a disposal of the asset, whether or not any capital sum by way of compensation or otherwise is received in respect of the destruction, dissipation or extinction.[55] If the Inspector is satisfied on a claim being made by the owner of an asset that the value of the asset has become negligible, he may allow the claim, whereupon the claimant is to be treated as having sold and immediately re-acquired the asset for a consideration equal to the value specified in the claim,[56] *i.e.* as if he had in fact disposed of it. It seems that in practice the Revenue treat the deemed sale as occurring in the chargeable period to which the claim relates. The time limit for making the claim is two years from the end of the chargeable period.[57] For the purposes of these provisions, a building can be regarded as an asset separate from the land on which it stands; but if a building is destroyed or its value becomes negligible, the person deemed to dispose of the building is to be treated as if he had also sold and immediately re-acquired the site of the building for a consideration equal to its market value at that time,[58] so any gain (or loss) on the site must be brought into the account in the same year of assessment as that in which the loss on the building is brought in. The abandonment of an option is in some cases[59] treated as a disposal of the option.

Roll-over relief is available in certain cases where compensation for the loss of an asset is applied in replacing the asset.[59a]

Mortgages, charges and hire-purchase

16–10 The transfer of an asset by way of security and its retransfer on redemption of the security involves no acquisition or disposal.[60] If a mortgagee or chargee (or receiver or manager) enforces the security, his acts are treated as those of the mortgagor or chargor.[61] If a person takes a transfer of property subject to a mortgage or charge, the amount of the liability assumed by him is treated as part of the cost of acquisition.[62] Thus, if P acquires an

---

53a. And see *Kirby* v. *Thorn EMI plc* in § 16–05.
54. C.G.T.A. 1979, s.21.
55. *Ibid.* s.22(1).
56. *Ibid.* s.22(2). For some guidance as to the meaning of "negligible," see [1972] B.T.R. "Current Tax Intelligence," at p. 405. And see *Williams* v. *Bullivant* (1983) 56 T.C. 159; (1983) S.T.C. 453; *Larner* v. *Warrington* (1985) S.T.C. 442.
57. See SP 12/1975 in (1975) S.T.I. 420.
58. C.G.T.A. 1979, s.22(3).
59. *Ibid.* s.137(4).
59a. *Ibid.* s.21.
60. *Ibid.* s.23(1).
61. *Ibid.* s.23(2).
62. *Ibid.* s.23(3).

asset for £5,000 which is charged to secure a debt of £1,000 which P takes over, P's cost of acquisition is £6,000.

If an asset is sold on hire-purchase, it is treated as disposed of at the beginning of the hire-purchase period, subject to later adjustment if the customer does not ultimately become the owner of the asset.[63]

Appropriations to and from stock-in-trade

16–11   A trader may acquire an asset otherwise than as trading stock and later appropriate the asset to the trade. A picture dealer might, for example, buy a painting for display in his office and later decide to include it among the items on sale to the public. If on a sale of the asset at its market value at the time of such appropriation, a chargeable gain or allowable loss would have accrued to him, the appropriation is treated as a disposal of the asset at market value, unless the trader elects to bring the asset into trading stock at its market value reduced by the amount of the chargeable gain or increased by the amount of the allowable loss.[64] By so electing the trader avoids any immediate charge to capital gains tax but any profit (or loss) on the eventual sale of the asset, or on the cessation of the trade, will be reflected in the profits (or losses) of the trade. The election applies only if the trader is chargeable to income tax in respect of the profits of the trade under Case I of Schedule D (or, if a company, carries on a trade, within the charge to corporation tax[65]). Conversely, if at any time an asset which is trading stock is appropriated by the trader for some other purpose, or is retained by him on the cessation of the trade, he is treated as having acquired the asset at that time for a consideration equal to the amount brought into the trading accounts in respect of it for tax purposes.[66] Thus the base value of the asset for purposes of capital gains tax is taken as the closing figure for income tax (or corporation tax) purposes. The practical application of these provisions is somewhat restricted in the case of stock-in-trade consisting of tangible movable property which is a wasting asset by an exemption which is discussed in § 16–44.

Capital distributions by companies

16–12   Where a person receives or becomes entitled to receive in respect of shares in a company any capital distribution from the company (other than a new holding[67]) he is treated as if he had in consideration of that capital distribution disposed of an interest in the shares.[68] "Capital distribution" means any distribution from a company, including a distribution in the course of dissolving or winding up the company, in money or money's worth except a distribution which in the hands of the recipient constitutes

---

63. *Ibid.* s.24.
64. *Ibid.* s.122(1), (3).
65. I.C.T.A. 1970, ss.250(3), 265(3).
66. C.G.T.A. 1979, s.122(2).
67. Defined *ibid.* s.77(1)(*b*).
68. *Ibid.* s.72(1).

income for the purposes of income tax.[69] Thus if a company goes into liquidation each shareholder is treated as disposing of an interest in his shares in consideration of the share of assets to which he becomes entitled in the liquidation. Each distribution in the course of winding up involves a part disposal by each shareholder. If the Inspector is satisfied that the amount of any capital distribution is small, as compared with the value of the shares in respect of which it is made, and he so directs, the occasion of the capital distribution is not treated as a disposal of the shares, but the amount or value of the capital distribution is deducted from any expenditure allowable as a deduction in computing a gain or loss on the disposal of the shares by the person receiving or becoming entitled to receive the distribution. A person who is dissatisfied with the refusal of the Inspector to give a direction may appeal to the Commissioners.[70] The Revenue treat an amount as small in relation to another amount if the first amount does not exceed 5 per cent. of the second amount.[71]

When, on a bonus or rights issue, the company making the issue sells fractional entitlements on the market and distributes the proceeds *pro rata* to the shareholders entitled, the distributions are treated as capital distributions.[72]

Demergers

16–12A   Section 117 of and Schedule 18 to the Finance Act 1980 introduced new provisions for facilitating certain transactions whereby trading activities carried on by a single company or group may be divided so as to be carried on by two or more companies not belonging to the same group or by two or more independent groups. Certain transfers in connection with such "demergers" which would otherwise constitute "distributions" are treated as "exempt distributions": see § 14–49A. Such exempt distributions are not capital distributions for the purposes of section 72 (see § 16–12); and sections 77 to 81 (see § 16–13) apply with modifications: see §§ 40–33 *et seq*.

Company re-organisations, etc.

16–13   Sections 77 to 88 of the Capital Gains Tax Act 1979 contain elaborate provisions which apply to the reorganisation or reduction of share capital, the conversion of securities and to company amalgamations. If, for example, there is a bonus issue or rights issue and shareholders are allotted shares or debentures in proportion to their existing holdings, the new shares or debentures are treated as acquired when the original shares were acquired and the total holding is treated as acquired for a price equal to the cost of the original shares plus any sum paid for the new holding.[73] Simi-

---

69. *Ibid.* s.72(5)(*b*). Exempt distributions under the demerger provisions (§ 40–33) are not capital distributions: F.A. 1980, Sched. 18, para. 19.

70. C.G.T.A. 1979, s.72(2)–(5)(*a*). For the Revenue's practice in charging tax where there is more than one distribution, see SP 1/1972.

71. I.R. Booklet, CGT 8 (1980), para. 118. *Cf.* F.A. 1986, s.54 in § 16–31.

72. C.G.T.A. 1979, s.73.

73. *Ibid.* ss.77–79. But see the proviso to s.79(1) added by F.A. 1981, s.91 in consequence of *I.R.C.* v. *Burmah Oil Ltd.* (1981) 54 T.C. 200; [1982] S.T.C. 30 (H.L.).

larly, if the rights attached to a class of shares are altered or there is a conversion of securities,[74] or a reduction of share capital (other than the repayment of redeemable shares), this can be achieved without any immediate liability to tax. If on a reorganisation or reduction of share capital a person becomes entitled to or receives a capital distribution from the company not forming part of the new holding, he is treated as having disposed of his original holding for a price equal to the amount of the distribution, the cost of the new holding being adjusted accordingly.[75] If the shares or debentures of an existing company are acquired by another company ("the take-over company") in exchange for shares or debentures of the take-over company, there is no new acquisition or disposal by the shareholders of the existing company. But this applies only if the take-over company holds or in consequence of the exchange will hold more than one-quarter of the ordinary share capital of the existing company or if the issue follows a general offer made in the first instance on a condition such that, if it were satisfied, the take-over company would hold more than one-quarter of the ordinary share capital of the existing company.[76] Schemes of arrangement can also be implemented without immediate tax liability.[77] Sections 87 and 88 of the Capital Gains Tax Act 1979 contain elaborate provisions to counter avoidance of tax by these provisions: see § 40–28. Section 460 of the Taxes Act 1970 may apply in some cases: see §§ 40–02 *et seq*.

A transfer of a business as a going concern to a company with the whole of its assets (or the whole of those assets other than cash) is not treated as a chargeable disposal of any of the assets to the extent that the consideration for the transfer consists of shares issued by the company.[78] The shares in such a case are treated as having taken the place of the assets. This provision enables a sole trader or partners to "convert" his or their business into a company without incurring an immediate liability to capital gains tax.

Debts

16–14   Where a debt is paid off (*i.e.* is satisfied) in whole or in part, this is generally treated as a disposal of the debt or part of it by the creditor at the time when the debt is satisfied.[79] No chargeable gain is treated as accruing on the disposal of a debt by the *original* creditor or his legatee (or by the original creditor's personal representative[80]), except in the case of a *debt on a security*.

---

74. C.G.T.A. 1979, s.82. There are special provisions which apply where there is a compulsory acquisition of shares (*e.g.* on the nationalisation of an industry) and government stock is issued in exchange: see *ibid.* s.84 and Sched. 6, para. 20(4) and F.A. 1976, s.54 and [1975] S.T.I. 348.

75. *Ibid.* s.79(2).

76. *Ibid.* s.85; and see § 16–16. Stamp duty aspects of company amalgamations are discussed in Chap. 33.

77. *Ibid.* s.86, and I.C.T.A. 1970, s.267, and see SP 5/85 in (1985) S.T.I. 295 stating the Revenue view as to what constitutes a reconstruction within these provisions.

78. *Ibid.* s.123.

79. *Ibid.* s.134(1), (2).

80. *Ibid.* s.134(1), (4), (5).

Thus if A borrows £5,000 from B on terms that B is entitled to a commercial rate of interest and a premium on repayment, B incurs no liability to capital gains tax on repayment of the debt by A or on an assignment of the debt by B to C, unless the debt is a debt on a security. (Conversely, if B is not repaid, B's loss is not an allowable loss unless the debt is a debt on a security).

But the position differs where an *assignee* of the debt (C in the example) receives satisfaction. Any gain of the assignee is a chargeable gain, unless the satisfaction is by way of a conversion of securities (*e.g.* on a conversion of loan stock into shares under a scheme of company reorganisation). There are provisions to prevent allowable losses being "manufactured" by an abuse of these rules.[81]

A debt is a debt on a security if a document is issued by the debtor (such as a loan stock certificate) which is either a marketable security or has such characteristics as enable it to be dealt in and, if necessary, converted into shares or other securities; but it is not necessary that the obligation should be secured.[82]

16–15 Where a creditor acquires property in satisfaction of his debt or part of it, the property is treated as disposed of by the debtor and acquired by the creditor for no more than its market value at the time of the creditor's acquisition thereof.[83] Thus if (in the above example) B accepted property having a market value of £4,500 in satisfaction of A's debt of £5,000, the base value of the property in B's hands would be £4,500 (not £5,000). If B had assigned the debt, no chargeable gain would have accrued because B was the original creditor: is B to be prejudiced if he takes property in satisfaction of the debt and assigns the property? The Act provides that where a chargeable gain accrues to B on a transfer of the property, this shall be reduced so as not to exceed the chargeable gain which would have accrued if B had acquired the property for a consideration equal to the amount of the debt. Thus if B disposes of the property for £5,200, B's chargeable gain is £200, not £700.

16–15A If A (not being a moneylender) invests money in B and suffers a loss of capital on his investment, no tax relief is available to A unless the debt due from B is a debt on a security: see § 16–14. Various devices were resorted to in an attempt to overcome this obvious injustice.[84] The injustice was, to an extent, remedied by section 49 of the Finance Act 1978 (now section 136 of the Capital Gains Tax Act 1979) as respects loans made (and guarantees given) after April 11, 1978, which treats an allowable loss as accruing where (i) money lent is used by the borrower wholly for the purposes of a trade carried on by him, not being a trade which consists of or includes the lending of money, (ii) the borrower is resident in the United Kingdom and

81. *Ibid.* s.134(4).

82. *Aberdeen Construction Group Ltd.* v. *I.R.C.* (1978) 52 T.C. 281; [1978] S.T.C. 127 (H.L.); *Cleveleys Investment Co.* v. *I.R.C.* (1972) 47 T.C. 300 and *Ramsay (W.T.) Ltd.* v. *I.R.C.* [1982] A.C. 300; (1979) 54 T.C. 101. And see SP 31/1970.

83. C.G.T.A. 1979, s.134(3).

84. See, *e.g. Harrison* v. *Nairn Williamson Ltd.* (1978) 51 T.C. 135; [1978] S.T.C. 67 (C.A.). For a useful discussion, see [1981] B.T.R. 156–161.

(iii) the borrower's debt is not a debt on a security. A loan which meets these conditions is referred to as "a qualifying loan." If the Inspector is satisfied, on a claim being made to him, that any outstanding amount of the principal of the qualifying loan has become irrecoverable, that the claimant has not assigned his right to recover that amount and that the claimant and the borrower were not each other's spouses[85] or companies in the same group[86] when the loan was made or at any subsequent time, the capital gains tax provisions take effect as if an allowable loss equal to the amount irrecoverable had accrued at the time when the claim is made. There are similar provisions which apply where a loss is suffered by a guarantor.

Value shifting[87]

16–16　　If a person having control of a company exercises his control so that value passes out of his shares or of those of a person with whom he is connected[88] into other shares, this is a disposal of the shares out of which value passes, notwithstanding that there is no consideration for the disposal; so also if value passes out of other rights over the company.

> In *Floor* v. *Davis*[89] it was held that the word "person" could, in this context, be read in the plural so as to make the provision apply where two or more persons cause value to pass out of shares. It was further held that deliberate inaction could constitute an "exercise" of control.

An adjustment of the rights and liabilities under a lease following the grant of a lease, such adjustment being favourable to the lessor, is treated as a disposal by the lessee of an interest in the property.

Similarly, the extinction or abrogation of a right or restriction over an asset involves a disposal.

Husband and wife[90]

16–17　　If, in any year of assessment, and in the case of a woman who in that year of assessment is a married woman living with her husband,[91] the man disposes of an asset to the wife, or the wife disposes of an asset to the man, both are treated as if the asset was acquired from the one making the disposal for a consideration of such amount as would secure that on the disposal neither a gain nor a loss would accrue to the one making the disposal. The disponee is treated as acquiring the asset for whatever is the cost of acquisition of the asset to the disponer. This general rule does not apply:

(a) if the asset was trading stock of the disponer or is acquired as trading stock of the disponee; or

(b) if the disposal is by way of *donatio mortis causa*.

---

85. *i.e.* "living together," see § 8–23.
86. Defined I.C.T.A. 1970, s.272.
87. C.G.T.A. 1979, s.25.
88. See *post*, § 16–18A.
89. [1980] A.C. 695; 52 T.C. 609; [1979] S.T.C. 379 (H.L.). See also § 16–07 and § § 40–28 *et seq.*
90. C.G.T.A. 1979, s.44.
91. See *ante*,§ 8–23.

The general rule stated above applies if the disposal occurs *after* separation but in the same year of assessment as that in which the separation occurs, provided the relationship of husband and wife subsists at the time of the disposal. Conversely, the general rule does not apply if the disposal occurs in a year of assessment throughout which husband and wife are no longer living together[91]; moreover, such a disposal will be between connected persons: see § 16–18A.

As to indexation allowance on disposals between spouses, see § 16–30B.

Partnerships

-17A   For capital gains tax purposes any dealings in partnership assets are treated as dealings by the individual partners and not by the firm as such.[92] The Board have issued a Statement of Practice[93] concerning the capital gains tax treatment of partnerships and the statements in this paragraph are based thereon. Each partner is regarded as owning a fractional share in the partnership assets (falling to be valued as a proportion of the market value of those assets) rather than as having a particular interest in the "partnership" falling to be valued as such. When any asset is disposed of by the partnership each partner is attributed with his fractional share of the gain accruing, either by reference to the allocation of asset surpluses under the partnership agreement or, in the absence of such allocation, by reference to his profit-sharing ratio. On a distribution of assets among the partners themselves (as, for example, on a dissolution), any partner not receiving a particular asset will be regarded as having disposed of his fractional share therein. Where there is a change in profit-sharing ratios (as on the introduction or retirement of a partner or on a merger), any disposal in underlying goodwill will be treated as made for a consideration equal to the partner's capital gains tax base cost, unless actual payment is made (whether made outside the partnership accounts or by adjustment in those accounts). Where partnership assets are revalued and a partner's share therein is subsequently reduced, he will be regarded as disposing of the fractional difference in the partnership assets. Likewise the partner whose share increases has his acquisition cost increased. Transactions between partners are not regarded as being made between connected persons[94] unless the partners are connected otherwise than by way of partnership (for example, father and son). Even in the latter case, however, the Revenue will not substitute market value on any transaction if nothing would have been paid had the parties been at arm's length.

Any lump sum paid to a partner on his leaving the partnership represents consideration for the disposal of his share in the underlying assets. Where, however, instead of receiving a capital payment, a retiring partner is to receive an annuity,[95] its capital value will not be treated as consideration

---

92. C.G.T.A. 1979, s.60(*b*).
93. SP 1/1975 in [1975] S.T.I. 17. This was extended by SP 1/1979.
94. C.G.T.A. 1979, s.63(4). See § 16–18A.
95. The Statement makes no reference to the possibility of such annuities becoming payable to the widow and dependants of a partner. Furthermore it does not expressly deal with the situation where one form of "rights" in a partnership is given up for another.

for the disposal of his share[96] in the partnership assets if it is no more than can be regarded as a reasonable recognition of his past work and effort.[97] Specific provision is made in the Statement for the pooling of expenditure and consequential elections.

3. Disposals by Way of Gift or Settlement and on Death

Gifts

16–18

Where a person disposes of an asset otherwise than by way of a bargain made at arm's length and in particular where he disposes of it by way of gift[98] or on a transfer into settlement by a settlor or by way of distribution from a company in respect of shares in the company, the disposal is deemed to be for a consideration equal to the market value of the asset. The person who acquires the asset in such a case is likewise treated as acquiring the asset at market value.[99] The rule also applies where a person acquires or, as the case may be, disposes of an asset wholly or partly for a consideration that cannot be valued, or in connection with his own or another's loss of office or employment or diminution of emoluments, or otherwise in consideration for or recognition of his or another's services or past services in any office or employment or of any other service rendered or to be rendered by him or another.[99] The rule does not apply to the acquisition of an asset if:

(a) there is no corresponding disposal of it, and
(b) there is no consideration in money or money's worth or the consideration is of an amount or value lower than the market value of the asset.[1]

At one time the rule did not apply where the disposal was by an "excluded person," such as a person who was neither resident nor ordinarily resident in the United Kingdom. Hence if trustees of a non-resident settlement disposed of an asset to a United Kingdom resident individual, the latter was not treated as acquiring the asset at market value even if the disposal gave rise to a charge to tax. The market value rule now applies where the disposal is made by an excluded person (as defined[1a]), unless both the disposer and the acquirer elect that it shall not do so.[1b] Disposals to charities and to certain bodies, such as the National Gallery, are the subject of a

---

96. Under C.G.T.A. 1979, s.31(3).
97. Provided the partner has been in the partnership for 10 years this requirement is treated as satisfied if the annuity is no more than two thirds of his average share in profits in the best three of the last seven years.
98. *Turner* v. *Follett* (1973) 48 T.C. 614; [1973] S.T.C. 148 (C.A.). The word "gift" can include any transfer of property: see *Berry* v. *Warnett* (1980) 55 T.C. 92 at p. 104H; and see § 16–21(2).
99. C.G.T.A. 1979, s.29A(1), added by F.A. 1981, s.90.
1. C.G.T.A. 1979, s.29A(2) added by F.A. 1981 s.90. For an explanation of this addition, see *Harrison* v. *Nairn Williamson Ltd.* (1978) 51 T.C. 135; [1978] S.T.C. 67 (C.A.). See [1981] B.T.R. 156–161.
1a. C.G.T.A. 1979, s29A(5).
1b. *Ibid.*, s.29A(3). The right of election only applies to disposals made after April 5, 1983 and before April 6, 1985. See (1984) S.T.I. 2–3 and 235.

special relief: see § 16–50. There are provisions under which donor and donee can elect to have the tax otherwise payable by the donor "held over" until the donee disposes of the asset. Hold-over relief is discussed in § 16–49.

There are elaborate provisions to prevent avoidance of capital gains tax by disposals at an undervalue; in particular, transactions between connected persons are assumed to be otherwise than by way of bargain at arm's length and an enquiry into open market value must be made.[2] Where a price is freely negotiated and the market moves in the vendor's favour before contract, the bargain may nevertheless be at arm's length.[3]

Although the donor or the vendor at an undervalue is chargeable with the tax payable under these provisions, the donee or purchaser can be assessed in some cases.[4]

There are special rules that apply where assets are disposed of in a series of linked transactions.[4a]

Connected persons

–18A   Section 63 of the Capital Gains Tax Act 1979 provides as follows:

"(1) Any question whether a person is connected with another shall . . . be determined in accordance with the following subsections of this section (any provision that one person is connected with another being taken to mean that they are connected with one another).

(2) A person is connected with an individual if that person is the individual's husband or wife, or is a relative, or the husband or wife of a relative, of the individual or of the individual's husband or wife.

(3) A person, in his capacity as trustee of a settlement, is connected with any individual who in relation to the settlement is a settlor, with any person who is connected with such an individual and with a body corporate which, under section 454 of the Taxes Act is deemed to be connected with that settlement ("settlement" and "settlor" having for the purposes of this subsection the meanings assigned to them by subsection (3) of the said section 454).

(4) Except in relation to acquisitions or disposals of partnership assets pursuant to bona fide commercial arrangements, a person is connected with any person with whom he is in partnership, and with the husband or wife or a relative of any individual with whom he is in partnership.

(5) A company is connected with another company—

(*a*) if the same person has control of both, or a person has control of one and persons connected with him, or he and persons connected with him, have control of the other, or

(*b*) if a group of two or more persons has control of each company, and the groups either consist of the same persons or could be regarded as consisting of the same persons by treating (in one or more cases) a member of either group as replaced by a person with whom he is connected.

(6) A company is connected with another person, if that person has control of it or if that person and persons connected with him together have control of it.

(7) Any two or more persons acting together to secure or exercise control of a

---

2. C.G.T.A. 1979, s.62. For "connected persons," see § 16–18A.
3. *Clark* v. *Follett* (1973) 48 T.C. 677 at p. 704F.
4. C.G.T.A. 1979, s.59. *Post*, § 16–25.
4a. See C.G.T.A. 1979, s.151; F.A. 1985, s.71 and Sched. 21.

company shall be treated in relation to that company as connected with one another and with any person acting on the directions of any of them to secure or exercise control of the company.

(8) In this section 'relative' means brother, sister, ancestor or lineal descendant."

The terms "company" and "control" are defined in section 155(1) of the Capital Gains Tax Act 1979.

Note that husband and wife are "connected persons" although they are not "living together" in the tax sense: see § 8–23. Thus a disposal made by a husband to his separated wife will be treated as a disposal at market value, unless the rule in § 16–17 applies.[5]

Free estate: deaths after March 30, 1971

16–19   On the death of an individual after March 30, 1971, the assets of which the deceased was competent to dispose[6] are deemed to be *acquired* on his death by the personal representatives or other person on whom they devolve for a consideration equal to their market value at the date of the death; but the assets are not treated as *disposed* of by the individual on his death.[7] Hence the death of an individual is not an occasion which gives rise to a charge to capital gains tax: assets of which the deceased was competent to dispose are subject only to capital transfer tax or inheritance tax[8] on his death and not to capital gains tax.[8a] But the death of an individual is an occasion which gives rise to a notional acquisition by the personal representatives at a cost equal to the market value of the assets of the deceased at the time of his death. This exemption from the charge to capital gains tax applies whether or not the assets are charged to capital transfer tax or inheritance tax.

> Thus if A dies owning quoted shares which cost £20,000 and which have a market value at death of £30,000, inheritance tax is leviable on the shares (unless the assets are exempt, *e.g.* as being left to a surviving spouse). A's personal representatives are treated for capital gains tax purposes as having acquired the shares at a cost of £30,000.

16–20   Is a subsequent disposal by personal representatives in the course of administration an occasion of charge? This depends on whether the disponee acquires as "legatee" or otherwise.

(1) On a person acquiring any asset as legatee, no chargeable gain accrues to the personal representatives: the legatee is treated as if the per-

---

5. For an example, see *Aspden* v. *Hildesley* (1982) 55 T.C. 609; [1982] S.T.C. 206.
6. Defined C.G.T.A. 1979, s.49(10) to mean assets of the deceased which he could if of full age and capacity have disposed of by his will, assuming all the assets are situated in England and the deceased was domiciled in England. Assets over which he has a power of appointment are excluded. The deceased's share in assets to which, immediately before his death, he was beneficially entitled as joint tenant is included: *ibid.* s.49(10).
7. *Ibid.* s.49(1). In *Larter* v. *Skone James* (1976) 51 T.C. 221; [1976] S.T.C. 220 it was held that "on the death" meant at the moment immediately after the death.
8. See *post* § 18–14.
8a. There is an exception in the case of "roll-up" funds: see § 7–34 and F.A. 1984, s.92(3), (4).

sonal representatives' acquisition of the asset had been his acquisition of it.[9] Hence a legatee's "acquisition cost" is the market value of the asset at the time of the deceased's death.[10] The expression "legatee" is widely defined to include any person taking under a testamentary disposition or on an intestacy or partial intestacy, whether he takes beneficially or as trustee; and a person taking under a *donatio mortis causa*[11] is treated as a legatee and as if his acquisition was made at the time of the donor's death.[12] Property appropriated by personal representatives in or towards satisfaction of a pecuniary legacy or any other interest or share in the property devolving under a testamentary disposition or intestacy is treated as appropriated to a person as legatee.[13] It should be noted that the exemption on acquisitions by legatees is not in express terms limited to disposals made prior to the completion of the administration period.[14]

(2) If personal representatives dispose of an asset otherwise than to a legatee, *e.g.* if they realise assets in order to pay capital transfer tax or inheritance tax, they are chargeable in respect of any gain which accrues on that disposal, subject to their right to relief in respect of allowable losses.[15] There is no provision under which unrelieved losses accruing on disposals by personal representatives can be made available for offset against gains of the deceased accruing before the death or gains of the beneficiaries entitled to the deceased's estate.[16]

Deeds of family arrangement, etc.

–20A   It often happens that beneficiaries under a will or intestacy agree between themselves, by a deed of family arrangement or similar instrument (*e.g.* formal correspondence), to vary the dispositions made under the will or created by the intestacy. The estate is then administered subject to the agreed variations. Section 68 of the Finance Act 1978 (see § 19–63) deals with the implications of such a variation as respects capital transfer tax and inheritance tax. Section 49(6) of the Capital Gains Tax Act 1979 provides that where within the period of two years after a person's death any of the dispositions (whether effected by will, under the law relating to intestacy or otherwise) of the property of which he was competent to dispose are varied, or the benefit conferred by those dispositions is disclaimed, by an instrument in writing made by the persons or any of the persons who benefit or would benefit under the dispositions, the variation or disclaimer shall not constitute a disposal for the purposes of capital gains

---

9. C.G.T.A. 1979, s.49(4).

10. Market value in the case of foreign assets means the value converted into sterling at the rate of exchange prevailing on the relevant date: see *Bentley* v. *Pike* (1981) 53 T.C. 590; [1981] S.T.C. 360.

11. A *donatio mortis causa* is a delivery of property in contemplation of the donor's death on the express or implied condition that the gift shall not be complete until the donor dies.

12. C.G.T.A. 1979 s.47(2). Thus if A makes a death-bed gift to B, this is not an occasion of charge nor is A's death an occasion of charge. B takes as his base cost the market value at death.

13. *Ibid.* s.47(3).

14. Completion of the administration is material to the matters discussed in §§ 9–10 *et seq.*

15. See § 16–37. For the rate chargeable, see § 16–02A.

16. This follows from the repeal of s.24(8) of the F.A. 1965, when it was replaced by F.A. 1969, s.24A and from the subsequent repeal of s.24A by F.A. 1971, Sched. 14, Pt. V.

tax; and the Act is to apply as if the variation had been effected by the deceased or, as the case may be, the disclaimed benefit had never been conferred.

This provision does not apply to a variation unless the person or persons making the instrument so elect by written notice given to the Board within six months after the date of the instrument or such longer time as the Board may allow. The section does not apply to a variation or disclaimer made for any consideration in money or money's worth other than consideration consisting of the making of the variation or disclaimer in respect of another of the dispositions. The section applies whether or not the administration of the estate is complete or the property has been distributed in accordance with the original dispositions. This provision is expressed to take effect from the date of the passing of the Act and not from April 11, 1978, as does a corresponding provision relating to capital transfer tax. By concession, however, both provisions will be applied from the earlier date.[17]

Settled property

16–21   (1) *Definition*. Settled property is widely defined in section 51 of the Capital Gains Tax Act 1979 as meaning, unless the context otherwise requires, "any property held in trust other than property to which section 46 above (nominees and bare trustees) applies."

Section 46 applies to assets held by a person (a) as nominee for another person; or (b) as trustee for another person absolutely entitled as against the trustee (or for two or more persons jointly so entitled); or (c) as trustee for any person who would be absolutely entitled as against the trustee but for being an infant or other person under disability (or for two or more persons who would be jointly so entitled, but for infancy, etc.). A person is so absolutely entitled as against the trustee where he has the exclusive right, subject only to satisfying any outstanding charge, lien or other right of the trustee to resort to the asset for payment of duty, taxes, costs and other outgoings, to direct how that asset shall be dealt with.[18] Assets which are subject to a unit trust scheme are treated separately from settled property[19] and from property to which section 46 applies (which may be described as "nominee property").

Property held for persons entitled in undivided shares is not settled property if the interest of each of the beneficiaries is not, *e.g.* contingent or subject to defeasance. Thus if land is held upon trust for X and Y in undivided shares (equal or unequal) the land is not settled property.[20]

---

17. See *post*, § 19–63.
18. C.G.T.A. 1979, s.46(2). And see *Tomlinson* v. *Glyns Executor & Trustee Co.* (1969) 45 T.C. 600 (C.A.); *I.R.C.* v. *Matthew's Executors* [1984] S.T.C. 386 (C.S.).
19. See *ibid.* s.51 and ss.92–98. Unit trust schemes are not settled property. And see s.61(4) regarding insolvents' assets.
20. *Kidson* v. *MacDonald* [1974] Ch. 339; 49 T.C. 503 (followed in *Harthan* v. *Mason* (1980) 53 T.C. 272; [1980] S.T.C. 94); but property held in common subject to the payment of an annuity is settled property: *Stephenson* v. *Barclays Bank Trust Co. Ltd.* (1975) 50 T.C. 374; [1975] S.T.C. 151. See also *Crowe* v. *Appleby* (1976) 51 T.C. 457; [1975] S.T.C. 502 (C.A.). See § 16–23, note 41. See *Frampton* v. *I.R.C.* (1985) S.T.C. at 193 fol.

In *Booth* v. *Ellard*,[21] B and 11 other taxpayers transferred their shares in X Limited to trustees to be held for 15 years on trusts set out in an agreement. Each shareholder restricted his right to dispose of the shares and to deal with his beneficial interest therein. *Held*, that the shares subject to the agreement were not "settled property": each of the beneficiaries was "absolutely entitled" because (a) their respective interests were concurrent and not successive and (b) their interests were qualitatively the same.

(2) *Property put into settlement.* Where property is transferred into settlement, this is treated as a disposal of the property thereby becoming settled property, whether the settlement is revocable or irrevocable and notwithstanding that the donor is interested as a beneficiary or is a trustee or the sole trustee of the settlement.[22] Thus the act of settling property may give rise to a chargeable gain or an allowable loss.[23] A settlor may (unilaterally) claim to have the gain held over: see § 16–49. A settlor and the trustees of his settlement are treated as "connected persons" (see § 16–18A) and accordingly a loss which accrues on the making of the settlement is deductible only from a chargeable gain accruing on some other disposal to the trustees, unless the settlement is for educational, cultural or recreational purposes.[24] Any stamp duty payable on the making of a settlement is an allowable expense in the capital gains computation.[25]

In *Berry* v. *Warnett*[26] B in March 1972 owned investments worth £219,880 on which an unrealised gain of £150,483 had accrued. B transferred the investments to a Guernsey company as his nominee. A Jersey company paid B full value (£14,500) for a reversionary interest in the investments expectant on B's death; and B then sold his retained life interest to a Bahamian company for £130,753. The transaction involving B, the Guernsey company and the Jersey company was completed by one tripartite deed which was executed on April 4, 1972. B sold his life interest to the Bahamian company in the next financial year, 1972–73. It was common ground that there was a "settlement" after the sale of the reversionary interest to the Jersey company and that the sale of the life interest to the Bahamian company gave rise to no charge to tax (see the exemption in § 16–24). The question arose whether the sale of the reversionary interest was a disposal of all the investments thereby becoming settled property, such disposal being deemed to be at market value (as the Crown contended) or was a mere part disposal for £14,500 (as B contended). *Held*, that the Crown's contention was right. There was a disposal by B of the legal title to the investments in March 1972—to be disregarded as being a transfer to a nominee. This became an effective disposal on April 4, 1972, when trusts were declared other than in favour of the settlor, thus making the investments "settled property." This was a disposal by B at (deemed) market value since the trustee acquired the investments otherwise than by way of bargain at arm's length. The existence of the bargain between B and a third party (the Jersey company) was irrelevant in this context.

---

21. (1980) 53 T.C. 393; [1980] S.T.C. 555 (C.A.).
22. C.G.T.A. 1979, s.53. S.53 was amended by F.A. 1981, s.86 to apply to a "transfer into" settlement and not a "gift in" settlement. This removes a difficulty revealed in *Berry* v. *Warnett* (below).
23. Payment of the tax due could at one time be postponed: see C.G.T.A. 1979, ss.8–9. But not in the case of disposals on or after April 6, 1984: F.A. 1984, s.63(1)(b).
24. *Ibid.* C.G.T.A. 1979, s.62(3).
25. See *post*, § 16–30. Ad valorem stamp duty on voluntary dispositions was abolished as from March 26, 1985: F.A. 1985, s.82(1), (8).
26. (1982) 55 T.C. 92; [1982] S.T.C. 396 (H.L.).

16–22   (3) *Disposals by trustees*. In relation to settled property, the trustees of a settlement are treated as being a single and continuing body of persons distinct from the persons who may from time to time be the trustees.[27] Hence a mere change of trustees gives rise to no disposal. A disposal by trustees of assets comprised in settled property may give rise to a chargeable gain or allowable loss on which the trustees will be assessed or may claim relief. In some cases trustees of settled property are *deemed* to have disposed of assets comprised in settled property. The following is a summary of these cases[28]:

(i) ABSOLUTE ENTITLEMENT AGAINST TRUSTEE. By section 54(1) of the Capital Gains Tax Act 1979, on the occasion when a person becomes absolutely entitled[29] to any settled property as against the trustee, all the assets forming part of the settled property to which he becomes so entitled are deemed to have been disposed of by the trustee, and immediately reacquired by him in his capacity as a trustee within section 46(1) of the Act, for a consideration equal to their market value. A person is absolutely entitled as against trustees when he has the exclusive right, subject only to satisfying any outstanding charge, lien or other right of the trustees to resort to the asset for payment of duty, taxes, costs or other outgoings, to direct how that asset shall be dealt with.[29] Market value means the price the assets might reasonably be expected to fetch on a sale in the open market.[30]

> Thus if assets are held upon trust for A contingently on his attaining the age of 25 years, the attainment of the specified age is an occasion of charge under section 54(1). The trustees are treated as having sold the property at its then market value. The point of the reference to section 46(1) is that the property ceases to be settled property on A becoming absolutely entitled thereto and any subsequent disposal by the trustees is treated for tax purposes as if it were a disposal by A and as if A's cost of acquisition was equal to the market value of the property on A's 25th birthday.

A person may become *absolutely* entitled although he is not *beneficially* entitled. Thus if trustees exercise a power of appointment or advancement so as to cause assets to be held on new trusts, the new trustees may become absolutely entitled as against the appointing trustees—and certainly will become so entitled if "no one will ever again need to refer to the original settlement except to confirm that it has ceased to exist."[31] The question is one of fact and degree. Some guidance may be found in the speech of Lord Wilberforce in *Roome* v. *Edwards*[32] where he said the following:

---

27. C.G.T.A. 1979, s.51(1), (2), (3). When settled property is divided between different trustees, as in the case of settled land, they are treated as together constituting and, so far as they act separately, as acting on behalf of a single body of persons: *ibid.* s.52(3).
28. For the special rules that apply where "hold-over relief" has been claimed, see § 16–49D.
29. C.G.T.A. 1979, s.46(2). The reference to becoming absolutely entitled as against the trustee includes the case where a person would become so entitled but for being an infant or other person under disability: *ibid.*, s.54(3).
30. C.G.T.A. 1979, s.150(1) and Sched. 6, Part I.
31. *Hoare* v. *Gardner*; *Hart* v. *Briscoe* [1979] Ch. 1; 52 T.C. 53; [1978] S.T.C. 89. See useful notes in [1978] B.T.R. pp. 1 and 118 and an article in [1980] B.T.R. 174. And see § 16–25A.
32. (1981) 54 T.C. 359 at p. 390B; [1981] S.T.C. 96 at p. 100. See also § 16–25A.

"Many settlements contain powers to appoint a part or a proportion of the trust property to beneficiaries: some may also confer power to appoint separate trustees of the property so appointed, or such power may be conferred by law (Trustee Act 1925, Section 37). It is established doctrine that the trusts declared by a document exercising a special power of appointment are to be read into the original settlement (*Muir* v. *Muir* [1943] A.C. 468). If such a power is exercised, whether or not separate trustees are appointed, I do not think that it would be natural for such a person as I have presupposed[33] to say that a separate settlement had been created: still less so if it were found that provisions of the original settlement continued to apply to the appointed fund, or that the appointed fund were liable, in certain events, to fall back into the rest of the settled property. On the other hand, there may be a power to appoint and appropriate a part or portion of the trust property to beneficiaries and to settle it for their benefit. If such a power is exercised, the natural conclusion might be that a separate settlement was created, all the more so if a complete new set of trustees were declared as to the appropriated property, and if it could be said that the trusts of the original settlement ceased to apply to it. There can be many variations on these cases each of which will have to be judged on its facts."

After this decision the Board of Inland Revenue issued a Statement of Practice 9/81 on the exercise of powers of appointment over settled property. The views expressed in that Statement had to be modified to some extent by the decision of the Court of Appeal in *Bond* v. *Pickford*[34] and, following consultations with the Law Society, the Revenue issued a revised Statement of Practice (SP7/84) which supersedes SP9/81. The text of the new Statement is as follows[34a]:

In *Roome & Denne* v. *Edwards*[34b] the House of Lords held that where a separate settlement is created there is a deemed disposal of the relevant assets by the old trustees for the purposes of CGTA 1979, s.54(1) (formerly FA 1965, s.25(3)). But the judgments emphasised that, in deciding whether or not a new settlement has been created by the exercise of a Power of Appointment or Advancement, each case must be considered on its own facts, and by applying established legal doctrine to the facts in a practical and commonsense manner. In *Bond* v. *Pickford* the judgments in the Court of Appeal explained that the consideration of the facts must include examination of the powers which the trustees purported to exercise, and determination of the intention of the parties, viewed objectively.

It is now clear that a deemed disposal under CGTA 1979, s.54(1) cannot arise unless the power exercised by the trustees, or the instrument conferring the power, expressly or by necessary implication, confers on the trustees authority to remove assets from the original settlement by subjecting them to the trusts of a different settlement. Such powers (which may be powers of advancement or appointment) are refered to by the Court of Appeal as 'powers in the wider form.' However, the Board considers that a deemed disposal will not arise when such a power is exercised and trusts are declared in circumstances such that—

(*a*) the appointment is revocable, or

---

33. This is "a person, with knowledge of the legal context of the word [settlement] under established doctrine and applying this knowledge in a practical and commonsense manner to the facts under examination."

34. [1983] S.T.C. 517 (C.A.).

34a. See [1984] S.T.I. 699. For SP 9/81 see the 15th edition of this book at § 16.22.

34b. [1982] A.C. 279; (1981) 54 T.C. 359 (H.L.).

(*b*) the trusts declared of the advanced or appointed funds are not exhaustive so that there exists a possibility at the time when the advancement or appointment is made that the funds covered by it will on the occasion of some event cease to be held upon such trusts and once again come to be held upon the original trusts of the settlement.

Further, when such a power is exercised the Board considers it unlikely that a deemed disposal will arise when trusts are declared if duties in regard to the appointed assets still fall to the trustees of the original settlement in their capacity as trustees of that settlement, bearing in mind the provision in CGTA 1979, s.52(1) that the trustees of a settlement form a single and continuing body (distinct from the persons who may from time to time be the trustees).

Finally, the Board accept that a Power of Appointment or Advancement can be exercised over only part of the settled property and that the above consequences would apply to that part."

16–22A *Exception on termination of life interest.* Where a person becomes absolutely entitled to assets forming part of settled property on the termination of a life interest[35] by the death of the life tenant, section 54(1) is modified[36] so as to accord with the general principle that there should be no charge to capital gains tax on a death but only a deemed acquisition at market value and an "uplift" in the capital gains tax "acquisition cost" or "base." On such an occasion no chargeable gain accrues on the disposal.[37]

Thus if assets are held upon trust for A for life, remainder to B absolutely, there is a notional disposal and re-acquisition at market value by the trustees on A's death under section 54(1) but no chargeable gain accrues on that disposal. The trustees start with a new "acquisition cost" for capital gains tax purposes equal to that market value.

16–22B Section 56(1A) of the Capital Gains Tax Act 1979 restricts the relief in § 16–22A where the life interest is in *part* only of the settled property: a chargeable gain accrues on the termination of the life interest but the gain is reduced by a proportion corresponding to the value of the property in which the life interest subsisted.

Assume that realty is held on trust as to half for A for life with remainder to B absolutely and as to the other half for C absolutely. A dies on or after April 6, 1982. On A's death there is a notional disposal by the trustees at market value of *all* the realty comprised in the settlement, because both B and C[38] then become absolutely entitled as against the trustees within section 54. A chargeable gain accrues (because s.56(1)(*a*) is made not to apply) but the chargeable gain attributable to the half share to which B becomes entitled is excluded in computing the tax chargeable.[39]

There is a special exception to meet the case where there is a "reverter to the disponer." We shall see in § 22–27 that if S transfers property to X for life, with no other dispositions, no inheritance tax is payable on X's death in respect of the property which then reverts to S. The exception is designed to prevent both inheritance tax and capital gains tax being

---

35. For definition, see § 16–23A and note that C.G.T.A. 1979, s.54(1) and s.55(1) apply on the termination by death of an annuity which is not a life interest: *ibid.* s.57.
36. This modification applies to deaths occurring after March 30, 1971.
37. C.G.T.A. 1979, s.56(1). But see § 16–49D (hold-over gains).
38. See *Crowe* v. *Appleby* (1976) 51 T.C. 457; [1976] S.T.C. 301 (C.A.) in note 41.
39. C.G.T.A. 1979, s.56(1A), inserted by F.A. 1982, s.84(2) in relation to interests terminating on or after April 6, 1982.

avoided by the use of this device. It is provided that if on the life tenant's death the property reverts to the disponer, the disposal and re-acquisition under section 54(1) of the Capital Gains Tax Act 1979 shall be deemed to be for such consideration as to secure that neither a gain nor a loss accrues to the trustee and shall, if the trustee had first acquired the property at a date earlier than April 6, 1965, be deemed to be at that earlier date.[39a]

> Suppose S purchases an asset in 1979 costing £50,000. In 1981 S grants a life interest in the asset (then worth £60,000) to X and the asset thus becomes "settled property." X dies in 1986 when the value of the asset is £70,000. No inheritance tax is payable on X's death: see § 22–27. But for the special exception, section 54(1), would apply on X's death and S would be treated as re-acquiring the asset at its then market value of £70,000. No gain would accrue on the death. By virtue of the exception, S is treated as re-acquiring the asset for £60,000.

A deemed disposal under section 54(1) of the Capital Gains Tax Act 1979 may produce an allowable loss. If the loss accrues to the trustees in respect of property to which a beneficiary becomes absolutely entitled as against the trustees or in respect of any property represented by that property (*e.g.* if the trustees have realised assets at a loss and invested the proceeds in the property being transferred to the beneficiary), the loss is treated as if it had accrued to the beneficiary when he becomes absolutely entitled if otherwise the loss would go unrelieved in the hands of the trustees, *i.e.* if no chargeable gains had accrued to the trustees from which the loss could be deducted. This rule applies whether the loss accrues to the trustees in the year of assessment in which the beneficiary becomes absolutely entitled or is carried forward from an earlier year.[40]

Where a deemed disposal gives rise to a chargeable gain, for which the trustees are accountable, there are provisions under which a beneficiary becoming absolutely entitled as against the trustees can be assessed in respect of so much of the gain as is attributable to the property to which he becomes so absolutely entitled: see § 16–25.

16–23   (ii) TERMINATION OF LIFE INTERESTS. Under section 55(1) of the Capital Gains Tax Act 1979, on the termination *on the death* of the person entitled to it, of a life interest in possession (see § 22–14) in all or any part[41] of

---

39a. C.G.T.A. 1979, s.56(1). But see § 16–49D (held-over gains).
40. *Ibid.* s.54(2).
41. "Part" includes an undivided fraction of a trust fund: *Pexton* v. *Bell* and *Crowe* v. *Appleby* (1976) 51 T.C. 457; [1976] S.T.C. 301 (C.A.). In *Crowe* v. *Appleby* T, by his will, directed that his residuary estate (which at all material times consisted of freehold land held on trust for sale) be held in trust for his five children in specified shares which were not all equal. Each child's share was to be held on protective trusts for such child for life, with remainders over. One child (C1) died in 1952 (before capital gains tax), his share devolving on his child (X) absolutely. A second child (C2) died in 1968–69, her share devolving on her children Y and Z absolutely. Each of C1 and C2 was life tenant of a $\frac{5}{30}$th part of the trust property. In 1969–70 the entire trust property was sold. *Held,* (i) that on C2's death there was a notional disposal, not of the whole of the trust property (as the Crown contended), but only of C2's $\frac{5}{30}$th share; (ii) that the entire trust property remained settled property at the time of the sale in 1969–70 notwithstanding the earlier deaths of C1 and C2, for neither X nor Y and Z had become absolutely entitled as against the trustees to the share which devolved on them. The trust fund was realty and they could not direct the trustees how to deal with the fund nor could they call for the immediate payment of their respective shares thereof. The trustees were accordingly chargeable to capital gains tax in respect of the gain accruing on the disposal of the whole of the fund.

settled property, the whole or a corresponding part of each of the assets forming part of the settled property and *not* ceasing at that time to be settled property are to be deemed at that time to be disposed of and immediately re-acquired by the trustee for a consideration equal to the whole or a corresponding part of the market value of the asset, but without any chargeable gain accruing.[42]

> Assume that property is settled on A for life, remainder to B for life, remainder to C absolutely. A dies after March 30, 1971. Under section 55(1), the trustees are deemed to have disposed of and immediately re-acquired the property on A's death for its market value but no chargeable gain accrues on that disposal. Hence there is an "uplift" in the capital gains base without any chargeable gain accruing. The same result will be achieved by the operation of section 54(1) on the subsequent death of B: see § 16–22(i).

16–23A   There is no deemed disposal where the termination of the life interest occurs *otherwise than on the death* of the life tenant, *e.g.* where it is terminated by surrender or through the exercise of a power in the settlement.[43] It should be noted that the above rule applies notwithstanding that the property is exempt from capital transfer tax on the death of the life tenant.

16–23B   "Life interest"[44–45] in relation to a settlement:

(a) includes a right under the settlement to the income of, or the use or occupation of, settled property for the life of a person other than the person entitled to the right or for lives:

> Thus if A, a life tenant, assigns his life interest to B, B has an interest during the life of A (an interest *pur autre vie*). B's interest is a "life interest";

(b) does not include any right which is contingent on the exercise of a discretion of the trustee or of some other person; and

(c) does not include an annuity, notwithstanding that the annuity is payable out of or charged on settled property or the income of settled property.

Position of the beneficiaries

16–24   No chargeable gain accrues on the disposal of an interest created by or arising under a settlement (including, in particular, an annuity or life interest, and the reversion to an annuity or life interest) by the person for whose benefit the interest was created by the terms of the settlement or by his legatee, except where that person acquired (or derived his title from one who acquired) his interest for a consideration in money or money's worth, other than consideration consisting of another interest under the settle-

---

42. C.G.T.A. 1979, s.55(1), as substituted by F.A. 1982, s.84(1); and see SP 11/1973 in [1973] S.T.I. 461. The statement in the text applies to deaths after March 30, 1971.
43. C.G.T.A. 1979, s.55(1) as substituted by F.A. 1982, s.84(1). This explains the repeal of C.G.T.A. 1979, ss.55(2) and 56(2).
44–45. C.G.T.A. 1979, s.55(4). A life interest in part of the income of settled property is treated as a life interest in a corresponding part of the settled property: *ibid.* s.55(1), and see *Pexton* v. *Bell*, at note 41, *ante*.

ment.[46] Where such a purchaser for a consideration in money or money's worth becomes as the holder of the interest absolutely entitled as against the trustee to any settled property, he is treated as disposing of the interest in consideration of obtaining that property.[47] This is without prejudice to the deemed disposal by the trustee under section 54(1) Capital Gains Tax Act 1979: see § 16–22(3)(i).

> Thus if property is settled upon trust for A for life, with remainder to B absolutely and B (or B's executor) sells the reversionary interest to P, no chargeable gain accrues to B (or B's executor); but P is chargeable in respect of any gain which accrues to him when (on A's death) P becomes absolutely entitled to the settled property and P is then treated as disposing of his interest.[47] This disposal by P is additional to the notional disposal by the trustees on P becoming absolutely entitled: see § 16–22.

If on a partition of settled property A surrenders his life interest in part of the property in consideration of an interest in capital, A is not treated as acquiring an interest by purchase: the consideration obtained by A is another interest under the settlement. Hence the exemption from capital gains tax for disposals of interests in settled property applies if A disposes of the interest so acquired by him. A life interest in settled property may be a wasting asset: see § 16–33.

6–24A *Special rule for interests in non-resident and migrant settlements.* Section 88 of the Finance Act 1981 qualifies the exemption in § 16–24 in relation to disposals on or after March 10, 1981 of interests in settlements which are (or become) non-resident settlements, *i.e.* where the trustees are neither resident nor ordinarily resident in the United Kingdom. The qualifications are as follows:

(1) Section 58(1) of the Capital Gains Tax Act 1979 does not apply to a disposal of an interest in settled property, other than a disposal treated under section 58(2) as made in consideration of obtaining the settled property, if at the time of the disposal the trustees are neither resident nor ordinarily resident in the United Kingdom.

> Thus if in the example in § 16–24 the settlement was non-resident, the disposal by B to P of the reversionary interest would not be exempt.

(2) If a gain accruing to a person ("the transferor") on a disposal of an interest in settled property is exempt under section 58(1) and the trustees subsequently become neither resident nor ordinarily resident in the United Kingdom, a chargeable gain is treated as accruing to the trustees immediately before they so "emigrate." The gain is equal to that which accrued to the transferor.

> Thus if in the example in § 16–24 the trustees become non-resident after B's disposal, a chargeable gain will accrue to the trustees equal to the exempt gain on B's disposal.

---

46. *Ibid.* s.58(1). The word "settlement" is not defined but it seems to be generally assumed that there is a settlement when there is "settled property" as defined in § 16–21. See, *e.g. Berry* v. *Warnett* in § 16–21.
47. *Ibid.* s.58(2).

No such chargeable gain is treated as accruing to the trustees under (2) if, before the end of the year in which they emigrate, the trustees have disposed of all the assets (and any interest in or right over or property derived from the assets) which, when the transferor disposed of his interest, constituted the settled property in which the interest subsisted. If the trustees retain some of the assets after the end of the year, the chargeable gain accruing to them is not to exceed the market value of those assets.[48]

There are provisions under which, if the trustees do not pay the tax within 12 months from the due date, this can be assessed on the transferor who then has a right of recovery against the trustees.[49]

Payment of the tax

16–25   Any capital gains tax which arises on a disposal (including a notional disposal) of settled property is assessed on the trustees of *that* settlement: see § 16–25A. If the tax is not paid within six months from the date when it becomes payable by the trustees, and before or after the expiration of that period of six months the asset in respect of which the gain accrued (or any part of the proceeds of sale of the asset) is transferred by the trustees to a person who as against the trustees is absolutely entitled to it, that person may at any time within two years from the time when the tax becomes payable be assessed and charged (in the name of the trustees) to the tax.[50] The beneficiary will generally have been required to indemnify the trustees in respect of their liability to capital gains tax.

There are provisions to enable tax assessed on the donor of assets and not paid by him to be recovered from the donee.[51]

Different settlements?

16–25A   Where trustees of a settlement appoint part of the settled property to be held on specified trusts for a beneficiary or beneficiaries, and retain the remainder of the settled property, a difficult question may arise whether there is a single settlement, *i.e.* whether the appointed property remains comprised in the "original" settlement. The question will assume importance, for example, if the trustees of the original settlement are or become non-resident and realise a chargeable gain on the disposal of assets, on which the Revenue cannot recover the tax, but the trustees of the appointed fund are resident in the United Kingdom. Can the Revenue assess the United Kingdom trustees in respect of the chargeable gains accruing on property which remained in the original settlement? This problem arose in *Roome* v. *Edwards*[52] where the House of Lords held that there was a single settlement for it was clear on the facts that the parties to the original settlement and the later appointment intended to treat the

---

48. F.A. 1981, s.88(3), (4).
49. *Ibid.* s.88(5), (6).
50. C.G.T.A. 1979, s.52(4).
51. *Ibid.* s.59.
52. (1981) 54 T.C. 359; [1981] S.T.C. 96 (H.L.): see § 16–22(3).

appointed fund as being held on the trusts of the original settlement, as added to and varied by the later appointment.

The question is closely allied to the question referred to in § 16–22(3) as to whether an appointment causes the appointee-trustees to become absolutely entitled as against the appointing trustees for the purposes of section 54(1) of the Capital Gains Tax Act 1979. If, notwithstanding an appointment, the property remains subject to the trusts of the original settlement, it must (it is thought) follow that section 54(1) does not apply to the appointment. Conversely, if the appointment creates a separate settlement, section 54 applies.

Non-resident settlements: attribution of gains to United Kingdom resident beneficiaries

16–26   A person who is neither resident nor ordinarily resident in the United Kingdom is outside the charge to capital gains tax: § 16–04. Section 80 of the Finance Act 1981, however, allows gains accruing to non-resident trustees to be attributed to United Kingdom resident beneficiaries who have received capital payments from the trustees. The section applies as respects chargeable gains accruing to the trustees of a settlement in a year of assessment during which the trustees are at no time resident or ordinarily resident in the United Kingdom, if the settlor or one of the settlors is at any time during that year (or was when he made his settlement[53]) domiciled and either resident or ordinarily resident in the United Kingdom. Section 80 applies to years of assessment in and from 1981–82 and supersedes earlier provisions.[54] The chargeable gains of the trustees may include gains accruing to a non-resident company in which the trustees have shares and which are attributed to the trustees under section 85 of the Finance Act 1981: see § 16–55.

There has to be computed for each year of assessment the amount on which the trustees would have been chargeable to tax if they had been resident or ordinarily resident in the United Kingdom; and this amount is called the *trust gains* for the year. The trust gains for a year are treated as chargeable gains accruing in that year to beneficiaries who receive (or who have previously received) *capital payments* from the trustees.[55]

"Capital payment"[56] means any payment which is not chargeable to income tax on the beneficiary or, in the case of a beneficiary who is neither resident nor ordinarily resident in the United Kingdom, any payment received otherwise than as income. "Payment" includes the transfer of an asset and the conferring of any other benefit and to any occasion on which

---

53. A settlement arising under a will or intestacy is treated as made by the testator or intestator at the time of his death: F.A. 1981, s.80(7). The "income tax" definitions of settlement and settlor now apply: see F.A. 1981, s.83(7) added by F.A. 1984, s.71. And see § 10–07.

54. See C.G.T.A. 1979, s.17 and F.A. 1981, s.80(8). For a remarkable case under the earlier provisions, see *Leedale* v. *Lewis* (1982) 56 T.C. 501; [1982] S.T.C. 835 (H.L.). For the circumstances in which tax assessed under s.17 for years up to and including 1983–84 can be deferred, see F.A. 1984, s.70 and Sched. 14; also [1984] S.T.I. 116–118 and 290.

55. F.A. 1981, s.80(2), (3).

56. *Ibid.* s.83. *Cf.* § 7–29 and § 10–43.

settled property becomes property to which section 46 of the Capital Gains Tax Act 1979 applies, *i.e.* if a beneficiary becomes absolutely entitled as against the trustee: see § 16–22(3). The amount of a capital payment made by way of loan and of any other capital payment which is not an outright payment of money is taken to be equal to the value of the benefit conferred by it (*cf.* § 7–29). A capital payment is to be regarded as received by a beneficiary from the trustees if:

(a) he receives it from them directly or indirectly; or

(b) it is directly or indirectly applied by them in payment of any debt of his or otherwise for his benefit; or

(c) it is received by a third person at the beneficiary's direction or by virtue of an assignment made by him;

and the person is treated as receiving a capital payment notwithstanding that it is received by him jointly with another.[56] Thus a beneficiary cannot avoid an attribution of gains under the section by, *e.g.* directing the trustees to apply the capital payment in discharging the beneficiary's bills (*cf.* § 10–43).

The attribution of chargeable gains to beneficiaries is made in proportion to, but is not to exceed, the amounts of the capital payments received by them. The beneficiary is not to be charged to tax on chargeable gains attributed to him unless he is domiciled in the United Kingdom at some time in that year.[57]

> *Example*
> In year 5 the trust gains (including trust gains carried forward from years 1–4) amount to £12,000. In year 5 capital payments are made to beneficiaries A, B and C amounting to £4,000, £6,000 and £10,000 respectively. The trust gains are divided between A, B and C in the same proportion, namely A: £2,400; B: £3,600; C: £6,000. Each of them is accordingly charged to capital gains tax if he is resident or ordinarily resident and domiciled in the United Kingdom.

Where no capital payment is made in a year, any trust gains of that year are carried forward and can be attributed to capital payments made in a later year, as in the example. Trust gains of one year may also be attributed to beneficiaries who receive capital payments in an earlier year.[58]

Once chargeable gains have been treated as accruing to a beneficiary in consequence of a capital payment, the payment is thereafter left out of account in attributing chargeable gains to beneficiaries. A capital payment cannot be assessed both under section 80 and section 45 of the Finance Act 1981: see § 7–29).[59]

Migrant settlements

16–26A   (1) *Exporting United Kingdom trusts.* We have seen that trust gains accruing to non-resident trustees in a year of assessment may be attributed to a beneficiary who receives a capital payment in an earlier year of assess-

---

57. *Ibid.* s.80(4), (6).
58. *Ibid.* s.80(3).
59. *Ibid.* s.45(6).

ment: see § 16–26. Section 81(1) of the Finance Act 1981 deals with the case where the settlement is a United Kingdom resident settlement at the time when the capital payment is made but non-resident at the time when there are trust gains. Briefly, a capital payment received by a beneficiary in a "resident period" (as defined) is disregarded for the purposes of section 80 (see § 16–26) if it was not made in anticipation of a disposal made by the trustees in a "non-resident period" (as defined). This provision is designed to meet the case where a trust is "exported" prior to the trustees disposing of trust assets and realising chargeable gains but where capital payments are made in anticipation of the exportation.

(2) *Importing non-resident trusts.* Section 81(2) of the Finance Act 1981 deals with the reverse situation where a non-resident settlement becomes resident and trust gains for the last year of the non-resident period are not (or are not wholly) attributed to beneficiaries. The trust gains (or the outstanding part of them) can be treated in such a case as chargeable gains accruing in the first year of the resident period to beneficiaries of the settlement who receive capital payments from the trustees in that year; and so on for the second and subsequent years until the amount treated as accruing to beneficiaries is equal to the amount of the trust gains for the last year of the non-resident period. A capital payment cannot be assessed both under section 81(2) and section 44 of the Finance Act 1981: see § 7–29.[59]

Transfers between settlements. Section 82 of the Finance Act 1981 contains provisions to counter the avoidance of tax by means of intersettlement transfers.

4. COMPUTATION OF GAINS OR LOSSES

16–27   The main rules which govern the computation of chargeable gains are to be found in sections 30 to 43 of the Capital Gains Tax Act 1979. The basic principles are stated in the following paragraphs.

General rules for assets acquired on or after April 5, 1965

16–28   The main rules relating to the computation of gains and losses may be summarised as follows:

16–29   1. In calculating the consideration for a disposal of assets there should be excluded any money or money's worth which is charged to income tax (or corporation tax) as income of the disponer or which is taken into account as a receipt in computing income or profits or gains or losses of the disponer.[60] Thus there is excluded that part of the premium on the grant of a lease which is chargeable as income under Schedule A: see § 6–16. The

---

60. C.G.T.A. 1979, s.31(1) and see s.43. As to corporation tax, see § 16–53.

special provisions which apply to certain sale and lease-back transactions are discussed in § 2–61.

Where the consideration for a disposal consists of a rentcharge or similar right to income, the capitalised value of the rentcharge or other income is taken into account.[61] The treatment of annuities payable to retired partners as consideration for the disposal of their interest in partnership assets is commented on in § 16–17A.

16–30 2. In calculating the gain accruing to a person on the disposal of an asset there may be deducted from the consideration[62]:

(a) the cost of acquisition of the asset (including any *incidental costs*) or, if the asset was not acquired, the expenditure incurred in producing it;

(b) expenditure incurred for the purpose of enhancing the value of the asset which is reflected in the state or nature of the asset at the time of disposal, and expenditure in establishing, preserving or defending the taxpayer's title to or right over the asset[63];

(c) the incidental costs of making the disposal.

Incidental costs means expenditure wholly and exclusively incurred for the purposes of the acquisition,[64] including fees, commission, or remuneration paid for the professional services of any surveyor or valuer, or accountant, or agent or legal adviser and costs of transfer or conveyance (including stamp duty), together with the costs of advertising to find a seller (in the case of acquisition) and costs of advertising to find a buyer and of valuation (in the case of disposal).[65] This rule is subject to the overriding qualifications that no deduction is allowed for expenditure which is otherwise allowed as a deduction in calculating liability to income tax or corporation tax or if, in the case of losses, it is covered by capital allowances; and that no deduction is allowed for any sum which would have been deducted if the asset to which the expenditure related had at all times been a fixed asset in use for the purposes of a trade.[66] This last qualification excludes normal maintenance expenditure, *e.g.* the cost of painting a house which is not a

---

61. *Ibid.* s.31(3) but see *post* § 16–35, as to the spreading of tax liability.
62. *Ibid.* s.32(1). For an article on the capital gains tax expenditure rules see [1978] B.T.R. 291 (R. Burgess). In *Stanton* v. *Drayton Commercial Investment Co. Ltd.* (1982) 55 T.C. 286; [1982] S.T.C. 585 (H.L.) D. agreed to buy a portfolio of investments for (say) £100,000 to be satisfied by the issue of 50,000 new shares in D. at £2. The agreement was conditional on the necessary resolutions for issue being passed and on a Stock Exchange quotation for the shares. The middle market price of the shares on the day of quotation was £1·50. On a subsequent disposal of part of the portfolio by D., *held* the cost was the contract price of £2, not the quotation price of £1·50.
63. *Ibid.* s.32(1). There is a scale of expenditure which the Inland Revenue allows to personal representatives for establishing title: see SP 7/81 in [1981] S.T.I. 501 (application from April 5, 1981).
64. See *I.R.C.* v. *Richard's Executors* (1971) 46 T.C. 626 (H.L.Sc.). Executors' costs of producing inventory to obtain confirmation of shares held to be expenditure wholly and exclusively incurred in establishing title thereto. See also *I.R.C.* v. *Chubb's Trustee* (1971) 47 T.C. 353 (Ct. of Sess.); *Cleveleys Investment Trust Co.* v. *I.R.C.* (1975) 51 T.C. 26; *Allison* v. *Murray* (1975) 51 T.C. 57; *Emmerson* v. *Computer Time International Ltd.* (1977) 50 T.C. 628 (C.A.); *Passant* v. *Jackson* (1986) S.T.C. 164.
65. C.G.T.A. 1979, s.32(2).
66. *Ibid.* s.33(1), (2).

principal residence. No deduction is allowable for the value of the tax-payer's personal labour and skill in enhancing the value of his own property.[67] No deduction is allowable more than once for any sum or for more than one sum.[68] No adjustment to take account of inflation is made in a computation of chargeable gains other than the statutory indexation in § 16–30B.[69]

16–30A   Sterling is the unit of assessment in which gains (or losses) are reckoned. Thus if assets are acquired or disposed of in some other currency, the cost or disposal consideration must be translated into the sterling equivalent at the relevant date.[70]

Indexation allowance

16–30B   The Finance Act, 1982 and Schedule 13 (as amended) provide for an "indexation allowance"—a complex but crude and limited form of relief from tax on gains attributable to inflation.[70a] The allowance applies only to disposals on or after April 6, 1982 (or after April 1, 1982 for companies).

The question whether an indexation allowance is available has to be determined in relation to each disposal. The first step is to see if (disregarding the indexation allowance) a gain or loss would accrue on the disposal. This is called the *"unindexed gain or loss."* If there is neither gain nor loss on the disposal, the unindexed gain or loss is nil. The second step is to determine the *relevant allowable expenditure* defined to mean

> "any sum which, in the computation of the unindexed gain or loss, was taken into account by virtue of paragraph (a) or paragraph (b) of sub-section (1) of Section 32 of [the Capital Gains Tax Act 1979]."

Thus it includes the items of expenditure falling under paragraphs (a) and (b) in § 16–30 but not the expenditure in paragraph (c). In determining the amount of relevant expenditure, account has to be taken of statutory provisions which increase, exclude or reduce the whole or any part of any item of expenditure falling within section 32 or which provides for it to be written down.

The indexation allowance is applied to each item of relevant allowable expenditure and is found by multiplying the item by a formula (expressed as a decimal and rounded to the nearest third decimal place) which, subject to a few exceptions, is

$$(RD - RI) \div RI$$

where RD is the retail prices index for the month in which the disposal occurs and RI is the retail prices index for March 1982 or the month in which the expenditure was incurred, whichever is the later. The Revenue

---

67. *Oram* v. *Johnson* (1980) 53 T.C. 319; [1980] S.T.C. 222.
68. *Ibid.* s.43 and Sched. 6, para. 12(4).
69. *Secretan* v. *Hart* (1969) 45 T.C. 701.
70. *Bentley* v. *Pike* [1981] S.T.C. 360 (1981) 53 T.C. 590; (where the "gain" was the result of the devaluation of the pound sterling against the German mark).
70a. F.A. 1982, ss.86–89 and Sched. 13; F.A. 1985, s.68 and Sched. 19. And see (1985) S.T.I. 217.

publish monthly tables showing the indexed rise to be used for disposals in the month.

Where there is an unindexed *gain*, the indexation allowance is deducted from the gain to give a reduced gain or a loss. Where there is an unindexed *loss*, the indexation allowances is added to the loss to give an increased loss. When the unindexed gain or loss is nil, there will be a loss equal to the indexation allowance.

Assets owned before March 31, 1982. For an asset owned by a person on March 31, 1982 and disposed of by that person on or after that date, he may claim to have the indexation allowance calculated as if he had acquired the asset for an amount equal to its market value at that date. The higher the then market value, the greater the allowance. The claim must be made within two years from the end of the year of assessment (or accounting period) in which the asset is disposed of, subject to the Revenue's power to extend the time limit. The claim does not affect any enhancement expenditure on the asset which was incurred after March 31, 1982.

16–30C There are a number of cases where an asset is treated as disposed of and acquired for a consideration such that neither gain nor loss accrues on the disposal. Examples are transfers between husband and wife (see § 16–17) and transfers between companies in the same group (see § 16–54). Where such a disposal occurs after April 5, 1982, the acquisition cost to the transferee will include any indexation allowance due in respect of the transferor's expenditure.

16–30D Where hold over relief (see § 16–49) or roll-over relief (see § 16–49E) is available, the amount to be held over or rolled over will take account of any indexation relief up to the date of the transfer.

Deductions: miscellaneous rules

16–31 There are a number of special provisions:

(i) Insurance premiums on a policy to cover the risk of damage or injury to, or loss or depreciation of, the asset are not deductible.[71]

(ii) Certain contingent liabilities are not allowed as a deduction unless they are enforced, when an appropriate adjustment in the tax liability is made. The restriction applies to the contingent liabilities of the assignor of a lease in respect of default by the assignee; to the liabilities of the vendor or lessor of land in respect of the covenants for quiet enjoyment; and to warranties given on the sale or lease of property other than land.[72]

In *Randall* v. *Plumb*[72a] V owned farmland. In consideration of the deposit with V of £25,000, V granted an option to enable a company to purchase V's land at

---

71. C.G.T.A. 1979, s.141.
72. *Ibid*. s.41.
72a. (1974) 50 T.C. 392.

an agreed price. The deposit was returnable in certain circumstances, *e.g.* if the company failed to obtain planning consent for the extraction of sand and gravel, etc. If the company exercised the option, the £25,000 was to be treated as part payment of the purchase price. It was conceded that V had received a capital sum derived from assets, with the consequence that there was a deemed disposal within s.20(1) and (3) of the Finance Act 1965: see § 16–08. The issue was whether the consideration for the disposal was £25,000 or some lesser sum. *Held*, that the possibility of V having to return the £25,000 could not be disregarded and a valuation should be made to take account of this possibility. Walton J. rejected the Crown's submission that only the contingencies referred to in C.G.T.A. 1979, ss.40(2) and 41 could be taken into account.

(iii) Expenditure incurred by a person absolutely entitled as legatee or as against trustees of settled property in relation to the transfer of the asset to him (including similar expenditure of the personal representatives or trustees) is allowable on a disposal by the beneficiary.[73]

(iv) No deduction is allowed for expenditure which has been or is to be met directly or indirectly by the Crown or any Government, public or local authority in the United Kingdom or elsewhere.[74]

(v) Income tax paid by the disponer of shares as a result of a statutory apportionment is deductible in computing the gain on the disposal of the shares, unless there has been an actual distribution of the amount apportioned.[75]

(vi) Overseas tax charged on the disposal of an asset is deductible so far as this fails to qualify for double taxation relief under section 10 of the Capital Gains Tax Act 1979.[76]

(vii) Interest is not deductible, except as provided by section 269 of the Income and Corporation Taxes Act 1970: see § 14–10.[77]

If capital allowances have been given in respect of expenditure on the asset, any such allowances (including renewals allowances) must be taken into account in computing the amount of any loss.[78]

16–31A   On the part disposal of an asset there are provisions for apportionment of expenditure between the part retained and the part disposed of.[79] The portion of the cost attributable to the part disposed is that arrived at by applying the fraction $\dfrac{A}{A + B}$ to the original total cost, where A equals the consideration for the part which is disposed of and B equals the market value of the part which is retained.

Suppose A owns an asset which cost £10,000 and that he disposes of a part for £7,000 at a time when the market value of the remainder is £13,000. The cost

---

73. C.G.T.A. 1979, s.47(1).
74. *Ibid.* s.42. But see F.A. 1981, s.48(7) as to the writing-off of government investment.
75. *Ibid.* s.74(1). See *ante*, § 15–53 and the Statement of Practice in [1977] S.T.I. 12, published as SP 2/1977.
76. *Ibid.* s.11.
77. *Ibid.* s.32(3).
78. *Ibid.* s.34.
79. *Ibid.* s.35.

attributable to the part disposed of is £10,000 $\times \dfrac{£7,000}{£7,000 + £13,000} = $ £3,500.
Consequently the amount of the gain is £7,000 − £3,500 = £3,500. The cost attributable to the part retained is £10,000 less £3,500 = £6,500.

Special rules of identification exist in the case of shares and securities.[80] There are special provisions which apply to small part disposals of land where the consideration does not exceed £20,000.[81]

16–32   3. *Wasting assets.* In the case of wasting assets not exempt from capital gains tax (see § 16–44), the original expenditure must be written down over the period between acquisition and disposal. The principle is that if a person has the enjoyment of a wasting asset over a period of years, he should not be able to claim loss relief based on the difference between buying and selling price; the buying price must be reduced to take account of the use and enjoyment of the asset.

16–33   Wasting asset is defined to mean an asset with a predictable life not exceeding 50 years, excluding freehold land.[82] "Life" in relation to tangible movable property means useful life, having regard to the purpose for which the asset was acquired or provided by the disponer.[83] Plant and machinery is in every case regarded as having a predictable life of less than 50 years, and in estimating its life it must be assumed that its life will end when it is finally put out of use as being unfit for further use, and that it is going to be used in the normal manner and to the normal extent and is going to be so used throughout its life as so estimated.[83] A life interest in settled property is not a wasting asset until the predictable expectation of the life tenant is 50 years or less.[84]

The expenditure incurred on the acquisition of a wasting asset, reduced by the residual or scrap value of the asset,[85] is to be treated as written off to nil at a uniform rate day by day over the life of the asset from the time of acquisition; and expenditure on the improvement of a wasting asset is to be treated as written off in the same manner from the time when it is first reflected in the state or nature of the asset.[86] There are provisions dealing with the case where the expenditure has qualified for capital allowances.[87]

16–34   In the case of leasehold interests,[88] whether of land or other property, the line of wastage is curved and the rate of wastage accelerates as the end of the term approaches. A lease of land is treated as a wasting asset only

---

80. *Ibid.* ss.64–70.
81. *Ibid.* s.107 ("small part disposals"). For disposals after April 5, 1986, the relief can be claimed where the disposal proceeds do not exceed 20 per cent. of the value of the holding. The £20,000 limit remains. See F.A. 1986, s.60.
82. *Ibid.* ss.155(1) and 37(1).
83. *Ibid.* s.37(1).
84. *Ibid.* s.37(1). This will be ascertained from actuarial tables approved by the Board.
85. Defined *ibid.* s.37(2), (3), as the predictable value at the end of the predictable life of the asset.
86. *Ibid.* s.38.
87. *Ibid.* s.39.
88. *Ibid.* Sched. 3.

when its duration is not more than 50 years but there are rules for determining the duration of a lease for this purpose. There is a table in the Act which sets out the rate at which the expenditure on a lease for 50 years is to be deemed to waste away and there is a formula for determining the amount of the original expenditure which is to be attributable to the consideration received on an assignment of the lease. Reference should be made to Schedule 3 to the Capital Gains Tax Act 1979 for the detailed provisions.

16–35   4. *For consideration payable by instalments.* Where an asset is sold for payments to be made by instalments, such as a rentcharge or other series of income payments, the consideration for the disposal is the capitalised value of the payments,[89] no discount being allowed in making the valuation for the postponement or for the risk that the payments might not be recovered. If any part of the consideration proves to be irrecoverable, such adjustment must be made (whether by way of discharge or repayment of tax or otherwise) as is required in consequence. It is provided that if the consideration or part of the consideration is payable by future instalments over a period exceeding 18 months, then, if the person making the disposal satisfies the Board that he would otherwise suffer undue hardship, the tax on the chargeable gain may, at his option, be paid by such instalments as the Board may allow over a period not exceeding eight years and ending not later than the time at which the last of the future instalments is payable.[90]

In *Coren* v. *Keighley*[91] V sold land to P for £3,750. The sale agreement provided that V should advance £2,250 on mortgage to P, repayable over 10 years at interest. The conveyance acknowledged the receipt by V of £3,750 and a legal charge, executed on the same day, acknowledged the advance to P. *Held* V was assessable to capital gains tax on the footing that he had received £3,750: this was not a sale by instalments.

In *Marren* v. *Ingles*[92] V sold shares in a company to P for a fixed price per share plus an amount to be determined later by reference to the company's profits. The Crown contended that there were two disposals by V: the first when the shares were sold, and the second when the amount was determined. *Held* there was a second disposal under C.G.T.A. 1979, s.20(1) (see § 16–08) because V then received a capital sum which was derived from "assets," namely, his right to receive the balance of the purchase price.

General rules for assets held on April 6, 1965

16–36   The Act charges capital gains tax only on gains which accrue after April 6, 1965. In the case of quoted shares or securities, the general rule is that the gain (or loss) is calculated by reference to their quoted market value on April 6, 1965, except that the calculation must be by reference to the orig-

---

89. *Ibid.* s.31(3).
90. *Ibid.* s.40(1). For the mode of testing hardship, see [1972] B.T.R. "Current Tax Intelligence," at pp. 404 and 441.
91. (1972) 48 T.C. 370.
92. (1980) 54 T.C. 76; [1980] S.T.C. 500 (H.L.).

inal cost price if this would show a smaller gain (or loss).[93] Where shares acquired on different dates are disposed of, the general rule is first in, first out. The rule for the valuation of land in the United Kingdom which has a development value is similar.[94]

In the case of other assets, the gain (or loss) is assumed to accrue at a uniform rate over the period of ownership; so that if, for example, an asset was acquired on April 6, 1962, and disposed of on April 6, 1966, one quarter of the total gain is chargeable because, out of the period of ownership of four years, one year fell after April 6, 1965[95]; but the disponer can elect to have his gain (or loss) computed by reference to the market value of the asset on April 6, 1965.[96] He cannot, however, get relief for a larger loss than the loss actually realised.[97] There are provisions for identifying unquoted shares which are disposed of with earlier acquisitions.[98]

The market value of assets means the price those assets might reasonably be expected to fetch on a sale in the open market.[99] The rules which determine the market value are substantially the same as those which apply for the purposes of capital transfer tax and inheritance tax.[1]

5. Losses

16–37 Generally, losses are computed in the same way as gains are computed[2]; and the provisions of the Act which distinguish gains which are chargeable gains from those which are not, or which make part of a gain a chargeable gain and part not, apply also to distinguish losses which are allowable losses from those which are not, and to make part of a loss an allowable loss and part not. References to the term "allowable loss" have to be construed accordingly.[3]

Capital gains tax is charged on the total amount of chargeable gains accruing to a person in a year of assessment, after deducting any allowable losses.[4] Allowable losses accruing in a year of assessment are deducted primarily from chargeable gains of that year and any surplus of unrelieved losses is carried forward to future years without time limit. Losses may not be carried back and relieved against gains of earlier years, except that allowable losses sustained by an individual in the year in which he dies may, so far as they cannot be deducted from chargeable gains accruing in

---

93. C.G.T.A. 1979, Sched. 5, paras. 1–3. The rule by which the market value of quoted securities is determined by reference to the official quotation does not apply "where in consequence of special circumstances prices so quoted are by themselves not a proper measure of market value": C.G.T.A. 1979, s.150(3) and Sched. 6, para. 2. See *Hinchcliffe* v. *Crabtree* [1972] A.C. 707; 47 T.C. 419 (H.L.).

94. *Ibid.* Sched. 5, para. 9, and see *Watkins* v. *Kidson* (1979) 53 T.C. 117; [1979] S.T.C. 464 (H.L.).

95. *Ibid.* Sched. 5, para. 11.

96. *Ibid.* Sched. 5, para. 12(1).

97. *Ibid.* Sched. 5, para. 12(2).

98. *Ibid.* Sched. 5, paras. 13–14.

99. *Ibid.* s.150 (valuation of shares not quoted on a stock exchange).

1. *Ibid.* s.153.

2. *Ibid.* s.29(1).

3. *Ibid.* s.29(2).

4. *Ibid.* s.4(1).

that year, be deducted from chargeable gains accruing to the deceased in the three years preceding the year in which the death occurs, taking chargeable gains accruing in a later year before those accruing in an earlier year.[5] Losses brought forward will be used only so far as necessary to reduce gains to an amount equal to the exempt amount for the year.[6] Losses incurred on a disposal to a connected person are generally only allowable against gains made on subsequent disposals to the same connected person.[7–9] Individuals resident or ordinarily resident within (but domiciled outside) the United Kingdom are taxed in respect of chargeable gains accruing from the disposal of assets situated outside the United Kingdom only on the amount received in the United Kingdom; and accordingly losses accruing on the disposal of assets situated outside the United Kingdom to any such individual are not allowable losses.[10] The treatment of losses in connection with settled property has already been mentioned.[11] Where in the case of a woman who in a year of assessment is a married woman living with her husband there is an allowable loss (whether of that year or carried forward from an earlier year) which would be deductible but for an insufficiency of chargeable gains, the loss is deductible from chargeable gains of the husband, unless either party makes application to the inspector before July 6, in the next following year of assessment.[12]

Capital losses on unquoted shares in trading companies

16–38   Section 37 of the Finance Act 1980 allows an individual who sustains an allowable loss (for capital gains tax purposes) to claim relief from income tax in place of the normal capital gains tax relief. This is discussed in § 12–10B.

"Manufactured" or "artificial" losses

16–38A   The Courts have considered a number of cases of tax-avoidance schemes involving attempts to manufacture "allowable losses" for set-off against chargeable gains. An individual, for example, who had realised (or was about to realise) a chargeable gain of £100,000 might buy from a "tax-house," for a fee, a "scheme" which would provide him with an (unreal) loss of the like amount. The *Ramsay*[13] case was concerned with an "off-the-peg" scheme. The *Burmah*[14] case was concerned with an "in-house" scheme. The House of Lords decided that such "manufactured" losses are not capable of being "allowable losses" of the kind for which relief is available; but it is now clear that the decisions in these cases have much wider implications. This is discussed in Chapter 36.

---

5. *Ibid.* s.49(2).
6. See § 16–02.
7–9. C.G.T.A. 1979, s.62(3). See § 16–21 (2).
10. C.G.T.A. 1979, ss.14(1) and 29(4).
11. See *ante.* § 16–22(3).
12. C.G.T.A. 1979, s.4(2). See § 16–04A.
13. (1981) 54 T.C. 101; [1981] S.T.C. 174 (H.L.).
14. (1982) 54 T.C. 200; [1982] S.T.C. 30 (H.L.).

6. Exemptions and Reliefs

The following is a summary of the principal exemptions and reliefs.

1. *Miscellaneous exemptions*

16–39   Private motor-cars are not chargeable assets[15]; thus no chargeable gain or allowable loss accrues on their disposal.[16] Saving certificates and government non-marketable securities (as defined[17]) are not chargeable assets.[18] Gains on the disposal of currency acquired for personal expenditure abroad are not chargeable gains.[19] Betting winnings and winnings from prizes are not chargeable assets.[20] Sums obtained by way of compensation or damages for any wrong or injury suffered by an individual in his person or in his profession or vocation are not chargeable gains.[21] Gains on disposals of certain gilt-edged securities are exempt from capital gains tax[22]; and a similar exemption now applies to gains on disposals of qualifying corporate bonds.[22a] Gains accruing to an authorised unit trust, an investment trust or a court investment fund are not chargeable gains.[23] A gain on the disposal of shares to which the business expansion scheme applies is not a chargeable gain.[23a]

2. *Life assurance and deferred annuities*

16–40   Where a person effects a policy of life assurance, whether on his own life or on that of some other person in whose life he has an insurable interest, the occasion of the payment of the sum assured or the occasion of the surrender of the policy are treated as a disposal by the policy holder of his rights under the policy in consideration of the amount then payable. Likewise, the occasion of the payment of the first instalment of a deferred annuity is treated as a disposal of the rights thereunder in consideration of the market value at that time of the right to that and further instalments of the annuity.[24] Similar provisions apply where the policy provides not for the payment of money but for the transfer of investments or other assets; the consideration for the disposal being in such case the market value of the assets at the time of the disposal.[25]

---

15. C.G.T.A. 1979, s.130.
16. *Ibid.* ss.19(4), 130.
17. *Ibid.* s.71.
18. *Ibid.* ss.71, 19(4), 130.
19. *Ibid.* s.133.
20. *Ibid.* s.19(4).
21. *Ibid.* s.19(5).
22. *Ibid.*, s.64. This applies to disposals after July 1, 1986: F.A. 1985, s.67(1). Before, the gilts had to be held for 12 months. "Gilt-edged securities" is defined and listed in C.G.T.A. 1979, s.64(1) and Sched. 2. And see (1985) S.T.I. 407.
22a. See F.A. 1984, s.64 and Sched. 13.
23. F.A. 1980, s.81(1).
23a. F.A. 1983, Sched. 5, para. 16 as substituted by F.A. 1986, Sched. 9, para. 15 in relation to shares issued after March 18, 1986: *ibid.*, para. 1(2).
24. C.G.T.A. 1979, s.143.
25. I.C.T.A. 1970, s.321.

It is provided that no chargeable gain shall accrue on a disposal in the circumstances mentioned in the preceding paragraph, except where the person making the disposal is not the original beneficial owner and acquired the rights or interests for a consideration in money or money's worth.[26] Thus if A takes out a policy of life assurance, no liability to capital gains tax arises on payment of the policy moneys to A, on a surrender of the policy, or on their payment to A's personal representatives on A's death, or on their payment to the trustees of a voluntary settlement to whom A transferred the policy. If A assigns the policy for money or money's worth, the exemption does not apply on payment of the policy moneys to the assignee. Furthermore A will be chargeable on the consideration received on, *e.g.* the disposal of his rights under a fire insurance policy which has matured, in so far as the property insured was a chargeable asset.[27]

3. *Private residences*

16-41 A gain which accrues on the disposal by an individual of a dwelling-house or part of a dwelling-house is not a chargeable gain if the house was the individual's only or main residence throughout his period of ownership (as defined[28]), or throughout the period of ownership except for all or any part of the last 24 months of that period.[29] If this condition is not satisfied throughout the period, a fraction of the gain is exempted corresponding to the period of occupation as a residence[30]; except that a period of absence not exceeding three years (or periods which do not together exceed three years) during which the dwelling-house was not the individual's only or main residence and throughout which he had no residence or main residence eligible for relief under the section are disregarded in certain circumstances.[31] This (and other provisions[31]) protect the person who is compelled to leave his normal residence, *e.g.* because of a temporary posting. If the gain accrues from the disposal of a dwelling-house, part of which is used exclusively for the purposes of a trade or business or of a profession or vocation, the gain is apportioned and the exemption applies to that part of the gain apportioned to the non-business portion.[32] There are provisions for apportionment where a residence is reconstructed or converted.[33]

---

26. C.G.T.A. 1979, s.143(1), (2).
27. *Ibid.* s.140(1). Reversing the decision in *I.R.C.* v. *Montgomery* (1974) 49 T.C. 679; [1975] S.T.C. 182. But see *Marren* v. *Ingles* in § 16–35.
28. *Ibid.* s.101(7) and s.102(4).
29. I.C.T.A. 1970, s.102(1). Period extended from 12 to 24 months as respects disposals after April 5, 1980; F.A. 1980, s.80(2), (3). The section applies to an individual's dwelling-house or part of a dwelling-house which is, or has at any time in his period of ownership been, his only or main residence, together with its garden or grounds up to a specified limit: see I.C.T.A. 1970 s.101(1)–(4). A bungalow to accommodate staff which is built in the grounds of a dwelling-house may itself fall within the exemption: see *Batey* v. *Wakefield* (1981) 55 T.C. 550; [1981] S.T.C. 521 (C.A.); and see *Green* v. *I.R.C.* (1982) 56 T.C. 10; [1982] S.T.C. 485 (C.A.), (caretaker's lodge).
30. *Ibid.* s.102(2).
31. *Ibid.* s.102(3) and 101(8) (temporary occupation of job-related living accommodation). See also Concessions D3 and D4.
32. *Ibid.* s.103(1) and as to apportionment, see s.101(9). See F.A. 1980, s.80(1) as to the effect of letting accommodation, *e.g.* to students and SP 14/80 in [1980] S.T.I. 748.
33. C.G.T.A. 1979, s.103(2).

The exemption applies to the individual's only or main residence and, in the case of a man and his wife living with him,[34] there can only be one residence or main residence.[35] A person with two or more residences may nominate one of them for exemption; and if he does not do so, the inspector may determine the matter, subject to the individual's right of appeal to the General or Special Commissioners.[36] Gains on the disposal of a residence provided for a dependent relative are in some cases exempt.[36a] The exemption applies to a disposal by a trustee of settled property of an asset which is the only or main residence of a person "entitled to occupy it under the terms of the settlement."[37]

In *Sansom* v. *Peay*[38] the exemption was held to apply where the occupation was that of beneficiaries under a discretionary settlement. Brightman J. said:

> " . . . looking at the matter *at the date of the disposal*, the beneficiaries were persons who, in the events which happened, were entitled to occupy the house and did occupy it under the terms of the settlement."

Relief is also given where personal representatives dispose of a house which before and after the deceased's death has been used as their only or main residence by individuals who under the will or intestacy are entitled to the whole or substantially the whole of the proceeds of the house either absolutely or for life.[39]

There is no exemption if the dwelling-house was acquired wholly or partly for the purpose of realising a gain from the disposal; nor is there any exemption in relation to a gain which is attributable to expenditure incurred during the period of ownership for the purpose of realising a gain from the disposal.[40]

If as a result of the breakdown of a marriage one spouse ceases to occupy his or her matrimonial home and subsequently as part of a financial settlement disposes of the home, or an interest in it, to the other spouse (or, if the transfer is after a divorce, ex-spouse) the home may be regarded for the purposes of section 101 of the Capital Gains Tax Act 1979 as continuing to be a residence of the transferring spouse from the date his (or her) occupation ceases until the date of transfer, provided that it has throughout this period been the other spouse's only or main residence. Thus if a married couple separate and the husband leaves the matrimonial home while still owning it, the exemption is given on a subsequent transfer to the wife, provided she has continued to live in the house and the husband has not elected that some other house should be treated for capital gains tax purposes as his main residence for this period.[41]

---

34. See § 8–23.
35. *Ibid.* s.101(6), (7).
36. *Ibid.* s.101(5).
36a. *Ibid.* s.105(1)–(6).
37. *Ibid.* s.104.
38. (1976) 52 T.C. 1; [1976] S.T.C. 494. An entitlement to occupy property may be an interest in possession for the purposes of capital transfer tax or inheritance tax: see § 22–20.
39. Concession D5.
40. *Ibid.* s.103(3).
41. Concession D6.

4. *Chattels sold for £3,000 or less*

16-42   A gain accruing on a disposal of an asset which is tangible movable property is not a chargeable gain if the amount or value of the consideration for the disposal does not exceed £3,000.[42] If the consideration exceeds £3,000, so much of it as exceeds five-thirds of the difference between the consideration and £3,000 is excluded from any chargeable gain.[43]

> Thus if an asset is sold for £3,300, the chargeable gain cannot exceed $\frac{5}{3} \times$ (£3,300 − £3,000) = £500.

There is a corresponding restriction on relief for losses. If a chattel acquired for more than £3,000 is disposed of for less than £3,000, the allowable loss is calculated as if the asset had been disposed of for £3,000.[44]

If two or more assets forming part of a set of articles (such as a set of chairs) are disposed of by the same seller to the same buyer,[45-46] whether on the same or different occasions, the two or more transactions are treated as a single transaction disposing of a single asset. Their value is therefore aggregated for the purpose of applying the exemption limit.

For wasting assets, see § 16–44.

5. *Works of art, etc.*

16-43   Gains which accrue on the disposal of works of art, etc., given or bequeathed to a body not established or conducted for profit are not chargeable gains if the asset would qualify for relief from inheritance tax under section 26(2) of the Capital Transfer Tax Act, 1984.[47] The Treasury may require an undertaking to be given and that undertaking must remain in force until the asset is disposed of.[48]

The exemptions referred to in this paragraph are withdrawn if the asset is later sold or if the undertaking referred to is not carried out.[49]

Any capital gains tax payable on a subsequent sale or a breach of the undertaking is allowed as a deduction from the amount chargeable to inheritance tax.[49]

6. *Exemption for tangible movables which are wasting assets*[50]

16-44   No chargeable gain is to accrue on the disposal of, or of an interest in, an asset which is tangible movable property and which is a wasting asset, *i.e.* even if the consideration exceeds the amount in § 16–42. An asset is a wasting asset if it has a predictable life of less than 50 years: see § 16–33. The exemption does not apply to a disposal of commodities of any description by a person dealing on a terminal market or dealing with or through a per-

---

42. *Ibid.* s.128(1). The section does not exempt certain gains on the disposal of commodities dealt in on a terminal market or of currency: *ibid.* s.128(6).
43. *Ibid.* s.128(2).
44. *Ibid.* s.128(3).
45.–46. Or to different buyers who are acting in concert or are connected persons: see *ibid.* s.128(4) and § 16–18A.
47. *Ibid.* s.147; and see *post* § 19–33.
48. *Ibid.* s.147.
49. See *post*, §§ 19–33 *et seq.*
50. *Ibid.* s.127.

son ordinarily engaged in dealing on a terminal market. The exemption does not apply to chattels used for the purposes of a trade in respect of which capital allowances are or could be claimed.

7. *Replacement of business assets: roll-over relief*

16–45   A relief may be claimed where business assets are sold and replaced by others. There is no exemption from the tax: relief is given by allowing the trader to deduct the gain from the cost of acquisition of the replacement and thus to defer payment of tax until the assets are disposed of and not replaced. The relief is thus a "roll-over" relief.

Section 115(1) of the Capital Gains Tax Act 1979 provides that if the whole of the consideration which a trader[51] obtains for the disposal of assets[52] (called "the old assets") used only for the purposes of the trade throughout the period of ownership is applied by him in acquiring other assets (called "the new assets") which on the acquisition are taken into use and used only for the purposes of the trade *and* the old assets and the new assets fall within the classes listed in section 118,[53] then the trader may claim to have the consideration so applied treated:

(a) as if the consideration for the disposal of the old assets were such as to produce neither gain nor loss;

(b) as if the cost of the new assets were reduced by the amount of the chargeable gain.

Section 116(1) of the Capital Gains Tax Act 1979 gives a limited relief where less than the whole consideration obtained for the old assets is applied in purchasing new assets, provided the amount not so applied does not exceed the gain on the disposal of the old assets (whether chargeable gain or not).

The relief is available only if the acquisition of the new assets takes place, or an unconditional contract for the acquisition is entered into, within 12 months before or not later than three years[54] after the disposal of the old assets; and in the case where there is an unconditional contract, the relief is given provisionally.[55]

16–46   The classes of assets listed in the section are as follows[56]:

(1) any building or structure in the nature of a building occupied (as well as used)[56a] only for the purposes of the trade and any land so occupied and used;

---

51. This includes a person who carries on a profession or vocation and the occupier of woodlands on a commercial basis: C.G.T.A. 1979, s.121(1), (2). See SP 5/86. Roll-over relief is also available to certain non-profit-making bodies formed to protect or promote the interests of traders and professional people: *ibid.* s.121(1)(*d*).
52. This includes an interest in assets: *ibid.* s.115(1).
53. See § 16–46. Where the new asset is a depreciating asset, see *ibid.* s.117(1).
54. *Ibid.* s.115(3).
55. *Ibid.* s.115(3). The Board may allow an extension of the period referred to. See SP 2/1973.
56. *Ibid.* ss.118, 119(1), (2).
56a. For the meaning of these words, see *Anderton* v. *Lamb* (1980) 55 T.C. 1; [1981] S.T.C. 43 (houses built for occupation by partners on farms *held* not to fall into class (1)). And see SP 2/1974.

(2) fixed plant or machinery not forming part of a building or structure[56a];

(3) ships, aircraft and hovercraft;

(4) goodwill.

The relief is withheld if the new assets are bought wholly or partly for the purposes of realising a gain on their disposal.[58]

There are provisions for apportionment if a building is used partly for the purposes of a trade[59] or if the old assets were not so used throughout the period of ownership[60] or if assets within the section are mingled with those outside it.[61]

Roll-over relief may be available in the case of property commercially let as furnished holiday accommodation.[62]

8. *Release on retirement from a family business*

16–47   The Finance Act 1985 introduces a new code of reliefs[62a] from capital gains tax which, subject to one exception,[63] applies to any disposal made on or after April 6, 1985. The new provisions are lengthy and complex and what follows is no more than an outline of the main rules.

Disposals by individuals

–47A   Relief from capital gains tax is given where a material disposal of business assets is made by an individual who, at the time of the disposal, has attained the age of 60 or has retired on ill-health grounds below the age of 60, *i.e.*, is able to satisfy the Board that he has ceased to be engaged in and, by reason of ill-health, is incapable of engaging in work of the kind he previously undertook in the business and is likely to remain permanently so incapable.[64] The maximum retirement relief is £100,000 where the qualifying period (meaning roughly the period during which the business has been carried on) is ten years or more; but the relief is given on a scale which rises from 10 per cent. where the qualifying period is precisely one year to 100 per cent. where it is ten years.[65] Retirement relief is available only against gains attributable to 'chargeable business assets,' as defined.[66]

---

57. The word "fixed" in the phrase "fixed plant and machinery" qualifies both plant and machinery: see *Williams* v. *Evans* [1982] S.T.C. 498 (earth moving machinery not fixed).

58. C.G.T.A. 1979 s.115(4).

59. *Ibid.* s.115(5).

60. *Ibid.* s.115(6).

61. *Ibid.* s.115(9). For the position where there is more than one trade, see *ibid.* s.115(7) and SP 8/81 in [1981] S.T.I. 502. For the position where a trade is transferred to a family company, see *ibid.* s.120. As to replacements in a group of companies, see I.C.T.A. 1970, s.276, and SP 1/1978 in [1978] S.T.I. 25.

62. F.A. 1985, sections 69–70 and Sched. 20 and see (1985) S.T.I. 2.

62a. See F.A. 1984, s.50 and Sched. 11, para. 2.

63. See *ibid.*, s.69(1).

64. See *ibid.*, s.69(1) and Sched. 20 para. 3(1).

65. See *ibid.*, Sched. 20, para. 13.

66. See *ibid.*, Sched. 20, Part II.

16–47B   For the relief to be available there has to be (i) a disposal of business assets which is (ii) a material disposal.

A *disposal of business assets* can arise in three situations[67]:

Situation (a): Where the individual disposes of the whole or part of a business. This includes a disposal by an individual of his interest in the assets of a partnership carrying on a business. A partnership business is treated as owned by each individual who is a member of the partnership, so a disposal by the firm of the business is treated as a disposal by each of the partners who is an individual.

Situation (b): Where the individual disposes of assets which, when the business ceased to be carried on, were in use for the purposes of the business. This meets the case where the business has collapsed and assets of the former business are being sold.

Situation (c): Where the individual disposes of shares or securities of a company. A disposal of shares is treated as made when a person receives a capital distribution from the company in respect of those shares *e.g.* in a liquidation: see § 16–12.

16–47C   The legislation takes each of these three situations and states the "relevant conditions" that have to be satisfied for a disposal to be a disposal to a *material disposal*.[68] The relevant conditions differ for each situation and have to be fulfilled for a period of at least one year. In Situation (a) the year ends on the date of the disposal of the business. In Situation (b) it ends with the date when the business ceased to be carried on. In Situation (c) it ends with "the operative date," which differs if, in the period before sale, there has been a cessation of business or the individual ceased to be a full-time working director.

A number of terms are used in stating the relevant conditions which are defined in paragraph 1 of Schedule 20. "*Family company*" means, in relation to an individual, a company the voting rights in which are (a) as to not less than 25 per cent. exercisable by the individual, or (b) as to more than 50 per cent. exercisable by the individual or a member of his family (defined) and, as to not less than 5 per cent., exercisable by the individual himself. A "*full-time working director*" in relation to one or more companies means a director who is required to devote substantially the whole of his time to the service of that company or, as the case may be, those companies taken together, in a managerial or technical capacity. A "*trading group*" means a group of companies (defined) the business of whose members, taken together, consists wholly or mainly of the carrying of a trade or trades (defined). A "*commercial association of companies*" means a company together with such of its associated companies (defined) as carry on businesses which are of such a nature that the businesses of the

---

67. *Ibid.*, s.69(2).
68. *Ibid.*, s.69(3)–(8).

company and the associated companies taken together may be reasonably considered to make up a single composite undertaking.

Situation (a)

–47D   In Situation (a)—disposal of a business—the relevant conditions to be fulfilled throughout the year ending with the date of the disposal are that the business should be owned either (i) by the individual (or partner) disposing of it or (ii) by a company which is a trading company and is either that individual's family company or a member of a trading group of which the holding company is that individual's family company; and where (ii) applies, the individual must be a full-time working director of the company or, if the company is a member of a group or commercial association of companies, of one or more companies which are members of the group or association. The alternatives in (i) and (ii) enable an incorporated business to be disincorporated and disposed of by individual members without loss of retirement relief.

Situation (b)

In Situation (b)—disposal of the assets of a ceased business—the relevant conditions are the same as in Situation (a). In addition, the individual making the disposal must have attained 60 or retired on ill-health grounds below 60 on or before the date when the business ceased to be carried on; and the disposal must take place within the "permitted period," defined as one year after the cessation or such longer period as the Board allows.

Situation (c)

In Situation (c)—the disposal of shares or securities—the relevant conditions are that, throughout the year, either

(a) the individual disposer owns the business which, at the date of disposal, is owned by the company or, if the company is the holding company of a trading group, by any member of the group; or

(b) the company is the individual's family company and is either a trading company or the holding company of a trading group and the individual is a full-time working director of the company or if the company is a member of a group or commercial association of companies, of one or more companies which are members of the group or association.

The alternatives in (a) and (b) enable an unincorporated business to become incorporated without loss of retirement relief.

–47E   *Associated disposals.*[69] An individual who disposes of a business, or assets, or shares or securities in a company in circumstances qualifying for retirement relief might also, at the same time, dispose of an asset owned by

---

69. See *ibid.*, s.70(6)–(8).

the individual personally and which has been in use for the purposes of the business. For example, a partner in a firm of solicitors might own the freehold of the property from which the firm carries on its business and might wish, when selling his share of the partnership assets, to sell his interest in the freehold. The Act contains provisions to enable such "associated disposals" to qualify for retirement relief.

Disposal by trustees[70–77]

16–48   We have seen that retirement relief may be available where an individual makes a material disposal of business assets. The relief is also available in certain circumstances where the individual is a beneficiary with an interest in possession (excluding a fixed term interest) in settled property, where the business assets from part of the settled property and where the trustees make the disposal of business assets at a time when the individual beneficiary (having been involved in the business) has attained the age of 60 or has retired on ill-health grounds below the age of 60.

The hold-over relief for gifts in § 16–49 may be available to defer any tax liability on such part of a chargeable gain as is not eligible for retirement relief.

9. Hold-over relief

16–49   We have seen that capital gains tax can in some cases be deferred where a trader (whether an individual, individuals, company or trustees) invests the proceeds of sale of an asset in another asset. The gain can be "rolled over" to that other asset: see §§ 16–45 *et seq.*

We now consider a relief which is available where one person disposes of an asset to another person otherwise than by way of bargain made at arm's length, *e.g.* on a gift or sale at an undervalue, and both parties (or in some cases the transferor alone) desire that the capital gains tax that would otherwise be payable on the disposal should be deferred until the transferee disposes of the asset. The liability to pay tax is "held over" until that event occurs. At one time "hold-over relief" was available only for disposals of business assets but the relief has been progressively extended and is now available (with exceptions) on the disposal of any asset, leaving the old business assets relief (see § 16–49E) to meet some of the exceptions.

Section 79 of the Finance Act 1980 (as extended)[78] enables an individual or the trustees of a settlement ("the transferor") to dispose of an asset to an individual or to the trustees of a settlement ("the transferee") without any immediate charge to capital gains tax: the charge to tax is held over until the transferee disposes of the asset without benefit of section 79 relief. Hold-over relief has to be claimed and is available only where the trans-

---

70–77. See *ibid.*, s.70(3)–(5).

78. The relief on the disposal of business assets (see § 16–49E) applied to disposals after April 11, 1978. Hold-over relief was first available only on disposals between individuals after April 5, 1980 (F.A. 1980, s.79). It was extended to disposals from an individual to trustees after April 5, 1981 (F.A. 1981, s.78). It has now been extended to disposals after April 6, 1982, *by* individuals or trustees *to* individuals or trustees (F.A., 1982, s.82), thereby rendering the provisions of the F.A. 1981 unnecessary.

feree is a resident or ordinarily resident in the United Kingdom; and a charge to tax arises if he ceases to be so resident: see § 16–49C. The claim must be made by both the transferor and the transferee, unless the transferor is an individual and the transferee is the trustee (or trustees) of a settlement, when the claim need be made by the transferor only.

16–49A The held-over gain on a disposal is the chargeable gain that would have accrued to the transferor on the disposal but for the relief; and where the relief is claimed its effect is that

(1) the amount of any chargeable gain which (apart from the section) would accrue to the transferor; and

(2) the amount which (apart from the section) would be the transferee's cost of acquisition

is reduced by an amount equal to the held-over gain.

> Assume A has an asset which cost A £30,000. A gives the asset to B, an individual. This has to be treated as a disposal at market value (§ 16–18). Assume the market value is £50,000. Assume that the indexation allowance to which A is entitled is nil and that the chargeable gain accruing to A on the disposal is therefore £20,000. A and B claim to have the gain held over. The effect is (i) the chargeable gain accruing on A's disposal (£20,000) is reduced by the held-over gain (£20,000) to nil; and (ii) B is treated as acquiring the asset for a consideration of £50,000 less £20,000 = £30,000.
>
> If, later, B sells the asset to P for £55,000, the chargeable gain accruing to B on that disposal is £55,000 less £30,000 (plus the indexation allowance to which B is then entitled). If B gives the asset to C and relief is again claimed, the tax liability is held over until C disposes of the asset. (If B or C die owning the asset, capital gains tax is avoided).

Section 79 of the Finance Act 1980 applies not only where A makes an outright gift to B (as in the example) but also where A sells the asset at an undervalue in a transaction which is "otherwise than under a bargain at arm's length." In such a case the held-over gain is reduced by the amount by which the consideration A receives exceeds A's cost of acquisition.

> Thus if, in the above example, A sells the asset (cost £30,000) to B for £35,000, the held-over gain is £20,000 less £5,000 = £15,000.

Any retirement relief due to the transferor under the provisions discussed in § 16–47 is given first, only the non-exempt excess being available for hold-over relief under section 79.

It should be noted that section 79 does not allow the holding over of *part* of a chargeable gain. In the example in § 16–49A, for example, A could not hold back a sufficient part of the chargeable gain of £20,000 to absorb his exempt amount for the year (£5,000 in 1982–83) or the amount of allowable losses available to A during the year.

16–49B Where a disposal in respect of which a claim is made under section 79 is a chargeable transfer for inheritance tax purposes, an amount in respect of the inheritance tax is deductible in computing the chargeable gain accruing to the transferee on his disposal of the asset. The amount of the inheritance tax which is deductible is whichever is the lesser of the tax chargeable on the transfer and the amount of the chargeable gain of the transferee. Thus the inheritance tax on the transfer is deductible save to the extent that this will create a capital gains tax loss for the transferee.

16–49C   *Emigration of the transferee.* If relief is given under section 79 of the Finance Act 1980 (see § 16–49) and the transferee becomes neither resident nor ordinarily resident in the United Kingdom without having previously disposed of the asset, a chargeable gain is deemed to accrue to the transferee of an amount equal to the held-over gain.[79] This applies only if the "emigration" occurs within six years after the transferee's acquisition of the asset. A disposal to a spouse of the transferee does not count as a previous disposal (so emigration of the transferee still "triggers" a charge under the section); but if that spouse makes a disposal, this is treated as a disposal by the transferee. If the tax assessed on the transferee is not paid within 12 months from the due date, the transferor can be assessed and charged in the name of the transferee to all or any part of that tax; but the transferor is entitled to recover any tax he pays from the transferee.

Deemed disposals by trustees of settled property

16–49D   A chargeable gain attributable to an asset may be held over on a disposal of that asset (with or without other assets) to trustees of a settlement.

There may subsequently be a deemed disposal of the asset by the trustees either:

(a) under section 54 of the Capital Gains Tax Act 1979 (see § 16–22) on a person becoming absolutely entitled to the asset as against the trustees (including the case where a life interest in settled property terminates and the settlement comes to an end); or

(b) under section 55 of the Capital Gains Tax Act 1979 (see § 16–23) where a life interest in settled property terminates and the property continues to be settled property.

(c) If the trustees of a United Kingdom resident trust cease to be so resident without having disposed of the asset: see § 16–49C. There are provisions to counter the avoidance of tax by the use of dual resident trusts.[79a]

In cases (a) and (b), the Act provides that no chargeable gain shall accrue on the disposal where the occasion of the charge is the termination of a life interest (see § 16–22B and § 16–23B). But for special provisions, capital gains tax could be avoided by putting a gainful asset into a specially created settlement with a life tenant having a short life-expectancy. It is accordingly provided that, as respect assets comprised in the settlement which have been the subject of hold-over relief, a chargeable gain shall

---

79. F.A. 1981, s.79.
79a. F.A. 1986, s.58.

accrue on a deemed disposal under section 54 or 55 (above) where a life interest terminates, but only as respects the assets which were the subject of the relief.[80]

10. *Relief for gifts of business assets*

16–49E   Section 126 of the Capital Gains Tax Act 1979 provides a relief which applies where an individual (called "the transferor") makes a disposal after April 11, 1978, otherwise than under a bargain at arm's length, to a person resident or ordinarily resident in the United Kingdom ("the transferee") of (a) an asset which is, or is an interest in, an asset used for the purposes of a *trade, profession or vocation*[81] carried on by the transferor or by a company which is his *family company* or (b) shares or securities of a *trading company*[82] which is the transferor's family company. The words in italics are defined as in § 16–47. The relief may also apply where business property or shares in a trading company are comprised in a settlement and the trustees of the settlement are transferors.

In consequence of the general hold-over relief for gifts which was introduced by section 79 of the Finance Act 1980 and later extended (see § 16–49), business assets hold-over relief, now applies only to disposal to *companies*.[83] Such transactions are thought to be unusual.

The relief enables business assets to be given away without any charge to capital gains tax arising until the donee sells those assets. The relief has to be claimed by the transferor and the transferee. Its effect is that the chargeable gain that would have accrued to the transferor but for section 126 (called the "held-over gain") is deducted from the transferor's chargeable gain and from the transferee's base cost.[84] Hence it operates in the same way as the relief in § 16–49.

Any retirement relief due to the transferor under the provisions in § 16–47 is given first, only the non-exempt excess being "held-over" under section 126.[85]

The relief applies to gifts of agricultural property which is not used for the purposes of a trade carried on as in (a), above, but only if a chargeable transfer of the property would qualify for relief from inheritance tax under the provisions discussed in §§ 19–40 *et seq.*

11. *Charities, etc.*

16–50   A gain which accrues to a charity and is applicable and applied for charitable purposes is not a chargeable gain.[86] When property held on charitable trusts ceases to be so held, there is a deemed disposal by the trustees

---

80. C.G.T.A. 1979, s.56A inserted by F.A. 1982, s.84(3) and applicable to interests terminating on or after April 6, 1982.
81. Trade, profession and vocation have the same meaning as in the Income Tax Acts (see § 2–01) and "trade" includes the occupation of woodlands on a commercial basis and with a view to the realisation of profits: C.G.T.A. 1979, s.126(7), (8).
82. C.G.T.A. 1979, s.124.
83. *Ibid.* s.126(4) and Sched. 4, paras. 2–3.
84. *Ibid.* s.126(2).
85. *Ibid.* Sched. 4, para. 1.
86. *Ibid.* s.145(1).

to themselves at market value on which a charge to capital gains tax may arise.[87]

A disposal to a charity, if made after March 21, 1972, is exempt from capital gains tax.[88] This applies to disposals by way of gift (including gifts in settlement) and sales for a consideration not exceeding the expenditure allowable for capital gains tax purposes. (Thus the exemption does not apply if an asset which is charged to secure £x is transferred to the charity in consideration of its undertaking to discharge the liability and £x exceeds the transferor's base cost.) The disposal and acquisition are treated as made for such a consideration as will secure that neither a gain nor a loss accrues on the disposal; and a gain accruing to the charity on a later disposal by it will be exempt from capital gains tax only if it is applicable and applied for charitable purposes. If not so exempt, the acquisition of the asset by the disponer will be treated as the charity's acquisition. The exemption on disposals to a charity applies also where, *e.g.* on the termination of a life interest, a charity becomes absolutely entitled as against the trustees.[89–90]

The exemption applies also to disposals to the bodies referred to in Schedule 6 to the Finance Act 1975 (gifts for national purposes): see § 19–21.

12. *Approved schemes*

16–51   A gain is not a chargeable gain if it accrues to a person from his disposal of investments held as part of an approved pension scheme.[91] A similar exemption applies to approved retirement annuity schemes.[92]

There is no chargeable gain on the disposal of any right to any allowance, annuity or capital sum payable out of any superannuation fund, or under any superannuation scheme, established solely or mainly for persons employed in a profession, trade, undertaking or employment, and their dependants.[93]

13. *Employee trusts*

16–51A   Section 13 of the Capital Transfer Tax Act 1984 (see § 19–70) exempts from inheritance tax dispositions made by close companies and individuals into trusts for the benefit of employees which satisfy certain stringent conditions. Section 149 of the Capital Gains Tax Act 1979 enables such transfers to be made without liability to capital gains tax.

14. *Double taxation relief*

16–52   Double taxation relief is granted against United Kingdom capital gains tax for any capital gains tax imposed on the same gains by another country. The relief is similar to that given for income tax.

---

87. *Ibid.* s.145(2).
88. *Ibid.* s.146(1), (2). See *Prest* v. *Bettinson* (1980) 53 T.C. 437; [1980] S.T.C. 607.
89.–90. *Ibid.* s.146(3).
91. F.A. 1970, s.21(7) and see §§ 39–08 *et seq.*
92. I.C.T.A. 1970, s.226(6).
93. C.G.T.A. 1979, s.144(*a*).

7. CHARGEABLE GAINS OF COMPANIES

16–53 The chargeable gains of companies are liable to corporation tax and not to capital gains tax.[94] The amount to be included in respect of chargeable gains in a company's total profits for any accounting period is the total gains accruing to the company in the period, after deducting allowable losses, including unrelieved losses brought forward from an earlier period.[95] The principles which determine whether a company has gains or losses and the amount thereof are the same as those which apply to persons other than companies.[96]

Only a part of the chargeable gains of a company is included in the total profits for an accounting period, for section 93(2) of the Finance Act 1972 directs that the chargeable gains to be so included shall be reduced by such fraction as Parliament may from time to time determine. The fraction for companies other than authorised unit trusts and investment trusts is one-seventh for the financial year 1986.[98] The reduction has the effect that a company's chargeable gains are taxed at 30 per cent. The exempt amounts referred to in § 16–02 and § 16–02A do not apply to companies. Gains accruing to an authorised unit trust, an investment trust or a court investment trust are not chargeable gains.[99]

Groups of companies

16–54 There are special provisions relating to capital gains of companies which are members of a group of companies (as defined). Broadly speaking, the disposal of an asset from one member-company of the group to another such company gives rise to no chargeable gain or allowable loss. A gain (or loss) arises only when the asset is disposed of outside the group or a company ceases to be a member of a group.[1]

Gains of non-resident companies

16–55 The circumstances in which a non-resident company is liable to capital gains tax are discussed elsewhere.[2] Section 15 of the Capital Gains Tax Act 1979 applies to a non-resident company which would be a close company if it were resident in the United Kingdom.

Every person who, at the time when a chargeable gain accrues to a company, is resident or ordinarily resident in the United Kingdom and holds shares in the company is treated as if a part of the chargeable gain had accrued to him.[3] That part is the proportion of the assets of the company to which that person would be entitled on a liquidation of the company at the

---

94. I.C.T.A. 1970, s.238(3).
95. *Ibid.* s.265(1).
96. *Ibid.* s.265(2), (3); for an exception, see F. (No. 2) A. 1975, s.58.
97. F.A. 1974, s.10(1).
98. F.A. 1984, s.18(3).
99. F.A. 1980, s.81(1), (7). For definitions see I.C.T.A. 1970, ss.358–9.
1. *Ibid.*, ss.272–279.
2. See *ante,* § 16–04.
3. C.G.T.A. 1979, s.15(1), (2).

time when the chargeable gain accrues to the company.[4] A part of the gain attributable to a person which is less than one-twentieth is disregarded.[5] Any amount which is distributed to the shareholder within two years from the time when the gain accrued is excepted from the charge, if that amount is subject to tax in the shareholder's hand.[6] Gains on the disposal of certain trading assets are excluded.[7]

As respects disposals accruing to a company on or after March 10, 1981, the persons to whom a chargeable gain can be attributed include trustees owning shares in the company who are at the time when the gain accrues neither resident nor ordinarily resident in the United Kingdom.[8] Such gains can be further attributed to beneficiaries who receive capital payments from the trustees, under section 80 of the Finance Act 1981: see § 16–26.

---

4. *Ibid.* s.15(3).
5. *Ibid.* s.15(4).
6. *Ibid.* s.15(4)(*a*). Adjustments will be necessary if an assessment has been made: *ibid.* s.15(6). The tax is deducted on an actual disposal of shares: *ibid.* s.15(7).
7. *Ibid.* s.15(5)(*b*).
8. F.A. 1981, s.85.

ADMINISTRATION, ASSESSMENTS AND BACK DUTY—CORPORATE AND NON-CORPORATE BODIES

CHAPTER 17

ADMINISTRATION, ASSESSMENTS AND BACK DUTY

1. ADMINISTRATION

17–01 INCOME tax, corporation tax and capital gains tax are under the care and management of the Commissioners of Inland Revenue who constitute the Board of Inland Revenue (hereinafter called "the Board"). Their principal office is at Somerset House, London. The day-to-day administration is carried out by inspectors and collectors of taxes who are full-time civil servants appointed by the Board who act under the direction of the Board.[1] Collectors, as their name implies, are responsible for the collection of the tax which is assessed by the inspector.

The general administration of the tax system underwent a major reform when the Income Tax Management Act 1964 came fully into force on April 6, 1965. That Act and later amending Acts were consolidated in the Taxes Management Act 1970.

2. RETURNS AND ASSESSMENTS

17–02 Any person may be required by a notice given to him by an inspector or other officer of the Board to deliver to the officer within the time limited by the notice a return of his income, computed in accordance with the Income Tax Acts and specifying each separate source of income and the amount from each source.[2] The return in every case must include a declaration by the person making the return that it is to the best of his knowledge correct and complete.[3] Liability to a penalty arises where a return of income is not made or is incorrect.[4] There is an obligation to provide information about chargeable gains,[5] including particulars of assets acquired, of the person from whom they are acquired and the consideration for the acquisition. A person chargeable to tax who has not delivered a return is required to give notice that he is chargeable not later than one year after the end of the year of assessment to which the return relates.[6]

Persons who receive income in a representative capacity (such as personal representatives and trustees) are under a similar obligation to make returns when required by notice to do so.[7]

---

1. Taxes Management Act (T.M.A.) 1970, s.1. Inspectors were called "surveyors" in earlier Acts.
2. T.M.A. 1970, s.8(1). Section 8 states what may be required in a return.
3. *Ibid.* s.8(7).
4. *Ibid.* ss.93–107. Generally as to penalties and interest, see the Board's practice in [1977] S.T.I. 110.
5. *Ibid.* s.12. See also ss.25–28. But see C.G.T.A. 1979, s.5(5) where chargeable gains do not exceed twice the exempt amount for the year.
6. T.M.A. 1970, s.7 and (for companies) s.10.
7. *Ibid.* s.8(2).

17–03   Employers are under a duty when required to do so to disclose the names and particulars of payments to employees.[8] The inspector has power to require every person carrying on a trade or business and every body of persons carrying on any other activity to make a return of payments for services rendered otherwise than by employees, including periodical or lump sum payments in respect of copyright. Payments not exceeding £15 and certain other payments are excluded.[9] There are extensive provisions which require the disclosure of payments of interest and rent.[10]

Companies

17–04   A company may be required to deliver to an inspector or other officer of the Board a return of its profits computed in accordance with the Corporation Tax Acts specifying the income taken into account in computing those profits, with the amount from each source, giving particulars of all disposals giving rise to chargeable gains or allowable losses, and giving particulars of all charges on income.[11] For partnership returns see § 11–03.

Claims

17–05   Section 42 of the Taxes Management Act 1970, and Schedule 2 set out the procedures for claiming reliefs and allowances and the rights of appeal from decisions on such claims.

Production of documents

17–06   Sections 20, 20A, 20B, 20C and 20D of the Taxes Management Act 1970, empower an inspector by notice in writing to require a person to deliver to him such documents as are in the person's possession or power as (in the inspector's reasonable opinion) contain, or may contain, information relevant to any tax liability to which the person is or may be subject, or to the amount of any such liability.[11a] The documents must be specified or described in the notice. Such a notice may also be directed to (for example) the taxpayer's spouse and any son or daughter of his and, where the taxpayer carries on or carried on a business, any other person concerned in the same business. Notices cannot be issued by an inspector save with the prior authority of the Board and with the consent of a General or Special Commissioner (who must be satisfied that the inspector is justified in using the powers conferred by the section). The Board also has powers to require the delivery of documents to one of its officers.

   In practice, the Board can enforce production of relevant books, etc., by

---

8. *Ibid.* s.15.
9. *Ibid.* s.16.
10. *Ibid.* ss.17–18 (interest); s.19 (rent) and see § 6–15.
11. *Ibid.* s.11.
11a. For a decision on the Revenue's powers under s.20C, see *I.R.C.* v. *Rossminster Ltd.* (1979) 52 T.C. 160; [1980] S.T.C. 42 (H.L.). And see *Monarch Assurance Co. Ltd.* v. *Special Commissioners* [1986] S.T.C. 311.

using its power to make an estimated assessment on the taxpayer.[12] The taxpayer must then either appeal or accept the assessment; and if he appeals, the appellate Commissioners have power to confirm the estimated assessment, unless it is shown by the appellant taxpayer to be excessive.[13] If the taxpayer appeals, the appellate Commissioners have power to issue a precept ordering *the appellant* to deliver *inter alia* all such books, accounts or documents in his possession or power which in the Commissioners' opinion contain or may contain information relating to the subject-matter of the appeal.[14]

Assessments

17–07   Assessments are made either by an inspector or the Board. Assessments are made by an inspector unless the Act otherwise provides.[15] If an inspector is satisfied that a return affords correct and complete information concerning the income of the taxpayer, he will make the assessment accordingly; but if the inspector is dissatisfied with any return, he may make an assessment to the best of his judgment.[16] This may be called an "estimated assessment."

17–08   If an inspector (or the Board) *discover*

  (a) that any profits which ought to have been assessed to tax have not been assessed, or

  (b) that an assessment to tax is or has become insufficient, or

  (c) that any relief which has been given is or has become excessive,

the inspector (or the Board) may make an assessment in the amount, or the further amount, which ought in his (or their) opinion to be charged.[17] It will be observed that such an assessment cannot be made unless there is first a *discovery* by the inspector (or the Board).[18] "An Inspector of Taxes 'discovers' (that income has not been assessed when it ought to have been), not only when he finds out new facts which were not known to him or his predecessor, but also when he finds out that he or his predecessor drew a wrong inference from the facts which were then known to him; and, further, when he finds out that he or his predecessor got the law wrong and did not assess the income when it ought to have been."[19] The time limits for making assessments are discussed later.[20] Leave of

---

12. *Ibid.* s.29(1), (2), (3).
13. *Ibid.* s.50(6). See, *e.g. Hellier* v. *O'Hare* (1964) 42 T.C. 155.
14. *Ibid.* s.51. *Cf.* the powers discussed in the previous paragraph, which are not restricted to *the appellant.*
15. *Ibid.* s.29(1). Before 1964, assessments were made by the Commissioners. The change in the law makes it unnecessary for an appellate court to send a case back to the Commissioners to amend the assessment: see *McMann* v. *Shaw* (1972) 48 T.C. 330.
16. *Ibid.* 1970, s.29(1).
17. *Ibid.* s.29(3).
18. *Cf.* I.T.A. 1952, s.41 (now repealed), and the cases thereon. See *Commercial Structures Ltd.* v. *Briggs* (1948) 30 T.C. 477 (C.A.); *Cenlon Finance Co. Ltd.* v. *Ellwood* [1962] A.C. 782; 40 T.C. 176; *Jones* v. *Mason Investments (Luton) Ltd.* (1966) 43 T.C. 570.
19. *Parkin* v. *Cattell* [1971] T.R. 177.
20. See *post*, §§ 17–19 *et seq.*

the General Commissioners or Special Commissioners is in some cases necessary before an assessment is made.[21]

An assessment is not void merely by reason of a formal defect or mistake.[22]

Relief for error or mistake

17–09   If a person who has paid tax charged under an assessment alleges that the assessment was excessive by reason of some error or mistake in a return he may, not later than six years after the end of the year of assessment within which the assessment was made (or of the accounting period in the case of a company), make a claim to the Board for relief.[23] The Board must consider the claim and may give such relief by way of repayment as is reasonable and just.[24] The Board must have regard to all the relevant circumstances of the case, and in particular whether the granting of relief would result in the exclusion from charge to tax of any part of the profits (as defined) of the claimant and assessments made on him in respect of chargeable periods other than that to which the claim relates.[25] There is a right of appeal to the Special Commissioners.[26] No relief is available under this provision in respect of the error or mistake as to the basis on which the liability of the claimant ought to have been computed where the return was in fact made on the basis or in accordance with the practice generally prevailing at the time when it was made.[27]

3. APPEALS

Appellate Commissioners

17–10   Tax appeals are heard by the General and Special Commissioners from whose decisions there is a further right of appeal to the High Court by way of case stated on a point of law only.

The General Commissioners are appointed locally for divisions.[28] In England and Wales they are appointed by and hold office during the pleasure of the Lord Chancellor. They receive no remuneration and the great majority of them have no special qualifications in law or accountancy or in tax matters generally. Thus they resemble the lay magistrates and appeals which raise difficult questions of law are usually not brought before them. The General Commissioners for every division appoint a Clerk (and in some cases an assistant Clerk in addition) to assist them.[29]

The Special Commissioners are appointed by the Lord Chancellor.[29a] They are full-time civil servants and are selected from persons with some

---

21. T.M.A. 1970, s.41.
22. *Ibid.* s.114. And see *Baylis* v. *Gregory* [1986] S.T.C. 22.
23. T.M.A. 1970, s.33(1).
24. *Ibid.* s.33(2), (3).
25. *Ibid.* s.33(3) and (5).
26. *Ibid.* s.33(4).
27. *Ibid.* s.33(2), proviso.
28. *Ibid.* s.2.
29. *Ibid.* s.3.
29a. *Ibid.* s.4. This provision came into force on January 1, 1985.

practical experience of tax matters obtained in government service or in private practice. Appeals which raise questions of law or which may be prolonged are usually brought before them. Questions as to the value of land are determined by the Lands Tribunal and as to the value of unquoted shares or securities by the Special Commissioners.[30]

Appeals are by a single Commissioner except when the Presiding Special Commissioner directs otherwise.[31]

General and Special Commissioners take an oath not to disclose any information received in the execution of their duties except for the purpose of those duties.[32]

Appeals to the Commissioners

17–11   A notice of assessment to tax must be served on the person assessed and must state the date on which it is issued and the time within which any appeal against the assessment may be made.[33] There is a right of appeal against every assessment and the appeal is commenced by giving notice in writing to the person issuing the assessment,[34] such notice to be given within 30 days after the date on which the notice of assessment was issued.[35] Some appeals lie only to the Special Commissioners,[36] but otherwise the appeal will be heard by the appropriate body of General Commissioners,[37] unless the appellant elects to bring the case before the Special Commissioners instead of the General Commissioners.[38] This right of election should be exercised by a notice combined (in the case of an appeal) with the notice of appeal, by a separate notice in writing to the Inspector or other officer of the Board within the time limited for bringing the proceedings.[39] If no such notice of election is given the appeal will be brought before the General Commissioners. This is subject to a power the General Commissioners now have to transfer a case to the special Commissioners because of its complexity or the length of time likely to be required for the hearing.[40]

The notice of appeal against any assessment must specify the grounds of appeal but, on the hearing of the appeal, the Commissioners may allow the appellant to put forward any ground not specified in the notice and take it into consideration if satisfied that the omission was not wilful or unreasonable.[41]

If an assessment is not appealed against within the time limit, it becomes

---

30. T.M.A. 1970, s.47.
31. *Ibid.* s.45. This provision came into force on January 1, 1985.
32. *Ibid.* s.6 and Sched. 1.
33. *Ibid.* s.29(5). For service, see *ibid.* s.115.
34. *Ibid.* s.31(2).
35. *Ibid.* s.31(1) read with F.(No. 2)A. 1975, s.67(1). For appeals to the Commissioners brought out of time, see T.M.A. 1970, s.49(1).
36. *Ibid.* ss.31(3) and 47(3).
37. *Ibid.* s.44.
38. *Ibid.* s.31(4).
39. *Ibid.* s.46(1).
40. *Ibid.* s.44(3).
41. *Ibid.* s.31(5).

final and conclusive and the amount assessed becomes payable on the due date.[42]

Once an assessment has been served on the person assessed, it cannot be lawfully altered except in accordance with the express provisions of the Taxes Act.[43] If, therefore, a person seeks to have an assessment altered, he must give notice of appeal and allow the appeal to be determined by the Commissioners (who can reduce or increase the assessment[43a]) or, under section 54 of the Taxes Management Act 1970, by agreement with the Inspector (see § 17–14). When an assessment states (a) the amount on which tax is chargeable and (b) the amount of tax, the Commissioners will normally discharge their duty to determine the assessment by reducing or increasing (a) without determining the figure in (b).[43b]

Once the appeal machinery has been set in motion, the appellant cannot withdraw the notice of appeal[44] and the Commissioners are bound to hear the appeal unless an agreement is reached under section 54.

The amount of tax covered by an assessment is deemed not to be finally determined until that assessment can no longer be varied, whether by any Commissioners on appeal or by the order of any court.[45]

Postponement of tax

17–12   The Tax Acts prescribe dates on which tax of different descriptions is due and payable.[46] Where there is an appeal against an assessment, the due date for payment was at one time deferred until the appeal was determined: hence it was often to the advantage of the taxpayer to appeal against the assessment for the sake of the interest earned on unpaid tax during the period of deferment. Section 55 and section 86 (§ 17–13) of the Taxes Management Act 1970[47] contain provisions to remove this advantage. The provisions of section 55 may be summarised as follows:

(1) An appellant who has grounds for believing that he is overcharged by an assessment and who wishes to appeal against the assessment may apply to the Commissioners to determine the amount of tax, payment of which should be postponed pending the determination of his appeal. The application for postponement is made by written notice to the Inspector (normally) within 30 days of the issue of the notice of assessment and must state the amount of the alleged overcharge and the grounds on which the appellant believes he is overcharged. The application for postponement is separate from the notice of appeal.

---

42. But see *ibid*. s.49 as to proceedings brought out of time.
43. *Ibid*. s.29(6).
43a. *Ibid*. s.50(6)–(7).
43b. *Ibid*. s.50(8).
44. *Ex p. Elmhirst* [1936] 1 K.B. 487; 20 T.C. 381: and see *Beach* v. *Willesden General Commissioner* (1981) 55 T.C. 63; [1982] S.T.C. 157.
45. T.M.A. 1970, s.118(4).
46. See I.C.T.A. 1970, s.4 (income tax); F.A. 1972, s.84(5) (advance corporation tax); C.G.T.A. 1979, s.7 (capital gains tax).
47. These sections were substituted for earlier provisions of T.M.A. 1970 by F.(No. 2)A. 1975, ss.45 and 46.

(2) If no application to postpone payment is made, the tax payable by the assessment is payable as if there were no appeal.

(3) If an application to postpone is made, it is heard and determined in the same way as an appeal; but this does not preclude the Commissioners from hearing the appeal itself. If the application is successful, the Commissioners will postpone payment of the tax which is prima facie overcharged until the determination of the appeal; but the remainder of the tax in respect of which payment is not postponed becomes due and payable as if it were tax charged by an assessment, notice of which was issued on the date of the Commissioners' determination and in respect of which no appeal was pending. If the Inspector and the taxpayer reach agreement as to the amount of tax payment of which should be postponed, this has the same effect as if the matter has been determined by the Commissioners.

(4) On the determination of the appeal itself,

    (a) any tax payable becomes due and payable as if it were tax charged by an assessment notice of which was issued on the date on which the Inspector issues to the appellant a notice of the total amount payable in accordance with the determination and in respect of which no appeal was pending; and

    (b) any tax overpaid must be repaid.

Interest on overdue tax

17–13   Section 86 of the Taxes Management Act 1970 provides that tax charged by an assessment to which the section applies shall carry interest at the prescribed rate (currently 8·5 per cent. per annum[48–49]) from "the reckonable date." This date is the date on which the tax becomes due and payable except that, where an application to postpone payment of tax has been made under section 55 (see § 17–12), the reckonable date is either:

(a) the date on which tax would have been due and payable if there had been no appeal; or

(b) the date mentioned in a Table in section 86(4), whichever is the later.

Example (i)

    X, a solicitor, is assessed under Case II of Schedule D for the year 1975–76 in the sum of £10,000. He disputes the assessment, considering himself overcharged by £3,000. The normal dates for payment of Schedule D tax are January 1, 1976, and July 1, 1976, in equal instalments: T.A. 1970, s.4(2). No application to postpone is made in respect of the tax on £7,000, which is accordingly due and payable on January 1, 1976, and July 1, 1976, and interest on that tax runs from these dates. An application to postpone is made as regards tax on £3,000 and, at the hearing of the application to postpone which is determined on October 6, 1976, X makes out a prima facie case of overcharge in respect of £2,000 but not in respect of the remaining £1,000.

48–49. The Income Tax (Interest on Unpaid Tax and Repayment Supplement) Order 1986 S.I. No. 1181 in [1986] S.T.I. 540.

Tax on the £1,000 is due and payable as if an unappealed notice of assessment were issued on October 6, 1976, *i.e.* within 30 days thereof. Interest in respect of tax on this £1,000 runs from July 1, 1976. Assume X pays the tax on £1,000 before the due date.

X's appeal is finally determined on June 1, 1977. If the appeal is unsuccessful, tax on the £2,000 falls due within 30 days of the determination. Interest runs from July 1, 1976.[50] If the appeal is successful, X is entitled to have the tax on the £2,000 repaid with interest calculated from April 5, 1977: see § 17–14.

Example (ii)

On March 1, 1978, T is assessed to income tax under Schedule D in respect of profits of the year 1974–75. The tax is due 30 days later, on March 31, 1978. There is no Table date applicable to this case, so interest on unpaid tax runs from March 31, 1978.

Repayment supplement

17–14   Where in the case of an individual, a partnership or United Kingdom trust or estate, the tax paid for a year of assessment is repaid after the end of the 12 months following that year of assessment and the amount repaid is not less than £25, the repayment is increased by an amount (called a "repayment supplement") equal to interest on the amount repaid at the rate of 8·5 per cent. per annum for the period (if any) between "the relevant time" and the end of the tax month in which the order for the repayment is issued.[51] Briefly, if the repayment is of tax that was paid after the end of the 12 months following the year of assessment for which it was payable, the relevant time is the end of the year of assessment in which the tax was paid; otherwise the relevant time is the end of the 12 months following the year of assessment to which the tax relates. "Tax month" means the period beginning with the sixth day of a calendar month and ending with the fifth day of the following calendar month.[52]

Assume T is assessed to capital gains tax for the year 1976–77 and the tax is due on (say) August 1, 1977. T appeals against the assessment and his appeal, which is determined more than one year after the end of the year 1976–77 (say on July 1, 1979) succeeds. T is entitled to a repayment supplement at the appropriate rate per annum from April 6, 1978, until July 5, 1979.

There are similar provisions which apply to companies.[53]

Settling appeals by agreement[54]

17–15   Where a person gives notice of appeal and, before the appeal is determined by the Commissioners, the Inspector or other proper officer of the Crown and the appellant come to an agreement, whether in writing or otherwise, that the assessment or decision under appeal should be treated as upheld without variation, or as varied in a particular manner or as dis-

50. Interest so runs on the excess if the amount of the assessment is increased: F.A. 1982, s.69 amending T.M.A. 1970, s.86.
51. F.(No. 2)A. 1975, s.47(1), (11) and (12).
52. *Ibid.* s.47(4) and (12).
53. *Ibid.* s.48.
54. T.M.A. 1970, s.54.

charged or cancelled, the like consequences are to ensue for all purposes as would have ensued if, at the time when the agreement was come to, the Commissioners had determined the appeal and upheld the assessment or decision without variation, had varied it in that manner or had discharged or cancelled it, as the case may be. Any such agreement is ignored if, within 30 days from the date when the agreement was come to, the appellant gives notice in writing that he desires to repudiate or resile from it. Where an agreement is not in writing the section does not apply unless the fact that an agreement was come to, and the terms agreed, are confirmed by notice in writing given by the Inspector or other proper officer of the Crown to the appellant or by the appellant to the Inspector or other proper officer. The effect of an agreement under section 510 is the same as if the point at issue had been determined on an appeal to the Commissioners.[54a] It is a question of fact whether, in any particular case, an "agreement" can be spelled out of negotiations between the Inspector and the appellant (or the person acting on his behalf in relation to the appeal).[55] An agreement under the section precludes any further assessment in relation to the matter in dispute.[56]

Conduct of appeals

17–16 At the hearing of an appeal before the Commissioners the appellant may appear by counsel or by a solicitor or accountant.[57] The Crown is usually represented by the Inspector. The proceedings are conducted in accordance with normal court procedure and the rules of evidence apply.[58] There are, however, no formal pleadings before the Commissioners. The Commissioners have power to summon any person (other than the appellant) to appear before them and to examine a witness on oath.[59] Where there are two Commissioners sitting who cannot agree, the normal practice is to discharge the assessment. The Commissioners have no power to make any order as to costs, so each party bears his own costs. As to the power to obtain information, see § 17–06.

Onus

17–17 Initially the onus lies on the taxpayer to adduce evidence showing that he has been overcharged by the assessment[60]; so where the taxpayer adduces no evidence on the basis of which the Commissioners can reduce this amount of the assessment, they must confirm it in the amount assessed.[61] Hence, when the quantum of the assessment is the only point in issue (as is

---

54a. *Cenlon Finance* v. *Ellwood* [1961] Ch.D. 634 at p. 649; 40 T.C. 189 at p. 195.
55. See *Cansick* v. *Hochstrasser* (1961) 40 T.C. 151; *Delbourgo* v. *Field* (1978) 52 T.C. 225; [1978] S.T.C. 234 (C.A.); *Scorer* v. *Olin Energy Systems Ltd.* [1984] S.T.C. 141 (C.A.).
56. *Cenlon Finance Co. Ltd.* v. *Ellwood* [1962] A.C. 782; 40 T.C. 176 (H.L.).
57. T.M.A. 1970, s.50(5) and see *Banin* v. *MacKinlay* [1984] S.T.C. 212 (taxpayer not attending but sending papers which the Commissioners would not read).
58. *Cooksey and Bibbey* v. *Rednall* (1949) 30 T.C. 514.
59. T.M.A. 1970 s.52(2). As to production of documents, see *Soul* v. *I.R.C.* (1963) 41 T.C. 517.
60. *Ibid.* s.50(6).
61. *Eke* v. *Knight* (1976) 51 T.C. 121; [1976] S.T.C. 1 and [1977] S.T.C. 198 (C.A.); *Nicholson* v. *Morris* (1976) 51 T.C. 95; [1976] S.T.C. 269 at p. 280.

common in a back-duty case) the onus may be said to lie solely on the tax-payer.[62] Where fraud, wilful default or neglect is alleged by the Crown, however, the onus lies on the Crown to prove such fraud, etc.[63]

Although the initial *evidential* onus lies on the taxpayer, this does not exonerate the Appeal Commissioners from satisfying themselves that the taxpayer is properly chargeable to tax nor the Crown from satisfying the Commissioners on this point.[64] For example, where the issue is whether activities of the taxpayer do, or do not, constitute the carrying on of a trade, and the taxpayer adduces facts consistent with either alternative, it is for the Crown to satisfy the Commissioners that the activities constitute the carrying on of a trade.[65]

Appeals from the Commissioners

17–18   Either the taxpayer or the Inspector (who usually represents the Crown before the Commissioners) may appeal from the Commissioners to the High Court.[66] If there is no appeal within the due time, the decision of the Commissioners is final.[67] The appeal is by way of case stated and lies only on a point of law. The limits on the power of the High Court to disturb the findings of the Commissioners have already been discussed.[68] No appeal to the High Court may be brought unless the appellant expresses dissatisfaction with the decision of the Commissioners immediately after the determination of the appeal.[69] If the decision is notified to the parties by letter, dissatisfaction should be expressed by way of immediate reply.

The appeal is commenced by notice in writing to the clerk to the Commissioners given within 30 days after the determination of the appeal requiring the Commissioners to state a case for the opinion of the High Court.[70] The case sets out the facts found by the Commissioners and their decision.[71] The case is prepared by the Commissioners and settled by the parties. If the case, when stated and signed, is defective, mandamus is the appropriate remedy.[72] The appellant must transmit the case to the High

---

62. *Haythornthwaite* v. *Kelly* (1927) 11 T.C. 657.
63. *Eagles* v. *Rose* (1945) 26 T.C. 427; *Barney* v. *Pybus* (1957) 37 T.C. 106. See also *Amis* v. *Colls* (1960) 39 T.C. 148 and *Hudson* v. *Humbles* (1965) 42 T.C. 380.
64. *Partington* v. *Att.-Gen.* (1869) L.R. 4 H.L. 100 at p. 122 (quoted in § 36–02); *Russell* v. *Scott* [1948] A.C. 422 at p. 433; 30 T.C. 394 at p. 424 *per* Lord Simonds; *D'Avigdor-Goldsmid* v. *I.R.C.* [1953] A.C. 347 at p. 361, *per* Viscount Simon; *Re Ralli's Settlement* [1965] Ch. 286 at p. 327, *per* Russell L.J.; *Hochstrasser* v. *Mayes* [1960] A.C. 376 at p. 389; *I.R.C.* v. *Reinhold* (1953) 34 T.C. 389 at pp. 393 and 396.
65. See *I.R.C.*. v. *Reinhold* (1953) 34 T.C. 389.
66. T.M.A. 1970, s.56(2).
67. *Ibid*. s.46(2).
68. See *ante*. § 2–03.
69. T.M.A. 1970, s.56(1), (2). As to the meaning of "immediately" in this section, see *R.* v. *General Commissioners of Income Tax, ex p. Clarke* (1971) 47 T.C. 691.
70. *Ibid*. s.56(2). A cost is £25. A *written* notice is obligatory: *R.* v. *Edmonton Income Tax Commissioners, ex p. Thomson* (1928) 14 T.C. 313.
71. *Ibid*. s.56(4).
72. In *Kirby* v. *Steele* (1946) 27 T.C. 370, Wrottesley J. (at p. 373) allowed the appellant to read affidavits supplementing a case; see also *Calvert* v. *Wainwright* (1947) 27 T.C. 475 at p. 477. In *Cannon Industries Ltd.* v. *Edwards* (1966) 42 T.C. 625, Pennycuick J. declined to allow affidavit evidence to be filed supplementing or contradicting the case stated. The High Court can send a case back to the Commissioners for amendment: T.M.A. 1970, s.56(7). The Queen's Bench Division will not amend a stated case on an application for mandamus: see *R.* v. *I.R.C.*, *ex p. Emery* (1980) 53 T.C. 555; [1980] S.T.C. 549.

Court within 30 days[73] after receiving it but there is no time-limit within which it must be set down.

The High Court may reverse, affirm or amend the determination of the Commissioners or may remit the case to them or make such other order as the court thinks fit.[74] The High Court has no power to make a consent order for the withdrawal of an appeal on terms giving effect to an agreement between the appellant and the respondent.[75]

From the High Court there is a further right of appeal to the Court of Appeal and thence, with leave, to the House of Lords.[76]

17–19 Notwithstanding that a case has been required to be stated or is pending before the High Court, tax must be paid in accordance with the determination of the Commissioners. If the High Court decides that too much tax has been paid, the amount overpaid will be refunded with interest; and if the High Court decides that too little tax has been charged, the amount undercharged is due and payable at the expiration of 30 days beginning with the date on which the Inspector issues to the other party a notice of the total amount payable in accordance with the order or judgment of the court.[77]

4. BACK DUTY

17–20 A "back duty case" arises when a taxpayer is found not to have disclosed his true income or has claimed reliefs or allowances to which he is not entitled or has otherwise evaded tax. There are three courses open to the Revenue in such a case:

(1) to commence criminal proceedings;
(2) to make assessments in respect of the tax lost to the Revenue, with interest;
(3) to claim penalties.

Each will be separately considered.

A. Criminal Proceedings

17–21 There are relatively few cases in which the Board take criminal proceedings. Section 5 of the Perjury Act 1911 makes it an offence knowingly and falsely to make any statement false in a material particular in any of the documents referred to in the section. The making of false statements or accounts knowing them to be false (including certificates of full disclosure

---

73. T.M.A. 1970, s.56(4), (5).
74. *Ibid*. s.56(6).
75. *Slaney* v. *Kean* (1969) 45 T.C. 415 (K. succeeded in appeal before General Commissioners; when case was stated, K. agreed Crown's appeal should be allowed. *Held*, court could not make consent order for withdrawal of appeal.) In such a case the Crown has therefore to satisfy the court that the appeal ought to succeed on its merits: see *e.g. Knight* v. *Parry* (1973) 48 T.C. 580; [1973] S.T.C. 56.
76. T.M.A. 1970, s.56(8). In some cases the appellant can "leapfrog" the Court of Appeal: see the Administration of Justice Act 1969.
77. *Ibid*. s.56(9).

such as are required by the Revenue in back duty cases) is a common law offence.[78]

B. *Assessments for Past Years*

17–22　Under section 34 of the Taxes Management Act 1970, an assessment can be made at any time not later than six years after the end of the chargeable period to which the assessment relates. In cases of fraud or wilful default,[79] there is generally no time limit (except in the case of assessments made against personal representatives[80]), but an assessment can be made only with leave of a General or Special Commissioner.[81]

　　The Revenue can make assessments for years before the six years referred to in section 34 (above) (called "normal years"), where the taxpayer was guilty of "neglect"; but leave of a General or Special Commissioner must first be obtained.[82] Neglect means—

> "negligence or a failure to give any notice, make any return or to produce or furnish any document or other information required by or under the Taxes Acts."[83]

Negligence, broadly speaking, means doing what a reasonable man would not do or failing to do what a reasonable man would do. The powers of the Revenue in cases of neglect are not as extensive as those which exist under section 34 (above) in cases of fraud or wilful default. The position in cases of neglect is as follows:

(1) *Assessments for "earlier years"*

17–23　　Where an assessment has already been made for a normal year for the purpose of making good to the Crown a loss of tax caused through fraud, wilful default or neglect, the Revenue can make assessments for any of the six years preceding the normal year (called "earlier years") provided the assessment is made not later than one year from the end of the year when the assessment for the normal year is finally determined, *i.e.* when no appeal is possible or outstanding.[84] No assessment may be made for the earlier year except to make good a loss of tax attributable to the taxpayer's neglect.[85]

> On November 5, 1982, assessments are made for 1976–77 (a normal year) when tax was lost through fraud, wilful default or neglect. Under section 37, the Revenue can make assessments for any one of the preceding six years, *i.e.*

---

78. *R.* v. *Hudson* (1956) 36 T.C. 561.
79. See *Clixby* v. *Pountney* (1967) 44 T.C. 515.
80. See *post*, § 17–25.
81. T.M.A. 1970, ss.36, 41. The Commissioner exercises an administrative function in deciding whether or not to grant leave under T.M.A. 1970, s.41, so natural justice does not require that the taxpayer should be heard: *Pearlberg* v. *Varty* (1972) 48 T.C. 14 (H.L.); *Nicholson* v. *Morris* (1977) 51 T.C. 95; [1977] S.T.C. 162 (C.A.).
82. *Ibid.* ss.37, 41.
83. *Ibid.* s.118(1).
84. *Ibid.* s.37(1), (3), (4). It is not necessary that the normal year assessment should state that its "purpose" was to recover tax attributable to fraud, etc., or that the Inspector should do so when the assessment is made. It is sufficient if there was tax lost as described in s.37(1) and that the normal year assessment recovered it: see *Thurgood* v. *Slarke* (1971) 47 T.C. 130.
85. *Ibid.* s.37(2).

1970–71 onwards, in which loss through neglect is proved if they do so before April 5, 1984.

It should be observed that no assessments can be made for an earlier year under section 37 unless tax is shown to have been lost through fraud, wilful default or neglect, in one of the normal years.

(2) Assessments for years before "earlier years"

17–24   If an assessment has been made for a year outside the normal six-year period, *i.e.* where there was fraud or wilful default, or neglect in an "earlier year," the Revenue can make an assessment for any of the previous six years in order to recover tax lost through the taxpayer's neglect; but such an assessment can be made only by leave of the General or Special Commissioners on proof of reasonable grounds for believing such neglect to have occurred.[86]

17–25   *Assessments on personal representatives.* Under section 40(1) of the Taxes Management Act 1970 an assessment on personal representatives must be made not later than three years from the end of the tax year in which the death occurs.[87]

Under section 40(2), assessments can be made (within the three years referred to) for any years of assessment ending not earlier than six years before the death, provided the assessment is to make good a loss of tax through fraud, wilful default or neglect. Leave of the General or Special Commissioners must first be obtained.[88]

> Death occurs on November 5, 1982. The Revenue can make assessments for the years 1986–87 to 1982–83, provided they do so before April 5, 1986.

These rules apply even if tax was lost through fraud or wilful default.

17–26   *Interest on tax recovered by assessment.* Section 88 of the Taxes Management Act 1970 gives the Revenue power to charge interest at "the prescribed rate" (currently, 11 per cent. per annum) on tax not paid at the due date by reason of the fraud, wilful default or neglect of the taxpayer. The Commissioners may at their discretion mitigate the interest chargeable.[89]

C. Penalties[90]

17–27   Reference should be made to Part X of the Taxes Management Act 1970 for details of the penalties chargeable for failure to make returns, making incorrect returns or accounts, and so on.

A common type of back-duty case is one in which a trader has submitted

---

86. *Ibid.* s.37(5), (6), (7) and s.41.
87. See *Harrison* v. *Willis Bros.* (1966) 43 T.C. 61 (C.A.), where A. and B. were partners trading as "A. and B. Bros." and, more than three years after B.'s death, an assessment was made on "A. and B. Bros. (A. and executors of B. deceased)." *Held*, the assessment was bad as against B. and his executors.
88. T.M.A. 1970, s.41.
89. *Ibid.* s.88(4); See § 17–13.
90. For the law before 1960, see *I.R.C.* v. *Hinchy* [1960] A.C. 748; 38 T.C. 625.

incorrect accounts to the Inspector, for which the penalty in respect of each year in which such accounts were rendered is (a) a sum not exceeding £50, plus (b) the amount of tax lost to the Revenue. Where there is fraud, the amount in (b) is doubled.[91]

The time-limit for proceedings

17–28   Under section 103 of the Taxes Management Act 1970 the normal time-limit for recovering penalties (even in proceedings against personal representatives) is six years from the date of the offence, with an extension in cases of fraud or wilful default to three years from the date of the final determination of the tax.

---

91. T.M.A. 1970, s.95.

PART 2

INHERITANCE

CHAPTER 18

THE MAIN CHARGING PROVISIONS

1. INTRODUCTION

18–01 INHERITANCE tax was introduced by the Finance Act 1986 as a replacement for capital transfer tax which had levied tax both on lifetime gifts and on a person's estate at death. The new tax, which is primarily a revision of capital transfer tax is concerned mainly to charge tax at death, bringing into charge additionally gifts which either were not made sufficiently far in advance of death or which failed to satisfy the strict rule requiring such gifts to be made unreservedly. Inheritance tax is also charged on gifts effected through trusts or companies. Whilst the new tax rules were introduced with effect from March 18, 1986, the name capital transfer tax applied to all charges made until the Finance Act 1986 received the Royal Assent.[1]

The new tax is parasitic on the previous system and has assumed the whole framework of the Capital Transfer Tax Act 1984 (now the Inheritance Tax Act 1984) with the superimposition of an exemption for gifts made more than seven years before the donor's death coupled with a complex set of anti-avoidance rules whose origin lies in the estate duty legislation which applied prior to 1975.

2. LIFETIME TRANSFERS

Chargeable transfers

18–02 Inheritance tax is charged on the value transferred by a *chargeable transfer*.[2] A chargeable transfer is any *transfer of value* made by an *individual*, other than an exempt transfer.[3] A transfer of value is defined[4] as:

> "a disposition (including a disposition effected by associated operations[5]) made by a person ("the transferor") as a result of which the value of his estate immediately after the disposition is less than it would be but for the disposition; and the amount by which it is less is the value transferred by the transfer."

Note that not every transfer of value (as defined) is a chargeable transfer: a transfer of value made otherwise than by an individual (*e.g.* by a company or by trustees) is not a chargeable transfer although, as will be seen later, certain dispositions made by trustees of settled property give rise to charges to tax *as if* they were chargeable transfers.[6] A transfer made by a company is not a chargeable transfer but may be a transfer of value

---

1. On July 25, 1986.
2. Inheritance Tax Act 1984, s.1. The I.H.T.A. 1984 is the name given to what was the Capital Transfer Tax Act 1984 by F.A. 1986, s.100(1). Unless otherwise stated all references in Chapters 18 to 26 are to the provisions of the I.H.T.A. 1984.
3. s.2(1). No disposition made prior to March 27, 1974 can be a transfer of value. Exempt transfers are discussed in §§ 19–01 *et seq.*
4. s.3(1).
5. See the definition of "disposition" in s.272.
6. See Chap. 22.

and, as such, may give rise to tax liability under provisions discussed in §§ 21–01 *et seq.*

18–02A Notwithstanding the general lifetime charge thus imposed by section 1 of the Act, the majority of transfers are exempted from charge by the provisions of section 3A[6a]:

> "(1) Any reference in this Act to a potentially exempt transfer is a reference to a transfer of value—
>
> > (*a*) which is made by an individual on or after 18th March 1986; and
> >
> > (*b*) which, apart from this section would be a chargeable transfer (or to the extent to which, apart from this section it would be such a transfer); and
> >
> > (*c*) to the extent that it constitutes either a gift to another individual or a gift into an accumulation and maintenance trust or a disabled trust";

If a transfer of value is a potentially exempt transfer and is made more than seven years before the death of the transferor it is an exempt transfer: if the transferor fails to survive seven years, the transfer has "proved to be a chargeable transfer" and tax is levied accordingly.[6b] Unless or until the transferor dies within that period, though, the transfer is treated as if it had already proved to be exempt[6c] so that tax is, at the very least, postponed until death.

18–03 It is important to grasp at the outset that inheritance tax is levied by reference to the diminution in value of the transferor's estate, not by reference to the increase in value of the transferee's estate. The difference may be illustrated by two examples:

> (i) A has a library of rare books including a number of volumes which form a set. A gives one volume out of the set to B. The diminution in the value of the set, on which tax may be levied, may greatly exceed the value of the single volume which B acquires.
>
> (ii) Similarly, if A with 52 per cent. of the shares of a company gives 3 shares to B, thereby reducing his holding to 49 per cent. and so losing control of the company, inheritance tax is levied on the diminution in the value of A's holding (which, again, will far exceed the value of the shares obtained by B).

Where the transferor pays[6d] the inheritance tax attributable to the transfer of value, the diminution in his estate will include the amount of the tax. This is because payment of the tax forms part of the cost to the transferor of making the transfer. Tax is consequently charged on the amount or

---

6a. Introduced by F.A. 1986, Sched. 19 para. 1.
6b. s.3A(4).
6c. s.3A(5), (6).
6d. This is likely to be of significance in future mainly in relation to gifts into settlement. Provision is made by Sched. 19, paras. 28–30 for liability in cases where the transferor dies within the seven year period to fall principally on the transferee. See § 24–02.

value of the property transferred plus the tax thereon paid by the transferor; and the amount of the tax is found by a grossing-up process. The reader might find it helpful to read now § 20–02 to 20–05 to see how the tax is charged.

18–04 The definition of transfer of value requires that there should be a *disposition*.[7] The word "disposition" is not defined[7a] but is a word of wide meaning. It is provided that where the value of a person's estate is diminished and that of another person's estate (or of settled property in which no interest in possession subsists) is increased by the first-mentioned person's omission to exercise a right, he shall be treated as having made a disposition at the time, or the latest time, when he could have exercised the right, unless it is shown that the omission was not deliberate.[8] Thus A's failure to pursue a just claim for damages against B or to pursue a claim for indemnity may constitute a chargeable transfer by A. So also, a deliberate omission to exercise an option or to vote at a company meeting may constitute a disposition. An omission to exercise a right would not be "deliberate" if, *e.g.* the person in question was able to prove that he was genuinely mistaken in thinking that he did not have the right.

The grant of a lease or tenancy

8–04A The grant of a lease or tenancy is a transfer of value if the interest in land out of which the grant takes effect is reduced in value in consequence of the grant. If the owner of an unencumbered freehold grants a tenancy at a market rent, there may nevertheless be a transfer of value, if, *e.g.* the diminution in the value of the freehold is not matched by the value of the right to receive the future rent.

By way of exception to the above rule, and to assist the farming community, section 16 provides that the grant of a tenancy of agricultural property (defined as in § 19–41) in the United Kingdom, the Channel Islands or the Isle of Man for use for agricultural purposes shall not be a transfer of value by the grantor if he makes it for full consideration in money or money's worth. The effect of this provision is thought to be that, provided the rent is a full market rent at the time of the grant, properly estimated and subject to review, there is no transfer of value, even if the value of the freehold is reduced.[8a] And see §§ 19–40 *et seq.*

Waiver of remuneration and dividends

18–04B A waiver or repayment of an amount of remuneration which, apart from the waiver or repayment, would be assessable to income tax under Schedule E (*i.e.* because the remuneration has already been earned and the

---

7. s.3(1): see § 18–02. Some guidance on the meaning of "disposition" may be found in the stamp duty cases in which the word "conveyance" has been considered: see §§ 28–03 *et seq.*
7a. The so-called "definition" contained in s.272 is of no real assistance.
8. s.3(3).
8a. There is some doubt about this, however: the Revenue are known to argue that for full consideration to be given, it is not enough that the tenant pay a full rent, since the market is known to bear the payment of a substantial premium as well.

employee is entitled to it: see § 3–06), but which, because of the waiver or repayment is not taxed under Schedule E, is not a transfer of value. But where the payer would have been entitled to a tax deduction had the remuneration actually been paid, the exemption from inheritance tax applies only if the payer gets no deduction or the amount is otherwise brought into charge to tax.[9]

A waiver of a dividend on shares is not a transfer of value provided the waiver is *within* 12 months before any right to the dividend has accrued.[10]

Associated operations

18–05   A series of "operations" which brings about a diminution in value in a person's estate will constitute a "disposition" where they are "associated operations" as defined in section 268(1): "disposition" includes a disposition effected by associated operations.[11] "Associated operations" means any two or more operations of any kind, being:

(a) operations which affect the same property, or one of which affects some property and the other or others of which affect property which represents, whether directly or indirectly, that property, or income arising from that property, or any property representing accumulations of any such income; or

(b) any two operations of which one is effected with reference to the other, or with a view to enabling the other to be effected or facilitating its being effected, and any further operation having a like relation to any of those two, and so on;

whether those operations are effected by the same person or different persons, and whether or not they are simultaneous. "Operation" includes an omission.[12]

> Thus if a husband (H) makes an exempt transfer of property to his wife (W) on condition that W shall transfer the property to X, the transfer to X may be treated as if H were the transferor, *e.g.* for the purposes of considering the possible application of the exemptions and reliefs discussed in Chapter 19.[13]

18–06   By way of qualification to this broad definition, the granting of a lease for full consideration in money or money's worth is not to be taken to be associated with any operation effected more than three years after the grant; and no operation effected on or after March 27, 1974, is to be taken to be associated with an operation effected before that date.[14]

> Assume L leases land to T for full consideration. After three years, when the

---

9. s.14: and see [1975] S.T.I. 394.
10. s.15.
11. s.272.
12. s.268(1).
13. Inland Revenue Press Notice of April 8, 1975: [1975] S.T.I. 191, commenting on s.268. See also *Rowland's Tax Guide 1983/84*, p. 444 and App. A95.
14. s.268(2).

rent being paid is no longer a full market rent, L sells his reversion to P for full consideration. L's sale cannot be "associated" with the lease so as to enable the Revenue to treat L as having made a transfer of value to P; *i.e.* on the basis that L could have obtained more from P if he had been able to increase the rent. If L sells the reversion to P within three years from the grant, the lease and subsequent sale can be treated as a single disposition, with the consequence that L will be treated as if he had sold the land unencumbered by the lease.

This example shows that the provisions relating to associated operations prevent a reduction in liability to inheritance tax by an operation or omission which reduces the value of the property disposed of.

18–07   Where a transfer of value is made by associated operations carried out at different times, it is treated as made at the time of the last of them; but where any one or more of the earlier operations also constitutes a transfer of value made by the same transferor, the value transferred by the earlier operations is to be treated as reducing the value transferred by all the operations taken together, except to the extent that the transfer constituted by the earlier operations but not that made by all the operations taken together is exempt under the relief for transfers between spouses: see §§ 19–02 *et seq.*[15]

> Assume a husband (H) owns 90 per cent. of the shares of a company. H wishes his son (S) to have an 80 per cent. holding. H gives his wife (W) a 40 per cent. holding because a transfer by W will attract a lower rate of inheritance tax. W and H then each give S a 40 per cent. holding. This is a gift by H to S of an 80 per cent. holding, effected by associated operations.

There are further examples in § 19–09.

18–07A   It seems that the provisions relating to "associated operations" cannot apply to transfers on death since they operate by an extension of the word "disposition." The charge to inheritance tax on death, however, does not require the effecting of a disposition, being imposed simply by means of a deemed transfer of value.[15a]

Meaning of estate

18–08   A chargeable transfer is one which diminishes the value of the transferor's "estate."[16] The expression "estate" is defined[17] as follows:

> " . . . a person's estate is the aggregate of all the property to which he is beneficially entitled, except that the estate of a person immediately before his death does not include excluded property."

18–09   The word "property" includes rights and interests of any description.[18] Property to which a person is not beneficially entitled, such as property held by him as trustee, is not part of his "estate." But it is not necessary

---

15. s.268(3).
15a. See § 18–14.
16. s.3(1).
17. s.5(1).
18. s.272.

that a person should *own* property in order to be treated as beneficially entitled to it. Thus a person is treated as beneficially entitled to property (not being settled property) over which he has a general power of appointment. Section 5(2) provides that:

> "A person who has a general power which enables him, or would if he were *sui juris* enable him, to dispose of any property other than settled property, or to charge money on any property other than settled property, shall be treated as beneficially entitled to the property or money; and for this purpose "general power" means a power or authority enabling the person by whom it is exercisable to appoint or dispose of property as he thinks fit."

The last four words in the subsection exclude the power or authority of a person having a power of attorney or as a mortgagee. The exclusion of powers over settled property means that if, for example, property is held upon trust for X for life and thereafter to such person or persons as X shall appoint, an appointment by X falls to be dealt with under the rules relating to settled property: see §§ 22–14 *et seq.* A person is not beneficially entitled to property to which he is entitled as a corporation sole.[19]

Dispositions without donative intent

18–10   Dispositions at market value are outside the ambit of the tax because they produce no diminution in the value of the transferor's estate. But if A sells property to B for £10,000 and there is evidence that A could have obtained (say) £14,000, this transaction may be explained either (i) on the basis that A intended to confer a benefit on B or (ii) on the basis that A made a bad bargain, having no intention of conferring any benefit on B. Tax is payable in the first but not the second of these cases.

18–11   This result is achieved by section 10(1) which provides that a disposition is not a transfer of value if it is shown that it was not intended, and was not made in a transaction intended, to confer any gratuitous benefit on *any* person *and* either:

(a) that it was made in a transaction at arm's length between persons not connected with each other,[20] or
(b) that it was such as might be expected to be made in a transaction at arm's length between persons not connected with each other.

Note that two conditions have to be satisfied for there not to be a transfer of value. As well as the transferor's (subjective) intention not to confer a benefit, the objective criteria in (a) or (b) have also to be satisfied.[21] The onus lies on the transferor to prove that the conditions have

---

19. s.271.
20. See s.270 which applies the definition of "connected persons" in C.G.T.A. 1979 s.63, with some modifications: see § 16–18A.
21. The application of section 10 to payments by employers to their employees or their dependants under certain accident insurance schemes is the subject of an Inland Revenue Press Release of January 6, 1976: see [1976] S.T.I. 4. Now see also Inland Revenue Press Release of July 9, 1986, extending the practice to Inheritance Tax.

been satisfied. If, in the example in § 18–10, A had sold the property to B for (say) £4,000, A would find it almost impossible to prove lack of donative intent. When a disposition is effected by associated operations (see § 18–05) the conditions have to be applied to the operations considered as a whole.

Transfers of money or property pursuant to an order of the court in consequence of a decree of divorce or nullity of marriage will often be exempt from inheritance tax as falling within section 10(1).

18–12   Section 10(1) does not apply:

(i) to certain acquisitions of reversionary interests,[22] as to which see § 22–101; or

(ii) to a sale of shares or debentures not quoted on a recognised stock exchange, unless a third condition is satisfied, *i.e.* that it is shown that the sale was at a price freely negotiated at the time of the sale *or* at a price such as might be expected to have been freely negotiated at the time of the sale.[22a] Thus a sale at a price predetermined by the articles of a company may give rise to a charge to inheritance tax.

Exempt transfers

18–13   A chargeable transfer is defined as a transfer of value made by an individual which is not an exempt transfer.[23] The cases in which transfers are "exempt transfers" are discussed in §§ 19–01 *et seq.*

Certain lifetime transfers for the maintenance, etc., of the transferor's family are expressed not to be transfers of value: see §§ 19–55 *et seq.*

Excluded property

18–13A   The Act provides that no account is to be taken of the value of excluded property which ceases to form part of a person's estate as a result of a disposition.[24] Excluded property is discussed in §§ 23–01 *et seq.* Property situated outside the United Kingdom in the beneficial ownership of an individual who is domiciled outside the United Kingdom is excluded property; so also are British Government securities in the beneficial ownership of persons neither domiciled nor ordinarily resident in the United Kingdom: see § 19–26.

These are the rules which govern the territorial scope of the legislation levying inheritance tax. Note that *domicile* is the key factor: an individual who is domiciled in the United Kingdom is liable to inheritance tax on property wherever situate; whereas an individual who is domiciled else-

---

22. s.55(2).
22a. s.10(2).
23. s.2(1).
24. s.3(2).

where is liable to inheritance tax only on property situated in the United Kingdom.

3. TRANSFERS ON DEATH

18–14 Death is the principal event on which inheritance tax is charged. In order to maintain the unity of the tax, the charge is imposed by deeming[25] the deceased to have made a single transfer of value immediately before his death, and by assuming that the value transferred thereby was equal to the value of his estate at that time (*i.e.* immediately before his death). The value of his estate is the price which it would fetch if sold in the open market at that time[26] (see § 20–17) less liabilities (see § 20–12) subject, however, to special rules which apply when the value of items included in his estate is affected by the death itself (see §§ 20–25 *et seq.*). "Excluded property" (see §§ 23–01 *et seq.*) does *not* form part of the deceased's estate at that time but otherwise his estate is taken to include all the property to which he was then beneficially entitled.[27] Thus it includes:

(a) property (other than settled property) over which the deceased had a general power of appointment or a special power if he was competent to appoint in his own favour. If the deceased was entitled to a lump sum payment under a superannuation scheme which he could have appointed to a third person but did not, this is taxable as part of his estate;

(b) policies of insurance, whether on the life of the deceased or of a third person, if the deceased was entitled to the sums payable thereunder;

(c) purchased annuities continuing after the deceased's death, but not those ceasing on his death (§ 20–25) nor those arising on his death in which he had no beneficial interest. There is a special rule which applies to annuities continuing on death and payable under approved retirement annuity schemes (see § 19–25);

(d) an undivided share and the severable share of a joint tenant;

(e) the share of a deceased partner in partnership property;

(f) an interest in possession in settled property (see § 22–17).

It also includes any property which the deceased has, at any time during his lifetime, given away subject to a "reservation"[27a]: see §§ 20–29 *et seq.*

Tax chargeable on death is attributed to the respective values of the items of property comprised in the deceased's estate in the proportions which they bear to the aggregate, subject to any provision reducing the amount of tax attributable to the value of any particular property and subject to any specific provisions of the deceased's will.[28] Deeds of family arrangement, disclaimers and other matters which may affect the devolution of property on death are considered in §§ 19–63 *et seq.*

---

25. s.4(1): and see § 20–25.
26. s.160: see §§ 20–17 *et seq.*
27. s.5(1).
27a. F.A. 1986, s.102(3).
28. s.265.

8–15   *Commorientes*. When it cannot be known which of two or more persons who have died survived the other or others, they are assumed to have died at the same instant.[29] Where this provision does not apply, because the order of deaths is known, quick succession relief may be available: see § 19–31.

4. RATES OF TAX

18–16   The rates of inheritance tax and the method of computing the charge to tax are considered in Chapter 20. On death, tax is imposed by reference to a Table set out in Schedule 1 to the Act. Chargeable lifetime transfers made more than seven years prior to a person's death are charged at half the rate which would apply on death; transfers in the final seven years being taxed at a percentage (never less than the corresponding lifetime rate) of the death rate: see § 20–03. Briefly, inheritance tax is charged at a rate which is determined by reference to the cumulative total of all chargeable transfers made during the previous seven years, except that the first "slice" of value transferred is tax free.[30] The exempt slice is £71,000 in the case of transfers made on or after March 18, 1986. For an example of the working of the tax, see § 20–04.

5. SETTLED PROPERTY

18–17   The rules which apply to transfers of settled property and interests in settled property are discussed in Chapter 22. Briefly, and at the risk of considerable inaccuracy, the legislation draws a distinction between settlements in which no person has an interest in possession, such as the common-form discretionary settlement, and other types of settlement in which a beneficiary has a vested interest, such as a life interest. In the case of discretionary settlements the legislature has sought to impose the same charge to tax as would be applicable if all the settled property were transferred once a generation. This is effected by the imposition of a charge at a reduced rate once every 7 years with, additionally, a proportionate charge on every occasion when property ceases to be held on the discretionary trusts. In the case of settlements in which a beneficiary has a vested interest, such as a life interest, the beneficiary is treated as the owner of so much of the settled property as corresponds to the value of his interest. Thus a life tenant entitled to the income of the fund is treated as entitled to the fund itself. A life tenant entitled to one-third of the income of a fund is treated as entitled to one-third of the fund, and so on.

---

29. s.4(2).
30. See the Table in § 20–02.

CHAPTER 19

RELIEFS AND RELATED PROVISIONS

1. EXEMPT TRANSFERS

19–01 SECTION 2(1) defines a chargeable transfer as any transfer of value made by an individual but which is not an exempt transfer. Since the tax is levied only on chargeable transfers it follows that dispositions which are exempt transfers are not subject to tax. Whilst Part II of the Act provides for those transfers which are properly "exempt," the Finance Act 1986 introduces a new concept of transfers which are "potentially exempt, " which is of vital importance in the application of inheritance tax. The effect of the new relief is to offer provisional exemption from tax, subject to the transferor surviving the gift by seven years. Exempt transfers proper are dealt with in §§19–02 to 19–23: it must be noted that of the exemptions described in those paragraphs, those numbered 2 to 5 are not available in respect of the deemed transfer of value on death: see §18–14; the limited application of certain exemptions to settled property is referred to in §22–31. Potentially exempt transfers are considered in §§19–30A *et seq.*

A transfer of value made by an individual which is exempt only to a limited extent is treated as an exempt transfer up to the limit of exemption and as a chargeable transfer beyond that limit.[1]

Details of certain exempt transfers are not required in returns made for the purposes of inheritance tax.[2]

1. *Transfers between spouses*

19–02 *Unlimited exemption.* A transfer of value is an exempt transfer to the extent that the value transferred is attributable to property which becomes comprised in the estate of the transferor's spouse or, so far as the value transferred is not so attributable, to the extent that that estate is increased.[3] The exemption applies to lifetime transfers and transfers on death and it applies whether or not the spouses are living together at the time of the transfer. Thus transfers between spouses which are made as part of the arrangements leading up to a decree absolute of divorce or nullity fall within the exemption whereas transfers made thereafter do not.[4] A transfer of value made by one spouse to a company of which the other spouse is sole shareholder is exempt because the latter's estate is thereby increased in value.

---

1. s.2(2).
2. [1976] S.T.I. 101.
3. s.18(1). The provision was introduced in this form by F.A. 1976, s.94 with effect from April 6, 1976. Previously a transfer was exempt "to the extent that the value of the estate of the transferor's spouse is increased." Thus, before the amendment, if H owned a valuable set of books and broke the set by giving one to W, the exemption only applied to the value of that book and not to the full diminution in the value of H's estate.
4. But see § 18–11.

9–03   The exemption does not apply if the disposition takes effect on the termination after the transfer of value of any interest or period or if it depends on a condition which is not satisfied within 12 months of the transfer, except that the exemption is not excluded by reason only that the gift is conditional on one spouse surviving the other for a specified period.[5] Property is for this purpose treated as given to a spouse if it is given to or held on trust for him.[6]

> Thus if a husband (H) gives property to A for life with remainder to his wife (W) absolutely, or to W after 60 days, the exemption does not apply; but if H gives property to W if she shall survive him by 60 days, which she does, the exemption applies.

19–04   *Limited exemption.* The unlimited exemption on inter-spouse transfers in § 19–02 does not apply if, immediately before the transfer, the transferor but not the transferee is domiciled in the United Kingdom. Then the value in respect of which the transfer is exempt (calculated as a value on which no tax is payable) is limited to £55,000 less any amount previously taken into account for the purposes of this limited exemption.[7] Thus if a series of transfers are made to a non-United Kingdom domiciled spouse, the exemption stops when £55,000 in value has been transferred.

     It follows that if one spouse wishes to transfer property to the other who is about to acquire a domicile of choice outside the United Kingdom, the transfer should be made before the domicile is acquired so as to obtain the benefit of the unlimited exemption.

19–05   Spouses may have separate domiciles as a result of section 1 of the Domicile and Matrimonial Proceedings Act 1973. In practice, spouses living together normally have the same domicile but there are situations in which this will not be the case. Suppose, for example, that H (who has a domicile of origin in Eire) married W (who has a domicile of origin in France) in 1968. They made their home in England where H acquired a domicile of choice (and W a domicile of dependency). In 1984 they decide to leave England to live abroad in circumstances where no one country has been selected as their permanent home. H and W will have abandoned[8] their English domicile with the consequence that their domiciles of origin revive,[9] so that H will have a domicile in Eire and W in France.

19–06   *Settled gifts.* A person who is beneficially entitled to an interest in possession in settled property is treated for inheritance tax purposes as beneficially entitled to the property in which the interest subsists: see § 22–17.

---

5. s.18(3).
6. s.18(4).
7. s.18(2). The original limit was £15,000. This was increased to £25,000 for transfers of value made after March 25, 1980 (F.A. 1980, s.86(2), (5)); and to £55,000 for transfers of value made after March 9, 1982 (F.A. 1982, s.90(1), (3)). Since that time no attempt has been made to maintain the link between the rise in the "nil-rate" band (see § 20–02) and the limited spouse exemption. It should also be noted that there is no 7-year cumulation period for s.18(2) relief—once a transfer has been made to a non-domiciled spouse, that gift must ever after be taken into account in determining the availability of the exemption.
8. For a recent case on the abandonment of domicile and s.1 of the 1973 Act, see *I.R.C.* v. *Duchess of Portland* [1982] Ch. 314.
9. See *Re Flynn (decd.)* [1968] 1 W.L.R. 103; [1968] 1 All E.R. 49.

It follows from this that if a person settles property, whether *inter vivos* or by will, on his spouse for life, the transfer into settlement is exempt from inheritance tax because the property becomes comprised in the estate of the transferor's spouse.

2. *The annual exemption*

19–07   Transfers of value made by a transferor in any one year are exempt to the extent that the values transferred by them (calculated as values on which no tax is payable)[10–11] do not exceed (as respects transfers on or after April 6, 1981) £3,000.[12] "Year" means a period of 12 months ending with April 5.[13] A transferor who does not "use" the relief in a year may carry forward the unused part and add it to the exempt amount in the next following year but not in a later year.[14]

> Thus if A makes transfers of £2,400 in the year ending April 5, 1986 (£600 of the exemption being unused), he can make exempt transfers of up to £3,600 (*i.e.* £600 + £3,000) in the year ending April 5, 1987. But the £600 unused in 1985–86 cannot be used after 1986–87.

A transfer of any form of property may qualify for this exemption, which applies to gifts in settlement as well as to direct gifts but not to transfers on death.[15] The exemption may also apply where tax is chargeable under section 52 (termination of interests in possession in settled property: see § 22–22 to § 22–24 and § 22–31). Husband and wife are separate chargeable individuals for the purposes of inheritance tax, so each of them is entitled to the annual exemption.

Since potentially exempt transfers ("PETs") are not immediately subject to inheritance tax, it would be to the disadvantage of the taxpayer were the annual exemption used to frank such transfers as being wholly exempt from tax. Accordingly the exemption is *not* to be applied to PETs *unless* they subsequently become chargeable[15a] (on the death of the transferor within the seven year period) when section 19 relief is granted by treating the PETs as having been made after all other non-exempt transfers of that year. This would appear to affect the inheritance tax computation of the following year as well since an unused annual exemption may have been carried forward under section 19(2) and applied in relief of a chargeable transfer of that year.

19–08   Where the values transferred in a year exceed the exempt amount, it becomes necessary to determine which transfers are exempt and which not exempt, because the transferee may (*e.g.* by agreement) be liable for

---

10–11. *i.e.* ignoring inheritance tax in calculating the £3,000 exemption.

12. s.19. The exemption was increased from £1,000 to £2,000 by F.A. 1976, s.93 but not so as to affect the operation of the exemption in relation to transfers made before April 6, 1976 and not so as to affect the amount which could be carried forward to the year of assessment beginning on that date. s.94(1), (7) increased the exemption to £3,000 as respects transfers made on or after April 6, 1981 but subject to the same limitations as before.

13. s.19(4).

14. s.19(2).

15. s.19(5).

15a. s.19(3A).

inheritance tax on the non-exempt transfer. The Act provides that the excess over the exempt amount—

(*a*) shall, as between transfers made on different days, be attributed, so far as possible, to a later rather than an earlier transfer, *i.e.* so as to exempt the earlier transfers; and

(*b*) shall, as between transfers made on the same day, be attributed to them in proportion to the values transferred by them.[16]

Thus if, in a year when the annual exemption stands at £3,000 A, on the same day, gives £800 in value to the trustees of the B trust and £3,000 to the trustees of the C trust, the excess of £1,400 is apportioned between the respective bodies of trusteees in the proportion 8 : 36.

19–09 *Associated operations.* If A sells an asset to B for (say) £20,000 but the price is left outstanding and A plans to release the debt at the rate of £3,000 a year, the sale and subsequent releases will be treated as associated operations, whether or not interest is payable by B on the amount outstanding. The transfer will be treated as made at the time of the last of the associated operations: see § 18–07. Thus if when A releases the last part of the debt the asset is worth £30,000, A is treated as then transferring £10,000.

But if A makes a gift to trustees on terms that they pay the inheritance tax by instalments, which A then finances by annual gifts equal to the amount of the annual exemption, these are not treated as associated operations. Hence an increase in the value of the gifted property does not affect the amount of tax attributable to A's gift.[17]

3. *Small gifts to same person*

19–10 Transfers of value made by a transferor in any one year by outright gifts to any one person are exempt if the values transferred by them (calculated as values on which no tax is chargeable[18]) do not exceed £250.[19] A year means the period 12 months ending with April 5.[19] Thus an individual can make any number of gifts in the course of a year in amounts of up to £250 per donee. This exemption is not available for gifts that exceed £250 by however small an amount; but such gifts may fall within the annual exemption in § 19–07.[20]

Note that the exemption applies only to "outright gifts to any one person." It is thought that a gift to trustees to hold on the trusts of a settlement falls outside this exemption,[21] although such a gift will fall within the

---

16. s.19(3).
17. See Inland Revenue Press Release of April 18, 1975 in [1975] S.T.I. 191.
18. *i.e.* ignoring inheritance tax in calculating the value transferred.
19. s.20. The limit of £250 was increased from £100 in the case of transfers of value made after March 23, 1980: F.A. 1980, s.86(3), (5).
20. As regards dispositions made before April 6, 1981 outright gifts were exempt "to the extent that" the values transferred did not exceed the amount of the exemption: hence the exemption was available in relation to the first slice of a larger gift.
21. See Dymond at para. 13.202 where the meaning of "outright" in this context is discussed.

annual exemption referred to in § 19–07. Transfers of value in the form of a free loan or free use of property are treated as outright gifts.[22] The small gifts exemption and the annual exemption are cumulative. Thus in any one year an individual can make any number of transfers of up to £250 per person in addition to transfers to *other* persons of up to the amount of the annual exemption.

4. *Normal expenditure out of income*

19–11   A transfer of value is an exempt transfer if, or to the extent that, it is shown:

(a) that it was made as part of the normal expenditure of the transferor; and

(b) that (taking one year with another) it was made out of his income; and

(c) that, after allowing for all transfers of value forming part of his normal expenditure, the transferor was left with sufficient income to maintain his usual standard of living.[23]

Expenditure is "normal" if it is habitual. Premiums which are reasonable in amount and which are regularly paid by an individual on a policy on his life for the benefit of a donee may fall within this exemption. Dispositions for the maintenance or education of the disponor's family (including dispositions under "income settlements": see §§ 10–10 *et seq.*) will generally be outside the scope of inheritance tax under section 11 (see § 19–55) but those which do not fall within that provision may well be exempted by section 21. The exemption applies to gifts in settlement as well as to outright gifts.

19–12   *Back to back policies.* A common method of estate duty avoidance involved the purchase by A for a capital sum of an annuity and the simultaneous purchase by A of a policy on A's life, expressed to be for the benefit of B. By this means A substituted dutiable capital with an annuity which ceased and so would not be dutiable on his death and also created an asset for B (the policy proceeds) by the payment of premiums constituting part of A's normal expenditure out of income. In this way dutiable capital of A was replaced by the benefit to B a non-dutiable policy. Section 21(2) now excludes the normal expenditure exemption by the following provision:

> "A payment of a premium on a policy of insurance on the transferor's life, or a gift of money or money's worth applied, directly or indirectly, in payment of such a premium, shall not for the purposes of this section be regarded as part of his normal expenditure if, when the insurance was made, or at any earlier or later time, an annuity was purchased on his life, unless it is shown that the purchase of the annuity and the making of any variation of the insurance or of any

---

22. s.29(3).
23. s.21(1).

prior insurance for which the first-mentioned insurance was directly or indirectly substituted, were not associated operations."

There is a special charge to inheritance tax on back to back arrangements: see § 21–09.

9–13   It has been the practice of the Revenue not to regard the purchase of an annuity and the effecting of a policy of assurance as "associated operations" if it is shown that the policy was issued after evidence of health had been obtained and the terms on which it was issued would have been the same even if the annuity had not been bought. Hence the normal expenditure exemption has been treated as not applying only if the purchase of the annuity enabled life cover to be obtained which would not otherwise have been available.

9–14   *Purchased life annuity.* The capital element in a purchased life annuity (see § 5–53) is *not* now to be regarded as income for the purposes of the normal expenditure exemption. This applies after April 5, 1975, but only to life annuities purchased after November 12, 1974.[24]

5. *Gifts in consideration of marriage*

9–15   There are three requisites for a gift to be in consideration of marriage: (i) it must be made on the occasion of a marriage; (ii) it must be conditional on the marriage taking place; and (iii) it must be made by a person for the purposes of or with a view to encouraging or facilitating the marriage.[25] It is a question of fact whether these requisites are present.

9–16   Transfers of value made by gifts in consideration of marriage are exempt to the extent that the values transferred by such transfers made by any one transferor in respect of any one marriage (calculated as values on which no tax is payable) do not exceed:

> (a) in the case of gifts satisfying the conditions in § 19–17 by a parent of a party to the marriage, £5,000;
> (b) in the case of other gifts satisfying those conditions, £2,500; and
> (c) in any other case, £1,000.

Any excess is attributed to the transfers in proportion to the values transferred.[26]

19–17   A gift may qualify for the £5,000 (or £2,500) exemption if:

> (a) it is an outright gift to a child or remoter descendant of the transferor; or

---

24. s.21(3), (4).
25. See the estate duty case of *Rennell* v. *I.R.C.* [1964] A.C. 173 and also *Re Park (decd.)* *(No. 2)* [1972] Ch. 385 which held that reference to the purpose or motive of a donor or settlor (*i.e.* condition (iii)) was wholly irrelevant in a case where the sole absolute beneficiary was a spouse of the marriage in question.
26. s.22(1).

(b) the transferor is a parent or remoter ancestor of either party to the marriage, and either the gift is an outright gift to the other party to the marriage or the property comprised in the gift is settled by the gift; or

(c) the transferor is a party to the marriage, and either the gift is an outright gift to the other party to the marriage or the property comprised in the gift is settled by the gift.[27]

19–18   The estate duty exemption for gifts in consideration of marriage was shown by the decision of the House of Lords in *Rennell* v. *I.R.C.*[28] to be much wider than had hitherto been supposed, for it was held to apply to a discretionary settlement for the benefit of a class which included issue of the settlor, who was the bride's father.[28a] This decision was nullified by section 53(1) of the Finance Act 1963, by provisions which are carried forward into inheritance tax which provide that a disposition shall not be treated as a gift made in consideration of marriage:

(a) in the case of an outright gift, if or in so far as it is a gift to a person other than a party to the marriage[29];

(b) in the case of any other disposition[29a] (*e.g.* a settled gift), if the persons who are or may become entitled to any benefit under the disposition include any person other than the following:

    (i) the parties to the marriage, issue[30] of the marriage, or a wife or husband of any such issue[30];

    (ii) persons becoming entitled on the failure of trusts for any such issue[30] under which trust property would (subject only to any power of appointment to a person falling within subparagraph (i) or (iii) of this paragraph) vest indefeasibly on the attainment of a specified age or either on the attainment of such an age or on some earlier event, or persons becoming entitled (subject as aforesaid) on the failure of any limitation in tail;

    (iii) a subsequent wife or husband of a party to the marriage, or any issue[30], or the wife or husband of any issue,[30] of a subsequent marriage of either party;

    (iv) persons becoming entitled under such trusts, subsisting under the law of England and Wales or of Northern Ireland, as are specified in section 33(1) of the Trustee Act 1925 (protective trusts),[30a] the principal beneficiary being a person

---

27. s.22(2). "Child" includes an illegitimate child, an adopted child and a step-child and "parent," "descendant" and "ancestor" are to be construed accordingly.

28. [1964] A.C. 173.

28a. *i.e.* the exemption was not limited to persons who were within the marriage consideration.

29. s.22(3).

29a. s.22(4).

30. References in the section to "issue" apply as if any person legitimated by a marriage, or adopted by the husband and wife jointly, were included among the issue of that marriage.

30a. Or s.34(1) of the Trustee Act (Northern Ireland) 1958.

falling within sub-paragraph (i) or (iii) of this paragraph, or under such trusts modified by the enlargement, as respects any period during which there is no such issue[30b] as aforesaid in existence, of the class of potential beneficiaries specified in paragraph (ii) of the said section 33(1);

(v) persons becoming entitled under trusts subsisting under the law of Scotland and corresponding with such trusts as are mentioned in sub-paragraph (iv);

(vi) as respects a reasonable amount of remuneration, the trustees of the settlement.

19–19 The exemption for gifts in consideration of marriage may also apply when tax is chargeable under section 52 (termination of interests in possession in settled property: see §§ 22–22 to 22–24).

6. *Gifts to charities*

19–20 Transfers of value to charities (as defined[31]) are exempt transfers.[31a] Where the value transferred (*i.e.* the loss to the transferor's estate) exceeds the value of the gift in the hands of the donee charity, the exemption nevertheless extends to the whole value transferred.[32] The exemption is unlimited in extent.[33] A gift of property to a charity out of a settlement in which no qualifying interest in possession exists may not be chargeable to inheritance tax: see § 22–99.

7. *Gifts to political parties*

19–20a Transfers of value to qualifying political parties (as defined[34]) are exempt transfers. Generally, no limit is placed on the exemption for such transfers but the exemption is limited to £100,000 in the case of gifts made on or within one year of the transferor's death.[34a] Where the value transferred (*i.e.* the loss to the transferor's estate) exceeds the value of the gift in the hands of the political party, the exemption extends (subject to the monetary limitation mentioned above) to the whole of the value transferred.[34b]

30b. See note 30, above.

31. s.272, which applies the definition contained in I.C.T.A. 1970 s.360: "any body of persons or trust established for charitable purposes only."

31a. s.23(2)–(5) denies the exemption where the transfer takes effect later or is conditional or where property is given for a limited period or may be used for other purposes.

32. See [1976] S.T.I. 145: Inland Revenue Press Release of April 15, 1976, now Statement of Practice 6/1976.

33. s.23(1). Unlimited exemption has been available in respect of transfers on or within one year of the transferor's death only since March 15, 1983. Originally, the exemption was limited in such circumstances to £100,000. It was increased to £200,000 for transfers of value made after March 25, 1980 and to £250,000 for such transfers made after March 8, 1982. Property given to a charity will, however, be "related property" for the purpose of valuing assets remaining in the transferor's estate: s.161(2)(*b*) and see § 20–19.

34. s.24(2).

34a. s.24(1). The restrictions imposed by s.23(2)–(5) on the exemption for gifts to charity (see note 31a above) are also applicable to the exemption for gifts to political parties.

34b. See [1976] S.T.I. 145: Inland Revenue Press Release of April 15, 1976, now Statement of Practice 6/1976.

8. *Gifts for national purposes, etc.*

19–21   A transfer of value is an exempt transfer to the extent that the value transferred by it is attributable to property which becomes the property of certain galleries, museums, national collections, university libraries, the National Trust, local authorities, Government departments or universities or university colleges in the United Kingdom.[35] As with the charities exemption in § 19–20, there is no financial limit on this exemption.

9. *Gifts for public benefit*

19–22   Transfers of value to a body not established or conducted for profit are exempt transfers if the Treasury so direct and if the property transferred falls into one of a number of categories which include[36]:

(a) land which in the opinion of the Treasury is of outstanding scenic or historic or scientific interest;
(b) a building (including the grounds used with it) for the preservation of which special steps should in the opinion of the Treasury be taken by reason of its outstanding historic or architectural or aesthetic interest and the cost of preserving it;
(c) an object which at the time of the transfer is ordinarily kept in, and is given with, a building within (b);
(d) a picture, print, book, manuscript, work of art or scientific collection which in the opinion of the Treasury is of national, scientific, historic or artistic interest; and
(e) property given as a source of income for the upkeep of any of the above.

The Treasury have wide powers to give directions and require undertakings to be entered into for the purpose generally of securing the preservation of the property or its character and reasonable access to it for the public.

Supplementary provisions

19–23   Where a transfer of value falls into one or more of the exemptions numbered 1, 6, 7, 8 or 9 above, but is not wholly exempt, sections 36 to 42 apply for the purpose of determining the extent of the exemption. Where the transfer is exempt up to a limit but not exempt as to the rest, these provisions (which are of considerable complexity) show how the non-exempt part is to be attributed to the gifts and how the exemption is to be allocated as between the gifts.

For accounting in respect of excepted transfers, see § 25–03A.

---

35. s.25 and Sched. 3. s.23(2)–(5) (see note 31a above) also applies to this exemption: s.25(2). Statement of Practice 6/1976 (see note 32 above) is also applicable to gifts for national purposes.
36. s.26. See also note 32 and the text thereto which also applies to this exemption. For the corresponding capital gains tax exemption, see C.G.T.A. 1979, s.147.

2. Miscellaneous Exemptions and Reliefs

1. *Death on active service, etc.*[37–38]

19–24   There is an exemption from the inheritance tax otherwise leviable on death where the deceased is certified by the appropriate authority as having died from a wound inflicted, accident occurring or disease contracted while he was a member of the armed forces, provided he was (i) on active service against an enemy or (ii) on other service of a warlike nature or which, in the opinion of the Treasury, involved the same risks as service of a warlike nature. The exemption also applies where the deceased died from a disease contracted at some previous time, the death being due to or hastened by the aggravation of the disease during a period when the deceased was on service as mentioned in (i) or (ii). The exemption also applies to members of certain women's services.

2. *Cash options under approved annuity schemes*[39]

19–25   Where under a contract or trust scheme approved by the Board under section 226 or 226A of the Income and Corporation Taxes Act or (before the commencement of that Act) under section 22 of the Finance Act 1956 (retirement annuities) an annuity become payable on a person's death to a widow, widower or dependant of that person, and under the terms of the contract or scheme a sum of money might at his option have become payable instead to his personal representatives, he is not, by virtue of section 5(2) (see § 18–09), to be treated as having been beneficially entitled to that sum. The sum of money is thus not chargeable to inheritance tax on death as property forming part of the deceased's estate.

3. *Government securities free of tax while in foreign ownership*[40]

19–26   Certain United Kingdom securities are issued by the Treasury subject to a condition for exemption from taxation so long as the securities are in the beneficial ownership of persons neither domiciled nor ordinarily resident in the United Kingdom. Such securities are "excluded property" if, not being settled property, they are in the beneficial ownership of such a person or, being settled property, such a person is beneficially entitled to a qualifying interest in possession in them.

> Thus if "exempt Government securities" are held by trustees upon trust for A for life with remainder to B absolutely and A is neither domiciled nor ordinarily resident in the United Kingdom, no inheritance tax is payable on the termination of A's interest in possession.

If the securities are settled property and no qualifying interest in possession subsists in them, as where Government securities are held on dis-

---

37–38. s.154.
39. s.152.
40. s.6(2) and s.48(4)(*a*).

cretionary trusts, the property is excluded property only if it is shown that all known persons for whose benefit the settled property or income from it has been or might be applied or who are or might become beneficially entitled[41] to an interest in possession in it are persons neither domiciled nor ordinarily resident in the United Kingdom.[41a] Where property is held on discretionary trusts for a class of persons which includes such non-domiciled, etc., persons and others, inheritance tax cannot be avoided by the trustees advancing or appointing part of the property into a second settlement for the exclusive benefit of the non-domiciled, etc., persons and investing such property in Government securities. This is because the conditions as to beneficial entitlement have to be satisfied as respects both the head settlement and the sub-settlement.[42] Where a close company is a beneficiary, the principle stated in § 22–51 applies.[43]

The extended definition of "domicile" in section 267 (see § 23–10) does not apply for the purposes of this provision.[44]

4. Overseas pensions[45]

19–27   The estate duty arrangements in relation to pensions formerly due from India, Pakistan and various ex-colonial governments are continued for inheritance tax.

5. Savings by persons domiciled in the Channel Islands or Isle of Man[46]

19–28   The Act treats as excluded property national savings certificates, premium savings bonds and certain other savings where the person beneficially entitled is domiciled in the Channel Islands or the Isle of Man.

The extended definition of domicile in section 267 (see § 23–10) does not apply for the purposes of this exemption.[46a]

6. Visiting forces and staff of allied headquarters[47]

19–29   The Act continues certain reliefs for members of overseas forces visiting this country and for the staff of allied headquarters. Certain property belonging to them is excluded property and the period of a visit to the United Kingdom is not treated as a period of residence in the United Kingdom or as creating a change of residence or domicile.

---

41. See *Von Ernst & Cie* v. *I.R.C.* [1980] S.T.C. 111 (C.A.). An unincorporated charity or a company with exclusively charitable objects is incapable of being "beneficially entitled" in this sense: only the objects of the trust fulfil this rôle.
41a. s.48(4)(*b*).
42. See ss.48(5), (6) as respects advances after April 19, 1978. See, generally, [1978] B.T.R. 133 at pp. 172–173.
43. s.101(1).
44. s.267(2).
45. s.153.
46. s.6(3).
46a. s.267(2)
47. s.155.

7. Double taxation relief [48–99]

19–30   Section 158 provides for double taxation agreements and double taxation relief in respect of inheritance tax.

3. POTENTIALLY EXEMPT TRANSFERS

19–30A   Where an individual makes a transfer of value[1] which would otherwise otherwise be a chargeable transfer[2] then, if the transfer is either a gift:

(a) to another individual; or

(b) into an accumulation and maintenance trust (see §§22–84 *et seq.*) or a disabled trust,[3]

that transfer will be "potentially exempt." Where the value transferred (*i.e.* the loss to the transferor's estate) exceeds the value of the gift received by the donee, the potential exemption extends to the whole value so transferred.[4] The exemption is only available under (a) above, it should be noted, where there is an *outright* gift to another individual.[5]

> Thus if property is settled by A upon trust for B for life, remainder to C absolutely, although the settled property is deemed to form part of B's estate in the same way as it would if he were an absolute owner (see §22–17), A's transfer is not potentially exempt and inheritance tax will (subject to the operation of any of the other exemptions) be a chargeable transfer liable to inheritance tax.

A PET becomes irreversibly exempt if the transferor survives his gift by seven years: if he fails to do so, the transfer becomes a chargeable transfer liable to inheritance tax.[6] Until the transferor dies, though, it is to be presumed that the exemption will be confirmed.[7]

> Thus if A, having made no previous chargeable transfers, gives £100,000 to B on July 1, 1986 (a PET) and settles £50,000 on trust for C for life, remainder to D absolutely (not a PET), the earlier gift does not form part of A's "cumulative total" for inheritance tax purposes unless and until he dies before July 1, 1993. Accordingly, the first £6,000 of the gift into settlement will be exempt from tax under section 19 and the remaining £44,000 will be charged to tax at the nil rate (see §20–02). If, however, A dies within seven years, the gift of £100,000 will prove to be a chargeable transfer, liable to inheritance tax at the rate in force in the year of A's death but computed by bringing the gift into his cumulative total for 1986/87. Tax on the gift into settlement will, correspondingly, be recomputed as a gift of £44,000 made by a person with a cumulative total of £100,000 (the settled gift retains its right to section 19 relief in precedence to the PET—see § 19–07).[8–48]

48–99. s.158.

1. s.3A. The provisions relating to PETs apply on and after March 18, 1986.

2. Where the transfer is already partly exempt and so is a chargeable transfer in part only, the PET provisions apply to the extent that the transfer would so otherwise be chargeable. s.19 (annual exemption) has been amended (see §19–07) so that relief under s.3A is given in priority to the relief afforded by that section.

3. Not dealt with in this book.

4. s.3A(2), (3). And see Statement of Practice 6/1976.

5. s.3A(2).

6. s.3A(3).

7. s.3A(6).

8–48. See Chap. 20 on the computation of the charge.

19–30B   The effect is, thus, to remove the charge to inheritance tax from outright gifts made at any time during a person's lifetime, except in the last seven years, and further to exempt gifts to favoured settlements made in the same period. Rules have been introduced (see §§20–29 *et seq.*) to ensure that advantage is not taken of the exemption to make gifts which effectively leave enjoyment with the transferor during his lifetime.

4. "QUICK SUCCESSION RELIEF"[49]

19–31   This relief applies on a death where the death which gives rise to the charge to inheritance tax, under section 4(1), was preceded by a chargeable transfer (called "the first transfer") made to the deceased not more than five years before his death which increased the value of his estate. The relief takes the form of a reduction in the tax chargeable on the later transfer, the reduction being a "percentage of the tax charged on so much of the value transferred by the first transfer as is attributable to the increase."

The percentage reduction varies with the period between the dates of the first and later transfers and is:

> 100 per cent. if the period is one year or less;
> 80 per cent. if the period is two years or less;
> 60 per cent. if the period is three years or less;
> 40 per cent. if the period is four years or less; and
> 20 per cent. if the period exceeds four years.

> Suppose A gives B £50,000 and dies within a year. B pays the inheritance tax due of £X. B himself dies $3\frac{1}{2}$ years after the date of A's gift, leaving an estate of £100,000. The inheritance tax on £100,000 will be reduced by 40 per cent. of £X.

19–32   The relief also applies on a lifetime transfer when the value transferred falls to be determined by reference to the value of settled property in which the transferor had an interest in possession, if the first transfer either was or included the making of the settlement or was made after the making of the settlement.

Example

> A settles £100,000 on trust for B for life, remainder to C absolutely, and pays the inheritance tax due of £Y. Within two years of the creation of the settlement, B surrenders his life interest, causing the acceleration of C's remainder. The tax payable by the trustees under section 52(1) (see §§22–23 *et seq.*) is reduced by 80 per cent. of £Y.

The relief in §§ 19–31 and 19–32 supersedes earlier provisions and applies when the later transfer is made on or after March 10, 1981.[50]

---

49. s.141.
50. The earlier provisions were s.30 and F.A. 1975, Sched. 5, para. 5.

5. Relief for Works of Art, Historic Buildings, etc.[51]

19–33   Provisions exist, applicable to transfers on death, lifetime transfers and transfers made by trustees of discretionary trusts, whose object is to encourage, by the conditional award of relief from inheritance tax, the ownership of pictures, collections and buildings, etc., which form part of the national heritage, in such a way as to preserve them for the enjoyment of all.

Section 30 makes a transfer of value an exempt transfer to the extent that the value transferred by it is attributable to property (a) which, on a claim made for the purpose, is designated by the Treasury under the powers given to it by section 31 (see below) and (b) with respect to which the requisite undertaking is given by such person as the Treasury thinks appropriate. Such a transfer is called a "conditionally exempt transfer."[52]

Section 31 allows the Treasury to designate the following:

     (a)   any pictures, prints, books, manuscripts, works of art, scientific collections or other things not yielding income which appear to the Treasury to be of national, scientific, historic or artistic interest;

     (b)   any land which in the opinion of the Treasury is of outstanding scenic or historic or scientific interest;

     (c)   any building for the preservation of which special steps should in the opinion of the Treasury be taken by reason of its outstanding historic or architectural interest;

     (d)   any area of land which in the opinion of the Treasury is essential for the protection of the character and amenities of a building mentioned in (c); and

     (e)   any object which in the opinion of the Treasury is historically associated with such a building as is mentioned in paragraph (c) above.

In the case of property within (a), the requisite undertaking is to keep the property in the United Kingdom and to take reasonable steps for its preservation and (save in the case of confidential documents) to secure reasonable access to the public.[52a] In the case of property within (b), the requisite undertaking is to maintain the land and to preserve its character and to secure reasonable access to the public.[53]

No exemption can be claimed for a lifetime transfer unless the transferor or his spouse (or both spouses between them) have been beneficially entitled to the property throughout the six years ending with the transfer

---

51. The Central Office of Information has published a basic guide to capital taxation and the national heritage which is reproduced in [1982] S.T.I. 352. The provisions dealt with in the following paragraphs replace more limited relief which was available only on death under the F.A. 1975. See the ninth edition of this book at § 19–33. Sched. 5 to the 1984 Act contains the rules which now deal with the subsequent treatment of property which was afforded relief under those earlier provisions.

52. s.30(2).

52a. Arrangements for satisfying the undertakings as to public access are set out in detail on Form 700A: see [1982] S.T.I. 350.

53. ss.31(2)–(4).

or, alternatively, the transferor acquired the property on a death which was itself a conditionally exempt transfer.[54]

This exemption does not apply to a transfer of value which is exempt under provisions relating to transfers between spouses (see § 19–02) or transfers to charities (see § 19–20).[55]

Chargeable events

19–34   Where the exemption under section 30(1) applies, the transfer is conditionally exempt (see § 19–33). Tax becomes chargeable under section 32 on the first occurrence thereafter of a *chargeable event* with respect to the property.[56] The following are chargeable events.

(1) *Non-observance of the undertaking.* Tax becomes chargeable if the Treasury are satisfied that the undertaking (see § 19–33) has not been observed in a material respect.[57] The person liable for the tax in that event is the person who, if the object were sold at the time the tax becomes chargeable, would be entitled to receive (whether for his own benefit or not) the proceeds of sale or any income arising from them.[57a]

(2) *Death, or disposal of the property.* Tax becomes chargeable if the person beneficially entitled to the property dies or the property is disposed of, whether by sale or gift or otherwise.[58] The person liable for the tax in the case of death is the person who, if the property were sold immediately after the death, would be entitled to receive (whether for his own benefit or not) the proceeds of sale or any income arising from them.[58a] The person liable for the tax on a disposal is the person by whom or for whose benefit the property is disposed of.[58b] There are two exceptions to this general rule:

(a) A death or disposal otherwise than by sale is not a chargeable event if it is itself a conditionally exempt transfer. This requires that the undertaking previously given with respect to the property be replaced by a corresponding undertaking given by such person as the Treasury think appropriate.[59]

> Thus if property which is accorded conditional exemption from inheritance tax on A's death passes to B and B dies, inheritance tax is payable unless B's personal representatives claim and obtain relief under section 30. Similarly, if C gives property to D and C's gift is accorded conditional exemption from inheritance tax, and D gives the property to E, inheritance tax is payable on

---

54. s.30(3). This qualification is designed to make it difficult for wealthy individuals to invest in assets forming part of the national heritage mainly for the purpose of avoiding inheritance tax.
55. s.30(4).
56. s.32(1). Where a chargeable event occurs this may extend to other conditionally exempt property associated with that which triggered the charge: see s.32(6), (7).
57. s.32(2).
57a. s.207(1).
58. s.32(3).
58a. s.207(1).
58b. s.207(2).
59. s.32(5).

D's gift unless D makes a successful claim for relief under section 30. The claimants in each case (B's personal representatives and D) would have to procure fresh undertakings from the appropriate persons.

(b) A death or disposal is not a chargeable event with respect to any property if the deceased's personal representatives within three years of the death (or, in the case of settled property, the trustees or the person next entitled) sell the property by private treaty (or give it) to one of the bodies mentioned in Schedule 3 (museums, etc.: see § 19–21) or apply it in satisfaction of the Board's claim for inheritance tax.[60]

Amount of the tax charge

19–35   Where tax becomes chargeable under section 32 (see § 19–34), it is charged on an amount equal to the value of the property at the time of the chargeable event (or the proceeds of sale in the case of an arm's length sale). If the relevant person (as defined),[61] is alive, tax is charged at the rates applicable to chargeable lifetime transfers (see § 20–02) as if he had made a transfer of value of that amount at the time of the chargeable event; if he is dead, tax is charged at the rates applicable to transfers on death and as if the amount had been added to the value transferred on his death and had formed the highest part thereof.[62]

The scheme of the legislation is to treat a conditionally exempt transfer followed by a chargeable event as if the transferor (or the relevant transferor) had made a non-exempt gift of property (valued, not at the date of the gift, but at the date of the chargeable event). Consistently with this concept, there are provisions in section 34 of the Act for reinstatement of the transferor's cumulative total by reference to the no-longer-exempt transfer.

> Assume A makes a conditionally exempt transfer of a Rembrandt to B. A later makes a non-exempt transfer into settlement of £80,000 and pays inheritance tax at the rate appropriate to that transfer. Later B sells the Rembrandt, *i.e.* there is a chargeable event and B is liable for the tax occasioned thereby. The proceeds of sale are £450,000. Under section 34, the rate or rates of tax applicable on any chargeable transfer made by A *subsequent* to the sale by B fall to be determined as if A had made a transfer of value of £450,000 at the time of the sale. If A is dead at the time of the sale by B, the amount transferred on A's death is increased by £450,000.

If the property is comprised in a settlement at the time of the sale, there are provisions for adding the taxable amount to the settlor's cumulative total of gifts in certain circumstances.[63]

Where after a conditionally exempt transfer of any property there is a chargeable transfer the value transferred by which is wholly or partly attributable to that property, any tax charged on that value so far as attributable to that property shall be allowed as a credit:

---

60. s.32(4).
61. In s.33(5).
62. s.33(1).
63. s.34(3).

(a) if the chargeable transfer is a chargeable event with respect to the property, against the tax chargeable in accordance with section 33 by reference to that event;

(b) if the chargeable transfer is not such a chargeable event, against the tax chargeable in accordance with section 33 by reference to the next chargeable event with respect to the property.[64]

Conditionally exempt and potentially exempt transfers

19–35A   Provision is made to ensure that the relief for PETs is given in priority to the more limited conditional exemption:

(a) No claim is to be made for conditional exemption in the case of any PET until that transfer proves chargeable on the subsequent death of the transferor.[65] Where that occurs, the lifetime transfer is exempted only to the extent that its value is attributable to property which has not subsequently been sold.[66] In determining whether property is suitable for designation for conditional exemption in such a case, the Treasury will consider the circumstances not as at the date of the transfer but as at the date of the transferor's death.

(b) But where, following a PET, any of the property which could have attracted conditional exemption is sold by private treaty to one of the bodies mentioned in Schedule 3 to the Act (see §19–21) or is applied in satisfaction of a claim for inheritance tax under section 230 (see §19–34) after the gift but before the transferor's death, the earlier transfer remains exempt from tax (to the extent of the property so sold) notwithstanding the death of the transferor within seven years.[67]

Settled property

19–36   Sections 78 and 79 provide an exemption from inheritance tax which would otherwise arise under provisions discussed later in this book (see §§ 22–41 *et seq.*) on distributions by trustees of a discretionary settlement of property designated by the Treasury under section 31 of the Act: see § 19–33.

Maintenance funds for historic buildings

19–37   Section 27, Schedule 4 and related sections contain provisions which enable property to be settled on trusts to secure the maintenance, repair or preservation of historic buildings, etc., without liability to inheritance tax. See also § 16–50A (capital gains tax).[67a]

---

64. s.33(7).
65. s.30(3B).
66. s.30(3C).
67. s.26A.
67a. For the special income tax treatment of such funds, see F.A. 1980, ss.52, 53.

6. MUTUAL AND VOIDABLE TRANSFERS

Mutual transfers

19–38   The relief for mutual transfers has been abolished by the Finance Act 1986 with effect from March 18, 1986.[68]

Voidable transfers[69–73]

19–38A   Where on a claim made for the purpose it is shown that the whole or any part of a chargeable transfer ("the relevant transfer") has by virtue of any enactment or rule of law been set aside as voidable or otherwise defeasible, *e.g.* on the bankruptcy of the transferor:

    (a) tax paid or payable by the claimant, both in respect of the relevant transfer or any other chargeable transfer made before the claim, that would not have been payable if the relevant transfer had been void *ab initio,* is repayable by the Board or, as the case may be, is not payable; and

    (b) the rate or rates of tax (including interest on tax) applicable to any chargeable transfer made after the claim by the person who made the relevant transfer is to be determined as if that transfer or part of it had been void.

Tax repayable carries interest (which is not income for any tax purposes) from the date on which the claim is made.

> Thus if A makes a voidable transfer in 1977 and a valid transfer in 1978, and the 1977 transfer is set aside, and a claim is made as respects the 1977 transfer in 1979, any tax paid on the 1977 transfer is repayable with tax-free interest from the date of the claim; and the tax paid on the 1978 transfer has to be recomputed as if the 1977 transfer had not been made, any overpaid tax being repayable with tax-free interest from the date of the claim.

7. RELIEF FOR BUSINESS PROPERTY

19–39   Section 104 provides that where the whole or part of the value transferred by a transfer of value is attributable to the value of any relevant business property, the whole or such part of the value transferred is to be reduced by a percentage (which varies according to the nature of the property transferred). The value transferred is calculated as a value on which no tax is chargeable: that is, inheritance tax is ignored when reckoning that value.

The relief applies to all transfers of value, including lifetime transfers, transfers on death and the amount on which tax is charged under the relevant property rules (see §§ 22–50 *et seq.*).[74] The relief does not have to be claimed.

Where the relief is given, inheritance tax is levied as if the value transferred were reduced by the appropriate percentage. Thus if A settles shares and the diminution in the value of A's estate is £100,000, but the 50

---

68. F.A. 1986, Sched. 23, Pt. X.
69–73. s.150.
74. s.103(1).

per cent. relief is available, A is treated as making a transfer of value of £50,000.

For the corresponding relief from capital gains tax, see § 16–49.

Relevant business property

19–39A   "Relevant business property" means, in relation to any transfer of value[75]:

> (a) property consisting of a business or an interest in a business, *e.g.* a partner's interest in a partnership business (including a business carried on in the exercise of a profession or vocation but excluding a business carried on otherwise than for gain);
> (b) shares or securities of a company which, by themselves or together with other shares or securities owned by the transferor, gave him control[76] of the company immediately before the transfer;
> (c) shares in a company not falling within (b) and not quoted on a recognised stock exchange (*i.e.* a minority holding of unquoted shares);
> (d) any land or building, machinery or plant which, immediately before the transfer, was used wholly or mainly for the purposes of a business carried on by a company of which the transferor then had control[76] or by a partnership of which he then was a partner. (In this case the relief applies only if the transferor's interest in the business or company immediately before the transfer was relevant business property.)[77]; and
> (e) any land or building which, immediately before the transfer, was used wholly or mainly for the purposes of a business carried on by the transferor and was settled property in which he was then beneficially entitled to an interest in possession.

19–39B   In *Fetherstonaugh* v. *I.R.C.*[78] the Court of Appeal decided that agricultural land held on trust and on which the tenant for life carried on a farming business as sole trader was "relevant business property." As a person with an interest in possession in such property he was, by section 49(1) (see §§ 22–14 *et seq.*), to be treated for all the purposes of capital transfer tax (as it then was) as beneficially entitled to the property itself. Accordingly, when he died, one of the assets which was to be considered to form part of his business under section 105(1)(*a*) was the trust land which he had farmed. Since assets falling within that provision attract relief at 50 per cent. it necessarily follows that section 105(1)(*e*)—which only attracts relief at 30 per cent.—is redundant.

In the case of woodlands managed on a commercial basis, both the land and trees may qualify as relevant business property under (a). The relief does not apply where the business (or the business carried on by the com-

---

75. s.105(1).
76. "Control" is defined by s.269.
77. s.105(6).
78. [1984] S.T.C. 261. See also S.P. 12/1980; and [1984] S.T.I. 651.

pany) consists wholly or mainly of dealing in securities, stocks or shares, land or buildings or making or holding investments[79]; except that the relief applies where the business is that of a market maker[79a] or discount house in the United Kingdom and to shares or securities in a holding company for one or more companies whose business is not within the exception.[80] It is in the context of business relief that the question whether a company is an investment company or a trading company assumes special significance.

There are special provisions which disallow the relief where property which would be relevant business property is subject to a binding contract of sale at the time of the transfer or where a company is in liquidation at the time when its shares are transferred.[81]

The value of a business is the value of the business assets (including goodwill) less liabilities incurred for the purposes of the business.

19–39C   Where both agricultural and business property relief would, prima facie, appear to be applicable, agricultural relief alone will be available even though it may well attract a lower percentage reduction than that would have been applicable had the taxpayer been able to claim business relief.

Amount of relief

19–39D   The amount of relief available depends on which of paragraphs (a) to (e) in § 19–39A applies. The reduction made in the value transferred where paragraphs (a) or (b) applies is 50 per cent. but 30 per cent. where one of paragraphs (c), (d) or (e) does so.[82] The relief is without financial limit.

In the case of a transfer of shares or securities, paragraph (b) in § 19–39A (and, consequently, the 50 per cent. relief) is not applicable if:

(a) the shares or securities would not have been sufficient without other property to give the transferor control of the company immediately before the transfer; *and*

(b) their value is later reduced on a sale by virtue of section 176.[83]

Section 176 affords relief where, on a person's death, he leaves a majority shareholding to two or more persons. The valuation at death will, of course, be considerably in excess of the aggregate of values of the minority shareholdings received by the legatees—and the transfer will obtain 50 per cent. business property relief. If, however, within three years of the death of the testator one of the legatees sells his shares at a price below that at which those shares were valued as part of the majority holding on death, he can make a claim that that lower price be substituted for that by reference

---

79. s.105(3).
79a. "Market maker" is a person who holds himself out at all normal times in compliance with Stock Exchange rules as willing to buy and sell securities at a price specified by him and who is recognised as doing so by the Council of the Stock Exchange—it approximates to an old-fashioned jobber.
80. s.105(4).
81. s.105(5).
82. s.104. But see § 19–39B on the relief actually available in respect of settled property which has been used in a business carried on by a beneficiary with an interest in possession.
83. s.105(2).

to which tax was payable on the deemed transfer on the earlier death. Since this has the effect of valuing that part of the transfer as if it were the transfer of a minority holding, it would not be appropriate for that transfer to obtain the 50 pr cent. relief and this section 105(2) provides.

At one time it was the practice of the Revenue to contend that the 50 per cent. relief was not available unless, as a result of the transfer, the transferor lost control of the company.

> Thus if X held 75 out of 100 issued shares in A Ltd., relief under section 105(1)(a) was considered to be available only if X transferred at least 25 of those shares away.

It is understood, however, that this unwarranted interpretation is no longer insisted upon.

Any exemptions or reliefs relating to transfers of value are given *after* business property relief.[84] Thus, the amount chargeable to tax on a lifetime settlement of relevant business property valued at £100,000 and qualifying for 50 per cent. relief (assuming the trustees pay the tax) is:

> £100,000 *less* £50,000 (business relief) *less* £3,000 (annual exemption) = £47,000.

If the donor pays the tax, the £47,000 is grossed up: see § 20–10.

Limitations on the availability of relief

19–39E   (i) *Minimum period of ownership.* To qualify for the relief the transferor must have owned the relevant business property throughout the two years immediately preceding the transfer.[85] Alternatively, it must have replaced other relevant business property and it, and the property it replaced, must have been owned for at least two years falling within the five years immediately preceding the transfer of value.[86] Where the transferor became entitled to the property on the death of his spouse, the deceased's period of ownership can be reckoned as part of the transferor's period of ownership.[87]

(ii) *Excepted assets.* In determining what part of the value transferred by a transfer of value is attributable to the value of any relevant business property that proportion of the value of such property which is attributable to "excepted assets" must be left out of account.[87a] An "excepted asset" is an asset which neither has been used wholly or mainly for the purposes of the business throughout the period of two years preceding the transfer or the whole of the period of ownership (if shorter), nor is required for future use in the business at the time of the transfer.[87b] Thus property which has been purchased for domestic use cannot obtain business relief on a transfer

---

84. Because the relief reduces the value transferred and not simply the amount of the chargeable transfer.
85. s.106.
86. s.107.
87. s.108.
87a. s.112(1).
87b. s.112(2).

simply because it has been entered in the accounts as an asset of the business.

Business property transfers within seven years of death

19–39F   Where a gift of relevant business property is made within seven years of the transferor's death, relief will not be available (so that adjustments will have to be made after death) unless certain additional conditions are satisfied. First[87c] the transferee must continue to own the property (or, in specified circumstances, replacement property) at the transferor's death—or, if earlier, at his own death. Secondly, that property must, at that later time, be relevant business property in the hands of the transferee.

> So, if X owned a controlling shareholding in Z Ltd., together with the factory in which Z Ltd. carried on its trade, and transferred the factory to his son, Y, business property relief would not be available in respect of that transfer on X's death within seven years unless Y had, prior to his father's death, acquired a controlling shareholding in the company. See §19–39A(d) above.

If the original property had been sold by the transferee before the transferor's death (or his own death, if earlier) relief can be sustained in relation to the earlier transfer if the transferee uses the proceeds of sale to acquire new qualifying property within 12 months of the sale,[87d] provided that both sale and purchase are effected in an arm's length sale or on terms similar to those which might be expected in such a sale.

There can be no charge to tax under these provisions unless the transferor dies within seven years of his gift: thus they will not apply simply because the transferee dies within that period. The provisions apply in two cases—first, where a PET proves chargeable and the transferee has disposed of the property; secondly, where the original transfer was a chargeable transfer (*e.g.* being made into settlement) and the trustees have subsequently turned the assets into cash. In each case, additional tax will become payable on the transferor's death by reference to an earlier transfer. Tax will not be payable, though, if the transferee retains the assets as relevant business property until the transferor's death but disposes of them thereafter but still within seven years of the original gift.

Payment of tax

19–39G   Tax on transfers of value of relevant business property can, in certain circumstances, be paid by interest-free instalments, provided the instalments are paid on the due dates: see §§ 25–26 *et seq.*

8. Relief for Agricultural Property

19–40   Sections 115 to 124B provide for relief from inheritance tax on transfers of value of agricultural property. These provisions, which apply to transfers of value made on or after March 10, 1981, supersede the old scheme of

---

87c. s.113A.
87d. s.113B. It is sufficient if the transferee enters into a binding contract to acquire such property within 12 months of the sale.

relief which is discussed in the thirteenth edition of this book at §§ 19–40 *et seq*. There are carry-over provisions from the old scheme which are summarised in § 19–48 below.

Definitions

19–41   The following definitions apply for the purposes of this relief:

Transfer of value includes an occasion when tax is chargeable under the relevant property rules in §§ 22–50 *et seq*. References to the value transferred by a transfer of value and to a transferor are to be construed as including respectively the amount on which tax is then chargeable and the trustees of the settlement concerned.[88]

Agricultural property means agricultural land or pasture and includes woodland and any building used in connection with the intensive rearing of livestock or fish if the woodland or building is occupied with agricultural land or pasture and the occupation is ancillary to that of the agricultural land or pasture. It also includes such cottages, farm buildings and farmhouses, together with the land occupied with them, as are of a character appropriate to the property.[89] Buildings used in connection with the activities of breeding and rearing horses on a stud farm are considered to be farm buildings[89a] "Agricultural property" does not, however, include farm animals or machinery.

Agricultural value in relation to agricultural property means the value of that property on the assumption that it is subject to a perpetual covenant prohibiting its use otherwise than as agricultural property.[90] Thus any development value which is attached to agricultural property is excluded from the definition of agricultural value.

Nature of relief

19–42   The relief for agricultural property applies to land in the United Kingdom which, for this purpose, is extended to include land in the Channel Islands and the Isle of Man.[91] The relief applies where the whole or part of the value transferred by a transfer of value is attributable to the agricultural value of agricultural property and it takes the form of a reduction by the *appropriate percentage* (see § 19–43) of the whole or that part of the value transferred which is attributable to the agricultural value.[92] The value transferred is for this purpose calculated as a value on which no tax is chargeable; that is, inheritance tax is ignored in reckoning the value transferred.[93] Note that the relief applies to a transfer of value, not a chargeable

---

88. s.115(1).
89. s.115(2). See *Lindsay v. I..R.C.* (1953) 34 T.C. 289. *Quaere* the position if the farmer continues to occupy the farmhouse and to continue farming after having, *e.g.* transferred such land to a partnership of which he is a member or having settled the land (other than the farmhouse).
89a. s.115(4): a declaratory amendment introduced by F.A. 1984, s.107.
90. s.115(3).
91. s.115(5).
92. s.116(1).
93. s.116(7).

transfer. Thus the annual exemption (see § 19–07) is ignored. There is no relief for that part (if any) of the value of land which represents its non-agricultural value, including any value attributable to the prospect of development for non-agricultural purposes. Agricultural relief does not have to be claimed. There are special provisions which disallow the relief where agricultural property is subject to a binding contract of sale at the time of the transfer.[93a]

The appropriate percentage

19–43   The appropriate percentage depends on the nature of the transferor's interest. The relief is:

   (i) 50 per cent. if the interest of the transferor immediately before the transfer carries the right to vacant possession or the right to obtain it within the next 12 months.[94] If the transferors are joint tenants or tenants in common (or in Scotland joint owners or owners in common) it is sufficient if the interests of all of them together carry that right.[95]

   (ii) 30 per cent. in any other case.[96]

Paragraph (i) applies to the interest of the freeholder in possession and the tenant farmer in possession. It also applies to the interest of the freeholder or leaseholder not in possession, but only in the exceptional case where he has the right to vacant possession because the tenant does not enjoy the protection of the Agricultural Holdings Acts, *e.g.* a tenant with grazing rights only. Paragraph (ii) applies to the interest of a reversioner with no such right to possession.

Where A, the owner of land, lets property to himself and B and C in order that the land may be farmed in partnership by A, B and C, both the 50 per cent. and the 30 per cent. relief will apply to a transfer of value of A's interest in the land. The 30 per cent. relief will apply to A's interest as freeholder, which will be valued on a tenanted basis taking account of any security of tenure conferred on B and C by the Agricultural Holdings Acts: the 50 per cent. relief will apply to A's interest in the land *qua* partner. The tenant's interest may have a substantial value even if the tenancy is at a full market rent.

The 30 per cent. relief is of great importance in practice because agricultural land is often owned by the head of a family (or by the trustees of a family settlement) but actually farmed by a farming partnership or (since the rate of corporation tax is lower than the rate of income tax) by a farming company with a tenancy of the land, the shares in which are owned by members of the family.

93a. s.124.
94. s.116(2).
95. s.116(6).
96. s.116(2). This relief was increased from 20 per cent. to 30 per cent. with effect in relation to transfers of value made on or after March 15, 1983: F.(No. 2)A. 1983, s.10.

Minimum period of occupation or ownership: the two-year and seven-year rules

19–44   By section 117 the relief does not apply to agricultural property unless either:

(a) it was occupied by the transferor for the purposes of agriculture throughout the period of two years ending with the date of the transfer; or

(b) it was owned by him throughout the period of seven years ending with that date and was throughout that period occupied (by him or another) for the purposes of agriculture.

(a) and (b) are referred to below as "the two-year rule" and "the seven-year rule" respectively.

Thus a freeholder or tenant who occupies and farms the land will qualify for the 50 per cent. relief after two years' continuous occupation; whereas a purchaser of a freehold or leasehold interest in land which continues to be farmed by others will qualify for the 30 per cent. relief only after seven years of continuous ownership. The seven-year rule is to prevent "death-bed" acquisitions of let agricultural land by persons wishing to avoid inheritance tax.

For the purposes of the two-year and seven-year rules, occupation by a company which is controlled by the transferor is treated as occupation by the transferor.[97] Thus land can be put into a farming company under the transferor's control without prejudicing the transferor's entitlement to agricultural relief on a later transfer of value (but the capital gains tax implications need to be carefully considered). In Scotland, occupation by a Scottish partnership is treated as occupation by the partners.[98-99] In the case of an English partnership, each partner occupies the partnership land through the agency of the others.

Replacements

19–45   What is the position if, before the end of the two-year period, the owner sells his interest in the land and re-invests the sale proceeds in other land? Must he wait two years before a transfer of value of the new farm qualifies for relief? Generally, the answer is in the negative, because section 118(1) provides that where the agricultural property occupied by the transferor on the date of the transfer replaced other agricultural property, the two-year rule shall be treated as satisfied if it, the other property and any agricultural property directly or indirectly replaced by the other property were occupied by the transferor for the purposes of agriculture for periods which together comprised at least two years falling within the five years ending with that date. Thus if, within the five years immediately preceding the gift of farm C, the transferor has owned and occupied (in this order) farm A for six months, farm B for twelve months and farm C for eight months, the

---

97. s.119(1).
98–99. s.119(2).

condition will be satisfied as respects farm C even if there were breaks between the periods of ownership. There is a similar provision which applies to the seven-year rule: here the rule is treated as satisfied if the properties have been owned by the transferor and occupied (by him or another) for periods together comprising at least seven years falling within the ten years ending with the transfer.[1] But relief under section 116 is not to exceed what it would have been had the replacement or any one or more of the replacements not been made.[2] Thus one cannot increase the amount of agricultural relief available by replacing an inexpensive farm by a more valuable one shortly before a transfer of value.

> *Example*
> A sells a farm, which he has owned and occupied for many years for £100,000 and buys another for £450,000. He dies within two years of the purchase, at which time the respective values of the farms are £140,000 and £500,000. Agricultural relief is limited to 50% × £140,000 = £70,000 and, thus, the agricultural value on the deemed transfer immediately before A's death is reduced from £500,000 to £430,000.

In applying this restriction on the relief available in respect of replacement farms, changes resulting from the formation, alteration or dissolution of a partnership are ignored.[3]

Successions

19-46   There are two cases in which the transferor can take credit for the period of someone else's occupation (or ownership) in applying the two year (or seven year) rule:

(1) *Succession on death of the spouse of the transferor.* Where the transferor became entitled to any property on the death of another person he is deemed to have owned it (and, if he subsequently occupies it, to have occupied it) from the date of the death. If that other person was his spouse he is also deemed to have occupied it for the purposes of agriculture for any period for which it was so occupied by his spouse, and to have owned it for any period for which his spouse owned it.[4]

> Thus if H devises agricultural property to his wife, W, and W subsequently makes a transfer of value, whether by lifetime transfer or on death, W can add the period of H's occupation or ownership to her own for the purposes of applying the two year or seven year rule, as appropriate.

Note that (1) does not apply if H makes a lifetime transfer to W. But the exception in the next paragraph may apply if W's transfer is made on death.

(2) *Succession to a donor.* If A transfers property to B (the earlier transfer) and B (or B's spouse) makes a subsequent transfer of value of the same property to C, and the earlier transfer but not the subsequent transfer satisfies the two-year (or seven-year) rule, as appropriate, the property

---

1. s.118(2).
2. s.118(3).
3. s.118(4).
4. s.120.

transferred is nevertheless eligible for relief provided either A's transfer or B's transfer was a transfer of value on death and provided B (or B's spouse or A's personal representatives) occupied the property for the purposes of agriculture at the time of his transfer. This rule enables a donee to take credit for his donor's qualifying period of occupation when he (the donee) makes a transfer of value,[5] whether a lifetime transfer or a transfer on death.[5a]

Shares and securities in farming companies

19–47   Transfers of shares or securities in a company which occupies or owns agricultural property will qualify for agricultural relief if:

(a) the agricultural property forms part of the company's assets and part of the value of the shares or securities transferred can be attributed to the agricultural value of the agricultural property; and

(b) the shares or securities gave the transferor control of the company immediately before the transfer.[6]

For this purpose a person has control of a company at any time if he then has the control of powers of voting on all questions affecting the company as a whole which if exercised would yield a majority of the votes capable of being exercised thereon. Where shares or securities are comprised in a settlement, any powers of voting which they give to the trustees are deemed to be given to the person beneficially entitled in possession to the shares or securities (except in a case where no individual is so entitled).[7]

Broadly speaking, it has to be shown that the company satisfies the conditions which the transferor himself would have had to satisfy if he had made the transfer of value. Thus the agricultural property must have been either:

(1) occupied by the company for the purposes of agriculture throughout the period of two years ending with the date of the transfer; or

(2) owned by the company throughout the period of seven years ending with that date and throughout that period occupied (by the company or another) for the purposes of agriculture.[8]

In either case the transferor must have owned the shares or securities throughout the period mentioned.[9] There are provisions to meet the case where the company replaces one asset with another.[10] There are also provisions which enable relief to be afforded where the shares in question replaced other shares or agricultural property eligible for relief.[10a]

For the purposes of conditions (1) and (2), a company is treated as hav-

---

5. s.121.
5a. But consider the application of ss.124A and 124B: see §19–48A.
6. s.122(1).
7. s.269.
8. s.123(1).
9. s.123(1)(*b*).
10. s.123(4).
10a. s.123(3).

ing occupied the property at any time when it was occupied by a person who subsequently controls the company.[11] Thus if the owner of agricultural property transfers the property to a company in exchange for shares, any agricultural relief available to the owner is unaffected *provided* he controls the company.

Carry over of old-scheme relief

19–48   Under the old scheme, relief was sometimes available at 50 per cent. on transfers of let agricultural property. This applied where the transferor had let the property to a partnership of which he was himself a member or to a company which he controlled.

> Thus if L let Blackacre Farm to L, M and N, who farmed in partnership, and L made a transfer of value of his freehold reversion in the farm, the 50 per cent. relief applied to that interest of L, which was valued on a tenanted and not on a vacant possession basis.

This generous treatment had its price, for the grant of the lease by L was treated under the old scheme as a transfer of value by L (but see § 18–04A).

Under the new scheme the grant of the tenancy by L may involve no transfer of value (see § 18–04A) but L's interest as owner has to be separated from his interest as a tenant, as explained in § 19–43.

Where land was let in such a case before March 10, 1981, and a transfer of value by L immediately before that date would have qualified for old scheme relief, the 50 per cent. relief continues as respects the interest to which L was entitled before that date, provided that L's interest did not at any time between March 10, 1981, and the date of the transfer of value carry a right to vacant possession of the land or the right to obtain it within the next 12 months, and did not fail to do so by reason of any act or deliberate omission of L during that period.[12]

Relief under the old scheme was limited to £250,000 of agricultural value and 1,000 acres. If, in the example, L had 2,000 acres before March 10, 1981, only 1,000 acres will qualify for the 50 per cent. relief; the remainder will qualify for the 30 per cent. relief.

Advisers will appreciate the importance of establishing the precise position as respects agricultural property owned on March 10, 1981, before recommending any action subsequently, and, in particular, of establishing that any pre-March 10, 1981, tenancy has not been terminated, *e.g.* by surrender and regrant.

For payment of inheritance tax by interest-free instalments: see §§ 25–26 *et seq.*

19–48A   Similar conditions apply to gifts of agricultural property made within seven years of the transferor's death to those relating to business property described in §19–39F above. Unless the following conditions are satis-

---

11. s.123(5).
12. s.116(2)(*b*) and (3).

fied,[12a] agricultural relief will retrospectively be denied in respect of the original transfer, requiring the collection of additional tax after the transferor's death:

(a) the transferee must own the original property (or a permitted replacement)[12b] throughout the period ending with the death of the transferor—or, if earlier, of the transferee himself; and

(b) the original property must be agricultural property (see §19–41) immediately before the relevant death and must have been occupied by someone for the purposes of agriculture throughout the period in question.

(c) If the original property took the form of shares in a farming company, then in substitution for (a) above, it is required that the company must continue to own the land which generated the agricultural relief on the orginal transfer.

9. WOODLANDS[13]

19–49 Sections 125 to 129 give relief where the value transferred by a chargeable transfer made on death is determined by reference to the value of woodlands. Woodlands may also qualify for business relief (see § 19–39), agricultural relief (see § 19–40) or, if of outstanding scenic interest, for conditional exemption (see § 19–33).

Nature of relief

19–50   The specific relief is available where any part of a deceased person's estate includes land in the United Kingdom on which trees or underwood are growing but which is not agricultural property as defined in § 19–40. Where the relief is given, the value of the trees and underwood are left out of account in determining the value transferred on death.[14]

Condition of relief

19–51   The relief is not available unless the deceased was beneficially entitled to the land throughout the five years immediately preceding his death or became beneficially entitled otherwise than for a consideration in money or money's worth, *e.g.* by gift or inheritance.[15]

The person liable for the tax on the death must claim the relief by giving written notice to the Board within two years of the death or such longer time as the Board may allow.[16]

12a. s.124A.
12b. s.124B.
13. There is a useful discussion of the advantages of investment in woodlands in *Tolley's Tax Planning 1982/83*, pp. 749–757.
14. s.125(2).
15. s.125(1)(*b*).
16. s.125(3).

Tax chargeable

19–52   If the value of trees or underwood is left out of account on a death and all or any part of the trees or underwood is subsequently disposed of (otherwise than to the disponor's spouse), whether together with or apart from the land on which they were growing, section 126 provides that tax is chargeable if the disposal occurs before any part of the value transferred on the death of any other person is attributable to the value of that land, *i.e.* if the disposal occurs before a death in connection with which relief is not given for the whole of the woodlands. The disponor is liable for the tax.[17] The relief in respect of woodlands thus takes the form of a deferred charge to tax and deferment can continue from one generation to another if, on each death, the relief is claimed and given. Tax is charged when there is a sale or lifetime transfer.

19–53   Tax is charged[17a] on the net proceeds of sale (less certain expenses[18]) if the disposal is a sale for full consideration in money or money's worth; and in any other case tax is charged on the net value of the trees or underwood at the time of the disposal. Tax is charged at the rate or rates at which it would have been chargeable on the death if the amount so chargeable (including any amount on which tax was previously chargeable under section 126 in relation to that death) had been included in the value transferred on death and the amount on which the tax is chargeable had formed the highest part of that value.[19] This is subject to the qualification that if business relief (see §§ 19–39 *et seq.*) would have been available on the death if "woodlands relief" had not been claimed, the value on which tax is chargeable is reduced by 50 per cent.; and for this purpose it is to be assumed that the statutory provisions conferring business relief were in force at the time of the death.[20] The death by reference to which tax is calculated is the last death prior to the event giving rise to the tax charge.

19–54   When the disposal on which tax is chargeable is a chargeable transfer, the value transferred is calculated as if the value of the trees or underwood had been reduced by the tax chargeable under section 126.[21] Where tax is charged on a disposal, it is not again charged in relation to the same death on a further disposal of the same trees or underwood.[22]

10. Lifetime Dispositions for Maintenance of Family[22a]

19–55   The exemptions referred to in this section are those which enable one party to a marriage to make provision for the other (by way of settlement or otherwise), or for a child of either party, on the occasion, for example, of a

---

17. s.208.
17a. s.127.
18. s.130(2).
19. s.128.
20. s.127(2).
21. s.129.
22. s.126(3).
22a. s.11.

decree of divorce or nullity; and those which enable provision to be made for the maintenance of a child not wholly in the care of the transferor, for an illegitimate child of his, or for the care of a dependent relative. The exemptions discussed below do not apply to deemed transfers on death.

19–56   A disposition is not a transfer of value if it is made by one party to a marriage in favour of the other party or of a child (including a step-child or adopted child[23]) of either party and is:

(a) for the maintenance of the other party, or

(b) for the maintenance, education or training of the child for a period ending not later than the year in which he attains the age of 18 or, after attaining that age, ceases to undergo full-time education or training.[24] ("Year" means any period of 12 months ending with April 5.[25])

19–57   The term "maintenance" is not defined nor is there any qualification as to the amount which may be provided. Contrast in this respect the exemption for a disposition in favour of a dependent relative (see § 19–60), which refers to "reasonable provision" for care and maintenance. It is thought, however, that a disposition in excess of the amount the court would order on an application for maintenance, etc., would fall outside the exemption and would be a transfer of value as regards the excess. Annual payments out of capital to pay for a child's education (which will fall outside the normal expenditure exemption in § 19–11) will be exempt under this provision; so also lump sum payments to schools under composition fee schemes.

19–58   Section 11 provides that dispositions for the maintenance of one's spouse are not transfers of value. It follows that section 18 (see § 19–56) which exempts transfers of value made by one spouse to the other is neither necessary nor applicable when section 11 itself is available. Section 18, though, is of great importance when one spouse makes a disposition of a capital nature in favour of the other—as, for example, when a husband transfers title in the matrimonial home to his wife. Clearly, section 11 was unnecessary as far as married couples are concerned, since section 18 could cope by exempting all dispositions by one party to the other. The true purpose of the section lies rather in its application to dispositions for the maintenance of an ex-spouse once a decree absolute has been made and the divorced couple are no longer husband and wife.[26] To this end, section 11(6) provides:

> "'Marriage', in relation to a disposition made on the occasion of the dissolution or annulment of a marriage, and in relation to a disposition varying a disposition so made, includes a former marriage."

---

23. s.11(6).
24. s.11(1).
25. s.11(6).
26. See *Fender* v. *St. John Mildmay* [1938] A.C. 1 (H.L.).

It is to be noted that the section requires that the disposition be made either on the occasion of the decree absolute or by variation of one made thereon. Even, therefore, if the wife is in no need of maintenance at the time of the decree it is necessary to ensure that the court orders nominal maintenance in order to secure the future application of the provision if the wife's circumstances change materially for the worse. Presumably this will be in the interests of the wife too, in order to prevent the application of the "clean break" principle.[26a]

9–59   A disposition in favour of a child (including a step-child or adopted child[27]) who is not in the care of a parent of his is not a transfer of value provided the child has been in the care of the person making the disposition for substantial periods before the child attains the age of 18. The disposition must be made for the purpose and for the period mentioned in (b) in § 19–56.[28]

9–60   A disposition is not a transfer of value if it is made in favour of a dependent relative (as defined[29]) of the disponor and is a reasonable provision for his care or maintenance.[30]

9–61   A disposition in favour of an illegitimate child of the person making the disposition is not a transfer of value if it is for the purpose and period mentioned in (b) in § 19–56.[31]

9–62   Where a disposition satisfies the conditions of the above exemptions to a limited extent only, so much of it as satisfies them and so much of it as does not satisfy them are treated as separate dispositions[32]; and where an exempt disposition is of an interest in possession in settled property, there is an exemption from the charge which would otherwise arise under section 52[32a]: see § 22–24.

11. DEEDS OF FAMILY ARRANGEMENT, ETC.

9–63   It frequently happens that beneficiaries under a will or on a intestacy agree between themselves, by a deed of family arrangement or similar instrument (*e.g.* formal correspondence), to vary the dispositions made under the will or created by the intestacy. The estate is then administered subject to the agreed variations. A common example of this is where a testator gives all his assets to his wife in the expectation that she will make whatever arrangements for their disposition seem most appropriate.

Section 142, which applies to any variation or disclaimer made on or after April 11, 1978, contains a provision which supersedes an earlier pro-

---

26a. See *Minton* v. *Minton* [1979] A.C. 593 at p. 608 (H.L.).
27. s.11(6).
28. s.11(2).
29. s.11(6).
30. s.11(3).
31. s.11(4).
32. s.11(5).
32a. s.51(2).

vision (now repealed) in section 47(1) of the Finance Act 1975 and no longer requires "a deed of family arrangement or similar instrument." Thus any written instrument will now suffice and assets can be redistributed in such a way as to introduce an object who was not an original beneficiary nor even a member of the deceased's family. Benefits can be redirected even if the redirector has accepted some advantage for himself.

The Revenue have announced[32b] that they will require certain conditions to be satisfied before they will accept that an instrument falls within section 142:

(a) the instrument must be in writing signed by the persons or some of the persons who benefit or would benefit under the dispositions of the property comprised in the estate of the deceased immediately before his death;

(b) the instrument must be made within two years of the death;

(c) the instrument must *clearly* indicate the dispositions that are the subject of it and must vary their destination as laid down by the deceased's will, or under the law relating to intestacy, or otherwise;

(d) a written notice electing that section 142 shall apply must be given to the Board within six months after the date of the instrument varying the dispositions; and

(e) the notice of election must refer to the appropriate statutory provisions.

They have also announced:

(i) that an election, once made, is irrevocable;

(ii) that it is not possible to take advantage of section 142 to redirect a benefit which has already passed to the transferor by means of an instrument falling within section 142; and

(iii) that they will look with disfavour on multiple instruments of variation.

Section 142 applies whether or not the administration of the estate is complete or the property concerned has been distributed in accordance with the original disposition.

Section 142 applies only to property which was comprised in the deceased's estate immediately before his death (see § 18–08), save that "excluded property" (see § 23–02) is included. Settled property to which the deceased was treated as beneficially entitled under section 49(1) (see § 22–17) is not included, so if property is held for A during the life of X and A predeceases X giving his interest *pur autre vie* to B, section 142 does not apply if B redirects his interest to C. Nor is it possible to rely on section 142 to "redirect" property which is deemed to form part of the estate of the deceased in consequence of his having reserved a benefit in respect of the gift, attracting the application of section 102 of the Finance Act 1986: see §§ 20–29 *et seq*.

32b. See [1985] S.T.I. 298.

Section 142 does not apply to a variation or disclaimer made for any consideration in money or money's worth, other than consideration consisting of the making, in respect of another of the dispositions, of a variation or disclaimer to which the section applies.[33]

Section 142 treats the variation as having been made by the deceased for the purposes of inheritance tax *but not otherwise.* If, for example, A gives his property to B but B wishes the property to pass to C, and a section 142 variation is made accordingly, there is a settlement *by B* for income tax purposes and a voluntary disposition *by B* for stamp duty purposes.

> Thus if H makes a will giving his entire estate to his wife, W, and W renounces her entitlement to (say) £60,000 in favour of her infant son, S, this is a settlement by W to which section 437 of the Income and Corporation Taxes Act 1970 applies and the income derived from the £60,000 is treated as the income of W for income tax purposes: see § 10–35.
> cd so much of it as does not satisfy them are treated as separate dispo instrument will require adjudication under section 12 of the Stamp Act 1891: see §28–45 and §30–01.
> For the similar provision applying to capital gains tax, see § 16–20A.

-64[33a]   There are certain other similar exemptions:

(1) Where property is left on discretionary trusts and, within two years after the death, the trustees distribute it by exercising their discretion: section 144 prevents a further charge to tax arising on the distribution, *i.e.* in addition to the charge on death; and it treats the distribution as having been made by the deceased's will. This enables a testator to settle property on discretionary trusts, leaving it to his trustees to decide on the disposition of the property. Provided the trustees make the distribution within two years of the death and before any interest in possession subsists in the property, there will be no adverse tax consequences. If the trustees (having power to do so) appoint the property to the settlor's spouse, the exemption in § 19–05 will apply and any tax paid on the death will be repayable.

(2) Where assets are left to a legatee subject to a request (not legally binding) that the legatee should distribute them in accordance with the testator's wishes: section 143 prevents a tax charge arising if the legatee carries out the testator's request within two years after the death. The transfer by the legatee is not a transfer of value and the provisions relating to inheritance tax apply as if the property transferred had been bequeathed by the testator's will.

(3) Where a variation results in property being held in trust for a person for a period which ends not more than two years after the death: section 142(4) provides that the disposition at the end of the period is to be treated as taking effect from its beginning (but not so as to

---

33. *Quaere* whether s.142(1) is excluded if litigation is compromised on terms that the plaintiff will withdraw his claim on condition that a variation is accepted.
33a. The next paragraph is § 19–68.

affect the application of the Act to any distribution or application of property during the period).

(4) On an intestacy, the surviving spouse may, under section 47A of the Administration of Estates Act 1925, elect to redeem his or her life interest for a capital sum. Section 145 provides that such an election is not a transfer of value: the surviving spouse is treated as having at all times been entitled to the capital sum, rather than the life interest.

(5) Where a person becomes entitled to an interest in settled property but disclaims the interest, then, if the disclaimer is not made for a consideration in money or money's worth, the inheritance tax provisions apply as if he had not become entitled to the interest.[34]

(6) The Inheritance (Provision for Family and Dependants) Act 1975 empowers the court to make a provision for the family and dependants of a deceased person out of the "net" estate and, in effect, to rewrite the deceased's will by changing the destination of property. Section 146 ensures that when such an order is made there will be the same charges to and exemptions from inheritance tax as if the will had been made in the terms of the order.

12. Dispositions Allowable for Income Tax or Conferring Retirement Benefits

19–68 By section 12(1) a disposition made by a person is not a transfer of value if it is allowable in computing that person's profits or gains for the purposes of income tax or corporation tax or would be so allowable if those profits were sufficient and fell to be so computed. Thus gifts to employees or former employees or their dependants which are deductible as a trade expense (see §§ 2–51 *et seq.*) are not transfers of value. Section 12(1) does not apply to gifts which are *not* deductible as a trade expense.

19–69 By section 12(2), contributions to approved retirement benefits schemes for employees and dispositions to provide benefits on or after retirement for an employee not connected with the disponor or, after death, for the employee's widow or dependants are exempt, provided, in the latter cases, the benefits are no greater than could be provided under an approved scheme. For the purposes of the provision the right to occupy a dwelling rent-free or at a rent less than might be expected to be obtained in a transaction at arm's length between persons not connected with each other is treated as a pension of an amount equal to the difference between the rent paid and the rent that might be obtained. Where a disposition satisfies the conditions to a limited extent only, so much of it as satisfies them and so much of it as does not satisfy them are treated as separate dispositions.[35]

---

34. s.93.
35. s.12(5).

13. DISPOSITIONS ON TRUST FOR BENEFIT OF EMPLOYEES[36]

19–70 Dispositions of property which a close company makes to trustees to be held on employee trusts of the description specified in section 86(1) are not transfers of value, if strict conditions are satisfied.[37] There is no "entry charge": see § 22–04. The trusts must permit the property to be applied for all or most of the persons employed by, or holding office with, the company or any one or more of its subsidiaries.[38]

The exemption does not apply[39] if the trusts permit any of the property to be applied at any time for the benefit of:

(a) a person who is a participator in the company making the disposition; or

(b) any other person who is a participator in any close company that has made a disposition whereby property became comprised in the same settlement, being a disposition which but for section 13 would have been a transfer of value; or

(c) any other person who has been a participator in any such company as is mentioned in paragraph (a) or (b) at any time after, or during the 10 years before, the disposition made by that company; or

(d) any person who is connected with any person within paragraph (a), (b) or (c).

The participators referred to do not include any participator who is beneficially entitled to less than 5 per cent. of any class of share capital or to less than 5 per cent. of the company's assets on a winding up.

It is thought that the conditions of exemption are so strict as to make the exemption of limited use.

---

36. For a useful discussion on employee trusts see *Tolley's Tax Planning 1982/83*, pp. 180–187. The impact of inheritance tax on a transfer of value made by a close company is discussed at §§ 21–01 *et seq.*.

37. s.13. See also C.G.T.A. 1979, s.149: see *ante*, § 16–51A.

38. s.13(1).

39. s.13(2).

CHAPTER 20

THE COMPUTATION OF THE CHARGE

1. GENERAL

20–01 Inheritance tax is charged on the value transferred by a transfer of value, that is to say, on any disposition which lessens the value of the transferor's estate; and the amount by which it is less is the measure of the value transferred. A comparison has therefore to be made between the value of the transferor's estate immediately before and immediately after the disposition. The following factors enter into the computation:

(1) the amount or value of the property which forms the subject of the disposition;

(2) tax and any other costs or expenses incurred by the transferor as a consequence of the disposition. (If it costs the transferor £2,000 in tax and other expenses to transfer assets worth £30,000, the loss to the transferor's estate by reason of the disposition is £32,000. This is the amount on which inheritance tax is payable.)

Section 2 of this chapter gives the rates of inheritance tax and explains the cumulative basis on which it operates. Section 3 of this chapter explains how tax and other expenses of the transfer are dealt with. Section 4 summarises the rules of valuation. These are similar to the rules which apply for capital gains tax but there are special provisions (called "related property" rules) to prevent avoidance of inheritance tax by splitting up valuable assets into a number of less valuable parts as, for example, by splitting a controlling shareholding in a company into a number of minority holdings. Section 5 deals with the problems of valuation on death associated with lifetime transfers in relation to which the donor has reserved a benefit.

2. RATES OF TAX

The statutory table

20–02 Inheritance tax is charged[1] at a rate or rates which are set out in a Table in Schedule 1 to the Act. The Table which applies to any chargeable transfer made on or after March 18, 1986, is as follows:

---

1. s.7.

TABLE OF RATES OF TAX

Portion of value		Rate of tax
Lower limit £	*Upper limit* £	*Per cent*
0	71,000	Nil
71,000	95,000	30
95,000	129,000	35
129,000	164,000	40
164,000	206,000	45
206,000	257,000	50
257,000	317,000	55
317,000	—	60

20–03   The Table applies, in the form set out above, to the transfer of value which a person is deemed to have made immediately before his death (§§ 18–14 *et seq.*). Chargeable transfers made during a person's lifetime are, except as explained below, charged at one–half of the rate which is set out in the Table.[1a] Where, however, the transfer is made in the seven years prior to the transferor's death,[1b] the following rates apply:

(a) if the transfer is made within three years of death, the rates set out in the Table apply;

(b) where the transfer is made more than three but not more than four years before the death, tax is charged at 80 per cent. of the death rates;

(c) where the transfer is made more than four but less than five years before, tax is charged at 60 per cent. of the death rates;

(d) where the transfer is made more than five but not more than six years before the death, at 40 per cent. of the death rates; and

(e) where the transfer is made more than six years before death but not more than seven, tax is charged at 20 per cent. of the death rates.

The above rules are subject always to the proviso that the tax payable shall not be less than that which would have been payable had the transferor survived the transfer by seven years.[1c] Effectively, this means that where the transfer was not potentially exempt, only paragraphs (a) to (c) will apply—transfers made not less than five years before the transferor's death will be subject to tax at 50 per cent of the death rates. Potentially exempt transfers alone will, therefore, benefit from paragraphs (d) and (e).

Indexation of rate bands

20–03A   Section 8 provides for indexation of the rate bands in the above Table: that is, the figures in the first two columns will increase by the same percentage as the retail prices index increases. (This is the general index of

---

1a. s.7(2).

1b. This rule applies both to PETs proved chargeable and to transfers which are not potentially exempt. Prior to March 18, 1986, death could only affect the tax charged on transfers made in the previous three years.

1c. s.7(5).

retail prices for all items published by the Department of Employment).
Thus if the retail prices index for December 1986 is higher than it was for
December 1985 by x%, the rate bands will increase by x%, such increases
applying to chargeable transfers made on or after April 6, 1987—and so on
from year to year, unless Parliament otherwise determines. If the increase
does not produce a multiple of £1,000, it is rounded up to the nearest
amount which is a multiple of £1,000. The Treasury is required each year
before April 6 to make an order specifying the new bands: in practice,
these orders are made on budget day.

The cumulative nature of the tax: the seven-year period

20–04   Capital transfer tax, when originally introduced, applied on a cumulative
basis to all chargeable transfers made by the taxpayer from his cradle to his
grave. Section 43(1) of the Finance Act 1981, however, imposed a limited
10–year cumulation period—transfers made more than 10 years before a
chargeable transfer were ignored in calculating the rate of tax payable on
the later disposition. With the introduction of inheritance tax, this period
has been reduced still further to seven years.[1d] Accordingly, only chargeable transfers made by the transferor within the period of seven years ending with the date of a transfer are now to be taken into account in
determining the appropriate rate of tax applicable to that transfer. The
revised system took effect on March 18, 1986 and the following example
will illustrate how tax will now be charged. Since exempt transfers are not
chargeable transfers (see § 18–02) exemptions and reliefs will be ignored
for the purposes of the example. Let it be assumed that A creates three
settlements on April 1, 1982, April 1, 1983 and April 1, 1984, transferring
respectively £105,000, £40,000 and £50,000.

Date of Transfer of value	Amount transferred	Cumulative total	Rate Bands	%		Tax
1.4.82	105,000		55,000	nil	nil	
			20,000	15	3,000	
			25,000	17·5	4,375	
			5,000	20	1,000	
		105,000				8,375
1.4.83	40,000		5,000	17·5	875	
			30,000	20	6,000	
			5,000	22·5	1,125	
		145,000				8,000
1.4.84	50,000		3,000	20	600	
			37,000	22·5	8,375	
			10,000	25	2,500	
	195,000					11,425

1d. s.7(1).

A cumulative record of all chargeable transfers made by the transferor in the immediately preceding seven years is needed to determine the tax payable on any later transfer.

20–05 On the death of a taxpayer inheritance tax may become payable in respect of earlier transfers in two cases. First, tax may be payable on PETs made within the previous seven years which have proved to be chargeable; secondly, the tax on chargeable transfers made during that period will have to be recomputed, taking account of the rules in section 7 relating to gifts made within seven years of death. Where a reduction in the rate at which tax is charged intervenes between transfer and death, the tax (or additional tax) is determined as if the most recent Table had applied at the time of the transfer.[2]

Transitionally, it is provided[2a] that nothing in the amendments to the 1984 Act made by the Finance Act 1986, Schedule 19 is to affect the tax chargeable on a transfer, notwithstanding that a death or other event occurs after March 17, 1986. Thus, for example, chargeable transfers made before March 18, 1986 will not be subject to further tax unless the transferor dies within *three* years of the transfer.

Example
A makes a gift of £100,000 to B on January 1, 1986. B agrees to pay the CTT on the transfer. On April 1, 1986, A gives £40,000 to C. On December 1, 1986, he settles £50,000 on interest in possession trusts. On January 2, 1988, A dies, possessed of an estate of £250,000.
It will be assumed that the 1986 Table of rates is still current in 1988.

Computation 1: tax paid on original transfers

Date of Transfer	Amount transferred	Cumulative total	Rate Bands			Tax
value				%		
1.1.86	100,000		67,000	nil	nil	
			22,000	15	3,300	
			11,000	17·5	1,925	
					———	5,225
		100,000				
1.4.86	40,000	— being a PET, the transfer is not immediately chargeable.				
		100,000				
1.12.86	50,000		29,000	17·5	5,075	
			21,000	20	4,200	
	———	———			———	
	190,000	150,000				9,275

When A dies on January 2, 1988, section 7 requires that the tax payable on any chargeable transfer made in the previous seven years be recomputed. The transitional provisions will, though, apply to preclude the recalculation of any transfers made more than three years before A's death (since less than three

---

2. Sched. 2, paras. 1A and 2.
2a. F.A. 1986, Sched. 19, para. 40.

years elapses between the introduction of inheritance tax and the date of his death). In each case of recomputation, the Table used will be that current in 1988.

Computation 2—the recomputation on death

Date of Transfer	Amount of transferred value	Cumulative total	Rate Bands	%	Tax
1.1.86	100,000		71,000	nil	nil
			24,000	30[2b]	7,200
			5,000	35	1,750
					8,950
		100,000			
1.4.86	40,000		29,000	35[2c]	10,150
			11,000	40	4,400
					14,450
		140,000			
1.12.86	50,000		24,000	40[2c]	9,600
			26,000	45	11,700
					21,300
		190,000			
2.1.88	250,000		16,000	45	7,200
			51,000	50	25,500
			60,000	55	33,000
			123,000	60	73,800
					139,500

Thus additional tax of £3,725 will be paid in respect of the transfer on January 1, 1986; tax of £14,450 will be paid in respect of the transfer of April 1, 1986 which has proved chargeable; and additional tax of £12,075 in respect of the settlement of December 1, 1986.

20–05A Section 131 reduces the tax (or additional tax) payable on transfers made within seven years of death if the value of the asset transferred falls between the date of the gift and death. In such a case the tax (or additional tax) may be calculated as if the value transferred was reduced by that diminution in value.[2d] Where the asset is sold before the transferor's death, the reduction is determined by reference to the proceeds of sale.

Special provisions apply to wasting assets.[2e]

Transfers of more than one property

20–05B Section 265 provides that where the value transferred by a chargeable transfer is attributable to the values of more than one property (an obvious example being the transfer which is deemed to occur on death) the tax

---

2b. No reduced rates were available in respect of any transfers which were subject to recomputation for the purposes of CTT.

2c. The reduced rates under s.7(4) do not apply to transfers within three years of death.

2d. Thus no relief is given in respect of the original element of grossing up.

2e. s.132.

which is chargeable is to be attributed to the various assets in proportion to their respective values (subject to any provision reducing the amount of tax which is to be attributed to the value of any particular asset). This is of importance where there are assets passing to a number of donees each of whom is to bear the tax on the items which he receives.

Transfers on the same day

20–05C   Section 266 provides that where the value transferred by more than one lifetime chargeable transfer made by the same person on the same day depends on the order in which the transfers are made, they are to be treated as made in the order which results in the lowest value chargeable. The effect is to treat transfers which are to be grossed up as made before transfers where the transferee is to bear the tax. Subject to this, the rate at which tax is charged on the values transferred by two or more such transfers is the effective rate at which tax would have been charged if those transfers had been a single chargeable transfer of the same total value.[3] These provisions do not apply to transfers made on death.[4]

Transfers reported late[4a]

20–05D   There are special provisions which apply where, for example, a transfer of value is made in 1984 and the appropriate amount of tax is paid thereon and the Revenue subsequently discover that an undisclosed transfer was made in (say) 1976, so that the cumulative total of earlier transfers by reference to which tax was charged on the 1984 transfer was understated: see § 25–30A.

3. LIABILITIES

20–06   Inheritance tax is charged on the value transferred by a disposition which reduces the value of the transferor's estate. The value transferred is the amount by which the estate is less.

A. *Liabilities resulting from the chargeable transfer*

20–07   A chargeable transfer may give rise to inheritance tax, capital gains tax, or stamp duty; and other incidental expenses may be incurred, such as conveyancing costs. All of these, if paid by the transferor, will reduce the value of his estate and, but for some express provision to the contrary, would enter into the computation of the value transferred on which inheritance tax is leviable. Section 5(4) requires that in determining the value of the transferor's estate immediately after the transfer, his liability (and in one

---

3. s.266(2). The "effective rate" is the rate determined by expressing the total tax payable as a percentage of the aggregate chargeable transfer.
4. s.266(3).
4a. s.264.

case his spouse's liability) to inheritance tax on the value transferred shall be taken into account but *not* his liability (if any) for any other tax or duty resulting from the transfer (*e.g.* capital gains tax or stamp duty). Section 164(*a*) likewise requires that incidental expenses incurred by the transferor in making the transfer shall be left out of account. Where tax is taken into account no allowance is made for the fact that it is not due immediately.[5]

20–08   It should be appreciated that the effect of taking a liability into account *immediately after* the transfer is to *increase* the diminution in value of the transferor's estate and so *increase* the value transferred which is chargeable to inheritance tax. The effect of section 5(4) is to require *inheritance tax* paid or payable by the transferor to be included in reckoning the amount on which such tax is payable: "grossing up" is required: see § 20–11. Where the transferee agrees to pay (or pays) the inheritance tax, there is no grossing up: see § 20–15.

> *Example*
> A settles property. The assets transferred by themselves diminish the value of A's estate by £100,000. In consequence of the settlement A incurs the following liabilities:
>
>   (i) incidental expenses;
>   (ii) capital gains tax; and
>   (iii) inheritance tax.
>
> The diminution in the value of A's estate (on which inheritance tax is payable) is £100,000 plus the amount of (iii) (see § 20–11) but the liabilities in (i) and (ii) are ignored.

20–09   By way of exception, capital gains tax borne by B in respect of A's chargeable gains, because A has failed to pay the tax, is treated for the purposes of inheritance tax as *reducing* the value transferred[6]; so also are A's incidental expenses if borne by B.[7]

> Thus if the trustees pay (i) and (ii) in the above example, the diminution in the value of A's estate is £100,000 *less* (i) and (ii) *plus* (iii).

The reason for this is that A's estate is "enriched" to the extent that the trustees meet A's liabilities.

20–10   *Hold-over relief.* Section 79 of the Finance Act 1980 introduced a general hold-over relief for gifts. This relief, and the position regarding inheritance tax, is discussed in § 16–49A.

20–11   *Grossing up for inheritance tax.*[8] In the case of some lifetime transfers, the inheritance tax on the disposition of property is paid by the transferor and has therefore to be taken into account in computing the value transferred in accordance with the basic principle stated in § 18–03. If A wishes

---

5. s.162(3)(*a*).
6. s.165. See also C.G.T.A. 1979, s.59: see § 16–18.
7. s.164(*b*).
8. Inheritance tax tables, including grossing up tables, are available from law bookshops.

to transfer a house into settlement and pays the tax the value transferred (on which tax is levied) is the value of the house plus the amount of the tax.

> Thus if A makes a lifetime transfer into settement of an asset worth £x, this is treated as a transfer of value of such an amount as, after deduction of inheritance tax calculated on that amount, leaves £x.

There is no grossing up in the case of a lifetime transfer if the transferee pays, or agrees to pay, the tax: see § 20–15. There are many advantages where the transferee pays the tax: there is no grossing up, so less tax is payable, and there are many cases in which the tax can be paid by instalments and (within limits) free of interest: see §§ 25–26 *et seq*.

20–12   The provisions discussed in § 20–07 relate to the taking into account of liabilities existing immediately after the transfer. Subject to those provisions and to the qualifications that follow, the general rule is that in determining the value of the transferor's estate at *any* time, his liabilities at that time shall be taken into account.[9] Thus in the case of a person's death, inheritance tax is payable on the value of the assets *less* liabilities.

B. *Other liabilities*

20–13   Except in the case of a liability imposed by law, only liabilities incurred by the transferor for a consideration in money or money's worth are taken into account.[10] Thus if A voluntarily charges his estate with the payment of £3,000 per annum to B for seven years, this liability is ignored in applying the inheritance tax rules to each payment which is made to B and in valuing A's estate on A's death.

20–14   A liability which falls to be discharged after the time at which it is to be taken into account is to be valued as at the time when it is to be taken into account.[11] Thus if, at the time of A's death, A owes £x to B, payable five years hence, the amount of £x has to be discounted to allow for the time before payment is due (unless the debt is for inheritance tax).

20–15   A liability in respect of which there is a right to reimbursement may be taken into account only to the extent (if any) that reimbursement cannot reasonably be expected to be obtained.[12] Thus if A owes B £x but A has the right to recover this amount from C, A's debt is left out of account if A can reasonably be expected to recover the debt from C. If A makes a transfer of value to trustees, A is primarily liable to pay the inheritance tax: see § 24–14; but if the trustees agree to bear the inheritance tax attributable thereto, A's right to reimbursement equals his liability to the Revenue for tax and so no grossing up is required.

---

9. s.5(3).
10. s.5(5).
11. s.162(2).
12. s.162(1).

20–16   Where a liability, such as a mortgage, is an incumbrance on any property, it must so far as possible be taken to reduce the value of *that* property.[12a] Where a liability is not an incumbrance on property in the United Kingdom and is a liability owed to a person resident outside and falling to be discharged outside the United Kingdom, it must so far as possible be taken to reduce the value of property outside the United Kingdom although not an incumbrance on such property.[13] These rules may be important as affecting the incidence of liability as between different transferees.

20–16A   Special rules limit the deduction of certain debts and incumbrances in the computation of the value of a person's estate at death: see §§ 20–28 *et seq.*

4. VALUATION

Open market value

20–17   Section 160 states that, except as otherwise provided, the value at any time of any property shall for the purposes of inheritance tax be the price which the property might reasonably be expected to fetch if sold in the open market at that time. No reduction is to be allowed on the ground that the whole property is hypothetically to be placed on the market at one and the same time.

Where there is no open market for the property, the existence of such a market must be assumed. Shares in private companies, for example, are necessarily subject to restrictions affecting their transfer; and often in family companies these restrictions include rights of pre-emption which make a minority holding virtually unmarketable. Nevertheless, for the purpose of valuation of such shares, it must be assumed that a free market exists but that the hypothetical purchaser, when registered, will hold the shares subject to the same restrictions on transfer as those which affected the hypothetical vendor.[14] The question in such cases is: how much would a hypothetical purchaser pay to stand in the vendor's shoes? The same principle applies when property is non-assignable.[15] The above principle of valuation applies, for example, to tenanted agricultural land which is subject to restriction on transfer or on parting with possession.

This is the rule as to valuation which applies for capital gains tax purposes and which applied for estate duty purposes. Market value as ascertained for the purposes of inheritance tax is to be taken to be the market value for the purposes of capital gains tax.[16] There is, however, a number of special provisions which apply for inheritance tax and which are considered in the following paragraphs.

Where the provisions relating to inheritance tax have to be applied on

---

12a. s.162(4).
13. s.162(5).
14. *I.R.C.* v. *Crossman* [1937] A.C. 26.
15. *Re Cassel* [1927] 2 Ch. 275.
16. C.G.T.A. 1979, s.153.

the *death* of an individual, the property to be valued is the whole of the property comprised in the deceased's estate: see § 18–14. Where the provisions have to be applied to a *lifetime transfer* by an individual, the inquiry is directed to finding the diminution in the value of the transferor's "estate" in consequence of that transfer, so the property to be valued is the actual property transferred or, if the transfer of property diminishes the value of other property of which it previously formed part, that other property. Thus in the example in § 18–03, the assets in the examples have to be valued before and after the transfers.

Restriction on freedom to dispose

20–18 Section 163 deals with the case where a contract, such as the grant of an option, excludes or restricts the right to dispose of property (thereby diminishing its value) and the property is later disposed of. The exclusion or restriction is taken into account on the later disposal only to the extent (if any) that consideration in money or money's worth was given for it; but if the contract itself was a chargeable transfer on which tax was charged (or was part of a series of associated operations which together were a chargeable transfer), a deduction is allowed for the value transferred thereby (calculated as if no tax had been chargeable on it) or by so much of it as was attributable to the exclusion or restriction.

Examples

(i) A grants B an option to purchase property at any time within three years for £20,000, its market value at the time of the grant. B exercises the option when the property is worth £39,000. No consideration was paid by B on the grant of the option. The option is ignored when it is exercised, so A makes a transfer of value of £19,000.

(ii) A grants B an option to purchase property at any time within three years for £20,000. The property is then worth £35,000. (This is a chargeable transfer by A and tax may be payable on the value transferred thereby of say, £15,000.) After two years B exercises the option, paying £20,000 when the property is worth £39,000. This is a further chargeable transfer by A. The value transferred by the contract (£15,000) is deductible from the value of the property. Thus the value transferred on the exercise of the option (assuming B pays the tax) is (£39,000—£15,000) less £20,000 = £4,000.

Where the contract was made before March 27, 1974, these provisions apply only if the first chargeable transfer is on death.[16a] Thus if after March 26, 1974, an option is exercised which was granted before that date, any diminution in the value of the grantor's estate resulting from the grant of the option is taken into account and the value transferred reckoned accordingly.

Section 163 will apply where a partnership agreement provides that, on the retirement or death of a partner, his share shall accrue to the continuing partners either without payment or for a sum less than the market value of his share; or where the continuing partners exercise an option conferred by the partnership agreement to acquire the share on such terms. The "restriction" imposed by the rights of the continuing partners must be

---

16a. s.163(2).

ignored in valuing the share transferred, save to the extent that full consideration in money or money's worth was given for it.

> In *Attorney General* v. *Boden*[17] (an estate duty case) a father and his two sons entered into a partnership agreement under which, on the father's death, his share of the goodwill was to accrue to the sons without payment. The sons were required to devote their time to the business and to be concerned in no other business. The father was obliged only to devote as much time as he thought fit. It was held that the sons had purchased for full consideration in the form of services the share of goodwill which accrued to them.

Valuation of related property

20–19   By section 161(2), property is related to the property comprised in a person's estate if either (a) it is comprised in the estate of his spouse[18]; or (b) it is or has within the preceding five years been the property of a charity, or held on trust for charitable purposes only (or has been the property of some other privileged body specified in sections 24, 25 or 26 (see §§ 19–20 to 19–22) and so became on an exempt transfer of value made by him or his spouse after April 15, 1976.

Section 161 prevents the owner of an asset avoiding inheritance tax by dividing up the asset into a number of less valuable parts by a transfer of part to the owner's spouse and/or to trustees of a discretionary or charitable settlement made by him or his spouse. But for the section an owner of (say) 90 per cent. of the shares in XYZ Limited could make an exempt transfer of half of his holding to his wife, with the consequence that each would have a 45 per cent. holding with an aggregate value less than the value of the owner's original 90 per cent. shareholding. Other property which may be reduced in value in this way includes, for example, an area of land which becomes less valuable when divided into a number of smaller units.

The Act provides that where the value of any property comprised in a person's estate would be less than the appropriate proportion of the value of the aggregate of that and any related property, the value shall be the appropriate proportion of the value of that aggregate. Thus in the example mentioned above the owner's 45 per cent. holding (if transferred) would be treated as having a value equal to one-half of the value of a 90 per cent. holding.

Section 176 provides a form of relief where property valued on death on a related property basis is sold within three years of the death at less than the value at the time of death.[18a]

Value of lessor's interest

20–20   A lease of property not granted for full consideration in money or money's worth is treated as a settlement in certain circumstances (for example a lease for life): see § 22–09. Where this applies, section 170 pro-

---

17. [1912] 1 K.B. 539.
18. See § 18–08. s.161 applies whenever and however the property came to be comprised in the spouse's estate.
18a. But see § 19–39D on the effect of s.176 on a claim for business property relief.

vides that the value of the lessor's interest in the property shall be taken to be a proportion of the value of the property, the proportion being that which the value of the consideration at the time the lease was granted bore to what would then have been the value of full consideration in money or money's worth.

Thus if L grants a lease for life to T for no consideration, the value of L's interest is taken to be nil if L subsequently transfers that interest. If L grants a lease to B at what was then 80 per cent. of full consideration. L's interest is treated as worth 80 per cent. of the value of the property. The balance represents the value of T's interest: see § 22–21. L's interest in the case of a lease which is treated as a settlement is not excluded property (see § 23–03) so a charge to inheritance tax may arise on any transfer of value by L.

Value of amounts due

20–21   In determining the value of a right to receive a sum due under any obligation, section 166 requires it to be assumed that the obligation will be duly discharged, except if or to the extent that recovery of the sum is impossible or not reasonably practicable and has not become so by any act or omission of the person to whom the sum is due. If, for example, X is entitled to a sum of money which a foreign exchange control authority will not allow to be remitted to the United Kingdom for five years, due account of this has to be taken in valuing the right.

Value of life policies, etc.

20–22   Section 167 provides for the valuation of certain life assurance policies and deferred annuities which are transferred otherwise than on the death of the life assured. Briefly, their value is not to be less than their total cost allowing for adjustment where there has been, *e.g.* a partial surrender. There are exceptions which apply to term policies and unit linked policies.

Farm cottages

20–23   Where agricultural property is valued and the property includes cottages occupied by persons employed solely for agricultural purposes in connection with the property (*i.e.* tied cottages), section 169 requires that no account be taken of the fact that the cottages are suitable for residential occupation by persons other than agricultural workers.

Open market price of unquoted shares and securities

20–24   In determining the price which unquoted shares or securities (*i.e.* those not quoted on a recognised stock exchange) might reasonably be expected to fetch if sold in the open market, section 168 requires it to be assumed that in that market there is available to any prospective purchaser all the information which a prudent prospective purchaser might reasonably require if he were proposing to purchase them from a willing vendor by private treaty and at arm's length.

Open market price of quoted shares and securities

20–24A   The market price of quoted shares and securities is found by applying the "quarter-up" rule, *i.e.* if the quotation is 104–106, the market price is found by adding to 104 one-quarter of the difference between 104 and 106 *i.e.* $104\frac{1}{2}$.

A special relief is available if shares or securities are sold within 12 months of a death for less than the market price at the time of death: see § 20–28.

In November 1980 the Stock Exchange introduced the Unlisted Securities Market. Securities dealt in on this market are not regarded by the Inland Revenue as "listed" or "quoted" for the purposes of the Taxes Acts; but they satisfy the tests of being "authorised to be dealt in" and "dealt in (regularly or from time to time)" on a recognised stock exchange. Where it is necessary for tax purposes to agree the open market value of such securities on a given date, initial evidence of their value will be suggested by the details of the bargains done at or near the relevant date. However other factors may also be relevant and the Shares Valuation Division of the Capital Taxes Office will consider whether a value offered on the basis of those bargains can be accepted as an adequate reflection of the open market value.[18b]

Value transferred on death

20–25   Inheritance tax is charged on the death of a person as if, immediately before his death, he had made a transfer of value equal to the value of his estate at that time. A valuation "immediately before" the death will take no account of changes in value which occur, or liabilities which arise, because of the death. It will take no account, for example, of any annuity purchased by the deceased which ceases on his death or the proceeds of an insurance policy taken out by a third person and which is payable on the deceased's death even though the former should be excluded and the latter included in computing liability to inheritance tax.

Section 171 meets this situation by providing that where, *by reason* of a person's death, the property comprised in his estate is added to or there is an increase or decrease in its value, any change having this effect is treated as having occurred *before* the death. The termination on death of any interest or the passing of any interest by survivorship does not fall within this rule: hence a terminated interest, such as a life interest or an interest passing by survivorship, is kept in charge to inheritance tax. It follows that an annuity ceasing on death which is payable out of settled property will give rise to tax because the deceased had an *interest* in that property; whereas an annuity ceasing on death which exists only in contract will give rise to no liability. Decreases in the value of unquoted shares by alterations in rights to take effect on the deceased's death also fall outside the rule so the full value of the shares (ignoring the alterations) is kept in charge to tax.[18c]

18b. SP 18/80 in [1980] S.T.I. 894.
18c. See s.171(2) and s.98(1).

Where on the death there is an undischarged liability to inheritance tax, it is deductible from the value of the estate only if the tax is actually paid out of the estate, and not by another liable person (such as the donee in the case of a lifetime transfer.)[19]

20–26　An allowance is made for reasonable funeral expenses including (by concession) a reasonable amount for mourning.[20]

20–27　Where, on a person's death, he was under a liability to make payments or transfer assets under a delayed transaction in respect of which section 262 (see § 21–07) has been applicable, that liability is taken into account in determining the size of the deemed transfer of value immediately before death *only after* the amount or value of the payments or assets have been reduced by the "chargeable portion" thereof (*i.e.* the amount determined under s.262(2)).[21]

20–27A　Where property is situated outside the United Kingdom, extra expense may be incurred in administering or realising the property and, where the expense is shown to be attributable to the situation of the property, an allowance is made against the value of the property of up to 5 per cent. of its value.[21a]

20–27B　There are special provisions which apply with respect to the valuation of qualifying investments which are sold at a loss within 12 months immediately following the date of the death.[21b] The provisions, which are of considerable complexity, are to be found in sections 178 to 189. Sections 190 to 198 contain relieving provisions where land is sold within three years of the death for less than its market value at the time of death. In both cases, a claim for reduction in the value of the deceased's estate as at the date of his death may be made.

Debts and incumbrances at death

20–28　It is the policy of inheritance tax to exempt from charge outright gifts made without reservation of benefit sufficiently far in advance of the transferor's death. It would, therefore, be possible to reduce the value of one's estate at death without suffering any lifetime detriment by the creation of "artificial debts."

> For example, suppose A gave property to B. Some time later, A repurchases the property for full consideration of (say) £100,000, giving B an IOU for the amount (which is left outstanding). Without provisions to the contrary, A would have reduced the value of his estate at death by £100,000—and, thus,

---

19. s.174(2).
20. s.172 and concession F1.
21. s.175.
21a. s.173.
21b. And see s.178(2) which applies when a quotation is temporarily suspended.

the inheritance tax payable by his personal representatives—at no lifetime detriment to himself, by the creation of a liability for, apparently, full consideration.

It is provided, therefore,[21c] that if in determining the value of a person's estate immediately before his death account has to be taken of any liability (whether in the form of a debt or an incumbrance on property of the deceased) that liability is to be abated to the extent that the consideration for the liability consisted of either:

(a) property derived from the deceased; or
(b) consideration from a third party who himself had at some time enjoyed the benefit of property derived from the deceased.

In the example given above, the liability would be fully abated since the whole of the consideration consisted of property derived from the deceased. If, on the other hand, B had at the same time lent A £50,000 at interest, so that at death A owed him (say) £240,000, that liability would be abated in proportion to the value of the original consideration which derived from A—*i.e.* 100 : 50, so that the deductible debt would be £80,000.

Further provision is made for the case where the deceased discharges an artificial debt before his death. Such a discharge is deemed to be a PET of an amount equal to the money or money's worth paid to effect it,[21d] and will be subject to inheritance tax in the usual way if the transferor does not survive the discharge by seven years.

5. Gifts with Reservation of Benefit

20–29 Section 102 of the Finance Act 1986 increases the size of a person's estate immediately before his death—and, thus, the inheritance tax payable under section 4 (see § 18–14) on the deemed transfer of value made at that time—by treating the deceased as beneficially entitled to any property which he has disposed of during his lifetime by way of a gift "subject to a reservation." The provision is modelled closely (but not precisely) on a corresponding rule of estate duty,[22] and the authorities relating to that rule will have considerable weight in the proper interpretation of its successor. A note of caution should be added, though: first, the manner in which courts interpret tax avoidance schemes has changed dramatically since the Finance Act 1894 was last in force and decisions based on the old approach must be reconsidered in the light of the decision of the House of Lords in *Furniss* v. *Dawson*[23] and similar such cases. Secondly, it remains to be seen whether the Capital Taxes Office will reintroduce its practices for estate duty—for example, in relation to joint tenancies.[24]

21c. F.A. 1986, s.103(1).
21d. *Ibid.*, s.103(5).
22. F.A. 1894, s.2(1)(c), applying s.38 of the Customs and Inland Revenue Act 1881.
23. [1984] S.T.C. 474. See Chap. 36.
24. See *Dymond's Death Duties* (15 ed.), Chap. XI.

20–30   In order for section 102 to apply, the original disposition must have been by way of *gift* and one of two alternative conditions must also be satisfied:

> (a) possession and enjoyment of the property was not bona fide assumed by the donee at, or before, the beginning of the "relevant period";
>
> (b) *at any time* in the "relevant period" the property was not enjoyed both to the entire exclusion of the donor (or virtually[25] to his entire exclusion) and of any benefit to him by contract or otherwise.[26]

20–31   "Gift" is not defined by the statute. In common parlance the word imports some element of bounty,[27] so that a fully commercial transaction involving a sale and leaseback by a taxpayer and an unconnected third party would not cause the application of section 102 in relation to the propery sold. There is, though, a fine line between a disposition which constitutes a gift with reservation of benefit and a sale of property, for example, in return for an annuity.[28]

20–32   The "relevant period" for the purposes of section 102 means the period of seven years before the donor's death (unless the gift is made later, when only the period between gift and death is "relevant"). This enables a donor to escape section 102 if he releases or surrenders all entitlement or enjoyment he might have over gifted property, provided that he does so more than seven years before his death. If property ceases to be subject to a reservation (for whatever reason), the donor is treated as having made a PET[29]: a surrender of a right of enjoyment of whatever nature will not, therefore, immediately be chargeable with inheritance tax, even though it has the effect of reducing the value of the estate of the donor. If the donor dies within seven years of the surrender, the double charge to tax will be avoided by regulations to be made under section 104 (see § 20–57).[30]

20–33   If, therefore, a donor is to avoid tax being charged on death by reference to property given away during his lifetime, the following conditions must be satisfied:

(1) *The donee must have assumed bona fide possession and enjoyment of the gifted property immediately upon the gift*

20–34   This requirement is satisfied if the donor transfers property to trustees for the donee, and also where the donor declares himself the sole trustee.[31] It is not satisfied if, for example, the donor of shares requires the donee to

---

25. This is new and may be taken to correspond to the previous practice that, for example, staying (at least temporarily) as a guest in a house given to another does not amount to joint enjoyment of the property.
26. s.97(1)(*a*), (*b*).
27. See *Re Earl Fitzwilliam's Agreement* [1950] Ch. 448.
28. *Att.-Gen.* v. *Johnson* [1903] 1 K.B. 617.
29. F.A. 1986, s.102(4).
30. This is also true where the original gift made subject to the reservation is within seven years of the donor's death: s.104(1)(*b*).
31. *Oakes* v. *Commr. of Stamp Duties* [1954] A.C. 57 at p. 72: see § 20–38.

sign a blank transfer which the donor retains; nor is it satisfied in the kind of transaction where the gift is in the terms: you (the donee) can have this but I (the donor) will keep it for the time being. This condition and the next condition (2) overlap and many of the decided cases draw no very clear distinction between them.

(2) *The donor must, from the date of the gift, be entirely excluded (a) from the gifted property, and (b) from any benefit by contract or otherwise: he must not resume enjoyment of the gifted property*

20-35   In order to determine whether or not the donor was excluded from, or had retained a benefit in, the *gifted property,* it is first necessary to ascertain the subject-matter of the gift. If, for example, A gives all his farms in Warwickshire except Ambridge Farm, there is no retention of any benefit by A. "What the donor keeps back is no gift."[32]

Similarly, if A reserves to himself a beneficial interest in property and gives the donee only such beneficial interest as remains after his own reserved interest has been satisfied, such reservation does not involve any benefit to the donor.[33]

> Thus, in *Munro* v. *Commissioner of Stamp Duties,*[34] the owner of a large area of land in New South Wales, on which he carried on the business of a grazier, agreed with his six children in 1909 that thereafter the business should be carried on by him and them as partners at will, the business to be managed by him, and each partner to get a share of the profits. In 1913 he transferred by way of gift to his children or to trustees for them all his rights, title and interest in the land. He remained a partner in the business until his death in 1929 and duty was then claimed in respect of the land, on the ground that it had not been retained by the donees to the entire exclusion of the donor or of any benefit to him. *Held,* that duty was not payable.

Lord Tomlin, delivering the judgment of the Privy Council, said (at p. 67):

> "What was comprised in the gift was, in the case of each of the gifts to the children and the trustees, the property shorn of the right which belonged to the partnership, and upon this footing it is in their lordships' opinion plain that the donee in each case assumed bona fide possession and enjoyment of the gift immediately upon the gift and thenceforward retained it to the exclusion of the donor. Further, the benefit which the donor had as a member of the partnership in the right to which the gift was subject was not in their lordships' opinion a benefit referable in any way to the gift. It was referable to the agreement of 1909 and nothing else . . . "

Munro's case was a gift of land subject to the rights of the donor under a pre-existing partnership agreement. If the donor had made an outright gift of the land and *subsequently* entered into a partnership agreement under which he assumed possession and enjoyment of the land, tax would clearly

---

32. *Wheeler* v. *Humphries* [1898] A.C. 506, *per* Lord MacNaghten at p. 509; *St. Aubyn* v. *Att.-Gen.* [1952] A.C. 15 *per* Lord Simonds at p. 29. See also *Potter* v. *I.R.C.* (1958) 37 A.T.C. 58, § 20–53, *post.*
33. *Oakes* v. *Commr. of Stamp Duties supra,* at p. 76.
34. [1934] A.C. 61 (P.C.).

have been payable. In this respect, *Munro's* case is distinguishable from the case of *Chick* v. *Commissioner of Stamp Duties.*[35]

20–36   Where the subject-matter of the gift is a limited interest in property, carved out of a larger interest owned by the donor, the interest which is retained is not a benefit reserved out of the gifted property.

> In *Commissioner of Stamp Duties* v. *Perpetual Trustee Co. Ltd.,*[36] shares were settled in 1917 upon trust during the minority of the settlor's son to apply income or capital for the maintenance, advancement or benefit of the son, as the trustees should think fit. On the son attaining the age of 21, the capital and any accumulations of income were to be transferred to the son absolutely. The settlor died in 1921 and his son attained 21 in 1931. *Held,* that the gifted property comprised the equitable interest in the shares. The resulting trust to the settlor in the event of his son failing to attain 21 was not, therefore, a benefit reserved.

20–37   If an individual landowner procures the grant of a lease to himself and thereafter makes a gift of or settles his interest in the land subject to that lease, the mere existence of the lease will not justify a claim for inheritance tax on the gifted reversionary interest. The subject-matter of the gift (applying the principles stated above) is the reversionary interest. But if the individual makes a gift of or settles his freehold interest in the land and *subsequently* takes a lease back, he thereby resumes enjoyment of the gifted property[37] and tax will be payable, subject to a statutory exception to this rule which applies where the lease is for full consideration.[38]

> In *Re Harmsworth, decd.*[39] A bequeathed an annuity to B on condition that B would, within a stated period after A's death, settle her own (B's) property on trust for B for life with remainder to C absolutely. B accepted the condition and settled the property. There was thus a gift of property from B to C. Harman L.J. said it was difficult to see how possession and enjoyment of an interest in remainder could be taken immediately on the gift but thought it was so taken because C became absolute owner of the remainder from the day the gift was made and could dispose of it or charge it and B had no further interest. Lord Denning M.R. differed on this point, holding that C would not secure possession and enjoyment until B's death when the interest would vest in possession. But on either view, B was not entirely excluded from the gifted property because she had the benefit of the annuity; and it has long been settled that the benefit need not be reserved out of the gifted property: *Att.-Gen.* v. *Worrall.*[40] The view expressed by Harman L.J. would seem to be more consistent with the authorities than the view of Lord Denning M.R.

Benefits reserved. Once the property which formed the subject-matter of the gift has been defined in accordance with the principles just stated, it is then necessary to inquire if the conditions of exclusion of the settlor have been satisfied. "Benefits reserved" may be grouped into three classes:

---

35. [1958] A.C. 435 (P.C.). See § 20–45.
36. [1943] A.C. 425 (P.C): *Cf. Oakes* v. *Commr. of Stamp Duties* [1954] A.C. 57: point (1) in § 20–38.
37. See *Chick* v. *Commr. of Stamp Duties* [1958] A.C. 435 (P.C.), § 20–45; and *Nichols* v. *I.R.C.* [1975] S.T.C. 278.
38. F.A. 1986, Sched. 20, para. 6. See § 20–45.
39. [1967] Ch. 826 (C.A.).
40. [1895] 1 Q.B. 99 (C.A.); see § 20–40.

20–38   (1) BENEFITS WHICH IMPAIR OR ENTRENCH UPON THE ENJOYMENT OF THE GIFTED PROPERTY. Two cases, both decisions of the Privy Council, illustrate benefits of this nature.

> In *Oakes* v. *Commissioner of Stamp Duties*[41] O, in 1924, settled a grazing property (which he owned) upon trust for himself and his four children as tenants in common in equal shares. The settlement deed gave O wide powers of management, including the right to reimbursement for expenses incurred as manager and the right to remuneration for all work done by him in managing the trust property. The balance of the profits was divided into five equal shares, one share to O and one share to each child. Children's shares were used for their maintenance and education during their minorities. This arrangement continued until O died in 1947. During the trust period O resided on the property with his family. The question arose whether, on O's death, the whole property passed or merely O's one-fifth share. *Held,* (i) that the right reserved by O to remuneration was a benefit within the section and that the whole property passed on his death; the right to remuneration was not a beneficial interest which was kept back on the execution of the settlement, for any remuneration had to come out of the trust property and therefore diminished the amount available for division among the tenants in common; (ii) that the advantage enjoyed by O in having the children's income available for their maintenance and education was not a benefit within the section; (iii) that it is not sufficient, to bring the case within the section, to take the situation as a whole and find that the settlor has continued to enjoy substantial advantages related to the settled property: it is necessary to consider the nature and source of each such advantage.

20–39   *Oakes'* case shows that the right to remuneration, albeit reasonable remuneration for services rendered, is a benefit to the person entitled to be remunerated. For this reason, it is sensible to include in deeds of settlement a clause expressly excepting the settlor from any right to be remunerated for services performed as trustee or otherwise.

> In *Commissioner of Stamp Duties* v. *Permanent Trustee Company,*[42] property was in 1924 settled on trust to apply such part of the trust income as the trustee should see fit for the maintenance, education and general support of the settlor's daughter until she should attain the age of 30 or marry, and on her attaining that age, to pay to her absolutely the balance of the trust fund, including accumulations of income. In 1938 the daughter married. Shortly afterwards, on her father's instructions, a new bank account was opened in the daughter's name and the bank was authorised by the daughter to allow her father to operate on the account in the fullest possible manner. In 1939 the trustees were instructed to pay all trust income into that account, and thereafter the settlor withdrew moneys from the account for his own purposes, such withdrawals being treated as interest-free loans made by the daughter. *Held,* that the daughter had not retained bona fide possession and enjoyment of the trust property to the entire exclusion of her father.

"The design and the result of the arrangement," said Viscount Simonds (at p. 525), "were that the daughter's possession and enjoyment were reduced and impaired precisely by the measure of the settlor's use and enjoyment of her income." It will be observed that the donor in this case resumed

---

41. [1954] A.C. 57 (P.C.).
42. [1956] A.C. 512 (P.C.).

enjoyment of the gifted property some fourteen years after the date of the gift, thereby bringing the whole of that property back into charge.

20–40 (2) COLLATERAL BENEFITS. The condition of exclusion of the donor is not necessarily satisfied merely because the donor no longer has any interest in the gifted property.

> In *Att.-Gen.* v. *Worrall*,[43] a father made a present to his son of about £24,000, secured on mortgage, and the son purchased the equity of redemption for a small sum. In return for his father's gift, the son covenanted to pay his father an annuity of £735 per annum during his life. In effect the son was returning to the father the income of the gifted property during the remainder of the father's life. It was held that the son had not obtained the enjoyment of the gifted property free from a benefit to the father.

20–41 It must not be supposed, however, that any and every benefit to the donor which is associated with a gift of property brings the case within the charge to inheritance tax.

> In *Att.-Gen.* v. *Seccombe*,[44] the owner of a farm gave it to his nephew who lived with him and who managed the farm. The donor continued for the remainder of his life to reside in the farmhouse and was maintained by his nephew. There was, however, no agreement or arrangement to this effect. *Held,* that the donee had assumed possession and enjoyment to the entire exclusion of the donor and of any benefit to him by contract or otherwise.

One explanation of this case is that the words "or otherwise" in the section must be construed *ejusdem generis* with the word "contract," and that the mere understanding which the parties had in *Seccombe's* case was not such a benefit. The decision has been criticised on the ground that the judge did not sufficiently recognise that the Act requires that the deceased should be excluded both from the gifted property and from any benefit, and that the words "by contract or otherwise" refer to the benefit and not to the property; even so, a line must be drawn somewhere.

20–42 There must, however, be considerable doubt whether *Seccombe* is still good law. The new legislation includes the words "virtually to the entire exclusion of the donor." Whilst it is thus clear that incidental enjoyment by the donor will not suffice to bring section 102 into operation, the phrase also suggests that anything in excess of "virtual exclusion" would be within the ambit of the section.

20–43 Moreover, specific provision is made for removing occupation of the donor from the application of section 102 in certain cases where, by old age or infirmity, the donor is no longer able to maintain himself.[45] If a number of stringent conditions are satisfied, the occupation will be ignored. The paragraph would, though, be of limited application if *Seccombe* were intended still to apply. The conditions are:

43. [1895] 1 Q.B. 99 (C.A.).
44. [1911] 2 K.B. 688.
45. F.A. 1986, Sched. 20, para. 6(1)(*b*).

(i) that the occupation results from a change in the circumstances of the donor which was unforseen by the donor at the time of the gift and which was not brought about by the donor in order to obtain relief under the paragraph.

The latter part of the condition would appear to apply only in cases where subsequent to the gift of the dwelling-house, an elderly donor decides to give away the rest of his estate to his children, intending to rely on filial affection for his provision therafter, with the intention that relief should be obtained in relation to his occupation of the dwelling-house under paragraph 6(1)(*b*).

(ii) that the change of circumstances occurs at a time when the donor is no longer able to maintain himself (through old age, infirmity or otherwise).

Thus, the change of circumstances does not have to be the onset of old age, etc.: indeed, especially in the case of old age, it is difficult to see how such a change could be said to be "unforseen." It would apply, though, for example, where the donor gave away his dwelling house in reliance on an offer of sheltered housing which subsequently fell through or proved unsatisfactory.

(iii) that the occupation represents reasonable provision by the donee for the care and maintenance of the donor; and

(iv) the donee is a relative of the donor or his spouse.

Generally, one would have expected the rule to be that the donor, in such circumstances as these, should be a relative of the donee or his spouse.

20–44   (3) BENEFITS BY ASSOCIATED OPERATIONS. Paragraph 6(1)(*c*) of Schedule 20 to the Finance Act 1986 provides that, in the case of a gift, a benefit which the donor obtains by virtue of any "associated operations"[46] of which the gift is one shall be treated as a benefit to the donor by contract or otherwise (and, thus, as falling within section 102). Most benefits which donors retain or secure directly or indirectly in connection with their gifts will fall within paragraph 6(1)(*c*), including, on a strict construction, benefits which are legally unenforceable. In estate duty, the practice of the Revenue was not to interpret the forerunner of the present provision in this way.[47] It would be most unwise to assume, though, that this practice will be resurrected.

Benefits obtained for full consideration

20–45   If the donor, having made an outright gift of property, subsequently resumes possession or enjoyment thereof, the property will continue to form part of the donor's estate at death however long after the gift the resumption of possession or enjoyment occurs. This is because the con-

---

46. As defined by s.268: see §§18–05 *et seq.*
47. See *Dymond's Death Duties* (15th ed.), p. 355.

dition requiring that the donor should be excluded from the gifted property will not have been satisfied.

> Thus in *Chick* v. *Commissioner of Stamp Duties*,[48] a father made an outright gift of property to one of his sons in 1934. Seventeen months later, the father, the donee son and another son entered into partnership as graziers on terms (*inter alia*) that the partnership business should be conducted on properties which included the gifted property. This arrangement continued until the father died in 1952. *Held,* that the donor had not been excluded from the gifted property which therefore passed on the donor's death. It was immaterial that the donor gave (if he did give) full consideration for his right as a member of the partnership to possession and enjoyment of the gifted property.

In consequence of the decision in *Chick* provision was made by statute (now F.A. 1986, Sched. 20, para. 6(1)(*a*)) that:

> "in the case of property which is an interest in land or a chattel, retention or assumption by the donor of actual occupation of the land or actual enjoyment of an incorporeal right over the land, or actual possession of the chattel shall be disregarded if it is for full consideration in money or money's worth."

Three points should be noted in connection with this provision. First, it applies only to gifts of interests in land or chattels. Secondly, the subsection applies only where the donor retains or assumes *actual* occupation of the land, or *actual* enjoyment of an incorporeal right (*e.g.* fishing rights) or *actual* possession of chattels. Constructive occupation or enjoyment will not suffice. Thirdly, the subsection gives no relief for partial consideration. In practice, it may be expected that the conditions of the subsection will be treated as satisfied if the consideration is full consideration at the time of retention or assumption of occupation, enjoyment or possession, even if it is not full consideration at some later time prior to the death.[49]

Specific exceptions to section 102

20–45A If or to the extent that the gift subject to the reservation of benefit is exempt under one of the following headings, it will also be excluded from the application of section 102[50]:

(a) transfers between spouses[51];
(b) small gifts exception[52];
(c) gifts in consideration of marriage[53];
(d) gifts to charities[54];
(e) gifts to political parties[55];
(f) gifts for national purposes[56];

---

48. [1958] A.C. 435 (P.C.).
49. See *Hanson's Death Duties* (10th ed.), Sixth supp., para. 1653.
50. F.A. 1986, s.102(5).
51. s.18, §§ 19–02 *et seq.*
52. s.20, § 19–10.
53. s.22, §§ 19–15 *et seq.*
54. s.23, § 19–20.
55. s.24, § 19–20A.
56. s.25, § 19–21.

(g) gifts for public benefit[57];

(h) maintenance funds for historic buildings[58];

(i) employee trusts.[59]

What property is dutiable?

20–46   Section 102(3) provides that inheritance tax on death is to be charged by including "property subject to a reservation" as part of the deceased's estate. It may happen, however, that A gives property to, or settles property upon, B subject to such a reservation but that B no longer has the property (or the trustees no longer do) on A's death. B may, for example, have sold or exchanged the subject-matter of the gift, or settled cash may have been used to purchase shares and the shares exchanged for other property—and so on. Is it then possible for section 102 to apply on A's death? Paragraphs 2 to 5 of Schedule 20 to the Finance Act 1986 contain elaborate provisions for identifying the property to be taken into account in computing the value of the deceased's estate as a result of section 102. The provisions are of extreme complexity and the following is no more than a brief outline. A distinction is drawn between absolute and settled gifts.

A. Absolute Gifts

(1) *Of money*

20–47   The sum given is treated as continuing to be the subject-matter of the gift, and thus as forming part of the deceased's estate, whatever the donee may have done with the money.[60]

(2) *Of property other than money*

20–48   (a) If the donee still has the property at the donor's death, that property forms part of the donor's estate, and is valued as at the date of death. If the gift was of shares or debentures, any bonus shares or debentures and any rights issue is also treated as having been comprised in the original gift[61] (subject to a deduction for any subscription price paid by the donee[62]). Where the property which passes by the gift is property attracting agricultural relief or business property relief in the hands of the donor (see §§ 19–39 *et seq.*), similar relief may be available on his death.[63] Such relief will not be available if the donee has subsequently disposed of the property prior to the death of the donor.

---

57. s.26, § 19–22.
58. s.27, § 19–37.
59. s.28.
60. F.A. 1986, Sched. 20, para. 2(2).
61. *Ibid.* para. 2(6).
62. *Ibid.* para. 3.
63. *Ibid.* para. 8.

20–49　　(b) If the donee no longer has the property at the donor's death, then:

(i) If the donee has sold, exchanged or otherwise disposed of the gifted property for full consideration in money, the money received is taxable (*i.e.* is treated as part of the donor's estate at death); but if for full consideration in property other than money, the substituted property is taxable instead.[64]

> For example, A gives a house to B subject to B paying an annuity to A. B exchanges the house for shares (for full consideration). On A's death, the shares are treated as forming part of A's estate. If B had sold the house for £150,000 (its market value at the time of sale), the £150,000 would be deemed to form part of A's estate at death, even if the money had later been used to purchase other property, or even though the house was worth £250,000 at A's death.

It thus is apparent that paragraph 2 permits the Capital Taxes Office to trace the original gifted property through any series of dispositions for full consideration by the donee, until a disposition is made for full consideration in money. At that moment the right to trace will terminate and the money will be treated as passing on the donor's death.

20–50　　(ii) If the donee has disposed of the property by way of gift, or otherwise than for full consideration, that disposal is ignored and the property is deemed to continue to be enjoyed by the donee unless the disposal was in favour of the donor.[65] The effect of this is that the substitution rules under paragraph 2(1) will not apply unless the property passes back to the donor—in which case the property in question will *actually* form part of the donor's estate at death (subject to any further gift of it) and the consideration (if any) given by the donor is substituted for the purposes of paragraph 2(1). In this latter case, it will be that consideration alone which will be *deemed* to form part of his estate at death.

20–51　　(iii) If the donee predeceases the donor, the substitution provisions apply as if he had not died and as if the acts of the donee's personal representatives were the donee's acts, and as if the property taken by any person under his will, or on his intestacy, were taken under a gift made by him at the time of his death.[66]

> A gives shares worth £50,000 to B subject to a reservation. B predeceases A, leaving the shares to C absolutely. At the time of B's death the shares are worth £75,000. A subsequently dies, when the shares are worth £125,000. The shares form part of A's estate, and are valued for the purposes of section 4 at £125,000. If B's personal representatives had sold the shares to C for full consideration, the cash of £75,000 would have been treated as forming part of A's estate.

---

64. *Ibid.* para. 2(1), (3).
65. *Ibid.* para. 2(4).
66. *Ibid.* para. 4.

20–52   (iv) If the donee settles the gifted property, or predeceases the donor having settled it by will or intestacy, the original donor is treated as having settled it himself at the date of the original gift[67]: see below.

20–53   The question may arise whether a gift is one of money or of property other than money. The following propositions may be advanced:

(1) If A contracts to buy Blackacre from B and directs B to convey Blackacre to C, this is a gift of Blackacre from A to C. Under the contract A acquires the right to dispose of Blackacre and he exercises that right by disposing of the property to C.[68]

(2) If A pays £100,000 to B and directs B to convey Blackacre to C, there being no contract under which A becomes entitled to Blackacre, this also is a gift of Blackacre. A acquires the right to dispose of Blackacre by the payment of money to B.

> In *Ralli Bros. Trustee Co. Ltd.* v. *I.R.C.*[69] A paid a premium to an insurance company for a policy of insurance on her life which she effected in the name of a trustee company which, under a previously executed settlement, had agreed to hold the policy and the policy moneys on trust for a member of A's family. *Held,* this was a gift of the policy and the moneys payable thereunder (which it was conceded was property in which A never had an interest) and not, as the Crown contended, of the premium.

(3) If C contracts to buy Blackacre from B and A pays the price, this is a gift of money from A to C. This is because A discharges C's liability to pay money to B.

(4) If A provides C with £100,000 to enable C to buy Blackacre from B, A having no dealings with B in the matter, this is a gift of money to C.

> In *Potter* v. *I.R.C.*[70] the deceased gave his son a crossed cheque for £10,000, drawn in favour of a company, for the express purpose of enabling his son to purchase shares in the company, which the son did. The deceased died within three years after his gift, when the shares were worth less than £10,000. The son contended that there was a non-aggregable gift of shares. It was held that the "property taken" under the gift was the £10,000 cash and not the shares. It followed that the gift was of property in which the deceased had an interest and was aggregable with the deceased's free estate.

B. Gifts by Way of Settlement (Whether of Money or Other Property)

20–54   (i) If a gift is made by way of settlement, but subject to a reservation, the rules in (A) above do not apply. Instead, the property comprised in the settlement at the time of the settlor's death is deemed to form part of his estate, except in so far as that property neither is, nor represents, nor is derived from, property originally comprised in the gift.[71] Accumulations of income are *not* considered to be derived from the gift, so that they are not aggregated with the settlor's estate.[72]

---

67. *Ibid.* para. 5(3).
68. *Potter* v. *I.R.C.* (1958) 37 A.T.C. 58 at p. 61 (C.S.).
69. [1968] Ch. 215.
70. (1958) 37 A.T.C. 58.
71. *Ibid.* para. 5(1).
72. *Ibid.* para. 5(5).

Thus if cash is settled by A, subject to a reservation, and the trustees use it to purchase shares, the shares (but not accumulated dividends) will be aggregated with A's estate on his death.

20–55   (ii) If the settlement terminates before the settlor's death, then the property in the settlement at termination is treated as having been comprised in the original gift (so that subsequent changes and substitutions will be dealt with under the rules in (A) above) except for property to which the settlor becomes absolutely and beneficially entitled. Such latter property is left out of account for the purposes of section 102: but if the settlor gives consideration for any of the property to which he becomes entitled, that consideration is treated as aggregable property.[73]

20–56   The substitution provisions in §§ 20–47 to 20–55 apply not only for the purposes of valuing the donor's estate at his death but also for computing the amount of the provisionally exempt transfer which occurs when property ceases to be subject to a reservation under section 102(4).[74]

The Double Charge to Tax

20–57   Certain events will be capable of causing two charges to inheritance tax to arise in respect of the same property. For example—

(a) A makes a transfer to B reserving a benefit, and dies within seven years. On his death, the PET will prove chargeable even though the value of the property so transferred continues to form part of his estate for the purposes of section 4.

(b) A makes a transfer to C which proves chargeable and his estate at death includes property acquired on a transfer of value made by C. This previously might have been dealt with under the mutual transfer provisions.

In such cases, regulations are to be made to avoid the duplication of inheritance tax.[75]

---

73. *Ibid.* para. 5(2).
74. Ibid. para. 1(1).
75. F.A. 1986, s.104.

CHAPTER 21

OTHER CHARGES

1. CLOSE COMPANIES

21–01   Inheritance tax is charged on the value transferred by a chargeable transfer, which is defined as a transfer of value made by an individual: see § 18–02. Hence a company is not chargeable to inheritance tax: but a company may make a disposition which is a transfer of value, the company's property being for this purpose treated as its "estate." Transfers of value by United Kingdom companies will be rare but may occur if, for example, assets are sold at an undervalue or purchased at an overvalue. Section 94 enables the Revenue, in effect, to treat a transfer of value made by a close company as if it had been made by its participators. It does so by apportioning the value transferred between them in accordance with their interests in the company. For this purpose "close company" means a company within the meaning of the Corporation Tax Acts which is, or would, if resident in the United Kingdom, be a close company for the purposes of those Acts (see §§ 15–07 *et seq.*)[1]; and "participator" has the meaning in § 15–02 except that a person who qualifies as a participator by reason only of being a loan creditor is excluded.[1]

It should be noted that the rules relating to potentially exempt transfers do not apply to transactions involving companies.

21–02   Section 94(1) provides that where a close company makes a transfer of value, tax is to be charged as if each individual to whom an amount is apportioned under the section had made a transfer of value of such amount as after deduction of tax (if any) would be equal to the amount so apportioned, less the amount (if any) by which the value of his estate is more than it would be but for the company's transfer. For this purpose his estate is treated as not including any rights or interests in the company: thus the measure of the liability is the value transferred by the company, not the amount by which the value of the participator's shares or other interest in the company is diminished in consequence of the transfer. The participator's estate will increase in value where the company's transfer is to the participator himself (or to another company in which the participator has an interest[2]): the exclusion of this increase is necessary to avoid a double charge to inheritance tax. It follows that where a company makes a transfer of value to one of several participators, an apportionment can be made to all of them; but the participator to whom the transfer was made gets credit to the extent to which his estate was enriched by the transfer.

A surrender for group relief of surplus advance corporation tax is not a transfer of value.[3]

---

1. s.102(1).
2. see s.95.
3. s.94(3).

21–03 Where an apportionment is made under section 94, the value transferred by the company's transfer is apportioned among the participators according to their respective rights and interests in the company immediately before the transfer, including rights and interests in the assets of the company available for distribution among the participators in the event of a winding up or in any other circumstances.[3a] Apportionments will not be made in respect of preference shares where this has only a small effect on their value.[4] An amount which is apportioned to a close company can be further sub-apportioned among its participators, and so on.[5] When the participators in a close company are trustees of a discretionary settlement, the relevant property rules take effect as if, on the making of the transfer by the company, the trustees had made a disposition to which paragraph (b) in § 22–65 applies.[6]

21–04 In two cases no apportionment is made[7]:

(a) where the value transferred by the company is attributable to any payment or transfer of assets to any person which falls to be taken into account in computing that person's profits or gains or losses for the purposes of income tax or corporation tax: thus if a company purchases an asset at an overvalue from a trader, no apportionment to any participators can be made in respect of that transfer of value;

(b) where the amount, if apportioned, would be apportioned to an individual domiciled outside the United Kingdom and the amount is attributable to the value of any property outside the United Kingdom.

"Golden handshakes," in the sense of payments made by a company for no consideration, may fall within the exemption in (a).

Liability for tax

21–05 The persons liable for the tax chargeable under section 94 are[8] the company and, so far as the tax remains unpaid after it ought to have been paid, the persons to whom any amounts have been apportioned and any individual (whether such a person or not) the value of whose estate is increased by the company's transfer; but

(a) a person to whom not more than 5 per cent. of the value transferred is apportioned is not as such liable for any of the tax[9] and the deemed transfer by him is left out of account where, on a subsequent transfer by that person, it becomes necessary to decide what previous transfers he has made[9a];

3a. s.102(2).
4. s.96.
5. s.94(2).
6. s.99.
7. s.94(2)(*a*) and (*b*).
8. s.202.
9. s.202(2).
9a. s.94(4).

(b) each of the other persons to whom any part of the value has been apportioned is liable only for such part of the tax as corresponds to that part of that value[9b]; and

(c) a person is not, as a person the value of whose estate is increased, liable for a greater amount than the amount of the increase.[10]

Alterations in capital as deemed dispositions

21–06 Section 98(1) provides that where there is at any time an alteration (including an extinguishment[11]) in a close company's share or loan capital not quoted on a recognised stock exchange or any alteration in any rights attaching to such shares or debentures, the alteration shall be treated as having been made by a disposition[11a] made at that time by the participators and shall not be taken to have affected the value immediately before that time of the shares or debentures not so quoted. Hence an alteration or extinguishment of share or loan capital by which value passes out of the shares may give rise to a charge to inheritance tax. (Compare the capital gains tax position: see § 16–16.)

2. Delayed Transfers of Value

21–07 Section 262 deals with the situation where a disposition made for a consideration in money or money's worth is a transfer of value (as in the case of a sale by the transferor at an undervalue or a purchase by the transferor at an overvalue) and any payments made or assets transferred by the transferor in pursuance of the disposition are made or transferred more than one year after the disposition is made. Supposing, for example, P agrees to buy an asset worth £20,000 from V for £35,000, payment to be made by five equal instalments of £7,000 payable over a five-year period. In such a case value is transferred by P in stages and section 262 imposes a tax charge in stages. It achieves this by providing that tax (if any) shall be charged as if (i) any payment made or asset transferred in pursuance of the disposition were a separate disposition made, without consideration, at the payment or transfer date; and (ii) as if the amount of the payment made or the value of the asset transferred on each of those separate dispositions were the chargeable portion of the payment or asset.[12]

21–08 The chargeable portion of any payment made or asset transferred at any time is such portion of its value at that time as is found by applying to it the fraction of which:

(a) the numerator is the value actually transferred by the disposition in (i) above, calculated as if no tax were payable on it; and

(b) the denominator is the value, at the time of that disposition, of the

---

9b. s.202(2).
10. s.202(3).
11. s.98(2).
11a. The disposition is deemed *not* to be a PET, so that inheritance tax may immediately become chargeable: s.98(3).
12. s.262(1)(*a*) and (*b*) and see § 20–26A.

aggregate of the payments made or to be made and assets transferred or to be transferred by the transferor in pursuance of it.[13]

Thus (in the example) P is treated as making five separate transfers of:

$$£7,000 \times \frac{£15,000}{£35,000} = £3,000$$

each of which may be potentially exempt.

3. Annuity Purchased in Conjunction with Life Policy

21–09 The nature of back to back insurance arrangements was mentioned briefly in § 19–12. Section 263 imposes a special charge in respect of back to back life policies where such policies are taken out with an annuity on the same life as part of an associated operation. In certain circumstances the person taking out the policy is treated as making a transfer of value.

---

13. s.262(2).

Chapter 22

SETTLED PROPERTY

1. Introduction

22–01 This chapter begins by considering the definition for inheritance tax purposes of the term "settlement" and related expressions. The settlement provisions in the legislation differentiate between:

(1) settled property in which some person is beneficially entitled to an interest in possession, such as a life interest or an annuity; and

(2) settled property in which there is no interest in possession, *e.g.* property held on discretionary trusts; and

(3) special classes of trust such as superannuation schemes, trusts for employees, protective trusts and trusts for the benefit of disabled persons, etc.

22–02 It is important to observe that the charges to tax are imposed by reference to settled *property* and *property* comprised in a settlement and not by reference to settlements as such. This is because a single settlement may direct that some property should be held on one class of trusts and other property on a different class of trusts; or the trusts on which property is held may change from time to time.

> Thus property comprised in the same settlement may be held as to part in trust for A for life with remainders over and as to the rest on discretionary trusts.

It should be noted that the rules relating to potentially exempt transfers do not apply to the deemed transfers of value made in respect of settled property nor on transfers into settlement made by an individual except, in the latter case, in respect of transfers into accumulation and maintenance settlements (§§ 22–84 *et seq.*) or a disabled settlement.

22–03 In the case of settled property falling within (1), it is inevitable that the interest in possession will at some time come to an end, either on death or by effluxion of time, if the holder of the interest has not previously disposed of it. The legislation makes the coming to an end of the interest (*e.g.* the death of a life tenant) the occasion of charge to inheritance tax. Where the interest is disposed of (*e.g.* where the life tenant surrenders his interest to the remainderman), this is treated as if it were the coming to an end of the interest.

In the case of settled property falling within (2) there is by definition no interest which will come to an end. In this case the principal charge to inheritance tax is a ten-year charge which is levied on the tenth anniversary of the commencement of the settlement and on subsequent anniversaries at ten-year intervals.

Property put into settlement: the "entry charge"

2–04   The disposition by which property becomes comprised in a settlement is a chargeable transfer unless either the transfer is exempt (or potentially exempt) or is not a transfer of value or the property is excluded property or falls to be left out of account under one of the reliefs, etc., discussed in Chapter 19. The charge to inheritance tax on property put into settlement may be described as "the entry charge." This chapter is, however, concerned with charges to inheritance tax on settled property which may arise *after* the property has become settled property.

The inheritance tax legislation provides that both the settlor and the trustees are liable for any inheritance tax payable when a settlor puts assets into a settlement by a lifetime transfer: see § 24–03. Where the trustees have power to pay, or do in fact pay, the inheritance tax the Inland Revenue used to take the view that the settlor has thereby an interest in the income or property of the settlement and that the income of the settlement should accordingly be treated as his for income tax purposes under the provisions discussed in § 10–39. The Board of Inland Revenue have now adopted a different practice and no longer treat the income of a settlement as that of the settlor for income tax purposes solely because the trustees have power to pay or do in fact pay inheritance tax on assets put into settlement. The change of practice applies to settlement income for 1981–82 and subsequent years of assessment.[1]

2. DEFINITION OF "SETTLEMENT" AND RELATED EXPRESSIONS

Settlement

2–05   The word "settlement" is defined[2] for purposes of inheritance tax as meaning any disposition or dispositions of property, whether effected by instrument, by parol or by operation of law (*e.g.* under the statutory provisions which apply on an intestacy), or partly in one way and partly in another, whereby the property is for the time being:

(a) held in trust for persons in succession (*e.g.* to A for life with remainder to B absolutely) or for any person subject to a contingency (*e.g.* to A if he shall attain the age of 25 years); or

(b) held by trustees on trust to accumulate the whole or part of any income of the property or with power to make payments out of that income at the discretion of the trustees or some other person, with or without power to accumulate surplus income (*e.g.* the common type of discretionary settlement); or

(c) charged or burdened (otherwise than for full consideration in money or money's worth paid for his own use or benefit to the person making the disposition), with the payment of any annuity or

---

1. SP 1/82 in [1982] S.T.I. 165.
2. s.43(1) and (2). In Scotland the word "settlement" also includes an entail and any deed charging an annuity on rents or other property: s.43(4). For the capital gains tax definition of "settled property" see *ante*, § 16–21.

other periodical payment payable for a life or any other limited or terminable period.

22–06   The definition includes property which would be so held or charged or burdened if the disposition or dispositions were regulated by the law of any part of the United Kingdom; or whereby, under the law of any other country, the administration of the property is for the time being governed by provisions equivalent in effect to those which would apply if the property were so held, charged or burdened.[3]

22–07   Note that the definition of settlement in § 22–05 requires a disposition or dispositions of property. The word "disposition" is not defined but it seems from the use of the term "whereby" and the sub-paragraphs (a) to (c) that follow that any instrument or court order, etc., which causes property to be held in trust or charged or burdened in one of the ways enumerated in the sub-paragraphs is a "disposition" whether or not any actual transfer of property is made. An instrument whereby A declares himself trustee of property for B for life is as much a settlement as is a disposition by A to trustees to hold upon trust for B for life. Thus if A voluntarily charges his property with the payment of an annuity to B during B's life, it is thought that this creates a settlement under sub-paragraph (c) and that a charge to inheritance tax will arise on the cesser of the annuity. Note that there is no settlement within the definition where property is charged with the payment of a perpetual annuity; nor where the annuity is granted for full consideration paid to the grantor.

> Thus if A sells Blackacre to B in consideration of an annual rentcharge secured on Blackacre and payable to A for life or for any other limited or terminable period, Blackacre is not settled property.

Annuities to retired partners

22–08   Where annuities payable to retiring partners are secured only by the personal covenants of continuing partners, there is no "settled property." The position is otherwise where such annuities are *charged* on property: then a charge to inheritance tax will arise on the coming to an end of an annuity, unless it can be shown that the persons paying the annuity obtained full consideration in money or money's worth. It is thought that this condition will normally be satisfied in the case of annuities of a reasonable amount provided under commercial partnership agreements for the benefit of partners and their widows.

Leases for lives

22–09   A lease of property which is for a life or lives, or for a period ascertainable only by reference to a death, or which is terminable on, or at a date ascertainable only by reference to, a death is treated as a settlement and

3. s.43(2).

the property as settled property unless the lease was granted for full consideration in money or money's worth.[4] Hence the rules relating to settled property cannot be avoided by the disponor granting a lease for life and not a life interest. Leases for a life or lives, etc., take effect as determinable leases for 90 years, as provided in section 149(6) of the Law of Property Act 1925. As to the valuation of the lessor's interest: see § 20–20. As to the valuation of the lessee's interest: see § 22–21.

Undivided shares

2–10   Property held for beneficiaries absolutely entitled in undivided shares is not settled property for the purposes of inheritance tax. Such property is not held for persons in succession.

Settlor

2–11   The expression "settlor" in relation to a settlement includes any person by whom the settlement was made directly or indirectly, and in particular (but without prejudice to the generality of these words) includes any person who has provided funds directly or indirectly for the purpose of or in connection with the settlement or has made with any other person a reciprocal arrangement for that other person to make a settlement.[5] "Settlor" is thus defined as in section 454(3) of the Taxes Act 1970.

Where more than one person is a settlor in relation to a settlement and the circumstances so require, the Act applies in relation to it as if the settled property were comprised in separate settlements.[6]

Trustee

2–12   The expression "trustee" in relation to a settlement of which there is no trustee in the ordinary meaning of the word means any person in whom the settled property or its management is for the time being vested.[7]

Excluded property[8]

2–13   We have seen that the value of "excluded property" is left out of account on a transfer of value by an individual, including the deemed transfer on death, so that excluded property falls outside the tax charge: see § 18–13. Section 6(1) provides that property situated outside the United Kingdom is excluded property if the person beneficially entitled to it is an individual domiciled outside the United Kingdom; and by section 48(1), a reversionary interest not acquired by purchase is excluded property unless it is one to which either the settlor or his spouse is beneficially entitled or it is the

---

4. s.43(3).
5. s.44(1). See §§ 10–07 *et seq.*
6. s.44(2).
7. s.45.
8. See, generally, Chap. 23.

interest expectant on the determination of a lease for lives treated as a settlement under the provision discussed in § 22–09.

In relation to settled property, section 48(3) provides that where property comprised in a settlement is situated outside the United Kingdom the property (but not a reversionary interest in the property) is excluded property unless the settlor was domiciled in the United Kingdom at the time the settlement was made. Section 6(1), above, applies to a reversionary interest in such property but does not otherwise apply.

Note that the key factors in relation to settled property are the domicile of the settlor at the time the settlement was made and the situation of the property at the time when the tax charge would otherwise arise. The domicile of the beneficiary is not a material factor except where the property disposed of is a reversionary interest, when the reversionary interest is excluded property under section 6(1), above, if the disponor is an individual domiciled outside the United Kingdom.

> Thus if S (being domiciled outside the United Kingdom) settles property on A for life with remainder to B absolutely, no charge to inheritance tax arises on A's death on property comprised in the settlement which is then situated outside the United Kingdom. The domiciles of S and A at the time of A's death are immaterial. If B gives his reversionary interest to C, this is a chargeable transfer by B, unless at the time B is an individual domiciled outside the United Kingdom and the settled property is situated outside the United Kingdom.

This example shows that a person domiciled outside the United Kingdom who intends to acquire a domicile in the United Kingdom should make any settlement he intends to make before he acquires the domicile.

3. SETTLED PROPERTY IN WHICH THERE IS A BENEFICIAL INTEREST IN POSSESSION

The meaning of interest in possession

22–14   The phrase "beneficially entitled to an interest in possession" is not defined in the inheritance tax legislation[9] and general principles of property law have to be applied. An interest in possession must be distinguished from an interest in remainder. If property is held by trustees upon trust for A for life with remainder to B absolutely, A has an interest in possession. B's interest does not vest in possession until A dies. If property is transferred to trustees upon trust for A if he attains the age of 25 years, A's interest in *capital* is contingent until he attains that age; but his interest in *income* vests in possession when he attains the age of 18 if by statute or otherwise he becomes entitled to the income on attaining that age.[10] In the case of property which produces no income (*e.g.* a settled life policy which has not yet matured), the person who would be entitled to the income if there were any (*e.g.* if the insurance company was in liquidation and the

---

9. See s.46 as to the position in Scotland.
10. Trustee Act 1925, s.31 as amended. See *Re Jones' Will Trusts* [1947] Ch. 48 and *cf. Att.-Gen.* v. *Power* [1906] 2 I.R. 272. See also [1975] S.T.I. 469.

trustees had invested the proceeds of the liquidation[11]) has an interest in possession.

The Board of Inland Revenue has stated the official view as to the nature of an interest in possession in the following terms.[12] "An interest in possession exists where the person having the interest has the immediate entitlement (subject to any prior claim by the trustees for expenses or other outgoings properly payable out of income) to any income produced by that property as the income arises; but that a discretion or power, in whatever form, which can be exercised after income arises so as to withhold it from that person negatives the existence of an interest in possession. For this purpose a power to accumulate income is regarded as a power to withhold it, unless any accumulations must be held solely for the person having the interest or his personal representatives. On the other hand the existence of a mere power of revocation or appointment, the exercise of which would determine the interest wholly or in part (but which, so long as it remains unexercised, does not affect the beneficiary's immediate entitlement to income) does not in the Board's view prevent the interest from being an interest in possession." This official view applies also for the purposes of section 55(1) of the Capital Gains Tax Act 1979: see § 16–23.

This official view has received judicial approval from the House of Lords.

> In *Pearson* v. *I.R.C.*[13] the capital and income of property was settled on trust for such one or more of S's children and their issue as the trustees should by deed appoint during a defined period. Pending appointment the trustees had power to accumulate all or any of the income. Subject thereto the trustees were to hold the capital and income on trust for S's children who attained 21 or married under that age, in equal shares. All three daughters of S had attained 21 by February 1974. In 1976 the trustees appointed £16,000 to a daughter, F. The Revenue claimed capital transfer tax on the appointment to F, on the footing that F thereby became entitled to an interest in possession at a time when no such interest subsisted: see § 22–46. *Held,* that the Revenue's claim was well founded since F had no interest in possession before the 1976 appointment. Until the appointment, F had only a right to such income as the trustees thought fit not to accumulate.

Further guidance on the meaning of "interest in possession" was provided by the High Court in *Moore & Osborne* v. *I.R.C.*[13a] where it was held that a sole beneficiary under a discretionary trust did not have such an interest since it was possible for further beneficiaries to come into existence. This was so even just before his death on which event the class would no longer be capable of increase.

See also § 22–100: "Protective trusts."

Where trustees exercise their powers so as to cause an interest in pos-

---

11. See *Re Midwood's Settlement* [1968] Ch. 238.
12. [1976] S.T.I. 75. Inland Revenue Press Release of February 12, 1976. The text of this release is also to be found in CTT 1 at p. 123.
13. [1981] A.C. 253; [1980] S.T.C. 318 (H.L.). Fox J. in the High Court, Buckley, Bridge and Templeman L.JJ. in the Court of Appeal and Lord Salmon and Lord Russell of Killowen in the House of Lords held that the Revenue's claim was ill-founded! For a useful note on the *Pearson* case, see [1982] B.T.R. 105 (John Jopling).
13a. [1984] S.T.C. 236.

session to cease to be such an interest, a tax charge may arise under the provisions discussed in § 22–23.

22–15   In 1979 the Inland Revenue published a Statement of Practice, 10/1979 which states, *inter alia*—

> "*Power for trustees to allow a beneficiary to occupy a dwelling house SP10/79*
>
> Many wills and settlements contain a clause empowering the trustees to permit a beneficiary to occupy a dwelling house which forms part of the trust property on such terms as they think fit. The Inland Revenue do not regard the existence of such a power as excluding any interest in possession in the property. . . . On the other hand, if the power is drawn in terms wide enough to cover the creation of an exclusive or joint right of residence, albeit revocable, for a definite or indefinite period, and is exercised with the intention of providing a particular beneficiary with a permanent home, the Revenue will normally regard the exercise of the power as creating an interest in possession. And if the trustees in exercise of their powers grant a lease for life for less than full consideration, this will also be regarded as creating an interest in possession in view of [sections 43(1)–(3) and 50(6) of the IHTA 1984].
>
> A similar view will be taken where the power is exercised over property in which another beneficiary had an interest in possession up to the time of the exercise."

In *Swales* v. *I.R.C.*,[13b] trustees of a discretionary settlement had arranged for the income of the trust fund to be paid direct to one of the beneficiaries for her own use by means of a standing order on their bank. Relying on *Sansom* v. *Peay*[13c] (which is the basis for the above Revenue practice) they sought to argue that the entitlement of the beneficiary was sufficiently permanent to create an interest in possession, subject to "revocation." The learned judge refused to accept *Sansom* v. *Peay* as authoritative or of any assistance for the purposes of Capital Transfer Tax, stating that it was concerned with different statutory provisions. There must in consequence, be some doubts as to the validity of the Revenue practice.

22–16   Where a person would have been entitled to an interest in possession in the whole or part of the residue of the estate of a deceased person if the administration of that estate had been completed, he is treated as if he had become entitled to an interest in possession in the unadministered estate (as defined) and in the property (if any) representing ascertained residue (as defined), or in a corresponding part of it, on the date as from which the whole or part of the income of the residue would have been attributable to his interest had the residue been ascertained immediately after the death of the deceased person.[14]

13b. [1984] S.T.C. 413.
13c. [1976] S.T.C. 494.
14. s.91.

Quantifying the interest in possession

2–17   A person beneficially entitled to an interest in possession in settled property is treated as beneficially entitled to the property in which the interest subsists,[15] apparently for all the purposes of inheritance tax.[16]

> Thus if Blackacre is held upon trust for A for life with remainder to B absolutely, A is treated as beneficially entitled to Blackacre and not merely to a life interest in it.

2–18   Where the person entitled to the interest is entitled to part only of the income (if any) of the property, the interest is taken to subsist in such part only of the property as bears to the whole of it the same proportion as the part of the income to which he is entitled bears to the whole of the income.[17]

> Thus if property is held upon trust to pay one-third of the income thereof to A for life, A is treated as having a beneficial interest in one-third of the property.

2–19   Where the beneficiary is entitled to an annuity of a fixed amount, or to the whole of the income of the property less a specified amount, he is treated as beneficially entitled to such part of the property as will produce that amount.[18] This is calculated by reference to the income yield of the property. The Treasury has power[19] to prescribe higher and lower rates which operate as limits beyond which variations in the actual income yield of the property are disregarded. The higher rate applies when the interest in the annuity comes to an end; the lower rate applies when the interest in the remainder of the property comes to an end. By the Capital Transfer Tax (Settled Property Income Yield) Order 1975,[20] which applies to interests in possession coming to an end after May 7, 1975, the rates are prescribed by reference to the Financial Times Actuaries Share Indices. The higher rate is the current yield from $2\frac{1}{2}$ per cent. Consols; the lower rate is the current gross dividend yield from the Financial Times Actuaries All Share Index. If no yield has been calculated for the date on which the property falls to be valued, the relevant Indices for the latest earlier date are used. Details of these yields can be obtained on any working day from the Capital Taxes Office.

2–20   Where the person entitled to the interest is not entitled to any income of the property but is entitled, jointly or in common with one or more other persons, to the use and enjoyment of the property, his interest is taken to subsist in such part of the property as corresponds to the proportion which

---

15. s.49(1).
16. See, for example, the decision of the Court of Appeal in *Fetherstonaugh* v. *I.R.C.* [1984] S.T.C. 261.
17. s.50(1).
18. s.50(2).
19. s.50(3), (4).
20. S.I. 1975 No. 610. See [1975] S.T.I. 260; S.I. 1980 No. 1000 substitutes a new upper limit, which is that shown in the Index for British Government Stock ("Irredeemables"). This applies to transfers of value made on or after August 15, 1980: see [1980] S.T.I. 511.

the annual value of his interest bears to the aggregate of the annual values of his interest and that or those of the other or others.[21]

22–21 Where a lease of property is treated as a settlement (see § 22–09), the lessee's interest in the property is taken to subsist in the whole of the property less such part of it as corresponds to the proportion which the value of the lessor's interest (see § 20–20) bears to the value of the property.[22]

The basis of the charge to tax

22–22 Sections 51 and 52 contain the principal provisions which apply for charging inheritance tax in the case of settled property in which some person has an interest in possession. If, though, property is held on trust for A for life with remainder over to B absolutely, and A dies, neither section 51 nor section 52 is applicable: instead, the value of the property in which A's interest in possession subsisted is taken into account in computing the deemed transfer of value under section 4 (see § 18–14). The events on the happening of which tax is chargeable under the above sections are, rather, the coming to an end of an interest in possession *during the lifetime* of the holder and the occurrence of certain other events which are treated as having had that effect. In each case the event gives rise to an assumed transfer of value by the person beneficially entitled to the interest who is, accordingly, treated as the "transferor" and as having made a transfer of his own property. The questions whether any exemptions or reliefs are available, or at what rate or rates tax is chargeable, or whether the settled property is excluded property, have all to be answered by reference to the personal circumstances of the transferor. The only respect in which the general rules do not apply is that the measure of the tax charge is related exclusively to the property comprised in the settlement. Questions as to the amount by which his "estate" is diminished in value do not arise.

The charging provisions

There are two basic rules of charge which are subject to a number of qualifications and exceptions which are referred to in § 22–25, below. The rules are as follows:

22–23 (1) Where at any time *during the life* of a person beneficially entitled to an interest in possession in any settled property his interest comes to an end, tax is chargeable as if at that time he had made a transfer of value and the value transferred had been equal to the value of the property in which his interest subsisted.[23] Where part only of an interest in settled property comes to an end, the value treated as transferred is the corresponding proportion of the property.[24]

---

21. s.50(5).
22. s.50(6).
23. s.52(1): and see s.3(4).
24. s.52(4)(*a*).

22–24   (2) Where a person beneficially entitled to an interest in possession in any settled property disposes of his interest, the disposal is not a transfer of value but is treated as the coming to an end of his interest.[25]

> Thus if property is settled on A for life with remainder to B absolutely and A assigns his interest by way of gift, this is not a transfer of value of A's life interest but is a transfer of value of the settled property itself.

Examples of the way in which these rules operate are given in §§ 22–32 *et seq*.

Exceptions

The basic charging rules stated in § 22–22 to § 22–24 take effect subject to the following exceptions:

(1) *Beneficial entitlement*

22–25   If the person whose interest in possession in the property comes to an end becomes, on the same occasion, beneficially entitled to the property or to another interest in possession in the property, tax is not chargeable unless the value of the property (or part) to which or to an interest in which he so becomes entitled is less than the value of the property in which his interest terminated. Tax is then chargeable on the difference.[26] For examples, see §§ 22–32 and 33.

(2) *Sales for full consideration*

22–26   If the interest in possession comes to an end by being disposed of by the person beneficially entitled thereto, and the disposal is for a consideration in money or money's worth of equal value to the property in which the interest subsisted, no tax is chargeable; but if its value is less, tax is chargeable as if the value of the property in which the interest subsisted were reduced by the amount of the consideration. Since it is unlikely that the value of a life interest (and, thus, the price someone will be willing to pay for it) will be as much as the value of the property in which the interest subsists, in practice such a disposal will always give rise to some charge to tax. For the purposes of this provision the value of a reversionary interest in the property or of any interest in other property comprised in the same settlement is left out of account.[27] For an example, see § 22–33.

(3) *Reverter to settlor*

22–27   If an interest in possession in settled property comes to an end during the settlor's life and on the same occasion the property in which the interest subsisted reverts to the settlor, no tax is chargeable unless the settlor or his

---

25. s.51(1). But disposals by way of disclaimer may be exempt: see § 19–66, and see also § 19–62.
26. s.53(2) and s.52(4)(*b*).
27. s.52(2).

spouse had acquired a reversionary interest in the property for a consideration in money or money's worth.[28]

> Thus if S transfers property to A for life, no tax is payable in respect of the property which on A's death reverts to S. This exception does not apply if S predeceases A.[28a]
>
> If S settles property on A for life with remainder to B absolutely and S purchases B's reversionary interest, this exception does not apply when on A's death the property reverts to S; nor does it apply if S's spouse purchases B's reversionary interest and transfers it to S, to whom it reverts on A's death.
>
> If as part of the financial arrangements on divorce H transfers the matrimonial home to his wife (W) until the children attain a certain age, the exception applies to the reverter of the property to H.

22–27A *Death.* If the occasion which brings the interest in possession to an end is the death of the person entitled thereto, and on that occasion the property reverts to the settlor, the value of the settled property is left out of account in determining the value of the deceased's estate immediately before his death for the purposes of section 4(1): see § 18–14.[29] Note that the subsection requires that the *value* of the settled property should be left out of account; but the *existence* of that property is not ignored.

> Thus if S transfers 52 per cent. of the issued ordinary shares in X Limited to A for life and, on A's death, A also has a personal holding of 10 per cent. of such shares, the value of the 52 per cent. holding is not chargeable to inheritance tax but the 10 per cent. holding has to be valued by aggregating with it the 52 per cent. holding. This is because the 52 per cent. holding forms part of A's estate immediately before his death: see § 22–17.

(4) *Reverter to spouse of settlor*

22–28 If an interest in possession in settled property comes to an end, whether on death or otherwise, and on the same occasion the settlor's spouse becomes beneficially entitled to the settled property, no tax is chargeable if the settlor's spouse is then domiciled in the United Kingdom.[30] "Spouse" includes the settlor's widow or widower, but only where the settlor died less than two years before the interest comes to an end.[31]

> Thus if H transfers property to trustees to hold upon trust for A for life with remainder to W (H's wife) absolutely, the transfer by H is not exempt because of A's intermediate life interest: see § 19–03; but no inheritance tax is payable if on the coming to an end of A's life interest W then becomes entitled to the property, provided she is then domiciled in the United Kingdom.

The effect is that there is only one occasion of charge to inheritance tax where an interest in possession is interposed in a transfer between spouses. This exception does not apply where either the settlor or his spouse had

---

28. s.53(3), (5), and s.54(1), (3). These provisions were amended to their present form by F.A. 1978, s.69. For a brief explanation for the amendments see [1978] B.T.R. 170; and see § 16–22 (capital gains tax).
28a. But see s.54(2).
29. s.54(1).
30. s.54(2).
31. s.54(2)(*b*).

acquired a reversionary interest in the property for a consideration in money or money's worth.[32]

> Thus if H (husband) settles property on A for life with remainder to B absolutely and his wife (W) acquires B's reversionary interest by purchase, a tax charge arises when W becomes entitled to the settled property on the termination of A's interest.

22–29   *Death.* The rule in § 22–27A applies also to the exception in § 22–28.[32a]

(5) *Surviving spouse exemption*

22–30   Where one party to a marriage died before November 13, 1974 (so that estate duty would have been leviable on his estate), and the other dies after March 13, 1975 (when estate duty law no longer applies), but the surviving spouse exemption would have applied on the second death if estate duty were then chargeable, the exemption will apply for inheritance tax purposes.[33] The exemption applies howsoever the surviving spouse's interest in possession comes to an end. The "surviving spouse exemption" was an exemption from estate duty which applied on the second-to-die of spouses where estate duty was paid on property passing on the death of the first-to-die and the survivor had only a limited interest, *e.g.* a life interest, in that property.[34]

(6) *Trustee's remuneration*

2–30A   Where a trustee is remunerated for his services by being given an interest in possession in settled property, and the interest does not represent more than a reasonable amount of remuneration, this is left out of account in valuing the estate of the trustee immediately before his death and no charge to inheritance tax is imposed when the interest comes to an end.[35]

(7) *The annual exemption and the exemption for gifts on marriage*

22–31   The annual exemption is discussed in § 19–07. The exemption for gifts in consideration of marriage is discussed in § 19–15. Both these exemptions may apply to events on the happening of which tax is chargeable under section 52: see § 22–22.[36]

> Thus if property is held upon trust for A for life with remainder to B absolutely and A surrenders his interest in the whole or part of the property to B, or A and B partition the property between them, the annual exemption may apply (or the marriage exemption if appropriate).

But the exemptions do not apply unless the transferor (A) gives the trustees notice informing them of the availability of the exemption; further, the exemptions apply only to the extent specified in the notice. The notice

---

32. s.54(3) and s.53(5)(*a*).
32a. s.54(2).
33. Sched. 6, para. 2. See also Chap. 26 below.
34. For details, see the 8th edition of this book, at § 23–54.
35. s.90.
36. s.57(1), (2).

must be given within six months after the transfer of value and must be in such form as the Board prescribes.[37]

The application of the charging provisions to concrete situations

(1) *Advancement*

22–32   If settled property is held upon trust for A for life with remainder to B absolutely and the trustees, in exercise of powers contained in the trust instrument, make an advance of capital to A, A's interest to this extent comes to an end: see § 22–23; but since A becomes beneficially entitled to the property advanced, no tax charge arises: see § 22–25. If the trustees advance capital to B, A's interest in the capital advanced comes to an end (see § 22–23) and a tax charge arises unless B is the settlor's spouse (see § 22–28), or A's spouse (see §§ 19–02 *et seq*).

(2) *Partition*

22–33   Assume that settled property is held upon trust for A for life with remainder to B absolutely. A and B agree to divide the fund between themselves in proportion to the respective values of their interests. Assume that A and B accordingly agree that the fund shall be divided as to one-third to A and two-thirds to B. A's interest in possession in two-thirds of the fund comes to an end (see § 22–23) and a tax charge arises (see § 22–25). If A pays the inheritance tax out of his one-third interest, A's interest comes to an end in two-thirds of the fund *plus* the tax thereon.

Similarly if A assigns the whole of his interest to B for its full value, A's interest is treated as coming to an end (see § 22–24); and a tax charge will arise if A assigns his interest to B for less than the full value of the property in which the interest subsists (see § 22–26).

(3) *Enlargement and reduction of interests*

22–34   If settled property is held upon trust for the children of X in equal shares and X has three children, the birth to X of a fourth child will reduce the share of each existing child from one-third to one-fourth. To this extent the beneficial interest of each of the three children comes to an end and a tax charge arises under § 22–23.

(4) *Interests pur autre vie*

22–35   The tax charge arises under § 22–23 where at any time *during the life of* the person beneficially entitled to an interest in possession, his interest comes to an end. If settled property is held upon trust for A during the life of X, a tax charge will arise on the termination of A's interest whether by the death of A, or by the death of X before A. If A dies before X and A's interest passes under his will or intestacy to B, a further charge to tax will arise on the termination of B's interest (subject to possible relief under § 19–31).

---

37. s.57(3), (4).

(5) *Failure of interest*

22–36   The tax charge arises when an interest in possession comes to an end: there is no tax charge when an interest fails before it vests in possession. Thus if property is held upon trust for A for life with remainder to B for life with remainder to C absolutely, and B predeceases A, no tax charge arises on B's death. So also, if property is held on trust for A if he shall attain the age of 25 years, and A dies aged 17, no tax charge arises; but if A dies after attaining the age of 18 years (when his interest vests in possession (see § 22–14)) a tax charge arises on A's subsequent death even before attaining the age of 25 years.

Depreciatory transactions

22–37   Since the tax charge under consideration is levied by reference to the value of the settled property at the time of the termination (or deemed termination) of the interest, any transaction which depreciates the value of the property before that time will result in a saving of tax. Section 52(3) accordingly provides that where a transaction is made between the trustees of the settlement and a person who is, or is connected with:

(a) the person beneficially entitled to an interest in the property; or
(b) a person beneficially entitled to any other interest in that property or to any interest in any other property comprised in the settlement; or
(c) a person for whose benefit any of the settled property may be applied,

and, as a result of the transaction, the value of the first-mentioned property is less than it would be but for the transaction, a corresponding part of the interest shall be deemed to come to an end unless the transaction is such that, were the trustee beneficially entitled to the settled property, it would not be a transfer of value.[38] A loan by trustees to a beneficiary may give rise to a tax charge under this provision. To take extreme examples, an unsecured interest-free loan which was not repayable on demand would depreciate the value of the settled property and so give rise to a charge under the section: a secured loan on commercial terms would not do so. A lease of trust property to a beneficiary on uncommercial terms is an example of a depreciatory transaction.

Close companies

(1) *Transfers of value by close companies*

22–38   Section 94 enables value transferred by a close company to be apportioned between the participators in certain circumstances: see §§ 21–01 *et seq*. Where the participators are trustees of settled property in which there is a qualifying interest in possession, section 99 enables the value trans-

---

38. *i.e.* if s.10 applied to the trustees.

ferred by the company to be apportioned through to the interest-holder. This is achieved by deeming there to be a termination of his interest.

(2) *Interests in possession vested in close company*

22–39   Where a close company is entitled to an interest in possession in settled property, the persons who are participators in relation to the company are treated as being the persons beneficially entitled to that interest according to their respective rights and interests in the company. Thus if the company's interest in possession comes to an end, or is treated as coming to an end, the participators can be treated as making transfers of value in proportion to their rights or interests in the company.[39]

Relief for successive charges on interest in possession

22–40[40]   There is a relief which applies where the termination of an interest in possession is quickly followed by another such termination: see § 19–31.

4. SETTLED PROPERTY IN WHICH THERE IS NO BENEFICIAL INTEREST IN POSSESSION

22–50   The Finance Act 1982 introduced new provisions (now contained in sections 58 to 85 of the Act) which apply to settled property in which no qualifying interest in possession subsists, called "relevant property." The meaning of "settled property" is discussed in § 22–05. The phrase "qualifying interest in possession" means[41] an interest in possession to which an individual is beneficially entitled or, in certain circumstances, an interest in possession to which a *company* is beneficially entitled. Property held on discretionary trusts is an example of relevant property.

22–51   There may be a qualifying interest in possession where a company is beneficially entitled in the following circumstances:

(1) Where the company is a close company (see §§ 15–07 *et seq.*). This is because an interest in possession to which a close company is entitled is treated as belonging to the participators in the company according to the respective values of their interests.[42] The word "participator" is defined as in section 303 of the Income and Corporation Taxes Act 1970, except that loan creditors are excluded[43]: see § 15–02. Where the participator is an individual, the interest in possession will be attributed to him. Where the participator is itself a close company, the interest will be attributed to the participators in that company, and so on. Where a participator is a trustee of settled property in which a person has an interest in possession, the interest will be attributed to that beneficiary[44]; hence, if he is an

---

39. s.101. See also *Brandenberg* v. *I.R.C.* [1982] S.T.C. 555.
40. The next paragraph is § 22–50.
41. s.59.
42. s.101.
43. s.102(1).
44. s.101(2).

individual, he will have a qualifying interest in possession; if he is not an individual, he may not have such an interest.

(2) Where the business of the company consists wholly or mainly in the acquisition of interests in settled property *and* the company acquired the interest in possession for full consideration in money or money's worth from an individual who was beneficially entitled to the interest.[45]

Thus if an individual with a life interest in settled property sells his interest to such a company, the rules applicable to "relevant property" will not then apply.

It is thought that the situation in paragraph (1) will rarely occur. Sales of interests in settled property whether vested or *in futuro* are not, however, uncommon.

22–52   The new provisions apply to events after March 9, 1982 but there are special provisions which apply to settlements which commenced before March 27, 1974.

Definitions

22–53   A number of definitions are used in this section of the book which do not appear in the legislation. Their use is intended to assist the reader in the understanding of legislation of an especially complex and tortuous variety.

"Relevant property rules" means the provisions contained in Chapter III, Part III of the 1984 Act which charge inheritance tax on "relevant property," *i.e.* property in which no qualifying interest in possession subsists.

"Pre-CTT settlement" means a settlement which commenced before March 27, 1974.

"Post-Estate Duty settlement" means a settlement which commenced after March 26, 1974.

"The settlor's pre-settlement cumulative total" means the cumulative total of chargeable transfers made by the settlor in the seven years preceding the commencement of the settlement.

"Initial value" means the value of the property comprised in the settlement immediately after its commencement.

"Depreciatory transaction" is used to describe the situation where the trustees of a settlement make a disposition as a result of which the value of the relevant property comprised in the settlement is less than it would be but for the disposition.

"The entry charge" means the charge to inheritance tax which arises when property is put into a settlement.

"Perpetual charitable trust" means settled property held for charitable purposes only without limit of time defined by a date or otherwise.

---

45. s.59(1), (2).

A "temporary charitable trust" means settled property held for charitable purposes for a specified time.

Sheltered property

22–54   There are nine cases of property in which no qualifying interest in possession subsists but which nevertheless is sheltered from the ordinary rules which apply to relevant property. The definition of relevant property excludes the following[46]:

(a) property held for charitable purposes, whether for a limited time or otherwise (see § 22–99);

(b) property held on accumulation and maintenance trusts (see §§ 22–84 *et seq.*);

(c) property held as a maintenance fund for heritage purposes;

(d) property held for the purposes of certain superannuation schemes;

(e) property held on trust for employees, etc. or on newspaper trusts;

(f) property held on protective trusts (see §§ 22–100);

(g) property held on certain trusts for disabled persons;

(h) property comprised in a trade or professional compensation fund[47]; and

(i) excluded property (see §§ 23–02 *et seq.*).

Categories (c), (d), (e), (g) and (h) are not discussed in this book.

The Relevant Property Rules

The following is a summary of the new provisions applicable to relevant property. The summary deals separately with (I) Post-Estate Duty settlements (see § 22–55 *et seq.*) and (II) Pre-CTT tax settlements (see §§ 22–77 *et seq.*). It is emphasised that the following is no more than a summary of the complex and detailed provisions contained in sections 58 to 85.

(I) The relevant property rules: post-Estate Duty settlements

A. *The entry charge*

22–55   The charge to tax on property which is put into settlement ("the entry charge") is discussed in § 22–04.

If no chargeable transfers have been made by the settlor in the seven years preceding the commencement of the settlement, a nil rate of inheritance tax is levied on the first tranche (currently £71,000) of property transferred into settlement. It will be seen later that the settlor's pre-settlement cumulative total (see § 22–53) has a special importance under the relevant property rules. Where the settlor or his spouse is beneficially entitled to an interest in possession in property immediately after it becomes comprised in a settlement, no inheritance tax is payable (see § 19–05); but the entry

---

46. s.58.
47. Defined, s.58(3).

charge is not avoided if the settlor or his spouse is merely an object of a discretionary trust with no qualifying interest in possession.

B. *The ten-year charge*

The amount charged

22–56   The principal charge on relevant property after the entry charge is a charge which is levied immediately before each ten-year anniversary on the value of relevant property then comprised in the settlement.[48] Where the trust fund comprises both relevant property and other property, tax is levied only on the relevant property and other property is taken into account in calculating the rate at which the relevant property is taxed. Business relief or agricultural relief (see § 19–39) may be available to reduce the amount on which inheritance tax is chargeable. For an example of the ten-year charge, see § 22–63.

"Ten-year anniversary" in relation to a settlement means the tenth anniversary of the date on which the settlement commenced and subsequent anniversaries at ten yearly intervals[49]; but no date falling before April 1, 1983, can be a ten-year anniversary.[50]

"The commencement of a settlement" is the time when property first becomes comprised in it.[51–52] Property which becomes comprised in a settlement in pursuance of a will or intestacy is taken to have become comprised in it on the death of the testator or intestate.

This is subject to a special rule which applies where there is an initial interest in favour of the settlor or his spouse. For example, if H settles property on W for life and, subject thereto, on discretionary trusts, no inheritance tax is payable on the creation of the settlement (see § 22–55); and accordingly the relevant property rules provide that the settlement shall be treated as made by W and as having commenced on W's death.[53]

The rate of charge

22–57/58   The rate at which inheritance tax is levied under the ten-year charge is 30 per cent. of the effective rate at which tax would be charged on a notional or "postulated" transfer, made immediately before the ten-year anniversary, by a notional transferor who has made certain transfers of value in the immediately preceding seven years.[54] The rationale for charging tax every ten years on events which are supposed to have occurred in the previous seven lies in the different functions of the two periods. The limited charge which is imposed every ten years approximates to the charge which would

---

48. s.64.
49. s.61(1).
50. s.61(3).
51–52. s.60.
53. s.80: and see s.61(2) which provides that ten-year anniversaries are calculated from the commencement of the real settlement. s.82: "excluded property" prevents abuse of these rules.
54. s.66(1).

ordinarily be imposed once every generation, on the death of an individual (assuming a generation to occur every 33 years). The seven year period is required because the deemed transfer is postulated to have been made by an individual transferor, whose cumulative total can only include gifts made in the previous seven years. As will be seen, however (see § 22–62), all transfers out of the discretionary trust which have been made in any of the ten years preceding the anniversary are deemed to have been made in the last seven—so that no loss of revenue is suffered by trustees making distributions in the three years next succeeding an anniversary. The tax is charged at lifetime rates so the highest possible levy is 30 per cent. of 30 per cent., which is 9 per cent. Two questions have to be answered to discover the effective rate: first, what is the amount of the postulated transfer of value (see § 22–59); secondly, what previous transfers of value must be assumed to have been made by the postulated transferor and during what seven-year period? (see § 22–62).

When the rate has been so determined it is applied to the value of the relevant property comprised in the settlement immediately before the ten-year anniversary (see § 22–56); but this is subject to an important exception. Where the relevant property in settlement immediately before the ten-year anniversary (i) was not relevant property throughout the period of ten years ending immediately before the ten-year anniversary or (ii) was not comprised in the settlement throughout that period, an adjustment has to be made because the ten-year charge "bites" only to the extent that conditions (i) and (ii) have been satisfied throughout the ten-year period. The adjustment is made by reducing the value attributable to the property which does not satisfy these conditions by $\frac{1}{40}$th for each of the successive quarters in the ten-year period which expired before the property became (or last became) relevant property comprised in the settlement.[55] "Quarter" means a period of three months.[56]

> Thus if relevant property in settlement at a ten-year anniversary and valued at £40,000 has been in settlement for only 8 quarters during the ten-year period its value is reduced by $\frac{32}{40}$ths to £8,000.

22–59   The postulated transfer is of an amount equal to the aggregate[57] of:

(a) the value of the relevant property comprised in the settlement *immediately before the ten-year anniversary,* irrespective for this purpose of the length of time during which it was relevant property comprised in the settlement, *i.e.* conditions (i) and (ii) in § 22–58 are ignored; and

(b) the value *immediately after the settlement commenced* of any part of the property then comprised in the settlement which was not then relevant property and has not subsequently become relevant property while remaining comprised in the settlement; and

---

55. s.66(2).
56. s.63.
57. s.66(3), (4).

(c) the value, immediately after a related settlement commenced, of the property then comprised in it.

22–60 Two settlements are *related settlements* if and only if the settlor is the same in each case and they commenced on the same day; except that two settlements are not related if all the property comprised in one or both of them was, immediately after the settlement commenced, held on perpetual charitable trusts (defined § 22–53).[58] A settlement of property on a temporary charitable trust (defined § 22–53) may be a related settlement. Note that settlements made by spouses on the same day are *not* related settlements.

22–61 As respects (b) and (c) in § 22–59, note that the amount of the postulated transfer and therefore the effective rate of tax will be greater if property which is not relevant property is mixed with relevant property in the same settlement or if other property (whether relevant property or not) is settled on the same day.

22–62 The postulated transfer of value is assumed[59] to be made immediately before the ten-year anniversary by a transferor who in the preceding seven years has made chargeable transfers of value equal to the aggregate of:

(a) the values transferred by any chargeable transfers made by the settlor in the period of seven years ending with the day on which the settlement commenced, disregarding transfers made on that day (*i.e.* the settlor's pre-settlement cumulative total); and
(b) the amounts on which any charges to tax were imposed under the proportionate charge (see § § 22–65 *et seq.*) in respect of the settlement in the *ten* years before the anniversary concerned.

Note from paragraph (a) that the settlor's pre-settlement cumulative total determines the effective rate of tax. It follows that an individual who proposes to make a number of transfers of value, including a settlement on discretionary trusts, should be advised to make the settlement *before* making other chargeable transfers.

Note from paragraph (b) that the deemed cumulative total of the last seven years of the notional transferor includes all amounts charged with the proportionate charge in any part of the ten years between anniversaries.

Example of a ten-year charge

22–63 Assume an individual already has a cumulative total of chargeable transfers amounting to £110,000. On May 1, 1986, he settles £60,000 on discretionary trusts. The entry charge to inheritance tax is:

---

58. s.62.
59. s.66(3), (5).

£19,000 @ 17.5%	=	£3,325
£35,000 @ 20%	=	£7,000
£6,000 @ 22.5%	=	£1,350

$$£11,675$$

Assume that during the ten years from May 1, 1986, to May 1, 1996, there are no distributions from the trust fund and that the value of the property held on discretionary trusts on May 1, 1996, is £125,000. The effective rate at which inheritance tax is charged is found by postulating a transfer of value on that day by a transferor who, in the preceding seven years, made chargeable transfers of £110,000.

Assume that the tax on a transfer of value of £125,000 made in 1996 by an individual with a cumulative total £110,000 is £24,000. The effective rate of inheritance tax is then:

$$\frac{24,000}{125,000} = 19.2\%$$

The tax payable on the ten-year anniversary is therefore—

$$30\% \text{ of } 19.2\% = 5.76\%$$
$$\text{of } £125,000 = £7,200.$$

Lifetime rates are applied on the ten-year anniversary.[60]

> *Note.* If, in the example, the discretionary settlement had been the first chargeable transfer made by the individual, the entry charge would be nil; and the ten-year charge would postulate a transferor making a first chargeable transfer equal to the value of the property in settlement on the ten-year anniversary.

Additions to settlements before the ten-year anniversary

22–64   There is a complex relieving provision which is designed to meet the case where transfers of value which increase the value of property comprised in a settlement are not intended to have that effect, *e.g.* where a family company whose shares are held on discretionary trusts gets into financial difficulties and, in order to keep the business going, cash is injected in order to pay off creditors. Such transfers can be disregarded in some cases.[61]

C. *The proportionate charge between ten-year anniversaries*

22–65   Since the principal charge on relevant property is the ten-year charge, it is necessary to have a "back-up" charge where the value of relevant property comprised in the settlement is reduced in advance of a ten-year anniversary by a deliberate act of the trustees, *e.g.* by appointments of capital to discretionary beneficiaries or transfers at an undervalue. Hence section 65 provides for a charge to tax:

> (a) where the property comprised in a settlement or any part of that property ceases to be relevant property (whether because it ceases to be comprised in the settlement or otherwise); and

---

60. s.66(3)(*c*).
61. s.67, and see the debates on the Finance Bill for 1982, Standing Committee A, col. 689.

(b) in a case in which paragraph (a) does not apply, where the trustees of the settlement make a disposition as a result of which the value of relevant property comprised in the settlement is less than it would be but for the disposition.

Paragraph (b) is treated as applying when shares in a close company are held on discretionary trusts and the company makes a transfer of value: see § 21–03.

For an example of the proportionate charge, see § 22–75.

22–66   Paragraph (a) will apply where relevant property is appointed out of settlement or an interest in possession is conferred in it. It will also apply to property which becomes sheltered property (see § 22–54) as by being appointed on accumulation and maintenance trusts, since such property is not relevant property (see § 22–54, paragraph (b)). Paragraph (b) catches what may loosely be described as "depreciatory transactions." Trustees are treated as making a disposition, *inter alia*, if they omit to exercise a right (unless it is shown that the omission was not deliberate); and the disposition is treated as made at the time or latest time when they could have exercised that right[62] (see § 18–04). "Disposition" includes a disposition effected by associated operations: see § 18–05.

A loan by trustees to a beneficiary may give rise to a tax charge under paragraph (b). To take extreme examples, an unsecured interest free loan which was not repayable on demand would depreciate the value of the settled property and so give rise to a charge: a secured loan on commercial terms would not do so. A lease of trust property on uncommercial terms, *e.g.* without normal rent review provisions, would likewise depreciate the value of the demised property.

Exceptions

22–67   The proportionate charge is not levied in the following cases:

1. If the event in question occurs in a quarter (*i.e.* during a period of three months) beginning with the day on which the settlement commenced or with a ten-year anniversary.[63]
2. Where trustees make (or incur a liability to make) a payment of costs or expenses, so far as they are fairly attributable to the relevant property.[64] The costs of a valuation may be included in this exception. It is thought that some difficulty may arise in practice in determining how attributions of costs and expenses should be made in some situations.
3. Where trustees make (or incur a liability to make) a payment which is (or will be) income of any person for any of the purposes of

---

62. s.65(9).
63. s.65(4).
64. s.65(5)(*a*). "Payment" includes a transfer of assets: s.63.

income tax or would for any of those purposes be income of a person not resident in the United Kingdom if he were so resident.[65] This is important: payments which are treated as income of the appointee (or which are treated as income of the settlor under one of the provisions discussed in Chapter 10) do not attract the proportionate charge to inheritance tax, even if they are payments out of capital.

4. Although dispositions at an undervalue are liable to inheritance tax under paragraph (b) in § 22–65, tax is not chargeable if the disposition is such that, if the trustees were beneficially entitled to the settled property, section 10 (dispositions not intended to confer gratuitous benefits) or section 16 (grant of tenancies of agricultural property) would prevent the disposition from being a transfer of value.[66]

5. Where the settlor was not domiciled in the United Kingdom when the settlement was made and settled property ceases to be situated in the United Kingdom and thereby becomes excluded property.[67]

6. Where the property ceases to be relevant property on becoming held on perpetual (but not temporary) charitable trusts.[68]

The amount charged

22–68   It will be recalled that in the case of individuals inheritance tax is levied by reference to the diminution in the value of the transferor's estate which results from the transfer of value: see § 18–03. The same principle is applied to the proportionate charge. Hence the general rule is that the amount on which tax is charged under section 65 is the amount by which the value of the relevant property comprised in the settlement immediately after the event in question is less than it would be but for the event.[69]

> Thus if trustees with a majority holding of shares in a private company make an appointment which deprives them of control, the amount of the proportionate charge to inheritance tax is not related to the value of the appointed shares but to the reduction in value of the trustees' holding of shares.

This is subject to the qualification that, if the tax is paid by the trustees out of the relevant property, grossing up is necessary; and inheritance tax is paid on the amount which, after deducting the tax, equals the amount on which tax would be chargeable if it had not been so paid (*i.e.* the diminution in the value of the settled property).[70]

Business relief or agricultural relief (see § 19–39 *et seq.*) may be available to reduce the amount on which inheritance tax is chargeable; and such relief is applied before grossing up.

---

65. s.65(5)(*b*).
66. s.65(6). And see §§ 18–10 and 18–04A.
67. s.65(7).
68. s.76.
69. s.65(2)(*a*).
70. s.65(2)(*b*).

The rate of charge

22–69   The rate of the proportionate charge to inheritance tax depends on whether the occasion of charge arises before the first ten-year anniversary or in between ten-year anniversaries. Each is considered separately.

(1) *Rate before first ten-year anniversary*[71]

22–70   The rate of charge preceding the first ten-year anniversary after the commencement of the settlement is the *appropriate fraction* of the *effective rate* at which tax would be charged on the value transferred by a postulated transfer made at the time of the appointment or transfer at an under-value.[72] The effective rate is found by postulating both a transfer (see § 22–73) and a transferor (see § 22–74).

22–71   The *appropriate fraction* is three-tenths of as many 40ths as there are complete successive quarters (*i.e.* periods of three months) in the period beginning with the day on which the settlement commenced and ending with the day before the occasion of charge.[73]

> Thus if a settlement of exclusively relevant property commences on January 1, 1982, and an appointment out of that property is made after 18 complete quarters, the appropriate fraction is $\frac{3}{10} \times \frac{18}{40}$ths of the amount. This fraction is then applied to the effective rate: see § 22–75.

22–72   An adjustment has to be made where the property coming out of settlement was not relevant property throughout the period referred to.[74]

> Thus if in the previous example eight quarters expired before the appointed property became relevant property, the appropriate fraction is $\frac{3}{10} \times \frac{10}{40}$ths.

22–73   The postulated transfer is one the value transferred by which is equal to the value, *immediately after the commencement of the settlement,* of the property then comprised in the settlement and of property then comprised in any related settlement (defined in § 22–60). This is the initial value: see § 22–53. Additions to the settlement are valued immediately after they become so comprised therein.[75]

> Note that the key factor in the equation is the value of all the property in the settlement (not only relevant property) at the start of the settlement—what may be called "the initial value."

22–74   The postulated transfer is assumed to be made by a transferor who in the seven years ending with the occasion of charge has made chargeable transfers with an aggregate value equal to the settlor's pre-settlement cumulative total.[76]

As with the ten-year charge, inheritance tax is levied at lifetime rates.[77]

---

71. s.68.
72. s.68(1).
73. s.68(2).
74. s.68(3).
75. s.68(4)(*a*), (5).
76. s.68(4)(*b*).
77. s.68(4)(*c*).

Example of the proportionate charge

22–75   Refer to the example in § 22–63. Assume that on May 15, 1987, the trustees appoint part of the trust capital to X. The appointment diminishes the value of the trust fund by £20,000, which is therefore the amount by reference to which inheritance tax is charged: see § 22–68. Four complete quarters have elapsed since the settlement commenced, so the appropriate fraction (see § 22–71) is:

$$3/10 \times 4/40 = 3/100.$$

The effective rate of inheritance tax on the £20,000 is found by postulating a transfer of value of £60,000 by a transferor who has made chargeable transfers of £110,000 in the seven years immediately preceding May 15, 1987: see § §22–73 and 22–74. Assume the tax on £60,000 at lifetime rates is £11,250, when the effective rate will be $\dfrac{11,250}{60,000} = 18.75\%$

The inheritance tax payable on the appointment is:

$$£20,000 \times \frac{3}{100} \times 18.75\% = \quad £112.50$$

(2) *Rate between ten-year anniversaries*[78]

22–76   The rate at which inheritance tax is charged in between ten-year anniversaries is the appropriate fraction of the rate at which it was charged on the last ten-year anniversary.[79]

The appropriate fraction is so many 40ths as there are complete successive quarters in the period beginning with the most recent ten-year anniversary and ending with the day before the occasion of charge.[80]

Adjustments (not summarised here) have to be made if there have been additions to the settlement on or after the last ten-year anniversary or if non-relevant property has become relevant property.[81]

II. The relevant property rules: pre-CTT settlements

22–77   The expression "pre-CTT tax settlement" is used in this book (but not in the legislation) to describe settlements which commenced before March 27, 1974, *i.e.* before either CTT or inheritance tax was levied on transfers of value: see § 18–02. The relevant property rules which came into effect as respects events after March 8, 1982, contain special provisions to deal with pre-CTT settlements. The relevant property rules outlined above apply to pre-CTT settlements subject to the following points.

---

78. s.69.
79. s.69(1).
80. s.69(4).
81. s.69(2), (3).

A. *The entry charge*

22–78   There will have been neither CTT nor inheritance tax in the creation of a pre-CTT settlement but later additions may give rise to an inheritance tax liability.

B. *The ten-year charge*

22–79   The inheritance tax position is as in § § 22–56 *et seq.* but note the following:

1. No date falling before April 1, 1983, can be a ten-year anniversary.[82] Thus the first ten-year charge for a settlement which commenced in 1962 or in 1972 will fall in 1992.

2. The notional transfer is of an amount equal to the value of the relevant property comprised in the settlement immediately before the ten-year anniversary, irrespective of the length of time during which it was relevant property.[83] Paragraphs (b) and (c) in § 22–59 do not apply.

3. The postulated transfer is not as stated in § 22–62 because paragraph (a), which has regard to the *settlor's* pre-settlement cumulative total does not apply. The postulated transfer is one made by the *trustees* and only (i) earlier "distribution payments" under the pre-1982 law and (ii) payments giving rise to the proportionate charge are taken into account (and only (ii) in the second or subsequent ten-year anniversary).[84]

22–80   *Example*

Assume a settlor created a settlement with £50,000 on April 30, 1972: the first ten-year anniversary would be April 20, 1992, at which time, say, the trust fund is worth £125,000. The effective rate at which inheritance tax would be charged on that amount would be calculated as if this were the first chargeable transfer made by the trustees (assuming no earlier distributions out of the settlement had been made).

C. *The proportionate charge*

22–81   1. The proportionate charge under section 65 is levied on the whole of the amount by which the value of the relevant property comprised in the settlement is diminished, as in the case of post-Estate Duty settlements: see § 22–68.

2. The rate of charge on events preceding the first ten-year anniversary is 30 per cent. of the effective rate.

3. The postulated transfer is not calculated by reference to the "initial value" of the settlement as in the case of post-Estate Duty settlements (see § 22–73) but by reference to the amount in paragraph 1, above.[85–86]

---

82. s.61(3).
83. s.66(6).
84. s.66(6).
85–86. s.68(6)(*a*).

4. The postulated transferor is not someone in the position of the settlor: hence the settlor's pre-settlement cumulative total is not relevant. The postulated transferor is one who in the seven years preceding the event has made chargeable transfers equal to the aggregate of:

(i) any amounts on which tax has been charged under section 65 (the proportionate charge) in respect of the settlement in the period of ten years ending with the day of the event, and

(ii) the amounts of any distribution payments made after March 26, 1974 but before March 9, 1982 and within the said period of ten years.[87]

22–82/83　　*Example*

Assume a discretionary settlement made in 1972 with a first distribution of capital in January 1987. The appointment diminishes the value of the trust fund by £85,000 which is, therefore, the amount by reference to which inheritance tax is charged: see § 22–68.

The effective rate of tax on the £85,000 is found by postulating a transfer of value of £85,000 (see § 22–81, para. 3) by a transferor whose only previous chargeable transfers are distributions out of the settlement (see § 22–81, para. 4).

Assume that the tax on a transfer of £85,000 is £3,000.

The effective rate is then: $\dfrac{3,000}{85,000} = 3.53\%$ and the charge on the distribution is

$30\% \times 3.53\% \times £85,000 = \quad \underline{\underline{£900}}$

5. ACCUMULATION AND MAINTENANCE SETTLEMENTS

22–84　The form of settlement considered in the section of the book that follows is often the most satisfactory and the most tax-efficient means whereby an individual can provide capital for beneficiaries who are his (or someone else's) children or remoter issue and at the same time give trustees power to either accumulate the income or to apply it for the maintenance, education or benefit of those beneficiaries. The income tax aspects of such settlements are referred to in § 37–14 and elsewhere in this book.

The disposition by which such a settlement is created may attract a liability to inheritance tax—the "entry charge" discussed in § 22–04—though that transfer, if made by an individual during his lifetime, will be potentially exempt: see § 19–30A—but such settlements enjoy substantial inheritance tax advantages thereafter, provided they satisfy the conditions for "accumulation and maintenance settlements" which are set out in section 71. Most of the problems that arise in satisfying these conditions arise in determining the extent to which trustees can be given a discretion as to the ultimate destiny of the income and/or capital. Great care has to be taken in drafting such settlements in regard to such matters as the period of accumulation, powers to vary the shares of prospective beneficiaries and

---

87. s.68(6)(*b*).

the application of the "class closing rules" *i.e.* determining the time at which eligibility for membership of a class of prospective beneficiaries closes. There are many pitfalls and it is wise to seek expert advice and often exceedingly unwise to rely on so-called "standard forms."

22–85   Section 71 applies to settled property if:

(a) one or more persons (referred to as "beneficiaries") will, on or before attaining a specified age not exceeding 25, become beneficially entitled to it, or to an interest in possession in it; and

(b) no interest in possession subsists in it and the income from it is to be accumulated so far as not applied for the maintenance, education or benefit of a beneficiary; and

(c) either:

(i) not more than 25 years have elapsed since the commencement of the settlement or, if it was later, since the time (or latest time) when the conditions stated in paragraphs (a) and (b) above became satisfied with respect to the property; or

(ii) all the persons who are or have been beneficiaries are or were either grandchildren of a common grandparent, or children, widows, or widowers of such grandchildren who were themselves beneficiaries but died before the time when, had they survived, they would have become entitled as mentioned in paragraph (a) above.

The effect of condition (c)(i) is to impose a time limit during which tax relief is available in the case of accumulation and maintenance settlements where the class of beneficiaries is not limited as in (ii). Condition (c) does *not* limit the duration of such settlements to 25 years: see § 22–88. Note that "beneficiaries" is defined by paragraph (a).

22–86   Settled property to which the conditions in § 22–85 apply is not relevant property (see § 22–54(b)); but the occasion of transforming relevant property into property held on accumulation and maintenance trusts is an occasion of charge to inheritance tax: see § 22–65. In applying the conditions "persons" includes unborn persons; but the conditions are treated as not satisfied unless there is *or has been* a living beneficiary.[88] A person's children include his illegitimate children, his adopted children and his stepchildren.[89] Hence if property is settled on the occasion of H's marriage for the children of H who attain the age of 25, and H then has no children, the conditions will not be treated as satisfied until a child is born: until then the property will be relevant property and the birth will be an occasion of charge to inheritance tax, since the property will then cease to be relevant property.

88. s.71(7).
89. s.71(8).

22–87   Where conditions (a) and (b) are satisfied at any time when there is only one beneficiary, they are not treated as ceasing to be satisfied on his death or on his attaining the specified age, if they would again be satisfied on the birth of another person. This explains the italicised words "or has been" in the above provision relating to unborn persons.

> Thus if property is settled upon trust for the children of X who attain the age of 25 and X has one child who dies before attaining that age, the conditions will be treated as continuing to be satisfied so long as X may have further children.

22–88   It is not necessary that the age for vesting of *capital* should be 25 or less because condition (a) is satisfied, whatever the age for vesting of capital, provided the beneficiaries will, on or before attaining a specified age not exceeding 25, become entitled to an interest in possession in the settled property, including a vested interest in *income*: see § 22–14. In settlements to which section 31 of the Trustee Act 1925 (as amended by the Family Law Reform Act 1969) applies, beneficiaries will acquire a vested interest in income on attaining the age of 18.[90]

22–89   Condition (a) is not satisfied unless it is certain that the beneficiaries will take a vested interest if the contingency is fulfilled. If, therefore, the trusts of the settlement contain provisions (whether express or incorporated by statute) which can defeat the beneficiary's contingent entitlement, section 71 will not apply. Hence, the existence of an overriding power of revocation and reappointment to persons who may not acquire interests in possession on or before attaining 25 will prevent condition (a) being satisfied.[91] In this regard, though, it should be noted that the presence of a power of advancement in form similar to that contained in section 32 of the Trustee Act 1925 (or its usual extension) will not negate the application of section 71.[91]

> Thus if property is settled on the occasion of H's marriage for the children of H contingently on attaining 25, a power conferred on the trustees to appoint *capital* to H's sister will offend condition (a), whereas a power to apply *income* for the benefit of H's sister will offend condition (b) in § 22–85.

22–90   Where there is a trust for accumulation and maintenance of a class of persons who become entitled to the property (or to an interest in possession in it) at a specified age not exceeding 25, condition (a) will not be offended by the existence of a power to vary or determine the respective shares of members of the class (even to the extent of excluding some members altogether) provided the power is exercisable only in favour of a person under 25 who is a member of the class.[92]

---

90. When the 1969 Act does not apply, vesting is postponed to the age of 21 years—and so s.71 will still apply. The 1969 does not apply to an interest under an instrument made before January 1, 1970: see Sched. 3, para. 5(1) to the Family Law Reform Act 1969. But the Act does apply to an interest made on or after that date even if the principal instrument was made before that date: see *Re Dickinson's Settlement* [1939] Ch. 27 and Statement of Practice E8 in Dymond, Vol. 2, p. 1281.

91. See *Lord Inglewood* v. *I.R.C.* [1983] S.T.C. 133.

92. Inland Revenue Press Release of September 2, 1977: [1977] S.T.I. 262.

22–91   The removal of an offending condition, *e.g.* by release of the power, will cause relevant property to cease to be such and will be an occasion of charge to inheritance tax.[92a]

22–92   By concession, the Board treat condition (a) as satisfied even if no age is specified in the trust instrument, if it is clear that a beneficiary will in fact become entitled to the settled property (or to an interest in possession in it) by the age of 25.[93] The concession will apply if, *e.g.*, the trust instrument provides for vesting in beneficiaries at the expiry of 21 years from the commencement of the settlement, if in fact the oldest beneficiary was aged three when the settlement was made.

Tax advantages

22–93   Where the conditions in § 22–85 are satisfied section 71(4) provides that inheritance tax shall not be charged under the section:

> (a) on a beneficiary's becoming beneficially entitled to, or to an interest in possession in, settled property on or before attaining the specified age; or
>
> (b) on the death of a beneficiary before attaining the specified age.

Hence when property is settled on accumulation and maintenance trusts satisfying the necessary conditions from the start, there is no ten-year charge to inheritance tax (because the property is not relevant property) and no proportionate charge if the property ceases to be settled property on the beneficiary becoming beneficially entitled at the specified age or dying before attaining that age.

When a charge will arise

22–94   A charge to tax under section 71 will arise:

> (a) where settled property ceases to be property held on accumulation and maintenance trusts; and
>
> (b) in a case where (a) does not apply, where the trustees make a disposition as a result of which the value of settled property held on such trusts is less than it would be but for the disposition.[94]

22–95   As regards (b), trustees are treated as making a disposition if they omit to exercise a right (unless it is shown that the omission was not deliberate) and the disposition is treated as made at the time or latest time when they could have exercised the right.[95]

Tax is not, however, to be charged under (b), if the disposition is such that, were trustees beneficially entitled to the property, section 10 (dispositions not intended to confer gratuitous benefit[96]: see § 18–11) or sec-

---

92a. As in *Lord Inglewood* v. *I.R.C.* [1983] S.T.C. 133.
93. See *White* v. *Whitcher* [1928] 1 K.B. 453; 14 T.C. 202.
94. s.71(3).
95. s.70(10), as applied by s.71(5).
96. s.70(4), as applied by s.71(5).

tion 16 (grant of tenancies of agricultural property: see § 18–04A) would prevent the disposition from being a transfer of value.

> Paragraph (a) will apply if, for example, property is settled on trust for all the children of A who shall attain the age of 25 and, subject thereto, to X absolutely, if X becomes entitled on failure of the accumulation and maintenance trusts.

22–96   Tax is not, however, charged in the circumstances set out in § 22–93 above or in respect of:

(a) a payment of costs or expenses (so far as they are fairly attributable to property to which the section applies), or

(b) a payment which is (or will be) income of any person for any of the purposes of income tax or would for any of those purposes be income of a person not resident in the United Kingdom if he were so resident,

or in respect of a liability to make such a payment.[97]

The measure of the tax charge

22–97   Where a tax charge arises under section 71, it is charged on the amount by which the value of property which is comprised in the settlement and to which the section applies is less immediately after the event giving rise to the charge than it would be but for the event.

Where, as in the above example, all the property formerly held on accumulation and maintenance trusts ceases to be so held, the charge will be on the value of the property comprised in the settlement.

There is no ten-year charge in the case of sheltered property.

22–98   The rate of charge is 0·25 per cent. for each of the first 40 complete successive quarters[97a] in the "relevant period," which is defined to mean the period beginning with the later of:

(a) the day on which the property in respect of which tax is chargeable became (or last became) property to which the section applies, and

(b) March 13, 1975.[98]

> Thus if in the case of a settlement made after March 13, 1975, the property has been held on accumulation and maintenance trusts for 20 successive quarters (*i.e.* periods of three months) before it ceases to be held on such trusts, the rate of charge is 5 per cent. The increase in the rate of charge diminishes after the first 40 quarters.[98a]

---

97. s.70(3).
97a. s.70(6).
98. s.70(8).
98a. *i.e.* although the *aggregate* rate of charge will continue to rise, it rises at a diminishing rate.

6. Other Sheltered Property

Charitable trusts

22–99   Transfers of value to exclusively charitable trusts are generally exempt from inheritance tax: see § 19–20. The relevant property rules do not apply to property held on charitable trusts even if the charitable trust is a temporary charitable trust[99] (defined § 22–53). For the purpose of these rules, where the trusts on which settled property is held require part of the income to be applied for charitable purposes, a corresponding part of the settled property is regarded as held for charitable purposes.[1]

But if property held for a temporary charitable purpose ceases to be so held or is the subject of a depreciatory transaction (otherwise than, for example, by an application for charitable purposes), a charge to tax arises under section 70.[2] This type of charge has been considered in connection with accumulation and maintenance settlements: see §§ 22–94 to 22–98.

Protective trusts

22–100   Generally speaking, a person who is a principal beneficiary under protective trusts to the like effect to those specified in section 33(1) of the Trustee Act 1925, will be considered to have an interest in possession.[3] The failure or determination[3a] of those trusts before the end of the trust period (which, for general trust purposes, will create or bring into effect discretionary trusts and, thus, prima facie, the "relevant property rules" for inheritance tax) will, however, be disregarded as far as inheritance tax is concerned[4] and the principal beneficiary will continue to be treated as beneficially entitled to an interest in possession.[5] There will, therefore, be no charge to tax under section 52 (see §§ 22–22 *et seq.*) on the failure or determination of the trusts, but distributions to other persons will give rise to a charge under that section.

These rules only apply to settlements where the interest failed or determined after April 11, 1978.[6] Trusts where such events occurred prior to that date are treated as partially sheltered trusts with charges to inheritance tax arising under the relevant property rules whenever a depreciatory transaction takes place or a distribution is made to someone other than the principal beneficiary.[7] In such a case the rules considered in relation to accumulation and maintenance trusts will apply: see §§ 22–94 *et seq.*

---

99. s.58(1)(*a*).
1. s.84.
2. s.70(2).
3. s.88.
3a. For the meaning of "failure or determination" see *Cholmondeley* v. *I.R.C.* [1986] S.T.C. 384.
4. s.88(2)(*a*).
5. s.88(2)(*b*).
6. s.73(1).
7. s.73(2).

7. THE PURCHASE OF A REVERSIONARY INTEREST

22–101 The estate of a person is the aggregate of all the property to which he is beneficially entitled other than excluded property. A reversionary interest acquired by purchase is not excluded property: see § 23–03. Nevertheless, section 55(1) provides that where a person entitled to an interest (whether in possession or not) in any settled property acquires a reversionary interest expectant (whether immediately or not) on that interest, the reversionary interest is not part of his estate. This is complementary to section 55(2) which provides that section 10(1) (see § 18–12) is not to apply to a disposition by which a reversionary interest is acquired on arm's length terms. The explanation for these somewhat obscure provisions is as follows.

22–102 Suppose property is settled on A for life with remainder to B absolutely. A has £50,000 of free estate and the settled property is worth £100,000. B's reversionary interest has a market value of £40,000. The aggregate value of A's estate for inheritance tax purposes is £150,000. If A purchases B's interest for £40,000, the value of A's estate would appear to be reduced to £110,000, *i.e.* £10,000 of free estate plus £100,000 of formerly settled property. The above provisions prevent tax being avoided in this way. First, section 55(2) causes A's payment of £40,000 to be treated as a chargeable transfer,[8] even though for full value: see § 18–12. Secondly, section 55(1) treats the reversionary interest as not part of A's estate. Thus A is treated as having an estate worth £100,000 plus £10,000 and as having made a chargeable transfer of £40,000.

There are numerous anti-avoidance provisions which apply to reversionary interests.[9]

---

8. Nor does such a transfer attract relief as a PET: see s.55(2), which precludes the application of s.3A in this case.

9. See, for example, ss.53(5), 54(3), 56(1), and 48(1), (2). See also [1981] B.T.R. 166 *et seq*.

CHAPTER 23

EXCLUDED PROPERTY

23–01 WE have seen that a transfer of value is defined as any disposition which diminishes the value of a person's estate but that no account is to be taken of the value of excluded property which ceases to form part of the estate: see § 18–13A. And although on the death of a person inheritance tax is charged as if, immediately before his death, he had made a transfer of value equal to the value of his estate immediately before his death, it is expressly provided that the estate of a person immediately before his death does not include excluded property: see § 18–08. Thus the value of excluded property is left out of account on all transfers of value, whether lifetime transfers or transfers on death. The question whether property escapes taxation as "excluded property" depends on whether it answers that description in the hands of the transferor (or the deceased), not whether it will answer that description in the hands of the transferee (or the beneficiary).[1]

1. MEANING OF EXCLUDED PROPERTY

23–02 (1) Subject to § 23–06, property situated outside the United Kingdom is excluded property if the person beneficially entitled to it is an individual domiciled outside the United Kingdom.[2] Thus an individual domiciled outside the United Kingdom will avoid inheritance tax by investing in assets situated outside the United Kingdom; and an individual who is about to acquire a domicile in the United Kingdom should consider making, *e.g.* settlements of assets before he does so.

23–03 (2) Subject to § 23–06, a reversionary interest (as defined) is excluded property unless (a) it has at any time been acquired (whether by the person entitled to it or by a person previously entitled to it) for a consideration in money or money's worth; or (b) it is one to which either the settlor or his spouse is or has been beneficially entitled[3]; or (c) is an interest expectant on the determination of a lease treated as a settlement by virtue of the provisions discussed in § 22–09.[4]

> Thus if property is settled on A for life with remainder to B absolutely, no inheritance tax is payable on a disposition by B of his reversionary interest before it falls into possession, unless B acquired his interest by purchase or by way of succession from a purchaser or is A's spouse.

---

1. *Von Ernst & Cie* v. *I.R.C.* [1980] S.T.C. 115.
2. s.6(1).
3. s.48(1): but exception (b) does not apply to a settlement created before April 16, 1976. The words "or has been" in exception (b) were inserted by F.A. 1981 and only have effect in respect of interests acquired after March 10, 1981.
4. s.48(1)(c). Exception (c) is required because the value in the lease is divided between lessee and reversioner, rather than completely being attributed to the estate of one of them: see §§ 20–20 and 22–21.

23–04   The rationale of excluding the reversionary interest is that inheritance tax will eventually be payable when the life interest comes to an end so the (then) reversioner will suffer the tax indirectly. The rationale of *not* excluding the reversionary interest acquired by purchase is that, without this exclusion, an individual could avoid tax by purchasing a reversionary interest for its market value (thereby reducing the value of his estate by the purchase price) and making a gift or settlement of the interest so purchased. The special provisions applicable to the purchase of reversionary interests by life tenants, etc. are considered in § 22–75.

23–05   A "reversionary interest" means a future interest under a settlement, whether it is vested or contingent (including an interest expectant on the termination of an interest in possession which, by virtue of section 50, is treated as subsisting in part only of any property).[5] It thus includes a future interest in remainder as well as a future interest in reversion. It also includes an interest which is expectant on the determination of a lease for life or lives treated as a settlement: see § 22–09.

23–06   (3) Section 48(3) provides that where property comprised in a settlement is situated outside the United Kingdom, the property (but not a reversionary interest in the property) is excluded property unless the settlor was domiciled in the United Kingdom at the time when the settlement was made. Thus if the settlor was domiciled outside the United Kingdom when the settlement was made, the property may be excluded property irrespective of the domicile of the beneficiary. The rule in § 23–02 is thus ousted except in the case of a reversionary interest, which is excluded property only if the beneficiary is an individual domiciled outside the United Kingdom.[6]

23–07   (4) Government securities in the beneficial ownership of persons neither domiciled nor ordinarily resident in the United Kingdom are excluded property: see § 19–26.

23–08   (5) Certain savings by persons domiciled in the Channel Islands or the Isle of Man are excluded property: see § 19–28.

There are special provisions to prevent an abuse of the "excluded property rules" by trustees of discretionary settlements.[6a]

2. The Situation of Property

23–09   Under English law all property, whether corporeal or incorporeal, has to be treated as situated somewhere. The following table shows briefly the main rules of English law for determining the situation of the assets mentioned; but where a Double Taxation Convention applies, reference must be made to the text of the Convention to see if there are different rules.

---

5. s.47.
6. s.48(3)(*b*).
6a. s.82.

Nature of property	*Where situate*
Land (including land subject to a mortgage) and other tangible assets.	Where the land or other asset is physically situated.
Debts.	
Simple contract debts.	Where the debtor resides.[7]
Specialty debts.	Where the specialty is situated.
Judgment debts.	Where the judgment is recorded.
Mortgages of land.	
If there is a personal obligation to repay the mortgage debt.	Same as for other debts (above).
If there is no such obligation but only a charge on the land.	Where the land is situate.
Securities.	
Bearer securities.	Where the document of title is situate.
Registered or inscribed securities.	Where the register is required to be kept.[8]
Bank balances.	Where the branch at which the debt is payable is situated.
Business assets, including a share in a partnership business and goodwill attached to a business.	Where the business is carried on.
Yacht situated in Great Britain but registered in Jersey.	Great Britain.[9]

Foreign Currency Accounts

23–09A   As respects deaths after March 8, 1982, a foreign currency account with a recognised bank in the United Kingdom is exempt from inheritance tax on death when the depositor was not domiciled in the United Kingdom immediately before his death, and was neither resident nor ordinarily resident there at that time. There is a corresponding exemption for deposits in the name of trustees for a beneficiary with a life interest.[10]

3. Extended Meaning of Domicile

23–10   The general meaning of the word "domicile" in English law is discussed in textbooks on private international law, to which reference should be made. For inheritance tax purposes, however, a person who would not otherwise be regarded as domiciled in the United Kingdom at any time (called "the relevant time") is to be treated[11] as domiciled in the United Kingdom at the relevant time if:

---

7. See *New York Life Insurance Co.* v. *Public Trustee* [1924] 2 Ch. 101, especially the judgment of Atkin L.J.; *English, Scottish & Australian Bank* v. *I.R.C.* [1932] A.C. 238 (H.L.).
8. See *Standard Chartered Bank Ltd.* v. *I.R.C.* [1978] 1 W.L.R. 1160; [1978] S.T.C. 272 (a case on duplicate registers: test is where in the ordinary course of affairs the owner would have dealt with the shares).
9. *Trustees Executors & Agency Co. Ltd.* v. *I.R.C.* [1973] Ch. 254; [1973] S.T.C. 96.
10. s.157.
11. s.267.

(a) he was domiciled in the United Kingdom within the three years immediately preceding the relevant time, *i.e.* three years' domicile outside the United Kingdom is needed to acquire a foreign domicile; or

(b) he was resident in the United Kingdom in not less than 17 of the 20 years of assessment ending with the year of assessment in which the relevant time falls.

23–11/12   For the purposes of (b), the question whether a person was resident in the United Kingdom in any year of assessment is to be determined as for the purposes of income tax (see §§ 7–17 *et seq.*), but without regard to any dwelling house available in the United Kingdom for his use: see § 7–19.[12]

23–13   The word "domicile" is normally construed in the legislation in this extended sense.[13] There is, however, an important exception which applies to exempt government securities: see § 19–26. Thus if a tax exile to whom section 267 applies makes a transfer of value of exempt government securities, the question whether this is a transfer of "excluded property" (see § 23–02) has to be answered by applying the ordinary tests applicable to domicile.

4. UNILATERAL RELIEF

23–14   When the same transfer of value attracts inheritance tax in the United Kingdom and a similar tax in a foreign country, relief may be available under treaties between the two countries but, where it is not, unilateral relief may be available. Where the relief is given, a credit is allowed for the foreign tax against the inheritance tax.[14]

---

12. s.267(4).
13. s.267(2).
14. See s.159 for details.

CHAPTER 24

LIABILITY AND INCIDENCE

WHERE a transfer of value is made or a charge arises in respect of "relevant property," there is a duty to deliver an account to the Board. The obligations with respect to the delivery of an account are discussed in §§ 25–02 *et seq.* The first section of this chapter shows who is liable to the Board for the tax found to be due and it will be seen that the person or persons so liable may not be the same person or persons as are liable to *deliver* an account. Thus in the case of a lifetime transfer, the transferor is the person required to deliver an account whereas the Board can recover the tax either from the transferor or the transferee or, in the case of transfer into settlement, from the settlor or the trustees or a beneficiary in respect of capital or income. When the tax has been paid to the Revenue the question next arises: who has to bear the tax? In the case of a chargeable transfer on death, for example, does the tax attributable to an item of property comprised in the deceased person's estate fall on the residuary fund or on a specific legatee or devisee of that property? This is discussed in the second section of this chapter.

1. LIABILITY

The persons liable to account to the Board for inheritance tax on the value transferred by a chargeable transfer are as follows; and where two or more persons are liable for the same tax, each is liable for the whole of it.[1] The basic rules in §§ 24–01 to 24–07 have to be read subject to qualifications in the paragraphs that follow.

(1) *Lifetime transfers*

24–01 Where the chargeable transfer is made by a disposition (including an omission treated as a disposition: see § 18–04) of the transferor, the persons liable are:

(a) the transferor and the transferee, *i.e.* any person the value of whose estate is increased by the transfer[2]; and

(b) so far as the tax is attributable to the value of any property, any person in whom the property is vested[3] (whether beneficially or other-

---

1. s.205.
2. s.199(1).
3. This includes any person who takes possession of, or intermeddles with, or otherwise acts in relation to, property so as to become liable as executor or trustee, and any person to whom the management of property is entrusted on behalf of a person not of full legal capacity: s.199(4). And see *I.R.C.* v. *Stype Investments (Jersey) Ltd.* [1982] S.T.C. 625: if A, an individual, appoints a foreign resident, B, to receive monies about to arise to A in England and A dies before the monies are payable and B procures payment of those monies to itself in such manner that the monies are submitted to another jurisdiction, so that B is unable to pay and account for the monies to the English personal representatives when finally constituted, B has intermeddled with the estate and constituted himself an executor de son tort, liable to pay inheritance tax in England: see *I.R.C.* v. *Stannard* [1984] S.T.C. 245.

wise) at any time after the transfer or who at any such time is beneficially entitled to an interest in possession in the property; and

(c) where by the chargeable transfer any property becomes comprised
in a settlement, any person for whose benefit any of the property or
income from it is applied.[4]

Note that the transferor is liable to account to the Board under (a) even
if, as between himself and the transferee, the latter has agreed to bear the
tax: and see § 20–15. Note that, in the case of a transfer into settlement,
the trustees are liable under (b).

24–02   Where a chargeable transfer is made within seven years of the transfer-
or's death, so that tax (in the case of PET) or extra tax becomes payable by
reason of his failure to survive the seven year period (see § 20–05), the
transferee is primarily liable for the tax (or extra tax): a secondary responsibility rests with the deceased's personal representatives.[5]

(2) *Transfers of settled property*

24–03   Where the chargeable transfer is one made under the settled property
rules (see Chap. 22) the persons liable are:

(a) the trustees of the settlement; and
(b) any person entitled (whether beneficially or not) to an interest in
possession in the settled property; and
(c) any person for whose benefit any of the settled property or income
from it is applied at or after the time of the transfer; and
(d) where the chargeable transfer is made during the life of the settlor
and the trustees are not for the time being resident in the United
Kingdom, the settlor.[6]

Trustees of a settlement are regarded as not resident in the United Kingdom unless the general administration of the settlement is ordinarily carried on in the United Kingdom *and* the trustees or a majority of them (and,
where there is more than one class of trustees, a majority of each class) are
for the time being resident in the United Kingdom.[7]

24–04   Where the chargeable transfer is made within seven years of the transfer-
or's death and extra tax becomes payable by reason of his failure to survive
the seven-year period, the settlor is not liable for the extra tax.[8] The persons listed in paragraphs (a)–(c) in § 24–03 are liable.

Thus if S settles property on A for life with remainder to B absolutely and A
assigns his interest to B and dies within seven years thereafter, S is not liable

---

4. s.199(1).
5. s.199(1), (2); s.204(6), (7) and (8).
6. s.201(1). The trustees are primarily liable: see § 24–14 and s.204(6)(*b*). Para. (*d*) does
not apply in relation to a settlement made before December 11, 1974 if the trustees were resident in the U.K. when the settlement was made and have not been so resident at any time
between that date and the time of the transfer: s.201(3).
7. s.201(5).
8. s.201(2).

for the extra tax. (In the example A is the assumed transferor by virtue of section 3(4): see § 22–22.) The trustees are primarily liable.

(3) *Transfers on death*

24–05   Where the chargeable transfer is made on the death of any person, under section 200, the persons liable are:

(a) the deceased's personal representatives (as defined)[9] as respects unsettled property and as respects settled United Kingdom land devolving on them as personal representatives[10];

(b) as respects other settled property, the trustees of the settlement;

(c) so far as the tax is attributable to the value of any property, any person in whom the property is vested[11] (whether beneficially or otherwise) at any time after the death or who at any such time is beneficially entitled to an interest in possession in the property;

(d) so far as the tax is attributable to the value of any property which, immediately before the death, was settled property, any person for whose benefit any of the property or income from it is applied after the death.[12]

For the purposes of these provisions, a person entitled to part only of the income of any property is deemed to be entitled to an interest in the whole of the property.[13]

(4) *Inter-spouse transfers*

24–06   Where a transferor is liable for any tax and, by another transfer of value made by him on or after March 27, 1974, any property became the property of a person who at the time of both transfers was his spouse, that person is liable for so much of the tax as does not exceed the market value of the property at the time of the spouse transfer.[14] This prevents a person escaping liability to pay inheritance tax on a chargeable transfer to one person by thereafter making an exempt transfer of the fund out of which tax on the first transfer would be payable to his (the transferor's) spouse.

> Thus if H gives property to his son (S) who is domiciled outside the United Kingdom and the rest of his property to his (H's) wife, W, and the tax cannot be recovered from H or S, the Revenue can seek recovery from W.

"Property"

24–07   References in the above paragraphs to "property" include references to any property directly or indirectly representing it.[15] Hence the tax charge is not avoided by selling the original property and reinvesting the proceeds of sale in other property.

---

9. s.272. This definition incorporates the provisions of s.199(4)(*a*)—executors de son tort, etc.: see note 3 above.
10. Settled land may now devolve on personal representatives: see note 20 below.
11. s.200(1)(*c*): and see note 3 above.
12. s.200(1)(*d*).
13. s.200(3): *cf.* § 22–18.
14. s.203.
15. See s.199(5), s.200(4) and s.201(6).

Exception from liability for purchasers

24–08   A purchaser of property, and a person deriving title from or under such a purchaser, is not liable for tax attributable to the value of the property purchased, unless the property is subject to an Inland Revenue charge.[16] "Purchaser" in this context means a purchaser in good faith for consideration in money or money's worth other than a nominal consideration and includes a lessee, mortgagee or other person who for such consideration acquires an interest in the property in question.[17]

> Thus if A makes a lifetime transfer of property to B who sells the property to a purchaser P, only A and B are liable for the tax on A's transfer notwithstanding (b) in § 24–01. Inland Revenue charges are referred to in § 25–31.

Special exemptions from liability in relation to objects and buildings forming part of the national heritage, woodlands, charities and political parties have been referred to elsewhere.[18]

Limitation of liability

24–09   The above paragraphs refer to various classes of person who may be liable for inheritance tax; but section 204 imposes some limit to their liability, as follows:

(1) *Personal representatives*

24–10   Generally a personal representative of a deceased person is not liable for tax attributable to the value of any property except to the extent of the assets he has received as personal representative or might have so received but for his own neglect or default.[18a] There is an exception as regards tax attributable to settled property consisting of land in the United Kingdom which devolves on or becomes vested in the personal representative: his liability is then limited to so much of that property as is at any time available in his hands for the payment of the tax or might have been so available but for his own neglect or default.[19] Settled land (within the meaning of the Settled Land Act 1925) may now devolve on personal representatives.[20]

(2) *Trustees*

24–11   A person is not liable for tax as trustee in relation to any property, except to the extent of:

(a) so much of the property as he has actually received or disposed of,

---

16. s.199(3).
17. s.272.
18. See Chap. 19.
18a. But see *I.R.C.* v. *Stannard* [1984] S.T.C. 245: s.204 does not alter the nature of the personal representative's liability, it merely limits it. If sued, therefore, an order can be made in the form de bonis propriis and a deficiency recovered against the estate of the personal representative unless he has pleaded plene administravit—otherwise he is taken to admit assets and s.204 is inoperable.
19. s.204(1).
20. This is the consequence of the repeal of s.53(3) of the Administration of Estates Act 1925 by Sched. 13 to F.A. 1975.

or as he has become liable to account for, to the persons beneficially entitled thereto; and

(b) so much of any other property as is for the time being available in his hands as trustee for the payment of the tax or might have been so available but for his own neglect or default.[21]

(3) *Vested or beneficial interest in property*

24–12 A person not liable for tax as personal representative or trustee but liable for tax as a person in whom property is vested, or as a person entitled to a beneficial interest in possession in any property, is not liable for tax except to the extent of that property.[22]

(4) *Beneficiaries*

24–13 A person liable for inheritance tax as a person for whose benefit any settled property, or income from any settled property, is applied is not liable for the tax except to the extent of the amount of the property or income so applied (reduced in the case of income by the amount of any income tax borne by him in respect of it and in the case of other property in respect of which he has borne income tax under section 478 of the I.C.T.A. 1970, or section 45 of the Finance Act 1981, by the amount of that tax).[24]

Primary and secondary liability

24–14 The person primarily liable for the tax in the case of a lifetime transfer is the transferor and, in the case of a chargeable transfer relating to a settlement, the trustees of the settlement. The other persons referred to above are liable only if the tax remains unpaid after it ought to have been paid.[25] Their liability is thus of a secondary nature. Where any part of the value transferred is attributable to the tax on it (*i.e.* where tax is taken into account in determining the diminution in the transferor's estate in consequence of the transfer), the person secondarily liable is liable to no greater extent than he would have been had the value transferred been reduced by the tax remaining unpaid.[26]

> Assume A makes a lifetime transfer of £40,000 to trustees and that the tax for which A is primarily accountable is £5,000, *i.e.* the value transferred by A is £40,000 + £5,000 = £45,000. If A pays none of the tax, the trustees' liability is calculated on the basis that the value transferred is £40,000. If A pays (say) £3,000 of the tax, leaving £2,000 unpaid, the trustees' liability is calculated on the basis that the value transferred is £40,000 + £3,000 = £43,000.

A is in both cases liable for the tax for which the trustees are is not liable.

---

21. s.204(2).
22. s.204(3).
23. s.204(4).
24. s.204(5).
25. s.204(6). As to when tax ought to be paid, see § 25–24.
26. s.204(6).

2. Incidence

(1) *Lifetime transfers*

24–15   The question who, as between donor and donee (or settlor and trustees), should bear the tax on a lifetime transfer is a matter they must decide between themselves and this decision will determine the amount by which the estate of the donor (or settlor) is diminished and, accordingly, the amount of tax payable. If A settles £100,000 and A agrees to or in fact pays the tax, having no right of reimbursement against the trustees, the £100,000 has to be grossed up as explained in § 20–10. There is no such grossing up if the trustees pay the tax.

(2) *Death*

24–16   Particular rules apply in the case of a transfer of value within seven years of the transferor's death. The transferor's personal representatives are liable only to the extent that the tax payable exceeds the liability of the other persons responsible for its payment (see § 24–07), save that they are also responsible for tax which remains outstanding for more than a year. Even then, their responsibility is restricted as mentioned in § 24–10.[26a]

Personal representatives have to deliver an account to the Board specifying to the best of their knowledge and belief all the property which formed part of the deceased's estate immediately before his death and the value of that property (see §§ 25–02 *et seq.*) and, on delivery of their account, must pay all the tax for which they are liable and may also pay tax for which they are not liable at the request of the persons who are liable (see § 25–24). Where, as is commonly the case, the deceased's estate comprises a number of different assets, the amount of tax attributable to each item is found by dividing the total tax payable between the various assets according to their respective values, but subject to any provision reducing the amount of tax attributable to the value of any particular property.[27]

Following the doubts which arose after the decision of *Re Dougal*[28] whether the rule in Scots law that realty does not carry its own liability to inheritance tax was applicable throughout the United Kingdom, legislation was introduced to clarify matters as regards deaths occurring after July 26, 1983. Section 211(1) now provides that where personal representatives are liable for inheritance tax, the tax is to be treated as part of the general testamentary and administration expenses of the estate. Accordingly, legacies and bequests will, in future, generally be free of inheritance tax which will, instead, fall on residue. Section 211(1) only applies, however, in so far as the tax is attributable to the value of property in the United Kingdom which vests in the personal representatives and which was not, prior to the deceased's death, settled property. Thus, unless the will otherwise pro-

---

26a. s.204(8).
27. s.265.
28. [1981] S.T.C. 514 (CS).

vides,[29–31] the only property liability for the tax on which will usually *not* fall on residue will be foreign property, settled property and property in which the deceased had an interest as a joint tenant.

Varying the incidence of tax

24–17 The incidence of inheritance tax can be varied by the testator by appropriate provisions in his will. The following example illustrates the effect of the normal rules:

> The property chargeable to inheritance tax on T's death is as follows: freehold property in England; leasehold property in England; foreign personalty; a joint interest in English freehold land; and shares in English companies. By his will T gives the freehold to A; the leasehold to B; the foreign personalty to C; and the residue of his estate to D. The total amount of tax payable is £50,000 which is apportioned rateably between the assets comprised in the estate.

The foreign personalty carries its own burden of tax, payable by C. Section 211(3) enables T's personal representatives, if they pay tax which does not fall on residue (see s.226(2)) to have that amount repaid to them by the person in whom the property to which the tax is attributable is vested. Tax on the freehold and leasehold property is a testamentary expense and is payable out of the residue given to D. Duty on the joint property (which passes to the surviving joint tenant and does not vest in T's personal representatives) is payable by the surviving joint tenant. Duty on the shares, which comprise the residuary estate, is payable out of residue. Much of the residuary estate given to D will therefore go in inheritance tax. (It is assumed in the example that none of the beneficiaries was T's wife: the problems that arise in the case of partially exempt transfers are discussed in § 24–20.)

The testator may, if he wishes, vary the incidence of tax by appropriate provisions in his will. Thus, in the example, if T wishes C to be relieved from the burden of tax, he can give the personalty "free of inheritance tax"; or he can provide that A and B should bear a rateable part of the tax, thereby freeing the residue from this liability. A testator who desires that realty should carry its own duty should now specifically so provide.

24–18 Under estate duty law it was held that when a testator wished to throw the burden of duty on to residue, a clause directing that "testamentary expenses" should be paid out of residue was insufficient to transfer estate duty which was a specific charge on property.[32] More specific provision was usually necessary, such as a direction to pay estate duty out of residue.[33] Section 211(2) provides that the general rules imposing a charge on residue have effect subject to a contrary intention shown by the deceased in his will. It is by no means certain, given the width of these words, whether the

---

29–31. s.211(2).
32. See *Re Owers* [1941] Ch. 17.
33. *Re Pimm* [1940] 2 Ch. 345; *cf. Re King* [1942] Ch. 413; *Re Phuler's Will Trusts* [1965] 1 W.L.R. 68; *Re Neeld, decd. (No. 2) (Note)* [1965] 1 W.L.R. 73n. (C.A.); *Re Walley* [1972] 1 W.L.R. 257; *Re Rosenthal* [1972] 1 W.L.R. 1273; *Re Williams* [1974] S.T.C. 123.

restrictive estate duty rules will continue to apply. Schedule 6, para. 1 provides that any provision in a document which refers to estate duty or death duties is to be taken as referring to inheritance tax: hence a provision in a will devising freehold property "free of death duties" or "free of estate duty" suffices to free the property from any liability which the property might otherwise bear in relation to inheritance tax. Similarly, section 100(1)(*b*) of the Finance Act 1986 provides that any reference in a document to capital transfer tax shall have effect as a reference to inheritance tax.[33a]

Partially exempt transfers

24–20   The rules[34] relating to the computation of inheritance tax payable on a gift which is only partially exempt are highly complex and the following remarks amount only to a description in outline of them. It should be noted that although the examples which will be given are all of transfers on death, the same rules can apply on other occasions, such as on the distribution of settled property.

There are three principles which have determined the structure of these rules:

(1) That gifts which are not exempt and do not bear their own tax must be grossed up.

(2) That specific gifts (*i.e.* gifts other than gifts of residue or of a share of residue) take precedence over gifts of residue, both as respects the attribution of limited exemptions and in the attribution of the value transferred by the overall transfer of value.[35]

(3) That if the Act provides that a transfer is exempt with respect to a particular specific gift, none of the tax shall fall on that gift: equally if it provides that the transfer is exempt with respect to a gift of a share of residue, none of the tax attributable to *residue* shall fall on that gift, in either case, notwithstanding the terms of the disposition itself.[36]

These rules have been modified by the Finance Act 1986 in the case of partially exempt transfers involving relevant business property or agricultural property.[36a] The purpose of the new section, section 39A is to ensure that the relief which is afforded in relation to transfers which include such property should, so far as possible, be attributed to the property which gave rise to it. This will be to the advantage of the Revenue in cases where the assets in question pass in circumstances where the gift of them would in any event be exempt, *e.g.* a farm left to one's spouse or to a charity: in other cases the taxpayer may be better off. It is fair to say that, to a great

---

33a. The next para. is § 24–20.
34. ss.36–42.
35. s.39.
36. s.41.
36a. See § 24–23.

extent, the new provision reflects a previous Revenue interpretation of somewhat ambiguous section.

As far as death is concerned, the transfer deemed to be made immediately before can be considered to be a transfer of specific gifts and of residue. If all specific gifts bear their own tax or are all free of tax, there will be little difficulty in computing and allocating the tax:

(i) If all specific gifts are free of tax, the value attributable to them must be determined by grossing up.[37]

> *Example*
> A, who has made no previous chargeable transfers, leaves £100,000 free of tax to his son S and the residue of his estate of £200,000 to his widow W.
> The £100,000 gift will have to be grossed up, making a gross gift of £113,769. S will, therefore, receive £100,000 and W £186,231 (£200,000 − £13,769). If A had made lifetime transfers within the last seven years, the legacy of £100,000 would have had to be grossed up at higher rates, reflecting those earlier transfers and the net residue received by W would be reduced accordingly.

(ii) If all specific gifts bear their own tax, grossing up is not necessary.[38]

> *Example*
> Assume, in the above example, that S's legacy is expressed by the will to bear its own tax. The tax on such a gift will be £8,950. S will, therefore, receive £91,050 and W, £200,000.

(iii) If the only part of the estate which is taxable is a part of the residue, computation and attribution will, again, be straightforward.

> *Example*
> X dies, leaving an estate of £250,000 of which £50,000 is left to charity and the residue to his son and widow in equal shares. If X has made no previous chargeable transfers, the chargeable part of his estate is determined by deducting the exempt £50,000 and dividing the residue in two: X's widow then receives an exempt £100,000 and his son, £91,050.[39]

24–21 (iv) If, though, some specific gifts bear their own tax while others do not, section 38(4) requires that, to the extent that those gifts do *not* bear tax, they must be grossed up at an assumed rate determined by section 38(5). This enables one to calculate the total chargeable part of the estate, on which tax is chargeable, and thence the tax itself. In order to do so, one must work through the following stages:

> (1) Gross up the value of the chargeable specific gifts not bearing their own tax at the rate that would be applicable if they were the only gifts being made by the deceased[40] (*i.e.* as with (ii) above).
> (2) Ascertain the relative proportions of exempt and chargeable parts of the estate,[41] *i.e.* add to the figure arrived at by carrying out stage (1) the value of the specific gifts bearing their own tax plus the value of any

---

37. s.38(1), (3).
38. s.38(1).
39. s.39 and s.41(*b*).
40. s.38(5)(*a*)(i).
41. s.38(5)(*a*)(ii).

exempt specific gifts. Deduct this from the total value of the estate: this gives the *notional* value of residue. Apportion this between the chargeable and exempt parts of residue. Add the value so found of the chargeable part of residue to the figure found at stage (1) and to the value of chargeable specific gifts bearing their own tax.

(3) Calculate the tax which would be payable on a transfer by the deceased of that notional chargeable part of the estate. Determine this as a percentage of the chargeable part.[42]

(4) Regross the *net* value of the chargeable specific gifts not bearing their own tax at the rate determined under stage (3) above.[43]

(5) Substitute this figure for the value arrived at in stage (1) in the computation carried out in stage (2). This recomputation will give the *actual* chargeable part from which the tax payable can be ascertained.[44]

24–22   *Example*

T's estate is valued at £300,000. Assume he made no chargeable transfers during his lifetime and that, by his will he gives legacies of £100,000 free of tax to his son S and £50,000, to bear its own tax, to his friend J. He leaves the residue of his estate to his widow W and his daughter D in equal shares. Tax on the legacy of £100,000 will, therefore, fall on residue.

In this case the problem is to ensure that W's exempt share of residue does not bear the tax attributable to D's taxable share (s.41(b): see § 24–20(3)). Following the stages set out in 24–21 above:

(1) The specific gift of £100,000 must be grossed up (s.38(1), (4), (5)): the grossed up sum attributable to such an amount is £113,769.

(2) The chargeable specific gifts are, therefore, £113,769 + £50,000. Notional residue is, therefore, £300,000 − £163,769 = £136,231 of which D's chargeable share is £68,115. The notional chargeable part of the estate is, thus, £163,769 + £68,115 = £231,884.

(3) The tax payable on such a transfer on death made by T (no grossing up this time) is £64,942. As a percentage of the notional chargeable part this is 28%. This is the "assumed rate": s.38(5)(a).

(4) Gross up the specific gift of £100,000 at the assumed rate of 28%:

$$£100,000 \times \frac{100}{100 - 28} = £138,889$$

(This computation can be effected without ascertaining the percentage as:

$$\frac{£100,000 \times 231,884}{231,884 - 64,942} \Bigg)$$

(5) Recomputing stage (2): the chargeable specific gifts are £138,889 + £50,000 = £188,889, leaving a residue of £111,111. Half of this (W's share) is exempt: £55,556. The chargeable part of the estate is, therefore, £188,889 + £55,556 (D's share) = £244,445.

24–23   The above calculations show the following:

---

42. s.38(5)(a), (b).
43. s.38(4).
44. s.38(1).

	£	£
Exempt part of estate (W's share)		55,555
Chargeable part of estate:		
(a) S's legacy	138,889	
(b) J's legacy	50,000	
(c) D's non-exempt share of residue	55,556	
		244,445
		300,000
Tax on chargeable part of estate (no grossing up)	71,223	

Actual rate of tax is (as opposed to the assumed rate) $\dfrac{71,223}{244,445} \times 100 = 29.14\%$

The final step is to determine the attribution of the tax and, thus, the distribution of the estate. This proceeds as follows:

1. The tax on S's legacy of £100,000, grossed up to £138,889 (section 38(1)) is £138,889 × 29.14% = £40,472
2. The tax on J's legacy is £50,000 × 29.14% = £14,570
3. The tax on D's share of residue is £55,556 × 29.14% = £16,189

Total tax = £71,231

4. The residue must now be calculated for the final time, taking into account the tax actually payable on S's legacy:

Z		£	£
	Total estate		300,000
	less S's legacy + tax thereon	140,472	
	less J's legacy	50,000	
			109,528

W's exempt share of residue is, therefore, £54,764: D's share, on which tax of £16,189 will be paid, is the same.

The estate will, therefore, be distributed as follows:

		£	£
S			£100,000
J		50,000	
	less	14,570	35,430
W			54,764
D		54,764	
	less	16,189	38,575
			71,231
Tax			
			300,000

Further complications are added where some of the assets passing under the partially exempt transfer are agricultural property or relevant business property. Section 39A (added by the Finance Act 1986, s.105) provides that, in such a case, the rules for the attribution of value contained in sections 38 and 39 are to be modified substantially:

(1) If there are *specific* gifts of agricultural or relevant business property, the value to be attributed to each of those gifts is to be reduced by the relief afforded in respect of that property under section 116 or section 104 respectively (see § 19–39 to § 19–48);

(2) the value of any other *specific* gifts is to be reduced by the "appropriate fraction,"

$$\frac{A}{B}, \text{ where:}$$

"A" is: the value transferred *less* the reduced value found under (1); and

"B" is: the unreduced value transferred *less* the value of gifts falling within (1) *before* reduction.

24–24 *Example*

A dies, leaving an estate of £600,000 as follows—

To his wife W, Blackacre Farm (with vacant possession), worth £200,000;

To his son S, a pecuniary legacy of £100,000; and

To his daughter, D, the residue of £300,000, including a controlling shareholding in A Ltd., worth £200,000.

The unreduced value transferred is, therefore, £600,000: the reduced value transferred (*i.e.* the actual value transferred) is £400,000. This value (*i.e.* of £400,000) is to be attributed thus—

(i) To the gift of Blackacre Farm, £100,000

(ii) To the legacy to S: £100,000 $\times \dfrac{(400,000-100,000)}{(600,000-200,000)} = $ £75,000.

(iii) To the residue of £300,000, therefore, will be attributed the remainder of the value transferred of £400,000 £225,000.

The effect of the provisions is, thus, to attribute the *whole* of the relief given to any specific gift of agricultural or business property to that particular gift, whilst attributing the relief afforded to agricultural or business property falling into residue proportionately between the other specific gifts and residue. So, here, the value of the other specific gifts and of residue were in the proportions 100 : 300, and the relief of £100,000 on the shares was accordingly divided 25 : 75.

CHAPTER 25

ADMINISTRATION AND COLLECTION

25–01   INHERITANCE tax is under the care and management of the Board.[1] Sections 215 to 261 provide for its administration and collection.

1. DELIVERY OF AN ACCOUNT

The duty to account: transfers on death

25–02   The personal representatives of a deceased person and every person who:

(a) is liable as transferor for tax on the value transferred by a chargeable transfer, or would be so liable if tax were chargeable on that value; or

(b) is liable as trustee[1a] of a settlement for tax on the value transferred by a transfer of value, or would be so liable if tax were chargeable on that value; or

(c) is liable as a donee for tax on the value transferred by a potentially exempt transfer which proves to be a chargeable transfer (even though the value is such that tax is not chargeable); or

(d) is liable as a person in whom property subject to a reservation is vested for the tax payable on the donor's death and which is attributable to that property; or

(e) is liable as trustee of a settlement for tax under the relevant property rules (see §§ 22–50, *et seq.*) or would be so liable if tax were chargeable on the relevant occasion;

are required[2] to deliver to the Board an account specifying to the best of their knowledge and belief all "appropriate property" and the value of that property.

25–03   Where the account is to be delivered by personal representatives, the appropriate property is all property which formed part of the deceased's estate immediately before his death[3]; but if the personal representatives, after making the fullest inquiries that are reasonably practicable in the circumstances, are unable to ascertain the exact value of any particular property, their account is in the first instance sufficient as regards that property if it contains a statement to that effect, a provisional estimate of the value of the property and an undertaking to deliver a further account of it as soon as its value is ascertained. The Board may from time to time give such

---

1. s.215. "The Board" means the Commissioners of Inland Revenue: s.272.
1a. See *I.R.C.* v. *Stype Trustees (Jersey) Ltd.* [1985] S.T.C. 394 on the liability of foreign trustees.
2. s.216(1).
3. s.216(3). A person who is an executor of the deceased only in respect of settled land in England and Wales is excluded from the application of the provision.

general or special directions as they think fit for restricting the property which may so be specified by personal representatives.[4]

Excepted estates.[5] With effect from September 1, 1981, an account need not be delivered in the estate (an "excepted estate") of any person who died on or after April 1, 1983, where:

(a) the total gross value of the estate for tax purposes does not exceed £40,000;

(b) the estate comprises only property which has passed under the deceased's will or intestacy, or by nomination, or beneficially by survivorship;

(c) not more than the higher of 10 per cent. of the total gross value or £2,000 consists of property situated outside the United Kingdom; and

(d) the deceased died domiciled in the United Kingdom and had made no lifetime gifts chargeable to inheritance tax.[6]

Excepted Transfers[6a]

(1) *Gifts*

25–03A   No account need be sent to the Inland Revenue of an "excepted transfer." This term covers a gift made by an individual on or after April 1, 1981 where:

(a) the amount of the gift and of any other chargeable transfers previously made by the individual in the same income tax year does not exceed £10,000; and

(b) the amount of the gift and of any other chargeable transfers made by the individual in the previous ten years does not exceed £40,000.

The Inland Revenue may subsequently require an account of such gifts in writing. In addition if an individual who has not reported a gift in the belief that it was covered by the exception later finds that it was not, he must deliver an account of it within six months of the time he discovers the omission.

(2) *Termination of an interest in possession in settled property*

We have seen in § 22–31 that an individual may allocate to the trustees of settled property in which he has an interest in possession the whole or part of the annual exemption and of any exemption for marriage gifts to which he may be entitled. The trustees can then apply these exemptions on

---

4. s.216(3)(*b*).

5. For details of this procedure see the Capital Transfer Tax (Delivery of Accounts) Regs. 1981 (S.I. 1980 No. 880) in [1981] S.T.I. 336 as amended by the Capital Transfer Tax (Delivery of Accounts) (No. 3) Regs. 1983 (S.I. 1983 No. 1039) in [1983] S.T.I. 330.

6. See the CTT (Delivery of Accounts) Regs. 1981 and the CTT (Delivery of Accounts) (No. 3) Regs. 1983.

6a. See the Inland Revenue Press Release of July 24, 1984 in [1984] S.T.I. 570.

the termination of that interest. If the value transferred by the termination is not greater than any exemption thus set against it ("an exempted termination") no account need be sent to the Inland Revenue. The Inland Revenue may require the trustees to account to them for any exempted termination but, unless they do so within six months of its date (and except in cases of fraud or failure to disclose material facts), the trustees will then be automatically discharged from the claim to tax (if any) in respect of that termination. The order applies in respect of terminations of interests on or after April 6, 1981.

5–03B   *No personal representatives.* Where there are no personal representatives of a deceased person because all property which formed part of his estate was such that no grant of representation or confirmation was required in the United Kingdom:

> (a) every person in whom any of the property vested (whether beneficially or otherwise) on or at any time after the deceased's death or who at any such time is beneficially entitled to an interest in possession in any such property; and
>
> (b) where any of the property is at any such time comprised in a settlement and there is no person within paragraph (a) above in respect of that property, every person for whose benefit any of that property (or income from it) is applied at any such time;

is required to deliver to the Board an account specifying to the best of his knowledge and belief the relevant property vested in him, in which he has an interest or which (or income from which) is applicable for his benefit, and the value of that property.[7]

The duty to account: transfers not on death

25–04   In other cases the appropriate property is any property to the value of which the tax is or would be attributable.[8]

25–05   Except in the case of an account to be delivered by personal representatives, a person is not required to deliver an account with respect to any property if a full and proper account of that property, specifying its value, has already been delivered to the Board by some other person who is or would be liable for the tax attributable to the value of the property, unless that other person is or would be liable with him jointly as trustee.[9] Thus delivery of an account by the transferee exonerates the transferor in the case of a lifetime transfer. No account is required for wholly exempt transfers.[10]

---

7. s.216(2).
8. s.216(4).
9. s.216(5).
10. See Form CAP C–5.

Time for delivering account

25–06   An account must be delivered:

   (a) in the case of an account to be delivered by personal representa-
       tives, before the expiration of the period of 12 months from the end
       of the month in which the death occurs, or, if it expires later, the
       period of three months beginning with the date on which the per-
       sonal representatives first act as such; and

   (b) In the case of a donee liable for tax on a PET which proves charge-
       able, before the expiration of twelve months from the end of the
       month in which the transferor's death occured; and

   (c) in the case of a person in whom property subject to a reservation is
       vested on the donor's death, the same time as in (b) above; and

   (d) in the case of an account to be delivered by a person when there are
       no personal representatives (see § 25–03B), before the expiration of
       the period of three months from the time when he first has reason to
       believe that he is required to deliver such an account; and

   (e) in the case of an account to be delivered by any other person, before
       the expiration of the period of 12 months from the end of the month
       in which the transfer is made or, if it expires later, the period of
       three months beginning with the date on which he first becomes
       liable for tax.[11]

25–07   A person liable for tax under section 32, section 79, section 126 or
Schedule 5 (see §§ 19–33 *et seq.* and § 19–52) must deliver an account
before the expiration of the period of six months from the end of the month
in which occurs the event by reason of which the tax is chargeable.[12]

Dispensing with accounts

25–07A   The Board can make regulations dispensing with the delivery of accounts
under section 216.[13]

Corrective and supplementary accounts

25–08   If a person who has delivered an account under the above provisions discovers at any time that the account is defective in a material respect by
reason of anything contained in or omitted from it he must, within six
months of that time, deliver a remedial account to the Board.[14]

Penalties

   There are penalties for failure to deliver an account under section 216
(see § 25–02) or section 217 (see § 25–08)[15] or for delivering incorrect
accounts, etc.[16]

---

11. s.216(6).
12. s.216(7).
13. s.256(1)(*a*).
14. s.217.
15. s.245.
16. ss.247 and 248.

2. RETURNS BY CERTAIN PERSONS ACTING FOR SETTLORS

25–09   Where any person, in a course of a trade or profession carried on by him, other than the profession of a barrister, has been concerned with the making of a settlement and knows or has reason to believe:

(a) that the settlor was domiciled in the United Kingdom; and
(b) that the trustees of the settlement are not or will not be resident in the United Kingdom;

he must, within three months of the making of the settlement, make a return to the Board stating the names and addresses of the settlor and of the trustees of the settlement.[17]

25–10   This requirement does not apply to:

(a) any settlement made by will; or
(b) any other settlement, if such a return in relation to that settlement has already been made by another person or if an account has been delivered in relation to it under section 216: see §§ 25–02 *et seq.*[18]

3. POWER TO REQUIRE INFORMATION AND INSPECT PROPERTY

25–11   The Board may by notice in writing require any person to furnish them within such time, not being less than 30 days, as may be specified in the notice with such information as the Board may require for the purposes of the inheritance tax provisions.[19] The notice may be combined with a notice relating to income tax.[20]

25–12   A barrister or solicitor is not obliged in pursuance of a notice under this provision to disclose, without his client's consent, any information with respect to which a claim to professional privilege could be maintained[20a]; except that:

(a) a solicitor may be so obliged to disclose the name and address of his client; and
(b) if his client is resident outside the United Kingdom and carries on outside the United Kingdom a business which includes the provision for persons in the United Kingdom of services or facilities relating to the formation of companies outside the United Kingdom, the making of settlements outside the United Kingdom, or the securing of control over, or the management or administration of, such com-

---

17. s.218(1). Trustees are not resident in the U.K., for the purposes of s.218, unless the general administration of the settlement is ordinarily carried on in the U.K. and the trustees, or a majority of them, are for the time being resident in the U.K.: s.218(3).
18. s.218(2).
19. s.219(1). For penalties see section 245(1)(*c*).
20. s.219(2).
20a. s.219(3).

panies or settlements, a solicitor may also be so obliged to disclose the names and addresses of persons in the United Kingdom for whom such services or the facilities have been provided in the course of that business.[21]

25–13   If the Board authorise any person to inspect any property for the purpose of ascertaining its value for the purposes of inheritance tax, the person having the custody or possession of the property must permit him to inspect it at such reasonable times as the Board may consider necessary. If any person wilfully delays or obstructs a person acting in pursuance of this provision he is liable on summary conviction to a fine.[22]

4. ASSESSMENT AND APPEALS

Notices of determination

25–14   Income tax, corporation tax and capital gains tax are generally charged by notices of assessment and appeals against assessments may be brought before the General or Special Commissioners. In the case of inheritance tax, however, the Board is empowered to give notice of determination of certain matters and an appeal lies against such a determination.

25–15   Where it appears to the Board that a transfer of value has been made, or where a claim has been made to the Board in connection with a transfer of value, the Board may give notice in writing to any person who appears to the Board to be the transferor or the claimant or to be liable for any of the tax chargeable on the value transferred, stating that they have determined the matters specified in the notice.[23] References here to transfers of value or to the values transferred by them include references to dispositions under the "relevant property" rules or to the amounts on which tax is chargeable in respect of them.[24]

25–16   The matters that may be specified in a notice in relation to any transfer of value are all or any of the following:

(a) the date of the transfer;
(b) the value transferred and the value of any property to which the value transferred is wholly or partly attributable;
(c) the transferor;
(d) the tax chargeable (if any) and the persons who are liable for the whole or part of it;
(e) the amount of any payment made in excess of the tax for which a person is liable and the date from which the rate at which tax or any repayment of tax overpaid carries interest; and

---

21. s.219(4).
22. s.220.
23. s.221(1).
24. s.221(6).

(f) any other matter that appears to the Board to be relevant for the purposes of the Act.[25]

25–17 A determination of any fact relating to a transfer of value will, if that fact has been stated in an account or return and the Board are satisfied that the account or return is correct, be made by the Board in accordance with that account or return; but may, in any other case, be made by the Board to the best of their judgment.[26] Thus the Board can make estimated determinations of value transferred in the same way that estimated assessments can be made for income tax purposes.

25–18 A notice of determination must state the time within which and the manner in which an appeal against any determination in it may be made.[27]

Conclusiveness of a notice

25–19 Subject to any variation by agreement in writing or on appeal, a determination in a notice is conclusive against the person on whom the notice is served; and if the notice is served on the transferor and specifies a determination of the value transferred by the transfer of value or previous transfers of value, the determination, so far as relevant to the tax chargeable in respect of later transfers of value (whether or not made by the transferor) is conclusive also against any other person, subject, however, to any adjustment under the provisions which may apply where too much or too little tax has been paid.[28]

Appeals

25–20 A person on whom a notice has been served may, within 30 days of the service, appeal against any determination specified in it by notice in writing given to the Board and specifying the grounds of appeal.[29] The appeal is to the Special Commissioners except in two cases:

(a) where it is agreed between the appellant and the Board (or, in default of agreement, if the High Court is satisfied on an application made by the appellant and gives leave) that the matters to be decided on the appeal are likely to be substantially confined to questions of law, the appeal may be to the High Court;

(b) any question as to the value of land in the United Kingdom must be determined by the Lands Tribunal.[30]

Many questions on inheritance tax are questions of construction and proceedings in the High Court (commenced by originating summons) are appropriate.

---

25. s.221(2).
26. s.221(3).
27. s.221(4).
28. s.221(5). See ss.240 and 241 as to adjustments.
29. s.222(1).
30. s.222(2), (3) and (5).

Appeals out of time

25–21   An appeal may be brought out of time with the consent of the Board or the Special Commissioners. The Board:

(a) must give that consent if satisfied, on an application for the purpose, that there was a reasonable excuse for not bringing the appeal within the time limited and that the application was made thereafter without unreasonable delay; and

(b) must, if not so satisfied, refer the application for determination by the Special Commissioners.[31]

Procedure before Special Commissioners

25–22   This is similar to the procedure where other taxes are involved. The Board may be represented by any of its officers; and any party to the appeal may be represented by a barrister, solicitor or any accountant who has been admitted a member of an incorporated society of accountants or, with the leave of the Special Commissioners, by any other person.[32] The Special Commissioners have wide powers to require the delivery of particulars and information, and to summon witnesses.[33]

The Special Commissioners may allow the appellant to put forward any ground of appeal not specified in the notice of appeal and may take it into consideration if satisfied that the omission was not wilful or unreasonable.[34] The Commissioners are required to confirm the determination appealed against unless they are satisfied that the determination ought to be varied or quashed.[35]

Statement of case

25–23   Within 30 days of the determination by the Special Commissioners of an appeal, any party to the appeal may question the determination on a point of law by a written request to the Special Commissioners to state and sign a case for the opinion of the High Court. The procedure and the powers and duties of the High Court with respect to such an appeal are similar to those in cases involving other taxes.[36]

5. Payment of Tax

25–24   Generally inheritance tax is due six months after the end of the month in which the chargeable transfer is made or, in the case of a transfer made after April 5 and before October 1 in any year otherwise than on death, at the end of April in the next year.[37]

---

31. s.223.
32. s.224(1).
33. s.224(2), (3). For penalties for disobedience see s.245(1)(*d*) and s.246.
34. s.224(4).
35. s.224(5).
36. s.225; and see §§ 17–11 *et seq.*
37. s.226(1).

Personal representatives must, on delivery of their account, pay all the tax for which they are liable and may also pay any part of the tax chargeable on the death for which they are not liable, if the persons liable therefor request them to make the payment.[38]

Extra tax payable by virtue of the transferor dying within seven years of the transfer (or one year in the case of a transfer to a political party) is due six months after the end of the month in which the death occurs.[39]

Tax chargeable under section 32 or section 79 or section 126 or under Schedule 5 to the Act is due six months after the end of the month in which the event by reason of which it is chargeable occurs.[40]

25–25   The Board have power in the first instance, and without prejudice to the recovery of the remainder of the tax, to accept or demand payment of an amount by reference to the value stated in an account or supplementary or corrective amount delivered to the Board.[41]

None of the above provisions authorises the recovery from, or requires the payment by, any person of tax in excess of his liability as limited by section 204: see §§ 24–09 *et seq.*[42]

Payment of tax by instalments

25–26   Section 227 contains elaborate provisions, which cannot be conveniently summarised, for tax to be paid by instalments where the value transferred is attributable to the value of land of any description, wherever situated, shares or securities giving control (as defined)[43] of a company and other shares or securities not quoted on a recognised stock exchange in respect of which certain conditions are satisfied. The provisions apply to transfers on death; and they apply to transfers otherwise than on death if either (a) the tax is borne by the person benefiting from the transfer or (b) the property is settled and remains in settlement after the transfer. If the property is sold before all instalments have been paid the balance of the tax becomes immediately payable. The relief is also available in relation to property transferred by a PET which proves chargeable provided that the donee still retains the qualifying property at the time of the donor's death.[43a]

25–27   Payment by instalments is by 10 yearly instalments and, generally, interest is chargeable on the whole of the unpaid tax at each instalment date. The rates of interest are 9 per cent. if the transfer was made on death or was a potentially exempt transfer and 11 per cent. in any other case.[44]

---

38. s.226(2).
39. s.226(3).
40. s.226(4) and see §§ 19–33 *et seq.* and § 19–52.
41. s.226(5).
42. s.226(6).
43. See s.228.
43a. s.227(1A).
44. S.I. 1985 No. 560. It is intended that the rate of 11 per cent. be reduced to 8½ per cent.: see [1986] S.T.I. 509.

25–28   Sections 227 and 229 provide for payment by instalments where the property transferred is a business or an interest in a business, and where there is a lifetime disposal of timber.

25–29   Section 234 provides that the instalments are to be free of interest where the value transferred represents shares or securities, a business or interest in a business, or the agricultural value of agricultural land. Excluded from this relief is tax on shares or securities in a company whose business is wholly or mainly dealing in shares or land or the making or holding of investments excluding land qualifying for agricultural relief. Land or buildings may qualify for this relief as business assets. There is an overriding limit of £250,000 on the value on which instalments may be interest-free which applies to chargeable transfers made before but not on or after March 10, 1981.[45]

Acceptance of property in satisfaction of tax

25–30   Section 230[46] gives the Board power to accept certain types of property, such as a work of art which the Ministers[46a] are satisfied is pre-eminent for aesthetic merit or historical value, in satisfaction of a claim for inheritance tax.

Transfers reported late

25–30A   Section 264 makes provision for cases where a transfer is not notified to the Board before the expiry of the period specified for the delivery of accounts (see § 25–06) and is not discovered until after the Board has accepted payment in full satisfaction of the tax on another transfer of value made by the transferor within the seven years after the earlier transfer.

In brief, the section increases the amount of tax payable on the transfer reported late to include the tax which would have been payable on the transfer had the Board had timeous notice of the earlier transfer. The section also makes provision for more complex cases where there have been several subsequent transfers or several unreported transfers which are later discovered.

Inland Revenue charge for unpaid tax

25–31   Where any tax charged on the value transferred by a chargeable transfer, or any interest on it, remains unpaid, a charge for the amount unpaid (called an Inland Revenue charge) is imposed in favour of the Board on:

(a) any property to the value of which the value transferred is wholly or partly attributable; and

---

45. See F.A. 1981, s.95.
46. See also s.231.
46a. Defined by s.230(5) as the Secretary of State and the Duchy of Lancaster.

(b) where the chargeable transfer is made by the making of a settlement or is made under the "relevant property" rules, any property comprised in the settlement.[47]

Property includes any property directly or indirectly representing it.[48]

25–32 Where the chargeable transfer is made on death, personal or movable property situated in the United Kingdom which was beneficially owned by the deceased immediately before his death and which vests in his personal representatives is not subject to the Inland Revenue charge; and for this purpose "personal property" includes leaseholds and undivided shares in land held on trust for sale, whether statutory or not; and the question whether any property was beneficially owned by the deceased is for this purpose determined without regard to section 49(1): see § 22–17.[49]

25–32A An Inland Revenue charge is also imposed on any property which has been the subject of a PET which proves chargeable unless it has been disposed of to a purchaser prior to the donor's death.[49a] In the latter event, the property representing that disposed of (*i.e.* generally, the proceeds of sale) will become the subject of the charge (see § 25–54).

25–33 The Inland Revenue charge imposed on any property takes effect subject to any incumbrance thereon which is allowable as a deduction in valuing that property for the purposes of the tax.[50]

25–34 A disposition of property subject to an Inland Revenue charge takes effect subject to that charge[51] unless the disposition is to a purchaser and, at the time of the disposition (as defined) certain conditions are satisfied, when the purchaser will take the property free from the charge; but the property for the time being representing it will instead be subject to the charge.[52] Thus if in the case of land in England or Wales the charge is not registered as a land charge or, in the case of personal property situated in the United Kingdom, the purchaser had no notice of the facts giving rise to the charge, the purchaser takes free from the Inland Revenue charge but the proceeds of sale in the hands of the vendor become subject to it. Where property subject to an Inland Revenue charge, or an interest in such property, is disposed of to a purchaser in circumstances where it does not then cease to be subject to the charge, it ceases to be subject to it on the expiration of the period of six years beginning with the later of the following dates:

(a) the date on which the tax became due; and
(b) the date on which a full and proper account of the property was first

---

47. s.237(1).
48. s.237(2).
49. s.237(3).
49a. s.237(3A).
50. s.237(5).
51. s.237(6).
52. s.238(1), (3).

delivered to the Board in connection with the chargeable transfer concerned.[53]

Certificates of discharge

25–35   A person liable for tax on the value transferred by a chargeable transfer which is attributable to the value of property specified in the application, may apply to the Board for a certificate to the effect that the Board is satisfied that tax has been, or will be, paid. The Board is bound to grant the certificate where the chargeable transfer is one made on death or the transferor has died. The certificate discharges *the property* shown in it from the Inland Revenue charge on its acquisition by a purchaser.[54]

There is a second form of certificate which merely discharges specified *persons* from liability for tax in respect of a specified transfer of value.[55]

The Board has power to make regulations for the issue of certificates of discharge.[56]

Dispositions under the "relevant property" rules (see §§ 22–55 *et seq*), are treated as transfers of value for the purposes of the above provisions.[57]

Certificates will not effectively discharge a person who has failed to disclose material facts.[58]

---

53. s.238(2).
54. s.239(1), (3)(*a*).
55. s.239(2), (2A), (3)(*b*).
56. s.256(1)(*b*).
57. s.239(5).
58. s.239(4).

INHERITANCE TAX, CAPITAL TRANSFER TAX AND ESTATE DUTY

26–01 SECTION 273 of and Schedule 6 to the Act contain various provisions to enable a proper transition to be made from estate duty to capital transfer tax, and, now, inheritance tax. Although estate duty is not leviable in respect of deaths occurring after March 12, 1975[1] it will be many years before these provisions become redundant.

This chapter is concerned only with those transitional matters for which provision has been made by the 1984 Act. For a full description of the rules which can now be considered to be spent, the reader is referred to Chapter 26 of the fifteenth edition of this book. It also deals with the transition from CTT to Inheritance Tax.

Interpretation

26–02 Paragraph 1 of Schedule 6 provides that references in any enactment, in any instrument made under any enactment or in any document (such as a will), whether executed before or after the passing of the Act to "estate duty" or "death duties" shall take effect, as far as possible, as if they included references to inheritance tax chargeable under section 4 of the Act: see §§ 18–14 *et seq.* An obvious example of such a reference is a provision in a will that a gift is (or is not) to bear such duties: see §§ 24–15 *et seq.*

The surviving spouse exemption[2]

26–03 For the purposes of inheritance tax, generally a transfer of value will be exempt to the extent that the value transferred by it is attributable to property which becomes comprised in the estate of the spouse of the transferor: see §§ 19–02 *et seq.* The subsequent transfer by the recipient spouse is, though, likely to be subject to inheritance tax. The estate duty rules, however, were to the opposite effect.[3] When a person died, leaving property to his spouse, that property would form part of the estate the value of which was subject to estate duty: but, by section 5(2) of the Finance Act 1894, on the subsequent death of the spouse, that property would be excluded from a second estate duty charge.

There will be many cases, therefore, where one spouse died prior to the abolition of estate duty and the other subsequently dies subject to the inheritance tax rules. Without some relieving provision tax would be chargeable on *both* deaths. Paragraph 2 of Schedule 6 provides, therefore, that if the first death occurred before November 13, 1974, property which

---

1. See F.A. 1975, s.49(1).
2. Sched. 6, para. 2.
3. See the 8th edition of this book, Chaps. 18 *et seq.*

would have obtained exclusion from estate duty under section 5(2) of the 1894 Act is to be left out of account on reckoning the deemed transfer of value immediately before the second death. Similar provisions apply where the property was settled property in which the surviving spouse had obtained an interest in possession from the other spouse.

Sales and mortgages of reversionary interests

26–04   Under estate duty, relief was given to a purchaser or mortgagee (for full consideration) of a reversionary interest, so that he would not be obliged to bear any increase in the amount of estate duty which was payable on the death of the preceding life tenant by reason of his interest in the settled property. Paragraph 3 of Schedule 6 is designed to maintain that relief in respect of such purchases or mortgages effected before March 27, 1974 when the life tenant dies after that date. The inheritance tax that the purchaser or mortgagee will become liable to pay will not exceed the amount of estate duty he would have paid had that tax continued to apply.

Conditionally exempt transfers

26–05   If an object obtained the estate duty equivalent of conditional exemption under section 78 of the Act (see §§ 19–33 *et seq.*), paragraph 4 of Schedule 6 provides that estate duty may still be charged under section 40(2) of the Finance Act 1930 on a chargeable sale which takes place after the introduction of inheritance tax.

Transition from CTT to inheritance tax

26–06   The transitional provisions relating to inheritance tax are to be found in the Finance Act 1986, Sched. 19, Pt. II.

Paragraph 40 provides that a death or other event occurring after March 18, 1986 is not to affect the tax chargeable before that date. This is necessary to prevent a lifetime transfer subjected to the less favourable CTT regime also suffering the more stringent charges on death under inheritance tax. Previously, it was the case that only transfers in the three years before death were liable to an increased charge on the demise of the transferor—now, the period of review has been extended to the last seven years (relieved only by the tapering provisions in section 7(4)—see § 20–03). The effect of paragraph 40 is, therefore, to preclude the recharge of gifts made prior to March 18, 1986 and more than three years before the transferor's death.

26–07   Paragraph 43 relates to settlements in which no interest in possession exists which have had a ten-year anniversary before the introduction of inheritance tax. The rate of tax charged on that anniversary would, without more, apply in relation to any proportionate charges made under section 65 in the subsequent ten years. As that rate is likely to be greater than might have been chargeable had inheritance tax been in force at the earlier anniversary, (since, under the new regime tax on the first ten year anniversary is calculated by reference to the cumulative total of chargeable transfers made by the settlor in only the past *seven* years), it is provided that for the purpose of the section 65 proportionate charge, the rate of tax is to be recalculated in accordance with the new rules. No repayment of tax will, however, follow from this recalculation in respect of the earlier section 64 charge.

PART 3

STAMP DUTIES

CHAPTER 27

INTRODUCTION

1. Sources and Administration

27–01   THE imposition of stamp duties is governed by the Stamp Act 1891,[1] as amended and supplemented by Revenue Acts and by annual Finance Acts.[1a] Many administrative provisions are contained in the Stamp Duties Management Act 1891, and some exemptions from duty are to be found in other Acts. The rules which govern the construction of revenue statutes will be discussed in a later chapter.[2]

27–02   The Stamp Act 1891 is in three Parts.[3] Part I begins with a section (s.1) which charges duty on the instruments set forth in the First Schedule, where there is a list of instruments, in alphabetical order, with the duty which each instrument attracts. The remaining sections of Part I (ss.2–17) contain detailed provisions as to the manner in which instruments should be stamped and the effect of failure to stamp. Part II (ss.18–111) amplifies some of the heads of charge in the First Schedule, dealing with them in the order in which they appear in the Schedule. Part III (ss.112–125) contains miscellaneous provisions. At the end of the First Schedule there is a list of instruments exempt from all duties. In addition to the statute law, there is a mass of case law, much of which dates from before 1891, but which is nevertheless useful because it aids in the interpretation of sections of older statutes which were repeated in the Act of 1891. In assessing the value of the older cases, though, it should be kept in mind that, until 1850, all questions of stamp duty were decided in open court upon an instrument being tendered in evidence, and that the Commissioners had no opportunity of being heard. Disputes as to the proper stamping of an instrument may still arise in this way[4] but there has, since 1850, been a procedure in existence by which the opinion of the Commissioners can be obtained as to the proper stamping of an executed instrument presented to them for "adjudication."[5] This opinion may then be challenged in the higher courts in proceedings in which the Commissioners are parties.

There is a number of extra-statutory concessions affecting stamp duties which are published in annual reports of the Commissioners. There are also Statements of Practice.

The administration of stamp duties is under the care and management of

---

1. In this book, "stamp duties" means those duties which are imposed by the Stamp Act 1891, as amended. Other taxes which may be levied by means of stamps are disregarded.
1a. The Inland Revenue has published a Consultative Document on the reform of stamp duties: see [1983] S.T.I. 133 at p. 138.
2. See *post*, Chap. 36.
3. For a judicial analysis of the S.A. 1891, see the judgment of Fletcher Moulton L.J. in *Maple & Co.(Paris) Ltd.* v. *I.R.C.* [1906] 2 K.B. 834.
4. See, *e.g. Re Waterhouse's Policy* [1937] 2 All E.R. 91.
5. The adjudication procedure is discussed *post*, §§ 27–41 *et seq.*

the Commissioners of Inland Revenue,[6] who delegate the day-to-day administration to the Controller of Stamps.

The process of stamping in outline

27–03   The stamp duties imposed by the Acts are of two kinds:

(1) *Fixed duties*, such as the duty of 50p on a deed of family arrangement.[6a] The amount of the duty does not depend on the consideration or other amount expressed in the instrument.

(2) *Ad valorem duties*, such as the duty of 50p for every £100 of the amount or value of the consideration on a transfer of shares.

Payment of the duty is indicated by a stamp which is impressed upon the instrument itself. The instrument must be presented to the Stamp Office[7] so that the stamp may be impressed thereon by the use of dies in the exclusive possession of the stamping authorities. The use of adhesive stamps is no longer permitted.[8] Where an impressed stamp is required, the normal practice (for example, in the case of a conveyance on sale) is that the purchaser's solicitor takes the instrument to the local stamp office where it is scrutinised by a clerk who marks in pencil the amount of the duty. The appropriate stamp is then impressed. It is the practice of solicitors not to erase the pencilled marking.

2. Basic Principles

27–04   The subject of stamp duties is one of some complexity; but there is a number of principles or rules which are of general application in stamp duty law and practice. These are as follows:

27–05   (1) *Stamp duty is charged on instruments, not on transactions*

This principle is fundamental and knows of only one exception—that of the stamp duty reserve tax.[8a] Unless that tax chargeable, if there is no instrument, there can be no duty. See also § 27–10.

27–06   (2) *The head of charge under which an instrument falls and, therefore, the amount of the duty, is determined by the nature of the transaction effected by the instrument*

In determining the nature of the transaction which is effected, the court will look to the substance of the instrument, not merely to its form.

---

6. Stamp Duties Management Act 1891, s.1.
6a. F.A. 1985, s.84(8). See § 28–15.
7. For details as to the location of the Stamp Offices, see Sergeant, p. 510.
8. See *post*, §§ 27–35 *et seq.*
8a. See §§ 28–50 *et seq.*

"In order to determine whether any, and if any what, stamp duty is chargeable upon an instrument, the legal rule is that the real and true meaning of the instrument is to be ascertained; that the description of it given in the instrument itself by the parties is immaterial, even although they may have believed that its effect and operation was to create a security mentioned in the Stamp Act, and they so declare."[9]

So, for example, an instrument described as a deed of dissolution of partnership may operate as a conveyance on sale[10]; and a covenant not to compete given by the vendor of a business to the purchaser may operate as an agreement to assign goodwill.[11]

This principle was considerd by Vinelott J. in a case concerned with the application to stamp duty of the new approach to the construction of tax avoidance schemes, *Ingram* v. *I.R.C.*[12]:

"Stamp duty is a tax on instruments. But . . . to determine whether an instrument falls within a chargeable category and the duty payable the Court must ascertain the substance of the transaction effected by it. The *Ramsay* principle requires that (in a case where the conditions described by Lord Brightman are satisfied) a composite transaction or series of transactions be treated as a single transaction achieving the preordained end."

In that case the appellant had acquired a freehold property by entering into an agreement for a long lease, and procuring the indirect conveyance of the freehold reversion. Applying the new approach, Vinelott J. held that the lease agreement was to be disregarded and the two sale agreements (of the freehold to, and from, an intermediate company) were to be treated as "accomplishing the transfer of the unencumbered freehold interest" for the consideration given both under the lease agreement and the sale agreement.

For the further discussion of the new approach, see Chapter 36.

27–07   (3) *If a transaction can be effected in more than one way, duty must be charged which is appropriate to the instrument actually used*[13]

27–08   (4) *The liability of an instrument to stamp duty depends on the circumstances which exist at the time when the instrument is executed*

Thus if property is transferred at a time when there is no subsisting agreement for the sale of that property to the transferee, the transfer is not dutiable as a conveyance or transfer on sale, even if the transfer is made in contemplation of a possible future sale. The application of this principle is demonstrated in the decision of the House of Lords in *Wm. Cory & Son*

---

9. *Limmer Asphalte Paving Co.* v. *I.R.C.* (1872) L.R. 7 Ex. 211 at pp. 214–215, *per* Martin B. See also *I.R.C.* v. *Duke of Westminster* [1936] A.C. 1 and *I.R.C.* v. *Europa Oil (N.Z.) Ltd.* [1971] A.C. 760; see *post*, § 36–03. See also *post*, § 28–48.
    10. *Garnett* v. *I.R.C.* (1899) 81 L.T. 633; see *post*, § 28–12.
    11. *Eastern National Omnibus Co.* v. *I.R.C.* [1939] 1 K.B. 161; see *post*, § 29–08.
    12. [1985] S.T.C. 835 at p. 851.
    13. Subject to the principle in *Ramsay* v. *I.R.C.* [1981] S.T.C. 174 and *Furniss* v. *Dawson* [1984] S.T.C. 153.

Ltd. v. *I.R.C.*,[14] which was nullified as regards instruments executed on or after August 1, 1965, by the Finance Act 1965.[15] The principle above stated is not, however, in any way abrogated by the provisions of the statute. Although the time of execution is the material time for determining the effect of an instrument for stamp duty purposes, the court will have regard to what is said and done thereafter in order to discover the true position when the instrument was executed.[16]

27–09 (5) *If an instrument is ineffective for the intended purpose, it is not liable to duty*

Thus, if an appointment of trustees is made by the wrong person, the instrument is not liable to duty; and if a stamp has already been impressed, the duty may be recoverable.[17]

27–10 (6) *A transaction effected orally normally attracts no duty*[18]

This follows from the principle already stated that stamp duty is a duty on instruments, not on transactions. Thus if a contract is concluded orally, or the title to property is transferred by delivery, duty is avoided. In some cases, to avoid duty, property which is not transferable by delivery can be converted into a deliverable state; for example, by severing fixtures before transfer.

Something may be deemed to be an instrument which would not otherwise be treated as such. Thus if shares are allotted for a consideration other than cash and the contract between the company and the allottee is not reduced to writing, section 88 of the Companies Act 1985 requires that particulars of the contract shall be delivered to the registrar of companies within one month after the allotment; and those particulars are deemed to be an instrument within the meaning of the Stamp Act 1891 and must be stamped with the same stamp duty as would have been payable if the contract had been reduced to writing. The Registrar may, as a condition of filing the particulars, require that the duty payable thereunder be adjudicated under section 12 of the Stamp Act 1891[19]: see § 27–41.

---

14. [1965] A.C. 1088 (H.L.). Discussed *post*, § 28–22. There is a number of other cases (cited in the *Cory* case) illustrating this principle. The principle was relied on by the Revenue in *Western United Investment Co. Ltd.* v. *I.R.C.* [1958] Ch. 392 at p. 398. *Cf. Combined Technologies Corporation plc* v. *I.R.C.* [1985] S.T.C. 348, where the reasoning of Vinelott J. (esp. p. 355e–f) ignores the principle in arriving at a decision adverse to the taxpayer. See also § 32–10A.

15. See *post*, § 28–23.

16. [1965] A.C. 1088 (H.L.), *per* Lord Reid at p. 1105.

17. See *post*, § 27–51.

18. Some transactions cannot be effected without the use of a written instrument. Thus (i) a deed is necessary to convey a legal estate in land (Law of Property Act 1925, s.52(1)); (ii) transfer of shares must be in writing (Companies Act 1985, s.183); (iii) a disposition of an equitable interest must be in writing (Law of Property Act 1925, s.53): see *Grey* v. *I.R.C.* [1960] A.C. 1, *post*, § 28–08. An exception to this principle exists in nthe stamp duty reserve tax: see §§ 28–50 *et seq.*

19. Companies Act 1985, s.88(4).

27–11   *Records of oral transactions.* If a transaction is effected without the use of a written instrument and subsequently a written record of that transaction is made, the written record is generally not liable to duty. This is because the transaction is not *effected* by the written instrument; the instrument merely records a transaction which has already been effected. There is an exception to this rule: under the principle established in *Cohen and Moore* v. *I.R.C.*,[20] the court will in certain circumstances treat an oral transaction and a subsequent written record thereof as one single transaction effected by the instrument. The facts of the case were as follows:

> Settlors orally declared that they would hold certain securities on trust until other trustees were appointed in their place. The securities were set forth in schedules to a draft deed and the trusts were set forth in the deed. Some five weeks after the verbal declaration of trust, the draft deed was executed reciting the verbal declaration and appointing trustees. *Held*, that the verbal declaration and the later deed formed one transaction and that the deed was liable to settlement duty.[20a]

"I think," said Finlay J., "that the transaction was really all one transaction and that, being one transaction, the whole was recorded in the document— the only document which has been drawn up—which is the settlement."[21] It should be noted that the deed was in draft at the time of the verbal declaration.[22]

27–12   (7) *The leading and principal objects rule*

"There is no better established rule as regards stamp duty than that all that is required is that the instrument should be stamped for its leading and principal object, and that this stamp covers everything accessory to this object."[23]

> *Examples*
> (i) The stamp on a lease covers an option to purchase the reversion.[24]
> (ii) The stamp on the creation of a settlement covers the appointment of the first trustees.
> (iii) The stamp on a conveyance or assent under seal covers any acknowledgment for production, undertaking for safe custody or any restrictive covenants.

If by virtue of the leading object principle the document is exempt from duty, an accessory provision is also exempt.

> *Example*
> The exemption from duty onn an assent not under seal covers any warranties as to title or acknowledgment for production.

27–13   (8) *Transactions effected by operation of law attract no duty*

> *Example*
> (i) On an appointment of a new trustee by deed (which is exempt from

---

20. [1933] 2 K.B. 126; and see *post*, § 28–18.
20a. Settlement duty was abolished by F.A. 1962, s.30. See § 30–14.
21. *Ibid.* at pp. 137–138.
22. Contrast *Grey* v. *I.R.C.* [1958] Ch. 375 at pp. 379–380 (on this point).
23. *Limmer Asphalte Paving Co.* v. *I.R.C.* (1872) L.R. 7 Ex. 211 at p. 217, *per* Martin B.
24. *Worthington* v. *Warrington* (1848) 5 C.B. 635. *Cf.* an option to purchase *other* property, which attracts a separate duty; see *post*, § 27–15, Example (ii).

duty[25]), no duty is chargeable by virtue of the implied vesting declaration under section 40 of the Trustee Act 1925.

(ii) No duty is attracted by the constructive trust for the purchaser which arises under a contract of sale.[26] *Cf.* the position where there is an express trust in the agreement.[27]

27–14   (9) *Documents containing separate instruments*

Sections 3 and 4 of the Stamp Act 1891 are intended to prevent evasion of duty by the use of one document to effect more than one transaction. Section 3(2) provides that:

> "If more than one instrument be written upon the same piece of material, every one of the instruments is to be separately and distinctly stamped with the duty with which it is chargeable."

By section 122(1), "instrument" includes every written document, and "material" includes every sort of material upon which words or figures can be expressed. In *Prudential Assurance Co. Ltd.* v. *I.R.C.*,[28] a memorandum indorsed on a life policy increasing the sum assured by the policy, following disclosure that the assured's age had been incorrectly stated, was held to be a separate instrument separately chargeable with duty by virtue of section 3(2). An alteration of an instrument after execution may in some cases constitute a new instrument requiring a fresh stamp.

27–15   (10) *Instruments to be separately charged with duty*

By section 4 of the Stamp Act 1891, except where express provision to the contrary is made by that or any other Act:

> "(*a*) An instrument containing or relating to several distinct matters is to be separately and distinctly charged, as if it were a separate instrument, with duty in respect of each of the matters;
>
> (*b*) An instrument made for any consideration in respect whereof it is chargeable with *ad valorem* duty, and also for any further or other valuable consideration or considerations, is to be separately and distinctly charged, as if it were a separate instrument, with duty in respect of each of the considerations."

The word "matters" in section 4(*a*) is not defined in the Act and some doubt has been expressed as to its proper interpretation. It is generally supposed, however, that it refers to the matters in respect of which duty is chargeable,[29] so that more than one duty is charged if the instrument either falls under more than one head of charge, or effects more than one transaction.[30] This principle does not contradict the "leading and principal objects rule" (see § 27–12) since it only applies where the matters are not simply accessory to a principal object. Examples of the application of section 4 which commonly arise in practice are as follows:

---

25. Duty under the head "Appointment" was abolished by F.A. 1985, s.85, Sched. 24.
26. *I.R.C.* v. *Angus & Co.* (1889) 23 Q.B.D. 579 (C.A.); see *post*, § 28–19.
27. *Chesterfield Brewery Co.* v. *I.R.C.* [1899] 2 Q.B. 7; see *post*, § 28–19.
28. [1935] 1 K.B. 101.
29. This view is supported by *Reversionary Interest Society Ltd.* v. *I.R.C.* (1906) 22 T.L.R. 740. *Cf.* Rowlatt J. in *Ansell* v. *I.R.C.* [1929] 1 K.B. 608 at p. 617.
30. *Lovelock* v. *Franklyn* (1847) 8 Q.B. 371; *cf. ante*, § 27–12, Example (i).

(i) A lease containing an option to buy land other than the demised land attracts lease duty and a 50p stamp in respect of the option (or *ad valorem* conveyance or transfer duty if there is separate consideration for it[31]).

(ii) In *Freeman* v. *I.R.C.*,[32] executors used one document to transfer to four residuary legatees shares in nine companies forming part of the testator's residuary estate. *Held,* that four transfer stamps were required.

27–16　(11) *If one transaction is effected by more than one instrument only one ad valorem duty can be charged if the ad valorem duty exceeds 50p*

This is important in connection with settlements of land and other property which are commonly effected by two instruments. The relevant provisions are discussed later.[33] Where there are several instruments of conveyance for completing the purchaser's title to property sold, only the principal instrument of conveyance is chargeable with *ad valorem* duty; the other instruments are chargeable with such *other* duty as they may be liable to, such duty not to exceed the *ad valorem* duty payable on the principal instrument.[34]

27–17　(12) *Choice of head of charge*

If an instrument falls under more than one head of charge in the Act, the Crown is entitled to claim duty under only one head, at its choice; but it may choose whichever head yields the most duty.

Examples
In *Speyer Bros.* v. *I.R.C.*,[35–38] certain notes issued by the United States of Mexico were both promissory notes and marketable securities for the purposes of the Stamp Act. *Held,* that they were liable to the higher duty imposed on marketable securities.

The principle in this paragraph must not be confused with the principle mentioned in § 27–15. *Speyer's* case, for example, was not a case of an instrument effecting more than one transaction; the instrument effected only one transaction but, looked at in different ways, it fell under more than one head of charge.

27–18　(13) *The contingency principle*

If the sum payable under an instrument is uncertain at the time of its execution, any *ad valorem* duty is assessed on the maximum which might become payable and which can be calculated in advance at the date of the instrument.

Example
A beer house is conveyed for £*x*, with an undertaking by the purchaser to pay £*y* if a spirit licence is obtained. *Ad valorem* conveyance or transfer duty is assessed on £*x* + £*y*.

---

31. See *post*, § 28–20.
32. (1871) L.R. 6 Ex. 101.
33. See *post*, §§ 30–16 *et seq.*
34. S.A. 1891, s.58(3); see § 28–47.
35–38. [1908] A.C. 92.

There are two leading cases on this principle.

> In *Underground Electric Railways Co.* v. *I.R.C.*,[39] A Ltd. agreed that *if* a sufficient number of stockholders in B Ltd. would exchange their ordinary stock for guaranteed stock, A Ltd. would guarantee 4 per cent. interest on such stock *if* the profits of B Ltd. were insufficient to pay interest at 4 per cent. It was known at the date of the deed that if the first condition was satisfied, and if B Ltd. made no profits, A Ltd. would have to make periodic payments of a maximum sum of £120,000. *Held*, that the deed was a primary security for the maximum which *might* be payable, namely £120,000, and was liable to bond covenant duty[40] thereon.

The instrument, said Warrington L.J., "is a security for the payment of a sum of money notwithstanding that events may happen which enable one or other of the parties to put an end to the obligation of which the security is a part and notwithstanding that in the event the obligation may not result in the recovery from the obligor of any particular sum of money."[41] The principle applies also to lease duty.[42]

27–19 *Minimum only calculable in advance.* If only a minimum sum payable can be calculated in advance, *ad valorem* duty is assessed on this minimum.[43]

> *Example*
> In assessing the *ad valorem* duty on a life policy, no account is taken of bonuses; but if a minimum bonus is provided, duty is assessed on this minimum.[44]

27–20 *Neither maximum nor minimum calculable in advance.* If neither a maximum nor a minimum can be calculated, no *ad valorem* duty can be charged, except where a sum can be ascertained which *might* be payable.

> *Example*
> In *Independent Television Authority and Associated-Rediffusion Ltd.* v. *I.R.C.*,[45] "A.-R." agreed to provide TV programmes for a fixed period of approximately nine years and to pay to the Authority a fee of £495,600 a year for $2\frac{1}{2}$ years and £536,900 thereafter. The agreement provided for an increase or decrease of such payments depending on variations in a certain index figure. *Held*, that *ad valorem* bond covenant duty[46] was payable on the total sum which *might* become payable under the agreement, namely over £4 million.
> "I take it, therefore, to be a well-settled principle," said Lord Radcliffe, at p. 443, "that the money payable is ascertained for the purposes of charge without regard to the fact that the agreement in question may itself contain provisions which will in certain circumstances prevent it being payable at all. If that is so, there is at least no better reason for adopting a different principle

---

39. [1914] 3 K.B. 210; affirmed [1916] 1 K.B. 306 (C.A.).
40. Bond covenant duty was abolished as from August 1, 1971, by F.A. 1971, s.64(1)(c); see *post*, § 27–53.
41. [1916] 1 K.B. 306 at pp. 318–320.
42. *Coventry City Council* v. *I.R.C.* [1979] Ch. 142; [1978] S.T.C. 151 (duty assessed on the maximum rent which could become payable).
43. See *Underground Electric Railways Co.* v. *I.R.C.* [1906] A.C. 21.
44. See *post*, § 34–03.
45. [1961] A.C. 427.
46. Bond covenant duty was abolished as from August 1, 1971, by F.A. 1971, s.64(1)(c); see *post*, § 27–53.

where there are found clauses which merely vary the amount to be paid according to specified contingencies."

3. THE CONSEQUENCES OF FAILING TO STAMP INSTRUMENTS

27–21 The act of failing to stamp a document, or of failing to stamp a document correctly, does not generally render any person liable to any action against him by the Revenue; nor does the want of the stamp invalidate the document.[47] In the ordinary case, the stamp authorities have no means of knowing when instruments are executed which are not duly stamped. The Stamp Act deals with the problem primarily in two ways:

- (*a*) by rendering unstamped (including insufficiently or improperly stamped) instruments inadmissible in evidence and generally useless, whilst they remain unstamped; and
- (*b*) by levying penalties when instruments are presented for stamping outside the time limits prescribed by the Act.

Each of these matters will be considered.

A. *Admissibility, etc., of Unstamped Instruments*

27–22 Section 14(4) of the Stamp Act 1891 provides that an instrument:

"shall not, except in criminal proceedings, be given in evidence or be available for any purpose whatsoever, unless it is duly stamped in accordance with the law in force at the time when it was first executed."

An instrument delivered as an *escrow* is only *executed*, for this purpose, when it becomes unconditional.[48] An instrument is not "duly stamped" if, though stamped, it bears the wrong kind of stamp. Thus, in *Ashling* v. *Boon*,[49] an instrument bearing an adhesive postage stamp appropriate to a receipt but which should have been stamped with an appropriated "bill or note" stamp as a promissory note was not allowed in evidence to prove payment of the money for which it was given. When an original document is inadmissible, secondary evidence of it is likewise inadmissible.

The rule against admissibility has no application to criminal proceedings (including proceedings before justices for recovery of a penalty) and it is arguable that it does not apply in proceedings before the General and Special Commissioners.[50] Further, an unstamped instrument has been admitted in evidence to prove an act of bankruptcy[51]; to prove fraud[52]; and it may be put to a witness to refresh his memory.[53]

---

47. In *Re Indo-China Steam Navigation Co.* [1917] 2 Ch. 100 at p. 106, Eve J. suggested *obiter* that the legal title to shares would not pass if the transfer was not properly stamped. This is generally thought to be wrong: Sergeant, p. 80.
48. See *Terrapin International Ltd.* v. *I.R.C.* [1976] 1 W.L.R. 665.
49. [1891] 1 Ch. 568.
50. See Monroe's *Stamp Duties*, (5th ed.), para. 22. The point was left open in *Sinclair* v. *I.R.C.* (1942) 24 T.C. 432 at pp. 442, 444.
51. *Re Gunsbourg* (1919) 88 L.J.K.B. 562.
52. *Re Shaw* (1920) 90 L.J.K.B. 204.
53. *Birchall* v. *Bullough* [1896] 1 Q.B. 325 (D.C.).

Collateral purpose

27–23   It was at one time thought that an unstamped instrument was admissible in evidence for a collateral purpose: thus, in *Fengl* v. *Fengl*,[54] in reliance on cases decided before 1891, it was argued that an unstamped separation deed (which clearly would not have been admissible in proceedings to enforce its provisions) was admissible in proceedings before justices on the issue of the voluntary nature of the separation. Sir Samuel Evans P., however, held that the old cases had been overruled by the very wide terms of section 14(4) of the Stamp Act 1891, making a document inadmissible in civil proceedings "for any purpose whatsoever." This view is supported by the decision of the Privy Council in *Ram Rattan* v. *Parma Nand*,[55] decided on comparable words in the Indian Stamp Act; so it now seems to be established[56] that an unstamped instrument is inadmissible even to prove some matter collateral to it.

The Revenue will not give effect to unstamped settlements, which are thus ineffective as a means of tax saving until and unless the instrument is stamped on payment of the appropriate penalty: see § 27–27.

Taking stamp objections

27–24   By section 14(1) of the Stamp Act 1891, if an instrument is produced in evidence in a civil court, the judge, arbitrator, or referee[57] is required to take notice of the omission or insufficiency of any stamp. He is thus under a statutory obligation to protect the Revenue, and it is not open to the parties to waive a stamp objection. The section further provides that if the instrument is one which may be legally stamped after execution,[58] it may be received in evidence on payment of the amount of the duty, of the penalty for stamping out of time, and of a further sum of £1. The usual practice is to allow an unstamped instrument to be put in evidence on a personal undertaking given by the solicitor of the party producing it to have it stamped and to pay the statutory penalty.[59]

Stamp objections by counsel

27–25   The General Council of the Bar has ruled that "save in revenue cases, it is unprofessional that a counsel should object to the admissibility of any document upon the ground that it is not, or is not sufficiently, stamped, unless such defect goes to the validity of the document; and counsel should not take part in any discussion that may arise in support of an objection on such a ground unless invited to do so by the court."[60]

If a dispute arises in the course of proceedings as to the proper stamp for

---

54. [1914] P. 274 (D.C.).
55. (1945) L.R. 73 Ind.App. 28.
56. But not, perhaps, in Scotland: *Watson* v. *Watson*, 1934 S.C. 374 at p. 379.
57. But not a Rent Tribunal: *R.* v. *Fulham, etc., Rent Tribunal* [1951] 2 K.B. 1 (D.C.).
58. See *post*, § 27–28.
59. *Re Coolgardie Goldfields Ltd.* [1900] 1 Ch. 475 at p. 477; *Parkfield Trust* v. *Dent* [1931] 2 K.B. 579.
60. Boulton, *Conduct and Etiquette at the Bar*, (6th ed.), p. 70.

an instrument tendered in evidence, the dispute must be settled in open court. It seems, however, that section 14(1) of the Stamp Act 1891 does not oblige the judge to try doubtful questions of stamp duty law, but merely requires that he should intervene in a clear case of omission or insufficiency of the stamp.[61] The modern practice in cases of doubt is to require an undertaking to have the instrument adjudicated.

Appeals

27–26   No appeal lies against the ruling of a judge[62] that an instrument is sufficiently stamped or requires no stamp[63]; but appeal lies from a ruling rejecting an instrument as insufficiently stamped.[64]

B. *Penalties for Stamping Out of Time*

27–27   The word "penalty" is commonly used to describe a punishment, in the form of a fine or other money payment, imposed by a court of criminal jurisdiction. The word is not used in this sense in the Stamp Act, for no criminal proceedings may be instituted for failure to stamp an instrument; nor is a penalty recoverable by civil action. A penalty is the price exacted by the Revenue for stamping an instrument out of time; the amount of the penalty increasing with the delay in the stamping of the instrument.

27–28   Section 15(1) of the Stamp Act 1891 provides that an unstamped or insufficiently stamped instrument may be stamped after execution[65] only on payment of:

  (1) the unpaid duty;
  (2) a penalty of £10; and
  (3) a further penalty, if the unpaid duty exceeds £10, of interest on such duty at 5 per cent. per annum from the date of first execution[65] of the instrument to the time when the interest equals the additional duty.

27–29   Section 15(2), however, contains different penalty provisions affecting the instruments listed in a Table in the section. This Table, as amended, is as follows:

---

61. See *Don Francesco* v. *De Meo*, 1908 S.C. 7.
62. But *semble* that a ruling of the Special Commissioners could be the subject of a case stated.
63. R.S.C., Ord. 59, r.11(5).
64. *The Belfort* (1884) 9 P.D. 215.
65. "Execution," in the case of instruments not under seal, refers to the act of signing: S.A. 1891, s.122(1). Often an instrument has to be executed by a number of parties and there is no means of telling when it was "first" executed. In practice, the stamp authorities accept the date which is inserted on the instrument as the date from which time starts to run. See a useful article by J. G. Monroe on "The Dating of a Document" [1960] B.T.R. 180.

Title of instrument as described in the First Schedule to the Act	*Person liable to penalty*
Bond, covenant, or instrument of any kind whatsoever.[66]	The obligee, covenantee or other person taking the security.
Conveyance on sale.	The vendee or transferee.
Lease or tack	The lessee.
Agreement for lease or tack chargeable under section 75.[67]	The person contracting for the lease or tack to be granted to him or another.
Unit trust instrument.	The trustees.[68]

It will be noted that not all the principal instruments liable to *ad valorem* duty are included in the Table. An instrument of the class referred to in the Table must (if not written on stamped material) be stamped within 30 days after its first execution,[69] unless:

(a) it was first executed out of the United Kingdom, when it must be stamped within 30 days of its arrival in the United Kingdom[70]; or

(b) it was lodged for adjudication, when it must be stamped within 14 days after notice of the assessment.[71]

The instruments in the Table can be stamped out of time only on payment of the unpaid duty, the penalties in (2) and (3) in § 27–28 and a further penalty equal to the stamp duty on the instrument. In addition, the person in the right-hand column of the Table is liable to a fine of £10 (even if the instrument is not presented for stamping).

Theory and practice

27–30   It seems clear from section 15 that the Stamp Act 1891 contemplates that all instruments executed in the United Kingdom will be stamped *before* execution, except for those instruments listed in section 15(2) which must be stamped (generally) within 30 days *after* execution. In practice, however, most impressed stamping is done after execution and the Commissioners (who have statutory power to mitigate or remit penalties)[72] will stamp most instruments presented within 30 days after execution without demanding the penalty prescribed by the Act.

C. *Other Sanctions for the Payment of Duty*

(a) *Recovery of stamp duty by action*

27–31   Duty cannot normally be recovered by action. Exceptionally, however, in the case of the following duties, proceedings in the High Court may be taken for the recovery of the duty as a debt due to the Crown:

---

66. This head of charge was abolished as from August 1, 1971, by F.A. 1971, s.64(1)(*c*); see *post*, § 27–53.
67. Inserted by F.A. 1984, s.111(4) with effect for any such agreement entered into on or after March 20, 1984.
68. Added to the Table by F.A. 1962, s.30(1).
69. See *ante*, § 27–28.
70. S.A. 1891, s.15(2)(*a*).
71. *Ibid.* s.15(2)(*b*).
72. *Ibid.* s.15(3)(*b*), amended by F.A. 1895, s.15.

(a) the capital duty in respect of chargeable transactions of capital companies[73];

(b) the duty payable on the assignment of a policy of life assurance where the policy moneys have been paid to the assignee without stamping the assignment.[74]

(b) *Fines*

27–32   Many sections of the Stamp Act impose fines,[75–76] which are recoverable as civil debts. Two of these sections merit special mention:

Section 5 of the Stamp Act 1891 provides that:

> "All the facts and circumstances affecting the liability of any instrument to duty, or the amount of the duty with which any instrument is chargeable, are to be fully and truly set forth in the instrument; and every person who, with intent to defraud Her Majesty,
>> (*a*) executes any instrument in which all the said facts and circumstances are not fully and truly set forth; or
>> (*b*) being employed or concerned in or about the preparation of any instrument, neglects or omits fully and truly to set forth therein all the said facts and circumstances;
> shall incur a fine of £25."

It is not always practicable or desirable to set forth in an instrument *all* the facts and circumstances affecting liability for duty; but no offence is committed unless an intent to defraud is present, so it is sufficient in practice to disclose material facts separately when presenting an instrument to the Commissioners for adjudication.

Section 17 of the Stamp Act 1891 provides that:

> "If any person whose office it is to enrol, register, or enter in or upon any rolls, books, or records any instrument chargeable with duty, enrols, registers, or enters any such instrument not being duly stamped, he shall incur a fine of £10."

Thus the secretary of a company incurs a fine if he registers an improperly stamped transfer of shares.[77] If the secretary refuses registration on the ground of the insufficiency of the stamp but the transferee questions his refusal, he should present the transfer for adjudication and, after adjudication, re-present it for registration. Mandamus is not the proper procedure.[78] The secretary or other officer concerned is entitled, when considering whether a transfer is duly stamped, to go behind the consideration stated in the transfer.

Thus in *Maynard* v. *Consolidated Kent Colliers Corporation*,[79] the stamp on a

---

73. F.A. 1973, s.47(7); see *post*, § 32–02.
74. S.A. 1891, s.118(2).
75–76. For a list of these sections, see Sergeant, (3rd ed.), pp. 7–8.
77. A master has been held vicariously liable for a fine imposed on his servant acting in the course of his duties: *Att.-Gen.* v. *Carlton Bank Ltd.* [1899] 2 Q.B. 158.
78. *R.* v. *Registrar of Joint Stock Companies* (1888) 21 Q.B.D. 131. As to the duties and liability of the registering officer, see the circular issued by the Revenue in Sergeant, pp. 77 *et seq.*
79. [1903] 2 K.B. 121 (C.A.).

transfer of shares was in accordance with the consideration stated on the face of the document, but it was found that the consideration actually given exceeded this amount. *Held*, that the directors were entitled to refuse registration of the transfer.

There is a two-year time limit for the recovery of fines, such two years being reckoned from the time when the fine is incurred.[80]

(c) *Conveyancing practice*

27–33   A purchaser is entitled to insist that every deed which forms a link in the vendor's title is duly stamped. This is because, by virtue of section 14(4) of the Stamp Act 1891, a purchaser cannot use an unstamped, or insufficiently stamped, deed for any purpose whatsoever, whether to defend his title or to attack a wrongdoer.

> Thus in *Whiting* v. *Loomes*[81] a mortgage deed was stamped with a 10s. deed stamp. *Held*, that a purchaser from the mortgagors was entitled to have the deed stamped before completion with the full *ad valorem* duty at the vendor's expense, notwithstanding that the mortgagee had consented to join in the conveyance.

"The court," said Lush J., "is not entitled to speculate whether the purchaser may or may not have occasion to use the deed. A purchaser is entitled to have every deed forming a step in his title in such shape that he can, if he need it, give it in evidence."

A purchaser is entitled to rescind the contract if the vendor refuses to stamp an unstamped instrument; and section 117 of the Stamp Act (which applies to instruments executed after May 16, 1888) invalidates any condition of sale framed with the view of precluding objection or requisition upon the ground of absence or insufficiency of stamp, or providing for the purchaser to undertake liability for the duty.

27–34   *Omnia rite esse acta.* There is a presumption that a document is duly stamped: *omnia praesumuntur rite et solemniter esse acta.* If, therefore, the consideration expressed in a deed which forms a link in the title appears to be inadequate, but the deed is stamped in accordance with the consideration therein expressed, the purchaser is not entitled to raise objection to the sufficiency of the stamp.[82]

A lost document is presumed to have been duly stamped[83] and the Commissioners will stamp a replica free of charge, or repay the duty if a replica has already been stamped.[84]

---

80. Inland Revenue Regulation Act 1890, s.22(2).
81. (1881) 17 Ch.D. 10 (C.A.); followed in *Maynard's* case (above).
82. *Re Weir and Pitt's Contract* (1911) 55 S.J. 536; and see (1954) 1 L.S. Digest 80, Opinion 268.
83. *Marine Investment Co.* v. *Haviside* (1872) L.R. 5 H.L. 624; and see Monroe's *Stamp Duties* (5th ed.), para. 57.
84. See Concession No. G1.

4. Method of Stamping

(1) *Impressed and adhesive stamps*

27–35 Payment of stamp duty must now be denoted by means of impressed stamps in all cases.[85] Stamp duty under the following headings, prior to their abolition, could be denoted by means of adhesive postage stamps:

(a) agreements under hand only[86];

(b) bills of exchange and promissory notes[87];

(c) receipts.[88–91]

Postage stamps are no longer valid for stamp duty purposes.

(2) *Denoting stamps*

–36/38 Where the duty with which an instrument is chargeable depends in any manner on the duty paid on another instrument, the payment of the last-mentioned duty will, on application to the Commissioners and production of both instruments, be denoted on the first-mentioned instrument.[92] The following denoting stamps are in use:

27–39 (a) *The duplicate denoting stamp.*[93] The duplicate or counterpart of an instrument is not duly stamped unless either:

(i) it is stamped as an original; or

(ii) it appears by some stamp impressed thereon that the full and proper duty has been paid on the original, *i.e.* unless the instrument is denoted.

The counterpart of a lease does not require denoting unless it is executed by the lessor. In addition to the denoting stamp, a duplicate must bear a fixed stamp under the head "Duplicate or Counterpart of any instrument chargeable with duty." This stamp is 50p (or the same as the original, if the stamp on the original is less than 50p).

27–40 (b) *The duty paid denoting stamp.* This is used on the following instruments:

(i) on a conveyance on sale, where *ad valorem* duty has already been paid on the agreement for sale under section 59 of the Stamp Act[94];

(ii) on a lease, where *ad valorem* duty has already been paid on the agreement for the lease under section 75(1) of the Stamp Act.[95]

The stamp in these cases bears the inscription: "Duty paid *ad valorem* £x."

---

85. S.A. 1891, s.2; see *post*, § 27–37.
86. *Ibid.* s.22; abolished as from August 1, 1970, F.A. 1970, Sched. 7.
87. F.A. 1961, ss.33(2); abolished as from February 1, 1971: F.A. 1970, Sched. 7.
88–91. S.A. 1891, s.101(2); abolished as from February 1, 1971: F.A. 1970, Sched. 7.
92. *Ibid.* s.11.
93. *Ibid.* s.72.
94. *Ibid.* s.59(3); see *post*, § 29–02.
95. See *post*, § 31–08.

The denoting stamp is obtained by leaving the instruments at the stamp office. The denoting stamp is, however, no guarantee that the original or principal instrument was duly stamped: a formal adjudication is necessary for this purpose.

The denoting stamp is used to counteract a device to avoid *ad valorem* duty on a conveyance of real property by using an agreement for a long lease: section 111(2) of the Finance Act 1984 provides, *inter alia*, that where an interest in land is conveyed or transferred subject to an agreement for a lease or tack for a term exceeding 35 years, it is not to be taken as duly stamped unless the duty paid on the agreement is denoted on the instrument transferring the interest. Thus it is not possible to keep hidden from the Land Registry the fact that *ad valorem* duty was not paid on the agreement for a lease and the purchaser will also take with notice of the fact.

(3) *Adjudication stamps*

27–41   Under section 12 of the Stamp Act 1891, any person may require the Commissioners to express their opinion with reference to any *executed* instrument on the questions: (a) whether the instrument is chargeable with any duty; and (b) with what amount it is chargeable.[96] If the Commissioners are of opinion that the instrument is not chargeable with duty, it will be stamped accordingly ("Adjudged not chargeable with any duty")[97]; otherwise, they will assess the duty and, when the instrument has been stamped in accordance with the assessment, they will add the adjudication stamp ("Adjudged duly stamped").[98]

27–42   *Appeals.* Any person who is dissatisfied with the assessment of the Commissioners may, within 21 days after the date of the assessment and *on payment of the duty* in conformity therewith, appeal to the High Court.[99] The appeal is by way of case stated and the Commissioners may be required to state and sign a case setting forth the question on which their opinion was required and the assessment made by them. In practice, the stated case is settled in draft by the Commissioners and then agreed with the appellant. The case will then be heard in the Chancery Division. It is the duty of the judge to determine the question submitted to him and to assess the duty, if any.[1] It may be necessary to call evidence, for example, as to the value of property.[2] If the court decides that the assessment of the Commissioners was wrong, the court will order that the duty (or the excess duty) be repaid, together with any fine or penalty paid in consequence of the erroneous

---

96. S.A. 1891, s.12(1).
97. *Ibid.* s.12(3).
98. *Ibid.* s.12(4).
99. *Ibid.* s.13. For a criticism of the adjudication procedure, see *E.C. (Holdings) Ltd.* v. *I.R.C.* (1959) 38 A.T.C. 73 at p. 74, *per* Roxburgh J.
1. S.A. 1891, s.13(3). The s.13 procedure was considered by Vinelott J. in *Ingram* v. *I.R.C.* [1985] S.T.C. 835 at p. 842.
2. See, *e.g. Speyer Bros.* v. *I.R.C.* [1906] 1 K.B. 318 (where evidence was heard on the question whether "gold coupon treasury notes" issued by the Mexican Government were capable of being dealt in according to the ordinary practice of the Stock Exchange).

assessment.[3] The court has power to award such interest as it may determine on the sum repaid.[4]

A further appeal from the order of the judge lies to the Court of Appeal and thence, with leave, to the House of Lords.

27–43 *Procedure for obtaining adjudication.* Briefly, the instrument on which adjudication is required must be presented or sent to the stamp office. According to the strict terms of section 5 of the Stamp Act 1891,[5] the instrument should itself set forth all the facts and circumstances affecting liability to duty; but this is not always practicable and indeed the Commissioners have power to obtain any information they require.[6]

27–44 *Effect of adjudication.* Any executed instrument can be presented for adjudication. In eight principal cases, adjudication is obligatory inasmuch that the instrument is not duly stamped without adjudication: see also § 27–10. These cases are:

(a) voluntary dispositions[7];

(b) conveyances and leases to charities[8];

(c) transactions exempt from capital duty within Part III of Schedule 19 to the Finance Act 1973[9];

(d) conveyances and transfers relieved from duty in connection with certain schemes of reconstruction and amalgamation of companies[10];

(e) conveyances and transfers relieved from duty as between associated companies[11];

(f) conveyances or transfers of property in contemplation of a sale thereof[12];

(g) conveyances in consideration of a debt.[13]

(h) documents executed solely for the purpose of effecting exempt distributions in connection with a demerger under the Finance Act 1980, Sched. 18.[13a]

In practice the court requires an undertaking that any orders made under the Variation of Trusts Act 1958 be adjudicated.[14] In other cases, however, adjudication is advantageous because it is generally conclusive as to the sufficiency of the stamp: the instrument is "admissible in evidence, and

---

3. S.A. 1891, s.13(4).
4. F.A. 1965, s.91, nullifying the decision in *Western United Investment Co. Ltd.* v. *I.R.C.* [1958] Ch. 392.
5. See *ante*, § 27–32.
6. S.A. 1891, s.12(2).
7. F.A. 1985, s.82(5).
8. F.A. 1982, s.129(2); see *post*, § 28–45/46.
9. F.A. 1973, s.47(6); see *post*, §§ 32–09 *et seq*.
10. F.A. 1986, ss.75 and 76 see §§ 33–02 *et seq*.
11. F.A. 1930, s.42(1), proviso; see *post*, § 33–10.
12. F.A. 1965, s.90(3); see *post*, § 28–23.
13. F.A. 1980, s.102(2); *post*, § 28–39.
13a. *Ibid*. para. 12(1A), (3).
14. For the practice, see Practice Note in [1966] 1 W.L.R. 345.

available for all purposes notwithstanding any objection relating to duty."[15] It is conclusive, therefore, as against a purchaser. But there are some exceptions to this rule of conclusiveness:

(a) an instrument which by law cannot be stamped after execution is not duly stamped, even if it bears an adjudication stamp impressed after execution[16];

(b) the court could probably go behind an adjudication stamp which was proved to have been obtained by fraud or misrepresentation[17];

(c) an adjudication stamp is not retrospective.

Thus in *Prudential Assurance Investment and Loan Association* v. *Curzon,*[18] a document was insufficiently stamped at the trial and objected to on this ground. After the trial and before the appeal, the instrument was adjudicated. *Held,* that this did not remove the objection to the sufficiency of the first stamp.

The procedure by adjudication and subsequent appeal is the normal procedure for obtaining an authoritative decision on some point of stamp duty law. Further, it has been used as a means of obtaining a determination of the court as to whether a body is a legal charity.[19]

(4) *Produced stamps*

27–45   The following instruments are not duly stamped, even if adjudicated, unless they are produced to the Commissioners and stamped with the "produced" (or "P.D.") stamp[20]:

(a) any conveyance on sale of the fee simple in land (including a conveyance of unregistered property where the consideration is under £30,000[21]);

(b) any lease or agreement for a lease of land for a term of seven years or more;

(c) any transfer on sale of such a lease (even if there are fewer than seven years to run);

(d) an instrument dutiable on issue as a bearer instrument.[22]

Where, however, there is a sale of registered land or an assignment or surrender of a registered lease, in either case being certified as made for a consideration not exceeding £30,000, the transferee is not obliged to pro-

---

15. S.A. 1891, s.12(5). But a "produced stamp" may be required; see *post,* § 27–45.

16. *Ibid.* s.12(6)(*b*); *Vallance* v. *Forbes* (1879) 6 R. (Ct. of Sess.) 1099.

17. Monroe's *Stamp Duties* (5th ed.), para. 65.

18. (1852) 8 Ex. 97. This was a case under the Stamp Duties Act 1850, s.14, where the "denoting" stamp therein referred to corresponds with the modern "adjudication" stamp. This decision has been applied in a case involving the validity of proxies presented at a meeting of shareholders: *Marx* v. *Estates and General Investments Ltd.* [1976] 1 W.L.R. 380; [1975] S.T.C. 671; see *post,* § 34–06.

19. *I.R.C.* v. *Baddeley* [1955] A.C. 572.

20. F.A. 1931, s.28.

21. See *post,* § 28–24.

22. F.A. 1963, s.60(3); see *post,* § 32–11.

duce the instrument to the Commissioners: instead, he must transmit it, together with the completed PD form to the Land Registry.[22a]

The object of the "produced" stamp is to give the authorities information about land values. A voluntary conveyance does not require a produced stamp; nor does a counterpart lease executed by the grantee or lessee only.

5. FOREIGN ELEMENT

(1) *The territorial limits of the Stamp Act*

27–46 Section 14(4) of the Stamp Act[23] (which states the consequences which follow where an instrument is not duly stamped in accordance with the law) applies to:

    (a) instruments executed in any part of the United Kingdom; and
    (b) instruments, wheresoever executed, relating to any property situate, or to any matter or thing done or to be done, in any part of the United Kingdom.

The subsection thus defines the territorial limits within which the Stamp Act operates.[24] A court order has been held to be "an instrument executed."[25]

With regard to (a), it will be noted that an instrument executed in the United Kingdom must be stamped, even though it operates abroad. Thus a conveyance of foreign land which is executed in England is inadmissible in evidence in the British courts unless it bears the *ad valorem* conveyance or transfer duty.[26]

The words in (b) were considered by the House of Lords in *I.R.C.* v. *Maple & Co. (Paris) Ltd.*[27] The facts were as follows:

> Property in France was transferred from one English company to another English company by an instrument (an *acte d'apport*) executed in France. The consideration for the transfer consisted of shares in the latter company which were to be issued and delivered to the former company in England. *Held,* that the instrument was liable to *ad valorem* duty as a conveyance on sale.

"The instrument," said Lord Macnaghten, "relates to the capital of the new company, out of which it was agreed that a specified number of shares should be appropriated and allotted to the old company. The share capital of the new company, if it was situate anywhere, was situate in England. In my opinion this instrument does relate to property situate in England. Be that as it may, it certainly relates to something to be done in England. It

---

22a. F.A. 1985, s.89; Stamp Duty (Exempt Instruments) Regs. 1985 (S.I. 1985 No. 1688).
23. See *ante*, § 27–22.
24. There are other sections which deal specifically with certain instruments executed abroad.
25. *Sun Alliance Ltd.* v. *I.R.C.* [1972] Ch. 133.
26. *Wright* v. *I.R.C.* (1855) 11 Ex. 458.
27. [1908] A.C. 22.

relates to the registration in the name of the old company of shares which were to be allotted in an English company as the consideration for the purchase of the French property."[28]

> In *Faber* v. *I.R.C.*,[29] an engineer executed a deed of covenant in Canada whereby he covenanted to pay to a Canadian company a proportion of the income from his profession (which he carried on in England), so long as he practised that profession. *Held,* that the deed related to something done or to be done in the United Kingdom (namely, the practice of the profession) and was liable to *ad valorem* duty.

If an instrument is executed abroad and relates wholly to property or matters abroad, the Stamp Act has no application.

If an instrument executed abroad conveys both foreign and English property, it is arguable (from s.4(*a*) of the Stamp Act) that it attracts duty only in respect of the English property: see § 27–15.

27–47   *Time for stamping.* It should be kept in mind that, although an instrument executed abroad may be liable to stamp duty, no penalty is payable until 30 days after it has been first received in the United Kingdom.[30] To avoid stamp duty, therefore, an instrument may be left outside the United Kingdom until such time as it is required within the United Kingdom.[31]

(2) *Conflict of laws*

27–48   The courts do not take notice of the revenue laws of a foreign state, except where they render an instrument void and not merely inadmissible.[32]

(3) *Double taxation relief*

27–49   No relief from stamp duty is given by the Stamp Act on instruments which are also dutiable in other countries.

27–50   There is an exception to this rule in the case of Northern Ireland and the Republic of Ireland[33]: If an instrument is dutiable in Great Britain and in Northern Ireland and is properly stamped in one of those countries, it is deemed to be properly stamped in the other; except that if the duty in such

---

28. [1908] A.C. 22 at p. 26.
29. [1936] 1 All E.R. 617.
30. See *ante*, § 27–29.
31. Furthermore it would appear to be possible to give secondary evidence of a document executed and retained abroad or, at least, of the effect of such a document: see *English, Scottish and Australian Chartered Bank* [1893] 3 Ch. 385 (C.A.).
32. *Bristow* v. *Sequeville* (1850) 5 Ex. 275; *Government of India* v. *Taylor* [1955] A.C. 491; *Brokaw* v. *Seatrain U.K. Ltd.* [1971] 2 Q.B. 476.
33. Government of Ireland Act 1920, s.29(1), as amended by the Irish Free State (Consequential Provisions) Act 1922 (Session 2), s.1. For text, see *Alpe on Stamps* (25th ed.), p. 400. As to bearer instruments, see F.A. 1963, s.61(9). The position is now governed by the Northern Ireland Constitution Act 1973 and the Northern Ireland Act 1974 under which, for the time being, stamp duties are levied by the U.K. government.

other country is higher, the instrument is not deemed to be duly stamped in that country unless the instrument is stamped for the excess. If an instrument is exempt from stamp duty in one country by virtue of a composition operating there, it is deemed to be stamped with the amount which would have been payable but for the composition.

There are similar provisions relating to the Republic of Ireland.[34]

6. STAMPS SPOILED OR WASTED

27-51 Section 9 of the Stamp Duties Management Act 1891 authorises the Commissioners to make an allowance where, in any of the cases listed in the section, a stamp is "spoiled." The following are examples of cases in which relief may be granted:

Examples
(i) A stamped instrument is found after execution to have been void *ab initio*. (But no relief is available under section 9 where a contract is voidable and is avoided; or where an instrument fails through non-fulfilment of a condition precedent.)

(ii) A stamped instrument is found after execution to be unfit, through error or mistake therein, for the purpose originally intended, *e.g.* where an appointment of trustees was made by the wrong person.

(iii) A stamped instrument becomes insufficient for the purpose for which it was intended through failure of some necessary party to sign it or to complete the transaction. But relief is available in this case only if the instrument has not been made use of for any purpose whatsoever.

(iv) Stamped material is, before execution, inadvertently spoiled or rendered unfit for the purpose intended.

Relief under section 9 is available only if the following conditions are satisfied[35]:

(a) the application for relief must be made within two years after the stamp has been spoiled or becomes useless or, in the case of an executed instrument, after the date of the instrument or, if not dated, after its execution[36];

(b) In the case of an executed instrument, no legal proceeding has been commenced in which the instrument could or would have been given or offered in evidence[37];

(c) In the case of an executed instrument, the instrument must be surrendered for cancellation.[37]

Relief, if granted, may take the form of a repayment in cash or the giving of stamps.[38]

The provisions in section 9 (above) should be contrasted with those in

---

34. Relief in respect of Double Taxation (Irish Free State Declaration) 1923 (S.R. & O. 1923 No. 406), Sched. Pt. III. The Stamp Act 1891 applies in the Republic but the rates of duty are different from those in the U.K., *e.g.* the duty on a conveyance on sale in the Republic is at the rate of £3 per cent. where the consideration exceeds £2,500.
35. Regulations have been made by the Commissioners as to the procedure for claiming relief. See Sergeant, *op. cit.* pp. 29–30.
36. Stamp Duties Management Act 1891, s.9(7), proviso (*a*).
37. *Ibid.* s.9(7), proviso (*b*).
38. *Ibid.* s.11, and see Concession G.2.

section 59 of the Stamp Act 1891,[39] which require that agreements for the sale of certain classes of property should be stamped as conveyances on sale but which direct the Commissioners to return the duty if the agreement is rescinded or annulled or for any other reason is not substantially performed or carried into effect. There are no conditions restricting the relief, such as those in (a), (b) and (c), above.

7. General Exemptions from all Stamp Duties

27–52   The following are the principal instruments which are exempt from all duties:

(1) *Under the Stamp Act 1891*

    (a) Transfers of shares in the Government or parliamentary stocks or funds.

    (b) Instruments for the sale, transfer, or other disposition, either absolutely or otherwise, of any ship or vessel, or any part, interest, share, or property of or in any ship or vessel.[40]

    (c) Testaments, testamentary instruments, and dispositions *mortis causa* in Scotland.

    (d) Instruments made by, to, or with the Commissioners of Works for any of the purposes of the Commissioners of Works Act 1852.

(2) *Under the Finance Act 1948, s.74*

Transfers of the stock of certain undertakings carried on under national ownership or control, when the Treasury so directs.

(3) *Under the Finance Act 1949, Schedule 8*

    (a) Instruments of apprenticeship etc.,

    (b) Articles of clerkship to a solicitor.

    (c) Bonds given pursuant to the directions of any Act, or of the Commissioners or the Commissioners of Customs, or any of their officers, for or in respect of any duties of excise or customs, or for preventing frauds or evasions thereof, or for any other matter or thing relating thereto.

    (d) Bonds on obtaining letters of administration in England or Ireland, or a confirmation of testament in Scotland.

    (e) Charterparties.

(4) *Under the Finance Act 1953, s.31*

Certain receipts given in connection with National Savings.

---

39. See *post*, § 29–03.
40. See *Deddington Steamship Co. Ltd.* v. *I.R.C.* [1911] 2 K.B. 1001 (C.A.).

(5) *Under the Finance Act 1959, s.30*

    (a) Cover notes, slips and other instruments usually made in anticipation of the issue of a formal policy, not being instruments relating to life insurance.

    (b) Instruments embodying alterations of the terms or conditions of any policy of insurance other than life insurance.

    (c) Policies of insurance on baggage or personal and household effects only, if made or executed out of Great Britain.

(6) *Under the Finance Act 1960, s.74*

Certain documents connected with the housing, training and health and efficiency of visiting forces.

(7) *Under the Finance Act 1963, s.65(3)*

Certain legal aid agreements and documents.

(8) *Under the Finance Act 1964, s.23*

Contracts of employment and memoranda thereof.

27–53 (9) *Under the Finance Act 1971, s.64(1) and (2)*

Section 64(1) abolished stamp duties under the following headings—

    (a) "Bond, Covenant, or Instrument of any kind whatsoever";

    (b) "Bond of any kind whatsoever not specifically charged with any duty"; and

    (c) "Mortgage, Bond, Debenture, Covenant."

Section 64(2) provides that, subject to the provisions concerned with instruments relating to several distinct matters[41] any instrument falling within any of the above headings is not to be chargeable with duty under any other heading in the First Schedule to the Stamp Act. An example is a transfer of a mortgage.[42] Thus a material distinction may arise between a transfer of a mortgage (which operates to transfer the debt) and a sale of an unsecured debt.[43]

---

41. See *ante*, § 27–15.
42. See *ante*, § 27–07.
43. See Law of Property Act 1925, s.114 and *Wale* v. *I.R.C.* (1879) 4 Ex.D. 270.

CHAPTER 28

CONVEYANCE OR TRANSFER DUTY

HEAD OF CHARGE[1]

28–01 THE Act imposes duty under two heads:

Head (1)

Conveyance or transfer on sale of any property.
Duty: *Ad valorem* on the amount or value of the consideration for the sale of £1 per £100 (or fraction of £100).[2]

Head (2)

Conveyance or transfer of any kind not hereinbefore described.
Duty: Fixed duty of 50p.

Conveyance or transfer duty is also charged on certain agreements (s.59; Chap. 29); and on certain conveyances or transfers made in contemplation of a sale.[3]

INTRODUCTION

28–02 These heads of charge are of great practical importance. Head (1), which has been described as "the most productive and the most complicated of all heads of charge,"[3] charges *ad valorem* duty on a conveyance on sale of any property. The basic rate of duty is £1 per £100 of the amount or value of the consideration, but no duty is payable where the consideration does not exceed £30,000 and the instrument contains a certificate of value.[4] This exemption does not apply on a transfer of stock or marketable securities,[5] other than Commonwealth government stock.[6] Generally, payment of conveyance or transfer duty is denoted by means of an impressed stamp on the instrument of conveyance. Transfers of shares are the most important class of instruments to attract this duty. Under the Stock Transfer Act 1963 the duty should be impressed on the Stock Transfer Form where that form alone is used and on the Brokers Transfer Forms if these forms are used. Transfers of loan stock are usually exempt from duty: see § 28–45(5).

---

1. S.A. 1891, Sched. 1. A third head was repealed by F.A. 1963, s.62(1), as from August 1, 1963.
2. For reduced rates, see *post*, § 28–24.
3. See *post*, § 28–23.
4. See *post*, § 28–24.
5. The expression "stock" includes (*inter alia*) any share in the stocks or funds of any foreign or colonial state or government, or in the capital stock or funded debt of any county council, corporation, company or society in the United Kingdom, or of any foreign or colonial corporation, company or society. It also includes a unit under a unit trust scheme (F.A. 1946, s.54(1)). The expression "marketable security" means a security of such a description as to be capable of being sold in any stock market in the U.K. (S.A. 1891, s.122), *e.g.* debentures in a public company.
6. See *post*, § 28–24.

1. WHAT IS A CONVEYANCE ON SALE?

28–03   Under section 54 of the Stamp Act 1891 the expression "conveyance on sale" includes every instrument, and every decree or order of any court or of any commissioners, whereby any property, or any estate or interest in any property, upon the sale thereof is transferred to or vested in a purchaser, or any other person on his behalf or by his direction. The expression "instrument" includes every written document.[7] If no instrument is used, as where the title to goods is transferred by delivery, no duty can be levied.[8]

An instrument is not a conveyance on sale under section 54 unless (a) it transfers property (b) upon a sale thereof.

What is a Sale?

28–04   A transaction is not a "sale" unless there is:

(1) *Mutual assent as to the sale and purchase of property.*[9] If this contractual element is absent, the transaction is not one of sale. It is for this reason that some assents escape liability to *ad valorem* duty.[10] However the general application of this principle must be doubted in view of the decisions in *Ridge Nominees Ltd.* v. *I.R.C.*[11] and *Sun Alliance Ltd.* v. *I.R.C.*[12] In the *Ridge* case an instrument executed on behalf of a dissentient shareholder which brought about a transfer of his shares under section 209 of the Companies Act 1948 (now ss.428–430, Companies Act 1985) was held to be a conveyance on sale; and in the *Sun Alliance* case the same conclusion was reached in regard to a court order under section 206 of the 1948 Act (now s.425).

Instruments effecting property transfers between spouses, whether in pursuance of an order of the court or in consequence of an agreement between the parties in connection witha decree of separation, divorce or nullity are exempted from charge under the heading "Conveyance or transfer on sale."[13]

(2) *A price in money paid or promised.*[14] It is this requirement which differentiates a sale from an exchange. An exchange is "a transaction in which property belonging to one person is transferred to another person in consideration of that other person's property being transferred to the first."[15] There is no "price" in the legal sense. Instruments which effect an exchange of real or heritable property are dutiable under a separate head of charge in the Stamp Act 1891.[16]

---

7. S.A. 1891, s.122.
8. But the F.A. 1963, s.67, prohibits the circulation of blank transfers pursuant to a sale of stock.
9. *Att.-Gen.* v. *Felixstowe Gaslight Co.* [1907] 2 K.B. 984.
10. See *post*, §§ 28–13 *et seq.*
11. [1962] Ch. 376 (C.A.).
12. [1972] Ch. 133.
13. F.A. 1985, s.13. After March 25, 1985, such instruments will attract fixed duty of 50p under the heading "Conveyance of any other kind."
14. *Benjamin on Sale*, (8th ed.), p. 2, quoted in *Littlewoods Mail Order Stores Ltd.* v. *I.R.C.* [1961] Ch. 597 at p. 631; [1963] A.C. 135 at p. 152 (H.L.).
15. *Viscount Portman* v. *I.R.C.* (1956) 35 A.T.C. 349; see *post*, § 28–48.
16. See *post*, §§ 28–47 *et seq.*

For the purposes of stamp duty, however, the following instruments are conveyances on sale:

    (a) A transfer of property in consideration of the transfer of any stock[17] or security, whether marketable or non-marketable.[18]

    (b) A transfer of property in consideration of a debt due to the transferee.[19]

    (c) An exchange of stock[20] or securities.[21]

A conveyance in consideration of marriage or of services is not a conveyance on sale.

The instrument must transfer property or an interest in property

28–05   An instrument cannot effectively transfer property unless the transferor has the interest which he purports to transfer: *nemo dat quod non habet.*

> Thus in *Limmer Asphalte Paving Co.* v. *I.R.C.*[22] the grant for value of an exclusive licence to carry on the business of asphalte paving in two counties, where the grantor had no right to make such a grant, was held not to be a conveyance of property.

"Property" has been defined as "that which belongs to a person exclusive of others and which can be the subject of bargain and sale to another."[23]

> In *Thames Conservators* v. *I.R.C.*[24] it was held that a grant of a permissive licence, revocable at will, to erect a jetty on the River Thames was not a conveyance of "property."

28–06   It is the instrument which operates in law to transfer property which attracts conveyance or transfer duty.[25]

> In *Oughtred* v. *I.R.C.*[26] trustees held shares on trust for A for life, with remainder to B absolutely.
>
> On June 18, 1956, it was orally agreed that B would on June 26 exchange his reversionary interest for certain shares (the "free" shares) owned by A beneficially, to the intent that A should become absolute owner of the settled shares.
>
> On June 26, 1956, three deeds were executed:
>
>   (i) A deed of release, reciting the earlier oral agreement and that the settled shares were "accordingly now held by the trustees" for A absolutely.

---

17. See note 5, *ante.*
18. s.55, *post,* § 28–33.
19. s.57, *post,* § 28–39.
20. See note 5, *ante.*
21. See *post,* § 28–49.
22. (1872) L.R. 7 Ex. 211.
23. *Potter* v. *I.R.C.* (1854) 10 Exch. 147 at p. 156.
24. (1886) 18 Q.B.D. 279. But this was a case under S.A. 1870, s.70, wherein the words "or any estate or interest in any property" do not appear in the definition of conveyance. Contrast S.A. 1891, s.54; see *ante,* § 28–03.
25. Lord Esher in *I.R.C.* v. *Angus* (1889) 23 Q.B.D. 579 at p. 589.
26. [1960] A.C. 206. And see *Henty and Constable (Brewers) Ltd.* v. *I.R.C.* [1961] 1 W.L.R. 1504 (C.A.); *Fitch Lovell Ltd.* v. *I.R.C.* [1962] 1 W.L.R. 1325.

(ii) A transfer by A of the free shares to B's nominee for a nominal consideration of 10s. (This instrument was stamped 10s.)

(iii) A transfer by the trustees to A of the legal title to the settled shares, also for a nominal consideration of 10s. (This instrument was stamped 10s. under Head (2) on the footing that it was not a conveyance *on sale* but a conveyance in which no beneficial interest passed.[27])

The issue was whether the transfer in (iii) was correctly stamped. It was held by a majority of the House of Lords that the transfer was liable to *ad valorem* duty as a conveyance on sale. If the legal title had remained vested in the trustees *ad valorem* duty would have been avoided.

28–07   It will be observed that the terms of the bargain and sale were that A should transfer the free shares to B in return for B's reversionary interest or, more precisely, for the legal title to the shares in which B's interest subsisted. The transfer by the trustees of the bare legal title to A was an implementation of B's part of the bargain and was therefore a conveyance "on sale."

"The parties to a transaction of sale and purchase may no doubt choose to let the matter rest in contract.[28] But if the subject-matter of a sale is such that full title to it can only be transferred by an instrument, then any instrument they execute by way of transfer of the property sold ranks for stamp duty purposes as a conveyance on sale notwithstanding the constructive trust in favour of the purchaser which arose on the conclusion of the contract."[29]

On the point (which was taken by the appellant) that the disputed transfer was made by the trustees and not by B, Lord Jenkins said (at p. 243):

"Where property sold is outstanding in some person other than the vendor, being a trustee for or nominee of the vendor so as to be bound to transfer the property according to the vendor's directions, then in my view a transfer by such person at the direction of the vendor is for the present purposes equivalent to a transfer by the vendor himself."

28–08   It was immaterial that no "beneficial interest" passed under the conveyance, this having already passed under the prior oral agreement.

In *Grey* v. *I.R.C.*[30] H transferred the bare legal title in 18,000 shares to trustees as his nominees. (This transfer was correctly stamped 10s. under head (2), since no beneficial interest passed to the trustees.[31]) He then had a subsisting equitable interest and later *orally* directed the trustees to hold 3,000 of the shares on trusts set forth in other settlements previously made on his grandchildren. (No stamp because no instrument.) Five weeks later, the trustees executed declarations (which H signed) reciting their title to the shares and H's oral directions, and acknowledging that they held the shares on the trusts of the other settlement. (Stamped 10s. as a declaration of trust.)

The question in *Grey's* case was whether the declaration executed by the

27. See *post*, § 28–44.
28. For an explanation of this phrase, see *post*, § 28–19.
29. [1960] A.C. 206, *per* Lord Jenkins at p. 241.
30. [1960] A.C. 1 (H.L.). See also *Vandervell* v. *I.R.C.* (1966) 43 T.C. 519 (H.L.) (*held* that s.53(1)(c) of the Law of Property Act 1925 did not apply where V caused the legal interest in shares to be transferred with the intention of simultaneously transferring the beneficial interest).
31. See *post*, § 28–44.

trustees and stamped 10s. was correctly so stamped. It was held that the oral directions given by H regarding the 3,000 shares were ineffective to dispose of his equitable interest (because writing is required by section 53(1)(c) of the Law of Property Act 1925); therefore the later declaration transferred H's equitable interest to the beneficiaries and was accordingly a conveyance.[32]

28–09 If a written instrument operates to transfer property, that instrument is liable to conveyance or transfer duty irrespective of the manner in which the instrument is described or of its form. This principle can be illustrated by considering particular transactions in which a conveyance or transfer of property is effected.

(a) *Partnership transactions*

28–10 Any instrument under which payment is made for a share of partnership assets is a conveyance on sale, whether payment is made by an incoming partner or to an outgoing partner.

> Thus in *Christie* v. *I.R.C.*[33] a retiring partner transferred his interest in the partnership property to the continuing partner at a price equal to the sum due to the retiring partner in respect of capital. *Held,* that this was a conveyance on sale.

But where the incoming partner merely brings in cash capital, this is not a sale unless there is a simultaneous withdrawal of capital by another partner, when it is the practice to charge *ad valorem* duty.

28–11 *Saving of duty on a dissolution.* Care must be taken in dissolving a partnership to avoid the use of an instrument which operates as a conveyance on sale.

> In *Garnett* v. *I.R.C.*[34] a deed of dissolution of partnership recited (a) that the retiring partner's credit was £41,752; (b) that the partnership realty had been conveyed to the continuing partner; (c) that the partnership chattels were in the possession of the continuing partner; and (d) that the continuing partner had given the retiring partner a promissory note for £41,752. The deed witnessed that the partnership was dissolved and that the retiring partner accepted the promissory note in satisfaction of his interest in the partnership.

It was held that the deed, notwithstanding that it purported to recite a conveyance of property which had already taken place, actually brought about a transfer of the interest therein referred to and was accordingly liable to duty as a conveyance on sale.

28–12 A mere withdrawal of capital by an outgoing partner does not operate as a conveyance on sale, if the capital is withdrawn under the terms of an instrument providing for the distribution of assets *in specie* on a dissolu-

---

32. Not a conveyance *on sale* but a conveyance by way of voluntary disposition: at that time chargeable as if it were a conveyance on sale.
33. (1866) L.R. 2 Ex. 46; 4 H. & C. 664 (a better report). See also *Phillips* v. *I.R.C.* (1867) L.R. 2 Ex. 399.
34. (1899) 81 L.T. 633.

tion. Such an instrument operates as a partition and is liable to a fixed duty of 50p.[35]

The following passage from *Lindley on Partnership*[36] was approved in *Garnett* v. *I.R.C.*[37] (at p. 637):

> "If the retiring partner, instead of assigning his interest, takes the amount due to him from the firm, gives a receipt for the money, and acknowledges that he has no more claims on his co-partners, they will practically obtain all they want; but such a transaction, even if carried out by deed, could hardly be held to amount to a sale; and no *ad valorem* stamp, it is apprehended, would be payable."

This suggests another method of avoiding duty on a dissolution.

(b) *Assents*

28–13   An assent under hand is normally exempt from duty; and an assent under seal is liable to a 50p stamp.[38] Where, however, a contractual element is present, the instrument operates as a conveyance on sale and is liable to the *ad valorem* duty. Accordingly, an assent by personal representatives to give effect to a contract of sale entered into by the deceased must be stamped as a conveyance on sale.[39] An assent appropriating property by personal representatives in or towards a pecuniary legacy (including the statutory legacy due to a surviving spouse on intestacy), however, is exempted from *ad valorem* duty, whether or not the consent of the legatee is required for the appropriation.[40–43] Similarly, appropriations to residuary legatees in satisfaction or part satisfaction of their share of residue, are not liable to *ad valorem* duty.

28–14   If an assent is made in favour of a residuary beneficiary and the value of the assented property exceeds the value of the beneficiary's entitlement, so that he pays a sum to make up the difference, duty is payable on the excess,[44] unless the residuary beneficiary is sole personal representative. The Revenue, it seems, take the view that a person cannot "sell" property to himself.

28–15   *Family arrangements.* Instruments executed by beneficiaries within two years of a person's death, which vary the dispositions effected by that death, are exempted from duty under the head "Conveyance or transfer on sale" by the Finance Act 1985, s.84(1) provided that the only consideration for the variation consists of another such variation.[45] The exemption will

---

35. *Macleod* v. *I.R.C.* (1885) 12 R. (Ct. of Sess.) 105. In *Henniker* v. *Henniker* (1852) 1 E. & B. 54 it was held that a partition was not a sale. See also *Cormack's Trustees* v. *I.R.C.*, 1924 S.C. 819.
36. (15th ed.), pp. 262–263 and Chap. 39.
37. (1899) 81 L.T. 633.
38. *Kemp* v. *I.R.C.* [1905] 1 K.B. 581; Administration of Estates Act 1925, s.36(11).
39. *G.H.R. Co.* v. *I.R.C.* [1943] K.B. 303.
40–43. F.A. 1985, s.84(4), (5), reversing the rule in *Jopling* v. *I.R.C.* [1940] 2 K.B. 282.
44. (1951) *Law Notes,* 51–52.
45. F.A. 1985, s.85(2).

not be available, therefore, where extraneous consideration is introduced in order to equate two such variations of differing value.

(c) *Receipts and acknowledgments*

28–16   A document, though described by the parties as a receipt, or acknowledgment, or memorandum, may nevertheless take effect as a conveyance.

> In *Horsfall* v. *Hey*[46] a document signed by both parties to the transaction recorded that "A has sold B all the goods, stock-in-trade, and fixtures in a certain shop for £50." *Held,* that notwithstanding the use of the past tense, the document meant: "A hereby sells to B" and was a conveyance on sale.

In *Garnett* v. *I.R.C.*,[47] as we have seen, a deed which in terms amounted to little more than a receipt and acknowledgment was held to be a conveyance on sale. Both *Horsfall* v. *Hey*[46] and *Garnett's* case[47] were relied on by Finlay J. in *Cohen and Moore* v. *I.R.C.*[48]

28–17   The authority of these cases may be questioned since the decision of the Court of Appeal in *Fleetwood-Hesketh* v. *I.R.C.*[49] The facts were as follows:

> Property was settled on a father for life, with remainder to his son in tail. The son disentailed with the consent of his father. Thereafter, an oral agreement was concluded by which the son purported to sell to the father for £160,000, and the father agreed to buy, the son's reversionary interest. The only written instrument relating to this transaction was an acknowledgment signed by the son stating that he had received from the father £160,000 and stating what the payment was for.

The Crown claimed that the instrument was liable to *ad valorem* conveyance or transfer duty either (a) as a conveyance on sale, or (b) as an agreement for sale under section 59 of the Stamp Act 1891.[50] Finlay J. (at first instance) held that the instrument was chargeable as a conveyance on the ground that it was a contemporaneous record of the transaction of sale. In the Court of Appeal, however, it was held that the instrument was chargeable under section 59; and only two of the three judges expressed opinions on the alternative claim, Romer L.J. holding that there was no conveyance on sale, and Maugham L.J. holding that there was.

28–18   It would seem, therefore, that a receipt or acknowledgment is chargeable with duty as a conveyance only if:

(1) It can be shown to have been the intention of the parties that the property should pass at the time of the execution of the document, and it did so pass; or

(2) the document, and the antecedent oral transaction under which the

---

46. (1848) 2 Ex. 778.
47. (1899) 81 L.T. 633; see *ante*, §§ 28–11 *et seq.*
48. [1933] 2 K.B. 126; see *ante*, § 27–11.
49. [1936] 1 K.B. 351 (C.A.). And see *Oughtred* v. *I.R.C.* [1960] A.C. 206 at p. 260.
50. See *post*, § 29–02.

property passed, can be shown to have been one single transaction under the principle established in *Cohen and Moore* v. *I.R.C.*[51]

(d) *Dispositions of equitable interests*

28–19　　An instrument by which A transfers an equitable interest to a purchaser is dutiable as a conveyance on sale,[52] even if it is in the form of a declaration of trust.

If, however, A agrees to sell a legal estate in land to B, the agreement itself operates to transfer an equitable interest to B, and A holds as bare trustee for B; but this is not a conveyance on sale: the very fact that the instrument is one of which equity will decree specific performance fixes it at once as an "agreement" and not as a "conveyance."[53]

This principle is frequently used to avoid stamp duty.

> Suppose, for example, that X wishes to convey land to XYZ Ltd., a company controlled by X. X agrees to sell the land to the company for a sum to be paid on the execution of the agreement; and the contract provides for completion to take place within (say) seven weeks. The contract is not liable to stamp duty and completion is postponed indefinitely. (If the contract provided for completion to take place (say) seven days after a notice given by the company to X, the Revenue might contend that the parties intended that the agreement should be the only instrument of title and that the agreement should be stamped as a conveyance.)
>
> The parties thus "let the matter rest in contract."[54] But although X is a constructive trustee for the company by virtue of the contract, a subsequent conveyance by X to the company of the legal estate is a conveyance on sale: it is not liable to the fixed duty of 50p as a conveyance passing no beneficial interest.[55]

(e) *Options*

28–20　　It was held in *George Wimpey & Co. Ltd.* v. *I.R.C.*[56] that the grant of an option over land was an instrument which vested an interest in property, on the sale thereof, in a purchaser within section 54 of the Stamp Act 1891: see § 28–03. Consequently *ad valorem* duty was chargeable on the consideration paid for the grant of the option. The grant of an option is, however, merely an offer to sell which, by operation of law, gives rise to an interest in the property. This decision can only be reconciled with the principle that a contract of sale is not chargeable under section 54[57] on the basis that the grant of an option is not capable of completion by conveyance or transfer. An option may, alternatively, be chargeable within section 60 of the Stamp Act 1891.[58]

---

51. [1933] 2 K.B. 126.
52. *Chesterfield Brewery Co.* v. *I.R.C.* [1899] 2 Q.B. 7. Wills J. held also that there was an agreement for the sale of an equitable interest dutiable under S.A. 1891, s.59; see *post*, § 29–02.
53. *I.R.C.* v. *Angus & Co.* (1889) 23 Q.B.D. 579 (C.A.), *per* Lord Esher M.R. at p. 591. And see § 27–13.
54. See the first passage from *Oughtred* v. *I.R.C.* [1960] A.C. 206 quoted *ante*, § 28–07.
55. *Oughtred* v. *I.R.C.* [1960] A.C. 206 (H.L.); see *ante*, § 28–06.
56. [1975] 1 W.L.R. 995; [1975] S.T.C. 248 (C.A.).
57. See *post*, § 28–13.
58. See *post*, § 28–38.

(f) *Miscellaneous cases*

28–21   A foreclosure order is a conveyance on sale by virtue of the Finance Act 1898, s.6. A family arrangement may be a conveyance[59]; and an amalgamation of companies usually involves a conveyance, whether it is effected by agreement[60] or otherwise, *e.g.* by Act of Parliament.

28–22   The liability of an instrument to stamp duty has to be determined at the moment when it is executed.[61] An instrument which transfers an interest in property at a time when there is no subsisting agreement for the sale of that property but which is executed in contemplation of a possible sale which may never take place is not a conveyance "on sale."

> Thus in *William Cory & Son. Ltd.* v. *I.R.C.*[62] the appellant company agreed in principle to purchase certain shares and a draft sale agreement was prepared fixing the completion date as November 1, 1957. On October 24, 1957, the appellant company demanded that the share-vendors grant the company an immediate option to purchase the shares and the option was duly granted. The option agreement dated November 1, 1957, provided that, in order to protect the rights of the appellant company, the share-vendors would forthwith transfer their shares to the appellant company, such shares to be held in trust for its registered holders but without passing any beneficial interest to them; and there were provisions for the re-transfer of the shares if the option lapsed. The shares were transferred in accordance with the option agreement and the option was exercised orally on November 8, 1957. *Held* (i) that the transfers of the shares were not conveyances or transfers on sale; and (ii) that the option agreement itself was merely an offer to sell: it was not an agreement for sale which attracted *ad valorem* duty under section 59 of the Stamp Act 1891.

28–23   The *Cory* decision revealed a device by which *ad valorem* duty on conveyances on sale could be avoided; and the Finance Act 1965 now provides that any instrument whereby property is conveyed or transferred to any person in contemplation of a sale of that property shall be treated for the purposes of the Stamp Act 1891 as a conveyance or transfer on sale of that property for a consideration equal to the value of that property.[63] The instrument must be presented for adjudication[64–65] and the value of the property will be determined by the Commissioners. Provision is made by section 90(5), Finance Act 1965 ensuring that the value of the property is not depressed by any right of reconveyance in the transferor in the event of the sale not proceeding. The provisions of the Act of 1965 came into force on August 1, 1965,[67] and apply to instruments executed on or after that date.

     If a conveyance or transfer of property in contemplation of a sale thereof is stamped in accordance with the section and the sale does not take place

---

59. *Bristol (Marquess)* v. *I.R.C.* [1901] 2 K.B. 336; *cf. Cormack's Trustees* v. *I.R.C.,* 1924 S.C. 819.
60. *Brotex Cellulose Fibres* v. *I.R.C.* [1933] 1 K.B. 158.
61. See *ante*, § 27–08.
62. [1965] A.C. 1088 (H.L.).
63. F.A. 1965, s.90(1), (4).
64–65. *Ibid.* s.90(3); and see *ante*, § 27–41.
66. Discussed *post*, § 30–08.
67. F.A. 1965, s.90(7).

and the property is re-conveyed or re-transferred to the vendor or trans-feror (or to a person to whom his rights have been transmitted on death or bankruptcy), or the sale takes place for a consideration which is less than the value in respect of which duty is payable under the section, the Commissioners will repay the duty (or excess duty) on a claim being made to them not later than two years after the making or execution of the dutiable instrument.[68]

It should be noted that section 90 of the Finance Act 1965 does not impose *ad valorem* duty on a mere option agreement: it applies only where property is conveyed or transferred in connection with the agreement. Further, it does not apply unless the property is conveyed or transferred in contemplation of a *sale*: it does not apply, for instance, where property is transferred as security for a loan if there is a subsequent sale to the transferee which was not in contemplation at the time of the transfer.

2. RATES OF DUTY AND CERTIFICATES OF VALUE

28–24   The current full rate of *ad valorem* conveyance or transfer duty is:

(1) 50p for every £50 (or part of £50) of the consideration, where the amount or value of the consideration does not exceed £500; and

(2) £1 for every £100 (or part of £100) of the consideration, where the amount or value of the consideration exceeds £500.

In either case, therefore, the full rate is, roughly, 1 per cent.

A reduced rate of duty, of 50p for every £100 (or part thereof) is imposed when the property transferred is stock or marketable securities.[69]

No duty is payable on instruments transferring property of a limited value, other than stock or marketable securities,[70–71] which are executed on or after March 20, 1984.[72]

The exemption is available where the amount or value of the consideration is £30,000 or less but is conditional on the instrument containing a certificate to the effect "That the transaction effected by the instrument does not form part of a larger transaction or series of transactions in respect of which the amount or value, or aggregate amount or value of the consideration exceeds £30,000."[73]

> Thus, if A conveys Blackacre to B for £28,000, the conveyance may be certified at £30,000, when B will pay no duty.

Once an instrument has been afforded exemption from *ad valorem* duty

---

68. *Ibid.* s.90(2); but see the proviso.

69. A rate, roughly, of $\frac{1}{2}$ per cent. introduced by F.A. 1986, s.64, with effect from October 27, 1986. Transitionally, though the rate applies to certain reconstructions, demergers and takeovers after March 24, 1986.

70–71. See the general exemption from duty in the case of loan capital referred to in § 28–45.

72. F.A. 1984, s.109. The section also removed the reduced rate applicable to transfers of stock, etc., to non-residents.

73. See F.A. 1958, s.34(1).

under this heading it will not then fall under the alternative heading "conveyance or transfer of any other kind."[74]

The object of the certificate of value is to prevent the avoidance of stamp duty by the artificial splitting up of transactions.

The words of the statutory certificate give rise to two problems:

(1) When does a transaction form part of a larger transaction or series of transactions?

(2) How is the amount or value of the consideration to be determined?

Is there a larger transaction or series?[75–76]

28–25   The type of problem which often arises in practice is as follows:

> A agrees to purchase two properties from B, each for £24,000. Each property is separately conveyed. If there was one transaction for £48,000, of which each conveyance formed a part, the duty on each conveyance @ £1 per £100 would be £480; but if there were two separate transactions, each conveyance would be certified at £30,000 and the duty would be nil.

Little guidance on this question is to be had from the cases, and none from the Act. It seems, however, that where there are simultaneous transfers of property by one transferor to one transferee, these must be taken to form one transaction if there is any degree of interdependence or linkage between the transactions. Thus, in the example above, if B could not (or would not) have purchased the one property without also purchasing the other, such interdependence would, it seems, be present.

Auction sales may be taken as an exception to this general rule, for in *Att.-Gen.* v. *Cohen*[77] it was held that if a purchaser buys separate lots of property by auction from one vendor, and there are separate contracts and conveyances, there is no series even if the contracts are for convenience evidenced by one memorandum. There would, however, be a series if the lots were included in one conveyance, or if several unsold lots were purchased in one block *after* an auction sale.[78]

What is the amount or value of the consideration?

28–26   All property which passes under the transaction or series must be taken into account in deciding if a certificate of value can be included, even property which is not included in any document; except that, under the Finance Act 1958, s.34(4), any *goods, wares or merchandise* may be disregarded, provided they are excluded from the conveyance and transferred by delivery. The consideration relating to all other items, whether foreign or not, including fixtures must be taken into account.[79] Trading stock and plant and machinery will fall within the words "goods, wares or merchandise"; cash in hand and cash on current or deposit account will not.

---

74. See a case which applies similar reasoning: *Att.-Gen.* v. *Lamplough* (1873) 3 Ex.D. 214.
75–76. See also *post*, § 28–28 (building plots); § 28–34 (periodical payments); § 28–42 (sub-sales).
77. [1937] 1 K.B. 478 (C.A.).
78. (1954) 51 L.S.Gaz. 369.
79. Statement by Controller of Stamps in [1979] B.T.R. 512.

Example

A agrees to sell his business as a going concern for £39,000. The consideration is apportioned between the assets as follows:

Land	£26,000
Goodwill	£3,000
Stock-in-trade	£10,000

Under section 34(4), the stock-in-trade can be disregarded for the purpose of certification, and a "not exceeding £30,000" certificate included, provided the stock is excluded from the actual conveyance (*i.e.* is transferred by delivery).
Note. If the land were to be conveyed separately, say, for £28,000, the conveyance could not be certified at £30,000, for the sale of the goodwill would form one transaction with the sale of the land.

The relief given by section 34(4) is valuable inasmuch that it enables the parties to deal with the stock or plant and machinery in the agreement (as they must, for tax purposes)[80–81] without thereby increasing the liability for stamp duty. Note that stamp duty can be saved on the sale of business assets (including cash) by "switching" the cash into stock or plant before the agreement is made. See also § 29–10.

3. CALCULATION OF THE CONSIDERATION FOR PURPOSES OF DUTY

28–27 The *ad valorem* duty payable under Head (1) in § 28–01 is not on the value of the property conveyed but on the "amount or value of the consideration for the sale." This is not necessarily the consideration stated in the instrument. Thus if land is acquired under compulsory powers and the payment to the vendor includes a sum for compensation for damage by severance or injurious affection, duty is charged on the total figure, even though no reference to the compensation payment is made in the conveyance of the land.

But under the Finance Act 1900, s.10, where a conveyance on sale is made for any consideration in respect whereof it is chargeable with *ad valorem* duty, and in further consideration of a covenant by the purchaser to make (or of his having previously made) any substantial improvement of or addition to the property conveyed to him, or of any covenant relating to the subject-matter of the conveyance, no duty is chargeable in respect of such further consideration.

There are cases where the assessment of *ad valorem* conveyance or transfer duty presents special problems. Some of these must now be considered.

(a) *Sales and leases of building plots and houses in the course of erection*

28–28 It is a common transaction for a person to purchase or to take a lease of land under an arrangement that the vendor or lessor will for additional consideration (by himself or his nominee) erect a house or other building on the land. The question then arises whether the cost of the house or building is to be treated as part of the cost of the land for stamp duty purposes.

If the building is completed before the date of the contract for the sale

---

80–81. See *ante*, §§ 2–34 *et seq.*

(or lease) of the land, the cost of the building is part of the cost of the land[82]; and if the land is conveyed (or leased) before the building is begun, the cost of the building is not part of the cost of the land.[83] So much seems clear from the cases. Where, however, at the date of the contract no house has been erected (or a house has been partly erected) and at the date of the conveyance (or lease) a house has been wholly (or partly) erected, the position (as appears from a statement issued by the Commissioners in August 1957) is as follows[84]:

28–29 "The Board have taken legal advice concerning the stamp duty chargeable on conveyances or leases of building plots in cases where at the date of the contract for sale or lease no house has been erected or a house has been partly erected on the site which constitutes or is included in the subject-matter of the sale or lease, and at the date of the conveyance or lease a house has been wholly or partly erected on the site.
The Board are advised that the law is as follows:

  (i) Subject to what is said under paragraph (iv) below, if under the contract for the sale or lease the purchaser or lessee is entitled to a conveyance or lease of the land in consideration only of the purchase price or rent of the site, the *ad valorem* duty on the conveyance or lease will be determined only by the amount of the purchase price or rent, although it may have been agreed that a house is to be built on the site at the expense of the purchaser or lessee.
    In such a case, the concurrent existence of a contract with the vendor or lessor or any other person for the building of a house on the site will not increase the stamp duty chargeable on the conveyance or lease.
  (ii) If under the contract the purchaser or lessee is not entitled to a conveyance or lease until a house has been built on the site at his expense and if the house is to be built by the vendor or lessor or by his agent or nominee, the payment of the building price by the purchaser or lessee will be part of the consideration for the conveyance or lease and the building price will be liable to *ad valorem* duty accordingly.
    (If the house is to be built by a person who is not the vendor or lessor or his agent or nominee, the payment of the building price will not form part of the consideration for the sale or lease except in so far as paragraph (iv) below applies.)
  (iii) When the position is as in paragraph (ii) above, and a purchaser or lessee not entitled to a conveyance or lease until a house has been erected at his expense in fact obtains a conveyance or lease when the house has been only partly erected, *ad valorem* duty is payable on the conveyance or lease on the proportionate amount of the building price attributable to the partial erection of the house computed as to the date of the conveyance or lease.
  (iv) (a) If, at the date of the contract, a house has been wholly or partly erected by the vendor or lessor or by his agent or nominee or by a builder not employed by the purchaser or lessee, it normally forms part of the subject-matter of the sale or lease and the consideration or apportioned consideration for that building (as existing at the date of the contract) is accordingly liable to *ad valorem* duty.

---

82. *M'Innes* v. *I.R.C.*, 1934 S.C. 424.
83. *Kimbers* v. *I.R.C.* [1936] 1 K.B. 132 (see *post,* § 28–30); *Paul* v. *I.R.C.* (1936) 15 A.T.C. 57.
84. (1957) 54 L.S.Gaz. 450.

(b) If, at the date of the contract, a house has been wholly or partly erected by the purchaser or lessee or by any person on his behalf the consideration or apportioned consideration for the house wholly or partly erected will not normally form part of the consideration for the sale or lease and accordingly will not be liable to *ad valorem* duty.

(c) This paragraph is subject to what is said in paragraphs (ii) and (iii) above.

(v) The contract referred to above may be contained in more than one instrument or it may be partly written and partly verbal. It includes any contractual arrangement between the parties.

These observations explain, so far as is possible in general terms, the view of the law at present adopted by the Board, but they have not, of course, the force of law, and are promulgated merely with the object of assisting the taxpayer. The Board are not bound by them, and the circumstances of any particular case may call for special consideration."

Certificates of value

28–30   The test for determining whether a purchase of land and a contract to build form part of one larger transaction or series is the same as the test for determining whether the cost of the building is to be reckoned as part of the cost of the land in assessing the *ad valorem* duty.

> In *Kimbers* v. *I.R.C.*[85] there was (i) a contract for the sale of land for £x, and (ii) a contemporaneous building contract for £y. The land was conveyed before the building was commenced. The conveyance was held to be properly stamped for £x, and it was not suggested that the conveyance formed one transaction with the building contract.

The matter was in issue in another case from which it emerges that the contracts will be treated as parts of a single transaction if they are so interlinked that, if the purchaser defaults on the building contract, he cannot enforce the contract for the sale of land.[86]

(b) *Special cases (ss.55–58)*

28–31   The Stamp Act makes special provision for the calculation of the consideration where this consists of foreign currency (s.6), stock[87] and securities (s.55), periodic payments (s.56), a debt (s.57) or where there is a sub-sale (s.58). Each of these provisions will now be separately considered.

Foreign currency

28–32   By section 6 of the Stamp Act 1891, where an instrument is chargeable with *ad valorem* duty in respect of any money in any foreign or colonial currency, duty is calculated on its value in British currency at the current rate of exchange on the day of the date of the instrument; and where the instrument contains a statement of the current rate of exchange and is

---

85. [1936] 1 K.B. 132.
86. *Paul* v. *I.R.C.* (1936) 15 A.T.C. 57.
87. See *ante*, § 28–02.

stamped in accordance therewith, it is to be deemed duly stamped unless and until the contrary is shown.

Consideration in stock[87] and securities

28–33　　If the consideration, or any part of the consideration, for a conveyance on sale consists of:

(a) any stock or marketable security,[87] the conveyance is to be charged in respect of the value of the stock or security[88];

(b) any security not being a marketable security (*e.g.* a debenture of a private company), the conveyance is to be charged in respect of the amount due at the date of the conveyance for principal and interest on the security.[89]

The transfer of the securities themselves, as consideration for the transfer of the other property, will only be subject to the fixed duty of 50p[90] since the other property cannot be regarded as consideration.[91] In (a), the duty must be calculated according to the "average price" on the Stock Exchange at the date of the conveyance.[92] If the conveyance contains a statement of the average price and is stamped in accordance therewith, it is deemed to be duly stamped until the contrary is shown.[93] If there is no average price, as where the shares are unquoted, the Commissioners must assess the value of the stock, etc., on the basis of any recent arm's length dealing or any other available evidence.

If on the formation of a company, property is conveyed in consideration of the issue of shares in the company, the Commissioners assess the *ad valorem* duty on the actual (not the nominal) value of the shares issued, which will be the value of the property conveyed.[94] The rule is the same where the consideration is to be satisfied by the transfer of shares recently issued.

> Thus if property worth £65,000 is sold to a company in consideration of the issue to the vendor of 100 £1 shares (being the whole of the company's nominal capital), the duty is payable on £65,000.[95]

Consideration consisting of periodical payments

28–34　　The effect of section 56 of the Stamp Act can be seen from the following table. Where the consideration (or any part of the consideration) for a conveyance on sale consists of the payments referred to in the left hand column, duty is charged on the sums in the right hand column.

---

88. S.A. 1891, s.55(1). As a consequence of this provision an "exchange" of securities constitutes two sales: *J. & P. Coats* v. *I.R.C.* [1897] 2 Q.B. 423 (C.A.).

89. S.A. 1891, s.55(2).

90. On "conveyances of any other kind" see § 28–43.

91. See note 88, above.

92. S.A. 1891, s.6(1).

93. *Ibid.* s.6(2). Consequently a subsequent purchaser cannot object to the conveyance as a document of title: *Re Weir & Pitt's Contract* (1911) 55 S.J. 536.

94. *Furness Railway Co.* v. *I.R.C.* (1864) 33 L.J.Ex. 173; *Carlyon Estates Ltd.* v. *I.R.C.* (1937) 46 T.C. 413; *John Foster & Sons* v. *I.R.C.* [1894] 1 Q.B. 516 (C.A.); see *post*, § 32–07.

95. *Carlyon Estates Ltd.* v. *I.R.C., supra*; see *post*, § 32–07.

	Consideration consisting of:	*Duty is chargeable on:*
s. 56 (1)	Money payable periodically for a definite period not exceeding 20 years, so that the total amount to be paid can be previously ascertained.	The total amount payable.
s. 56 (2)	Money payable periodically for a definite period exceeding 20 years or in perpetuity or for any indefinite period not terminable with life.	The total amount "which will or may, according to the terms of sale, be payable" during the 20 years following the date of the instrument.
s. 56 (3)	Money payable periodically during any life or lives.	The amount which will or may, according to the terms of sale, be payable during the 12 years following the date of the instrument.

Example

A conveyance in consideration of a perpetual yearly rentcharge is chargeable with *ad valorem* conveyance or transfer duty under section 56(2) on the total amount payable during the 20 years after the date of the conveyance.[96] A conveyance in consideration of a lump sum and a life annuity to the vendor should be stamped on the lump sum and under section 56(3).[97]

A sum which is payable only on a contingency such as sufficiency of profits, may nevertheless fall within section 56.[98]

28–35   A grant of a lease in consideration of a rent, or the transfer of part of leasehold property with an apportionment of the liability for the rent, is outside section 56[99] since the rent does not form part of the consideration for the grant or assignment but is, rather, part and parcel of the thing demised.[99a]

28–36   Section 56(2) was considered in *Western United Investment Co. Ltd.* v. *I.R.C.*,[1] where the facts were as follows:

On May 9, 1956, W agreed to purchase shares and to pay for them by 125 yearly instalments of £44,000 each, total £5½ million. The agreement provided (cl. 3) that if W defaulted in payment of any instalment, all the unpaid instalments were to become immediately payable. On June 1, 1956, the transfer of shares to W was executed.

The Revenue contended, *inter alia*, that the transfer was liable to conveyance or transfer duty at £2 per cent. (the then applicable rate) on

---

96. Where at the time of the conveyance, the property conveyed is already subject to a rentcharge or an annuity, s.56 does not apply. See S.A. 1891, s.57, *post*, § 28–39, Example (ii).
97. *Cf. Martin* v. *I.R.C.* (1904) 91 L.T. 453.
98. See the Contingency Principle, *ante*, § 27–18. A case on s.56(2) is *Underground Electric Railways Ltd.* v. *I.R.C.* [1906] A.C. 21.
99. *Swayne* v. *I.R.C.* [1900] 1 Q.B. 172 (C.A.).
99a. *Ibid.* at p. 176.
1. [1958] Ch. 392. For the income tax sequel to this case, see *Vestey* v. *I.R.C.* [1962] Ch. 861: see § 5–27.

£5½ million on the ground that, under clause 3, the whole £5½ million "*might* according to the terms of sale" be payable within 20 years. Upjohn J. (at p. 404) rejected this contention:

> "Clause 3 is in a literal sense a term of the sale in that it is an undoubted term of the contract of sale. But it is a term of the contract which only comes into operation if the terms of sale be broken. The terms of sale for the purposes of section 56, in my judgment, are the terms of sale upon which the parties contemplate that the property will be paid for, *i.e.* 125 annual instalments of £44,000. The terms of sale do not, in my judgment, comprehend terms of the contract of sale which come into operation if, but only if, the agreed terms of sale are broken."

The duty assessable was, therefore, only that applicable to the sum of 20 annual instalments.

28–36A The phrase "money payable periodically" has been considered in relation to section 56(2). In *Blendett Ltd.* v. *I.R.C.*[1a] a lease at a premium of £240,500 provided for the paymennt of £50,000 on execution and the balance 23 years later. The Court of Appeal rejected the taxpayer's claim to pay duty on only £50,000 under section 56(2). Lord Templeman said "I find no trace of money being payable periodically. I find two separate payments which complete the total premium of £240,500." The Crown's claim for duty on that total amount was accordingly upheld.

28–37 *Certificates of value.* It seems that, if property is conveyed in consideration of the payment of (say) £36,000 by 30 annual instalments of £1,200 so that duty is chargeable under section 56(2) on the total, 20 annual instalments (£24,000), the conveyance can be certified as for a consideration "not exceeding £30,000."

Sale of an annuity

28–38 Under section 60 of the Stamp Act 1891 where, on the sale of an annuity or other right not before in existence,[2] such annuity or other right is not created by actual grant or conveyance, but is only secured by bond, covenant, contract or otherwise, such instrument is chargeable as a conveyance.

> Thus if A contracts to provide B with £x a year in consideration of a lump sum payment by B of £y, the contract must be stamped as a conveyance on sale, the *ad valorem* duty being assessed on the purchase price, *i.e.*, £y.

The grant of an option for £x may be dutiable as a conveyance on sale under section 60 rather than under section 54.[3] In practice, most life annuities are purchased from insurance companies and are "purchased life annuities" within the Taxes Acts.[4] Such annuities are not chargeable under section 60 but are charged at the rate of 5p per £10, or part thereof, of the

---

1a. [1984] S.T.C. 95 (C.A.).
2. See *Great Northern Ry.* v. *I.R.C.* [1901] 1 K.B. 416 at p. 426.
3. See *William Cory & Son Ltd.* v. *I.R.C.* [1965] A.C. 1088 and *George Wimpey & Co. Ltd.* v. *I.R.C.*, [1975] S.T.C. 248 *ante*, § 28–20.
4. See *ante*, §§ 3–53 *et seq.* (tax).

annuity.[5] Again, section 60 does not apply to a voluntary disposition of an annuity (which formerly attracted bond covenant duty); nor to a transaction whereby a loan is repaid by way of an annuity (which formerly attracted mortgage duty).

Consideration in the form of a debt

28-39   If property is conveyed to any person in consideration (wholly or in part) of a debt due to him, the debt is deemed to be the whole (or part, as the case may be) of the consideration for the transfer.[6]

> Thus if A accepts Blackacre, worth £36,000, in satisfaction of a debt of £34,000, the conveyance of Blackacre must be stamped on £34,000.

Prior to the Finance Act 1980, s.102, if the debt exceeded the value of the property conveyed in satisfaction, the property was deemed to have been sold for the greater amount. This rule attracted considerable criticism,[7] in consequence of which section 102 was eventually introduced, reducing the consideration to the value of the property conveyed.[8]

> So, if in the above example, Blackacre were worth £34,000 and the debt stood at £36,000, the conveyance of the one in satisfaction of the other would be deemed to be made for consideration of £34,000 and no more.

If property is conveyed subject either certainly or contingently to the payment or transfer of any money or stock,[9] whether being or constituting a charge or incumbrance upon the property or not, the money or stock is deemed to be the whole (or part, as the case may be) of the consideration.

> *Examples*
>   (i) If mortgaged property is conveyed for £24,000, duty is assessed on the aggregate amount of the purchase price (£24,000) and the amount of the mortgage debt, including any interest then due, whether the purchaser assumes personal liability for the mortgage debt or not.
>   (ii) If a fee simple is conveyed subject to an annuity previously charged on the property, duty is assessed on the aggregate of the purchase price and the value of the annuity calculated under section 56, above.
>   (iii) If on the sale of a business the purchaser agrees to discharge the vendor's debts, whether secured or unsecured, duty is assessed on the aggregate of the purchase price and the amount of the debts.[10]

The effect of this provision in section 57 of the Stamp Act 1891 is that wherever a purchaser assumes a liability of the vendor to a third party (in consequence whereof he will, of course, pay less for the property), the liab-

---

5. Under Head 3 of bond covenant duty in S.A. 1891, Sched. 1 (as extended by F.A. 1956, s.38(1)). This head of charge was not repealed by F.A. 1971, s.64(1)(*a*).
6. S.A. 1891, s.57.
7. See, for example, *Huntington* v. *I.R.C.* [1896] 1 Q.B. 422, *per* Wright J.
8. The instrument must be adjudicated: see § 27–41; and see also F.A. 1981, s.107 in § 30–05 (purchase of local authority and public sector dwellings at a discount); and F.A. 1984, s.110 (extension of s.107 relief to other cases).
9. See *ante*, § 28–02, note 5.
10. And see *post*, §§ 29–09 *et seq.*

ility must be reckoned as part of the consideration, even if the liability is contingent.

28–40   Liabilities which are inherent in the nature of property conveyed are not, however, within section 57.

> Thus if leasehold property is assigned, the assignee's covenant to pay the rent apportioned to the property so assigned is not treated as part of the consideration of the sale[11]; and if partly paid shares are transferred, no duty is in practice claimed in respect of the liability to pay future calls.

Apportionment of consideration

28–41   If property is contracted to be sold for one consideration and is conveyed to a purchaser (or to separate joint purchasers) in parts by different instruments, the consideration must be apportioned as the parties think fit and duty charged accordingly.[12]

28–42   *Sub-sales.* If a person, having contracted to purchase property but not having obtained a conveyance thereof, contracts to sell it to another person to whom the property is immediately conveyed, the conveyance must be charged in respect of the consideration moving from the sub-purchaser.[13]

> *Examples*
>   (i) A contracts to sell property to B for £32,000. B contracts to sell the property to C for £35,000, whereupon A (acting on B's directions) conveys the property direct to C. C must pay duty on £35,000. (B pays no duty, for there is no "conveyance" to him).
>   (ii) Facts same as in (i), except that B contracts sub-sales to a number of purchasers of different parts of the property. Each sub-purchaser must pay duty on the consideration moving from him.

It follows that a purchaser who intends to resell the property can avoid stamp duty by avoiding completion.[14] Steps have been taken, however, to counteract a more complex form of avoidance, involving sub-sales. Section 112 of the Finance Act 1984 amends section 58(4) so that it should not apply in cases where the chargeable consideration moving from the sub-purchaser is less than the value of the property immediately before the sale to him.

> The scheme which the provision is designed to counteract operated as follows: A agreed to sell land to B for full consideration. B entered into an agreement with C to sell on for a nominal consideration together with an agreement by C that he would grant B a long lease. A then conveyed the property direct to C: section 58(4) supposedly operated to reduce the dutiable amount to the nominal consideration paid by C on the sub-sale. The agreement for a long lease was not at that time chargeable with *ad valorem* duty.[14a] It may be noted that

---

11. *Swayne* v. *I.R.C.* [1900] 1 Q.B. 172 (C.A.); affirming [1899] 1 Q.B. 335.
12. S.A. 1891, s.58(1) and (2).
13. *Ibid.* s.58(4). Strict compliance with this subsection is necessary to take advantage of it; thus it does not apply if the original purchaser obtains a conveyance before contracting to sub-sell: *Fitch Lovell* v. *I.R.C.* [1962] 1 W.L.R. 1325 at pp. 1341–1342.
14. But see *Escoigne Properties Ltd.* v. *I.R.C.* [1958] A.C. 549, *post*, § 33–10.
14a. Now see F.A. 1984, s.111.

the Revenue have stated that they do not accept the efficacy of the scheme under the old law.[14b]

The Act does not provide for the case where a purchaser, having contracted to purchase property for one undivided consideration, sub-sells part only of the property, so that part is conveyed direct to the sub-purchaser and the remainder to the purchaser. It is now settled,[15] however, that the conveyance to the sub-purchaser must be charged in respect of the consideration moving from him, and that the conveyance of the remainder must be charged on an apportioned part of the original purchase price, and not on the difference between that price and the amount paid by the sub-purchaser. The apportionment is made by reference to the relative values of the parts.

Example
A contracts to sell two identical properties of equal value to B for a total consideration of £50,000. B contracts to sub-sell one property to C for £27,000 and A conveys direct to C. The conveyance to C must be charged on £27,000 and can be certified as "not exceeding £30,000." The conveyance of the other property, although it will acknowledge the receipt of only £23,000, must be charged on £25,000 and, since it forms part of a larger transaction for £50,000, cannot be certified as "not exceeding £30,000."

Furthermore the Act does not provide for the case where a purchaser, having contracted to purchase property, agrees to transfer it in exchange for the transfer of another property from another person. Here it is considered that, since the only conveyance or transfer is one of exchange and not of sale, no *ad valorem* duty is payable on the original purchase price.[15a]

4. HEAD (2): CONVEYANCES LIABLE TO A FIXED DUTY OF 50P

28–43 The second head of charge in § 28–01 levies a fixed duty of 50p on "any conveyance or transfer of any kind not hereinbefore described." The charge extends to:

"Every instrument, and every decree of any court or of any commissioners, whereby any property on any occasion, except a sale or mortgage, is transferred to or vested in any person . . . "[16]

excepting, of course, conveyances which are chargeable with duty under Head (1).

28–44 The following are examples of instruments which are chargeable under Head (2):

(1) A conveyance in consideration of marriage or services. These are not conveyances *on sale* because there is no price.
(2) A conveyance under which no beneficial interest passes and which is

---

14b. See [1984] S.T.I. 230–231. And see *Ingram* v. *I.R.C.* [1985] S.T.C. 835, § 27–06.
15. *Maples* v. *I.R.C.* [1914] 3 K.B. 303.
15a. Under the heading "exchange or excambion," *ad valorem* duty will be payable on the subsequent transfers. See § 28–47.
16. S.A. 1891, s.62.

not made on or in contemplation of a sale.[17-18] A conveyance to a nominee is an example of such a conveyance; but if A agrees to sell land to B who thus acquires an equitable title to the land, the subsequent conveyance to B is a conveyance on sale.[19]

(3) A conveyance for effectuating the appointment of a new trustee[20] or the retirement of a trustee, whether or not a new trustee is appointed.[21]

(4) A transfer by a liquidator of the assets of the company *in specie* to shareholders, in satisfaction of their rights in a winding up; or a transfer by trustees to beneficiaries on a distribution of trust funds.

An exchange or partition of property may be dutiable under this head: see § 28-47.

5. EXEMPTIONS AND RELIEFS FROM CONVEYANCE OR TRANSFER DUTY

28-45/46 The General Exemptions from all stamp duties have already been referred to.[22-23] Other conveyances which are exempt are:

(1) certain conveyances in connection with the reconstruction and amalgamation of companies[24];

(2) certain conveyances between associated companies[25-26];

(3) transfers of shares in building societies[27-28];

(4) transfers of *loan capital*[29] carrying no conversion rights into or rights of acquisition of shares or other securities,[29a] the interest on which does not exceed a reasonable commercial return and does not fall to be determined to any extent by reference to the results of a business or to the value of any property: see § 32-01. Also excluded from the exemption is loan capital giving the right to the payment of a premium on redemption which is not reasonably comparable with other such capital listed in the Official List of the Stock Exchange;

(5) any transfer to a stock exchange nominee.[30] There are other special provisions dealing with stock exchange transactions.[31]

(6) Conveyances to charities or Trustees of the National Heritage

---

17-18. F.A. 1965, s.90; see *ante*, § 28-23.
19. *Oughtred* v. *I.R.C.* [1960] A.C. 206 (H.L.); see *ante*, § 28-06.
20. S.A. 1891, s.62, proviso.
21. F.A. 1902, s.9.
22-23. See *ante*, § 27-52.
24. See *post*, § 33-01 *et seq.*
25-26. See *post*, §§ 33-09 *et seq.*
27-28. Building Societies Act 1962, s.117.
29. F.A. 1986, s.79(4) "Loan capital" is defined by s.78(7) (made applicable by s.79(12)) as "any debenture stock, corporation stock, or funded debt issued by a body corporate or any other body or persons, or any capital raised by such a body if the capital is borrowed or has the character of borrowed money (whether in the form of stock or otherwise); or stock or marketable securities issued by the government of any country or territory out of the United Kingdom." For the meaning of "funded debt" see *Reed International Ltd.* v. *I.R.C.* [1976] A.C. 336; [1975] S.T.C. 427. And see *Agricultural Mortgage Corpn. Ltd.* v. *I.R.C.* [1978] Ch. 72; [1978] S.T.C. 11 (C.A.).
29a. The Inland Revenue issued a Statement of Practice on March 13, 1984 that loan stock which can only be converted into other unconvertible loan stock does fall with the scope of the exemption.
30. F.A. 1976, s.127(1).
31. F.A. 1986 ss.81-85.

Memorial Fund in the case of instruments executed on or after March 22, 1982.[32]

6. EXCHANGE AND PARTITION

28-47 An instrument which effects an exchange of realty for realty (or a partition of realty) attracts a fixed stamp of 50p under the head of charge "Exchange or Excambion" in the Stamp Act 1891; except that if more than £100 is paid for equality, the principal instrument effecting the transaction must be stamped as a conveyance on sale for the sum paid for equality.[33] The parties can decide for themselves which of the instruments is to be deemed the principal instrument.[34] Any other instrument will be liable to a duty of 50p, if *ad valorem* duty is paid on the principal instrument or nil if *ad valorem* duty on the principal instrument is at the nil rate.

> *Examples*
> A exchanges his freehold (value £40,000) for B's freehold (value £76,000), A paying £36,000 for equality. The deed of exchange must be stamped on the £36,000 equality money. (There will be a duplicate deed bearing the duplicate denoting stamp.)
> If £100 or a lesser sum is paid for equality, the instrument bears a 50p stamp under the head of charge "Exchange or Excambion."

An exchange of leasehold for leasehold, or of leasehold for freehold, is outside this head of charge but is not on this account a conveyance on sale.[35]

> Thus in *Littlewoods Mail Order Stores Ltd.* v. *I.R.C.*,[35] a freehold property owned by one company was exchanged for a leasehold property owned by another company. There was no equality money. It was held that the instrument effecting this transaction was not a deed of exchange for the purposes of the Stamp Act; that it was not a conveyance *on sale*, because there was no price in money[36]; but that it was a "conveyance of any kind not hereinbefore described"[37] and attracted a duty of 50p.

28-48 Where equality money is paid in such a case, the instrument is *pro tanto* a conveyance on sale.[38]

If an instrument, though described by the parties as an exchange, effects a transaction of a different nature, it must be stamped accordingly.[39]

> Thus if A contracts to sell Blackacre (freehold) to B, and B contracts to sell Whiteacre (freehold) to A, and the two contracts of sale are completed by an instrument which is described as an exchange, the instrument must be stamped as effecting two conveyances on sale.

An opinion of the Controller of Stamps has been given on the following practice, where A has entered into a contract with B to sell A's house for

---

32. F.A. 1982, s.129. The instrument must be adjudicated: see *ante*, § 27-44.
33. S.A. 1891, s.73.
34. *Ibid.* s.73; s.61(2).
35. *Littlewoods Mail Order Stores Ltd.* v. *I.R.C.* [1963] A.C. 135 (H.L.).
36. See *ante*, § 28-04.
37. See *ante*, § 28-44.
38. See *Littlewoods Mail Order Stores Ltd.* v. *I.R.C.* [1963] A.C. 135, *per* Viscount Simonds at p. 151.
39. *Viscount Portman* v. *I.R.C.* (1956) 35 A.T.C. 349.

(say) £23,200 and has also entered into a contract with C to buy C's house for (say) £33,200. The transaction is sometimes carried into effect by (1) C conveying his house to A in exchange for A's house and £10,000, and (2) C conveying A's former house to B for £23,200. The Controller's opinion is that in this case the first conveyance would attract duty as a conveyance of C's house for £33,200 and as conveyance of A's house for £23,200 and that a certificate of value on the footing that £10,000 was paid for equality of exchange would be inappropriate.[40]

28–49   An exchange of stock or securities constitutes a sale for purposes of stamp duty[41] but it may well attract the exemption referred to in § 28–45/46 (5).

The stamp duty reserve tax

28–50   As part of the continuing reform of stamp duties following the Green Paper of March 1983, the duty on share transactions was reduced by the Finance Act 1986 to $\frac{1}{2}$ per cent.: correspondingly, however, the base on which such duty is levied was widened. And, in order to ensure that the broadening of that base was fully effective, a new tax, the stamp duty reserve tax, was introduced.

The tax is charged whenever an agreement for the transfer of "chargeable securities"[42] is made for valuable consideration,[43] unless, before the expiry of the period of two months from the date when the agreement became unconditional, two requirements have been satisfied:

(i) the appropriate instrument or instruments, transferring the securities to the purchaser or his nominee, have been executed; and

(ii) the instrument (or instruments) or transfer has been duly stamped.

28–51   Whilst the tax is partly designed as an anti-avoidance provision, its principal intent is to bring into charge to duty "closing transactions" made within a stock exchange account—that is to say, those cases where a person has avoided duty on share transactions by selling the shares in the same account as that in which he purchased them.

Exceptions to the charge

28–52   Stamp duty reserve tax is not levied on agreements—

(a) for the sale of stocks, etc. any instrument of transfer of which would itself would be exempt from duty (*e.g.* gilt edged securities)[44]

---

40. (1960) 57 L.S.Gaz. 451.

41. *J. & P. Coats* v. *I.R.C.* [1897] 2 Q.B. 423 (C.A.). This is because a conveyance on sale is a transfer of property for money (see *ante*, § 28–04) and, by reason of s.55 of the S.A. 1891 (see *ante*, § 28–33) stock is the equivalent of money.

42. "Chargeable securities" are defined by s.99(3)–(5) as meaning stocks, shares, loan capital and units under a unit trust scheme other than shares, etc., which are not registered in a register kept in the U.K. which have been issued by a body corporate which itself is not registered in the U.K. and further excluding shares, etc., which are exempt from all stamp duties (*e.g.* gilt edged securities).

43. F.A. 1986, s.87.

44. *Ibid.*, s.99(5).

(b) to transfer unit trusts to the managers of the scheme[45]

(c) to transfer stock chargeable under the head "Bearer instrument"

28–53   The tax will fall due on the expiry of the two month period, when it will be payable by the purchaser[46] at a rate of 50p for each £100 or part thereof.[47] Provision is made, however, for the repayment or cancellation of the tax if, within six years of the agreement for sale becoming unconditional, the relevant conditions mentioned in § 28–50 above become satisfied. In such a case, if the tax had actually been paid, it will become repayable, together with interest at a rate to be fixed by the Treasury.[48]

---

45. *Ibid.*, s.90.
46. *Ibid.*, s.91.
47. *Ibid.*, s.87(6).
48. *Ibid.*, s.92.

CHAPTER 29

SECTION 59 AND THE SALE OF A BUSINESS

29-01 ON a sale of land, the contract of sale bears no stamp and the subsequent conveyance is stamped *ad valorem*. Payment of the *ad valorem* duty can be avoided if the purchaser dispenses with the conveyance and relies on the equitable title acquired by purchase, but in normal circumstances the purchaser requires the legal estate and a formal conveyance is therefore necessary.[1] But on a sale of goodwill or of an equitable interest in property different considerations arise. In such cases, where the contract is specifically enforceable, the title which the purchaser acquires under the contract is, for all practical purposes, as good as the title which he would acquire under a formal assignment and, indeed, it is the usual practice to dispense with a formal assignment. Section 59 of the Stamp Act 1891, however, prevents any loss of stamp duty to the Revenue by providing that any contract or agreement[2] for the sale of:

29-02
(1) Any equitable estate or interest in any property whatsoever; or
(2) any estate or interest in any property except:
    (i)   land;
    (ii) property locally situate out of the United Kingdom;
    (iii) goods, wares or merchandise;
    (iv) stock (including shares) or marketable securities[3]; or
    (v) any ship or part of a ship;

shall be charged with the same *ad valorem* duty (to be paid by the purchaser) as if it were an actual conveyance on sale of the property agreed to be sold.[4] A subsequent conveyance or transfer (if any) is not then chargeable with any duty but the Commissioners will, on application, *either* impress a duty paid denoting stamp on the conveyance or transfer *or*, on production of the contract or agreement duly stamped, transfer the *ad valorem* duty to the conveyance.[5]

29-03 A contract or agreement which, though liable to the *ad valorem* duty, bears no stamp is nevertheless deemed to be duly stamped for all purposes, if a conveyance or transfer is presented for stamping within six months after the first execution of the agreement, or within such longer period as the Commissioners may think reasonable in the circumstances of the case.[6]

If a contract is stamped *ad valorem* under section 59 and the contract is

---

1. Law of Property Act 1925, s.52(1). In some cases, *e.g.* on the "conversion" of a partnership into a limited company, it may be convenient to dispense with a formal conveyance and leave the legal estate in the former partners. But see *Escoigne Properties Ltd.* v. *I.R.C.* [1958] A.C. 549; *post*, § 33–10.
2. This does not include an agreement granting an option to purchase: *William Cory & Son Ltd.* v. *I.R.C.* [1965] A.C. 1088 (H.L.), discussed *ante*, § 28–22.
3. See *ante*, § 28–02, note 5.
4. For rates of duty, certificates of value, etc., see *ante*, §§ 28–24 *et seq*.
5. S.A. 1891, s.59(3).
6. *Ibid.* s.59(5) as amended by F.A. 1970, Sched. 7, para. 1(3)(*b*); but there may be a penalty for late stamping: see *ante*, § 27–27.

afterwards rescinded or annulled, or for any other reason is not substantially performed or carried into effect, the Commissioners must return the duty.[7]

9–03A Where shares are allotted for a consideration other than cash, and the contract under which the transaction takes place is not in writing, section 88(3) of the Companies Act 1985 requires that particulars of the contract should be delivered to the Registrar within one month after the allotment, and the particulars are deemed to be an instrument within the Stamp Act 1891: and see § 32–03 *et seq.*

1. Exceptions to Section 59 of the Stamp Act 1891

29–04 There are three exceptions in section 59 which require special mention.[8]

(1) *Land*

29–05 A contract for the sale of an *equitable* interest in land is within section 59, even if the land is situate outside the United Kingdom.[9] A contract for the sale of a *legal* estate or interest in land is excepted from the section, notwithstanding the equitable title which the purchaser acquires on exchange of contracts.

(2) *Property locally situate outside the United Kingdom*

29–06 It was at one time supposed that intangible property, such as debts, patents and other things in action, could have no "local situation."[10] The earlier cases which supported this view were overruled by the House of Lords in *English, Scottish and Australian Bank Ltd.* v. *I.R.C.,*[11] where it was held that a contract for the sale of debts owed by debtors resident outside the United Kingdom was a contract for the sale of property "locally situate out of the United Kingdom" and was therefore within the exception. It can now be taken as settled that a locality, albeit fictitious, must be imputed to all things in action. An agreement for the sale of the goodwill of a business carried on abroad, with customers abroad, has been held to fall within the exception.[12]

(3) *Goods, wares or merchandise*

29–07 An agreement for the sale of trading stock or plant or machinery attracts no stamp duty if the items fall within the words "goods, wares or merchandise." Moreover, such items can be included in the sale agreement yet be disregarded for the purposes of a certificate of value, if they are excluded from the actual conveyance.[13]

---

7. S.A. 1891, s.59(6). Contrast the relief under the Stamp Duties Management Act 1891, *ante*, § 27–51.

8. See generally Sergeant, pp. 137 *et seq.*

9. *Farmer & Co.* v. *I.R.C.* [1898] 2 Q.B. 141. If the contract was executed outside the U.K., the liability to stamp it in the U.K. would not arise until such time (if ever) that it was brought to the U.K.: see *ante*, § 27–46 *et seq.*

10. See Sergeant, p. 139.

11. [1932] A.C. 238.

12. *I.R.C.* v. *Muller & Co.'s Margarine* [1901] A.C. 217.

13. F.A. 1958, s.34; see *ante* § 28–26.

The interest of an owner under a hire-purchase agreement is not within the exception[14]; but the interest of a pawnbroker in the goods pawned is within it.[15] In practice, the Revenue treat cash in hand and cash on current account (but not cash on deposit) as falling outside section 59.[16]

2. PROPERTY WITHIN SECTION 59 OF THE STAMP ACT 1891

29–08   A contract for the sale of any of the following items is clearly caught by section 59 (except where the property is locally situate out of the United Kingdom) and is liable to *ad valorem* conveyance or transfer duty:

(1) *Goodwill.*[17] If A contracts to sell the goodwill of his business and the business premises, the contract is liable to no duty in respect of the premises and to *ad valorem* duty in respect of the goodwill, which must be separately valued for this purpose.[18] In practice, and to save the expense of valuing goodwill, the Commissioners are prepared to stamp the contract *ad valorem* in respect of both the goodwill and the premises. The conveyance is then charged with a fixed duty of 50p and should be adjudicated (or denoted).

The liability for duty in respect of goodwill cannot be avoided by the purchaser taking from the vendor a covenant not to compete; for such a covenant has been held to constitute an agreement for the sale of goodwill, though not so worded.[19]

(2) *Bookdebts.*

(3) *Cash on deposit.* This is a debt due from a bank to its customer.[20] Cash in hand, cash in current account, bills and notes, are in practice treated as falling outside section 59: see § 29–07.

(4) *Patents, licences, trade marks, copyrights and "know-how."*

(5) *Benefit of pending contracts.*

(6) *Tenant's and trade fixtures on leasehold property.*[21]

(7) *The interest of an owner under a hire-purchase agreement.*[22]

(8) *Equitable interests in freehold and leasehold property.*

3. STAMP DUTY ON THE PURCHASE OF A BUSINESS

29–09   Where a contract of sale includes items within section 59 and items not caught by the section, the consideration must be apportioned; and the apportionment must be a bona fide apportionment based on the commer-

---

14. *Drages* v. *I.R.C.* (1927) 46 T.C. 389.
15. *Riley (Arthur) Ltd.* v. *I.R.C.* (1931) 46 T.C. 402.
16. S.A. 1981, s.59 applies to "property" and the official view is that cash in hand and cash on current account are not "property": see *St. Aubyn* v. *Att.-Gen.* [1952] A.C. 15, *per* Lord Simonds at p. 32.
17. *Benjamin Brooke & Co.* v. *I.R.C.* [1896] 2 Q.B. 356.
18. *West London Syndicate Ltd.* v. *I.R.C.* [1898] 2 Q.B. 507 (C.A.).
19. *Eastern National Omnibus Co. Ltd.* v. *I.R.C.* [1939] 1 K.B. 161; see *ante*, § 27–06. A bare agreement not to compete in consideration of a money payment is void: *Vancouver Malt, etc.* v. *Vancouver Breweries* [1934] A.C. 181.
20. *Foley* v. *Hill* (1848) 2 H.L. Cas. 28.
21. Fixtures on freehold property are, of course, part of the freehold and thus within the exceptions to s.59.
22. *Drages* v. *I.R.C.* (1927) 46 T.C. 389.

cial value of the respective properties. An apportionment should be made on Form 22, supplied by the Stamp Office.

Methods of saving duty

29–10   By careful planning, a considerable amount of stamp duty can be saved on the take-over of a business as a going concern. For example:

The state of A's business is as follows:

Liabilities	£	*Assets*	£
Secured creditors	9,000	Freehold	20,000
Trade creditors	9,000	Goodwill	4,000
		Stock	9,000
		Bookdebts	8,000
Excess of assets over liab-		Bank: Current A/C	1,000
ilities	27,000	Bank: Deposit A/C	3,000
	£45,000		£45,000

B will purchase the business for £27,000 and will take over the liabilities to secured and trade creditors.

The total consideration for stamp duty purposes is:

	£
Purchase price	27,000
Liabilities taken over[23–24]	18,000
	£45,000

This £45,000 must be apportioned between the assets (as in the account, above).

The sale agreement. Ad valorem duty is payable on the sale agreement (under section 59) on the following items:

	£	
Goodwill	4,000	
Bookdebts	8,000	
Cash on deposit	3,000	
	£15,000	*Ad val.* duty: £150[25]

The other items attract no duty.

The transfer. The conveyance of the freehold for £20,000 would attract conveyance or transfer duty at £1 per cent. The stock-in-trade and cash in hand would in practice be transferred by delivery, without any instrument of transfer. The duty would be thus on the

	£	
Freehold	20,000	*Ad. val.* duty: £200[25]
Total ad valorem duty:		£350

23–24. See S.A. 1891, s.57, *ante*, § 28–39.

25. No certificate of value can be included in either the sale agreement or the transfer for there is one larger transaction for more than £30,000 (even ignoring the value of the stock).

29–11   In order to save duty, the following arrangements should be made:

    (1) Cash on deposit (£3,000) should be transferred to current account before the date of agreement. This takes it out of section 59.

    (2) There should be no agreement to transfer bookdebts (£8,000). These should be retained by the vendor[26] and, when collected, used to discharge so far as possible the liabilities (which also should so far as possible be retained by the vendor).[26] On the figures given, the vendor should retain the bookdebts (£8,000) plus £1,000 from cash in hand, to discharge the liabilities to the trade creditors. This achieves a double saving of duty, both in respect of the bookdebts (s.59) and the liabilities (s.57).

If this is done, the property agreed to be taken over will be:

Liabilities	£	*Assets*	£
Secured creditors	9,000	Freehold	20,000
		Goodwill	4,000
Excess of assets over liab-		Stock	9,000
ilities	27,000	Bank: Current A/C	3,000
	£36,000		£36,000

The total consideration for stamp duty purposes is then:

		£
Purchase price		27,000
Liabilities taken over (s. 57) ..		9,000
		£36,000
less		
*Stock	9,000	
*Cash in hand	3,000	
		12,000
		£24,000 *Ad val.* Duty: £0

(*Transferred by delivery, so as to avoid stamp duty.)

A certificate of value not exceeding £30,000 should be included in both documents since there is one transaction not exceeding that amount. Consequently it has been possible not only to reduce the consideration on which duty is chargeable but also the rate of duty applicable.

---

26. Or, more usually, by the purchaser as agent for the vendor. There may be fiscal disadvantages in excluding bookdebts which should be carefully weighed against the prospective saving of stamp duty. Thus relief from capital gains tax on the transfer of a business to a company is available only where *all* the assets (or all the assets other than cash) are transferred: see *ante*, § 16–13.

The vendor cannot insist on the purchaser taking a conveyance of the freehold and an assignment of goodwill in one instrument, nor can the vendor object if the purchaser does not require a written assignment of goodwill.

Treatment of cash

29–13   It should be noted that even where cash in hand or cash on current account is included in the sale agreement, so that it must be mentioned on Form 22, no stamp duty is payable on the cash because it falls outside section 59 of the Stamp Act 1891 (see § 29–07); but the cash cannot be disregarded in determining the certificate of value to be included in the conveyance—because cash is not excepted from section 34(4) of the Finance Act 1958: see § 28–26.

Thus if the assets sold are made up of:

		£
1.	Goodwill	29,200
2.	Loose plant	10,000
3.	Cash in hand	900
		40,100

no *ad valorem* duty is payable on items 2 and 3 but the amount conveyed for certification purposes is the sum of items 1 and 3 (*i.e.* £30,100).

CHAPTER 30

VOLUNTARY DISPOSITIONS AND SETTLEMENTS

1. VOLUNTARY DISPOSITIONS

30–01   PRIOR to March 26, 1985, voluntary conveyances or transfers attracted *ad valorem* duty in accordance with the provisions of section 74 of the Finance (1909–10) Act 1910. That duty has, however, been abolished with effect from that date by section 82 of the Finance Act 1985. In future, instruments effecting voluntary transfers will be chargeable only under the head "Conveyance of any other kind."

It will, though, still be necessary to submit such instruments to the Commissioners for adjudication under section 12 of the Stamp Act as being duly stamped.[1] It may be anticipated that, in accordance with an announcement made by the Inland Revenue at the time of publication of the Finance Bill, the Commissioners will eventually, exercise the enabling power conferred on them by section 87 of the Finance Act 1985 to make regulations exempting such instruments from adjudication, provded that they carry a certificate that they are duly stamped. As yet, though, the appropriate regulations have not been promulgated.

2. SETTLEMENT DUTY AND UNIT TRUSTS

30–02   The charge to stamp duty under the heading "Settlement" in the Stamp Act 1891 was abolished as from August 1, 1962, by section 30 of the Finance Act 1962. Prior to its abolition it had applied to:

(a) marriage settlements;
(b) voluntary settlements where property was transferred without an instrument chargeable as a voluntary disposition (*e.g.* settlements of cash, bearer securities or renounced shares); or
(c) instruments which otherwise escaped duty (*e.g.* a transfer of government stock or funds).[2]

Such settlements now escape stamp duty entirely.

30–03   Section 30 of the Finance Act 1962 added a new head of charge to Schedule 1 to the Stamp Act 1891 as follows:

"UNIT TRUST INSTRUMENT." Any trust instrument of a unit trust scheme (within the meaning of the Finance Act 1946, ss.53–57):

For every £100 (or fractional part of £100) of the amount or value of the property subject to the trusts created or recorded by the instrument . . . 25p."

A unit trust scheme is widely defined in the Finance Act 1946 to mean any arrangements made for the purpose, or having the effect, of providing, for

---

1. F.A. 1985, s.82(5).
2. See, *e.g. Ansell* v. *I.R.C.* [1929] 1 K.B. 608.

persons having funds available for investment, facilities for the participation by them, as beneficiaries under a trust, in any profits or income arising from the acquisition, holding, management or disposal of any property whatsoever.[3]

It will be recalled that the units (including sub-units)[3] are "stock" for the purposes of stamp duty.[4]

---

3. F.A. 1946, s.57(1). This definition was extended by the F.A. 1963, s.65.
4. See *ante*, § 28–02, note 5. The characteristics of "stock" are usefully listed in Monroe's *Stamp Duties*; see (5th ed.) para. 272.

CHAPTER 31

LEASE DUTY

31–01 LEASES of land are chargeable under the head "Lease or Tack" in the Stamp Act 1891.[1] The Act contains no definition of "lease" which must be taken to have the meaning ascribed to it under the general law. The instrument must therefore confer a right to exclusive possession for a period that is definite or capable of definition. These requirements of the general law are fully discussed in the standard works on the law of property[2]; but with regard to stamp duty, the following points should be noticed:

(1) An instrument which takes effect as a *licence*, even though described as a lease, is not subject to lease duty. A mere licence in consideration of periodical payments now attracts no duty whatsoever.[3] Whether an instrument takes effect as a licence or lease depends on the substance of the transaction and not merely on the form of the instrument.[4]

(2) Lease duty applies only to leases of "lands, tenements or heritable subjects." A hiring of chattels in consideration of periodical payments, even if described as a lease, is outside the charge; nor would it have attracted bond covenant duty.[5] A lease of incorporeal hereditaments, including sporting rights, is within the charge.

The head of charge

31–02 The general scheme of the Stamp Act 1891 is to charge fixed duties on certain short-term leases at low rents, and *ad valorem* duties on leases for more than a year and on periodic tenancies. The sub-heads of charge in the Stamp Act are as follows:

(1) Lease for any definite term less than a year:

(a) of a furnished dwelling-house or apartment where the rent for such term exceeds £500[6] .... £1[7]

(b) of any lands, except or otherwise than as aforesaid .... Same as on a lease for a year at the rent reserved for the definite term.

---

1. Sched. 1. "Tack" is the Scottish equivalent of "Lease." "Shared ownership" leases granted by local authorities and others may be dutiable as conveyances on sale: see F.A. 1980, s.97 as amended by F.A. 1981, s.108 for details.
2. Megarry and Wade; *Law of Real Property* (5th ed.), pp. 632–645.
3. Prior to August 1, 1971, such an instrument would have attracted bond covenant duty. That duty was abolished by F.A. 1971, s.64(1).
4. See *Addiscombe Garden Estates Ltd.* v. *Crabbe* [1958] 1 Q.B. 513 (C.A.).
5. F.A. 1958, s.35(1). See note 3, above.
6. £500 substituted for £400 by F.A. 1982, s.113(3)(a).
7. Note that stamp duty on a furnished letting might be saved by making the term one year less one day.

(2) Lease for any other definite term, or for any indefinite term:

(a) where there is a "premium" moving either to the lessor or to any other person: *ad valorem* duty is charged on the premium.
(See "Duty on the premium": below.)
(b) where the consideration, or any part thereof, is any rent: *ad valorem* duty is charged on the rent.
(See "Duty on the rent": below.)

(3) Leases of any other kind not hereinbefore described[8–9]:

If no "premium"; term not over 35 years or indefinite; and rent not exceeding the rate (or average rate) of £100 per annum:
Fixed duty of £2.

31–03   *Meaning of "premium."* The word "premium" does not appear in the Act and is used in § 31–02 as a convenient abbreviation for the phrase "consideration, moving either to the lessor or to any other person, consisting of money, stock[10] or security" which is used in the Act. The phrase includes, for example, a fixed sum payable by the tenant in lieu of decorating whether such sum be payable at the beginning or at the end of the term. Again, where the tenant undertakes to bear the lessor's solicitors' costs, such costs are "consideration" within the Act, but it is the practice of the Commissioners to ignore them.[11]

Note that *ad valorem* duty is payable on a premium whether it is payable to the lessor or to any other person.

Thus if T takes a lease of land from L in consideration of a premium payable to B, a builder, duty is payable on the premium even though B is not a party to the lease.[12] The amount of the premium should be stated in the lease.[13]

Leases of building plots and houses in the course of erection, and the question whether a certificate of value can be included, have already been discussed.[14]

31–04   *Duty on the premium.* Where a premium is payable, the *ad valorem* duty thereon under sub-head (2) is as on a conveyance on sale for the same amount.[15] The nil rate will apply where a certificate of value is included in the lease, provided the rent (or the average rent) does not exceed £300 per annum.[16] The usual form of the certificate is as follows:

8–9. A mining lease for royalties would attract duty under this head. A lease at a fixed rent plus a royalty is charged both on the fixed rent and on the royalty.
  10. Defined in S.A. 1891, s.122(1); and see *ante*, § 28–02, note 5.
  11. [1959] 56 L.S.Gaz. 95.
  12. *Cf. Att.-Gen.* v. *Brown* (1849) 3 Ex. 662. In the common case, T is the builder's nominee under a building agreement and L is the ground landlord granting the lease by direction of the builder.
  13. See S.A. 1891, s.5; *ante*, § 27–32.
  14. See *ante*, § 28–28.
  15. See *ante*, § 28–01.
  16. F.A. 1963, s.55(2); £300 substituted for £250 by F.A. 1982, s.128(2).

"It is hereby certified that the transaction hereby effected does not form part of a larger transaction or of a series of transactions in respect of which the amount or value, or the aggregate amount or value, of the consideration other than rent exceeds £30,000."

31–05   *Duty on the rent.*[17] The *ad valorem* duty on the rent, under sub-head (2), is as follows:

(a) Term not exceeding seven years or indefinite:
  Rent not exceeding £500 per annum .... nil
  Rent exceeding £500 per annum .... 50p per £50 or part thereof ..... (£1%)

(b) Term exceeding seven years but not 35 years .... £1 per £50 or part thereof ..... (£2%)

(c) Term exceeding 35 years but not 100 years .... £6 per £50 or part thereof .... (£12%)

(d) Term exceeding 100 years .... £12 per £50 or part thereof .... (£24%)

There is a sliding scale for (b), (c) and (d) where the rent does not exceed £500 per annum.[17]

31–06   In 1891, a lease for life or for a term determinable on marriage would have fallen under (a), but such leases now take effect as leases for 90 years determinable after the death (or marriage) of the lessee[18] and fall, therefore, under (c). It seems that the only leases for an "indefinite term" are periodic tenancies. A lease for a fixed term and thereafter until determined is treated as a lease for the fixed term plus a further period until the earliest date when the lease can be determined.[19] The following are leases for a definite term:

(i) A lease for a fixed term, with an option to renew for a further term. This should be stamped as a lease for the original term only,[20] no additional duty being attracted by virtue of the option.[21] If, however, the option is exercised, the instrument exercising the option should be stamped as an agreement for a lease.[22]

Thus if L grants a lease to T for 35 years, with an option (or options) for an additional term or terms not exceeding 35 years each, the lease duty on the original lease is £2 per cent. of the rent. If the option is exercised, the instrument is again stamped at £2 per cent. of the rent.

(ii) A lease for a fixed term liable to earlier determination on notice.[23]

---

17. For details, see F.A. 1982, s.128(3) amending the Table in S.A. 1891 as respects instruments executed on or after March 22, 1982. For the charge on conditional or contingent rent, see *Coventry City Council* v. *I.R.C.* [1978] S.T.C. 151; see *ante* § 27–18.
18. Law of Property Act 1925, s.149(6). See also *Earl of Mount Edgcumbe* v. *I.R.C.* [1911] 2 K.B. 24.
19. F.A. 1963, s.56(3).
20. *Hand* v. *Hall* (1877) 2 Ex.D. 355 (lease for less than three years with option to tenant to remain for a further three-and-a-half years. *Held*, to create a term for less than three years).
21. See *ante*, § 27–12.
22. See *post*, § 31–08.
23. *Earl of Mount Edgcumbe* v. *I.R.C.* [1911] 2 K.B. 24; *Cummins Engine Co. Ltd.* v. *I.R.C.* [1981] 1 W.L.R. 1363; [1981] S.T.C. 604 (C.S.).

31–07   Where the rent is progressive, it must be averaged over the term for the purpose of assessing the duty.

> *Example*
>   Land is leased for seven years at a rent of £150 per annum for two years; £300 per annum for the next two years; and £400 per annum for the remaining three years. The average rental is £300.

An instrument granting a reversionary lease is liable to the same stamp duty as an instrument which grants a non-reversionary lease. The device of granting a 21-year lease[24–25] and a 35–year reversionary lease, with options for renewal, is used to avoid high rates of *ad valorem* duty on long leases.

An instrument increasing the rent reserved under another instrument duly stamped as a lease is itself dutiable as a lease or tack in consideration of the additional rent payable[26] but no additional duty would appear to be payable on the sum paid by the landlord to secure such additional rent.

Agreement for a lease

31–08   An agreement for a lease, provided that the agreement is specifically enforceable and is registered as an estate contract, is almost as good as a lease, at all events so far as the original lessee is concerned.[27] The Stamp Act 1891, as amended, though, contains provisions which prevent loss of stamp duty by the use of such agreements. Section 75(1) provides that an agreement for a lease[28] is to be charged with the same duty as would be payable if it were an actual lease for the term and consideration mentioned in the agreement. Section 75(2) allows, however, that where duty has been so paid and subsequently a lease is granted substantially in conformity with the agreement, the *ad valorem* duty which would be payable is reduced by the duty already paid on the agreement itself.

Prior to March 20, 1984, a variety of schemes was in currency which relied on the use of an agreement for a lease in excess of 35 years (which was, at that time, outside the scope of section 75(1)) in order to depress the value of the freehold which was actually the subject-matter of the transaction. So, in the simplest case, H would enter into an agreement for a 999-year lease with the owner of the property, V, for a premium equal to the value of the property and at a peppercorn rent. V would then sell the freehold reversion to H's wife W for its full value of £1 which supposedly alone attracted *ad valorem* duty (at the nil rate). The Revenue do not accept that such schemes were successful,[28a] but nevertheless have taken steps to counteract this and other similar devices in section 111 of the Finance Act 1984.[29] In future, *ad valorem* duty will be payable on all agreements for

---

24–25. A reversionary lease must take effect within 21 years from the date of the instrument which creates it: Law of Property Act 1925, s.149(3).
    26. S.A. 1891, s.77(5). See *Gable Construction Co. Ltd.* v. *I.R.C.* [1968] 1 W.L.R. 1426.
    27. For a discussion on the subject see Cheshire's *Modern Law of Real Property* (11th ed.), pp. 373 *et seq.* and Megarry and Wade, *Law of Real Property* (5th ed.), pp. 638 *et seq.*
    28. As amended by F.A. 1984, s.111.
    28a. In the first reported case on such schemes the Revenue's view prevailed: see *Ingram* v. *I.R.C.* [1985] S.T.C. 835, §27–06.
    29. See *ante*, § 27–40.

leases, of whatever length,[30] and the duty paid will then be required to be denoted on any instrument which seeks to convey the freehold subject to the agreement.[30a]

The Stamp Act contains no provisions for the recovery of the duty if the agreement is afterwards rescinded or annulled.[31] Relief may, however, be available in some cases under the Stamp Duties Management Act 1891.[32]

Other matters

31–09   (1) *Service charges, etc.* Charges made by a lessor for heating, lighting, cleaning or other services (*e.g.* porterage, lifts, etc.) attract stamp duty as follows:

    (a) if reserved as rent, they attract lease duty;

    (b) if they are fixed contributions payable under covenant only, they attract no duty.[33]

If the charges cannot be ascertained in advance, no *ad valorem* duty is payable.[34]

31–10   (2) *Penal rents.* Where a lease contains a provision for a penal rent, or an increased rent in the nature of a penal rent (*e.g.* in the event of a breach of covenant by the lessee), no duty is payable in respect of such provision.[35] Similarly, no duty is payable in respect of the surrender or abandonment of an existing lease of the same premises.[35]

31–11   (3) *Covenants to improve the demised premises.* A lease for a consideration which attracts *ad valorem* duty and in further consideration either:

    (a) of a covenant by the lessee to make (or of his having previously made) any substantial improvement of or addition to the demised property; or

    (b) of any covenant relating to the matter of the lease,

attracts no further duty in respect of the covenants in (a) or (b).[36]

31–12   (4) *Instruments withdrawing a notice to quit.* Where notice to determine a tenancy is given and is subsequently withdrawn by agreement between the parties, the instrument withdrawing the notice operates as an agreement for a new tenancy and must be stamped accordingly.[37]

---

30. S.A. 1891, s.75(1) as amended by F.A. 1984, s.111(1).
30a. F.A. 1984, s.111(2).
31. *Cf.* S.A. 1891, s.59(6), *ante*, § 29–03.
32. See *ante*, § 27–51.
33. Prior to August 1, 1971, they attracted bond covenant duty. And see [1981] B.T.R. C161.
34. See *ante*, § 27–20. But a fixed duty of £2 is charged: see (1962) 59 L.S.Gaz. 44.
35. S.A. 1891, s.77(1).
36. *Ibid.* s.77(2), as amended by Revenue Act 1909, s.8. Contrast F.A. 1900, s.10, *ante*, § 28–27.
37. *Freeman* v. *Evans* [1922] 1 Ch. 36 (C.A.).

Method of stamping leases

31–13   Leases must bear an impressed stamp.
For the stamping of duplicates and counterparts, see § 27–39.
For the produced stamp, see § 27–45.

CHAPTER 32

SHARE CAPITAL, BEARER INSTRUMENTS AND COMPOSITIONS

1. CHARGEABLE TRANSACTIONS OF CAPITAL COMPANIES

Background

32–01   Capital duty under section 112 or section 113 of the Stamp Act 1891 (on statements relating to nominal share capital of limited companies) was abolished as from August 1, 1973.[1] The duties on loan capital[2] under section 8 of the Finance Act 1899 and on marketable securities[3] under Schedule 1 to the Stamp Act 1891 were abolished with effect from January 1, 1973.[4] Thus there is no longer any charge to stamp duty on the creation of issue of any such securities: nor, as a rule, is the transfer of loan capital subject to duty under the heading "Conveyance or transfer on sale."[5]

There is, however, a new charge to duty which takes the place of the former share capital duty and is effective from August 1, 1973. This charge is found in sections 47 and 48 of, and Schedule 19 to, the Finance Act 1973 and conforms with the United Kingdom's obligations under an EEC directive. The new duty may be called "capital companies duty."

The effect of these provisions is that it is more expensive to capitalise a company by issuing shares (on which capital companies' duty is payable) than by issuing loan stock (on which no duty is payable). Further, transfers of shares attract *ad valorem* conveyance or transfer duty whereas transfers of loan stock may be exempt: see § 28–45(4).

32–02   Under section 47 of the Finance Act 1973, stamp duty at the rate of £1 for every £100 (or fraction of £100) is payable on the statement required when a qualifying *capital company* undertakes a *chargeable transaction*.

Capital company

A capital company is[6]:

   (1) a limited liability company or limited partnership incorporated in the United Kingdom;

---

1. F.A. 1973, s.49(1)(*a*). The similar duty under the Limited Partnerships Act 1907, s.11 was also abolished from that date: F.A. 1973, s.49(1)(*b*).
2. Loan capital is defined in F.A. 1899, s.8(5), as: "any debenture stock, . . . corporation stock . . . or funded debt, by whatever name known, or any capital raised by any . . . corporation, company, or body of persons formed or established in the United Kingdom, which is borrowed, or has the character of borrowed money, whether it is in the form of stock or in any other form, and whether the loan thereof is secured by a mortgage, marketable security or other instrument, or is unsecured but does not include . . . any overdraft at the bank or other loan raised for a merely temporary purpose for a period not exceeding 12 months . . ." This definition is, in effect, preserved by F.A. 1973, s.49(9). *Cf.* the definition in F.A. 1986, s.78(7): § 28–46 n. 29.
3. The expression "marketable security" is defined in S.A. 1891, s.122 as "a security of such a description as to be capable of being sold in any stock market in the United Kingdom."
4. F.A. 1973, s.49(2) and (3).
5. See now F.A. 1986, s.79, which replaces, with amendments, F.A. 1976, s.126..
6. F.A. 1973, s.48(1).

(2) a company incorporated according to the law of another member state of the EEC;

(3) any other corporation or body of persons whose shares or assets can be dealt in on a Stock Exchange within the EEC; or

(4) any other corporation or body of persons operating for profit whose members have both the right to dispose of their shares to third parties without prior authorisation and limited liability.

A unit trust (whether authorised or not) is not a capital company; nor is an unlimited company, whether or not it has a share capital. Unlimited companies are often used in order to avoid stamp duty; but where there is a share capital, some restriction on the transfer of shares is required in order to fall outside (4).

The charge under section 47 of the Finance Act 1973 applies only if the capital company has its place of effective management or its registered office in Great Britain (but in the latter case only if its place of effective management is outside the EEC).[7]

Chargeable transactions

32–03   The transactions giving rise to the charge under section 47 are set out in paragraph 1 of Schedule 19 to the Finance Act 1973 and are as follows:

(1) *Formation* of a capital company.[8] Duty is charged as follows:

(a) if the formation is the consequence of the conversion of a corporation or body of persons into a capital company, the duty is charged on the actual value[9] of the net assets of that company immediately after the conversion[10];

(b) in all other cases duty is charged on the actual value of net assets of any kind contributed by the members.[11]

If, however, in either event, the value of the net assets is less than the nominal value of the shares at the relevant time, duty is charged on that nominal value.[12] The charge does not extend to the conversion of a capital company into a different type of capital company or to the alteration of a company's memorandum or articles.[13]

32–04   (2) *Increase in capital* by the contribution of assets of any kind[14]; *e.g.* if share capital is *issued* for money or money's worth, but not if there is a bonus issue. There is a similar charge where assets are contributed in return for rights (*e.g.* voting rights) similar to those attaching to shares.[15]

---

7. F.A. 1973, s.47(1).
8. *Ibid.* Sched. 19, para. 1(*a*).
9. Presumably this means market value. See *Advokatrådet p/p P. Conradsen A/S v. Ministry of Fiscal Affairs* [1979] E.C.R. 2221, on the question of what expenses may be deducted in the computation of "actual value."
10. F.A. 1973, Sched. 19, para. 4(2).
11. *Ibid.* Sched. 19, para. 4(1).
12. *Ibid.* Sched. 19, para. 7(1).
13. *Ibid.* Sched. 19, para. 2(1)(*b*).
14. *Ibid.* Sched. 19, para. 1(*b*).
15. *Ibid.* Sched. 19, para. 1(*c*).

The charge is on either the actual value of net assets contributed or the nominal value of the shares, whichever is the greater.[16] The charge applies to the conversion of loan stock into share capital and the issue of shares in satisfaction of a debt owed by the company.[17]

> In *Cambridge Petroleum Royalties Ltd.* v. *I.R.C.*[18] shares of 20p each were issued in 1972 (*i.e.* before capital duty was introduced) at a premium of 80p per share and on terms that half these amounts were payable on issue. In 1975 the company made a call in respect of the balance of 50p per share. The Revenue claimed capital duty. *Held*, that the claim was unjustified. The undertaking each shareholder gave in 1972 to pay the balance when called on was itself a contribution of assets, and the fulfilment of that undertaking did not "increase" the company's assets.

32–05   (3) *Conversion of an unlimited company to a limited company.*[19] Since an unlimited company is not a capital company its conversion to limited liability status is a chargeable event. This head of charge likewise extends to an increase in the amount contributed by a limited partner. The charge is on the net assets of the company immediately before the transaction (or the part thereof that represents the share in the company's net assets that has become unlimited).[20]

32–06   (4) *Transfer to Great Britain of the place of effective management or registered office* of a capital company, unless that company is subject to a similar charge to duty (*i.e.* as that contained in s.47) in another Member State of the EEC.[21] The charge is on either the actual value of net assets belonging to the company at the time of the chargeable transaction or the nominal value of its shares at that time whichever is the greater.[22] There is an alternative charge, which lies within the discretion of the Commissioners, who may assess duty on the basis of the actual value of the shares in the company at the time of the chargeable transaction.[23] Hence the repatriation of a non-United Kingdom resident company to Great Britain may trigger a charge to capital companies' duty unless precautionary steps are taken beforehand.

Relief from conveyance or transfer duty[24]

32–07   If the chargeable transaction falls within either (1) or (2) in § 32–03 and 32–04 and assets are conveyed or transferred to the capital company in consideration of the issue of shares in that capital company, no conveyance or transfer duty is payable on the conveyance or transfer of such assets except on:

---

16. *Ibid*. Sched. 19, paras. 4(1), 7(1)(*a*) and 11 (schemes of arrangement).
17. *Ibid*. Sched. 19, para. 2(2).
18. [1982] S.T.C. 325.
19. F.A. 1973, Sched. 19, para. 1(*d*).
20. *Ibid*. Sched. 19, para. 5.
21. This appears to be the effect of F.A. 1973, Sched. 19, para. 1(*e*)-(*h*). And see § 32–02.
22. *Ibid*. Sched. 19, paras. 6(1) and 7(2).
23. *Ibid*. Sched. 19, para. 6(2).
24. *Ibid*. Sched. 19, para. 13.

(i)   stock or securities,[25] or

(ii) the whole or any part of an undertaking,[26] or

(iii) any estate or interest in land.

These exceptions would appear to have the effect of denying relief in most circumstances. The only circumstances in which the relief would appear to apply would be on a conveyance or transfer of assets (in consideration of the issue of shares) of such things as know-how, patents, copyrights or trademarks (*i.e.* intellectual property). Thus if A conveys land to B Limited for £100,000 to be satisfied by the issue of shares in B Limited, credited as fully paid, B Limited (if a capital company) is liable both to capital companies' duty and conveyance or transfer duty. The position is therefore the same as if A had subscribed cash for the shares and B Limited had applied the cash in purchasing the land from him.

Stamping

32–08   A statement containing prescribed particulars of the chargeable transaction must be delivered within one month of the date of that transaction.[27] This statement must be delivered to the Registrar of Companies where the transaction is[28]:

(1)   the formation of a limited liability company under the Companies Act 1985;

(2)   an allotment of shares in respect of which a return must be delivered under section 88(2) of that Act (and see § 29–03A);

(3)   a registration or change in contribution or liability of a limited partnership under section 8 or 9 of the Limited Partnerships Act 1907.

In the case of all other chargeable transactions the statement must be delivered to the Commissioners. It is this statement (Form PUC 1 or 6) that bears the duty payable. Duty is charged at the rate of £1 per £100 (or fraction of £100)[29] and failure to comply with these provisions leads to a fine of 5 per cent. per month of the duty chargeable.[30]

Exemptions from duty

32–09   (1) *An increase in capital following a reduction.*[31] An increase in issued capital is exempt from duty if it occurs within four years of a reduction in nominal capital, but only if that reduction was "as a result of losses sustained." The exemption is applied to any number of increases during this four-year period but only to the extent of the amount of the reduction is attributable to the losses.

---

25. Such transfers may now, however, be exempt under the provision discussed in § 28–45(4).

26. See *Baytrust Holdings Ltd.* v. *I.R.C.* [1971] 1 W.L.R. 1333, § 33–02 n. 2.

27. F.A. 1973, s.47(1).

28. *Ibid.* s.47(2).

29. *Ibid.* s.47(5).

30. *Ibid.* s.47(7).

31. *Ibid.* Sched. 19, para. 9.

32–10   (2) *Reconstructions, amalgamations, takeovers, etc.* Paragraph 10 of
Schedule 19 to the Finance Act 1973 replaces the exemption from capital
duty previously contained in section 55 of the Finance Act 1927. The conditions for obtaining relief from capital companies' duty are as follows:

(a) there is a chargeable transaction whereby a capital company
acquires:
  (i) not less than 75 per cent. of the issued share capital of
  another capital company,[32–33] or
  (ii) the whole or any part of the undertaking of another capital
  company[32–33];
(b) the acquired capital company[32–33] is effectively managed or registered in a country within the EEC;
(c) the consideration (disregarding such part as consists of the assumption or discharge of liabilities of the acquired company and other
than as mentioned in (d) below) consists of shares issued[34] by the
acquiring company either, in case (i) above, to the shareholders in
the acquired company in exchange for shares held by them,[35] or, in
case (ii) above, to the acquired company or its shareholders;
(d) any balance of consideration other than shares must consist wholly
of cash which must not exceed 10 per cent. of the nominal amount
of the shares issued as consideration.

A company which makes a general offer to acquire not less than 75 per
cent. of the share capital of an existing company should, if it wishes to
obtain relief from capital companies' duty on *all* the consideration shares it
issues, make its offer conditional on receipt of the requisite number of
acceptances and issue no shares until the condition is satisfied. If the company declares the offer unconditional before the "not less than 75 per
cent." test is satisfied, and consideration shares are issued during the
period before the test is satisfied, relief from capital companies, duty will
be restricted.

If the transaction is within (a)(i) above (*i.e.* an acquisition of shares) the
exemption is lost if, within the period of five years[36] after the chargeable
transaction, the acquiring company:

(a) ceases to retain 75 per cent. of the acquired company's shares; or
(b) disposes of any of the shares in the acquired company which it held
immediately after the occurrence of the chargeable transaction.

In either event any transfer is to be disregarded if it is itself an exempt

---

32–33. The relief also applies where the *acquired* company is not a capital company within
the definition in § 32–02, *ante*, but is a corporation or body of persons treated as a capital
company in another EEC Member State: F.A. 1973, Sched. 19, para. 10(6).

34. The consideration shares must be registered in the names of the acquired company or
its shareholders: *Oswald Tillotson Ltd.* v. *I.R.C.* [1933] 1 K.B. 134 (C.A.).

35. The Commissioners have expressed the view that the vendors must be the registered
holders of the shares in the acquired company and that the mere renunciation of renounceable
letters of allotment cannot constitute part of a transaction of "exchange."

36. This provision is more restrictive than that which existed under F.A. 1927, s.55(1)(A)
but otherwise the conditions for obtaining relief are less stringent.

transaction or is effected in the course of winding up the acquiring company. If the exemption is lost by virtue of these provisions duty is payable within one month of the event that led to the exemption being lost and the provisions relating to fines apply accordingly.

Conveyance or transfer duty.

32–10A   Note that § 32–10 is concerned with the question whether capital companies' duty under section 47 of the Finance Act 1973 is payable on the issue of shares by the acquiring company. The question whether conveyance or transfer duty is payable on the transfer *to* the acquiring company of *shares* in (a)(i) or *undertaking* in (a)(ii) must be answered by reference to section 55 of the Finance Act 1927: see § 33–05. Relief under section 55 depends on there being a *reconstruction or amalgamation*. Relief from capital companies' duty does not.

Demergers

32–10B   Section 117 of and Schedule 18 of the Finance Act 1980 have introduced provisions to facilitate certain transactions whereby trading activities carried on by a single company or group may be carried on by two or more independent groups., Particular transactions effected in connection with such "demergers" are treated as "exempt distributions"—see §§ 14–49A and 16–12A. To this end, Schedule 18 provides that a document relating to a chargeable transaction carried out solely for effecting such an exempt distribution is not subject to capital duty.[36a]

This exemption was considered by Vinelott J. in *Combined Technologies Corpn. Ltd.* v. *I.R.C.*[36b] The learned judge there held that the relief only extended to instruments which effected transactions forming part of an "exempt distribution" and did not encompass instruments which effected steps preceding such a distribution, even if they were essential if the distribution was to take place.

2. BEARER INSTRUMENTS

32–11   Section 59 of the Finance Act 1963[37] introduced into the Stamp Act 1891 a new head of charge on "Bearer instruments." The charge is imposed on the instruments listed in the left-hand column of the following table and the amount of duty is shown in the right-hand column:

(1) Inland bearer instrument (other than deposit certificate for overseas stock).	Duty of an amount equal to three times the transfer duty.[38]

36a. F.A. 1980, Sched. 18, para. 2.
36b. [1985] S.T.C. 348.
37. Amended by F.A. 1970, s.32 and Sched. 7, para. 6(2), (3), as from August 1, 1970.
38. This means the duty which would be chargeable under the heading "Conveyance or Transfer on sale" in respect of an instrument in writing transferring the stock constituted by or transferable by means of the inland or overseas bearer instrument in question for a consideration equal to the market value of that stock: F.A. 1963, s.59(3).

(2) Overseas bearer instrument (other than deposit certificate for overseas stock or bearer instrument by usage).	Duty of an amount equal to three times[38a] the transfer duty.[38]
(3) Instruments excepted from paragraph (1) or (2) of this heading.	Duty of 10p[39] for every £50 or part of £50 of the market value.
(4) Inland or overseas bearer instrument given in substitution for a like instrument duly stamped *ad valorem* (whether under this heading or not).	Duty of 10p.[39]

Exemptions

32–12

(1) Instrument constituting, or used for transferring, stock which is exempt from all stamp duties on transfer by virtue of General Exemption (1) in the First Schedule to the Stamp Act 1891[40] or of any other enactment.

(2) Renounceable letter of allotment, letter of rights or other similar instrument where the rights under the letter or instrument are renounceable not later than six months after the issue of the letter or instrument.

(3) No duty is chargeable on the issue on or after August 1, 1967, of any instrument which relates to stock expressed in the currency of a territory outside the scheduled territories, or on the transfer on or after that date of the stock constituted by, or transferable by means of, any such instrument.[41]

(4) No duty is chargeable under the heading "Bearer instrument" on the issue of any instrument by a designated international organisation or on the transfer of the stock constituted by, or transferable by means of, any instrument issued by such an organisation.[41a]

The designation is effected by the Treasury and may be made in respect of any organisation of which the United Kingdom is a member and where the membership agreement provides for exemption from tax for the organisation.

No duty is chargeable under the heading "Bearer Instrument" on the issue of any instrument which relates to loan capital, or on the transfer of the loan capital constituted by, or transferable by means, such an instrument.[41b]

Definitions

32–13   The instruments referred to in the left-hand column of the table in § 32–11 are defined as follows:

(a) "Inland bearer instrument" means[42] any of the following instruments

---

38a. Substituted by F.A. 1986, s.65(1).
39. See F.A. 1964, Sched. 11, para. 2.
40. See *ante*, § 27–51, para. (a).
41. See F.A. 1967, s.30, for details.
41a. F.A. 1984, s.126(1), (3)(c).
41b. F.A. 1986, s.79(2).
42. F.A. 1963, s.59(2).

issued by or on behalf of any company or body of persons corporate or unincorporate formed or established in the United Kingdom, that is to say:

   (i) any marketable security[43] transferable by delivery;

   (ii) any share warrant or stock certificate to bearer and any instrument to bearer (by whatever name called) having the like effect as such a warrant or certificate;

   (iii) any deposit certificate to bearer;

   (iv) any other instrument to bearer by means of which any stock can be transferred.

(b) "Overseas bearer instrument" means[42] an instrument issued otherwise than by or on behalf of any such company or body of persons as is mentioned in paragraph (a) above, being an instrument described in sub-paragraphs (i) to (iv) of that paragraph or a bearer instrument by usage.

(c) "Deposit certificate" means[42] an instrument acknowledging the deposit of stock and entitling the bearer to rights (whether expressed as units or otherwise) in or in relation to the stock deposited or equivalent stock; and "deposit certificate for overseas stock" means a deposit certificate in respect of stock of any one company or body of persons not being such a company or body as is mentioned in paragraph (a) above.

(d) "Bearer instrument by usage"[43] means an instrument not described in sub-paragraphs (i) to (iv), above, which is used for the purpose of transferring the right to any stock, being an instrument delivery of which is treated by usage as sufficient for the purpose of a sale on the market, whether that delivery constitutes a legal transfer or not.

(e) "Stock"[44] includes securities, and references to stock include references to any interest in, or in any fraction of, stock or in any dividends or other rights arising out of stock and any right to an allotment of or to subscribe for stock; "transfer" includes negotiation, and "transferable," "transferred" and "transferring" are to be construed accordingly; and a bearer instrument by usage used for the purpose of transferring the right to any stock is to be treated as transferring that stock on delivery of the instrument, and as issued by the person by whom or on whose behalf it was first issued, whether or not it was then capable of being used for transferring the right to the stock without execution by the holder.

Payment of duty

32–14   The duty payable under the head "Bearer Instrument" in § 32–11 is chargeable *on issue* in the case of:

   (a) any instrument issued in Great Britain; and

   (b) any instrument issued by or on behalf of a company or body of persons corporate or unincorporate formed or established in Great Britain, not being a foreign loan security;

---

43. Defined *ante*, § 32–01, note 3.
44. F.A. 1963, s.59(4).

and "foreign loan security" means a security issued outside the United Kingdom in respect of a loan which is expressed in a currency other than sterling and is neither offered for subscription in the United Kingdom nor offered for subscription with a view to an offer for sale in the United Kingdom of securities in respect of the loan.[45]

In cases not covered by the previous paragraph, the duty is chargeable *on transfer* in Great Britain of the stock constituted by or transferable by means of the instrument, if—had the transfer been effected by an instrument which was *not* a bearer instrument—the instrument would have been chargeable as a conveyance on sale.[46]

Ascertainment of market value

32–15   Where an instrument is chargeable *on issue*, the market value of the stock constituted by or transferable by means of that instrument is to be taken for the purposes of section 59 of the Finance Act 1963 to be:

(a) where the stock was offered for public subscription (whether in registered or in bearer form) within 12 months before the issue of the instrument, the amount subscribed for the stock;

(b) in any other case, the value of the stock on the first day within one month after the issue of the instrument on which stock of that description is dealt in on a stock exchange in the United Kingdom or, if stock of that description is not so dealt in, the value of the stock immediately after the issue of the instrument.[47]

Where an instrument is chargeable *on transfer* of the stock constituted by or transferable by means of that instrument, the market value of that stock is to be taken to be the value of that stock:

(a) in the case of a transfer pursuant to a contract of sale, on the date when the contract is made;

(b) in any other case, on the day preceding that on which the instrument is presented to the Commissioners for stamping, or, if it is not so presented, on the date of the transfer.[48]

3. COMPOSITIONS

32–16 The Stamp Act 1891 and later Acts contained provisions by which certain bodies might, if they wished, compound for the duty payable on transfers of their stock. Transfers covered by the composition were then exempt

---

45. *Ibid.* s.60(1). The instrument must be produced to the Commissioners before issue and must bear a particular stamp denoting this. Within six weeks after issue (or such longer time as the Commissioners allow) a statement must be delivered to the Commissioners and duty paid on delivery thereof. There are penalties for non-compliance: *ibid.* s.60(3), (4) and (7).
46. *Ibid.* s.60(2). As to method of stamping and penalties for transferring instruments not duly stamped, see *ibid.* s.60(5), (6) and (7).
47. *Ibid.* s.61(1).
48. *Ibid.* s.61(2).

from duty. Such compositions were of two types: (1) the once for all composition under section 65 of the Finance Act 1971 and (2) composition by periodical payments. With the general abolition of transfer duty on loan capital (see § 28–45(4)) all such composition provisions have now ceased to have effect.[49]

---

49. See F.A. 1976, s.126(4).

CHAPTER 33

COMPANIES

THIS chapter deals with the reliefs from *ad valorem* conveyance or transfer duty which are available in the case of company reconstructions and amalgamations and transfers between associated companies. It does not deal with the reliefs from "capital companies duty": see §§ 32–09 *et seq.*

1. RELIEFS ON RECONSTRUCTION AND AMALGAMATION

33–01   Until recently, relief was available in a wide variety of circumstances falling within the classification "reconstruction or amalgamation," provided that either the conditions specified by section 55 of the Finance Act 1927 or those contained in sections 78–80 of the Finance Act 1985 were satisfied. With limited exception, all such relief has now been removed by section 74 of the Finance Act 1986. The withdrawal of the relief stems partly from the abuse of the system by devices such as the "Preftrick," which avoided the strict conditions of section 55 and partly from its diminished significance in consequence of the reduction of the duty charged on the transfer of securities from 2 per cent. to $\frac{1}{2}$ per cent. The residual reliefs deal with particularly favoured forms of reconstructions and amalgamations involving the transfer of undertakings—which would otherwise have attracted *ad valorem* duty at a rate of 1 per cent, and certain paper-for-paper share exchanges.

Reconstructions without real change of ownership

33–02   Section 75 of the Finance Act 1986[1] affords complete relief from stamp duty under the heading "Conveyance or transfer of sale" in any case where one company ("A Co.") acquires the whole or part of an undertaking carried on by another company ("T Co.") in pursuance of a scheme for the reconstruction of T Co. It appears that if all the other requirements of section 75 are satisfied, the scheme will inevitably be a "reconstruction." The section will not be satisfied, though, unless the transaction involves the transfer of an "undertaking": that is to say, a business or enterprise undertaken by T Co.: thus the mere transfer of assets is *not* a transfer of part of an undertaking.[2]

Conditions for relief

33–03   Relief is only granted if—

   (a) A Co. has its registered office in the United Kingdom[3]
   (b) the consideration for the acquisition consists only of—

---

1. The relief is available with effect from March 25, 1986.
2. See the judgment of Plowman J. in *Baytrust Holdings Ltd.* v. *I.R.C.* [1977] 1 W.L.R. 1333 at p. 1354: "A greengrocer's business is no doubt to sell fruit, but the pounds of applies which you buy can hardly be described as a purchase of part of the greengrocer's business."
3. *Ibid.* s.75(4).

    (i) the issue of shares in A Co. to *all* the shareholders in T Co.; and

    (ii) (optionally) the assumption or discharge by A Co. of liability of T Co.[4]

The requirement that there should be an *issue* of shares is only satisfied by actual registration of the shareholders of T Co. as holders of the new shares. No relief will be given if the shares are allotted on renounceable letters of allotment and then wholly or partly renounced in favour of outside purchasers[5] (or even other existing shareholders); nor if the new shares are registered in the names of nominees as trustees for the existing shareholders.[6] Furthermore, the person to whom the shares are issued must at the time of issue become the beneficial owner of the shares—a condition which is not satisfied if he is not free to deal with them as he wishes, *e.g.* by reason of some prior commitment to transfer them to another.[7]

Further requirements are—

  (c) the acquisition must—
      (i) be effected for bona fide commercial reasons; and
      (ii) not form part of a scheme or arrangement one of the main purposes of which is the avoidance of stamp duty, income tax, corporation tax or capital gains tax[8]; and
  (d) after the acquisition—
      (ii) each of the shareholders in A Co. must be a shareholder in T Co. and vice versa; and
      (ii) each shareholder must own the same proportion of shares in each company.

It would seem, therefore, that the sole intention of the provisions is to enable companies to syphon businesses off into new sister companies owned by precisely the same shareholders, in exactly the same proportions, as before.

33–04   Finally, in order to qualify for relief under section 75, the instrument in respect of which the relief is sought must be transmitted to the Commissioners to be adjuicated not chargeable under section 12 of the Stamp Act 1891.

Third party acquisitions

33–05   Section 76 of the Finance Act 1986 *reduces* the duty chargeable under the heading "Conveyance or transfer on sale" from 1 per cent to $\frac{1}{2}$ per cent. in certain cases where one company ("A Co.") acquires the whole or part

---

    4. *Ibid.* s.75(4)(*a*), (*b*).
    5. *Oswald Tillotson* v. *I.R.C.* [1933] 1 K.B. 134 (C.A.).
    6. *Ibid. per* Finlay J. The Court of Appeal left the point open but support for this view of Finlay J. may be found in *Murex* v. *I.R.C.* [1933] 1 K.B. 173.
    7. *Baytrust Holdings Ltd.* v. *I.R.C.* 1 W.L.R. 1333 at p. 1354 *et seq.*
    8. On the meaning of "issue," see § 33–03.

of the undertaking of another company "(T Co.") principally in consideration of the issue of shares in A Co.

Conditions for relief

33–06   The reduction is only available if—

(a) A Co. has its registered office in the United Kingdom; and
(b) the consideration of for the acquisition consists of—
   (i) the issue[8] of shares in A Co. either to T Co. or to all or any of its shareholders; and
   (ii) (optionally) cash not exceeding in amount 10 per cent. of the nominal value of the shares so issued or the assumption or discharge of liabilities of T Co.[9]

A reduced rate of duty is also available when A Co. in similar circumstances acquires from a creditor "relevant debts" owned by T Co. In this context, "relevant debts" are bank debts, trade debts, and other debts which were incurred by T Co. more than two years prior to their assignment to A Co.

In each of the above cases, the reduced rate of duty is not payable unless the instrument effecting the transfer or assignment has been adjudicated.

33–07   As a result of a non-government amendment there was reintroduced into the stamp duty legislation a total exemption from duty under the head "conveyance or transfer on sale" in the case of instruments transferring shares on a takeover in certain very limited circumstances.[10]

33–08   Section 77 of the Finance Act 1986 affords the exemption in cases where the following conditions are satisfied:

(a) the registered office of the acquiring company (A Co.) is in the U.K.;
(b) the transfer forms part of an arrangement by which A Co. is to acquire the *whole* of the issued share capital of the target company, T Co.;
(c) the acquisition is for bona fide commercial reasons and is not designed to avoid any of a wide range of specified taxes;
(d) the *only* consideration for the transfer of the shares in T Co. is the *issue* of shares in A Co.: in other words, the transaction must be a pure paper-for-paper exchange involving, for example, no partial cash consideration;
(e) there is no value shifting in the holdings of the shareholders in T Co. as a result of the arrangements.

The section applies in relation to instruments executed on or after August 1, 1986.

---

9. s.76(3) F.A. 1986, s.76(3).
10. The section applies in relation to instruments executed on or after August 1, 1986.

2. TRANSFERS BETWEEN ASSOCIATED COMPANIES

33–09 Relief from conveyance or transfer duty is given under section 42 of the Finance Act 1930 on an instrument by which one company transfers property to an associated company where the association is so close that the transfer is virtually a mere change in "nominal ownership." It is apparently not necessary that the companies should be incorporated in England or Scotland[11–27]; nor need the transfer be in connection with a scheme of reconstruction or amalgamation. Relief under section 42 is frequently sought in connection with schemes of reconstruction to which paragraph 10 of Schedule 19 to the Finance Act 1973 (see § 32–10) does not apply. No relief is available in the case of instruments executed before August 1, 1967, if either company is an unlimited company.

Conditions of relief

33–10 To obtain relief under section 42 of the Finance Act 1930 it must be shown to the satisfaction of the Commissioners of Inland Revenue[28]:

(a) that the effect of the instrument is to convey or transfer a beneficial interest in property from one body corporate to another; and

(b) that the bodies in question are "associated," that is to say, either:

   (i) one of the bodies is the beneficial owner of not less than 90 per cent. of the issued share capital of the other (*i.e.* transfers between parent and subsidiary); or

   (ii) not less than 90 per cent. of the issued share capital of each of the bodies is in the beneficial ownership of a third such body (*i.e.* transfers between subsidiaries of the same parent company).[29]

The ownership referred to is ownership directly or through another body corporate or other bodies corporate, or partly directly and partly through another body corporate or other bodies corporate.[30] The relief will not apply if one of the companies is in liquidation since its assets (including any shares it owns in other companies) will be held on trust for its creditors and members.[31]

The instrument must be adjudicated.[32]

Condition (a) was considered in *Escoigne Properties Ltd.* v. *I.R.C.*,[33] where the facts were as follows:

11–27. *Nestlé Co. Ltd.* v. *I.R.C.* [1953] Ch. 395 at p. 399.

28. F.A. 1930, s.42, as amended by F.A. 1967, s.27(2), in the case of instruments executed on or after August 1, 1967. Or, on appeal, to the satisfaction of the court: *Leigh Spinners Ltd.* v. *I.R.C.* (1956) 46 T.C. 425 at p. 434.

29. F.A. 1930, s.42(2), substituted by F.A. 1967, s.27(2).

30. *Ibid.* s.42(3), substituted by F.A. 1967, s.27(2). F.A. 1938, Sched. 4, Pt. I, is to be applied for the purposes of determining the amount of capital held through other bodies corporate, with the substitution of references to issued share capital for references to ordinary share capital.

31. *I.R.C.* v. *Olive Mill Ltd.* (1963) 41 T.C. 77.

32. F.A. 1930, s.42(1), proviso. See *ante*, § 27–41.

33. [1958] A.C. 549.

X agreed to sell property to A Ltd. but no conveyance was executed. X thus became a constructive trustee for A Ltd. A Ltd. later agreed to sell the property to B Ltd. (its wholly owned subsidiary) whereupon X conveyed the property to B Ltd. by direction of A Ltd. *Held*, that B Ltd. was not entitled to relief under section 42.

Condition (b) requires that the body in question should be "beneficial owner" of not less than 90 per cent. of the issued share capital of the other body. If a company owns shares which an outsider (not an associated company) has a contractual right to acquire, the company is not "beneficial owner," whether the contract be conditional[34] or unconditional.[35] Furthermore, it may be that on the grant of a simple option to purchase a shareholder ceases to be "beneficial owner."[36] The words "90 per cent. of the issued share capital" refer to nominal, not actual, value.[37]

Many problems arise in practice where inter-group transfers are to be made *after* a public announcement that negotiations for a sale of companies in the group have been completed.

Further conditions of relief

33–11   After the Finance Act 1930, an ingenious device came into use by which duty-free transfers could be made between companies which were not associated. This device involved the formation of a "dummy-bridge company" and the use (and abuse) of the relieving provisions in section 42.[38] Section 50 of the Finance Act 1938 was designed to prevent the use of this device. That section was substituted as respects instruments executed on or after August 1, 1967, by section 27(3) of the Finance Act 1967, which requires that the claimant for relief under section 42 must satisfy the Commissioners that the instrument in respect of which relief is claimed was not executed in pursuance of or in connection with an arrangement[39] under which either:

(a) the consideration, or any part of the consideration, for the conveyance or transfer was to be provided or received directly or indirectly, by a person other than a body corporate which at the time of the execution of the instrument was associated with either the transferor or the transferee (meaning, respectively, the body from whom and the body to whom the beneficial interest was conveyed or transferred); or

(b) the said interest was previously conveyed or transferred, directly or indirectly, by such a person; or

---

34. *Leigh Spinners Ltd.* v. *I.R.C.* (1956) 46 T.C. 425.

35. *Parway Estates Ltd.* v. *I.R.C.* (1958) 45 T.C. 135 (C.A.). And see *Holmleigh (Holdings) Ltd.* v. *I.R.C.* (1958) 46 T.C. 435; *Wood Preservation Ltd.* v. *Prior* (1968) 45 T.C. 112 and *Baytrust Holdings Ltd.* v. *I.R.C.* [1971] 1 W.L.R. 1333 at p. 1354. For a recent case on the meaning of "beneficial ownership," see *Burman* v. *Hedges & Butler Ltd.* (1978) 52 T.C. 501; [1979] S.T.C. 136.

36. See Sergeant, p. 548 and the cases there cited.

37. *Canada Safeway Ltd.* v. *I.R.C.* [1973] Ch. 374.

38. See Lord Denning in *Escoigne Properties Ltd.* v. *I.R.C.* [1958] A.C. 549 at pp. 567–568.

39. As to "arrangement," see the income tax case of *Crossland* v. *Hawkins* [1961] Ch. 537; 39 T.C. 493 (C.A.) and see *ante*, § 10–08.

(c) the transferor and the transferee were to cease to be associated by reason of a change in the percentage of the issued share capital of the transferee in the beneficial ownership of the transferor or a third body corporate.

Without prejudice to the generality of paragraph (a) above, an arrangement is to be treated as within that paragraph if it is one whereunder the transferor or the transferee, or a body corporate associated with either, was to be enabled to provide any of the consideration, or was to part with any of it, by or in consequence of the carrying out of a transaction or transactions involving, or any of them involving, a payment or other disposition by a person other than a body corporate so associated.

33–12   In *Shop and Store Developments Ltd.* v. *I.R.C.*,[40] a company transferred properties to its wholly owned subsidiary company for a price which was satisfied by the issue, credited as fully paid, of shares in the subsidiary company, such shares being issued on renounceable letters of allotment. Immediately following the issue of these shares the company renounced some of them to an issuing house for cash and it was admitted that all these transactions were part of an arrangement. *Held*, that the "consideration" in section 50 of the Finance Act 1938 (of which paragraph (a) in § 32–11 is an amended version) denoted the consideration received by the company for its properties and that *this* was provided by the subsidiary company and not by the issuing house: accordingly the conveyances to the subsidiary company were exempt from *ad valorem* duty.

In consequence of this decision, section 50 of the Finance Act 1938 was replaced by section 27(3) of the Finance Act 1967. The conveyance in the *Shop and Store* case would not now be exempt, because paragraph (a), above, would apply by reason of the added words "or received."[41]

33–13   The provisions of the Finance Act 1938, corresponding to paragraph (b) in § 33–11 were considered in *Littlewooods Mail Order Stores Ltd.* v. *I.R.C.*,[42] where the facts which are relevant to the present discussion were as follows:

In 1947, L had granted a 99-year lease of premises to A Ltd. (Littlewoods) at a rent of £23,444 per annum. The lease had about 80 years to run. An ingenious scheme was devised by which the subsidiary of A Ltd. would acquire the freehold of the premises by payment of a rent of £42,450 per annum over a period of about 22 years. On six successive days various instruments were executed of which the first two were as follows:

(i) December 8: L granted to A Ltd. a lease for 22 years and 10 days at £6 per annum. This operated as a surrender of the existing 99-year lease.

---

40. [1967] A.C. 472 (H.L.).
41. Similarly, if a company wishing to sell property to an outsider conveys that property to a wholly owned subsidiary of the vendor company, leaving the purchase price unpaid, and then sells the shares of the subsidiary company to the outsider, paragraph (a) applies. See *Curzon Offices Ltd.* v. *I.R.C.* [1944] 1 All E.R. 606: *cf. Times Newspapers Ltd.* v. *I.R.C.* [1973] Ch. 155.
42. [1963] A.C. 135 (H.L.). In *Escoigne Properties Ltd.* v. *I.R.C.* [1958] A.C. 549, the House of Lords held unanimously that paragraph (b) applied on the facts stated: see *ante*, § 33–10.

(ii) December 9: A Ltd. assigned the new lease to B Ltd., its wholly owned subsidiary.

It was held that the transaction in (i), namely, the grant of the new lease by L, was a "conveyance" and that the instrument in (ii) was executed in connection with an arrangement under which the beneficial interest in the property (*i.e.* the new leasehold term) was "previously conveyed . . . directly or indirectly" by a non-associated company. The exemption from duty on conveyances between parent and subsidiary did not, therefore, apply.

Consideration provided by outsiders

33–14   If a company conveys property to its subsidiary and the purchase price is to be provided by an outsider, clearly no relief is available because the requirement in (a) in § 33–11 is not satisfied. What, however, is the position if the outsider merely loans the purchase price or guarantees its payment? Can such a person be said to have "provided" the consideration "directly or indirectly"?

In *Curzon Offices v. I.R.C.*,[43] A Ltd. transferred property to B Ltd., its wholly owned subsidiary, under an arrangement by which (i) an outsider, X Ltd., not associated with A Ltd. or B Ltd., was to guarantee a bank advance to enable B Ltd. to pay part of the purchase price, and (ii) part of the purchase price was to be left on mortgage. X Ltd. was to acquire the whole of the issued share capital of B Ltd. on the day after the transfer.

The relief from stamp duty was refused to B Ltd. because X Ltd. had (so it was held) provided part of the consideration. It was not, however, decided in this case that the guarantee of the advance by X Ltd. would of itself constitute a provision of consideration; nor was it suggested that the bank advance constituted such a provision. Part of the purchase price remained on mortgage and if A Ltd. called upon B Ltd. to pay off the mortgage, then either (a) X Ltd. would provide it directly out of its own resources, *i.e.* under its guarantee; or (b) X Ltd. would provide the money out of the resources of B Ltd. its wholly owned subsidiary, thereby diminishing the value of X Ltd.'s own shares in B Ltd. and indirectly providing part of the consideration.

33–15   It is the practice of the Commissioners, in claims for relief under section 42, to require a statutory declaration from a solicitor concerned in the transaction as to the matters on which they require to be satisfied.

3. DEMERGERS

33–16   Section 117 of and Schedule 18 to the Finance Act 1980 have introduced new provisions for facilitating certain transactions whereby trading activities carried on by a single company or a group may be carried on by two or more companies not belonging to the same group or by two or more independent groups. Certain transactions in connection with such "demergers"

---

43. [1944] 1 All E.R. 606 (C.A.); affirming [1944] 1 All E.R. 163; 22 A.T.C. 406.

are treated as 'exempt distributions' see §§ 14–49A and 16–12A. A document executed solely for the purpose of effecting an exempt distribution is chargeable with stamp duty under the head "Conveyance or Transfer on Sale" at the *reduced* rate of 50p for every £100 (or part of £100) of the amount or value of the consideration for the sale to which the document gives effect.[44] The instrument must be adjudicated.[45]

---

44. F.A. 1980, Sched. 18, para. 12 (1A as inserted by F.A. 1986, s.73(4). For a decision on what documents are "executed solely for the purpose of an exempt distribution" see *Combined Technologies Corpn. Ltd.* v. *I.R.C.* [1985] S.T.C. 348; § 32–10A.
45. F.A. 1980, Sched. 18, para. 12(1A)) as inserted by F.A. 1986. s.73(5).

CHAPTER 34

MISCELLANEOUS COMMERCIAL DOCUMENTS

1. POLICIES OF INSURANCE

34–01   THE stamp duty on policies of insurance has been greatly simplified by section 30 of the Finance Act 1959, as amended by section 32 of the Finance Act 1970. Now, duty is leviable under a single charge:

(a) *Policies of life insurance*

34–02   The expression "policy of life insurance" is defined in the Stamp Act 1891 as:

> "a policy of insurance upon any life or lives or upon any event or contingency relating to or depending upon any life or lives except a policy of insurance . . . for any payment agreed to be made upon the death of any person only from accident or violence or otherwise than from a natural cause."[1]

Thus the ordinary endowment policy is included, *i.e.* the policy which provides for payment of the sum assured on survival to a certain age or date; but the accident policy is excluded. In some cases, an endorsement on a policy may operate as a separate policy, on a principle already discussed.[2] A policy which is taken out under the Married Women's Property Act 1882, s.11, is within the section and attracts no further duty by reason of the endorsement that it is for the benefit of wife or children; but if it contains a declaration of trust, it will attract additional duty as a declaration of trust.

34–03   *Rates of duty.* Duty is levied under the head of charge "Policy of Life Insurance" in the Stamp Act 1891.[3] The duty is an *ad valorem* duty reckoned on the amount of the "amount insured." Bonuses are not taken into account in calculating the "amount insured" unless there is a guaranteed minimum.[4] The rates of duty on life policies are as follows:

Where the amount insured exceeds £50 but does not exceed £1,000	5p for every £100 or part of £100 of the amount insured.
Where the amount insured exceeds £1,000	50p for every £1,000 or part of £1,000 of the amount insured.

These rates are subject to an exception made by section 47 of the Finance Act 1966,[5] which levies a maximum duty of 5p on a policy of life assurance if the period of cover does not exceed two years and the policy contains no provision whereby it might become available for a period exceeding two years. The purpose of this exception is to enable insurance companies to

---

1. S.A. 1891, s.98(1), as amended.
2. See *ante*, § 27–14.
3. A new head of charge was substituted by F.A. 1970, s.32 and Sched. 7, para. 17.
4. See the Contingency Principle, *ante*, § 27–18.
5. As amended by F.A. 1970, s.32 and Sched. 7, para. 17(2).

issue short-term life policies (as distinct from accident policies) to travellers without any *ad valorem* stamp duty.

A policy of life insurance which is made solely in connection with the re-insurance of a risk to which a policy duly stamped under the heading "policy of life insurance" relates is chargeable with duty under that heading only if it is under seal, with a maximum charge of 50p.[6]

There is a concession allowing repayment of stamp duty on policies which are cancelled under sections 65 and 66 of the Insurance Companies Act 1974.[7]

There is a relief from stamp duty where a new qualifying policy is issued to replace another on the occasion of a change in the life or lives assured.[8]

(b) *Policies of insurance, other than life assurance*

34-04   This head of charge has now been abolished.[9]

2. LETTERS OR POWERS OF ATTORNEY, ETC.

34-05   This head has now been abolished.[10]

---

6. F.A. 1970, Sched. 7, para. 17(3). This charge has survived the abolition of the general charge of 50p under the head "Deed of any other kind."
7. Concession G5. See [1980] S.T.I. 9.
8. F.A. 1982, s.130; explained in [1982] S.T.I. 143.
9. F.A. 1970, Sched. 7, para. 1(2)(*b*).
10. See F.A. 1985, s.85.

PART 4

VALUE ADDED TAX

CHAPTER 35

VALUE ADDED TAX

1. INTRODUCTION

35–01 VAT is charged on the supply of goods and services in the United Kingdom and on the importation of goods into the United Kingdom made on or after April 1, 1973.[1]

The main provisions relating to the tax are to be found in the Value Added Tax Act 1983[2] and in a substantial body of orders and regulations made thereunder. All these provisions are, however, subject to the terms of the EEC Sixth Council Directive on VAT which has direct effect in the United Kingdom.[3]

> Thus in *P.J. Parkinson*[3a] the VAT Tribunal held that a supply of fishing rights which would have been subject to tax at the standard rate under section 47(5) was exempt from VAT in consequence of the direct application of Article 13.B of the Sixth Directive.

35–02 Tax is charged at two rates depending on the classification of the goods or services supplied, viz. the zero rate and the positive rate of 15 per cent. The Treasury may, by order, increase or decrease the positive rate of tax by a percentage not exceeding 25 per cent.[4] When a taxable person makes a supply for a consideration, the tax is deemed to form part of that consideration,[5] *i.e.* if the supply is chargeable at the positive rate, three-twenty-thirds of the consideration charged is tax. The Act thus affords no right to charge an amount of VAT on any supply—the taxable person must, instead, ensure that the consideration to which he is contractually entitled has been computed so as to take account of that liability.[6]

The tax is under the care and management of the Commissioners of Customs and Excise.[7]

35–03 VAT is a tax on the final consumption of goods or services which is collected by instalments. The tax is charged on the "value added" by a taxable person at each stage in the process of production. In practical terms, the

---

1. See V.A.T.A. 1983, s.1 and Sched. 10, para. 4.
2. References in this chapter to statutory provisions are references to the V.A.T.A. 1983 as amended unless otherwise stated. The V.A.T.A. 1983 came into force on October 26, 1983, consolidating the previous legislation, which was contained mainly in F.A. 1972, Pt. 1.
3. At least to the extent that its terms are unconditional and precise. On the effect of Community legislation, see Art. 189 of the Treaty of Rome: *Staatssecretaris Van Financien* v. *Co-operative Aardappelenbewaarplaats G.A.* (1981) 3 C.M.L.R. 337; and *Book Club Associates* v. *Commissioners of Customs and Excise* [1983] V.A.T.T.R. 34 at p. 49.
3a [1985] V.A.T.T.R. 219. See also *Direct Cosmetics* v. *Commissioners* [1983] V.A.T.T.R. 194, [1985] S.T.C. 479.
4. s.9.
5. s.10(2).
6. Nevertheless s.42 automatically adjusts the amount of consideration payable under a contract when the rate of tax chargeable in respect of such a supply changes before the supply is made, unless the contract otherwise provides.
7. In this chapter referred to simply as the Commissioners.

"value added" is the profit (including wages) of the taxable person computed by reference to invoices supplied and received. Thus, in effect, the instalment of tax due at each stage is the amount chargeable on the difference between the cost of acquisition and the proceeds of sale. Whenever a taxable person supplies goods or services to another taxable person he charges him the basic cost of the goods or services plus the amount of VAT thereon, and must give him a tax invoice showing the amount of these items.[8] A taxable person will thus have taxable "inputs" (the supplies to him) and taxable "outputs" (the supplies by him) and he must account to the Commissioners for the difference between his "input tax" and his "output tax" (or, if the former exceeds the latter, he can reclaim the excess). The tax is not borne by the taxable person: he simply passes the burden on by adding the amount of the tax to his bill so that it forms part of the contractual consideration for the supply. The ultimate non-business consumer bears the tax since he cannot deduct it as an "input." Eventually, therefore, VAT is simply a form of sales tax borne by the final non-business consumer. A simple example, where tax is payable at the positive rate, may illustrate the principle.

35–04   *Example*

B is a cabinet maker who, in a particular accounting period, purchases timber from A at a basic (net of VAT) price of £1,000 and fittings from C at a basic price of £300. In the same period he sells finished cabinets to D, a retailer, at a basic price of £6,000. The position, as regards B, would then be as follows:

	£ BASIC		£ VAT
Payments (inputs)			
Timber	1,000	+	150
Fittings	300		45
	———	+	——
	1,300		195
	———	+	——
Sales (outputs)			
Cabinets	6,000		
	———	+	900
			——

B would then account to the Commissioners for £705.

35–05   In theory, the £705 represents the tax on B's "added value" (his profit and the wages paid). It will be seen, however, that the timber and fittings do not have to be used in the construction of the particular cabinets sold in this period. Rather, there is a simple balancing of output invoices for the period against input invoices of the same period. Plainly, there may be many other taxable inputs for the period the tax on which may be deducted: for example, accountancy and legal services, telephone bills, stationery and equipment purchased. This simple balancing of invoices for the period is called the "tax from tax" system (that is the deduction of "input tax" from "output tax").

---

8. Sched. 7, para. 2(1).

35–06   This system applies to taxable persons throughout the process of production. On the final sale to a non-business consumer the VAT is added to the basic price but a tax invoice is not given. Thus, in the above example, D, the retailer, will have received an invoice charging £6,000 (basic) plus £900 (VAT). In the same period he may have sold goods (whether the cabinets or not) for a basic price of £15,000 to which he would have added VAT of £2,250. From that £2,250 he may deduct all his taxable inputs (including the £900) and will only have to account to the Commissioners for the difference. The same is true, of course, for A and C. The final (non-business) consumer will, however, neither receive a tax invoice nor be able to recover the VAT.

35–07   It will be seen that the effect of this process is that the final consumer of a cabinet bears a tax of 15 per cent. on its retail price, although that tax has been collected at various stages (and in various accounting periods) from the taxable persons concerned in its production and sale.

35–08   Tax is not charged on exempt supplies[9] nor on supplies by persons who are not taxable persons.[10] This may be beneficial in that it gives such a supplier a competitive edge over taxable persons in dealings with non-business consumers but usually this will be far outweighed by its disadvantages. An exempt person must absorb the VAT on the goods and services supplied to him for the purposes of his business and he will be unable to pass the burden on to taxable persons to whom he makes supplies.

Example
    Thus, taking the example in § 35–04 above. Assume that B's sales never exceed £5,000 in a quarter. His position would then be:

	£ BASIC		£ VAT
Payments			
Timber	1,000	+	150
Fittings	300		45
		+	
	1,300		195
		+	
Sales			
Cabinets	5,000	+	—

B thus has unabsorbed tax of £195. Since he will sell to D, a registered taxable person, his supplies, which are free of VAT, are not at a commercially lower price, for D would, in any event, have been able to absorb any tax on supplies to him.

Correspondingly, a taxable person who makes some taxable supplies and some exempt supplies will only be able to recover a proportion of the input tax he suffers.

9. s.17 and Sched. 6, *post*, § 35–52.
10. s.2 and Sched. 1, *post*, §§ 35–12 *et seq*.
11. s.16 and Sched. 5, *post*, §§ 35–64 *et seq*.

35–09   The Act provides that the supply of certain kinds of goods or services is "zero-rated."[11] The effect of this is that the taxable person pays no tax on his outputs but is nevertheless entitled to treat the supply as if it were a taxable supply: he may, therefore, recover all the tax he has suffered on his inputs without restriction. One particularly advantageous aspect of VAT is that exports are zero-rated[12] and are, therefore, subject to no tax whatsoever. All the elements of tax suffered by an exporter can be identified under the invoice system and, accordingly, all the VAT suffered directly or indirectly in the production of exports can be reclaimed.

2. The Scope of the Charge

35–10   There are two heads of charge: on taxable supplies and on the importation of goods.

A. *Taxable Supply*

35–11   Tax is chargeable on the taxable supply of goods or services in the United Kingdom made by a taxable person in the course or furtherance of any business carried on by him.[13]

A "taxable supply" is any supply of goods or services in the United Kingdom other than an exempt supply. The term, therefore, simply excludes the exemptions set out in Schedule 6 to the Act.[14]

It is necessary to consider the meaning of the following terms:

(1) taxable person;

(2) supply;

(3) goods or services;

(4) in the course or furtherance of a business;

(5) in the United Kingdom.

35–12   (1) *Taxable person*

A person who makes or intends to make taxable supplies is a taxable person while he is or is required to be registered under Schedule 1 to the Act.[15] It follows that even though a person is not so registered he will yet be liable to account for VAT if he makes any taxable supplies.

Registration

35–13   A person is liable to be registered:

(a) after the end of any quarter if the value of his taxable supplies:
   (i) in that quarter has exceeded £7,000; or
   (ii) in the four quarters then ending has exceeded £20,500.[16]

---

12. s.16(6).
13. s.2(1).
14. s.2(2). As to Sched. 6, see §§ 35–52, *post.*
15. s.2(2).
16. Sched. 1, para. 1(*a*), as amended by the VAT (Increase of Registration Limits) Order 1986, with effect from March 19, 1986. The power of the Treasury to amend such limits is granted by Sched. 1, para. 12.

Even though a person exceeds the £7,000 limit in one quarter he is still not liable to be registered if he can satisfy the Commissioners that the value of his taxable supplies in that and the next three quarters will not in aggregate exceed £20,500.

(b) at any time, if there are reasonable grounds for believing that the value of his taxable supplies in the period of one year beginning at that or any later time will exceed £20,500.

35–14   In determining whether a person is liable to register, the Commissioners will consider the aggregate value of his taxable supplies from all his business activities. Once registered, that registration will apply to all such activities carried on by that particular person. Thus, he is not entitled to separate registrations in respect of separate businesses[17] nor is he entitled to register in respect of some only of his businesses. Indeed, no distinction is drawn between a person making or receiving supplies in his capacity as trader and in that of trustee of his business' pension fund. Accordingly, he can set the input tax paid on supplies made to him as trustee against his personal liability to account for output tax.[18] This principle may, indeed, be carried further so that the taxpayer will not be entitled to separate registration in respect of another business carried on by him solely in the capacity of a trustee. This derives from the fact that the charge to tax under section 2 of the Act is laid on a "taxable person" and so would appear to encompass all taxable supplies made by him in whatever capacity.

A taxable person makes only one supply and thus will be able to deduct the inputs of one business from the outputs of another.[18a]

Aggregation of supplies

35–14A   Section 10 of the Finance 1986 confers on the Commissioners power to direct that a number of persons be treated as a single taxable person, liable to registration as such. The power will be exercised where the persons between them carry on a business which has been divided artificially in order to avoid a liability to be registered (for example, by ensuring that the value of taxable supplies made by each person never exceeds the registration limits).[18b]

Discretionary registration

35–15   A person who makes or satisfies the Commissioners that he intends to make taxable supplies, though not in an amount rendering him liable to be registered, may yet request that he be treated as so liable and thus be registered.[19] Such registration is in the discretion of the Commissioners[20] who

---

17. See *Commissioners* v. *Glassborow* [1975] Q.B. 465 and *post*, § 35–23.
18. See *Commissioners* v. *British Railways Board* [1976] 1 W.L.R. 1036; [1976] S.T.C. 359.
18a. Nevertheless, this principle is to some extent limited by the rule that only supplies made in course or furtherance of a business are taxable supplies: *Apple and Pear Development Council* [1986] S.T.C. 192; *Whitechapel Art Galleries* [1986] S.T.C. 156: see § 35–40.
18b. See [1986] S.T.I. 585.
19. Sched. 1, para. 11(1)(*b*).
20. An appeal lies against the refusal of the Commissioners to the VAT Tribunal: s.40(1)(*i*).

require to be satisfied that the trader has a "compelling and continuing business need for registration" and that the income derived from the taxable supplies contributes or will contribute substantially to the trader's livelihood.[21] Such registration might be advantageous to a taxpayer since it would enable him to recover VAT on his inputs. A person who sold direct to the general public would be unlikely to wish to do so; persons selling or supplying services to other taxable persons, however, would be in a better financial position if they were to register.[22] The provision is not of widespread application, though, since it is difficult to envisage a wholesaler whose taxable supplies do not exceed £20,500. There will, however, be a number of barristers in this position. A barrister, strictly, supplies services to the solicitor who instructs him and not to the lay client. If he is registered for VAT he may deduct the tax on his inputs, for example, in his telephone bills and on his purchases of stationery and office furniture, from the tax added to his own fees. The latter tax will be input tax which the solicitor can, in turn, set off against the VAT which he will charge on the final fee to the lay client. If the barrister is not a taxable person, he will have to absorb the tax on his inputs or charge a higher fee, whilst the solicitor will have to pay VAT on the aggregate of his own and the barrister's services with no corresponding deductible output.[23]

A corresponding *exemption* from registration is available where all the supplies which a person would make are zero-rated. If such exemption is granted he remains under a continuing obligation to inform the Commissioners if circumstances change.[24]

Cancellation of registration

35–16   The criteria for determining whether a person has ceased to be liable to be registered are somewhat more stringent than those applicable on initial registration. A registered person will only cease to be liable to be registered:

1.(a) after the end of any quarter if he has been registered for the whole of the two years then ending and the value of his taxable supplies in each year has been £20,500 or less—unless there are reasonable grounds for believing that the value of his taxable supplies in the year then beginning will exceed £20,500;

(b) at any time if the Commissioners are satisfied that the value of his supplies in the period of one year then beginning will be £19,500 or less.[25]

---

21. Customs and Excise leaflet 700/1/85, para. 8.
22. On this see *ante*, § 35–08.
23. Costs incurred by a solicitor on supplies *to him* to enable him to provide his services to the client form part of the solicitor's inputs and, therefore, when charged to the client attract tax at the positive rate as being in respect of legal services, albeit that the costs themselves may have been exempt or zero-rated: *Rowe and Maw* v. *Commissioners* [1975] 1 W.L.R. 1291.
24. Sched. 1, para. 11(1)(a), and 11(2).
25. Sched. 1, para. 2, as amended by the VAT (Increase of Registration Limits) Order 1986, with effect from June 1, 1986, and Sched. 1, para. 9.

2. on his giving notice that he has ceased to make taxable supplies—such notice must be given within 10 days of the date on which he does so.[26]

35–17　　　It has been said[27] that the value of supplies for the purpose of determining the application of the deregistration provisions should be computed *net* of VAT. The Commissioners require, however, that the value of taxable turnover (*including* VAT) be taken as the appropriate measure.[28]

> *Example*
> A, a registered person for VAT has in each of the two years in the period ending on June 30, 1986, made taxable supplies of £20,700, inclusive of VAT. If the value of his supplies for the purpose of Schedule 1, para. 2 are computed *net* of VAT he is entitled to be deregistered, since the value of his supplies in each year will not have exceeded £20,500. The Commissioners, though, will not grant him deregistration because in their view the provision requires them to determine the value of his supplies at £20,700.

The Commissioners may cancel the registration of any person who has ceased to be liable to be registered and who fails to make returns or to account for any tax due.[29]

Special cases

35–18　　　(1) *The Crown*.[30] VAT is chargeable on any taxable supplies made by the Crown by way of business. The Treasury has power to subject supplies made by Government departments to VAT if those supplies appear to be similar to supplies made by other persons in the course of carrying on a business.

35–19　　　(2) *Local Authorities*.[31] Local authorities which make taxable supplies are required to register even though their value falls below the £20,500 registration limit.

35–20　　　(3) *Groups of companies*.[32] Although companies may be closely associated, unless and until a group has been registered as such by the Commissioners, each company will be a separate taxable person[33] for VAT purposes and disposals between group members will be chargeable to tax as if they were wholly at arm's length.[33a] This is of little consequence when every group member is a fully taxable person but it can lead to a serious leakage of tax if the recipient company makes no taxable outputs or is partially exempt. Relief is available, however, if the companies make an appli-

---

26. Sched. 1, paras. 7 and 8. On the effect of a temporary cessation of a business see *David Wickens Properties Ltd.* v. *Commissioners* [1982] V.A.T.T.R. 143.
27. See *H. R. Short* v. *Commissioners* [1983] V.A.T.T.R. 94 at p. 105.
28. Customs leaflet 700/11/85, para. 3.
29. Sched. 1, para. 10.
30. s.27.
31. s.28.
32. s.29.
33. Subject to the turnover requirements; see *ante*, §§ 35–13 *et seq* And subject to the application of F.A. 1986, s.10: see § 35–14A.
33a. See, for example, *Tarmac Roadstone Holdings Ltd.* [1985] S.T.C. 830.

cation[34] to the Commissioners to be treated as a group for VAT. Once the application has been accepted the group is treated as a single entity for VAT by deeming one member of the group, the "representative member," to be carrying on the businesses of the other members as well.[35] Accordingly,[36] supplies by one member of a group to another will be disregarded and any taxable[37] supplies made by any group member to persons outside the group will be treated as made by the representative member.

35–21   Two or more companies can be treated as a group if one controls each of the others, one person controls them all, or two or more individuals carrying on business in partnership control all of them. "Control" in this context will exist if one person holds over 50 per cent. of the nominal share capital, controls the composition of the Board of Directors, or is the holding company of a person who has such control.[38]

An application for group treatment may be made in respect of part of a group only. Further applications can also be made at a later date to add further members to the group, to remove a member, to change the representative member or to discharge group registration altogether.[39]

35–22   If a company carries on business in various divisions, the registration of the company may, if the company so requests and the Commissioners see fit, be made in the names of those divisions.[40] The Commissioners are of the opinion, though, that this option is not available to render companies partially exempt. The effect of such registration is simply administrative, enabling separate divisions of an unwieldy company to submit separate returns, when it would be difficult to collate the necessary information in time to enable a single return to be made. It has no effect, however, on the registration limits—all divisions must be registered, whatever the total value of an individual division's turnover may be: furthermore, VAT is not charged on inter-divisional transfers.

35–23   (4) *Partnerships*.[41] Partnerships are to be registered in the partnership name and no account is taken of a change of partners. If two partnerships are comprised of exactly the same persons there can be only one registration.[42] The liability to pay the tax is governed by section 9 of the Partnership Act 1890, but if a person is a partner for part of a period only, he will be regarded as a continuing partner only until the change is notified to the

---

34. This should be made not less than 90 days before the date on which it is desired that group registration should take effect: s.29(7). Retrospective registration *can* be granted by the Commissioners: *Commissioners* v. *Save & Prosper Group Ltd*. [1979] S.T.C. 205, although they are generally unwilling to exercise this power.

35. All group companies are, however, jointly and severally liable for any tax due from the representative member.

36. s.29(1).

37. Thereafter, the registration limits will be determined by reference to group turnover. In certain circumstances, therefore, it can be advantageous *not* to apply for group treatment.

38. See s.29(8). Control can also be given by statute to, for example, a public corporation.

39. s.29(5).

40. s.31.

41. s.30.

42. See *Commissioners* v. *Glassborow* [1975] Q.B. 465 and, *ante* § 35–14.

Commissioners and his liability in the period for tax on supplies made by the firm will be limited to such proportion of the firm's liability as may be just.[43]

A notice served on a partnership in its registered name is valid as against all the partners.[44]

(2) *Supply*

5–24   Supply "includes all forms of supply"—for example sale, hire-purchase, exchange or part exchange but, save in exceptional circumstances, nothing is a supply unless it is done for a consideration. The authorities are agreed that "supply" is a word of the widest import.[45] So, in *Carlton Lodge Club* v. *Commissioners*[46] it was held that the words "supply of goods or services" simply meant the furnishing or serving of goods or services and were not limited to the supply of goods or services by way of sale. In a later case,[47] Griffiths J. held: " 'supply' is the passing of possession in goods pursuant to an agreement whereby the supplier agrees to part with and the recipient agrees to take possession. By 'possession' in this context is meant control over the goods, in the sense of having the immediate facility for their use."

Thus the passing of possession under a contract for sale which was void on the ground that the goods which were the subject of the sale were stolen, was still a taxable supply of goods for the purpose of VAT.

Notional supplies

A. *Self-supply*

5–25   Generally speaking, there can only be a supply for the purposes of VAT if there is both a supplier and a recipient.[48] This requirement can be taken to be satisfied, however, where an unincorporated body furnishes goods or services to one of its members[49] or where a partnership's services or facilities are utilised by one of the partners.[50] The legislation also provides a particular exception to the usual rule in the case of a self-supply.

5–26   An exempt person suffers a hidden tax on goods and services supplied to him for the purposes of his business since he is unable to recover the input tax which has been charged. The same will be true of a partially exempt businessman as regards the exempt part of his activities. To ameliorate this difficulty he might decide to produce some goods—or effect some services—himself. In order to prevent anticipated avoidance of tax by such

43. s.30(2) and (5).
44. s.30(4). *Cf. Blyth Elfords* v. *Commissioners* [1985] V.A.T.T.R. 204.
45. *Commissioners* v. *Oliver* [1980] 1 All E.R. 353.
46. [1974] 3 All E.R. 798; [1974] S.T.C. 507.
47. *Commissioners* v. *Oliver* [1980] 1 All E.R. 353.
48. If there is a transfer of the whole property in goods from A to B, that is a supply by A to B and cannot be a supply by A to any other person: *Sooner Foods Ltd.* v. *Commissioners* [1983] S.T.C. 376.
49. *Carlton Lodge Club*, note 46, above.
50. *Border Flying Co.* v. *Commissioners* [1976] V.A.T.T.R. 132.

means, the Treasury has been given power[51] to treat such self-supplies as taxable on their open market value. Orders have been made in respect of stationery[52] and motor cars.[53] No orders have, as yet, been made in respect of supplies of services.

B. *The reverse charge*[54]

35–27   Where a taxable person who belongs in the United Kingdom receives[55] a supply of certain kinds of services made by a person who belongs[56] in a country other than the United Kingdom the Act treats the recipient as if he personally had supplied the services to himself in the course or furtherance of his business for a consideration equal to that for which the services were supplied to him.[57] Thus he must account to the Commissioners for output tax at a rate equal to 15 per cent of the value of the supply[58] but may, correspondingly, claim credit for input tax. If the recipient only makes taxable supplies the two items will be self-cancelling but a proportion of the deemed input tax will be irrecoverable if he is partially exempt. The services to which these rules apply are set out in Schedule 3 to the Act and, in brief, are as follows:

(a) transfers and assignments of copyright, patents, licences, trade-marks and similar rights;

(b) advertising services;

(c) services of consultants, engineers, lawyers, accountants, etc. (but excluding any services relating to land);

(d) refraining from pursuing any business activities;

(e) banking, financial and insurance services[58a];

(f) the supply of staff;

(g) the hiring of goods—other than of the means of transport[58b];

(h) procuring any of the above.

C. *Supplies made otherwise than for a consideration*

35–28   Any transaction which is not made for a consideration is, supposedly, not a "supply" for the purposes of VAT.[59] Although this is true if the matter is one of the furnishing of services,[60] the rule is severely undermined as

---

51. s.3(5), (6), (8).

52. VAT. (Special Provisions) Order 1981, art. 14.

53. VAT. (Cars) Order 1980. This order only applies in the rare case where the trader has been able to reclaim input tax on the car and then removes it from his stock, *e.g.* a demonstration car. On the meaning of "motor car" see *Commissioners* v. *Jeynes* [1984] S.T.C. 30.

54. s.7 and Sched. 3.

55. Where the taxable person has business establishments both within and outside the U.K. the supply is deemed to be received at that where the supply is most directly used: s.8(4). This will determine where the recipient "belongs" for the purposes of the section.

56. See §§ 35–45 *et seq.*

57. See s.11 for the manner of determining the "consideration."

58. s.10(2) is inapplicable.

58a. See *Culverpalm Ltd.* v. *Commissioners* [1984] V.A.T.T.R. 199. In light of that case the Commissioners have decided to treat rent collection services supplied to overseas persons in respect of U.K. properties as subject to VAT at the standard rate from July 1, 1985.

58b. Thus the liability of such supplies will be determined by reference to the location of the customer, rather than the place where the goods were used.

59. s.3(2)(*a*).

60. "Services" in their non-technical sense. Power does exist to derogate from the rule even in the case of services: see s.3(4), (6) but it has not been exercised.

regards the supply of goods. A taxable person is deemed to have made a supply of goods in the course or furtherance of his business if:

    (a) goods cease to be business assets on a transfer or disposal (whether or not made for a consideration and whether made to himself or to another)[61]; or

    (b) he ceases to be a taxable person—unless the goods did not originally attract input tax or the business is transferred as a going concern to, or is carried on by, another taxable person.[62]

Thus, save in the instances mentioned, there is a charge to VAT on the aggregate value of all the goods of a business on discontinuance or deregistration. Technically, the valuation should be at the cost to the taxable person of their acquisition[63] but by concession[64] their value can be taken to be what he would have paid for them had he purchased them in their used state.

35–29   A taxable person is also deemed to have made a taxable supply in the course or furtherance of his business (on this occasion, a supply of services) if goods which are business assets are put to any private use by him or by others.[65]

D. *Supplies by or through another person*

35–30   (i) *Agents.*[66] Where an agent arranges a supply, the supply is deemed to be made by or to the principal whom he represents. Accordingly, the agent neither makes nor receives the supply which he has arranged—although he will himself be making a separate supply of agency services to his principal. It is, thus, the principal who must account for output tax or who can claim input tax relief on the supply. If the supplies are made through an agent who issues invoices in his own name, the Commissioners can, though, treat each as a supply made by the seller to the agent together with a further supply by the agent to the purchaser.[67]

35–31   (ii) *Persons exercising a power of sale.* Where a judgment creditor or a mortgagee exercises a power of sale to dispose of goods belonging to a taxable person, it is the latter who is deemed to have made the supply.[68]

---

61. Sched. 2, para. 5(1). The subparargraph does not apply, however, in the case of the gift of goods costing less than £10 in the course or furtherance of a business or to gifts of industrial samples to a customer or potential customer. On the meaning of "gift" see *GUS Merchandise Corp. Ltd.* v. *Commissioners* [1981] S.T.C. 569. Where the supply is for no consideration, its value is deemed to be the cost of the goods to the person making the supply: Sched. 4, para. 7.

62. Sched. 2, para. 7. There is also a *de minimis* exception if the tax recovered would not exceed £250.

63. Sched. 4, para. 7.

64. Concession A.1, Customs and Excise Notice 748.

65. Sched. 2, para. 5(3): if otherwise than for a consideration, the value of the supply is taken as the full cost of providing the services: see Sched. 4, paras. 8 and 10.

66. On the meaning of "agency" for VAT see *Commissioners* v. *Johnson* [1980] S.T.C. 624.

67. s.32(4).

68. Sched. 2, para. 6.

(3) Goods or services[69]

35–32   There is no definition of goods in the Act, although certain transactions are to be treated as a supply of goods.[70] Presumably, the term "goods" covers all tangible movables but not choses in action. The Act draws a distinction between a dealing with goods which effectively transfers all proprietary rights in the assets to another person—which it specifies is a supply of goods[71] and one which only affords limited beneficial enjoyment of goods—which it treats as a supply of services. Thus a transfer of an undivided share or of possession (*i.e.* under a bailment, hiring or letting) is a supply of services[72]—unless that transfer of possession is under an agreement which contemplates that the whole property in the goods will pass in the future, *e.g.* a hire-purchase transaction.[73] In obedience to the requirements of the EEC Sixth Council Directive on VAT, the Act also provides that the following should be deemed to be a supply of goods:

(a) the supply of any form of power, heat, refrigeration or ventilation[74]; and

(b) the granting, assignment or surrender of a major interest in land. A major interest in land means the fee simple or a tenancy for a term certain[75] under a lease for a period exceeding 21 years.[76]

35–33   The Act further provides that where a person produces goods by applying a treatment or process to another person's goods he is treated as supplying goods, not services.[77] This would, for example, apply to a tailor who made a suit from a customer's own cloth but not to the laundry which subsequently cleaned the suit. Subject to these rules, section 3(2)(*b*) provides:

"anything which is not a supply of goods but is done for a consideration (including, if so done, the granting, assignment or surrender of any right) is a supply of services."

35–34   Thus, although leases for less than 21 years and choses in action are not treated as goods, any dealing with them for consideration constitutes a supply of services.[78]

35–35   Section 3(2)(*b*) is of considerable importance in determining the proper description of any particular supply. In any contract what a person receives is a bundle of rights in return for the consideration he provides. Neverthe-

---

69. The distinction between goods and services can be important since an importation or a gift of goods (but not ordinarily of services) may be chargeable to VAT, and the factors determining the time of supply are different. See *ante*, §§ 35–28 and *post*, §§ 35–49 *et seq.*
70. Sched. 2.
71. Sched. 2, para. 1(1).
72. *Ibid.* para. 1(1)(*a*), (*b*).
73. *Ibid.* para. 1(2).
74. Sched. 2, para. 3.
75. For the meaning of "term certain" in the context of a time-sharing agreement see *Cottage Holiday Associates Ltd.* v. *Commissioners* [1983] S.T.C. 278 and *post*, §§ 35–74.
76. s.48(1). This provision and the last are based on Art. 5 of the Directive and are strange notions within the concept of English law. A major interest in land is brought within the scope of the charge so that its grant, after the construction of a building, can be zero-rated; see *post*, § 35–74.
77. Sched. 2, para. 2. The tax, however, would only be imposed on the "service charge": see *post*, § 35–86.
78. Generally speaking, though, such supplies will be exempt; Sched. 6, Groups 1 and 5: see *post*, §§ 35–52, 35–57.

less, the effect of the subsection is that it is what is *done* for that consideration which is relevant for VAT purposes. Accordingly, if the rights obtained are the rights to receive particular goods or services, the supply will be deemed to be of those goods or services, and the bundle of contractual rights will be ignored. In other cases, however, the supply will constitute the service of granting a right simpliciter.

So in *British Railways Board* v. *Commissioners*,[79] a student paid £1·50 for a rail identity card entitling her to the benefit of reduced price rail travel. The Court of Appeal held that what the Board supplied her in consideration of the payment of £1·50 was not the *right* to obtain supplies of rail travel at reduced prices but transport by rail itself. Accordingly, the supply was zero-rated under Schedule 5, group 10, item 4.[80]

35–36 Where, on the other hand, a person receives a number of benefits for a single payment, the supply must be apportioned. So, in *Commissioners* v. *Automobile Association*,[81] the Court held that a person who paid a membership subscription to the A.A. received a supply of books, which was a zero-rated supply of goods,[82] together with other benefits amounting to a positive-rated supply of services and that it was, therefore, necessary to apportion the membership fee between them.

Since the A.A. case the Tribunal has on several occasions been called on to decide how an apportionment should be made in appropriate cases. It has consistently held that where consideration has been given for a number of severable supplies it should be divided between the various supplies in proportion to their cost.[82a]

35–37 The Treasury has power to make orders treating any transaction as a supply of goods, or of services, or as neither.[83] This power has been exercised so that the exchange of a reconditioned item for an article of a similar nature is treated as a supply of services[84] with the effect that tax is only charged on the payment for the exchange and not on the full value of the reconditioned article. Using the same power, the Treasury has taken certain supplies entirely outside the scope of the tax by providing that they shall be considered to be neither a supply of goods nor of services[85]:

    (a) the disposal of certain specified kinds of goods by finance houses, insurance companies or mortgagees (after repossession under finance agreements, etc.);

---

79. [1977] 1 W.L.R. 588; [1977] S.T.C. 221. And see *Spigot Lodge Ltd.* v. *Commissioners* [1985] S.T.C. 255.
80. See *post*, § 35–77.
81. [1974] 1 W.L.R. 1447; [1974] 1 All E.R. 1257. Under s.47(2)(*a*) the provision by a club, association or organisation (for a subscription or other consideration) of the facilities or advantages available to members is the carrying on of a business; see *post*, § 35–42.
82. See Sched. 5, Group 3; *post*, § 35–69.
82a. *River Barge Holidays Ltd.* Lon/77/345.
83. s.3(3).
84. See VAT (Special Provisions) Order 1981, art. 13.
85. (a) *ibid*. arts. 10 and 11; (b) Sched. 4, para. 6; and VAT (Treatment of Transactions) Order 1973 and VAT (Trading Stamps) Order 1973; (c) VAT (Special Provisions) Order 1981, art. 12(1); (d) *ibid*. art. 12(2); and (e) VAT (Treatment of Transactions) Order 1986.

(b) certain transactions in trading stamps;

(c) the supply of business assets in the course of the transfer of the whole or part of a business as a going concern by one taxable person to another or by a non-taxable person to any other person;

(d) the assignment of hire purchase and conditional sale agreements to a bank or other financial institution;

(e) certain supplies by a pawnee to a pawnor of items pledged where property had subsequently passed to the pawnee.

(4) *In the course or furtherance of a business*

35–38   Section 47 provides that the term "business" "*includes* any trade, profession or vocation." Although this would appear to follow closely the wording of Schedule D Cases I and II, the provision would not seem to have the extended meaning of "adventure or concern in the nature of trade."[86] Thus, an isolated transaction which might be taxable under Case I of Schedule D will not bring the taxpayer within the scope of VAT[87]:

> "The use of the words 'in the course of' suggests that the supply must not be merely in sporadic or isolated transactions but continued over an appreciable tract of time and with such frequency as to amount to a recognisable and identifiable activity of the particular person on whom the liability is to fall"[88]

Nevertheless, the definition is in some respects far wider than that applicable for income tax: the Courts have consistently asserted that section 47(1) is simply inclusive[89] and is not restricted to the activities of persons who would be within the charge to income tax. Thus, an investment business consisting of the purchase, development and letting of a building would be a business for the purposes of VAT.[90]

35–39   The width of this definition can be appreciated from an examination of *Commissioners* v. *Morrison's Academy*.[91] There, a company was formed with the object of providing boarding house accommodation for the pupils of a private school. The company's affairs were so managed that neither a profit nor a loss would accrue. The Court of Session held that the company was liable to account for VAT on the value of supplies of such accommodation. The proper approach in deciding whether a person carried on a business for VAT was to consider the activities in the course of which taxable supplies were made. If those activities were predominantly concerned with the making of taxable supplies to consumers for a consideration, the taxpayer was in the "business" of making taxable supplies, which supplies were made in the course or furtherance of a business. It followed that there was need neither for a "commercial purpose" nor the intention of making a profit before a business could exist for the purposes of VAT.

---

86. Cf. I.C.T.A. 1970, s.526(5).

87. See *ante*, §§ 2–05 *et seq*.

88. *Per* Lord Cameron in *Commissioners* v. *Morrison's Academy Boarding House Association* [1977] S.L.T. 197; [1978] S.T.C. 1.

89. *Ibid. passim*.

90. The definition does not, however, extend to a person building a house for his own occupation: see *R.A. Archer* v. *Commissioners* [1974] V.A.T.T.R. 1—although such persons are now entitled to a refund of the tax paid on the goods used in the construction of the building: s.21.

91. See, note 88, above.

35–40   Although the phrase is thus of wide import, there are certain somewhat ill-defined limitations. First, there can be no business for VAT purposes which does not involve the carrying on of an activity or function which includes the making of some supplies recognised for VAT. A body which makes no such supplies cannot, therefore, apply to be registered in order to reclaim VAT on its inputs, simply because it carries on its functions in a businesslike manner.[92] Secondly, the word "business" excludes any activity which is carried on merely for pleasure and enjoyment, even though the participants contribute towards the costs incurred by one of their number in providing the activity in question.[93] Nor will activities in furtherance of a charitable or benevolent purpose constitute a business if not conducted commercially, or for some consideration.[94] Finally, a distinction must be drawn between a "business" and an organisation which, in a business-like way provides voluntary services to the community, even though it requires payment to cover expenses.[95]

> Thus in *Commissioners* v. *Apple and Pear Development Council*,[95a] the Council's activities fell into two main categories—those which were financed by an annual charge levied on all growers in the United Kingdom in accordance with statute, and a promotion scheme which was funded by subscriptions of growers who voluntarily joined the scheme. The Court of Appeal held that the Council could only recover the input tax which was attributable to the latter scheme, since in that case alone did it provide services for a consideration. The House of Lords agreed, but referred the case to the European Court on the question whether the statutory charge itself was "consideration" for the purposes of VAT.

35–41   Clearly, in these circumstances, the largest body of persons whose supply of services will not constitute a taxable supply in the course or furtherance of a business is that of employees and others subject to income tax under Schedule E. Nevertheless, section 47(4) derogates from this principle where, in the course or furtherance of a trade or profession, a person accepts an office. In this case, any services supplied by him as holder of that office are treated as supplied in the course or furtherance of his business. This provision would seem to cover the accountant who was an auditor or a solicitor who was a company registrar.[96] It will not apply, though, to a practising solicitor or to any other taxable person who took up a part-time *employment*.

35–42   Certain other types of transaction are deemed to be the carrying on of a business[97]:

---

92. Nevertheless, a statutory body which does make some supplies may be liable to be registered: *National Water Council* v. *Commissioners* [1979] S.T.C. 157.

93. *Commissioners* v. *Lord Fisher* [1981] S.T.C. 238.

94. *Commissioners* v. *Royal Exchange Theatre Trust* [1979] 3 All E.R. 797; [1979] S.T.C. 728; *Yoga for Health Foundation* v. *Commissioners* [1983] V.A.T.T.R. 297.

95. *Greater London Transfusion Services* v. *Commissioners* [1983] V.A.T.T.R. 241, where the service provided blood donors to London hospitals. *Quaere* whether the supply was exempt as a supply of blood: Sched. 6, Group 7, item 6: *cf. Commissioners* v. *British Railways Board* [1977] 1 W.L.R. 588, *ante*, § 35–35.

95a. [1985] S.T.C. 383 (C.A.); [1986] S.T.C. 192 (H.L.). And see also *Whitechapel Art Galleries* [1986] S.T.C. 156.

96. See *I.R.C.* v. *Brander and Cruickshank* [1971] 1 W.L.R. 212; 46 T.C. 574, *ante*, § 3–03.

97. s.47(2).

(a) *the provision by a club, association or organisation for a subscription or other consideration of the facilities or advantages available to its members.* Such associations (*e.g.* sports clubs) are not subject to income tax or corporation tax on supplies to their members by virtue of the mutuality principle[98] but will be subject to VAT both on subscriptions received[99] and goods sold.[1] Bodies having objects in the public domain of a political, religious, philanthropic, philosophical or patriotic nature and which call for subscriptions from their members are not, however, to be treated *for that reason alone* as carrying on business[2] provided that the subscriptions paid to them obtain no facility or advantage other than the right to participate in the management of the body or to receive reports on its activities. Thus, a distinction must be drawn between subscriptions which are, in reality, donations or contributions towards the furtherance of the aims of an association or charity (which would not be taxable) and subscriptions paid for securing something substantial for the subscriber in return (which would be taxable).

35–43 Membership benefits supplied in return for subscriptions by trades unions and professional organisations are exempt[3] but other benefits supplied by such bodies for separate consideration (*e.g.* in trade union clubs) are subject to the tax.[4]

(b) *The admission, for a consideration, of persons to any premises.* This applies to theatres, cinemas, funfairs, casinos and the like.

These provisions would apply to fund-raising businesses or activities carried on by charities—as opposed to transactions in furtherance of the charitable purpose.[5]

"or furtherance of a business"[6]

35–44 The words "or furtherance" were added with effect from January 1, 1978. They are intended to emphasise that any purchases or sales subsidiary to the main purpose of a business still fall within the scope of the tax.

> Thus, in *Ridley* v. *Commissioners*[7] the sale of sporting rights, an asset which had never been used for the purposes of the trade of the taxpayer (farming), was still considered to be a supply in the course or furtherance of that trade

---

98. See *ante*, §§ 2–16 *et seq.*
99. See, for example, *Exeter Golf Club* v. *Commissioners* [1981] S.T.C. 211, *post*, § 35–86.
1. Subject to the £20,500 registration limit: see *ante*, §§ 35–13 *et seq.* This provision has been held to apply to the Club Cricket Conference in providing the facilities of a fixture bureau and an umpires' panel; [1973] V.A.T.T.R. 53; and see *Royal Highland and Agricultural Society of Scotland* [1976] V.A.T.T.R. 38.
2. s.47(3).
3. Sched. 6, Group 9. Prior to January 1, 1978, such organisations had a right to elect to be treated as taxable or exempt. Now, such bodies, if within the scope of the Group, will be exempt and thus will be unable to recover tax on their inputs.
4. Subject to the minimum turnover requirements; see *ante*, §§ 35–13 *et seq.*
5. On the introduction of the tax, however, the Chancellor of the Exchequer stated that favourable consideration would be given to the registration of local branches of charities, so that they could come within the exemption limits. The manner in which the Commissioners exercise this consideration is set out in Customs Leaflet No. 701/1/84 "Charities."
6. s.2(1).
7. [1983] V.A.T.T.R. 81. (*Cf. RWK Stirling* v. *Commissioners* [1983] V.A.T.T.R. 232.

since the funds so obtained were to be used to assist the finances of the business by reducing the overdraft.

So, too, a professional person who disposed of (or, on retirement appropriated to personal use) some office furniture would make a supply which attracted tax, albeit that he was not in the business of selling furniture. In this context, section 47 further provides that, as from January 1, 1978, the disposal of a business as a going concern, or anything done in connection with its termination, shall be deemed to be in the course or furtherance of the business.[8]

(5) *In the United Kingdom*

35–45   Subject to the reverse charge mentioned above,[9] if goods or services are not supplied in the United Kingdom there can be no charge to VAT. Section 6 sets out principles for determining the place of supply. As far as goods are concerned, the place of supply depends on the situation of the goods prior to the supply. Thus, goods in the United Kingdom, or which are to be removed *from* the United Kingdom are treated as supplied *in* the United Kingdom: correspondingly, goods situated outside the United Kingdom, or which are to be brought *to* the United Kingdom, are considered to be supplied *outside* the United Kingdom and, therefore, are not within the scope of VAT on supplies. The place where buyer and seller "belong" is, thus, irrelevant when determining the liability of a supply of goods to VAT. The provisions relating to services are more complicated. Services are generally deemed to be supplied in the country where the supplier "belongs" and the following rules apply to determine where that may be.[10]

35–46   It will be found to be:

(a) the country where he has a business establishment[11] or some other fixed establishment,[12] provided that he has no other such establishment elsewhere;

(b) the country which is his usual place of residence[13] if he has no business establishment anywhere;

(c) if he has business establishments in more than one country, that in which is the establishment most directly concerned with the supply.

The Treasury has power[14] to specify where a supply of services is made.[14a]

---

8. s.47(5), (6); see also the excluding provisions in the VAT (Special Provisions) Order 1981, art. 12(1), *ante*, § 35–37.

9. See *ante*, § 35–27.

10. s.8.

11. By s.8(5)(*a*), a person carrying on business in a country through a branch or agency situated there is deemed to have a business establishment in that country.

12. In *Binder Hamlyn* v. *Commissioners* [1983] V.A.T.T.R. 171, the Tribunal held that a registered company office, maintained in order to comply with the Companies Act 1985, constituted "some other fixed establishment" for the purposes of s.8, although it did not amount to a "business establishment."

13. "Usual place of residence" in relation to a body corporate, means the place where it is legally constituted: s.8(5)(*b*).

14. s.6(6).

14a. See, for example, the VAT (Hiring of Goods) Order 1985 (S.I. 1985 No. 799).

35–47   In consequence of these rules, the travel agent, barrister, solicitor, or accountant, with his sole business establishment in the United Kingdom, would prima facie, be liable to VAT on services rendered to overseas clients. Where such a person has establishments both in the United Kingdom and elsewhere, he must determine with which establishment the service is most directly concerned and, if this is in the United Kingdom, the supply will be within the charge to tax. Such services will, however, normally be zero-rated.[15]

35–48   Since the Isle of Man has also adopted VAT it can, in effect, be regarded as part of the United Kingdom for the purpose of the tax.[16]

B. *Importation*

35–49   Tax on the importation of goods is charged and payable as if it is a duty of customs.[17]

This rule applies to the importation of goods by any person (whether taxable or not). At the time that goods are removed from customs bond both import duty and VAT become payable. The value on which VAT is so payable is determined as follows:

(1) If the goods are imported at a price in money payable as on a transfer of the property and for no other consideration, the value is an amount equal to the price plus import duties payable plus the cost of the freight and insurance to the place of importation.[18] If, however, the price was less than market value, and the parties were connected persons and the importer is not entitled to a credit for the input tax, market value is substituted.[19]

(2) If (1) above does not apply, the value is the open market value of the goods as determined in accordance with Community legislation plus (so far as not already included) import duties and the cost of freight and insurance.[20]

35–50   The open market value of the goods is their value on the date when they came out of customs bond into the United Kingdom. Any sale of the goods whilst they remain in bond will not attract VAT.[21] The Treasury has power to grant relief in whole or in part from VAT on the importation of goods, so as to give effect to international agreements. It is the Commissioners, however, who are given the power to make provision for the remission or repayment of VAT in whole or in part on goods which have previously been exported and on goods which are to be re-exported.[22]

---

15. Under Sched. 5, Group 9: "International services."
16. See VAT (Isle of Man) Order 1982 and VAT (Isle of Man) (No. 2) Order 1982.
17. s.2(4). Zero rated goods are not, however, subject to VAT on importation: s.16(3).
18. s.11(2). For the purpose of tax on importation, therefore, the price is taken to be VAT-exclusive. *cf.* s.10(2): "value of supply," *ante*, § 35–02 and *post*, § 35–86.
19. Sched. 4, para. 2.
20. s.11(3).
21. See Sched. 5, Group 15, *post*, § 35–82.
22. s.19(2), (3).

35–51   VAT on importation becomes due at the time and place of the entry of the goods into the United Kingdom. It is possible to delay payment for a period, averaging a month, if adequate security for the subsequent payment of the tax is provided to the satisfaction of the Commissioners.[23] Such tax will thus become payable at a time other than that of the making of a tax return: fully taxable traders will, though, be able effectively to gain delayed relief from the tax by set-off in their next return.

35–51A   No VAT will be payable on the temporary importation of goods solely for repair, renovation, modification or other such treatment so long as the goods are re-exported within six months (or such longer period as the Commissioners may allow) and do not at any time pass into the ownership of a United Kingdom resident. Correspondingly, VAT *will* be charged on the re-importation of goods into the United Kingdom which have been sent abroad for such treatment. The charge in this latter case will be based on the cost of repairs *plus* duty and freight—but *not* on the value of the goods themselves.[23a]

3. EXEMPTIONS

35–52   VAT is charged only on taxable supplies made by taxable persons.[24] A "taxable supply" is defined as a "supply of goods or services made in the United Kingdom *other than an exempt supply*."[25] A supply of goods or services is an exempt supply if it is of a description specified in Schedule 6 to the Act.[26] The Treasury is given wide powers[27] to vary the Schedule by addition or deletion. The exemptions are as follows:

35–53   (1) *Land.* The grant, assignment or surrender of any interest in or right over land or of any licence to occupy land is, subject to certain specified exceptions, an exempt supply.[28] So, neither the sale of land nor the receipt of rent will attract VAT. Excluded from the exemption, however, are the provision of hotel or holiday accommodation,[28a] the grant of facilities for camping in tents or caravans, of parking facilities, game and fishing rights,

---

23. This system of "postponed entry," introduced by F.A. 1984, Sched. 6 as ss.37A and 37B of the Customs and Excise Management Act 1979 with effect from November 1, 1984, replaces the more generous system of postponed accounting which previously enabled payment to be delayed for up to 11 weeks.
23a. VAT (General) Regulations 1985, regs. 44 and 48.
24. s.2(1).
25. s.2(2).
26. s.17(1).
27. s.17(2).
28. An agreement conferring a franchise to sell goods at a particular place may still constitute a licence to occupy land: *British Airports Authority* v. *Commissioners* [1977] 1 W.L.R. 302; on the other hand, a subscription to a sports club (where members own the land in common) is not paid for the grant of an interest in land but for the facilities provided by the club: *Trewby* v. *Commissioners* [1976] 1 W.L.R. 932; [1976] S.T.C. 122 and *Commissioners* v. *Little Spain Club Ltd.* [1979] S.T.C. 170. The distinction derives from the proper analysis of the legal rights conferred under the agreement: *British Railways Board* v. *Commissioners* [1977] 1 W.L.R. 588.
28a. On the provision of hotel accommodation see § 35–92. On the meaning of holiday accommodation, see Group 1, Note 1, Sched. 6 and *Court Barton Property Plc.* [1985] V.A.T.T.R. 148.

rights to fell timber, of storage and mooring facilities for ships or aircraft, and the provision of exhibition space.

Certain supplies of land are zero-rated.[29]

35–54 (2) *Insurance*. Exemption is given to the provision of insurance and re-insurance by persons permitted[30] to carry on insurance business, and to the making of insurance arrangements and the handling of insurance claims.

Some supplies of insurance are zero-rated.[31]

35–55 (3) *Postal Services*. The conveyance of postal packets (other than tele-grams or datapost packets) and services connected therewith are exempt if supplied by the Post Office. The telephone service is not exempt.

35–56 (4) *Betting, gaming and lotteries*. The provision of facilities for the placing of bets, or for the playing of games of chance and the granting of a right to take part in a lottery are exempt from VAT. Such activities will, however, be subject to betting and gaming duties. Club subscriptions and admission fees are not so exempt: a gaming club which imposes such charges will, therefore, only be partially exempt. Amusements and facilities provided at such places as fairgrounds are not exempt.[32]

35–57 (5) *Finance*. Exemption is afforded to any dealings with money,[33] securities for money, foreign exchange and the granting of credit. The exemption applies to the services of money and mortgage brokers (except in respect of the issue of Exchange securities such as certificates of deposit[34]) but not those of stockbrokers. Stockjobbers, however, are exempt. The exemption only applies to the money transactions of banks—whose advisory services will be standard-rated: banks are, therefore, partially exempt traders.[35] Nor does the exemption extend to the supply of coins or notes as collectors' items or for investment purposes: such supplies are taxable.

35–58 (6) *Education*. This exemption applies to the provision of education and research (and of goods and services incidental thereto to the persons receiving the education) by schools[36] and universities. The exemption extends to the provision of education or research[37] by other organisations if of a similar kind[38] and if otherwise than for profit.

The Commissioners consider that the provision of meals in such institu-

---

29. See *post*, §§ 35–74 *et seq.*
30. By the Insurance Companies Act 1982, s.2.
31. See *post*, § 35–76.
32. Special rules apply to determine the nature and value of the supply made to a person playing a "gaming machine": see s.13.
33. This would include the assignment of a chose in action.
34. See *Commissioners* v. *Guy Butler (International) Ltd.* [1977] Q.B. 377 (C.A.).
35. See *post*, § 35–101.
36. The provision of the service of teaching by freelance tutors is considered to be made to the institution concerned, rather than to the pupils and, therefore, is standard-rated.
37. And, again, of goods and services incidental thereto supplied to the students.
38. See *Church of Scientology of California* v. *Commissioners* [1979] S.T.C. 297.

tions is incidental to the education provided and the VAT Tribunal has held that the same is true of parking facilities.[39]

The exemption is also applicable to the provision of facilities by a youth club or association of youth clubs—but presumably not to the provision of accommodation or meals by, for example, the Youth Hostel Association.

35–59   (7) *Health and Welfare*. Exempted are the supply of services (and the supply of goods in connection therewith) by registered medical practitioners, dentists, opticians, nurses, midwives, hearing-aid dispensers and similar persons. Thus the supply of spectacles is exempt if made as part of the service of the optician, for example after an eye test, but the retailing of sunglasses would not attract the exemption. The supply of services (but not the supply of goods)[40] by a chemist is also exempt. The exemption further applies to the provision of care and medical or surgical treatment (and the supply of goods in connection therewith) in a hospital or other approved institution such as a private registered nursing home.

The exemption also covers the supply of welfare services by charities and public bodies. "Welfare services" has a wide meaning, encompassing the provision of care and treatment to the sick and elderly, the protection of the young and the provision of spiritual welfare by religious institutions.

35–60   (8) *Burial and cremation*. The services of undertakers are exempt and the Commissioners also consider the supply of a coffin (though not a headstone) in connection therewith as falling within this Group.[41]

35–61   (9) *Trades unions and professional bodies*. Exemption is granted to the supply to its members of services (and goods connected therewith) which are referable to its aims and which are available without any payment other than a membership subscription, by trade unions, professional associations, associations for the advancement of knowledge, and associations formed for the purpose of making representations to Government, etc. The exemption does not extend to the provision of social activities undertaken by such bodies.

35–62   (10) *Sports competitions*. The granting of a right to enter such a competition is exempt if the consideration is used wholly towards the provision of prizes or if the right is granted by a non-profit-making organisation.

35–63   (11) *Works of art*. Exemption is afforded to the disposal of works of art and other objects which are accepted in lieu of tax debts or which are sold by private treaty to approved public galleries or institutions under the "douceur arrangements."[42]

---

39. *Re R. A. Archer (No. 2)* [1975] V.A.T.T.R. 1. Now that the scope of the tax is extended to supplies in the course *or furtherance* of a business it would seem that educational establishments will, prima facie, be chargeable to VAT in respect of disposals of goods that are no longer required for the purposes of their business.

40. But see Sched. 5, Group 14; *post*, § 35–81.

41. The exemption does not extend to the service of clearing a graveyard: *Re UFD Ltd.* [1981] V.A.T.T.R. 199.

42. That is to say, where the value of the exemption from capital taxation on the disposal to the institution is shared between the individual and the institution.

4. Zero Rating

35–64 If a supply of goods or services is zero rated, no tax is chargeable on the supply, although the transaction is treated as a taxable supply in all other respects.[43] The taxable vendor is thus able to recover the input tax he suffered but the purchaser receives the supply entirely free from VAT. The descriptions of the supplies which are zero rated are contained in section 16 and Schedule 5 to the Act.

35–65 Section 16(3) provides that, save as otherwise provided, goods of a description falling within Schedule 5 are to be excepted from tax not simply on their supply but also on their importation into the United Kingdom. Section 16(6) further provides that a supply of any type of goods is zero rated if the Commissioners are satisfied that the prescribed conditions have been fulfilled and that the goods have been exported by the vendor or are to be used as stores on a voyage or flight terminating outside the United Kingdom. Regulations exist to afford zero-rating to special cases of export of goods and services.[44]

35–66 The other matters which are zero-rated are set out in Schedule 5.[45] They are as follows:

35–67 (1) *Food*. A sale of food, animal feeding stuffs, seeds and live animals of a kind generally used as food for human consumption (but not alcohol, fruit juices, pet foods, sweets, crisps, chocolates, etc.) is zero rated. A supply of food in the course of catering, however, is not zero rated. Broadly speaking, the distinction is between the purchase of food and the purchase of a meal. The Schedule states that "a supply of anything in the course of catering includes any supply of it for consumption on the premises on which it is supplied and[46] any supply of hot food for consumption off those premises." All such supplies are, therefore, standard rated.

35–68 (2) *Sewerage services and water*. Sewerage services and water, other than distilled water, deionised water and bottled water, are zero rated.

35–69 (3) *Books*.[47] brochures, pamphlets, leaflets,[48] newspapers,[49] sheet music, maps and other articles supplied with them and not separately accounted for are supplied at the zero rate. Zero rating is not extended, however, to any charge made for the delivery of such items.

---

43. s.16(1).

44. See VAT General Regs. 1985, regs. 49–57.

45. The Treasury has power to amend the Schedule by order: s.16(4).

46. Added by F.A. 1984, Sched. 6, Part 1. The legislation thus effectively abandoned the previously important distinction between food supplied for consumption on and off the premises. On the supply of hot food see *Pimblett Ltd.* v. *Commissioners* [1985] V.A.T.T.R. 210.

47. The question whether these words extend to the supply of a binder for a loose-leaf work has come before the Tribunal no fewer than four times. The result of these cases appears to be that if the binder is supplied separately, it will not be zero rated: *Re Marshall Cavendish Ltd.* [1973] V.A.T.T.R. 65.

48. On the meaning of the word "leaflet" see *Cronsvale Ltd.* v. *Commissioners* [1983] V.A.T.T.R. 313.

49. A property guide, mainly consisting of advertisements, is not a newspaper or periodical falling within this Group: see *Geoffrey E. A. Snushall* v. *Commissioners* [1982] S.T.C. 537.

–70/71   (4) *Talking books for the blind and handicapped and wireless sets for the blind.* This covers *specially adapted* magnetic tape, tape recorders, and ancilliary items supplied to the RNIB, the National Listening Library and other similar charities. It also covers the supply of a radio or cassette recorder to a charity for gratuitous loan to the blind.

35–72   (5) *News services.* This group does not include the supply of photo-graphs.[50]

35–73   (6) *Fuel and power.* Coal, electricity, heat and air conditioning are zero rated as is domestic heating oil. Petrol and oil used in road vehicles, though, are subject to the tax.

35–74   (7) *Construction of buildings, etc.* This group consists of:

    (i) the granting, by a person constructing a building,[51] of a major inter-est in, or in any part of, the building or its site.[52] The effect of this provision is to enable a person who owns a site and who arranges for the construction thereon of a building, to deduct his input tax attributable thereto (including the fees of architects and surveyors) if subsequently he sells the freehold or grants a lease in excess of 21 years[53] (whether or not at a rack rent).

    (ii) The supply of services in the course of construction or demolition (but not repair or maintenance or alteration[54]) of any buildings or of any civil engineering work[55] other than the services of an architect or surveyor.

    (iii) The supply by a person supplying services within (ii) above[56] of materials, builder's hardware or other articles ordinarily installed as

---

50. A news clipping service is not zero rated: *Re Newsclip (U.K.) Ltd.* [1975] V.A.T.T.R. 67.

51. The item also applies where the interest is granted by someone on the builder's behalf—for example by trustees for a building partnership: Group 8, Note 1.

52. In *Re Stapenhill Developments Ltd.* [1984] V.A.T.T.R. 1, the Tribunal held that Group 8, item 1 does *not* require that there be a completed building on the land, the word being "constructing": the sale of land with partially dug foundations did not, however, fall within the provision.

53. The grant of a time-sharing lease for one week per annum for 80 years is not the grant of a "tenancy for a term certain exceeding 21 years" as required by Group 8: *Cottage Holiday Associates Ltd.* v. *Commissioners* [1983] S.T.C. 278.

54. After June 1, 1984, the supply of such services in connection with the alteration of a building is no longer zero rated, unless the building is a listed building: F.A. 1984, Sched. 6, Pt. II and Group 8A: "Protected buildings." On the distinction between the enlargement of an existing building and the construction of a new one, see *Great Shelford Free Church* [1985] V.A.T.T.R. 123—but consider [1985] S.T.I. 333.

55. In order for a supply to be zero rated in this connection, it is not sufficient for it to be in the course of a civil engineering work: rather, it must be made in the course of *the construction of a* civil engineering work: *En-tout-cas Ltd.* v. *Commissioners* [1973] V.A.T.T.R. 101 and *GKN Birwelco Ltd.* v. *Commissioners* [1983] V.A.T.T.R. 128. The decision in *En-tout-cas* was subsequently restricted by Treasury order—although not in a manner affecting this aspect of the decision. In consequence, supplies in the course of the construction of a civil engineer-ing work in the garden or grounds of a private dwelling (*e.g.* a swimming pool or tennis court) are not zero rated: Group 8, Note 2(*b*). Note 2(*a*) also excludes, with effect from June 1, 1984, the construction of a secondary, non-residential building (such as a separate garage) within the garden or grounds of a private residence: see F.A. 1984, Sched. 6, para. 5.

56. Sched. 5, Group 8, item 3.

fixtures by builders in connection with those services.[57] Excluded from this treatment is fitted furniture, other than kitchen units, and domestic electrical and gas appliances, other than those used to provide space heating or water heating.[58]

35–75   A similar distinction is drawn where a builder constructs houses or flats on his own land for sale or long lease: he is not entitled to deduct input tax paid on the supply to him of articles not ordinarily installed as fixtures by builders or, now,[59] of the majority of fitted furniture or gas or electrical appliances.

When zero rating is available, it is applicable regardless of the fact that the supplier is a sub-contractor making supplies to a main contractor. There are also provisions whereby a person constructing a building for his own occupation (and thus not making taxable supplies) can recover the tax he suffers on supplies made to him.[60]

35–76   (8) *International services*. The following services are zero rated when supplied by persons belonging in the United Kingdom:

(a) The supply of services relating to foreign land. This embraces architectural and surveying services and possibly conveyancing.

(b) The letting on hire of any means of transport for use in a place outside the EEC which are exported by the lessor or which are otherwise outside the EEC.[61]

(c) The supply of services relating to cultural, artistic, sporting or entertainment activities, where those services are performed outside the United Kingdom.

(d) The supply of services of valuing goods or carrying out work on goods where the goods are situated outside the United Kingdom and the service is supplied abroad.

(e) The supply of any service comprised in Schedule 3 where the supply is received by a person who belongs in another Member State of the EEC for the purposes of a business carried on by him.

(f) The supply of any services contained in Schedule 3[62] (excluding insurance) and the supply of insurance and reinsurance by authorised insurers[63] when made to a person who belongs *outside* the EEC (whether received by him for the purposes of a business carried on by him or not).

---

57. As regards "articles ordinarily installed" see *Commissioners* v. *Smitmit Design Ltd.* [1982] S.T.C. 525.

58. Sched. 5, Group 8, Note 2A, as inserted by F.A. 1984 Sched. 6, para. 6. And see *Robert Dale & Co. (Builders) Ltd.* v. *Commissioners* [1983] V.A.T.T.R. 61.

59. VAT (Special Provisions) Order 1981, Art. 8, as substituted by the VAT (Special Provisions) (Amendment) (No. 2) Order 1984.

60. s.21.

61. The hiring of goods other than transport is dealt with by Schedule 3 which provides for such supplies to be taxed at the location of the customer: see § 35–27. And see Group 9, items 5 and 6.

62. For a full list of these services see *ante*, § 35–27.

63. See Sched. 5, Group 2.

(g) The supply of certain types of insurance in connection with the carriage of passengers or of goods to or from a place outside the EEC.

(h) The supply by the Export Credit Guarantee Department (or another person making a similar supply) of insurance in connection with the export of goods out of the EEC.

(i) The supply of financial services of certain kinds falling within Schedule 6, Group 5,[64] where those services are related to the export of goods or the transhipment of goods whose ultimate destination is outside the EEC.

(j) The supply to a foreigner of work carried out on goods acquired within or imported into the United Kingdom and which are then exported.

(k) The supply of services in procuring for another any export of goods or any of the services described in (a)–(f) and (j) above or in procuring any supply of goods or services made outside the United Kingdom.

35–77   (9) *Transport.* In outline, this Group zero rates the supply of, or chartering, letting on hire, repair or maintenance of, ships and aircraft (excluding yachts and light aircraft), the transport of passengers,[65] pilotage, salvage and ancilliary services. Supplies by travel agents would be included in this Group, although an apportionment would have to be made in respect a supply of services which includes not only transportation but also accommodation, as for example a package holiday. Taxis are not zero rated.[66]

35–78   (10) *Caravans and houseboats.* The supply of caravans which are of a size in excess of that which can be used on the roads, and thus which can only be used as homes, and of houseboats which are designed or adapted for use as homes and which are incapable of self-propulsion, is zero rated.

35–79   (11) *Gold.* Gold supplied between Central Banks and members of the London Gold Market is zero rated.

35–80   (12) *Bank Notes.* Bank notes are zero rated.

35–81   (13) *Drugs, medicines and aids for the handicapped, etc.* This Group zero rates the supply of any goods by a chemist on a doctor's or a dentist's prescription and the general supply of items designed or adapted solely[67] for

---

64. See *ante*, § 35–57.

65. In *British Railways Board* v. *Commissioners* [1977] 1 W.L.R. 588 the question arose whether a payment securing the right to cheap fares was itself consideration for the supply of transport: the Court of Appeal held that it was the first part of a two part tariff paid for the supply of transport and therefore fell to be zero rated, see *ante*, § 35–35.

66. Group 10, item 4 only catches the transport of passengers in a vehicle designed or adapted to carry not less than 12 passengers.

67. See, for example, *Princess Louise Hospital* v. *Commissioners* [1983] V.A.T.T.R. 191. The Group has now been extended to include certain items of particular use to handicapped persons which have not been specially adapted for their use, *e.g.* vertical lifts and distress alarm systems.

use by the chronically sick or handicapped either to a handicapped person or to a charity which makes such items available to handicapped persons.

35–82   (14) *Imports, exports, etc.* This group zero rates the supply of goods whilst in customs bond, the transfer by a taxable person of goods or services to another place of business of his outside the United Kingdom, and supplies to overseas bodies in connection with defence projects.

35–83   (15) *Charities.* The supply of new and secondhand goods which are donated to or sold by a charity established for the relief of distress is zero rated, as is the provision of parts and accessories for, and the repair and maintenance of, such goods. The Group also zero rates the export of any goods by a charity.

35–84   (16) *Clothing and footwear.* This covers articles designed as clothing or footwear for young children and which is not suitable for use by an older person. There is no definition of "young children." It also zero rates protective boots and helmets for industrial use and crash helmets.

35–85   *Terminal Markets.*[68] For the market in futures there is a "tax free" ring for sales and purchases and no tax will be chargeable unless and until the goods are delivered. Consequently these activities are zero rated.

5. COMPUTATION

The value of a supply

35–86   In the simple case of a supply for a consideration in money, the value of the supply is that consideration less the amount of the tax.[69] Thus, where the supply is charged with tax at the positive rate of 15 per cent., the tax amounts to three-twenty-thirds of the consideration.[70] In other cases, *i.e.* where the consideration does not consist, or wholly consist, of money, the value of the supply is its open market value less the amount of the tax chargeable.[71] If, however, there is no consideration for a supply of goods— as where the supplier makes a gift—the value of the supply is taken to be the cost of the goods to the supplier,[72] unless that cost did not exceed £10, when no VAT is charged.[73] This latter provision might cover, for example,

---

68. s.34 and Regulations made thereunder: VAT (Terminal Markets) Order 1973 as amended.
69. s.10(2). On cases where apportionment is necessary, see § 35–36.
70. s.9(1).
71. s.10(3), (5): and see *Davies* v. *Commissioners* [1975] 1 W.L.R. 204; [1975] S.T.C. 28 for the effect of this provision where the price is discounted under a cheque trading arrangement: it would seem that tax is charged on the full amount and not on the price less commission. For the valuation of consideration taking the form of an interest-free loan, see *Commissioners* v. *Exeter Golf and Country Club Ltd.* [1981] S.T.C. 211. There is no rule, though, that the consideration must move from the recipient to the supplier: *Largs Golf Club* v. *Lord Advocate* [1985] S.T.C. 226.
72. Sched. 4, para. 7. See *Teknequip Ltd.* [1985] V.A.T.T.R. 167. This does not apply, though, when the supply is made to a connected person: see *post*, § 35–87.
73. Sched. 2, para. 5; see *ante*, § 35–28.

a gift of a watch to a retiring employee: it would not apply, though, to the supposedly "free gift" given as an inducement, which would be taxable by reference to its market value.[74] On the other hand, parts supplied "free" under a guarantee given on the sale of goods would not be subject to a charge to VAT since they will be considered to be covered by the charge made on the original sale.

Gifts of services are not, at present, charged to VAT.[75]

35–87   The above rules are subject to the qualification that if a supply is made for a consideration in money which is less than its open market value, to a person who is connected with the supplier and who is not entitled to full credit for input tax in respect of the supply then, in order to avoid the loss which would otherwise result, the Commissioners are empowered to direct that the value of the supply be taken to be its open market value.[76] Such a direction cannot be made more than three years after the time of the supply but it can be made in respect of further prospective supplies. The provision is, in fact, somewhat limited in extent. Plainly, it cannot apply to gifts of services—which are entirely outside the scope of the tax—but equally it is inapplicable to *gifts* of goods: it is thus restricted to supplies of goods for inadequate monetary consideration. It has further been provided that the provision is not to apply to the supply of food, beverages or hotel or other accommodation to employees—when the value of the supply is restricted to the consideration actually charged,[77] less tax.

35–88   Another similar anti-avoidance provision allows the Commissioners, where a taxable person carries on his business (or part of it) by supplying goods to a number of non-taxable persons for sale by retail, to give directions securing that the value of the supply made by him be taken to be its open market value on a sale by retail.[78] This covers direct selling through domestic outlets—for example, sales by exempt persons at coffee mornings. The object is to ensure that VAT is charged on the retail mark-up and thus to prevent an unfair marketing advantage accruing through the use of exempt retail outlets. This provision will only apply, however, to *business organisations* adopting such a sales strategy and not, for example, to charity coffee mornings.

Secondhand goods

35–89   VAT also applies to the supply of secondhand goods by taxable persons: but the Treasury has, in the exercise of its powers,[79] made orders restricting the amount on which tax is chargeable to the dealer's margin, instead of

---

74. *Bodyshop Supply Services Ltd.* [1984] V.A.T.T.R. For the meaning of "gift" see *GUS Merchandise Corp.* v. *Commissioners* [1981] S.T.C. 569.
75. Although the Treasury has power, under s.3(4), to specify that the gratuitous supply of a particular service is to be treated as a taxable supply, it was stated during the Committee stage of the Finance Bill in 1977 that there was no present intention to invoke the provision: no orders have yet been made.
76. Sched. 4, para. 1.
77. Sched. 4, para. 10.
78. Sched. 4, para. 3.
79. s.18.

the full resale price, in areas where a substantial amount of competition from non-registered individuals can be anticipated: the secondhand car trade, works of art and antiques, motor cycles, caravans, board and outboard motors, electronic organs, aircraft, firearms and, most recently, horses and ponies.

Discounts and credit sales

35–90   If goods are sold (or imported) under terms that allow for a cash discount, the value of the supply is the discounted sum even though the purchaser fails to pay within the specified time and thus subsequently pays the higher price.[80] If discounts are offered by quantity, there will be an adjustment of tax at the end of the period to give effect to the discount obtained. So, too, if goods are sent out in returnable containers (*e.g.* a bottle) on which a deposit is paid, the value of the container, or the amount of the deposit, is not taken into account in determining the value of the supply unless the container is not returned.

35–91   Where, on the other hand, a sale is made on credit, the value of the supply is the cash price for the goods, disregarding the interest element.

Long-stay accommodation[81]

35–92   Where hotel or similar accommodation is provided to an individual for his own use (whether alone or with others) for a period exceeding four weeks, the value of that part of the supply which is made after the initial four week period is reduced to such part thereof as is attributable to the provision of facilities *other* than the right to occupy the accommodation. The legislation requires, though, that the value of such other facilities be considered to be at least 20 per cent. of the whole. The provision is designed to afford service flat occupiers and long-term hotel guests similar relief from VAT on accommodation to that given to house dwellers.[82]

Book tokens, etc.

35–93   The consideration given for items such as book tokens and record tokens is disregarded for VAT purposes except to the extent (if at all) that it exceeds the value of the token itself.[83]

The time of supply

35–94   The time of supply can have an effect on the value of the supply. First, the rate of tax chargeable may be varied: when this occurs, the rate of tax applicable to a contract is that in force when the supply is made and not, if different, that at the date of the contract.[84] This is equally true if, by

---

80. Sched. 4, paras. 4, and 5.
81. Sched. 4 para. 9. The paragraph was amended by s.11 FA 1986 to preclude its use in the case of block supplies by hoteliers to tour operators of hotel rooms for a season.
82. Rents are exempt under Sched. 6, Group 1; see *ante*, § 35–53.
83. Sched. 4, para. 6.
84. See s.42 and *ante*, § 35–02.

amendment, a particular kind of supply ceases to be (or becomes) exempt or zero rated between contract and "tax point."[85] Secondly, the duty to account for tax on a supply only arises one month after the end of the prescribed accounting period in which it was made. If the tax point of the supply falls after the end of that period, liability to account will be postponed for three months.

Section 4 specifies the basic tax points:

(i) a supply of goods is treated as taking place:
   (a) at the time when they are removed from the supplier's premises;
   (b) if the goods are not to be removed, when they are made available to the person to whom they are supplied;
   (c) if they are taken on approval, or on sale or return, when it becomes known that a supply has taken place (or will take place): if matters are unresolved after a year, the supply is deemed to take place on the first anniversary of removal;

(ii) a supply of services occurs when the services are performed.[86] If a service is performed over a period it is considered that this would be when the service is completed.

If, however, a tax invoice is given or a payment made (other than in a case falling within (i)(c) above) prior to one of these specified events the time when the earlier event occurs is the tax point.[87] But if a tax point is given within 14 days *after* the relevant occasions mentioned in (i) and (ii) above, or such longer period as the Commissioners may specify, then the time when the invoice is given will be the tax point unless the taxable person elects to adhere to the basic rules of delivery and performance.[88] Special rules apply when the rate of tax is changed or a relevant zero rating or exempting provision is amended: the taxable person can elect that the supply be treated as made at the time of the basic tax point under (i) or (ii) above, regardless of when payment is made or a tax invoice is issued.[89]

35–95   Thus in all ordinary cases, it will be the time when the tax invoice is issued that will be the tax point. This is sensible, since such an invoice represents money in the recipient's hands as an input: nevertheless, it would have been much simpler to have made the earlier of tax invoice and payment the sole determinant.

35–96   Where a supply is made for a consideration the whole or part of which is determined or payable periodically or at the end of any period or which is only determined when the goods are appropriated for any purpose, the tax

---

85. The name the Commissioners give to the occasion on which tax is chargeable.

86. The services of a barrister or advocate are treated as performed on the occasion when his fee is received, or a tax invoice is issued, whichever is the earlier: save that all the services for which fees are outstanding are deemed to be performed on the day on which he ceases to practise: VAT (General) Regs. 1985, reg. 25.

87. s.5(1). See *Dolomite Double Glazing Ltd.* [1985] V.A.T.T.R. 183.

88. s.5(2).

89. s.41.

point will be determined by reference to regulations made by the Commissioners.[90] This provision will apply mainly to hiring arrangements[91] where the tax will be imposed on the service charge.

35–97   Where the consideration for a supply of services is not ascertainable at the time when they are performed (as is often the case with royalties) then a further supply is deemed to take place whenever a payment is received or a tax invoice is issued.[92]

Bad debts

35–98   The liability to pay VAT is imposed on the taxable person and arises at the time of supply.[93] It can happen, therefore, that a taxable person who has made a taxable supply finds himself liable to account to the Commissioners for the tax on the supply and yet unable to recover the consideration from the defaulting debtor. Limited relief is available[94] allowing a refund of tax paid if the taxable person can establish:

(a) that his debtor is insolvent (*i.e.* has been adjudged bankrupt has entered into a deed of arrangement or composition or scheme for the benefit of his creditors or, being a company, is the subject of a creditors' voluntary winding up or is being wound up under an order of the court or a certificate has been issued as to the insufficiency of the corporate assets to satisfy unsecured creditors); and

(b) he has proved in the insolvency (the refund is restricted to that VAT inherent in any deficiency); and

(c) that the value of his supply did not exceed open market value; and

(d) that, if the supply was of goods, property in those goods passed to the purchaser.

No analogous relief is available, however, where a purchaser makes a payment in advance for goods which are never supplied to him owing to the subsequent insolvency of the "supplier." Usually, a credit would be available against a person's output tax but such a credit only arises in respect of "input tax," which is defined as "tax on the supply to him of any goods or services." Since *ex hypothesi*, there will have been no such supply, there can be no input tax and, thus, no credit.[95]

Calculation

35–99   Having determined the value of a taxable supply, the taxable person adds on VAT at the appropriate rate and charges his customer the total amount. If his customer is also a taxable person he must give him a tax

---

90. s.5(9).
91. These are supplies of services: Sched. 2, para. 1(1)(*b*)—thus the applicable statutory regulation is VAT (General) Regs. 1985, reg. 23.
92. VAT (General) Regs., 1985, reg. 24.
93. s.2(3).
94. Under s.22 and the VAT (Bad Debt Relief) Regs. 1985.
95. *Theotrue Holdings Ltd.* v. *Commissioners* [1983] V.A.T.T.R. 88.

invoice showing the amount of these items.[96] Although this tax is technically due at the moment of supply[96a] it is accounted for by returns made for each accounting period. The total amount of tax payable on the taxable supplies made by him in an accounting period is called output tax: from this he may deduct input tax, that is tax he has paid on the supply to him of goods or services used or to be used for the purpose of any business carried on by him[97] or tax paid on the importation of any goods by him for the same purpose.[98] He must also show that the supply is made to him and not to any other person.[99] If goods or services are supplied to a taxable person and are used partly for business purposes and partly for other purposes the supply is apportioned so that only the part referable to his business is allowed as an input tax credit.[1] He then accounts to the Commissioners for the difference between output and input tax or, if the input tax exceeds the output tax, claims a repayment.[2] Where input tax exceeds output tax for a prescribed accounting period the Commissioners must pay a supplement to the trader if they fail to issue written instructions directing repayment of the excess within 30 days after the receipt of a properly completed return for the period.[2a]

The Treasury has power to make orders disallowing the deduction of input tax in cases specified in the order.[3] Such orders have been made in respect of business cars, entertainment expenses and luxury fittings such as washing machines, fitted carpets, televisions and cookers in zero rated buildings.

35–100   Regulations have been made whereby persons carrying on business in a Member State of the EEC can recover VAT suffered by them on purchases, etc., made in the United Kingdom.[4] Similar provisions pertain in the other Member States for the benefit of taxable persons who belong in the United Kingdom.

Partial exemption

35–101   The fundamental principle running through the legislation is that credit for input tax is only available if and in so far as that tax is attributable to onward taxable supplies (whether those supplies are chargeable at the posi-

---

96. Sched. 7, para. 2; and see VAT (General) Regs. 1985, regs. 12–16.
96a. s.2(3).
97. A credit is allowed for such a proportion of the tax on goods acquired by a person intending to carry on a business as the Commissioners consider in all the circumstances to be fair and reasonable: s.15(1)(c) and VAT (General) Regs. 1985, reg. 37.
98. s.14(3). It should be noted that as from January 1, 1978, the words "used or to be used" have been added, although it is not considered that this represents a significant change from the previous provision.
99. See *Manchester Ship Canal Co.* v. *Commissioners* [1982] STC 351 where services relating to a pension scheme were held to be supplied to the employing company and not to the trustees of the scheme. See also *R. Wiseman & Sons* [1985] V.A.T.T.R. 168.
1. s.14(4).
2. s.14(5). If he so desires, the taxable person may have his input tax credit held over to a subsequent period: s.14(6).
2a. The supplement will be the greater of £30 or 5 per cent. of the sum due for repayment. The system commences on October 1, 1986. And see the VAT (Repayment Supplement) (No. 2) Regs. 1985.
3. VAT (Special Provisions) Order 1981, arts. 8 and 9 and s.14(10).
4. s.23 and VAT (Repayment to Community Traders) Order 1980.

tive or zero rate). In the ordinary case, a taxable person will be able to deduct all his input tax because all his outputs will be so taxable. Where, however, a person makes some exempt supplies an apportionment must be made. Examples of such persons are chemists[5] and banks.[6] The system of apportionment is not prescribed by the Act itself but is left to regulations made by the Commissioners.[7] Provision is made whereby exempt supplies can be disregarded if they do not exceed certain stated amounts.[8] Where apportionment is necessary the taxable person will only be able to deduct that proportion of his input tax which equals the percentage of the value of his supplies which consist of taxable supplies.

> Thus, a trader whose supplies consist as to 80 per cent. of exempt supplies and as to 20 per cent. of taxable supplies, will only be able to deduct 20 per cent. of his input tax as a credit against his output tax.

The Commissioners will, however, allow an alternative method to be used if it can be shown to achieve a fair attribution.

Refund of tax

35–102   (1) Section 20 provides that certain bodies can claim a refund of tax on goods or services supplied to them or goods imported by them for the purpose of their non-business activities. For the purpose of their business activities the normal input/output mechanism operates. Consequently, these bodies will only suffer tax on supplies to them or goods imported by them for the purpose of an exempt business carried on by them. Where, however, in the opinion of the Commissioners, their exempt supplies represent an insignificant proportion of the whole, the whole of the tax may be refunded. The bodies to which this provision applies are local authorities, various statutory bodies providing similar services, police authorities, passenger transport authorities, the BBC and Independent Television News Ltd.

(2) Under section 36 the Commissioners have power to give refunds of tax to traders who make only exempt supplies, on the purchase of plant and machinery.[9–10]

(3) Under section 23, the Commissioners may provide for the repayment of tax to persons carrying on business in a Member State of the EEC other than the United Kingdom if such tax would be input tax of theirs if they were taxable persons belonging in the United Kingdom. The section provides for the extension of such scheme to persons outside the EEC if a Community Directive so requires. So far, regulations under this section have been made only for the benefit of Community traders.[11]

---

5. Sched. 6, Group 7; see *ante* § 35–59.
6. Sched. 6 Group 5; see *ante* § 35–57.
7. See the VAT (General) Regs. 1985, regs. 29–37.
8. Under reg. 35, exempt supplies will be disregarded if less than £200 per month, or than 1 per cent. of the value of all his supplies, or than both £8,000 per month and 50 per cent. of the value of all his supplies, or than £16,000 and 25 per cent. of the value of all his supplies. The purpose is to exclude the partial exemption rules in minor cases.
9–10. No such order has yet been made.
11. See VAT (Repayment to Community Traders) Order 1980 and *ante* § 35–100.

(4) A person constructing a new home otherwise than in the course or furtherance of a business carried on by him can obtain a refund of the tax on goods supplied to him for the construction in respect of which he would have been entitled to a credit had he been trading.[12]

Income tax and corporation tax

35–103 There are no express provisions in the Act dealing with the deduction of VAT under Schedule D, Cases I and II, for income and corporation tax purposes. Nevertheless, money expended wholly and exclusively for the purposes of a trade or profession is under section 130 of the Income and Corporation Taxes Act 1970 deductible in computing the profits of the business chargeable to tax.[13] If the taxpayer is a fully taxable person for VAT he will not have to take the tax into account at all for such purposes since he will actually suffer no tax by virtue of the input/output credit system. If, though, he is exempt or partially exempt he will be able to claim the total price (including VAT) of the goods and services purchased (in so far as he has been unable to obtain input tax credit in respect of the supplies) in computing his profits for income or corporation tax. In such a case he is the ultimate consumer and the unrelieved tax will be part of the price for the goods or services.

6. COLLECTION AND ENFORCEMENT

35–104 The Commissioners are empowered to make regulations requiring the tax to be paid by reference to such periods (which are known as "prescribed accounting periods" and are generally of three months' duration) and at such time and in such manner as they may determine.[14] In particular, the regulations may prescribe the form of accounts to be kept and of returns to be made and may require that tax invoices be given with (or within a prescribed period after) every taxable supply to a taxable person.[15] Every taxable person must keep such records as the Commissioners may require for a period of up to six years.[16]

Assessments

35–105 If a trader makes correct returns at the proper time, it will not be necessary for the Commissioners to raise formal assessments on him: for he will be obliged to pay the tax due when he makes his return. When, however, a person fails to make a required return, or to keep proper records, or where the Commissioners are of the opinion that his returns are incorrect or incomplete, they are empowered[17] to make estimated assessments. Assessments will also be necessary if the taxable person has improperly claimed

---

12. s.21; see *ante*, § 35–74.
13. See *ante*, § 2–57.
14. s.14(1) and Sched. 7, para. 2.
15. *Ibid.* and see VAT (General) Regs. 1985, Pt. III.
16. Sched. 7, para. 7.
17. Sched. 7, para. 4. See *Van Boeckel* v. *Commissioners* [1981] S.T.C. 290.

sums by way of repayment of a supposed excess of input tax over output tax.

35–106 Inputs are not strictly matched in accounts with their corresponding output.[18] It is possible, therefore, for a taxable person to claim input tax credit on an asset supposedly acquired for the purposes of his business which is then diverted to his own personal use. The Commissioners are entitled to require a taxable person to give an account of goods in respect of which he has claimed a tax credit: if he fails to give a satisfactory explanation of their whereabouts, the Commissioners can treat him as having made an onward supply of the goods and assess him to the tax that he would have accounted for on such a supply.[19]

Generally, a separate assessment should be made by the Commissioners for each prescribed accounting period but a "global assessment" may be raised in a case where it is not possible to identify a specific period for which the tax claimed is due.[20]

35–107 Prima facie, the period within which assessments must be raised are stricter than the comparable ones for income tax. An assessment of an amount due for a prescribed accounting period may not be made after the later of:

(a) two years after the end of the prescribed accounting period; and
(b) one year after evidence of facts, sufficient in the opinion of the Commissioners to justify the making of an assessment, comes to their knowledge.[21]

If such evidence comes to the knowledge of the Commissioners after an assessment has been made, they are entitled to make a further assessment.

35–108 These rules have, however, been interpreted liberally: merely because the Commissioners have evidence which suggests that an *investigation* should be conducted does not mean that they have enough to justify the making of an *assessment*. Thus, until the Commissioners know precisely what value of supplies has not been returned, they are not in a position to justify making an assessment.[22] What is more, it has also been held that a Tribunal is not entitled to decide what facts justify the making of an assessment—this is entirely in the discretion of the Commissioners[23]—all the Tribunal can do is to determine when the last of those facts came to the

---

18. See *ante*, § 35–99.
19. Sched. 7, para. 4(6).
20. *S. J. Grange Ltd.* v. *Commissioners* [1979] 1 W.L.R. 239; [1979] S.T.C. 183, as interpreted by *International Languages Centres Ltd.* v. *Commissioners* [1983] S.T.C. 394. For further proceedings in the latter case, see [1986] S.T.C. 279.
21. Sched. 7, para. 4(5).
22. See *GUS Merchandise Corp.* v. *Commissioners* [1978] V.A.T.T.R. 28.
23. *Cumbrae Properties (1963) Ltd.* v. *Commissioners* [1981] S.T.C. 799, following the decision of the House of Lords in *Commissioners* v. *J. H. Corbitt (Numismatists) Ltd.* [1981] A.C. 22; [1980] S.T.C. 231.

knowledge of the Commissioners—although it can interfere if the Commissioners' failure to make an earlier assessment was perverse.

5–109   The Commissioners cannot, by use of global assessment, seek to extend the limitation period. Accordingly, when such an assessment is raised, covering a number of prescribed accounting periods, the period of two years laid down by Schedule 7, para. $4(5)(a)$ runs from the end of the *earliest* period included in the assessment.[24]

5–110   Although the Commissioners thus have considerable latitude in the time within which they may make an assessment nevertheless, even where facts come to their knowledge belatedly, they may not as a general rule raise an assessment more than six years after the prescribed accounting period in question. Exceptionally, however, the Commissioners are empowered to make assessments within *twenty* years of the relevant period if tax has been lost through conduct of the taxpayer amounting to dishonesty or for which he could have been convicted of fraud.[25] If reliance is place on this power, the Commissioners will have to justify its use in any subsequent proceedings before the VAT Tribunal.

5–111   Tax due from any person is recoverable as a debt due to the Crown.[26] In any proceedings brought for its recovery, a certificate of the Commissioners to the effect that a person was or was not registered, that a return was not made, or that tax was not paid, is prima facie evidence of those facts.[27]

Compliance provisions

5–112   In accordance with the recommendations of the Keith Committee on Tax Enforcement Powers, the failure of a taxpayer (otherwise than fraudulently)[28] to comply with the requirements of the V.A.T.A. 1983 has ceased to be a criminal offence. Instead, a range of penalties has been introduced by the Finance Act 1985 to encourage taxable persons carry out their statutory obligations, to make proper returns and promptly to pay tax due. These provisions are of extreme complexity and the description below does little more than outline the main features of the scheme.

Penalties

1. *Dishonesty*[28a] A person guilty of dishonest conduct for the purpose of evading VAT is to be liable to a penalty equal to the tax which he has sought to evade or the amount of an unwarranted refund which he has dishonestly claimed. Section 13(4) offers the dishonest taxpayer an incentive

---

24. *S. J. Grange Ltd.* v. *Commissioners* [1979] 1 W.L.R. 239; [1979] S.T.C. 183.
25. F.A. 1985, s.22.
26. Sched. 7, para. 6.
27. Sched. 7, para. 11.
28. See § 35–117 in relation to the criminal offence of the fraudulent evasion of VAT.
28a. F.A. 1985, s.13, effective from July 25, 1985.

to cooperate—if he does so, the penalty will be reduced to half that which would otherwise have been imposed.

2. *Breach of registration requirements*[28b] Where a person fails to comply with a requirement that he notify the Commissioners of his liability to register under V.A.T.A. 1983, Sched. 1, or where an unregistered person issues a tax invoice, a penalty is imposed equal to 30 per cent. of the "relevant tax" or, if greater, £50. The "relevant tax" is the VAT for which he is liable in the periods in which he should have been registered or the VAT which was charged in the improper invoices. No penalty will be imposed if the taxpayer can demonstrate a "reasonable excuse."

3. *Breach of regulatory provisions*[28c] Fixed monetary penalties are prescribed where a taxable person fails to notify the Commissioners of his ceasing to make taxable supplies (see § 35–16) or to comply with the requirements relating to the keeping and preservation of records (see § 35–109) or *any* rule or regulation in subordinate legislation made under the Act *other* than the procedural rules relating to appeals to VAT Tribunals (§ 35–121). Again, a taxpayer who has a reasonable excuse is excepted from liability to the penalty.

The default surcharge[28d]

A "surcharge" is payable by a taxable person who fails to make a return, or promptly to pay the tax due under a return, during a period in which he is subject to a "surcharge liability notice." Such a notice will be served on a taxpayer who has been in default (by failing to make returns, etc.) for two prescribed accounting periods ending within a year of one another. The surcharge period then runs from the date on which the notice is served until the anniversary of the end of the second prescribed accounting period in which he was in default; further occasions of default during the currency of the notice will, though, cause its extension. Since the surcharge payable depends on the number of accounting periods in which the taxable person has been in default during the surcharge period, this has the supplementary effect of increasing his potential liability.

A "reasonable excuse" defence exists to the surcharge—if the taxable person can demonstrate that the return or the tax in question was sent at a time such that it was reasonable to expect the Commissioners to receive it within the prescribed time limits, or that there was reasonable excuse for failing to do so, the default will be ignored for the purposes of section 19.[28e]

28b. F.A. 1985, s.15, effective from July 25, 1985. For an example of the operation of the section, see *L. R. Rhodes* v. *Commrs.* [1986] V.A.T.T.R. 72.

28c. F.A. 1985, s.17, effective from July 25, 1985.

28d. F.A. 1985, s.19, effective from October 1, 1986.

28e. It is a matter of no little interest how the decision in *Aikman* v. *White* [1986] S.T.C. 1 will affect the operation of this provision.

Example

   X is in default in respect of a period ending on March 30, 1987 and again in respect of a period ending on December 31 in that year. The Commissioners are entitled to serve a surcharge liability notice on him. This they do on February 2, 1988. X's surcharge period runs from that date until December 31, 1988. If, during that period, he fails to make returns on time or to pay tax promptly, he will be liable to a surcharge as specified by section 19(4). Thus, if X fails to make his return for the period to September 30, 1988, by October 31 he will (subject to the due diligence exception) be liable to a surcharge of the greater of £30 and 5 per cent. of the tax outstanding for that period, *and,* under section 19(3), the Commissioners will be entitled to extend the surcharge period to September 30, 1989. Any further default during the period will be met with an increased surcharge and a further prolongation of the period, until a year has elapsed during which he has not been in default.

Security

35–113   The Commissioners have power to require a taxable person, as a condition of his supplying goods or services under a taxable supply (and, thus, at all) to give security for the payment of any tax which may become due from him.[29] Furthermore when making a repayment of or allowance for any input tax to any person they may require him to produce such documents relating to the tax as may have been supplied to him and, if they think it necessary for the protection of the revenue, the giving of such security for the amount of the payment as may appear appropriate.[30] It is thought that these powers are only used in cases involving an exceptional repayment of input tax. The security required is a bond.

   An apparent "time-trap" exists where a taxpayer wishes to appeal against a direction of the Commissioners that he give security within a specified period—usually of 30 days—since his appeal will not be heard before the date by which he is obliged to obey the direction. In such a case, the taxpayer should make an application under rule 19(1) of the VAT Tribunal Rules 1986 requesting the extension of the period for compliance with the Commissioners' notice.[30a]

Information

35–114   The Commissioners have power to require taxable persons to furnish them with information and to produce documents[31] relating to supplies made or the goods supplied. The information relating to the supply of services which a taxable person can be required to disclose is limited, however, to that relating to the consideration for the supply and the name and address of the person to whom it is made.[32] Thus a professional man cannot be required to disclose confidential information.

---

29. Sched. 7, para. 5(2). See *Power Rod (U.K.) Ltd.* v. *Commissioners* [1983] V.A.T.T.R. 334 for a case where the Commissioners properly exercised this power.
30. Sched. 7, para. 5(1).
30a. *Gayton House Holdings Ltd.* [1984] V.A.T.T.R. 111.
31. Sched. 7, para. 8.
32. Sched. 7, para. 8(3).

35–115   Power also exists to take samples with a view to determining how the goods or materials from which they are derived ought to be or have been treated for the purposes of VAT.[33]

Entry and search

35–116   There are wide powers of entry to business premises for persons acting under the authority of the Commissioners[34] so that a series of spot checks can be instituted. If there are reasonable grounds to suspect that an offence in connection with the tax has been committed a magistrate may issue a warrant authorising the entry and search of premises; a person acting under that warrant may seize and remove any documents or other things found on the premises reasonably required for evidence, and may search any person found there whom he reasonably believes is in possession of such documents.[35]

Offences

35–117   The fraudulent evasion of the tax is a criminal offence subject to a penalty of £1,000 or three times the amount of the tax, whichever is the greater, or imprisonment for a term not exceeding seven years, or both.[36] There are similar penalties for false statements or the use of documents which are false in a material particular.[37] When a person's conduct *must have* involved the commission by him of one or more of these offences then, whether or not the particulars of the offence are known, he is guilty of the offence and subject to the usual penalties.[38] The purpose of this latter provision is presumably to place the burden of proving matters peculiarly within his own knowledge on the taxable person. The safeguard is that the Court must be satisfied that he *must* have committed an offence.

Appeals

35–118   Owing to the peculiar nature of VAT—in particular, the fact that it will generally be beneficial for a person to be registered as a taxable person— the occasions when a taxpayer may feel aggrieved by a decision of the Commissioners will be far more numerous than simply those when an assessment has been issued. Section 40 accordingly provides a long list of matters against a decision of the Commissioners on which the taxpayer may appeal to the Value Added Tax Tribunal, the principal categories of which are as follows:

    (a) registration and deregistration;
    (b) the tax payable on a supply or importation;

---

33. Sched. 7, para. 9.
34. Sched. 7, para. 10.
35. Sched. 7, para. 10(3).
36. s.39(1).
37. s.39(2).
38. s.39(3). On the framing of indictments under the subsection, see *R.* v. *Asif* [1985] S.T.I. 317.

(c) the amount of input tax in respect of which a taxable person is entitled to credit;

(d) the availability of refunds;

(e) assessments;

(f) the imposition of penalties and surcharges under the Finance Act 1985.

Rules exist[38a] enabling the Commissions and a taxable person to settle VAT appeals by agreement.

5–119   There are, however, decisions of the Commissioners over which the VAT Tribunal has only limited jurisdiction. Matters which are within the discretion of the Commissioners were, originally, considered to be wholly outside the competence of the Tribunal.[39] Jurisdiction in such matters has, though, now been granted by section 40(6)[40] so that the Tribunal will interfere with the exercise of a discretion by the Commissioners if, but only if: " . . . the appellate tribunal reaches the clear conclusion that there has been a wrongful exercise of discretion, in that no weight, or no sufficient weight, has been given to relevant considerations."[41] In other words, if the Commissioners have exercised their discretion in a way in which no reasonable panel of Commissioners could have acted.

5–120   Before an appeal can be entertained by the Tribunal, however, the appellant is required to have made all the returns which he should have made—even if those returns would be nil returns. If the returns, when made, show that he is liable to account to the Commissioners for VAT, that tax *must* be paid before his case can be heard: furthermore, unless the appellant can satisfy the Commissioners or the Tribunal that he would otherwise suffer hardship, he must also pay any tax which is in dispute.

5–121   The procedural rules relating to the manner and time in which appeals are to be brought and to the conduct of the appeal are contained in subordinate legislation.[42] Under those rules, an appeal must be brought by serving notice at the appropriate Tribunal centre before the expiry of 30 days after the *date of the letter* containing the disputed decision of the Commissioners.[43] The Commissioners may, however, notify the taxpayer in writing that his time for appeal should continue while further negotiations take place: in order to set time running again, the Commissioners will send a further letter stating that 21 days after its date the time for appealing will expire. A certain amount of leniency is displayed by the Tribunal in these

38a. F.A. 1985, s.25. See § 17–15 for a discussion of the income tax rules of which the section is almost an exact replica.

39. *Commissioners* v. *J. H. Corbitt (Numismatists) Ltd*. [1981] A.C. 22; [1980] S.T.C. 231.

40. *Pinetree Housing Association Ltd*. v. *Commissioners* [1983] V.A.T.T.R. 227; *Blue Boar Property etc., Ltd*. v. *Commissioners* [1984] V.A.T.T.R. 12.

41. *Charles Osenton & Co*. v. *Johnston* [1942] A.C. 130 at p. 138.

42. See VAT Tribunal Rules 1986; V.A.T.A. 1983, Sched. 8, para. 9. The 1986 Rules replace the 1972 rules with effect from July 1, 1986.

43. VAT Tribunal Rules 1986, r. 4.

matters which has power to extend any time limit relating to an appeal of its own volition.[44]

35–122   Generally, the hearing of the appeal will be in public, although the Tribunal may accede to the request of a party thereto that it be heard in private.[45] There is no restriction on the person who may present the case— each party may appoint whomsoever he wishes.[46] If a party fails to appear at the hearing the Tribunal may dismiss the appeal or the application—the offending party has 14 days from the decision of the Tribunal being drawn up, however, to apply for the hearing to be reinstated, which the Tribunal may do on whatever terms it considers to be just.[47] At the end of an appeal, the Tribunal has power to award costs[48]: although these will generally follow the event, it is the practice of the Commissioners not to seek an award in their favour save in appeals against penalties and in exceptional cases of vexatious litigants.[48a]

35–123   Appeals from the VAT Tribunal are made to the Divisional Court of the Queens Bench Division of the High Court. Such appeals are limited, however, to points of law.[49]

---

44. And see *Commissioners* v. *Holvey* [1978] Q.B. 310 where Pain J. expressed disquiet about the shortness of the period given for appealing.

45. VAT Tribunal Rules 1986, r. 24.

46. *Ibid*. r. 25.

47. *Ibid*. r. 26.

48. *Ibid*. r. 29. On the award of interest see *R. Porter* v. *Commissioners* [1985] V.A.T.T.R. 255.

48a. See the statement of practice, [1986] S.T.I. 574 and *Wimpey Group Services Ltd.* v. *Commissioners* [1984] V.A.T.T.R. 66.

49. Tribunals and Inquiries Act 1971, s.13 as made applicable to VAT by the Tribunals and Inquiries (VAT Tribunal) Rules 1972. The Commissioners will, it should be noted, seek costs if successful in the High Court.

PART 5

TAX PLANNING

"It may seem hard that a cunningly advised taxpayer should be able to avoid what appears to be his equitable share of the general fiscal burden and cast it on the shoulders of his fellow citizens. But for the Courts to try to stretch the law to meet hard cases (whether the hardship appears to bear on the individual taxpayer or on the general body of taxpayers as represented by the Inland Revenue) is not merely to make bad law but to run the risk of subverting the rule of law itself. Disagreeable as it may seem that some taxpayers should escape what might appear to be their fair share of the general burden of national expenditure, it would be far more disagreeable to substitute the rule of caprice for that of law. The most famous warning in the history of our fiscal law is constituted by *The Case of Ship Money* (1637) 3 St. Tr. 825. It could be strongly argued that it was contrary to fiscal equity that the financial burden of providing warships (or their money equivalent) for the defence of the whole realm should fall exclusively on the inhabitants of maritime towns and districts, to the exoneration of inland citizens: yet such, it seems, was the law of the land; and the Judges who appear to have stretched the law have not escaped the censure of history. So I think that counsel for the taxpayers was justified, when frankly admitting that your Lordships were concerned with unmeritorious tax avoidance schemes, in drawing attention to *Commissioners of Inland Revenue* v. *Duke of Westminster* [1936] A.C. 1. There Lord Tomlin, at page 19, cited Coke (4 Inst. 41) on the danger of "substituting 'the incertain and crooked cord of discretion' for 'the golden and streight metwand of the law.' " And Lord Russell of Killowen, at page 24, cited Lord Cairns in *Partington* v. *Attorney-General* (1869) L.R. 4 H.L. 100, at page 122:

> If the person sought to be taxed comes within the letter of the law he must be taxed, however great the hardship may appear to the judicial mind to be. On the other hand, if the Crown, seeking to recover the tax, cannot bring the subject within the letter of the law, the subject is free, however apparently within the spirit of the law the case might otherwise appear to be'

—although I do not take either great Judge as meaning that the "letter" of the law was to be interpreted in exclusion of the resolutions in *Heydon's Case* (1584) 3 Co. Rep. 7a."

Per Lord Simon of Glaisdale in *Ransom* v. *Higgs* (1974) 50 T.C. 1 at p. 94.

"Under our constitution the imposition of taxation is a matter for Parliament. Indeed within Parliament itself it is a matter in which the House of Commons has a predominant role. The only function of the courts in this sphere is to interpret and apply the legislation enacted by Parliament in accordance with relevant legal principles. Among the relevant legal principles is the principle that the courts are bound to seek to ascertain the true nature of a transaction and to give effect to it. That, to my mind, is the real basis of the *Ramsay* principle. (I choose the phrase 'true nature', but other expressions such as 'reality' or 'substance'—in the sense in which I understand the latter term to have been used by Lord Bridge in *Furniss* v. *Dawson*—will do just as well)."

Per Warner J. in *I.R.C.* v. *Bowater Property Development* (1985) S.T.C. at p. 798.

Chapter 36

Introduction

1. Introduction

36–01 THE first four parts of this book have been devoted to a statement of the fundamental principles of income and capital gains taxation, inheritance tax, value added tax and stamp duties. In the part that follows some aspects of these subjects are considered in relation to problems of tax planning. The words "tax" and "taxation" are used in this part of the book to refer to all forms of taxation.

36–02 Tax planning means arranging a client's affairs so that no more tax is payable than is necessary. The need for tax planning arises because, in both family and business life, there is often more than one method of achieving the same end-result; and "tax planning" describes the technique of selecting the method which is least costly in tax. Inevitably tax planning involves "tax avoidance" in the sense that less tax is payable than would have been payable without the planning; but tax avoidance of this kind is not only unobjectionable: it is commonsense. Indeed, most individuals embark on an exercise in tax planning at some stage in their lives. This arises on the purchase of a house, the provision of life assurance for dependants, and the making of a will. Separation and divorce often demand a substantial exercise in tax planning.

36–03 A father, with a high income, may wish to make an allowance to his unmarried son, aged 18, who has no income. He can make a voluntary allowance; alternatively, he can covenant by deed to make the allowance. In the first case the father gets no tax relief on the payments he makes but the son pays no tax, since a voluntary allowance is not "income." In the second case the father gets relief from tax at the basic rate (but not at the higher rates), provided the covenant is to run for a period which might exceed six years and is irrevocable; the son has a taxable income (and will suffer basic rate income tax by deduction: see § 5–30) but will be able to reclaim from the Revenue so much of the tax suffered by deduction as exceeds his true liability, taking into account the single person's allowance.

> Thus in 1986–87 a son (with no other income) who was paid £2,600 under an appropriately drafted deed of covenant, and who suffered tax at the basic rate of 29 per cent. on this amount by way of deduction, would be able to reclaim an amount equal to 29 per cent. of £2,335 (the single person's allowance), *i.e.* £677.15. There will be an overall saving or "avoidance" of tax resulting from the father's alienation of income to his son.

36–04 This example shows that "tax avoidance" may be no more than the result of choosing one of two equally acceptable methods of achieving a desired result. In the world of commerce, where transactions are much more complex, the range of alternative methods is much wider.

36–05   Tax planning is an important function, for the burden of tax is nowadays so great that taxation must be regarded as one of the major costs of production; and enterprising and productive schemes are often made possible only by intelligent tax planning. In other cases legislation is so hasty and ill-conceived, essential reforms are so long delayed,[1] or the consequences of legislation (unforeseen by legislators) are so immoral that taxpayers have to rely on the concoction of "schemes" to avoid what would otherwise be a manifestly unjust or even absurd result. The comments of Lord Reid[2] can often be made of sections of Finance Acts:

> "I have suggested what may be a possible meaning but if I am wrong about that I would not shrink from holding that the sub-section is so obscure that no meaning can be given to it. I would rather do that than seek by twisting and contorting the words to give to the sub-section an improbable meaning. Draftsmen as well as Homer can nod, and Parliament is so accustomed to obscure drafting in Finance Bills that no one may have noticed the defects in this sub-section."

36–06   It is often said that recent decisions of the Courts—notably the decisions of the House of Lords in the *Ramsay* and *Dawson* cases—have removed the possibility of tax planning, because planning implies "avoidance" and any steps taken with avoidance in mind can now be treated as a fiscal nullity. This is wrong, as will be seen from the later pages of this chapter. Tax planning is alive and well and will remain so, so long as taxpayers enjoy freedom of choice as to the way in which they conduct their business, family and other transactions, including *e.g.* charitable giving.

2. Basic Rules

36–07   All forms of taxation are imposed by Parliament: there is no rule of common law or of equity which makes a person liable to tax. "Tax is the creature of statute." The function of the court in relation to all statutes is to interpret their meaning and "the fundamental rule of interpretation to which all others are subordinate is that a statute is to be expounded according to the intent of them that made it."[3] This intention must be discovered from the actual words used in the statute, taking the statute as a whole and the words in the context in which they appear[4]; and in this respect no distinction is made between taxing statutes and other statutes. The court will not allow speeches made during the course of parliamentary debates, reports of Royal Commissions or official circulars to be admitted in evi-

---

1. Tax avoidance implies the receipt of something in one form in preference to another. To say that a non-smoker "avoids" tax by not smoking or that a person "avoids" an accident when he stands in a road in which there is no traffic is to use the word in a different sense. See the discussion on "tax advantage" in § 40–10.

2. Consider, *e.g.* I.C.T.A. 1970, s.451 (see *ante*, §§ 10–30 *et seq.*), and the remarks of Lord MacDermott in *Potts' Executors* v. *I.R.C.* [1951] A.C. 443 at p. 466; 32 T.C. 211 at p. 236; see also *I.R.C.* v. *De Vigier* (1964) 42 T.C. 25 (H.L.); *Bates* v. *I.R.C.* [1968] A.C. 483; 44 T.C. 225 (H.L.). No attempt was made to remedy the defects of s.451 until F.A. 1981.

2a. *Associate Newspapers Group Ltd.* v. *Fleming* (1972) 48 T.C. 382 at p. 406C.

3. Maxwell, *The Interpretation of Statutes* (11th ed.), p. 1.

4. *Colquhoun* v. *Brooks* (1889) 14 App.Cas. 493; 2 T.C. 490; *I.R.C.* v. *Wesleyan and General Assurance Society* (1948) 30 T.C. 11, *per* Lord Greene M.R. at p. 16; *Mangin* v. *I.R.C.* [1971] A.C. 739 *per* Lord Donovan at p. 746.

dence as an aid to interpretation.[5] The purpose of a statutory provision must be found in the terms of the statute itself. Furthermore, where the words are clear, the court must give effect to them, however inconvenient or undesirable the result may be.[6] Where an Act of Parliament contains a provision which imposes a charge to tax (called a "charging section"), the section will be strictly construed in the sense that the taxpayer will be given the benefit of any doubt as to the scope of the charge: clear words must be used to create a liability to tax.[7] This emphasis on the letter of the law was explained by Rowlatt J. as follows:

> "In a taxing Act one has to look merely at what is clearly said. There is no room for any intendment. There is no equity about a tax. There is no presumption as to a tax. Nothing is to be read in, nothing is to be implied. One can only look fairly at the language used."[8]

Lord Cairns stated the rules as follows:

> "If the person sought to be taxed comes within the letter of the law he must be taxed, however great the hardship may appear to the judicial mind to be. On the other hand, if the Crown, seeking to recover the tax, cannot bring the subject within the letter of the law, the subject is free, however apparently within the spirit of the law the case might otherwise appear to be."[9]

In *Hochstrasser* v. *Mayes* Viscount Simonds said[10]:

> "It is for the Crown, seeking to tax the subject, to prove that the tax is exigible, not for the subject to prove that his case falls within exceptions which are not expressed in the Statute but arbitrarily inferred from it."

3. THE WESTMINSTER DOCTRINE

36–08 Before a statute can be applied in relation to any given transaction, the first step is to ascertain the effect of the transaction as between the parties, that is, the rights and obligations created by the transaction must be determined in accordance with general principles of law. An important case which illustrates this point in the field of revenue law is *I.R.C.* v. *Duke of Westminster*,[11] where the facts were as follows:

> Deeds of covenant were executed by the Duke in favour of employees. The deed in each case provided that the payments were to be without prejudice to any claim for remuneration to which the employee might thereafter be entitled but it was understood by the employee that he was not expected to make any such claim so long as the amount received under the covenant and any other payments he received equalled his current salary.

---

5. *Assam Railways and Trading Co.* v. *I.R.C.* [1935] A.C. 445; but see *Escoigne Properties Ltd.* v. *I.R.C.* [1958] A.C. 549, *per* Lord Denning at p. 566.

6. *Re Robb's Contract* [1941] Ch. 463 (C.A.). This decision was nullified by F.A. 1942, s.44, which amended F. (1909–10) A. 1910, s.74(6).

7. *Russell* v. *Scott* [1948] A.C. 422 at p. 433; 30 T.C. 375 at p. 424, *per* Lord Simon.

8. *Cape Brandy Syndicate* v. *I.R.C.* [1921] 1 K.B. 64 at p. 71; 12 T.C. 358 at p. 366. But see *Bennion on Statutory Interpretation* at pp. 242 and 621.

9. *Partington* v. *Att.-Gen.* (1869) L.R. 4 H.L. 100 at p. 122.

10. (1959) 38 T.C. 673 at p. 706. See also *I.R.C.* v. *Reinhold* (1953) T.C. 389 and Russell L.J. in *Re Rallis Settlement* [1965] Ch. 286 at p. 327 (C.A.).

11. [1936] A.C. 1; 19 T.C. 490. For reaffirmations of the principle in this case, see *I.R.C.* v. *Europa Oil (N.Z.) Ltd.* [1971] A.C. 760, *per* Lord Wilberforce at p. 771; *Ramsay* v. *I.R.C.* (1981) 54 T.C. 101 at p. 185A, *per* Lord Wilberforce.

The Revenue contended that although the transaction was in the *form* of the grant of an annuity or annual payment, in *substance* the transaction was an agreement by the employee to continue in service at his normal salary and should be treated as such for tax purposes. This contention was rejected by the Court of Appeal and the House of Lords. Lord Tomlin stated the position as follows[12]:

> " . . . it is said that in revenue cases there is a doctrine that the court may ignore the legal position and regard what is called 'the substance of the matter,' and that here the substance of the matter is that the annuitant was serving the Duke for something equal to his former salary or wages, and that therefore, while he is so serving, the annuity must be treated as salary or wages. This supposed doctrine . . . seems to rest for its support upon a misunderstanding of language used in some earlier cases. The sooner this misunderstanding is dispelled and the supposed doctrine given its quietus, the better it will be for all concerned . . . Every man is entitled if he can to order his affairs so that the tax attaching under the appropriate Acts is less than it otherwise would be. If he succeeds in ordering them so as to secure this result, then, however unappreciative the Commissioners of Inland Revenue or his fellow taxpayers may be of his ingenuity, he cannot be compelled to pay an increase in tax. This so-called doctrine of the 'substance' seems to me to be nothing more than an attempt to make a man pay notwithstanding that he has so ordered his affairs that the amount of tax sought from him is not legally claimable."

Lord Russell of Killowen said this[13]:

> "If all that is meant by the doctrine is that having once ascertained the legal rights of the parties you may disregard mere nomenclature and decide the question of taxability or non-taxability in accordance with the legal rights, well and good. . . . If, on the other hand, the doctrine means that you may brush aside deeds, disregard the legal rights and liabilities arising under a contract between parties, and decide the question of taxability or non-taxability upon the footing of the rights and liabilities of the parties being different from what in law they are, then I entirely dissent from such a doctrine."

The language used by the parties to a transaction is not conclusive as to the nature of their legal relationship.[14] On the other hand, the nature of the transaction may be determined by the form selected by the parties[15] or even by the stamp which an instrument bears.[16]

Sham transactions

36–09   In the *Westminster*[16a] case Lord Tomlin said "the substance is that which results from the legal rights and obligations of the parties ascertained upon ordinary legal principles"—hence the form of the transaction as revealed by the documents determines its substance; but he added:

> "There may, of course, be cases where documents are not bona fide nor

---

12. [1936] A.C. 1 at pp. 19–20; 19 T.C. 490 at p. 520 and see § 36–43.
13. *Ibid.* at pp. 25 and 524, respectively.
14. *I.R.C.* v. *Wesleyan and General Assurance Society* [1948] 1 All E.R. 555 at p. 557; 30 T.C. 11 at p. 24 (H.L.), *per* Viscount Simon.
15. *Ruskin Investments* v. *Copeman* [1943] 1 All E.R. 378.
16. *Re McArdle* [1951] Ch. 669.
16a. [1936] A.C.1; 19 T.C. 490.

intended to be acted upon but are only used as a cloak to conceal a different transaction. No such case is made or even suggested here."

The nature of a "sham" was considered by Diplock L.J. in *Snook* v. *London & West Riding Investments Limited*[17] where he said—

"it means acts done or documents executed by the parties to the sham which are intended by them to give to third parties or to the Court the appearance of creating between the parties legal rights and obligations different from the actual legal rights and obligations (if any) which the parties intend to create. But one thing, I think, is clear in legal principle, morality and the authorities . . . that for acts or documents to be a 'sham,' with whatever legal consequences flow from this, all the parties thereto must have a common intention that the acts or documents are not to create the legal rights and obligations which they give the appearance of creating."

The question whether a document or transaction is a "sham" in this sense is substantially a question of fact for the Commissioners.[18] The court will disregard, *i.e.* refuse to give effect to, a document or transaction which is a sham.[19] A sham transaction is inherently worthless and needs no statute to nullify it.

4. THE RAMSAY AND BURMAH CASES

The Ramsay case

36–10   In the *Westminster* case there was one transaction only, namely, the grant of an annuity; and the issue was whether the annuity could be treated as salary or wages: see § 36–08. The House of Lords has recently[20] considered the scope of the *Westminster* doctrine in relation to composite transactions in the form of complex "schemes" designed to produce an "allowable loss" of an amount specified by the purchaser of the scheme, for offset against chargeable gains of a similar amount. The details of the scheme employed in the *Ramsay* case are unimportant but Lord Wilberforce described the scheme as follows[21]:

"The scheme consists, as do others which have come to the notice of the courts, of a number of steps to be carried out, documents to be executed, payments to be made, according to a timetable, in each case rapid: see the attract-

---

17. [1967] 2 Q.B. 786 at p. 802 and see the discussion on "artificial" and "fictitious" transactions in *Seramco Trustees* v. *Income Tax Commissioner* [1977] A.C. 287 (J.C.). This definition of "Sham" was approved in *Ramsay Ltd.* v. *I.R.C.* [1982] A.C. 300 at p. 337. See *Sherdley* v. *Sherdley* [1986] S.T.C. 266 (C.A.) where, in a divorce case, a father with custody, care and control of the children applied for an order to be made against himself for periodical payments to be made to the children and it was said that this would amount to a sham. See also *Ingram* v. *I.R.C.* [1985] S.T.C. at pp. 843–844 where Vinelott J. discusses a conclusion of the commissioners in a stamp duty case that a lease agreement which the parties intended should never proceed to completion was a "sham."

18. See, *e.g. I.R.C.* v. *Garvin* (1981) 55 T.C. 24 at 62 A–E; [1980] S.T.C. 295 at p. 300.

19. See *Napier* v. *National Business Agency* [1951] 2 All E.R. 284; 30 A.T.C. 181; *Gray* v. *Lewis* [1982] A.C. 300; (1873) 8 Ch.App. 1035.

20. *W. T. Ramsay Ltd.* v. *I.R.C.* ("the *Ramsay* case") [1982] A.C. 300; (1981) 54 T.C. 101; *Eilbeck* v. *Rawling* (1981) 54 T.C. 101; [1981] S.T.C. 174 (H.L.); *I.R.C.* v. *Burmah Oil Company Ltd.* (1981) 54 T.C. 200; [1982] S.T.C. 30 (H.L.) *Furniss* v. *Dawson* [1984] A.C. 474; [1984] S.T.C. 153 (H.L.).

21. (1981) 54 T.C. 101 at p. 183G.

ive description by Lord Justice Buckley in *Rawling*.[22] In each case two assets appear, like particles in a gas chamber[23] with opposite charges, one of which is used to create the loss, the other of which gives rise to an equivalent gain which prevents the taxpayer from supporting any real loss, and which gain is intended not to be taxable. Like the particles, these assets have a very short life. Having served their purpose they cancel each other out and disappear. At the end of the series of operations, the taxpayer's financial position is precisely as it was at the beginning, except that he has paid a fee, and certain expenses, to the promoter of the scheme."

36–11 The *Westminster* principle, said Lord Wilberforce[24]

" . . . is a cardinal principle, but it must not be overstated or overextended. While obliging the court to accept documents or transactions, found to be genuine, as such, it does not compel the court to look at a document or a transaction in blinkers, isolated from any context to which it properly belongs. If it can be seen that a document or transaction was intended to have effect as part of a nexus or series of transactions, or as an ingredient of a wider transaction intended as a whole, there is nothing in the doctrine to prevent it being so regarded: to do so is not to prefer form to substance, or substance to form. It is the task of the court to ascertain the legal nature of any transaction to which it is sought to attach a tax or a tax consequence and if that emerges from a series or combination of transactions, intended to operate as such, it is that series or combination which may be regarded. For this there is authority in the law relating to income tax and capital gains tax—see *Chinn* v. *Hochstrasser*[25]: *I.R.C.* v. *Plummer*.[26]

For the commissioners considering a particular case it is wrong, and an unnecessary self limitation, to regard themselves as precluded by their own finding that documents or transactions are not 'shams', from considering what, as evidenced by the documents themselves or by the manifested intentions of the parties, *the relevant transaction is*. They are not, under the *Westminster* doctrine or any other authority, bound to consider individually each separate step in a composite transaction intended to be carried through as a whole. This is particularly the case where (as in *Rawling*) it is proved that there was an accepted obligation once a scheme is set in motion, to carry it through its successive steps. It may be so where (as in *Ramsay* or in *Black Nominees Limited* v. *Nichol*) there is an expectation that it will be so carried through and no likelihood in practice that it will not. In such cases (which may vary in emphasis) the commissioners should find the facts and then decide as a matter (reviewable) of law whether what is in issue is a composite transaction, or a number of independent transactions."

36–12 A key feature of the schemes discussed in the *Ramsay* case is succinctly expressed in two sentences from the speeches of Lord Wilberforce and Lord Fraser:

"At the end of the series of operations, the taxpayer's financial position is precisely as it was at the beginning, except that he has paid a fee, and certain expenses, to the promoter of the scheme" (Lord Wilberforce).
"The essential feature of both schemes was that, when they were completely

---

22. (1981) 54 T.C. 101 at p. 157; [1980] S.T.C. 192.
23. The better view is that particles do not interact in the manner described except in a *vacuum* chamber.
24. (1981) 54 T.C. 101 at p. 185 A–F.
25. [1981] A.C. 533; 54 T.C. 311 (H.L.).
26. [1980] A.C. 896; 54 T.C. 1 (H.L.).

carried out, they did not result in any actual loss to the taxpayer" (Lord Fraser).

The schemes were thus "self-cancelling." Furthermore, there was no third person whose tax position was affected by the operations. They were "off-the-peg" tax avoidance schemes with no enduring legal consequences.

The Burmah case

36–13   The *Burmah* case,[27] like the *Ramsay*[28] case, concerned the "manufacture" of an allowable loss, but differed because the "scheme" was evolved within the group and not bought "off-the-peg" from a "tax house." The facts, briefly expressed, were as follows:

> Burmah Oil (P) had two subsidiary companies, S1 and S2. In 1968 P sold certain stock in British Petroleum (BP) to S1, the purchase price being left outstanding. In 1971, for good commercial reasons, and when the value of the stock had fallen by £160 million, S1 sold the BP stock back to P. S1 realised a loss of about £160m. on this transaction, which was its only business transaction. At this stage S1 owed P £160m. and was insolvent to this extent. P was thus in the situation of having a bad debt of £160m. which, not being a debt on a security (see § 16–14), was not an "allowable loss" for the purposes of capital gains tax.
>
> In 1971 P put in effect the following scheme which was designed to transmute its loss on its investment in S1 into an "allowable loss". The steps in the scheme were planned to take place according to a pre-set timetable; draft minutes and letters were prepared in advance; and it was clear that the scheme, once started, would proceed to completion.
>
> *Step 1*: P made a loan of £160m. to S2 which S2 loaned to S1. S1 repaid P. Thus S2 was indebted to P in place of S1.
>
> *Step 2*: S1 had a rights issue of new shares. P subscribed £160m. The subscription moneys were used to repay S2, who repaid P. The rights issue was "geared" to produce the required figure of £160m. After Step 2, S1 was in a position to file a declaration of solvency.
>
> *Step 3*: S1 went into members voluntary liquidation and P claimed that the subscription money of £160m. was part of the cost of acquisition of its shares in S1 and that P realised an "allowable loss" of about 160m.

Lord Fraser, with whom the other Law Lords agreed, formulated the relevant question as follows[29]:

> "The question . . . is whether the present scheme, when completely carried out, did or did not result in a loss such as the legislation is dealing with, which I may call for short, a real loss."

It was held that it did not. The question, so expressed, was the same question as arose in the *Ramsay* case.

36–14   The following points should be noticed in connection with this decision:
1. It was accepted that the loss of £160m. on the purchase and resale of the BP stock was a real loss arising from a transaction which was carried

---

27. (1981) 54 T.C. 200; [1982] S.T.C. 30 (H.L.).
28. (1981) 54 T.C. 101; [1981] S.T.C. 174 (H.L.).
29. (1981) 54 T.C. at 220H; [1982] S.T.C. 30 at p. 38b.

out for good commercial reasons and that the debt of £160m. owed to P was a real debt.

2. Throughout the scheme S retained the BP stock. If it had sold that stock it would have realised an "allowable loss," but the scheme was devised to enable P to incur an allowable loss for the purposes of capital gains tax without actually selling BP stock and without affecting the cost to P of acquiring that stock.

3. The entire scheme was masterminded by P and each of Steps 1 and 2 involved a sum of about £160m. going round in a circle and returning to its source, in each case P. Lord Fraser said this[30]:

> "The result was that although Burmah (P) apparently suffered the loss of almost the whole price that it had paid for the new shares, except for the cash balance returned on liquidation, it suffered no real loss because it got back all the money except the capital duty [on the new shares]. Moreover, it still had the BP shares which it could have realised in the open market at a loss on their original purchase price. If the argument for Burmah is right, this would be one more case in which the taxpayer had achieved the apparently magic result of creating a tax loss that was not a real loss."

4. Although the rights issue was "geared" to produce a loss of £160m. (which was equivalent to the previous loss in value of the BP stock), it could have been geared to produce any other figure.

5. The change in the position of P from creditor to contributor could not affect any third party and could have no enduring effect since the dissolution of S1 was an integral part of the scheme.

36–15 *Ramsay* and *Burmah* are authority for the proposition that there is no legal principle which compels the Court to examine separately each step in a series of operations which are planned in advance and are intended, when embarked upon, to proceed to completion. The Court is not confined to a single-step approach. On the contrary, it is entitled to look at the operations as a whole in deciding the tax consequences of the transactions. Thus in relation to multi-stage schemes designed to create losses, the Court is entitled to ask whether, looking at the steps as a whole, the loss which is said to result to the taxpayer is the kind of loss which is an "allowable loss" for capital gains tax purposes. The *Ramsay* and *Burmah* cases do not decide that the Court should disregard or ignore the steps in a composite transaction; it must be regard all the steps, but as a whole. This approach (said Lord Wilberforce) does not introduce a new principle: it is to apply to new and sophisticated legal devices the undoubted power and duty of the Courts to determine their nature in law and to relate them to existing legislation:

> "To force the Courts to adopt, in relation to closely integrated situations, a step by step, dissecting approach which the parties themselves may have negated, would be a denial rather than an affirmation of the true judicial process. In each case the facts must be established, and a legal analysis made:

---

30. *Ibid.* at p. 28.

legislation cannot be required or even be desirable to enable the court to arrive at a conclusion which corresponds with the parties' own intentions."[31]

Hence in the *Burmah* case Lord Fraser said[32] the *ratio* of the decision in *Ramsay* was to be found in the following words of Lord Wilberforce:

"The capital gains tax was created to operate in the real world, not that of make-belief. As I said in *Aberdeen Construction Group Ltd.* v. *I.R.C.* it is a tax in gains (or I might have added gains less losses), it is not a tax on arithmetical differences. To say that a loss (or gain) which appears to arise at one stage in an indivisible process, and which is intended to be cancelled out by a later stage, so that at the end of what was brought as, and planned as, a single continuous operation, is not such a loss (or gain) as the legislation is dealing with, is in my opinion, well and indeed essentially within the judicial function."

36–16   Lord Diplock said in the *Burmah* case[33]:

"It would be disingenuous to suggest, and dangerous on the part of those who advise on elaborate tax avoidance schemes to assume that *Ramsay's* case did not mark a significant change in the approach adopted by this House in its judicial role to a pre-ordained series of transactions (whether or not they include the achievement of a legitimate commercial end) into which there are inserted steps that have no commercial purpose apart from the avoidance of a liability to tax which in the absence of those particular steps would have been payable. The difference is in approach. It does not necessitate the overruling of any earlier decisions of this House; but it does involve recognising that Lord Tomlin's oft quoted dictum in the *Westminster* case 'every man is entitled if he can to order his affairs so as that the tax attaching under the appropriate Acts is less than it otherwise would be', tells us little or nothing as to what methods of ordering one's affairs will be recognised by the Courts as effective to lessen the tax that would attach to them if business transactions were conducted in a straightforward way."

This passage in Lord Diplock's speech heralds what has been called "the new approach" to tax planning. This is further discussed in the later sections of this Chapter: see §§ 36–19 *et seq*.

5. The Dawson Case

36–17   The facts in *Furniss* v. *Dawson*[34] were as follows:

The shareholders in A Limited (members of the Dawson family) received a cash offer for their shares from Wood Bastow and agreed in principle to accept the offer. Chargeable gains would accrue, and an immediate liability to capital gains tax would arise, on a disposal of the shares for cash. In order to defer (but not avoid) this liability the Dawson family shareholders incorporated a company in the Isle of Man (Greenjacket) and exchanged their shares in A Limited for shares in Greenjacket. This was step 1 of the transaction and it was claimed that this was an exchange, exempt from capital gains tax by reason of the roll-over relief given by the Finance Act 1965, Schedule 7, paragraph 6.[35] Greenjacket then sold the shares in A Limited to Wood Bastow an the cash

---

31. (1981) 54 T.C. 101 at 187D; [1981] S.T.C. 174 at p. 182a.
32. (1981) 54 T.C. 200 at p. 220 D-E; [1982] S.T.C. 30 at p. 37h.
33. (1981) 54 T.C. 200 at p. 214 D.
34. [1984] A.C. 474 (C.A. and H.L.); 55 T.C. 324.
35. Now C.G.T.A. 1979 s.85; mentioned *ante*, § 16–13.

proceeds were duly paid to Greenjacket. This was step 2 of the transaction. No chargeable gain accrued on the sale by Greenjacket which occurred immediately after the acquisition from the Dawson family.

It should be noted that there was no evidence that the cash was, *e.g.* loaned by Greenjacket to the Dawson family shareholders or that there was a scheme which included the making of such loans. The case was decided on the basis that the cash was paid to, and remained with, Greenjacket and that Greenjacket was the beneficial owner of it.

36–18   The Special Commissioners found that Greenjacket became the beneficial owner of the shares in A Limited on completion of the exchange agreement and that step 1 qualified for roll-over relief. The Special Commissioners also found that Greenjacket was not contractually bound to sell the shares in A Limited to Wood Bastow. The Crown failed before the Special Commissioners.

After the Special Commissioners gave their decision, the *Ramsay* case (see § 36–10) was decided in the House of Lords and the Crown announced[36] that it would contend that the Dawson family disposed of their shares to Wood Bastow and that the intermediate disposal to Greenjacket should be disregarded. The *Burmah* case (see § 36–13) was then heard in the House of Lords and Vinelott J. deferred giving his decision in the *Dawson* case until after the judgments in the *Burmah* case had been delivered.

36–19   The question for Vinelott J. was how far the "new approach" referred to by Lord Diplock in the *Burmah* case (see § 36–16) justified the Crown's submission. After a careful review of the authorities (including the dissenting judgment in *Floor* v. *Davis*: see § 16–07B) the judge fastened on the important point that the transaction in the *Dawson* case had enduring legal consequences in a way that the circular self-cancelling transactions in the other case did not. The *Westminster* doctrine required that those consequences should not be disregarded. Even if the two stages in the transaction in *Dawson* were treated as parts of a single composite transaction, there were enduring legal consequences which could not be ignored: Greenjacket existed; it became the beneficial owner first of the shares in A Limited and then of the proceeds of sale; and the Dawson family and continued to be shareholders in Greenjacket:

> "The Court cannot . . . ignore those enduring consequences and either disregard the exchange agreement or treat the sale agreement as if it had been entered into by Greenjacket as nominee or agent for the Dawson family shareholders. To do so would be to divorce the facts existing in the real world and to substitute for them facts assumed to exist in an unreal fiscal world. That, it seems to me, is precisely what the Court is forbidden by the decision in the *Westminster* case to do."[37]

---

36. The Crown served a notice under R.S.C., Ord. 91, r.4: see [1984] A.C. 474 at p. 524B. Note that the notice was served *after* the Commissioners had made their findings of fact.
37. (1984) 55 T.C. 324 at p. 347 H.

36–20   The Court of Appeal (affirming the decision of Vinelott J.) said the
transactions involved two disposals—the one to, and the other by, Greenjacket; and there was nothing in the *Ramsay* case which compelled the
court to treat the two disposals as if they were once.

36–21   The House of Lords unanimously allowed the Crown's appeal. Lord
Brightman (with whose speech Lord Fraser and Lord Roskill entirely
agreed) said the following[38]:

> "My Lords, in my opinion the rationale of the new approach is this. In a pre-
> planned tax-saving scheme, no distinction is to be drawn for fiscal purposes,
> because none exists in reality, between (i) a series of steps which are followed
> through by virtue of an arrangement which falls short of a binding contract, and
> (ii) a like series of steps which are followed through because the participants are
> contractually bound to take each step seriatim. In a contractual case the fiscal
> consequences will naturally fall to be assessed in the light of the contractually
> agreed results. For example, equitable interests may pass when the contract for
> sale is signed. In many cases equity will regard that as done which is contracted to
> be done. *Ramsay* says that the fiscal result is to be no different if the several steps
> are pre-ordained rather than pre-contracted. For example, in the instant case tax
> will, on the *Ramsay* principle, fall to be assessed on the basis that there was a
> tripartite contract between the Dawsons, Greenjacket and Wood Bastow under
> which the Dawsons contracted to transfer their shares in the operating com-
> panies to Greenjacket in return for an allotment of shares in Greenjacket, and
> under which Greenjacket simultaneously contracted to transfer the same shares
> to Wood Barstow for a sum in cash. Under such a tripartite contract the Dawsons
> would clearly have disposed of the shares in the operating companies in favour of
> Wood Bastow in consideration of a sum of money paid by Wood Bastow with the
> concurrence of the Dawsons to Greenjacket. Tax would be assessed, and the
> base value of the Greenjacket shares calculated, accordingly. *Ramsay* says that
> this fiscal result cannot be avoided because the preordained series of steps are to
> be found in an informal arrangement instead of in a binding contract. The day is
> not saved for the taxpayer because the arrangement is unsigned or contains the
> words 'this is not a binding contract.'
>
> The formulation by Lord Diplock in *Inland Revenue Commissioners* v. *Bur-
> mah Oil Co. Ltd.* [see, § 36–16] expresses the limitations of the *Ramsay* prin-
> ciple. First, there must be a pre-ordained series of transactions; or, if one likes,
> one single composite transaction. This composite transaction may or may not
> include the achievement of a legitimate commercial (i.e., business) end. The
> composite transaction does, in the instant case; it achieved a sale of the shares
> in the operating companies by the Dawsons to Wood Bastow. It did not in
> *Ramsay*. Secondly, there must be steps inserted which have no commercial
> (business) *purpose* apart from the avoidance of a liability to tax—not 'no busi-
> ness *effect*.' If those two ingredients exist, the inserted steps are to be dis-
> regarded for fiscal purposes. The court must then look at the end result.
> Precisely how the end result will be taxed will depend on the terms of the tax-
> ing statute sought to be applied."

In the second paragraph of this passage, Lord Brightman refers to two limitations or ingredients or "requirements"[38a] that have to be present before
the *Ramsay* principle can be applied. These two requirements are now
examined:

---

38. [1984] A.C. 474 at pp. 526–527; 55 T.C. at p. 400 H.
38a. See *I.R.C.* v. *Bowater Property Developments* [1985] S.T.C. 783 at p. 797; (facts in
§ 36–27).

(1) *A pre-ordained series of transactions*

36–22   *Ramsay* decides that where a document or transaction is intended to have effect as part of a series of transactions, its legal nature and any tax consequences should be determined by looking at the transaction as a whole. *Ramsay* rejects the need for a "step by step" approach. If there is a contract between a number of parties, the fiscal consequences depend on the contractually agreed results; the *Ramsay* principle states that the fiscal result is no different if the several steps are pre-ordained rather than pre-contracted.

The *Ramsay* principle applies only if there is a pre-ordained series of transactions (Lord Brightman) or a composite transaction (Lord Wilberforce) or if the transactions are planned as a single scheme (Lord Fraser). It is thought all these phrases have the same meaning.[39] The *Ramsay* principle does not apply to a number of independent transactions. Nor does it apply to a transaction which does not involve a series of steps, such as a common form deed of covenant (see § 36–40) or the covenant in the *Westminster* case: and in this connection a distinction can be drawn between a series of transactions and a single transaction which (say) involves a series of payments.

36–23   It is for the Commissioners to find the facts and to decide (their decision on this point being reviewable on appeal) if there is a pre-ordained series of transactions.

In *Ewart* v. *Taylor*,[40] Vinelott J. said that:

" . . . in all the cases in which the Crown have succeeded in establishing that a series of transactions should be regarded as steps in a single composite scheme the scheme has been conceived as a single integrated scheme in the sense that the parties entered into it *on the understanding that the scheme would be carried through as a whole or not at all*, and that if as a result of some unforeseeable event (adopting Lord Wilberforce's analogy) the machinery had become jammed, or (adopting Lord Russell's analogy) the stylus had stuck in a groove before the record had been fully played, each of the parties would have been obliged (though without being contractually bound) to assist in restoring everyone to his original position, at least so far as that could be done without exposing any party to any fiscal or other penalty."

36–24   It is not altogether clear what importance should be attached to the concept of a tripartite contract which appears in the judgment of Lord Brightman (see § 36–21); but a close study shows that Lord Brightman expresses this as the *effect* of applying *Ramsay* to, and not the *test* for determining the existence of, a pre-ordained series of transactions. On facts such as those in *Dawson*, is it to be said that there can only be a pre-ordained series of transactions if, at the moment when assets are transferred to Greenjacket, the entire arrangement with the ultimate purchaser or purchasers is then capable of being expressed in contractual terms? Is it necessary, for

---

39. Lord Bridge used the phrase "a series of inter-dependent transactions" (*ibid*. p. 517C) and, later, "interlocking, interdependent and predetermined transactions" (*ibid*. p. 517G).
    40. [1983] S.T.C. 721 at p. 772j.

example, that all the terms of the bargain with the ultimate purchaser or purchasers should have been agreed upon?

36–25 If A transfers property to B with no ultimate purchaser in mind but merely as a piece of tax planning and in the hope or expectation that some purchaser might or will materialise, or that a compulsory purchase order might be made, it is thought that the *Ramsay* principle cannot be applied A's transfer if a purchaser (C) later emerges and B sells to C. The transfers from A to B and from B to C will be independent transactions and their fiscal consequences have to be judged accordingly.

36–26 If A transfers property to B in anticipation of a sale to C on terms which have already been negotiated with C (as in the *Dawson* case) but the sale to C goes off and the property is later sold (perhaps on different terms) to D, it is thought the *Ramsay* principle will not ordinarily apply to the transfer by A. A more difficult problem will arise if there is a change of circumstances after the transfer from A to B and the deal with C has to be renegotiated and takes place on terms different from those which were originally envisaged. The decision if there was truly all one transaction will be a matter of judgment for Commissioners.

36–27 The question whether there was a "single composite transaction having the two requirements stipulated by Lord Brightman (see § 36–21) has arisen in a number of recent cases:

> In *Craven* v. *White*,[40a] on July 19, 1976, the taxpayers (A) transferred shares in a supermarkets company (Queensferry) to B in exchange for shares issued by B, a newly incorporated Isle of Man company. (A claimed that this was a reorganisation of the share capital of Queensferry giving rise to no tax liability). The transfer to B was made in anticipation of a sale of the Queensferry shares by B to C but there was a strong possibility that the sale to C would not take place. No agreement for sale, contractual or non-contractual, existed at the time of the transfer to B; furthermore, a merger with D was under active consideration, it being intended at the time of the transfer in July that B should act as a holding company in the merger. The Queensferry shares were in fact sold by B to C for over £2m. in August 1976 and B made interest-free loans of the entire sale proceeds to A between 1977 and 1981. The Crown claimed that the transfer from A to B was a fiscal nullity and that A should be treated as having disposed of the Queensferry shares to C, there being a single composite transaction. *Held*, that there was no such transaction because "looking at the facts found by the Special Commissioners . . . it is impossible to conclude that there was no likelihood in practice in July 19 that the sale to C would not be completed". Further, A had a commercial purpose in mind (merger) in transferring the shares to B. Hence neither of the two requirements stipulated by Lord Brightman were present.
>
> In *I.R.C.* v. *Bowater Property Developings Ltd.*,[40b] A, a member of the Bowater group, was negotiating in 1980 for the sale of certain land ("Crafts Marsh") to C, a company outside the group. In March 1980 A agreed to sell

---

40a. [1985] S.T.C. 531.
40b. [1985] S.T.C. 783. See also *Baylis* v. *Gregory* [1986] S.T.C. 22. These cases and *Craven* v. *White* (above) are to be heard by the Court of Appeal early in 1987.

the land to five companies within the Bowater group ("the B Companies") as beneficial tenants in common in equal undivided shares, the sole purpose being to take advantage of the £50,000 exemption from development land tax that each of the five companies could claim. In May 1980 A sent a draft contract to C, naming the B Companies as vendors. In July 1980 C replied that it no longer wished to proceed, due to the effect of the economic situation on C's business. In 1981 circumstances had changed, negotiations were resumed and in November 1981 sales were completed at a higher price and on different terms from those first negotiated. The Revenue claimed that there was a single composite transaction and that the first transfer from A to B should be treated as a fiscal nullity. *Held,* that Lord Brightman's first requirement was not satisfied. "The crucial fact . . . is that it had not been pre-ordained or pre-arranged, at the time of the first transaction, that the second transaction would follow. It could not be said at that time that there was no "likelihood in practice" that the second transaction would not follow. When it followed, 19 months later, it followed as an independent transaction."

In these cases the courts have rejected the proposition advanced by the Crown that any transaction can be disregarded if it is a step taken with a view to avoiding tax in a certain event and that event happens. As Vinelott J. said in *Ingram* v. *I.R.C*:[40c]

"That would clearly involve an extension of the *Ramsay* principle as developed in *Dawson*. That principle as stated by Lord Brightman is confined to a case where the transaction is 'pre-ordained' *in that the end achieved is that intended when the first step in the transaction is taken*".

(2) *Business purpose*

36–28   The *Ramsay* principle was held to apply in the *Dawson* case because the exchange of shares with Greenjacket (step 1) served

"no commercial (business) purpose apart from the avoidance of a liability to tax."

The words "apart from' recognise that a decision to mitigate or defer tax may itself be a commercial decision.[41] It seems from the words of Lord Brightman that the *Ramsay* principle will not apply if the inserted steps have (and achieve) *some* business or commercial purpose apart from the avoidance of a liability to tax. But it is not enough that the transaction has a business *effect*: see § 36–31. *Craven* v. *White* in § 36–27 is an example of a case where the business purpose requirement was held to be satisfied.

36–29   If in *Dawson* the whole of the cash proceeds had been required to purchase another business in place of the business being sold and the share-vendors had decided, for commercial reasons, that the new business should be acquired by Greenjacket, it is arguable that the business/commercial test would be satisfied.[42]

40c. [1985] S.T.C. 835 at p. 850 e. italics supplied.
41. *I.R.C.* v. *Brebner* [1967] 2 A.C. 18; 43 T.C. 705 (H.L.). "No commercial man in his senses is going to carry out commercial transactions except upon the footing of paying the smallest amount of tax involved" (*per* Lord Upjohn).
42. *Cf. Clark* v. *I.R.C.* (1978) 52 T.C. 482 in § 40–02.

36–30   Not all transactions in which steps are introduced for the purpose of deferring or reducing tax are business or commercial transactions in the ordinary sense of the term. Many transactions are carried out for family, domestic or matrimonial reasons or to benefit charity. The word "business' has been held to have a wide meaning in other contexts and it is to be hoped that the courts will recognise that a wide variety of such transactions can properly be described as business transactions.[43]

36–31   *Business effect.* Lord Brightman draws a distinction between business purpose and business effect. This echoes the point made by Vinelott J. in the High Court that the transaction in the *Dawson* case had "enduring legal consequences": see § 36–19. It is no defence to an assessment based on *Ramsay* or *Dawson* that there were enduring legal consequences. *Ramsay* and *Burmah* were cases involving circular self-cancelling transactions which, by definition, had no such consequences; but the *Dawson* case shows that there is now a doctrine of fiscal nullity which can be applied despite the business effect of the transactions. In *Dawson* Lord Brightman said:

> "In the instant case the inserted step was the introduction of Greenjacket as a buyer from the Dawsons and as a seller to Wood Bastow. That inserted step had no business purpose apart from the deferment of tax, although it had a business effect. If the sale had taken place in 1964 before capital gains tax was introduced, there would have been no Greenjacket."[43a]

The effect of applying the Ramsay principle

36–32   It might be expected that applying the words of Lord Wilberforce in *Ramsay* to the facts of the *Dawson* case would lead to the consequences that step 1 was not such an amalgamation as falls within the relieving provisions in Schedule 7 to the Finance Act 1965,[44] because Parliament did not intend that those provisions should provide roll over relief in circumstances such as those in *Dawson*, but that no *disregarding* of any part of the transaction was called for. Lord Wilberforce had not mentioned disregarding in *Ramsay*: see § 36–15. But this "constructional" or "interpretational" approach seems to have been ruled out in the *Dawson* case by the Commissioners' own findings of fact.[45]

Dawson requires that, where there is a pre-ordained series of transactions aimed to achieve an end result, *steps* in the series which are found to have been inserted for no business/commercial purpose should be disregarded and tax law applied accordingly. The "relevant transaction" to which tax law is applied is therefore an edited version of the original. In the *Dawson* case, the relevant transaction was identified as a sale by the Daw-

---

43. See, *e.g. I.R.C.* v. *Marine Steam Turbine Co. Ltd.* [1920] 1 K.B. 193 at pp. 202–203; 12 T.C. 174 at pp. 179–180. And see the so-called "predication test" referred to in *Newton*'s case [1958] A.C. 450 at p. 466.

43a. [1984] A.C. 474 at p. 527F; and see *ibid.* at p. 525B–D.

44. See now C.G.T.A. 1979, s.85. The 1977 Act amendment is *ibid.* ss.87–88.

45. On this approach, see the interesting judgments in *Stubart Investments Ltd.* v. *The Queen* (1984) 84 D.T.C. 6305.

sons of their shares in A Limited to Wood Bastow, the cash proceeds being paid at the direction of the Dawsons to Greenjacket. Step 1 (the exchange of shares with Greenjacket) was disregarded because it served no business/commercial purpose. The tax consequence of the decision therefore was that there was a chargeable disposal and not, as had been hoped, a disposal qualifying for roll-over relief. Further, the chargeable disposal was a disposal by the Dawson family and not by Greenjacket.[46]

36–33   It is impossible to escape the conclusion that, in *Dawson*, the vendors were treated for the purposes of the assessment before the court as having carried out a different transaction from the transaction they actually carried out; indeed, they were treated as having carried out the transaction they went out of their way to avoid carrying out.[46a] They were treated as having sold their shares for cash; in fact, the right to the cash was foregone in order to achieve a deferment of tax liability.

36–34   It is interesting to see how the "disregarding" point was put in argument in the *Dawson* case[47]:

> "The Crown does *not* contend that the transfer to Greenjacket ought to be disregarded in the sense of treated as if it did not happen, but contends that it should be disregarded in the sense that it is not the relevant disposal. Likewise, the Crown does *not* contend that the taxpayers ought to be taxed *as if* they had transferred the shares directly in a single step to the ultimate purchaser, but contends that they ought to be taxed on the basis that they transferred them by two steps to the ultimate purchaser, those two steps being planned and implemented as the component elements of a single transaction, together constituting the relevant disposal for the purposes of the capital gains tax."

Then later[48]:

> "The interposition of Greenjacket had a commercial *effect*, since it led to the receipt by it of the proceeds of sale, but that was no part of the taxpayers *purpose*. It was merely the price that the taxpayers reluctantly had to pay in order to obtain the hoped-for tax advantages of the scheme."

The practitioner who has to live with the immensely detailed text of the capital gains tax legislation must be forgiven if he senses an element of double-talk in this presentation. When is a disposal not a disposal?

36–35   *Dawson* did not decide that the *existence* of Greenjacket should be disregarded for fiscal purposes. The decision simply requires that *steps* in a series of transactions should be disregarded, in the sense that they have no relevance in determining the real transaction which is to be taxed. Income received by Greenjacket and dividends paid by Greenjacket would be taxed in the ordinary way; and it was recognised that a sale by the Dawsons of their shares in Greenjacket might give rise to capital gains tax, if the

---

46. Thus open assessments on the equivalent of Greenjacket in any similar scheme must be discharged.
46a. See *Ingram* v. *I.R.C.* [1985] S.T.C. at p. 850 b.
47. [1984] A.C. 474 at p. 510 F–G.
48. *Ibid*. at p. 512 B–C.

value of B Limited increased after the exchange. If Greenjacket had been a close company and had loaned the cash proceeds to participators, an assessment could be made on Greenjacket under section 286 of the Income and Corporation Taxes Act 1970 see (§ 15–25) and on its directors under section 66 of the Finance Act 1976: see § 3–49. Monstrous results can arise as a result of these sections when the sale of shares occurred before *Dawson* was decided and assessments have been kept open pending the decision in that case which, of course, changes the law retrospectively.

36–36 *Young* v. *Phillips*[49] is an interesting example of the effect of applying the *Dawson* case to a complex series of transactions. The facts may be briefly summarised as follows:

> A and B were resident in the United Kingdom but domiciled in South Africa. A and B owned all the shares in an English company (E Co.) which had substantial revenue reserves. A and B were concerned about the possible impact of capital transfer tax on the business of E Co. and decided to transfer their shares in E Co. to an overseas company. The following scheme was carried out in order to avoid capital gains tax. A new company in Jersey (J Co.) was incorporated. Initially A and B were not directors or shareholders. The reserves of E Co. were capitalised and applied in paying for new preferred ordinary shares which were issued to A and B on renounceable letters of allotment. A and B were then appointed directors of J Co. J Co. resolved to purchase the new preferred ordinary shares in E Co. from A and B for about £1.3 million. It was resolved that the unissued shares of J Co. be issued to A and B at a premium of over £1.3 million. A and B went to Jersey where they renounced their preferred ordinary shares to J Co., which was duly registered as a member. A and B were paid for their shares in E Co. and paid E Co. the amount of the premium.

A and B resisted assessments to capital gains tax on the ground that they had disposed of assets (rights to have shares allotted) which were situated outside the United Kingdom.[50] Their objection was rejected, it being held that they disposed of a chose in action situated in the United Kingdom. However, the Crown had an alternative contention based on the *Dawson* case which was dealt with by Nicholls J. as follows (summarising):

> Before the scheme was initiated A and B owned all the shares in E Co. After the scheme had been carried through they still owned their original shares in E Co. but, by their direction, new shares in E Co. had been issued to J Co. in exchange for shares in J Co. issued to A and B. That was the relevant transaction or, using Lord Brightman's phrase, the end result. Value therefore shifted out of A and B's original shares in E Co. so as to cause a "disposal", (see § 16–16). But the process by which this was achieved, including the issue of shares by J Co., could not be disregarded because it was the relevant transaction. Paragraph 6(2) of Schedule 7 the Finance Act 1965 applied because J Co. issued shares in exchange for more than 25 per cent. of the ordinary shares in E Co. But this did not assist A and B because the amendment in Finance Act 1977 gave rollover relief only where the transaction did not have tax avoidance as a main purpose.[51] The scheme was here designed to avoid capital gains

49. [1984] S.T.C. 520.
50. C.G.T.A. 1979, s.14; see *ante*, § 16–04.
51. See note 35 above.

tax. *Dawson* was distinguishable because, in that case, the issue of shares formed no part of the relevant transaction and could therefore be disregarded.

36–37   At the risk of some inaccuracy, the *Dawson* case requires the court to decide what the taxpayer ends up with after the series of transactions to see how that end result could have been achieved more expensively in tax terms if steps had not been inserted; but it does not allow the court to treat the taxpayer as ending up with something different from what he in fact has. The point may be illustrated by referring to a common method of avoiding capital transfer tax for individuals resident in, but domiciled outside, the United Kingdom, who have substantial assets in the United Kingdom. Such individuals may be advised to form an overseas company and to transfer assets to that company in exchange for shares registered in the books of that company. The objective is to remove assets from the ambit of United Kingdom capital transfer tax by "transmuting" those assets into "excluded property": see § 18–13A. (*Young* v. *Phillips* employed this device but also aimed to avoid capital gains tax as a sale). Both the conditions referred to by Lord Brightman are satisfied: there is a pre-ordained series of transactions and (presumably) no business/commercial purpose is served through the transactions involving the overseas company, yet it is difficult to see how either *Ramsay* or *Dawson* could frustrate the transaction. Applying the "before and after approach" of Nicholls J. in *Young* v. *Phillips* (see § 36–36), before the scheme is initiated the individual owns assets situated in the United Kingdom. After the scheme, the individual owns (in their place) shares situated outside the United Kingdom; the overseas company owns the assets. *That* is the end result and *that* is the relevant transaction. There is no other transaction which can be disregarded.

6. The Future: Random Thoughts

36–38   Lord Scarman said in the *Dawson* case that "the law in this area [of tax planning] is in an early stage of developments." Lord Bridge said "the drawing of precise boundaries will need to be worked out on a case by case basis." In the *Burmah* case Lord Diplock, after quoting Lord Tomlin's well known dictum that every man is entitled to order his affairs so that the tax attaching under the appropriate Acts is less than it otherwise would be (see § 36–08) added that this:

> "tells us little or nothing as to what methods of ordering one's affairs *will be recognised by the Courts as effective* to lessen the tax that would attach to them if business transactions were conducted in a straightforward way."

Lord Scarman spoke of "unacceptable tax avoidance," curiously contrasting it with "unacceptable tax evasion"—curious, because evasion is a *criminal* offence—adding that "the law will develop from case to case" and referring also to the "map making process." Lord Wilberforce spoke in *Ramsay* of "the emerging principles" of the law. It is anyone's guess how the law will develop: it is possible that the Courts will frustrate those forms of tax planning which it finds unacceptable and that principles will have to be worked out for determining what is or is not acceptable, and what "tax avoidance" really is. (see § 36–39(5)). Let it be hoped that the rule of caprice does not take the place of the rule of law.[52]

36–39   The following are no more than random and disjointed thoughts on the "new approach" or, as it is called in Commonwealth cases, the "doctrine of fiscal nullity":

(1) The doctrine formulated by Lord Brightman in the *Dawson* case is narrowly confined to multi-stage, composite transactions in which steps are deliberately inserted for tax avoidance purposes. On one view, the decision may be said to have only limited effect. This view is borne out by the decisions in § 36–27. Revenue claims that the doctrine applies should not be accepted without very careful examination. Sabre-rattling by Inspectors is not appropriate.[53]

(2) The doctrine is of universal application and may be invoked by the taxpayer in appropriate cases. It may become relevant in litigation to which the Revenue is not a party, *e.g.* in divorce proceedings, where the means of a spouse have to be determined and that spouse has carried out a tax planning exercise to which the doctrine might apply.

(3) Although *Ramsay*, *Burmah* and *Dawson* were concerned with capital gains tax, the doctrine is susceptible of application to all other taxes. In the *Ingram* case it was applied to stamp duty.

(4) A re-examination of all anti-avoidance provisions in taxing statutes would be welcome, following the decision in the *Dawson* case. The statement made by the Chief Secretary to the Treasury (see § 36–40) refers to a possible pruning out of some provisions.

(5) The new approach invites a re-examination of the nature of tax avoidance. What is tax avoidance? If a statute enables X to obtain a tax deduction for complete year of assessment if he does something the day before the year ends but not if he does it a day later, and his decision to choose the former is motivated solely by tax considerations, is this tax avoidance?[54] If the answer is No and the reason is that X is merely exercising a choice which the statute confers on him, why was the scheme in the *Dawson* case branded as objectionable tax avoidance? Is the act of transferring a partnership business to a company to take advantage of the low rate of corporation tax tax avoidance? Problems of his kind have engaged the attention of the Courts of Australia over many years in considering the (now replaced) section 260 of the Income Tax Assessment Act 1936–1981, producing a wealth of case law to which some reference might usefully be made. The decisions are collected in the recent decision of the High Court of New Zealand in *Challenge Corporation Ltd.* v. *I.R.C.*[55]

---

52. See the quotations immediately before the start of this chapter.
53. See text of letter from the I.R.C. the I.C.A.E.W. in [1985] S.T.I. 574 (para. 24).
54. Decisions of the Full High Court in Australia show that if a taxpayer organises his affairs in order to attract the tax consequences for which the Act makes specific provision, and does so deliberately for the purpose of obtaining the tax advantage, this is not "tax avoidance" for the purposes of s.260. This is the "doctrine of choice": see *Keighery Pty. Ltd.* v. *Federal Commissioner of Taxation* (1957) 100 C.L.R. 66; *Casuarina Pty. Ltd.* v. *Federal Commission of Taxation* (1971) 71 A.T.C. 4068.
55. (1984) 6 N.Z.T.C. 61807.

Cold comfort: parliamentary statement by the Chief Secretary to the Treasury

36–40 The following statement has been made in the House of Commons by the Chief Secretary to the Treasury:

> "I should also touch on the implications of the recent decision of the House of Lords in *Furniss* v. *Dawson*. I am aware of the acute interest in that case. Taken with the decision in Ramsay's case it is now clear that the widespread assumptions based on the Duke of Westminster's case in the 1930s—that the courts will always look at the form rather than the substance of a transaction or various transactions—is no longer valid.
>
> The House of Lords made it clear that this is an evolving area of law, but the emerging principles do not in any way call in question the tax treatment of covenants, leasing transactions and other straightforward commercial transactions. Nor is there any question of the Inland Revenue challenging for example, the tax treatment of straightforward transfers of assets between members of the same group of companies. I also assure the House that, in accordance with normal practice, the Inland Revenue will not seek to reopen cases when assessments were properly settled in accordance with prevailing practice and became final before that decision.
>
> The Board of Inland Revenue will also see whether clearance for types of case of special importance or general guidance for the benefit of taxpayers and their advisers can be given. The principle in *Furniss* v. *Dawson* should lead in future to great simplicity in our tax system and will, I hope, enable us in time to prune out provisions which owe their existence to the complexities of a high rate—some might say a confiscatory rate—tax system with a multiplicity of special reliefs. I am sure that the whole House will welcome that."

The word "straightforward" which appears in two places in this statement is taken from Lord Diplock's speech in the *Burmah* case: see § 36–16. Many business and commercial transactions involve great complexity and there are a number of different ways of achieving the same end result. It is not always obvious which way should be regarded as "straightforward".

Guidance Note TR 588

36–40A On June 10, 1985 a meeting took place between representatives of the Inland Revenue, the Institute of Chartered Accountants and the Law Society at which a number of areas of difficulty arising from the *Dawson* case were identified. Following this meeting, the Revenue wrote a letter indicating its views on certain matters and the full text of the letter (which is too long to reproduce here) was published in the form of a Guidance Note by the Institute.[56] Paragraphs of this Guidance Note are referred to elsewhere in the book, under the appropriate headings.

Chapter 37

GIFTS, SETTLEMENTS AND WILLS

1. Outright Gifts

37–01   An outright gift may now give rise to a number of different charges to tax, all of which have been considered in detail elsewhere in this book. An outright gift is a disposal for the purposes of the tax on capital gains and a charge to tax may arise unless the gift is exempt from the charge.[1] The donor is treated as disposing of, and the donee as acquiring, the gifted asset at its market value at the time of the gift. The charge to tax falls on the donor; but there are provisions under which the donee can be assessed, subject to his right, if he pays the tax, to recover an equal amount from the donor or his personal representatives.[2] There are provisions under which donor and donee can elect to have the donor's gain held over until the donee disposes of the asset: see § 16–49A.

37–02   An outright gift is also a transfer of value and will, for the purposes of inheritance tax, be a potentially exempt transfer unless the gift is properly exempt or the property given is excluded property. If the donor fails to survive his gift by seven years, inheritance tax will be payable by the donee. Capital gains tax may also be payable on the gift, on the gain which is deemed to accrue on the deemed disposal at market value (see §16–18): but if inheritance tax subsequently becomes payable on the transfer proving chargeable, whilst that tax will be charged on the diminution in the value of his estate, any capital gains tax he may have paid will be left out of account.[3]

Inheritance tax is so charged that later gifts made in a period of seven years, and in particular, in the last seven years before death, will be more expensive than earlier gifts. Thus though it will be advantageous to make outright gifts before the approach of death, care should always be taken as to the order in which gifts are made, especially if some are settled.[4]

37–03   Although gifts made well before death will attract no inheritance tax, they do suffer capital gains tax: gifts on death, however are liable to inheritance tax but not capital gains tax. In some instances, the saving of capital gains tax will outweigh the potential inheritance tax charge—for example, where the property is to pass to one's spouse, or where the estate is of little value. For this and other reasons donors should be cautious in taking advantage of the relief by which capital gains tax can be held over—see §16–49 and §16–49A.

---

1. See *ante*, § 16–18.
2. C.G.T.A. 1979, s.59.
3. See §§ 20–06 *et seq.*
4. See § 22–64A.

37–04   Although transfers between husband and wife are in many cases exempt from both inheritance tax and capital gains tax it may not be good tax planning for a wealthy husband to transfer property to his equally wealthy wife: for this will merely increase the tax payable on *her* death. Instead, it is sensible, wherever possible, to divest oneself of as much of one's estate as it is felt is superfluous to that needed to preserve one's standard of living, in favour of one's children and grandchildren—and to do so as early as possible. In this context, though, careful attention should be paid to the satisfaction of the rules precluding the making of gifts with reservation of benefit.[5] As long as the marriage is satisfactory, steps should be taken after this to achieve some equalisation of estates.

37–05   If the gifted property is trading stock of the donor's trade, the donor may incur liability to tax through the operation of the rule in *Sharkey* v. *Wernher*.[6] No charge to capital gains tax will arise in such a case, though inheritance tax might be payable were the donor to die shortly thereafter.

Gifts to directors or employees may be taxable under the rules of Schedule E as emoluments of an office or employment.[7]

2. Income Settlements

37–06   Income settlements in the form of "deeds of covenants" are a useful means of alienating income from one taxpayer to another. If A, having an income of £10,000, covenants to pay £1,000 to B, the covenanted amount becomes income of B (charged at the basic rate by deduction at source) and B can reclaim from the Revenue the amount of overpaid tax. A secures tax relief at the basic rate in the manner described in §§ 5–33 *et seq*. See Computations B and C in § 8–69.

37–07   The gross amount payable under an income settlement is no longer deductible in computing the liability of the covenantor to higher rate income tax, except[8] in the cases of:

(1) annual payments made under a partnership agreement to or for the benefit of a former member, or to the widow or dependants of a deceased former member of the partnership, being payments made under a liability incurred for full consideration or under the provisions in § 10–14;

(2) certain annual payments applied in acquiring a business; and

(3) certain payments made by one party to a marriage to the other, after the dissolution or annulment of the marriage or while they are separated: see Chapter 38;

(4) annual payments to charities.

---

5. See § 20–29.
6. See § 2–46.
7. See § 3–09.
8. See I.C.T.A. 1970, s.457; see, §§ 10–17 *et seq*.

37–08   Income settlements continue to be useful in tax planning where the covenantee's income is not fully absorbed by personal reliefs, or where the covenantee is exempt from income tax (as in the case of a charity), provided the covenant is so drafted as not to cause the income to be treated as the income of the covenantor under one or other of the provisions considered in §§ 10–04 *et seq.* The settlement must be for a period which might exceed six years (three years in the case of charitable covenants) and must not be "revocable" in the extended income tax sense.[9] Further, the covenantor must have sufficient income taxed at the basic rate for section 52 of the Taxes Act 1970 to apply and for section 53 of that Act not to apply. Covenants are a sensible method whereby a parent can provide for a child undergoing university education, where the parent's income disqualifies him from obtaining a local authority grant: consideration should be given, however, to the effect of any income or capital settlement on a beneficiary's entitlement to grant, where his parent's income is within the usual limits.[10] Income settlements play a major role in cases of separation and divorce: see Chapter 38.

3. Capital Settlements

37–09   A capital settlement is a settlement of income-producing property, often for the benefit of the settlor's children and/or remoter issue. For the purposes of inheritance tax, capital settlements are classified according to the trusts on which the settled property is held. The legislation distinguishes (i) settled property in which there is a beneficial interest in possession; (ii) settled property in which there is no beneficial interest in possession; and (iii) settled property held on special trusts, such as trusts for accumulation and maintenance. It will be convenient under this heading to mention briefly some considerations which will affect the use of each type of settlement in the future. Their use in connection with arrangements made on separation and divorce is referred to in Chapter 38.

A. Settled Property in Which There is a Beneficial Interest in Possession

37–10   Settlements were made long before any form of taxation existed and there will continue to be numerous occasions when individuals will wish to distribute their wealth so as to delay the vesting of capital and, meanwhile, to confer limited interests in income, whether by way of life interest or annuity. It will be remembered that, in addition to capital gains tax, inheritance tax may be payable on the making of a settlement[11] and that the legislation treats each holder of an interest in possession as the beneficial owner of the fund in which his interest subsists. Inheritance tax is accordingly payable on the termination, or deemed termination, of each interest

---

9. See § 10–26.
10. See the Local Education Authority Award Regs. 1978 (S.I. 1978 No. 1097).
11. This is subject to held-over relief from capital gains tax (see § 16–49A) and the exemptions and reliefs generally applicable to both taxes.

in possession, for however short a time that interest endures (subject only to quick succession relief).[12] Hence, in drafting this kind of settlement, a succession of interests in possession should be avoided; and instead of annuities being charged on settled property, they should where possible be secured by personal covenant or purchased. The uplift in the nil rate inheritance tax band to £71,000, coupled with the 7-year cumulation period may increase the use of settlements in financial planning.

37–11   A reversionary interest is generally excluded property and can be extinguished before it vests in possession without any charge to tax. Such an interest should be extinguished where its duration is likely to be short or where the combination of a low income yield and a high capital fund will produce overburdensome tax.

B. Settled Property in Which There is No Interest in Possession

1. Use in the future

37–12/13   The discretionary trust is the commonest form of settlement which falls under this head. Whilst such settlements do suffer from the regular imposition of a charge to inheritance tax on each ten-year anniversary, the revision of the manner in which charges are levied on them by the Finance Act 1982 led to a revival in their previously waning popularity. It remains to be seen whether that popularity will continue after the introduction of the potentially exempt outright gift.

C. Accumulation and Maintenance Settlements

37–14   "Accumulation and maintenance settlement" conveniently describes a settlement under which the capital is destined to vest in a person or persons contingently on attaining a specified age. Section 31 of the Trustee Act 1925 usually applies to English settlements of this type with the consequence that beneficiaries become entitled to the income (and therefore acquire an interest in possession) on attaining the age of 18 years,[13] before which time the income can either be applied for the maintenance, education or benefit of the beneficiary or beneficiaries, or accumulated. Such trusts are particularly favoured. No inheritance tax is charged on their creation (provided the settlor survives seven years), although capital gains tax may be payable. Furthermore, section 71 of the Inheritance Tax Act 1984 (see §§22–74 *et seq.*) prevents any charge to inheritance tax either on distributions in favour of a beneficiary or when a beneficiary's interest vests in possession. Note that it is not necessary for the purposes of the section that the interest in *capital* should vest when or before the beneficiary attains the age of 25 years; it is sufficient if his interest in *income* so vests.[14] Income which is accumulated attracts no higher rate income tax but only income

---

12. See §§ 12–14 *et seq.*
13. See notes to § 22–68.
14. This view has been confirmed in an Inland Revenue Press Release in [1975] S.T.I. 469.

tax at the basic rate plus additional rate tax of 16 per cent., *i.e.* 45 per cent. in 1986–87. This rate applies to the whole of the income and is a relatively high rate. Income which is applied for a child's maintenance, education or benefit is treated as the child's income (and can be reduced by personal reliefs), except where the settlor is the child's parent and the child is under 18 years and unmarried, when the income is treated as the parent's income. Settlements of this kind will continue to be widely used in tax planning as a means of saving for children and grandchildren. They are especially useful as a vehicle for holding shares in a family company which are expected to grow in value.

4. WILLS

37–15   There are many problems of a fiscal nature which may arise during the course of advising clients about to make their wills. Before advice can be given an inventory should first be made of the client's estate and the value of each item estimated. The amount of inheritance tax likely to be paid on death should then be estimated. The client's wishes as to the disposition of each item of property can then be considered in relation to the tax payable and the funds available to meet it. Against this background the client may wish to consider (i) the extent to which the burden of inheritance tax might be reduced, *e.g.* by *inter vivos* dispositions; and (ii) ways and means of funding the payment of the tax on death, *e.g.* by insurance policies. It cannot be stressed too strongly that the aim must be to provide the client with a draft will which is satisfactory both from a personal and fiscal point of view. Although there is a two-year period after the death in which it may be possible to rectify matters, where the will is deficient in tax-planning terms, without adverse capital gains tax[15] or inheritance tax[16] consequences, this may well be costly in income tax.[17]

The advantage of being able to make lifetime gifts free from inheritance tax has to be weighed against the fact that capital gains tax is payable on lifetime disposals but not on death. It is true that a donor can make an election to have the deemed gain made on a lifetime gift "held over"[18]: the asset so transferred will not, however, benefit from the "free uplift" which is available to assets passing on death.

The consequences of making gifts "free of tax" or "free of duty" are considered in §§ 24–17 *et seq.* The exemptions from inheritance tax have been considered in detail in Chapter 19 but the following general comments are relevant in the present context:

37–16   (1) The exemption for transfers between spouses (see § 19–02) enables one spouse to transfer an absolute or limited interest in property to the other, either *inter vivos* or by will, free of the tax. If a husband (H) gives

---

15. See *ante*, § 16–20A.
16. See *ante*, § 19–63.
17. See *ante*, § 19–63.
18. See *ante*, §§ 16–49 and 16–49A.

property to his wife (W) absolutely or for life, and H dies first, no inheritance tax is payable on H's death on the property given to W; but inheritance tax will be payable on W's death, whether she has a life interest or an absolute interest in the property.

Nevertheless, although it might, therefore, seem advisable to leave all one's estate to one's spouse by will, to do so might well be to take a very short-sighted view. If, for example H has an estate of £500,000 and W an estate of her own of £300,000, then on H's death leaving all his property to W no tax will be payable: on W's subsequent death, though, inheritance tax of some £400,300 will be suffered. If H were instead simply to equalise the two estates, tax would be paid on each death of £160,300, a total of £320,600. Too much can be made of the principle of the equalisation of estates, as well, though: if, for example, there is a great disparity in the ages of the spouses a far larger proportion of the joint estates should be passed to the surviving spouse—both on the basis that tax postponed is tax saved (consider the interest which might accumulate on £160,300, if W were to survive 10 or 15 years) and because it will be possible for the survivor to make *inter vivos* transfers, taking advantage of potential exemption.

Clearly, every case will be dependent on its own facts: the only hard and fast rules are that, in any estate of substance, the nil-rate band of each party should be fully utilised in making gifts to the children, and that each should seek to make as many lifetime gifts in cash as possible.

37–16A (2) Even if financial circumstances are such as to enable the testator to leave some part of his estate away from his spouse, the property so available should not necessarily be given to the children, who may already be sufficiently wealthy in their own right. Thought should instead be given to missing out the next generation and leaving the property to the testator's grandchildren. To this end, it may be advisable to create accumulation and maintenance trusts in favour of a class of grandchildren, since the size of the class may well be uncertain at the time of the testator's death.

37–16B (3) It is possible to leave tax-planning to one's executor-trustees so that the estate can be distributed in accordance with the needs of the potential dependants at that time, rather than at the time when the will was executed. Section 144 of the Inheritance Tax Act 1984 allows distributions from a discretionary trust created by will which are made within two years of the testator's death to be made without any charge to inheritance tax. This provision is more effective than relying on the exemption granted to deeds of family arrangement by section 142 since:

(a) the trust will obviate the need to rely on the generosity of a more fortunate beneficiary who cannot, of course, be forced to enter into a deed of family arrangement;

(b) a deed of family arrangement made by a surviving spouse in favour of infant children of the marriage will be a settlement for income tax purposes and, thus, with income tax disadvantages.[19]

---

19. See I.C.T.A. 1970, ss.137, 138, *ante*, § 10–37.

37–17 (4) The exemption for transfers not exceeding £3,000 in each year (§ 19–07) is useful as a means of dissipating an estate in annual stages.

37–18 (5) The "normal expenditure out of income" exemption (see § 19–11) can be used to fund the payment of premiums on a policy which the payer has effected for the benefit of a third person, *e.g.* to enable that person to pay inheritance tax on the payer's death.

37–19 (6) A marriage is a convenient opportunity to make tax-free transfers of a limited amount: see § 19–15.

37–20 (7) Investment in exempt government securities may be a useful method of saving inheritance tax for persons neither domiciled nor ordinarily resident in the United Kingdom or for trustees holding property on trust for such persons: see § 19–26.

37–21 (8) Above all, the maximum use should be made of potential exemption.

CHAPTER 38

ASPECTS OF MATRIMONIAL FINANCE

1. THE TAXATION OF HUSBAND AND WIFE WHEN LIVING TOGETHER

38–01 IT was explained in § 8–23 that the separate incomes of husband and wife are generally aggregated for the purpose of determining the total tax payable. By section 37 of the Income and Corporation Taxes Act 1970, a woman's income chargeable to income tax, so far as it is income for a year of assessment or part of a year of assessment during which she is a married woman living with her husband, is deemed for tax purposes to be his income and not to be her income. By way of exception to this general rule, husband and wife can jointly elect for the wife's earnings (as defined) to be charged to tax separately from their other income: see § 8–29. This exception was introduced to "encourage" wives with an earning capacity to resume, or continue, work. Care should be taken before making such an election since, from the wife's *earned* income, there have to be deducted her reliefs, *e.g.* for interest or annuities paid by her. Her investment income is, however, treated as her husband's income. Problems may therefore arise if her reliefs exceed her earned income. This right of election should not be confused with the separate provision, discussed in § 8–26, under which either husband or wife may apply to be separately *assessed*. An application for a separate assessment does not alter the total amount of tax payable by the two spouses: its only effect is that each spouse is liable for his or her own tax. Section 39 of the Income and Corporation Taxes Act 1970 provides for the same reliefs and allowances to apply as if there were no separate assessment. It also provides for the allocation of the reliefs and allowances between husband and wife. The reliefs and allowances available to spouses are discussed in §§ 8–42 *et seq*. See also Computation D in § 8–69.

38–02 The exemption from capital gains tax on disposals between husband and wife applies only to disposals made in a year of assessment during which the woman is a married woman living with her husband: see § 16–17. Hence disposal made after separation may not be exempt from capital gains tax, subject to the concession referred to in § 38–21 below.

38–03 Transfers between spouses are normally exempt from inheritance tax, formerly capital transfer tax, if made while the marriage subsists, whether or not the spouses are living together: see § 19–02.

What constitutes living together

38–04 A married woman is treated for tax purposes as "living with her husband" unless either:

(a) they are separated under an order of a court of competent jurisdiction or by deed of separation; or

(b) they are in fact separated in such circumstances that the separation is likely to be permanent.

The Revenue treat the separation as likely to be permanent if the parties have been living apart for one year. For the position where one spouse is resident, outside or absent from the United Kingdom, see § 8–23.

2. SEPARATION

38–05   If, throughout a year of assessment, husband and wife are not living together (see § 38–04), the income of each of them is separately charged and separately assessed to tax. The man is entitled to the personal relief appropriate to a married man if he wholly maintains his wife and is *not* entitled to deduct any sum paid for her maintenance in computing his total income. Accordingly, if husband and wife are separated and the wife is wholly maintained out of payments made by the husband on a voluntary basis, he is entitled to the personal relief appropriate to a married man. If he maintains her under a court order or under an enforceable agreement, he is entitled to the personal relief appropriate to a single man: see § 8–42.

As regards capital gains tax and inheritance see § 38–02 and § 38–03, above.

Periodical payments

38–06   Where husband and wife live separately, the husband will normally provide for his wife and children by means of periodical payments; and he may do so either voluntarily or under an enforceable agreement.

38–07   Where voluntary payments are made, the payee incurs no tax liability (because voluntary payments are not "income") and the payer gets no tax relief on the payments. A husband making voluntary payments continues to be entitled to the personal relief appropriate to a married man: see § 8–42. The payments are exempt from inheritance tax under the exemption discussed in § 19–02 ("transfers between spouses").

38–08   Where payments are made under an enforceable agreement, whether an agreement *inter partes* or a deed poll, and whether orally or in writing, periodical payments are annual payments within Case III of Schedule D: see § 5–04. If the husband agrees to pay his wife a gross amount of (say) £200 a month, the husband deducts tax at the basic rate (as explained in §§ 5–30 *et seq.*). The wife thus "suffers" tax at the basic rate by deduction at source. If by reason of her reliefs and allowances the wife is not liable to tax at so high a rate, she can recover the difference from the Revenue by means of a repayment claim. Conversely, if she has other income, the grossed up amount of the periodical payments (£200 monthly) is brought into the computation of her total income as explained in § 8–18. The husband may deduct the gross amount payable to his wife in computing his total income and so obtain relief from income tax at the higher rates: see §§ 8–31 *et seq.* Because of this he is entitled only to the personal allowance

appropriate to a single person: see § 8–42. See Computations B and C in
§ 8–69.

Agreements for a net sum

38–09   The example in § 38–08 illustrates the position where the agreement provides for a gross sum of £200 monthly. The disadvantage of expressing a
periodical payment as a gross sum is that the net amount after tax will
increase or decrease as the basic rate of tax deceases or increases. It is
often more convenient for a net sum to be specified which will remain constant whether or not the basic rate changes. The husband may, for
example, agree to pay his wife such a sum as after deduction of tax at the
basic rate will leave her with £270 monthly. If the basic rate is 30 per cent.,
this represents a gross income of £400 monthly. If the basic rate is 50 per
cent., it represents a gross income of £200. Where the formula "such a sum
as after deduction of tax" is used, this means tax at the basic rate and not
tax at the higher rates: the reference to "deduction" can refer only to tax at
the basic rate because tax at the higher rates cannot be suffered by deduction.

Agreements to meet expenses

38–10   The parties to an agreement may wish to include a provision under which
the husband is to meet the expense of keeping the matrimonial home or of
educating the children. If the husband pays the bills he is entitled to no tax
relief on expenditure so incurred because payment of bills does not put his
wife in receipt of an income. (This would be so even if he were bound by a
court order to pay the bills: the obligation would be as to the *application* of
his income and not its disposition, *cf.* § 38–19.) If, on the other hand, the
husband agrees to pay his wife such a sum as after deduction of tax at the
basic rate will provide her with an amount equal to the amount of the
expenses, which she then bears out of the income so provided, the husband
is entitled to tax relief on the grossed up amount of the sums paid.

Mortgage interest

38–10A   Mortgage interest is eligible for tax relief if the mortgaged property is the
only or main residence of the borrower or of his separated spouse; but the
relief is available only on loans up to £30,000: see § 8–60A. Thus if after
separation the wife continues to occupy the matrimonial home on which
the husband has borrowed (say) £25,000, the husband's borrowing limit for
the purchase of a residence for his own occupation is £5,000. Where the
former matrimonial home is owned in equal shares and there is a joint
mortgage, the husband's tax position will be alleviated if his wife covenants
in the separation agreement to pay (say) half the mortgage interest and the
husband agrees to provide her with an amount of income equal to the interest so paid. This, in the example, would increase the husband's borrowing
limit (with tax relief) from £5,000 to £15,000; and he would also obtain tax
relief on the amount paid to his wife.

Provision for children

38–11   Where under a separation or similar agreement a husband agrees to make a periodical payment to his child, the transaction is a "settlement" with the consequence that the amount so paid is deemed to be income of the husband if at the time of payment the child is unmarried and under the age of 18 years: see § 10–23. Where, however, the child is either married or has attained the age of 18 years, the appropriate amount is treated as income of the child and the father is entitled to relief from tax at the basic rate (but not at higher rates: see § 10–13. The exception in § 10–16 does not apply). Court orders directing payments direct to a child are not treated as settlements: see § 10–09.

Agreements to consent to divorce

38–12   Separating spouses may wish to have included in a separation agreement a provision that if one spouse petitions for divorce after two years of separation, the other will consent to a decree being granted for the purposes of section 1(2)(*d*) of the Matrimonial Causes Act 1973. It is arguable that such a clause would enable a husband (by petitioning for divorce after two years) to terminate his obligations to make periodical payments *under the agreement* so as to make the separation agreement "a revocable settlement" within section 445 of the Income and Corporation Taxes Act 1970 and thus deprive the husband of tax relief on payments made thereunder: see § 10–26.

Maintenance orders and small maintenance orders

38–13   Periodical payments made to a wife under a maintenance order are treated in the same way as periodical payments made to a wife under an enforceable agreement, except for special provisions which apply to "small maintenance payments": see § 5–05.

3. DIVORCE, ETC.

Orders for periodical payments

38–14   The court has wide powers under Part II of the Matrimonial Causes Act 1973 to make orders for periodical payments (secured or unsecured) in cases of divorce, nullity or judicial separation and also in cases of neglect to maintain. Magistrates' courts can order unsecured maintenance under section 11 of the Domestic Proceedings and Magistrates' Court Act 1978.

38–15   A court order, not being an "agreement" within section 106(2) of the Taxes Management Act 1970, may lawfully provide for a "tax free" sum: see § 5–48. An order to pay £x "free of tax" means an order to pay such a sum as after deduction of tax at the basic rate will leave £x, *i.e.* the amount stated is treated as the net amount. Where no reference to tax is made in the order, the amount stated is the gross amount.

38–16   Payments made under a court order which do not exceed £48 weekly or £208 monthly are "small maintenance payments" and are made without deduction of tax: see § 5–05. Where the payments are not small maintenance payments the tax position of the payer and payee respectively are as stated in §§ 38–08 *et seq*.

38–17   Some of the problems which arise where there is a foreign element in the transaction have been referred to in § 5–43.

Whose income?

38–18   A court order which directs payment to be made *direct* to any individual is treated by the Revenue as *not* being a settlement to which the provisions of section 437 of the Income and Corporation Taxes Act 1970 apply: see § 10–09.[1] Thus if an order provides for periodical payments to be made to a child, the payments are treated as income of the child and not as income of any other person. If, however, periodical payments are ordered to be made to the wife for the maintenance of the child, the payments are income of the wife.[2] An order in the latter form is plainly undesirable if the wife has (or comes to have) an income in her own right but when the child has no income.

> In *Morley-Clarke* v. *Jones*[2a] the husband (H) who divorced his wife in 1969 was ordered to pay her a weekly sum for the maintenance of their child. The payments were treated as income of the wife.[2b] When later the wife started to earn income, this arrangement was no longer tax-efficient. In 1980 the wife obtained an order by consent varying the 1969 order so that H would make payments to the child direct; the 1980 order was back-dated to 1969. The wife claimed to have the earlier assessments (treating the maintenance payments as her income) reduced to nil, on the basis that the 1980 order changed the tax position retrospectively. *Held,* that the 1980 order could not alter the fact that the sums actually paid to the wife were her taxable income at the time the payments were made.

The single person's allowance in 1986–87 is £2,335 and an order for payments up to this amount can be made in favour of a child without making the child liable for any tax (assuming this is the child's only income). Some care is needed in deciding whether or not the order should be made to the child direct or to the parent who has care and control.[3]

Under section 2 of the Domestic Proceedings and Magistrates' Courts Act 1978 magistrates can order that payments be made direct to a child. Such an order can be back-dated to a date not earlier than the date of the

---

1. See *Yates* v. *Starkey* [1951] Ch. 465; 32 T.C. 38.
2. *Stevens* v. *Tirard* [1940] 1 K.B. 204; 23 T.C. 321 (C.A.): " . . . the payment of money to a wife on the condition that she is not accountable for the expenditure of the money, but is only bound properly to maintain the children, is inconsistent with the view that the money is the children's money in their own right": *per* Lawrence J. at p. 326.
2a. [1985] S.T.C. 660 (C.A.).
2b. See note 2, *supra*.
3. See J. E. Adams "Children's Maintenance—Tax and Welfare Benefit Advantages of Direct Payments" (1975) 72 L.S.Gaz. 750.

application. Where an order, whether original or varying an existing order, does in fact provide for payments to the spouse or to the child for a period prior to the date of that order, the Inland Revenue will accept that such payments can be taken into account for tax purposes provided (a) the payments do not relate to a period before the date of application for the order or the variation order, as the case may be; (b) the parties agree; and (c) there has been no undue delay by the parties in pressing the application.[4] Thus the same tax consequences follow as respects both parties as if the order had been made and took effect from the date to which it is back-dated. And see § 5–05 (small maintenance payments).

Divorce: payment of school fees

38–19   Orders to make periodical payments in respect of children often include an element on account of school fees. Difficulty has arisen in the past in determining how exactly the school fees should be paid, *i.e.* whether by the father direct or by the mother out of payments made under the order. An arrangement was made with the Inland Revenue[5] and is now embodied in a Statement of Practice[6] whereby school fees may be paid directly to the school by the father and tax relief allowed on the part of the payment made in respect of them if the order directing payment contains the following formula:

> "that that part of the order which reflects the school fees shall be paid to the [headmaster] [bursar] [school secretary] as agent for the said child and the receipt of that payee shall be a sufficient discharge."

Provided this order reflects what is happening in practice, tax relief will be given to the payer for these payments which form part of the taxable income of the child. The school fees will be payable in full out of the *net* amount due under the maintenance order *after* tax at the basic rate has been deducted from the total amount payable. In the Revenue's view, the onus is on the parties themselves to produce evidence, where requested, that the person receiving the school fees has agreed to act as agent for the child and that the contract for the payment of the fees (which will most easily be proved if in writing) is between the child (not the spouse making the payments) and the school.[6] There is no requirement that the order of the court should specify the *amount* of school fees to be paid.[7]

8–19A   Difficulties have arisen with regard to the practice referred to in § 38–19 as a result of the decision of the Court of Appeal in *Sherdley* v. *Sherdley*[8] where the Court of Appeal decided that the matrimonial courts should not make orders in accordance with the formula in the Statement of Practice.[9] These facts in the case were as follows:

---

4. SP 6/81 in [1981] S.T.I. 492. But see *Morley-Clarke* v. *Jones, supra.*
5. [1980] S.T.I. 259.
6. SP 15/80 in [1980] S.T.I. 749. And see the Practice Direction in [1983] 1 W.L.R. 800. The form of contract is in [1982] S.T.I. 442.
7. [1982] S.T.I 66 (HC Written Answer).
8. [1986] S.T.C. 266 (C.A.).
9. See note 6, *supra.*

In divorce proceedings the father (F) had obtained custody, care and control of his three children aged 13, 11 and 9. The children were all at fee-paying schools and F was paying the fees. F applied to the court for an order *against himself* that he should make periodical payments to the school as agent for each child, in accordance with the procedure in § 38–19. *Held*, the divorce court should make no such order.

The Master of the Rolls described the notion of three young children appointing the headmaster or bursar as their agent as "cloud cuckoo land" and used the word "sham" in reference to the transaction. Neill J. said the divorce courts should not make orders the tax courts might disregard and thought the *Ramsay* principle applied, apparently on the basis that F's application was a "step" in a "composite transaction": see §36–21. Balcombe J. saw no objection to the court making the order which was most beneficial to the child, even if this involved a saving of tax. He could see no objection to the agency concept which worked satisfactorily in practice but thought it would be preferable if some less artificial scheme could be devised.

Capital provision

38–20   Part II of the Matrimonial Causes Act 1973 empowers the court to order a lump sum provision in favour of a party to the marriage or a child of the family or to make a property adjustment order directing, for example, the transfer of the matrimonial home from husband to wife, or the making of a settlement, or the variation of an existing settlement. The taxes on capital gains and transfers of capital have to be kept in mind when considering orders of this kind.

38–21   As regards capital gains tax, it will be remembered that the exemption which applies to transfers between spouses does not apply in years of assessment after the year in which the parties separate: see § 16–17. There is, however, a limited concession which applies only to the matrimonial home. Where as a result of a breakdown of the marriage one spouse ceases to occupy his or her matrimonial home and subsequently as part of a financial settlement disposes of the home, or an interest in it, to the other spouse (or, if the transfer is after divorce, ex-spouse), the home may be regarded for the purposes of section 102 of the Capital Gains Tax Act 1979 (exemption or relief from capital gains tax on an individual's main residence: see § 16–41) as continuing to be a residence of the transferring spouse from the date his (or her) occupation ceases until the date of transfer, provided that it has throughout this period been the other spouse's only or main residence. Thus where a married couple separate and the husband leaves the matrimonial home while still owning it, the usual capital gains tax exemption or relief will be given on the subsequent transfer to the wife, provided she has continued to live in the house and the husband has not elected that some other house should be treated as his main residence for this period.[10]

---

10. Concession D6 quoted in [1973] S.T.I. 450.

38–22   As regards inheritance tax, transfers between spouses, *i.e.* prior to decree absolute, are exempt from the tax: see § 19–02. Transfers of property made after decree absolute may qualify for exemption from inheritance tax under one of the other exemptions in Chapter 19. Dispositions in favour of a child of the family may be exempt from inheritance tax under the exemption discussed in § 19–55.

Settlements

38–23   Where there are young children, the court may order that the wife be permitted to remain in occupation of the matrimonial home for a specified period, that it be then sold and that the proceeds of the sale be then divided in specified proportions. An order in this form creates a "settlement" for the purposes of inheritance tax and capital gains tax. Under the settlement the wife has an "interest in possession" as explained in § 22–14. The transfer into settlement in such case is exempt from inheritance tax under the exemption discussed in § 19–55 and from capital gains tax under the concession referred to in § 38–21. On the termination of the wife's interest in possession, no inheritance tax is payable in respect of so much of the settled property as reverts to the settlor husband: see § 22–27. It is thought that the exemption in § 19–55 applies to that part of the settled property which passes to the wife. The husband is liable to capital gains tax on any increase in the value of the matrimonial home between the date of the transfer into settlement and the deferred sale.

CHAPTER 39

PROBLEMS RELATED TO OFFICES AND EMPLOYMENTS

1. GENERAL MATTERS

39–01 THE taxation of emoluments under Schedule E has been considered.[1] At the outset it was pointed out that a difficult question sometimes arises, in the case of individuals who undertake a number of different engagements at the same time, whether each engagement constitutes a different office or employment or whether they together constitute a single profession or vocation within Schedule D.[2] Where claims for expenses are concerned, the rules of Schedule D are more favourable to the taxpayer than the rules of Schedule E and it is sometimes practicable so to arrange matters that an individual is brought under Schedule D; but it should not be assumed that Schedule D is always to be preferred. The "golden-handshake" provisions of Schedule E[3] are more favourable to the taxpayer than the corresponding rules of Schedule D[4]; and the rules of Schedule E provide more opportunity than is sometimes realised for tax-free "fringe-benefits."[5]

39–02 Normal remuneration paid to directors and employees of trading concerns is deductible in computing profits for tax purposes. Excessive remuneration may be disallowed.[6] Pensions and salary which are, in reality, annual payments, may be taxed as such.[7] The Revenue tend to restrict the amount of director's remuneration allowable by way of management expenses, especially in the case of companies with pure investment income.[8]

39–03 In the case of directors and employees with £8,500 a year or more the statutory provisions relating to expenses allowances and benefits in kind must be carefully watched.[9]

39–04 Considerable care is required in drafting service agreements for directors, especially where these certain provisions for pensions or other retirement benefits. It is not always appreciated that a service agreement providing retirement benefits for a single director may be a "retirement benefits scheme" to which the provisions of section 23 of the Finance Act

---

1. See *ante*, Chap. 3.
2. See *ante*, § 3–03.
3. See *ante*, §§ 3–24 *et seq*.
4. See *ante*, §§ 2–25 *et seq*.
5. See *ante*, §§ 3–14 *et seq*.
6. See *ante*, § 2–59.
7. See *ante*, § 5–04.
8. See *ante*, § 6–32.
9. See *ante*, §§ 3–40 *et seq*.

1970 apply.[10] This may result in a wholly unexpected tax liability. A service agreement which is a vehicle for providing a pension for a director's widow in circumstances where the prosperity of the company is in no way enhanced may be *ultra vires* and void.[11]

39–05   A payment which is made in connection with the termination of an office or employment, and which is not otherwise chargeable to tax, is chargeable to tax under Schedule E by virtue of section 187 of the Income and Corporation Taxes Act 1970, subject to a limited exemption from tax.[12] A payment which is chargeable to tax apart from the section does not qualify for this exemption. The question whether such a payment is deductible depends, in the case of a trading company, on the general principles applicable to Schedule D expenses and, in particular, on whether the payment is made wholly and exclusively for the purposes of the company's trade.[13] A payment made by way of compensation to an employee who is wrongfully dismissed will be allowed as a deduction if there is a genuine pre-estimate of the damage he suffers; and even where the employee could be rightly dismissed, a sum paid to secure his voluntary retirement might be allowed.[14] Where the shares of the person to be compensated are being acquired, the compensation will be disallowed if it represents consideration for the shares.[15]

39–06   If an award of damages by the court is based on income which has been lost to the claimant and that income would have been taxable if received by the claimant, the court will take tax into account in assessing damages under the rule in *Gourley's* case.[16] Tax will not be taken into account by the court if the sum awarded is itself chargeable to tax. Thus in an action for damages for wrongful dismissal, the *Gourley* principle applies in the case of an award of less than £25,000[17]; and where the award exceeds £25,000, it applies to the tax-free £25,000.[18-20]

[The next paragraph is 39–08.]

2. APPROVED PENSION SCHEMES

39–08 Many of the tax problems which arise where a pension scheme exists have been discussed elsewhere in this book. These problems can be summarised as follows:

---

10. See *ante*, §§ 3–30 *et seq*.
11. *Re W. & M. Roith Ltd.* [1967] 1 W.L.R. 432; but see *Re Horsley & Weight Ltd.* [1982] Ch. 442 (C.A.).
12. See *ante*, §§ 3–25 *et seq*.
13. See *ante*, §§ 2–51 *et seq*. Note especially § 2–66.
14. See *Mitchell* v. *B. W. Noble Ltd.*, *ante*, § 2–55.
15. See *ante*, § 2–66.
16. *British Transport Commission* v. *Gourley* [1956] A.C. 185 (H.L.). For a statement of the conditions to be satisfied, see *London & Thames Haven Oil Wharves Ltd.* v. *Attwooll* (1966) 43 T.C. 491 at p. 515 (C.A.); and see *Raja's Commercial College* v. *Gian Singh & Co. Ltd.* [1977] A.C. 312; [1976] S.T.C. 282 (J.C.).
17. *Parsons* v. *B.N.M. Laboratories* [1964] 1 Q.B. 95.
18–20. *Bold* v. *Brough, Nicholson & Hall Ltd.* [1964] 1 W.L.R. 201.

(1) Problems which concern the employer[21]:

    (a) whether annual contributions made by the employer are deductible in computing profits under Schedule D;

    (b) whether an initial contribution to establish the pension fund is similarly deductible;

    (c) whether the income of the pension fund is subject to tax;

    (d) whether pensions are deductible in computing profits;

(2) Problems which concern employees[22]:

    (a) whether the employee's contributions are deductible in computing emoluments under Schedule E;

    (b) whether contributions of the employer are to be treated as additional emoluments of the employee;

    (c) whether pensions are taxable;

    (d) whether benefits paid on the death of the employee are subject to inheritance tax;

It is generally to the advantage of the employer and the employees that the pension scheme should be approved by the Commissioners of Inland Revenue and the main types of approved scheme are now considered. The setting up of pension schemes and matters relating to them is nowadays a matter for pension specialists, and only a brief outline of the subject is given in this book.

Approved retirement benefits schemes

39–09   Under section 19 of the Finance Act 1970 the Board are under an obligation to approve a retirement benefits scheme provided the following conditions are satisfied:

    (a) the scheme is bona fide established for the sole purpose of providing "relevant benefits"[23] payable to the employee or to his widow, children, dependants or personal representatives;

    (b) the scheme is recognised by the employer and employees to whom it relates and every employee who is, or has a right to be, a member of the scheme has been given written particulars of all essential features of the scheme which concern him;

    (c) there is a person resident in the United Kingdom responsible for discharging the duties imposed on the administrator of the scheme under the Act;

    (d) the employer is a contributor to the scheme;

    (e) the scheme is established in connection with some trade or undertaking carried on in the United Kingdom by a person resident in the United Kingdom;

    (f) in no circumstances, whether during the subsistence of the scheme

---

21. Discussed *ante*, § 2–78.
22. Discussed *ante*, §§ 3–28 *et seq*.
23. Defined F.A. 1970, s.26(1).

or later, can any employee's contributions under the scheme be repaid.

39–10 There are certain other conditions which must be satisfied in practice: broadly speaking, (i) contributions by the employee should not exceed 15 per cent. of his salary; (ii) the benefits payable to the employee must consist only of benefits payable on or after retirement at a specified age not earlier than 60 or later than 70, or on earlier retirement through incapacity; (iii) the aggregate value of the relevant benefits payable on or after retirement after 40 or more years' service must not exceed two-thirds of his final remuneration; and (iv) the lump sum benefits payable on or after retirement must not exceed three-eightieths of his final remuneration for each year of service up to a maximum of 40 (the overall limit for 40 years' service being, therefore, $\frac{120}{80}$ths).

There are provisions whereby the Revenue have a discretion to approve a scheme even if it does not satisfy one or more of the prescribed conditions.[24]

If an employer pays a sum to provide benefits for any employee pursuant to a retirement benefits scheme, that sum is deemed to be income of the employee assessable under Schedule E (if not otherwise chargeable to income tax as income of the employee). Where the retirement benefits scheme is approved, the employee is exempted from this charge to tax.

However, to obtain the maximum tax benefits, the scheme should be an "exempt approved scheme." Under the provisions of section 21 of the Finance Act 1970, an "exempt approved scheme" is one which is approved and which is established under irrevocable trusts.

39–11 Where the retirement benefit scheme is an "exempt approved scheme" the consequences are as follows:

(a) The investment income of the fund is exempt from tax, and capital gains on the disposal of investments are not chargeable gains for the purposes of capital gains tax.

(b) The employer's contributions to the fund are deductible in computing profits: ordinary annual contributions being deductible in the year when they are paid and other contributions being treated as the Board direct. An initial contribution to establish a pension fund will normally be spread over a period of not more than 10 years.

(c) Employees' contributions (if they are "ordinary annual contributions"[25]) are deductible in computing emoluments under Schedule E in the year when they are paid; no allowance is given under section 19 or 20 of the Taxes Act 1970 in respect of any payments which qualify for relief under section 21 of the Finance Act 1970.

(d) An annuity paid out of the fund to a person residing in the United

---

24. *Ibid.* s.20. Booklet IR 12 gives guidance as to the manner in which the Board exercise their discretion [1979] S.T.I. 402, at p. 404.
25. "Back contributions" are not "ordinary annual contributions": *Kneen* v. *Ashton* [1950] 1 All E.R. 982; 31 T.C. 343.

Kingdom will be treated as an emolument falling under Schedule E to which PAYE will apply instead of as an annual payment under section 53 of the Income and Corporation Taxes Act 1970.[26]

39–12/13   Where contributions are returned to the employee (as, for when he leaves the employment), they are taxed at one-half of the basic rate in the year of repayment, the administrator of the fund being charged to tax under Case VI of Schedule D on that amount.[27] Where contributions are repaid to the employer (as on a winding up of the pension fund), if the scheme relates to a trade, profession or vocation carried on by the employer the repaid contributions are treated as a receipt of the trade, etc., and if the scheme does not relate to a trade, profession or vocation, they are assessed on the employer under Case VI of Schedule D.[28–29]

Retirement annuities

39–14   Before the Finance Act 1956, self-employed persons, controlling-directors of controlled companies and employees who were not in pensionable employment were unable to provide for their old age out of untaxed income, as were employees who were members of an approved pension scheme. The Finance Act 1956 introduced provisions by which an individual could make arrangements to secure a retirement annuity, either from an insurance company or through a professional body, and obtain a measure of tax relief in respect of the premiums or contributions paid by him. These provisions (as extended by s.20 of and Sched. 2 to the Finance Act 1971) are now in sections 226–229 of the Income and Corporation Taxes Act 1970 (as amended by ss.31 to 33 of the Finance Act 1980).[30]

39–15   Section 226 of the Income and Corporation Taxes Act 1970 gives tax relief to an individual chargeable to income tax in respect of relevant earnings (as defined) from any trade, profession, vocation, office or employment who pays a premium or other consideration (called "a qualifying premium") under an annuity contract approved by the Board as having for its main object the provision for the individual of a life annuity in old age or under a contract approved under section 226A of the Act. Section 226A allows the Board to approve (a) a contract the main object of which is the provision of an annuity for the wife or husband of the individual, or for any one or more dependants of the individual and (b) a contract the sole object of which is the provision of a lump sum on the death of the individual before he attains the age of 75. A number of conditions have to be satisfied before approval will be granted. Approval can in some cases be obtained for a retirement annuity contract which enables the individual to transfer the value of his accrued benefits to another life office.[31]

---

26. F.A. 1970, Sched. 5, Pt. II, para. 1.
27. *Ibid.* Sched. 5, Pt. II, para. 2.
28–29. *Ibid.* para. 4.
30. The Inland Revenue published notes for guidance on the changes introduced by the F.A. 1980 in [1980] S.T.I. 625. See also SP 9/80: Investigation settlements and retirement annuity relief in [1980] S.T.I. 624.
31. F.A. 1978, s.26.

Under section 227(1) of the Income and Corporation Taxes Act 1970, relief is given in respect of a qualifying premium paid by an individual only on a claim being made for the purpose. Where relief is given, the amount of the premium may be deducted from or set off against the *relevant earnings* (as defined[32]) of the individual for the year of assessment in which the premium is paid. There are provisions for carry forward in the event of an insufficiency of relevant earnings in any one year.

There are limits to the tax relief which is obtainable. Generally, the amount which may be deducted in respect of a contract (including a contract approved under section 226A) must not exceed $17\frac{1}{2}$ per cent. of the individual's *net relevant earnings* (as defined[33]) for the year. For 1982–83 and subsequent years of assessment, the percentage of net relevant earnings which may be deducted is increased for older contributors (roughly the "over 50" age group).[34] Not more than 5 per cent. of the individual's net relevant earnings for the year may be deducted in respect of a contract approved under section 226A.

Approval will be given for a contract which gives the individual the right to receive, by way of commutation of part of the annuity payable to him, a lump sum not exceeding three times the annual amount of the remaining part of the annuity.

---

32. I.C.T.A. 1970, s.227(4).
33. *Ibid*. s.227(5). Charges on income are not now deducted from relevant income for the purposes of computing net relevant earnings.
34. F.A. 1982, s.38.

CHAPTER 40

TAX AVOIDANCE

40–01 PART XVII (ss.460–496) of the Income and Corporation Taxes Act 1970, is entitled Tax Avoidance. Many of the anti-avoidance provisions contained in Part XVII have been mentioned earlier in this book including:

(1) a group of sections (ss.478–481) designed to prevent avoidance of United Kingdom tax by transferring assets abroad[1];

(2) a section (s.482) which makes it a criminal offence without the consent of the Treasury *inter alia* for a body corporate resident in the United Kingdom to cease to be so resident or for the trade or business, or part of the trade or business, of a United Kingdom resident company to be transferred to a person not so resident[2];

(3) sections (ss.483–484) designed to prevent avoidance of tax by the sale of "tax loss companies"[3];

(4) sections (ss.485–486) to prevent avoidance of tax by transactions between associated companies, such as sales at an undervalue or overvalue[4];

(5) a section (s.491) restricting the amount of rent which is deductible in the case of certain sale and lease-back transactions[5];

(6) a section (s.496) entitled "transactions associated with loans or credit" which, *inter alia*, deals with "disguised interest."

The recent decisions of the House of Lords in the cases of *Ramsay, Burmah Oil* and *Dawson* are considered in §§ 36–10 *et seq.*

In this chapter, four groups of the remaining anti-avoidance provisions in Part XVII of the 1970 Act are considered, the topics dealt with being those which are of such importance in practice as to merit special mention; but nothing more than a bare outline of the relevant provisions is attempted.

1. CANCELLATION OF TAX ADVANTAGES: SECTION 460

40–02 Section 460 of the Income and Corporation Taxes Act 1970 (formerly s.28 of the Finance Act 1960), applies where in certain circumstances stated in the section and in consequence of a transaction in securities or of the combined effect of two or more such transactions, a person is in a position to obtain, or has obtained, a tax advantage. Tax advantage includes the avoidance of a possible assessment to tax. The section does not apply if the person in question shows that the transaction or transactions were carried out either for bona fide commercial reasons or in the ordinary course of making or managing investments *and* that none of them had as their main

---

1. See *ante*, § 7–26.
2. See *ante*, § 7–22.
3. See *ante*, § 14–30.
4. See *ante*, § 2–44.
5. See *ante*, § 2–62.

object, or one of their main objects, to enable tax advantages to be obtained.[6] Note that there are two "limbs" to this exemption. Further, the section does not apply if the transaction or transactions in securities were carried out and any change in the nature of any activities carried on by a person, being a change necessary in order that the tax advantage should be obtainable, was effected before April 5, 1960.[7]

In *Clark* v. *I.R.C.*[8] the taxpayer (a farmer) needed £50,000 to buy an adjoining farm. He regarded the chance to buy this farm as the opportunity of a lifetime as the resultant entity could be farmed more efficiently. He was minded to raise the cash by selling to an outsider his shares in a family investment company ("Highland"), the principal asset of which was a holding of shares in one quoted company ("Caledonian"). The taxpayer was persuaded by his father not to do this: the father was anxious that family control of Caledonian should be preserved. Instead the taxpayer sold his Highland shares to another family company, Equity. (For the application of s.460 to such a transaction, see *I.R.C.* v. *Cleary* in § 40–10.) On an appeal against a notice under section 460, Fox J. held that the sale was carried out for bona fide commercial reasons, that is, the taxpayer's need to raise cash in order to buy the adjoining farm. He held the Special Commissioners were wrong in holding that the commercial reason must be connected with the taxpayer's interest in companies concerned in or affected by the transaction. So to hold would be inconsistent with the decision in the *Brebner* case.

It is important to note that the Special Commissioners held that the transaction did not have as its main object or one of its main objects to enable tax advantages to be obtained. There was no appeal against this finding of fact. Hence the court was concerned with only one limb of the exemption.

When the taxpayer decided to sell his Highland shares to Equity, his brother (who was the only other shareholder) decided to do likewise. The brother had no need for cash but he thought it would be imprudent to be left with a 50 per cent. holding, the value of which might be reduced. The Commissioners discharged the notice against him on the ground that his was a transaction "in the ordinary course of making or managing investments" and the Crown abandoned this appeal.

Procedure

40–03   The procedure under section 460 is initiated by the service by the Board of a notice under subsection (6), notifying the person in question that the Board have reason to believe that the section might apply to him in respect of a transaction or transactions specified in the notice. The person in ques-

---

6. I.C.T.A. 1970, s.460(1). For a case falling within this exemption, see *I.R.C.* v. *Brebner* [1967] 2 A.C. 18; 43 T.C. 705 (H.L.). In that case the extraction of cash from the company in a non-taxable form was an integral part of a commercial scheme. See also *Goodwin* v. *I.R.C.* (1976) 50 T.C. 583 (H.L.). *Cf. Hague* v. *I.R.C.* (1968) 44 T.C. 619 (C.A.); *I.R.C.* v. *Horrocks* (1968) 44 T.C. 645; *Hasloch* v. *I.R.C.* (1971) 47 T.C. 50.

7. I.C.T.A. 1970, s.460(1), proviso. See *Greenberg* v. *I.R.C.* [1972] A.C. 109; 47 T.C. 240.

8. (1978) 52 T.C. 482; [1978] S.T.C. 614.

tion may, on receipt of the notice under subsection (6), make a statutory declaration to the effect that the section does not apply to him stating the facts and the circumstances upon which his opinion is based. The declaration must be made within 30 days of the issue of the notice[9] but, in practice, the Board may agree within the period of 30 days to accept a declaration some days after the period of 30 days has expired. Where several notices are served on shareholders of the same company in respect of the same transaction, it is common practice to deliver a principal declaration by one shareholder together with supporting declarations by the other shareholders. On receipt of the declaration, the Board may decide to take no further action on the matter; but if they decide otherwise, they must send the declaration to the Tribunal constituted under the section together with a certificate stating that the Board see reason to take further action in the matter.[9] In addition, the Board may send to the Tribunal a counter-statement replying (in effect) to the taxpayer's declaration.[10] Proceedings before the Tribunal are in private and the taxpayer has no opportunity at this stage of seeing or commenting on the counter-statement.[11] The function of the Tribunal is to determine from the statutory declaration and any counter-statement whether or not there is a prima facie case for proceeding in the matter and it may reasonably be assumed in all save the most unusual cases that a prima facie case for proceeding will be found. If the Tribunal finds a prima facie case for proceeding (or if no statutory declaration is made within the time specified), the Board serve a further notice under subsection (3) of section 460 which, for the first time, specifies the manner in which it is proposed to counteract the tax advantage. A person to whom a subsection (3) notice is given may within 30 days thereafter give notice of appeal to the Special Commissioners on the ground that section 460 does not apply and/or that the adjustments proposed to be made are inappropriate.[12] Proceedings before the Special Commissioners are conducted in the same way as ordinary appeals against an assessment. If the appellant or the Revenue is dissatisfied with the decision of the Special Commissioners, the dissatisfied party may require the case to be reheard by the Tribunal.[12] Proceedings before the Tribunal are conducted in substantially the same way as are proceedings before the Special Commissioners. There is a right of appeal by way of Case Stated on a point of law to the High Court from the Special Commissioners or from a rehearing by the Tribunal.[13]

Conditions for the operation of the section

40-04   Three conditions[14] must exist before section 460 of the Income and Corporation Taxes Act 1970 applies. First, there must be a transaction or transactions in securities. Secondly, the person in question must be in a

---

9. I.C.T.A. 1970, s.460(6).
10. *Ibid*. s.460(7).
11. See *Wiseman* v. *Borneman* [1971] A.C. 297 (H.L.).
12. I.C.T.A. 1970, s.462(2).
13. *Ibid*. s.462(3).
14. *Ibid*. s.460(1).

position to obtain, or have obtained, a tax advantage in consequence of the transaction in securities or of the combined effect of two or more such transactions. Thirdly, the tax advantage must be obtained in one of the circumstances mentioned in section 461. Each of these three conditions requires separate consideration:

40–05   (1) *Transaction in securities*. The phrase "transaction in securities" is defined[15] as including transactions, of whatever description, relating to securities, and in particular:

(i) the purchase, sale or exchange of securities;

(ii) the issuing or securing the issue of, or applying or subscribing for, new securities;

(iii) the altering, or securing the alteration of, the rights attached to securities.

40–06   In *I.R.C.* v. *Parker*[16] it was held that the particular instances referred to in (i), (ii) and (iii) do not in any way restrict the meaning to be given to the general words which precede them and that the redemption of debentures was accordingly a transaction in securities. Where shares are sold for cash the act of payment by the purchaser is a transaction in securities; and the payment of a dividend may also be such a transaction.[17]

40–07   Section 460(2) provides that

" . . . for the purposes of this chapter a tax advantage obtained or obtainable by a person shall be deemed to be obtained or obtainable by him in consequence of a transaction in securities or of the combined effect of two or more such transactions, if it is obtained or obtainable in consequence of the combined effect of the transaction or transactions and of the liquidation of a company."

40–08   This subsection is aimed at various types of company reconstruction. Suppose that A Limited carries on a business, has distributable reserves of £100,000 and has cash or other liquid assets of the same amount. The shareholders of A Limited form a new company, B Limited, and A Limited (or its liquidator) sells the business of A Limited to B Limited in consideration of an allotment of shares in B Limited credited as fully paid up. The cash or liquid assets are left in A Limited, which then goes into liquidation. In such circumstances section 460 applies and the shareholders of A Limited are treated as if the assets received by them in the liquidation of A Limited (less the amount of cash subscribed for the shares and excluding the shares in B Limited) represented the net amount of a dividend.[18] It is assumed in the example that the shareholders in both companies are the same and hold

---

15. *Ibid.* s.467(1). Securities includes shares and stock and (generally) the interest of a member in a company not limited by shares: *ibid.* s.467(1).

16. [1966] A.C. 141; 43 T.C. 396 (H.L.); for the facts, see *post*, § 40–09. Loans may be transactions in securities which confer a tax advantage: see *Williams* v. *I.R.C.* (1980) 54 T.C. 257; [1980] S.T.C. 535 (H.L.).

17. See *Greenberg* v. *I.R.C.* [1972] A.C. 109; 47 T.C. 240 (H.L.).

18. For the computation of liability, see *post*, §§ 40–13 *et seq.*

their shares in the same proportions. A notice under section 460 would probably not be issued to a shareholder of A Limited who had no shares in B Limited.

In *I.R.C.* v. *Joiner*,[19] a members' voluntary liquidation was preceded by a liquidation agreement, the purpose of which was to vary the shareholders' rights to receive surplus assets in a liquidation in such a way that the taxpayer could both continue to carry on the business of the company and receive surplus cash. The liquidation agreement was held to constitute a transaction in securities and the tax advantage to be the combined effect of that transaction and the liquidation.

40–08A   *Liquidation.* At one time it was supposed that the liquidation of a company was not a transaction in securities because it involves no alteration of the rights attached to securities: it merely gives effect to pre-existing rights. But after the decision of the House of Lords in the *Greenberg*[20] case, in which some of their Lordships expressed the view that a payment of a dividend might be a transaction in securities, the Revenue were advised that a distribution to a shareholder in the liquidation of a company is a transaction in securities. In 1960 an assurance was given to the House of Commons[21] that an ordinary liquidation was outside section 460 and, on March 21, 1973, Mr. John Nott assured the House "that the Inland Revenue have not sought and will not seek to apply the provisions of section 460 of the Income and Corporation Taxes Act 1970 to ordinary liquidations." In answer to a further parliamentary question asked on April 19, 1973, Mr. John Nott said that the Inland Revenue

> "do not propose any change of practice in relation to an ordinary liquidation, that is to say the bona fide winding up of a business as a distinct entity, whether the business with its concomitant goodwill then comes to an end or is taken over by some other concern which is under substantially different control. On the other hand the Inland Revenue would not regard as 'ordinary' a liquidation which is part of a scheme of reconstruction which enables the old business to be carried on as before with substantially the same shareholders, directly or indirectly, in control. Section 460 does not of course apply where a taxpayer can show that the transaction or transactions were carried out for bona fide commercial reasons or in the ordinary course of making or managing investments and that the main object or one of the main objects was the obtaining of a tax advantage."

A further "explanation" of the official practice was given to the Standing Committee dealing with the Finance Bill 1973 on May 16, 1973.[22] The effect of the Revenue's statements appears to be that every distribution in every liquidation of a company to which section 460 applies will be regarded as falling within section 460 unless the taxpayer can satisfy the Board (or the Special Commissioners on appeal) that the distribution formed part of a transaction carried out for bona fide commercial reasons,

---

19. (1975) 50 T.C. 449; [1975] S.T.C. 657 (H.L.).
20. See note 16, above.
21. *Hansard*, May 25, 1960, col. 511.
22. [1973] S.T.I. 263.

etc.; but having regard to the decisions in *Hague* and *Horrocks*[23] it seems unlikely that the "bona fide commercial test" could ever be satisfied in regard to most voluntary liquidations. In the author's opinion no liquidation or reduction of capital should now be carried out without prior clearance under section 464 of the Act except where it is certain beyond doubt that the company is a company to which section 460 cannot apply: see § 40–11.

In *I.R.C.* v. *Joiner*[24] Goulding J. and the House of Lords declined to decide in the Revenue's favour the point which was forcefully argued by the Crown that, since the *Greenberg* case, every distribution in a liquidation is a "transaction in securities" for the purposes of section 460. The *Joiner* case was decided against the taxpayer on the narrower ground referred to in § 40–08. If section 460 applies to ordinary liquidations, the statutory provision in section 460(2) (see § 40–07), which was introduced by way of amendment by section 25(5) of the Finance Act 1962, is otiose and it is difficult to see why it was not omitted from the consolidation amendments made by the Finance Act 1969. Viscount Dilhorne and Lord Diplock expressed firm opinions in the *Joiner* case that the liquidation of a company could not itself be regarded as a transaction in securities.

40–09   (2) *Tax advantage.* The phrase "tax advantage" is defined[25] as a relief or increased relief from, or repayment or increased repayment of, tax, or the avoidance or reduction of an assessment to tax or the avoidance of a possible assessment thereto, whether the avoidance or reduction is effected by receipts accruing in such a way that the recipient does not pay or bear tax on them, or by a deduction in computing profits or gains.

> In *I.R.C.* v. *Parker*,[26] a company in May 1953 capitalised £35,002 of its accumulated profits and applied the same in paying up in full at par debentures which were duly issued to the members. The debentures conferred no charge on any of the company's assets nor did they carry interest. It was a condition of the issue of the debentures that the company might at any time after the death of the registered holder or after the expiration of seven years from the date of the debentures, whichever was earlier, give notice of its intention to pay off the debentures on the expiration of six months from the giving of the notice. In July 1960 the company gave notice of intention to redeem the debentures which were duly redeemed in January 1961. A notice was duly served on a debenture holder under section 460 (then section 28 of the Finance Act 1960), and the Revenue contended that the amount repaid to the debenture holder should be treated for the purposes of the section as if it represented the net amount of a dividend.

The House of Lords held, by a majority, that section 460 applied. The debenture holder received in a capital form (*i.e.* by way of redemption of his debenture) moneys which, apart from the capitalisation in 1953, would have been available for distribution by way of dividend; a possible assessment to surtax was thereby avoided and a tax advantage was obtained.

---

23. See *ante*, § 40–02, note 6.
24. (1975) 50 T.C. 449.
25. I.C.T.A. 1970, s.466(1).
26. [1966] A.C. 141; 43 T.C. 396 (H.L.).

Further, it was held (by a majority) that the tax advantage was obtained in 1961 when the debentures were redeemed and not in 1953 when the profits were capitalised and the taxpayer received a mere acknowledgment of indebtedness which could be redeemed at the company's discretion.

40–10   In *I.R.C.* v. *Cleary*,[27] the taxpayers had 50 per cent. each of the shares of two companies, A Limited and B Limited. B Limited had a balance on profit and loss account of £180,000 of which £130,000 was represented by cash at the bank. The taxpayers sold their shares in A Limited to B Limited for £121,000 in cash (being their market value). The Revenue contended that the taxpayers had secured a tax advantage by receiving from B Limited as the price for their shares assets which were available for distribution by way of dividend and that they had thereby avoided surtax on £121,000 grossed up at the standard rate of tax. The House of Lords unanimously upheld the Revenue's contention.

It will be observed that the definition of "tax advantage" includes the avoidance of a *possible* assessment to tax. The point of the *Cleary* case was that B Limited had paid out cash which, in view of the amount of the revenue reserve, could have been distributed by way of dividend; so the shareholders avoided a possible assessment to surtax. In fact, however, the revenue reserve of B Limited was unaffected by the transactions in securities: all that happened was that a sum of cash in the balance sheet of B Limited was replaced by shares in A Limited. On a subsequent distribution of assets by B Limited, whether in cash or *in specie*, a further liability to tax would arise until the revenue reserve of £180,000 was exhausted. It is difficult in these circumstances to see what tax advantage was secured by the transactions in the *Cleary* case. In a recent case it has been suggested that a person secures a tax advantage if there is any conceivable way in which the transaction could have been carried out more expensively in tax terms.[28]

40–10A   *Sales of shares for cash.* It was at one time thought that section 460 would not apply where a major shareholder in a company to which paragraph D applied (see § 40–11) and which had reserves available for distribution by way of dividend sold his shares to an "outsider" for cash. This thinking was based on the belief that the seller obtained no tax advantage, since the seller could not have received the sale proceeds *from the purchaser* in the form of a dividend. This view has now been shown to be wrong.

Thus in *I.R.C.* v. *Wiggins*[29]

> W. Limited carried on the business of selling and restoring picture frames. In 1955, W. Limited acquired, for £50, a frame with a picture in it. About 10 years later the picture was found to be by Poussin and to be worth about £130,000. W. Limited entered into negotiations with K. Limited to sell the picture. The following scheme was devised to enable the shareholders in W. Limited (call them T) to realise the Poussin with liability only to capital gains tax. First, W. Limited sold the bulk of its stock (excluding the Poussin) to C. Limited, a company also owned by T; and the staff of W. Limited took

---

27. [1968] A.C. 766; 44 T.C. 399 (H.L.).

28 *Anysz* v. *I.R.C.*, *Manolescue* v. *I.R.C.* (1977) 53 T.C. 601; [1978] S.T.C. 296. See also *Williams* v. *I.R.C.* (1980) 54 T.C. 257 (H.L.) and *Emery* v. *I.R.C.* [1981] 54 T.C. 607.

29. (1978) 53 T.C. 639; [1979] S.T.C. 244. For a full analysis of the case-law, see *I.R.C.* v. *Garvin* (1981) 55 T.C. 24 (H.L.) *per* Buckley L.J.

employment with C. Limited. Secondly, K. Limited purchased the share capital of W. Limited (the assets of which then included the Poussin) for £45,000. This price took account of the fact that K. Limited would get no tax deduction for the cost of the shares in W. Limited, as it would if it had purchased the Poussin itself. The Revenue served section 460 notices on T, contending that T obtained a tax advantage in receiving £45,000 from K. Limited, that this represented the value of trading stock of W. Limited and that it was received "in connection with the distribution" of profits within section 461D: see § 40–11. The sale of stock was such a distribution.

The Special Commissioners held that the transaction fell within the circumstances prescribed in section 461D (see § 40–11) but held that T obtained no tax advantage since the £45,000 received by T could not have been received *from K. Limited* otherwise than as capital. Walton J. allowed the Crown's appeal, holding that T obtained a tax advantage because what T received from K. Limited in a capital form could (but for the avoidance scheme) have been received from W. Limited by way of dividend. The condition that the receipt should be "in connection with the distribution of profits" was satisfied since the scheme was designed to obtain in a capital form the profit attributable to the Poussin.

Every agreement for the sale of shares should now be made subject to a clearance being obtained under section 464 (see § 40–15), except where it is certain beyond doubt that the company is a company to which section 460 cannot apply (see § 40–11); and the application for clearance should give full particulars of any scheme intended to be employed for saving or deferring liability to stamp duty or capital gains tax (and see § 40–31).

40–11   (3) *The prescribed circumstances.* Section 461 prescribes five circumstances in which the section applies. Paragraphs A, B and C are aimed at dividend-stripping transactions of various types and are not further considered. The circumstance mentioned in paragraph D is:

"That in connection with the distribution of profits of a company to which this paragraph applies,[30] the person in question so receives as is mentioned in paragraph C (1) above such a consideration as is therein mentioned."

The consideration referred to is a consideration which either—

"(i) is, or represents the value of, assets which are (or apart from anything done by the company in question[31] would have been) available for distribution by way of dividend,[32] or (ii) is received in respect of future receipts of the company, or (iii) is, or represents the value of, trading stock of the company, and the said person so receives the consideration that he does not pay or bear tax on it as income."

---

30. The paragraph applies to (a) any company under the control of not more than five persons, and (b) any other company which does not satisfy the condition that its shares or stock or some class thereof (disregarding debenture stock, preferred shares or preferred stock), are authorised to be dealt in on a stock exchange in the United Kingdom, and are so dealt in (regularly or from time to time); but the paragraph does not apply to a company under the control of one or more companies to which the section does not apply; and see *I.R.C.* v. *Garvin* (1981) 55 T.C. 24 (H.L.)

31. *e.g.* a capitalisation of reserves.

32. This means assets *legally* available for distribution, not assets which are available in a commercial sense: *I.R.C.* v. *Brown* (1971) 47 T.C. 217 (C.A.). See now Companies Act 1980, ss.39 *et seq*.

This paragraph was held to apply in the *Parker*[33] and *Cleary*[34] cases. In the *Parker*[35] case the debenture holder had in 1962, on redemption of his debentures, received a consideration representing the value of assets which, but for the capitalisation in 1953, would have been available for distribution by way of dividend; and he received it "in connection with the distribution of profits." The word "distribution" in this context includes application in discharge of liabilities. In the *Cleary*[36] case, the payment of cash by B Limited was a transfer of assets and was therefore a distribution of profits in the sense in which those words are expanded by section 467(2).

40–12 Paragraph E of section 461 prescribes the circumstance:

> "That in connection with the transfer directly or indirectly of assets of a company to which paragraph D applies[37] to another such company, or in connection with any transaction in securities in which two or more companies to which paragraph D applies are concerned, the person in question receives non-taxable consideration[38] which is or represents the value of assets available for distribution[38] by such a company and which consists of any share capital or any security (as defined by section 237(5) of this Act) issued by such a company."

So far as this paragraph relates to share capital other than redeemable share capital, it does not apply unless and except to the extent that the share capital is repaid (in a winding up or otherwise).[39] The following are examples of cases to which paragraph E would apply. A Limited which carries on a business has cash or other liquid assets which the shareholders wish to extract. A new company (B Limited) is incorporated to which A Limited transfers its business in consideration of an allotment of ordinary shares and its liquid assets in consideration of debentures or redeemable preference shares. A Limited is then liquidated. Similarly, if the assets of an existing company are "hived off" into a number of newly formed subsidiary companies for a consideration which includes debentures or redeemable preference shares in a subsidiary company, paragraph E will apply to any distribution of such debentures or redeemable preference shares to members of the existing company; but it will not apply to distributions of ordinary shares.

It has been held,[40-44] *inter alia*, that where a person receives a non-taxable consideration under the first limb of paragraph E of section 461 by virtue of a transfer of assets between companies to which paragraph D applies, representing the value of assets available for distribution by such a company, and also consisting of share capital, the Revenue cannot rely on paragraph D so as to deprive the taxpayer of the benefit of the deferment of tax liability specifically provided by paragraph E (2).

---

33. [1966] A.C. 141; 43 T.C. 396 (H.L.); for the facts, see *ante*, § 40–09.
34. [1968] A.C. 766; 44 T.C. 399 (H.L.); for the facts, see *ante*, § 40–10.
35. See *ante*, § 40–06.
36. See *ante*, § 40–10.
37. See note 30 above.
38. Defined in I.C.T.A. 1970, s.461(3).
39. I.C.T.A. 1970, s.461, para. E (2).
40-44. *Williams* v. *I.R.C.* (1980) 54 T.C. 257; [1979] S.T.C. 598 (C.A.).

Computation of liability

40–13   Where a United Kingdom resident company transfers or pays to its
shareholders a fund which could have been (but was not) distributed by
way of dividend, the tax advantage to a recipient shareholder is (it is
thought) determined by (i) ascertaining the amount of the assessment that
could have been made on that shareholder if the company had utilised the
fund in making a qualifying distribution and paying the ACT applicable
thereto and (ii) by then seeing what advantage the shareholder obtained by
receiving the fund in a non-taxable form.

Thus if a fund of £5,000 is transferred to a United Kingdom resident individual who would be entitled to a tax credit, the shareholder is treated as
having received income chargeable under Schedule F made up of a qualifying distribution of £3,500 and a tax credit of £1,500 (assuming a rate of
ACT of 3/7ths). The tax advantage is therefore equal to the higher rate tax
that would have been payable by the shareholder on a qualifying distribution of £5,000. A shareholder who is a United Kingdom resident individual
whose income is insufficiently large to suffer higher rate income tax obtains
no tax advantage, because the basic rate tax liability would be reduced by
the equivalent tax credit. A shareholder who is a non-resident company is
liable to neither higher rate income tax nor basic rate income tax and therefore obtains no tax advantage. Shareholders who are United Kingdom resident trustees obtain a tax advantage equal to additional rate tax on £5,000.

Return of sums paid by subscribers

40–14   The assets to which paragraphs C, D and E apply "do not include assets
which (while of a description which under the law of the country in which
the company is incorporated is available for distribution by way of dividend) are shown to represent a return of sums paid by subscribers on the
issue of securities."[45] Thus section 460 does not apply to assets representing capital (*e.g.* a share premium account) even though such assets are distributable by way of dividend under the relevant foreign law.

Clearances

40–15   There is a procedure whereby particulars of a proposed transaction may
be sent to the Board and the Board asked to give a clearance for the transaction.[46–47] No appeal lies against a refusal to give a clearance. Section 460,
as interpreted by decisions of the House of Lords, has become a draconian
provision and the manner in which the section has been administered has
given cause for concern. Applications for clearance under section 464 have
to be submitted at the same time as applications under section 40 or 41 of
the Finance Act 1977: see § 40–32. As to sales of shares, see § 40–10A. As
to demergers, see § 40–33. As to companies purchasing their own shares,
see § 14–76 *et seq.*

---

45. I.C.T.A. 1970, s.461, para. C (2).
46–47. *Ibid.* s.464.

2. Artificial Transactions in Land: Sections 488–490

40–16 Section 488 of the Income and Corporation Taxes Act 1970, was enacted "to prevent the avoidance of tax by persons concerned with land or the development of land." Its purpose, expressed in general terms, is to tax as income all *quasi*-dealing profits derived directly or indirectly by the exploitation of land or any interest in land. The marginal note refers to "artificial" transactions in land but this is something of a trap: there is nothing "artificial" in selling shares in a land-owning company, yet this is the very type of transaction to which the section might apply. Section 488(2) provides that the section applies whenever—

(a) land, or any property deriving its value from land (including (i) any shareholding in a company, or any partnership interest, or any interest in settled property, deriving its value directly or indirectly from land, and (ii) any option, consent or embargo affecting the disposition of land[48]), is acquired with the sole or main object of realising a gain from disposing of the land, or

(b) land is held as trading stock, or

(c) land is developed with the sole or main object of realising a gain from disposing of the land when developed,[49]

and any gain of a capital nature[50] is obtained from the disposal of the land in the circumstances next mentioned.

40–17 The section applies to a disposal "by the person acquiring, holding or developing the land, or by any connected person."[51] A company is connected with another person if that person has control of it or if that person and persons connected with him together have control of it,[52] and any two or more persons acting together to secure or exercise control of a company are treated in relation to that company as connected with one another[53]; so that, for example, section 488 will apply where a company owns land to which (a), (b) or (c) in § 40–16 applies and shares in the company are sold by a person connected with the company, *e.g.* any of the shareholders of a closely controlled company. The section will not apply to sales of shares by members of a quoted company, merely by reason of the company's ownership of land falling within (a), (b) or (c). The section also applies "where any arrangement or scheme is effected as respects the land which enables a gain to be realised by any indirect method, or by any series of transactions, by any person who is a party to, or concerned in, the arrangement or scheme."[54] Thus it would apply if land was disposed of by, for example,

---

48. I.C.T.A. 1970, s.488(12).
49. See *ante*, § 2–11A.
50. A gain is of a "capital nature" if, apart from the section, it is not chargeable as income. The section does not apply to a gain realised before April 15, 1969: I.C.T.A. 1970, s.488(14). And see note 60, below. For recent decisions on s.488, see *Yuill* v. *Wilson* (1980) 52 T.C. 674; [1980] S.T.C. 460 (H.L.) and *Chilcott* v. *I.R.C.* (1981) 55 T.C. 446; [1982] S.T.C. 1.
51. I.C.T.A. 1970, s.488(2). The question whether a person is connected with another is to be determined in accordance with s.533 of the Act: *ibid.* s.488(12). See § 16–18A.
52. *Ibid.* s.533(6).
53. *Ibid.* s.533(7).
54. *Ibid.* s.488(2). See also *ibid.* s.489.

the method employed in the case of *Associated London Properties Ltd.* v. *Henriksen.*[55]

40–18   Briefly, where the section applies, the gain (determined in accordance with the section) is treated as income chargeable to tax under Case VI of Schedule D.[56] The section applies to all persons, whether resident in the United Kingdom or not, if all or any part of the land in question is situated in the United Kingdom.[57]

40–19   There is an exemption from the section where a company holds land as trading stock and there is a disposal of shares in that company; but the exemption applies only where all land held by the company is disposed of in the normal course of its trade so as to procure that all opportunity of profit in respect of the land arises to the company.[58] This is an exceedingly badly drafted provision and its meaning is not clear.

> Suppose that A Ltd. is a property dealing company owning two trading assets, Blackacre and Whiteacre. X and Y, who are brothers, together own the whole of the issued capital of A Ltd. On the sale of the shares, X and Y (if not dealers in shares) would be assessed to tax under Case VI of Schedule D by virtue of section 488(2). But if subsequently A Ltd. sold Blackacre *and* Whiteacre in the normal course of trade and for full market value, section 488 would cease to apply with the consequence (apparently) that X and Y would be entitled to recover the tax paid by them under Case VI.

It is not clear what the position is if the sale by the company occurs more than six years after the year of assessment in which the sale of the shares takes place. *Quaere* whether X and Y can claim repayment and are assessable to capital gains tax. The practical answer may be that X and Y should take a covenant from the purchaser of the shares to procure that the company will dispose of all its trading stock in the ordinary course of its trade within a period not exceeding six years from the time of the agreement.

40–20   There is a procedure of limited value by which, in certain circumstances, a person who considers that paragraph (a) or paragraph (c) of section 488(2), set out in § 40–16, might apply to him can seek a clearance from the Inspector.[59] A clearance under section 488 will in practice preclude an assessment under Case I of Schedule D.

3. Sales of Income Derived from the Personal Activities of an Individual: Sections 487 and 489

40–21   Schemes of an elaborate nature have existed for some years to enable high tax payers, especially entertainers, to "capitalise" their future earnings.

---

55. (1944) 26 T.C. 46; see *ante*, § 2–13.
56. I.C.T.A. 1970, s.488(3), (6)–(8).
57. *Ibid.* s.488(13).
58. *Ibid.* s.488(10).
59. *Ibid.* s.488(11).

Briefly, the individual would form a company, subscribe for shares, and enter into a contract giving the company the benefit of his services for a specified period for a salary. He would then sell the shares in the company to a public non-close company, often in consideration for the issue of loan stock redeemable over a period of years and related in some way to the company's earnings. The Finance Act 1969 contained provisions for taxing under Case VI of Schedule D, as income, the capital amounts received in such circumstances but, as is so frequently the case with anti-avoidance legislation, the relevant provisions are expressed in such wide terms as to include transactions far removed in concept from the transaction which is legislated against. The provisions of the 1969 Act are now in section 487 of the Income and Corporation Taxes Act 1970, which is expressed to apply where:

40–22   "(*a*) transactions or arrangements are effected or made to exploit the earning capacity of an individual in any occupation by putting some other person in the position to enjoy all or any part of the profits or gains or other income, or of the receipts, derived from the individual's activities in that occupation, or anything derived directly or indirectly from any such income or receipts, and

(*b*) as part of, or in connection with, or in consequence of, the transactions or arrangements any capital amount[60] is obtained by the individual for himself or for any other person, and

(*c*) the main object, or one of the main objects, of the transactions or arrangements was the avoidance or reduction of liability to income tax."

40–23   In the conventional scheme at which the section was aimed, the individual's service agreement with the company provided for a salary which, even if substantial, was very much less than the expected earning capacity of the individual; and in that sense the service agreement was an arrangement by which the company was able to "exploit" the earning capacity of the individual it employed. It is thought that paragraph (a) in § 40–22 would not apply in a case where an individual was employed at a full commercial rate.

40–24   The section provides that references to any occupation are references "to any activities of any of the kinds pursued in any profession or vocation, irrespective of whether the individual is engaged in a profession or vocation, or is employed by or holds office under some other person."[61] In the case of the conventional scheme at which the section was aimed, the individual was commonly an entertainer pursuing a vocation who, prior to the implementation of the scheme, had been charged to tax under Case II of Schedule D; but the section is made to apply to a person who, while pursuing "Case II activities," had chosen from the start to do so as a director or employee of a company.

---

60. "Capital amount" means any amount in money or money's worth, which apart from ss.487–488, does not fall to be included in any computation of income for purposes of the Tax Acts, and other expressions including the word "capital" are to be construed accordingly: I.C.T.A. 1970, s.489(13).
61. I.C.T.A. 1970, s.487(3).

40–25   Section 487(4) provides that the section shall not apply to a capital amount obtained from the disposal (a) of assets (including any goodwill) of a profession or vocation, or a share in a partnership which is carrying on a profession or vocation, or (b) of shares in a company, so far as the value of what is disposed of, at the time of disposal, is attributable to the value of the profession or vocation as a going concern, or as the case may be to the value of the company's business, as a going concern. Thus the section will not ordinarily apply if, for example, a solicitor sells his partnership share for a capital sum. It is provided, however, that if the value of the profession, vocation or business as a going concern is derived to a material extent from prospective income or receipts derived directly or indirectly from the individual's activities in the occupation, and for which, when all capital amounts are disregarded, the individual will not have received full consideration, whether as a partner in a partnership or as an employee or otherwise, section 487(4) should not exempt the part of the capital amount so derived.

40–26   Where the section applies, the capital amount is treated for all the purposes of the Income Tax Acts as earned income of the individual which arises when the capital amount is receivable, and which is chargeable to tax under Case VI of Schedule D.[62] An amount is not regarded as receivable by a person until that person can effectively enjoy or dispose of it.[63]

40–27   The section applies to all persons, whether resident in the United Kingdom or not, if the occupation of the individual is carried on wholly or partly in the United Kingdom.[64]

4. ASPECTS OF CAPITAL GAINS TAX AVOIDANCE

40–28   There are a number of provisions in the legislation relating to capital gains tax by which tax liability is deferred in what may loosely be called "paper for paper" transactions. Many of these provisions have been used in the past in schemes of tax avoidance and the Capital Gains Tax Act 1979 contains anti-avoidance provisions. Some of these are now considered.

Share exchanges

Assume that X owns 30 per cent. of the issued share capital of Company A. Company B offers to acquire X's shares in Company A and to issue shares in Company B in exchange. X accepts the offer. This transaction involves a disposal by X for money's worth but section 85 of the Capital Gains Tax Act 1979 treats the two companies as if they were the same company and the exchange as if it were a re-organisation of that company's

---

62. *Ibid.* s.487(2).
63. *Ibid.* s.489(13).
64. *Ibid.* s.487(7).

share capital. The effect of this is that the transaction is not treated as involving any disposal of the shares in Company A owned by X or any acquisition of the new holding in Company B; instead, the original shares and the new holding are treated as the same asset, acquired as the original shares were acquired. This means that X is to be treated for capital gains tax purposes as having acquired the shares in Company B at the time when, and at the price on which, he purchased the shares in Company A. Hence any gain (or loss) which has accrued in respect of X's holding of shares in Company A is deferred or "rolled over" until X makes a disposal of the shares in Company B.

Schemes of reconstruction or amalgamation

40–29   The following is an example of an amalgamation of assets. Company A owns a portfolio of investments which Company P wishes to acquire, issuing its own shares in exchange. Company A arranges to go into members' voluntary liquidation and its members enter into an agreement with the liquidator, that the liquidator will transfer the assets of Company A (after satisfying liabilities) to Company P and that the members of Company A will accept in the liquidation, in satisfaction of their rights as members, shares issued by Company P. This is a scheme of amalgamation. Two questions arise which affect the charge to tax on capital gains: (i) Is the transfer of assets from Company A to Company P exempt from tax by reason of section 267(1) of the Income and Corporation Taxes Act 1970? This section applies where, *inter alia*, any scheme of reconstruction or amalgamation[66] involves the transfer of the whole or part of a company's business to another company and the transferor company receives no part of the consideration for the transfer (otherwise than by the transferee company taking over the whole or part of the liabilities of the business); (ii) Can the members of Company A defer any liability to capital gains tax on their holdings in Company A under section 86 of the Capital Gains Tax Act 1979? This section refers to the case where, under any arrangement between a company and the persons holding shares in or debentures of the company or any class of such shares or debentures, being an arrangement entered into for the purposes of or in connection with the scheme or reconstruction or amalgamation,[66] another company issues shares or debentures to those persons in respect of and in proportion to (or as nearly as may be in proportion to) their holdings of the first mentioned shares or debentures. Where this section applies, the transaction is treated as if it were a share exchange: see § 40–28.

The transaction in the last example involves an element of tax avoid-

---

65. Difficulty frequently arises in practice in determining what is, or is not, a scheme of reconstruction. Schemes of partition are so regarded for capital gains tax purposes: see SP5/85 in [1975] S.T.I. 295; but this seems inconsistent with stamp duty cases: see *e.g. Brooklands Selangor Ltd.* v. *I.R.C.* [1970] 1 W.L.R. 429 in § 33–02 and *Baytrust Holdings Ltd.* v. *I.R.C.* [1971] 1 W.L.R. 1333. Since there is now a clearance procedure requiring the Board to determine what is or is not a scheme of reconstruction, it is to be hoped that the Capital Gains Tax and Stamp Duty Departments of the Inland Revenue will sing in unison. Note that the new clearance procedure for "demergers" covers stamp duty: see *post*, §§ 40–33 *et seq.*

ance. The alternative procedure would have been for Company A to go into members' voluntary liquidation and to distribute its assets in the form of cash to enable its shareholders to re-invest in Company P; but this transaction would have involved two liabilities to capital gains tax, one on the company and the other on its members. The scheme mitigates this dual liability.

Avoidance provisions

40–30   Section 87 of the Capital Gains Tax Act 1979 provides that neither section 85 (share exchanges) nor section 86 of the 1979 Act (reconstructions and amalgamations) shall apply unless the transaction in question is effected for bona fide commercial reasons and does not form part of a scheme or arrangements of which the main purpose, or one of the main purposes, is avoidance of liability to capital gains tax or corporation tax. Section 267(3A) of the Income and Corporation Taxes Act 1970 is in similar terms. However, section 87 is expressed not to affect the operation of sections 85 and 86: (i) in any case where the person to whom the shares or debentures are issued does not hold more than 5 per cent. of, or of any class of, the shares in or debentures of the acquired company or (ii) in any case where, before the issue is made, the Board have on the application of *either company* notified the applicant that the Board are satisfied that the exchange, reconstruction or amalgamation will be effected for bona fide commercial reasons and will not form part of any such scheme or arrangements as are there mentioned. The sections apply when the issue or transfer takes place after April 19, 1977.

Applications for clearance

40–31   Applications for clearance under section 88 of the Capital Gains Tax Act 1979 have to be in writing and to contain particulars of the operations to be effected. The Board has 30 days within which to require the applicant to furnish further particulars for the purpose of enabling the Board to make their decision (such period being further extended if further particulars are required). The Board have to notify their decision to the applicant within 30 days of receiving the application or, if they require further particulars, within 30 days of the notice requiring such particulars being complied with. If the Board are not satisfied that the transaction will be effected for bona fide commercial reasons, etc., or do not notify their decision within the time specified, the applicant may require the matter to be referred to the Special Commissioners. An application for clearance under the section is void if it does not fully and accurately disclose all facts and considerations material for the decision.

40–32   An Inland Revenue Press Release on April 19, 1977,[66] requires that applications for clearance under section 88 of the Capital Gains Tax Act 1979 should be made separately from (but cross-referenced to) any clear-

---

66. [1977] S.T.I. 88.

ances or consents being sought under sections 464 (see § 40–15), 482 see § 7–24) or 488 (see § 40–20) in respect of the same scheme. The applications are required to give full particulars of the proposed scheme and of all companies directly involved, the tax districts and references to which the company's accounts are submitted; and they must be accompanied by copies of accounts for the last two years for which accounts have been prepared.

5. DEMERGERS

40–33 This chapter is entitled "Tax Avoidance" and it might be said that the provisions to facilitate "demergers" in the Finance Act 1980 have little to do with avoidance. This is true, up to a point, but the legislation draws much inspiration from the belief that demerging abounds with avoidance possibilities and many of the provisions are of an anti-avoidance nature. Be that as it may, this is a convenient point in the book at which to summarise the legislation. Section 117 and Schedule 18 to the Finance Act 1980 were introduced to facilitate certain transactions whereby trading activities carried on by a single company or group may be divided so as to be carried on by two or more companies not belonging to the same group or by two or more independent groups. A simple example of the type of transaction envisaged is the following:

> A Limited carried on two separate trades, the X trade and the Y trade. The shareholders of A Limited are two families: the X family and the Y family. The shareholders desire that the X trade should be carried on by a new company (X Ltd.) owned by the X family and that the Y trade should be carried on by a new company (Y Ltd.) owned by the Y family.

The demerger of the trades in such a case would involve the formation of two new companies, X Ltd. and Y Ltd., the transfer of the X and Y trades from A Limited to the new companies and the transfer of the shares in the new companies to the X and Y families in the form of a "distribution."[67]

40–34 The definition of "exempt distribution" in Schedule 18 covers all the transfers involved in such a demerger that might otherwise constitute "distributions" for the purposes of the provisions discussed in §§ 14–40 *et seq.* The Schedule is, however, full of conditions which are designed to ensure that the reliefs which are given apply only to the segregation of trades of trading companies and that the demerged companies remain trading companies. The segregation of a property or investment portfolio from a trade gets neither blessing nor relief.

40–35 No attempt is made to summarise the numerous conditions that have to be satisfied. Paragraph 7(1) of Schedule 18 to the Finance Act 1980 requires that the distribution must be made

> "wholly or mainly for the purpose of benefiting some or all of the trading

---

67. Statement of Practice SP 13/80 in [1980] S.T.I. 663 shows how the Revenue will apply certain of the demerger provisions in practice. See also [1981] S.T.I. 194.

activities which before the distribution are carried on by a single company or group and after the distribution will be carried on by two or more companies or groups."

Further, paragraph 7(2) requires that the distribution does not form part of a scheme or arrangement the main purpose or one of the main purposes of which is

"(a) the avoidance of tax (including stamp duty);
(b) without prejudice to (a), the making of a chargeable payment (as defined in paragraph 13); or
(c) the acquisition by any person or persons other than members of the distributing company of control of that company, of any other relevant company or of any company which belongs to the same group as any such company; or
(d) the cessation of a trade or its sale after the distribution."

The reference to "chargeable payment" in (b) is designed to ensure that the scheme involves no extraction of cash made otherwise than for bona fide commercial reasons.

Where the numerous conditions in the Schedule are satisfied, any distributions involved are exempt distributions (see § 14–49A); and there are exemptions from capital gains tax (see § 16–12A) and stamp duty (see § 33–15).

INDEX